MW00784148

REMEDIES
CASES AND MATERIALS
Seventh Edition

By

Doug Rendleman
Huntley Professor of Law
Washington & Lee University

AMERICAN CASEBOOK SERIES®

Mat #40327959

Thomson/West have created this publication to provide you with accurate and authoritative information concerning the subject matter covered. However, this publication was not necessarily prepared by persons licensed to practice law in a particular jurisdiction. Thomson/West are not engaged in rendering legal or other professional advice, and this publication is not a substitute for the advice of an attorney. If you require legal or other expert advice, you should seek the services of a competent attorney or other professional.

American Casebook Series and West Group are trademarks registered in the U.S. Patent and Trademark Office.

ISBN–13: 978–0–314–15861–1
ISBN–10: 0–314–15861–8

 *TEXT IS PRINTED ON 10% POST CONSUMER RECYCLED PAPER*

Summary of Contents

Table of Contents

Table of Cases

The principal cases are in bold type. Cases cited or discussed in the text are roman type. References are to pages. Cases cited in principal cases and within other quoted materials are not included.

*

REMEDIES
CASES AND MATERIALS

*

Chapter 1

REMEDIAL GOALS

A. INTRODUCTION

The techniques a student will learn in Remedies are two: how to select a remedy; and, once a remedy is selected, how to measure it. Learning these techniques will teach the student important lessons about how lawyers and judges find common-sense solutions to clients' and litigants' problems by developing a new idea or, better yet, by adopting an old idea to the solution.

A student's study of substantive law leads to an important conclusion—that a defendant is, or is not, liable for violating a plaintiff's property right, committing a tort, breaching a contract, or some other infraction. The student's study of procedure, the mechanics of litigation, pleading, discovery and proof, teaches the student how the court decided the liability issue. The student's Remedies course fills the important gap between substance and procedure and answers a crucial question: what does the court do for the successful plaintiff?

This Remedies course will show only a little concern for the substantive elements leading to the defendant's liability; we will concede the plaintiff her substantive right against the defendant without belaboring it. Our line of departure is the idealistic statement "For every wrong there is a remedy."

The court's basic remedial alternatives are relatively few and roughly classifiable. To begin with, the court's judgment itself may be a declaration of rights that resolves the dispute without further implementation.

We can look at a court's capabilities from two sides: what the court may do *for* the plaintiff, and what it may do *to* the defendant.

First, what may a court do on behalf of the winning plaintiff?

The court may:

(a) Grant the plaintiff specific relief, usually specific performance or an injunction. The judge may order a defendant who breached a contract to perform it. If the defendant took the plaintiff's property, the judge may order the defendant to restore it. If the defendant is committing a tort or some other misconduct, the judge may order him to cease. Specific relief is often an equitable remedy, so the plaintiff may have to qualify for it.

(b) Award the plaintiff substitutionary relief, in other words money damages. Compensating the plaintiff's loss is the basic principle of common law damages. The court may award the plaintiff a money judgment to compensate the loss she sustained.

1

Editor's Definition: When this book uses the word "award," it does not mean "prize," like an Academy Award, it means "adjudicate, decide after consideration."

(c) Award the plaintiff restitution. A court will call the plaintiff's recovery based on the defendant's gain or unjust enrichment restitution.

Second, what consequences may a civil court impose on the losing defendant? The classification differs. A civil court may not imprison the defendant as punishment. The court may:

(a) Require the defendant to transfer title or possession of property.

(b) Order the defendant to do something.

(c) Prohibit the defendant from doing something.

(d) Direct that the defendant be confined to coerce him to obey any of the above except an order to pay the plaintiff money.

(e) Enter a money judgment that the defendant pay the plaintiff money to compensate the plaintiff, to prevent the defendant's unjust enrichment, or to punish the defendant.

Some of the court's remedies are called "specific," sometimes "in personam" remedies. These remedies operate against the defendant's person.

Other remedies are called "substitutional," sometimes "in rem" remedies. These remedies operate against the defendant's property.

Our system of remedies is divided into equitable remedies and legal remedies. The principal equitable remedies are the injunction, specific performance, and the constructive trust; equitable remedies are associated with the expressions "specific" and "in personam" relief. The court's major legal or common law remedy is money damages; money damages are associated with the terms "substitutional" and "in rem" relief.

The merger of equity and law has ameliorated without eliminating the hazards of the distinctions in the preceding paragraph. Two major differences between a court's equitable remedy and its legal remedy remain: (a) A party lacks a right to a jury trial for an equitable remedy, an injunction, specific performance, or a constructive trust, in contrast to a party's right to a jury to hear and decide factual issues for money damages. (b) The judge's will enforce an in personam equitable order by holding the defendant in contempt, in contrast to the plaintiff's collection of money damages with a writ of execution, garnishment, and judgment lien.

Courts continue to recite the rubric that before the judge will grant the plaintiff an injunction or other equitable remedy, she must persuade the judge that her legal remedy, damages, is inadequate, or that without an injunction, she will suffer irreparable injury.

We now turn to the goals sought to be achieved. Anyone may use the civil justice system to summon the government's power to investigate a wrong, to hold the wrongdoer responsible and to account, and to implement a remedy. A court will seldom discuss or consciously articulate remedial goals. One of the purposes of our study of Remedies will be to isolate and examine remedial goals to evaluate our present remedial structure. A lawyer will select the remedy that will best advance a client's interest. Economic, moral, and administrative values influence the court's remedial choices. The views that our society takes of individual rights, property, and the demands of commerce will affect a court's remedial goals.

B. TORT REMEDIAL GOALS

1. *Prevent a Tort From Occurring*. The best remedy to protect a plaintiff from the defendant's threatened tort is an injunction, a judge's order that prohibits the defendant's future misconduct.

2. *Restore the Status Quo*. Another of the court's remedial goals is to put things back the way they were before the defendant's tort. If the defendant wrongfully seized the plaintiff's property, the judge can require the defendant to return it. Although restitution or restoration is not available for a plaintiff's personal injury, it is a recognized and legitimate remedial goal for a property tort.

3. *Compensate the Plaintiff for the Loss*. The compensation or indemnity principle dominates common law tort damages remedies. If the defendant's tort injured the plaintiff, the court can award the plaintiff damages which will compensate plaintiff's loss, as nearly as money can. A court may order the defendant to pay money damages for a plaintiff's physical or mental injury, pain and suffering, lost income, and loss of property value.

4. *Deter Future Torts*. Those who apply market economic analysis to legal problems stress the effect of a plaintiff's actual or potential compensatory damages recovery to structure potential defendants' incentives to take precautionary measures to prevent future mishaps.

5. *Establish, Declare, and Vindicate the Plaintiff's Rights*. A court following the common law torts tradition may establish and vindicate a plaintiff's important rights and reprobate the defendant's misconduct. Those who subscribe to the corrective justice school emphasize the court's function of holding a wrongdoer to account for the wrong.

Under a declaratory judgment statute, a court may declare what the parties' legal relations are. A judge's declaratory judgment of parties' rights may resolve some tort controversies, such as a defendant's threatened invasion of a plaintiff's property rights. A declaratory judgment differs from an injunction, for it neither commands nor forbids anything.

A court may award nominal damages to a plaintiff for a defendant's tort to vindicate the plaintiff's rights. A court may use both compensatory damages and punitive damages to single out a defendant's wrongs and to emphasize the plaintiff's rights.

6. *Punish Wrongdoers*. A court's punitive damages judgment will punish the defendant for an aggravated wrongful act and deter similar acts in the future.

C. REMEDIAL GOALS IN CONTRACT BREACHES

1. *Fulfill Plaintiff's Expectancy of Gain*. The court may provide plaintiff the potential benefit she would have achieved if defendant had performed the contract. This may consist specific performance to prevent or overcome the defendant's breach; but if specific performance is not available, money damages must fulfill the plaintiff's expectancy goal, so far as money can.

2. *Special Damages to Restore Plaintiff's Losses and Reliance Expenditures.* Damages compensate the plaintiff for her losses and for expenditures she incurred in reliance upon the contract.

3. *Restitution.* The court's rescission of a contract or agreement followed by restitution will restore the plaintiff and the defendant to their respective situations prior to the transaction by having each return the part performance he or she received from the other.

4. *Punish or Deter the Defendant.* A common law court attains its goal of deterrence or prevention by granting the plaintiff's expectation and special damages; a market economist may say that measure will deter defendants' breaches that the law should prevent. A court will almost never award a plaintiff punitive damages when a defendant breaches a contract.

5. *Declare or Terminate Parties' Contractual Rights or Duties.* A court may grant a declaratory judgment either before or after a party's breach.

D. REMEDIAL GOALS FOR UNJUST ENRICHMENT

1. *Restore the Benefits Defendant Unjustly Holds, Restitution.* "Unjust enrichment" describes a separate substantive area as extensive as *either* tort or contract. Although the unjust enrichment concept is primordial, courts have evolved a unified body of doctrinal and remedial rules only recently under the heading of "Restitution." In short, the defendant's unjust enrichment is the substantive law, restitution to the plaintiff is the remedy.

Because a defendant's "unjust enrichment" frequently results from that defendant's tort or breach of contract, lawyers often think of restitution as a tort or contract remedy; in this sense, restitution is a remedial goal for both defendants' contract breaches and their torts.

In addition, a court's restitution award to the plaintiff based on the defendant's unjust enrichment is an important freestanding remedy. A substantive law of unjust enrichment giving rise to the plaintiffs' remedy of restitution emerges from the defendant's enrichment in the absence of any tort or breach of contract.

This casebook largely ignores the substantive law of contract, property, and tort; however, we include material that a separate course on "Restitution" might cover. In Chapter 4, we devote special attention to Unjust Enrichment–Restitution both as a remedy and as a substantive doctrine.

2. *Punishment and Deterrence.* Restitution serves subordinate goals of punishment and deterrence when the court compels the defendant to disgorge benefits which exceed the plaintiff's harm.

E. THE HISTORICAL BACKGROUND OF MODERN REMEDIES

Introduction

Once we have stated the goals of contract, tort, and restitution remedies and determined the injured plaintiff's options, the court's choice of an appropriate remedy for a plaintiff's injury ought to be straightforward. Unfortunately, the court's choice is often difficult. Most states' constitutions or statutes say that the common law of England is the rule of decision in state courts. These states inherited the common law "forms of action" and the division between law and equity.

The dual system with Common Law and Chancery courts, each with its own remedies, complicated the injured plaintiff's choice of remedy. What might otherwise require the judge to ask a pragmatic question about which remedy best achieves the court's and the plaintiff's remedial goals for a particular defendant's breach is complicated by forcing the judge to inquire into the relationship between legal and equitable remedies.

Editor's Observation: The word "equity" has so many different meanings that, so far as possible, this book refers to the Court of Equity as the "Court of Chancery," and the judge there is often the "Chancellor." This is an attempt to eliminate one of the multiple meanings of the word "equity" and to reserve that term for equitable doctrines, but more particularly for equitable remedies.

Because history has a significant impact on modern remedies, let's next summarize some of the common law forms of action and explain the system of equity. These distinctions will remain important in the chapters that follow.

1. ACCOMMODATION OF REMEDIAL GOALS WITHIN THE COMMON LAW SYSTEM: A SUMMARY OF COMMON LAW ACTIONS

a. *Torts–Property*

1. *Specific Restitution of Property.* Real Property. The old real actions such as writs of right and writs of entry, which dated back to the Norman Conquest, provided for the plaintiff's specific recovery of real property. When procedural complexities destroyed their effectiveness, the old writs were supplanted by the writ of *ejectment.* Originally developed to recover possession of a leasehold estate, the courts extended *ejectment* with a series of ingenious and elaborate fictions to provide an expeditious procedure for adverse claimants to try title to land. Today an owner uses *ejectment* to recover possession of land.

Personal Property. An owner's remedies to recover personal property from a defendant were more limited and less familiar. *Detinue* developed from the writ of *debt* as a distinct form of action for the wrongful detention of a specific chattel. Devised to be used against an unfaithful bailee, *detinue* was extended to include a chattel a defendant wrongfully withheld. In addition to other procedural disadvantages, the judgment in *detinue* let the defendant either return the chattel or pay the plaintiff its value. *Replevin,* another action to recover plaintiff's personal property, originated to test the lawfulness of a landlord's distraint; today replevin is typically available across the board to retrieve the plaintiff's personal property from a defendant.

Today *ejectment* and *replevin* survive; *"detinue"* may draw a blank expression, except in old fashioned states like Virginia. These remedies are governed by statutes which attain the remedial goal without the common law technicalities, though due process decisions make a plaintiff's prejudgment recapture a less summary remedy.

2. *Compensatory Damages.* Damages are the common law's principal tort remedy, a "substitutional" remedy, that is money for harm.

Trespass in its various forms provided damages for a defendant's intentional injuries to the plaintiff's person (*vi et armis*), for taking the plaintiff's chattels (*de bonis asportatis*), and for invasion of the plaintiff's realty (*quare clausum fregit*)—today *trespass to land*.

Trespass on the case was used to compensate the plaintiff for injuries ranging from indirect and negligent injuries to the person to nuisances and various business torts. The action of *trover* for the defendant's conversion of the plaintiff's chattels yielded compensatory damages. While *trespass* and *trover,* and even *trespass on the case,* are described in the past tense, do not assume that these labels have vanished from current usage.

3. *Punishment.* From earliest times, the common law courts regarded punishing a tortfeasor to be a legitimate remedial objective. Damages, said Lord Mansfield, are designed not only to compensate the injured plaintiff but also to punish the defendant and to deter defendants' future misconduct and to show the jury's "detestation" of the act itself. Courts' explicit decisions to impose punitive damages to punish and deter defendants began in the eighteenth century. Today a court will award a plaintiff punitive damages only when the defendant's misconduct surpasses an uncertain level of meanness, wantonness, or maliciousness.

4. *Prevention.* The Common Law court's inability to prevent a defendant's tort was a major deficiency of the common law system of substitutional money damages. This inability created judicial business for Chancery and its remedies, the injunction and specific performance. Deterrence results indirectly, however, from potential tort defendants' realization that liability to a plaintiff for compensatory damages and perhaps punitive damages might follow its tortious misconduct.

5. *Declaration of Rights, Obligations and Status.* The Common Law court lacked a remedy with the sole purpose of determining parties' rights or status. The incidental effect of a court's decision in *ejectment* is to adjudicate title; but the court's judgment itself orders the plaintiff's to take possession. A court also declares litigants' rights through an award of nominal damages. Thus in a plaintiff's action of *trespass to land,* the plaintiff without actual injury may recover nominal damages to vindicate her property rights.

b. Contract Breaches

The courts developed common law actions to meet the needs of commerce to enforce consensual obligations. The writs were *account, covenant, debt,* and *assumpsit.*

Account, which dates from the thirteenth century, was a plaintiff's common law action for the defendant's breach of a fiduciary obligation. Originally it was directed toward bailiffs of manors. Nudged by statutes, courts extended it to guardians, partners, and the like. It withered for two reasons: (a) the weight of a cumbersome procedure that involved double litigation; and (b) Chancery's special claim over fiduciaries.

Covenant was originally the plaintiff's only method to recover unliquidated damages for the defendant's breach of what today we would term an executory contract. By the end of the thirteenth century, the courts had narrowed its focus to an instrument under seal; *covenant* did not lie if *debt* was applicable, where a sum certain was due, until the end of the sixteenth century.

Debt was one of the oldest personal actions. *Debt* would lie to enforce a defendant's legal duty created by contract, custom, or record, so long as the defendant's duty was to pay the plaintiff a sum certain. In this context, contract meant either a specialty, an obligation under seal, or a simple contract where one party's consideration had been exchanged for the other's promise to pay. *Debt* was also the plaintiff's proper remedy to recover statutory penalties (a duty created "by custom") and to collect money judgments, the so-called *"debt on a record."*

Assumpsit is the most important and most complicated contractual form of action. *Assumpsit* derives from the amorphous writ of *trespass on the case* as shown by the original name of the action, *case sur assumpsit*. Precise classifications as contracts or torts was no more characteristic of the fifteenth century English legal system than it is of ours today. Thus the plaintiff could characterize the defendant's breach of contract as deception and hence tortious, a choice that still affects a plaintiff's remedies for deceit and breach of warranty.

While England developed into a nation of traders and shopkeepers, its courts separated *assumpsit* from *trespass on the case* and *assumpsit* became a distinct form of action for defendants' contractual breaches. The courts first allowed *trespass on the case* for a defendant's breach of an express promise supported by consideration consisting of either detriment to the promisee or the exchange of mutual promises. The court's decision in Slade's Case in 1602 extended *assumpsit* to any action in which *debt* would lie on a simple contract. The court implied a second promise to pay the debt upon which the action of *assumpsit* could be premised; it meant that *assumpsit* would lie where someone promised to pay a sum certain upon receipt of a benefit, the quid pro quo. This form of action became known as *indebitatus assumpsit,* "being indebted, he promised." If the defendant received either goods or services in a transaction where both parties anticipated payment but no fixed sum of money had been agreed upon, *indebitatus assumpsit* was improper since *debt* would not lie.

Having discovered in Slade's Case how natural it was to imply a promise, the common law courts extended *assumpsit* by inferring the defendant's promise to pay the plaintiff reasonable value. The courts achieved this goal with the *quantum* counts which permitted a plaintiff to sue in *assumpsit* to recover either the reasonable value of services (*quantum meruit*) or the reasonable value of goods and materials (*quantum valebant*).

Assumpsit assumed two forms:

1. *Special assumpsit* was a plaintiff's action on a simple express contract, supported by consideration, whether executory or partially executed. In strict common law pleading, if the contract was under seal, it was a specialty in common law terms, and *special assumpsit* would not lie; the plaintiff's proper writ was either *debt* or *covenant*.

2. *General assumpsit* described an action where the plaintiff employed generalized formulations known as common counts. The common counts are forms of declarations in *indebitatus assumpsit;* with excess verbiage deleted, they are known today. The six common counts are: for *goods sold and delivered,* for *work done,* for *money lent,* for *money paid by the plaintiff to the use of the defendant,* for *money had and received,* and for *money due on an account stated.* The courts used *money had and received* and work done, *quantum meruit,* to develop legal restitution, also called contract implied by law and quasi-contract.

One thing a student should avoid is the notion that the writs and forms of action were dysfunctional from the beginning, a form of legal derangement. "[S]ince the mechanism of change within the common law had been to allow one writ to do the work formerly done by another, the whole process came to be seen as an irrational interplay between the 'forms of action.' It was not. It was the product of men thinking." S.F.C. Milsom, Historical Foundations of the Common Law 36 (2d ed. 1981).

Against this background, we will next examine how common law courts attain the various remedial goals. Courts have achieved these goals by particularizing the rules for measuring damages.

1. *The Expectancy*. The court's dominant goal for damages for breach of contract is to award the plaintiff's expectancy. The normal "benefit of the bargain" measure of damages is the potential gain the plaintiff would have enjoyed had the defendant not breached the contract.

2. *Special Damages and Reliance Expenditures*. The court's goal is to compensate in the conventional sense, including the plaintiff's losses from the breach plus her expenditures in reliance upon the agreement.

3. *Restitution*. One of the court's restitutionary goals for a breached contract is to return the parties to their original positions, the reverse of the aim of fulfilling the plaintiff's expectancy; the court may grant rescission followed by restitution. In addition, one of the plaintiff's remedies for a defendant's breached contract is restitution.

4. *Punishment and Prevention*. The Common Law courts defaulted this goal for a defendant's breach of contract. Punitive damages are virtually excluded. Deterrence of future breaches occurs because of the litigation itself and the attainment of the other goals.

c. Unjust Enrichment—Restitution

1. *Restoration of Benefits*. The court's goal is to compel the defendant to return unjust gain. The common law possessory actions, *ejectment* and *replevin*, suffice to a point.

Where it became necessary to value defendant's unjust enrichment in money, common law courts utilized the common counts of *general assumpsit, money had and received* and *quantum meruit*. This development led to the body of doctrine called contracts implied by law or quasi-contract.

2. *Punishment and Prevention*. The court bases restitution on the defendant's unjust enrichment, not the plaintiff's detriment. Earlier courts disclaimed punishment except for the effect of measuring the plaintiff's recovery in a way that may exceed her losses. Some courts have imposed punitive damages in addition to restitution.

d. Conclusion

This sketch of the way Common Law courts adopted their methods to attain remedial goals discloses deficiencies, notably (a) the lack of remedies to prevent specific future harm; and (b) the lack of remedies to afford specific relief except for the possessory actions of *ejectment* and *replevin*.

To understand how solutions to these imperfections were supplied, we turn
to

2. THE HISTORY AND DEVELOPMENT OF THE CHANCERY COURT

After the Norman conquest in 1066, the king of England retained a
residuary but overriding jurisdiction to adjudicate a dispute outside the common
law court system. That jurisdiction was limited to disputes where the common
law remedies were inadequate. That doctrine is still with us in the fading notion
that a court cannot grant a plaintiff an equitable remedy unless her legal remedy
is inadequate or, in different words with the same meaning, unless she will
encounter irreparable injury. S.F.C. Milsom, Historical Foundations of the
Common Law, Chapter 4 (2d ed. 1981).

During the thirteenth century people presented petitions or "bills" to the
king seeking redress for grievances "as of grace." While the monarch forwarded
most of these to the Common Law courts, an exceptional petition went to the
king's council. The council dealt with individual grievances and, in turn, delegated some to the royal secretariat or Chancellor, an office associated with the
administration of justice because it had developed the original common law
writs. The Chancery was in the king's chapel, and most of the medieval
Chancellors were also church officials, bishops and archbishops.

Soon petitioners began to send their bills directly to the Chancellor.
Through delegation and gradual development, the executive department evolved
into the full-fledged Court of Chancery.

Chancery's informal process lacked the language and forms of the common
law writs. By the fifteenth century, unable to develop and promulgate new
common law writs, the Chancellors issued decrees in disputes. In theory, if the
common law fell short, Chancery would render complete justice according to the
law of the land. The Common Law courts' solutions did fall short because of the
rigidity and hardening of the forms of action and the writ system and because of
evidence rules that prevented the Common Law court from considering the
merits. Chancery, a court of conscience, prided itself on not sending a deserving
plaintiff out without a remedy.

Chancery procedure. Liberated from the common law forms of action and
rules of evidence, a Chancery petitioner began a suit in equity by a bill which
initiated a subpoena to the defendant and informal pleading. Lacking a jury, the
Chancellor received the parties' evidence by written deposition.

Chancery procedure had several advantages. Chancery litigation was less
expensive and relatively quick. It bypassed local tribunals where corrupt officials
or favoritism might frustrate justice. A Chancellor who could order the defendant to produce important documents might consider all relevant evidence to get
to the bottom of a dispute. The Chancellor's favorite plaintiffs in the formative
period were the weak, the poor, and the oppressed.

Substantive equity. Chancery courts developed several separate substantive
areas of equity doctrine, for example uses and trusts, as well as mortgages.
Enforcing a lien is still considered an equitable matter. There were separate
equitable defenses: examples include laches and unclean hands. Chancery also
had broad principles known as "Maxims of Equity," for example, "He who seeks
equity must do equity."

Equitable remedies. A Chancery decree is directed to the defendant personally; it orders or forbids the defendant's conduct. In contrast, a Common Law court's judgment stated that the plaintiff was entitled to recover a specific amount of money from the defendant; the defendant was not ordered to pay, but the plaintiff could take further steps to collect, or execute, the judgment.

Milsom says of "the nature of equitable decrees: [that] results were not declared to be so; instead parties were told to make them so." Historical Foundations of the Common Law 90 (2d ed. 1981). The Chancellor might require a defendant to perform a contract specifically or to discharge a fiduciary obligation. The injunction was the Chancellor's chief remedy; specific performance was also important. The availability of specific relief drew plaintiffs' lawsuits to Chancery based on the claim that the plaintiff's legal remedy was inadequate. The modern Chancellor, for example, will grant specific performance of a defendant's contract to sell real property as a matter of course. So long as the Chancery court granted injunctions and specific relief, the pressure on common law courts to develop personal remedies was kept to a minimum.

The injunction became the Chancellor's most effective remedy. To enforce an injunction, the Chancellor could fine or imprison a stubborn defendant or sequester his property pending obedience. Chancery court decrees operated in personam, on the person of the defendant. Moreover, early Chancellors often declined to give a plaintiff damages. In a system where possible conflicts in rulings may have led to confrontation, the Chancery court's in personam orders had a strategic advantage which obviated many of the conflicts. Personal enforcement through specific orders to the parties kept Chancery on a different plane, one external to the Common Law court.

Discretion. Another contrast between the Common Law court and the Chancery court developed. The Common Law court applied a body of rules to a set of facts. In contrast, the Chancellor decided an individual dispute flexibly and with less concern for formal rules. Chancellors stressed factual, contextual decisions and de-emphasized the mechanical application of rules to facts. This type of adjudication may be called "equitable,"—an "equity" decision in Aristotle's sense corrects the abuses of a general law when it fails to provide for a just result in an individual case. Ethics, Vol. 10.

"The discussion about the relative importance in a legal system of certainty and abstract justice is unending," Milsom wrote, "but it begins at a definite stage of development, namely when the law is first seen as a system of substantive rules prescribing results upon given states of fact. In England this discussion was at once institutionalized; certainty resided in the common law courts, justice in the chancellor's equity." Historical Foundations of the Common Law 94 (2d ed. 1981).

Disadvantages. Many charged that the Chancellor's informality, lack of formal rules, and emphasis on conscience led to vagueness and unpredictability. If the Chancery was not a court of law but a court of conscience, it was the Chancellor's conscience, potentially ad hoc, arbitrary, and subjective. John Seldon's joke about "roguish" equity from the middle of the seventeenth century bears repeating: "Equity is according to the conscience of him that is Chancellor, and as that is larger or narrower so is Equity. Tis all one as if they should make the standard for the measure we call a foot to be the Chancellor's foot. What an uncertain measure would this be! One Chancellor has a long foot, another a short foot, a third an indifferent foot." The Table–Talk of John Selden 64 (Singer ed. 1847 [1689]).

From the late fifteenth century, the availability of Chancery to plaintiffs encouraged the Common Law courts to improve tort and contract, mostly through the writs of trespass on the case and assumpsit.

By 1600, Chancery was a regular court with its own procedure, and Chancellors began to develop precedents. Powerless Chancery litigants became scarce. Chancery litigation focused on real property; under declining feudalism, Chancellors adjudicated uses or trusts of land. The Chancellor could not interfere with an owner's possession; but he could issue an injunction, order specific performance, grant relief from penal bonds, and recognize the debtor's equity of redemption in a mortgage.

The Common Law courts declined to accept fraud as a defense to a plaintiff's action on a sealed instrument. The fraud victim's only remedy was in Chancery, an injunction to forbid the defendant from collecting the debt or judgment. The Chancellor would grant what is called a "common" injunction against a plaintiff who had won an improper judgment at common law by "fraud." The Chancellor did not reverse or negate the plaintiff's common law judgment; he merely threatened imprisonment if the plaintiff-judgment creditor collected the judgment from the defendant. Remnants of the "common" injunction exist today: An interpleader is an injunction forbidding potential plaintiffs from suing the stakeholder anywhere but in the interpleader action. And a federal judge may grant a plaintiff a *Younger* injunction forbidding the state authorities from maintaining an unconstitutional state criminal prosecution.

Chancellors' use of "common" injunctions to enjoin procedures in other courts led to disharmony between Chancery and the Common Law courts and to a clash in 1616. Lord Ellesmere antagonized the Common Law courts' judges by entertaining Chancery actions after the Common Law courts had entered judgments. Sir Edward Coke, bridling at Ellesmere's presumption to reopen cases already decided by Common Law courts, commenced to issue habeas corpus to release litigants imprisoned by Ellesmere for contempt for violation of common injunctions. When James I took the matter up in 1616, Coke had fallen into disfavor and Ellesmere with his ally Francis Bacon completed his descent. In addition to dismissing Coke, the king issued a decree confirming the Chancery court's ability to hear a Common Law court defendant's suit after a Common Law courts' judgment.

A recalibration of sorts occurred in 1617 when Ellesmere died and Bacon who succeeded him as Chancellor undertook to refurbish judicial relations. The king's decree came to be perceived as contrary to law; but with improved relations, lawyer-Chancellors refined the principles of equity. The difficulty of seeking legal remedies in common law courts and equitable remedies in Chancery persisted.

A system of Chancery precedent developed. There was hostility to the idea that similar disputes might be treated differently. The press of business led to routines, including routine rules. Chancery became a court of record with reported decisions. The rules of mortgages and trusts were as specific as any common law rules. Equity followed the law in tort and contract. Known rules hardened into binding precedents, and binding precedents hardened into rigidity. Lord Eldon in 1818 observed that "Nothing would inflict on me greater pain in quitting this place than the recollection that I had done anything to justify the reproach that the equity of this court varies like the chancellor's foot." Gee v. Prichard, 2 Swan. 402, 414 (1818).

Chancery courts and equitable doctrines had exercised a creative force in the Middle Ages; this force was long since spent in the nineteenth century. Chancery's hardening of the litigation arteries led to the merger or fusion of the common law and equity and to abolition of the separate court of Chancery. The merger of equity and law did not occur overnight; for court reform, then as now, is not for the short-winded.

Chancery, which evolved as an escape valve from the constraint of the common law writs and procedure, developed its own defects which came to predominate over its virtues. The nineteenth-century Chancery Court that Dickens described in Bleak House was characterized by corruption, verbosity, complexity, delay, and expense which benefitted the lawyers and bureaucrats and forced litigants into despair. Many lawsuits lasted 30 years. Too much centralization and too many administrative duties led to delegation and early forms of alternative dispute resolution. A piecework system of paying fees fed the delay and expense.

Reformers' unarticulated aspiration was to merge or assimilate Chancery and Common Law courts into one court which retained the best features of both while it eliminated the worst features of its predecessors. Positive features of Chancery were discovery, bench trials, in personam remedies, and specific remedies—the injunction and specific performance. Chancery deficiencies were inabilities to decide questions of law, to try factual issues to a jury, and to award damages.

Common law courts' positive features were clear rules, jury trials, and money damages. Law courts needed to simplify pleading, to compel discovery, to entertain equitable defenses, and to grant injunctions and specific performance.

The United Kingdom which developed the dual Chancery and common law courts emerged from "fusion" with a single trial court of general jurisdiction with a Chancery Division. The irony of merger there is that the Chancery bar and the Chancery Division are devoted to property law, the one area that demands certainty and specific rules, belying the notion that equity consists of applying discretion to particular circumstances to mete out individualized justice based on conscience. J.H. Baker, An Introduction to English Legal History 115 (2002).

English law came to its North American colonies in the seventeenth century. Lawrence Friedman, A History of American Law 95–101 (2005). To evolve the system of pleading the common law writs and the separate Court of Chancery was possible; to import that system and to adopt it wholesale would have been insane. Colonial status led, however, the colonies to adopt the mother country's institutions. Lawyers were trained in England; English texts, including Blackstone, were influential. Fortunately, the colonies' primitive conditions in the seventeenth and eighteenth centuries impeded excessive refinements. A modern sense of separation of powers was absent. There was no clear distinction between trial courts and appellate courts; and final appeals often went to a legislature.

After the American Revolution, the Seventh Amendment in the federal Constitution's Bill of Rights "preserved" the civil jury in "Suits at common law." Judges were elected, lay judges sat in many courts, and lawyers often lacked legal training except through apprenticeship. George Wythe and St. George Tucker at William and Mary endeavored to harmonize law to the new republic. Anglophiles like Chancellor Kent and Justice Story exercised a conservative influence.

Reform began in 1799. Georgia abolished the forms of action and moved to factual pleading, uniting the common law and equity, and to one form of civil action. States lacked a separate system of Equity, because Chancery was identified with royal absolutism and adjudication without a jury. Massachusetts, Pennsylvania, North Carolina, and Georgia added equity powers to law courts. Lawrence Friedman, A History of American Law 97–98 (2005). In courts of general jurisdiction, the same judge decided both law and equity. Legislatures passed statutes allowing litigants at law to employ equitable defenses. Many legislators held the idealistic view that an average citizen without a lawyer could plead facts under codes.

The Field Code in New York in 1848 was a watershed event: "The distinction between actions at law and suits in equity, and the forms of action of all such actions and suits heretofore existing are abolished; and there shall be in this state, hereafter, but one form of action, for the enforcement or protection of private rights and the redress or prevention of private wrongs, which shall be denominated a civil action." The procedure after merger retained many of the best features of pre-merger Chancery procedure, joinder, interpleader, counterclaims, and the remedies of specific performance and injunction.

Law and Equity were, however, incompletely merged because of the jury. The unification movement left unmerged the constitutional right to a jury trial in an action at law, the lack of a jury trial in Chancery-equity, and the difficulty of telling the difference. Constitutions and bills of rights preserved the historic separation. The choice between the jury's populism and the judge's dour elitism permeates civil remedies. The common people in the jury box express the community's moral judgment and conscience. Critics, however, emphasize the jury system's expense, complexity, and delay; moreover, a jury, they assert, may be emotional to the point of irrationality, unpredictable, and extravagant with a defendant's money.

The structure of ideas beneath the early Common Law forms of action persists because the old writs were based on abiding distinctions between property, tort, contract, and restitution. That the language of the law expresses the distinctions imperfectly, often badly, should not surprise anyone. Legal development is ragged and piecemeal; change is pressed forward, not by any reformer's urge for overarching consistency, but by an adversary system fueled by an individual lawyer's desire to win a client's case.

Law and Equity are not categories of the real world. The law-equity distinction is not functional, but substantively meaningless and procedurally disruptive. Two foundation ideas rose from merger's ashes, one remedial, the other substantive. The remedial idea is the court's personal order to a defendant, specific performance or an injunction. The substantive idea is the court's need for a general fairness default to technical rules. The core ideas in the division between substitutionary and specific remedies remain significant. An equitable remedy, the injunction in particular, is the tool of an activist judiciary.

The Federal Rules of Civil Procedure were the twentieth century's major contribution to clarity in the remedial system. The Rules' purpose, in the words of Rule 1, is "the just, speedy, and inexpensive determination of every action."

Law and equity are merged by the words of Rule 2: "There shall be one form of action to be known as 'civil action.'" Rule 38 preserves the litigants' right to a jury trial as the Constitution or statute commands.

Procedural devices formerly available in Chancery court are available across the board; these devices include joinder, discovery, the class action, and interpleader. The principles of substantive equity remain in effect in all actions. The court will grant the winning plaintiff the legal or equitable remedy she is entitled to regardless of the relief her complaint seeks. Rule 54(c).

Most of the states, where the vast majority of civil litigation occurs, have merged their courts and adopted all or parts of the federal rules. Never quick to adopt an innovation, Virginia finally merged its separate courts in 2005, effective in 2006.

Chapter 2

MODERN DAMAGES

The Jury and Damages. The injured plaintiff's principal civil remedy is money damages. The money damages that the defendant pays to the plaintiff perform two functions: (a) The plaintiff is compensated for her loss, that is the money damages will substitute, so far as money can, for the plaintiff's substantive interest that the defendant's breach impaired. (b) Damages deter the particular defendant, as well as other potential defendants; the possibility of paying damages in the future encourages them to take reasonable precautions to prevent future liability.

The lay jury is a constant presence in damages litigation because the federal and the states' constitutions require a jury to assess damages. The Seventh Amendment to the United States Constitution and comparable provisions in state constitutions cloak the civil jury in constitutional raiment. The federal Seventh Amendment provides: "In Suits at common law, where the value in controversy shall exceed twenty dollars, the right of trial by jury shall be preserved, and no fact tried to a jury shall be otherwise re-examined in any Court of the United States, than according to the rules of the common law." Although the Seventh Amendment does not apply to the states' court systems, state constitutions have their own civil jury sections. The Virginia Constitution's Article 1, Section 11 provides: "In controversies respecting property, and in suits between man and man, trial by jury is preferable to any other, and ought to be held sacred." Many state court systems have stronger traditions of jury trial than the federal system.

Our system of civil procedure through pleading, discovery, motions for summary judgment, and pretrial conferences focuses the litigants' attention on a jury trial as a discrete event. The political choice of the jury is based in history. "The founders of our nation considered the right of trial by jury in civil cases an important bulwark against tyranny and corruption, a safeguard too precious to be left to the whim of the sovereign, or, it might be added, to that of the judiciary." wrote Justice Rehnquist in his dissenting opinion in Parklane Hosiery v. Shore, 439 U.S. 322, 343 (1979).

The jury serves as the community's conscience in two distinct issues: first, the jury decides whether the defendant is liable to the plaintiff; and, second, if so, the jury sets the amount of the plaintiff's damages. The jury's role in pricing plaintiff's damages will hold our interest throughout this chapter.

"In the process of gaining public acceptance for the imposition of sanctions, the role of the jury is highly significant. The jury is a sort of ad hoc parliament

15

convened from the citizenry at large to lend respectability and authority to the process. * * * Any erosion of citizen participation in the sanctioning system is in the long run likely * * * to result in a reduction in the moral authority that supports the process." Judge Gibbons dissenting in In re Japanese Electronic Products Antitrust Litigation, 631 F.2d 1069, 1093 (3d Cir.1980).

Immediately after paying homage to the jury, a court will often step back and express ambivalence about the jury's role. Witness Justice O'Connor dissenting: "The jury system has long been a guarantor of fairness, a bulwark against tyranny, and a source of civic virtues. * * * But jurors are no infallible guardians of the public good. * * * Arbitrariness, caprice, passion, bias, and even malice can replace reasoned judgment and law as the basis for jury decisionmaking. Modern judicial systems therefore incorporate safeguards against such influences. * * * Courts long have recognized that jurors may view large corporations with great disfavor. * * * [J]uries may feel privileged to correct perceived social ills stemming from unequal wealth distribution by transferring money from 'wealthy' corporations to comparatively needier plaintiffs." TXO Production Corp. v. Alliance Resources Corp., 509 U.S. 443, 473, 490, 491 (1993).

If the plaintiff's damages are a jury decision, but if jurors are susceptible to impermissible influences, then the judge must channel and check the jury's discretion. Many damages issues lurk in the judge's other rulings. Which plaintiff is entitled to have a jury pass on which contentions? What evidence will the jury hear and consider? Will the trial judge submit the issues of the defendant's liability and the plaintiff's damages to the jury? How will the judge define the damages issues in the instructions to the jury? After the jury sets a plaintiff's damages, what form will the trial judge's and appellate courts' post-verdict judicial review take?

Whether the jury is a paragon or a pariah, most litigants in fact forgo a jury trial. The parties settle the great majority of damages lawsuits, leaving only a few to be tried to juries.

Several features of our civil justice system structure the litigants' private negotiation that usually leads them to settle: The plaintiff's contingency fee contract with her lawyer means that her attorney's fee will be paid from any settlement or recovery. Since potential defendants carry liability insurance, the defendant's insurance company chooses the lawyer who will defend the lawsuit, and the insurance carrier will indemnify the defendant for covered claims. In litigation, the plaintiff and the defendant develop and present facts with a minimum of judicial participation. The amount of the plaintiff's damages, which are numerical steps on a continuum from zero to infinite dollars, is more susceptible to compromise than the yes-no dichotomy of the defendant's liability.

The rules of procedure and evidence support the parties' incentives to settle litigation. The rules for pretrial conferences explicitly facilitate the parties' settlement. Fed.R.Civ.P. 16(a)(5), (c). The parties' settlement offers and negotiations are not admitted as evidence. Fed.R.Evid. 408. A litigant who rejects an opponent's settlement offer and receives a less-favorable judgment may be compelled to pay the adversary's costs. Fed.R.Civ.P. 68.

If most lawsuits are settled, may a lawyer safely forget about a jury trial and the damages rules? No, emphatically. The lawyers' predictions about the way a trial will come out determine litigants' pretrial bargaining positions. The parties will settle in light of the rules for the defendant's liability and the plaintiff's damages that potentially apply in a jury trial. A lawyer must understand the applicable damages rules from the beginning. And the trials that do occur have heightened importance because they set the standards for the private bargaining in the lawsuits that other litigants settle.

The damages lawsuits that parties try to juries are, however, not typical of all lawsuits. Look for these features in the decisions in this Chapter: one side is intransigent or has a reputation to protect, the outcome is uncertain, or the stakes are unusually high.

The chapter begins with property damages cases and several cases on personal injury damages. Two defenses to—or limitations on—a plaintiff's damages are avoidable consequences and collateral source. Punitive damages and attorney fees are often major parts of the plaintiff's money recovery; but neither compensates the plaintiff in the sense of recovery of money to substitute for her impaired substantive interest. Later Chapters develop remedies to protect and vindicate a plaintiff's property and contractual rights.

Actual and potential defendants fear jumbo verdicts. Critics who think the jury is expensive, emotional, irrational, and unpredictable argue for legislative and judicial tort reform to halt what they refer to as the "liability crisis" created by "runaway" jury verdicts. Many of the damages doctrines in this Chapter are on the tort reformer's agenda. The controversial doctrines include damages for pain and suffering, punitive damages, and the American Rule which requires each side to pay its own attorney fees. The groups that oppose tort reform almost unanimously praise the civil jury. The Chapter concludes with tort reform.

A. THE NATURE OF LEGAL DAMAGES

GAVCUS v. POTTS

United States Court of Appeals, Seventh Circuit, 1986.
808 F.2d 596.

FAIRCHILD, SENIOR CIRCUIT JUDGE. Constance Gavcus brought an action in district court against members of the Potts family for trespass and unlawful removal of silver coins from her home. The jury returned a special verdict finding an unauthorized removal of property and awarding Mrs. Gavcus the cost of installing new locks and an alarm, attorney's fees incurred in a prior action concerning the silver coins, and punitive damages. The district court set aside the jury's damage awards and entered judgment for Mrs. Gavcus for nominal damages of one dollar. Mrs. Gavcus appeals from that judgment.

Mr. Gavcus died in March of 1981. Lillian Potts was Mr. Gavcus' daughter by a prior marriage and was a residual beneficiary under her father's will. Lillian's family attended his funeral and left several days afterwards after staying with Mrs. Gavcus in her home. The Potts returned to Mrs. Gavcus' home the day after they left and, in her absence, removed a large quantity of silver coins valued at more than $150,000. The deputy who investigated the removal of the coins contacted Mrs. Potts, who later returned the coins to the sheriff's office. A couple of weeks later, Mrs. Gavcus hired an attorney to get the coins back for her. The attorney initiated a proceeding pursuant to § 968.20 of the Wisconsin Statutes [Editor's Note: This was an action under the Wisconsin criminal code to recover seized property.] for return of the coins. * * * The circuit court determined that the coins belonged to Mrs. Gavcus individually and ordered their return. * * * Mrs. Gavcus then brought the suit at bar for damages, including the attorney fees she incurred in the prior litigation.

Mrs. Gavcus did not claim any physical injury to the real property. The court did allow her to offer evidence of the cost of new locks and the burglar alarm she installed after the removal of the coins, and of the amount of attorney's fees incurred in the earlier litigation. Apparently the district court had some doubt as to the propriety of these items of damage and chose to admit the evidence and submit questions concerning those items in a special verdict, and to address the legal questions after the verdict was returned. The appeal arises from the court's determination that these items were not properly recoverable as damages. The jury had awarded by special verdict $3,126 for the cost of locks and a burglar alarm and $12,000 in attorney's fees.

Nominal compensatory damages can be awarded when no actual or substantial injury has been alleged or proved, since the law infers some damage from the unauthorized entry of land. Additionally, compensatory damages can be awarded for actual or substantial injury to realty. These latter damages are generally measured by the cost of restoring the property to its former condition or by the change in value before and after the trespass. Consequential damages can also be recovered for a trespass, since a trespasser is liable in damages for all injuries flowing from his trespass which are the natural and proximate result of it. One such compensable result of a trespass is personal injury to the owner of the land. If a trespass causes mental distress, the trespasser is liable in damages for the mental distress and any resulting illness or physical harm. [citations]

The installation of locks and a burglar alarm was not a repair of physical damage, and the cost was not recoverable as compensation for injury to property. Mrs. Gavcus' theory is that the trespass had caused an impairment of her sense of security and that the installation became reasonably necessary on account of that impairment.

We reject the theory, however, for two reasons. * * * [First,] there was a failure of proof as to the nature, extent, and causation of any emotional distress, or cost of required treatment.

Second, assuming that she could have proved that the trespass caused increased nervousness, uneasiness, and worry, she cites no authority, nor was any authority found, which shows that the cost of an improvement to property intended to alleviate distress of that type would be properly allowable as damages. * * *

In Wisconsin, attorney's fees incurred in a prior action are allowable as damages in a subsequent action only if the prior litigation was the natural and proximate result of the subsequent defendant's wrongful act and involved the plaintiff and a third party. [citations] Thus, to recover the $12,000 in attorney's fees which the jury awarded, Mrs. Gavcus must show that (1) because of the defendants' unlawful removal of the coins, (2) she became involved in litigation with a third party. We will first examine the requirement that the prior litigation involve a third party.

For a plaintiff to receive attorney's fees for prior litigation, the prior litigation must have been between the plaintiff and a third party; it cannot have been between the same parties that are involved in the subsequent lawsuit. [citations] * * *

Mrs. Gavcus asserts that the sheriff was the required third party. The sheriff, however, did not actively participate in the litigation, and seems to have been a mere stakeholder. By September of 1981, Mrs. Potts had appeared in the probate proceeding, seeking a determination of the title to the silver coins. Apparently, had the coins been the joint property of both Mr. and Mrs. Gavcus or an asset of the estate, Mrs. Potts' residual share would have been increased. Sometime between mid-March and December 1, 1981, the silver coins were transferred from the sheriff's possession to the possession of the personal representative. At the end of July, 1982, a trial was held on the issue of the ownership of the silver. The circuit court found that the coins were Mrs. Gavcus' individual property, obtained either through her own efforts or as gifts from Mr. Gavcus and ordered them returned to Mrs. Gavcus pursuant to her attorney's motion under § 968.20. The attorney's fees were incurred in this litigation over ownership of the coins. Whether the silver was owned jointly by Mr. and Mrs. Gavcus, was an asset of the estate, or was owned individually by Mrs. Gavcus was the essence of this entire dispute. The dispute was between Mrs. Potts and Mrs. Gavcus, both of whom were beneficiaries and both of whom are involved as parties in the case at bar. Since both the prior and present actions are between the same parties, attorney's fees are not recoverable. * * *

Even if the litigation over ownership had involved a third party, Mrs. Gavcus did not fulfill the other requirement for recovery of attorney's fees—the requirement that the prior litigation was a natural and proximate result of a wrongful act by the defendant. To fulfill this requirement, Mrs. Gavcus must show that the defendants' unauthorized removal of the coins caused her to enter into the litigation. Analysis of the facts shows that the prior litigation was not proximately caused by the defendants' removal of the coins.

Mrs. Potts knew of the coins' existence prior to her removal of them from the Gavcus home. The litigation was caused by her claim that the coins were jointly owned by her father and Mrs. Gavcus or were the property of the estate, not by her resort to self-help to obtain possession of them. Since the prior litigation did not result from the taking of the silver, the second part of the test is not met and attorney's fees cannot be awarded.

Attorney's fees are not available because the prior action was not against a third party and was not naturally and proximately caused by the Potts' conduct. Both parties agree that the award of punitive damages could not be sustained unless compensatory damages had been awarded. [citation]

The judgment appealed from is AFFIRMED.

Notes

1. Suppose that Mrs. Gavcus had testified that after her home was invaded she was sleepless, anxious, and depressed. Suppose further that her doctor had testified that Mrs. Gavcus needed the locks and alarms to sleep. Would the court have been more likely to have approved her recovery of the expense? Perhaps

2. *Punitive Damages.* Although the defendants may have committed intentional torts, they escape virtually unscathed. The purposes of punitive damages are to punish wrongdoers and to deter them and others from future misconduct. Would awarding Mrs. Gavcus punitive damages punish and deter these defendants? Would an award of punitive damages to her also vindicate the policies of forbidding conversion and trespass? Would they reimburse some of her litigation expense? If the

jury finds defendants' misconduct to have been sufficiently aggravated to warrant punitive damages, should the court require plaintiff to prove actual damages as a prerequisite for the plaintiff to recover punitive damages? No

1. PROOF OF THE EXISTENCE OF DAMAGES

DURA PHARMACEUTICALS, INC. v. BROUDO

Supreme Court of the United States, 2005.
544 U.S. 336.

JUSTICE BREYER delivered the opinion of the Court. A private plaintiff who claims securities fraud must prove that the defendant's fraud caused an economic loss. 15 U.S.C. § 78u–4(b)(4). We consider a Ninth Circuit holding that a plaintiff can satisfy this requirement—a requirement that courts call "loss causation"—simply by alleging in the complaint and subsequently establishing that "the price" of the security "*on the date of purchase* was inflated because of the misrepresentation." In our view, the Ninth Circuit is wrong, both in respect to what a plaintiff must prove and in respect to what the plaintiffs' complaint here must allege.

I. Respondents are individuals who bought stock in Dura Pharmaceuticals, Inc., on the public securities market between April 15, 1997, and February 24, 1998. They have brought this securities fraud class action against Dura and some of its managers and directors (hereinafter Dura) in federal court. In respect to the question before us, their detailed amended complaint makes substantially the following allegations:

(1) Before and during the purchase period, Dura (or its officials) made false statements concerning both Dura's drug profits and future Food and Drug Administration (FDA) approval of a new asthmatic spray device.

(2) In respect to drug profits, Dura falsely claimed that it expected that its drug sales would prove profitable.

(3) In respect to the asthmatic spray device, Dura falsely claimed that it expected the FDA would soon grant its approval.

(4) On the last day of the purchase period, February 24, 1998, Dura announced that its earnings would be lower than expected, principally due to slow drug sales.

(5) The next day Dura's shares lost almost half their value (falling from about $39 per share to about $21).

(6) About eight months later (in November 1998), Dura announced that the FDA would not approve Dura's new asthmatic spray device.

(7) The next day Dura's share price temporarily fell but almost fully recovered within one week.

Most importantly, the complaint says the following (and nothing significantly more than the following) about economic losses attributable to the spray device misstatement: *"In reliance on the integrity of the market, [the plaintiffs]* * * * *paid artificially inflated prices for Dura securities" and the plaintiffs suffered "damage[s]" thereby.*

The District Court dismissed the complaint. In respect to the plaintiffs' drug-profitability claim, it held that the complaint failed adequately to allege an appropriate state of mind, *i.e.,* that defendants had acted knowingly, or the like.

In respect to the plaintiffs' spray device claim, it held that the complaint failed adequately to allege "loss causation."

The Court of Appeals for the Ninth Circuit reversed. In the portion of the court's decision now before us—the portion that concerns the spray device claim—the Circuit held that the complaint adequately alleged "loss causation." The Circuit wrote that "plaintiffs establish loss causation if they have shown that the price *on the date of purchase* was inflated because of the misrepresentation." (emphasis in original). It added that "the injury occurs at the time of the transaction." Since the complaint pleaded "that the price at the time of purchase was overstated," and it sufficiently identified the cause, its allegations were legally sufficient.

Because the Ninth Circuit's views about loss causation differ from those of other Circuits that have considered this issue, we granted Dura's petition for certiorari. [citations] We now reverse.

II. Private federal securities fraud actions are based upon federal securities statutes and their implementing regulations. Section 10(b) of the Securities Exchange Act of 1934 forbids (1) the "use or [employment] * * * of any * * * deceptive device," (2) "in connection with the purchase or sale of any security," and (3) "in contravention of" Securities and Exchange Commission "rules and regulations." Commission Rule 10b–5 forbids, among other things, the making of any "untrue statement of material fact" or the omission of any material fact "necessary in order to make the statements made * * * not misleading."

The courts have implied from these statutes and Rule a private damages action, which resembles, but is not identical to, common-law tort actions for deceit and misrepresentation. [citations] And Congress has imposed statutory requirements on that private action. *E.g.,* 15 U.S.C. § 78u–4(b)(4).

In cases involving publicly traded securities and purchases or sales in public securities markets, the action's basic elements include:

(1) *a material misrepresentation (or omission),* [citation];

(2) *scienter, i.e.,* a wrongful state of mind, [citation];

(3) *a connection with the purchase or sale of a security,* [citation]

(4) *reliance,* often referred to in cases involving public securities markets (fraud-on-the-market cases) as "transaction causation," see Basic Inc. v. Levinson, 485 U.S. 224 248–249 (1988) (nonconclusively presuming that the price of a publicly traded share reflects a material misrepresentation and that plaintiffs have relied upon that misrepresentation as long as they would not have bought the share in its absence);

(5) *economic loss,* 15 U.S.C. § 78u–4(b)(4); and

(6) *"loss causation," i.e.,* a causal connection between the material misrepresentation and the loss, [citation].

Dura argues that the complaint's allegations are inadequate in respect to these last two elements.

A. We begin with the Ninth Circuit's basic reason for finding the complaint adequate, namely, that at the end of the day plaintiffs need only "establish," *i.e.,* prove, that "the price *on the date of purchase* was inflated because of the misrepresentation." In our view, this statement of the law is wrong. Normally, in cases such as this one (*i.e.,* fraud-on-the-market cases), an inflated purchase price will not itself constitute or proximately cause the relevant economic loss.

For one thing, as a matter of pure logic, at the moment the transaction takes place, the plaintiff has suffered no loss; the inflated purchase payment is offset by ownership of a share that *at that instant* possesses equivalent value. Moreover, the logical link between the inflated share purchase price and any later economic loss is not invariably strong. Shares are normally purchased with an eye toward a later sale. But if, say, the purchaser sells the shares quickly before the relevant truth begins to leak out, the misrepresentation will not have led to any loss. If the purchaser sells later after the truth makes its way into the market place, an initially inflated purchase price *might* mean a later loss. But that is far from inevitably so. When the purchaser subsequently resells such shares, even at a lower price, that lower price may reflect, not the earlier misrepresentation, but changed economic circumstances, changed investor expectations, new industry—specific or firm—specific facts, conditions, or other events, which taken separately or together account for some or all of that lower price. (The same is true in respect to a claim that a share's higher price is lower than it would otherwise have been—a claim we do not consider here.) Other things being equal, the longer the time between purchase and sale, the more likely that this is so, *i.e.,* the more likely that other factors caused the loss.

Given the tangle of factors affecting price, the most logic alone permits us to say is that the higher purchase price will *sometimes* play a role in bringing about a future loss. It may prove to be a necessary condition of any such loss, and in that sense one might say that the inflated purchase price suggests that the misrepresentation (using language the Ninth Circuit used) "touches upon" a later economic loss. But, even if that is so, it is insufficient. To "touch upon" a loss is not to *cause* a loss, and it is the latter that the law requires. 15 U.S.C. § 78u–4(b)(4).

For another thing, the Ninth Circuit's holding lacks support in precedent. Judicially implied private securities—fraud actions resemble in many (but not all) respects common-law deceit and misrepresentation actions. [citations] The common law of deceit subjects a person who "fraudulently" makes a "misrepresentation" to liability "for pecuniary loss caused" to one who justifiably relies upon that misrepresentation. Restatement (Second) of Torts § 525, p. 55 (1977) (hereinafter Restatement of Torts). And the common law has long insisted that a plaintiff in such a case show not only that had he known the truth he would not have acted but also that he suffered actual economic loss. See, *e.g.*, Pasley v. Freeman, 3 T.R. 5:1, 100 Eng. Rep. 450, 457 (1789) (if "no injury is occasioned by the lie, it is not actionable: but if it be attended with a damage, it then becomes the subject of an action"). * * *

Finally, the Ninth Circuit's approach overlooks an important securities law objective. The securities statutes seek to maintain public confidence in the marketplace. See United States v. O'Hagan, 521 U.S. 642, 658 (1997). They do so by deterring fraud, in part, through the availability of private securities fraud actions. [citation] But the statutes make these latter actions available, not to provide investors with broad insurance against market losses, but to protect them against those economic losses that misrepresentations actually cause. * * *

The statutory provision at issue here and the paragraphs that precede it emphasize this last mentioned objective. Private Securities Litigation Reform Act of 1995. The statute insists that securities fraud complaints "specify" each misleading statement; that they set forth the facts "on which [a] belief" that a statement is misleading was "formed"; and that they "state with particularity facts giving rise to a strong inference that the defendant acted with the required state of mind." 15 U.S.C. §§ 78u–4(b)(1), (2). And the statute expressly imposes on plaintiffs "the burden of proving" that the defendant's misrepresentations "caused the loss for which the plaintiff seeks to recover." § 78u–4(b)(4).

The statute thereby makes clear Congress' intent to permit private securities fraud actions for recovery where, but only where, plaintiffs adequately allege and prove the traditional elements of causation and loss. By way of contrast, the Ninth Circuit's approach would allow recovery where a misrepresentation leads to an inflated purchase price but nonetheless does not proximately cause any economic loss. That is to say, it would permit recovery where these two traditional elements in fact are missing.

In sum, we find the Ninth Circuit's approach inconsistent with the law's requirement that a plaintiff prove that the defendant's misrepresentation (or other fraudulent conduct) proximately caused the plaintiff's economic loss. We need not, and do not, consider other proximate cause or loss-related questions.

B. Our holding about plaintiffs' need to *prove* proximate causation and economic loss leads us also to conclude that the plaintiffs' complaint here failed adequately to *allege* these requirements. We concede that the Federal Rules of Civil Procedure require only "a short and plain statement of the claim showing that the pleader is entitled to relief." Fed. Rule Civ. Proc. 8(a)(2). And we assume, at least for argument's sake, that neither the Rules nor the securities statutes impose any special further requirement in respect to the pleading of proximate causation or economic loss. But, even so, the "short and plain statement" must provide the defendant with "fair notice of what the plaintiff's claim is and the grounds upon which it rests." Conley v. Gibson, 355 U.S. 41, 47 (1957). The complaint before us fails this simple test.

As we have pointed out, the plaintiffs' lengthy complaint contains only one statement that we can fairly read as describing the loss caused by the defendants' "spray device" misrepresentations. That statement says that the plaintiffs "paid artificially inflated prices for Dura's securities" and suffered "damage[s]." The statement implies that the plaintiffs' loss consisted of the "artificially inflated" purchase "prices." The complaint's failure to claim that Dura's share price fell significantly after the truth became known suggests that the plaintiffs considered the allegation of purchase price inflation alone sufficient. The complaint contains nothing that suggests otherwise.

For reasons set forth in Part II–A, *supra,* however, the "artificially inflated purchase price" is not itself a relevant economic loss. And the complaint nowhere else provides the defendants with notice of what the relevant economic loss might be or of what the causal connection might be between that loss and the misrepresentation concerning Dura's "spray device." * * *

[I]t should not prove burdensome for a plaintiff who has suffered an economic loss to provide a defendant with some indication of the loss and the causal connection that the plaintiff has in mind. At the same time, allowing a plaintiff to forgo giving any indication of the economic loss and proximate cause that the plaintiff has in mind would bring about harm of the very sort the statutes seek to avoid. Cf. H.R. Conf. Rep. No. 104–369, p. 31 (1995) (criticizing "abusive" practices including "the routine filing of lawsuits * * * with only a faint hope that the discovery process might lead eventually to some plausible cause of action"). It would permit a plaintiff "with a largely groundless claim to simply take up the time of a number of other people, with the right to do so representing an *in terrorem* increment of the settlement value, rather than a reasonably founded hope that the [discovery] process will reveal relevant evidence." Blue Chip Stamps v. Manor Drug Stores, 421 U.S. 723, 741 (1975). Such a rule would tend to transform a private securities action into a partial downside insurance policy. See H.R. Conf. Rep. No. 104–369, at 31.

For these reasons, we find the plaintiffs' complaint legally insufficient. We reverse the judgment of the Ninth Circuit, and we remand the case for further proceedings consistent with this opinion. It is so ordered.

Notes

1. The tort of misrepresentation that evolved from the common law form of action "trespass on the case" retains the rule that damages are a substantive element of the plaintiff's tort cause of action: no damages, no cause of action. Threatened future harm to the plaintiff will not suffice for a damages action. The plaintiff may not prove that a defendant violated a technical right and recover nominal damages. Contrast the tort of trespass to land which evolved from the "trespass" form of action, as in *Gavcus*, where actual damages are not a substantive element and the plaintiff may sue a defendant for a technical violation and recover nominal damages.

2. *Procedure Revisited.* In *Dura,* for the first time, the Court encountered a complaint that flunked Rule 8(a). There is a difference between formal and substantive insufficiency. A plaintiff's formally insufficient complaint fails to give the defendant adequate notice of a viable legal theory. In a substantively insufficient complaint, plaintiffs' adequately pleaded theory fails to state a claim. Is the complaint in *Dura* formally or substantively insufficient? Plaintiffs may amend a complaint that the defendant hasn't answered. But how?

3. *Loss Causation.* The Supreme Court focuses on loss causation: Defendants' misrepresentation caused the plaintiff's loss.

Suppose that defendants' false statements have inflated the market value of the stock. Why has Buyer no loss when he buys? Would it suffice for Buyer to allege that Dura stock's price fell when the truth became known? Why may Buyer not have a loss when he sells? Must Buyer negate all alternative explanations? Is the purpose of the securities statutes to prevent a stock buyer's loss, or to prevent a stock buyer's loss caused by an issuer's misrepresentation?

4. *Tort Reform?* *Dura* makes it easier for a defendant to defeat a securities class action. In fraud-on-the-market litigation, a shareholder-plaintiff must connect the defendants' misrepresentation with plaintiffs' loss in value. Since many things can cause a stock's price to decline, plaintiffs must show more than an inflated price to connect the defendants' misrepresentation with the plaintiffs' loss.

5. *Looking Ahead.* Uncertainty frequently complicates the plaintiff's recovery of damages. Since the plaintiff's negligence action evolved from the "trespass on the case" form of action, it also retained the rule that damages are a substantive element of the plaintiff's tort. The plaintiff may sue the defendant for an injunction, the subject of the next chapter, if she is at risk of irreparable injury in the future. But the plaintiff may not prove that a defendant negligently violated a technical right and recover nominal damages.

Here is a problem to carry us through the following material to Henry v. Dow Chemical. Plaintiff Henrico has been exposed to defendant's Powco's known carcinogen, for example asbestos or dioxin. Although she has no present physical injury, for as long as 40 years Henrico must live with an enhanced risk of developing a serious disease and perhaps a premature death. Plaintiff who cannot now present expert evidence that she is has a 51% probability of cancer will not be able to recover for that. Pollock v. Johns–Manville Sales Corp., 686 F.Supp. 489 (D.N.J. 1988); Mauro v. Raymark Industries, Inc., 116 N.J. 126, 561 A.2d 257 (1989).

Henrico is at risk, she is afraid, and she expects medical expenses for tests. For her recovery for her increased risk, see Youst v. Longo which is next. In the decision in the Note that follows Youst v. Longo, the *Ayres* Court took up her emotional distress; the Court made a crucial distinction between another plaintiff, one with a physical injury, and one like her, without injury. In Henry v. Dow Chemical, the next case, the Michigan court dealt with her medical expenses for tests.

YOUST v. LONGO

Supreme Court of California, 1987.
43 Cal.3d 64, 233 Cal.Rptr. 294, 729 P.2d 728.

Lucas, Justice. Is a racehorse owner entitled to tort damages when the harness driver of another horse negligently or intentionally interferes with the owner's horse during a race, thereby preventing the owner from the chance of winning a particular cash prize? It is a well-settled general tort principle that interference with the *chance* of winning a contest, such as the horserace at issue here, usually presents a situation too uncertain upon which to base tort liability. We agree that application of this principle should govern here. * * *

Plaintiff Harlan Youst entered his standardbred trotter horse, Bat Champ, in the eighth harness race at Hollywood Park in Inglewood, California. Also entered in the race was The Thilly Brudder, driven by defendant, Gerald Longo. During the race, defendant allegedly drove The Thilly Brudder into Bat Champ's path and struck Bat Champ with his whip, thereby causing the horse to break stride. Bat Champ finished sixth while The Thilly Brudder finished second. The Board reviewed the events of the race and disqualified The Thilly Brudder, which moved Bat Champ into fifth place, entitling plaintiff to a purse of only $5,000.[1]

Plaintiff filed a complaint for damages asserting [intentional interference with prospective economic advantage]. Plaintiff sought as compensatory damages the difference in prize money between Bat Champ's actual finish and the finish which allegedly would have occurred but for defendant's interference. Plaintiff requested compensatory damages in three alternative amounts, namely, the purse amount for either first, second or third place (less the fifth place prize of $5,000 which Bat Champ has already received). Ascertainment of the amount of actual damages apparently would require a finding as to the position in which Bat Champ would have finished but for defendant's interference. Punitive damages of $250,000 were also sought. * * *

Each of the three counts in the complaint purports to state a claim for loss of prospective economic advantage, rather than for physical personal injury or property damage. The torts of negligent or intentional interference with prospective economic advantage require proof of various elements as a prerequisite to recovery. However, as a matter of law, a threshold causation requirement exists

---

1. [Footnotes renumbered.] The purse for the race was $100,000 distributed as follows: the   winner received $50,000; second place received $25,000; third place received $12,000; fourth

for maintaining a cause of action for either tort, namely, proof that it is reasonably *probable* that the lost economic advantage would have been realized but for the defendant's interference. * * *

Determining the probable expectancy of winning a *sporting* contest but for the defendant's interference seems impossible in most if not all cases, including the instant case. Sports generally involve the application of various unique or unpredictable skills and techniques, together with instances of luck or chance occurring at different times during the event, any one of which factors can drastically change the event's outcome. In fact, certain intentional acts of interference by various potential "defendant" players may, through imposition of penalties or increased motivation, actually allow the "victim" player or team to prevail. Usually, it is impossible to predict the outcome of most sporting events without awaiting the actual conclusion.

The Restatement Second of Torts specifically addresses the speculative nature of the outcome of a horse race. The relevant comment is contained in a "Special Note on Liability for Interference With Other Prospective Benefits of a Noncontractual Nature." The comment states that various possible situations may justify liability for interference with prospective economic benefits of a noncommercial character. Special mention is given to "[c]ases in which the plaintiff is wrongfully deprived of the expectancy of winning a race or a contest, when he has had *a substantial certainty or at least a high probability of success.* For example, the plaintiff is entered in a contest for a large cash prize to be awarded to the person who, during a given time limit, obtains the largest number of subscriptions to a magazine. At a time when the contest has one week more to run and the plaintiff is leading all other competitors by a margin of two to one, the defendant unjustifiably strikes the plaintiff out of the contest and rules him ineligible. In such a case there may be sufficient certainty established so that the plaintiff may successfully maintain an action for loss of the prospective benefits. *On the other hand, if the plaintiff has a horse entered in a race and the defendant wrongfully prevents him from running, there may well not be sufficient certainty to entitle the plaintiff to recover.* * * * " (Rest.2d Torts, § 774B, special note, pp. 59–60, italics added.)

As indicated by the Restatement comment, certain contests may have a higher probability of ultimate success than others. To this end, the cases cited by the Court of Appeal here, awarding damages to competitors in contests, are distinguishable because in each case there was a high probability of winning.[2] In addition to the Restatement position, one older case has specifically held that the loss of a chance to win a prize purse at a trotting horse race was too speculative to support tort liability. (See Western Union Tel. Co. v. Crall (1888) 39 Kan. 580, 18 P. 719.)

Applying the foregoing analysis to the instant case, it seems clear that plaintiff's complaint fails adequately to allege facts showing interference with a *probable* economic gain, i.e., that Bat Champ would have won this horserace, or

---

place received $8,000, and fifth place received $5,000.

2. Nor are we persuaded by the Court of Appeal's argument that damages should be allowed for the value of the lost chance of benefit. (See Schaefer, Uncertainty and the Law of Damages (1978) 19 Wm. & Mary L.Rev. 719.) Under this approach, plaintiff would not recover the full value of the lost prize but that value discounted by the probability of winning in the absence of defendant's interference. We believe this calculation is incorporated in the basic analysis for interference with prospective economic advantage; the speculative nature of the chance of winning is examined in establishing the first element of the tort as opposed to determining specific damages after recognizing a cause of action. In the instant case, the potential economic advantage is simply too speculative to allow *any recovery.*

at least won a larger prize, if defendant had not interfered. Here, the complaint only alleged in conclusory terms that defendant's wrongful interference resulted in a lost "opportunity" to finish higher in the money. The complaint merely indicated that defendant's maneuvers and whipping forced Bat Champ to break stride and fall out of contention.[3]

We conclude, as a matter of law, that the threshold element of probability for interference with prospective economic advantage was not met by the facts alleged. * * *

Notes

1. *Nothing or All?* Would the plaintiff in *Youst* have succeeded if he had convinced the court that, if not nobbled, "Bat Champ" would have had a "high probability" of a better finish? Should the judge instead admit the expert's evidence, instruct the jury that the law does not compensate speculative injury, and let the jury decide? The idea of a specific breaking point leads to the "all-or-nothing" approach, a methodology that denies any recovery for a less-than-even chance.

2. *Lost Chance.* Academic writers favor allowing the plaintiff to recover the value of the lost chance regardless of the exact probabilities involved. The *Youst* court cites Professor Schaefer's thoughtful article in a footnote, but it rejects his reasoning.

Earlier decisions which adopted the "value of the chance" approach to uncertainty issues were breach of contract cases where the plaintiff lost a chance for a prize in a contest. The best known is Chaplin v. Hicks, 2 K.B. 786 (1911) where the plaintiff, one of 50 contestants for 12 prizes in a beauty contest, lost any chance of winning because she was not properly notified of appearance time. Another is Kansas City, Mexico & Orient Railway v. Bell, 197 S.W. 322 (Tex.Civ.App. 1917). A railroad breached a contract to deliver hogs in time for a contest and the plaintiff received a second instead of a possible first prize. Mange v. Unicorn Press, 129 F.Supp. 727 (S.D.N.Y. 1955) is a third. Plaintiff's answer to a puzzle contest was erroneously marked "wrong." If the answer had not disqualified him, he would have become one of a pool of 23,548 contestants to compete for 210 prizes including a $307,500 first prize. Figure the value of that chance. Finally consider McDonald v. John P. Scripps Newspaper, 210 Cal.App.3d 100, 257 Cal.Rptr. 473 (1989). A disappointed contestant in a spelling bee sued alleging that the contest officials allowed an ineligible candidate to compete. In dismissing the complaint, the trial judge stated, "I see a gigantic causation problem * * * common sense tells me this lawsuit is nonsense."

If a plaintiff could be compensated for the value of a lost chance according to the statistical probability value of that chance, the substantive requirement of "damages" for the *existence* of a cause of action would be virtually eliminated. Anything over 0% chance would keep the plaintiff in court. The prospect of increased litigation has less appeal to the judiciary than to statistically minded analysts. But read on.

3. *Lost Chance to Survive.* A wrongful death plaintiff who cannot prove that more probably than not their decedent would have survived except for the defendant's negligence may argue for recovery based on the value of the decedent's chance

---

3. Presented in plaintiff's opposition to the demurrer were the following additional facts: "As the horses entered in the eighth race rounded the last turn, Bat Champ *began to make his move* to the lead of the group. As his move progressed, Defendant drove his horse into Bat Champ's path and thereafter whipped Bat Champ with his whip. Bat Champ's advance was halted, his stride broken and his *chances* at finishing 'in the money' ended." (Italics added.) Further, at oral argument, plaintiff asserted that the alleged interference took place 100 yards from the finish line. However, despite these asserted facts, Bat Champ's chance of placing higher in the purse money remained highly speculative.

of survival that the defendants' negligence caused him to lose. How to measure that value was the issue in Smith v. State Department of Health and Hospitals, 676 So.2d 543 (La.1996).

After an x-ray revealed a mediastinal mass, defendants failed to follow-up or to treat Benjamin Smith, and his fatal cancer was not diagnosed until 15 months later. After Smith died, his family sued defendant for wrongful death. Defendant argued that no damages were caused because Smith's death was likely anyway.

The intermediate appellate "court concluded that the evidence preponderated to show that the Department's negligence was a substantial factor in depriving Smith of a ten percent chance of surviving for five years. Fixing the total damages at $764,347, the court reduced this amount proportionate to the lost ten percent chance of survival and awarded a total of $76,434 to Mrs. Smith and her two minor children."

The Louisiana supreme court, aware that "little attention has been given to the complex issue we focus on today of the appropriate methodology for calculating the value of the loss of a chance of survival," "recognized three possible methods of valuation of the loss of a chance of survival in professional malpractice cases."

"The first, and the method we adopt today in this decision, is for the factfinder—judge or jury—to focus on the chance of survival lost on account of malpractice as a distinct compensable injury and to value the lost chance as a lump sum award based on all the evidence in the record, as is done for any other item of general damages.

"The second method, as advocated by plaintiffs, is to allow full survival and wrongful death damages for the loss of life partially caused by malpractice, without regard to the chance of survival. We reject this argument, agreeing with the court of appeal that full recovery is not available for deprivation of a chance of survival of less than fifty percent. To allow full recovery would ignore the claimants' inability to prove by a preponderance of the evidence that the malpractice victim would have survived but for the malpractice, which is a requirement for full recovery.

"The third method, and the method adopted by the court of appeal in this case, is to compute the compensable chance as 'the percentage probability by which the defendant's tortious conduct diminished the likelihood of achieving some more favorable outcome.' Joseph H. King, Jr., Causation, Valuation and Chance in Personal Injury Torts Involving Preexisting Conditions and Future Consequences, 90 Yale L.J. 1353, 1382 (1981). * * *

"Our point of disagreement with the court of appeal's method * * * is its rigid use of a precise mathematical formula, based on imprecise percentage chance estimates applied to estimates of general damages that never occurred, to arrive at a figure for an item of general damages that this court has long recognized cannot be calculated with mathematical precision. [citations] When these total hypothetical damages are reduced by a numerical factor determined from evidence of percentage rates of survival for certain periods after discovery of the disease at various stages of the disease, the uncertainty progresses geometrically. * * *

"The jury will be allowed to consider an abundance of evidence and factors, including evidence of percentages of chance of survival along with evidence such as loss of support and loss of love and affection, and any other evidence bearing on the value of the lost chance. The jury's verdict of a lump sum amount of damages can be tested on appeal for support in the record by reviewing the percentage chances and the losses incurred by the tort victim and his or her heirs, and any other relevant evidence, thus providing assurance against speculative verdicts."

The dissenter favored the percentage-probability test and maintained that "the majority's approach * * * allows the jury to simply arrive at a damage figure without properly explaining the basis of the figure. This 'rabbit-out-of-the-hat' approach will be virtually impossible to review on appeal under the manifest error standard. The reviewing court will have little idea of what chance of survival the jury determined was lost, thus little basis to determine if the jury was manifestly erroneous."

4. What are our problem plaintiff Henrico's prospects of recovering for her risk of cancer under Youst v. Longo and the lost chance decisions?

5. *Recovery for the Plaintiff's Fear of Cancer.* Under the Federal Employers' Liability Act, may a plaintiff whose asbestosis was caused by exposure on the job to the defendant's asbestos include damages for fear of cancer as part of his pain and suffering damages? The Supreme Court said yes. The Court distinguished an earlier decision that an exposed but disease-free plaintiff may not recover for emotional distress. However, the present plaintiff's "emotional distress claims brought on by a physical injury" was one where "pain and suffering recovery is permitted." Once a defendant is liable for any of plaintiff's physical harm, it is also liable for the plaintiff's "genuine and serious" emotional distress from the harm or from the defendant's conduct that caused the harm. Thus the plaintiff's pain and suffering recovery included recovery for fear of cancer. On the other hand, for plaintiff's "stand-alone emotional distress claims not provoked by any physical injury" the majority said that "recovery is sharply circumscribed by the zone-of-danger test." Norfolk & Western Railway v. Ayers, 538 U.S. 135 (2003).

Questions? (a) Where does *Ayers* leave problem plaintiff Henrico's claim for fear of developing cancer? (b) Two Railroad employees Paul and Pete are equally exposed to asbestos. Paul develops asbestosis, but Pete does not. Paul and Pete have equal probabilities of developing cancer. Both Paul and Pete fear cancer. Under *Ayers*, Paul, the one with asbestosis, recovers for fear of cancer, but his fellow employee Pete does not. Are these results consistent? fair?

6. *Medical Monitoring.* Problem plaintiff Henrico's future risk could have come about in several ways, a dangerous worksite, a disaster, a defective product, or the industrial pollution in Henry v. Dow Chemical below. Plaintiffs have several possible substantive theories for a toxic tort—strict liability for hazardous activity, nuisance, trespass, or negligence. The latter is plaintiffs' substantive theory in Henry v. Dow Chemical.

The plaintiff's present and future expense of dealing with her future risk comes under the remedial tag of medical monitoring. Although the plaintiff's medical monitoring remedy is neither recovery for increased risk of a serious malady nor recovery for emotional distress, it is related to both as follows: Defendant has breached its legal duty by releasing a harmful substance; plaintiff has been exposed to defendant's harmful substance; plaintiff, although lacking present symptoms, has an increased risk of developing a serious disease in the future; early detection and attention through medical monitoring will both reduce the plaintiff's ongoing emotional distress and ameliorate the disease's future onset. But someone has to pay for the regimen of early detection and attention. On the one hand, the plaintiff may have medical insurance. On the other hand, the court may employ the medical monitoring remedy to pass this cost to the defendant.

A court may use the medical monitoring remedy to require the defendant to pay for the plaintiffs' medical attention; that facilitates plaintiffs' ability to have disease diagnosed and treated promptly; and by requiring the defendant to internalize the cost of the danger, it deters pollution. Redland Soccer Club, Inc. v. Department of the Army, 548 Pa. 178, 696 A.2d 137, 146–47 (1997).

Medical monitoring lawsuits have been plaintiff class actions. A class action and either a contingency fee contract or a common fund attorney fee recovery will suffice to attract a specialist law firm to maintain the complex litigation.

Lawyers and judges have developed three sub-types of medical monitoring remedies: (a) Defendant pays a lump sum to each individual plaintiff for her future medical attention. (b) Plaintiffs' doctors send medical monitoring bills to defendant. (c) A court-supervised medical monitoring program like the plaintiffs in Henry v. Dow Chemical below sought: when people in the plaintiff class are vulnerable and at risk because of the defendant's pollution or contamination, the court orders the defendant to set up a supervised program to examine and observe the plaintiffs to detect major health problems early.

The three types of medical monitoring remedies involve different procedures. The first type, lump sum damages, would be a federal Rule 23(b)(3) damages class. The third type, seeking a court-supervised program, would be a federal Rule 23(b)(2) class action for an injunction. Procedures for notice and preclusion differ. We usually think of a jury trial for damages, a (b)(3) plaintiff class, but not for an equitable remedy under (b)(2); but courts' solutions have not been so neat, some requiring a jury trial for some parts of a (b)(2) medical-monitoring trial.

If the plaintiffs in Henry v. Dow Chemical are seeking an equitable remedy, why did your editor put the decision in the Damages chapter instead of in the Equity chapter that follows? *Henry* deals with the damages concepts that we are studying; plaintiffs suffer a "loss" that doesn't qualify as a legal "injury" or "damages." And the equitable remedy plaintiffs sought would require the defendant to pay money.

HENRY v. DOW CHEMICAL COMPANY

Supreme Court of Michigan, 2005.
473 Mich. 63, 701 N.W.2d 684.

CORRIGAN, J. The 173 plaintiffs in this matter have asked to represent a putative class of thousands in an action against defendant, The Dow Chemical Company. Their core allegation is that Dow's plant in Midland, Michigan, negligently released dioxin, a synthetic chemical that is potentially hazardous to human health, into the Tittabawassee flood plain where the plaintiffs and the putative class members live and work.

This situation appears, at first blush, to have the makings of a standard tort cause of action. But closer inspection of plaintiffs' motion for class certification reveals that one of plaintiffs' claims is premised on a novel legal theory in Michigan tort law and thus raises an issue of first impression for this Court.

In an ordinary "toxic tort" cause of action, a plaintiff alleges he has developed a disease because of exposure to a toxic substance negligently released by the defendant. In this case, however, the plaintiffs do not allege that the defendant's negligence has actually caused the manifestation of disease or physical injury. Instead, they allege that defendant's negligence has created the *risk* of disease—that they *may* at some indefinite time in the future develop disease or physical injury because of defendant's allegedly negligent release of dioxin.

Accordingly, the plaintiffs have asked the circuit court to certify a class that collectively seeks the creation of a program, to be funded by defendant and supervised by the court, that would monitor the class and their representatives for possible future manifestations of dioxin—related disease. The defendant moved for summary disposition, arguing that plaintiffs' medical monitoring claim was not cognizable under Michigan law. The circuit court denied this motion. * * *

We now reverse the circuit court order denying the motion and remand for entry of summary disposition in favor of defendant on plaintiffs' medical monitoring claim. Because plaintiffs do not allege a *present* injury, plaintiffs do not present a viable negligence claim under Michigan's common law. * * * We therefore remand this matter to the circuit court for entry of summary disposition in defendant's favor on plaintiffs' medical monitoring claim.

FACTS AND PROCEDURAL HISTORY. Defendant, The Dow Chemical Company, has maintained a plant on the banks of the Tittabawassee River in Midland, Michigan, for over a century. The plant has produced a host of products, including, to name only a few, "styrene, butadiene, picric acid, mustard gas, Saran Wrap, Styrofoam, Agent Orange, and various pesticides including Chlorpyrifos, Dursban and 2, 4, 5–trichlorophenol." Michigan Department of Community Health, Division of Environmental and Occupational Epidemiology, *Pilot Exposure Investigation: Dioxin Exposure in Adults Living in the Tittabawassee River Flood Plain, Saginaw County, Michigan,* May 25, 2004, p. 4.

According to plaintiffs and published reports from the MDEQ, [Michigan Department of Environmental Quality] defendant's operations in Midland have had a deleterious effect on the local environment. In 2000, General Motors Corporation was testing soil samples in an area near the Tittabawassee River and the Saginaw River when it discovered the presence of dioxin, a hazardous chemical believed to cause a variety of health problems such as cancer, liver disease, and birth defects. By spring 2001, the MDEQ had confirmed the presence of dioxin in the soil of the Tittabawassee flood plain. Further investigation by the MDEQ indicated that defendant's Midland plant was the likely source of the dioxin. [citation]

In March 2003, plaintiffs moved for certification of two classes in the Saginaw Circuit Court. The first class was composed of individuals who owned property in the flood plain of the Tittabawassee River and who alleged that their properties had declined in value because of the dioxin contamination. The second group consisted of individuals who have resided in the Tittabawassee flood plain area at some point since 1984 and who seek a court-supervised program of medical monitoring for the possible negative health effects of dioxin discharged from Dow's Midland plant. This latter class consists of 173 plaintiffs and, by defendant's estimation, "thousands" of putative members.

Defendant moved * * * for summary disposition of plaintiffs' medical monitoring claim. The Saginaw Circuit Court denied this motion, and denied defendant's subsequent motions for reconsideration and for a stay of proceedings. * * * [T]he defendant sought emergency leave to appeal in this Court. * * * [O]n June 3, 2004, we stayed the proceedings below and granted defendant's application for leave to appeal.

In January 2005, defendant entered into a settlement agreement with the MDEQ regarding dioxin contamination in the Tittabawassee River valley. [citation] The agreement, which was reached after months of negotiation, provides that defendant will fund extensive cleanup efforts aimed at minimizing residents' exposure to dioxin.

STANDARD OF REVIEW. We review de novo the circuit court's denial of defendant's motion for summary disposition. * * * A movant is entitled to summary disposition [citation] if "[t]he opposing party has failed to state a claim on which relief can be granted." [citation] * * *

ANALYSIS. I. * * * Plaintiffs' theory is that Dow negligently released dioxin into the Tittabawassee flood plain and that, as a result, plaintiffs must incur the costs of intensive medical monitoring for the possible health effects of elevated exposure to dioxin. Thus, at its core, plaintiffs' medical monitoring claim is one of negligence. It is usually held that in order to state a negligence claim on which relief may be granted, plaintiffs must prove (1) that defendant owed them a duty of care, (2) that defendant breached that duty, (3) that plaintiffs were injured, and (4) that defendant's breach caused plaintiffs' injuries. [citations] * * *

Here, defendant argues that plaintiffs have not established any present physical injuries, and have therefore failed to state a valid negligence claim. We agree. As an initial matter, it is necessary for us to determine the exact nature of plaintiffs' claim. We must decide whether plaintiffs are in fact seeking compensation for future injuries they *may* suffer, or for present injuries they *have* suffered.

If plaintiffs' claim is for injuries they may suffer in the future, their claim is precluded as a matter of law, because Michigan law requires more than a merely speculative injury. This Court has previously recognized the requirement of a present physical injury in the toxic tort context. In Larson v. Johns–Manville Sales Corp., 427 Mich. 301, 314, 399 N.W.2d 1 (1986), for example, we held that a cause of action for asbestosis, which typically is manifest between ten and forty years after exposure, arises only when an injured party knows or should know that he has, in fact, developed asbestosis. Similarly, we held that a cause of action for asbestos-related lung cancer arises only when there has been a "discoverable appearance" of cancer. Thus, *Larson* squarely rejects the proposition that mere exposure to a toxic substance and the increased risk of future harm constitutes an "injury" for tort purposes. It is a *present* injury, not fear of an injury in the future, that gives rise to a cause of action under negligence theory.

Here, it is clear that plaintiffs do not claim that they have suffered any present physical harm because of defendant's allegedly negligent contamination of the Tittabawassee flood plain. Indeed, plaintiffs in their arguments to this Court expressly deny having any present physical injuries.

Plaintiffs have not cited an exception to the rule that a present physical injury is required in order to state a claim based on negligence. Nor, indeed, does the dissent. We can therefore reach only one conclusion: if the alleged damages cited by plaintiffs were incurred in anticipation of possible future injury rather than in response to present injuries, these pecuniary losses are not derived from an injury that is cognizable under Michigan tort law.

However, if plaintiffs' claim is that by virtue of their potential exposure to dioxin they have suffered an "injury," in that any person so exposed would incur the additional expense of medical monitoring, then their claim is also precluded as a matter of law, because Michigan law requires an actual injury to person or property as a precondition to recovery under a negligence theory.

As noted in this opinion, the elements that a plaintiff in a negligence action must prove are usually summed up in the familiar four-part test: (1) duty, (2) breach, (3) causation, and (4) damages. Although these four elements are usually the primary focus of a negligence analysis, it has always been implicit in this analysis that in order to prevail, a plaintiff must also demonstrate an actual *injury* to person or property. Indeed, such injury constitutes the essence of a plaintiff's claim. * * *

While the courts of this state may not have always clearly articulated this injury requirement, nor finely delineated the distinction between an "injury" and the "damages" flowing therefrom, the injury requirement has always been present in our negligence analysis. It has simply always been the case in our jurisprudence that plaintiffs alleging negligence claims have also shown that their claims arise from present physical injuries. We are not aware of any Michigan cases in which a plaintiff has recovered on a negligence theory without demonstrating some present physical injury. * * *

Plaintiffs effectively urge us to expand our common-law jurisprudence by concluding that the traditional four-part test can be met without also satisfying the requirement of a present physical injury, no doubt aware that we have never before been squarely presented with such a claim. Until now, there has never been a need for this Court to articulate specifically the injury requirement. But in light of the novel nature of plaintiffs' claims, however, it has become necessary for us to do so today. We therefore reaffirm the principle that a plaintiff must demonstrate a present physical injury to person or property *in addition to* economic losses that result from that injury in order to recover under a negligence theory.

This requirement does not constitute a change in the common law of this state. While we have from time to time allowed for the development of the common law as circumstances have required, [citation] the injury requirement has always been an implicit part of a negligence action in Michigan. Had we been presented in 1869 with an action against a blacksmith by local residents alleging that the blacksmith's emissions caused them the fear of physical injury *someday,* we have little doubt that this Court would have expressly articulated the injury requirement at that time. However, such a case has never before been presented to this Court, so it falls to us today to articulate what this Court has always assumed: present harm to person or property is a necessary prerequisite to a negligence claim.

The requirement of a present physical injury to person or property serves a number of important ends for the legal system. First, such a requirement defines more clearly who actually possesses a cause of action. In allowing recovery only to those who have actually suffered a present physical injury, the fact-finder need not engage in speculations about the extent to which a plaintiff possesses a cognizable legal claim. [citation] Second, such a requirement reduces the risks of fraud, by setting a clear minimum threshold—a present physical injury—before a plaintiff can proceed on a claim. By requiring a prospective plaintiff to make a showing of an actual physical injury, present tort law thus excludes from the courts those who might bring frivolous or unfounded suits. In particular, the fact-finder need not be left wondering whether a plaintiff has in fact been harmed in some way, when nothing but a plaintiff's own allegations support his cause of action.

Finally, and perhaps most significantly, the requirement of a present physical injury avoids compromising the judicial power. The exercise of the "judicial power" by this Court, Const. 1963, art. 6, § 1, contemplates that there will be standards—legally comprehensible standards that guide the judicial branch's resolution of the matters brought before it. The present physical injury requirement establishes a clear standard by which judges can determine which plaintiffs have stated a valid claim, and which plaintiffs have not. In the absence of such a requirement, it will be inevitable that judges, as in the instant case, will be required to answer questions that are more appropriate for a legislative than a judicial body: How far from the Tittabawassee River must a plaintiff live in order to have a cognizable claim? What evidence of exposure to dioxin will be required to support such a claim? What level of medical research is sufficient to support a claim that exposure to dioxin, in contrast to exposure to another chemical, will give rise to a cause of action?

Here, it is apparent that the only "injuries" alleged by the putative representatives of the medical monitoring class are "the losses they have and will suffer as they are forced to monitor closely their health and medical condition because of their exposure to Dow's Dioxin [sic] pollution." Thus, plaintiffs have arguably stated a present *financial* injury, i.e., damages. From this description, however, it is apparent that plaintiffs do not claim that they suffer from *present physical* injuries to person or property. Rather, plaintiffs allege that they *may* develop dioxin-related illnesses in the future. At best, then, the only "injury" from which plaintiffs suffer at present is a *fear of future illness*. They seek an "equitable remedy" of a medical monitoring program not in order to redress actual or present injury to their persons but instead to screen for possible future injury. * * *

It is no answer to argue, as plaintiffs have, that the need to pay for medical monitoring is *itself* a present injury sufficient to sustain a cause of action for negligence. In so doing, plaintiffs attempt to blur the distinction between "injury" and "damages." While plaintiffs arguably demonstrate economic losses that would otherwise satisfy the "damages" element of a traditional tort claim, the fact remains that these economic losses are wholly derivative of a *possible, future* injury rather than an *actual, present* injury. A financial "injury" is simply not a present physical injury, and thus not cognizable under our tort system. Because plaintiffs have not alleged a present physical injury, but rather, "bare" damages, the medical expenses plaintiffs claim to have suffered (and will suffer in the future) are not compensable. * * *

Here, as noted, the only noneconomic injury alleged by plaintiffs is their fear of future physical injury. Plaintiffs' fear, however reasonable, is still not enough to state a claim of negligence. Even if we were to construe plaintiffs' claim broadly as one for emotional distress, our common law recognizes emotional distress as the basis for a negligence action only when a plaintiff can also establish *physical* manifestations of that distress. Thus, plaintiffs have not established a present, legally cognizable injury.

Plaintiffs advance their claim as if it satisfies the traditional requirements of a negligence action in Michigan. In reality, plaintiffs propose a transformation in tort law that will require the courts of this state—in this case and the thousands that would inevitably follow—to make decisions that are more characteristic of those made in the legislative, executive, and administrative processes. * * * [W]e are not prepared to acquiesce in this transformation. * * *

II. Having determined that plaintiffs' claim cannot stand under our current law of negligence, we turn now to plaintiffs' core argument—that we should *modify* the common law of negligence in order to permit their medical monitoring claim to proceed.

This Court is the principal steward of Michigan's common law. [citations] Acting in this capacity, we have on occasion allowed for the development of the common law as circumstances and considerations of public policy have required. But * * * our common-law jurisprudence has been guided by a number of prudential principles. [citation] Among them has been our attempt to "avoid capricious departures from bedrock legal rules as such tectonic shifts might produce unforeseen and undesirable consequences," a principle that is quite applicable to the present case.

Plaintiffs have asked us to recognize a cause of action that departs drastically from our traditional notions of a valid negligence claim. Beyond this enormous shift in our tort jurisprudence, judicial recognition of plaintiffs' claim may also have undesirable effects that neither we nor the parties can satisfactorily predict. For example, recognizing a cause of action based solely on exposure— one without a requirement of a *present* injury—would create a potentially limitless pool of plaintiffs. * * *

Litigation of these preinjury claims could drain resources needed to compensate those with manifest physical injuries and a more immediate need for medical care. It is less than obvious, therefore, that the benefits of a medical monitoring cause of action would outweigh the burdens imposed on plaintiffs with manifest injuries, our judicial system, and those responsible for administering and financing medical care. Because such a balancing process would necessarily require extensive fact-finding and the weighing of important, and sometimes conflicting, policy concerns, and because here we lack sufficient information to assess intelligently and fully the potential consequences of our decision, we do not believe that the instant question is one suitable for resolution by the judicial branch.

We are certainly not alone in our reluctance to engage in the delicate balancing of costs and benefits that plaintiffs' proposed expansion of the common law requires. Many of these concerns were noted by the United States Supreme Court in Metro–North Commuter R. Co. v. Buckley, 521 U.S. 424 (1997). (holding that the Federal Employers' Liability Act does not permit recovery of future medical monitoring costs). There, the Court observed that judicial recognition of mere exposure to a toxic substance as a sufficient trigger for tort liability could lead to a stampede of litigation that would divert resources from more immediate and compelling claims, such as those brought by individuals with actual disease or injury, to less meritorious claims. * * *

We share the concerns raised by the United States Supreme Court in *Buckley.* Simply put, judicial recognition of a medical monitoring cause of action may do more harm than good—not only for Michigan's economy but also for "other potential plaintiffs who are not before the court and who depend on a tort system that can distinguish between reliable and serious claims on the one hand, and unreliable and relatively trivial claims on the other." *Buckley.*

Even if this Court were institutionally equipped to gauge the potential costs and benefits of sanctioning a medical monitoring cause of action, plaintiffs have done little to help us understand the ramifications that a decision in their favor might have for Michigan. When pressed at oral argument to address the potential costs and benefits of plaintiffs' proposed cause of action, for example, plaintiffs' counsel was unable to hazard a guess at how Michigan's economy might be affected. * * *

This * * * goes to the heart of why we are reluctant to alter the common law of negligence in the manner proposed by plaintiffs: however much equity might favor lightening the economic burden now borne by parties exposed to dioxin in the Tittabawassee flood plain, we have no assurance that a decision in plaintiffs' favor—which would create a hitherto unrecognized cause of action with a potentially limitless class of plaintiffs—will not wreak enormous harm on Michigan's citizens and its economy. Such a decision necessarily involves a drawing of lines reflecting considerations of public policy, and a judicial body is ill-advised to draw such lines given the limited range of interests represented by the parties and the resultant lack of the necessary range of information on which to base a resolution. * * *

We would be unwise, to say the least, to alter the common law in the manner requested by plaintiffs when it is unclear what the consequences of such a decision may be and when we have strong suspicions, shared by our nation's highest court, that they may well be disastrous.

III. * * * [T]here is a stronger prudential principle at work here: the judiciary's obligation to exercise caution and to defer to the Legislature when called upon to make a new and potentially societally dislocating change to the common law.

Ours, after all, is a government founded on the principle of separation of powers. In certain instances, the principle of separation of powers is an affirmative constitutional bar on policy-making by this Court. In other cases, however, the separation of powers considerations may operate as a *prudential* bar to judicial policy-making in the common-law arena. This is so when we are asked to modify the common law in a way that may lead to dramatic reallocation of societal benefits and burdens. As shown above, plaintiffs have sought a radical change in our negligence jurisprudence and have provided no guidance on how this proposed change might affect Michigan. In effect, we have been asked to craft public policy in the dark. This problem alone ought to make any reasonably prudent jurist extremely wary of granting the relief sought by the plaintiffs.

In addition to the problems presented by the legal question whether a medical monitoring cause of action exists, we are faced with the more practical questions of *how* such a monitoring program would work. For example, a threshold concern would likely be the determination of eligibility for participation in such a program. Such a determination involves the consideration of a number of practical questions and the balancing of a host of competing interests—a task more appropriate for the legislative branch than the judiciary.

Of equal concern would be the administration of such a program. The day-to-day operation of a medical monitoring program would necessarily impose huge clerical burdens on a court system lacking the resources to effectively administer such a regime. Nor do the courts possess the technical expertise necessary to effectively administer a program heavily dependent on scientific disciplines such as medicine, chemistry, and environmental science. The burdens of such a system would more appropriately be borne by an administrative agency specifically created and empowered to administer such a program. The court system, in our view, is simply not institutionally equipped to establish, promulgate operative rules for, or administer such a program.

The propriety of judicial deference to the legislative branch in expanding common-law causes of action is further underscored where, as here, the Legislature has already created a body of law that provides plaintiffs with a remedy. * * *

In this case, the Legislature has already provided a method for dealing with the negligent emission of toxic substances such as dioxin. The Natural Resources and Environmental Protection Act (NREPA), [citation], empowers the MDEQ to deal with the environmental and health effects of toxic pollution. * * *

[T]he Legislature has authorized the MDEQ to address precisely the sort of environmental and health risks occasioned by Dow's alleged emission of dioxin into the Tittabawassee flood plain. Not only is the MDEQ specifically authorized under the NREPA to undertake "health assessments" and "health effect studies," [citation] but the department is also empowered to take "other actions that may be necessary to prevent, minimize, or mitigate injury to the public health, safety, or welfare, or to the environment." [citation] Indeed, as plaintiffs' counsel acknowledged at oral arguments, the MDEQ *has* been involved in the remediation of the Tittabawassee dioxin contamination and has engaged in a pilot medical monitoring program of residents.

Plaintiffs believe, however, that the MDEQ's response has been insufficient—that the department lacks the funding necessary to engage in medical monitoring on the scale they would prefer. It is apparent, therefore, that the plaintiffs are asking this Court to create a new remedy—a cause of action for medical monitoring—where the Legislature has already signaled its preference with respect to the appropriate form a remedy should take. In deference to the policy-making branch of our government, we decline to create this alternative remedial regime.

IV. We have established that plaintiffs' medical monitoring claim is not cognizable under our current law and that recognition of this claim would require both a departure from fundamental tort principles and a cavalier disregard of the inherent limitations of judicial decision-making. For these reasons, defendant is entitled to summary disposition of plaintiffs' medical monitoring claim. We need address only one remaining argument: plaintiffs' contention that their request for a medical monitoring program is not subject to summary disposition * * * because it is a claim for equitable, as opposed to legal, relief.

Plaintiffs' reliance on the nature of the relief they seek essentially puts the cart before the horse. Regardless of what sort of remedy a plaintiff requests, we must nevertheless determine whether that remedy is supported by a valid claim. As the Kentucky Supreme Court recently observed, "It is not the remedy that supports the cause of action, but rather the cause of action that supports a remedy." Wood v. Wyeth–Ayerst Labs., 82 S.W.3d 849, 855 (Ky., 2002). Here, plaintiffs have pleaded a cause of action based on a theory of negligence and have argued that we should expand the common law of torts in order to permit their medical monitoring claim to proceed. Plaintiffs never attempt to characterize their claim as an equitable cause of action, and point to no case law where a similar tort-based claim is held to create an equitable cause of action.

* * * [P]laintiffs' claim is not cognizable under our current law of negligence and is not within a permissible expansion of the common law. Neither, perforce, is the claim based in equity. A court cannot "create substantive rights under the guise of doing equity," or "confer rights" where none exists. Stein v. Simpson, 37 Cal.2d 79, 83 (1951). Therefore, regardless of whether the relief plaintiffs seek is equitable or legal in nature, defendant was entitled to summary

disposition regarding plaintiffs' medical monitoring cause of action because plaintiffs have not stated a valid cause of action.

V.   Although the dissenting opinion is passionately argued and, no doubt, well-intentioned, it is rooted in a number of fundamental misconceptions about the applicable law and about our majority opinion. Some of these errors have already been noted and need no further discussion. But three particular inaccuracies in the dissent warrant special mention.

First, the dissent argues that our holding makes "plaintiffs' physical health * * * secondary to defendant's economic health." But our opinion does no such thing. We take no position on whether defendant should or should not pay for the costs of monitoring for dioxin-related disease. Rather, we hold that plaintiff has not stated a claim under our current tort law and that the determination whether that law should change to accommodate plaintiffs' claims belongs, in our view, to the people's representatives in the Legislature. * * *

Second, the dissenting opinion casts our opinion as one leaving injured plaintiffs without a remedy. * * * But our opinion does not hold that a party who actually contracts a dioxin-related disease will be foreclosed from recovery. On the contrary, assuming such a person could show physical harm and causation, the four elements of a traditional negligence claim would be met. Upon such a showing, that person would be entitled to full compensation for the injury in the same manner as any other person injured by another's negligence.

The dissent's overwrought rhetoric aside, the question is not *whether* an injured party should recover for Dow's contamination of the environment but *when* a party may be considered "injured" under Michigan tort law and recover for Dow's negligence. Justice Cavanagh may prefer a system in which polluters' resources are doled out on a first-come, first-served basis. He may be comfortable with the notion that such a regime runs the risk of diverting limited resources from those devastated by cancer, birth defects, and other dioxin-related diseases to those who have yet to manifest dioxin-related illness. He is entitled to these beliefs. But his beliefs are not reflected in our common law of negligence and, given the potential repercussions of his first-come, first-served notions of justice, his vision should be turned into law, if at all, by the Legislature.

This point leads to the dissenting opinion's third and most troubling error: Justice Cavanagh's complete disregard for the effects that our decision may have on those other than the parties at bar. For example, the dissent asserts that our concerns about the effects that a decision in plaintiffs' favor might have are unfounded given the nature of the relief that plaintiffs request. * * * The dissent asserts, in effect, that we need not trouble ourselves about recognizing plaintiffs' proposed cause of action because they seek a medical monitoring program rather than a cash payment. What this argument ignores, of course, is that medical monitoring is not without cost.

Moreover, the dissent overlooks the fact that recognizing a cause of action before manifest injury in this case will allow *other* causes of action for negligence before manifest injury. The dissent's disdain for our "concerns about financial impact" can be sustained only by disregarding the effect that these other preinjury actions might have on the state's economy. To recognize a medical monitoring cause of action would essentially be to accord carte blanche to any moderately creative lawyer to identify an emission from any business enterprise anywhere, speculate about the adverse health consequences of such an emission, and thereby seek to impose on such business the obligation to pay the medical costs of a segment of the population that has suffered no actual medical harm.

Worse still is the dissenting opinion's failure to consider the possible human toll of its approach. Indeed, our dissenting colleague is offended at our suggestion that allowing these plaintiffs to recover might limit resources available to those who show manifest physical injury:

"I can think of no greater misdeed than to actually argue that allowing *these plaintiffs* to seek the equitable remedy of requiring this defendant to pay for the *costs* of necessary medical monitoring tests somehow would divert resources from children with birth defects. This is fabrication at its most unforgivable— refusing to acknowledge that providing plaintiffs with the opportunity to merely seek an equitable remedy is well with the bounds of judicial discretion and will not devastate the economy or cause sick children to die." (emphasis in original).

This is an argument that can be sustained only if one believes that we live in a world in which every tortfeasor has unlimited resources to compensate those affected by its negligence. Ours, of course, is not that sort of world. Those who do wrong necessarily have a limited capacity to compensate those who suffer from their wrongdoing. * * *

Our nation's experience with asbestos litigation has shown that this concern was well-founded. It is therefore quite puzzling that our dissenting colleague would show such a blithe disregard for the real-world effects of his invocation of equity in this case.

Equity is indeed an instrument of justice. But when it is exercised without due regard for the interests of those who are not before the Court, its invocation can lead to great injustice. It is precisely because a decision in plaintiffs' favor may have sweeping effects for Michigan's citizens and its economy that we believe this matter should be handled by those best able to balance these competing interests: the people's representatives in the Legislature.

CONCLUSION. We conclude that the trial court erred in denying defendant's motion for summary disposition regarding plaintiffs' medical monitoring claim. The cause of action proposed by plaintiffs is not cognizable under Michigan law. Accordingly, we remand this matter to the Saginaw Circuit Court for entry of an order of summary disposition in defendant's favor with regard to plaintiffs' medical monitoring cause of action.

MICHAEL F. CAVANAGH, J. (*dissenting*). The proper issue in this case is whether defendant must pay for plaintiffs' medical monitoring costs. However, rather than simply address this basic issue, the majority chooses to use this case as a vehicle to raise fears about the economy and hypothesize that providing medical monitoring to these plaintiffs would result in our state's economic disaster. The majority erroneously presents this case as one in which it must choose between an equitable remedy for plaintiffs and the economic viability of defendant and of our state. Because the dichotomy the majority has constructed is a false one, I must dissent.

At its core, this case is about rights and responsibilities. Defendant is undeniably responsible for years of actively contaminating the air, water, and soil that surrounds plaintiffs' homes. Defendant is undeniably responsible for the suffering that plaintiffs must endure as they face years of wondering if the contamination that they and their children have been exposed to will result in devastating illnesses and their untimely deaths. Thus, the issue is who should pay for plaintiffs' medical monitoring costs under the unique circumstances of this case when it is clear that defendant is responsible for the wrong that prompted the need for plaintiffs to be medically monitored. Stated differently, where defendant has contaminated the environment, should plaintiffs, defendant, or the taxpayers of the state of Michigan pay plaintiffs' medical monitoring costs? Whatever the majority's intent, the result of disregarding the only question properly posed in this case is that plaintiffs' physical health is inexcusably deemed secondary to defendant's economic health.

I. PLAINTIFFS PRESENT A REASONABLE CLAIM FOR MEDICAL MONITORING COSTS. Plaintiffs are owners and residents of property located within the one-hundred-year flood plain of the Tittabawassee River in Saginaw County. The Michigan Department of Environmental Quality (MDEQ) found as much as 7,300 parts per trillion (ppt) of dioxin in the flood plain, which substantially exceeds Michigan's cleanup standard of ninety ppt for direct residential contact. * * * After the MDEQ conducted testing, it determined that defendant was the source of the pollution. Because of the health risks that plaintiffs may face, plaintiffs seek a court-supervised medical monitoring program that is administered by qualified health professionals. * * *

Exposure to dioxin can cause cancer, liver disease, birth defects, miscarriages, and reproductive damage, as well as other illnesses. Children are more significantly affected by dioxin than adults. Dioxins do not break down easily. Once dioxin is released into the environment, it stays in the environment for an extremely long time. When dioxin gets into a person's body, it stays indefinitely in a person's blood and body fat. Because dioxin stays in the body for a long time, the adverse effects of dioxin exposure may not be immediate.

Plaintiffs' counsel stated at oral argument that a pilot study of the community conducted by the Michigan Department of Community Health found that fifty to eighty percent of the people tested have dioxin levels that put them in the 75th to the 95th percentile compared to the national average for their age and gender.

The majority notes that defendant has entered into a settlement agreement [with MDEQ] in which "defendant will fund extensive cleanup efforts aimed at minimizing residents' exposure to dioxin." The specifics of this agreement indicate that defendant is willing to pay for items such as landscaping some homes to cover exposed soil and augmenting some ground cover in public parks; however, defendant remains unwilling to pay for any necessary medical monitoring costs as a result of its dioxin contamination.

II. PLAINTIFFS' CLAIM FOR MEDICAL MONITORING WARRANTS EQUITABLE RELIEF. Plaintiffs' request for a court-supervised medical monitoring program that is administered by qualified health professionals is undoubtedly reasonable. Plaintiffs merely request that defendant pay the cost of medical monitoring to ensure that dioxin-related illnesses are caught at their earliest. Plaintiffs simply seek to minimize the devastating effects of illnesses caused by defendant's acts.

The majority * * * argues that plaintiffs' rights have not been actually violated and they have suffered no injuries and, therefore, no damages. With this, I vehemently disagree. Plaintiffs have suffered actual harm and damages— the heightened exposure to dioxin that they received because of defendant's acts is akin to an injury. Plaintiffs were exposed to dioxin at *over eighty times* the level deemed safe for direct residential contact. Plaintiffs were advised that routine activities, such as flower gardening and lawn work, could further increase their risk of dioxin exposure. [citation] Plaintiffs were further advised that they should avoid allowing their children to play in the soil to avoid further contamination. If it were not for defendant's acts, plaintiffs would not be obliged to incur the expenses involved in additional testing for early detection of any illnesses caused by the increased dioxin exposure. In this case, the exposure itself and the need for medical monitoring constitute the injury. [citation]

Plaintiffs can also offer facts sufficient to establish causation, contrary to the majority's assertion. As noted by the majority, defendant's Midland plant was identified as the "principal source of dioxin contamination in the Tittabawassee River sediments and the Tittabawassee River flood plain soils." Given the facts, it is entirely reasonable for plaintiffs to argue that they would not have to undergo medical monitoring tests for dioxin poisoning but for the actions of defendant. To argue that there are insufficient facts to support plaintiffs' argument is a willful avoidance of the record.

Notably, my belief that these plaintiffs should be allowed to seek equitable relief does not mean that I advocate that *any* exposure allows a person to bring a claim for medical monitoring costs. That position would indeed be imprudent. However, in this case, a candid review of the facts indicates that plaintiffs' heightened exposure has caused them harm and plaintiffs have no adequate legal remedy. While plaintiffs may not have yet developed dioxin-related illnesses, the fact remains that they are at a much greater risk because of defendant's acts. As such, their long-term exposure to dioxin has caused a change in the medical monitoring that plaintiffs would otherwise be prescribed. For example, according to reasonably accepted medical practice, doctors do not generally prescribe testing to determine a patient's dioxin level. However, in this case, because of the prolonged exposure to high levels of dioxin, a doctor may, according to accepted scientific principles, find that such tests are reasonably necessary to best monitor and treat a patient. When these tests are ordered, defendant should be responsible for paying the costs of the tests because defendant is responsible for the *need* for the tests.

Plaintiffs do not, as the majority asserts, advocate for "a cause of action that departs drastically from our traditional notions of a valid negligence claim" and seek a "radical change" in negligence law. Also, contrary to the majority's assertion, Larson v. Johns–Manville Sales Corp., 427 Mich. 301, 304–305 (1986), does not affect the decision before the Court today. *Larson* dealt with the statute of limitations for causes of action for asbestosis and cancer related to asbestos exposure. This Court held that a cause of action for asbestosis or cancer related to asbestos exposure accrues when a person learns or should learn that he has developed asbestosis or cancer, not when he was first exposed to asbestos. This was necessary because the underlying claims in *Larson* were wrongful death actions premised on *asbestosis and cancer*. A person cannot bring a wrongful death claim for asbestosis until the victim *actually has asbestosis*. But *Larson* has no effect on whether plaintiffs can seek an equitable remedy for a court-supervised medical monitoring program that is administered by health professionals.

Medical monitoring is recognized in a number of jurisdictions. [citations] Moreover, because of the latent nature of most illnesses resulting from exposure to dioxin, plaintiffs may not be able to establish an immediate physical injury of the type contemplated by a traditional tort action. [citations] But merely because an illness is latent does not mean that plaintiffs have not been injured and suffered damages.

A plaintiff who is involved in an automobile accident and suffers no observable physical injury but nevertheless undergoes medically necessary diagnostic tests to determine whether internal injuries exist is no doubt entitled to recover the costs of the examination. If accepted medical practice also deemed it necessary to perform such tests in the future, in order to detect the onset of any subsequently developing injury caused by the accident, the costs of the continued tests would be recoverable. * * * The outcome should be the same when the operative incident is toxic exposure rather than collision and the potential future harm is disease rather than physical impairment. Miranda v. Shell Oil Co., 17 Cal.App.4th 1651, 1657 (1993).

Because of the established facts in this case, a court-supervised medical monitoring program that is administered by qualified health professionals is a viable and equitable remedy for plaintiffs to seek that is nonpreclusive of any future damages claim. [citation] An equitable remedy is necessary because there is no adequate legal remedy for plaintiffs. [citations] "The absence of precedents, or novelty in incident, presents no obstacle to the exercise of the jurisdiction of a court of equity, and to the award of relief in a proper case." 30A CJS, Equity, Effect of Absence of Precedents, § 10. "The essence of a court's equity power lies in its inherent capacity to adjust remedies in a feasible and practical way to eliminate the conditions or redress the injuries caused by unlawful action." Freeman v. Pitts, 503 U.S. 467, 487 (1992).

It is within the sound discretion of the courts whether to offer equitable relief. [citation] Regardless of how plaintiffs may have characterized their pleadings, "[t]he court has equitable jurisdiction to provide a remedy where none exists at law, even if the parties have not specifically requested an equitable remedy, whenever the pleadings sufficiently give notice of a party's right to relief and demand for judgment." 30A CJS, Equity, Lack of Remedy at Law as Ground and Limit of Jurisdiction, § 18; [citations] However, contrary to the majority's assertion, plaintiffs indeed ask for equitable relief as it relates to medical monitoring. Plaintiffs' complaint states that they have no adequate remedy at law and they seek "equitable/injunctive relief in the form of a medical monitoring program."

While the majority argues that the separation of powers precludes it from allowing plaintiffs to proceed, I strongly disagree. The majority's framing of the issue and its subsequent argument allow it to claim that "[w]e take no position on whether defendant should or should not pay for the costs of monitoring for dioxin-related disease." The majority's argument is essentially that its hands are tied because the Legislature has not acted. But this argument ignores a basic tenet of our system of jurisprudence—courts have the inherent power to provide equitable remedies. [citations] The majority's steadfast insistence that it cannot allow plaintiffs to proceed because the Legislature has not acted allows the majority to sidestep the issue, instead of explicitly stating and supporting its position that these plaintiffs are unworthy of relief.

Because principles of equity are firmly entrenched in our justice system, plaintiffs' position would not require this Court to depart from longstanding principles fundamental to our justice system. "The purpose of equity is to do complete justice in a case where a court of law is unable, because of the inflexibility of the rules by which it is bound, to adapt its judgment to the special circumstances of the case." 27A Am. Jur. 2d, Equity, Nature, Purpose, and Distinguishing Features, § 2. "[E]quity is the perfection of the law, and is always open to those who have just rights to enforce where the law is inadequate." Grand Lodge of the Ancient Order of United Workmen of the State of Michigan v. Child, 70 Mich. 163, 172 (1888). Allowing plaintiffs to merely *proceed* to seek a court-supervised medical monitoring program under equity principles certainly does not stray from the foundations of Anglo–American law.

III.   EQUITABLE RELIEF PROPERLY PLACES THE RESPONSIBILITY FOR ANY MEDICAL MONITORING COSTS ON DEFENDANT, THE PARTY RESPONSIBLE FOR IMPOSING THE COSTS ON PLAINTIFFS. Throughout its opinion, the majority invokes the fear of a ruined economy to support its decision. But the majority's prediction of a ruined economy falters after examining the true nature of the equitable relief that plaintiffs are seeking. Notably, allowing plaintiffs to seek medical monitoring costs would not result in a windfall for plaintiffs. [citations] Notably, these *plaintiffs would receive no money whatsoever.* Payments for doctor-prescribed testing would be made through a court-supervised fund. This fund would only compensate plaintiffs for medical monitoring costs actually incurred after the monitoring was ordered by a qualified health professional. The only "benefit" that a plaintiff would receive is payment for tests ordered by a doctor that are above and beyond what would generally be ordered for that plaintiff.

This is in contrast to the relief sought in Metro–North Commuter R. Co. v. Buckley, 521 U.S. 424, 439–441 (1997). In *Metro–North,* an employee sought a change in the common law that would permit a lump-sum damages award for medical monitoring costs. * * * As Justice Ginsburg, concurring in part and dissenting in part, in *Metro–North,* noted, "If I comprehend the Court's enigmatic decision correctly, Buckley [the employee] may replead a claim for relief and recover for medical monitoring, but he must receive that relief in a form other than a lump sum."

Notably, the majority's concerns about financial impact can actually be alleviated to a great degree by allowing plaintiffs' practical, proactive approach. A court-supervised medical monitoring program administered by qualified health professionals would provide early detection to plaintiffs and likely *lessen* the fiscal damages that defendant would be liable for if dioxin-related illnesses are discovered later. The early detection of illnesses may allow treatment to proceed in a more reasonable manner, often with more options for the person affected than if detection had been delayed. [citations] Plaintiffs' counsel clearly articulated just such an example of the benefits of medical monitoring:

> Let me give you a very clear example of how medical monitoring would work in an instance like this. Say there's a woman of child bearing age and her blood is tested for high levels of dioxin and she is found to have high levels of dioxin, 95th percentile or so in her body. Medical doctors who are familiar with dioxin contamination say well one of the possible results of having high levels of dioxin contamination in your blood is that you may have depressed thyroid function. So they do a very simple test, a standard test for thyroid function and find out that there is depression of thyroid function. She is then treated and birth defects that are linked to depressed thyroid function do not happen to her [child]. She does not have a child with a birth defect because that preventative measure prevented that irreparable harm. * * *

Notably, the majority fails to mention that plaintiffs would not be *forced* to engage in medical monitoring tests if they chose not to. A court-supervised medical monitoring program would allow plaintiffs to make a choice, and those who choose to be monitored and who meet the requirements set forth by qualified health professionals could be monitored. * * *

Also, contrary to the majority, I do not believe that an equitable remedy should be refused merely because administering the remedy may be inconvenient or even difficult. * * * Indeed, the desegregation of our nation's schools was certainly not an easy task, yet the United States Supreme Court found that overseeing this process was an appropriate equitable remedy for the courts. Brown v. Bd. of Ed. of Topeka, 349 U.S. 294, 300 (1955) ("Traditionally, equity has been characterized by a practical flexibility in shaping its remedies and by a facility for adjusting and reconciling public and private needs."). I certainly believe that a court in our state, just as courts have done in other states, can determine a suitable way to administer a medical monitoring program. [citations]

Finally, not content to merely present this case as one in which allowing plaintiffs to seek an equitable remedy would devastate the economy of Michigan, the majority also seeks to pit plaintiffs against "those devastated by cancer, birth defects, and other dioxin-related diseases." While the majority accuses the dissent of countless transgressions, I can think of no greater misdeed than to actually argue that allowing *these plaintiffs* to seek the equitable remedy of requiring this defendant to pay for the *costs* of necessary medical monitoring tests somehow would divert resources from children with birth defects. This is fabrication at its most unforgivable—refusing to acknowledge that providing these plaintiffs with the opportunity to merely seek an equitable remedy is well within the bounds of judicial discretion and will not devastate the economy or cause sick children to die.

IV. A FURTHER REVIEW OF THE ECONOMIC CONSIDERATIONS OF PLAINTIFFS' CLAIM INDICATES THAT EQUITABLE RELIEF IS PROPER. At its core, this is not a complex case. Defendant contaminated the environment with dioxin. Because of defendant's conduct, plaintiffs require medical monitoring to ensure that the negative effects of defendant's acts can be best countered. Medical monitoring costs money. Plaintiffs, defendant, or the taxpayers of the state of Michigan must pay the costs. Because plaintiffs only require medical monitoring as a result of defendant's conduct, it seems clear that it is reasonable that defendant pay the costs. The theory behind a claim for medical monitoring is simple. When a plaintiff is exposed to a hazardous substance, it is often sound medical practice to seek periodic medical monitoring to ascertain whether the plaintiff has contracted a disease. Because this need for medical monitoring was caused by a defendant's tortious acts or omissions, a defendant may be required to pay the cost of monitoring. This is not meant to punish defendant; it merely seeks to hold defendant to the reasonable standard that a polluter pays for the costs of polluting. "The mere fact that a wrongdoer may suffer, however, will not deter equity from granting relief to an injured party." 27A Am. Jur. 2d, Equity, § 102.

The majority's decision that plaintiffs cannot seek equitable relief is indefensible when one realizes that its position leaves plaintiffs who cannot afford to pay for doctor-prescribed medical monitoring with no recourse. * * * As plaintiffs' counsel stated, researchers conducting the pilot studies "have been besieged by people begging to have their blood tested and particularly begging to get their children tested because it's very difficult to do that by yourself. * * * it's really, really hard for individuals to get them done because it's cost prohibitive and beyond that it's just not available to them as individuals."

Whatever its intent, the majority's result protects a wrong-doing corporation at the expense of the health of the people wronged. But we cannot turn a blind eye to defendant's repeated contamination of our state's environment because holding defendant accountable may negatively affect its profits. If defendant cannot produce its product without behaving responsibly, then it has no business operating within our state. The lives of the people in the affected area are worth more than defendant's financial well-being, even if it were indeed at stake. And contrary to the majority's position, I am fully aware of the "real-world effects" of today's decision, as plaintiffs most certainly will be as well. The "real-world effects" are that defendant, the party responsible for plaintiffs' need for medical monitoring, will not bear any of the costs of its wrongdoing. Rather, the burden now falls on plaintiffs' shoulders.

The decision to turn our backs on plaintiffs because we have not yet faced a case so egregious violates the trust that the people of the state of Michigan have placed in us. * * * Where a claim is equitable in nature, exercising discretion may be necessary to ensure that an unconscionable decree is not entered. Kratze v. Independent Order of Oddfellows, 442 Mich. 136, 142 (1993). And that discretion most certainly should be exercised in this case.

While no one can say with certainty which plaintiffs will contract illnesses, suffer, and die because of their increased exposure to dioxin, this does not mean that plaintiffs cannot seek an equitable remedy. The unfortunate reality is that dioxin causes cancer, birth defects, and other illnesses. The prolonged exposure of plaintiffs to such high levels of dioxin puts them at a vastly increased risk. When a qualified health professional believes that it is in a patient's best interest to administer medical testing that would not be required if it were not for defendant's acts, this Court should not deny plaintiffs the ability to seek this modest remedy.

V. THE "REMEDY" OFFERED BY THE NATURAL RESOURCES AND ENVIRONMENTAL PROTECTION ACT DOES NOT PRECLUDE PLAIN-TIFFS' CAUSE OF ACTION. The majority states that the Legislature has already provided plaintiffs with a remedy because the "Natural Resources and Environmental Protection Act (NREPA) empowers the MDEQ to deal with the environmental and health effects of toxic pollution." While the MDEQ *may* take responsive action, it is not *required* to take action. Further, the fact that the MDEQ may choose to take responsive action to minimize injury to the public health does not absolve defendant of its responsibility to plaintiffs. While the majority repeatedly claims to be concerned about the effect on Michigan's economy if plaintiffs are allowed to bring a claim against defendant, the majority's approach shifts the costs resulting from defendant's actions to Michigan taxpayers. The MDEQ's ability to act does not eliminate defendant's responsibility to plaintiffs or eliminate the fact that plaintiffs can seek a court-supervised medical monitoring program funded by defendant. * * *

Finally, the concern of the MDEQ is *public* health, but what the MDEQ may deem appropriate to protect the public as a whole, even assuming sufficient funds were available in the budget, is not necessarily what may be in an individual plaintiff's best medical interest. Further, the MDEQ does not purport that its study can be extrapolated to provide relevant information to other people in the affected areas. * * * The majority's insistent and inexplicable refusal to hold defendant accountable for its acts allows defendant to escape responsibility for its actions and leaves plaintiffs with no adequate remedy.

VI. CONCLUSION. Today, the majority holds that defendant's egregious long-term contamination of our environment and the resulting negative health effects to plaintiffs are just another accepted cost of doing business. But as long as defendant is not held responsible for the decisions it makes, it behooves corporations like defendant to continue with business practices that harm our residents because the courts will shield them from liability by claiming that they are powerless to act. And it is the people of our state who will pay the costs—with their money and with their lives—of allowing defendant to contaminate our environment with no repercussions. Sadly, this Court has resorted to a cost-benefit analysis to determine and, consequently, degrade the value of human life, and this is an analysis that I cannot support. * * * Today, our Court has shirked its duty to protect plaintiffs and the people of our state, thereby leaving defendant's practices and interests unassailed. As such, I must respectfully dissent.

Notes

1. *Damages v. Injunction*? The court will enter a damages judgment to force defendant to pay damages to compensate plaintiff for past injury. The judge grants an injunction to forbid defendant from injuring the plaintiff in the future.

A plaintiff without a present injury may seek an injunction "quia timet," which means "because he fears." A judge will grant the injunction if the plaintiff's risk passes the required threshold of "imminence." Another type of injunction is "reparative." The judge says, in effect, to the defendant, "You made a mess, now you clean it up."

2. *Tort*? Will a judge grant an injunction for a tort? A tort is a substantive cause of action; an injunction is one remedy for a winning tort plaintiff.

3. *Personal Injury*? Will a judge grant an injunction to prevent plaintiff's personal injury? Probably the most common modern-day injunction forbids the defendant from continuing domestic or other personal violence and abuse. Similarly, an injunction in a defendant's nuisance or trespass on plaintiff's land, will prevent plaintiff's future personal injury.

4. *Creative Equity*? The Michigan court's decision in *Henry* allows us to compare the majority's view that medical monitoring is for the legislature with the dissent's position that the court of Chancery has the power to order medical monitoring with a court-supervised program. We return to the courts' eternal debate about the Chancery's creativity in the Equity chapter.

5. Suppose that the courts in Henrico's state have not ruled on whether to allow plaintiffs a cause of action for medical monitoring. Should they allow her to maintain one?

6. *Market Share*. When plaintiff was injured by a drug's side effects, but plaintiff could not prove which of many manufacturers supplied the defective drug, the court found each manufacturer responsible for plaintiff's injuries and limited damages against each particular manufacturer to its share of the market. Sindell v. Abbott Laboratories, 26 Cal.3d 588, 163 Cal.Rptr. 132, 607 P.2d 924, cert. denied, 449 U.S. 912 (1980).

B. PROVING THE AMOUNT OF DAMAGES

The Quantum of Proof. Uncertainty plagues the calculation of the plaintiff's damages. A list of the usual uncertainties may help at the outset.

1. The court can determine many of plaintiff's pecuniary damages that have accrued before trial with some confidence about their accuracy—lost wages, medical expenses, the value of damaged property, and expectancy and reliance damages for breach of contract. Plaintiff's lost business profit is famously difficult to prove and recover; this casebook's business-profit decision is Mindgames v. Western Publishing in the chapter on breach of contract.

2. Pecuniary damages which will accrue in the future, impaired earning capacity and future medical expenses in personal injury cases or lost future profits of a business, are more intractable.

3. Some forms of plaintiff's compensatory damages are inherently uncertain. These include nonpecuniary damages, such as the plaintiff's pain and suffering and mental anguish. The jury must translate the evidence into pecuniary form under instructions that can be described as uncertain.

4. The Utah court discussed the important distinction between the fact and the amount of damages: "To prove damages, the plaintiff must prove two points. First, it must prove the fact of damages. The evidence must do more than merely give rise to speculation that damages in fact occurred; it must give rise to a reasonable probability that the plaintiff suffered damage as result of a breach. Second, the plaintiff must prove the amount of damages. The level of persuasiveness required to establish the *fact* of loss is generally higher than that required to establish the *amount* of a loss. [citations] It is, after all, the wrongdoer, rather than the injured party, who should bear the burden of some uncertainty in the amount of damages. While the standard for determining the amount of damages is not so exacting as the standard for proving the fact of damages, there still must be evidence that rises above speculation and provides a reasonable, even though not necessarily precise, estimate of damages. [citations] The amount of damages may be based upon approximations, if the fact of damage is established, and the approximations are based upon reasonable assumptions or projections. [citations]" Atkin Wright & Miles v. Mountain States Telephone and Telegraph Co., 709 P.2d 330 (Utah 1985).

The Utah court mentioned a principle that may assist a plaintiff to recover uncertain damages: the tortfeasor, not the plaintiff, "should bear the burden of some uncertainty in the amount of damages." A related principle holds that a defendant who is responsible for the uncertainty of plaintiff's proof of damages risks the worst-case scenario. This comes from Armory v. Delamirie, a familiar Property casebook case. A goldsmith conned a chimney sweeper's boy out of a "jewel" that the boy had found. The trial judge instructed the jury "unless the defendant did produce the jewel and shew it not to be of the finest water, they should presume the strongest against" the jeweler. "The jury awarded the sweep the value of the best jewels." Armory v. Delamirie, 1 Strange 505, 93 Eng.Rep. 664, 664 (K.B. 1722).

The principle applies even in antitrust where the damages "presumed" against the defendant may be trebled. Bigelow v. RKO Radio Pictures, 327 U.S. 251, reh'g denied, 327 U.S. 817 (1946).

Washington v. American Community Stores and Childs v. United States deal with lost future earnings. Pain and suffering and lost enjoyment of life follow in Loth v. Truck-a-way and McDougald v. Garber.

1. PLAINTIFF'S LOST CAPACITY TO EARN

WASHINGTON v. AMERICAN COMMUNITY STORES CORP.

Supreme Court of Nebraska, 1976.
196 Neb. 624, 244 N.W.2d 286.

WHITE, CHIEF JUSTICE. This is an appeal from a jury verdict and judgment in the sum of $76,000 [quite a bit at the time, Editor]. arising out of a motor vehicle collision. The trial court directed a verdict against the defendant on the issue of liability. * * *

The accident took place April 11, 1972. The plaintiff was then 24 years old [life expectancy, 49.9 years] and had been actually employed by the state as an adult parole officer since he was graduated from college in December 1971. At the outset we point out that there is no dispute concerning the permanency of the plaintiff's injury nor the fact that the injury disabled the plaintiff from pursuing the wrestling sport. * * *

[T]he basic thrust of the defendant's contention in this appeal is that the court should not have submitted the plaintiff's loss of earning capacity to the jury. It is argued that the evidence is based upon speculation and conjecture, that evidence of contingent, uncertain future possibilities, and uncertain future happenings, is speculative and conjectural and therefore incompetent, and the verdict is excessive.

* * * The plaintiff had attended the University of Nebraska at Omaha and he has compiled an outstanding record as an intercollegiate wrestler. He won first place in his weight division in the NAIA wrestling tournament his sophomore and senior years, was second once, and placed third in his freshman year. His collegiate record was 103 wins and 4 losses. * * * Expert testimony on his behalf was that before his injury he was a prime candidate for the 1972 United States Olympic team and had the qualifications to become a great international wrestler and to win a medal. There was evidence that those who compete in the Olympics and win a medal have a much better opportunity to secure employment in the coaching or professional wrestling fields. * * * At the time of the injury he was in excellent physical condition and had consistently demonstrated the training habits required to successfully compete in the Olympic trials. The plaintiff testified that prior to the accident he intended to try to make the United States Olympic team. The plaintiff offered no evidence of his earnings at the time of the injury or at the time of the trial that were derived from his wrestling skills. * * * There was evidence offered and rejected that supports a finding that as a coach he could have received earnings in the range of $16,000 to $20,000 per year. * * *

The defendant nevertheless argues that the evidence is insufficient and that the instructions submitting the issue are in error because there was no evidence of his earnings from the wrestling sport or profession at the time of the injury or at the time of trial. This argument has been rejected by this court ever since Bliss v. Beck, 80 Neb. 290, 114 N.W. 162, in which this court held that a married woman could recover for her diminished earning capacity, and that it was not necessary that she actually engaged in business on her own account, or intended to do so before her injury. It is settled law in Nebraska that loss of earning capacity, as distinct from loss of wages, salary, or earnings, is a separate element of damage. It is equally well settled that a loss of past earnings is an item of special damage and must be specifically pleaded and proved. Impairment of earning capacity is an item of general damage and proof may be had under general allegations of injury and damage. [citation] Proof of an actual loss of earnings or wages is not essential to recovery for loss of earning capacity. [citations] Recovery for loss or diminution of the power to earn in the future is based upon such factors as the plaintiff's age, life expectancy, health, habits, occupation, talents, skill, experience, training, and industry. From our quite detailed review of the facts, it is clear that there was ample evidence to sustain the findings of the jury as to the talents, skill, experience, training, and industry in the pursuit of the wrestling sport and preparation for professional occupation and career in this area. The other evidence as to plaintiff's age, life expectancy, health, and habits sustains the presence of all these elements required as to the proof of loss of earning capacity.

The defendant complains that the proof of prospective earnings of a coach or a professional wrestler fell short of adequacy and was insufficient to support the verdict. As we have pointed out such specific evidence is unnecessary for the plaintiff to recover under a general allegation of damage. But, more importantly, in this case the plaintiff offered evidence of the earning capacity of coaches and wrestlers. He specifically offered to prove that the average starting salary of a collegiate wrestling coach was approximately $20,000 per year, and that a good professional wrestler would average $500 to $1,000 per week. The defendant objected to this testimony and it was excluded by the court. The defendant is now in no position to complain of the insufficiency of the evidence. A party who objects to the evidence and causes it to be excluded, cannot obtain a reversal of the judgment as unsupported for want of the evidence so excluded. [citation] There is no merit to this contention. * * *

Affirmed.

MORAN, DISTRICT JUDGE. I respectfully dissent. There was no evidence of plaintiff's earnings from any source at the time of the injury or at the trial. I contend that the plaintiff had the duty to produce this evidence.

Notes

1. *Washington's Lost Life.* What would Washington's life have been like if the defendant had not committed the tort? Plaintiff's proof develops Washington's hypothetical world that, because of his injury, cannot exist. What is the difference between Washington's hypothetical prevented world and his post-injury real world?

2. *Washington's Lost Chance.* Should the jury resolve the uncertainty about the amount of Washington's future lost earning capacity with a statistical valuation of his "lost chance"? If Washington had one chance in five of making the Olympic team, should he receive 20% of the anticipated benefit of Olympic participation? Elmer J. Schaefer, Uncertainty and the Law of Damages, 19 Wm. & Mary L.Rev. 719 (1978).

3. *Introduction to Childs v. United States.* The following decision is under the Federal Tort Claims Act, (FTCA), which waives the United States government's

sovereign immunity for a federal employee's tort. A FTCA trial occurs in federal district court before the judge without a jury. State substantive tort law governs. For us, one advantage of the trial to the judge is his detailed narrative of factfinding which would be absent from a jury's general verdict.

The *Childs* lawsuit is for wrongful death. All states have wrongful death and survival statutes. Generalization about wrongful death damages, though perilous, is necessary. In theory the plaintiff sues under the wrongful death statute to force the tortfeasor to compensate the decedent's survivors; the plaintiff uses the survival statute to preserve the decedent's cause of action for losses she sustained before death. State statutory schemes vary widely; there are in addition specialized statutes like the Federal Employers Liability Act, the Death on the High Seas Act, the Jones Act, and Longshoremen and Harbor Workers' Compensation Act. A state Workers' Compensation act may provide financial benefits to dependents of an employee killed at work. The various statutory schemes include startlingly different calculations of the amount of possible damages.

Questions you should ask about wrongful death and survival statutes include:

1. Beneficiaries. Who are the beneficiaries? The decedent's estate? Her heirs? Her next of kin? Others? Does a wrongful death action survive a beneficiary's death? How will the judgment be apportioned among several beneficiaries?

2. Procedure. What procedure governs the action? What statute of limitations? Who are the parties? Does the wrongful death cause of action mesh with the survival action?

3. Measurement of Damages. How does the statute define compensatory damages? Does it allow damages that are "just?" Does it restrict plaintiff's recovery to "pecuniary damages?" If recovery is limited to "pecuniary damages," are they defined? May plaintiff recover for the decedent's pain and suffering before death? How will the future damages be discounted to present value? Do damages include pre-judgment interest? Do income taxes affect damages? May plaintiff recover punitive damages?

When reading Childs v. United States, ask how the combination of the FTCA and the Georgia statutory scheme affected the answers to these questions in the deaths of Debra and General Gordon.

Notice several other things in Judge Nangle's careful decision. How did the plaintiffs plan and present evidence to tell a convincing story about the lost futures of the missing lives? Did the evidence bring a measure of certainty to an inherently uncertain task? How did the defendant answer plaintiff's evidence? What role did the parties' fact witnesses and expert witnesses play? What evidence appealed to the emotions? What to the rational? How important is individualized evidence compared to statistical and composite evidence? Is there, either in the parties' presentations or in the judge's decision, any indication of racial or sexual stereotyping?

The lengthy decision was shortened by eliminating some legal analysis, the discussion of pain and suffering damages, and all but one paragraph about Ashley Scott, a passenger killed in the fatal crash.

CHILDS v. UNITED STATES

United States District Court, S.D. Georgia, 1996.
923 F.Supp. 1570.

NANGLE, DISTRICT JUDGE. * * * On November 10, 1992, Ashley Latrise Scott ("Ashley"), Debra Reese Gordon ("Debra") and her unborn child, General Gordon ("General"), were traveling in Debra's automobile through an intersection in downtown Savannah, Georgia, when a United States Postal Service ("USPS") truck wrongfully entered the intersection and struck Debra's automobile. The force of the collision pushed the automobile head-on into another truck that was sitting at the intersection. Ashley, Debra and General died almost immediately after the collision.

Plaintiffs brought the above-captioned actions against the United States of America ("USA" or "Government") under the Federal Tort Claims Act ("FTCA"), 28 U.S.C. § 2671 et seq., seeking damages for decedents' wrongful death, * * * and funeral and medical expenses. * * *

[T]he Government admitted that it is vicariously liable for the negligent acts of the Government employee operating the USPS truck. * * * The parties have further stipulated that * * * the estates of Debra and General Gordon are entitled to a total of $8,794.00 for funeral and medical expenses, as well as expenses related to the damage done to Debra's vehicle. Remaining for resolution, then, is the question of damages as to plaintiffs' wrongful death claims * * * .

Debra Gordon was a 33-year-old female who was, at the time of her death, eight months pregnant with General Gordon. Debra was in relatively good physical health and, according to the Mortality Table for 1949, Ultimate, had a life expectancy at the time of her death of 46.80 years. General Gordon, who upon autopsy appeared to be a healthy fetus, had, according to the same table, a life expectancy of 73.18 years.

Debra grew up in a large, close-knit family on a farm in Millen, Georgia. Debra's mother, plaintiff Rosa Reese, and her father, General Reese, were married for 53 years, and Debra was one of eight children. Debra remained extremely close to all of her family, enjoying the counsel, advice, society and companionship of her mother and siblings until the time of her death. Debra was generally regarded as the favorite child in the family and the moving force in assuring that the family remained close.

Debra attended Jenkins County High School in Millen, Georgia, where she was an excellent student. She was on the Student Council, was vice-president of the National Honor Society, was president of the Foreign Language Club and was very active in the Future Business Leaders of America. Debra was also very popular at school.

After graduating from high school, Debra attended college for approximately three years, during which time she studied to become a nurse. Many of Debra's siblings, and almost all of her nieces and nephews, have attended college or have college degrees.

Debra did not, however, attain a nursing degree. Instead, she began working at M & M Foods, a grocery store in Savannah, Georgia, that subsequently became Kroger Foods. Debra worked her way up to produce manager in 1983 and held that position until the time of her death in 1992. She worked at Kroger for a total of 13 years.

Debra was an exceptional employee who took great pride in her work. The Court heard testimony from two of Debra's former superiors at Kroger. Both testified that she was the best produce manager that they had ever worked with, and one of the witnesses indicated that he had rated Debra's job performance as high as any employee he had ever rated at Kroger. In sum, Debra was an extremely successful produce manager: her department was consistently profitable and she had an excellent relationship with both her co-workers and the store's customers. Both witnesses also indicated that Debra could have advanced into upper management in the company if she had been so inclined.

Debra's personal life centered around church and family. She regularly attended the church. * * * Debra liked people and was extremely outgoing and friendly with those in her life.

Debra was married for five years but did not have any children from that marriage. In 1985, her husband committed suicide. Thus, at the time of her death, Debra was an unmarried widow living alone in her own home in Savannah, Georgia. She knew that she was going to give birth to a boy out of wedlock and had decided to name the child after her father, General Reese. Debra did not, however, disclose the identity of the father of General to anyone, and General's father remains unknown to this date. Thus, although General clearly would have been the beneficiary of the love, care and companionship of Debra and her family, he was apparently going to be born into a home in which the father would be completely absent.

Economic Testimony. The Court heard testimony from * * * economic experts, each of whom attempted to place an economic value on the loss associated with the decedents' deaths based upon their lost future income, fringe benefits and household services. * * * Francis W. Rushing, Ph.D., a Professor of Economics at Georgia State University, testified on behalf of plaintiff Reese as to the economic loss associated with the deaths of Debra and General. For the Government, David R. Kamerschen, Ph.D., a Professor of Economics at the University of Georgia, testified as to the lost economic value of each of the decedent's lives. [The experts relied on Census and Bureau of Labor Statistics figures; the footnotes were deleted.]

In valuing the decedents' lost future income, all * * * experts used the following four elements in making their calculations: (1) base-year or entry-level income; (2) income growth rate; (3) worklife expectancy; and (4) discount rate. The base-year income is the decedent's initial actual or projected before-tax income. The income growth rate reflects the fact that the base-year income will grow over time as a result of inflation, productivity gains and progression in one's career. The worklife expectancy is the probable length of time a person would have remained in the workforce, taking into account periods of voluntary and involuntary unemployment. Finally, because income earned in the future is less valuable than income earned today, the discount rate is used to calculate the present value of a decedent's future income loss.

In addition to these elements, Dr. Kamerschen's appraisals include two other elements: personal tax offset and personal expense/consumption offset. These elements simply reflect the fact that some portion of the decedents' income would be lost to the decedent's personal consumption and to income taxes and would not, therefore, be available to the decedents' survivors. Plaintiffs, as set forth below, contend that neither offset is warranted under the FTCA or Georgia law; thus, * * * Dr. Rushing [did not include] these elements in [his] appraisals.

In valuing decedents' lost fringe benefits, which include items such as health insurance, pension benefits and social security, each expert simply took a percentage, ranging from 15% to 20%, of the present value of the decedents' lost income. The final element included in some of the experts' appraisals is lost household services, which reflects the fact that the decedents' uncompensated household labor services have been lost. Thus, the experts attempt to place an economic value on the decedents' contributions to a household by first determining the number of hours in a year that the decedents would have spent doing uncompensated household labor and then multiplying this number by the minimum wage in 1993, which was $4.25 per hour. They grow this figure and then discount it back to present-day value in the same way that they do for decedents' lost income.

Although each expert employed essentially the same appraisal technique, their calculation of the decedents' total economic loss, not surprisingly, varied substantially. Their conclusions are set forth below. * * *

In appraising Debra's lost future income, Dr. Rushing uses her actual income in 1992 on an annualized basis, which is $24,196.00. He then grows this figure at the annual average rate of pay raise that Debra enjoyed at Kroger— 5.6%—over her expected worklife, which he assumes is 32 years. This worklife expectancy is based upon his assumption that Debra would have worked without interruption until she retired at age 65. Debra was 33 years of age at the time of her death; thus, Dr. Rushing arrives at a 32–year worklife expectancy by subtracting 33 from 65, her assumed age of retirement. Dr. Rushing testified that he did not use the worklife table because Debra's actual work history is a better indicator of her worklife expectancy. Dr. Rushing then discounts these future cashflows back to present-day value (he chose July 1, 1995) using the 5% discount rate to arrive at $890,139.00 as the present value of her lost future wages.

Likewise, Dr. Kamerschen uses $24,196.00 as Debra's base-year income. He also calculates a growth rate for Debra based upon her earnings history at Kroger; however, his calculation is based upon a geometric average, whereas Dr. Rushing's is based upon an arithmetic average. Thus, Dr. Kamerschen calculates a slightly lower growth rate of 5.41%.

In contrast to Dr. Rushing, Dr. Kamerschen relies upon the worklife tables in arriving at Debra's expected worklife. He assumes a worklife for Debra of 20.99 years, which is the average of (1) an active black female 33.3 years of age (19.09 years); and (2) an active black female 33.3 years of age with 15 or more years of schooling (22.89 years). He thus grows Debra's income for 20.99 years at 5.41% per year and then discounts these cashflows back to present-day value using the 5% discount rate to arrive at a present value for her lost income of $556,770.00. [H]e then subtracts 30% for taxes and 50% for personal consumption to arrive at $194,870.00 as the present value of her lost net income.

In order to calculate Debra's lost fringe benefits, Dr. Rushing spoke with Kroger representatives to find out what fringe benefits were available to its employees. Based upon these discussions, Dr. Rushing chose 19.6% as the appropriate percentage of Debra's lost future income for calculating her lost fringe benefits. Thus, multiplying $890,139.00 by 19.6%, Dr. Rushing arrives at $174,467.24 as the value of her lost fringe benefits. Dr. Kamerschen, on the other hand, takes 15% of his calculation for Debra's lost gross income— $556,770.00—to arrive at $83,516.00 as the value of Debra's lost fringe benefits.

As to Debra's lost household services, Dr. Rushing assumes that she would have provided such services during the first 18 years of General Gordon's life. Thus, he values Debra's lost household services in the first year of General Gordon's life as $4,618.90, based upon 20.9 hours of such services per week valued at the minimum wage rate of $4.25 per hour. He then grows this figure at

4.3% (this figure represents Dr. Rushing's calculation of the annual inflation rate in the United States for the period 1950 to 1993) for a period of 18 years and then discounts these future cashflows back to present value using the 5% discount rate. He thus calculates the present value of Debra's lost household services as $82,088.00.

Dr. Kamerschen agrees that lost household services are properly attributed to Debra for the first 18 years of General's life. He finds the value of her lost household services in the first year of General's life to be $5,950.50, based upon the assumption that she would have rendered 1,400 hours per year of such services valued at the minimum wage of $4.25 per hour. He grows this yearly figure for 18 years at an annual growth rate of 6.36% and then brings these cashflows back to present-day value using the 5% discount rate to arrive at a total value for her lost household services of $119,757.00.

Thus, the total present economic loss associated with Debra's death, according to Dr. Rushing, is $1,147,694.00, based upon lost future income of $890,139.00, lost fringe benefits of $174,467.24 and lost household services of $82,088.00. Dr. Kamerschen, on the other hand, calculates the total economic loss associated with her death as $398,142.00, based upon lost net income of $194,870.00, lost fringe benefits of $83,516.00 and lost household services of $119,757.00.

In appraising General's lost future income, Dr. Rushing assumes, based upon General's family background, that he would have attained either a two-year or four-year college degree. Thus, he calculates General's lost income based upon two different profiles: one based upon two years of college and the other based upon four years. Based upon these profiles, Dr. Rushing estimates the 1992 starting income for a male with an associate degree and a male with a bachelor's degree. He then grows the starting salary for an associate degree holder to the year that General would enter the workforce—2013—at the annual rate of 4.3%. He performs the same calculation for a bachelor degree holder, growing the starting salary for such a graduate to the year 2015, which is the year that General would have entered the workforce under this scenario. This, according to Dr. Rushing, yields General's starting salary in 2013 with an associate degree, and his starting salary in 2015 with a bachelor's degree. He then continues to grow the associate degree starting income for the worklife expectancy of an associate degree holder, 37.6 years, and the bachelor degree starting income for the worklife expectancy of a bachelor degree holder, 38.3 years. Finally, he discounts these future cashflows back to present-day value using the 5% discount rate. Based upon these calculations, Dr. Rushing concludes that the present-day value of General's lost future income is $1,136,830.00, assuming he would have attained an associate degree, and $1,441,752.00, assuming he would have attained a bachelor degree.

Dr. Kamerschen, on the other hand, * * * calculates the weighted average of the actual historical before-tax income for black males of all education levels in the United States, which is $16,990.00 in 1993 dollars. Dr. Kamerschen assumes that General would have entered the workforce at age 20 and would have a worklife expectancy of 35.22 years, which is an average of the worklife expectancies for 20–year old black males of all educational levels. Thus, he grows $16,990.00 until the year General would be 20 years old, and then continues to grow it for 35.22 years, his worklife expectancy. Dr. Kamerschen then discounts these future cashflows back to present value using the 5% discount rate to get

$866,710.00 as the present value of General's lost future income. After deducting 30% of this figure for income taxes and a further 50% from the resulting figure to account for General's personal consumption, Dr. Kamerschen arrives at $303,349.00 as the present value of General's lost net income.

As to General's lost fringe benefits, Dr. Rushing takes 19.6% of General's lost income, which is $222,819.00 under the associate degree scenario and $282,583.00 under the bachelor degree scenario. Dr. Kamerschen, on the other hand, takes 15% of his estimate of General's lost gross income, $866,710.00, to arrive at $130,007.00 as the lost value of General's fringe benefits. Both experts concluded that lost household services were inappropriate in the case of an unborn child.

Thus, Dr. Rushing's appraisal of the total present economic loss associated with General's death, assuming he would have attained a two-year college degree, is $1,359,649.00, based upon lost future income of $1,136,830.00 and lost fringe benefits of $222,819.00. Under his assumption that General would have attained a four-year college degree, Dr. Rushing finds the total loss to be $1,724,335.00, based upon lost future income of $1,441,752.00 and lost fringe benefits of $282,583.00. Dr. Kamerschen, on the other hand, calculates the total economic loss associated with General's death as $433,355.00, based upon lost future net income of $303,349.00 and lost fringe benefits of $130,007.00.

In evaluating the experts' testimony as to the economic loss associated with the decedents' deaths, the Court is constrained to point out that virtually all hypotheses and projections relating to the decedents' lives are necessarily speculative. No triers of fact, be they jurors or judges, can predict the future. The wisest of sages acknowledge this. All history proves that it is simply not possible to anticipate the vagaries of life. Predicting who will live a long and enjoyable life or an unhappy and fretful life, who will suffer from illnesses, both mild and serious, who will have to spend extra time to care for a loved one, who will spend time in the Peace Corps, a kibbutz or other service organization, who will fail and who will succeed and who will either enjoy or suffer through life, is a game for fools.

Genes and luck play a significant role in all of our lives and there is no way to factor such matters into life's equation. Perhaps the horrible accident of November 10, 1992, that brings us together in this case is a most sad, but most apt, example of this. Any one of us who has attended a 40th, or even 50th, reunion of a grade school or high school or college class can attest to the unpredictability of life. Some of the most charismatic and promising of our then colleagues died young, or suffered long illness or suffered through other unfortunate and unhappy events. Others, perhaps even those deemed least likely to succeed, have led rather successful, apparently useful lives. Very few members of the human race in our great country, whether male or female, white or black or yellow, of whatever ethnic composition, escape the unpredictable vagaries of life. Life's cup is both half empty and half full.

Valuing the life of a human being is, then, a profoundly difficult task and is made all the more difficult in these cases by the fact that there is no clear economic loss associated with the death of * * * General. Unlike Debra, who had an earnings history and therefore a clear monetary loss when she died, * * * General was an unborn fetus who not only had no earnings history at the time of his death, but had not even taken his first breath on this earth. Thus, the mathematical precision by which * * * experts value the economic loss associated with * * * General's death is illusory; there simply is no factual basis for the assumptions that underlie their calculations. * * *

Thus, because no one can know what * * * General's educational and occupational achievement would have been, the experts were at liberty to make assumptions consistent with the interests of the party for which they were testifying. Plaintiffs' experts were optimistic in their assumptions about * * * General's schooling, starting salary and expected worklife, while defendant's expert was very conservative in his assumptions about these critical elements. It is not surprising, then, that * * * Dr. Rushing's appraisal of the economic loss associated with General's death exceeds Dr. Kamerschen's appraisal by more than $1 million. This remarkable disparity in opinion brings to mind an observation made by the Supreme Court many years ago: "Experience has shown that opposite opinions of persons professing to be experts may be obtained to any amount." Winans v. New York & E.R. Co., 62 U.S. (21 How) 88, 101 (1858). * * *

Dr. Rushing's appraisal of $1,359,649.00 to $1,724,335.00 as the range of economic loss associated with General's death is premised upon the extremely optimistic assumption that General would have attained either a two- or four-year college degree and would have had a starting salary and worklife commensurate with these levels of education. These assumptions are exceedingly optimistic in light of the fact that absolutely nothing is even known about General's basic personal attributes, not to mention the more subtle qualities that are vital to an individual's success: academic capabilities, work ethic, ability to get along and gain rapport with people, etc.

Turning to Dr. Kamerschen's appraisals of * * * $433,355.00 for General, the Court would first note that his deduction of 30% of the decedents' lost income to account for their personal taxes and 50% from the resulting figure to account for * * * personal expenses is contrary to the Court's construction of Georgia law and the FTCA, as more fully explained below. Accordingly, the appropriate figure to look at in Dr. Kamerschen's appraisals is his calculation of decedents' lost gross income, which brings his appraisal of General's [economic loss] up to $996,717.00.

Dr. Kamerschen attempts to avoid the pitfalls inherent in making specific assumptions by calculating a blended salary and worklife expectancy for Ashley based upon the salaries and worklife expectancies for all black females and for General based upon the salaries and worklife expectancies for all black males. In so doing, however, he arrives at figures that are not consistent with Ashley's and General's respective backgrounds. His projections of Ashley's starting salary and expected worklife are significantly lower than his projections for General. His projection for Ashley's salary of $13,202.00 is $3,788.00 less than the $16,990.00 starting salary he projects for General. Likewise, his projection of Ashley's expected worklife of 28.15 years, is 7.7 years less than the worklife he projects for General. [This occurs] even though Ashley's short personal history clearly indicates that she had an aptitude for school and an ability to gain rapport with people. General, on the other hand, has no personal history and was to be raised in a single-parent home, without knowing his father, by a mother who did not graduate from college.

Finally, there is a question as to the reliability of Dr. Kamerschen's worklife expectancy calculations. The Department of Labor report on which he relies in making his calculations suggests that it is improper to combine worklife expectancies based upon gender and worklife expectancies based upon race, as Dr. Kamerschen does in calculating all of the decedents' blended worklife expectancies. In other words, the author of the report tested for the effect of race and for the effect of gender upon a person's worklife expectancy. She did not, however, test for the combined effect of both race and gender "because the sample is too limited to develop reliable joint probabilities." Thus, Dr. Kamerschen's worklife expectancies are based upon a calculation deemed to be imprudent by the author of the report.

In sum, the appraisals of economic loss associated with * * * General's death are little more than speculation by witnesses whose underlying assumptions have been obviously influenced by the interests of the party for whom they have testified. For this reason, the Court will give very limited credibility to the expert testimony on the economic loss associated with * * * General's death.

Plaintiffs contend that they are entitled, under the FTCA and Georgia's wrongful death statute, to two distinct elements of recovery for the wrongful deaths of * * * Debra and General: 1) the tangible, economic value of their lives, as shown by the testimony of their experts; and 2) the intangible, non-economic value of the their lives as shown by the testimony of the decedents' family, friends, co-workers, teachers and ministers.

Plaintiffs further contend that their recovery should not be reduced by either the personal taxes or expenses (i.e. consumption) that decedents would have incurred had they lived. [The judge agreed with plaintiffs' contentions.] * * *

The FTCA provides that "[t]he United States shall be liable [for torts committed by its employees while acting within the scope of their employment] in the same manner and to the same extent as a private individual under like circumstances, but shall not be liable for interest prior to judgment or for punitive damages." 28 U.S.C. § 2674. Because the United States is liable in the same manner and to the same extent as a private individual, its liability is determined under the laws of the state in which the act or omission giving rise to the cause of action arose, [citations] which in this case is the State of Georgia.

Recovery in Georgia for the wrongful death of an individual is governed by Georgia's wrongful death statute, O.C.G.A. §§ 51–4–1 through 51–4–5. There is no dispute that the right of recovery under this statute * * * for the wrongful death of Debra resides with her mother, plaintiff Rosa Reese. See O.C.G.A. §§ 19–7–1, 51–4–4. Furthermore * * * the right of recovery for General's wrongful death resides with plaintiff Rosa Reese, as the administrator of General Gordon's estate.

The Georgia wrongful death statute provides for the recovery of "the full value of the life of the decedent," see O.C.G.A. §§ 51–4–2,–3, and–5(a), which is defined as "the full value of the life of the decedent without deducting for any of the necessary or personal expenses of the decedent had he lived." O.C.G.A. § 51–4–1(1). The Court of Appeals of Georgia has held that the "full value of life" is comprised of two categories of damages:

(1) those items having a proven monetary value, such as lost potential lifetime earnings, income, or services, reduced to present cash value ... or

(2) lost intangible items whose value cannot be precisely quantified, such as a parent's society, advice, example and counsel as determined by the enlightened conscience of the jury.

Consolidated Freightways Corp. of Del. v. Futrell, 201 Ga.App. 233, 410 S.E.2d 751, 752 (1991). * * * [The judge held that despite the "or" between (1) and (2) in the quoted material, a wrongful death plaintiff could recover both types of damages under appropriate proof.]

The fact-finder is thus vested with discretion in applying these components to the particular facts before it, and this discretion is especially wide in the case of a young child:

> [A]s to infants of tender years, it is impossible to give evidence of the pecuniary value of the probable loss, and therefore the question of damages for loss on account of impairment of future earning capacity is left to the sound judgment, experience, and conscience of the jury without any proof thereof whatever* * * * "The value to a parent of the services of a minor child is not determinable solely from evidence as to the amount of money the child earns or is capable of earning during its minority. The value of a child's services may be determined from all the evidence, including evidence as to the age and precocity of the child, its earning capacity, and the services rendered by it, the circumstances of the family and the living conditions, and from experience and knowledge of human affairs on the part of the jury."

Collins v. McPherson, 91 Ga.App. 347, 85 S.E.2d 552, 554 (1954). * * *

It is apparent from the foregoing that Georgia law permits this Court, as the fact-finder in these two cases, wide latitude in calculating the "full value" of the lives of * * * Debra and General. The Court may consider the economic losses associated with the decedents' deaths, as well as any non-economic, intangible losses that the Court deems relevant in determining the full value of the their lives. * * *

Applying the law to the facts found by this Court, the following are the Court's conclusions as to the full value of * * * Debra's and General's lives, expressed, of course, in monetary terms, the only method of valuation available to the Court.

Debra, of course, is the decedent about whom the most is known. She had an exceptionally close relationship with all of her family, and she was also very close to her co-workers and friends at church. She also loved her job and was clearly very good at it. Debra's life was not, however, without difficulty. Her husband had committed suicide and she was about to become a single, unmarried mother who, for reasons of her own, disclosed to no one the identity of General's father.

Because Debra had a regular earnings history when she died, there is a clear economic loss associated with her death. Dr. Rushing appraises this loss at $1,147,694.00, while Dr. Kamerschen's appraises it at $760,043.00. The $387,651.00 differential in their appraisals is largely explained by the disparity in their assumptions about Debra's worklife expectancy. Dr. Rushing assumed that Debra would have worked every year of her life until age 65, thus yielding a worklife expectancy of 32 years. Dr. Kamerschen, on the other hand, used a worklife expectancy of 20.99 years, which is a blended worklife expectancy for black females 33.3 years of age. This calculation is * * * based upon a combination of worklife expectancies for females and for African Americans, which is a combination that the author of the report cautions against.

Dr. Kamerschen's calculation ignores the fact that Debra had worked continuously since she began working for Kroger (M & M Foods), that she was an exceptional employee and that she would be the sole source of support for her child. The Court thus concludes that Dr. Rushing's assumption that Debra would work every year of her life until age 65 is more realistic in this instance. As a single mother she likely would have had no other choice.

As to Debra's lost fringe benefits, the Court concludes that Dr. Rushing's appraisal, though seemingly high, is the better of the two appraisals because the percentage of income that he chose is based upon his discussions with Kroger officials. Finally, as to Debra's lost household services, the Court, on this more speculative item, concludes that both of their appraisals of this loss are too high. Based upon these conclusions as to the economic loss associated with Debra's death, and taking into account the intangible components of Debra's life, the Court concludes that the full value of Debra's life is $1,350,000.00.

Obviously, one can only speculate as to the kind of person that General would have been, his life having been taken before anyone could know him. It is clear that he would have had a loving, caring mother who would have done her best to provide him with all of the things that he would have needed in life. He also would have had a large and caring family from which he could seek advice, counsel and companionship. He was, on the other hand, facing the disadvantage of being raised by a single, working mother, with no father in the home. Taking these intangible components of General's life into account, as well as the evidence of the economic loss associated with his death, the Court concludes that the full value of General's life is $1,083,000.00. * * *

[Judgment was entered for $8,794.00 for decedents' medical and funeral expenses, as well as property damage to Debra's vehicle; $1,350,000.00 for the wrongful death of Debra Gordon; and $1,083,000.00 for the wrongful death of General Gordon.]

Notes

1. *September 11 Compensation.* Less than a fortnight after the terrorist attacks on September 11, 2001, Congress responded with a compensation system for those injured and for the nearly 3,000 deaths. Congress created a judicial remedy, which few utilized, and a no-fault administrative remedy funded by the United States, which 98% of the families pursued. 49 U.S.C. § 40101.

The Attorney General appointed Kenneth Feinberg as Special Master to administer the program, to set the ambit and rules for the awards, and to individualize the victims' losses. The Special Master and 450 employees wrapped up their work in mid–2004 and filed a Final Report of the Special Master for the September 11th Compensation Fund of 2001.

We will compare the administrative system for the 9/11 survivors' "wrongful death" claims with the litigated wrongful death damages in Childs v. United States and other cases below. The Special Master's book about his experience is Kenneth Feinberg, What is Life Worth?: The Unprecedented Effort to Compensate the Victims of 9/11 (2005). The book is quoted below with page numbers. Mr. Feinberg gave a speech to the American Law Institute on May 17, 2005, which, when quoted, is cited as (ALI speech).

Before returning to the Gordons' wrongful deaths, however, it is important to observe something that will come up again below: in contrast to common-law damages rules, Congress's 9/11 legislation required reduction of victims' recovery by subtracting collateral source payments, including pensions and life insurance.

2. *Averages.* "Statistical charts, such as the mortality tables and work-life expectancy tables prepared by the United States Department of Labor, compile averages and are often deemed authoritative, particularly in the absence of contradictory particularized evidence. * * * These tables are not binding on the fact finder. * * * Moreover, the statistical charts are updated on average every 10 years and therefore exhibit a lag in reflecting changing work and mortality patterns." Earl v. Bouchard Transportation Co., Inc., 735 F.Supp. 1167, 1175 (E.D.N.Y. 1990), (Weinstein, J.), affirmed, 917 F.2d 1320 (2d Cir.1990).

3. *Lost Income.* Plaintiff recovers for lost capacity to earn, not for lost actual wages. (Washington relied on lost potential income.) Projecting Debra Gordon's lost income forward was a satisfactory and safe way for plaintiff to prove her lost capacity to earn. Does the plaintiff's factual evidence about Debra Gordon's life simply build up to the expert's economic testimony? General Gordon's recovery was for his lost capacity to earn. A homemaker, a student, an unemployed person, or a child who lacks income may also recover for lost capacity.

4. *Length of Debra Gordon's Working Life.*

(a) *Continuous Employment?* Should a judge or the jury shorten a young woman like Debra's worklife for a time out of the labor market to raise children? Calculating the lost earning capacity of a woman injured badly at the age of 19½, one judge observed, "There was a likelihood of marriage and motherhood in her future. Marriage probably would have interrupted her career, but with her training she could have resumed her career, if it had become necessary or desirable during or after marriage." Frankel v. United States, 321 F.Supp. 1331, 1338 (E.D.Pa.1970), affirmed sub nom. Frankel v. Heym, 466 F.2d 1226 (3d Cir.1972).

(b) In contrast, another court wrote, "In an environment where more and more women work in more and more responsible positions, and where signs of the changing times are all around us, it can no longer automatically be assumed that women will absent themselves from the work force for prolonged intervals during their child-bearing/child-rearing years." Reilly v. United States, 863 F.2d 149, 152–154, 167 (1st Cir.1988).

(c) The lengths of the September 11 victims' work-lives were based on actuarial data that assumed an employed 25-year-old victim would have worked for another 33.6 years, a figure that declined with age. An employed 65-year-old's work life was 4.2 years. Although a woman's statistical work-life expectancy is lower than a man's, the 9/11 calculation used male data for both sexes.

Should the factfinder consider an income table based on sex or race, male or female, African or Asian or European or Hispanic, etc.? Another possibility is to use a "blended" or unisex, human race statistical table.

(d) How persuasive is the judge's decision setting Debra Gordon's work life?

(e) *Retirement Age?* There is no mandatory retirement age for most employees. Why assume Debra Gordon would have retired at age 65?

5. *Debra's Future Prospects.* (a) Why assume that Debra Gordon would not have remarried? Should plaintiff have developed Debra's professional scenario to include additional education, promotions, and professional advancement?

(b) Special Master Feinberg quotes a victim's mother: "Mr. Feinberg, you're about to calculate an award for my daughter. Now my daughter was a first-year associate at a law firm in the World Trade Center, but I'm telling you something right now, I'm here to tell you, don't you calculate economic loss on the basis of her first-year salary. She was going to become a partner in this firm in six years. Not only that, I'm telling you that in the eighth year they would have changed the name of the firm and added her name to the letterhead." * * *

"Well, Mrs. Jones, I mean, you know, these young associates, they leave after a couple—"

"Don't tell me. You never met my daughter. * * * My daughter was going to be named partner in this firm so I want a calculation at $500,000 or $600,000 a year, not $110,000 a year. Don't tell me. You never met my daughter." (ALI Speech)

"[W]hat" Feinberg wrote in his book, "could I possibly say to a mother determined to write her dead daughter's future, a future that would never be?" (p. 89.)

(c) The limits on a victim's rosy future is more evident in Waldorf v. Shuta, 896 F.2d 723, 726, 742–43 (3d Cir.1990). "Waldorf failed to provide the evidentiary foundation, the 'prerequisites for employment,' for the jury to consider his future earnings as an attorney. He was a 24-year-old high school drop-out who had obtained his high school equivalency diploma in the military. He had worked as a paralegal in the military, but had been unable to find employment as a paralegal in civilian life; he had entered and dropped out of the New York Police Academy; he had been refused admission to a four-year degree program and had completed one year of a two-year Associate Degree Program at the College of Staten Island. At the time of the accident, he was taking six courses, three of which were photography, tennis and acting. While there is no reason to doubt Waldorf's aspiration to become a lawyer, no credible evidence had been presented that he had the ability to become a lawyer. At the time of the accident, he did not possess the qualifications, and it is not at all certain that he would have been admitted to law school. * * * There was no credible evidence as to Waldorf's ability and qualifications as an attorney, and the district court erred in allowing the jury to consider whether to grant him future earnings as an attorney. Such consideration was unduly speculative." Waldorf's lawsuit, which stemmed from an accident in 1982, was not over in 1998, the final time it is reported. Waldorf v. Shuta, 142 F.3d 601 (3d Cir. 1998).

(d) The September 11 victims' yearly increases in income assumed 2% inflation and 1% gain in productivity. A component for "life-cycle or age-specific increase" declined with the victim's age: an 18-year-old's projected growth rate was 9.7% yearly, which slowly declined to 3% beginning at age 52.

(e) Should the judge have based his calculation for Debra's "growth" on similar figures?

(f) Suppose a female victim's parents were members of a religious sect that de-emphasized education, encouraged early arranged marriages and large families, and openly discouraged women from working outside the home. Should the court admit this evidence to support low damages for her lost capacity to earn?

6. *Household Labor*. (a) *Duration*. Does a mother's "household" services to her son end when he reaches 18?

(b) *Amount*. The parties' experts and the judge started with the then minimum wage. Should the judge have valued Debra Gordon's "household labor" at the minimum wage? Was $4.25 too low?

Consider two other techniques. One way to assess the contributions of a parent-spouse who is not employed outside the home is to consider the economic value of each component of the decedent's activity. Another is the deceased's earning capacity on the open job market: "Courts have had difficulty determining damages in cases involving disabled housewives. To value a housewife's services by adding up the amounts that would be required to hire providers of the various components of these services (cleaning, child care, cooking, etc.)—the 'replacement cost' approach—although the one most commonly used by courts is unsatisfactory because it ignores opportunity cost. The minimum value of a housewife's services, and hence the cost to the family if those services are eliminated, is the price that her time would have commanded in its next best use. Suppose that she had been trained as a lawyer and could have earned $100,000 working for a law firm but chose instead to be a housewife and that the various services she performed as a housewife could have been hired in the market for $20,000. Since she chose to stay home, presumably her services in the home were considered by the family to be worth at least $100,000; if not, the family could have increased its real income by her working as a lawyer and hiring others to perform he household functions. Therefore the loss when she was disabled was at least $100,000." Richard Posner, Economic Analysis of Law § 6.11 (6th ed. 2002) (footnotes omitted).

(c) Debra Gordon had a full-time job and also performed household labor. Is "opportunity cost" appropriate to value her household labor? Ann Estin, Love and Obligation: Family Law and the Romance of Economics, 36 Wm. & Mary L.Rev. 989, 1026–35 (1995).

7. *Taxes and Personal Consumption.* A September 11 victim's base for earnings started with her after-tax income; then her share of household consumption was subtracted from that. The personal-consumption percentage declined with higher income and more dependants. Although a victim's salary grew, her tax and consumption were set on the date of her death.

The judge decided not to subtract Debra Gordon's taxes and consumption from her income. This was favorable to the plaintiffs. But was it less accurate?

8. *Wrongful Death of a Child.* In an earlier age and a rural economy, a child was an economic asset to a family. Limiting his parents' wrongful death damages to their "pecuniary loss" prevented speculative and conjectural recovery. That has changed.

For most contemporary urban families, a minor child is a substantial expense item; the family's childraising expense may total several hundred thousand dollars through college, not to mention law school. Except in a law-school classroom hypothetical, however, no-one has suggested that, under a reverse variation of the "pecuniary loss" rule, the dead child's parents ought to pay a tortfeasor who liberates them from the expense.

Nevertheless, measuring parents' economic loss for a minor child's death is a significant challenge. The parents' recovery for loss of the child's society and companionship has been controversial. In Illinois, in the wrongful death of stillborn child, there is a rebuttable presumption that the parents may recover for loss of society which, the court ruled, falls within the scope of "pecuniary injury." Seef v. Sutkus, 145 Ill.2d 336, 583 N.E.2d 510 (1991).

Should the jury consider the victim's filial piety? If a boy's parents were Chinese, might they argue that their damages should be increased for the loss of an eldest son because, following the custom of "Bau–Da" or filial piety, he would have provided for them in retirement? For a "yes" answer under Canadian law, see Lai v. Gill, [1980] SCR 431; Sum Estates v. Kam [1997] BCJ No. 2645 (CA).

The Michigan court measured the parents' recovery by the value of their investment in the dead child, "the expenses of birth, of food, of clothing, of medicines, of instruction, of nurture and shelter." Wycko v. Gnodtke, 361 Mich. 331, 339, 105 N.W.2d 118, 122 (1960).

In addition to the parents' investment in money, what about letting them recover for their investment of time spent rearing the child before his death? "This method of valuation becomes less reliable as the child gets older, because then the parents will have recouped more of their investments in the form of intangible services (e.g., being bright, cute, cuddly) rendered them by the child. On the other hand, the older the child, the easier it is to predict his market earnings." Richard Posner, Economic Analysis of Law § 6.12 (6th ed. 2002). If the parents do recover for the time they spent rearing the child, should the court measure its value by the cost of procuring a substitute or by alternative prices for their services?

How should the jury consider the victim's social class? The *Childs* plaintiffs developed General's cousins' educational achievement. Should evidence of a minor child's lost capacity to earn include his parent's education, occupation, and income; the stability of his family life; his I.Q., education, and motivation; his siblings and birth order? This evidence might be admitted and considered in Canada. Houle v. Calgary (City) (1985) 60 AR 366 (CA). Are these avenues of inquiry "the trappings that build and perpetuate class?" Jeff Berryman, Accommodating Ethnic and Cultural Factors in Damages for Personal Injuries. (forthcoming). Should a court base wrongful death recovery on the victim's family members' or on his individual accomplishments?

9. *Grief.* Even more controversial than recovery for the parents' loss of their child's positive attributes has been their recovery for their loss in trauma, sorrow, mental distress, and grief for the lost child. The court allowed this recovery in Dawson v. Hill & Hill Truck Lines, 206 Mont. 325, 671 P.2d 589 (1983). The Nebraska Supreme Court declined the invitation. Nelson v. Dolan, 230 Neb. 848, 434 N.W.2d 25 (1989).

A family's "noneconomic" loss for a 9/11 victim's pain and suffering and the family's emotional distress was calculated at $250,000 for each decedent; $100,000 was added for each spouse and dependent. These figures were based on federal programs for military and law-enforcement personnel killed while on duty. (p. 75–76.)

10. *Money?* The death of a close family member is a dire event in every life; the survivors of sudden and violent deaths, like Debra's and General's, suffer the most distressful consequences.

The survivors' grief process reveals their raw emotions and may last a long time; it takes many and changing forms, including depression and its associates, anger and frustration.

(a) Kenneth Feinberg: "Mrs. Jones, you've got three more months to file this claim. You are going to receive about $3 million, Mrs. Jones. Sign the application. I'll help you fill it out."

"Go away, Mr. Feinberg. I lost my son. This is all about numbers? Just go away. Leave the application on the kitchen table."

"Mrs. Jones, you don't get it. You're compounding the felony. Set up a foundation in your son's name. Take the $3 million tax free."

"Thank you for coming, Mr. Feinberg. Leave it on the kitchen table." She never filed.

"My biggest disappointment in this program: there were 13 families who did nothing. They never entered the program. They never filed a lawsuit. I met with those 13 families separately, and I learned something about clinical depression." (ALI speech).

(b) Mere money is the only remedy that a lawyer and a court can offer a bereaved survivor. The judicial remedy of money is, however, a seriously second-best solution for a victim's family members' expectations, hopes, and needs. In addition to being unable to restore the world as it was before the casualty, the legal system is unable to satisfy the victim's survivors by securing an admission of fault and an apology from the wrongdoer. Indeed the plaintiffs' lawyer's goal of a hefty cash settlement will almost certainly include the defendant's explicit non-admission of fault or liability. Moreover, the plaintiffs' money settlement means that the victim's survivors will lack the closure of the "day in court" some of them desire. And yes, family members do sometimes fight about money.

(c) *"I hear you."* The Special Master conducted a series of open meetings and private conferences. "The [September 11] fund," he wrote, "could only be successful if claimants were given the opportunity to be heard." (p. 44.) Although someone criticized almost every one of his measurements, people who have been consulted and heard feel better, or less bad, about a decision.

11. *Standing is who.* A person's legal eligibility or "standing" to sue a tortfeasor for a wrongful death and to share the money may not coincide with that person's economic and emotional "standing" with the deceased person. A state statute may include wrongful death recovery for the victim's bitterly estranged spouse or sibling but exclude a longtime domestic partner of the same or different sex.

(a) *The Courts.* An unmarried male cohabitant who was not qualified to sue for wrongful death as a spouse or "domestic partner" under the California statutes lacked standing to sue for the wrongful death of his female partner. Moreover, the state's wrongful death and domestic partner statutes, so construed, did not, the court held, violate equal protection. Holguin v. Flores, 122 Cal.App.4th 428, 18 Cal.Rptr.3d 749 (2004).

A same-sex partner who had a Vermont civil union with the decedent lacked standing to maintain a New York wrongful death action, the court held, because he was not a statutory "spouse" or "distributee." Moreover, the statute, so construed, did not violate equal protection. Langan v. St. Vincent's Hospital, 25 A.D.3d 90, 802 N.Y.S.2d 476 (2005).

(b) *September 11.* The Special Master based a person's eligibility to receive a September 11 award on the United States state or foreign-nation law of the victim's domicile; but a foreign nation's law that allowed multiple spouses or barred women from recovery was not implemented. (p. 69–70.)

The 9/11 awards did not adhere literally to states' statutes' that excluded relationships that were not formalized.

The Special Master regularly encountered serious hostility between a decedent's parents and his or her fiancée. Sometimes he mediated; sometimes he delayed; "sometimes, however, family peace required that I add an additional amount and earmark it solely for the fiancée or same-sex partner"; sometimes "even this did not work * * * [because] there was just too much bad blood." (p. 69.)

Kenneth Feinberg: In walks the same-sex partner. "Mr. Feinberg, we were together for 11 years. You should treat me like a spouse."

"Biological parents, what do you say to that?"

"She was coming home to live. That 11–year thing, that was ending, and but for 9/11 she was going to break up and come home."

"Same-sex partner, what do you say to that?"

"Is that what they said? Let me tell you something. Eleven years ago when we moved in together they disowned her, and they didn't speak to her for 11 years. Now they come looking for the money? Outrageous." (ALI speech)

(c) Debra's friends and fellow employees who lost her unique human qualities are not in the picture, nor is her employer, Kroger, which lost a capable and loyal manager. General's father remained unknown. Under the Georgia statute, General's grandmother and aunts shared the wrongful death judgments.

(d) *Where There's a Will.* Would it be sounder public policy to follow the decedent's will, if there is one, in distributing a wrongful death judgment? Only 20% of the 9/11 victims had a will.

12. *Wrongful Death, General Gordon.* Is the judge humble enough about the uncertainty of projecting General Gordon's lost life into the future? Are the experts' economic projections of General Gordon's life fantasy cloaked in the false certainty of invented numbers? What compensatory purpose does the judgment for General Gordon's wrongful death serve? What deterrence purpose? Are other forms of recovery more appropriate?

13. *Alternatives.* If projecting General's unbegun life trajectory is a little too imprecise for you, what are the alternatives? To begin with, for the purposes of the Fourteenth Amendment, a fetus is not a person, the Supreme Court held in Roe v. Wade, 410 U.S. 113 (1973). A legislature or court must ask whether it is appropriate to have a different legal definition of a "person" for wrongful death.

(a) The traditional rule was: no wrongful death for the death of a fetus. Dietrich v. Inhabitants of Northampton, 138 Mass. 14 (1884). As recently as 2004, the Texas court held that a fetus was not a "person" within that state's wrongful death and survival statutes. Fort Worth Osteopathic Hospital, Inc. v. Reese, 148 S.W.3d 94 (Tex. 2004).

(b) Most jurisdictions allow wrongful death recovery if the fetus was "viable." Farley v. Sartin, 195 W.Va. 671, 466 S.E.2d 522 (1995).

(c) Arizona allows the parents to recover for the wrongful death of a viable fetus. But, in 2005, in a couple's suit against a reproductive clinic, the appellate court refused "to expand the meaning of 'person' in the wrongful death statute to include a three-day-old eight-celled cryopreserved pre-embryo." The court left the couple with other theories, negligence, fiduciary breach, and breach of the bailment contract. Jeter v. Mayo Clinic Arizona, 211 Ariz. 386, 121 P.3d 1256 (App.2005).

(d) Georgia is in a subcategory that allows wrongful death recovery for the death of an embryo.

(e) A final alternative when a tortfeasor kills an unborn fetus or embryo is to let the parents recover for mental anguish. New Jersey's courts decline to cover a stillborn fetus under wrongful death and survival statutes; but they do recognize the mother's tort recovery in her individual capacity for emotional distress and mental suffering. Giardina v. Bennett, 111 N.J. 412, 545 A.2d 139 (1988).

After rejecting constitutional attacks, the federal court observed that "New Jersey has chosen to draw a bright line that eliminates the nearly impossible problems of proof inherent in such actions when injury to a fetus is at issue." Alexander v. Whitman, 114 F.3d 1392, 1406 (3d Cir.1997).

14. *Funeral Expenses.* Even though the government stipulated to them in Childs v. United States, a victim's funeral expenses are somewhat incongruous as wrongful death damages because the defendant did not cause, but merely accelerated, its victim's funeral. After a trial for the wrongful death of an infirm 87-year-old, a Wisconsin jury returned a zero verdict for funeral expenses even though "undisput-

ed evidence at trial established that the funeral expenses totaled $7,610.10." Quoting Horace, the state supreme court said, "Eventually, we all must die. But that fact does not mean that a fact-finder may refuse to award funeral and burial expenses when the victim of the medical malpractice is elderly and, in the absence of medical malpractice, was likely to die sooner than a younger victim. The malpractice was a cause of the death and the tortfeasor is liable, as a matter of law, for reasonable funeral and burial expenses." Lagerstrom v. Myrtle Werth Hospital–Mayo Health System, 285 Wis.2d 1, 700 N.W.2d 201, 223–224 (2005).

15. *Reduction to Present Value.* The chapter will return to the lump-sum rule, interest, and reduction to present value; but the topics are important enough to summarize here.

A plaintiff's damages judgment is a lump sum which includes damages for plaintiff's lost future income. The court determines the plaintiff's loss period or worklife in years and the earnings that the victim would have lost in each year. If a victim's earnings loss is, say, $25,000 for each of 40 years, a judgment for $1,000,000 would over-compensate her family because their entire loss does not occur in the first year. If the family received the whole amount of her future earnings in the first year, they could invest it and spend the interest; the principal sum would remain intact at the end of the loss period. At a 5% interest rate, interest on a $1,000,000 judgment would yield $50,000 per year forever and leave the principal sum. So the court reduces or discounts the lump sum to present value. The plaintiff should recover an amount sufficient to supply the expected periodic payments for the loss period. Each year the plaintiff will be able to draw out part of the principal plus the interest that the principal has earned during that year. When the loss period ends, the lump sum should be gone. To reduce the lump sum to present value, the court discounts it by assuming the rate of interest rate that it will be expected to earn. The higher the interest rate, the more interest the lump sum earns and the smaller the lump sum plaintiff needs. Present value tables in books and computer programs are used to couple amounts and interest rates to periodic payments. Assuming a compounded interest rate of 5%, the present value of $25,000 per year for 40 years is $428,977.

The example is simpler than the future pecuniary losses in the principal case which the experts adjusted for productivity gains and inflation. The issues and assumptions in the calculation include the length of the loss period, the victim's professional advancement, and her industry's productivity gains. A statute setting Georgia's interest rate for present value calculations eliminated that issue for Debra and General Gordon. Ga.Code § 51–12–13 (1996).

An important issue during a period of inflation is whether and how to increase the lump sum to accommodate to future inflation and the accompanying decline in the money's purchasing power. See Jones & Laughlin Steel Corp. v. Pfeifer, 462 U.S. 523, 533–48 (1983); Beaulieu v. Elliott, 434 P.2d 665, 671 (Alaska 1967).

A September 11 victim's lost future income was discounted to present value based on mid- to long-term U.S. Treasury securities' after-tax yields which varied with the victim's age. The government assumed that younger victims' survivors would make longer-term investments. A victim under 36 had a discount rate of 5.1%, 4.2 after tax. For those over 54, it was 4.2%, after tax, 3.4%.

16. *What's a Life Worth?* (a) Special Master Kenneth Feinberg quotes Senator Tom Daschele who was then Senate minority leader. Daschele observed, "Do you want to put a value on human life right now? I don't." (p. 37.)

(b) Economists rush in where senators fear to tread? "Valuing human lives sounds like an ethical or even a metaphysical undertaking, but all that's actually involved is determining the value that people place on avoiding small risks of death.

From data on wage premia in dangerous occupations, the response of housing prices to proximity to hazardous sites, seatbelt use, cigarette smoking, and other behavior toward risk of death, actual or perceived, economists can calculate how much money the average person would demand to incur a given such risk. Division of the 'price' charged to bear a given risk by the risk yields the value-of-life estimate. So if the risk of death is one in ten thousand and the price demanded to bear the risk is $500, the value of life would be $5 million ($500 ÷ .0001). There have been many studies of risk-taking and risk-avoiding behavior; they yield a range of estimates of the value of (U.S.) life from around $4 million to $9 million, with a median of $7 million." Richard Posner, Guido Calabresi's *The Costs of Accidents*: A Reassessment, 64 Md.L.Rev. 12, 17 (2005).

(c) Has everyone been listening to the economists? In the September 11 disbursal, more than $7,000,000,000 was distributed, including 2,880 death claims to survivors. "I was convinced," Mr. Feinberg wrote, "that I should use my discretion to *narrow the gap* between high-end and low-end awards." (p. 47) One narrowing technique was to ignore victims' yearly compensation above $231,000, that is in the top 2% of incomes. (p. 73.) The death awards ranged from $250,000 to $7,100,000; the median was $1,700,00, the mean $2,100,000. Not many exceeded $3,000,000. (p. 52.)

(d) Speaking for himself, in retrospect, Special Master Kenneth Feinberg thinks that, in any future system, "all eligible claimants should receive the same amount." Uniform payouts are a cinch to calculate and easier to administer.

Also—"economic distinctions among claimants [are] guaranteed to promote divisiveness." (p. 183–185.) "A firefighter's widow stands up to me and says, 'My husband died a hero. He saved 30 lives. You're going to give him $1.4 million, and you're giving $5 million to the accountant who worked for Enron! Where's the justice, Mr. Feinberg?'" (ALI speech)

(e) Should the family of a victim with six children and 30 more working years receive the same amount as the wealthy widow of an 82-year-old retired stockbroker?

17. *A Low–Value Life?* A trial lawyer may say that every life is worth at least $1 million. After the Special Master subtracted collateral sources and exercised his discretion, the minimum September 11 award was $250,000.

Back to Savannah: Set there, John Berendt's popular book "Midnight in the Garden of Good and Evil," centered on Joe Williams shooting Danny Hansford, a volatile, violent hustler. Williams's murder trials ended in the fourth and final one with his acquittal on self-defense. A sub-plot was Hansford's mother's wrongful death lawsuit.

Williams speaking: "But Danny's mother takes the prize with her ten-million dollar lawsuit against me. After all the anguish and grief Danny had caused her, after she'd thrown him out of the house and gotten police protection from him, Danny was suddenly her beloved dead son, miraculously transformed from a dangerous liability into an asset worth ten million dollars. Lord knows what it will cost me to defend myself against her lawsuit."

In the end, "because [Williams] had been found innocent of any crime in Danny Hansford's death, his insurance company would step in and settle with Hansford's mother." Chapters 18, p. 254–55; 28, p. 371 (1994). We don't learn how much.

Allowing the defendant to argue for reduced damages because, before the accident, the plaintiff had "led a life of crime and laziness" was the Canadian court in Rodzinski v. Modern Dairies Ltd. [1949] 2WWR 456 (Man.KB).

Let's try two hypothetical wrongful death cases: Is every life worth $1 million or at least $250,000?

(a) Bill Kilen, a five-year-old infantile autistic child had been enrolled for two years at Stonecreek School, a residential care facility for handicapped children. Bill had not developed any communication or relationship skills, and he was a "runner" who needed to be watched and sometimes tethered for his own safety. An autistic child almost always puts a heavy emotional strain on his parents and family. The admissions evaluations in Stonecreek School's file show that Bill would spend his entire life either in a residential facility or at home with a full-time caretaker. In January, tragically, Bill bolted from his group, crawled under a fence, and drowned in Stonecreek. Bill's caretaker was inattentive enough to support a finding of negligence.

The state wrongful death statute allows the plaintiff to recover "the full value of the [decedent's] life." Stonecreek's owner thinks a starting settlement offer of $50,000 might lead the Kilens to settle for under $100,000, perhaps for about $75,000. What kind of case on damages might the Kilens mount? What are Stonecreek's prospects for a quick five-figure settlement?

(b) Four-year-old Jessica's mother, Marie Keller, had been supporting her serious cocaine addiction by prostitution and shoplifting. Marie was on her way to meet a producer of internet porn videos to sell Jessica's services for a kiddy-porn video when an intoxicated driver's vehicle jumped the curb and killed her.

Since Jessica's father is unknown, she has been placed with foster parents, a loving and capable couple who have said they may be interested in adopting her. You are her legal guardian. The tortfeasor's insurance company has offered $25,000 to settle for Marie's death. The same "full-value" statute governs.

18. *The Jury.* Although a federal district judge sets the damages in an FTCA trial, a jury calculates the plaintiff's damages in most personal injury and wrongful death trials. Can a juror be expected to follow all the experts' assumptions and calculations? Will a judge do better? Which is the best suited for the task?

2. PAIN AND SUFFERING

In addition to past and future damages for lost earnings and medical expenses, a personal injury plaintiff recovers compensatory damages for her pain and suffering.

A plaintiff's pain and suffering damages are premised on the idea that a victim who has been through a harrowing experience has lost more than her earnings and medical bills. Pain is physical: tissue damage stimulates a person's nerves and this hurts. Suffering describes the way a person processes or perceives pain; suffering can take several forms, among them grief, bereavement, fear, and frustration.

Instead of ignoring the plaintiff's intangible loss, the decision to award the victim money recognizes the plaintiff's pain and suffering, albeit in a different form, and singles out the defendant's misconduct for public acknowledgment.

Courts, legislatures, and commentators often refer to pain and suffering damages as "noneconomic." Are they? Pain and suffering "losses impose opportunity costs. People will pay to avoid them and demand payment to risk incurring them." Richard Posner, Economic Analysis of Law § 6.12 (6th ed. 2002). Is it more accurate to refer to pain and suffering as economic, but nonpecuniary?

1. *Justification*? What justifies a plaintiff's recovery for her pain and suffering?

(a) *Compensation*: A person's pain and suffering does not occur in money; money damages can neither replace nor repair them. Does the *Consorti* court, quoted below, think that the cancer-victim plaintiff is under-compensated? Of a $12,000,000 verdict for his pain and suffering, which the trial judge had declined to reduce, but which the appellate court reduced to $3,500,000, the appellate court observed, "reasonable people [plaintiff's] age, in good mental and physical health, would not have traded one-quarter of his suffering for a hundred million dollars, much less twelve. * * * While the law seeks by reasonable compensation to make a plaintiff whole, we must recognize that compensation for suffering can be accomplished only in a symbolic and arbitrary fashion. There are at least two serious shortcomings to the endeavor. First, money awards do not make one whole; they do not alleviate pain. Second, there is no rational scale that justifies the award of any particular amount, in compensation for a particular amount of pain." Consorti v. Armstrong World Industries, 72 F.3d 1003, 1009 (2d Cir. 1995). The Supreme Court vacated the appellate court's opinion, quoted above, and ultimately the trial judge described Consorti's ordeal and set his pain and suffering damages at $5,000,000. In re Joint Eastern and Southern District Asbestos Litigation, 9 F.Supp.2d 307 (S.D.N.Y. 1998). We return to Consorti below to deal with the trial judge's and appellate court's post-verdict judicial review.

(b) *Substitutes*: An economist may strain to explain that a plaintiff can use the money from pain and suffering damages to purchase a substitute or a distraction: a former athlete who has lost a foot can buy a television and watch others run.

(c) *Deterrence*: A potential defendant has the possibility of being required to pay an injury victim's pain and suffering damages built into its safety expenditures to prevent future fatalities.

(d) *Litigation Finance*: Under the American Rule each side pays its own attorney fees; a winning plaintiff will not recover her attorney's fees as part of her damages. But under the United States courthouse culture, generally understood, a plaintiff's verdict for pain and suffering damages is camouflaged attorney fees. So long as accident victims use contingency fee contracts to retain attorneys and so long as attorneys receive a percentage of the settlement or recovery, pain and suffering damages will be used to pay the plaintiff's attorney. Pain and suffering damages will persist through the pre-no-fault era.

(e) Do you think plaintiffs are over- or under-compensated for pain and suffering? If the jury values plaintiff's post-injury life in uninjured terms, will the verdict be under-compensatory because the money is worth less to the injured and disabled victim who cannot enjoy an uninjured lifestyle?

2. *Subjectivity*: Each of us endures a bad experience differently. In the courtroom, a plaintiff's pain and suffering is individual to that particular plaintiff. Each juror is different. The juror cannot see the plaintiff's pain, and the plaintiff cannot communicate it in words. Converting pain and suffering into a dollar figure is expensive and difficult. Valuations vary; prediction is precarious. A plaintiff's tort recovery for her nonpecuniary loss uses market language and methodology to treat the plaintiff's casualty and injury as a market transaction, albeit an involuntary one.

Uncertainty, subjectivity and the risk of exorbitant judgments lead potential defendants to argue for principles to confine pain and suffering damages and to make them more predictable.

The judicial quest for principles to confine pain and suffering occurs in several stages, admission of evidence, jury instructions, limitations on argument, and post-verdict judicial review. One response has been tort reform, the statutory cap, which we return to below.

3. *Components*. What is included in pain and suffering?

(a) The victim's "anguish and terror felt in the face of impending injury and death."

(b) The victim's "tangible physiological pain * * * at the time of injury and during recuperation."

(c) The victim's "enduring loss of enjoyment of life [as one] who is denied the pleasures of normal personal and social activities because of his permanent physical impairment." 2 American Law Institute, Enterprise Responsibility for Personal Injury: Approaches to Legal and Institutional Change 199–200 (1991).

(d) The ALI report also classifies as pain and suffering what others call the derivative damages category of consortium, "the immediate emotional distress and long-term loss of love and companionship resulting from the injury or death of a close family member."

4. *Proof*. What evidence may a plaintiff introduce to prove her pain and suffering? How do jurors relate to a plaintiff's pain in general and as an element of damages? Science lacks an objective way to measure a person's subjective experience of pain. Perhaps a juror has a migraine headache or lower back pain or knows someone with chronic pain syndrome. Another juror may, however, hear plaintiff's evidence with disbelief or doubt and think that she may be malingering.

Plaintiff's pain-and-suffering testimony is prominent but risky because it is interested and potentially exaggerated. It will touch on plaintiff's life before the incident, the incident itself, the therapy following the incident, and how the injury impairs her ability to conduct normal and enjoyable activity. Testimony may focus on the quality of plaintiff's daily cycle of home, family, and work life.

A physician-expert can assess the level of pain from the way plaintiff describes it. A health-care provider may test plaintiff's functions to diagnose and treat; these tests can be used to describe how injuries affect plaintiff's activities. Plaintiff's friends and family members can explain and corroborate how the injury affected the plaintiff. When plaintiff's spouse testifies that the injury affects spousal relationships and family responsibilities, damages for plaintiff's pain and suffering blend into the spouse's consortium recovery. Summaries of lay and expert testimony which was sufficient to convince a skeptical judge to enter large verdicts for flight attendants' post traumatic stress disorder with depression are reported in In re Air Crash Disaster at Charlotte, N.C., 982 F.Supp. 1101 (D.S.C. 1997); 982 F.Supp. 1115 (D.S.C. 1997).

A vocabulary surplus exists for plaintiff's pain and suffering damages. The court below uses "general damages" to describe plaintiff Loth's pain and suffering damages in contrast to "special damages" for her pecuniary damages. The professional vocabulary for pain and suffering also includes "noneconomic," and "nonpecuniary." Loth's expert Stanley Smith adds "hedonic" damages for the lost enjoyment of life part of her pain and suffering. This book tries to stay with pain and suffering, but a student should expect to read and hear differing terms for the same ideas.

LOTH v. TRUCK–A–WAY CORP.

California Court of Appeal, 1998.
60 Cal.App.4th 757, 70 Cal.Rptr.2d 571 (reh'g denied, review denied).

ORTEGA, ACTING PRESIDING JUSTICE. In this personal injury lawsuit arising from an automobile accident, the jury awarded the plaintiff substantial general damages, which was not in itself remarkable. What was unusual, however, was plaintiff's expert economist's testimony on "hedonic" damages, or damages to compensate for the loss of enjoyment of life.

"The term hedonic damages itself was first suggested by economist Stanley Smith in the case of Sherrod v. Berry [(N.D.Ill. 1985) 629 F.Supp. 159, reversed on other grounds (7thCir. 1988) 856 F.2d 802]. Hedonic damages derives its name from the Greek word 'hedonikos' meaning pleasure or pleasurable. As interpreted by the courts around the United States, hedonic damages means either a loss of enjoyment of life or loss of life's pleasures." Price, *Hedonic Damages: To Value a Life or Not to Value a Life?* (1993) 95 W.Va.L.Rev. 1055, 1056.) Smith is the same economist who testified as plaintiff's hedonic damages expert in this case. * * *

The admissibility of such testimony appears to be a question of first impression in California. We conclude the expert's testimony on hedonic damages was inadmissible as a matter of law and its admission was prejudicial. We reverse the judgment and remand for a new trial on damages.

FACTUAL & PROCEDURAL BACKGROUND. On June 29, 1994, plaintiff Shereen Loth was on a business trip driving north on Interstate 5. Plaintiff's small car was struck by a 24–wheel tractor-trailer rig owned by defendant Truck–A–Way. * * *

Plaintiff walked away from the accident but her car was seriously damaged. She continued her trip in a rental car, but she had suffered a concussion, was disoriented, and was unable to handle her business affairs. (Plaintiff, a design school graduate, owns a small but growing business that manufactures and markets lingerie throughout California and in Las Vegas.) Plaintiff cut short her business trip and flew home.

Two days after the accident, plaintiff went to her doctor complaining of headaches, low back pain, and a stiff neck. Between July 1994 and March 1995, plaintiff saw five other doctors including a neurologist, a psychiatrist, and an orthopedic surgeon. She had disabling neck pain, headaches, severe low back pain, groin pain, and shooting pains down her legs. She received physical therapy which lessened her headaches, neck pain, and upper back pain, but failed to improve her low back pain, groin pain, and shooting pains down her left leg. A soft tissue injury specialist gave her cortisone shots in the lower back and sacroiliac joint, but she felt no lasting relief. She had six chiropractic sessions that were of no help. According to plaintiff's medical experts, she has exhausted her treatment options other than taking pain medications with dangerous potential side effects.

Plaintiff sued Truck–A–Way and its employee driver for personal injuries, property damage, and lost earnings. Defendants conceded liability at trial, and the only issue for the jury was damages.

Plaintiff asked the jury for $208,479 in special damages, comprised of medical damages (past and future) of $27,635, temporary lost earnings of $147,675, and property damage and miscellaneous expenses of $3,507. (Those figures do not total $208,479, but that is what the jury was told both orally and in writing.)

As for pain and suffering, plaintiff asked for an unspecified amount of damages, including compensation for loss of enjoyment of life. Plaintiff, who was 27 when the accident occurred, was a star high school varsity athlete in volleyball, softball, and basketball. Before the accident, she worked 10 to 11–hour days (including a night shift as a cocktail waitress), played softball and volleyball three nights a week, and exercised at the gym every day. After the accident, she could not sit at a sewing machine for longer than an hour without pain, could not function as a cocktail waitress, could not play organized sports, and could no longer water or snow ski, jog, or golf. Her social life, which had previously revolved around her athletic activities, was severely impaired. Driving a car now causes her jaw to hurt. To prevent her jaw from clenching, she must drive with her mouth agape. She has constant lower back pain that increases with activity and sometimes shoots down her leg. She had hoped to get married and have children, but her condition has made her fearful of having children and her "sexual spontaneity is gone."

Over defendants' objection, plaintiff's expert economist Stanley V. Smith testified he had computed the basic economic value of life (apart from one's earnings from employment). Defendants raised numerous grounds * * * for excluding Smith's testimony. They included: (1) there is no consensus among experts in the field that a scientific method for computing hedonic damages exists. [citations] (2) the method of computing hedonic damages is not a matter for which expert testimony is admissible under Evidence Code section 801; (3) Smith's testimony would be more prejudicial than probative and would enflame the jury (Evid.Code, § 352); (4) the evidence is inadmissible under California law which prohibits a separate instruction on loss of enjoyment of life damages (Huff v. Tracy (1976) 57 Cal.App.3d 939) and precludes a double recovery for pain and suffering and loss of enjoyment of life; and (5) the evidence is speculative and invades the province of the jury to compute the amount of general damages.

Smith relied upon three types of studies of: (1) the amount society is willing to pay per capita on protective devices such as seat belts, smoke detectors, etc., (2) the risk premiums employers pay to induce workers to perform hazardous jobs, and (3) the cost/benefit analyses of federally mandated safety projects and programs. Based on those studies, Smith calculated the value of an average person's remaining 44–year life expectancy at $2.3 million, which he described as a baseline figure. Smith adjusted the baseline figure to account for plaintiff's longer than average remaining life expectancy of 53 years. He multiplied the adjusted baseline figure by various percentages reflecting plaintiff's possible degrees of disability to calculate various possible hedonic damage awards. For example, Smith told the jury that in plaintiff's case, a 33 percent loss of enjoyment would be worth $1,684,000, a 10 percent loss of enjoyment would be worth $510,000, and a 5 percent loss of enjoyment would be worth $255,000. Smith gave the jury a table to assist it in making its mathematical calculations.

Defendants, having failed to prevail on their objections to Smith's testimony, offered no expert testimony to refute Smith's assertions.

In closing argument, plaintiff's counsel specifically referred to Smith's testimony, and pointed out the absence of conflicting expert testimony on the formula for computing hedonic damages. Plaintiff's counsel stated: "Now I want you to compare the experts. Stan Smith testified. He wrote the book literally on this kind of damages. He's tops in his field. There's been no contradiction of anything that he said."

Defendants' closing argument urged the jury to disregard plaintiff's claim of a lower back injury. Defense counsel conceded plaintiff had incurred a soft tissue injury to the neck and a concussion, but argued her other injuries were not related to the accident. As for pain and suffering damages, defense counsel argued that the jury needed no expert testimony to calculate an award. Counsel pointed out Smith's $2.3 million baseline figure did not take into account "any unique personalities, likes, interests of any one of us. I think each one of us is a * * * distinct individual, and I think it's almost sacrilegious or almost impossible to place value on human life. That's going to be a tough job for you, and that's something that you are going to have to decide in this matter." Counsel urged the jury to ignore Smith's testimony, which he characterized as "just too speculative."

The jury returned a general verdict for plaintiff for $890,000. After the trial court denied defendants' motion for new trial or remittitur, defendants appealed from the judgment.

CONTENTIONS ON APPEAL. Defendants contend Smith's testimony on hedonic damages was inadmissible and the amount of the judgment was unsupported by the record.

DISCUSSION. In California, a pain and suffering award may include compensation for the plaintiff's loss of enjoyment of life. Loss of enjoyment of life, however, is only one component of a general damage award for pain and suffering. It is not calculated as a separate award.

"California case law recognizes, as one component of general damage, physical impairment which limits the plaintiff's capacity to share in the amenities of life. (Henninger v. Southern Pacific Co., (1967)) 250 Cal.App.2d 872, 883 (loss of both legs); Purdy v. Swift and Co., (1939) 34 Cal.App.2d 656, 658 (impairment of taste and smell); Scally v. W.T. Garratt & Co., (1909) 11 Cal.App. 138 (loss of ability to pursue musical studies). The California decisions rarely employ the 'enjoyment of life' rubric, yet achieve a result consistent with it. No California rule restricts a plaintiff's attorney from arguing this element to a jury. Damage for mental suffering supplies an analogue." (Huff v. Tracy).

"There are four views as to the recovery of damages for loss of enjoyment of life (hedonic damages): (1) such damages are not recoverable; (2) such damages are recoverable as a part of the damages for pain and suffering; (3) such damages are recoverable as an element of the permanency of injury; and (4) such damages are recoverable as a separate element of damages." (3 J. Stein, Stein on Personal Injury Damages (1992) Mental Anguish, § 3:18:1)

Much of the debate has focused on whether the plaintiff must have been conscious or aware of the injury to recover hedonic damages. * * * In New York, the highest state court held that hedonic damages are not recoverable independently of pain and suffering damages and reversed an award of hedonic damages to a comatose plaintiff. (McDougald v. Garber [Editor: below in this casebook.] But a New Jersey court held in Eyoma v. Falco (A.D.1991) 435, 589 A.2d 653, that pain and suffering damages may be awarded where the patient was comatose.

There is "[n]o definite standard or method of calculation * * * prescribed by law by which to fix reasonable compensation for pain and suffering." (BAJI No. 14.13 (8th ed. 1994)) As our Supreme Court stated, "One of the most difficult tasks imposed upon a jury in deciding a case involving personal injuries is to determine the amount of money the plaintiff is to be awarded as compensation for pain and suffering. No method is available to the jury by which it can objectively evaluate such damages, and no witness may express his subjective opinion on the matter. In a very real sense, the jury is asked to evaluate in terms of money a detriment for which monetary compensation cannot be ascertained with any demonstrable accuracy. As one writer on the subject has said, 'Translating pain and anguish into dollars can, at best, be only an arbitrary allowance, and not a process of measurement, and consequently the judge can, in his instructions, give the jury no standard to go by; he can only tell them to allow such amount as in their discretion they may consider reasonable. * * * The chief reliance for reaching reasonable results in attempting to value suffering in terms of money must be the restraint and common sense of the jury.' " (Beagle v. Vasold (1966) 65 Cal.2d 166, 172.)

The jury must impartially determine pain and suffering damages based upon evidence specific to the plaintiff, as opposed to statistical data concerning the public at large. The only person whose pain and suffering is relevant in calculating a general damage award is the plaintiff. How others would feel if placed in the plaintiff's position is irrelevant. It is improper, for example, for an attorney to ask jurors how much "they would 'charge' to undergo equivalent pain and suffering." (Beagle v. Vasold) "This so-called 'golden rule' argument is impermissible." (Brokopp v. Ford Motor Co. (1977) 71 Cal.App.3d 841, 860.)

Attorneys may, however, ask the jury to measure the plaintiff's pain and suffering on a "per diem" basis. (Beagle v. Vasold) The court in *Beagle* explained that while the "per diem" argument is permissible, the "golden rule" argument is not: "In holding that counsel may properly suggest to the jury that plaintiff's pain and suffering may be measured on a 'per diem' basis, we do not imply that we also approve the so-called 'golden rule' argument, by which counsel asks the jurors to place themselves in the plaintiff's shoes and to award such damages as they would 'charge' to undergo equivalent pain and suffering."

"The appeal to a juror to exercise his subjective judgment rather than an impartial judgment predicated on the evidence cannot be condoned. It tends to denigrate the jurors' oath to well and truly try the issue and render a true verdict according to the evidence. (Code Civ. Proc., § 604.) Moreover, it in effect asks each juror to become a personal partisan advocate for the injured party, rather than an unbiased and unprejudiced weigher of the evidence. Finally, it may tend to induce each juror to consider a higher figure than he otherwise might to avoid being considered self-abasing." (Neumann v. Bishop (1976) 59 Cal.App.3d 451, 484–485.)

In this case, plaintiff did not make an impermissible "golden rule" argument, but she did something similar. She asked the jury to accept $2.3 million as the baseline value of life and to give her a percentage of that figure (adjusted for her age) as hedonic damages. The baseline figure, however, is not based upon an analysis of any particular individual's life. It is based upon benchmark figures such as the amount society spends per capita on selected safety devices, or the amount employers pay to induce workers to perform high risk jobs. We perceive no meaningful relationship between those arbitrarily selected benchmark spending figures and the value of an individual person's life. Moreover, our Supreme Court has rejected the notion that pain and suffering damages may be computed by some mathematical formula. (Beagle v. Vasold) Smith's hedonic damages formula, however, purports to do just that.

Defendants objected to Smith's testimony on several grounds. One objection was based on the prohibition against separately instructing the jury on general damages for pain and suffering and damages for loss of enjoyment of life (Huff v. Tracy).

Defendants raised no claim of instructional error on appeal. In this case, the jury received the following standard instructions on pain and suffering damages:

> "The defendants having admitted liability, you must award plaintiff damages in an amount that will reasonably compensate for each of the following elements of claimed loss or harm, provided that you find it was or will be suffered by plaintiff and was or will be caused by such defendant[s'] conduct." (Based on BAJI No. 14.01 (8th ed.1994).)

> "The amount of such award shall include: [¶] Medical expenses [¶] Loss of earnings [¶] Loss of use of property [¶] Costs of repair or replacement [¶] Loss of employment [¶] Loss of business or employment opportunities [¶] Pain and suffering [¶] Inconvenience [¶] Mental suffering [¶] Emotional distress." (Based on BAJI No. 14.01 (8th ed.1994).)

> "Reasonable compensation for any pain, discomfort, fears, anxiety and other mental and emotional distress suffered by the plaintiff and of which injury was a cause and for similar suffering reasonably certain to be experienced in the future from the same cause. [¶] No definite standard or method of calculation is prescribed by law by which to fix reasonable compensation for pain and suffering. Nor is the opinion of any witness required as to the amount of such reasonable compensation. Furthermore, the argument of counsel as to the amount of damages is not evidence of reasonable compensation. In making the award for pain and suffering you shall exercise your authority with calm and reasonable judgment and the damages you fix shall be just and reasonable in the light of the evidence." (Based on BAJI No. 14.13 (8th ed.1994).)

Separate instructions on pain and suffering and loss of enjoyment of life are prohibited because they could mislead a jury to award double damages for the same injury. Defendants argued below that Smith's testimony was inadmissible as a matter of law because of its potential for misleading the jury to award double damages. We find the objection was valid and we conclude, as a matter of law, Smith's testimony should have been excluded on that ground.

In cases involving more severe injuries where the plaintiff shows the jury a "day in the life" videotape to support a pain and suffering award, the admission of expert testimony on hedonic damages would present an even stronger danger that the jury would award double damages. As was stated in Jones v. City of Los Angeles (1993) 20 Cal.App.4th 436: "The videotape best describes the problems Ms. Jones encounters on a daily basis in a way mere oral testimony may not convey to the jurors. The videotape also best demonstrates the everyday problems a person with paraplegia encounters as a result of an injury of this kind. Moreover, the videotape is the most effective way to explain to the jury the extent of the assistance and medical attention required as a result of being rendered a paraplegic.''

Our conclusion is consistent with that of other courts. * * *

In addition, Smith's testimony should have been excluded for another reason. Defendants also objected on the ground that the method of computing hedonic damages is not a matter for which expert testimony is admissible under Evidence Code section 801. That objection was also sound.

A plaintiff's loss of enjoyment of life is not "a subject that is sufficiently beyond common experience that the opinion of an expert would assist the trier of fact[.]" (Evid.Code, § 801, subd. (a).) No amount of expert testimony on the value of life could possibly help a jury decide that difficult question. A life is not a stock, car, home, or other such item bought and sold in some marketplace.

Smith's impersonal method of valuing life assumes that for the most part, all lives have the same basic value. That has democratic appeal, but Smith used no democratic processes in reaching that conclusion or selecting which benchmark figures to consider in setting the baseline figure. There is no statute Smith could have turned to for guidance. Our Legislature has not decreed that all injured plaintiffs of the same age and with the same degree of disability should recover the same hedonic damages; nor has it assigned set values in tort cases for the loss of an eye, ear, limb, or life. Moreover, our judicial law prohibits trial counsel from referring to the amounts of jury verdicts in other cases. [citations] Because counsel may not ask the jury to give the same amount of damages as in another case, it would be inconsistent to permit an expert witness to do so.

The figures Smith included in his baseline calculation have nothing to do with this particular plaintiff's injuries, condition, hobbies, skills, or other factors relevant to her loss of enjoyment of life. The studies Smith used may help explain how much consumers will pay for safer products, or how much society should pay for government-mandated safety programs, but they shed no light on how to value this particular plaintiff's pain and suffering following the automobile accident. It is speculative, at best, to say the amount society is willing to spend on seat belts or air bags has any relationship to the intrinsic value of a person's life or the value of an injured plaintiff's pain and suffering. By urging the jury to rely upon a baseline value supported by factors having nothing to do with this plaintiff's individual condition, Smith's testimony created the possibility of a runaway jury verdict.

That is not to say, however, that we believe the verdict was so large as to shock the conscience or suggest it was the result of passion or prejudice. Plaintiff testified she has substantial pain, cannot indulge in her passion for sports, and has lived a comparatively drab existence following the accident. On this record, we cannot say, as a matter of law, that a verdict of $890,000 is in any way excessive.

Our present system of requiring the jury to determine, without the benefit of a mathematical formula, the amount of a general damages award is not without its faults. But unless and until the Legislature devises a method for computing pain and suffering damages, a plaintiff may not supply, through expert testimony or otherwise, her own formula for computing such damages. Just as no judge may give the jury a standard for determining pain and suffering damages [citation], no expert may supply a formula for computing the value of life and, by extrapolation, the value of the loss of enjoyment of life. That calculation, at present, must be left to the sound discretion of the jury.

We note other jurisdictions have also excluded Smith's hedonic damages expert testimony. [citations]

Having determined Smith's testimony was inadmissible as a matter of law, we turn to the issue of prejudice. We must examine all the evidence to determine whether it is reasonably probable that a different result would have been reached absent the error. [citations] If so, reversal is required.

Because loss of enjoyment of life is simply one component of pain and suffering damages, presenting the jury with a formula for separately calculating hedonic damages created a risk of double recovery for pain and suffering and loss of enjoyment of life. The jury heard plaintiff's testimony regarding the drastic lifestyle changes she had made because of her injuries, and was told it could award "[r]easonable compensation for any pain, discomfort, fears, anxiety and other mental and emotional distress suffered by the plaintiff and of which injury was a cause and for similar suffering reasonably certain to be experienced in the future from the same cause." Plaintiff's testimony alone was sufficient to support a general damages award that included compensation for loss of enjoyment of life. But there was more than just plaintiff's testimony. The jury also heard Smith's expert testimony on how much a life is worth and how to calculate hedonic damages by multiplying that figure by the percentage of plaintiff's disability.

While the judge correctly instructed the jury there is no single mathematical formula for computing pain and suffering damages, the instruction was insufficient to cure the error of admitting Smith's testimony. Plaintiff's counsel's argument that Smith's testimony was unrefuted rendered the instruction a mere wink and a nod. It is reasonably probable and almost a certainty the jury awarded a double recovery. Accordingly, the admission of Smith's testimony was prejudicial.

DISPOSITION. We reverse the judgment and remand for a new trial on damages. * * *

Notes

1. Issues include: Is plaintiff's lost enjoyment of life freestanding or part of her pain and suffering. Whether to admit an expert's evidence of plaintiff's "hedonic" loss. Whether lost enjoyment of life can be recovered on behalf of someone who is in a coma or dead.

2. An example of valuing hedonic damages from an earlier decision: "Assume that a person purchases a safety device for $700 and that device reduces the probability of his death from 7 in 10,000 to 5 in 10,000. By reducing his chance of dying by 2/10,000ths, or one chance in 5,000 at a cost of $700, economists would say that he valued his life at $3,500,000. In effect, if 5,000 people spent $700 each on air bags, one life would be saved at a total cost of $3,500,000. These figures are not the actual figures from air bag studies, but just sample figures to show how the analysis is done, in simple terms." Ayers v. Robinson, 887 F.Supp. 1049, 1052 (N.D.Ill.1995). Judge Shadur rejected the testimony.

3. Other courts have respond to the issues in different ways. In Mississippi, for example, a plaintiff's lost enjoyment of life is an element of his damages that is

separate from his pain and suffering. Moreover, Stan Smith's expert testimony is admissible to prove plaintiff's lost enjoyment of life. Kansas City Southern Railway Co. v. Johnson, 798 So.2d 374 (Miss. 2001).

4. In *Loth*, did the California pattern jury instruction on pain and suffering focus the jury's judgment on the absence, in Loth's post-injury life, of the positive features of her pre-injury life? Is the phrase "loss of enjoyment of life" ambiguous because it emphasizes the negative and fails to distinguish between the negative and the absence of the positive?

5. Although the *Loth* court praises the jury's "restraint and common sense," does it force the jury to exercise that restraint and common sense in the dark?

6. The jury combined all of Loth's damages into one figure in a lump-sum "general verdict." Might a special or itemized verdict form that breaks the plaintiff's damages into categories have clarified the issues for the jury, the trial judge, and the court of appeal?

7. *Closing Argument on Pain and Suffering*:

(a) *The "Golden Rule."* A Golden Rule measurement of the plaintiff's pain and suffering asks jurors to put themselves in plaintiff's predicament and to return a verdict for the amount they would want if they had plaintiff's injuries. Courts forbid Golden Rule arguments either in summation or in instructions. Why?

(b) *A Specific Amount.* "Plaintiff's counsel, in summation, asked for a specific dollar amount [$1,500,000] as damages." Defendants now urge us to adopt a per se rule prohibiting counsel from suggesting a specific sum as damages. We decline to do so.

While at least one circuit has such a rule, [citation] we favor a more flexible approach. It is best left to the discretion of the trial judge, who may either prohibit counsel from mentioning specific figures or impose reasonable limitations, including cautionary jury instructions. [citation] Here, counsel reviewed the evidence on damages and asked for an award of $1,500,000. The court instructed the jury that damages should be awarded 'only upon and only in proportion to a showing as to the nature, duration and severity of his condition.'

"Although the jury's award of $750,000, exactly half of the demand by plaintiff's counsel, suggests that the jurors may have been influenced by counsel's mention of a particular dollar amount, in context, the closing and the charge to the jury do not support defendants' claim that the jury was *unfairly* influenced."

Lightfoot v. Union Carbide Corp., 110 F.3d 898, 912–13 (2d Cir. 1997).

(c) *Per Diem or Unit of Time.* "In recent years the question has received consideration in a number of jurisdictions. The weight of authority favors allowing use in argument of a mathematical formula such as suggesting amounts on a per diem basis when damages for pain and suffering are involved. * * *"

"Authorities opposing per diem amount arguments as to damages for pain and suffering give varied reasons: (1) that there is no evidentiary basis for converting pain and suffering into monetary terms; (2) that it is improper for counsel to suggest a total amount for pain and suffering, and therefore wrong to suggest per diem amounts; (3) that to do so amounts to the attorney giving testimony, and expressing opinions and conclusions on matters not disclosed by the evidence; (4) that juries frequently are misled thereby into making excessive awards, and that admonitions of the court that the jury should not consider per diem arguments as evidence fail to erase all prejudicial effect; (5) that following such argument by plaintiff, a defendant is prejudiced by being placed in a position of attempting to rebut an argument having no basis in the evidence, with the result that if he does not answer plaintiff's argument in kind he suffers its effect on the jury, but if defendant does answer in kind he thereby implies approval of the per diem argument for damage determination for pain and suffering.

"Authorities approving such arguments give numerous reasons: (1) that it is necessary that the jury be guided by some reasonable and practical considerations; (2) that a trier of the facts should not be required to determine the matter in the abstract, and relegated to a blind guess; (3) that the very absence of a yardstick makes the contention that counsel's suggestions of amounts mislead the jury a questionable one; (4) the argument that the evidence fails to provide a foundation for per diem suggestion is unconvincing, because the jury must, by that or some other reasoning process, estimate and allow an amount appropriately tailored to the particular evidence in that case as to the pain and suffering or other such element of damages; (5) that a suggestion by counsel that the evidence as to pain and suffering justifies allowance of a certain amount, in total or by per diem figures, does no more than present one method of reasoning which the trier of the facts may employ to aid him in making a reasonable and sane estimate; (6) that such per diem arguments are not evidence, and are used only as illustration and suggestion; (7) that the claimed danger of such suggestion being mistaken for evidence is an exaggeration, and such danger, if present, can be dispelled by the court's charges; and (8) that when counsel for one side has made such argument the opposing counsel is equally free to suggest his own amounts as inferred by him from the evidence relating to the condition for which the damages are sought." Ratner v. Arrington, 111 So.2d 82, 88–89 (Fla.App. 1959).

(d) *How Much Per Diem is Too Much?* The jury verdict for plaintiff Charles Westbrook was $925,000. "In reviewing the entire argument in context as we must, we also note that the jury appears to have adopted counsel's unit of time argument which urged the jury to evaluate a long period of pain and suffering, or loss, as a multiple of its smaller time equivalents. * * *

"[C]ounsel used $1.00 per waking hour as a sum which would adequately compensate Charles Westbrook for his future pain, suffering, and mental anguish. Again, counsel did his arithmetic and arrived at a figure of $298,711.20. According to our calculations, counsel must have used 18 as the number of waking hours in a day to arrive at this figure. Similarly, counsel set $1.00 per waking hour as the worth attributable to Westbrook's loss of the capacity to enjoy life and reached a total of $298,711.20 over 45.6 years. Consequently, for pain, suffering, mental anguish, and restrictions on leisure activities caused by the accident, counsel calculated a damage figure of $597,000. * * *

"Counsel then calculated for the jury that $597,000 for pain, suffering, mental anguish and loss of life's enjoyment, plus $328,000 for lost earnings, totaled $925,000. It is the exact figure the jury awarded.

"It is difficult to evaluate whether awards for pain and suffering are excessive. Here, the jury was not asked to delineate the portion of damages awarded for lost earnings and the amount awarded for pain and suffering. However, because Westbrook's request was granted to the penny, we can safely assume that $597,000 represented damages for pain, suffering and diminished capacity to enjoy life, while $328,000 was intended to compensate for lost earnings. Looking at the lost earnings sum alone, we are drawn to notice the extreme generosity of this award. * * *

"Breaking down a large time span into its smaller parts of weeks, days or even hours holds a great appeal to a juror looking for a more understandable and manageable way to approach the task of fixing damages. However, this court has found such arguments impermissible because they tend to produce excessive verdicts.

Baron Tube Co. v. Transport Insurance Co., 365 F.2d 858 (5th Cir.1966) (en banc). This tendency came to fruition in Charles Westbrook's case.

"In *Baron Tube,* this court stated: '[T]he [unit of time] argument cannot be supported by evidence because pain and suffering cannot be measured in dollars on a unit of time basis; that the amount of such damages must necessarily be left, without mathematical formula, to the sound discretion of the jury, because there is no mathematical rule by which the equivalent of such injuries in money can be legally determined; that such arguments create an illusion of certainty in the jury's mind which does not and cannot in fact exist; and that the whole argument is designed and framed to present an appeal to the jurors to put themselves in the plaintiff's shoes.'

"The court went on, however, to recognize that such arguments are 'not improper where accompanied by a suitable cautionary instruction' to protect against an excessive verdict. The en banc court further emphasized its holding by stating that while a trial judge has much discretion in the means employed to protect against excessive verdicts, a cautionary instruction should have been given to ameliorate the effects of a unit of time argument. 'We hasten to reiterate that these matters, *except for requiring a cautionary instruction,* are left to the discretion of the trial court.' (emphasis added).

"No cautionary instruction was given in this case. * * * That the jury awarded precisely the amount of money the formula produced is conclusive evidence that the jury adopted the unit of time formula. Thus, we are convinced that the size of this award is, in part, directly attributable to an uncorrected unit of time argument. This implicates the concerns expressed in *Baron Tube.* We caution that we do not read *Baron Tube* to hold a unit of time argument reversible per se. Rather, such argument may be allowed when couched with proper safeguards or otherwise cured." Westbrook v. General Tire and Rubber Co., 754 F.2d 1233, 1239–40, reh'g denied, 760 F.2d 269 (5th Cir.1985):

(e) More questions about lost enjoyment of life damages and the per diem argument follow:

Is the *Loth* court's analogy comparing the hedonic expert's evidence to a lawyer's forbidden "Golden Rule" argument persuasive? Would an analogy to a lawyer's permitted per diem closing argument be more apt?

(f) A "day in the life" videotape is the most personalized form of plaintiff's pain-and-suffering evidence. Even though the judge's instruction tells the jury that the lawyers' arguments are not evidence, is a lawyer's per diem argument impersonal and not individualized?

(g) In addition to the *Loth* court's stated reasons to exclude the expert's hedonic evidence, is the court also concerned that the evidence would simply lead to excessive recovery? Shereen Loth's case is not further reported.

McDOUGALD v. GARBER

Court of Appeals of New York, 1989.
73 N.Y.2d 246, 538 N.Y.S.2d 937, 536 N.E.2d 372.

WACHTLER, CHIEF JUDGE. * * * On September 7, 1978, plaintiff Emma McDougald, then 31 years old, underwent a Caesarean section and tubal ligation at New York Infirmary. Defendant Garber performed the surgery; defendants Armengol and Kulkarni provided anesthesia. During the surgery, Mrs. McDougald suffered oxygen deprivation which resulted in severe brain damage and left her in a permanent comatose condition. * * *

A jury found all defendants liable and awarded Emma McDougald a total of $9,650,102 in damages, including $1,000,000 for conscious pain and suffering and a separate award of $3,500,000 for loss of the pleasures and pursuits of life. The balance of the damages awarded to her were for pecuniary damages—lost earnings and the cost of custodial and nursing care. Her husband was awarded $1,500,000 on his derivative claim for the loss of his wife's services. On defendants' posttrial motions, the Trial Judge reduced the total award to Emma McDougald to $4,796,728 by striking the entire award for future nursing care ($2,353,374) and by reducing the separate awards for conscious pain and suffering and loss of the pleasures and pursuits of life to a single award of $2,000,000. * * *

Also unchallenged are the awards in the amount of $770,978 for loss of earnings and $2,025,750 for future custodial care—that is, the pecuniary damage awards that survived defendants' posttrial motions.

What remains in dispute, primarily, is the award to Emma McDougald for nonpecuniary damages. At trial, defendants sought to show that Mrs. McDougald's injuries were so severe that she was incapable of either experiencing pain or appreciating her condition. Plaintiffs, on the other hand, introduced proof that Mrs. McDougald responded to certain stimuli to a sufficient extent to indicate that she was aware of her circumstances. Thus, the extent of Mrs. McDougald's cognitive abilities, if any, was sharply disputed.

The parties and the trial court agreed that Mrs. McDougald could not recover for pain and suffering unless she were conscious of the pain. Defendants maintained that such consciousness was also required to support an award for loss of enjoyment of life. The court, however, accepted plaintiffs' view that loss of enjoyment of life was compensable without regard to whether the plaintiff was aware of the loss. Accordingly, because the level of Mrs. McDougald's cognitive abilities was in dispute, the court instructed the jury to consider loss of enjoyment of life as an element of nonpecuniary damages separate from pain and suffering. The court's charge to the jury on these points was as follows:

> "If you conclude that Emma McDougald is so neurologically impaired that she is totally incapable of experiencing any unpleasant or painful sensation, then, obviously, she cannot be awarded damages for conscious pain * * *.

> "It is for you to determine the level of Emma McDougald's perception and awareness. Suffering relates primarily to the emotional reaction of the injured person to the injury. Thus, for an injured person to experience suffering, there, again, must be some level of awareness. If Emma McDougald is totally unaware of her condition or totally incapable of any emotional reaction, then you cannot award her damages for suffering. If, however, you conclude that there is some level of perception or that she is capable of an emotional response at some level, then damages for pain and suffering should be awarded * * *.

> "Damages for the loss of the pleasures and pursuits of life, however, require no awareness of the loss on the part of the injured person. Quite obviously, Emma McDougald is unable to engage in any of the activities which constitute a normal life, the activities she engaged in prior to her injury * * * Loss of the enjoyment of life may, of course, accompany the physical sensation and emotional responses that we refer to as pain and suffering, and in most cases it does. It is possible, however, for an injured person to lose the enjoyment of life without experiencing any conscious pain and suffering. Damages for this item of injury relate not to what Emma

McDougald is aware of, but rather to what she has lost. What her life was prior to her injury and what it has been since September 7, 1978 and what it will be for as long as she lives."

We conclude that the court erred, both in instructing the jury that Mrs. McDougald's awareness was irrelevant to their consideration of damages for loss of enjoyment of life and in directing the jury to consider that aspect of damages separately from pain and suffering. * * *

Damages for nonpecuniary losses are, of course, among those that can be awarded as compensation to the victim. This aspect of damages, however, stands on less certain ground than does an award for pecuniary damages. An economic loss can be compensated in kind by an economic gain; but recovery for noneconomic losses such as pain and suffering and loss of enjoyment of life rests on "the legal fiction that money damages can compensate for a victim's injury" (Howard v. Lecher, 42 N.Y.2d 109, 111, 397 N.Y.S.2d 363, 366 N.E.2d 64). We accept this fiction, knowing that although money will neither ease the pain nor restore the victim's abilities, this device is as close as the law can come in its effort to right the wrong. We have no hope of evaluating what has been lost, but a monetary award may provide a measure of solace for the condition created.

Our willingness to indulge this fiction comes to an end, however, when it ceases to serve the compensatory goals of tort recovery. When that limit is met, further indulgence can only result in assessing damages that are punitive. The question posed by this case, then, is whether an award of damages for loss of enjoyment of life to a person whose injuries preclude any awareness of the loss serves a compensatory purpose. We conclude that it does not.

Simply put, an award of money damages in such circumstances has no meaning or utility to the injured person. An award for the loss of enjoyment of life "cannot provide [such a victim] with any consolation or ease any burden resting on him * * * He cannot spend it upon necessities or pleasures. He cannot experience the pleasure of giving it away" (Flannery v. United States, 4th Cir., 718 F.2d 108, 111, cert. denied 467 U.S. 1226).

We recognize that, as the trial court noted, requiring some cognitive awareness as a prerequisite to recovery for loss of enjoyment of life will result in some cases "in the paradoxical situation that the greater the degree of brain injury inflicted by a negligent defendant, the smaller the award the plaintiff can recover in general damages." The force of this argument, however—the temptation to achieve a balance between injury and damages—has nothing to do with meaningful compensation for the victim. Instead, the temptation is rooted in a desire to punish the defendant in proportion to the harm inflicted. However relevant such retributive symmetry may be in the criminal law, it has no place in the law of civil damages, at least in the absence of culpability beyond mere negligence.

Accordingly, we conclude that cognitive awareness is a prerequisite to recovery for loss of enjoyment of life. We do not go so far, however, as to require the fact finder to sort out varying degrees of cognition and determine at what level a particular deprivation can be fully appreciated. With respect to pain and suffering, the trial court charged simply that there must be "some level of awareness" in order for plaintiff to recover. We think that this is an appropriate standard for all aspects of nonpecuniary loss. No doubt the standard ignores analytically relevant levels of cognition, but we resist the desire for analytical purity in favor of simplicity. A more complex instruction might give the appearance of greater precision but, given the limits of our understanding of the human mind, it would in reality lead only to greater speculation.

We turn next to the question whether loss of enjoyment of life should be considered a category of damages separate from pain and suffering.

There is no dispute here that the fact finder may, in assessing nonpecuniary damages, consider the effect of the injuries on the plaintiff's capacity to lead a normal life. Traditionally, in this State and elsewhere, this aspect of suffering has not been treated as a separate category of damages; instead, the plaintiff's inability to enjoy life to its fullest has been considered one type of suffering to be factored into a general award for nonpecuniary damages, commonly known as pain and suffering.

Recently, however, there has been an attempt to segregate the suffering associated with physical pain from the mental anguish that stems from the inability to engage in certain activities, and to have juries provide a separate award for each [citations].

Some courts have resisted the effort, primarily on the ground that duplicative and therefore excessive awards would result (see, e.g., Huff v. Tracy, 57 Cal.App.3d 939, 944, 129 Cal.Rptr. 551, 553). Other courts have allowed separate awards, noting that the types of suffering involved are analytically distinguishable [citations]. Still other courts have questioned the propriety of the practice but held that, in the particular case, separate awards did not constitute reversible error [citations].

We do not dispute that distinctions can be found or created between the concepts of pain and suffering and loss of enjoyment of life. If the term "suffering" is limited to the emotional response to the sensation of pain, then the emotional response caused by the limitation of life's activities may be considered qualitatively different. But suffering need not be so limited—it can easily encompass the frustration and anguish caused by the inability to participate in activities that once brought pleasure. Traditionally, by treating loss of enjoyment of life as a permissible factor in assessing pain and suffering, courts have given the term this broad meaning.

If we are to depart from this traditional approach and approve a separate award for loss of enjoyment of life, it must be on the basis that such an approach will yield a more accurate evaluation of the compensation due to the plaintiff. We have no doubt that, in general, the total award for nonpecuniary damages would increase if we adopted the rule. That separate awards are advocated by plaintiffs and resisted by defendants is sufficient evidence that larger awards are at stake here. But a larger award does not by itself indicate that the goal of compensation has been better served.

The advocates of separate awards contend that because pain and suffering and loss of enjoyment of life can be distinguished, they must be treated separately if the plaintiff is to be compensated fully for each distinct injury suffered. We disagree. Such an analytical approach may have its place when the subject is pecuniary damages, which can be calculated with some precision. But the estimation of nonpecuniary damages is not amenable to such analytical precision and may, in fact, suffer from its application. Translating human suffering into dollars and cents involves no mathematical formula; it rests, as we have said, on a legal fiction. The figure that emerges is unavoidably distorted by the translation. Application of this murky process to the component parts of nonpecuniary injuries (however analytically distinguishable they may be) cannot make it more accurate. If anything, the distortion will be amplified by repetition.

Thus, we are not persuaded that any salutary purpose would be served by having the jury make separate awards for pain and suffering and loss of enjoyment of life. We are confident, furthermore, that the trial advocate's art is a sufficient guarantee that none of the plaintiff's losses will be ignored by the jury.

The errors in the instructions given to the jury require a new trial on the issue of nonpecuniary damages to be awarded to plaintiff Emma McDougald. * * *

Titone, Judge (d)issenting). The majority's holding represents a compromise position that neither comports with the fundamental principles of tort compensation nor furnishes a satisfactory, logically consistent framework for compensating nonpecuniary loss. Because I conclude that loss of enjoyment of life is an objective damage item, conceptually distinct from conscious pain and suffering, I can find no fault with the trial court's instruction authorizing separate awards and permitting an award for "loss of enjoyment of life" even in the absence of any awareness of that loss on the part of the injured plaintiff. Accordingly, I dissent. * * *

The capacity to enjoy life—by watching one's children grow, participating in recreational activities, and drinking in the many other pleasures that life has to offer—is unquestionably an attribute of an ordinary healthy individual. The loss of that capacity as a result of another's negligent act is at least as serious an impairment as the permanent destruction of a physical function, which has always been treated as a compensable item under traditional tort principles (e.g., Simpson v. Foundation Co., 201 N.Y. 479, 95 N.E. 10 [loss of sexual potency]). Indeed, I can imagine no physical loss that is more central to the quality of a tort victim's continuing life than the destruction of the capacity to enjoy that life to the fullest.

Unquestionably, recovery of a damage item such as "pain and suffering" requires a showing of some degree of cognitive capacity. Such a requirement exists for the simple reason that pain and suffering are wholly subjective concepts and cannot exist separate and apart from the human consciousness that experiences them. In contrast, the destruction of an individual's capacity to enjoy life as a result of a crippling injury is an objective fact that does not differ in principle from the permanent loss of an eye or limb. * * *

Significantly, this equation does not suggest a need to establish the injured's awareness of the loss. The victim's ability to comprehend the degree to which his or her life has been impaired is irrelevant, since, unlike "conscious pain and suffering," the impairment exists independent of the victim's ability to apprehend it. Indeed, the majority reaches the conclusion that a degree of awareness must be shown only after injecting a new element into the equation. Under the majority's formulation, the victim must be aware of the loss because, in addition to being compensatory, the award must have "meaning or utility to the injured person." This additional requirement, however, has no real foundation in law or logic. "Meaning" and "utility" are subjective value judgments that have no place in the law of tort recovery, where the primary goal is to find ways of quantifying, to the extent possible, the worth of various forms of human tragedy.

Moreover, the compensatory nature of a monetary award for loss of enjoyment of life is not altered or rendered punitive by the fact that the unaware injured plaintiff cannot experience the pleasure of having it. The fundamental distinction between punitive and compensatory damages is that the former exceed the amount necessary to replace what the plaintiff lost [citation]. As the Court of Appeals for the Second Circuit has observed, "[t]he fact that the compensation [for loss of enjoyment of life] may inure as a practical matter to third parties in a given case does not transform the nature of the damages" (Rufino v. United States, 2nd Cir., 829 F.2d 354, 362).

Ironically, the majority's expressed goal of limiting recovery for nonpecuniary loss to compensation that the injured plaintiff has the capacity to appreciate is directly undercut by the majority's ultimate holding, adopted in the interest of "simplicity," that recovery for loss of enjoyment of life may be had as long as the injured plaintiff has " 'some level of awareness,' " however slight. Manifestly, there are many different forms and levels of awareness, particularly in cases involving brain injury. Further, the type and degree of cognitive functioning necessary to experience "pain and suffering" is certainly of a lower order than that needed to apprehend the loss of the ability to enjoy life in all of its subtleties. Accordingly, the existence of "some level of awareness" on the part of the injured plaintiff says nothing about that plaintiff's ability to derive some comfort from the award or even to appreciate its significance. Hence, that standard does not assure that loss of enjoyment of life damages will be awarded only when they serve "a compensatory purpose," as that term is defined by the majority.[1]

In the final analysis, the rule that the majority has chosen is an arbitrary one, in that it denies or allows recovery on the basis of a criterion that is not truly related to its stated goal. In my view, it is fundamentally unsound, as well as grossly unfair, to deny recovery to those who are completely without cognitive capacity while permitting it for those with a mere spark of awareness, regardless of the latter's ability to appreciate either the loss sustained or the benefits of the monetary award offered in compensation. In both instances, the injured plaintiff is in essentially the same position, and an award that is punitive as to one is equally punitive as to the other. Of course, since I do not subscribe to the majority's conclusion that an award to an unaware plaintiff is punitive, I would have no difficulty permitting recovery to both classes of plaintiffs.

Having concluded that the injured plaintiff's awareness should not be a necessary precondition to recovery for loss of enjoyment of life, I also have no difficulty going on to conclude that loss of enjoyment of life is a distinct damage item which is recoverable separate and apart from the award for conscious pain

1. Another problem with the majority's analysis is the absence of any discussion about the time frame to be used in measuring the award of damages for plaintiff's loss of enjoyment of life. Damages for "pain and suffering" are directly correlated to the plaintiff's experience of "pain and suffering" and thus are routinely awarded only for that period of time during which the injured had sufficient cognitive powers to have that experience. Damages for loss of enjoyment of life, in contrast, are awarded as a monetary replacement for the plaintiff's diminished ability to participate in the pleasures and pursuits of healthy living during the remainder of his or her natural life span. Thus, a legitimate question exists as to whether the plaintiff is entitled to recover an award representing his entire lifetime's loss notwithstanding that he was conscious of the loss for only a few moments before lapsing into cognitive oblivion. Furthermore, in view of the majority's conclusion that an award is not truly compensatory if it cannot be enjoyed by the injured party, an additional question arises as to whether the cognitive capacity of the plaintiff must be measured at the time when the award is to be given rather than at some earlier point before the commencement of trial.

and suffering. The majority has rejected separate recovery, in part because it apparently perceives some overlap between the two damage categories and in part because it believes that the goal of enhancing the precision of jury awards for nonpecuniary loss would not be advanced. However, the overlap the majority perceives exists only if one assumes, as the majority evidently has, that the "loss of enjoyment" category of damages is designed to compensate only for "*the emotional response* caused by the limitation of life's activities" and "*the frustration and anguish caused by* the inability to participate in activities that once brought pleasure" (emphasis added), both of which are highly *subjective* concepts.

In fact, while "pain and suffering compensates the victim for the physical and mental discomfort caused by the injury; * * * loss of enjoyment of life compensates the victim for the limitations on the person's life created by the injury", a distinctly *objective* loss (Thompson v. National R.R. Passenger Corp.). In other words, while the victim's "emotional response" and "frustration and anguish" are elements of the award for pain and suffering, the "limitation of life's activities" and the "inability to participate in activities" that the majority identifies are recoverable under the "loss of enjoyment of life" rubric. Thus, there is no real overlap, and no real basis for concern about potentially duplicative awards where, as here, there is a properly instructed jury.

Finally, given the clear distinction between the two categories of nonpecuniary damages, I cannot help but assume that permitting separate awards for conscious pain and suffering and loss of enjoyment of life would contribute to accuracy and precision in thought in the jury's deliberations on the issue of damages. * * * In light of the concrete benefit to be gained by compelling the jury to differentiate between the specific objective and subjective elements of the plaintiff's nonpecuniary loss, I find unpersuasive the majority's reliance on vague concerns about potential distortion owing to the inherently difficult task of computing the value of intangible loss. My belief in the jury system, and in the collective wisdom of the deliberating jury, leads me to conclude that we may safely leave that task in the jurors' hands.

For all of these reasons, I approve of the approach that the trial court adopted in its charge to the jury. Accordingly, I would affirm the order below affirming the judgment.

Notes

1. *Economic?* The majority opinion refers to "noneconomic losses such as pain and suffering and loss of enjoyment of life." Does that statement equate nonpecuniary with noneconomic?

2. *Justification.* The majority and dissenting opinions debate whether damages must have "meaning or utility to the injured person." If the payment is intended to deter, to structure potential defendants' future incentives to reduce and avoid risk, it achieves that purpose when exacted; who receives the payment and how they spend it are irrelevant. Does barring comatose Emma McDougald from recovering damages for loss of enjoyment of life undercut deterrence?

3. *Flannery.* The majority opinion cites Flannery v. United States. The *Flannery* court had reasoned that a permanently comatose person's recovery of damages for lost enjoyment of life could not be compensatory damages and therefore constituted the punitive damages that are forbidden under the Federal Tort Claims Act. In

1992 the Supreme Court, rejecting the *Flannery* court's approach, defined punitive damages for FTCA purposes narrowly to include only damages to punish and deter. Molzof v. United States, 502 U.S. 301 (1992).

4. *Lost Enjoyment.* Should plaintiff's pain and suffering, the negative, be separated from her lost of enjoyment of life, the absence of the positive?

5. *The Tort Victim's Pre-death Fear, Anguish, and Pain and Suffering.* The law is currently is a state of ferment.

(a) Here is the judge's decision in Debra Gordon's case. "It is undisputed that Debra died within minutes of the collision. Consequently, any pain and suffering that she might have experienced was momentary and fleeting. Accordingly, the Court concludes that an award of damages for pain and suffering is inappropriate in this case." Childs v. United States, 923 F.Supp. 1570 (S.D.Ga.1996).

(b) The New York courts approach a victim's final minutes differently. A drowning child experienced six to seven minutes, which the jury valued at $6,000,000. " '[R]ecovery for noneconomic losses such as pain and suffering * * * rests on the legal fiction that money damages can compensate for a victim's injury. We accept this fiction, knowing that although money will neither ease the pain nor restore the victim's abilities, this device is as close as the law can come in its effort to right the wrong' (McDougald v. Garber). However, as also noted in *McDougald*: 'Translating human suffering into dollars and cents involves no mathematical formula; it rests as we have said on a legal fiction. The figure that emerges is unavoidably distorted by the translation.'

"To obtain the 'benefit' of this legal fiction the law requires as a 'prerequisite to recovery' that the victim of a tort have 'cognitive awareness' (McDougald v. Garber); and therefore the plaintiff has the 'threshold burden of proving consciousness for at least some period of time following an accident in order to justify an award of damages for pain and suffering' (Cummins v. County of Onondaga, 84 N.Y.2d 322, 324 (1994). This burden can be satisfied by direct or circumstantial evidence [citation], but '[m]ere conjecture, surmise or speculation is not enough to sustain a claim for [pain and suffering] damages' (Cummins v. County of Onondaga).

"Often when unconsciousness or death occurs shortly after a tort, it is difficult, sometimes impossible, to determine if a decedent suffered or was actually conscious of any pain. In those instances, the jury, as well as the reviewing court, must rely upon inferences drawn from sparse circumstances in order to determine the degree of consciousness. [citations] 'In determining damages for conscious pain and suffering experienced in the interval between injury and death, when the interval is relatively short, the degree of consciousness, severity of pain, apprehension of impending death, along with duration, are all elements to be considered' (Regan v. Long Is. RR Co., 128 A.D.2d 511 [2nd Dept.1987]). Obviously, if death is immediate and the record is barren of any circumstantial evidence of consciousness, a pain and suffering award will not be upheld. * * *

"Other Relevant Damage Awards. The cases dealing with these types of non-economic awards are either distinguishable, or too few, or too remote in time to provide meaningful guidance as to what would be considered reasonable compensation for the non-economic damages sustained herein. But see, [citations] Dontas v. City of New York, 183 A.D.2d 868, 584 N.Y.S.2d 134 [2d Dept. 1992]. [citations] * * *

"It is evident that plaintiff adduced sufficient evidence from which the jury could conclude that the decedent suffered a most terrible and prolonged demise over a period of approximately six minutes, during which he suffered physical pain, terror, and knowledge of his impending death. As noted above, the degree of consciousness, severity of pain, and duration of apprehension of impending death are all key elements to be considered. Although the City relies on the case of Dontas v. City of New York, [verdict as to damages for conscious pain and suffering in favor of a 16 year-old boy who drowned, was reduced from $2,000,000 to $50,000], it was observed by the Second Department in that case that the courts were limited by the testimony of the 'experts from both sides [which] indicated that a drowning victim would lose consciousness in just a *few* minutes.' Even apart from the terror-filled period prior to going under for the last time, the evidence in this cases supports a conclusion that plaintiff was conscious for a longer period of time, during which he was engaged in a death struggle to extricate himself from currents which buffeted his body and which undoubtedly terrified him and gave him a keen awareness of impending death. It is important to note that in many of the wrongful death/pre-impact terror cases, which have upheld and sustained significant awards of damages for minimal conscious pain and suffering, the pre-impact terror was measured in seconds; whereas in the case under consideration the pre-death terror and awareness of death is measured in multiple minutes. The Court concludes that reasonable compensation for this horrible experience, and the conscience pain and suffering endured thereby, should not be less than two million, ($2,000,000) dollars."

Following adjustment for a settlement and appellate review, the dead child's pain and suffering damages in this lawsuit were set at $1,250,000. Maracallo v. Board of Education of City of New York, 2 Misc.3d 703, 769 N.Y.S.2d 717, 721–23, 727 (N.Y.Sup.Ct.2003); 21 A.D.3d 318, 800 N.Y.S.2d 23 (2005).

6. *Post-verdict Judicial Review of a Jury Verdict for a Plaintiff's Pain and Suffering.* The trial process includes the judge's rulings on the admission of evidence and submission to the jury, the judge's instructions to the jury, and the jury's deliberation, leading to its verdict. After the jury's damages verdict for the plaintiff, the defendant will move for a new trial, perhaps asserting legal error or inadmissable evidence, and for remittitur of excessive damages or a new trial unless the plaintiff accepts a reduced amount.

The next stage, post-verdict judicial review, includes both the trial judge's ruling on defendant's post-verdict motions and appellate review.

Because the civil jury enjoys constitutional stature, the trial judge cannot simply reduce the jury's damages verdict to a "correct" amount. Since "determination of an award of damages lies within the province of the jury, a court's outright reduction of a jury's award without offering the plaintiff the option of a new trial on damages denies the plaintiff his constitutional right to a jury trial." Lightfoot v. Union Carbide Corp., 110 F.3d 898, 914 (2d Cir.1997). Instead the trial judge or appellate court will let the plaintiff choose between a new trial and reduced damages.

A court's conditional new-trial order, effective unless the plaintiff accepts the reduced figure, is usually called a "remittitur." The judicial decision to offer the defendant a new trial unless it agrees to additional damages is called an "additur." The Seventh Amendment right to a jury trial, the Supreme Court held in 1935, prevents a federal trial judge from using additur, but use of remittitur is appropriate. Dimick v. Schiedt, 293 U.S. 474 (1935).

(a) *Tests.* Courts have reviewed the size of a jury's verdict under a standard of whether it "shocked" the judicial conscience. Another approach requires the court to ask whether the jury verdict reveals "passion or prejudice." These standards are at once imprecise and subjective. Most courts administer them to defer to the jury's verdict.

More concerned about predictability and uniformity, the New York legislature's tort-reform statute required its courts to ask whether a verdict "deviates materially from what would be reasonable compensation." CPLR 5501(c). The United States Supreme Court held that a federal district judge could, consistently with the Seventh Amendment, apply the New York standard to review verdicts in diversity cases. Gasperini v. Center for Humanities, Inc., 518 U.S. 415 (1996).

(b) *Consorti.* The review can be complicated. As part of the ongoing asbestos tragedy, the jury set cancer-victim Consorti's pain and suffering damages at $12,000,000. Judge Sweet, the federal trial judge, conducted a comparative analysis and applied a post-verdict judicial review of whether the verdict shocked the conscience before declining to reduce it.

The court of appeals's conscience was shocked, however; moreover applying the stricter New York post-verdict judicial review statute, the appellate court thought that Consorti's pain and suffering verdict "deviates materially." from "reasonable compensation." The appellate court's remarks are quoted above. p. 69.

Down went Consorti's pain and suffering verdict to $3,500,000. Rejecting the court of appeals's application of the post-verdict judicial review standards, however, the United States Supreme Court vacated and remanded. Under *Gasperini*, the Court held, the federal *trial* judge applies the state post-verdict judicial review standard, but the federal *court of appeals* reviews the trial judge's decision by asking whether the trial judge's decision was an abuse of discretion. Back went Consorti's pain and suffering damages to trial Judge Sweet who, in 1998, meticulously examined similar decisions and described Consorti's ordeal in heart-rending detail before setting the pain and suffering damages at $5,000,000. In re Joint Eastern and Southern District Asbestos Litigation, 9 F.Supp.2d 307 (S.D.N.Y. 1998). Not an observer of these gyrations, however, was plaintiff Consorti who had died shortly after the trial in 1993.

(c) The difficulty any factfinder has in quantifying a plaintiff's non-pecuniary damages, especially pain and suffering, interact with any judicial or legislative effort to develop uniform and predictable standards that prevent an occasional crushing verdict. Comparisons with other awards founder. Each plaintiff's case is factually unique. The judge and the appellate court owe some deference to the initial factfinder, usually a jury with constitutional status. What is a similar case? How much deviation is allowed? Decisions become flatfooted and mechanical or sink into a Serbonian bog of contradiction.

(d) An interested student who is prepared for some technicality may read Judge Weinstein's post-verdict judicial review of pain and suffering damages in Geressy v. Digital Equipment Corp., 980 F.Supp. 640, 655–63 (E.D.N.Y.1997).

7. *"Insurance" for Pain and Suffering.* Often a tort plaintiff's injuries grew out of a transaction with the source of her injuries. Two examples are a buyer's products liability suit against a seller or manufacturer and a patient's malpractice suit against a health professional. Viewing the tort system as a compulsory insurance system, the buyer and the patient are "insured" because each pays for "insurance coverage" through the price or the fee. Economists have quarreled about whether product buyers and patients want to pay the portion of the charge that "buys" their "insurance" against pain and suffering. Those who think not urge policymakers to abolish pain and suffering damages. Professors Croley and Hanson suggest that people who are, as economists calculate, rational maximizers really do want pain and suffering "insurance." Steven Croley & Jon Hanson, The Nonpecuniary Costs of Accidents: Pain-and-Suffering Damages in Tort Law, 108 Harv.L.Rev. 1785 (1995).

The argument is whether to abolish pain and suffering damages because it is forced insurance coverage that most people don't want. Should a court require someone who caused an accident to bear a cost which includes a jury's estimate of an injured person's pain and suffering? Are litigation finance and augmented deterrence goals of pain and suffering damages? Is the economist's "insurance" argument likely to founder in the practical world when confronted with the roles a plaintiff's pain and suffering damages play in compensating her attorney and in setting standards for deterrence?

8. *Final Questions.* One of this section's underlying themes has been whether to base a plaintiff's recovery of compensatory damages on individualized calculations, to give the plaintiff what the plaintiff lost, or, on averaged data, to give the plaintiff what an average or composite victim would have lost.

Can we generalize about the choice between individualized and averaged recovery? Do carefully individualized damages calculations compensate a plaintiff better? From the point of view of a potential defendant, will averaged damages payments create the "correct" amount of expenditures to deter or prevent future injuries? Does it matter whether an insurance mechanism is part of the way a potential future defendant's incentives are structured? Are averaged payouts easier and less expensive to administer because they lack the protracted and expensive procedure of proving individual damages? But is resolving the dispute through averaging fair to an injured victim?

This material has taken you on lengthy, sometimes complex, detours into economics, accounting, and statistics. Attempts to round off the rough edges have not always succeeded. Do these technical disciplines produce precise solutions to compensatory damages problems? Is a background in literature, history, and the humanities really just as helpful? More to the point, what role should technical sciences play in aiding, qualifying, or superceding the way a jury expresses the community's conscience in setting an injured plaintiff's damages?

C. LIMITATIONS ON DAMAGES RECOVERY

1. AVOIDABLE CONSEQUENCES

Plaintiff's religiously motivated decision to decline medical treatment reminds us, in a little different form, of the broader question of individualized versus averaged measurement of damages. Will the plaintiff recover what she lost or what a "reasonably prudent person" with her injuries would have lost? How much will the government through a judge and jury second-guess a victim's choices to submit to or to decline medical procedures? In reading the following decision, observe the way the majority and dissent treat the issues of (a) evaluating the reasonableness of plaintiff's excuse, and (b) applying the "eggshell skull" doctrine to plaintiff's injuries.

WILLIAMS AND ROBBINS v. BRIGHT

New York Supreme Court, Appellate Division, 1997.
658 N.Y.S.2d 910, 230 A.D.2d 548.
appeal dismissed, 90 N.Y.2d 935, 664 N.Y.S.2d 273, 686 N.E.2d 1368 (1997).

WALLACH, J. Plaintiff Robbins was a passenger in an automobile driven by her 70–year old father on an upstate highway. An eyewitness saw the car veer off the road at about 65 mph and turn over in a culvert on adjoining farmland. There was circumstantial evidence that the driver, who had driven with this plaintiff and other family members early that morning from New York City to Plattsburgh and was returning the same day, had fallen asleep at the wheel. This was conduct that the jury found to be both negligent and a proximate cause of the accident. On this appeal, defendants, who include the lessors of the vehicle, do not seriously contest liability; the main issue is the trial court's treatment of plaintiff Robbins' alleged failure to mitigate damages due to her religious beliefs as a Jehovah's Witness.

The central question for us, on appellate review, is not merely the admeasurement of plaintiff's damages under the application of traditional tort law standards, but the broader controversy involving plaintiff's beliefs and their proper effect upon her monetary award. That, in turn, obliges us to grapple with grave constitutional issues ordinarily not involved in a motor vehicle accident— even one as tragic and catastrophic as this one.

For a hundred years it has been settled law in this state that a party who claims to have suffered damage by the tort of another is bound "to use reasonable and proper efforts to make the damage as small as practicable" (Blate v. Third Ave. R.R. Co., 44 App.Div. 163, 167), and if an injured party allows the damages to be unnecessarily enhanced, the incurred loss justly falls upon him. [citation]

Plaintiff Robbins suffered a severely damaged right hip, as well as a painful injury to her left knee. Her own expert testified that if these injuries were not alleviated by well recognized and universally accepted surgical procedures, her prognosis was for a wheelchair-bound life because of the inevitability of necrotic development in the bone structure of these limbs. Moreover, all the experts agreed that the surgical intervention available to this plaintiff (52 years of age at the time of the accident) offered her the prospect of a good recovery and a near normal life. However, Robbins, a devout Jehovah's Witness, presented proof (chiefly from her own hospital records) that she was obliged to refuse these recommended surgeries because her church prohibits the blood transfusions they would necessarily entail.

In accordance with settled law, the New York pattern jury instruction on the subject of damage mitigation refers to the actions of "a reasonably prudent person" and measures the duty to mitigate in accordance with that standard:

> "A person who has been injured is not permitted to recover for damages that could have been avoided by using means which a reasonably prudent person would have used to (cure the injury, alleviate the pain). * * * If you find that the plaintiff is entitled to recover in this action, then in deciding the nature and permanence of her injury and what damages she may recover for the injury, you must decide whether in refusing to have an operation the plaintiff acted as a reasonably prudent person would have acted under the circumstances."

Although the trial court acquainted the jury with the existence of that standard, it charged that in this case the standard to be applied was something very different:

> You have to accept as a given that the dictates of her religion forbid blood transfusions. And so you have to determine * * * whether she * * * acted reasonably as a Jehovah's Witness in refusing surgery which would involve blood transfusions. Was it reasonable for her, not what you would do or your friends or family, was it reasonable for her given her beliefs, without questioning the validity or the propriety of her beliefs?

[The jury's verdict for plaintiff was for "damages of $163,244.81 for past medical and hospital bills, $1,500,000 for past pain, suffering and disability,

$3,982,900 for future hospital, medical and nursing and home care expenses, and $4,000,000 for future pain, suffering, disability and loss of enjoyment of life." The trial judge found the verdict for pain and suffering to be excessive. Past pain and suffering was reduced to $1,000,000 and future pain and suffering to $2,750,000. Plaintiff accepted the reduction. Editor.]

In abandoning the "reasonably prudent person" test in favor of a "reasonable Jehovah's Witness" standard, over defendants' objection, the trial court perceived the issue as involving this plaintiff's fundamental right to the free exercise of her religion, protected by the First Amendment to the United States Constitution and article I, § 3 of our State Constitution. The First Amendment prohibits any law "respecting an establishment of religion, or prohibiting the free exercise thereof." Essentially, the court held that if the jury were permitted to assess this plaintiff's refusal to accept additional surgery without total deference to her religious beliefs, it would unlawfully restrain "the free exercise" of her Jehovah's Witness faith and would thus be constitutionally prohibited. In effect, this plaintiff's religious beliefs were held, as a matter of law, to relieve her of any legal obligation to mitigate damages under the same standard required of all other persons similarly situated who do not share similar religious convictions.

Prior to this action, New York courts have rarely dealt with the issue of a plaintiff whose medical care was limited by her religious beliefs. Virtually all of the handful of jurisdictions to have considered the question have adopted the test of the reasonably prudent person instead of the formulation employed here. [citations]

In our view, the analysis of the trial court contained many flaws. The first error was in defining the fundamental issue as whether any jury verdict could be permitted to conflict with this plaintiff's "religious belief that it may be better to suffer present pain than to be barred from entering the Kingdom of Heaven." The dissent finds this quotation from the trial justice's opinion "misleading," although resort to the official State law reports leaves us hard pressed to imagine how this citation could be confused with the jury instruction quoted verbatim earlier. The confusion, if any, lies somewhere else.

With all due deference, this is not the question that should have been presented; to put it in this manner inevitably skews the result. A second error, although not central to the focus of this analysis, was in the trial court's effort to extend the application of the "eggshell skull" doctrine—traditionally limited to a plaintiff's pre-existing physical condition, [citation] mental illness, [citation] or psychological disability [citation]—to include this plaintiff's religious beliefs.

No one suggests that the State, or, for that matter, anyone else, has the right to interfere with that religious belief. But the real issue here is whether the consequences of that belief must be fully paid for here on earth by someone other than the injured believer. According to the trial court, the State has little interest in enforcing its general rule of damage mitigation simply to rescue a wrongdoer from the full consequences of his tortious conduct. This simplistic formulation has little application to the realities of this case. Here, the "wrongdoer," who fell asleep at the wheel, paid for his "fault" with his life. The respondents in damages ((d)efendant car leasing company and its insurance carrier) must answer for the harm under the derivative liability imposed by Vehicle and Traffic Law § 388, which expresses the State's interest in cost allocation among that segment of the public that pays automobile insurance premiums.

Of course, the State does not have any interest in the question of who wins this lawsuit, or the extent to which one party prevails over the other. But the State does have a compelling interest in assuring that the proceedings before its civil tribunals are fair, and that any litigant is not improperly advantaged or disadvantaged by adherence to a particular set of religious principles. The State also has a compelling interest, by constitutional command under the Fourteenth Amendment, to extend equal protection of the law to every person haled before its courts. A derivative tortfeasor is certainly entitled to no less equal protection, in this regard, than an individual under criminal indictment. * * *

The trial court's instruction to the jurors on mitigation directed them to pass upon the reasonableness of plaintiff Robbins' objection, on religious grounds, to a blood transfusion. The fallacy in this instruction was that the jury never received any evidence pertaining to the rationale of her religious convictions, nor how universally accepted they may have been by members of her faith. True, there were entries in her medical records that she refused blood transfusions because she was a Jehovah's Witness, and there was brief testimony (in the context of presenting her diminished physical capabilities) that she attended Jehovah's Witness prayer services. But there was no evidence of the basis for the religious prohibition of blood transfusions. The charge thus created a sham inquiry; instead of framing an issue on how plaintiff Robbins' religious beliefs impacted on mitigation, the court foreclosed the issue in her favor without any supporting evidence. Let us recall, the jurors were told that they must ask themselves whether this plaintiff's refusal to accept a blood transfusion was reasonable, "given her beliefs, without questioning the validity" of those beliefs. Having thus removed from the jury's consideration any question as to the validity (that is to say, the reasonableness) of plaintiff Robbins' religious convictions, the court effectively directed a verdict on the issue.

Of course, the alternative—the receipt of "expert" testimony on this subject—presents an even worse prospect. Such evidence, if any conflict developed, would present a triable issue as to whether the conviction against transfusions was heretical—or orthodox i.e., "reasonable"—within the Jehovah's Witness faith.

The State may not endorse religion or any particular religious practice. [citation] The trial court, in accepting the sincerity of plaintiff Robbins' beliefs as a given and asking the jury to consider the reasonableness of her actions only in the context of her own religion, effectively provided government endorsement to those beliefs. American courts have no business endorsing or condemning the truth or falsity of anyone's religious beliefs. The admonition delivered by Justice Douglas more than a half century ago, in United States v. Ballard, 322 U.S. 78, 86–87, bears repeating:

> Freedom of thought, which includes freedom of religious belief, * * * embraces the right to maintain theories of life and of death and of the Hereafter which are rank heresy to followers of the orthodox faiths. Heresy trials are foreign to our constitution. Men may believe what they cannot prove. They may not be put to the proof of their religious doctrines or beliefs * * * [I]f those doctrines are subject to trial before a jury charged with finding their truth or falsity, then the same can be done with the religious

beliefs of any sect. When the triers of fact undertake that task, they enter a forbidden domain.

Aside from the usefulness of Justice Douglas' obiter dictum in defining this "forbidden domain," we cannot agree with the dissent's position that the trial judge's charge should be upheld as "more favorable to the defendants than the opinion and holding in United States v. Ballard." The defendants in this Federal mail fraud prosecution had distributed, among other things, writings referring to their personal meetings with—and dictated instructions received from—Jesus and Saint Germain. The trial court advised the jury that the issue for determination would not be whether those dubious events had actually occurred, but whether the defendants believed, in good faith, that they had occurred. The jury instruction, approved by the Supreme Court majority, was addressed to whether or not the Ballards had the requisite mens rea to support a criminal conviction. Such an element of mail fraud has little relevance to the principles of tort law at stake here.

Even under the three-pronged formula of Lemon v. Kurtzman, 403 U.S. 602, 612–13, this State action by the trial court impermissibly entered the "forbidden domain." Under that test, a challenged governmental action, in order to pass constitutional muster, must have a secular purpose, its principal or primary purpose may not advance or inhibit religion, and it may not foster excessive entanglement with religion. No secular court can decide—or, for that matter, lead a jury to decide—what is the reasonable practice of a particular religion without setting itself up as an ecclesiastical authority, and thus entangling it excessively in religious matters, in clear violation of the First Amendment. * * *

In espousing the objective standard and remanding this matter for a new trial, we take note of an obvious problem with strict adherence to the pattern jury instruction that is provided as a general guide. We conclude that the unmodified application of that formulation would work an injustice in this case, as well as in others of a similar nature. It seems apparent to us that a person in plaintiff Robbins' position must be permitted to present to the jury the basis for her refusal of medical treatment; otherwise, the jury would simply be left with the fact of her refusal, without any explanation at all. Once such evidence is (as it should be) received, the court is called upon to instruct the jurors as to how such evidence should affect their deliberations. Addressing this issue, we hold that the pattern jury instruction must be supplemented here with the following direction:

> In considering whether the plaintiff acted as a reasonably prudent person, you may consider the plaintiff's testimony that she is a believer in the Jehovah's Witness Faith, and that as an adherent of that faith, she cannot accept any medical treatment which requires a blood transfusion. I charge you that such belief is a factor for you to consider, together with all the other evidence you have heard, in determining whether the plaintiff acted reasonably in caring for her injuries, keeping in mind, however, that the overriding test is whether the plaintiff acted as a reasonably prudent person, under all the circumstances confronting her.

The so-called "reasonable believer" charge * * * has found some support in other jurisdictions. [citations] Our modification of the PJI charge is intended to strike a fair balance between the competing interests of these parties. And in pursuit of that goal, we reiterate that the court is not to permit the introduction of any "theological" proof, by way of either expert or lay testimony, as to the validity of religious doctrine, nor should the court issue any instructions whatsoever on that score. * * *

Accordingly, the judgment of Supreme Court, New York County * * * which after a jury verdict, awarded plaintiff Robbins damages for her personal injuries * * * should be reversed, on the law and the facts, without costs, and the matter remanded for new trial on damages alone.

ROSENBERGER, J. (dissenting) I respectfully dissent and would affirm the judgment appealed. The trial judge charged the jury in a manner more favorable to the defendants than the opinion and holding in Unites States v. Ballard, quoted and cited by the majority, would require.

Ballard involved a mail fraud prosecution in which the defendants allegedly misrepresented certain religious beliefs as part of a fraudulent scheme to sell memberships and literature and to solicit donations. The trial court recognized that it would be a violation of the Establishment Clause of the First Amendment to factor the reasonableness of religious beliefs in the legal determination of whether or not the defendants had been proven guilty. It, therefore, instructed the jurors that they were only to inquire whether the defendants "honestly and in good faith believe[d]" what they preached in determining whether they were guilty or not. If they found that the defendants had a good faith belief in what they espoused, they were not to go on to consider the reasonableness or validity of that belief. This instruction was upheld upon First Amendment scrutiny by the United States Supreme Court.

The majority states that the Court in *Ballard*, dealt only with the issue of mens rea in a criminal case. I, of course, see the issue quite differently. * * *

Although the majority writes that that issue "has little relevance to the principles of tort law at stake here," I am unaware of any doctrine or holding which limits the application of the First Amendment to the United States Constitution to criminal law. Basic principles of constitutional law do not change depending upon whether the context of a case is civil or criminal.

Although the issue of religion enters this case in the context of the plaintiff's duty to mitigate damages, the trial court used language to obviate a Constitutional violation in the instructions here under review. The pattern jury instruction as to the legal doctrine of avoidable consequences, or the duty to undertake reasonable efforts to minimize consequential damages, though neutral on its face, would have been discriminatory as applied to a practicing Jehovah's Witness whose religion forbids the acceptance of blood transfusions. [citation]

The trial court's adapted charge reveals that it appropriately created an instruction that meets the state's interest in minimizing tort damages to those reasonably incurred, in the situation of an incidental burden placed upon plaintiff's practice of her religious beliefs as a Jehovah's Witness (see, *Ballard*.) * * * As relevant, the court's charge stated:

> Now, in making your determination as to whether [plaintiff] has acted reasonably to mitigate damage, I will instruct you that under no circumstances are you to consider the validity or reasonableness of her religious beliefs. * * * [W]e cannot have a situation in which jurors in passing on the reasonableness of somebody's conduct, pass upon whether their religious beliefs are reasonable or not reasonable.
>
> What is reasonable for [an] adherent of one religion may appear totally unreasonable to someone who has different beliefs, but you may not pass

upon the validity of anyone else's beliefs. That is out of bounds for you. You have to accept as a given that the dictates of her religion forbid blood transfusions. And so you have to determine in assessing the question of damages, damages past and damages future, whether she, Mrs. Robbins, acted reasonably as a Jehovah's Witness in refusing surgery which would involve blood transfusions. Was it reasonable for her, not what you would do or your friends or family, was it reasonable for her given her beliefs, without questioning the validity or propriety of her beliefs.

The charge in this case did not take the issue of whether Mrs. Robbins acted reasonably away from the jury. The trial judge instructed this jury at least five times that whether she acted reasonably in refusing surgery was a matter to be decided by them. In doing so, the court gave an instruction more favorable to the defendants than was proper under the standard set forth by the Supreme Court of the United States in United States v. Ballard.

The sincerity and good faith of the plaintiff's beliefs were not contested at trial or on appeal by the defendants. Realistically, they could not have been successfully challenged. The evidence showed that she stated that she would refuse blood transfusions in conformity with her religious belief at her first contact with a physician after the accident. She maintained her resolve even upon being informed that it could cost her her life. Nonetheless, the trial judge in his charge instructed the jury to consider her sincerity and good faith, when he told the jurors that "from the evidence, you may or may not conclude that the observance of her religion was very important to her." There was no exception to this portion of the charge, which was in conformity with United States v. Ballard.

The majority finds fault with the instruction that the jury "may not pass on the validity of anyone else's beliefs"; it would have the jury hear evidence and determine whether the refusal to submit to a blood transfusion was orthodox, or reasonable, within the Jehovah's Witness faith. This inquiry crosses an impermissible First Amendment Establishment Clause boundary.

As the Supreme Court has noted in West Virginia Board of Education v. Barnette (319 U.S. 624, 642):

> [F]reedom to differ is not limited to things that do not matter much. That would be a mere shadow of freedom. The test of its substance is the right to differ as to things that touch the heart of the existing order. If there is any fixed star in our constitutional constellation, it is that no official, high or petty, can prescribe what shall be orthodox in politics, nationalism, religion, or other matters of opinion or force citizens to confess by word or act their faith therein.

The trial court's adaptation of the pattern jury charge recited above was an appropriate accommodation of plaintiff's religious beliefs. * * * As Justice O'Connor noted in her concurrence in Wallace v. Jaffree, 472 U.S. 38, 83:

> The solution to the conflict between the Religion Clauses lies * * * in identifying workable limits to the government's license to promote the free exercise of religion. The text of the Free Exercise Clause speaks of laws that prohibit the free exercise of religion. On its face, the Clause is directed at government interference with free exercise. Given that concern, one can plausibly assert that government pursues Free Exercise Clause values when it lifts a government-imposed burden on the free exercise of religion. If a

[rule] falls within this category, then the standard Establishment Clause text should be modified accordingly. It is disingenuous to look for a purely secular purpose when the manifest objective of a [rule] is to facilitate the free exercise of religion by lifting a government imposed burden. Instead the [court] should simply acknowledge that the religious purpose of such a [rule] is legitimated by the Free Exercise Clause.

The majority also questions the validity of asking "whether any jury verdict could be permitted to conflict with this plaintiff's 'religious belief that it may be better to suffer present pain than to be barred from entering the Kingdom of Heaven.' "It goes on to observe: "With all due deference, this is not the question that should have been presented; to put it in this manner inevitably skews the result." This "question" is not a quote from the jury charge. It is a quote from the trial court's decision upholding its instructions. It is, therefore, misleading for this Court to state that the manner of the question skewed the resulting response. This question was never put to the jury, and the manner in which the actual question was put to the jury was, as seen from the quoted portions of the charge, quite different.

The jury charge was in conformity with our tort system, allowing for an assessment of the actual situation of a victim of negligence, rather than assigning a certain value to a designated injury * * * The concept of the "eggshell plaintiff" has not been limited to physical infirmities. [citations]

As the majority opinion has emphasized, the monetary damages to plaintiff will be paid, not by the deceased tortfeasor, but by an insurance carrier. This observation, carried to its logical extension, would substantially diminish the concept linking fault and monetary responsibility for damages in most tort claims. Be that as it may, the danger that the cost of such accidents, borne by insurance carriers, would be passed on to the general public in the form of greater premiums is unsupported by data evincing a high frequency of religious refusals to accept certain medical care. * * *

In sum, to have the leasing company and insurance carrier reimburse this plaintiff for the loss she has suffered is in accord with First Amendment requirements that "Congress shall make no law respecting an establishment of religion, or prohibiting the free exercise thereof," which applies to both state legislative and judicial action. [citations] It is also in conformity with the more broadly drafted Article 1, section three of the New York Constitution, which guarantees all State citizens "free exercise and enjoyment of religious profession and worship, without discrimination or preference"; as well as Article 1, section eleven, which directs that "[n]o person shall, because of * * * creed or religion, be subjected to any discrimination in his civil rights by any other person or by any firm, corporation, or institution, or by the state or any agency or subdivision of the state."

This plaintiff should not be subjected to the intrusiveness and indignity of having the reasonableness of her religious beliefs examined and determined by a jury. This basic protection is afforded her by not one, but two constitutions. * * *

Notes

1. *Questions.* One way to begin is to ask whether a court can reject all of a plaintiff's religious excuses for her failure to avoid the consequences of a defendant's tort. Does taking away plaintiff's damages penalize her religious practice?

May a "reasonable person" be a Jehovah's Witness? That answers itself as "yes." Would a "no" answer stigmatize a person's religious belief as unworthy? Does the court's "supplemental" jury instruction allow the jury to find plaintiff's refusal of transfusions to be unreasonable?

A court will respect an individual's autonomy to reject a medical procedure. Should that respect for autonomy extend to compelling someone else to compensate her for the increased costs of her choice?

A tortfeasor may pay higher damages because of the way plaintiff's religious beliefs affect her decisions. May that require the tortfeasor to subsidize the plaintiff's religious practice? More generally, the insurance system, often funded by mandatory liability insurance, compensates the plaintiff. How does that differ from a tax to support a religion?

2. *Plaintiff's Career Path.* What substitute employment, if any, must a plaintiff accept to avoid the consequences of a disabling injury? On the one hand, the legal standard ought to encourage an injured plaintiff to reallocate her resources productively. On the other hand, the new employment is crucial to plaintiff's career path and self-image.

(a) In Walmsley v. Brady, 793 F.Supp. 393, 395 (D.R.I. 1992), a disabled veterinarian who had specialized in equine surgery was unable to follow her favored career path. Defendants thought she should recover lost capacity to earn based on a future administering an animal clinic. Judge Pettine planned to instruct the jury as follows:

> Loss of earnings relates to the field in which the plaintiff was trained. If she can no longer practice in the specialized field in which she had planned to practice, you must then inquire and determine whether or not such a deprivation has resulted in a loss of earning capacity when juxtaposed against what she can do now as a veterinarian. The plaintiff is not required to mitigate damage to such an extent as to alter her professional career path to an unreasonable degree. As to reasonableness, the plaintiff is not required to accept alternative employment even though she could earn more money in said employment, provided that the higher paying job is unreasonably different from her chosen occupation.

Under this instruction may Dr. Walsmley recover for lost capacity to earn even if she earns more after the injury than before?

(b) Another defendant argued that a burn victim with one usable arm had not avoided consequences because he declined employment other than in his previous line of work. "Before the accident," the West Virginia court wrote, "[plaintiff] was a strong able-bodied laborer with a grade school education and an IQ in the low 80s. Now [plaintiff] has a grade school education, an IQ in the low 80s, but has only one arm and no longer can do heavy manual labor. Yet [defendant] claims that [plaintiff] could have obtained other employment after he was laid off * * * but that he did not attempt to do so. Perhaps [plaintiff] should have looked for work as a door stop in Southern California. We think not." A little more plausibly, "Before the accident, Mr. Helmick performed manual labor such as digging ditches. Unfortunate as the circumstances are, there is not a great need in West Virginia for one-armed ditch diggers." Recovery as totally disabled was sustained. Helmick v. Potomac Edison Co., 185 W.Va. 269, 406 S.E.2d 700, 708, cert. denied, 502 U.S. 908 (1991).

(c) *A Contrast.* Assuming that plaintiff was unfit for sea duty, he "is not entitled to recover for the rest of his life what he would have earned at sea; the law requires him to mitigate his damages by finding other employment." Even though he has not sought work, "I find that the accident caused Williams to be out of work from April 7, 1986 through June, 1987. After that time, plaintiff was no longer fully disabled.

Even if he was unfit for sea duty after that time, he could have mitigated his damages by finding another line of work." Williams v. United States, 712 F.Supp. 1132, 1140 (S.D.N.Y.1989).

(d) Some Remedies students may remember a well-known case from Contracts, Parker v. Twentieth Century–Fox Film, where the court found "Big Country, Big Man" was not suitable, comparable, or substantially similar employment for Shirley MacLaine after the studio breached her contract for "Bloomer Girl." It's below.

3. *Lost Use.* A plaintiff whose vehicle is damaged may seek lost use damages for the period it is out of service. Suppose the defendant denies liability altogether. If repairs are not performed, plaintiff's claim for lost use damages mounts during settlement negotiations. A reasonable period of time to complete repairs limits plaintiff's lost use period; when the lost use period is protracted, defendant may argue that plaintiff failed to take prudent measures to avoid the consequences. The owner may respond that defendant's stubborn refusal to make a reasonable settlement offer prevented her from avoiding consequences by repairing the vehicle. Courts often exacerbate the dilemma of a defendant who denies liability by extending plaintiff's lost use period beyond the reasonable repair period when plaintiff lacks the money to pay for repair or when defendant's refusal to pay was itself unreasonable. Urico v. Parnell Oil Co., 708 F.2d 852 (1st Cir.1983).

4. *Buckle Up.* Numerous decisions discuss whether, if an automobile accident victim has failed to buckle available seat and shoulder belts, the evidence of nonuse should be excluded or whether the jury should consider it under the head of contributory negligence, comparative negligence, assumption of the risk, or avoidable consequences. A student writer surveys the legislation and decisions and quotes the Earl of Andrews's statement in 1683 before His Majesty's Order of Scribes: "Quoth what fool darest upon the highways of this realm without properly strapping his ass to his cart." Note, Caveat Viator: Safety is No Longer the Only Good Reason for Oregonians to "Buckle Up," 67 Or.L.Rev. 901, 904 (1988).

The law remains unsettled. A Utah statute forbade evidence of a plaintiff's failure to wear a seatbelt on the issues of avoidable consequences, contributory negligence, and comparative negligence. The Utah court rejected a constitutional attack. The statute, Justice Durham wrote, "is quite consistent with a common law tort principle commonly referred to as the 'thin skull' or 'eggshell skull' doctrine: one who injures another takes the injured as she finds him. [citations] Under this doctrine the defendant has to pay for all injuries, even if a given plaintiff is more vulnerable to injury than others." Ryan v. Gold Cross Services, Inc., 903 P.2d 423, 428 (Utah 1995).

The Florida court traced a complex series of court decisions and statutes. Failure to use a seatbelt, it held, is evidence of comparative negligence. Not buckling up is pre-accident conduct which is unlike declining an operation after the injury. The lack of restraint affects plaintiff's "second collision" with the inside of the vehicle, not the "first collision" between plaintiff's and defendant's vehicle. Ridley v. Safety Kleen, 693 So.2d 934 (Fla.1996).

Crisp distinctions between avoidable consequences to reduce damages and the defenses of contributory negligence, comparative negligence, assumption of risk, and last clear chance are not always maintained.

5. *At Lease.* When a tenant breaches a lease, the avoidable consequences doctrine encourages the landlord to take reasonable measures to find a substitute tenant. The history of avoidable consequences in tenants' breaches of leases has been the history of characterization, choosing between real property and contract law. Basing the formerly dominant rule on the real-property doctrine that a lease is a

conveyance for a term, courts did not recognize the avoidable consequences doctrine. A landlord might do nothing after a tenant breached and yet collect the full rent for the full term of a long, but breached, lease. The policy of encouraging landlords to rerent to prevent physical deterioration and economic waste led courts to discard the real property characterization and treat leases like other contracts for the purpose of recognizing avoidable consequences. Jack I. Bender & Sons v. Tom James Co., 37 F.3d 640 (D.C. Cir.1994). Sommer v. Kridel, 74 N.J. 446, 378 A.2d 767 (1977) is familiar to many Property veterans.

6. *Positive Recovery for Avoidable Consequences.* A plaintiff may recover the expense of reasonable measures to avoid future consequences of defendant's breach. (a) If a tenant breaches a lease, for example, the landlord may recover its expense of advertising the vacancy and its broker's commissions for finding a substitute tenant. (b) If a neighbor pollutes and causes a nuisance, damaging adjoining land, the property owner may clean up the pollution on her own property and recover cleanup expense from the polluter. Enfield v. Atlantic Richfield Co., 790 F.Supp. 1080 (W.D.Ok.1989). (c) A trade libel plaintiff recovered for the value of the time its employees spent attempting to reverse or avert the damage the defamation caused to its reputation in the government-contracting community. Comdyne I, Inc. v. Corbin, 908 F.2d 1142, 1146 (3d Cir.1990).

7. *Proof, Burden of Proof.* If, for example, a personal-injury plaintiff's operation is successful, and her employment resumes, then her earnings damages period ceases. She may recover for the medical bills as an expense of minimizing damages. But she cannot prove any earnings losses after her employment resumes; a plaintiff's avoided consequence is damage that does not occur. The defendant's avoidable consequences defense comes up when defendant charges that the plaintiff should have taken steps to stop damages from mounting, but unreasonably did not.

Ordinarily avoidable consequences operates like an defendant's affirmative defense to the amount of the plaintiff's damages. Plaintiff proves damages. The defendant has the burden to prove that plaintiff was unreasonable in failing to avoid the consequences of its breach. This may place on defendant the burden to produce evidence peculiarly within plaintiff's knowledge, which, defendant may argue, unfairly reverses the ordinary burden of producing evidence. Because of plaintiff's superior access to the evidence, the court may place on plaintiff the burden of showing that it adopted reasonable measures to minimize damages. Novelty Textile Mills, Inc. v. C.T. Eastern, Inc., 743 F.Supp. 212, 218–19 (S.D.N.Y.1990). This may be part of the plaintiff's burden to prove the amount of damages. Or it may convert avoiding the consequences into an element of the basic "duty" that the plaintiff must satisfy to assert a cause of action. D.R. Mobile Home Rentals v. Frost, 545 N.W.2d 302 (Iowa 1996). One court thought the public policy was strong enough to prevent the tenant from contracting away the requirement that the landlord show reasonable diligence to relet. Drutman Realty Co. v. Jindo Corp., 865 F.Supp. 1093 (S.D.N.Y.1994).

8. *Prejudgment Measures and Avoidable Consequences.* A successful employment discrimination plaintiff may recover "front pay," her future lost wages. Before a final decision after a full hearing, the judge may grant plaintiff a preliminary injunction ordering the defendant to "reinstate" her in the disputed position. Reinstatement stops plaintiff's lost wages from accruing and converts what might have been a successful plaintiff's ultimate recovery of lost wages into an avoided consequence. Legault v. aRusso, 842 F.Supp. 1479 (D.N.H. 1994).

A preliminary injunction cannot aim a plaintiff with physical injury back along her former career trajectory. Even though some lawsuits for damages take a decade to reach trial, a judge will usually refuse to grant a preliminary injunction for plaintiff's interlocutory compensation. Arguing that a judge should be able to issue a preliminary injunction to order a defendant to pay a plaintiff before trial is Rhonda Wasserman, Equity Transformed: Preliminary Injunctions to Require the Payment of Money, 70 B.U. L.Rev. 623 (1990).

9. *Terminology: Mitigation of Damages—Avoidable Consequences*. The expression "mitigation of damages" technically describes the ways a *defendant* may decrease a plaintiff's damages. The same expression is frequently used to describe what more correctly is termed "avoidable consequences," the steps plaintiff should take to prevent her damages from mounting. "Minimize damages" or "avoidable consequences," is preferred, but "mitigation of damages," though a little imprecise, is too entrenched in the legal vocabulary to budge.

[handwritten margin note: Use the phrase "avoidable consequences"]

10. The majority opinion in *Williams* said, "Of course, the State does not have any interest in the question of who wins this lawsuit, or the extent to which one party prevails over the other." Do you agree?

2. COLLATERAL SOURCE RULE

Definitions and an Example: To illustrate the collateral source rule, here is an example of a collateral source payment and contractual subrogation drawn from first-party or collision insurance: Deffy negligently damages Lindsey's Studebaker. Lindsey's collision insurer, Onestate, pays her loss claim for repairing the car. Onestate's payment to Lindsey is from a "collateral source," one unrelated to Deffy. The common-law collateral source rule forbids defendant Deffy from using Onestate's collateral source payment to Lindsey to reduce her damages. So far, so good for Lindsey, who may sue Deffy and end up being paid twice for her injured Studebaker. But if Lindsey's insurer Onestate "subrogates" to Lindsey's tort claim against tortfeasor Deffy, then, in law, Onestate is substituted for Lindsey as a potential tort creditor of Deffy.

The collateral source rule, which doesn't always involve insurance, may over-compensate a plaintiff. Under the collateral source rule, even though "everyone involved in the case expects the Shriners Hospital, which is treating the child, will continue to provide all necessary care free of charge, * * * a plaintiff who has been compensated in whole or in part by a source independent of the tortfeasor is nevertheless entitled to a full recovery against the tortfeasor, to prevent the tortfeasor from gaining a windfall." Moulton v. Rival Co., 116 F.3d 22, 27 (1st Cir.1997).

What does economic analysis tell us about the collateral source rule and deterrence? If the defendant can reduce the damages it pays plaintiff by the amount of insurance plaintiff receives, will that affect its incentive to spend up to plaintiff's loss discounted by the probability of recurrence to prevent future accidents? Yes. If plaintiff receives money from both her insurance carrier and a tortfeasor, will that be a windfall? No. Richard Posner, Economic Analysis of Law § 6.13 (6th ed. 2002).

Tort reformers seek to reduce what they consider to be plaintiff's over-compensation with tort-reform statutes changing the collateral source rule. Under an earlier Illinois statute, the money that a plaintiff received through disability benefits and reimbursed medical expenses was simply subtracted from his damages. "Plaintiff is not entitled to recover those amounts * * * for which he has already received compensation from a collateral source." Cohan v. Garretson, 282 Ill.App.3d 248, 667 N.E.2d 1325, 1335 (1996). Turnbull v. USAir, Inc., 133 F.3d 184 (2d Cir.1998) (New York statute).

The legal landscape for plaintiff's collateral source receipts, even within a single state, can be complex. A plaintiff's potential for double recovery has spurred more than half of the states' legislatures to change the common-law collateral source rule. Some tort-reforming legislatures have passed statutes abolishing the common-law collateral source rule outright, others have modified it. The Wisconsin court takes up one of the second group of statutes in the following decision.

LAGERSTROM v. MYRTLE WERTH HOSPITAL–MAYO HEALTH SYSTEM

Supreme Court of Wisconsin, 2005.
285 Wis.2d 1, 700 N.W.2d 201.

SHIRLEY S. ABRAHAMSON, C.J. This is an appeal from a judgment and order of the Circuit Court for Dunn County. * * * Following a jury's verdict, the circuit court entered judgment in the amount of $55,755 plus costs in favor of Klover Lagerstrom, individually as surviving spouse of Vance H. Lagerstrom and as Special Administrator of the Estate of Vance H. Lagerstrom, deceased, referred to collectively as the estate, against Myrtle Werth Hospital–Mayo Health System, ABC Insurance Company, its insurer, Red Cedar Clinic–Mayo System, and DEF Insurance Company, its insurer, referred to collectively as the defendants. The circuit court's order denied a post-verdict motion. * * * [T]he estate appealed.

The * * * issue presented is whether the circuit court erred under Wis. Stat. § 893.55(7) in admitting evidence of collateral source payments in this medical malpractice action, in refusing to admit evidence of the estate's potential obligation to reimburse Medicare, [a United States government social-insurance program for medical expenses of those over 65], and in instructing the jury that it may, but need not, consider the collateral source payments in determining the reasonable value of the medical services rendered. * * *

I. For purposes of this appeal the facts are undisputed. The defendants conceded that they were negligent in their care and treatment of the decedent and committed malpractice by inserting a feeding tube into the passageway of the decedent's lung rather than into the stomach and inserting fluids. * * *

The decedent's wife initiated a wrongful death medical malpractice action under ch. 655 as the surviving spouse and as the special administrator of the decedent's estate.

Counsel for the estate communicated with Medicare in regard to various medical expenses that Medicare paid. Communications from Medicare indicate that Medicare would rely on its statutory right to reimbursement. Medicare was therefore not joined in the action.

The estate introduced evidence about the reasonable value of the medical services rendered to the decedent. The amount was approximately $89,000. The defendants, over the estate's objections, presented evidence and argued to the jury that the out-of-pocket charges incurred by the estate were only $755, with the remaining medical expenses paid through collateral sources, such as Medicare, medical provider write-offs pursuant to Medicare regulations, and private insurance. The circuit court instructed the jury that the estate's total out-of-pocket expense for medical services was $755.

The jury was instructed that the law does not require it to reduce the sum it determines to be the reasonable value of the medical services caused by the defendants' negligence to reflect payments made by other sources. The jury was further instructed, however, that it may reduce, if it so decides, the amount awarded for the reasonable value of medical services by the amount of collateral source payments.

The circuit court limited the estate's argument to the jury regarding the estate's obligation to reimburse Medicare. The estate could not argue that the estate had potential liability to Medicare. Rather, the estate was forced to argue that the estate could, if it wished, voluntarily repay Medicare.

The circuit court gave the jury special verdict questions with separate instructions on each element of damages. * * *

The jury answered the separate verdict questions on damages, awarding the estate $20,000 for the decedent's pain and suffering and awarding the surviving spouse $35,000 for the loss of society and companionship. The jury awarded the estate $755 for medical expenses. * * *

The focus of the appeal is the circuit court's admission of evidence of collateral source payments for the purpose of determining the reasonable value of the medical services, its refusal to admit evidence of the estate's potential obligation to reimburse Medicare, and its instruction to the jury that it may consider the collateral source payments in awarding damages for the medical expenses.

The estate's central objection to Wis. Stat. § 893.55(7) is that in permitting evidence of collateral benefits and in not providing guidance regarding the fact-finder's consideration of this evidence, the legislature has unlawfully delegated public policy and equitable considerations to juries on a case-by-case basis without any guidelines. The estate challenges the constitutionality of § 893.55(7) on several grounds, including violation of separation of powers, right to trial by jury, and equal protection and due process guarantees. State courts are divided about the constitutionality of legislative enactments declaring collateral source payments admissible as evidence. [citations] We conclude that under a proper interpretation of § 893.55(7), these constitutional issues do not arise. * * *

II. The primary issue presented is the interpretation of Wis. Stat. § 893.55(7). * * * The statute reads as follows:

Evidence of any compensation for bodily injury received from sources other than the defendant to compensate the claimant for the injury is admissible in an action to recover damages for medical malpractice. This section does not limit the substantive or procedural rights of persons who have claims based upon subrogation.

* * * We determine the meaning of Wis. Stat. § 893.55(7) in light of (A) the text of the statute; (B) the legislative history of the statute; (C) the legislative goal in adopting the statute; and three concepts of law embodied in the statute; namely, (D) the valuation of medical services; (E) the collateral source rule; and (F) subrogation. * * *

A. We examine first the text of Wis. Stat. § 893.55(7). It is only 50 words long, yet covers a large area of the law of damages in medical malpractice cases. Although the instant case involves medical expenses, the statute appears to encompass all damages in a medical malpractice action and to make evidence of all collateral source payments admissible in regard to all damage claims.

Although the statute speaks of compensation to the claimant, the instant case demonstrates that the statute also encompasses payments, write-offs, or forgiveness made directly to health care providers rather than to the claimant. Also, even though the statute uses only the phrase "bodily injury," unlike Wis. Stat. § 893.55(4)(b) and (e), which use both "bodily injury" and "death," it is broad enough to include wrongful death actions.

The statute does not limit the nature of the collateral source payments and thus on its face seems to encompass payments such as those from federal and state governments, life insurance, income continuation plans, and volunteer services, some of which are ordinarily excluded by similar statutes in other states. [citation]

The only limitation stated in Wis. Stat. § 893.55(7) is that it does not limit the substantive or procedural rights of persons who have claims based upon subrogation. The legislature obviously attempted to make the statute conform to the rules of subrogation.

The text of the [Wisconsin] statute does not address numerous issues in relation to medical expenses, the subject of this appeal. First and foremost, the text does not state the purpose for which the evidence of collateral source payments is admissible. The statute does not require that a fact-finder or circuit court reduce the reasonable value of the medical services rendered to account for the collateral source payments. The collateral source rule denies a tortfeasor credit for payments or benefits conferred upon the plaintiff by any person other than the tortfeasor. Many states abrogating the collateral source rule by statute require the fact-finder or court to reduce the reasonable value of medical services by the amount of collateral source payments. Rudolph v. Iowa Methodist Med. Ctr., 293 N.W.2d 550 (Iowa 1980) (statute requires mandatory reduction in award to account for collateral source payments). [citations]

The [Wisconsin] statute is silent about the admissibility of evidence about the expenses a victim incurred to acquire the collateral source payments, such as premiums or other expenditures. For example, the Arizona statute that allows evidence of certain collateral source payments also allows the plaintiff to introduce evidence of expenses paid to secure the collateral source payments. The plaintiff may also introduce evidence of the collateral source provider's right to recovery against the plaintiff as reimbursement or under subrogation. The statute further provides that "unless otherwise expressly permitted to do so by statute, no provider of collateral benefits * * * shall recover any amount against the plaintiff as reimbursement for such benefits nor shall such provider be subrogated to the rights of the plaintiff." Ariz.Rev.Stat. Ann. § 12–565 (West 2003). The [Wisconsin] statute neither prohibits nor allows the admission of such evidence.

The [Wisconsin] statute explicitly states that it does not limit the rights of subrogees but says nothing about the rights of reimbursement. The statute is silent about whether a victim may introduce evidence of subrogation or the victim's obligation to reimburse a collateral source. For example, Indiana's statute that allows the admission of proof of collateral source payments other than certain enumerated payments allows admission into evidence of proof of the amount of money the plaintiff is required to repay. See Ind.Code Ann., § 34–44–1–2 (West 1998). The [Wisconsin] statute neither prohibits nor allows the admission of such evidence.

The [Wisconsin] statute is silent about whether the parties may argue to the fact-finder about the public policies underlying the collateral source rule, such as preventing tortfeasors from benefitting from payments inuring to the victim and deterring tortfeasors. Similarly, the statute does not say whether the public policies underlying subrogation, such as the prevention of double recovery, can be argued to the jury. The statute neither prohibits nor allows such arguments. In sum, the text of the statute raises more questions than it answers.

Even though the legislature did not clearly articulate how fact-finders and courts are supposed to use and apply Wis. Stat. § 893.55(7), and even though the language of the statute does not express a complete abrogation of the collateral source rule in medical malpractice actions, we must interpret Wis. Stat. § 893.55(7) to give effect to the legislature's explicit language allowing the admission of evidence of collateral source payments in medical malpractice actions under chapter 655.

B.   The legislative history of Wis. Stat. § 893.55(7) provides some guidance in interpreting the statute.

An early draft of the bill that became Wis. Stat. § 893.55(7) included a sentence requiring that collateral source payments reduce an award of damages: "The award of damages under ch. 655 shall be reduced by any compensation that the injured party received from sources other than the defendant to compensate him or her for the injury." This sentence does not appear in the enacted statute.

[Most of the court's lengthy and detailed discussion of legislative documents is omitted below.]

Not all insurance companies have the same interests in regard to the collateral source rule and subrogation. * * * Insurance companies insuring a victim of medical malpractice for the victim's medical expenses want to retain the collateral source rule and subrogation rights so that they can be reimbursed by the tortfeasor for the payments they made for the victim's medical expenses. In contrast, insurance companies insuring a health care provider tortfeasor want to eliminate the collateral source rule so that they can pay a victim less money for the victim's medical expenses; these insurance companies want to eliminate subrogation so that they need not pay a victim's insurance company for medical expenses the victim's insurance company paid. The abolition of the collateral source rule (and subrogation) results in an anomaly: The victim's insurance company compensates the victim for medical expenses and the tortfeasor's insurance company is relieved of paying the victim's medical expenses.

The legislature apparently added the last sentence of the statute as some sort of compromise to take into account the divergent interests of different insurance companies. The compromise is, however, unintelligible in the context of Wis. Stat. § 893.55(7).

"As a rule of evidence, [the collateral source rule] precludes introduction of evidence regarding any benefits the plaintiff obtained from sources collateral to the defendant. As a rule of damages, it precludes the defendant from offsetting the plaintiff's receipt of collateral compensation against the * * * judgment." See Linda J. Gobis, Note, Lambert v. Wrensch: Another Step Toward Abrogation of the Collateral Source Rule in Wisconsin, 1988 Wis. L.Rev. 857, 861

The most reasonable explanation of the statute on the basis of the legislative history is that Wis. Stat. § 893.55(7) became simply a modification of the evidentiary aspect of the collateral source rule, not the substantive aspect. * * *

C.   The legislative goals are not explicitly set forth in the statute. Section 893.55(7) was adopted in the 1995–96 session to modify the 1975 Liability and Patients Compensation Act, which created chapter 655 in the Wisconsin Statutes, along with other provisions governing medical malpractice actions, effective July 1975. Chapter 655 was adopted in reaction to a perceived crisis in medical malpractice. [citations]

The immediate goal of Wis. Stat. § 893.55(7) was arguably to provide fact-finders with information about the collateral source payments in the hope that victims would not obtain double recovery as a result of the increased prevalence of both publicly and privately provided medical expense insurance. [citations] The ultimate goal of § 893.55(7) would be to reduce health care providers' insurance premiums as a result of a reduction of victims' recoveries.

We therefore examine possible interpretations of Wis. Stat. § 893.55(7) with the legislative history and goals in mind, along with three key legal concepts implicated in Wis. Stat. § 893.55(7): the valuation of reasonable medical expenses; the common law collateral source rule; and subrogation. We shall discuss these three concepts in turn and then finally set forth our interpretation of § 893.55(7) in light of the text, the legislative history, the legislative goal and these concepts.

D.   In calculating damages, a person injured by medical malpractice may recover the reasonable value of the medical services reasonably required by the injury. Thoreson v. Milwaukee & Suburban Transp. Co., 56 Wis.2d 231, 243 (1972). We have recognized that in "most cases [the reasonable value of medical services] is the actual expense, but in some cases it is not. But the test is the reasonable value, not the actual charge, and therefore there need be no actual charge." Thoreson v. Milwaukee & Suburban Transp. Co. It is not a controversial proposition that the recovery is for the value of the services, not for the expenditures actually made or the obligations incurred. That medical and nursing services are rendered gratuitously "should not preclude the injured party from recovering the value of the services as part of his compensatory damages." Thoreson v. Milwaukee & Suburban Transp. Co.

The defendants argue that Wis. Stat. § 655.009(2), enacted in 1975, changed the standard for determining the reasonable value of medical services in medical malpractice cases. Section 655.009(2) provides that "[t]he court or the jury, which ever is applicable, shall determine the amounts of medical expense payments previously incurred and for future medical expense payments."

We are not persuaded that this statute changes the long-standing rule that the "reasonable value of medical services" is the reasonable value of medical services rendered, without limitation to amounts paid. This long-standing rule has been applied in both chapter 655 medical malpractice actions and in other actions as the method for determining the reasonable value of medical services.

The most logical interpretation of Wis. Stat. § 655.009(2) is that the court or jury should determine past and future medical expenses based on the common-law standard for determining such damages. We agree with the amicus curiae brief of the Wisconsin Academy of Trial Lawyers that if the legislature had intended in 1975 to make the measure of damages in medical malpractice actions "payments" for medical services actually made by the victim, it need not have adopted Wis. Stat. § 893.55(7) to modify the collateral source rule.

E. We next examine the second, related principle implicated by Wis. Stat. § 893.55(7), the well-recognized common law collateral source rule. The collateral source rule helps claimants recover the "reasonable value of the medical services, without limitation to the amounts paid." Koffman v. Leichtfuss, 246 Wis.2d 31, 37, 630 N.W.2d 201, 205 (2001). Regardless of the method of financing the victim's medical expenses, a tortfeasor's liability is the reasonable value of the treatment rendered without limitation to the amounts actually paid by the victim. * * *

The policy basis for the collateral source rule is that a tortfeasor who is legally responsible for causing an injury should not be relieved of his or her obligation to compensate the victim simply because the victim has the foresight to arrange, or good fortune to receive, benefits from a collateral source for injuries and expenses. An underlying justification for the rule is that should a windfall arise because of an outside payment, the party to profit from that collateral source should be the injured person, not the tortfeasor. The collateral source rule also ensures that the liability of similarly situated tortfeasors is not dependent on the relative fortuity of the manner in which each victim's medical expenses are financed. Koffman v. Leichtfuss. Moreover, although some plaintiffs may get duplicate recovery, many successful plaintiffs are far from fully compensated, considering, for example, attorney fees and costs.

Furthermore, the collateral source rule is designed to deter wrongdoing; the rule "deter[s] negligent conduct by placing the full cost of the wrongful conduct on the tortfeasor." Ellsworth v. Schelbrock, 235 Wis.2d 678, 684, 611 N.W.2d 764, 767 (2000).

Those critical of the collateral source rule argue that the rule allows a victim a double recovery: a payment by the tortfeasor and a payment by a collateral source. * * *

The collateral source rule works in conjunction with subrogation and reimbursement. Plaintiffs do not necessarily actually receive a double recovery even if they collect fully from both the tortfeasor and the collateral source, because a collateral source may have a right of subrogation or reimbursement. [citation]

Wisconsin Stat. § 893.55(7) explicitly provides that it does not limit the substantive or procedural rights of persons who have claims based upon subrogation. As we explained previously, the legislature did not mandate that a fact-finder offset collateral source payments in determining the reasonable value of medical services to protect subrogation. Subrogation helps reduce an insurer's losses and makes it at least theoretically possible for an insurer to limit premium charges accordingly. The protection of subrogation has therefore been used to justify the collateral source rule. The relationship of § 893.55(7) to the collateral source rule and subrogation dictates to a large extent the interpretation of the statute.

F. We turn now to the third legal principle embodied in the statute, subrogation. By virtue of payments made on behalf of the victim (the subrogor), a payor (subrogee) sometimes obtains a right to recover these payments in an action against a tortfeasor and is a necessary party in an action against the tortfeasor. [citation] Subrogation exists to ensure that the loss is ultimately placed upon the wrongdoer and to prevent the victim (the subrogor) from being unjustly enriched through a double recovery, namely recovering from both the paying party (the subrogee) and the tortfeasor. [citation] An entity with a subrogation right can waive the right to subrogation in favor of reimbursement. [citation] Successful plaintiffs thus must sometimes reimburse sources of collateral payments out of tort recoveries. The principles of subrogation therefore are applicable when the right is asserted as a reimbursement.

Subrogation ordinarily works in tandem with the collateral source rule to further the goals of both rules. The collateral source rule prevents benefits received by the victim from inuring to the tortfeasor, and subrogation prevents the victim from receiving a double recovery because the payor of the benefits may recover the payments from the tortfeasor or the victim. In other words, when the risk of double recovery on the part of the victim does not exist because the payor may seek subrogation, the collateral source rule applies. [citation]

In other states with statutes admitting collateral source payments in evidence, subrogation rights are explicitly not protected, and the payor of the collateral source payments (the subrogee) is prohibited from receiving reimbursement. [citations] In contrast, the Wisconsin legislature chose in Wis. Stat. § 893.55(7) to protect the substantive or procedural rights of persons who have claims based upon subrogation. This choice is clear on the face of the statute and in the legislative history, as we previously explained.

Any interpretation of § 893.55(7) must therefore take into account that the statute does not limit the rights of claims based on subrogation.

III.   With these principles in mind, we interpret Wis. Stat. § 893.55(7).

The text of § 893.55(7) renders admissible evidence of any compensation for bodily injury received from sources other than the defendant to compensate the claimant for bodily injury in a medical malpractice damage action. The text does not direct the fact-finder how to consider or use evidence of collateral source payments. The Wisconsin statute, unlike statutes in other states, does not require an offset or reduction of any malpractice award by the amount of collateral source payments.

According to the legislative history, the first sentence of Wis. Stat. § 893.55(7) modifies the collateral source rule by merely allowing evidence regarding other sources of compensation to be presented to the jury in a medical malpractice action. Wisconsin Stat. § 893.55(7) modified, but did not abrogate, the long-standing common-law collateral source rule that the reasonable value of medical services is the full value of the medical services, not limited by any collateral source payments.

The rights of persons whose claims are based on subrogation are not limited by Wis. Stat. § 893.55(7), as the last sentence in the statute makes clear. The sentence in the original draft of the statute requiring that [medical malpractice] damages * * * shall be reduced by any compensation the injured party received from sources other than the defendant made insurance companies worry that their subrogation rights would be adversely affected, and the sentence was therefore eliminated.

In order for subrogation (or reimbursement) and the collateral source rule to work in tandem to prevent a victim's double recovery and protect subrogation, Wis. Stat. § 893.55(7) must be interpreted to require courts to instruct juries to consider the collateral source payments only in determining the reasonable value of the medical services rendered.

An alternative interpretation of Wis. Stat. § 893.55(7), that is, to allow a fact-finder to offset the collateral source payments, leaves many questions unanswered that the legislature could not have intended this court to answer. The statute is silent about the parties' ability to introduce evidence or argue about the obligation to repay collateral sources. The statute is silent about the admissibility and consideration by the fact-finder of expenses the victim incurred to acquire the collateral source payments. The statute is silent about the ability of the parties to argue to the fact-finder the public policies underlying the collateral source rule and subrogation. * * * With so many unresolved issues regarding a fact-finder's ability to make discretionary off-sets, we must conclude that the legislature intended that the jury not do so.

We conclude that the text of § 893.55(7) explicitly allows evidence of collateral source payments to be introduced in medical malpractice actions. We further conclude that if evidence of collateral source payments from sources including Medicare, other state or federal government programs, medical insurance or write-offs, and discounted or free medical services is presented to the fact-finder, then the parties must be allowed to furnish the jury with evidence of any potential obligations of subrogation or reimbursement. Because the text does not inform a fact-finder what to do with the evidence, in interpreting the statute and determining what a fact-finder must do with the evidence we consider the text of the statute, the legislative history, the legislative goal, and three common-law concepts encompassed in medical malpractice actions and Wis. Stat. § 893.55(7), namely reasonable value of medical services, the collateral source rule, and subrogation. We conclude that the circuit court must instruct the fact-finder that it must not reduce the reasonable value of medical services on the basis of the collateral source payments. Although the jury is instructed not to use the evidence of collateral source payments to reduce the award for medical services, evidence of collateral source payments may be used by the jury to determine the reasonable value of medical services.

The facts of this case illustrate that our interpretation of Wis. Stat. § 893.55(7) fulfills the legislative policies and objectives. In this case, Medicare was not a party but has rights of reimbursement from the parties. The concepts of reimbursement and subrogation are similar.

If the estate recovers an award for the value of the medical services rendered, the estate would not necessarily have a double recovery because it would have an obligation to reimburse Medicare. In the instant case, the attorney for the estate received three lengthy letters * * * from Medicare, each advising the attorney in boldface type of the estate's obligation to reimburse Medicare for Medicare payments out of any recovery or settlement it receives as a result of the litigation. Because Medicare may seek reimbursement, to protect Medicare's right of reimbursement, the collateral source rule should apply. That is, the fact-finder should be advised of the estate's potential obligation to Medicare and the fact-finder should not reduce an award to the estate by the collateral source payments by Medicare because of the potential obligation to repay Medicare. [citation] * * * [T]he jury may hear evidence of collateral source payments and evidence relevant thereto to determine the reasonable value of the medical services but must not use the collateral source payments as an offset to determine the reasonable value of the medical services.

Because the circuit court failed to advise the jury that it must not reduce its award for the reasonable value of medical expenses by the amount of the collateral source payments, we reverse the circuit court's judgment and order and remand the cause for a new trial in accordance with this decision on the issue of the hospital and medical expenses.

IV.   Irrespective of the interpretation of Wis. Stat. § 893.55(7) adopted, the circuit court committed prejudicial error. * * *

According to the record, Medicare explicitly asserted its intention to seek reimbursement for its payments.

Nevertheless, the circuit court barred the estate from introducing evidence of its potential obligation to reimburse Medicare and further barred the estate from arguing to the fact-finder that it would not be getting a double recovery if the fact-finder awarded it the full reasonable value of medical services.

According to the calculation of the reasonable value of medical services rendered, the collateral source rule and subrogation (or reimbursement), the risk of double recovery on the part of the estate did not necessarily exist in the present case. * * *

The circuit court ruled that the estate could, if it wished, argue that the estate "could reimburse Medicare." It could not argue that the estate might be required to do so.

The instruction given did not advise the jury of the estate's potential obligation to reimburse Medicare. * * *

The estate was clearly prejudiced when the circuit court barred the estate from introducing evidence about its potential obligation to Medicare and gave an instruction that did not refer to the estate's potential obligation to reimburse Medicare. The result was that the estate recovered only $755 for medical expenses although it may have to reimburse Medicare for a significantly larger sum. * * *

The defendants * * * argue that the difficulties facing the estate stem not from Wis. Stat. § 893.55(7) or the instructions but from the estate's failure to name Medicare as a party. The defendants contend that had Medicare been named as a party, the statute presumably would have worked as intended: Evidence of Medicare's payments would have been admitted and subject to cross-examination; Medicare would have been on the verdict and the issue of the estate's obligation to Medicare would no longer exist. The defendants assert that they too have a potential liability to Medicare, and that they would be subject to double liability if the jury awarded greater medical expenses to the estate than the $755 awarded. In sum, according to the defendants, neither party should have been allowed to argue specifically about Medicare because Medicare was not a party. Yet Medicare considerations were important, once its payments were submitted to the jury.

The effect of the circuit court errors on the estate was significant. The jury was not informed of the crucial fact that the estate may be responsible to Medicare for all or part of $89,000. By not allowing the jury to hear evidence that Medicare could recover a sum in excess of $755 from the estate, the circuit court committed reversible error.

Irrespective of the proper interpretation of Wis. Stat. § 893.55(7), we conclude that the circuit court erred in not admitting evidence of the estate's potential obligation to reimburse Medicare. Accordingly, we reverse the circuit court's judgment and order and remand the cause for a new trial on the issue of the hospital and medical expenses. * * *

The judgment and order of the circuit court are reversed and the cause is remanded.

PATIENCE DRAKE ROGGENSACK, J. (concurring in part and dissenting in part). * * * I dissent from the majority opinion's conclusion that evidence admitted pursuant to § 893.55(7) could not be used by a fact-finder to abrogate Wisconsin's collateral source rule in this case.

The legislature enacted Wis. Stat. § 893.55(7) in order to reduce health care providers' insurance premiums by reducing medical malpractice jury verdicts through the use of evidence of expenses that the plaintiff has incurred, but has not paid. In order to achieve the legislature's purpose, when third parties with rights of subrogation or direct action have not been joined, a jury must be able to reduce the damages awarded to a plaintiff for amounts the plaintiff has not paid, thereby abrogating the collateral source rule under those circumstances. Because the United States government was not joined in the lawsuit, the case before us presents a fact-finder's reduction of health care expenses for amounts the Lagerstroms have not paid, which I conclude is permissible under § 893.55(7). Accordingly, because I would affirm the judgment of the circuit court, * * * I do not join the majority opinion. * * *

The interpretation of § 893.55(7) begins with the plain meaning of the words chosen by the legislature. * * * When a statute is ambiguous, the legislature is presumed to intend the interpretation that advances the purpose of the statute. [citation]

Here, both parties agree that Wis. Stat. § 893.55(7) is ambiguous, although they differ in regard to what its meaning should be. The majority opinion concludes the statute provides for the admission of evidence of payments by others. * * * But once admitted, the majority opinion holds that this evidence cannot be used as a subtraction from the damages to be awarded a successful plaintiff because to do so would abrogate the collateral source rule. In my view, that second conclusion is not reasonable. As I explain below, it cuts against the legislative purpose behind the enactment of § 893.55(7), that of reducing the size of damage awards in medical malpractice actions through the abrogation of the collateral source rule when doing so will prevent windfalls or double recoveries by the plaintiff.

In 1975, the legislature first responded to what it perceived as a crisis in the provision of health care. * * * Accordingly, § 893.55(7) must be read in the context of a comprehensive legislative scheme to reduce health care costs through containment of the size of awards in medical malpractice cases.

Accordingly, I interpret Wis. Stat. § 893.55(7) as permitting a reduction of damages awarded to a successful plaintiff in a medical malpractice action by amounts that a plaintiff has incurred, but has not paid, for health care services. In order to accomplish the legislative purpose for which § 893.55(7) was enacted, a reduction should occur when write-offs have occurred or when third-party payers with rights of reimbursement or subrogation were not joined in the action. This is fair to plaintiffs who will be made whole, and it is fair to defendants who will not be required to give windfalls or double recoveries to plaintiffs. However, when third parties with subrogated rights or rights of direct action due to their payment of the injured party's medical expenses are joined in the lawsuit and their rights are adjudicated in that lawsuit, a reduction in the amount the tortfeasor is found to owe for what those parties paid would not be appropriate. Stated otherwise, when the parties who paid medical expenses claim for repayment in the lawsuit, the award of damages will include compensation for those parties, as well as for the injured party.

In the case before us, Lagerstrom paid only $755 for medical services, yet Lagerstrom sought $89,375.78 from the jury. Medicare paid $64,759.40 and received provider write-offs of $23,861.38 for a total participation of $88,620.78 as payment for Vance Lagerstrom's health care services. Lagerstrom was made whole by the jury's verdict because everything Lagerstrom paid was repaid by the damages that were awarded. Yet, Lagerstrom appeals. Lagerstrom seeks all that Medicare paid. * * * In support of that position, Lagerstrom asserts * * * that [s]he has potential liability to Medicare for the payments that Medicare made. I disagree. * * *

While the collateral source rule may permit a windfall to a plaintiff when the claim is not based on medical malpractice, [citation] the purpose of Wis. Stat. § 893.55(7) was to modify the collateral source rule in medical malpractice actions. Accordingly, Lagerstrom is due only so much in reimbursement for health care expenses as Lagerstrom paid. That is sufficient to make Lagerstrom whole. * * *

In regard to the * * * contention, that Lagerstrom should recover the $64,759.40 that Medicare paid, I * * * disagree. Lagerstrom purposefully refused to name the United States government as a party, either as a defendant or as an involuntary plaintiff, pursuant to Wis. Stat. § 803.03. Accordingly, as I explain below, the judgment in this case does not affect any claim the United States government has by virtue of the Medicare payments that were made.

The record reflects that on July 30, 2001, the United States government gave notice to Lagerstrom's attorney that "Medicare's regulations require that your client pay Medicare back within 60 days of your receipt of settlement or insurance proceeds." Medicare had then paid $64,759.40. The record also reflects that the defendants attempted to get Lagerstrom to name the United States as a necessary party, * * * but Lagerstrom resisted and prevailed. The jury verdict dated February 2003 did not adjudicate the interests of the United States. * * * Accordingly, a lawsuit by the United States government against the tortfeasor's insurer has not been precluded by this lawsuit. However, there is no basis for a claim against Lagerstrom under the jury's clearly itemized verdict. * * *

Since Lagerstrom refused to name the United States government as a party to the action, both the plaintiff and the defendants were treated similarly in regard to the arguments each could make to the jury. That is, Lagerstrom could argue to the jury that if it included in the damages amounts that Medicare paid, it would repay those amounts to the United States government, and the insurer could argue that amounts paid by Medicare should not be included in the verdict because it remained obligated to Medicare for those same amounts. Therefore, I agree that the circuit court properly instructed the jury. * * *

[T]he instruction given followed the purpose set out by the legislature in enacting Wis. Stat. § 893.55(7). The reduction the jury made prevented a windfall to Lagerstrom, and it prevented a double recovery that could have occurred because Lagerstrom refused to name the United States government as a party and thereby adjudicate its interests. Accordingly, a new trial is not appropriate. Lagerstrom was made whole by the jury's verdict. That the United States government still may have a right of action for the Medicare payments it made, is not unfair to Lagerstrom. Lagerstrom is left with the choice [s]he made, as are the defendants who may be required to deal with [the government] about what is yet due to Medicare.

Therefore, for the reasons set out above, I would affirm the judgment of the circuit court. * * *

DAVID T. PROSSER, J. (dissenting). The plaintiff-appellant challenges the constitutionality of Wis. Stat. § 893.55(7). She also claims that the admission of "prejudicial evidence of collateral source payments so that [she] was awarded only her out-of-pocket medical expenses instead of the reasonable value of the medical expenses incurred" entitles her to a new trial as to medical expense damages. The majority opinion reformulates the issues, and then eviscerates a key component of the medical malpractice statute. Because the court's decision countermands legitimate legislative action, I respectfully dissent.

The collateral source rule * * * has been part of Wisconsin common law since at least 1908. [citation] * * *

From the outset, the collateral source rule recognized the unfairness in relieving a tortfeasor from full liability for injuries the tortfeasor caused simply because the injured party had the foresight to purchase or bargain for insurance or other benefits, or because the injured party received other "compensation" from a collateral source. Over the years, however, the collateral source rule has tended to inflate jury verdicts and lead to double recovery for plaintiffs. The rule sometimes provides an extra source of economic damages, and this may be significant when noneconomic damages have been capped by legislation. Indeed, some litigants have used the rule as a means to get around the cap on noneconomic damages. Using this strategy, double recovery is not an occasional byproduct of the rule; it is the desired objective. * * *

Whatever the merits of the collateral source rule in the court's past cases, the case at hand presents new issues. Unlike past cases, this case involves medical malpractice, which is governed by a unique set of statutes. In 1995 the legislature created Wis. Stat. § 893.55(7), which modifies the collateral source rule in medical malpractice cases. Thus, the principal issue is how the modified rule affects medical expenses in medical malpractice cases. * * *

In 1995 the legislature specifically addressed the collateral source rule in medical malpractice cases. The Act created Wis. Stat. § 893.55(7). * * *

Subsection (7) modifies the collateral source rule by allowing evidence of other compensation to be presented to the jury in a medical malpractice action. It does not *require* an offset or a reduction of a malpractice award by the amount of any other payments, but it *permits* the jury to make such a reduction after considering evidence of other compensation. Admitting this information into evidence negates the principle that the jury should "wholly disregard" the fact of other compensation. * * *

Subsection (7) is different from Wis. Stat. § 655.009(2) and Wis. Stat. § 893.55(5) because, by its terms, it is not limited to evidence of payments for medical expenses. It is broad enough to cover all kinds of compensation from collateral sources for medical malpractice. Some of this compensation will have no right of subrogation or reimbursement, which indicates that the patient *would* receive double recovery under the collateral source rule in the absence of the statutory modification. * * *

The majority opinion acknowledges that the collateral source rule has been modified. But it jumps to the conclusion that "the modification of the collateral source rule is a modification of the rules of evidence to allow evidence of the other payments; the modification is not an explicit modification of the substantive collateral source rule that a collateral source payment does not reduce an award of medical expenses." The opinion goes on to hold that "the circuit court must instruct the fact-finder that it must not reduce the reasonable value of medical services on the basis of the collateral source payments."

These startling conclusions render Wis. Stat. § 893.55(7) a nullity. * * *

[The majority] correctly notes that subsection (7) encompasses all damages in a medical malpractice action and makes evidence of all collateral source payments admissible in regard to all damage claims. * * *

The majority opinion also argues that "the text of the statute raises more questions than it answers." This contention, designed to open the door to statutory interpretation, sums up four paragraphs in which the majority poses questions that the statute does not address. Posing questions that will be answered by the circuit court or jury on a case-by-case basis is nothing more than a ploy to create ambiguity in the statute to justify statutory construction.

[T]he majority looks at legislative history and notes that an early draft of 1995 Assembly Bill 36 contained the sentence: "The award of damages under ch. 655 shall be reduced by any compensation that the injured party received from sources other than the defendant to compensate him or her for the injury." This sentence is deleted from the final draft. * * *

There is a perfectly reasonable explanation for deletion of the sentence from the first draft. The authors of the bill opted to permit juries to weigh the facts and then decide whether to reduce damage awards by all or part of the amount of collateral source payments. * * * This flexibility anticipates juries balancing the equities in widely varying fact situations, and taking into account special circumstances like Medicare reimbursement. * * *

The majority complains that the legislative history does not make clear how the admissibility of collateral source payments to a plaintiff "impacts our case law defining 'reasonable value of medical services' as the reasonable value of medical services rendered, without limitation to amounts paid, or how that modification affects the collateral source rule and subrogation." I believe it does. The statute permits the jury to consider collateral source payments in a medical malpractice case in determining damages. Subsection (7) preserves the substantive and procedural rights of persons who have claims based on subrogation. Those rights are established outside the statute. Persons who have claims based on subrogation or reimbursement must assert their claims at an appropriate time in an appropriate manner, neither of which is limited by subsection (7). The court is then required to respond in a way that both accurately informs the jury and protects subrogation rights. * * *

The majority accurately states two of the legislature's goals, namely, (1) to provide fact-finders with information about the collateral source payments in the hope that patients will not obtain double recovery; and (2) ultimately, to reduce health care providers' insurance premiums. The obvious goal *not* stated by the majority is to allow juries to take other compensation into account in determining the amount of damage awards. * * *

[H]aving stated at least some of the legislative goals, the majority sets out to undermine them. It begins with a discussion of "the valuation of reasonable medical expenses." The majority writes: "In calculating damages, a person injured by medical malpractice may recover the reasonable value of the medical services reasonably required by the injury."

The majority dismisses Wis. Stat. § 655.009(2), saying it does not change "the long-standing rule that the 'reasonable value of medical services' is the reasonable value of medical services rendered, without limitation to amounts paid." This is not correct. The majority does not point to any authority to substantiate its conclusion that the reasonable value of medical services has no relationship to *actual payments where actual payments have been made* in the medical malpractice context. * * *

Contrary to the majority opinion, there is substantial evidence that damages for past medical and hospital expenses have been tightly controlled over the years by Wisconsin judges, in keeping with § 655.009(2) ("the amounts of medical expense payments previously incurred"). * * *

[T]he reasonable value of medical services has not been measured consistently as the *highest* reasonable cost for those services, *particularly in medical malpractice cases.* The "highest value" approach is a recent phenomenon. * * *

Even if Wis. Stat. § 655.009(2) and Wis. Stat. § 893.55(7) were to be interpreted as requiring the full, undiscounted value of medical services, this does not negate the admitted modification of the collateral source rule in § 893.55(7) for medical malpractice cases.

The majority's discussion of the collateral source rule is an unpersuasive denial of the fact that the legislature has acted to modify the rule. For instance, the discussion of the policy basis for the collateral source rule is beside the point, inasmuch as the legislature had a different policy objective in mind: containing the liability costs of health care providers by discouraging double recovery. * * *

This brings us to subrogation. Subrogation has been defined as the "substitution of one party for another whose debt the party pays, entitling the paying party to rights, remedies, or securities that would otherwise belong to the debtor." Ruckel v. Gassner, 253 Wis.2d 280, 286, 646 N.W.2d 11, 14 (quoting *Black's Law Dictionary* 1440 (7th ed.1999)). Subrogation rights are often embodied in contracts, such as insurance policies. Sometimes subrogation is protected by statute or derived from operation of law. * * *

There are multiple ways to handle subrogation claims. * * * Wisconsin Stat. § 893.55(7) does not attempt to catalog all the possibilities or to determine the procedure to be followed in each situation.

The majority writes that "[a]ny interpretation of § 893.55(7) must * * * take into account that the statute does not limit the rights of claims based on subrogation." This is not in dispute. It does not follow, however, that "Wis. Stat. § 893.55(7) must be interpreted to require courts to instruct juries to be instructed to consider the collateral source payments only in determining the reasonable value of the medical services rendered." Such an instruction ignores situations in which there is absolutely no right of subrogation or reimbursement. * * *

The majority opinion asserts that Wis. Stat. § 893.55(7) leaves many questions unanswered. * * * In my view, it is the majority opinion that muddles the law and creates confusion. I can fathom no reason why a jury should not be permitted to receive any evidence or hear any argument on collateral source payments that will help it make a reasonable determination of medical malpractice damages, after taking into account subrogation and/or reimbursement rights and anything the plaintiff contributed to earn the payments. Under Wis. Stat. § 893.55(7), the jury must be *permitted* not to award double recovery to the plaintiff in a medical malpractice case.

First, the plaintiff is not entitled to recover medical expense damages from the defendants for any value of medical services provided by Myrtle Werth Hospital that exceeds the actual Medicare payments to Myrtle Werth because any such damages would not only be double recovery for the plaintiff but also double liability for the tortfeasor-defendants. Such liability is simply not part of the collateral source rule.

Second, *if* the jury were permitted to consider the full reasonable value of medical services provided by Luther Hospital, Lakeside Nursing Home, St. Joseph's Hospital, and any other post-malpractice provider * * * , the jury must be given authority to award damages or not to award damages for the "value" exceeding actual Medicare payments. The jury should not be instructed to disregard actual payments by Medicare or actual costs to Mr. Lagerstrom in determining the award of damages for past medical expenses. The jury should be fully informed of the facts, including facts about reimbursement.

Third, Medicare reimbursement amounts should be determined by the court and inserted in the special verdict. Mrs. Lagerstrom argues that Medicare has statutory reimbursement rights. * * * She quotes 42 C.F.R. § 411.24 (2004) to the effect that: "If the beneficiary or other party receives a third party payment, the beneficiary must reimburse Medicare within 60 days." The Wisconsin Academy of Trial Lawyers argues in its amicus brief that: "The federal government is expressly granted statutory rights of reimbursement. * * * The government may seek to exercise these rights against any and all amounts recovered, regardless of their designation by the jury. Consequently, if a jury reduces or eliminates an award for medical expenses paid by Medicare, plaintiffs face the very real likelihood of a 'double loss.' This is because Medicare may assert its right of recovery against the entirety of the award."

If these representations are accurate, Medicare could assert its right of reimbursement against the plaintiff's award for the deceased's actual medical costs, the award for pain and suffering, and the award for wrongful death.

[T]here appears to be a basis for such a conclusion in the Code of Federal Regulations, even though the July 30, 2001, communication from the Health Care Financing Administration to Mrs. Lagerstrom's attorney demands reimbursement for "overpayment." This dilemma illuminates why Medicare should have been joined as a plaintiff in this litigation. * * * In any event, Medicare could *not* force Lagerstrom to repay *more* than the judgment amount. [citation]

In my view, upon remand, the circuit court should award Medicare the precise amount of money it paid for post-malpractice medical services, plus interest, minus a proportionate share of the cost incurred by Mrs. Lagerstrom in securing this reimbursement amount. This would protect all damages awarded to Mrs. Lagerstrom. * * *

There is no need to order a new trial on the issue of hospital and medical expenses. * * *

For the reasons stated above, I respectfully dissent.

Notes

1. *Home Court Advantage?* Did the Wisconsin healthcare providers and their liability insurer lose in the legislature or in the court?

2. *Party Time!* The Medicare branch of the United States government had asserted an interest in being reimbursed from plaintiff-Lagerstrom's recovery from the defendants; Medicare was a major character in *Lagerstrom*, but one that remained offstage. Adjudicating the dispute without Medicare as a party is awkward for the parties and the court. The plaintiff had not joined Medicare. Medicare probably could have intervened as a plaintiff to protect its claim. But it hadn't. As a nonparty in *Lagerstrom*, Medicare is not bound or precluded by the result. The majority opinion says that Medicare was a "necessary" party plaintiff. A "necessary" party is one who *should* be joined in the action, but who may be excused. To be distinguished from a "necessary" party is an "indispensable" party; the latter *must* be joined for a lawsuit to proceed.

A subrogated payor is substituted for its payee, becomes the "real party in interest" in a lawsuit, and may exercise all its payee's legal rights. An insurance company that would rather litigate in its insured's costume may use a ruse like a "loan receipt" to avoid party status.

What should we make of it? What comes next? Instead of a "necessary" party should Medicare have been an "indispensable" one? Should the court have adjudicated the dispute without the government as a party?

3. *Reasonable vs. Written-off?* Defendants in other appeals have argued that plaintiffs' medical-expense damages should be limited to the amount the healthcare providers accepted under agreements between healthcare providers and Medicare, Medicaid or private insurance companies. The tortfeasor, courts have held, must pay plaintiff the "reasonable value" of medical services, not the lower "written-off" amount actually paid. See, e.g., Bynum v. Magno, 106 Hawai'i 81, 101 P.3d 1149, 1160 (2004).

The Virginia court implemented this by holding that the amounts "written off" by the provider were a collateral source payment from plaintiff's insurance carrier; thus the tortfeasor could not introduce evidence that supports deducting either the insurance payments to plaintiff or the amount the insurance carrier actually paid the provider from plaintiff's medical-expense damages. Acuar v. Letourneau, 260 Va. 180, 531 S.E.2d 316 (2000).

Are these decisions straightforward applications of the evidence branch of the collateral source rule? Should a court treat Medicare or Medicaid payments from the federal or state government differently than private insurance payments? In *Lagerstrom*, is the "reasonable value" pill harder to swallow because the health care provider is also the tortfeasor?

4. *Malingering.* At trial, defendant Castelletti introduced evidence of payments plaintiff Proctor received from disability insurance "on the ground that it was probative of Proctor's malingering." Proctor appealed a judgment for $7000:

"Evidence of malingering is arguably probative. * * * In sum, collateral source evidence should not be admitted because of the potential that the jury will misuse the evidence in a manner that is prejudicial to the plaintiff. It should not matter that the stated purpose of introducing the evidence is, arguably, probative. The excessive prejudicial nature of the evidence mandates its exclusion. That is, no matter how probative the evidence of a collateral source may be, it will never overcome the substantially prejudicial danger of the evidence." Proctor v. Castelletti, 112 Nev. 88, 90, 911 P.2d 853, 854 (1996).

5. *An End to Subrogation*? Suppose the deceased had maintained a whole-life policy of insurance on his life that named his wife as beneficiary. If, after his death, the life insurance company had paid the policy proceeds to his widow, it would not be subrogated to her claim for wrongful death. Life insurance policies do not contain subrogation clauses, and the court would probably view the whole-life policy as an investment rather than a contract of indemnity.

6. *September 11.* Congress's legislation for the 9/11 victims required reduction of their awards by collateral source payments, including their pensions and life insurance. Special Master Kenneth Feinberg observed that subtraction of all collateral source payments from survivors' awards "turned a tort-based compensation system into a type of social welfare program, a 'public safety net' designed to guarantee that no 9/11 family would be made destitute by the tragedy." In the end, the Special Master did not consider private charity as a collateral source, and payments to the victims' families by workers' compensation insurers that would subrogate were not subtracted. (pp. 36, 71, 81).

7. The Wisconsin court's *Lagerstrom* decision touches on two topics that will come up later, (a) tort reform and (b) restitution.

(a) *Tort Reform.* The Wisconsin legislature's tort reform that focused on medical malpractice began in 1975. In 1995, it enacted the collateral-source statute that the *Lagerstrom* court construes. The dissent refers to other tort-reform statutes, in particular to a cap on "noneconomic" damages. The Wisconsin cast of judicial characters returns below in the Tort Reform section of this chapter playing the same roles in a decision on the state's "noneconomic" or pain-and-suffering damages cap.

(b) *Restitution.* Justice Abramson's majority opinion says that a collateral source payor's successful subrogation prevents the plaintiff's unjust enrichment by double recovery. Subrogation is a topic of restitution; Chapter 4 of this book returns to restitution. "Equitable subrogation" is the legal doctrine of subrogation which is distinguished from subrogation under a contract. The new restatement of restitution has a section on equitable subrogation which takes up the collateral source rule in comment b. Restatement (Third) of Restitution and Unjust Enrichment § 26 (Tent. Draft No. 2, (2002)).

8. *Plaintiff's Tax Writeoff.* Investors who purchased limited partnership shares in a motel deducted the partnership's large losses from their income tax. After the motel failed, the investors successfully sued the seller under the federal securities statutes arguing misrepresentations and omissions. Should the court award them the purchase price plus interest or that amount minus the tax benefits they received? The Supreme Court declined to offset the plaintiffs' tax benefits; the offset, the Court emphasized, would undercut the securities law's goal of deterring misrepresentation. Randall v. Loftsgaarden, 478 U.S. 647 (1986).

9. *Collateral Sources and Plaintiff's Benefit From the Defendant's Breach.* Because of the opportunities it may reveal, defendant's violation of the plaintiff's rights may, by itself, leave her better off than before. The state of the law is one of disarray.

(a) *Rule.* "The benefits rule provides that if a defendant's tortious conduct confers a benefit, as well as a harm, upon the plaintiff, the jury may weigh the value of the benefit against the claimed harm." Gits v. Norwest Bank Minneapolis, 390 N.W.2d 835, 837 (Minn.App.1986).

(b) *Rule "Applied."* After the plaintiff was driven from his residence when the defendant brought in a gusher nearby, the appellate court observed: "In the matter of the injury to the [plaintiff's] realty, the court specially found, by specific items, what it would cost to restore the premises to their original condition, and allowed the aggregate amount as damages. [Defendant] does not dispute the accuracy of the court's figures, but contends that the discovery of oil in its well gave a new value to the property of the [plaintiffs]—a value as oil property, greatly in excess of its previous value as residential property—and that the restoration of the property to its original condition will add nothing to its value for its new use. Wherefore, the value being greater after the 'blowout' than it was before, [defendant] argues, the [plaintiffs] suffered no loss by reason of the injury to the realty. We are not impressed with [defendant's] argument on this point." Green v. General Petroleum Corp., 205 Cal. 328, 334–38, 270 P. 952, 955–56 (1928).

If the plaintiffs pocket the damages and sell their residence to an oil company, what purpose has their recovery served?

(c) *The Mother Country.* In England, someone who was wrongfully convicted of a crime may be compensated from public funds for the improper punishment. A prisoner who was found to have been wrongfully convicted was released. The British government argued that, to prevent his recovery for a loss which he had not suffered, his saved living expenses while incarcerated should be subtracted from the amount he was to be paid for the miscarriage of justice. Not from his pain and suffering, it maintained, but merely from his lost wages. "[T]he claimant would have had to pay for his own living expenses out of those earnings," said the court of appeal in its opinion accepting the government's deduction. "All the unpleasant aspects of involuntary incarceration are, or should be, taken into account in [the pain and suffering] part of the award." Independent Assessor v. O'Brien and Hickey, [2004] EWCA Civ. 1035, quotations from para. 103.

Is this deduction similar to subtracting the victim's personal consumption from a September 11 award?

(d) *Four Examples of Benefits.* (1) A contractor breaches a contract for a scrubber to reduce pollution from a company's factory; before the company relets the contract, a scientist discovers a way to reduce the factory's pollution substantially for one third of the "original" cost; the company adopts the scientist's innovation and saves several million dollars.

(2) After a tortfeasor negligently kills her spouse, plaintiff remarries; instead of being unemployable and an unmitigated jerk like the deceased, the new husband, a law student, is a jewel of the first water.

(3) Professional negligence leads to a woman's pregnancy; but instead of being the unwanted child they had taken medical precautions to prevent, the baby turn out to be cute, cuddly, and the center of his parents' lives.

(4) Defendant kidnaps plaintiff. After being released, plaintiff writes a best-selling book recounting her harrowing experience. Plaintiff's book earns royalties.

Are the new (1) contract, (2) husband, (3) baby, and (4) book royalties benefits from collateral sources? If the four "victims" do sue, is each defendant entitled to a credit for the benefit to each plaintiff?

D. ENHANCEMENT AND ADJUSTMENT OF COMPENSATORY DAMAGES

1. PREJUDGMENT INTEREST

This will continue and expand the material after Childs v. United States, p. 66.

"The following hypothetical case illustrates the injustice of denying prejudgment interest. Suppose A inflicts precisely the same amount of damage of any type on B and C at the same moment, evaluated by juries as $1,000 each. If C wins his judgment a year later than B and does not get prejudgment interest for the year, C recovers less than B for the same injury; C has been deprived of the use value of $1,000 for one year while B has enjoyed the use value. Interest is the market, or in the case of the legal rate, the legislative evaluation of the use value of money. B obviously has not gotten too much for he had a right to be made whole immediately upon being injured, and B and C should get the same amount for the same injury, so C must have gotten too little. Only by awarding prejudgment interest from the time the cause of action accrues, when a plaintiff is entitled to be made whole, can the sort of injustice which happened to C in the hypothetical case be avoided. We are also influenced by the policy consideration that failure to award prejudgment interest creates a substantial financial incentive for defendants to litigate even where liability is so clear and the jury award so predictable that they should settle." State v. Phillips, 470 P.2d 266, 274 (Alaska 1970).

Interest measures the time value of money. The plaintiff's request for prejudgment interest on a judgment arises from the delay between the plaintiff's injury and the defendant's payment. The litigation process often takes several years. If the court determines in 2005 that plaintiff had damages from her injury in 2000, then, in retrospect, defendant has had the use of "plaintiff's" money during that five-year period, in effect an involuntary interest-free loan.

To compensate plaintiff accurately and to structure deterrence efficiently, defendant should pay interest. Economic theory supports interest adjustments to place both plaintiff and defendant where they would have been financially had defendant paid plaintiff immediately. Interest adjustments also remove defendant's incentive to delay litigation and to withhold offers to settle. Interest on the judgment from the time the plaintiff's claim arose until judgment is called prejudgment interest; interest on the judgment from the date of judgment until defendant pays it is called postjudgment or judgment interest. Distinguish both from contract interest, which is interest a debtor agrees to pay a creditor.

Despite the persuasive arguments for prejudgment interest, the law remains in a jumble. It defies easy generalization because many jurisdictions' legislatures have addressed statutes specifically to the issue; a detailed study of the possibilities for interest in each lawsuit is imperative. Nevertheless, some general ideas follow the caution that you may encounter refinements not herein indicated.

The common-law interest rules were a complicated series of specious reasons for a court to decline to award plaintiffs prejudgment interest most of the time. The liquidated-unliquidated rule had two sides. The liquidated side required the defendant to pay prejudgment interest only on a plaintiff's claims that was either certain or clearly ascertainable with a calculation, that is a "liquidated" claim. The unliquidated side declined to charge the defendant interest on the plaintiff's uncertain, incalculable, that is "unliquidated" claim. The plaintiffs' damages judgments for the torts in this chapter are unliquidated.

Several reasons were given not to charge a defendant with prejudgment interest. They appear to stem from an anachronistic aversion to interest left over from the medieval era, a view of interest as a punishment or sanction instead of compensation, and a mindset of viewing interest from the defendant's perspective, charging interest only if the defendant could know or determine exactly what it owed. Large judgments, fluctuating interest rates, and increased financial sophistication brought plaintiff's recovery of prejudgment interest out of the realm of arcane esoteria and into the arena of public debate.

Some reforms followed. The trend is in the direction of adding prejudgment interest to all money judgments. Two methods of judicial improvement tinker with the liquidated-unliquidated rules: (a) a court may expand the category of what can be calculated or ascertained; and (b) a court may restate rules as discretion.

The trend toward prejudgment interest is ragged and not always rational. Prejudgment interest lacks headline impact; the return of lower and more stable interest rates beginning in the 1980s has been accompanied by a lack of legislative zeal to reform the law. Statutes, once passed, tend to petrify legal development; if the legislature once got interest wrong, it tends to stay wrong. A court lacks the legislature's ability to study the whole problem and state the solution systematically and definitively. In litigation, prejudgment interest is usually a secondary issue for both parties; judicial changes respond to particular parts of particular disputes.

Professor Michael Knoll's article, A Primer on Prejudgment Interest, 75 Tex.L.Rev. 293 (1996), applies financial principles to answer questions about how a jurisdiction ought to calculate prejudgment interest to compensate and deter with fairness and efficiency.

Should a plaintiff's judgment include prejudgment interest? Yes, for the reasons above. In retrospect, a plaintiff's money judgment is a forced loan from the plaintiff to the defendant that accrues on the date of the plaintiff's injury. Defendant's payment of the judgment should put both plaintiff and defendant where they would have been, financially, if defendant had paid plaintiff on the date of the injury. Prejudgment interest compensates plaintiff for the defendant's use of the amount that, looking back, was plaintiff's all along. The difference between a liquidated and an unliquidated amount, which views prejudgment interest from the defendant's perspective, is not relevant to the reasons to charge the defendant prejudgment interest; courts and the legislature should repudiate the distinction.

Should a plaintiff's judgment for past nonpecuniary injuries like pain and suffering bear prejudgment interest? Yes, so long as the damages are to compensate. To avoid duplication, a court should discount plaintiff's future damages to present value to the date of *injury* and compute prejudgment interest at the defendant's cost to borrow.

"Simple" interest is calculated on the original amount for each base period; "compound" interest is calculated on the base amount plus the interest from the prior period. Should the prejudgment interest a defendant pays be simple or compound? Compound, since the defendant does not pay each installment of interest to the plaintiff but keeps it until the whole judgment is paid.

What is the correct interest rate for a defendant's prejudgment interest? Usually the defendant's cost to borrow an equivalent amount without collateral, that is unsecured, a rate the court may adjust during the interest period. The prime rate is a default rate if the court lacks knowledge of the defendant's cost to borrow. If the plaintiff is a small business or individual that lacks ability to diversify the risk, prejudgment interest may exceed defendant's cost to borrow. Income tax affects both the size of the judgment and the amount defendant pays, and the court should also take it into account.

Even if the judgment when granted makes the defendant insolvent and reduces it to bankruptcy? Yes, but if the judgment, had it been granted immediately, had that effect, the court may lower the defendant's prejudgment interest rate.

What if the defendant does not pay the plaintiff right away? The plaintiff's judgment ought to continue to earn postjudgment interest during delay and appeals. Postjudgment interest statutes exist and often set the rates. The set rates are often too low; in any event, they are contrary to Professor Knoll's argument for interest at the defendant's cost to borrow.

Reduction to present value is interest in reverse: where the plaintiff receives money now for a loss, for example, her wages, that will occur in the future, reduction of the future damages to present value adjusts the lump sum for the interest it will earn before she needs the amounts.

2. PUNITIVE DAMAGES

TUTTLE v. RAYMOND, III

Supreme Judicial Court of Maine, 1985.
494 A.2d 1353.

VIOLETTE, JUSTICE. * * * On July 6, 1977, the plaintiff, Hattie Tuttle, was seriously injured when a Lincoln driven by the defendant, Ralph Raymond, III, struck the Plymouth in which she was a passenger. The force of the impact sheared the Plymouth in half. Based on the evidence presented at trial, the jury could have found that the defendant was driving at an excessive speed in a 25 mile per hour zone when he struck the Plymouth, and that the defendant went through a red light just before the impact.

The defendant conceded liability at trial and focused instead on the amount of damages the jury should properly award. From the outset of the litigation, the defendant asserted both that punitive damages should not be recognized under the law of Maine and that, in any event, the facts of this case did not generate the issue of punitive damages. Nevertheless, the trial court submitted this issue to the jury, and refused to disturb the jury's decision to award [$50,000 compensatory damages and] $22,000 in exemplary damages.

Vigorous criticism of the doctrine of punitive damages is hardly a recent development in the field of jurisprudence. Arguments against the availability of such awards have been circulating for one hundred years and longer. [citations] During those hundred years, commentators have exhaustively analyzed the doctrine. [citations] Nonetheless, a substantial majority of jurisdictions today allow common law punitive damages in appropriate cases as a recovery beyond the amount necessary to compensate the plaintiff, for the purpose of deterrence or punishment or both. [citations]

The law of Maine on this issue is in accord with the position of this substantial majority. Since adopting the doctrine of punitive damages in Pike v. Dilling, 48 Me. 539 (1861), this Court has frequently and consistently reaffirmed the availability of such awards at common law under the appropriate circumstances. [citations] "It would be simplistic to characterize [this position] as mere blind adherence to an outmoded principle. Rather, the doctrine of punitive damages survives because it continues to serve the useful purposes of expressing society's disapproval of intolerable conduct and deterring such conduct where no other remedy would suffice." Mallor and Roberts, [Punitive Damages: Toward a Principled Approach, 31 Hastings L.J. 639, 641 (1980)].

The defendant in the case at bar contends that we should nevertheless abandon the judicially created rule of punitive damages in this state. In support of this position, the defendant proffers several arguments, which we consider seriatim. After careful consideration, we conclude that the doctrine of punitive damages retains its viability, and we refuse to abrogate the availability of exemplary awards at common law in Maine.

One objection raised by the defendant is that the civil law is ill-suited to accomplish the goals that purportedly justify the doctrine of punitive damages. The defendant contends that the proper function of the civil tort law is to make plaintiffs whole, and that grave problems arise when it is used to extract from defendants something beyond full compensation for the victim. The defendant asserts that the primary purpose allegedly served by the doctrine of punitive damages, deterrence through punishment, is more properly left to the criminal law with its attendant procedural safeguards.

The bright line that the defendant attempts to interpose between the civil and the criminal law is in fact artificial. The courts of this country historically have not restricted the civil law to a compensatory function. In 1851, the United States Supreme Court, relying on over a century of judicial precedent, observed: "By the common as well as by statute law, men are often punished for aggravated misconduct or lawless acts, by means of a civil action, and the damages, inflicted by way of a penalty or punishment, given to the party injured." Day v. Woodworth, 54 U.S. (13 How.) 363, 371 (1851). Use of the civil law to shape social behavior is both logical and desirable. There are many instances where the criminal law alone is inadequate to achieve the desired deterrent effect. For instance, even when the defendant's conduct violates a criminal statute, it may be a crime that is rarely prosecuted, or the maximum applicable penalty may not correspond to the actual outrageousness of the conduct and the defendant's ability to pay. Of course, where a criminal sanction does constitute an adequate deterrent in a given case, there is no justification for adding a civil penalty in the form of punitive damages. This potential problem, however, does not require the wholesale abrogation of the doctrine of punitive damages. A more sensible solution is to allow the fact finder to consider evidence of any criminal punishment imposed for the conduct in question as a mitigating factor on the issue of punitive damages,[1] a step already taken by this Court. See Hanover Insurance Co. v. Hayward, 464 A.2d 156, 159 (Me.1983).

1. [Footnotes renumbered.] We note that, despite our decision in Hanover Insurance Co. v. Hayward, 464 A.2d 156 (Me.1983), the trial court in this case excluded evidence of the fact that the defendant was convicted and punished criminally for the same conduct that gave rise to

Furthermore, the lack of certain procedural safeguards, which are required in criminal prosecutions,[2] does not render the civil law unfit to serve this deterrent function. The statute books provide many examples where penalties, in the form of multiple damages payable to a private party, are imposed in civil actions for the purpose of discouraging undesirable conduct.[3] The absence of these procedural safeguards presents no constitutional bar to the imposition of punitive damages in a civil action. [citations] The reason for requiring such safeguards in the criminal arena, the threat to the defendant of incarceration or other substantial stigma, does not justify their application in actions for punitive damages.

In a related argument, the defendant criticizes the doctrine of punitive damages because it permits a person to be punished twice for the same offense. The defendant observes that in the case at bar he was *both* convicted and fined in a criminal proceeding *and* assessed with punitive damages in a subsequent civil proceeding based upon the same conduct. The defendant contends that the assessment of an exemplary award in addition to criminal punishment for the same conduct offends the constitutional prohibition against placing a defendant twice in jeopardy. * * *

"In the constitutional sense," jeopardy is a technical term that encompasses only the risk inherent in proceedings that are "essentially criminal." [citation] Accordingly, a civil action for punitive damages cannot infringe on a defendant's constitutional right to be free from double jeopardy. [citations] A claim for punitive damages is based upon a *private* wrong, and is clearly distinguishable from a criminal prosecution, which is brought solely on the behalf of the public. [citations] The state and federal constitutional prohibitions against double jeopardy present no bar to actions for punitive damages. * * *

Another objection to punitive damages raised by the defendant is that they bestow a windfall upon the plaintiff. As the defendant observes, such damages are awarded in Maine in excess of any amount necessary to compensate the plaintiff. [citation] The defendant contends that a plaintiff injured by a tort is entitled to be made whole, and not to be put in a better position than if the tort had never occurred. [citations]

this civil litigation. A defendant is entitled to have the jury consider such evidence when it decides whether to assess punitive damages and, if so, in what amount. Because of our disposition of this case, however, we need not decide whether the trial court's exclusion of this evidence constitutes reversible error.

2. As stated by one commentator, who was obviously uncomfortable with the notion of punitive damages:

Again, when assessed exemplary damages, the accused [sic] is really punished for a criminal offense without the safeguards of a criminal trial. He is summoned into court to make compensation for a purely private injury, with no issue upon a criminal charge presented; punishment by fine is inflicted without indictment or sworn information; the rules of evidence as to criminal trials are rejected; the doctrine of reasonable doubt is replaced by the rule of preponderance of evidence; the defendant is compelled to testify against himself; and, though in crimi-

nal offenses the law fixes a maximum penalty which is imposed by the court, the jury is entirely free to assess exemplary damages, subject only to the power of the court, unwillingly exercised, to set aside the verdict. The procedure and principles of criminal law are disregarded. * * * Willis, Measure of Damages When Property Is Wrongfully Taken by a Private Individual, 22 Harv.L.Rev. 419, 421 (1909).

3. See e.g., 10 M.R.S.A. § 1322 (1980) (providing for treble damages, attorney's fees, and costs for willful violation of Fair Credit Reporting Act); 14 M.R.S.A. § 6034 (1980) (providing for double damages, attorney's fees, and costs for willful retention of security deposit in violation of law); 15 U.S.C. § 15 (1976) (providing for treble damages, attorney's fees, and costs for violation of antitrust laws); 15 U.S.C. § 72 (1976) (providing for treble damages, attorney's fees, and costs for unfair competition in importing trade).

We find, however, that the extra recovery afforded to plaintiffs by punitive damages, rather than constituting a "windfall," serves a useful purpose. The potential for recovering an exemplary award provides an incentive for private civil enforcement of society's rules against serious misconduct.[4] As noted earlier, the civil law effectively augments the criminal law in deterring intolerable conduct. The doctrine of punitive damages encourages the use of civil actions by private parties in response to such conduct, especially when the prospective compensatory recovery is low or the expected cost of litigation is high.[5]

The defendant next argues that the doctrine of punitive damages invites abuse because there is no objective standard by which to determine the amount of a proper award. According to the defendant, the jury is left to speculate concerning the appropriate amount of punitive damages in a given case, with the result of arbitrary and excessive awards. The defendant contends that this is a flaw in the doctrine that outweighs any justification for allowing exemplary awards.

In fact, however, the lack of any precise formula by which punitive damages can be calculated is one of the important assets of the doctrine. "Punitive damages * * * can be individualized to provide a deterrent that will be adequate for each case." Mallor and Roberts, at 657. Such flexibility can ensure a sufficient award in the case of a rich defendant and avoid an overburdensome one where the defendant is not as wealthy. Flexibility is also necessary to avoid situations where the potential benefits of wrongdoing could outweigh a known maximum liability. In short, "[a]lthough a quantitative formula would be comforting, it would be undesirable." Mallor and Roberts, at 666.

We, of course, do not advocate the availability of punitive damages on a completely open-ended basis. The trial court must reject a claim for punitive damages as a matter of law unless the plaintiff presents adequate proof that the defendant acted in a sufficiently culpable manner. Further, even after the plaintiff has satisfied his prima facie burden on the issue of exemplary damages, the fact finder must weigh "all relevant aggravating and mitigating factors" presented by the parties, including the egregiousness of the defendant's conduct, the ability of the defendant to pay such an award, and any criminal punishment imposed for the conduct in question. After such consideration, an exemplary award is "within the *sound* discretion of the fact finder." *Hanover Insurance Co.* (emphasis added). If the fact finder awards punitive damages that are excessive

---

4. The defendant contends that this incentive is in fact a drawback because plaintiffs will attempt to maximize their recoveries without any regard as to what amount of punitive damages would serve as a just and sufficient deterrent. This, however, is not so much a problem inherent in the doctrine of punitive damages as it is a byproduct of our chosen adversary system of justice. We use this system because potential excesses, such as the one raised by the defendant, are hopefully cured by an equally zealous and competent advocate on the opposing side, an impartial jury as a fact finder, and a wise and wary judge overseeing the entire proceeding.

5. In Wangen v. Ford Motor Co., 97 Wis.2d 260, 294 N.W.2d 437 (1980), the defendant argued that, in order to avoid giving the plaintiff a windfall, the court should award any punitive damages to the public. After noting that this

argument had "a certain equitable ring" to it, the Wisconsin Supreme Court ultimately rejected it. The court stated:

"The 'windfall criterion' overlooks that the payment of punitive damages to the injured party is justifiable as a practical matter, because such damages do serve to compensate the injured party for uncompensated expenses, e.g., attorneys' fees and litigation expenses, and that the windfall motivates reluctant plaintiffs to go forward with their claims. If punitive damages were paid to the public treasury, fewer wrongdoers would be punished because the injured would have no inducement to spend the extra time and expense to prove a claim for punitive damages once an action had been brought."

A Maine author has suggested that punitive damages could be split between plaintiffs and the state pursuant to legislative action. [citation]

in light of the relevant factors, the trial court or this Court can intervene. [citations]

We also observe that the lack of precision in measuring appropriate exemplary awards is not a trait unique to the doctrine of punitive damages. Compensatory awards for intangible harm, such as pain and suffering, and emotional distress, are likewise not subject to any exact standard for determining an appropriate amount.

In conclusion, we are not persuaded that we should abolish common law punitive damages in Maine.[6] It may well be, as the defendant argues, that the doctrine of punitive damages no longer serves any purpose for which it was originally intended.[7]

> "This argument, however, fails to account for the fact that many legal doctrines serve purposes that differ from those for which they originally were developed. * * * So long as a doctrine continues to serve a necessary policy goal, the fact that it has diverged from its original function does not provide a basis for abolishing the doctrine. The pertinent question is whether punitive damages continue to serve a rational policy."

Mallor & Roberts, (emphasis added). We conclude that they do.

Although we reject the defendant's contention that we should abolish common law punitive damages in Maine, we perceive cogent reasons for avoiding an overbroad application of the doctrine. Notions of fairness and efficiency weigh against allowing exemplary awards where the stated goal of deterring reprehensible conduct would be furthered only marginally or not at all. Rather, punitive damages should be available based only upon a limited class of misconduct where deterrence is both paramount and likely to be achieved. With this in mind, we turn to a re-examination of the type of tortious conduct that can justify an exemplary award in Maine.

It is generally accepted that mere negligence cannot support an award of punitive damages. Beyond that, however, there has been some variation in describing the quality of tortious conduct necessary to support an exemplary award. Recent decisions of this Court have indicated that Maine law recognizes the availability of punitive damages based upon "wanton, malicious, reckless or grossly negligent conduct." [citations]

Such a standard is overbroad. Whatever qualitative difference exists between mere negligence and "gross" negligence, it is insufficient to justify allowing punitive damages based upon the latter class of conduct. "Gross"

---

6. We note that, although our opinion today provides a careful evaluation of a longstanding doctrine, many issues concerning the availability of punitive damages, which are not raised by this case, remain for future consideration and resolution. These issues include, inter alia, whether one can insure against the assessment of punitive damages, whether one can be vicariously liable for punitive damages, and the application of punitive damages in products liability and multiple plaintiff litigation. It should be clear that our decision not to abandon the doctrine of punitive damages does not eliminate the need for future definition and modification of it.

7. Some theorize that punitive damages initially compensated plaintiffs for intangible harms, which were not cognizable under the existing common law. [citation] Of course, modern tort law now allows compensatory damages for such intangible injuries, eliminating that particular basis for punitive damages. It has also been suggested that punitive damages first arose in cases involving "affronts to the honor of the victims," as a means of satisfying insulted plaintiffs and preventing them from resorting to violent forms of self-help, such as dueling. [citation] It is not so clear that this function of the doctrine of punitive damages has become obsolete. In any event, it is not the primary justification given for exemplary awards today.

negligence simply covers too broad and too vague an area of behavior, resulting in an unfair and inefficient use of the doctrine of punitive damages. A similar problem exists with allowing punitive damages based merely upon "reckless" conduct. "To sanction punitive damages solely upon the basis of conduct characterized as 'heedless disregard of the consequences' would be to allow virtually limitless imposition of punitive damages." [citation] A standard that allows exemplary awards based upon gross negligence or mere reckless disregard of the circumstances overextends the availability of punitive damages, and dulls the potentially keen edge of the doctrine as an effective deterrent of truly reprehensible conduct.

We therefore determine that a new standard is needed in Maine. "If one were to select a single word or term to describe [the] essence [of conduct warranting punitive damages], it would be 'malice.' "[citations] Indeed, the *malicious* commission of a tort is a common thread running through many of the decisions in which this Court has upheld an award of punitive damages. [citations] We therefore hold that punitive damages are available based upon tortious conduct only if the defendant acted with malice.

This requirement of malice will be most obviously satisfied by a showing of "express" or "actual" malice. Such malice exists where the defendant's tortious conduct is motivated by ill will toward the plaintiff. [citations] Punitive damages will also be available, however, where deliberate conduct by the defendant, although motivated by something other than ill will toward any particular party, is so outrageous that malice toward a person injured as a result of that conduct can be implied. We emphasize that, for the purpose of assessing punitive damages, such "implied" or "legal" malice will not be established by the defendant's mere reckless disregard of the circumstances.

We recognize that in some other jurisdictions the malice necessary to support an award of punitive damages can be implied from a mere reckless disregard of the circumstances. [citations] We adopt a narrower view in order to reduce the vagueness and uncertainty surrounding the concept of implied malice in this context. As we indicated earlier, by allowing punitive damages based only upon this more certain and more culpable class of conduct, the efficiency and the fairness of the doctrine as a deterrent is increased.

In the case at bar, the evidence shows that the plaintiff was seriously injured by the defendant's reckless operation of an automobile. The plaintiff contends that such conduct on the part of the defendant is sufficient to support an award of punitive damages. Under the standard we announce today, it clearly is not. We certainly do not condone the defendant's conduct; nor do we fail to appreciate the tragic injuries imposed upon the plaintiff as a result of that conduct. We have determined, however, that deterrence—recognized by this Court as "*the* proper justification" for punitive damages [citations]—cannot justify imposing an exemplary award in addition to compensatory damages and possibly criminal sanctions based solely upon a defendant's reckless disregard of the circumstances. Because the defendant's conduct was not accompanied by malice, either express or implied, we vacate the award of punitive damages.

Our stated goal of avoiding an overbroad application of the doctrine of punitive damages leads us to consider another issue raised by the defendant, namely, the standard of proof that should govern a claim for an exemplary award. Presently in Maine, a plaintiff must prove his case for punitive damages by a preponderance of the evidence. See McKinnon v. Tibbetts, 440 A.2d 1028,

1031 (Me.1982). The defendant urges us to abandon that rule, and to impose instead the more stringent proof requirement of clear and convincing evidence upon a plaintiff seeking an exemplary award. * * *

This Court recently noted that "although the preponderance [of the evidence] standard normally prevails in a civil case, appellate courts in a large number of categories of litigation have found compelling reasons for requiring a higher form of proof." Taylor v. Commissioner of Mental Health, 481 A.2d 139, 150 (Me.1984). In *Taylor,* we listed a wide variety of cases where the United States Supreme Court, the Law Court, or a court of some other jurisdiction has imposed the requirement of clear and convincing evidence upon the party bearing the burden of proof. Under this standard of proof, we observed, "the party with the burden of persuasion may prevail only if he can 'place in the ultimate factfinder an abiding conviction that the truth of [his] factual contentions are "highly probable." ' "

We conclude that such a higher standard of proof is appropriate for a claim for punitive damages. It should be obvious from our discussion that, although punitive damages serve an important function in our legal system, they can be onerous when loosely assessed. The potential consequences of a punitive damages claim warrant a requirement that the plaintiff present proof greater than a mere preponderance of the evidence. Therefore, we hold that a plaintiff may recover exemplary damages based upon tortious conduct only if he can prove by clear and convincing evidence that the defendant acted with malice. * * *

Judgment amended by vacating award of punitive damages; as so amended, judgment affirmed.

Notes

1. *Abolition.* Louisiana, Massachusetts, New Hampshire, and Washington lack common-law punitive damages; their jurisprudence allows a plaintiff to recover punitive damages only when a statute provides for them. Nebraska's state constitution forbids all punitive damages, statutory and common law. As the Maine court points out, the rest of the United States states' courts and the federal courts allow a plaintiff to recover punitive damages in limited circumstances.

2. *The Misconduct Threshold.* What quality of a defendant's misconduct is necessary for a jury to impose punitive damages?

(a) In a prison inmate's civil rights suit against a guard, the jury awarded the plaintiff $5000 punitive damages. Smith v. Wade, 461 U.S. 30, 41, 46–49, 56 (1983).

"The rule in a large majority of jurisdictions was that punitive damages (also called exemplary damages, vindictive damages, or smart money) could be awarded without a showing of actual ill will, spite, or intent to injure. * * *

"The same rule applies today. The Restatement (Second) of Torts (1979), for example, states: 'Punitive damages may be awarded for conduct that is outrageous, because of the defendant's evil motive *or his reckless indifference to the rights of others.*' § 908(2) (emphasis added). Most cases under state common law, although varying in their precise terminology, have adopted more or less the same rule, recognizing that punitive damages in tort cases may be awarded not only for actual intent to injure or evil motive, but also for recklessness, serious indifference to or disregard for the rights of others, or even gross negligence. * * *

"Smith's argument, which he offers in several forms, is that an actual-intent standard is preferable to a recklessness standard because it is less vague. He points out that punitive damages, by their very nature, are not awarded to compensate the injured party. [citations] He concedes, of course, that deterrence of future egregious conduct is a primary purpose of both § 1983, [citations] and of punitive damages. [citations] But deterrence, he contends, cannot be achieved unless the standard of conduct sought to be deterred is stated with sufficient clarity to enable potential defendants to conform to the law and to avoid the proposed sanction. Recklessness or callous indifference, he argues, is too uncertain a standard to achieve deterrence rationally and fairly. A prison guard, for example, can be expected to know whether he is acting with actual ill will or intent to injure, but not whether he is being reckless or callously indifferent.

"Smith's argument, if valid, would apply to ordinary tort cases as easily as to § 1983 suits; hence, it hardly presents an argument for adopting a different rule under § 1983. In any event, the argument is unpersuasive. While, *arguendo,* an intent standard may be easier to understand and apply to particular situations than a recklessness standard, we are not persuaded that a recklessness standard is too vague to be fair or useful. * * *

"We hold that a jury may be permitted to assess punitive damages in an action under § 1983 when the defendant's conduct is shown to be motivated by evil motive or intent, or when it involves reckless or callous indifference to the federally protected rights of others. We further hold that this threshold applies even when the underlying standard of liability for compensatory damages is one of recklessness. Because the jury instructions in this case are in accord with this rule, the judgment of the Court of Appeals is affirmed."

In the plaintiff's § 1983 civil rights action, the defendant was entitled to a qualified privilege that protected him from liability for even compensatory damages unless his misconduct was "reckless." The Court allowed the same threshold for compensatory damages and punitive damages because punitive damages are discretionary with the factfinder, not "a matter of right, no matter how egregious the defendant's conduct."

Also, a successful plaintiff in an action under § 1983, the civil rights act, recovers attorney fees pursuant to 42 U.S.C. § 1988.

(b) Many courts follow Tuttle v. Raymond's strict approach to the misconduct threshold to authorize punitive damages. Owens–Illinois v. Zenobia, 325 Md. 420, 601 A.2d 633 (1992) (actual malice); Masaki v. General Motors Corp., 71 Haw. 1, 7, 780 P.2d 566, 571 (1989) (conscious wrongdoing).

(c) A majority of courts follow Smith v. Wade; they authorize punitive damages for a defendant's conscious or reckless disregard.

Does the Tuttle v. Raymond court distinguish clearly between intentional misconduct and conscious disregard of consequences?

Several states let the jury award punitive damages based on the defendant's gross negligence. Do the *Tuttle* court's reasons to reject punitive damages based on the defendant's gross negligence persuade you?

Which threshold is better?

3. *Insurance Against Punitive Damages.* Observers worry that insurance may create a "moral hazard" because a person with insurance may be more likely to engage in risky activities, knowing that his insurance company will foot the bill. Should a court or an insurance company allow Ralph Raymond, III or the prison guards in Smith v. Wade to insure against their potential liability for punitive damages?

Liability insurance policies typically exclude from coverage one of the usual prerequisites for punitive damages, an insured's intentional tort. Insurance companies were surprised to learn that their promise in a liability policy, "to pay on behalf of the insured all sums which the latter shall become legally obligated to pay as damages because of bodily injury or property damage," could include punitive damages. See Dayton Hudson Corp. v. American Mutual Liability Insurance Co., 621 P.2d 1155 (Okl.1980), where the "policy promised to pay damages because of false arrest committed in the conduct of the insured's business."

The insurance industry has not adopted specific exclusions for punitive damages. In Floyd's Sales & Service, Inc. v. Universal Underwriters Insurance Co., 910 F.Supp. 464, 465 (D.Neb. 1995), the policy insured against "punitive damages where insurable by law."

Should a court should permit a potential tort defendant to insure against punitive damages? The issue is one of public policy in addition to policy language. Some decisions oppose insurance for punitive damages; they reason that a potential defendant's insurance coverage diminishes punitive damages' ability to punish and deter. The leading decision is Northwestern National Casualty Co. v. McNulty, 307 F.2d 432 (5th Cir.1962).

But a court's moral sense is diminished if: a jury imposes consumer-protection punitive damages for products liability, an employer-defendant is vicariously liable for a supervisor's misconduct, or a defendant's tort was unintentional. Many decisions find that standard policy language includes coverage of punitive damages. The leading decision that allows coverage rejects the idea that insurance against punitive damages undermines deterrence and punishment. Lazenby v. Universal Underwriters Insurance Co., 214 Tenn. 639, 383 S.W.2d 1 (1964).

4. *Clear and Convincing*. More than half of the states have, either through statute or, as in *Tuttle*, by decision, raised the plaintiff's punitive damages burden of proof from a preponderance to clear and convincing evidence. The argument is in *Tuttle*: to acknowledge retribution, to check power, and to enhance protection before punishing.

Will requiring the plaintiff to establish the defendant's liability for punitive damages by "clear and convincing" evidence make any difference?

5. *Defendant's Wealth*. "The wealth of the defendant is also relevant [evidence at trial], since the purposes of exemplary damages are to punish for a past event and to prevent future offenses, and the degree of punishment or deterrence resulting from a judgment is to some extent in proportion to the means of the guilty person." Restatement (Second) of Torts § 908 comment e (1979).

California *requires* evidence of defendant's wealth. Plaintiff bears the burden of proof to show defendant's financial condition as a prerequisite to recovering punitive damages. Adams v. Murakami, 54 Cal.3d 105, 284 Cal.Rptr. 318, 813 P.2d 1348 (1991).

Does the jury's consideration of defendant's wealth invite the jury to punish the defendant for its status, for who it is, and dissipate the jury's focus on what the defendant has done? Answering "Yes" are Kenneth Abraham and John Jeffries, Jr., Punitive Damages and The Rule of Law: The Role of Defendant's Wealth, 18 J. Legal Stud. 415 (1989). In contrast, "to the extent that punitive damages correct for underdeterrence resulting from the use of purely compensatory damages, current law permitting juries to take defendants' wealth into account * * * may be theoretically correct." Jennifer Arlen, Should Defendants' Wealth Matter?, 21 J. Legal St, 413, 428–29 (1992).

6. *Punitive Damages Beyond Torts*? May a plaintiff recover punitive damages only for a defendant's tort? Does the plaintiff's "form of action" matter as much as the need to punish and deter defendant's misconduct? Consider punitive damages for the defendant's breach of contract or added to an injunction or to restitution.

(a) *Punitive Damages in Contracts*. One court said: "However valid these [punitive] policy objectives might be in respect to pure torts involving conduct of an extraordinary and outrageous character, they have little relevance in the area of contract law, where breaches of contract do not ordinarily engender as much resentment or mental or physical discomfort as do torts of the former variety. Hence, the rule has developed that punitive damages may never be recovered in pure breach of contract suits [citations] on the theory that it is sufficient to provide pecuniary compensation to the aggrieved party without the necessity of assuaging his feelings or allaying community outrage by means of exemplary damages. * * * A further reason for prohibiting recovery for punitive damages in pure contract cases is that the mere availability of such a remedy would seriously jeopardize the stability and predictability of commercial transactions, so vital to the smooth and efficient operation of the modern American economy." The plaintiff must present an independent tort as a base for punitive damages. General Motors Corp. v. Piskor, 281 Md. 627, 638–39, 381 A.2d 16, 22 (1977).

Only a few courts approve awarding punitive damages to a contract plaintiff. One involved defendant's breach of a covenant not to compete. Although the defendant's egregious conduct might be considered unfair competition, the court chose to base punitive damages solely on the breach of a covenant. Davis v. Gage, 106 Idaho 735, 682 P.2d 1282 (App.1984).

That a plaintiff may usually not recover punitive damages for breach of a contract is a powerful incentive for the plaintiff to characterize the defendant's contract-related misconduct as a tort.

(b) *Punitive Damages in Chancery—Equity*. Courts have been departing from the traditional rule that the Court of Chancery possessed neither the power nor the "equitable jurisdiction" to impose punitive damages on a defendant. The merged court, with the "power" to grant punitive damages, may have the duty to award them in order to afford the plaintiff complete relief.

(c) *Punitive Damages with Restitution*. Restitution is traditionally disassociated from punitive damages. The first Restatement of Restitution does not refer to punitive damages. Professor George Palmer's four-volume Restitution treatise has no index entry for punitive damages. Why?

Even "legal," restitution, courts have said, is governed by "equitable" principles. Restitution's traditional vocabulary impeded a court's analysis that included awarding the plaintiff punitive damages; the plaintiff's waiver of a defendant's tort to sue it in assumpsit justified denying punitive damages because the plaintiff had selected a "quasi-contract." These reasons are not entirely persuasive.

As suggested above, the barriers that restricted punitive damages to the common law court and excluded them from Chancery are coming down. And the contract characterization of legal restitution is widely recognized as a legal fiction at best, a fallacy at worst.

A court measures both restitution and punitive damages to deter profitable misconduct by taking the defendant's benefit or profit.

When deciding how to measure a plaintiff's restitution, a court will often examine the defendant's mental state. If the defendant's wrongdoing was conscious, the court will choose a higher measure of recovery to take all the defendant's benefit, the better to deter misconduct. Olwell v. Nye & Nissen Co. p. 835. BASF Corp. v. Old World Trading Co., Inc., 41 F.3d 1081, 1095–96 (7th Cir.1994).

To help set the size of a punitive damages verdict, the jury may hear evidence and receive instructions to measure punitive damages to strip any profit from the defendant, even to exceed the profit so that the defendant recognizes a loss.

Should a defendant, after being compelled to disgorge profits as restitution, also pay the plaintiff punitive damages? A defendant may assert that charging him profit which exceeds plaintiff's losses already has an element of punishment and deterrence. In Ward v. Taggart the court affirmed restitution plus punitive damages. Punitive damages will, the court said, "discourage oppression, fraud, or malice by punishing the wrongdoer * * * where restitution would have little or no deterrent effect, for wrongdoers would run no risk of liability to their victims beyond that of returning what they wrongfully obtained." Ward v. Taggart, 51 Cal.2d 736, 743, 336 P.2d 534, 538 (1959).

7. *Discharge in Bankruptcy.* Suppose a defendant files bankruptcy to shed a damages judgment.

A compensatory damages judgment for a defendant's negligent tort or breach of contract will be discharged in the defendant's bankruptcy. The Supreme Court allowed a defendant to discharge a medical malpractice judgment. Kawaauhau v. Geiger, 523 U.S. 57 (1998).

Exceptions to a debtor's bankruptcy discharge include a debt that is "for willful and malicious injury by the debtor to another entity or to the property of another entity;" 11 U.S.C. § 523(a)(6).

The required degree of defendant's willfulness and malice as well as the effect in the bankruptcy court of a state court's decision is subject to pulling and hauling. A plaintiff's judgment for punitive damages, however, will usually survive an individual defendant's bankruptcy. Cohen v. de la Cruz, 523 U.S. 213 (1998), involved a trebled judgment for a bankruptcy debtor's "actual fraud." The Court's reasoning appears to include punitive damages within the category of debts not discharged, even though the decision does not deal specifically with them.

8. *Post-verdict Judicial Review of Punitive Damages Verdicts for Excessiveness.*

(a) *State Excessiveness Review.* After the jury's verdict that plaintiff will recover punitive damages, the defendant usually files a post-verdict motion for remittitur-conditional new trial on the ground of excessiveness. The trial judge will decide whether to approve, reduce, or eliminate the punitive damages. There are two common law tests for excessiveness of punitive damages. The judge may ask whether the size of the punitive damages verdict either (a) shows passion, prejudice, or partiality; or (b) shocks the judicial conscience. Remember also New York's statutory test, whether the verdict's amount "deviates materially from what would be reasonable compensation," which the Supreme Court approved for compensatory damages in diversity actions in federal court. Gasperini v. Center for Humanities, Inc. Note 6, p. 89.

Inadequacy Review. Claiming the same power to increase punitive damages that exists for compensatory damages, a trial judge granted plaintiffs a new trial solely on punitive damages unless the defendant agreed to $5,000 punitive damages for each student-victim of a teacher's sexual abuse. Micari v. Mann, 126 Misc.2d 422, 481 N.Y.S.2d 967 (Sup.Ct.1984).

(b) *Constitutional Excessiveness.* The first of a series of constitutional decisions was Browning–Ferris Industries v. Kelco Disposal, Inc., 492 U.S. 257 (1989). The Eighth Amendment to the United States Constitution forbids "excessive fines." A defendant that the jury had mulcted $6,000,000 punitive damages in addition to $51,146 compensatory damages sought post-verdict relief under the Eighth Amendment. The Excessive Fines Clause, the Supreme Court decided, does not limit civil punitive damages. But the Court's opinions hinted that the Fourteenth Amendment's Due Process Clause might prohibit excessive punitive damages.

Next was Pacific Mutual Life Insurance Co. v. Haslip, 499 U.S. 1 (1991). Rejecting Pacific Mutual's argument that an $840,000 punitive damages verdict was the "product of unbridled jury discretion and violative of its due process rights," the Court affirmed. Alabama's punitive damages satisfied due process because of the judge's instructions to the jury and post-verdict judicial review by both the trial judge and the state supreme court.

The third was TXO Production Corp. v. Alliance Resources Corp., 509 U.S. 443 (1993). The defendant asserted that a punitive damages-compensatory damages ratio of 526/1 created a substantive due process violation. In a jigsaw puzzle of an opinion, the Supreme Court found no due process violation. Justice Scalia, who views due process analysis as flawed, nevertheless thought the decision insulated most punitive damages verdicts. "[T]he great majority of due process challenges to punitive damages awards can henceforth be disposed of simply with the observation that 'this is no worse than *TXO*.' " Consider whether the Alabama Supreme Court in the next principal decision may have relied on Scalia's remark in reducing Dr. Gore's punitive damages.

In its fourth effort, Honda Motor Co. Ltd. v. Oberg, 512 U.S. 415 (1994), the Court gave defendant's post-verdict remittitur motion constitutional significance. It compelled states to include in post-verdict judicial review a factual evaluation of the jury's punitive damages verdict for excessiveness.

These decisions set the stage for round five.

BMW OF NORTH AMERICA, INC., v. GORE

Supreme Court of the United States, 1996.
517 U.S. 559.

JUSTICE STEVENS delivered the opinion of the Court. * * * In January 1990, Dr. Ira Gore, Jr. purchased a black BMW sports sedan for $40,750.88 from an authorized BMW dealer in Birmingham, Alabama. After driving the car for approximately nine months, and without noticing any flaws in its appearance, Dr. Gore took the car to "Slick Finish," an independent detailer, to make it look " 'snazzier than it normally would appear.' " Mr. Slick, the proprietor, detected evidence that the car had been repainted. The top, hood, trunk, and quarter panels of Dr. Gore's car were repainted at BMW's vehicle preparation center in Brunswick, Georgia. The parties presumed that the damage was caused by exposure to acid rain during transit between the manufacturing plant in Germany and the preparation center. Convinced that he had been cheated, Dr. Gore brought suit against BMW of North America (BMW), the American distributor of BMW automobiles. Dr. Gore alleged, inter alia, that the failure to disclose that the car had been repainted constituted suppression of a material fact.[1] The complaint prayed for $500,000 in compensatory and punitive damages, and costs.

---

1. [Footnotes renumbered] Alabama codified its common-law cause of action for fraud in a 1907 statute that is still in effect. The statute provides: "Suppression of a material fact which the party is under an obligation to communicate constitutes fraud. The obligation to communicate may arise from the confidential relations of the parties or from the particular circumstances of the case." Ala.Code § 6–5–102 (1993). * * *

At trial, BMW acknowledged that it had adopted a nationwide policy in 1983 concerning cars that were damaged in the course of manufacture or transportation. If the cost of repairing the damage exceeded 3 percent of the car's suggested retail price, the car was placed in company service for a period of time and then sold as used. If the repair cost did not exceed 3 percent of the suggested retail price, however, the car was sold as new without advising the dealer that any repairs had been made. Because the $601.37 cost of repainting Dr. Gore's car was only about 1.5 percent of its suggested retail price, BMW did not disclose the damage or repair to the Birmingham dealer.

Dr. Gore asserted that his repainted car was worth less than a car that had not been refinished. To prove his actual damages of $4,000, he relied on the testimony of a former BMW dealer, ["the former owner of the Birmingham dealership sued in this action"] who estimated that the value of a repainted BMW was approximately 10 percent less than the value of a new car that had not been damaged and repaired. To support his claim for punitive damages, Dr. Gore introduced evidence that since 1983 BMW had sold 983 refinished cars as new, including 14 in Alabama, without disclosing that the cars had been repainted before sale at a cost of more than $300 per vehicle. Using the actual damage estimate of $4,000 per vehicle, Dr. Gore['s attorney in summation to the jury] argued that a punitive award of $4 million would provide an appropriate penalty for selling approximately 1,000 cars for more than they were worth.

In defense of its disclosure policy, BMW argued that it was under no obligation to disclose repairs of minor damage to new cars and that Dr. Gore's car was as good as a car with the original factory finish. It disputed Dr. Gore's assertion that the value of the car was impaired by the repainting and argued that this good-faith belief made a punitive award inappropriate. BMW also maintained that transactions in jurisdictions other than Alabama had no relevance to Dr. Gore's claim.

The jury returned a verdict finding BMW liable for compensatory damages of $4,000. In addition, the jury assessed $4 million in punitive damages, based on a determination that the nondisclosure policy constituted "gross, oppressive or malicious" fraud. See Ala.Code §§ 6–11–20, 6–11–21 (1993).

BMW filed a post-trial motion to set aside the punitive damages award. The company introduced evidence to establish that its nondisclosure policy was consistent with the laws of roughly 25 States defining the disclosure obligations of automobile manufacturers, distributors, and dealers. The most stringent of these statutes required disclosure of repairs costing more than 3 percent of the suggested retail price; none mandated disclosure of less costly repairs. Relying on these statutes, BMW contended that its conduct was lawful in these States and therefore could not provide the basis for an award of punitive damages.

BMW also drew the court's attention to the fact that its nondisclosure policy had never been adjudged unlawful before this action was filed. Just months before Dr. Gore's case went to trial, the jury in a similar lawsuit filed by another Alabama BMW purchaser found that BMW's failure to disclose paint repair constituted fraud. Yates v. BMW of North America, Inc., 642 So.2d 937 (Ala. 1993). While awarding a comparable amount of compensatory damages, the Yates jury awarded no punitive damages at all. * * * Before the judgment in this case, BMW changed its policy by taking steps to avoid the sale of any refinished vehicles in Alabama and two other States. When the $4 million verdict was returned in this case, BMW promptly instituted a nationwide policy of full disclosure of all repairs, no matter how minor.

In response to BMW's arguments, Dr. Gore asserted that the policy change demonstrated the efficacy of the punitive damages award. He noted that while no jury had held the policy unlawful, BMW had received a number of customer complaints relating to undisclosed repairs and had settled some lawsuits. Finally, he maintained that the disclosure statutes of other States were irrelevant because BMW had failed to offer any evidence that the disclosure statutes supplanted, rather than supplemented, existing causes of action for common-law fraud.

The trial judge denied BMW's post-trial motion, holding, inter alia, that the award was not excessive. On appeal, the Alabama Supreme Court also rejected BMW's claim that the award exceeded the constitutionally permissible amount. The court's excessiveness inquiry applied the factors articulated in Green Oil Co. v. Hornsby, 539 So.2d 218, 223–224 (Ala.1989), and approved in Pacific Mut. Life Ins. Co. v. Haslip, 499 U.S. 1, 21–22 (1991). Based on its analysis, the court concluded that BMW's conduct was "reprehensible"; the nondisclosure was profitable for the company; the judgment "would not have a substantial impact upon [BMW's] financial position"; the litigation had been expensive; no criminal sanctions had been imposed on BMW for the same conduct; the award of no punitive damages in Yates reflected "the inherent uncertainty of the trial process"; and the punitive award bore a "reasonable relationship" to "the harm that was likely to occur from [BMW's] conduct as well as ... the harm that actually occurred."

The Alabama Supreme Court did, however, rule in BMW's favor on one critical point: The court found that the jury improperly computed the amount of punitive damages by multiplying Dr. Gore's compensatory damages by the number of similar sales in other jurisdictions. Having found the verdict tainted, the court held that "a constitutionally reasonable punitive damages award in this case is $2,000,000," and therefore ordered a remittitur in that amount. The court's discussion of the amount of its remitted award expressly disclaimed any reliance on "acts that occurred in other jurisdictions"; instead, the court explained that it had used a "comparative analysis" that considered Alabama cases, "along with cases from other jurisdictions, involving the sale of an automobile where the seller misrepresented the condition of the vehicle and the jury awarded punitive damages to the purchaser."[2]

Because we believed that a review of this case would help to illuminate "the character of the standard that will identify constitutionally excessive awards" of punitive damages, we granted certiorari.

Punitive damages may properly be imposed to further a State's legitimate interests in punishing unlawful conduct and deterring its repetition. [citations] In our federal system, States necessarily have considerable flexibility in determining the level of punitive damages that they will allow in different classes of cases and in any particular case. Most States that authorize exemplary damages afford the jury similar latitude, requiring only that the damages awarded be

2. * * * In light of the Alabama Supreme Court's conclusion that (1) the jury had computed its award by multiplying $4,000 by the number of refinished vehicles sold in the United States and (2) that the award should have been based on Alabama conduct, respect for the error-free portion of the jury verdict would seem to produce an award of $56,000 ($4,000 multiplied by 14, the number of repainted vehicles sold in Alabama).

reasonably necessary to vindicate the State's legitimate interests in punishment and deterrence. See *TXO*, *Haslip*. Only when an award can fairly be categorized as "grossly excessive" in relation to these interests does it enter the zone of arbitrariness that violates the Due Process Clause of the Fourteenth Amendment. Cf. *TXO*. For that reason, the federal excessiveness inquiry appropriately begins with an identification of the state interests that a punitive award is designed to serve. We therefore focus our attention first on the scope of Alabama's legitimate interests in punishing BMW and deterring it from future misconduct.

No one doubts that a State may protect its citizens by prohibiting deceptive trade practices and by requiring automobile distributors to disclose presale repairs that affect the value of a new car. But the States need not, and in fact do not, provide such protection in a uniform manner. Some States rely on the judicial process to formulate and enforce an appropriate disclosure requirement by applying principles of contract and tort law. [citations] Other States have enacted various forms of legislation that define the disclosure obligations of automobile manufacturers, distributors, and dealers. [citations] The result is a patchwork of rules representing the diverse policy judgments of lawmakers in 50 States.

That diversity demonstrates that reasonable people may disagree about the value of a full disclosure requirement. Some legislatures may conclude that affirmative disclosure requirements are unnecessary because the self-interest of those involved in the automobile trade in developing and maintaining the goodwill of their customers will motivate them to make voluntary disclosures or to refrain from selling cars that do not comply with self-imposed standards. Those legislatures that do adopt affirmative disclosure obligations may take into account the cost of government regulation, choosing to draw a line exempting minor repairs from such a requirement. In formulating a disclosure standard, States may also consider other goals, such as providing a "safe harbor" for automobile manufacturers, distributors, and dealers against lawsuits over minor repairs.

We may assume, arguendo, that it would be wise for every State to adopt Dr. Gore's preferred rule, requiring full disclosure of every presale repair to a car, no matter how trivial and regardless of its actual impact on the value of the car. But while we do not doubt that Congress has ample authority to enact such a policy for the entire Nation, [citations] it is clear that no single State could do so, or even impose its own policy choice on neighboring States. * * *

We think it follows from these principles of state sovereignty and comity that a State may not impose economic sanctions on violators of its laws with the intent of changing the tortfeasors' lawful conduct in other States. Before this Court Dr. Gore argued that the large punitive damages award was necessary to induce BMW to change the nationwide policy that it adopted in 1983. [citations] But by attempting to alter BMW's nationwide policy, Alabama would be infringing on the policy choices of other States. To avoid such encroachment, the economic penalties that a State such as Alabama inflicts on those who transgress its laws, whether the penalties take the form of legislatively authorized fines or judicially imposed punitive damages, must be supported by the State's interest in protecting its own consumers and its own economy. Alabama may insist that BMW adhere to a particular disclosure policy in that State. Alabama does not have the power, however, to punish BMW for conduct that was lawful where it occurred and that had no impact on Alabama or its residents. [citations] Nor may Alabama impose sanctions on BMW in order to deter conduct that is lawful in other jurisdictions.

In this case, we accept the Alabama Supreme Court's interpretation of the jury verdict as reflecting a computation of the amount of punitive damages "based in large part on conduct that happened in other jurisdictions." As the Alabama Supreme Court noted, neither the jury nor the trial court was presented with evidence that any of BMW's out-of-state conduct was unlawful. "The only testimony touching the issue showed that approximately 60% of the vehicles that were refinished were sold in states where failure to disclose the repair was not an unfair trade practice." The Alabama Supreme Court therefore properly eschewed reliance on BMW's out-of-state conduct, and based its remitted award solely on conduct that occurred within Alabama. The award must be analyzed in the light of the same conduct, with consideration given only to the interests of Alabama consumers, rather than those of the entire Nation. When the scope of the interest in punishment and deterrence that an Alabama court may appropriately consider is properly limited, it is apparent—for reasons that we shall now address—that this award is grossly excessive.

Elementary notions of fairness enshrined in our constitutional jurisprudence dictate that a person receive fair notice not only of the conduct that will subject him to punishment but also of the severity of the penalty that a State may impose. [citations] Three guideposts, each of which indicates that BMW did not receive adequate notice of the magnitude of the sanction that Alabama might impose for adhering to the nondisclosure policy adopted in 1983, lead us to the conclusion that the $2 million award against BMW is grossly excessive: the degree of reprehensibility of the nondisclosure; the disparity between the harm or potential harm suffered by Dr. Gore and his punitive damages award; and the difference between this remedy and the civil penalties authorized or imposed in comparable cases. We discuss these considerations in turn.

Perhaps the most important indicium of the reasonableness of a punitive damages award is the degree of reprehensibility of the defendant's conduct. As the Court stated nearly 150 years ago, exemplary damages imposed on a defendant should reflect "the enormity of his offense." Day v. Woodworth, 13 How. 363, 371 (1852). * * * This principle reflects the accepted view that some wrongs are more blameworthy than others. Thus, we have said that "nonviolent crimes are less serious than crimes marked by violence or the threat of violence." Solem v. Helm, 463 U.S. 277, 292–293 (1983). Similarly, "trickery and deceit," *TXO*, are more reprehensible than negligence. * * *

In this case, none of the aggravating factors associated with particularly reprehensible conduct is present. The harm BMW inflicted on Dr. Gore was purely economic in nature. The presale refinishing of the car had no effect on its performance or safety features, or even its appearance for at least nine months after his purchase. BMW's conduct evinced no indifference to or reckless disregard for the health and safety of others. * * *

Dr. Gore contends that BMW's conduct was particularly reprehensible because nondisclosure of the repairs to his car formed part of a nationwide pattern of tortious conduct. Certainly, evidence that a defendant has repeatedly engaged in prohibited conduct while knowing or suspecting that it was unlawful would provide relevant support for an argument that strong medicine is required to cure the defendant's disrespect for the law. Our holdings that a recidivist may be punished more severely than a first offender recognize that repeated misconduct is more reprehensible than an individual instance of malfeasance. [citations]

In support of his thesis, Dr. Gore advances two arguments. First, he asserts that the state disclosure statutes supplement, rather than supplant, existing remedies for breach of contract and common-law fraud. Thus, according to Dr. Gore, the statutes may not properly be viewed as immunizing from liability the nondisclosure of repairs costing less than the applicable statutory threshold. Second, Dr. Gore maintains that BMW should have anticipated that its failure to disclose similar repair work could expose it to liability for fraud.

We recognize, of course, that only state courts may authoritatively construe state statutes. As far as we are aware, at the time this action was commenced no state court had explicitly addressed whether its State's disclosure statute provides a safe harbor for nondisclosure of presumptively minor repairs or should be construed instead as supplementing common-law duties. A review of the text of the statutes, however, persuades us that in the absence of a state-court determination to the contrary, a corporate executive could reasonably interpret the disclosure requirements as establishing safe harbors. [The Court's discussion of specific state statutes is omitted.] We simply emphasize that the record contains no evidence that BMW's decision to follow a disclosure policy that coincided with the strictest extant state statute was sufficiently reprehensible to justify a $2 million award of punitive damages.

Dr. Gore's second argument for treating BMW as a recidivist is that the company should have anticipated that its actions would be considered fraudulent in some, if not all, jurisdictions. This contention overlooks the fact that actionable fraud requires a material misrepresentation or omission. [citations] This qualifier invites line drawing of just the sort engaged in by States with disclosure statutes and by BMW. We do not think it can be disputed that there may exist minor imperfections in the finish of a new car that can be repaired (or indeed, left unrepaired) without materially affecting the car's value. There is no evidence that BMW acted in bad faith when it sought to establish the appropriate line between presumptively minor damage and damage requiring disclosure to purchasers. For this purpose, BMW could reasonably rely on state disclosure statutes for guidance. In this regard, it is also significant that there is no evidence that BMW persisted in a course of conduct after it had been adjudged unlawful on even one occasion, let alone repeated occasions.

Finally, the record in this case discloses no deliberate false statements, acts of affirmative misconduct, or concealment of evidence of improper motive, such as were present in *Haslip* and *TXO*. We accept, of course, the jury's finding that BMW suppressed a material fact which Alabama law obligated it to communicate to prospective purchasers of repainted cars in that State. But the omission of a material fact may be less reprehensible than a deliberate false statement, particularly when there is a good-faith basis for believing that no duty to disclose exists.

That conduct is sufficiently reprehensible to give rise to tort liability, and even a modest award of exemplary damages, does not establish the high degree of culpability that warrants a substantial punitive damages award. Because this case exhibits none of the circumstances ordinarily associated with egregiously improper conduct, we are persuaded that BMW's conduct was not sufficiently reprehensible to warrant imposition of a $2 million exemplary damages award.

The second and perhaps most commonly cited indicium of an unreasonable or excessive punitive damages award is its ratio to the actual harm inflicted on the plaintiff. See *TXO, Haslip*. The principle that exemplary damages must bear a "reasonable relationship" to compensatory damages has a long pedigree. * * * Our decisions in both *Haslip* and *TXO* endorsed the proposition that a comparison between the compensatory award and the punitive award is significant.

In *Haslip* we concluded that even though a punitive damages award of "more than 4 times the amount of compensatory damages," might be "close to the line," it did not "cross the line into the area of constitutional impropriety." *TXO*, following dicta in *Haslip*, refined this analysis by confirming that the proper inquiry is " 'whether there is a reasonable relationship between the punitive damages award and the harm likely to result from the defendant's conduct as well as the harm that actually has occurred.' " Thus, in upholding the $10 million award in *TXO*, we relied on the difference between that figure and the harm to the victim that would have ensued if the tortious plan had succeeded. That difference suggested that the relevant ratio was not more than 10 to 1.

The $2 million in punitive damages awarded to Dr. Gore by the Alabama Supreme Court is 500 times the amount of his actual harm as determined by the jury. Moreover, there is no suggestion that Dr. Gore or any other BMW purchaser was threatened with any additional potential harm by BMW's nondisclosure policy. The disparity in this case is thus dramatically greater than those considered in *Haslip* and *TXO*.

Of course, we have consistently rejected the notion that the constitutional line is marked by a simple mathematical formula, even one that compares actual and potential damages to the punitive award. *TXO*.[3] Indeed, low awards of compensatory damages may properly support a higher ratio than high compensatory awards, if, for example, a particularly egregious act has resulted in only a small amount of economic damages. A higher ratio may also be justified in cases in which the injury is hard to detect or the monetary value of noneconomic harm might have been difficult to determine. It is appropriate, therefore, to reiterate our rejection of a categorical approach. Once again, "we return to what we said ... in *Haslip*: 'We need not, and indeed we cannot, draw a mathematical bright line between the constitutionally acceptable and the constitutionally unacceptable that would fit every case. We can say, however, that [a] general concer[n] of reasonableness ... properly enter[s] into the constitutional calculus.' " *TXO*, (quoting *Haslip*). In most cases, the ratio will be within a constitutionally acceptable range, and remittitur will not be justified on this basis. When the ratio is a breathtaking 500 to 1, however, the award must surely "raise a suspicious judicial eyebrow." *TXO*, (O'Connor, J., dissenting).

Comparing the punitive damages award and the civil or criminal penalties that could be imposed for comparable misconduct provides a third indicium of excessiveness. As Justice O'Connor has correctly observed, a reviewing court engaged in determining whether an award of punitive damages is excessive should "accord 'substantial deference' to legislative judgments concerning appropriate sanctions for the conduct at issue." Browning–Ferris Industries of Vt.,

---

3. Conceivably the Alabama Supreme Court's selection of a 500 to 1 ratio was an application of Justice SCALIA's identification of one possible reading of the plurality opinion in *TXO*: any future due process challenge to a punitive damages award could be disposed of with the simple observation that "this is no worse than *TXO*." As we explain in the text, this award is significantly worse than the award in *TXO*.

Inc. v. Kelco Disposal, Inc., (O'Connor, J., concurring in part and dissenting in part). * * * In this case the $2 million economic sanction imposed on BMW is substantially greater than the statutory fines available in Alabama and elsewhere for similar malfeasance.

The maximum civil penalty authorized by the Alabama Legislature for a violation of its Deceptive Trade Practices Act is $2,000; [citations] other States authorize more severe sanctions, with the maxima ranging from $5,000 to $10,000. [citations] * * *

The sanction imposed in this case cannot be justified on the ground that it was necessary to deter future misconduct without considering whether less drastic remedies could be expected to achieve that goal. The fact that a multimillion dollar penalty prompted a change in policy sheds no light on the question whether a lesser deterrent would have adequately protected the interests of Alabama consumers. In the absence of a history of noncompliance with known statutory requirements, there is no basis for assuming that a more modest sanction would not have been sufficient to motivate full compliance with the disclosure requirement imposed by the Alabama Supreme Court in this case.

We assume, as the juries in this case and in the *Yates* case found, that the undisclosed damage to the new BMW's affected their actual value. Notwithstanding the evidence adduced by BMW in an effort to prove that the repainted cars conformed to the same quality standards as its other cars, we also assume that it knew, or should have known, that as time passed the repainted cars would lose their attractive appearance more rapidly than other BMW's. Moreover, we of course accept the Alabama courts' view that the state interest in protecting its citizens from deceptive trade practices justifies a sanction in addition to the recovery of compensatory damages. We cannot, however, accept the conclusion of the Alabama Supreme Court that BMW's conduct was sufficiently egregious to justify a punitive sanction that is tantamount to a severe criminal penalty.

The fact that BMW is a large corporation rather than an impecunious individual does not diminish its entitlement to fair notice of the demands that the several States impose on the conduct of its business. Indeed, its status as an active participant in the national economy implicates the federal interest in preventing individual States from imposing undue burdens on interstate commerce. While each State has ample power to protect its own consumers, none may use the punitive damages deterrent as a means of imposing its regulatory policies on the entire Nation.

As in *Haslip*, we are not prepared to draw a bright line marking the limits of a constitutionally acceptable punitive damages award. Unlike that case, however, we are fully convinced that the grossly excessive award imposed in this case transcends the constitutional limit.[4] Whether the appropriate remedy requires a new trial or merely an independent determination by the Alabama Supreme Court of the award necessary to vindicate the economic interests of Alabama consumers is a matter that should be addressed by the state court in the first instance.

4. Justice Ginsburg expresses concern that we are "the only federal court policing" this limit. The small number of punitive damages questions that we have reviewed in recent years, together with the fact that this is the first case in decades in which we have found that a punitive damages award exceeds the constitutional limit, indicates that this concern is at best premature. In any event, this consideration surely does not justify an abdication of our responsibility to enforce constitutional protections in an extraordinary case such as this one.

The judgment is reversed, and the case is remanded for further proceedings not inconsistent with this opinion.

It is so ordered.

[JUSTICE BREYER's concurring opinion joined by JUSTICE O'CONNOR and JUSTICE SOUTER is omitted.]

JUSTICE SCALIA, with whom JUSTICE THOMAS joins, dissenting.

Scalia
dissent

Today we see the latest manifestation of this Court's recent and increasingly insistent "concern about punitive damages that 'run wild.'" *Haslip*. Since the Constitution does not make that concern any of our business, the Court's activities in this area are an unjustified incursion into the province of state governments.

In earlier cases that were the prelude to this decision, I set forth my view that a state trial procedure that commits the decision whether to impose punitive damages, and the amount, to the discretion of the jury, subject to some judicial review for "reasonableness," furnishes a defendant with all the process that is "due." I do not regard the Fourteenth Amendment's Due Process Clause as a secret repository of substantive guarantees against "unfairness"—neither the unfairness of an excessive civil compensatory award, nor the unfairness of an "unreasonable" punitive award. * * *

[The majority opinion] though dressed up as a legal opinion, is really no more than a disagreement with the community's sense of indignation or outrage expressed in the punitive award of the Alabama jury, as reduced by the State Supreme Court. * * *

In truth, the [majority opinion's three] "guideposts" mark a road to nowhere; they provide no real guidance at all. * * * One expects the Court to conclude: "To thine own self be true."

JUSTICE GINSBURG, with whom THE CHIEF JUSTICE joins, dissenting.

Ginsburg dissent

The Court, I am convinced, unnecessarily and unwisely ventures into territory traditionally within the States' domain, and does so in the face of reform measures recently adopted or currently under consideration in legislative arenas. The Alabama Supreme Court, in this case, endeavored to follow this Court's prior instructions; and, more recently, Alabama's highest court has installed further controls on awards of punitive damages. I would therefore leave the state court's judgment undisturbed, and resist unnecessary intrusion into an area dominantly of state concern.

The respect due the Alabama Supreme Court requires that we strip from this case a false issue: no impermissible "extraterritoriality" infects the judgment before us; the excessiveness of the award is the sole issue genuinely presented. * * *

[T]he Court will work at this business alone. It will not be aided by the federal district courts and courts of appeals. It will be the only federal court policing the area. The Court's readiness to superintend state court punitive damages awards is all the more puzzling in view of the Court's longstanding reluctance to countenance review, even by courts of appeals, of the size of verdicts returned by juries in federal district court proceedings. And the reexamination prominent in state courts [citations] and in legislative arenas, [citations] serves to underscore why the Court's enterprise is undue.

Notes

1. *Back Home in Alabama.* The Alabama court took a little less than a year to respond to the Supreme Court's remand with its "further proceedings not inconsistent." BMW of North America, Inc. v. Gore, 701 So.2d 507 (Ala.1997). Excerpts follow with comments.

The United States Supreme Court, the Alabama court observed, "seems to hold that the presumption of validity Alabama extends to a jury verdict must yield to a more meaningful judicial review of that verdict when it is challenged by a tortfeasor as excessive."

The "Court's [three] guideposts are not intended to exclude judicial consideration of other factors that might bear on the question of excessiveness. * * * We see the three guideposts as factors to be emphasized in a judicial review of a punitive damages award" under state law. Thus the Alabama court assimilated the "guideposts" into Alabama's pre-existing standards of judicial review.

Due process requires two kinds of "adequate notice" for punitive damages: adequate notice to the tortfeasor the misconduct "could subject him to punishment" and "adequate notice of the severity of the penalty that might be imposed." Alabama's state statutes and common law satisfied both prerequisites.

Reprehensibility: "[W]hile BMW's conduct was reprehensible enough to justify the imposition of punitive damages, it was not so reprehensible as to justify the imposition of a $2 million penalty." Reprehensibility "encompasses considerations such as" the duration of [the defendant's] conduct, the degree of the defendant's awareness of any hazard * * * his conduct has caused or is likely to cause, * * * any concealment or 'cover-up' of that hazard, and the existence and frequency of similar past conduct. * * * Alabama statutes also require that a court consider whether the defendant has been guilty of the same or similar acts in the past and that it consider the efforts made to remedy the wrong. [citation] To these considerations, the Supreme Court in *BMW* adds two others that principally determine reprehensibility: (1) the defendant's awareness of his actions or omissions causing harm and (2) the quality and quantity of rights of others that were disregarded by the defendant.``

Ratio: "[W]e reject the easy answer of adopting one ratio that would apply to all and would therefore give a wrongdoer precise notice of the penalty that his misconduct might incur. To do so would frustrate the purpose of punitive damages, which is to punish and deter a defendant's misconduct. A ratio that could be deemed reasonable in many cases might well be insufficient in cases where the defendant has reaped great profit from its conduct, or where its conduct is particularly reprehensible." So much for the ratio?

Civil Penalty: "Because the legislature has set the statutory penalty for deceitful conduct at such a low level, [$2,000 under the deceptive trade practices act] there is little basis for comparing it with any meaningful punitive damages award, particularly where the defendant is wealthy and the profit gained from the fraudulent act is substantial. In this case, the maximum statutory penalty does not even remove the profit BMW realized from the sale of the damaged automobile to Gore. Accordingly, a consideration of the statutory penalty does little to aid in a meaningful review of the excessiveness of the punitive damages award."

In another decision on remand following *BMW*, the Alabama court adopted a consumer-protection theory of punitive damages. Alabama's weak regulation of the insurance industry means that consumers will seek redress through litigation instead of the regulatory process. Indeed low "sanctions for comparable misconduct" almost warrant high punitive damages. Life Insurance Company of Georgia v. Johnson, 701 So.2d 524, 531 (Ala.1997). So much for the civil penalty? √

The Alabama court also analyzed several factors from pre-*BMW* Alabama common law beginning with:

Defendant's Wealth: "[A] consideration of the defendant's wealth must necessarily be open-ended; however, we suggest that a trial court might consider whether a punitive damages award that exceeds 10% of the defendant's net worth crosses the line from punishment to destruction, particularly where the defendant's conduct is not highly reprehensible. Thus, the fact that a punitive damages award exceeds 10% of the defendant's net worth could suggest that the award should be reduced."

Plaintiff's Litigation Expense: "[T]he costs associated with this trial were substantial. However, where other * * * factors do not support a large punitive damages award, substantial litigation costs borne by the plaintiff will not alone justify the award."

Criminal Sanctions: "No criminal sanctions were imposed upon BMW for its conduct, so this factor is irrelevant here."

Other Civil Lawsuits: "Several other civil actions have been filed that are based upon the same conduct by BMW. We must view this fact as weighing against the punitive damages award."

Conclusion. "We agree that the $2 million award of punitive damages against BMW was grossly excessive. For guidance in determining the amount of punitive damages that would be proper, we have looked to comparable cases of fraud in the sale of an automobile." The court compared two Alabama decisions. "The trial court's order denying BMW's motion for a new trial is affirmed on the condition that the plaintiff file with this Court within 21 days a remittitur of damages to the sum of $50,000; otherwise, the judgment will be reversed and this cause remanded for a new trial."

Justice Almon, concurring, stressed, "the deterrent effect of the original award, which changed BMW's national policy in a way that benefitted purchasers of its automobiles, has been unduly minimized as this case has proceeded through successive stages of review."

Justice Cook, concurring, noted that a punitive damages judgment of $50,000 is "slightly less" than Dr. Gore's economic damage, $4,000, "multiplied by 14, the number of repainted vehicles sold in Alabama."

Justice Houston "would remand to allow the trial judge to apply the revised standard, because the trial judge should have the first opportunity to order remittitur of an excessive award to a constitutionally permissible amount." He looked for a "special justification that, I believe, is necessary to uphold a punitive damages award in excess of three times the compensatory damages award." Here there was economic harm without danger to physical health or to safety. "After this action was filed, the Legislature, during its 1993 Regular Session, enacted Act No. 93–203, Ala. Acts 1993 (now codified at Ala.Code 1975, § 8–19–5), to require manufacturers to disclose those repairs costing more than the greater of $500 or 3% of the manufacturer's suggested retail price. Consequently, because the cost of refinishing the plaintiff's vehicle was less than 3% of the manufacturer's suggested retail price, the conduct for which BMW is being punished would not even be tortious if it occurred today." Nevertheless "after considering [BMW's] pattern or practice of nondisclosure, as well as the reasonable costs associated with the plaintiff's prosecution of this action, I agree with the majority that $50,000 is a constitutionally permissible amount under the facts of this case."

Justices of the Alabama Supreme Court are elected. Justice See, not participating, noted, "It is not surprising that the *BMW* case intruded into my 1996 campaign for this office. During the campaign, I restricted my comments on this case to the published opinions of this Court and the United States Supreme Court. Nonetheless, because of the high profile of the *BMW* case, and because of its prominent role during the campaign, I believe it is in the best interests of this Court that I recuse myself from this case."

2. *Ratio—Reprehensibility*. Suppose a wealthy defendant does something seriously bad, intending specifically to hurt the plaintiff; but, by accident, he injures the plaintiff only slightly. Is the Supreme Court's ratio "guidepost" consistent with its reprehensibility "guidepost"? Is the proper ratio (a) punitive damages to plaintiff's actual harm or (b) punitive damages to plaintiff's actual harm plus potential harm?

If the plaintiff recovered nominal damages plus punitive damages, is the ratio irrelevant? For a police officer's misuse of official power, malicious prosecution, the jury verdict for $1 nominal compensatory damages was buttressed by $200,000 of punitive damages. "In *Gore* a 500 to 1 ratio was 'breathtaking.' However, in a § 1983 case in which the compensatory damages are nominal, a much higher ratio can be contemplated while maintaining normal respiration. Since the use of a multiplier to assess punitive damages is not the best tool here, we must look to the punitive damages awards in other civil rights cases to find limits and proportions. * * * [I]n police misconduct cases sustaining awards of a similar magnitude, the wrongs at issue were far more egregious." The court remitted punitive damages to $75,000. Punishment-deterrence were slanted because, not only was the City planning to pay all damages, but the jury was told. Lee v. Edwards, 101 F.3d 805, 811–812 (2d Cir.1996).

3. *Civil Penalty*. Touching on both ratio and civil penalty is the Wisconsin court's decision in Jacque v. Steenberg Homes. Over the owners' protest, the defendant crossed their land to deliver a mobile home. For the offence, the government imposed a $30 citation. The civil jury, after finding no actual damages, returned a verdict for the plaintiffs for $1 nominal damages and for $100,000 punitive damages. Ignoring the *Gore* Court's analysis as "largely irrelevant," the Wisconsin court approved $100,000 punitive damages with $1 nominal damages. When the plaintiffs lacked compensatory damages and the government's sanction was low, perhaps trivial, punitive damages will create an incentive for future victims to sue, remove the profit from the defendant's illegal activity, and serve to deter improper behavior in the future. Jacque v. Steenberg Homes, Inc., 209 Wis.2d 605, 563 N.W.2d 154 (1997).

4. *Empirical Studies of Verdicts*. In June 1997, the Rand Institute for Civil Justice released a study of jury verdicts including punitive damages in California, New York state, Chicago, Houston, and St. Louis. Some of the findings follow. The author is Stephen Carroll.

Verdicts for punitive damages occurred in less than four percent of civil jury trials. The percentage rate had gone down in the 1990s.

But the amounts had gone up. Since the late 1980s, the average punitive damages verdict in the jurisdictions studied has more than doubled, from $3,300,000 to $7,600,000.

Punitive damages are most frequent in litigation where the plaintiff's harm was financial, that is insurance, employment, sales, leases, and property improvement. Personal injury and products liability comprise smaller parts of the punitive damages docket.

Alabama juries returned punitive damages verdicts more frequently than other juries studied, and Alabama plaintiffs' punitive damages were a larger percentage of the total verdicts.

"[J]uries rarely award [punitive] damages and award them especially rarely in products liability and medical malpractice cases. * * * When juries do award punitive damages, they do so in ways that relate strongly to compensatory awards." Theodore Eisenberg et al, Juries, Judges, and Punitive Damages: An Empirical Study, 87 Cornell L.Rev. 743, 745 (2002).

Moreover, trial judges and appellate courts reduce or parties settle almost all jumbo punitive damages verdicts. Kip Viscusi, The Blockbuster Punitive Damages Awards, 53 Emory L.J. 1405 (2004).

The studies do not reflect the Supreme Court's further dose of intense post-verdict judicial review in State Farm v. Campbell below.

5. Between *Gore* and its *State Farm* decision that follows, the Supreme Court held that a Court of Appeals should conduct its constitutional due-process review of a district court jury's punitive damages verdict de novo instead of using the more deferential abuse-of-discretion standard of review usually accorded to findings of fact. De novo appellate review of the due-process issue is consistent with the Seventh Amendment's Re-examination Clause because, the Court maintained, a jury's decision to grant punitive damages is not the usual finding of fact but a conclusion that expresses its moral condemnation of the defendant's misconduct. The appellate court reviews the findings of fact below with the clearly erroneous test. Cooper Industries, Inc. v. Leatherman Tool Group, Inc., 532 U.S. 424, 436–41, n.14 (2001).

STATE FARM MUTUAL AUTOMOBILE INSURANCE. CO. v. CAMPBELL

Supreme Court of the United States, 2003.
538 U.S. 408.

JUSTICE KENNEDY delivered the opinion of the Court. * * * The question is whether, in the circumstances we shall recount, an award of $145 million in punitive damages, where full compensatory damages are $1 million, is excessive and in violation of the Due Process Clause of the Fourteenth Amendment to the Constitution of the United States.

[The Campbells' bad-faith insurance lawsuit began in 1981 when Curtis Campbell turned out to pass six vans on a two-lane highway. One person was killed in the accident and another permanently disabled. In the victims' lawsuit, State Farm, Campbell's insurance company, rejected its own staff's advice and refused to settle for Campbell's policy limit, $50,000, "assuring the Campbells that 'their assets were safe, that they had no liability for the accident, that [State Farm] would represent their interests.'" After the jury returned a verdict of $185,849, State Farm refused to cover the $135,849 excess liability and its counsel told the Campbells, "You may want to put for sale signs on your property to get things moving." Campbell retained his own lawyer for the appeal. However, after the Utah Supreme Court rejected Campbell's appeal, State Farm did pay the whole judgment including the excess liability.

[The Campbells sued State Farm for bad faith, fraud, and intentional infliction of emotional distress. Although the United States Supreme Court decided BMW v. Gore before the damages phase of their bad-faith trial, the Campbell's evidence on punitive damages featured extensive testimony about two decades of State Farm's allegedly tortious settlement practices in several states. The jury's verdict for the Campbells was for "$2.6 million in compensatory damages and $145 million in punitive damages, which the trial court reduced to $1 million and $25 million respectively." The Utah Supreme Court reinstated the jury's $145 million punitive damages award. More facts emerge below in the shortened opinion.]

Under the principles outlined in BMW of North America, Inc. v. Gore, this case is neither close nor difficult. It was error to reinstate the jury's $145 million punitive damages award. We address each guidepost of *Gore* in some detail.

"[T]he most important indicium of the reasonableness of a punitive damages award is the degree of reprehensibility of the defendant's conduct." *Gore.* * * * [W]e must acknowledge that State Farm's handling of the claims against the Campbells merits no praise. The trial court found that State Farm's employees altered the company's records to make Campbell appear less culpable. State Farm disregarded the overwhelming likelihood of liability and the near-certain probability that, by taking the case to trial, a judgment in excess of the policy limits would be awarded. State Farm amplified the harm by at first assuring the Campbells their assets would be safe from any verdict and by later telling them, postjudgment, to put a for-sale sign on their house. While we do not suggest there was error in awarding punitive damages based upon State Farm's conduct toward the Campbells, a more modest punishment for this reprehensible conduct could have satisfied the State's legitimate objectives, and the Utah courts should have gone no further.

This case * * * was used as a platform to expose, and punish, the perceived deficiencies of State Farm's operations throughout the country. * * *

A State cannot punish a defendant for conduct that may have been lawful where it occurred. *Gore.* * * * Nor, as a general rule, does a State have a legitimate concern in imposing punitive damages to punish a defendant for unlawful acts committed outside of the State's jurisdiction. * * *

Here, the Campbells do not dispute that much of the out-of-state conduct was lawful where it occurred. * * * Lawful out-of-state conduct may be probative when it demonstrates the deliberateness and culpability of the defendant's action in the State where it is tortious, but that conduct must have a nexus to the specific harm suffered by the plaintiff. A jury must be instructed, furthermore, that it may not use evidence of out-of-state conduct to punish a defendant for action that was lawful in the jurisdiction where it occurred. *Gore.* * * *

For a more fundamental reason, however, the Utah courts erred * * *: The courts awarded punitive damages to punish and deter conduct that bore no relation to the Campbells' harm. A defendant's dissimilar acts, independent from the acts upon which liability was premised, may not serve as the basis for punitive damages. A defendant should be punished for the conduct that harmed the plaintiff, not for being an unsavory individual or business. Due process does not permit courts, in the calculation of punitive damages, to adjudicate the merits of other parties' hypothetical claims against a defendant under the guise of the reprehensibility analysis. * * * Punishment on these bases creates the possibility of multiple punitive damages awards for the same conduct; for in the usual case nonparties are not bound by the judgment some other plaintiff obtains. *Gore* (BREYER, J., concurring) ("Larger damages might also 'double count' by including in the punitive damages award some of the compensatory, or punitive, damages that subsequent plaintiffs would also recover"). * * *

The reprehensibility guidepost does not permit courts to expand the scope of the case so that a defendant may be punished for any malfeasance, which in this case extended for a 20–year period. In this case, because the Campbells have shown no conduct by State Farm similar to that which harmed them, the conduct that harmed them is the only conduct relevant to the reprehensibility analysis.

Turning to the second *Gore* guidepost, we have been reluctant to identify concrete constitutional limits on the ratio between harm, or potential harm, to the plaintiff and the punitive damages award. * * * We decline again to impose a bright-line ratio which a punitive damages award cannot exceed. Our jurisprudence and the principles it has now established demonstrate, however, that, in practice, few awards exceeding a single-digit ratio between punitive and compensatory damages, to a significant degree, will satisfy due process. In *Haslip,* in upholding a punitive damages award, we concluded that an award of more than four times the amount of compensatory damages might be close to the line of constitutional impropriety. We cited that 4–to–1 ratio again in *Gore.* * * * While these ratios are not binding, they are instructive. They demonstrate what should be obvious: Single-digit multipliers are more likely to comport with due process, while still achieving the State's goals of deterrence and retribution, than awards with ratios in range of 500 to 1, or, in this case, of 145 to 1.

Nonetheless, because there are no rigid benchmarks that a punitive damages award may not surpass, ratios greater than those we have previously upheld may comport with due process where "a particularly egregious act has resulted in only a small amount of economic damages." *Gore* (positing that a higher ratio *might* be necessary where "the injury is hard to detect or the monetary value of noneconomic harm might have been difficult to determine"). The converse is also true, however. When compensatory damages are substantial, then a lesser ratio, perhaps only equal to compensatory damages, can reach the outermost limit of the due process guarantee. The precise award in any case, of course, must be based upon the facts and circumstances of the defendant's conduct and the harm to the plaintiff. * * *

In the context of this case, we have no doubt that there is a presumption against an award that has a 145–to–1 ratio. The compensatory award in this case was substantial; the Campbells were awarded $1 million for a year and a half of emotional distress. This was complete compensation. The harm arose from a transaction in the economic realm, not from some physical assault or trauma; there were no physical injuries; and State Farm paid the excess verdict before the complaint was filed, so the Campbells suffered only minor economic injuries for the 18–month period in which State Farm refused to resolve the claim against them. The compensatory damages for the injury suffered here, moreover, likely were based on a component which was duplicated in the punitive award. Much of the distress was caused by the outrage and humiliation the Campbells suffered at the actions of their insurer; and it is a major role of punitive damages to condemn such conduct. Compensatory damages, however, already contain this punitive element. * * *

The remaining premises for the Utah Supreme Court's decision bear no relation to the award's reasonableness or proportionality to the harm. They are, rather, arguments that seek to defend a departure from well-established constraints on punitive damages. While States enjoy considerable discretion in deducing when punitive damages are warranted, each award must comport with the principles set forth in *Gore*. Here the argument that State Farm will be punished in only the rare case, coupled with reference to its assets (which, of course, are what other insured parties in Utah and other States must rely upon for payment of claims) had little to do with the actual harm sustained by the Campbells. The wealth of a defendant cannot justify an otherwise unconstitutional punitive damages award. *Gore.* * * *

The third guidepost in *Gore* is the disparity between the punitive damages award and the "civil penalties authorized or imposed in comparable cases." * * * Great care must be taken to avoid use of the civil process to assess criminal penalties that can be imposed only after the heightened protections of a criminal trial have been observed, including, of course, its higher standards of proof. Punitive damages are not a substitute for the criminal process, and the remote possibility of a criminal sanction does not automatically sustain a punitive damages award.

Here, we need not dwell long on this guidepost. The most relevant civil sanction under Utah state law for the wrong done to the Campbells appears to be a $10,000 fine for an act of fraud, an amount dwarfed by the $145 million punitive damages award. * * *

An application of the *Gore* guideposts to the facts of this case, especially in light of the substantial compensatory damages awarded (a portion of which contained a punitive element), likely would justify a punitive damages award at or near the amount of compensatory damages. The punitive award of $145 million, therefore, was neither reasonable nor proportionate to the wrong committed, and it was an irrational and arbitrary deprivation of the property of the defendant. The proper calculation of punitive damages under the principles we have discussed should be resolved, in the first instance, by the Utah courts.

The judgment of the Utah Supreme Court is reversed, and the case is remanded for further proceedings not inconsistent with this opinion. *It is so ordered.*

[Justices Scalia, Thomas, and Ginsberg dissented separately. The three justices agreed that *Gore* was incorrect; instead the federal Constitution and its Due Process Clause should play no substantive role in states' punitive damages. "I am also of the view," Justice Scalia added, "that the punitive damages jurisprudence which has sprung forth from BMW v. Gore is insusceptible of principled application; accordingly, I do not feel justified in giving the case *stare decisis* effect." Excerpts from Justice Ginsberg's dissent follow.]

The large size of the award upheld by the Utah Supreme Court in this case indicates why damages-capping legislation may be altogether fitting and proper. Neither the amount of the award nor the trial record, however, justifies this Court's substitution of its judgment for that of Utah's competent decisionmakers. In this regard, I count it significant that, on the key criterion "reprehensibility," there is a good deal more to the story than the Court's abbreviated account tells.

Ample evidence allowed the jury to find that State Farm's treatment of the Campbells typified its "Performance, Planning and Review" (PP&R) program; implemented by top management in 1979, the program had "the explicit objective of using the claims-adjustment process as a profit center." "[T]he Campbells presented considerable evidence," the trial court noted, documenting "that the PP&R program * * * has functioned, and continues to function, as an unlawful scheme * * * to deny benefits owed consumers by paying out less than fair value in order to meet preset, arbitrary payout targets designed to enhance corporate profits." * * *

Evidence the jury could credit demonstrated that the PP&R program regularly and adversely affected Utah residents. * * * State Farm manager Bob Noxon, Summers testified, resorted to a tactic of this order in the Campbell case when he "instruct[ed] Summers to write in the file that Todd Ospital (who was killed in the [Campbell] accident) was speeding because he was on his way to see a pregnant girlfriend." In truth, "[t]here was no pregnant girlfriend." * * * While overseeing the Campbell case, Brown ordered adjuster Summers to change the portions of his report indicating that Mr. Campbell was likely at fault and that the settlement cost was correspondingly high. * * *

The trial court further determined that the jury could find State Farm's policy "deliberately crafted" to prey on consumers who would be unlikely to defend themselves. In this regard, the trial court noted the testimony of several former State Farm employees affirming that they were trained to target "the weakest of the herd"—"the elderly, the poor, and other consumers who are least knowledgeable about their rights and thus most vulnerable to trickery or deceit, or who have little money and hence have no real alternative but to accept an inadequate offer to settle a claim at much less than fair value."

The Campbells themselves could be placed within the "weakest of the herd" category. The couple appeared economically vulnerable and emotionally fragile. At the time of State Farm's wrongful conduct, "Mr. Campbell had residuary effects from a stroke and Parkinson's disease."

To further insulate itself from liability, trial evidence indicated, State Farm made "systematic" efforts to destroy internal company documents that might reveal its scheme, efforts that directly affected the Campbells. For example, State Farm had "a special historical department that contained a copy of all past manuals on claim-handling practices and the dates on which each section of each manual was changed." Yet in discovery proceedings, State Farm failed to produce any claim-handling practice manuals for the years relevant to the Campbells' bad-faith case. * * *

Documents retained by former State Farm employee Samantha Bird, as well as Bird's testimony, showed that while the Campbells' case was pending, Janet Cammack, "an in-house attorney sent by top State Farm management, conducted a meeting * * * in Utah during which she instructed Utah claims management to search their offices and destroy a wide range of material of the sort that had proved damaging in bad-faith litigation in the past—in particular, old claim-handling manuals, memos, claim school notes, procedure guides and other similar documents." "These orders were followed even though at least one meeting participant, Paul Short, was personally aware that these kinds of materials had been requested by the Campbells in this very case."

Consistent with Bird's testimony, State Farm admitted that it destroyed every single copy of claim-handling manuals on file in its historical department as of 1988, even though these documents could have been preserved at minimal expense. Fortuitously, the Campbells obtained a copy of the 1979 PP&R manual by subpoena from a former employee. Although that manual has been requested in other cases, State Farm has never itself produced the document.

"As a final, related tactic," the trial court stated, the jury could reasonably find that "in recent years State Farm has gone to extraordinary lengths to stop damaging documents from being created in the first place." State Farm kept no records at all on excess verdicts in third-party cases, or on bad-faith claims or attendant verdicts. State Farm alleged "that it has no record of its punitive damage payments, even though such payments must be reported to the [Internal Revenue Service] and in some states may not be used to justify rate increases." Regional Vice President Buck Moskalski testified that "he would not report a punitive damage verdict in [the Campbells'] case to higher management, as such reporting was not set out as part of State Farm's management practices."

The Court dismisses the evidence describing and documenting State Farm's PP&R policy and practices as essentially irrelevant. * * * Once one recognizes that the Campbells did show "conduct by State Farm similar to that which harmed them," it becomes impossible to shrink the reprehensibility analysis to this sole case, or to maintain, at odds with the determination of the trial court, that "the adverse effect on the State's general population was in fact minor." * * *

"Other acts" evidence concerning practices both in and out of State was introduced in this case to show just such "deliberateness" and "culpability." The evidence was admissible, the trial court ruled: (1) to document State Farm's "reprehensible" PP&R program; and (2) to "rebut [State Farm's] assertion that [its] actions toward the Campbells were inadvertent errors or mistakes in judgment." Viewed in this light, there surely was "a nexus" between much of the "other acts" evidence and "the specific harm suffered by [the Campbells]."

When the Court first ventured to override state-court punitive damages awards, it did so moderately. * * * In a legislative scheme or a state high court's design to cap punitive damages, the handiwork in setting single-digit and 1–to–1 benchmarks could hardly be questioned; in a judicial decree imposed on the States by this Court under the banner of substantive due process, the numerical controls today's decision installs seem to me boldly out of order.

I remain of the view that this Court has no warrant to reform state law governing awards of punitive damages. *Gore,* (GINSBURG, J., dissenting). Even if I were prepared to accept the flexible guides prescribed in *Gore,* I would not join the Court's swift conversion of those guides into instructions that begin to resemble marching orders. For the reasons stated, I would leave the judgment of the Utah Supreme Court undisturbed.

Notes

1. *Home Cooking in Utah.* In its "further proceedings not inconsistent," the Utah Supreme Court ignored the suggestion of a 1/1 ratio in the United States Supreme Court majority opinion's next-to-last paragraph. Instead the Utah court set the Campbell's punitive damages at $9,018,780.75, nine times their compensatory damages. The United States Supreme Court denied certiorari. Campbell v. State Farm, 98 P.3d 409 (Utah 2004), cert. denied, 543 U.S. 874 (2004).

2. *Does Deterrence Survive?* The Supreme Court's majority opinion narrows a defendant's punitive-damages "reprehensibility" by excluding almost all of its out-of-state misconduct and its misconduct that did not affect the plaintiff. Does the majority opinion's treatment undermine a state's ability to impose punitive damages to deter potential defendants' future misconduct?

Sounds like it!

3. *Civil Procedure Revisited.* Is the Court in *Gore* and *State Farm* returning to the rigid views of state territorial sovereignty established in 1878 in Pennoyer v. Neff. But didn't the Court reject those views in International Shoe v. Washington?

4. *Breadth of State–Sovereignty Analysis.* In both *Gore* and *State Farm*, the United States Supreme Court dealt with state courts that applied state tort law; in both, the Court ruled that the defendants' out-of-state misconduct was out of the state court's bounds.

A federal court may grant a plaintiff punitive damages for her federal claim, employment discrimination for example. Should a federal court deciding on punitive damages for a plaintiff's federal claim apply the *Gore-State Farm* state-sovereignty analysis?

In *Mathias*, the next decision, the federal court applied state tort law under its diversity jurisdiction, but defendant's extra-territorial misconduct was not involved. Should a federal court, deciding a plaintiff's state-law claim for punitive damages, consider the defendant's out-of-state misconduct?

A state court may apply federal substantive law in a civil rights, discrimination, or F.E.L.A case. Should a state court deciding on punitive damages for a plaintiff's federal claim apply the *Gore-State Farm* state-sovereignty analysis?

5. A judge who is sentencing a recidivist criminal may consider his prior convictions on unrelated, indeed dissimilar, charges and his convictions in other states. When a civil jury is setting a defendant's civil punitive damages, however, the *Gore-State Farm* Court limited its consideration of the defendant's misconduct unrelated to plaintiff and of its out-of-state misconduct. What accounts for the difference? The lack of criminal procedural protections for imposing punitive damages on a defendant? The lack of a statutory maximum amount of punitive damages? The fact that other civil plaintiffs may sue the defendant later and recover more punitive damages? A conservative Court that is less interested in protecting an individual criminal defendant than in shielding a civil defendant that is a business corporation engaged in nationwide commerce?

6. *Consumer-Protection Punitive Damages.* Although impaired and reckless driving is a widespread problem, Tuttle v. Raymond involved one victim suing one tortfeasor. On the other hand, in *Gore* and *State Farm*, an individual plaintiff sued a business over what both plaintiffs claimed was the defendants' widespread abuse. The next several Notes take up specialized problems of using punitive damages for consumer protection. Like BMW, the defendants are corporations. Consumer-protection punitive damages grow out of an individual plaintiff suing a business-corporation defendant for products liability, predatory business practice, or fraud.

7. *Vicarious Liability for Punitive Damages.* When will an employer be responsible its employee's tort leading to punitive damages?

(a) *The Restatement View.* The California Supreme Court adopted language from several lower court cases that "while an employer may be liable for an employee's tort under the doctrine of *respondeat superior,* he is not responsible for punitive damages where he neither directed nor ratified the act. California follows the rule laid down in the Restatement of Torts, § 909; it provides that punitive damages can properly be awarded against a principal because of the act by an agent, if but only if, '(a) the principal authorized the doing and the manner of the act, or (b) the agent was unfit and the principal was reckless in employing him, or (c) the agent was employed in a managerial capacity and was acting in the scope of employment, or, (d) the employer or manager of the employer ratified or approved the act.' " Agarwal v. Johnson, 25 Cal.3d 932, 950, 160 Cal.Rptr. 141, 152, 603 P.2d 58, 69 (1979).

(b) *Broader Exposure.* Other courts are more willing to charge the employer with punitive damages for an employee's tort.

Alabama's threshold for an employer's responsibility for punitive damages was whether the employee had acted within the scope of employment. In Pacific Mutual Life Insurance Co. v. Haslip, 499 U.S. 1, 11–13 (1991), the Supreme Court declined to find that it violated due process. The scope-of-employment rule advanced important policies; deterrence and prevention; and encouragement of care in selecting, training, and supervising employees. Alabama's legislature in turn narrowed the employer's responsibility to resemble the Restatement's above. Ala.Code § 6–11–27.

The court in Arizona allowed vicarious liability for punitive damages for an employee's misconduct "in furtherance of the business and within the scope of employment." Hyatt Regency Phoenix Hotel Co. v. Winston & Strawn, 184 Ariz. 120, 129, 907 P.2d 506, 515 (App.1995), review denied, (1996).

Stroud v. Denny's Restaurant, Inc., 271 Or. 430, 532 P.2d 790 (1975). A corporation is liable for punitive damages, regardless of whether the employee is classified as "menial" rather than "managerial," so long as the employee acts within the scope of employment.

(c) *Florida Variation.* If the employee's conduct rises above the willful-and-malicious liability threshold for punitive damages and if the employer was independently negligent, then the jury may impose punitive damages on the employer. Schropp v. Crown Eurocars, Inc., 654 So.2d 1158 (Fla.1995).

8. *"Innocent" Defendants.* Punitive damages, a corporate defendant may argue, are really borne by shareholders who are personally without malice or callousness, and who do not manage the corporation.

Critics focus on punitive damages' effect in products liability and professional malpractice litigation. They charge that possible punitive damages overdeter. Punitive damages erode a business's willingness to research and develop new products, may prompt a business to remove a useful product from the market, and lead many doctors to practice "defensive medicine" and to take other excessive and wasteful precautions. Do you think that a potential defendant's consideration of actual plus possible harm leads to overdeterrence?

(a) The goal of punitive damages ought to be to encourage an efficient level of corporate monitoring of agents, not to punish. Accordingly a court should decline to let a plaintiff recover punitive damages against a corporate defendant for an employee's torts except to adjust compensatory damages upward for the probability of apprehension. Higher punitive damages recovery will lead to inefficiency because of excessive monitoring, higher prices, and increased litigation costs. If the court intends to punish an individual, charging a wealthy defendant more makes sense; but this is untrue for a corporation because the innocent shareholders suffer the detriment. Daniel Fischel & Alan Sykes, Corporate Crime, 25 J. Legal Stud. 319, 348–49 (1996).

(b) A court in one of the personal injury and wrongful death actions against manufacturers of asbestos products responded to the defendant's innocent-shareholders argument:

"We are not dissuaded from allowing punitive damages because this cost will ultimately be borne by 'innocent' shareholders. Punitive damage awards are a risk that accompanies investment. Shimman v. Frank, 625 F.2d 80 (6th Cir.1980) did not establish a contrary rule. In that case we reduced, but did not eliminate, an award of punitive damages against a union; we noted that 'the ones who will end up paying for the punitive damages award are the union members. For this reason, courts should be slow to award huge punitive damages awards against unions.' The case of a union member and shareholder are, however, not wholly analogous. Individual workers only seldom can choose which union to belong to; a group of workers cannot change bargaining agents overnight. Investors may typically place their money where they choose and withdraw it when they wish. The prospect of ultimate liability for punitive damages may encourage investors to entrust their capital to the most responsible concerns." Moran v. Johns–Manville Sales Corp., 691 F.2d 811, 817 (6th Cir.1982)

(c) Government entities are not vicariously liable for punitive damages. Why not?

9. *Overkill: Multiple Punitive Damages for Mass Torts.* The ultimate sum of punitive damages separately won by individual victims of a "mass tort" may reach menacing proportions as jury verdicts against the tortfeasor continue to come in. Does the magnitude of a tortfeasor's misconduct and the large number of its victims reduce the amount of punitive damages that a particular plaintiff may recover? The argument has two dimensions: (a) the amount of punishment to impose for defendant's misconduct may, in the hands of successive juries, become excessive; and (b) an earlier successful punitive-damages plaintiff may take the defendant's money for her punitive damages and leave the other victims who sue later no money for even their compensatory damages. Courts have not been sympathetic.

In Palmer v. A.H. Robins Co., 684 P.2d 187 (Colo.1984), the court upheld $600,000 compensatory damages and $6,800,000 punitive damages in a single products liability case against the manufacturer of the Dalkon Shield. The court remarked that the record was devoid of a showing of past punitive damages verdicts that would make this award oppressive enough to raise a colorable due process claim. It suggested that where an adequate showing is made, the trial court could simply instruct the jury, at defendant's request, to consider the amount of past punitive verdicts imposed on the defendant. *Query:* Is defense counsel likely to request this?

When Johns–Manville filed for Chapter 11 reorganization in August 1982, it pointed out that in 1981 and the first half of 1982, litigation had resulted in ten punitive damages verdicts against it at an average of $616,000. This, of course, was still early in the unfolding scenario. The fifth circuit in Hansen v. Johns–Manville Products Corp., 734 F.2d 1036 (5th Cir.1984), after noting the foregoing data, nevertheless held that Texas law did not preclude adding another $300,000 (reduced from $1,000,000) in punitive damages in the wrongful death case before it.

Several ameliorative techniques have been suggested. They include caps on punitive damages, limiting punitive damages to the first successful plaintiff, and giving a defendant credit for earlier payments of punitive damages. The judge may allow the defendant to tell a later jury about earlier punitive damages verdicts in hope that they will be compassionate. Might the news about an earlier jury encourage the later jury to follow the leader?

One state in the federal system cannot solve the riddle of multiple punitive damages; for state A cannot prevent other victims from suing the defendant in states B and C where jurisdiction over the defendant exists, and state A cannot bar states B and C from applying their own law. Consolidation of punitive damages actions in one lawsuit in United States court is difficult in a federal system. Federal legislation has been suggested. Jon Koenig, Punitive Damage "Overkill" After TXO Production Corp. v. Alliance Resources: The Need for a Congressional Solution, 36 Wm. & Mary L.Rev. 751 (1995).

Later Litigation. In another asbestos case, the court said that earlier punitive damages verdicts for the same misconduct are relevant to the amount needed to punish and deter defendant. Potential future punitive damages verdicts are also relevant, but less weighty than past verdicts. But this evidence must be presented to the jury at the trial to be considered on appeal. The adversary process should function to determine whether earlier verdicts were for different misconduct, paid by defendant's insurance carrier, or settled or appealed. To protect the defendant from prejudice from this evidence, the trial may be bifurcated; the jury may consider punitive damages first at a liability stage and later at an amount stage. The judge may give limiting instructions. Stevens v. Owens–Corning Fiberglas Corp., 49 Cal. App.4th 1645, 57 Cal.Rptr.2d 525 (1996).

In yet another asbestos lawsuit, the defendant had shown how much it had already been punished and argued against more punishment as excessive. Repetitive punitive damages verdicts to successive plaintiffs did not, the court held, violate due process. Owens–Corning Fiberglas Corp. v. Rivera, 683 So.2d 154 (Fla.App.1996).

Under deterrence theory, the jury may measure the punitive damages the defendant pays and the plaintiff recovers by considering the injury the defendant inflicted on others; the jury may base a punitive damages verdict on an argument that the jury should punish the defendant for all its victims. *Gore* took this issue up; most of the defendant BMW's other "victims" were out of Alabama and may not even have been "victims" at all.

10. *Societal Damages.* Except that a named class-action plaintiff recovers for all victims, a plaintiff's action for consumer-protection punitive damages may resemble a class action, particularly when the jury seems to measure the defendant's punitive damages by its total misconduct that affects all of its "victims." In *Gore* and *State Farm* the Court finds error in the size of each plaintiff's punitive damages judgment.

When a business through repeated misconduct injures multiple victims, Professor Sharkey proposes to overcome the Court's problems yet to retain deterrence by transmogrifying punitive damages into societal damages—the plaintiff recovers for other victims, but this part of the recovery takes the form of compensatory damages and will be distributed to those victims. Catherine Sharkey, Punitive Damages as Societal Damages, 113 Yale L.J. 347 (2003).

11. *An Improper Reason to Reduce Punitive Damages.* The jury found that decedent died because of Playtex's failure to warn her of the fatal risk of toxic shock syndrome from its tampons; the jury verdict was $1,525,000 compensatory damages plus $10,000,000 punitive damages. "After the entry of judgment and apparently in response to the trial court's suggestion, Playtex represented that it was discontinuing the sale of some of its products, instituting a program of alerting the public to the dangers of toxic shock syndrome, and modifying its product warning. The trial court thereupon ordered the punitive damage award reduced to $1,350,000." * * *

"Under both federal and Kansas law, remittitur is not proper unless the amount of damages awarded is so excessive that it shocks the judicial conscience. [citations] * * *

"In this case, the judge reviewed his notes on the evidence supporting the award of punitive damages at the post-trial hearing and stated that he was 'satisfied there was sufficient evidence there' and 'that the jury's answers were intelligently drawn, they were not drawn out of passion or prejudice, they understood this evidence.' The judge also stated that 'the amount of the verdict does not bother me, nor shock my conscience, and in light of the findings this jury made I'm not surprised with it.' He then declared that had O'Gilvie been allowed to seek punitive damages of $20,000,000, an award for that amount would not have been a surprise to him and would not have been remitted.

"Notwithstanding the court's ruling that the punitive damages verdict was supported by the evidence, was not excessive, and did not shock its conscience, it assured counsel for Playtex that substantial modification or complete remittitur would be forthcoming if Playtex should decide to remove its super-absorbent tampons from the market. In so doing, the court stated its view that this verdict was only the beginning, and that other cases would follow.

"We find no authority in either the relevant federal or state law that would permit a trial court to remit a punitive damage award under the circumstances of this case." O'Gilvie v. International Playtex, Inc., 821 F.2d 1438, 1440–41, 1448–49 (10th Cir.1987), cert. denied, 486 U.S. 1032 (1988).

12. *Detour—Taxation of Punitive Damages* Did the O'Gilvie plaintiffs have to pay tax on punitive damages? The "yes" answer came in O'Gilvie v. United States, 519 U.S. 79 (1996). The punitive damages were not excludable from their gross income as "damages on account of personal injuries." In the meantime, Congress has amended the statute to clarify that punitive damages are taxable income, except where only punitive damages are allowed for wrongful death. 26 U.S.C. § 104(a)(2), (c). Also, apart from damages for medical care, emotional distress damages are taxed with punitive damages. So much for compensation?

13. *Punitive Damages–Capital Punishment.* Quoting an earlier decision, the Alabama court said, "the punitive damages award should sting, but ordinarily it should not destroy." Life Insurance Co. of Georgia v. Johnson, 684 So.2d 685, 697 (Ala.1996), on remand from the United States Supreme Court, 701 So.2d 524 (Ala.1997).

A corporation which cannot be sentenced to jail can only be punished by taking its money. If punishment of unforgivable corporate misconduct is the goal, why not take it all?

Is Tobacco Next? Taking up the arguments for and against consumer-protection punitive damages and discussing punitive damages in tobacco litigation in an article whose lengthy title is its summary is Cynthia Mabry, Warning! The Manufacturer of This Product May Have Engaged in Cover–Ups, Lies, and Concealment: Making the Case for Limitless Punitive Awards in Products Liability Lawsuits, 73 Ind.L.J. 187, 224–26 (1997).

MATHIAS v. ACCOR ECONOMY LODGING

United States Court of Appeals, Seventh Circuit, 2003.
347 F.3d 672.

POSNER, CIRCUIT JUDGE. The plaintiffs brought this diversity suit governed by Illinois law against affiliated entities * * * that own and operate the "Motel 6" chain of hotels and motels. One of these hotels (now a "Red Roof Inn," though still owned by the defendant) is in downtown Chicago. The plaintiffs, a brother and sister, were guests there and were bitten by bedbugs, which are making a comeback in the U.S. as a consequence of more conservative use of pesticides. [citations] The plaintiffs claim that in allowing guests to be attacked by bedbugs in a motel that charges upwards of $100 a day for a room and would not like to be mistaken for a flophouse, the defendant was guilty of "willful and wanton conduct" and thus under Illinois law is liable for punitive as well as compensatory damages. [citations] The jury agreed and awarded each plaintiff $186,000 in punitive damages though only $5,000 in compensatory damages. The defendant appeals, complaining primarily about the punitive-damages award. It also complains about some of the judge's evidentiary rulings, but these complaints are frivolous and require no discussion. * * *

The defendant argues that at worst it is guilty of simple negligence, and if this is right the plaintiffs were not entitled by Illinois law to any award of punitive damages. It also complains that the award was excessive—indeed that any award in excess of $20,000 to each plaintiff would deprive the defendant of its property without due process of law. The first complaint has no possible merit, as the evidence of gross negligence, indeed of recklessness in the strong sense of an unjustifiable failure to avoid a *known* risk, [citations] was amply shown. In 1998, EcoLab, the extermination service that the motel used, discovered bedbugs in several rooms in the motel and recommended that it be hired to spray every room, for which it would charge the motel only $500; the motel refused. The next year, bedbugs were again discovered in a room but EcoLab was asked to spray just that room. The motel tried to negotiate "a building sweep [by EcoLab] free of charge," but, not surprisingly, the negotiation failed. By the spring of 2000, the motel's manager "started noticing that there were refunds being given by my desk clerks and reports coming back from the guests that there were ticks in the rooms and bugs in the rooms that were biting." She looked in some of the rooms and discovered bedbugs. The defendant asks us to disregard her testimony as that of a disgruntled ex-employee, but of course her credibility was for the jury, not the defendant, to determine.

Further incidents of guests being bitten by insects and demanding and receiving refunds led the manager to recommend to her superior in the company that the motel be closed while every room was sprayed, but this was refused. This superior, a district manager, was a management-level employee of the defendant, and his knowledge of the risk and failure to take effective steps either to eliminate it or to warn the motel's guests are imputed to his employer for purposes of determining whether the employer should be liable for punitive damages. [citations] The employer's liability for compensatory damages is of course automatic on the basis of the principle of respondeat superior, since the district manager was acting within the scope of his employment.

The infestation continued and began to reach farcical proportions, as when a guest, after complaining of having been bitten repeatedly by insects while asleep in his room in the hotel, was moved to another room only to discover insects there; and within 18 minutes of being moved to a third room he discovered insects in that room as well and had to be moved still again. (Odd that at that point he didn't flee the motel.) By July, the motel's management was acknowledging to EcoLab that there was a "major problem with bed bugs" and that all that was being done about it was "chasing them from room to room." Desk clerks were instructed to call the "bedbugs" "ticks," apparently on the theory that customers would be less alarmed, though in fact ticks are more dangerous than bedbugs because they spread Lyme Disease and Rocky Mountain Spotted Fever. Rooms that the motel had placed on "Do not rent, bugs in room" status nevertheless were rented.

It was in November that the plaintiffs checked into the motel. They were given Room 504, even though the motel had classified the room as "DO NOT RENT UNTIL TREATED," and it had not been treated. Indeed, that night 190 of the hotel's 191 rooms were occupied, even though a number of them had been placed on the same don't-rent status as Room 504. One of the defendant's motions in limine that the judge denied was to exclude evidence concerning all other rooms—a good example of the frivolous character of the motions and of the defendant's pertinacious defense of them on appeal.

Although bedbug bites are not as serious as the bites of some other insects, they are painful and unsightly. Motel 6 could not have rented any rooms at the prices it charged had it informed guests that the risk of being bitten by bedbugs was appreciable. Its failure either to warn guests or to take effective measures to eliminate the bedbugs amounted to fraud and probably to battery as well. [citations] * * * There was, in short, sufficient evidence of "willful and wanton conduct" within the meaning that the Illinois courts assign to the term to permit an award of punitive damages in this case.

But in what amount? In arguing that $20,000 was the maximum amount of punitive damages that a jury could constitutionally have awarded each plaintiff, the defendant points to the U.S. Supreme Court's recent statement that "few awards [of punitive damages] exceeding a single-digit ratio between punitive and compensatory damages, to a significant degree, will satisfy due process." The Court went on to suggest that "four times the amount of compensatory damages might be close to the line of constitutional impropriety." State Farm Mutual Automobile Ins. Co. v. Campbell. Hence the defendant's proposed ceiling in this case of $20,000, four times the compensatory damages awarded to each plaintiff. The ratio of punitive to compensatory damages determined by the jury was, in contrast, 37.2 to 1.

The Supreme Court did not, however, lay down a 4-to-1 or single-digit-ratio rule—it said merely that "there is a presumption against an award that has a 145-to-1 ratio," State Farm Mutual Automobile Ins. Co. v. Campbell—and it would be unreasonable to do so. We must consider why punitive damages are awarded and why the Court has decided that due process requires that such awards be limited. The second question is easier to answer than the first. The term "punitive damages" implies punishment, and a standard principle of penal theory is that "the punishment should fit the crime" in the sense of being proportional to the wrongfulness of the defendant's action, though the principle is modified when the probability of detection is very low (a familiar example is the heavy fines for littering) or the crime is potentially lucrative (as in the case of trafficking in illegal drugs). Hence, with these qualifications, which in fact will figure in our analysis of this case, punitive damages should be proportional to the wrongfulness of the defendant's actions.

Another penal precept is that a defendant should have reasonable notice of the sanction for unlawful acts, so that he can make a rational determination of how to act; and so there have to be reasonably clear standards for determining the amount of punitive damages for particular wrongs.

And a third precept, the core of the Aristotelian notion of corrective justice, and more broadly of the principle of the rule of law, is that sanctions should be based on the wrong done rather than on the status of the defendant; a person is punished for what he does, not for who he is, even if the who is a huge corporation.

What follows from these principles, however, is that punitive damages should be admeasured by standards or rules rather than in a completely ad hoc manner, and this does not tell us what the maximum ratio of punitive to compensatory damages should be in a particular case. To determine that, we have to consider why punitive damages are awarded in the first place. [citation]

England's common law courts first confirmed their authority to award punitive damages in the eighteenth century, [citation] at a time when the institutional structure of criminal law enforcement was primitive and it made sense to leave certain minor crimes to be dealt with by the civil law. And still today one function of punitive-damages awards is to relieve the pressures on an overloaded system of criminal justice by providing a civil alternative to criminal prosecution of minor crimes. An example is deliberately spitting in a person's face, a criminal assault but because minor readily deterrable by the levying of what amounts to a civil fine through a suit for damages for the tort of battery. Compensatory damages would not do the trick in such a case, and this for three reasons: because they are difficult to determine in the case of acts that inflict largely dignitary harms; because in the spitting case they would be too slight to give the victim an incentive to sue, and he might decide instead to respond with violence—and an age-old purpose of the law of torts is to provide a substitute for violent retaliation against wrongful injury—and because to limit the plaintiff to compensatory damages would enable the defendant to commit the offensive act with impunity provided that he was willing to pay, and again there would be a danger that his act would incite a breach of the peace by his victim.

When punitive damages are sought for billion-dollar oil spills and other huge economic injuries, the considerations that we have just canvassed fade. As the Court emphasized in *Campbell,* the fact that the plaintiffs in that case had been awarded very substantial compensatory damages—$1 million for a dispute over insurance coverage—greatly reduced the need for giving them a huge award of punitive damages ($145 million) as well in order to provide an effective remedy. Our case is closer to the spitting case. The defendant's behavior was outrageous but the compensable harm done was slight and at the same time difficult to quantify because a large element of it was emotional. And the defendant may well have profited from its misconduct because by concealing the infestation it was able to keep renting rooms. Refunds were frequent but may have cost less than the cost of closing the hotel for a thorough fumigation. The hotel's attempt to pass off the bedbugs as ticks, which some guests might ignorantly have thought less unhealthful, may have postponed the instituting of litigation to rectify the hotel's misconduct. The award of punitive damages in this case thus serves the additional purpose of limiting the defendant's ability to profit from its fraud by escaping detection and (private) prosecution. If a tortfeasor is "caught" only half the time he commits torts, then when he is caught he should be punished twice as heavily in order to make up for the times he gets away.

Finally, if the total stakes in the case were capped at $50,000 (2 x [$5,000 + $20,000]), the plaintiffs might well have had difficulty financing this lawsuit. It is here that the defendant's aggregate net worth of $1.6 billion becomes relevant. A defendant's wealth is not a sufficient basis for awarding punitive damages. State Farm Mutual Automobile Ins. Co. v. Campbell; BMW of North America, Inc. v. Gore. That would be discriminatory and would violate the rule of law, as we explained earlier, by making punishment depend on status rather than conduct. Where wealth in the sense of resources enters is in enabling the defendant to mount an extremely aggressive defense against suits such as this and by doing so to make litigating against it very costly, which in turn may make it difficult for the plaintiffs to find a lawyer willing to handle their case, involving as it does only modest stakes, for the usual 33–40 percent contingent fee.

In other words, the defendant is investing in developing a reputation intended to deter plaintiffs. It is difficult otherwise to explain the great stubbornness with which it has defended this case, making a host of frivolous evidentiary arguments despite the very modest stakes even when the punitive damages awarded by the jury are included. * * *

All things considered, we cannot say that the award of punitive damages was excessive, albeit the precise number chosen by the jury was arbitrary. It is probably not a coincidence that $5,000 + $186,000 = $191,000/191 = $1,000: i.e., $1,000 per room in the hotel. But as there are no punitive-damages guidelines, corresponding to the federal and state sentencing guidelines, it is inevitable that the specific amount of punitive damages awarded whether by a judge or by a jury will be arbitrary. (Which is perhaps why the plaintiffs' lawyer did not suggest a number to the jury.) The judicial function is to police a range, not a point. See BMW of North America, Inc. v. Gore.

But it would have been helpful had the parties presented evidence concerning the regulatory or criminal penalties to which the defendant exposed itself by deliberately exposing its customers to a substantial risk of being bitten by bedbugs. That is an inquiry recommended by the Supreme Court. See BMW of North America, Inc. v. Gore. But we do not think its omission invalidates the award. We can take judicial notice that deliberate exposure of hotel guests to the health risks created by insect infestations exposes the hotel's owner to sanctions under * * * Chicago law that * * * are comparable in severity to the punitive damage award in this case. * * * [A] Chicago hotel that permits unsanitary conditions to exist is subject to revocation of its license, without which it cannot operate. [citation] We are sure that the defendant would prefer to pay the punitive damages assessed in this case than to lose its license. AFFIRMED.

Notes and Questions

1. Was the Campbells' dispute with State Farm really about their "insurance coverage"?

2. How significantly will the *State Farm* decision's "single-digit" multiple figure in future lower-court decisions?

3. Is the *Mathias* court more faithful to the deterrence justification for punitive damages than the *State Farm* Court?

4. Does the jury's $191,000 total of damages for each Mathias show that it was punishing the defendant for misconduct unrelated to the plaintiffs? How well does the court deal with that issue?

5. Did the *Mathias* court get the Supreme Court's message in BMW v. Gore and State Farm v. Campbell? Or, was the Court's message in *Gore* and *State Farm* too fuzzy to be effective? Does the *Mathias* decision show that the Court will be unable to administer its *Gore* and *State Farm* guideposts?

Professor Roberts argues that the ratio guidepost is inconsistent with the reprehensibility guidepost particularly where the plaintiff has a small pecuniary injury and the wealthy defendant's misconduct merits large reprehensibility. Caprice Roberts, Ratios, (Ir)rationality & Civil Rights Punitive Awards, 39 Akron L.Rev. ___ (2006).

6. In discussing the policy justifications for punitive damages in *State Farm*, the Supreme Court listed only punishment and deterrence as reasons to take the punitive damages money away from the defendant. The court in *Mathias*, like the court in Tuttle v. Raymond, above, discusses in addition reasons to give the punitive damages money to the plaintiff: to create an incentive for a tort victim to sue and to finance the plaintiff's litigation as well as to give the tort victim an alternative to violent retaliation against the wrongdoer. Are these courts' broader views of punitive

damages policies superior to the Supreme Court's more attenuated and circumscribed view?

7. The Supreme Court has decided that a plaintiff's punitive damages under state law are limited by the Due Process Clause and has established "guideposts." Reconsider the way the Alabama court responded in *Gore,* the Utah court in *State Farm,* and the federal court of appeals in *Mathias.* Answer the following questions?

(a) Did the Supreme Court muddle existing law? Do the Court's decisions contain clear guidance to either courts or legislatures deciding future punitive damages issues?

(b) Do the Supreme Court's decisions ignore important federalism policies? Will they weaken state judicial and legislative efforts to reform punitive damages? Are federal substantive due process limits on state punitive damages law unwise?

(c) Is every punitive damages verdict now susceptible to reversal for constitutional excessiveness? Having twice reversed "grossly excessive" state punitive damages verdicts, will the Supreme Court be swamped by requests to review state decisions?

3. ATTORNEY FEES

The "American Rule" and Exceptions. In the United States, under the "American Rule," both winning and losing litigants bear their own expenses, including attorney fees. One effect is that the prevailing plaintiff's recovery often falls short of full compensation. Another is the contingency fee contract which lets a plaintiff's attorney have a percentage share of any settlement or recovery.

A plaintiff's remedy should put her where she would have been absent the defendant's wrong. Suppose a negligent tree maintenance company cuts down Paula's shade trees which were worth $6,000. The damages rule for a defendant's negligent injury to the plaintiff's property is diminished market value, but no emotional distress damages. Paula hires a lawyer and sues. The verdict is for $6,000. If the lawyer worked 10 hours at $200 per hour or if a contingency fee contract calls for 1/3, then after the fee, Paula recovers only an effective $4,000, $2,000 short of her pre-tort position. If her trees' value was $600, it is not worth suing for if the tortfeasor refuses to settle.

What can its friends say on behalf of the American Rule? A loser-pays system, one that requires the loser to pay the winner's lawyer's bill, the Supreme Court observed, brings with it "the possible deterrent effect that fee shifting would have on poor litigants with meritorious claims, the time, expense, and difficulty of litigating the fee question, and the possibility that the principle of independent advocacy might be threatened by having 'the earnings of the attorney flow from the pen of the judge before whom he argues.'" Summit Valley Industries v. Local 112, United Brotherhood of Carpenters and Joiners of America, 456 U.S. 717, 725 (1982).

The Court's point that fee shifting would obstruct a potential plaintiff's access to justice could be met by one-way fee shifting, that is letting a successful plaintiff, but not a successful defendant, recover her attorney fees; one-way shifting reduces a plaintiff's cost to litigate without penalizing someone who sues unsuccessfully.

The American Rule is one of tort reformers' agenda items. How did a rule that leads to under-compensation for a plaintiff get on the tort reform agenda? Tort reformers seek to reverse the American Rule and to require the loser to pay all or part of the winner's attorney fees. This loser-pays rule, they argue, will deter frivolous litigation, give defendants a respite, and clear congested court dockets.

Law and economics scholars, however, predict that a loser-pays rule will increase the judicial system's administrative costs; for under the American Rule, litigants settle to avoid future litigation costs; but under loser-pays, a likely winner who knows the loser will pay all of her litigation costs has less incentive to settle. With one-way fee shifting, a winning plaintiff recovers attorney fees.

The principal exceptions to the American Rule are found in contracts, statutes, and judicial doctrines. These exceptions determine whether one party will pay the other's attorney fees and, if so, the amount.

Contract. When a contract calls for the breaching party to pay the non-breaching party's attorney fees, as many form contracts and leases do, a judge will award attorney fees to the nonbreaching party.

Statute. Congress has created more than 100 exceptions in statutes ranging from the Civil Rights Act, 42 U.S.C. § 1988, to the Copyright Act, 17 U.S.C. § 116. State legislatures have been equally active. Many statutes shift attorney fees one way, only to the prevailing plaintiff; one-way fee shifting promotes compensation for the winning plaintiff without hampering access to court. Under existing civil procedure rules, a judge may assess attorney fees because of a litigant's misuse or abuse of the judicial process. Fed.R.Civ.P. Rules 11, 16, 26, and 37. Always check the relevant statutes and procedural rules.

Judicially Created Exceptions. The major court-created exception is the "common fund" doctrine which is treated at length below. Another, the bad-faith-litigation exception, has been controversial.

If the jurisdiction doesn't have an authorizing rule or statute and if an attorney or litigant asserts frivolous claims or pursues frivolous or abusive pretrial tactics, may a court require him to pay his opponent's attorney fees? Answers vary.

(a) Yes, said the United States Supreme Court. Under the bad-faith exception to the American Rule, a federal district judge has inherent power to sanction a litigant's abusive, bad-faith litigation misconduct by requiring the abuser to pay his opponent's attorney's fees. Chambers v. NASCO, Inc., 501 U.S. 32 (1991).

(b) The New York Court of Appeals disagreed. "Existing remedies for such conduct, such as disciplinary proceedings for attorneys, contempt or possibly criminal proceedings if perjury is involved, or seeking redress in a separate action for damages on theories of malicious prosecution or abuse of process have not proved effective to deter frivolous litigation in the past. * * * The fact is that the most practicable means for establishing appropriate standards and procedures which will provide an effective tool for dealing with this problem is by plenary rule rather than by ad hoc judicial decisions. Thus in the case now before us sanctions cannot be imposed because at the time the petitioner instituted the proceeding, there was neither a statute nor a court rule authorizing the imposition of sanctions for frivolous actions." A.G. Ship Maintenance Corp. v. Lezak, 69 N.Y.2d 1, 4, 6, 511 N.Y.S.2d 216, 217–19, 503 N.E.2d 681, 682–84 (1986).

(c) Another judicially-created exception to the American Rule charges the defendant with the plaintiff's attorney fees when defendant's breach of contract or tort leads plaintiff into litigation with a third party, Peters v. Lyons, 168 N.W.2d 759 (Iowa 1969). The court in Gavcus v. Potts, p. 17, found this exception inapplicable to plaintiff Gavcus. Finally, a plaintiff's lawyer's bill is an item of malicious prosecution damages.

None of the exceptions to the American Rule will apply to a typical personal injury. Should the victim's damages which include her doctor's bill also include her lawyer's bill?

The "common fund" exception to the American Rule follows:

Judge Broderick defined the common fund theory: "The Supreme Court has recognized that a 'litigant who recovers a common fund for the benefit of persons other than himself or his client is entitled to a reasonable attorney's fee from the fund as a whole.' *Boeing Co. v. Van Gemert*, 444 U.S. 472, 478 (1980). This common fund doctrine rests on the perception that individuals who profit from a lawsuit 'without contributing to its costs are unjustly enriched at the successful litigant's expense.' *Boeing Co.* To prevent this inequitable result, a court may assess fees against the entire fund and thereby spread litigation costs proportionately among those whom the suit benefits. Similarly, the Third Circuit has noted that in the class action context, attorneys who create a settlement fund are entitled to recover fees against that fund. 'The award of fees under the equitable fund doctrine is analogous to an action in quantum meruit; the individual seeking compensation has, by his actions, benefitted another and seeks payment for the value of the service performed.' Lindy Bros. Builders v. American Radiator & Standard Sanitary Corp., 487 F.2d 161, 165 (3d Cir.1973)." Sala v. National Railroad Passenger Corporation, 128 F.R.D. 210, 212 (E.D.Pa. 1989).

1. *The Common Fund Theory as Restitution.* Normally when someone receives an unsolicited benefit, not conferred under a contract, a court will decline to grant restitution to the "volunteer" who furnished it.

(a) Ann, a lawyer and property owner, sues the city; the court voids the city's method of appraising Ann's home for property tax. The court's decision establishes a precedent. The city, in response, reappraises all the houses in Ann's subdivision. Every property owner in the subdivision receives a reduced tax bill. Were the property owners enriched? Unjustly? Should each property owner pay Ann an attorney fee for her efforts?

(b) A testator with four children wills her entire estate to a charity. One child retains a lawyer under a contingency fee contract to break the will. The lawyer succeeds. The estate passes under the state intestacy statute equally to all four children. May the lawyer recover an attorney fee from the other three children under the common fund theory? In a similar case, the court, refusing to grant restitution, emphasized the lawyer's contract with his client and the lack of a contract with the others. Felton v. Finley, 69 Idaho 381, 209 P.2d 899 (1949). But, if the three siblings accepted inheritances, weren't they enriched unjustly? John Dawson, Lawyers and Involuntary Clients: Attorney Fees From Funds, 87 Harv.L.Rev. 1597 (1974).

(c) Judge Broderick applied the common-fund doctrine in *Sala* which was a Rule 23 (b)(3) damages class action. Do class action plaintiffs differ from the first two problems? A member of a Rule 23 (b)(3) plaintiff class receives notice with three pieces of advice. (i) You have an opportunity to "opt out" of the class. (ii) If you do not opt out, you will be bound by the judgment. (iii) If you do not opt out, you may appear through counsel. Is that advance notice a sufficient reason to charge a class member up to 33% of the settlement? The judge must approve both a settlement and an attorney fee. Although it didn't in 1989, Rule 23 now provides for a "reasonable" lawyer's fee "authorized by law." Rule 23(h).

2. *Limitations on Common Fund Recovery.* (a) In a later phase of the litigation about the flooded tunnel in Chicago's Loop, the attorneys for the class plaintiffs sued the opt-out plaintiffs for attorney fees. The class plaintiffs' attorneys argued that they had benefitted the opt-out group, apparently through creating a precedent and by providing other opportunities for "coat-tailing."

The appellate court disagreed: it thought class members were free to exit a plaintiff class, leaving behind any responsibility for attorney fees; it rejected common fund recovery because class counsel had created no fund; and it refused quantum meruit recovery when there was no attorney-client relationship. In re Chicago Flood Litigation, 289 Ill.App.3d 937, 682 N.E.2d 421 (1997).

(b) *Private Attorney General.* The common-fund doctrine is a foundation for a "private attorney general" who litigates successfully and implements a strong public policy to request attorney fees. Under the common-fund theory, the court carves the litigating plaintiff's attorney fees out of the benefitting plaintiffs' recovery. However under the private-attorney-general theory, the litigation does not create any "common fund" so the defendant pays plaintiff's attorney's fee.

(i) *Federal Court.* The United States Supreme Court rejected the plaintiffs' argument that an equitable exception to the American Rule exists in United States court for a "private attorney general" who litigates successfully and creates a significant public benefit. Alyeska Pipeline Service Co. v. Wilderness Society, 421 U.S. 240 (1975). Following the *Alyeska* decision, however, Congress created a statutory exception by enacting the Civil Rights Attorney's Fees Act of 1976 to allow statutory attorney fees under the federal civil rights acts. 42 U.S.C. § 1988.

(ii) *State Court.* Where litigants vindicated a public policy based on a constitutional theory, the California Supreme Court authorized plaintiffs to recover their attorney fees under California law based on the private attorney general theory. Serrano v. Priest, 20 Cal.3d 25, 141 Cal.Rptr. 315, 569 P.2d 1303 (1977) denied Clowes v. Serrano 432 U.S. 907 (1977), cert., aff'd, Serrano v. Unruh, 32 Cal.3d 621, 186 Cal.Rptr. 754, 652 P.2d 985 (1982). The California legislature passed a statute that allows attorney fees where successful litigation results in a significant pecuniary or nonpecuniary benefit to the public. Cal.Civ. Proc.Code § 1021.5.

3. *A Zero-sum Game.* Under a fee-shifting statute, the plaintiff class recovers legal fees from the defendant. In a "classic" common fund, plaintiffs first pay their lawyers, then the plaintiffs seek recompense from the fund. However, under the modern common fund doctrine, the plaintiff class's lawyers usually seek their fee payment directly from the resulting common fund. Also, in a class-action common fund under federal Rule 23(h), the class lawyers recover their fees directly from the fund.

Under the common fund doctrine, the plaintiffs' attorneys' fees are paid from the plaintiffs' recovery, fee sharing, rather than being paid by the defendant, fee shifting. A class action may be settled for two sums, a recovery for the plaintiff class and a fund for plaintiffs' attorney's fees. Johnston v. Comerica

Mortgage Corp., 83 F.3d 241 (8th Cir.1996). Where a class action is settled for one sum, however, is the difference between fee sharing and fee shifting blurred?

4. *Interests in Conflict.* Because a class lawyer's collusive settlement with the defendant might compromise the interests of the class members, or some of them, for high attorney fees, lawyers' recovery of attorney fees in a settled class action poses a potential conflict between members of the plaintiff class and their class lawyer.

5. *Amchem.* Protection of class members was one of the reasons the Supreme Court disapproved a settlement-only class action for a class of plaintiffs exposed to asbestos. Plaintiff class actions of tort victims like the constitutional tort plaintiffs in Nilsen v. York County, below, appear to be permitted under this decision. Amchem Products, Inc. v. Windsor, 521 U.S. 591, 624 (1997).

Amount? "Although it is well established that attorneys' fees may be drawn from a fund in court," Judge Broderick continued in *Sala,* "there is some controversy regarding the proper method by which the amount of compensation should be calculated." We turn to that "controversy." We will focus on the judge's choice between two measurement techniques, the lodestar and the percentage of recovery. "Every fee award, however, is necessarily fact specific." J/H Real Estate Inc. v. Abramson, 951 F.Supp. 63, 67 (E.D.Pa.1996).

6. *Lodestar Rising.* Where a statute calls for attorney fees, most courts favor the lodestar measure over the percentage of recovery. The judge computes a lawyer's lodestar fees by multiplying the number of hours the lawyer reasonably worked on a lawsuit by a reasonable hourly billing rate for such services. The judge bases the lawyer's billing rate on the given geographical area, the nature of the services provided, and the lawyer's experience.

What advantages does lodestar measurement have? "Courts generally regard the lodestar method, which uses the number of hours reasonably expended as its starting point, as the appropriate method in statutory fee shifting cases. Because the lodestar award is de-coupled from the class recovery, the lodestar assures counsel undertaking socially beneficial litigation (as legislatively identified by the statutory fee shifting provision) an adequate fee irrespective of the monetary value of the final relief achieved for the class.

"This de-coupling has the added benefit of avoiding subjective evaluations of the monetary worth of the intangible rights often litigated in civil rights actions. Outside the pure statutory fee case, the lodestar rationale has appeal where * * * the nature of the settlement evades the precise evaluation needed for the percentage of recovery method. The lodestar method has the added benefit of resembling modes of fee determination in conventional bipolar litigation. On the other hand, the lodestar method has been criticized as giving class counsel the incentive to delay settlement in order to run up fees while still failing to align the interests of the class and its counsel, and for not rewarding counsel incrementally for undertaking the risk of going to trial. [citation]

"Courts use the percentage of recovery method in common fund cases on the theory that the class would be unjustly enriched if it did not compensate the counsel responsible for generating the valuable fund bestowed on the class. [citation] Because these cases are not presumed to serve the public interest (as evidenced by the lack of a fee statute), there is no social policy reason that demands an adequate fee. Instead, the court apportions the fund between the class and its counsel in a manner that rewards counsel for success and penalizes it for failure." In re General Motors Corp. Pick–Up Truck Fuel Tank, 55 F.3d 768, 821 (3d Cir.1995).

7. *Lodestar Descending*. What are the arguments against using lodestar measurement in a common-fund case? "First, calculation of the lodestar increases the workload of an already over-taxed judicial system. Second, the elements of the lodestar process are insufficiently objective and produce results that are far from homogenous. Third, the lodestar process creates a sense of mathematical precision that is unwarranted in terms of the realities of the practice of law. Fourth, the lodestar is subject to manipulation by judges who prefer to calibrate fees in terms of percentages of the settlement fund or the amounts recovered by the plaintiffs or of an overall dollar amount. Fifth, although designed to curb certain abuses, the lodestar approach has led to others. Sixth, the lodestar creates a disincentive for the early settlement of cases. The report * * * added 'there appears to be a conscious, or perhaps, unconscious, desire to keep the litigation alive despite a reasonable prospect of settlement, to maximize the number of hours to be included in computing the lodestar.' Seventh, the lodestar does not provide the district court with enough flexibility to reward or deter lawyers so that desirable objectives, such as early settlement, will be fostered. Eighth, the lodestar process works to the particular disadvantage of the public interest bar. Ninth, despite the apparent simplicity of the lodestar formulation, considerable confusion and lack of predictability remain in its administration." Johnston v. Comerica Mortgage Corp., 83 F.3d 241, 245 n.8(8th Cir.1996).

Judge Williams stated it in efficiency and cost-effectiveness terms. "The lodestar method will not necessarily reveal poor economic decisions; whereas the percentage of the fund will. That is, where the lodestar calculation results in fees that are noticeably disproportionate to the fund available for distribution, there is a good possibility that inefficient decisions were made along the way. The percentage of the fund method provides an efficient check on the attorney's judgment because it informs the court that the professionals could have regulated their expenses better—without requiring the court to micromanage the litigation." Gaskill v. Gordon, 942 F.Supp. 382, 386 (N.D.Ill.1996).

8. *How High the Lodestar*? Litigation over the amount of statutory attorney fees, particularly under Civil Rights Acts, is one of the legal profession's most popular indoor sports. Grendel's Den, Inc. v. Larkin may be somewhat atypical except for the court's nit-picking concerning the number of hours, the proper hourly charge, and the reasonableness of expenses.

Having prevailed in a civil rights action in the Supreme Court in Larkin v. Grendel's Den, 459 U.S. 116 (1982), the successful attorneys applied for fees. Some of the issues the court examined were: whether a professor must support a request for attorney fees with contemporaneous time records; whether Professor Tribe spent too much time reading opponents' briefs, writing briefs, and preparing for oral argument; whether Professor Tribe's "relevant community" for fee rate was that of "nationally prominent constitutional law scholars" or "the Boston Market" and his prior charges; and the proper amount for hotel board and room in Washington, D.C. to prepare to present the oral argument before the Supreme Court. Grendel's Den, Inc. v. Larkin, 749 F.2d 945, 949, 952–57 (1st Cir.1984)

In 2004, a federal judge in Rhode Island measured an abortion-litigation lawyer's attorney fee by Rhode Island, not New York, rates. The work, voiding a Rhode Island partial-birth-abortion statute, was not, the judge maintained, specialized enough to warrant summoning a New Yorker to the Ocean State. Rhode Island Medical Society v. Whitehouse, 323 F.Supp.2d 283 (D.R.I.2004).

9. *Percentage of Recovery, Ascending or Descending?* Should attorney fees in common fund cases always be based on the percentage of recovery instead of the lodestar?

Plaintiffs' class actions for defendants' improper maintenance of residential mortgage escrow accounts were settled. Defendants agreed to injunctions changing future mortgage servicing practices. For damages, each named plaintiff received $2000, class members received 60, 68, and 75 cents each. Defendants established funds for attorney fees which totaled $157,000 and "agreed not to oppose the request for attorney fees." "Given the relatively small cash rebate and the dispute as to the value of the injunctive relief, the district court's decision to apply the lodestar approach was not an abuse of discretion." And the lodestar will be appropriate on remand. Johnston v. Comerica Mortgage Corp., 83 F.3d 241, 243, 246 (8th Cir.1996).

10. *What Percentage of the Recovery?* Under percentage-of-recovery measurement, the percentage may vary from case to case.

(a) Less than three percent. The attorneys' request for 2.829% of a settlement that would eventually pay out $114,500,000 was approved as "reasonable." Local 56, United Food and Commercial Workers Union v. Campbell Soup Co., 954 F.Supp. 1000, 1005 (D.N.J.1997).

(b) Thirty-eight percent. "[T]he court has struggled to do justice to the class members and the professionals. Many of the class members lost their entire life savings when they decided to invest with Gordon and Boula. However, through the efforts of these professionals, much of the money has been recovered." Gaskill v. Gordon, 942 F.Supp. 382, 388 (N.D.Ill.1996).

11. *Contingent Multiplier?* May the court raise lodestar measurement when the issues litigated were complex and the prospect of success sometimes dim?

In the Clean Water Act's statutory fee recovery, an attorney with a contingency fee contract recovers under the lodestar. The lodestar may not be enhanced by a contingent multiplier. An "enhancement for contingency would likely duplicate in substantial part factors already subsumed in the lodestar." In particular, lodestar measurement reflects the difficulty of establishing the merits through a higher number of hours and a higher hourly rate for an experienced and skilled attorney. City of Burlington v. Dague, 505 U.S. 557, 562 (1992).

Dague does not apply to common fund-percentage of recovery attorney fee awards. Local 56, United Food and Commercial Workers Union v. Campbell Soup Co., 954 F.Supp. 1000, 1004 n. 6 (D.N.J.1997). Can't the judge enhance these anyway by raising the percentage?

12. *Dawson's Diagnosis.* Professor John Dawson published his article, "Lawyers and Involuntary Clients in Public Interest Litigation" before the Supreme Court's decision in *Alyeska*, and before the modern class action had gathered the momentum it now reveals and expanded into mass torts. Dawson thought that the common-fund attorney-fee theory and percentage-of-recovery measurement were profoundly misguided.

"There is," he wrote, "a certain irony in the conclusion to which one is driven—that the lawyer's best hope of being overpaid is to succeed in litigation that promotes some interest beyond that of his client, especially an important public interest." The percentage-of-recovery measurement theory, he argued, distorts both restitution and contract. It borrows restitution's vocabulary of preventing unjust enrichment and uses it "not to aid, but to becloud, analysis." It is a bridge between a real contingency fee contract based on agreement and a bogus one "imposed without consent, by court order" which exacts fees from involuntary clients. In short, according to Dawson, the attorneys are unjustly enriched. Dawson embraced lodestar measurement as superior to percentage of recovery. John Dawson, Lawyers and Involuntary Clients in Public Interest Litigation, 88 Harv.L.Rev. 849, 854, 869, 871, 925–29 (1975).

NILSEN v. YORK COUNTY

United States District Court, District of Maine, 2005.
400 F.Supp.2d 266.

HORNBY, DISTRICT J. I. INTRODUCTION. This is an award of attorney fees and expenses, out of a $3.3 million class action settlement for arrestee strip searches at the York County [Maine] Jail. Although I approved final settlement in my Orders of August 18 and September 8, 2005, I reserved ruling on the motion for attorney fees. I conclude that the preferred method for determining a reasonable attorney fee is a market-mimicking analysis. Although the market data here is scant, it leads me to award 25% of the settlement, $825,000. Final expenses remain to be determined. But it appears that approximately $2,400,000 * * * will go to the class members. There are approximately 7,500 class members. From claims filed it appears that with a participation rate of approximately 17.78%, over 1,300 persons will directly benefit from this common fund.

II. PROCEDURAL BACKGROUND. Individuals processed at York County Jail ("Jail") filed a lawsuit under 42 U.S.C. § 1983. They claimed that the Jail violated the Fourth Amendment by maintaining a policy of "strip searching" arrestees without individualized suspicion. After extensive discovery by the parties, I granted the plaintiffs' motion for class certification under Federal Rule of Civil Procedure 23(b)(3). Certification was appealed and affirmed. [citation] The parties then began discussions with a mediator. They subsequently filed a notice of voluntary settlement.

The settlement agreement, largely funded by defendants' insurance, requires York County to establish a common fund of $3.3 million in satisfaction of all its liabilities (including attorney fees). Although not part of the common fund created, there is additional value in the requirement that York County maintain a written policy prohibiting challenged strip searches, value akin to that of injunctive relief, which will benefit future arrestees.

The fund is to be distributed to class members after deduction of costs and fees. The agreement also provides that the plaintiffs' lawyers will ask the Court to award attorney fees out of the fund, in the amount of 30%, along with reimbursement for costs and expenses. Obviously the agreement does not and cannot dictate what amount I will actually award.

I held a preliminary hearing on the proposed settlement, and approved class-wide notice. Prior to the final fairness hearing, the plaintiffs submitted a Motion for Attorney's Fees and Litigation Expenses. After the final fairness hearing, I approved the settlement in all respects but one, and gave the parties the opportunity to amend. At that time I reserved ruling on the request for attorney fees and expenses. The parties amended the settlement to cure the offending term, and on September 8, 2005, I granted final approval of the settlement. The motion for attorney fees, therefore, is now ripe for decision.

The plaintiffs' lawyers have asked me to award attorney fees, using the "percentage-of-funds" method, in the amount of 30% of the total settlement fund. * * * As the settlement fund is worth $3.3 million, they are asking for $990,000. (On the basis solely of hourly rates and hours spent, the lawyers estimated in June, 2005, that they would accrue somewhat less than $520,000 by the time everything is complete, although that estimate may now be higher. * * *

III. ANALYSIS. A. ATTORNEY FEES. Under the Federal Rules of Civil Procedure, in a class action I may award "reasonable attorney fees and nontaxable costs authorized by law." Fed.R.Civ.P. 23(h). Had this lawsuit proceeded to a successful judgment for the plaintiffs, they could have recovered from the defendant York County reasonable attorney fees and costs under 42 U.S.C § 1988, on top of any damages they received. Instead, York County settled the lawsuit before trial for a lump sum of $3.3 million, covering all its liabilities, including attorney fees. That settlement amount reflects both the class members' compensable injuries *and* their statutory claim to attorney fees. Unless the lawyers who have produced the successful outcome are paid, the class members will be unjustly enriched. [citations] By the terminology of some of the caselaw, this settlement is a "common fund," and the common fund doctrine allows me to award attorney fees from it. [citations]

Making a fair fee award from a common fund in a class action settlement is a difficult determination for a judge. There are no adversarial presentations to test the fee claim, and our legal system does not ordinarily expect judges to behave as inquisitors, gathering testimony and collecting information on their own.

Presented with an unopposed request, therefore, I depend upon my own analysis and secondary research—against a backdrop of popular dissatisfaction with large and highly publicized fees. [citation] But the lawyers here are highly skilled and experienced civil rights attorneys. Their professional performance was exemplary; they represented the class members' interests zealously, achieving an excellent result for the class under the circumstances. For these reasons, they deserve a reasonable fee that duly recognizes their professional excellence and performance and provides an appropriate incentive for lawyers to take on future meritorious cases on behalf of a client class. At the same time, they do not deserve a windfall at the expense of the class and I do not want the size of the award to encourage frivolous litigation that benefits primarily lawyers.

In candor, I simply do not know the precise fee award that meets those concerns. I can only detail the process I have used.

(1) Method: Lodestar or Percentage-of-Funds. In the First Circuit [which includes Maine], courts have discretion to award fees from a common fund "either on a percentage of the fund basis or by fashioning a lodestar." In re Thirteen Appeals Arising out of the San Juan Dupont Plaza Hotel Fire Litig., 56 F.3d 295, 307 (1st Cir.1995).

If this case had proceeded to judgment, I would be bound to use the lodestar in determining any fee award against the defendant York County, as it is the strongly preferred method in fee-shifting cases. * * * [citations] The Circuits generally have concluded that common fund principles govern, however, where a fee shifting case settles before judgment. [citations] * * *

As between the two methods, the First Circuit has noted that the percentage-of-funds method is the prevailing practice, and that it may have distinct advantages over the lodestar approach. In re Thirteen Appeals. According to the Third Circuit, the percentage-of-funds method is preferred in common fund cases "because it allows courts to award fees from the fund in a manner that rewards counsel for success and penalizes it for failure." In re Rite Aid Corp. Sec. Litig., 396 F.3d 294, 300 (3d Cir.2005). I shall use the percentage-of-funds method here—*i.e.,* is the total fee reasonable when examined as a percentage of recovery?

(2) The Limited Role of the Lodestar. As I have previously recognized, the "lodestar approach (reasonable hours spent times reasonable hourly rates, subject to a multiplier or discount for special circumstances, plus reasonable disbursements) can be a check or validation of the appropriateness of the percentage-of-funds fee, but is not required." In re Compact Disc I, 216 F.R.D. 197, 215–6 (D.Me.2003). Here, the lodestar figure is lower than the requested percentage fee, approximately $520,000 vs. $990,000.

When the lodestar cross-check shows that the percentage fee is lower than the fees the lawyers have accrued on a time-and-services basis, it is relatively easy to support a percentage-based fee. [citations] But what if the percentage fee is higher than the lodestar (as it is here), maybe substantially higher? * * *

I conclude that [I may] award a percentage attorney fee (so long as it is reasonable) from a common fund in a class action settlement even if the fee effectively represents a multiplier of the lodestar amount. * * *

(3) The Reasonableness of the Requested Percentage. In a class action, any fee I award must be reasonable. Fed.R.Civ.P. 23(h). Thus, I must determine whether the 30% requested is reasonable under the circumstances, bearing in mind that my role takes on special importance because there are no adversaries here to dispute the fee and because I must act as a fiduciary of the class. In re Rite Aid Corp. Sec. Litig., (when determining fees, judges "must protect the class's interest by acting as a fiduciary"). First Circuit cases give no guidance on how to determine whether a given percentage is reasonable. First, therefore, I canvass the approaches of other Circuits.

(a) Other Circuit Approaches. The majority of Circuits review percentage-of-funds fee awards by using multifactor tests in which the district court must examine and set forth findings on each factor. [citations] * * *

It is easy to see that the multifactor tests largely overlap. Almost all include factors related to the lodestar amount (time and labor), the complexity and difficulty of the case, the quality of the lawyers or the representation (including skill, standing, and efficiency), the size of the fund (including the value of the benefit to the class), and the risk of nonpayment or contingency of the case. Additionally, [four circuits] add comparison to other awards in similar cases, and [two other] Circuits also look to whether there are objections. * * *

Three other circuits do not mandate specific multifactor tests. Instead, the Ninth Circuit uses a benchmark of 25%, from which deviation is permitted upon consideration of various case-specific factors. [citation] The Eighth Circuit and the District of Columbia Circuit have not ruled on the appropriate way to review a percentage-of-funds fee award, and have not engaged in any extended discussion of reasonableness. But both those circuits have pointed to "benchmark" percentage ranges to justify the reasonableness of particular fees. [citations]

The Seventh Circuit determines reasonableness through a market-mimicking approach with the goal of awarding a fee that is the "market price for legal services, in light of the risk of nonpayment and the normal rate of compensation in the market" at the outset of the case. In re Synthroid Mktg. Litig., 264 F.3d 712, 718 (7th Cir.2001). According to the Seventh Circuit, reasonableness is not an ethical or philosophical question; "it is not the function of judges in fee litigation to determine the equivalent of the medieval just price. It is to determine what the lawyer would receive if he were selling his services in the market rather than being paid by court order." In re Cont'l Ill. Sec. Litig., 962 F.2d 566, 568 (7th Cir.1992). This approach emulates the incentives of a private client-attorney relationship; the market price should take into account "the risk of nonpayment," "quality of performance," "the amount of work," and "the stakes of the case." For the Seventh Circuit, the key inquiry is what a private plaintiff would have negotiated with the lawyers, if they had bargained at arm's length at the outset of the case.

The Seventh Circuit approach presents special concerns in the context of class actions, of course, for generally no contract exists between lawyers and the class. At least two of the named plaintiffs in this case *did* sign contracts with one of the law firms, agreeing to a contingency fee of one-third of the recovery. After all, attorney fees in a class action require court, not client, approval. Thus, there is no readily apparent source of information about the market. That is the major criticism leveled at the Seventh Circuit approach: that for some fee-shifting class action claims, any "market" is simply illusory and speculative, and that instead of any sort of privately negotiated fee, for many noncommercial cases the fee is set entirely by judicial reference to what is reasonable. [citations] While the Seventh Circuit has recognized that this is a legitimate concern, it retorts that a "consider-everything," factor-based method of setting fees "assures random and potentially perverse results," and that a "list of factors without a rule of decision is just a chopped salad ." *In re Synthroid Mktg. Litig.*

(b) The Method I Shall Adopt in this Case. My decision on attorney fees is of great importance to the lawyers and class members in this case. Every dollar I award the lawyers is a dollar that the class members will not recover and vice-versa. It also has great importance for future lawyers and plaintiff classes in this District, for in the absence of First Circuit law, they deserve an intelligible and predictable standard. I hope that an ongoing exposure to attorney fee requests in these class actions has begun to inform my thinking. I shall try to explain fully the rationale for my award for guidance in future attorney fee cases.

In past awards from common funds, I have recognized the difficulty and arbitrariness of assessing the reasonableness of a given fee. [citation] *In re Compact Disc I,* 216 F.R.D. at 216 ("Although some of the cases and commentaries call upon district judges to give a precise analysis of how they choose the percentage, I do not know how to do so in any meaningful way that would defend 10% over 11% or 9%, etc."). In none of those cases did I specify a methodology for determining reasonableness; rather, I referred more generally to finding the particular percentages reasonable under the circumstances. [citations] In each of them, the fee I awarded was lower than the lodestar figure accrued by the lawyers at the time of settlement. [citations] Today, in the first case in which I have been asked to award a percentage that is *higher* than the lodestar, I shall identify a specific methodology.

The path of least resistance is to employ the multifactor approach to reasonableness. The majority of circuits use it and the fee-seeking lawyers have used it here. It will support virtually any percentage fee I award in a range from 16% to 33–1/3%.

But the preceding statement is the first and primary reason I reject the multifactor approach. It offers little predictability to either the awarding court, or the lawyers who seek fee awards. [citation] In this case, for example, it would support equally a fee award of 16%, 20%, 25%, 30%, or 33–1/3%. That is not a rule of law or even a principle. Instead, it allows uncabined discretion to the fee-awarding judge. A judge who likes lawyers and remembers the hazards of practice can be generous; a judge who cares more about public reaction or who never used contingent fees in practice can be stingy. A district judge using the multifactor analysis has an instinctive notion, consciously or unconsciously, of what is an appropriate fee (a fee *"Gestalt,"* as it were). The multifactor analysis merely supports the judge's instinctive view. And on review, appellate courts then take comfort from the weighing and juggling of the various considerations. But the factors do not produce a result or even a substantive standard of reasonableness. At the very least, the market-mimicking approach is situated outside the judge's *Gestalt,* in a somewhat more objective realm. It is difficult to contradict the judge's statement about the case's complexity or lack thereof, the difficulties of discovery, the quality of the lawyering, etc. These are all highly subjective judgments.

The second reason I reject the multifactor approach is that some of the factors seem inconsistent with the reason for using a percentage-of-funds method in the first place, which is designed to create incentives for the lawyer to get the most recovery for the class by the most efficient manner (and penalize the lawyer who fails to do so). [citations] Why, then, should we adjust the percentage depending upon whether the lawyer was efficient, how much time the lawyer put into the case, etc.?

The third reason I reject the factor-based approaches is that they consume significant lawyer and judicial resources, a consideration that has led to the criticism (and in some quarters, the abandonment) of the lodestar method in favor of the percentage-of-funds method. [citation]

I believe that in setting a fee, a judge, consciously or unconsciously, necessarily compares what lawyers typically get paid for equivalent services— *i.e.,* the market price. The judge may do that based on recollections from when that judge was a lawyer, from information generated in other cases, or from general lawyer/judge gossip, but inevitably the judge takes such information into account. The Seventh Circuit appropriately makes this measure explicit, rather than a *Gestalt* lurking behind the multifactor review. Making the standard explicit, in turn, allows the lawyers or objectors to provide evidence to correct judicial misimpressions. This standard obviates, at least to a certain extent, the need to assign a value to an attorney's work based on nothing more than a subjective judgment regarding that work. It gives a court a background against which to work by requiring courts to look to evidence regarding the sorts of fees and costs generated in analogous suits funded by paying clients.

There is good reason for using a market-oriented approach. If a consumer wanted to determine a reasonable plumber's, mechanic's or dentist's fee, the consumer would have to look to the market. Why should lawyers be different? Perhaps more important, the market is the implicit if not explicit standard when a jury awards damages that include reasonable medical expenses in a personal injury case. We do not use a multifactor approach then. We even look at the market to a degree in lodestar cases, because we purport there to look at market rates for what a lawyer can charge as an hourly rate.

I therefore adopt the methodology of the Seventh Circuit as most reflective of what a judge does instinctively in setting a fee as well as most amenable to predictability and an objective external constraint on a judge's otherwise uncabined power. * * * The market-mimicking approach has its own shortcomings but it is better than the fuzzier alternatives.

Unfortunately, in this case I do not have direct data on the market price for civil rights class action lawyers, or for strip search class action cases inside or outside of Maine. To some degree, that is unavoidable for the reasons already described: the class action "market" is controlled by judges. That is why this is a market "mimicking" approach. But there should be contextual market information available, such as what lawyers charge as percentage fees for various types of litigation. As I suggest later, I shall probably ask for such information in future cases. Moreover, because I have not used this method of testing reasonableness previously and because First Circuit caselaw is silent, in fairness I will re-open the question if the lawyers wish to present additional evidence and arguments addressing it. If they do so request, however, I shall also consider appointing a special master under Fed.R.Civ.P. 53, or an independent expert under Fed.R.Evid. 706, and also entertain the defendant's offer to reveal information about its attorney fee arrangements.

In the meantime, I look to such evidence as is available to suggest what hypothetical negotiation would have produced at the outset as an agreed-to fee for a case such as this.

(1) Standard Contingency Fees. First, I consider standard contingency fees and the limitations imposed upon them by statutes or regulations. Although there is considerable variation by type of case and by stage of litigation, one-third of the amount recovered is considered by most to be the general standard in personal injury litigation. [citation] At least two of the named plaintiffs in this case did negotiate contracts for a straight contingency fee of one-third of the recovery. * * * Obviously such agreements bind neither the class nor the court, but they are of modest limited evidentiary value on what the market might produce. Nevertheless, the paramount question remains what the lawyer would hypothetically charge in a *class action* specifically. The class action provides for the possibility of a significantly larger recovery that, despite the inherent increased complexity, may induce the lawyer to take the case for a lower percentage charge. Thus, while this information is relevant, it does not compel a particular result.

Looking to other facets of contingent fee practice, I observe that Maine statutes limit the contingency fee in medical malpractice claims to what is ultimately a lower percentage. 24 M.R.S.A. § 2961(1) (2000) (in medical malpractice actions, total contingent fee that may be contracted is 33.33% of first $100,000 of recovery, 25% of next $100,000, and 20% of any amount over $200,000). For the amount recovered here, the blended fee would be 20.6%. Maine also places declining limits on attorney fees in proceedings before the Workers Compensation Board. 39–A M.R.S.A. § 325(4)(B) (2001) (if case tried to completion, fees may not exceed 30% of benefits accrued; for lump-sum settlements post-expenses, fees restricted to 10% of first $50,000, 9% through 6% of the next increments of $10,000, and 5% of any amount over $90,000). For the award requested here, the blended fee would be 5.1%. I am not aware of any other Maine caps on what a lawyer can charge a client.

For certain claims, Federal statutes also limit the amount that a lawyer may collect from a client. For example, courts may approve contingency fees to a maximum of only 25% of past due benefits awarded to a successful plaintiff in Social Security proceedings. [citation] The Federal Tort Claims Act allows courts to approve contingency fees from the successful plaintiff's recovery to a maximum of 25% if the fund is created through judgment, or 20% if through settlement. [citation]; *see also* Veterans' Benefit Act, [citation] (20% of past due benefit). Several other federal statutes are less generous and allow a maximum of only 10% of the recovery to go toward attorney fees. *See, e.g.,* War Claims Act, [citation] (10% of award).

Both the state and federal percentage caps are instructive, for they represent constraints on the fee a lawyer may recover in certain legal arenas. Sometimes, the maximum allowable percentage then becomes the market norm in that arena, rather than merely the upper ceiling. At the same time, I recognize that there is no statutory cap for attorney fees in civil rights cases like this one.

(2) Awards in Other Cases. For other strip search class actions resulting in a common fund settlement, the lowest percentage awarded as a fee that I have discovered was 16% ($1 million of a $6.25 million common fund). [citation] The highest percentage explicitly awarded by a court was 33.33%, or $3,833,333 of an $11.5 million fund. [citation] Other cases seem to be distributed fairly evenly within that range. [Judge Hornby summarized several decisions in an Appendix which is omitted.]

Median attorney fee awards in other class actions generally (*i.e.,* not limited to strip searches) range within a few percentage points on either side of 30%. Thus, a survey of 1,120 common fund class actions found that the median award of attorney fees and expenses was 31.6% of the fund for cases in which the class recovery ranged from $3 million to $5 million. [citation] According to a recent Federal Judicial Center study of 621 class actions, an award of 29% for attorney fees and expenses was "typical." [citation] An earlier Federal Judicial Center study found that median fee rates "ranged from 27% to 30%." [citation]

(3) The Award Here. Maine practice is certainly relevant. This is a Maine lawsuit, with a Maine defendant, and mostly Maine plaintiffs. Therefore, to the extent I know them, I consider both the general range of contingent fee agreements and the limits that Maine has placed statutorily on contingent fee recovery for certain kinds of cases.

I can glean here that the Maine legislature concluded that 20.6% is a reasonable fee for medical malpractice cases of this magnitude. It appears that lawyers continue to take such cases with that fee limitation. On the other hand, there is no limit for civil rights lawsuits like this one, and therefore the lawyers are able to bargain for a higher contingent fee in individual civil rights cases. It is hard to generalize which kind of lawsuit has the higher risk and the greater complexity. Arguably, a personal injury percentage is not a very good measure for a civil rights case. [citation] This critique may be particularly apt when a civil rights case is likely to result in mainly injunctive, rather than monetary, relief. A lawyer who agrees to litigate a case likely to result in injunctive relief would conceivably conduct arm's length negotiation in a very different manner than the typical personal injury case; he or she might eschew the percentage-of-funds method entirely and instead opt for an hourly or flat-fee arrangement.

Since the [Maine Med-mal] 20.6% fee limit stays the same regardless of how much the recovery exceeds $200,000, the medical malpractice lawyer has the opportunity to generate a huge fee with a huge award that may not be available in civil rights class actions like this one. Fees, of course, are ordinarily negotiated at the outset of the litigation before the size of recovery is known. Thus, those factors suggest that the market fee hypothetically negotiated for a civil rights class action might be somewhat higher than the 20.6% effective rate for medical malpractice cases of this size.

The workers compensation limits are unduly low for a civil rights class action. Workers compensation is largely an administrative proceeding, generally without complex factual issues, extensive discovery, or difficult arguments such as class certification, liability is strict, and the legislature has tried to reduce lawyer involvement. The medical malpractice numbers are more instructive and persuasive; like class actions, that cause of action includes complex factual and legal issues, as well as substantial barriers to recovery. Therefore, I put little weight on the workers compensation fee limits.

The Federal numbers are somewhat relevant. This was primarily a federal cause of action with a statutory fee award available at a successful conclusion. However, the federal limits from other statutes may be too restrictive, for many of the claims at stake under those statutes are administrative and straightforward. Those limits may also reflect a legislative desire that attorney fees not diminish certain statutory entitlements. Therefore, I conclude that the higher end of the federal 10%–25% range is more relevant than the lower end. I also recognize as I did before that without a federal statutory cap for this type of case, the lawyers hypothetically are able to negotiate for a higher percentage. A primary difficulty with all these numbers is that lawyers customarily practice in one of these fields or another, not across fields. Thus, the numbers have limited relevance.

I also consider that two of the named plaintiffs agreed to one-third contingency fees, and that a one-third contingency fee agreement is widely recognized in personal injury litigation. I draw no firm conclusions from that data, because the two individual contracts were signed before class status existed, and the individuals, contemplating their own individual recovery, had little incentive to bargain for a lower fee that might be available in a class action. I have already explained why the general contingency fee agreement is of limited help for the peculiarities of class actions.

Other judicial fee awards are relevant to some extent. Other courts' awards necessarily affect the expectations of lawyers and, therefore, what they might agree to in voluntary negotiation. [citation] What they show here is that lawyers continue to take such cases in the face of fee awards ranging from 16% to 33–1/3%. Human nature suggests, therefore, that lawyers taking such a case might hope for 33 1/3% but recognize that it might be as low as 16%.

The above analysis leads me to an attorney fee award here of 25% ($825,-000). This percentage is at the higher end of the federal statutory limitation range, somewhat above the effective Maine malpractice limit, much higher than the Maine workers compensation percentage, lower than the standard one-third contingent fee and lower than the two fee agreements entered into before this became a class action. The percentage is in the mid-range of court awards in strip search cases, and it is more than 6% lower than the average award in general class actions with recoveries of this size. * * * I do recognize that the fact that my award falls within the range of other judicial awards serves mostly to give me comfort against embarrassing comparisons. It does not really show what the lawyers would have agreed to in an arm's length negotiation. Like my fee award, most of those awards were not adversarially tested (unless there were active and skilled objectors).

I am not confident that 25% truly is a good approximation of the market-mimicking rate. I could be wrong in either direction. On the information I have, I just don't know. Ironically, therefore, on this record my use of the Seventh Circuit's market-mimicking analysis may not be much better than the multifactor approach. But I hope that it will generate better evidence of the attorney fee market in future cases and more rational and predictable awards.

My reduction from the lawyers' requested 30% is no reflection whatsoever upon the quality of representation, or the nature of this litigation; these lawyers were excellent. Further, it is not a criticism of the percentage that they requested, given the precedents that they cite from other jurisdictions.

In future class actions that involve court-awarded attorney fees from a common fund, I will expect to receive evidentiary materials bearing on what lawyers negotiate for contingent fees or otherwise in comparable cases. I may well request detail about the percentages that would apply at different settlement stages of the case. [citation] I may also consider using my authority under Fed.R.Evid. 706 to appoint an expert to advise me on the attorney fee market. Finally, I may at least consider ordering lawyers to propose fee arrangements at the outset.

B. LITIGATION COSTS AND CLAIMS ADMINISTRATION EXPENSES. In class action litigation, a district court may award reasonable costs. Fed. R.Civ.P. 23(h). * * * Because I have not awarded the requested 30%, I direct the lawyers to promptly file with the court documentation of accrued and projected litigation costs and claims administration expenses, which I will then review. * * *

IV. CONCLUSION. I award 25% of the settlement in attorney fees, specifically $825,000. * * * SO ORDERED.

Notes

1. From the "fairness" hearing on the strip-search settlement in Nilsen v. York County we learn that after a premium to named plaintiff, deponents, etc., class members' recovery was one-size-fits-all. Every class member received the same amount, including those with multiple arrests-searches. Moreover, the judge rejected as unconstitutional double payments to women with "two zones of privacy," and the fee decision reflects that the final settlement was apparently unisex. Nilsen v. York County, 382 F.Supp.2d 206, 220 (D.Me.2005). In *Nilsen*, no class member opposed either the settlement or the attorney fee motion. Each participating class member's share is $1,719.90.

Many of the class members had a silent partner. The Maine authorities having found that 284 class members owed child support and related debts, corralled $463,000 of the recovery. CBS News: Maine Deadbeats Pay Back Strip–Search Cash. Augusta Maine, January 24, 2006.

2. *Rite Aid.* Nilsen v. York County is a "small" class action. In re Rite Aid, which Judge Hornby cites, is on the other end of the class action size continuum. A plaintiff class of 300,000 investors sued for violations of the Securities Exchange Act of 1934 and Rule 10b–5. A first settlement was worth $193 million. The source of the fee petition was a second settlement of $126.6 million with outside auditors KPMG LLP and former executives. Plaintiffs' lawyers requested 25%, $31.6 million, from the KPMG settlement fund. Over objection from two class members, the district judge approved the lawyers' request, leading to an appeal.

(a) *Sliding Scale.* Court of appeals: In this "mega-fund" case, should the trial judge have applied a declining percentage "sliding-scale" reduction that decreased the fee percentage on the higher reaches of the settlement?

"The [trial] court did not abuse its discretion in declining to apply a 'sliding scale' reduction, nor in viewing the size of the fund to be a factor weighing in favor of approval of the fee request."

Editor's Aside: Won't a more proficient lawyer create a larger settlement? Does the "sliding-scale" technique fail to reward, indeed does it punish, a skilled lawyer's proficiency? And does it encourage quick but modest settlements?

(b) *Multiplier.* A lodestar cross-check on the percentage of fund leads to a "multiplier"—an increase or decrease of the lodestar amount. In *Nilsen*, the lawyers' percentage fee was 1.6 (the multiplier) times the lodestar amount. A high multiplier, in turn, helps the judge test whether the lawyers' percentage-of-recovery fee is too large.

Rite Aid Court of Appeals: "Here, the District Court approved a lodestar cross-check multiplier of 4.07, using an average hourly billing rate of $605, the combined hourly rates of the senior-most partners at lead co-counsel firms, and 12,906 billed hours. * * * [The objector] contends the District Court improperly applied the billing rates of only the most senior partners of plaintiffs' co-lead counsel, resulting in an artificially low multiplier. On this point, we agree. In performing the lodestar cross-check, the district courts should apply blended billing rates that approximate the fee structure of all the attorneys who worked on the matter." In re Rite Aid Corp. Securities Litigation, 396 F.3d 294 (3d Cir.2005).

Back in the district court, Judge Dalzell applied a recalculated "blended" figure in the lodestar cross-check. With the recalculated lodestar, $4,549,824.75, the multiplier was 6.96. "Having computed the multiplier," the judge concluded that the original "amount of $31,660,328.75 (the 'Fee Award'), which constitutes twenty-five percent of the Settlement Fund of $126,641,315.00" was "reasonable." For "this case appears to involve the largest class recovery on record against an auditor in a 10b–5 action," and "through the exercise of their considerable skill, plaintiffs' counsel obtained a historic recovery for the class in a rare and complex kind of case where victory at trial would have been, at best, remote and uncertain." In re Rite Aid Corp. Securities Litigation, 362 F.Supp.2d 587, 589–90 (E.D.Pa.2005).

3. *Questions.* Compare the courts' measurements of attorney fees in *Nilsen* and *Rite Aid.* What percentage of the settlement was each group of lawyers asking for? Each of the judges used a lodestar cross-check. What were the "multipliers"?

A United States court of appeals reviews a trial judge's decision setting lawyers' fees for an abuse of discretion. In *Rite Aid*, the court of appeals disapproved the unblended rate the trial judge used for the lodestar cross-check; the appellate court did not disapprove the 4.07 multiplier. Wasn't the court of appeals suggesting to the trial judge that the attorney fees were too high? If so, did the trial judge get the message? Do the lodestar cross-check and the multiplier reveal excessive fees? Do attorney fees that are almost seven times the lawyers' usual hourly rates mean that the trial judge should have reduced the plaintiffs' lawyers' percentage, either across the board or on the settlement's higher reaches? Or, might the trial judge have applied the lodestar method of measuring attorney fees?

4. An attorney fee decision in the Michael Milken–Drexel Burnham Lambert litigation was "balanced." After the class litigation was settled for over $54,000,000, plaintiffs' counsel asked for percentage of recovery, 25%, to yield $13,500,000. However, the lodestar, as finally calculated, led to $2,100,000, about 4%. The court of appeals approved lodestar measurement, without any multiplier. "[E]ither the lodestar or the percentage of the recovery methods may properly be used to calculate fees in common fund cases." Goldberger v. Integrated Resources, Inc., 209 F.3d 43, 45 (2d Cir.2000).

5. *Pigs Get Fed, Hogs Get Slaughtered.* If a winner's attorney fee request is excessive, the judge may deny the fee request entirely. First State Insurance Group v. Nationwide Mutual Insurance Company, 402 F.3d 43 (1st Cir.2005).

6. *Settlement Waives Fee.* Plaintiffs brought a § 1983 class action claiming that the state had provided deficient health and education services to handicapped children. The state agreed to a settlement conditioned upon an attorney fee waiver. The Supreme Court ruled that it was not an abuse of discretion for the district judge to approve a settlement which included a complete fee waiver. Evans v. Jeff D., 475 U.S. 717 (1986), reh'g denied, 476 U.S. 1179 (1986). What are the implications of this decision for Civil Rights lawyers?

7. *What Are You Going to Give for It?* The problem of setting attorney fees in a class action may be that fee-setting occurs at the end of the lawsuit rather than at its beginning. One suggestion is to let the competitive "market" regulate fees by having the judge conduct an "auction" at the beginning of a class's action for damages. "Auction" here means that the judge solicits sealed "bids" to evaluate to select the plaintiff class's law firm. The judge selects the "winning" firm after competition based on the competing firms proposed percentage "prices," qualifications, and other services.

8. *Who Won?* Under many federal fee-shifting statutes, a "prevailing party" will receive a statutory attorney fee.

A plaintiff may achieve a favorable result without a favorable court ruling. Before 2001, using the catalyst theory of "prevailing," most federal courts focused on whether the plaintiffs got what they wanted rather than on whether they won in court.

Buckhannon Board & Care Home operated assisted living facilities that were not in compliance with a West Virginia statute. After the West Virginia authorities issued orders closing its facilities, Buckhannon sued them in United States court maintaining that the state statute violated federal statutes. During discovery, the West Virginia legislature repealed the state statute. The federal judge dismissed Buckhannon's lawsuit as moot.

Dealing later with Buckhannon's fee petition, the United States Supreme Court considered whether a plaintiff that was enjoying the result it desired without having secured any judicial ruling was a "prevailing" plaintiff. The Court rejected the catalyst theory. It held that the clear meaning of "prevailing party" required court-ordered relief or a "judicial imprimatur," for example the judge's approval of a consent decree. Even when you get what you want, you don't always get all you want: No attorney fees for the legislative winner. Buckhannon Board & Care Home, Inc. v. West Virginia Department of Health & Human Resources, 532 U.S. 598 (2001).

What judicial action is a qualifying "judicial imprimatur"? Dealing with the division in authority on whether a plaintiff who secures a preliminary injunction qualifies as a "prevailing party" to recover her attorney fees, is Bart Forsyth, Preliminary Imprimaturs: Prevailing Party Status Based on Preliminary Injunctions, 60 Wash. & Lee L.Rev. 927 (2003).

Some federal fee-shifting statutes authorize a plaintiff to recover attorney fees "whenever appropriate." Not requiring "prevailing party" success, these statutes may preserve the catalyst theory or something that resembles it. Ohio River Valley Environmental Coalition v. Timmermeyer, 363 F.Supp.2d 849 (S.D.W.Va.2005).

The United States Supreme Court's interpretation of the federal fee-shifting statute is not binding on a state court. After *Buckhannon*, the California Supreme Court reaffirmed its adherence to the catalyst approach to determining whether a successful public-interest plaintiff was eligible to recover attorney fees under the state private-attorney-general statute. Graham v. DaimlerChrysler Corp., 34 Cal.4th 553, 21 Cal.Rptr.3d 331, 101 P.3d 140, 148–49 (2004).

E. TORT REFORM

Tort reform, really mostly personal-injury damages reform, is, like our system of civil remedies, both complex and controversial. The following material summarizes tort reform and several related damages issues.

Concern to compensate the injured and to spread losses dominated tort doctrinal development during the first six decades of the twentieth century. The worm began to turn with rising insurance premiums for drivers, health care providers, and manufacturers. Law and economics of the market economics school focused professional attention more on deterrence and less on compensation and corrective justice. The tort system, reformers argued, is characterized by delay, high transaction costs, (translation—attorney fees), and lottery-like results in the form of erratic extremely high payouts.

The movement for no-fault began in the 1960s. Under a no-fault compensation statute, each driver's insurance pays his or her own pecuniary losses but typically nothing for pain and suffering. Early and full monetary recovery extricates accident victims from the litigation morass. Universal no-fault has not yet arrived. Tort reformers have focused on other goals.

Tort reformers' overarching goal is straightforward: to decrease the number of plaintiffs' damages judgments and to reduce the amounts of the judgments that remain. Several of tort reformers' major targets are the collateral source rule, pain and suffering damages, joint and several liability, and punitive damages. All but joint and several liability are damages reforms. Both of this section's principal decisions deal with plaintiffs' challenges to caps on damages. Lesser tort reform agenda items are to substitute the English or loser-pays attorney fees rule for the American Rule, to replace lump sum damages judgments with periodic payments, to limit the contingency fee contract, and to restrict class actions.

Tort reformers' agenda items are related, even synergistic. The personal injury litigation system combines the collateral source rule, pain and suffering damages, and punitive damages with plaintiff's contingency fee contract, defendant's insurance company, and the American Rule for attorney fees. Subtracting plaintiffs' collateral source payments from damages and reducing damages for pain and suffering will decrease plaintiff's total recovery and, along with that, plaintiff's attorney's fee.

Who are the players in tort reform? Tort reformers are a loose coalition of actual and potential tort defendants and their allies who seek to limit liability exposure for professional service providers, manufacturers, and their insurers. Opponents of tort reform include consumer groups and lawyers who represent plaintiffs, as well as the plaintiffs themselves. The stakes are high, and the battles, fought on several fronts, are intense. Thirteen amicus briefs were filed in Best v. Taylor Machine.

Tort reformers seek both legislative and judicial change. The legal profession usually thinks of the common law of torts as created and maintained by courts but existing at the sufferance of an elected legislature that can change tort law at any time. Although the doctrine of stare decisis usually leads a court to follow precedent, judicial changes in the common law occur from time to time. One example in this chapter is the Maine court's decision in Tuttle v. Raymond to raise the defendant's misconduct threshold for punitive damages to the higher level of "malice" and to set the plaintiff's burden of proof at "clear and convincing evidence."

From the Contract With America in the 1990s to the president's State of the Union address in 2006, proponents of tort reform have argued for federal tort-reform legislation maintaining that the system of justice is not functioning because of runaway juries, elected judges, greedy lawyers, a litigation explosion, and frivolous lawsuits. Tort reform issues have also been debated in state judicial elections and state initiative elections.

Both the courts and the legislature are, in turn, subject to the constitutions, federal and state, as definitively interpreted by, surprise!, surprise!, the courts. The United States Constitution and state constitutions are available to a litigant both for judicial tort reform and to check legislative tort reform. The United States Supreme Court's Constitutional decisions setting due process limits on state common law punitive damages culminating in *BMW* and *Campbell* are judicial tort reform. The principal decisions in this section, Best v. Taylor Machine and Gourley v. Nebraska Methodist Health System, and many of the decisions in the Notes are state courts' decisions under state constitutions.

The division of tort reform labor between the legislature and the courts varies from one jurisdiction to another. The Maine court's tort reforms have legislative origins in other states. The Alabama legislature, for example, established that state's misconduct threshold for punitive damages, "oppression, fraud, wantonness or malice," and its burden of proof, "clear and convincing," in a statute. Ala.Code §§ 6–11–20 (1993).

In Tuttle v. Raymond, in a footnote which seems to commend the idea to the legislature, the Maine court had mentioned dividing punitive damages between the plaintiff and the government. Ignoring that division of responsibility, Alabama's state Supreme Court judicially instituted a split of punitive damages between the plaintiff and the state's general fund. Life Insurance Co. of Georgia v. Johnson, 684 So.2d 685, 696 (Ala.1996); after reconsideration on remand from the United States Supreme Court for further consideration in light of BMW v. Gore, the Alabama court decided that Constitutionally mandated post-verdict judicial review overcame the need to divide punitive damages between the plaintiff and the government. Life Insurance Co. of Georgia v. Johnson, 701 So.2d 524, 534 (Ala.1997).

Plaintiffs' pain and suffering damages are a significant tort reform target. Critics charge that plaintiffs' pain and suffering recovery constitutes a primary part of the high transaction costs that plague the personal injury system and erode American business's ability to compete. Plaintiffs' recovery for pain and suffering, they maintain, skews an injured person's incentives to utilize health care excessively and drives up health-care costs. A statute capping the amount of a plaintiff's pain and suffering damages makes verdicts less capricious.

But, tort reform opponents ask, are caps fair to the plaintiffs most likely to encounter them, women, the young, the elderly, and the most seriously injured victims? For these plaintiffs have long and serious encounters with pain, as well as expensive attorney fees.

Professor Sharkey studied the way statutory caps on "noneconomic" damages affect verdicts and published the results in a useful article with all kinds of information about tort reform. Cathy Sharkey, Unintended Consequences of Medical Malpractice Caps, 80 N.Y.U. L.Rev. 391 (2005). Based on the idea that the boundaries between the categories of personal injury damages may be permeable, she examined the "crossover effect": In a state with a cap on plaintiffs' noneconomic damages, plaintiffs' lawyers and juries will learn how to augment plaintiffs' pecuniary damages. From the medical malpractice verdicts in the trials that she studied, Professor Sharkey concluded that noneconomic damages caps did not affect plaintiffs' overall compensatory damages totals. (Id. at 445, 469, 472, 478) What did affect the verdicts? First, no surprise, the severity of the plaintiff's injury. (Id. at 471) Two other, less expected, factors also increase the size of plaintiffs' malpractice verdicts: if the jurisdiction's judges are elected in partisan elections and if the jurisdiction has a screening panel for a malpractice case. (Id. at 474) Contrary to what an observer might expect, lower verdicts are associated with the common-law collateral source rule and a patient compensation fund. (Id. at 475) Nor do caps lead to lower malpractice insurance rates; even though the lawyers and the judge don't tell the jurors about the cap, the cap might "anchor"—be the jurors' reference point or "floor" to start thinking about an amount. (Id. at 408, 422–28) Medical professionals' insurance premiums may reflect insurance companies' investment decisions. Professor Sharkey thinks that a cap on a plaintiff's total damages "might be more effective than noneconomic damages caps." (Id. at 415).

This casebook has two principal decisions on damages caps: Best v. Taylor Machine, on a cap on pain and suffering for all plaintiffs, and Gourley v. Nebraska Methodist Health Systems, on a total, across-the-board, cap on a plaintiff's medical malpractice damages. Following *Gourley* is an excerpt from a decision striking down the Wisconsin cap on pain and suffering in medical malpractice.

BEST v. TAYLOR MACHINE WORKS

Supreme Court of Illinois, 1997.
179 Ill.2d 367, 689 N.E.2d 1057.

JUSTICE McMORROW delivered the opinion of the court: * * * Plaintiff, Vernon Best, was injured on July 24, 1995, while he was operating a forklift for his employer, Laclede Steel Company, in Alton, Illinois. The forklift was designed and manufactured by Taylor Machine Works (Taylor) and sold by Allied Industrial Equipment Corporation (Allied). Best sustained injuries when the forklift's mast and support assembly collapsed while Best was moving slabs of hot steel. As a result of the collapse, flammable hydraulic fluid manufactured by Lee Helms, Inc. (Helms), ignited and engulfed Best in a fireball. While on fire, Best leaped from the cab of the forklift and fractured both heels. Best also suffered second and third degree burns over 40% of his body, including his face, torso, arms and hands.

Best filed a product liability action seeking damages against Taylor, Allied and Helms. * * * In his amended complaint, Best seeks compensatory damages for all injuries. Best alleges that he has and will incur noneconomic damages in excess of $500,000. He also seeks declaratory and injunctive relief against Public Act 89–7 on the grounds that the Act violates the Illinois Constitution. * * *

The circuit court ruled that 15 specific provisions of Public Act 89–7 were unconstitutional and that the Act as a whole was unconstitutional. * * * [Defendants appealed.]

Plaintiffs challenge the $500,000 limit on compensatory damages for noneconomic injuries set forth in section 2–1115.1 of the Code of Civil Procedure. Section 2–1115.1(a) provides:

"In all common law, statutory or other actions that seek damages on account of death, bodily injury, or physical damage to property based on negligence, or product liability based on any theory or doctrine, recovery of non-economic damages shall be limited to $500,000 per plaintiff. There shall be no recovery for hedonic damages." * * *

The statute defines "non-economic damages" as "damages which are intangible, including but not limited to damages for pain and suffering, disability, disfigurement, loss of consortium, and loss of society." 2–1115.2(b). * * *

The cap on compensatory damages for noneconomic injury is, as the parties acknowledge, at the heart of Public Act 89–7. The key role of this cap is reflected in the preamble to the Act, which contains 18 specific "findings" and eight listed "purposes" based on those findings. Eight of the 18 findings in the preamble pertain to noneconomic damages. These findings declare that: (1) limiting noneconomic damages will improve health care in rural Illinois, (2) more than 20 states limit noneconomic damages, (3) the cost of health care has decreased in those states, (4) noneconomic losses have no monetary dimension, and no objective criteria or jurisprudence exists for assessing or reviewing noneconomic damages awards, (5) such awards are highly erratic and depend on subjective preferences of the trier of fact, (6) highly erratic noneconomic damages awards subvert the credibility of such awards and undercut the deterrent function of tort law, (7) such awards must be limited to provide consistency and stability for all parties and society and (8) "a federal executive branch working group" determined that limiting noneconomic damages was the most effective step toward legislative reform of tort law because it reduces litigation costs and expedites settlement.

In addition to the above legislative "findings," the preamble to Public Act 89–7 states legislative "purposes" which relate to the limit on noneconomic damages. These purposes may be summarized as follows: reduce the cost of health care and increase accessibility to health care, promote consistency in awards, reestablish the credibility of the civil justice system, establish parameters or guidelines for noneconomic damages, protect the economic health of the state by decreasing systemic costs, and ensure the affordability of insurance.

The preamble also declares, "It is the public policy of this State that injured persons injured through negligence or deliberate misconduct of another be afforded a legal mechanism to seek compensation for their injuries."

In the circuit court, defendants maintained that the Act and its specified goals represent a return to fairness, predictability, responsibility and rationality in the tort arena. Specifically, defendants argued that the limit on noneconomic damages provides rationality to the system of awarding damages for personal injury.

Plaintiffs, in their motion for partial summary judgment, challenged the legislature's use of chiefly anecdotal evidence to justify the Act. An example which was cited frequently in the legislative debates is the infamous McDonald's spilled coffee case. [citation] As one author has noted, the facts of this case were presented to the public in a skewed fashion. M. Rustad, Nationalizing Tort Law: The Republican Attack on Women, Blue Collar Workers and Consumers, 48 Rutgers L. Rev. 673, 720–21 (1996). In that case, it was reported that an 81-year-old woman received a $2.9 million punitive damages verdict for injuries incurred after she spilled hot coffee in her lap. However, less widely reported was that the verdict was reduced by the court to $480,000, the elderly woman underwent numerous skin graft operations for third degree burns, and McDonald's had prior knowledge of hundreds of similar scalding incidents. Also, the excessive award was for punitive, not compensatory, damages.

Citing a 1992 report from the National Center for State Courts, plaintiffs noted that businesses, not private personal injury plaintiffs, constitute the most active group of litigants in the state. Plaintiffs further argued that the uncontested empirical evidence that they presented in conjunction with their motion clearly shows that the legislative "findings" listed in the preamble do not provide a rational justification for the limitation of compensatory damages for noneconomic injuries. In support, plaintiffs submitted several affidavits with their motion for summary judgment on the constitutionality of section 2–1115.1.

Neil Vidmar, Professor of Social Science and Law at Duke Law School in Durham, North Carolina, submitted an affidavit in which he explains that many of the assertions about medical malpractice litigation contained in the preamble of Public Act 89–7, as well as statements made at the hearing and debates which preceded its passage, have no empirical basis and were based on unsubstantiated perceptions or unreliable data. * * * Vidmar states that he is aware of no reliable evidence in the formal studies which indicate that a limit on noneconomic damages corresponds to a significant impact on the cost or availability of health care or that noneconomic damages and the costs of liability insurance are directly linked.

In a separate affidavit, Marc Galanter, Evjue–Bascom Professor of Law at the University of Wisconsin Law School, agrees that there is little evidence, apart from anecdotes, to support the perceived deleterious effects of the present civil litigation system. * * * He maintains that the only consequences which clearly flow from the passage of Public Act 89–7 are increased profitability of insurance companies and a reduction in the payments to the most seriously injured tort victims. According to Galanter, court filings in the law division of the circuit court of Cook County have actually declined during the period from 1980 to 1994. Galanter asserts that arguments which rely on systemic costs of the civil litigation system and its negative effect on health care and jobs are purely speculative. Similarly, he states that the salutary effects attributed to the type of tort reform attempted in Public Act 89–7 are largely speculative. Galanter concludes that when comparing isolated instances or anecdotal evidence against the reliable empirical data that does exist, it is apparent that the findings which form the basis for Public Act 89–7 are erroneous.

In addition to the above affidavits, plaintiffs offered the joint affidavit of Stephen Daniels, M.A., Ph.D., a senior research fellow at the American Bar Foundation in Chicago, and Joanne Martin, M.M., J.D., an assistant director of the same foundation. Their affidavit summarizes the key empirical findings of scholarly literature and compares them to the factual underpinnings of Public Act 89–7. Like Vidmar and Galanter, Daniels and Martin state that the facts which form the stated intention or goals of Public Act 89–7 are not substantiated by the empirical data and critical analyses found in published, scholarly literature. Daniels and Martin summarize data which show that only a tiny fraction of accidental deaths and injuries are pursued through the litigation system as claims for compensation. They further maintain, based on studies, that jury awards are not erratic or capricious, but rather relate closely to the severity of the particular injury. * * *

In this court, plaintiffs challenge the constitutionality of the damages cap, section 2–1115.1, on the basis that it violates the special legislation clause of the Illinois Constitution. Plaintiffs maintain that for individuals whose injuries are minor or moderate, the limit will rarely, if ever, be implicated. Instead, the limit is imposed only when a jury or trial court finds, and the reviewing court agrees, that an award of compensatory noneconomic damages in excess of $500,000 is required to make the plaintiff whole. According to plaintiffs, section 2–1115.1 impermissibly penalizes the most severely injured individuals, whose pain and suffering, disfigurement, and other noneconomic injuries would be most likely to result in a compensatory award in excess of $500,000 but for the statutory limit. Similarly, plaintiffs reason, the damages cap arbitrarily benefits certain tortfeasors, who are relieved of liability for fully compensating plaintiffs. Thus, plaintiffs maintain, section 2–1115.1 constitutes special legislation.

The special legislation clause of the Illinois Constitution provides:

"The General Assembly shall pass no special or local law when a general law is or can be made applicable. Whether a general law is or can be made applicable shall be a matter for judicial determination." Ill. Const.1970, art. IV, § 13. * * *

According to plaintiffs, section 2–1115.1 contains three arbitrary classifications that have no reasonable connection to the stated legislative goals: (1) the limitation on noneconomic damages distinguishes between slightly and severely injured individuals, (2) the limitation on noneconomic damages arbitrarily distinguishes between individuals with identical injuries, and (3) the limitation arbitrarily distinguishes types of injury. At oral argument, plaintiffs offered examples illustrating how the limitation on noneconomic damages is disconnected from the stated legislative purposes of providing rationality and consistency to jury verdicts.

In the first example, it is assumed that three plaintiffs are injured as a result of the same tortfeasor's negligence. Plaintiff A is injured moderately, and suffers pain, disability and disfigurement for a month. Plaintiff B is severely injured and suffers one year of pain and disability. Plaintiff C is drastically injured, and suffers permanent pain and disability. For purposes of this example, it is further assumed that a jury awards plaintiffs A and B $100,000 in compensatory damages for noneconomic injuries. Plaintiff C receives $1 million for his permanent, lifelong pain and disability.

In the above hypothetical, section 2–1115.1 fails to provide consistency or rationality to a jury's seemingly inconsistent decision to award plaintiffs A and B the same amount for very different noneconomic injuries. Therefore, the legislative goal of providing consistency is not met by the damages cap. With respect to plaintiff C, section 2–1115.1 arbitrarily and automatically reduces the jury's award for a lifetime of pain and disability, without regard to whether or not the verdict, before reduction, was reasonable and fair.

The tortfeasors in this example are also treated differently, without any justification. The tortfeasor who injures plaintiffs A and B is liable for the full amount of fairly assessed compensatory damages. In contrast, section 2–1115.1 confers a benefit on the similarly situated tortfeasor who injures plaintiff C. This tortfeasor pays only a portion of fairly assessed compensatory damages because of the limitation in section 2–1115.1. Therefore, the statute discriminates between slightly and severely injured plaintiffs, and also between tortfeasors who cause severe and moderate or minor injuries.

Plaintiffs suggest that section 2–1115.1 creates a second arbitrary legislative classification by distinguishing between injured individuals who suffer identical injuries. For example, we are asked to assume that an individual loses his leg due to a defectively manufactured forklift today, and he loses his other leg in a car accident the following year. Both injuries are caused by the negligent conduct of others. The injured individual brings two different actions against two different defendants, and a jury assesses compensatory damages for noneconomic injuries at $400,000 in each case. Section 2–1115.1 would allow the plaintiff to recover both verdicts in full. However, if the same plaintiff lost both legs in a single accident due to the negligence of another, and if the jury fairly assessed $800,000 in compensatory damages for noneconomic injuries, then the cap in section 2–1115.1 would eliminate a substantial portion of that tortfeasor's liability, without regard to the facts of the case.

To illustrate the third arbitrary classification created by the limitation on noneconomic damages in personal injury actions, plaintiffs argue that section 2–1115.1 improperly discriminates among types of injuries. Plaintiffs maintain that the legislative statements concerning the supposed difficulties of assessing damages for noneconomic injuries apply equally to all tort claims for pure noneconomic loss, and not just those involving death, bodily injury or property damage. Other torts that remain unaffected by the legislation at issue are invasion of privacy, defamation, intentional infliction of emotional distress, negligent infliction of emotional distress, damage to reputation and breach of fiduciary duty. The speculative nature of noneconomic damages for these torts, which do not involve personal injury, is not addressed by the cap in section 2–1115.1.

Plaintiffs maintain that the above illustrations demonstrate the arbitrariness of the classifications created by section 2–1115.1, in violation of the prohibition against special legislation. Plaintiffs contend that the classifications contained within section 2–1115.1 allow certain culpable tortfeasors to escape liability for a portion of fairly assessed compensatory damages, while requiring others to pay the full amount of assessed damages. Similarly, certain injured plaintiffs are denied compensatory damages, while other similarly situated injured plaintiffs are awarded full compensation, without any rational justification for the distinction.

Defendants raise a series of related arguments in opposition to plaintiffs' contention that section 2–1115.1 is arbitrary and not rationally related to a legitimate government interest. Defendants contend that plaintiffs' arguments are "fatally flawed" in that they are based on the erroneous assumption that noneconomic injuries, which are difficult to assess, should be monetarily compensable. Defendants further argue that section 2–1115.1 is rationally related to the legislative goal of reducing systemic costs of the civil justice system, which may be accomplished "one step at a time"; that the General Assembly has the power to change the common law; and that other jurisdictions have upheld statutory limitations on damages similar to section 2–1115.1. We address each of defendants' arguments in turn.

At oral argument, in rebuttal, defendants stated that "it is not true that money can compensate for noneconomic damages, [or] at least the legislature could find that is the case." Defendants do not dispute the general proposition that noneconomic injuries are "real." Rather, defendants argue that noneconomic damages are "inherently unmeasurable." Thus, according to defendants, the legislature's adoption of an "objective" limitation on noneconomic damages is reasonable and must be upheld as a legitimate exercise of legislative judgment.

Defendants' argument contradicts the statute under consideration. Subsection (b) of section 2–1115.1 defines noneconomic loss or noneconomic damages as "damages which are intangible, including but not limited to damages for pain and suffering, disability, disfigurement, loss of consortium and loss of society." Subsection (c) provides that "compensatory damages" or "actual damages" are "the sum of the economic and noneconomic damages." Section 2–1115.1 itself demonstrates that the legislature believed that remuneration is an appropriate means by which to compensate tort victims for their noneconomic injuries. Therefore, the application of a limit to the noneconomic damages of some, but not all, injured plaintiffs is not justified by the difficulty of assessing such damages.

We do not disagree with defendants' assertion that damages for noneconomic injuries are difficult to assess. We simply determine that it does not follow that the difficulty in quantifying compensatory damages for noneconomic injuries is alleviated by imposing an arbitrary limitation or cap on all cases, without regard to the facts or circumstances. Further, the preamble to Public Act 89–7 states that "[i]t is the public policy of this State that persons injured through the negligence or deliberate misconduct of another be afforded a legal mechanism to seek compensation for their injuries." There is universal agreement that the compensatory goal of tort law requires that an injured plaintiff be made whole. * * * [T]he $500,000 limit does not reestablish the credibility of the tort system, and does nothing to assist the trier of fact in determining appropriate damages for noneconomic injuries. The limitation actually undermines the stated goal of providing consistency and rationality to the civil justice system.

We reject defendants' argument that the damages cap in section 2–1115.1 should be upheld because reform can be undertaken "one step at a time." * * * [T]his court has rejected the "one step" rationale to support a classification if the classification is arbitrary. [citation] We need not address this justification further.

Defendants also argue that the legislative interest in reducing the "systemic costs of tort liability" is sufficient to overcome plaintiffs' special legislation challenge. The "systemic costs of tort liability" are not defined in Public Act 89–7 and we are uncertain as to the meaning and scope of these terms. Even if we assume that the reduction of these undefined systemic costs is a legitimate state interest, we do not discern how the limiting of noneconomic damages in personal injury actions may be considered rationally related to the achievement of that interest. * * * In the instant case, we are unable to discern any connection between the automatic reduction of one type of compensatory damages awarded to one class of injured plaintiffs and a savings in the systemwide costs of litigation. Even assuming that a systemwide savings in costs were achieved by the cap, the prohibition against special legislation does not permit the entire burden of the anticipated cost savings to rest on one class of injured plaintiffs. [citations] We therefore reject defendants' systemic costs rationale as a basis for upholding section 2–1115.1.

Defendants additionally argue that the General Assembly has the power to change the common law and, therefore, the limitation on compensatory damages is constitutional. For example, defendants cite to the Worker's Compensation Act as an instance of the legislature's valid exercise of the police power in limiting liability of an employer for injuries sustained by an employee during the course of his or her employment. [citations]

Plaintiffs do not dispute that the legislature has the power to change the common law, and we do not question defendants' argument insofar as it stands for the general principle that the General Assembly may alter the common law and change or limit available remedies. This principle is well grounded in the jurisprudence of this state. [citations] However, defendants' argument assumes too much. The legislature is not free to enact changes to the common law which are not rationally related to a legitimate government interest. The General Assembly's authority to exercise its police power by altering the common law and limiting available remedies is also dependent upon the nature and scope of the particular change in the law. We hold in the case at bar that the statutory cap on compensatory damages for noneconomic losses is arbitrary.

Finally, defendants support their contention that the limitation on noneconomic damages in section 2–1115.1 is constitutional by referring to several other state court decisions which have upheld damage limitations. [citations]

However, other jurisdictions have held statutory damages caps unconstitutional. [citations]

The statutory caps on damages which have been enacted by other states vary considerably in scope and effect. Similarly, the state constitutional provisions and precedents under which these damage caps have been challenged are unique to each jurisdiction. Although the decisions from other states may be instructive in some respects, we believe that these decisions are of limited assistance in answering the specific question of whether section 2–1115.1 offends the special legislation clause of the Illinois Constitution. We hold that it does.

Plaintiffs also assert that section 2–1115.1 violates the separation of powers clause by improperly delegating to the legislature the power of remitting verdicts and judgments, which is a power unique to the judiciary. See Ill. Const.1970, art. VI, § 1 (judicial power is vested in the supreme, appellate and circuit courts). According to plaintiffs, because section 2–1115.1 limits damages for noneconomic injuries, the section violates the constitutional separation of powers doctrine by invading the province of the judiciary and imposing a "one-size-fits-all 'legislative remittitur.' " Plaintiffs argue that the cap on damages contravenes the traditional authority of the courts to assess, on a case-by-case basis, whether a jury's damages award is excessive.

Defendants disagree with plaintiffs' characterization of the operation of section 2–1115.1 as a legislative remittitur. They argue that the damages cap merely "sets an outer parameter by which wholly subjective damages are limited" and in no respect displaces traditional judicial functions. * * *

For over a century it has been a traditional and inherent power of the judicial branch of government to apply the doctrine of remittitur, in appropriate and limited circumstances, to correct excessive jury verdicts. [citations]

The practice of ordering a remittitur of excessive damages has long been recognized and accepted as part of Illinois law. [citations] The remittitur doctrine has been acknowledged as promoting both the administration of justice and the conclusion of litigation. * * *

Case law reflects that the application of remittitur should be considered on a case-by-case basis because the evidence and circumstances supporting verdicts must be carefully examined before a jury's assessment of damages is reduced. [citations]

In the case at bar, we conclude that section 2–1115.1 undercuts the power, and obligation, of the judiciary to reduce excessive verdicts. In our view, section 2–1115.1 functions as a "legislative remittitur." Unlike the traditional remittitur power of the judiciary, the legislative remittitur of section 2–1115.1 disregards the jury's careful deliberative process in determining damages that will fairly compensate injured plaintiffs who have proven their causes of action. The cap on damages is mandatory and operates wholly apart from the specific circumstances of a particular plaintiff's noneconomic injuries. Therefore, section 2–1115.1 unduly encroaches upon the fundamentally judicial prerogative of determining whether a jury's assessment of damages is excessive within the meaning of the law.

We additionally note that the cap provision of section 2–1115.1 forces the successful plaintiff to forgo part of his or her jury award without the plaintiff's consent, in clear violation of the well-settled principle that a trial court does not have authority to reduce a damages award by entry of a remittitur if the plaintiff objects or does not consent. [citations] A plaintiff's refusal to consent to remittitur will result in the ordering of a new trial. [citations]

In the case at bar, we conclude that section 2–1115.1 invades the power of the judiciary to limit excessive awards of damages. The courts are constitutionally empowered, and indeed obligated, to reduce excessive verdicts where appropriate in light of the evidence adduced in a particular case. Section 2–1115.1, however, reduces damages by operation of law, without regard to the specific circumstances of individual jury awards. Although legislative limits upon certain types of damages may be permitted, such as damages recoverable in statutory causes of action, we hold that the cap in section 2–1115.1 violates the separation of powers clause of the Illinois Constitution.

In summary, we hold that the compensatory damages cap of section 2–1115.1 violates the constitutional prohibition against special legislation and also violates the separation of powers clause. Because we have so determined, we decline to address the parties' additional arguments questioning the validity of section 2–1115.1 as violating the right to a jury trial and the right to a certain remedy under the Illinois Constitution.

JUSTICE MILLER, dissenting in part: * * * Contrary to the majority's holding, I would conclude that the limit on noneconomic losses contained in the Act does not violate the special legislation prohibition of the Illinois Constitution, for the provision at issue readily satisfies the requirements of the rational basis test. Reform of the civil justice system is surely a legitimate governmental goal, and imposing a $500,000 limit on the recovery of noneconomic damages is rationally related to those ends. * * *

Some will argue that the amount selected by the legislature in the provision at issue here is too low. Although that might be a valid objection to the Act as an expression of public policy, for each of us would probably set the limit at a greater or lesser level, it is not a constitutional defect in the legislation. Like a repose statute, the limit on the recovery of noneconomic losses reflects the balance struck by the legislature between an individual's interest in compensation for his or her own injuries, and the public's interest in an affordable system of tort law.

Again, to uphold the statute we need not be convinced of the correctness of the legislature's judgment-we need only find that the question is debatable and that the legislature has adopted a rational means of achieving the desired ends. * * *

In deciding that the cap on noneconomic losses is invalid special legislation, the majority tests the provision against specially selected hypothetical cases that are obviously designed to illustrate defects in the statute. The legislature, however, makes no pretense that the reform measures at issue here are a panacea for all the ills, perceived or otherwise, in our system of tort law. Nor is it necessary that legislation like this have such miraculous effect. Under rational basis review, we ask only whether the means chosen by the legislature are rationally related to the purposes of the law. In contrast to the examples posited by the majority, one could as easily select hypothetical cases that support and sustain the remedy devised by the legislature. * * *

Perhaps uncertain of its own conclusion, the majority opinion goes on to consider an alternative argument against the limit on noneconomic damages, hoping to persuade the reader by prolixity, if not by force of reasoning. Here, the majority finds that the limit on the recovery of noneconomic damages functions as a legislatively imposed remittitur and for that reason violates the separation of powers doctrine. The majority's discussion of this additional argument is entirely unnecessary, given the majority's prior holding that the same measure is invalid special legislation. On the merits, I disagree with the majority's conclusion that the cap on noneconomic damages improperly intrudes on the judicial power of remittitur. The challenged provision does not represent a finding about the evidence of any particular case, and it does not detract from the power of a court to reduce an award of damages in appropriate circumstances. Remittitur pertains to judges and juries, not the legislature; by characterizing the cap on damages as a remittitur, the majority is simply erecting and demolishing a strawman. The majority's broad holding on this question means, in essence, that the legislature may never impose a limit on damages, at least in common law actions. Given the implications of this holding and the absence of any need to discuss the issue, I would not join this part of the majority opinion even if I agreed with the court that the caps provision was invalid special legislation.

Notes

1. The Illinois legislature passed a targeted malpractice $1,000,000–$500,000 cap on noneconomic damages in 2005. Expect challenges. 735 Ill. Comp. Stat. 5/2–1706.5 (2005).

2. *Tort Reform and the Jury.* (a) Workers' compensation, the granddaddy of tort reform, removed most employee-employer damages claims from the jury. "If these provisions [in the workers compensation act] relating to compensation are to be construed as definitely fixing the amount which an employer must pay in every case where his liability is established by statute, there can be no doubt that they constitute a legislative usurpation of the functions of the common law jury." Ives v. South Buffalo Ry. Co., 201 N.Y. 271, 291–92, 94 N.E. 431, 438 (1911). Although the quoted sentence may be technically dictum, the state constitution was amended; workers compensation supplanted the jury trial. N.Y. Const. Art. 1, § 18.

(b) A different judicial approach was evident in 1992 in Maryland. A $350,000 statutory limitation on recovery of "noneconomic" damages does not, the Free State's court held, interfere with the jury's right to determine damages properly. The litigants' constitutional right to a jury prevents the judge from taking the jury's function. But it does not prevent the legislature from removing a cause of action from the judicial arena. The legislature, which had the power to abolish a common law cause of action completely, could abolish a cause of action for noneconomic damages over $350,000. Murphy v. Edmonds, 325 Md. 342, 601 A.2d 102 (1992). The Maryland legislature has raised the cap.

3. *A Juryfree Administrative Agency?* May Congress or perhaps a state legislature establish a specialized administrative agency to administer "public rights" and exclude lay jurors? "The Seventh Amendment was declaratory of the existing law, for it required only that jury trial in Suits at common law was to be 'preserved.' It thus did not purport to require a jury trial where none was required before. Moreover, it did not seek to change the factfinding mode in equity or admiralty nor to freeze equity jurisdiction as it existed in 1789, preventing it from developing new remedies where those available in courts of law were inadequate." Atlas Roofing Co. v. Occupational Safety and Health Review Commission, 430 U.S. 442, 459 (1977).

Are agencies the tort reform solution?

4. *Other Tort Reform Agenda Items.*

(a) *Joint and Several Liability.* Each of numerous liable defendants is responsible to the plaintiff for the full amount of his damages. Norfolk & Western Railway v. Ayers, 538 U.S. 135 (2003). The purposes are to assure that plaintiff is compensated, to spread the loss around, and to encourage settlement. Critics argue that the joint-and-several rule encourages a plaintiff to seek a defendant with maximum ability but minimum culpability.

In a part of *Best* not included above, the Illinois court held that the tort reform statute which eliminated joint and several liability in actions for death, bodily injury, or property damage, and replaced it with proportionate several liability, was unconstitutional special legislation.

(b) *Post-verdict Judicial Review.* Heightened post-verdict judicial review of the size of a plaintiff's damages verdict is a tort reform technique that asks the trial judge and appellate courts to check the jury's proclivity to be generous with defendant's money. More careful post-verdict judicial review of jury verdicts is found in the New York statute the Supreme Court approved for diversity jurisdiction in *Gasperini*, Note 6, pp. 88–89.

Judicial development of post-verdict judicial review occurred in *BMW* and *Campbell*. pp. 133, 145.

(c) *Periodic Payments*. Periodic payments of a damages judgment changes the common law's preference for a lump-sum judgment. Several states have adopted some form of periodic payment statute, usually for bodily injury damages in particular types of cases.

New York has a periodic payment system for a damage judgment for personal injury, injury to property or wrongful death that exceed $250,000. N.Y.Civ.Proc. & R. § 5041 (McKinney Supp.1990). The statute sets out a method for computing and paying future amounts through an annuity contract. If the injured plaintiff dies, a portion of the annuity payment terminates. See Frey v. Chester E. Smith and Sons, Inc., 751 F.Supp. 1052 (N.D.N.Y.1990).

After the decision in Williams and Robbins v. Bright, p. 90, Judge Greenfield ordered the defendant to pay a lump sum of the installments which had accumulated between the verdict and the judgment instead of beginning installments. "[T]he plaintiff," the judge observed, need not wait because she "faces the prospect of years of appeals on constitutional questions of first impression." Williams v. Bright, 167 Misc.2d 179, 181, 637 N.Y.S.2d 915, 917 (1995). The appellate court approved this part of Judge Greenfield's decision. Williams v. Bright, 230 A.D.2d 548, 658 N.Y.S.2d 910, 916 (1997).

The California Supreme Court rejected due process and equal protection challenges to a California statute that sets periodic payments for medical malpractice damages for "future damages." American Bank and Trust Co. v. Community Hospital of Los Gatos–Saratoga, Inc., 36 Cal.3d 359, 204 Cal.Rptr. 671, 683 P.2d 670 (1984).

A Model Statute. The National Conference of Commissioners on Uniform State Laws in 1980 proffered a Model Periodic Payment of Judgments Act. Defendant's periodic payments, proponents claim, protect an unsophisticated plaintiff from investment risks and save her investment counseling fees. In theory, defendant benefits by purchasing an annuity for a fixed sum to cover the judgment, while being able to terminate payments if the actual event calls for their cessation. Model Periodic Payment of Judgments Act, 14 U.L.A. 20; Henderson, Designing a Responsible Periodic–Payment System for Tort Awards: Arizona Enacts a Prototype, 32 Ariz.L.Rev. 21 (1990).

(d) *Negotiated Tort Reform: A Structured Settlement*. The litigants can remove the uncertainty in future personal injury damages with a privately negotiated agreement called a structured settlement which calls for installments payable as the plaintiff's expenses accrue. Streams of annuity payments totaling large sums can assure plaintiff's security and remove the plaintiff's investment risk at a cost far lower than the total of payments. The issues are how to assure future payments, when to pay plaintiff's attorney fee, and how to accommodate to the interest rate, inflation, and taxes.

5. *Medical Malpractice Reform*. Observers of the tort reform scene have divided tort reform into three waves. The third wave which the nation is now encountering is, like the first wave in the 1970s, focusing on plaintiffs' damages for medical malpractice. The Nebraska court's *Gourley* decision and the Wisconsin court's *Ferdon* decision which is summarized following *Gourley*, are plaintiffs' state-constitutional challenges to tort-reform legislation targeted at medical malpractice.

GOURLEY EX REL. GOURLEY v. NEBRASKA METHODIST HEALTH SYSTEM, INC.

Supreme Court of Nebraska, 2003.
265 Neb. 918, 663 N.W.2d 43.

PER CURIAM. Neb.Rev.Stat. § 44–2825(1) of the Nebraska Hospital–Medical Liability Act limits recoverable damages in medical malpractice actions to $1,250,000. The district court determined that the damages limitation was unconstitutional because it denied the appellees Colin M. Gourley and his parents, Michael J. Gourley and Lisa A. Gourley, equal protection of the law and a right to a jury trial. The appellants, Michelle S. Knolla, M.D., and Obstetricians–Gynecologists, P.C., doing business as the OB/GYN Group, contend that the district court erred in determining that § 44–2825(1) was unconstitutional. * * *

I. NATURE OF CASE. The Gourleys brought this medical malpractice action against * * * Knolla; [and] * * * OB/GYN Group. * * * The Gourleys sought damages for injuries sustained by Colin because of the alleged negligent care Lisa received during her pregnancy. A jury awarded the Gourleys $5,625,000, and the district court entered judgment for the Gourleys in that amount and against Knolla and the OB/GYN Group.

II. BACKGROUND. During her pregnancy, Lisa received prenatal care from Knolla, an obstetrician and gynecologist employed with the OB/GYN Group. On November 15, 1993, in the 36th week of her pregnancy, Lisa informed Knolla that she noticed less movement from the twin fetuses she was carrying. Knolla assured Lisa that this was common and that everything appeared to be normal. Two days later, Lisa called the OB/GYN Group to again report a lack of fetal movement and was told to come to the office to meet with Dietrich. Dietrich's examination revealed that one of the fetuses suffered from bradycardia, a decrease in the fetus' heart rate, and a lack of amniotic fluid. Dietrich instructed Lisa to proceed to Methodist Hospital for examination by Robertson, who was employed by Perinatal Associates.

During his examination, Robertson determined that an immediate cesarean section should be performed. Shortly thereafter, Colin and his twin brother, Connor, were delivered. Colin was born with brain damage and currently suffers from cerebral palsy and significant physical, cognitive, and behavioral difficulties.

The Gourleys filed suit alleging that Knolla and the OB/GYN Group failed to monitor Lisa and Colin while they were under their care. * * *

The jury found Knolla and the OB/GYN Group to be 60 percent and 40 percent negligent, respectively. The jury awarded the Gourleys $5,625,000. * * *

The court * * * concluded that the cap on damages in § 44–2825(1) violated equal protection under Neb. Const. art. I, § 3. The court also concluded that § 44–2825(1) violated the Gourleys' right to a jury trial under Neb. Const. art. I, § 6. * * * The court * * * entered judgment for the Gourleys and against Knolla and the OB/GYN Group, jointly and severally, in the full amount of $5,625,000. Knolla and the OB/GYN Group appeal.

III. ASSIGNMENTS OF ERROR. Knolla and the OB/GYN Group assign that the district court erred in * * * declaring unconstitutional the damages cap of the Nebraska Hospital–Medical Liability Act, § 44–2825. * * *

The Gourleys argue that the cap violates principles of (1) special legislation, (2) equal protection, (3) open courts and right to a remedy, (4) right to a jury trial, (5) taking of property, and (6) separation of powers. The Gourleys rely solely on provisions of the state Constitution.

The Gourleys do not argue that the cap violates substantive due process or deprives them of life, liberty, and the pursuit of happiness as listed in their motion for new trial. Other than arguing equal protection, the Gourleys do not argue that Neb. Const. art. I, § 3, applies to their case. The Gourleys also did not argue to the trial court that the cap is unconstitutional as applied, nor do they make that argument on appeal.

When specific constitutional questions are presented, courts will not search for constitutional authority that was not raised and argued by the parties to overthrow a legislative enactment. [citations] Thus, we will consider only the specific constitutional arguments that the Gourleys raise and argue. Because we are asked to review numerous alternate grounds for finding the cap unconstitutional, we generally address the constitutional issues concerning the Gourleys' contentions.

Statutory Provisions and Background. The Nebraska Hospital–Medical Liability Act was created to address a perceived medical liability crisis. The act created a medical review panel, capped the amount of damages that could be recovered, and created the Excess Liability Fund. Neb.Rev.Stat. §§ 44–2801 et seq. Under the act, health care providers that do not opt out of the act's coverage must file proof of financial responsibility with the Director of Insurance and pay surcharges for the excess liability fund. §§ 44–2821 and 44–2824. The act allows patients to opt out of the act's coverage. § 44–2821(3). Section 44–2825 provides:

(1) The total amount recoverable under the Nebraska Hospital Medical Liability Act from any and all health care providers and the Excess Liability Fund for any occurrence resulting in any injury or death of a patient may not exceed * * * (c) one million two hundred fifty thousand dollars for any occurrence after December 31, 1992.

(2) A health care provider qualified under the act shall not be liable to any patient or his or her representative who is covered by the act for an amount in excess of two hundred thousand dollars. * * * [A]ny amount due from a judgment or settlement which is in excess of the total liability of all liable health care providers shall be paid from the Excess Liability Fund.

Special Legislation. The Gourleys contend that § 44–2825(1) is unconstitutional special legislation because it provides a special privilege to health care professionals while placing a burden on the most severely injured plaintiffs.

Neb. Const. art. III, § 18, provides:

The Legislature shall not pass local or special laws in any of the following cases, that is to say:

* * * *

Granting to any corporation, association, or individual any special or exclusive privileges, immunity, or franchise whatever. * * * In all other cases where a general law can be made applicable, no special law shall be enacted.

We described the purpose of the constitutional safeguard against special legislation in Haman v. Marsh, 237 Neb. 699, 709, 467 N.W.2d 836, 844–45 (1991), as follows:

> By definition, a legislative act is general, and not special, if it operates alike on all persons of a class or on persons who are brought within the relations and circumstances provided for and if the classification so adopted by the Legislature has a basis in reason and is not purely arbitrary. * * * General laws embrace the whole of a subject, with their subject matter of common interest to the whole state. Uniformity is required in order to prevent granting to any person, or class of persons, the privileges or immunities which do not belong to all persons. * * * It is because the legislative process lacks the safeguards of due process and the tradition of impartiality which restrain the courts from using their powers to dispense special favors that such constitutional prohibitions against special legislation were enacted.

Thus, the focus of the prohibition against special legislation is the prevention of legislation which arbitrarily benefits or grants "special favors" to a specific class.

A legislative act constitutes special legislation if it creates an arbitrary and unreasonable method of classification. * * *

We have consistently stated that the test for determining the constitutionality of classifications is as follows:

> "A legislative classification, in order to be valid, must be based upon some reason of public policy, some substantial difference of situation or circumstances, that would naturally suggest the justice or expediency of diverse legislation with respect to objects to be classified. Classifications for the purpose of legislation must be real and not illusive; they cannot be based on distinctions without a substantial difference." "Classification is proper if the special class has some reasonable distinction from other subjects of a like general character, which distinction bears some reasonable relation to the legitimate objectives and purposes of the legislation. The question is always whether the things or persons classified by the act form by themselves a proper and legitimate class with reference to the purpose of the act."

State ex rel. Douglas v. Marsh, 207 Neb. 598, 609, 300 N.W.2d 181, 187 (1980). [citations]

We note that a special legislation analysis is similar to an equal protection analysis, and often the two are discussed together because, at times, both issues can be decided on the same facts. [citation] As a result, language normally applied to an equal protection analysis is sometimes used to help explain the reasoning employed under a special legislation analysis. But the focus of each test is different. The analysis under a special legislation inquiry focuses on the Legislature's purpose in creating the class and asks if there is a substantial difference of circumstances to suggest the expediency of diverse legislation. This is different from an equal protection analysis under which the state interest in legislation is compared to the statutory means selected by the Legislature to accomplish that purpose. Under an equal protection analysis, differing levels of scrutiny are applied depending on if the legislation involves a suspect class. [citations]

This court has upheld the constitutionality of the Nebraska Hospital Medical Liability Act. Prendergast v. Nelson, 199 Neb. 97, 256 N.W.2d 657 (1977), [which was a physician's attack on the medical review panel.] Discussing equal protection, we first held there was a reasonable basis for the classification. Then, in response to the argument that the medical review panel constituted a special privilege for the health care provider and imposed an undue burden on the seriously injured patient, we stated:

> In this respect it must be remembered the Nebraska procedure is an elective one. Under the election, the act guarantees the claimant an assured fund * * * for the payment of any malpractice claim he [or she] may have. Under the common law remedy [the claimant] had no such guarantee. * * *

> Additionally, the claimant is assured of a procedure which will provide him access to an impartial medical review panel to determine whether the health care provider met the applicable standard of care. In return, claimant by his election agrees to the [cap]. * * * [T]he classification rests on reasons of public policy and a substantial difference between medical care providers and other tort-feasors. Suffice it to say that the constitutional safeguard is offended only if the classification rests on grounds wholly irrelevant to the achievement of the state's objective. * * * Nothing in the act suggests, as defendant infers, that the legislation involved was enacted for the relief of the medical care provider. The enactment was, and so appears to us to be, in the public interest. This is paramount. * * *

[E]ven before *Prendergast* was decided, this court recognized the Legislature's concern over the rising cost of malpractice insurance and the substantial difference between medical practitioners and other tort-feasors. When holding that the statute of limitations for malpractice actions did not constitute special legislation, we stated:

> There are substantial reasons for legislative discrimination in regard to this field. We have seen in recent years the growth of malpractice litigation to the point where numerous insurance companies have withdrawn from this field. Insurance rates are practically prohibitive so that many professional people must either remain unprotected or pass the insurance charges along to their patients and clientele in the form of exorbitant fees and charges. This unduly burdens the public which requires professional services.

Taylor v. Karrer, 196 Neb. 581, 586, 244 N.W.2d 201, 204 (1976). * * *

[I]n 2000, this court quoted and relied on language from *Prendergast,* stating that in *Prendergast,* we were "dealing with the fundamental right to adequate medical care" and affirming " 'the right of the Legislature to exercise the police power to promote the general health and welfare of the citizens of this state.' " Bergan Mercy Health Sys. v. Haven, 260 Neb. 846, 857, 620 N.W.2d 339, 348 (2000). We also quoted *Prendergast* as follows:

> "Defendant * * * assumes the legislation was enacted to relieve doctors or insurance companies of some of their burden. We do not accept defendant's premise. Doctors and insurance companies are able to protect themselves against financial burdens by passing the cost on to their patients. Because they were doing so, [they] created part of the problem. The Legislature deemed it necessary to exercise its police power to make available qualified medical services at reasonable prices for the Nebraska public. We find no constitutional violation of this effort."

Thus, we have recognized on repeated occasions that the classification in the Nebraska Hospital–Medical Liability Act is based upon a reason of public policy.

Further, we have recognized the existence of a substantial difference of situation or circumstances that justified diverse legislation for the classification.

The Gourleys argue, however, that § 44–2825(1) was not justified. The Gourleys point out that there was disagreement in the Legislature at the time § 44–2825(1) was enacted and conflicting testimony at the hearing on the motion for new trial. Thus, they argue that there never was an insurance crisis and that lifting the cap would have little effect on the cost of medical services. The Gourleys essentially ask that we independently review the wisdom of enacting the cap. We decline to do so. * * *

It is commonly held that courts will not reexamine independently the factual basis on which a legislature justified a statute, nor will a court independently review the wisdom of the statute. [citations] This court does not sit as a superlegislature to review the wisdom of legislative acts. [citations]

Also, all reasonable intendments must be indulged to support the constitutionality of legislative acts, including classifications adopted by the Legislature. If the Legislature had any evidence to justify its reasons for passing the act, then it is not special legislation if the class is based upon some reason of public policy, some substantial difference of situation or circumstances, that would naturally suggest the justice or expediency of diverse legislation concerning the objects to be classified. See Prendergast v. Nelson. We reach this determination by considering what the Legislature could have found at the time the act was passed.

It is not this court's place to second-guess the Legislature's reasoning behind passing the act. Likewise, "it is up to the legislature and not this Court to decide whether its legislation continues to meet the purposes for which it was originally enacted." * * * Because we give deference to legislative factfinding and presume statutes to be constitutional, any argument that the record contains evidence that the act was not wise or necessary when it was enacted does not change the analysis. * * *

At the committee hearing, the Legislature heard from both proponents and opponents of the act. There was testimony from witnesses indicating that there was a problem recruiting physicians in the state and that increases in medical malpractice insurance were raising the cost of medical care. Public Health and Welfare Committee Hearing, L.B. 703, 84th Leg., 2d Sess. (Jan. 27, 1976). There was also testimony that a cap would not affect the cost of medical care, and some expressed the belief that the act was nothing more than a boon for insurance companies. Generally, the proponents of the act expressed concern that an insurance crisis existed, but admitted that it was likely impossible to know if a cap on damages would solve the problem. Based on the information before it, the Legislature generally believed that a damages cap would solve the problem, especially when combined with the medical review panel and the Excess Liability Fund. Thus, the Legislature set out a specific statement of findings and intent in the Nebraska Hospital–Medical Liability Act. In § 44–2801, the Legislature stated:

(1) The Legislature finds and declares that it is in the public interest that competent medical and hospital services be available to the public in the State of Nebraska at reasonable costs, and that prompt and efficient methods be provided for eliminating the expense as well as the useless expenditure of time of physicians and courts in nonmeritorious malpractice claims and for efficiently resolving meritorious claims. It is essential in this state to assure continuing availability of medical care and to encourage

physicians to enter into the practice of medicine in Nebraska and to remain in such practice as long as such physicians retain their qualifications. (2) The Legislature further finds that at the present time under the system in effect too large a percentage of the cost of malpractice insurance is received by individuals other than the injured party. The intent of sections 44–2801 to 44–2855 is to serve the public interest by providing an alternative method for determining malpractice claims in order to improve the availability of medical care, to improve its quality and to reduce the cost thereof, and to [e]nsure the availability of malpractice insurance coverage at reasonable rates.

Here, the Legislature had evidence to justify their reasons for passing the act. The class is based upon reasons of public policy and substantial differences of situation or circumstances that suggested the justice or expediency of diverse legislation.

Other states have also expressed agreement that a cap on damages for medical malpractice does not constitute special legislation. [citations]

To the extent that other courts have found damages caps to constitute special legislation, those cases do not conform to our legal precedent and are unpersuasive. [citations] We conclude that the cap does not violate principles prohibiting special legislation.

Equal Protection. The Gourleys next contend that the cap violates the equal protection clause of the Nebraska Constitution. They first argue that the cap affects fundamental rights and ask that this court apply a "searching" or rigorous review.

Neb. Const. art. I, § 3, states: "No person shall be deprived of life, liberty, or property, without due process of law, nor be denied equal protection of the laws." * * *

The Equal Protection Clause does not forbid classifications; it simply keeps governmental decisionmakers from treating differently persons who are in all relevant respects alike. [citation] In any equal protection challenge to a statute, the degree of judicial scrutiny to which the statute is to be subjected may be dispositive. If a legislative classification involves either a suspect class or a fundamental right, courts will analyze the statute with strict scrutiny. Under this test, strict accordance must exist between the classification and the statute's purpose. The result the Legislature seeks to effectuate must be a compelling state interest, and the means employed in the statute must be such that no less restrictive alternative exists. On the other hand, if a statute involves economic or social legislation not implicating a fundamental right or suspect class, courts will ask only whether a rational relationship exists between a legitimate state interest and the statutory means selected by the Legislature to accomplish that end. Upon a showing that such a rational relationship exists, courts will uphold the legislation. [citations] Some legislative classifications, such as those based on gender, are reviewed under an intermediate level of scrutiny. [citation]

A majority of jurisdictions apply a rational basis or other similar test and determine that a statutory cap on damages does not violate equal protection. [citations] A few jurisdictions have applied a heightened standard under their state constitution. [citations]

The Gourleys contend that a heightened level of scrutiny should be applied to this case because the cap affects fundamental rights such as the right to a jury trial, full remedy, property, and medical care. They also argue that the cap affects a suspect class because plaintiffs with damages awards over the cap are "saddled with disabilities." * * * We disagree that a heightened level of scrutiny should be applied.

The right of access to the courts is important, but that right is impaired only by state action that limits or blocks access to the courts. [citation] The damages cap at issue does not limit access to the courts. Instead, it limits a plaintiff's recovery in court. Further, access to the courts to pursue redress for injuries is not the type of fundamental right which requires heightened scrutiny. [citation] In addition, the classification created by § 44–2825 is not based on suspect criteria. Instead, the Gourleys' interest in unlimited damages is economic. [citations] We find no merit in the argument that plaintiffs with damages awards over the cap are a suspect class. * * * Because the interests at issue are economic, we apply the rational basis test.

Under the rational basis test, the Equal Protection Clause is satisfied as long as there is (1) a plausible policy reason for the classification, (2) the legislative facts on which the classification is apparently based may rationally have been considered to be true by the governmental decisionmaker, and (3) the relationship of the classification to its goal is not so attenuated as to render the distinction arbitrary or irrational. [citation] The rational relationship standard is the most relaxed and tolerant form of judicial scrutiny under the Equal Protection Clause. [citation] Thus, when determining whether a rational basis exists for a legislative classification, courts look to see if any state of facts can be conceived to reasonably justify the disparate treatment which results. [citation]

As with their arguments about special legislation, the Gourleys contend that the act was unwise and unnecessary. But as we already discussed, we will not second guess the conclusions of the Legislature. Further, in economics and social welfare, a statute does not violate the Equal Protection Clause merely because the classifications made by its laws are imperfect. [citation] The fact that other schemes could have been selected does not mean that the scheme chosen is constitutionally infirm. [citation] As long as the classification scheme chosen by the Legislature rationally advances a reasonable and identifiable governmental objective, a court must disregard the existence of other methods that other individuals might have preferred. [citation] Social and economic measures run afoul of the Equal Protection Clause only when the varying treatment of different groups or persons is so unrelated to the achievement of any combination of legitimate purposes that a court can only conclude that the Legislature's actions were irrational. [citation]

The district court concluded that § 44–2825 was unconstitutional partially because it is a cap on all damages instead of a cap on only noneconomic damages. This does not change the analysis. A statute will not offend equal protection if a rational relationship exists between a legitimate state interest and the statutory means selected by the Legislature to accomplish that end. We note that other courts have upheld statutes that cap all damages. [citations]

Here, the Legislature was concerned about a perceived insurance crisis that could affect the ability of the state to recruit and retain physicians and increase the costs of medical care. Reducing health care costs and encouraging the provision of medical services are legitimate goals which can reasonably be thought to be furthered by lowering the amount of medical malpractice judgments. [citation]

We have previously recognized these goals as legitimate legislative concerns. Prendergast v. Nelson. Also, a rational relationship exists between the concern and the statutory means selected by the Legislature to accomplish its goal. We note that § 44–2825 was generally based on an Indiana act. [citation] In Johnson v. St. Vincent Hospital, 273 Ind. 374, 404 N.E.2d 585 (1980), the Indiana Supreme Court upheld the damages cap in the Indiana act, and it noted that the act established a form of government-sponsored insurance, set limitations upon liability, and placed the burden upon persons injured by the industry. The court then stated:

> An insurance operation cannot be sound if the funds collected are insufficient to meet the obligations incurred. It must, however, be accepted that the badly injured plaintiff who may require constant care will not recover full damages, yet at the same time we are impressed with the large amount which is recoverable and its probable ability to fully compensate a large proportion of injured patients. In the same vein, badly injured patients would have little or no chance of recovering large sums of money if the evil the act was intended to prevent were to come about, i.e., that an environment would develop in the State in which private or public malpractice insurance were unavailable or unused. Of some relevance here is also the fact that after suit and recovery against a health care provider is completed, there continues a total life-time dependency upon other health care providers for vital treatment of the residuum of illness from the prior negligence and of new and unrelated illnesses. Thus to the extent that the limitation upon recovery is successful in preserving the availability of health care services, it does so to the benefit of the entire community including the badly injured plaintiff.

Although one may disagree with this reasoning, the Nebraska Legislature heard similar comments when it was considering enacting § 44–2825.

Finally, we note that some jurisdictions have held that a cap on damages violates equal protection. In some cases, the jurisdiction applied a heightened level of scrutiny, which we reject. [citations] Another is unclear about the level of scrutiny. [citation] Several fail to give deference to the Legislature and engage in judicial factfinding, which we also reject. [citation] Another requires the provision of a replacement remedy, quid pro quo, to limit recovery of damages, which we reject and which will be discussed when dealing with the open courts provision of the Nebraska Constitution. [citation] We find these cases unpersuasive. Thus, we conclude that the cap on damages in § 44–2825 satisfies principles of equal protection.

Open Courts and Right to Remedy. The Gourleys contend that § 44–2825 violates the open courts provision of the Nebraska Constitution and denies them their right to a remedy. They argue that common-law rights and remedies that were in place at the time the constitution was adopted are protected from legislative change.

Neb. Const. art. I, § 13, provides: "All courts shall be open, and every person, for any injury done him or her in his or her lands, goods, person, or reputation, shall have a remedy by due course of law and justice administered without denial or delay. * * * "

A majority of jurisdictions have held that a cap on damages does not violate the open courts and right to remedy provisions of their state constitution.

[citations] A minority of courts have held that a cap on damages violates a state constitution's open courts or right to remedy provision. [citations]

It has long been the law of Nebraska, however, that the Legislature is free to create and abolish rights so long as no vested right is disturbed. [citation] When upholding the constitutionality of the review panel provision of the act, we stated in Prendergast v. Nelson:

> Basically the contention is that the Legislature is powerless to alter a common law right. The law itself as a rule of conduct may be changed at the will or even at the whim of the Legislature unless prevented by constitutional limitations. * * * The Constitution does not forbid the creation of new rights, nor the abolition of old ones recognized by the common law, to attain a permissible legislative object.

Thus, we have held that no one has a vested interest in any rule of the common law or a vested right in any particular remedy. [citation]

The Gourleys contend that rights that were in place when the constitution was adopted are an exception to these rules. In the alternative, they contend that the Legislature cannot change a remedy without providing an adequate replacement, or quid pro quo. We disagree. * * *

In Nebraska, the common law of England was adopted by statute. Neb.Rev. Stat. § 49–101. Thus it exists here by legislative enactment and may be repealed. [citation] Section 44–2825(1) also does not bar access to the courts or deny a remedy. Instead it redefines the substantive law by limiting the amount of damages a plaintiff can recover. Although plaintiffs have a right to pursue recognized causes of action in court, they are not assured that a cause of action will remain immune from legislative or judicial limitation or elimination. [citation]

We have also held that if a common-law right is taken away, nothing need be given in return. Prendergast v. Nelson. Because the Legislature can eliminate a common-law cause of action entirely, it can also alter the remedy for a cause of action without providing a replacement remedy, or quid pro quo. We conclude that § 44–2825(1) does not violate Neb. Const. art. I, § 13.

Jury Trial. The Gourleys contend that the cap violates their right to a trial by jury. Knolla and the OB/GYN Group counter that the Legislature can abolish a common-law cause of action and that therefore, it follows that it can limit the amount of damages that can be recovered.

Neb. Const. art. I, § 6, provides: "The right of trial by jury shall remain inviolate." * * *

Courts are split on whether a cap on damages violates the right to a jury trial. The majority of courts hold that a cap does not violate the right to trial by jury. [citations] Other courts have applied language that is generally the same as the Nebraska Constitution and have concluded that a cap on damages does violate a plaintiff's right to a jury trial. [citations] We disagree with the reasoning of those courts.

The purpose of article I, § 6, is to preserve the right to a jury trial as it existed at common law and under the statutes in force when the constitution was adopted. [citations] The primary function of a jury has always been factfinding, which includes a determination of a plaintiff's damages. [citation] The court, however, applies the law to the facts. Section 44–2825 provides the remedy in a medical malpractice action. The remedy is a question of law, not fact, and is not a matter to be decided by the jury. [citations] Instead, the trial court applies the remedy's limitation only after the jury has fulfilled its factfinding function. [citations]

Further, as we have discussed, the Legislature has the right to completely abolish a common-law cause of action. [citation] If the Legislature has the constitutional power to abolish a cause of action, it also has the power to limit recovery in a cause of action. [citation] We conclude that § 44–2825 does not violate the right to a jury trial.

Taking of Property. The Gourleys next contend that the cap acts to take property in violation of Neb. Const. art. I, § 21. They argue that a cause of action and a jury's determination of damages are property.

Article I, § 21, states: "The property of no person shall be taken or damaged for public use without just compensation therefor." Article I, § 21, applies to vested property rights. [citation]

As previously discussed, we have held that a person has no property and no vested interest in any rule of the common law or a vested right in any particular remedy. [citation] Further, courts have rejected the argument that a cause of action and determination of damages are property. [citations] The cap on damages in § 44–2825 does not violate Neb. Const. art. I, § 21. We conclude that the Gourleys' argument is without merit.

Separation of Powers. The Gourleys contend that § 44–2825 violates the separation of powers provision of Neb. Const. art. II, § 1. They argue that the cap legislatively transfers their property to another, acts as a legislative remittitur, and acts as a legislative judgment on damages.

We have already stated that a person has no property and no vested interest in any rule of the common law or a vested right in any particular remedy. [citation] The Gourleys' argument about the legislative transfer of property is without merit. We also find no merit in the argument that the cap acts as a legislative judgment of damages. As we have discussed, the Legislature may abolish a common-law right or remedy. For the same reasons the cap does not violate the right to a jury trial, it also does not act as a legislative determination of the amount of damages in any specific case.

We note that one court has held that a cap on damages improperly delegates to the Legislature the power to remit verdicts and judgments. Best v. Taylor Mach. Works. In *Best,* the court concluded that the determination whether a verdict was excessive was a discretionary function of the trial court and that a cap on damages improperly delegated that function to the Legislature.

Other courts, however, have determined that a cap on damages does not violate principles of separation of powers. [citations] Most of these courts have specifically disagreed with the reasoning that a cap acts as a legislative remittitur. [citations] * * *

We agree that the damages cap does not act as a legislative remittitur or otherwise violate principles of separation of powers. The cap does not ask the Legislature to review a specific dispute and determine the amount of damages. Instead—without regard to the facts of a particular case—the cap imposes a limit on recovery in all medical malpractice cases as a matter of legislative policy. We have stated repeatedly that the Legislature may change or abolish a cause of action. Thus, the ability to cap damages in a cause of action is a proper legislative function. [citations] We determine that the cap on damages does not violate art. II, § 1. * * *

CONCLUSION. We reverse that portion of the district court's judgment finding that § 44–2825(1) is unconstitutional and affirm the judgment in all other respects. The district court shall enter judgment for the Gourleys in the amount of $1,250,000.

CONNOLLY, J., concurring. * * * [T]he dissent would apply to a special legislation analysis a level of scrutiny comparable to the intermediate scrutiny test employed in an equal protection analysis. This is incorrect because, as the majority opinion states, the special legislation test is not a heightened test. Instead, it is simply a different test from that of equal protection. The rule advocated by the dissent introduces principles of equal protection into a special legislation analysis. Under the dissent's rule, legislation that was subject to a rational basis review under equal protection would always receive heightened scrutiny under a special legislation analysis. The effect would be a back door way of using an equal protection analysis to find legislation that passes muster under equal protection to be unconstitutional. A special legislation analysis has a different focus from an equal protection analysis and should not be used as a second equal protection clause under which everyone gets heightened scrutiny.

GERRARD, J., concurring. In 1976, a precipitous process in the final stage of legislation led to the enactment of the Nebraska Hospital–Medical Liability Act. The act in significant instances unfairly deprives the Gourleys of the full measure of *economic damages* that is the most fundamental element of a meaningful recovery for negligently injured people. In a number of cases, people injured through no fault of their own will be unable to even collect their proven medical expenses. While I reluctantly concur with the per curiam opinion's conclusion that the act does not violate any of the provisions of the Nebraska Constitution that have been raised, briefed, and argued in this case, it would be injudicious to sit idly by and silently concur in a matter of such importance to so many parties. I, therefore, write separately to express my serious concerns about the public policy upon which the act is purportedly based and whether the act adequately protects the substantive due process rights of injured persons.

ECONOMIC AND NONECONOMIC DAMAGES. The Nebraska Hospital–Medical Liability Act, Neb.Rev.Stat. § 44–2801 et seq. limits an injured person to a total recovery of $1,250,000 for any single occurrence of medical professional malpractice. See § 44–2825(1). This limitation on total recovery ignores the distinctions to be made between different measures of damages and, as in the present case, can result in the inability of injured persons to recover even the expenses for their medical care. This unwarranted restriction on economic damages is, in my view, a fundamental flaw.

There are two separate types of compensatory damages, economic and noneconomic. Economic damages include the cost of medical care, past and future, and related benefits, i.e., lost wages, loss of earning capacity, and other such losses. Noneconomic losses include claims for pain and suffering, mental anguish, injury and disfigurement not affecting earning capacity, and losses which cannot be easily expressed in dollars and cents. [citations] While both economic and noneconomic damages are intended to compensate plaintiffs for their injuries, they do so in fundamentally different ways. Money damages are, at best, an imperfect means of compensating plaintiffs for intangible injuries.

The effects of economic losses, on the other hand, can be fully ameliorated by the payment of money damages.

In other words, while the legal system cannot undo pain and suffering, it can and should provide that medical expenses be fully paid. * * *

Noneconomic damages are generally the largest portion of a medical liability settlement. [citation] More significantly, unbridled noneconomic damages have been said to present the primary threat to maintaining reasonable malpractice premiums, because such awards are based on highly subjective perceptions and resist actuarial prediction. [citations]

Recognizing these basic principles, the substantial majority of states that have enacted limitations on medical malpractice damages have limited noneconomic damages, but allowed complete recovery for economic losses. [citations] Similarly, several courts upholding the constitutional validity of such limitations have, in so doing, noted the distinction between economic and noneconomic damages. [citations] * * *

EXCESS LIABILITY FUND. * * * [T]here is little suggestion that the Legislature fully considered how the different aspects of the act would interact. The primary concern of the Legislature seems to have been the problem of increasing malpractice insurance premiums, and it is evident that the cap on total damages was intended to reduce those premiums. However, an examination of the statutory scheme demonstrates that there is no significant relationship between the cap on total recovery and malpractice insurance premiums, because of the intervening effect of the Excess Liability Fund.

Under the act, a qualified health care provider shall not be liable to any patient for an amount in excess of $200,000 arising from any occurrence. See § 44–2825(2). Instead, subject to the overall limit established by § 44–2825(1), any amount due from a judgment in excess of the total liability of all liable health care providers shall be paid from the Excess Liability Fund. See § 44–2825(3). Health care providers are required to maintain professional liability insurance in the amount of $200,000 per occurrence. See § 44–2827.

To compensate for judgments above $200,000 per qualified health care provider, but below the cap on total recovery, the act creates the Excess Liability Fund (hereinafter the Fund), which is supported by a surcharge levied on all qualified health care providers. See § 44–2829. The amount of the surcharge is established by the Director of Insurance and is intended to maintain a reserve in the Fund "sufficient to pay all anticipated claims for the next year and to maintain an adequate reserve for future claims." See § 44–2830. * * *

The effect of this scheme is to attenuate, if not almost completely sever, the relationship between the cap on total recovery and malpractice insurance premiums. Malpractice insurance premiums are established based on actuarial principles which generally evaluate, inter alia, the risk of liability and the predicted value of successful claims. [citation] Because of the Fund, however, the exposure of malpractice insurance carriers is limited to $200,000 arising out of any single occurrence for any single care provider. It is that figure, and not the cap on total liability, which must provide the primary basis for actuarial determinations of malpractice insurance premiums.

The cap on total recovery, then, has some, but minimal, bearing on the market cost of medical malpractice insurance. The cap on total recovery does not serve to limit the liability of malpractice insurers; instead, it limits the liability of the Fund. Unfortunately, the Legislature, in enacting the act, does not seem to have reflected on whether each of the specific provisions of the act were necessary or warranted in light of the remaining provisions. When considering the public policy rationale for the cap on total liability—and, more particularly, the cap on economic damages—the question is, To what extent can a limitation on recovery for proven economic losses be justified by a need to limit the potential liability of the Fund?

SUBSTANTIVE DUE PROCESS. In my view, this question, when placed in its proper constitutional framework, implicates the constitutional right to substantive due process of law. There is a substantial overlap between the tests applied under due process and equal protection analysis. [citation] The distinction is that equal protection and special legislation analyses are focused on the classes created by a statute and whether there is justification for making such classifications and treating those classes differently. [citation] Due process, on the other hand, questions the justification for abrogating a particular legal right, and the appropriate scrutiny is determined by the importance of the right that is at issue. [citation] Thus, while the act does not create suspect classifications, and there may be some rational basis for treating health care tort-feasors differently from other tort-feasors, whether economic damages may be taken from negligently injured persons is a separate issue and calls for a different constitutional analysis. Because my concerns regard the nature of the basic right that has been taken—the right to recover for proven economic damages—those concerns are properly addressed by a due process analysis.

However, as the per curiam opinion correctly determines, the issue of substantive due process has not been brought before this court, and we are precluded from deciding, on the record and briefing before us, whether the act comports with that constitutional mandate. Nonetheless, my judicial responsibilities compel me to express my serious reservations regarding the act's satisfaction of constitutional due process, for the benefit of other litigants, the members of the Legislature, and their constituents, the public.

The Nebraska Constitution provides that "[n]o person shall be deprived of life, liberty, or property, without due process of law. * * *" Neb. Const. art. I, § 3. The concept of due process embodies the notion of fundamental fairness and defies precise definition. [citation] The primary purpose of that constitutional guaranty is security of the individual from the arbitrary exercise of the powers of government. [citation] The Legislature may not, under the guise of regulation, set forth conditions which are unreasonable, arbitrary, discriminatory, or confiscatory. [citation] * * *

[M]easures adopted by the Legislature to protect the public health and secure the public safety and welfare must still have some reasonable relation to those proposed ends. [citations] There must be some clear and real connection between the assumed purpose of the law and its actual provisions. [citation] * * *

[T]he question [is] whether the right to recover for economic losses is important enough to merit heightened scrutiny under the Nebraska Constitution. Although this court, because of the limitation on the issues presented, has no occasion in this case to determine the appropriate level of scrutiny to be applied in a due process analysis of a cap on economic damages, it is worth noting that several courts have concluded the right to recover damages for personal injury is essential, and caps on damages are subject to heightened judicial scrutiny in making constitutional determinations. [citations] As explained by the Supreme Court of South Dakota:

> Medical bills, lost wages, and prescription costs are tangible damages, whereas pain and suffering and like damages are largely intangible. Unbridled noneconomic damage awards present a real threat to maintaining reasonable malpractice insurance premiums, because such awards are unpredictable and based on highly subjective perceptions. * * * In truth, however, the * * * flat cap on total damages potentially cuts not only fat, but muscle, bone and marrow. If a malpractice patient's hospital bill, for example, exceeds the cap, then the patient can recover nothing for the remaining medical bills, future bills, past and future income lost, prescriptions, etc.

Matter of Certif. of Questions of Law, 544 N.W.2d 183, 200 (S.D.1996). The right to such recovery "is a substantial property right, not only of monetary value but in many cases fundamental to the injured person's physical well-being and ability to continue to live a decent life." Condemarin v. University Hosp., 775 P.2d 348, 360 (Utah 1989).

The facts of the instant case demonstrate the callous effect of denying recovery for economic damages. The record shows that Colin suffered severe brain damage and will, for the rest of his life, be afflicted by cerebral palsy and extensive physical, cognitive, and behavioral deficiencies. The economic evidence presented by the Gourleys sets forth the expenses likely to be incurred over the course of Colin's life because of his disabilities, including medications, care, and medical treatment and equipment. The Gourleys' expert testified, without contradiction, that the expenses for Colin's care will total $12,461,500.22 over the course of his life. This figure has a present value of $5,943,111, of which the jury awarded $5 million. In short, it is undisputed that the Gourleys will recover, because of § 44–2825(1), less than one-fourth of Colin's medical expenses alone.

This effect on the quality of life of an injured child, incurred because of a statutory limitation on the right to collect economic damages, must be balanced against the act's only direct effect: the maintenance of the Fund. The evidence in this case does not indicate that the Fund requires financial protection. In fact, the evidence is far to the contrary. In 1998, the surcharge for qualified health care providers was 5 percent. The balance in the Fund at the end of 1998 was $62,625,074, and the estimated liabilities of (i.e., potential claims against) the Fund at that time were $24,014,000. Between 1990 and 1998, the amount of total claims paid in any given year ranged from a low of $1,795,069 in 1990 to a high of $4,197,308 in 1991. In 1998, the Fund *earned* over three times more than it paid out in claims, even disregarding the additional funds obtained through the surcharge (which, it should be noted, was only one-tenth of the surcharge permitted under the act).

Given the stark comparison between the assets of the Fund and the potential poverty that can result from forcing negligently injured persons to find their own means of paying for catastrophic medical expenses, it may ultimately be determined that the act, in capping recovery for economic damages, is unconstitutional as applied to plaintiffs whose proven economic damages exceed the cap. This would not render the act completely inoperative, but would prelude application of the cap where it would prevent a complete recovery of economic damages. [citations] * * *

However, the discretion of the Legislature is circumscribed, as always, by the Nebraska Constitution, particularly where the abrogation of fundamental rights is concerned. The effect of the act on a substantial right—recovery of economic damages—is especially troubling, and potentially unreasonable, when balanced against the negligible effect that such recovery would have on the Fund.

The parties in this case have not presented the question whether the act, as applied, violates substantive due process, and I agree with the per curiam opinion's determination that we should not overthrow a legislative enactment on the basis of authority not raised and argued by the parties. The per curiam opinion expressly reserves ruling on such issues, which means that some of the most important questions about the act remain, for the time being, unanswered. This does not, however, prevent the Legislature from considering whether the act, in its current form, is fair, wise, or necessary, nor should it preclude legislative changes to protect both the constitutional validity of the act and the well-being of the citizens of Nebraska.

CONCLUSION. As previously stated, I concur, albeit grudgingly, in the per curiam opinion's conclusions regarding the constitutional challenges to the act. I join in the opinion of the court regarding the other issues presented. I remain deeply troubled by the public policy choices reflected in the act, particularly the denial of economic recovery to negligently injured persons. It is pointedly unfair, and may well prove unconstitutional, for the law of this state to safeguard a surplus of tens of millions of dollars in the Excess Liability Fund by denying negligently injured persons money for needed medical care and potentially condemning them to undue poverty. But, because this case does not afford us the opportunity to decide that constitutional question, I reluctantly concur in the judgment of the court.

HENDRY, C.J., * * * dissenting. I concur with Justice Gerrard insofar as he suggests that the cap on damages imposed by Neb.Rev.Stat. § 44–2825(1) may violate substantive due process rights of injured persons. I write separately, however, to state that * * * I believe the Gourleys lack standing to challenge the Nebraska Hospital–Medical Liability Act as unconstitutional special legislation in violation of Neb. Const. art. III, § 18. * * *

I believe that the general class of persons standing in the same relation to the privilege would be all other health care professionals who are not "health care providers" as defined by the act, but who nonetheless may be liable "for bodily injury or death on account of alleged malpractice, professional negligence, failure to provide care, breach of contract, or other claim based upon failure to obtain informed consent for an operation or treatment." Neb.Rev.Stat. § 44–2822. Such individuals could include, for example, optometrists [citations]; dentists [citations]; and chiropractors [citation].

I therefore conclude that the only persons who would have standing to assert that § 44–2825(1) is unconstitutional special legislation are such members of the general class who do not benefit from the privilege of the cap on damages pursuant to § 44–2825(1). [citations] Because in my view the Gourleys lack standing, I reserve judgment as to whether § 44–2825(1) violates Neb. Const. art. III, § 18, until the proper party, together with an adequate and proper record, is before the court. * * *

McCORMACK, J., * * * dissenting. * * * I respectfully dissent from the per curiam opinion's analysis of the constitutionality of Neb.Rev.Stat. § 44–2825(1).

(the cap). I would find that the cap is special legislation in violation of Neb. Const. art. III, § 18. * * *

SPECIAL LEGISLATION. Neb. Const. art. III, § 18, provides:

The Legislature shall not pass local or special laws in any of the following cases, that is to say: * * * Granting to any corporation, association, or individual any special or exclusive privileges, immunity, or franchise whatever. * * * In all other cases where a general law can be made applicable, no special law shall be enacted. * * *

It is because the legislative process lacks the safeguards of due process and the tradition of impartiality which restrain the courts from using their powers to dispense special favors that such constitutional prohibitions against special legislation were enacted.

A legislative act constitutes special legislation, violative of Neb. Const. art. III, § 18, if it creates an arbitrary and unreasonable method of classification. * * *

The tests applied in an equal protection case are well known. If a statute involves economic or social legislation not implicating a fundamental right or suspect class, courts will ask only whether a rational relationship exists between a legitimate state interest and the statutory means selected by the Legislature to accomplish that end. [citation] * * * Upon a showing that such a rational relationship exists, courts will uphold the legislation. [citation] The intermediate scrutiny test requires that a party seeking to uphold a statute that classifies individuals must show that the classification serves important governmental objectives and that the discriminatory means employed are *substantially* related to achievement of those objectives. See Mississippi University for Women v. Hogan, 458 U.S. 718 (1982). Finally, if a legislative classification involves either a suspect class or a fundamental right, courts will analyze the statute with strict scrutiny. Under this test, strict congruence must exist between the classification and the statute's purpose. The end the Legislature seeks to effectuate must be a compelling state interest, and the means employed in the statute must be such that no less restrictive alternative exists. [citation]

In Haman v. Marsh, 237 Neb. 699, 713, 467 N.W.2d 836, 846 (1991), we described special legislation as being a "narrower" test than equal protection. We further explained that "[t]he test of validity under the special legislation prohibition is *more stringent* than the traditional rational basis test." The level of scrutiny required by the above-mentioned test is "more stringent" because of the requirement that classifications be based upon some *"substantial"* difference of situation or circumstances. [citations]

Because the test of validity under the special legislation prohibition is more stringent than the traditional rational basis test, I would apply a level of scrutiny comparable to the intermediate scrutiny test. It is well known that the degree of judicial scrutiny to which the statute is to be subjected may be dispositive. [citation] That has proved to be the case in other states that have analyzed caps. Those states that have subjected caps to the minimal rational basis test have, as one might expect, found their caps to be constitutional. [citations] However, caps have generally been unable to survive a more stringent level of scrutiny. [citations]

In analyzing a special legislation claim, we must determine (1) the privilege created by the statute, (2) the particular class which is singled out to receive the privilege, (3) the persons within the general class that is made the subject of the legislation who stand in the same relation to the privilege as the particular class, and (4) whether a substantial difference exists between the particular class and the general class. [citation]

The cap grants a privilege to all health care providers whose negligence causes catastrophic damages, i.e., damages in excess of $1,250,000, because they are liable for less than 100 percent of the damages they cause. The general class standing in the same relation to these health care providers is all other professional service providers who commit malpractice and cause catastrophic damages and who are liable for 100 percent of the damages they cause. Is there a substantial difference between these two classes? I do not believe that there is. Each class provides services to the public. Each class is subject to actions brought by the public for malpractice committed in the course of providing those services to the public. Each class is financially burdened by those actions which prove to be successful. Each class may impose the costs of those successful actions on the public at large. Yet the Legislature has chosen to provide a benefit to one subset of the general class by exempting those health care providers whose negligence causes damages in excess of $1,250,000 from full liability for their negligent actions. Thus, I conclude that the cap is unconstitutional special legislation in violation of Neb. Const. art. III, § 18.

As Justice Gerrard discusses in greater detail, I am equally concerned by the fact that the cap applies to *all* damages, whether economic or noneconomic. Several states have struck down statutes that impose a cap on all damages. [citations] The majority of states with caps in effect today limit only the noneconomic damages a person may recover and do not limit recovery for economic damages. [citation] As the per curiam opinion notes, evidence offered at trial indicates that the Gourleys' economic damages, reduced to present value, is a minimum of $5,943,111. The jury failed to award even this amount, instead awarding $5 million in economic damages and $625,000 in noneconomic damages. However, by applying the cap and slashing the Gourleys' award to $1,250,000, the Gourleys receive an award which will cover only a fraction of their expenses over the course of Colin's lifetime and, in effect, receive nothing for their pain and suffering. [citation] If Nebraska followed the majority of states with caps that limited only noneconomic damages, the Gourleys would have been able to recover a large percentage of the expenses they will be burdened with for the rest of Colin's life. Had a valid challenge to the cap been preserved on substantive due process grounds, I would find that the cap violates that constitutional mandate as well for the reasons expressed by Justice Gerrard in his concurring opinion.

One of the stated purposes of the Nebraska Hospital–Medical Liability Act is to "[e]nsure the availability of malpractice insurance coverage at reasonable rates." Neb.Rev.Stat. § 44–2801(2) (Reissue 1998). As the per curiam opinion states, "the proponents of the act expressed concern that an insurance crisis existed, but admitted that it was likely impossible to know if a cap on damages would solve the problem. Based on the information before it, the Legislature generally believed that a damages cap would solve the problem." Now, 27 years after enactment of the cap, the information available indicates otherwise. [A lengthy discussion of malpractice insurance rates and physicians' incomes is omitted.]

I respectfully dissent from the per curiam opinion's conclusion that the cap is constitutional.

Notes

1. The Nebraska legislature seems to have responded to Justice Gerrard's warning in the last two paragraphs of his opinion by raising the cap to $1,750,000 for "any occurrence after December 31, 2003."

2. *Constitutional Surplus.* In addition to the federal Constitution's Due Process and Equal Protection Clauses, state constitutions contain their own similar clauses. Since the clauses are in state constitutions, however, each state supreme court has the last, unreviewable, word on what its Due Process and Equal Protection Clause mean.

3. *The United States Constitution.* Plaintiffs' federal constitutional challenges to state damages-capping statutes have not succeeded. In Smith v. Botsford General Hospital, the federal court of appeals applied a Michigan cap to a plaintiff's damages in a federal statutory tort. The court cursorily rejected the plaintiff's jury trial and equal protection challenges. The federal court's jury trial reasoning was similar to the *Gourley* court's: if the legislature can abolish a cause of action, it can retain the cause of action and merely limit a plaintiff's damages. The court's equal-protection analysis was brief: the legislature's goal of controlling the cost of health care is economic regulation leading to rational-basis review. Smith v. Botsford General Hospital, 419 F.3d 513 (6th Cir.2005).

The wise plaintiff will argue that a tort-reform statute violates the state's constitution.

4. *State Constitutions.* State supreme courts' interpretations, although not "bound," by, are influenced by the United States Supreme Court's decisions and by other state supreme courts' decisions under their separate but similarly or identically worded clauses. But that's not all.

The state courts' tort-reform decisions introduce us to state constitutional provisions without a federal constitutional counterpart like the ban on "special legislation," the requirement of "open courts," and the "right to a remedy." Once again, each state supreme court has the final word on what its constitution means. Once again, the state courts, although influenced, are not "bound," by other state courts' interpretations. Even though the string citations are removed to shorten the decisions for law-school study, the reader will be struck by the parallel lines of state authority on both sides of most issues. It gets worse.

5. *The Multi–Floored Constitution.* The United States Supreme Court has developed three levels of equal-protection decisions: strict, intermediate, and rational basis. The reader may be pardoned for thinking that due process, equal protection, special legislation, open-court, and right-to-a-remedy are swirling together. Stirring the three levels into the mix may seem to create the height of confusion. Hang on to your hat for a fourth, rational basis with teeth.

6. The separate opinions in *Gourley* seem to agree that a cap on noneconomic damages would be constitutional. However, the Illinois court had not accepted a general cap before *Gourley*, and the Wisconsin court didn't accept a targeted malpractice cap on noneconomic after *Gourley*. In July of 2005, the Wisconsin Supreme Court decided Ferdon ex rel. Petrucelli v. Wisconsin Patients Compensation Fund, 284 Wis.2d 573, 701 N.W.2d 440 (2005).

Matthew Ferdon was injured during birth and suffered a partially paralyzed and deformed right arm. After his malpractice trial against the negligent physician, the jury's verdict included $700,000 for Matthew's "noneconomic" damages.

The Wisconsin legislature had enacted a special Chapter for medical malpractice. We studied the *Lagerstrom* case which dealt with the Chapter's collateral source and subrogation section, p. 102. The Chapter also established a Fund, which Ferdon had sued as a defendant. More to the point, Ferdon's noneconomic damages exceeded the Chapter's cap. The issue the court faced in *Ferdon* was whether the statutory cap on a malpractice plaintiff's noneconomic damages of $350,000, adjusted for inflation to $410,322, violated the equal protection guarantee in the Wisconsin state Constitution

The court invalidated the cap. It divided along the same lines as it had in *Lagerstrom*, Chief Justice Abrahamson writing the majority opinion, Justices Prosser and Roggensack dissenting in separate opinions. The opinion is complex and lengthy. "No other court evaluating a cap on noneconomic damages in [a] medical malpractice case has considered (or at least has not cited) the amount of statistical data and evidence this court has cited in this case," dissenting Justice Prosser observed. The main points in *Ferdon* follow.

"The parties disagree," Chief Justice Abrahamson wrote in her opinion for the majority, "about which level of judicial scrutiny should apply in this case. Matthew Ferdon invites this court to use the strict scrutiny standard in reviewing the statutory $350,000 cap. He argues that the noneconomic damages cap implicates the fundamental right to a trial by jury and the right to a remedy protected by the state constitution. The Fund argues that strict scrutiny is unwarranted and that the proper level of review is rational basis review. * * *

"We agree with the Fund that rational basis, not strict scrutiny, is the appropriate level of scrutiny in the present case. This court has stated that Wis. Stat. chapter 655 does not deny any fundamental right and does not involve a suspect classification. [citations] In the context of wrongful death medical malpractice actions, this court has previously held that '[c]apping noneconomic wrongful death damages does not violate any fundamental right. * * * [citation] * * * Similarly, in examining whether the appointment of six-member compensation panels effectively denied suing patients access to the courts, thereby violating their rights to a jury trial as preserved in Article I, Section 5 of the Wisconsin Constitution, this court held that chapter 655 did not involve fundamental rights or suspect classifications. [citation] As for Article I, Section 9, '[t]his court has never construed the right [to a remedy provision] to be fundamental.' [citation] * * *

"The rational basis test is 'not a toothless one.' [citation] 'Rational basis with teeth,' sometimes referred to as 'rational basis with bite,' focuses on the legislative means used to achieve the ends. [citation] This standard simply requires the court to conduct an inquiry to determine whether the legislation has more than a speculative tendency as the means for furthering a valid legislative purpose. * * *

"Constitutional law scholar Professor Gerald Gunther wrote, * * * that rational basis with teeth is *not* the same as 'intermediate scrutiny.' " [citation] * * *

"The main classification is the distinction between medical malpractice victims who suffer over $350,000 in noneconomic damages, and medical malpractice victims who suffer less than $350,000 in noneconomic damages. That is, the cap divides the universe of injured medical malpractice victims into a class of severely injured victims and less severely injured victims. Severely injured victims with more than $350,000 in noneconomic damages receive only part of their damages; less severely injured victims with $350,000 or less in noneconomic damages receive their full damages. In other words, the statutory cap creates a class of fully compensated victims and partially compensated victims. Thus, the cap's greatest impact falls on the most severely injured victims. * * *

"Young people are most affected by the $350,000 cap on noneconomic damages, not only because they suffer a disproportionate share of serious injuries from medical malpractice, but also because many can expect to be affected by their injuries over a 60– or 70–year life expectancy. This case is a perfect example. Matthew Ferdon has a life expectancy of 69 years; he was injured at birth. An older person with a similarly serious medical malpractice injury will have to live with the injury for a shorter period. Yet both the young and the old are subject to the $350,000 cap on noneconomic damages. * * *

"The legislature enjoys wide latitude in economic regulation. But when the legislature shifts the economic burden of medical malpractice from insurance companies and negligent health care providers to a small group of vulnerable, injured patients, the legislative action does not appear rational. Limiting a patient's recovery on the basis of youth or how many family members he or she has does not appear to be germane to any objective of the law."

The majority identified and examined legislative objectives in setting the cap, among them: assuring that medical providers' liability insurance is available and reasonably priced; reasonable Fund Assessments; lowering the overall cost of medical care; attracting health care providers to Wisconsin, and retaining them once there; and preventing unnecessary tests and other "defensive medicine."

"If the legislature's objective was to ensure that Wisconsin people injured as a result of medical malpractice are compensated fairly, no rational basis exists for treating the most seriously injured patients of medical malpractice less favorably than those less seriously injured. No rational basis exists for forcing the most severely injured patients to provide monetary relief to health care providers and their insurers. * * *

"A rationale sometimes offered for limiting recovery for noneconomic damages is that it is difficult to place a monetary value on such a loss, that money is an imperfect compensation for intangible injuries, and that sympathetic juries may award excessive sums for noneconomic damages. Yet no one contends that the legislature determined that when someone is injured through medical malpractice, the maximum reasonable compensation for noneconomic damages is $350,000. Apparently, $350,000 was selected not necessarily in relation to what constitutes reasonable compensation for the victim, but rather was arrived at as a result of its relation to the other legislative objectives such as lowering medical malpractice premiums and health care costs."

After an extensive and detailed examination, the majority held that none of the legislative objectives supported the classification in the cap.

Finally, "the Fund (and the amici who support the Fund's position) argue that striking down the $350,000 cap on noneconomic damages for common-law medical malpractice actions will mean the end to caps in a variety of other contexts. This 'the sky is falling' argument is unpersuasive. We rest our decision on equal protection grounds. Thus, the decision is limited to the statutes [citations] at issue in the instant case and the facts and rationales motivating and supporting the enactment of the statutes."

Justice Crooks concurred: "I am convinced that the current cap on noneconomic medical malpractice damages is unconstitutional. The stated legislative objectives, when reviewed in accord with a rational basis test, provide insufficient justification for that cap under the equal protection clause and, further, the $350,000 cap is too low to satisfy the right to a jury trial as guaranteed in Article I, Section 5, when considered in conjunction with the right to a remedy in Article I, Section 9 of the Wisconsin Constitution. * * *

"Wisconsin can have a constitutional cap on noneconomic damages in medical malpractice actions, but there must be a rational basis so that the legislative objectives provide legitimate justification, and the cap must not be set so low as to defeat the rights of Wisconsin citizens to jury trials and to legal remedies for wrongs inflicted for which there should be redress."

Justice Prosser dissented: "Caps on noneconomic damages are part of a broad legislative strategy to keep health care affordable and available in a way that will benefit Wisconsinites as a whole. Even when this strategy works exactly as intended, it has the effect of limiting the noneconomic damages for some patients. * * *

" 'Our form of government provides for one legislature, not two.' Flynn v. DOA, 216 Wis.2d 521, 529 (1998). This court is not meant to function as a 'super-legislature,' constantly second-guessing the policy choices made by the legislature and governor. * * *

"Today, a majority of this court utilizes several unacceptable tactics to invalidate a legislative act.

"First, the majority relies on the Wisconsin Constitution, not the United States Constitution, to nullify legislation. This tactic assures that the court's decision will receive minimal scrutiny from legal scholars and no review by the United States Supreme Court.

"Second, the majority alters the test for reviewing the constitutionality of legislation on equal protection grounds, where the legislation does not affect a fundamental right. It moves from a 'rational basis' test, long established in our law, to an intermediate scrutiny test which it euphemistically labels 'rational basis with teeth.'

"Third, the majority lays the groundwork for invalidating other damage caps and preventing the legislature from responding to this decision. When the court insulates its decisions from review by the United States Supreme Court and response by other branches of state government, it is effectively destroying the checks and balances in our constitutional system. * * *

"[T]he opinion gives rational basis a 'makeover,' and it reappears as 'rational basis with teeth.' * * * The 'rational basis with teeth' standard is actually closer to the 'intermediate level of scrutiny' than to rational basis review. * * *

"Constitutional law scholar Laurence Tribe describes rational basis with bite as 'covertly heightened scrutiny,' and warns that 'covert use [of heightened scrutiny] presents dangers of its own.' [citation] * * * In future cases, the majority will be able to rely on 'rational basis with teeth' to invalidate legislation that does not suit the majority's fancy. * * *

"I strongly disagree with the majority's conclusion that the legislature did not have a rational basis to enact the cap on noneconomic damages in medical malpractice actions. * * *

"The majority takes a novel approach to nullifying the damage cap. Instead of concentrating its fire on Wisconsin's enactment of the damage cap, the majority attacks the effectiveness of *any* cap on noneconomic damages *anywhere,* and concludes that no such cap has had any effect at all on any of the five legislative objectives it deduced. * * *

"The breadth of this holding is staggering. It means that, contrary to the majority's narrow statement of the issue, it will be very difficult for Wisconsin legislators to re-enact a cap on noneconomic damages in the future. The majority has attempted to insulate its ruling from legislative reaction and redress by making its ruling so broad. * * *

"Wisconsin's patients compensation system guarantees unlimited coverage of economic damages obtained in a settlement or at trial. It requires doctors to purchase liability insurance coverage and requires health care providers to pay annual assessments into the Fund. Thus, a cap helps ensure predictable and certain compensation for medical malpractice patients.

"By contrast, plaintiffs in other kinds of tort cases, even wrongful death suits in which there is a statutory cap, sometimes may be able to prove more than a million dollars in noneconomic damages but they are rarely able to recover that amount from defendants. That is why underinsured motorist coverage is so important in motor vehicle accidents. * * *

"The majority belittles Ferdon's $410,000 award in noneconomic damages to supplement his $403,000 award for future medical expenses. *This money will be paid.* How many motorists purchase $500,000 in liability coverage in the event they injure another motorist, or $500,000 in underinsured motorist coverage for situations in which they are injured by another driver? If Ferdon were to suffer an equivalent injury in a work-related accident, would workers' compensation payments even come close to the total payment in this case?"

The dissenting opinion, citing numerous studies and "a small dose of common sense," disagreed with the majority opinion's conclusion that the legislature's objectives did not support the cap: "Given the standard of review, which it faithfully claims is the 'rational basis' test, the majority should not be able to ignore the mountain of evidence supporting the effectiveness of caps."

The Legislature Strikes Back. In its 2006 session the Wisconsin legislature capped a med-mal plaintiff's "noneconomic" damages at $700,000. The governor signed the bill.

7. *Damages Caps and Tort Law as a Law of Redress.* Taking a "public law" view of torts, Professor John Goldberg conceives of tort law as a law that guarantees a plaintiff's right to redress: "a special set of due process rights that entitle individuals to certain governmental structures and certain bodies of law." A plaintiff, who has a due process right to a legal system that allows redress for a tortfeasor's wrong, should, he maintains, be able to sue a wrongdoer to vindicate her rights and interests to secure redress from another who has wrongfully injured her.

Get to the point—Are caps constitutional? A total cap like Nebraska is "odious." A pain and suffering cap is not unconstitutional, but that targeted cap may be unconstitutional for a homemaker or an elderly plaintiff because it will effectively eliminate the plaintiff's claim. John Goldberg, The Constitutional Status of Tort Law: Due Process and the Right to a Law for the Redress of Wrongs, 115 Yale L.J. 524, 621–22 (2005).

8. *Proposed Tort Reforms of Punitive Damages.* Tort reformers dislike punitive damages and seek principles of confinement to prevent abuses. Both of this chapter's punitive damages decisions, Tuttle v. Raymond, p. 122, and BMW v. Gore, p. 133, are judicial tort reform. Summaries of legislative tort reforms of punitive damages follow.

(a) *Have the Judge Set the Amount.* An irrational and exorbitant jury verdict, reformers contend, may be based on plaintiff's lawyer's emotional appeal, jurors' hostility against enterprise, and their misplaced sympathy for plaintiffs. After the jury determines that the defendant is liable for punitive damages, proponents argue, the judge ought to determine the amount. A judge will be better at deciding dispassionately how much will suffice to punish and deter a tortfeasor. A judge's review of comparable punitive damages verdicts will lead to more a predictable and consistent decision.

Jury members, a study of mock juries concluded, collectively reflect a social consensus on when someone's misconduct crosses the threshold that qualifies a defendant for punitive damages. But different juries produce erratic and scattered results when they convert this moral consensus into dollar amounts. The jury's group deliberative process tends to increase their verdict, which is "typically higher, and often far higher, than the median judgment of the same jury's individual members before deliberation began." The study favors assigning the punitive damages to the judge. Cass R. Sunstein et al., Punitive Damages: How Juries Decide (2002)

The proposal to have the judge set the amount of punitive damages may violate the litigants' state constitutional right to a jury trial on the amount of damages. Reviewing a statute assigning to the judge the power to set the amount of punitive damages, the Ohio court commended the jury's "salutary restraint" on "evil passions" and struck the legislation down because it violated the litigants' right to a jury trial. Litigants have a common-law right to a jury to assess the amount of punitive damages. The court assumed that assessing and measuring plaintiff's "common law" damages are the jury's function, asked whether jury trial existed at common law, found common law juries passing on punitive damages, and invalidated the state's tort reform statute. Zoppo v. Homestead Insurance Co., 71 Ohio St.3d 552, 644 N.E.2d 397 (1994).

A contrary decision on whether judicial assessment of punitive damages interfered with the constitutional right to a jury trial is Smith v. Printup, 254 Kan. 315, 866 P.2d 985 (1993). Plaintiffs received punitive damages at the jury's discretion which, the Kansas court held, does not qualify as a right under the state constitutional guarantee of a jury trial.

Also, after the North Carolina legislature capped punitive damages at treble the plaintiff's compensatory damages or $250,000, whichever is larger, the state supreme court upheld the cap against a tort plaintiff's state constitutional attack on several grounds, separation of powers, including a legislative remittitur, right to a jury trial, unconstitutional taking of property, due process and equal protection, open courts, and void for vagueness. Rhyne v. K–Mart Corp., 358 N.C. 160, 594 S.E.2d 1 (2004).

(b) *Bifurcation.* Separating the jury's consideration into stages is called bifurcation, even though trifurcation sometimes occurs. Defendant argues that the same jury ought not consider its substantive liability, plaintiff's compensatory damages, its liability for punitive damages, and the amount of punitive damages in one trial. Although evidence of a defendant's wealth or income is relevant to setting the amount of punitive damages, to prevent prejudice, this wealth evidence should be withheld from the jury until after a plaintiff's verdict on liability. A jury will decide both whether the defendant is liable for punitive damages and the amount of them but at separate times.

One common technique has two stages. In the first, the jury decides on defendant's substantive liability, the amount of plaintiff's compensatory damages, and whether the defendant may be liable for punitive damages. If the answers in the first stage are affirmative, a second stage follows where, after hearing more evidence, the same jury will set the amount of defendant's punitive damages.

In Minnesota, if a plaintiff seeks punitive damages, any party may request bifurcation. If so, a separate proceeding before the same judge or jury will determine whether to impose punitive damages and how much. Minn.Stat.Ann. § 549.20(4).

Bifurcation simplifies the litigation. In addition it keeps evidence of defendant's wealth from the jury when it is deciding liability and setting the plaintiff's compensatory damages, but it places relevant wealth evidence before the jury when it is deciding how large punitive damages ought to be.

(c) *A Cap*. Several states have caps to limit the amount of punitive damages. These caps come in various forms, multiples or ratios, absolute caps, caps in certain substantive areas, like professional malpractice, and variations which depend on defendant's income or size. Caps guide and confine jurors' discretion; they make punitive damages more predictable.

The Alaska court held that the state's punitive damages cap does not violate any of three state constitutional provisions—equal protection, jury right, and takings. Reust v. Alaska Petroleum Contractors, 127 P.3d 807 (Alaska 2005). As discussed above, the North Carolina court declined to disapprove a statutory cap on punitive damages. The court rejected plaintiff's contentions that the cap violated the Tarheel state's constitutional provisions on separation of powers-legislative remittitur, right to a jury trial, unconstitutional taking of property, due process and equal protection, open courts, and void for vagueness. Rhyne v. K–Mart Corp., 358 N.C. 160, 594 S.E.2d 1 (2004).

If, however, the goal of punitive damages is to punish a wrongdoer and to deter its and others' misconduct, then a cap limits the court's ability to reach its goal of punishment commensurate with the defendant's misconduct. An absolute cap on punitive damages may reduce the effect of society's response to the defendant's most egregious misconduct and shrink a jumbo-sized defendant's punishment to a nick. If punitive damages are a multiple of compensatory damages and the victim has low compensatory damages from a wealthy defendant's misconduct that had a high potential for harm, then punitive damages may not achieve their goal of punishing and deterring.

(d) *Diverting or Splitting Punitive Damages*. Giving the government some of the punitive damages achieves the public policy goals of punishment and deterrence without creating a "windfall" for a private plaintiff. Eight states have split-recovery statutes that divert part of a plaintiff's punitive damages verdict to the government. And in a common-law decision, the Ohio court established a split-recovery system in that state. Dardinger v. Anthern Blue Cross & Blue Shield, 98 Ohio St.3d 77, 781 N.E.2d 121 (2002).

If, however, giving the punitive damages to the plaintiff increases her incentive to pursue a wrongdoer, then a split-recovery scheme will reduce a potential plaintiff's motivation to become a bounty hunter.

There are several split-recovery issues: What percentage is diverted? Are plaintiff's litigation expenses subtracted before applying the percentage? What state agency receives the money? Candidates are the general fund and various victim-compensation funds. Is splitting the recovery general or limited to one type of defendant or substantive theory, for example malpractice?

Splitting punitive damages between the plaintiff and the government may have an unintended consequence: it might stimulate jurors' and judges' redistributionist zeal to mulct corporate, out-of-state, and notorious defendants. Policymakers seeking to reduce plaintiffs' punitive damages windfalls may end up increasing the amount of punitive damages defendants pay.

Giving part of the plaintiff's punitive-damages money to the government blurs the difference between a public criminal fine and private civil damages. Punitive damages escaped the Supreme Court's scrutiny under the Excessive Fine Clause of the Eighth Amendment because the plaintiff received the money instead of the government. Browning–Ferris Industries of Vermont, Inc. v. Kelco Disposal, Inc., 492 U.S. 257 (1989). A government's receipt of punitive damages under a split-recovery statute invites reawakened judicial inquiry under the Excessive Fines Clause. Observers have mentioned several additional constitutional problems in split-recovery systems: double jeopardy, procedural due process, and a taking of plaintiff's property, the judgment. Catherine Sharkey, Punitive Damages as Societal Damages, 113 Yale L.J. 347, 375–89 (2003).

State courts decisions responding to plaintiffs' constitutional attacks on split-recovery statutes go both ways, though probably more have approved than have disapproved the statutes.

(i) The Indiana court held that a statute diverting 75% of a plaintiff's punitive damages verdict to the state victims' compensation fund was not an unconstitutional taking. "The lawyer and the client get to play the hand the legislature deals them, no more and no less." Cheatham v. Pohle, 789 N.E.2d 467, 475 (Ind.2003).

(ii) Missouri's supreme court upheld a statute that divided punitive damages equally between the plaintiff and the state. "Placing reasonable limitations on common law causes of action is within the discretion of the legislative branch and does not invade the judicial function." Fust v. Attorney General, 947 S.W.2d 424, 430–31 (Mo.1997).

(iii) The Alaska court held that diversion of 50% of punitive damages to the state not an unconstitutional taking. Reust v. Alaska Petroleum Contractors, 127 P.3d 807 (Alaska 2005).

(iv) On the other hand, the Utah court held that the 1989 version of a split-recovery statute was an unconstitutional taking. The statute had been amended in the meantime, perhaps curing the defects the court identified. Smith v. Price Development, 125 P.3d 945 (Utah 2005).

9. *System Reform*? The civil remedies system is so complex that reformers ought to examine the interrelated parts together. Many damages rules have secondary consequences or purposes; for example plaintiff's pain and suffering damages, collateral source recovery, and punitive damages create a fund that is available to compensate her lawyer without reducing her total recovery below her lost wages and medical expense.

The American Law Institute's 1991 Reporters' Study, Enterprise Responsibility for Personal Injury: Approaches to Legal and Institutional Change, examined the whole tort-personal injury system and made several controversial recommendations. The citations are to page numbers in Volume II.

(a) *Pain and Suffering*. To retain plaintiffs' pain and suffering damages, but to reserve them for "victims who suffer significant injuries." The factfinder will set the plaintiff's amount of pain and suffering damages from "meaningful guidelines," perhaps formulated in the legislature, "based on a scale of inflation-adjusted damage amounts attached to a number of disability profiles that range in severity." (p. 229–30)

(b) *Collateral Source*. To reverse the collateral source rule. "A plaintiff's tort recovery should be reduced by the amount of present and estimated future payments from all sources of collateral benefits except life insurance." Insurers lose all subrogation rights. (p. 182)

(c) *Punitive Damages*. To reform punitive damages. A plaintiff's punitive damages against an "enterprise" defendant where deterrence is more important than retribution ought to be based on "clear and convincing evidence" of a management decision in "reckless disregard" of others' safety. Ideas for setting the amount of plaintiff's punitive damages include bifurcation; admitting evidence of defendant's profit from the tort, but not its overall wealth; consideration of having the judge determine the amount; a compensatory damages—punitive damages ratio but with an absolute ceiling as a safety valve for when defendant's "especially egregious wrongdoing" inflicts "only modest harm." Finally, for a defendant's mass torts from a single course of conduct a "national mandatory class action" to determine and distribute punitive damages. (pp. 264–65)

(d) *Attorney Fees.* To compensate a successful plaintiff for her attorney fees. A plaintiff's recovery for loss items already paid by a collateral source, pain and suffering compensation, and punitive damages are now sources of funds that a successful plaintiff can use for her attorney fees without cutting into her recovery for lost wages and medical expenses. If plaintiff's recovery of expenses already paid by a collateral source is eliminated, if pain and suffering damages are scheduled, and if punitive damages are limited, then that fund will shrink or disappear. The project recommends a new item of tort damage, one-way attorney fee shifting: "[P]revailing claimants [should] be entitled as a general rule to recover reasonable attorneys' fees and litigation expenses from defendants." (p. 268.) A plaintiff's attorney fees will be measured by a percentage of her recovery; the project would leave the percentage to the judge who would instruct the jury that fee-shifting will occur.

Plaintiff's recovery of attorney fees will be coupled with an offer-of-settlement rule: when a defendant offers to settle for a certain amount and the plaintiff rejects the offer, then, if the plaintiff recovers less than the offer, she must pay the defendant's post-offer costs. Moreover, when plaintiff has engaged in frivolous or groundless litigation, a winning defendant will recover its attorney fees.

Some litigation will be ineligible for attorney fee shifting. Examples include plaintiff's suit for an injunction or some other form of specific relief, for specific amounts like liquidated damages, and some wrongful death actions where the judge must approve any settlement.

(e) *Prejudgment Interest.* Addressing the common-law rule that denied plaintiff recovery of prejudgment interest on "unliquidated," or almost all tort, damages, the reporters' study proposes plaintiff's "recovery of compound interest at market rates on all compensatory damages already suffered at the time of the award, with such interest accruing from the time of the loss." (p. 269)

(f) *Joint and Several.* To supplant joint and several liability, "multiple defendants would be liable in proportion to their negligence or equitable contribution to the plaintiff's losses." What about the plaintiff's losses from insolvent or absent defendants? Those defendants' shares will be allocated "among available solvent defendants as well as the plaintiff in proportion to each party's negligence or equitable contribution to the plaintiff's loss." (p. 157)

What do you think?

Chapter 3

EQUITABLE REMEDIES—
THE INJUNCTION

This chapter examines the remedies that we have traditionally considered to be equitable; it focuses on one, the injunction. After the defendant has violated the plaintiff's substantive rights, a court may award her damages, the subject of the prior chapter, to compensate her for harm that has already occurred. On the other hand, a judge may grant an injunction, an equitable remedy, to prevent a defendant's future harm to plaintiff, to assure she, in fact, receives her substantive entitlement.

A court has several equitable remedies; these include an injunction, a constructive trust and a resulting trust, an equitable lien, subrogation, accounting for profits, equitable rescission, reformation, and specific performance. The court's Big Three equitable remedies are the injunction, the constructive trust, and specific performance. While this chapter will emphasize the injunction, it will touch on the judge's other equitable remedies as its progress requires. The constructive trust is more comfortable in the Restitution Chapter. And specific performance is best analyzed with the plaintiff's other remedies for a breached contract in Chapter 6.

"Equity" is a common word in legal and lay language. This chapter uses "equity" in the technical sense of an equitable remedy. When the more specific names for an equitable remedy can be substituted for the words "equitable," "equitable remedy" or "equitable jurisdiction," this book tries to say injunction, constructive trust, or specific performance instead.

Even after procedural merger of the courts of chancery and the common law, a lawyer must be alert to equity-law distinctions which remain important in various contexts, statutory, remedial, procedural, and substantive. Some brief reviews of Supreme Court decisions will illustrate the lawyer's need for vigilance.

Bowen v. Massachusetts was a horrendously complicated administrative law decision. One question was whether a federal district judge's reversal of a Department of Health and Human Services's disallowance of Medicaid reimbursements was "relief other than money damages" which was forbidden under the statute that waives the government's sovereign immunity. The Supreme Court examined several distinctions, held the trial judge's declaratory judgment-injunction up to the light, and decided that it was more like "an equitable action for specific relief" which was permitted to the federal district judge under the statute. Bowen v. Massachusetts, 487 U.S. 879, 892–95 (1988).

Quackenbush v. Allstate Insurance involved the labyrinthine complexities of federal court abstention under the doctrine of Burford v. Sun Oil Co., 319 U.S. 315 (1943). *Burford* abstention to dismiss or remand, the Supreme Court decided, was appropriate for the federal district court when the plaintiff's federal action was an equitable or discretionary one, not, however, when the plaintiff's action was for money damages. Quackenbush v. Allstate Insurance Co., 517 U.S. 706 (1996).

The Supreme Court has decided several lawsuits involving the meaning of "equitable" in the ERISA statute that governs federal regulation of employee benefits and pensions. That statute empowers the federal judge to grant a successful ERISA plaintiff "appropriate equitable relief."

In its first decision, the Court determined that the judge could not award a ERISA plaintiff either consequential, (the term this book uses is "special") damages or punitive damages. For they were not "equitable." Massachusetts Mutual Life Insurance Co. v. Russell, 473 U.S. 134, 144 (1985).

Going a little further in its second decision, the Court held that the ERISA statute's limitation to "appropriate equitable relief" excluded the plaintiff from recovering compensatory money damages. Money damages are, the majority said, "the classic form of legal relief," not allowable as "equitable relief."

Justice Scalia's majority opinion includes a notable boner. Although Chancery did accord money relief, the opinion read the words "equitable relief" to "refer to those categories of relief that were typically available in equity (such as injunction, mandamus, and restitution, but not compensatory damages)." Mertens v. Hewitt Associates, 508 U.S. 248, 256 (1993). One of Justice Scalia's "typical" examples is incorrect, for mandamus is legal relief; a second is half-incorrect and misleading, for restitution has both legal and equitable forms; moreover the idea that compensatory damages were not "typically available in equity" may also be inaccurate since Chancery courts frequently awarded a successful plaintiff compensatory damages.

The Court's third ERISA remedies decision was an insurance company's restitution claim for subrogation; the insurance company, having paid its insured's expenses, was seeking to be substituted for the insured for the appropriate portion of the insured's tort recovery. The subrogation plaintiff attempted to bring its claim within "restitution" in the Court's examples of typical equitable claims, quoted in the prior paragraph. Justice Scalia, taking another tack, discovered legal restitution and, emphasizing the money relief that the plaintiff was seeking, found that "a judgment imposing a merely personal liability upon the defendant to pay a sum of money" was "quintessentially an action at law," excluded from the "equitable relief" the court was qualified to grant to a plaintiff under the ERISA statute. Great West Life & Annuity Insurance Co. v. Knudson, 534 U.S. 204, 210, 214 (2002).

In her concurrance in a later ERISA case, this one about ERISA's preemption of state law, Justice Ginsberg emphasized that an ERISA plaintiff's remedies were being ground down between the jaws of an "encompassing interpretation" of ERISA preemption of plaintiffs' state law causes of action and the Court's "cramped construction" of federal "equitable" remedies available under ERISA to the plaintiff. She maintained that the Court's misunderstanding was so profound and the injustice to plaintiffs so stark that either the Court or Congress should simply start again from the beginning and forge a new ERISA remedial structure. Aetna Health Inc. v. Davila, 542 U.S. 200, 222 (2004).

Professor John Langbein has written persuasively that the Court's ERISA remedies decisions went awry from the very beginning because the statute's "equitable relief" means trust and fiduciary law which allow a plaintiff to recover all forms of make-whole or compensatory damages. John H. Langbein, What ERISA Means By "Equitable": The Supreme Court's Trail of Error in Russell, Mertens, and Great West, 103 Colum.L.Rev. 1317 (2003).

In November of 2005, while this edition was being prepared, the Court agreed to hear another ERISA case, Mid Atlantic Medical Services v. Sereboff, 407 F.3d 212 (4th Cir.), cert. granted, 126 S.Ct. 735 (2005). In *Sereboff*, an ERISA fiduciary, having paid for the defendant's medical attention, sought to be subrogated to the defendant's tort recovery. The court of appeals, recognizing the contrary decisions in other circuits, "applied" *Knudson*, above, and discerned that this time the plaintiff's remedy of subrogation was "equitable," to wit an equitable lien or constructive trust. The Supreme Court affirmed while this edition was in page proof. The fiduciary's remedy was "equitable" because it was "a constructive trust or equitable lien on a specifically identifiable fund." Sereboff v. Mid Atlantic Medical Services, 126 S.Ct. 1869, 1874 (2006). We will mention these decisions when we study the difference between legal restitution and equitable restitution in the Restitution chapter.

As developed in Chapter 1, the courts in the United States descend from the courts of common law and Chancery or Equity in medieval England. This book uses the name Chancery for the court and Chancellor for the judge in order to eliminate one confusing meaning of equity. In any event, the courts of the common law and Chancery are now in some fashion merged.

Medieval Chancery was a separate judicial system developed by the Chancellors in response to rigid or unsatisfactory legal rules. Early Chancellors prided themselves on the flexibility to dispense with legal rules that created injustice. A frequent and familiar contemporary usage is that "equity" means fairness and describes a court's discretion to make an individual exception to an austere rule when the rule will lead to an inequitable result. Equitable discretion accompanies equitable remedies and will be examined in this chapter.

Equity has procedural and substantive meanings in legal language. The medieval Chancellors developed distinctive procedures for Chancery. The modern versions of Chancery procedure's most valuable features are discovery, the class action, and interpleader. These have become parts of merged civil procedure; we do not consider them to be separately equitable today. One crucial procedural difference between common law or "legal" and Chancery or "equitable" procedure remains: litigants have a right to summon a jury for factfinding at their trial in a suit under the "common law," but none if the action is under equity.

Today several substantive fields are classified as equitable because the medieval Chancellors developed them. The Chancellors' most important substantive contributions were to trusts, mortgages, and bankruptcy. Contemporary "equitable" substantive subjects include quiet title, partition, liens and mortgages, trusts, fiduciaries, guardianships, dissolution of marriages, and adoptions. Equitable substantive rules have worked their way into statutory and general law. Most lawyers think of them not as equitable remedies but as distinct branches of substantive law with equitable features like discretion and the absence of a jury.

[handwritten marginal note: No jury for Divorce]

Equitable remedies, an injunction or specific performance, and the legal remedy, damages, are "concurrently" available to plaintiffs in contracts, torts, property, and constitutional law. In these concurrent areas, a court may award a successful plaintiff either an injunction or compensatory damages. Limitations on the court's "equitable jurisdiction" and the inadequacy prerequisite for an equitable remedy operate in concurrent areas where either a legal or an equitable remedy may be appropriate.

Accustomed to thinking of the court's jurisdiction over the person and subject matter jurisdiction, most modern readers will be unfamiliar with the idea of "equity jurisdiction." A court has subject matter jurisdiction when the constitution or statutes say this court can do something about this kind of dispute. Today a court with general jurisdiction decides what used to be called actions at law and suits in equity.

When two courts divided the business, the test of whether the court had "equity jurisdiction" sounded like a subject-matter jurisdiction test. "Equity jurisdiction" combined two kinds of issues: (a) does the plaintiff have a proper basis for coming into equity?; and (b) should the judge exercise equitable jurisdiction by granting the plaintiff an equitable remedy? Properly answered today these questions are addressed to the judge's wisdom and fairness, not to the judge's basic power to decide. The question of whether the judge should grant plaintiff an injunction is complicated enough without combining it with the question of whether the judge has the power to decide the lawsuit at all. In other words, the court's "equity jurisdiction" is not jurisdictional. Zechariah Chafee, Some Problems of Equity 301–306 (1950).

Nevertheless, for decades courts pronounced rules about whether to grant plaintiff an injunction or other equitable remedy in terms of whether "equitable jurisdiction" existed. And in 1999, the Supreme Court hinged a decision on the federal court's lack of "equitable jurisdiction." The federal court lacked statutory "equitable jurisdiction" to grant a plaintiff an asset-freezing injunction because the district judge in 1999 has the "equity jurisdiction" that the English High Court exercised in 1789, the time of the new federal constitution and the Judiciary Act of 1789. Grupo Mexicano de Desarrollo, S.A. v. Alliance Bond Fund, Inc., 527 U.S. 308 (1999).

Judges sorted damages-legal remedy from the injunction-equitable remedy with the inadequacy prerequisite and other limitations on "equitable jurisdiction." Before granting her an injunction, the court required the plaintiff to demonstrate that her legal damages remedy, if granted, will be inadequate or that without an injunction, she will suffer an irreparable injury. The question of whether the inadequacy test still means what it sounds like will be examined below.

If money damages will be inadequate relief for the plaintiff, then the judge ought to accelerate the response to her grievance to expedite her opportunity to enjoy the interest she presumably cannot be satisfactorily compensated for. The availability to the plaintiff of immediate or prompt interlocutory relief, a temporary restraining order, (TRO), or a preliminary injunction, secures for plaintiff the opportunity to enjoy promptly the very interest the substantive law guarantees. The plaintiff's fast procedural track to a preliminary injunction is developed in this chapter.

A judge uses contempt to enforce an injunction. The judge's chief goal is to secure the plaintiff's substantive entitlement. The story of contempt is the story of how much power to achieve that goal will be focused on the judge.

The Chapter begins by examining the way the courts shaped the traditional maxims or sayings of Chancery to forge the injunction into the formidable remedy it is today. The Chapter closes with the reaction to the modern injunction which it calls Injunction Reform.

A. TRADITIONAL MAXIMS ASSIST AND LIMIT INJUNCTIONS

1. EQUITY ACTS IN PERSONAM

"The rule that 'Equity acts in personam' is the lanthern that guides us through the entire labyrinth of equity jurisprudence."[1] From the defendant's perspective, a common feature of an injunction, a constructive trust, and specific performance is the personal response or conduct each requires from the defendant. The judge commands the defendant's conduct, enjoins the defendant to do or to forbear specified conduct, to execute the constructive trust by conveying to plaintiff, or to perform the contract specifically. For in personam relief to work, the judge will wield contempt against a recalcitrant or disobedient defendant. The plaintiff's ability to enjoy in fact the interest the substantive law guarantees begins when the defendant behaves as the law expects. To light our way through the "labyrinth of equity," we pick up the "lanthern" of in personam equitable relief at the beginning of this chapter and carry it before us throughout.

If the money damages in the prior chapter starred a jury as factfinder and led to a money judgment collected impersonally, then an equitable injunction in this chapter features a judge who acts as factfinder and continues to be involved in drafting personal orders and administering contempt. In contrast to an in personam equitable order, the plaintiff collects a "legal" judgment for money damages impersonally: the judgment winner's usual collection techniques are the writ of execution, garnishment, and the judgment lien; the sheriff satisfies the plaintiff's unpaid money judgment by seizing and selling the defendant's property without, however, involving the defendant personally. The law, in traditional vernacular, "acts in rem." The plaintiff's collection of a money judgment is left to other courses in law school. Contempt to enforce an injunction will be examined below.

"In the infancy of the court of chancery, while the chancellors were developing their system in the face of a strong opposition, in order to avoid a direct collision with the law and with the judgments of law courts, they adopted the principle that their own remedies and decrees should operate *in personam* upon defendants and not *in rem*. The meaning of this simply is, that a decree of a court of equity, while declaring the equitable estate, interest, or right of the plaintiff to exist, did not operate by its own intrinsic force to vest the plaintiff with the legal estate, interest, or right to which he was pronounced entitled; it was not itself a legal title, nor could it either directly or indirectly transfer the title from the defendant to the plaintiff. A decree of chancery spoke in terms of personal command to the defendant, but its directions could only be carried into effect by his personal act. It declared, for example, that the plaintiff was

---

1. H. Hanbury and D. Yardley, English Courts of Law 96 (5th ed.1979).

equitable owner of certain land, the legal title of which was held by the defendant, and ordered the defendant to execute a conveyance of the estate; his own voluntary act was necessary to carry the decree into execution; if he refused to convey, the court could endeavor to compel his obedience by fine and imprisonment." I Pomeroy, Equity Jurisprudence, § 428, page 469 (1881).

Hanbury and Yardley described equitable remedies and contempt a little more colorfully. The Chancellor "could grant specific performance, that is to say, order the defendant to perform a contract according to its terms, or injunction, that is to say, order him to desist from conduct prejudicial to the plaintiff; and, like a skillful fisherman, would never let him go, once hooked, but could always jerk him back to obedience by the threat or fact of personal constraint." H. Hanbury & D. Yardley, English Courts of Law 95–96 (5th ed., 1979).

Suppose the defendant is in another jurisdiction, a place with a legal system of its own. The next three cases test the traditional maxim "Equity acts in personam" in the crucible of disputes that cross state lines and national borders.

A court, to begin with, may grant a land buyer a specific performance decree which orders the defendant-seller to convey land in another jurisdiction. Historic litigation in England between William Penn and Lord Baltimore concerned then-colonial land. Penn v. Lord Baltimore, 1 Ves.Sen. 444 (1750).

A plaintiff may ask the court to enjoin the defendant's extra-territorial misconduct. A court with personal jurisdiction over the defendant is able to order that defendant, in personam, to act or refrain from acting in another state. Reebok International Ltd. v. Sebelen, 959 F.Supp. 553, 558–59 (D.P.R. 1997).

An International Example. "In this trademark case, Calvin Klein Industries, Inc. seeks a preliminary injunction restraining the distribution or sale of sportswear bearing the Calvin Klein label. Calvin Klein entered into a manufacturing contract with defendants BFK Hong Kong, Ltd. and its director, James Langford, but after several delays in delivery, Calvin Klein refused to accept the merchandise, citing tardiness and deviation from other manufacturing requirements. As a result, the garments remain in Pakistan, and Calvin Klein seeks an injunction prohibiting defendants from trying to sell them independently. * * *

"The only remaining issue, therefore, pertains to the necessary scope of the injunction, specifically, whether, having found plaintiff entitled to a preliminary injunction on sales in the United States, this court also may enjoin sale of these garments abroad. The Lanham Act ordinarily supports injunctions only against sales in the United States, where the trademark is registered. However, the law may reach abroad, and apply extraterritorially, under certain circumstances. Steele v. Bulova Watch Co., Inc., 344 U.S. 280, 289 (1952). In *Bulova,* the Supreme Court applied the Lanham Act to bar the defendant from selling infringing watches in Mexico, because the sales had an effect on United States commerce and because certain acts relating to the manufacture of the watches had occurred in the United States. Finding that Congress intended to make the Lanham Act's reach coextensive with the Commerce Clause, *Bulova* holds that under the statute 'a United States District Court has jurisdiction to award relief to an American corporation against acts of infringement and unfair competition consummated in a foreign country by a citizen and resident of the United States.'

"In determining whether such relief is appropriate, however, the following factors are to be considered: 1) whether defendant's conduct has a substantial effect on United States commerce; 2) whether the defendant is a United States citizen; and 3) whether extraterritorial enforcement of the trademark will encroach upon foreign trademark rights. * * *

"Consideration of the relevant factors supports the issuance of an extraterritorial injunction in this case. There is no dispute that defendant possesses no rights under foreign law with which an injunction against it might conflict. Although defendant Langford is not a United States citizen, the evidence indicates that he resides in New York, and is the controlling force behind BFK, a New York corporation. Therefore, both Langford and BFK may be treated as United States citizens for the purpose of this discussion. * * *

"The final factor for consideration—the effect of foreign, infringing sales on United States commerce—also supports Calvin Klein's application for a preliminary injunction. Effects on domestic commerce may include certain harms to plaintiff, as a domestic corporation, such as diversion of sales, [citation] or harm to licensees. [citation] In addition, a substantial effect on commerce may be found where the defendant's activities are supported by or related to conduct in United States commerce. In *Bulova,* for example, diversion of sales to consumers, who could find cheap, imitation watches just over the Mexican border, as well as the defendant's purchase of component parts in the United States, constituted sufficient effects on commerce.

"Calvin Klein is entitled to injunctive relief against infringing sales where such sales would divert Calvin Klein's sales, or would harm licensees. Because the garments at issue were manufactured under a contract made in New York, for delivery to New York, the remedies for breach of that contract necessarily have some effect on commerce. Calvin Klein claims that, because of its worldwide advertising and use of authorized licensees, any sale of the garments will irreparably damage Calvin Klein directly, by undermining Calvin Klein's good will and reputation for quality manufacture, or indirectly, by depriving Calvin Klein licensees of their exclusive rights. Such injuries would have a substantial effect on United States commerce, and, therefore, are enjoinable under the Lanham Act.

"Accordingly, defendants are preliminarily enjoined from selling the infringing goods in the United States, and in such other markets as Calvin Klein may demonstrate that it has established its presence, through either direct sales or licensees. Additionally, defendants must make reasonable efforts to ensure that those to whom they sell the goods do not resell or otherwise introduce the goods into territories in which Calvin Klein has a presence, as described above." Calvin Klein Industries, Inc. v. BFK Hong Kong, Ltd., 714 F.Supp. 78, 78–80 (S.D.N.Y. 1989).

Another court enjoined that defendant's sale of counterfeit shoes in Mexico. Reebok International Ltd. v. Marnatech Enterprises, Inc., 737 F.Supp. 1515, 1521 (S.D.Cal.1989), aff'd 970 F.2d 552, 559, 563 (9th Cir. 1992).

As we might expect, there are some qualifications on the outer fringes. The United States Supreme Court turned down a creditor-plaintiff's asset-freezing injunction against its debtor-defendant in Mexico. Justice Scalia's majority opinion turned on the federal court's lack of statutory "equitable jurisdiction" to grant a plaintiff an asset-freezing injunction, not on the court's in personam jurisdiction to affect a defendant's conduct in another country. The defendant had consented to initial personal jurisdiction in New York. Grupo Mexicano de Desarrollo, S.A. v. Alliance Bond Fund, Inc., 527 U.S. 308 (1999).

Suppose a United States plaintiff sues a foreign-nation defendant seeking an injunction against the defendant's trademark infringement in the foreign nation. Jazz-musician Cecil McBee sued a Japanese defendant who was selling a "Cecil McBee" line of clothes to teenage girls in Japan and maintaining a Japanese-language Website with that name. When a plaintiff seeks an injunction against the foreign activity of a foreign defendant, the court of appeals held, the plaintiff must show a "substantial effect" on United States commerce to attain Lanham Act subject matter jurisdiction. The defendant's only sales in the United States were to McBee, apparently intended to establish personal jurisdiction over the defendant. Since McBee had already lost in Japan, he apparently has to accept teenage Japanese girls wearing provocative garments named after him. McBee v. Delica, 417 F.3d 107 (1st Cir. 2005).

Enjoining litigation in another jurisdiction, called an anti-suit injunction, increases the possibility of a policy conflict between the two states. In Wells v. Wells, 36 Ill.App.3d 91, 93, 343 N.E.2d 215, 217 (1976), the court said that the power to enjoin a suit in another state "is a matter of great delicacy invoked with great restraint in order to avoid distressing conflicts and reciprocal interference with jurisdiction."

TABOR & CO. v. McNALL

Appellate Court of Illinois, Fourth District, 1975.
30 Ill.App.3d 593, 333 N.E.2d 562.

CRAVEN, JUSTICE. Tabor & Company, a Nevada corporation authorized to do business in Illinois, contracted with * * * McNall Bros. Grain Service, for the purchase and delivery of a large amount of grain. McNall is a Wisconsin corporation, but the grain was to be delivered to the buyer Tabor in LaSalle, Illinois. The contracts for this delivery, seven in all, were negotiated by phone between the Wisconsin office of McNall Bros. and the Illinois office of Tabor, and confirmed in writings sent from Tabor to McNall.

McNall performed partially, then defaulted. On June 4, 1974, Tabor filed a complaint on the contract in the circuit court of Macon County, Illinois. On June 18, 1974, McNall filed a suit in the circuit court of Rock County, Wisconsin, admitting default on the contract and seeking to limit its damages. McNall thereafter filed a limited appearance in the Illinois court, contesting that court's jurisdiction on the grounds that McNall had insufficient business contacts with Illinois to support such jurisdiction. The accompanying motion to quash service of process was denied August 2, 1974.

On August 27, 1974, Tabor petitioned the Illinois court to enjoin McNall from proceeding further with the suit in Wisconsin. At the same time, Tabor filed a petition for writ of prohibition in the Supreme Court of Wisconsin in an attempt to arrest the progress of the circuit court action there. On September 10, 1974, the Supreme Court of Wisconsin denied the request for a writ of prohibition.

Finally, on October 11, 1974, the Illinois court issued a writ of temporary injunction restraining McNall from proceeding further with the action in Rock County, Wisconsin. The order noted that there was no just reason for denying its enforcement or appeal. The McNalls nevertheless proceeded with their action in the Wisconsin court which proceeded to a verdict on October 16, 1974. On November 8, Tabor filed a petition for rule to show cause why McNall should not be held in contempt of court for violating the temporary injunction. The McNalls then appealed the order enjoining them from proceeding in Wisconsin, contending [among other things] that the trial court was in error in enjoining them from pursuing the Wisconsin action. * * *

The McNalls' * * * contention is that the trial court judge issued the temporary injunction solely to protect the earlier acquired jurisdiction of the Illinois court, and that such is an insufficient justification for enjoining a foreign court proceeding. The trial court made no finding that the Wisconsin proceeding would be likely to result in fraud or oppression, or that any equity appeared to require intervention. On the contrary, the trial court specifically found that the McNalls had filed suit in Wisconsin to protect themselves, not to harass Tabor.

Trial court reasoning

The only reason for intervention suggested by the trial court is a fear that Wisconsin law might not afford the Illinois defendant the protection he deserves:

> "THE COURT: We are all aware, and we are getting more firsthand knowledge all the time, apparently as a result of the—I hesitate to use the word, but the socialistic background of the State of Wisconsin, the Farmers' Labor Party and the Lafollettes and all the rest, they do have some pretty strange laws up there that I sometimes fail to comprehend, as witness this law suit where a plaintiff can come in and state under oath that he has breached his contract but I want my damages mitigated, it seems a little foreign to our experience here."

Such reasoning does not constitute sufficient basis for enjoining prosecution of a foreign suit:

> "It is not enough that there may be reason to anticipate a difference of opinion between the two courts, and that the courts of a foreign state would arrive at a judgment different from the decisions of the courts in the state of the residence of the parties. [citation] It is not inequitable for a party to prosecute a legal demand against another in any forum that will take legal jurisdiction of the case, merely because that forum will afford him a better remedy than that of his domicile. To justify equitable interposition it must be made to appear that an equitable right will otherwise be denied the party seeking relief. [citation]" (Royal League v. Kavanagh, 233 Ill. 175, 183, 84 N.E. 178, 181.)

Nor is it sufficient that the suit in Illinois was instituted before the suit in Wisconsin:

> "A party has the legal right to bring his action in any court which has jurisdiction of the subject-matter and which can obtain jurisdiction of the parties. Should he begin two suits within the same jurisdiction, the pendency of the suit first brought may be pleaded in abatement of the later proceeding. This is not true of suits brought in different jurisdictions upon the same cause of action. The mere pendency of a suit in a sister state or in a court of the United States cannot be pleaded in abatement of a proceeding in a state court. * * * [I]t is only where it clearly appears that the prosecution of an action in a foreign state will result in a fraud, gross wrong, or oppression, that a court of equity will interfere with the general right of a party to press his action in any jurisdiction in which he may see fit and in as many of them as he chooses and restrain him from the prosecution of such a suit." (Illinois Life Insurance Co. v. Prentiss, 277 Ill. 383, 387, 115 N.E. 554, 556.)

The trial judge did not cite, nor does the record disclose, any facts to show why an injunction is necessary to avert "fraud, gross wrong or oppression." Consequently, it was error to enjoin the McNalls from proceeding in a foreign court.

Finally, Tabor contends that McNalls, by violating the injunction of the circuit court of Illinois, deprived themselves of the "clean hands" required from one who seeks equity. We have been advised of no authority which would bar them from seeking reversal of the order they disobeyed. The rule to show cause why they should not be cited for contempt is not before this court.

The circuit court erred in the issuance of the injunction.

Reversed.

Notes

1. *Dueling Injunctions.* Under the rules which give an injunction in personam force, if the forum court enjoins a litigant from litigating in another state, then only the litigant is enjoined; the forum court cannot affect the out-of-state court itself, even if it does have personal jurisdiction over the litigant. The out-of-state court may in turn enjoin the other litigant from litigating back in the forum court. Is this a reason for a court not to enjoin out-of-state litigation in the first place? In James v. Grand Trunk Western Railroad Co., 14 Ill.2d 356, 152 N.E.2d 858 (1958), cert. denied, 358 U.S. 915 (1958), the Illinois court issued an injunction prohibiting enforcement of a Michigan decree enjoining the prosecution of a wrongful death action in Illinois for an accident in Michigan. Might both parties be subject to contempt for pursuing a remedy in court?

2. *Effect of Anti-suit Injunction.* Suppose an out-of-state court has enjoined the litigants from pursuing litigation in the forum. If one party continues, what effect should the forum court extend to the other court's injunction? (a) The court might decide that the other court's injunction is in personam which means it operates only on the enjoined defendant and subjects him to contempt by the other court. (b) The court may follow comity either to recognize or to refuse to recognize the out-of-state injunction. (c) The court may accord full faith and credit to the out-of-state injunction.

(a) *Contempt of the Out-of-State Court.* The idea that an out-of-state violation is contempt of the court which granted the injunction grows out of quotation from Hanbury and Yardley above that the Chancellor, once the defendant was "hooked," "could always jerk him back to obedience by the threat or fact of personal constraint." The Supreme Court recognized the forum court's power to hold the defendant in contempt for his out-of-state violation in Baker v. General Motors, which is discussed below.

(b) *Comity.* Some courts recognize an out-of-state injunction "strictly as a matter of comity." Fuhrman v. United America Insurors, 269 N.W.2d 842, 847 (Minn.1978). See Lowe v. Norfolk & Western Railway Co., 96 Ill.App.3d 637, 645, 421 N.E.2d 971, 978 (1981). A forum court's comity analysis is flexible; the court considers many variables including whether the out-of-state judgment is consistent with forum public policy. When a forum court analyzes an out-of-state anti-suit injunction under comity, it usually decides that forum litigation may proceed as if the out-of-state court had not enjoined it.

A different approach was evident in Smith v. Walter E. Heller & Co., 82 Cal.App.3d 259, 271, 147 Cal.Rptr. 1, 8 (1978). A New York federal district judge, after finding a California lawsuit to be duplicative and pursued in bad faith to harass, enjoined the litigant from maintaining the California action. The litigant pursued the California action by requesting a default. The California trial judge dismissed the California action. Affirming, the California court of appeal said that "The comity which one court owes to another of concurrent jurisdiction should always prevent the one from lending itself as an instrument in permitting a contempt of the process of the other." *Most sound reasoning*

A United States court will receive a foreign-*nation*'s court's injunction under the doctrine of comity; for the Constitution's Full Faith and Credit Clause only applies to a sister-*state* judgment. The United States court will decline to recognize and extend comity to a foreign-nation injunction which is based on substantive law that is repugnant to United States "public policy." Enjoined in France from disseminating Nazi merchandise on its auction site, Yahoo! sued in the United States for declaratory judgment that the French injunction was repugnant to United States policy of favoring free-expression. In 2006, however, the court of appeals's en banc decision turned Yahoo! down without a firm majority opinion. Yahoo! Inc. v. La Ligue Contre Le Racisme et L'Antisemitisme, 433 F.3d 1199 (9th Cir. 2006). Since the internet transcends national boundaries, expect foreign-nation injunctions to continue to create international conflicts.

(c) *Full Faith and Credit*. The federal Constitution's Full Faith and Credit Clause requires a state to recognize and give effect to a sister state's judgment. In the words of the statute implementing that clause, a state's judgments "shall have the same full faith and credit in every court * * * as they have by law or usage in the courts of such State * * * from which they are taken." 28 U.S.C. § 1738.

Under the Full Faith and Credit Clause, the forum accepts an out-of-state money judgment even though it may be based on substantive law that is contrary to forum public policy. Fauntleroy v. Lum, 210 U.S. 230 (1908). Do out-of-state injunctions differ?

In 1998, the United States Supreme Court decided its first full faith and credit case involving an out-of-state injunction, Baker v. General Motors Corp., 522 U.S. 222 (1998). The Court's answers to our questions above are complex and require a little detour.

To settle post-employment litigation, General Motors and Elwell entered into a Michigan consent injunction which forbade Elwell from testifying in litigation against GM. However, in apparent violation of the Michigan decree, Elwell testified in Missouri in the Bakers' wrongful death litigation against GM. Reversing the trial court's $11.3 million jury verdict for the Bakers, the Eighth Circuit Court of Appeals decided that the Michigan consent injunction would receive full faith and credit in the Missouri lawsuit. A unanimous Supreme Court thought not. Although it did hold that injunctions in general are entitled to full faith and credit, the Court said that this particular consent decree was not.

First, a forum state's injunction is entitled to full faith and credit in another state. It did not matter that the Michigan decree was contrary to Missouri's public policy. A court may apply a public policy exception and decline to choose another state's substantive law which it finds repugnant. But once a sister-state judgment exists, there is no public policy exception to the full faith and credit due to that judgment; a state must allow a judgment creditor to collect a sister-state money judgment even though the sister-state substantive law the judgment is based on is repugnant to the collection state's public policy.

Second, the Missouri court may not decline full faith and credit on the ground that the Michigan injunction is equitable. The Court has accorded full faith and credit to equity decrees; for example, an equitable decree compelling the defendant to pay money is the equivalent of a judgment at law and, under full faith and credit, it is entitled to nationwide recognition.

Third, despite the first two points, GM cannot employ the Michigan decree in the Missouri lawsuit to bar Elwell's testimony there. Full faith and credit means that the Missouri court must apply Michigan's domestic preclusion doctrines to Michigan's judgment. But the Missouri court may employ its own enforcement mechanisms to Michigan's judgment.

Moreover the Michigan court lacks authority to forbid Elwell's testimony in a Missouri court; a Michigan order that prohibits a witness's testimony in Missouri litigation interferes with a lawsuit under Missouri's jurisdiction. A Michigan court cannot employ a domestic Michigan injunction to extend a Michigan injunction's reach beyond the dispute between Elwell and GM to exclude evidence in the Bakers' Missouri lawsuit against GM; for the Bakers who brought the Missouri lawsuit were nonparties to the Michigan litigation, never subject to the Michigan court's jurisdiction. "Michigan has no authority to shield a witness [Elwell] from another jurisdiction's [Missouri's] subpoena power in a [Missouri] case involving persons and causes outside Michigan's governance. Recognition, under full faith and credit, is owed to dispositions Michigan has authority to order. But a Michigan decree cannot command [Elwell's] obedience elsewhere [in Missouri] on a matter the Michigan court lacks authority to resolve."

From this language and perspective, we can answer one of our questions, tentatively concluding that the Court's unhappiness with an injunction that affects out-of-state litigation means that State A probably isn't required to extend full faith and credit to State B's anti-suit injunction against a defendant's litigation in state A. Of an anti-suit injunction, an Illinois court observed, "this court need not, and will not, countenance having its right to try cases, of which it has proper jurisdiction, determined by the courts of other States, through their injunctive process." James v. Grand Trunk Western Railroad Co., 14 Ill.2d 356, 372, 152 N.E.2d 858, 867 (1958), cert. denied, 358 U.S. 915 (1958). Does Baker v. General Motors vindicate the Illinois court's observation? Analysis of an anti-suit injunction under "comity" seems appropriate.

Finally, what did the Court have to say about Elwell's responsibility to obey the Michigan order? The court that granted the injunction will administer any sanctions for breach of it. Elwell, it seems, may be vulnerable to Michigan contempt proceedings. This is a surprising answer to State A's other question about State B's anti-suit injunction: defendant's violation in State A may lead to contempt in State B.

Questions about *Baker*. Was the Michigan court prudent in the first place to enter an injunction which, contrary to the usual rules of litigation, appeared to forbid Elwell from testifying in litigation outside Michigan? Is the Supreme Court's decision focused on an injunction decree that forbids a defendant from participating in litigation? For example what if the Michigan injunction had been based on a business seller's covenant not to compete with his buyer? If GM does charge Elwell with contempt in Michigan, should the Michigan court really consider that his testimony under a Missouri subpoena could be contemptuous?

3. *Statutes*. A statute prohibits a federal court from enjoining state court litigation. 28 U.S.C. § 2283 (1994). Even if the lawsuit falls within an exception in the statute, the federal judge may still refuse injunctive relief because of the abstention doctrines in Younger v. Harris, discussed below. Similarly a state court is prohibited from enjoining federal proceedings except where necessary to protect property under its control. General Atomic Co. v. Felter, 434 U.S. 12 (1977). California reinforces this policy by statute. Cal.Civ.Code § 3423(b).

4. *A Foreign–Nation Anti-suit Injunction.* The Full Faith and Credit Clause does not apply to an injunction issued by a court in another nation. The court declining to enjoin litigation in Malaysia, observed that "a foreign antisuit injunction should issue only when the foreign proceeding 1) threatens the jurisdiction of the United States court, or 2) evades strong public policies of the United States." Berkshire Furniture Co., Inc. v. Glattstein, 921 F.Supp. 1559, 1561 (W.D.Ky.1995).

In Laker Airways Ltd. v. Sabena, Belgian World Airlines, the court upheld a United States court's counter anti-suit injunction in antitrust litigation:

"The district court's injunction was within its discretion even though the United Kingdom courts have issued in personam injunctions stopping Laker from proceeding against British Airways and British Caledonian. Long experience derived from this country's federal system teaches that a forum state may, but need not, stay its own proceedings in response to an antisuit injunction against a party before the court. * * * In suits involving states, even the Full Faith and Credit Clause does not compel recognition of an antisuit injunction. * * * The same result is reached here *a fortiori,* since the mandatory policies of the [clause] do not apply to international assertions of exclusive jurisdiction. The antisuit injunction was a necessary and proper vehicle to protect the [district court's] jurisdiction and prevent the evasion by KLM and Sabena of important domestic laws governing the conduct of business within the United States * * *. KLM and Sabena do not dispute the power of the United States District Court to issue the injunction. They contend rather that [it] abused its discretion." The court also rejected the argument of paramount sovereignty, that Laker Airways' nationality required deference to the courts of the United Kingdom. Laker Airways Ltd. v. Sabena, Belgian World Airlines, 731 F.2d 909, 933–34 (D.C. Cir.1984),

5. *Enjoining a Litigant's Multi–Lawsuit Harassment.* An injunction prohibiting a litigant from filing multiple groundless lawsuits to abuse and harass defendants and others presents a different problem which courts solve with different rules. Tidik v. Ritsema, 938 F.Supp. 416, 426–27 (E.D.Mich.1996).

6. *Land or Property in Another State.*

(a) *The Local–Action Rule.* The distinction between a transitory and a local action is often important to a plaintiff who is selecting the venue for property litigation. Most lawsuits are transitory; the plaintiff may sue the defendant on a transitory cause of action in any court with subject matter and personal jurisdiction. The local-action rule forbids a court from entertaining an action for trespass to out-of-state land or for title or ownership of out-of-state land. The reasons courts give for the rule are that land records and property law expertise are found at the land's situs. Moreover a plaintiff can usually use a long arm statute to sue the defendant at the situs.

Although the local-action rule dates from John Marshall's opinion as Circuit Judge in Livingston v. Jefferson, 15 Fed.Cas. 660 (C.C.D.Va. 1811) (No. 8, 411), both the rule's contours and even whether it is one of venue or jurisdiction are indistinct. Following the rule, even though a plaintiff seeks a judgment for damages for trespass to land against a defendant over whom the court has obtained personal jurisdiction, the court will refuse to proceed if the land is in another state. Classification of a trespass-to-land action as local is a historical anomaly, explainable only by the intricacies of laying venue under the common law system of pleading. This anachronistic rule has been rejected by judicial decision in several states and by legislation in others. Eugene Scoles, Peter Hay, Patrick Borchers & Symeon C. Symeonides, Conflict of Laws § 7.7 (Fourth Edition 2004).

(b) *Does Equity Act In Personam?* Where the local action rule exists, can it be reconciled with the forum court's power to grant a plaintiff in personam relief against a defendant when that relief affects out-of-state land? Penn v. Lord Baltimore, 1 Ves.Sen. 444 (1750). Suppose the plaintiff asks the court to compel the defendant who is personally before the court to execute a conveyance of out-of-state land. In 1810 Chief Justice Marshall established what may be called the equitable corollary to the local-action rule: "in a case of fraud, or trust, or of contract, the jurisdiction of a court of chancery is sustainable, wherever the person be found, although lands not within the jurisdiction of that court may be affected by the decree." Massie v. Watts, 10 U.S. (6 Cranch) 148, 160 (1810).

Where defendant has a "personal obligation" under a "contract" to convey foreign land to plaintiff, Massie v. Watts enables the Chancellor to decree specific performance. The "trust" Massie v. Watts refers to may be a constructive one. Materese v. Calise, below, involves a constructive trust.

To be distinguished from the in personam relief with an "indirect" effect on the foreign land, as in Massie v. Watts, is an "unmixed question of title" where, because relief would affect the out-of-state land "directly," the court will decline relief. Connell v. Algonquin Gas Transmission Co., 174 F.Supp. 453, 457 (D.R.I.1959).

A plaintiff filed a Texas lawsuit charging defendant with breach of contractual fiduciary duties and asking the Texas court to impose a constructive trust on land in Colorado; the Texas federal court decided that, although the local-action rule was one of subject matter jurisdiction, not venue, the plaintiff's suit was transitory, not local. Thus the Texas court had subject matter jurisdiction. Keller v. Millice, 838 F.Supp. 1163 (S.D.Tex.1993).

Another plaintiff asked a California court to declare that California resident defendants were constructive trustees of land located in Illinois. Upholding the plaintiff's complaint, the court of appeal observed that, "Equity acts in personam, not in rem. After the court has obtained jurisdiction of the parties it may, by decree operating in personam against them, control their actions with respect to property situated without its jurisdiction whenever such action is necessary for it to effect a complete disposition of the controversy." The court said that the decree "does not of itself affect title of the realty in [the state of the situs.]" In *Mills,* the court also ruled that plaintiff was entitled to a decree establishing an equitable lien on the Illinois property. Mills v. Mills, 147 Cal.App.2d 107, 116–17, 305 P.2d 61, 67–68 (1956).

(c) *Beyond In Personam Relief.* What if the defendant, a breaching land seller or a constructive trustee, refuses to execute the court-ordered conveyance? Under pure in personam theory, the Chancellor could not act directly on the land's title, for that would constitute the anomaly of Chancery or Equity acting in rem. Instead, traditionally, the Chancellor would "jerk" defendant "back to obedience by the threat or fact of personal constraint," in plain English, imprison the defendant until he executed the deed. When recalcitrant defendants vowed to rot in jail forever rather than convey land, legislatures subordinated in personam theory to effective relief for plaintiffs; statutes and procedural rules were enacted either providing for an effective deed by an appointed commissioner or granting the judgment effect to convey the land. In Matarese v. Calise, below, the trial court's decree provided that if defendant failed to comply, plaintiff "could apply to the court for the appointment of a commissioner to make the conveyance in the name of the defendant."

Federal Rule of Civil Procedure 70 authorized either type of procedure: "Judgment for Specific Acts; Vesting Title. If a judgment directs a party to execute a conveyance of land or to deliver deeds or other documents or to perform any other specific act and the party fails to comply within the time specified, the court may direct the act to be done at the cost of the disobedient party by some other person appointed by the court and the act when so done has like effect as if done by the party. On application of the party entitled to performance, the clerk shall issue a writ of attachment or sequestration against the property of the disobedient party to compel obedience to the judgment. The court may also in proper cases adjudge the party in contempt. If real or personal property is within the district, the court in lieu of directing a conveyance thereof may enter a judgment divesting the title of any party and vesting it in others and such judgment has the effect of a conveyance executed in due form of law. When any order or judgment is for the delivery of possession, the party in whose favor it is entered is entitled to a writ of execution or assistance upon application to the clerk.''

A California judge may authorize a clerk to execute a deed to land in a foreign jurisdiction. In Phelps v. Kozakar, 146 Cal.App.3d 1078, 194 Cal.Rptr. 872 (1983), the only limitation the court was willing to recognize was lack of jurisdiction over the property owners.

(d) *Rule 70's Travels Out of State.* A commissioner's deed or judgment under Rule 70 or the equivalent will be effective in the forum state. The courts of a state where land is located have exclusive subject matter jurisdiction over internal land. What effect should a court where the property is located accord to a decree from another state of the United States? Courts at the situs of the land will recognize a deed from another state executed under the other state's court order and threat of contempt. Under an earlier, more traditional, view of full faith and credit, however, a court's decree did not operate directly to convey foreign land; moreover, the court could not appoint someone to make a conveyance for a recalcitrant defendant. Fall v. Eastin, 215 U.S. 1 (1909).

Modern courts tend, however, tend to find ways to accept reliable out-of-state decrees that affect forum land; the court will cite preclusion, comity, or full faith and credit. In a quiet title action the Michigan court granted full faith and credit to a Massachusetts decision that plaintiff did not own Michigan land. McKay v. Palmer, 170 Mich.App. 288, 427 N.W.2d 620 (1988). See also Matter of Estate of Mack, 373 N.W.2d 97 (Iowa 1985). Orders to convey land are routinely enforced by courts of the state where the land is located. In re Wiswall's Estate, 11 Ariz.App. 314, 464 P.2d 634 (1970), reh'g denied, 12 Ariz.App. 26, 467 P.2d 250 (1970). Restatement (Second) of Conflicts of Law § 102 (1971).

A North Carolina decision bucks the modern tide by denying full faith and credit to a Kansas judgment that purported to affect title to North Carolina land. Buchanan v. Weber, 152 N.C.App. 180, 567 S.E.2d 413, writ denied, 356 N.C. 433, 572 S.E.2d 427 (2002).

In Matarese v. Calise, below, the land is in another nation, beyond the reach of full faith and credit.

MATARESE v. CALISE
Supreme Court of Rhode Island, 1973.
111 R.I. 551, 305 A.2d 112.

PAOLINO, JUSTICE. This case is before us on the defendant's appeal from a judgment entered in the Superior Court ordering the defendant to convey to the plaintiff certain real estate located in Forio, Ischia, Italy. * * *

The plaintiff was a businessman in the town of Forio on the island of Ischia which is located off the coast of Naples. The defendant was born in Italy but was an American citizen. * * * He came to this country from Forio in 1955. * * *

The property involved in this case was formerly owned by one Anna Coppa DiMaio, who was born in this country and had never been to Italy. Her brother,

Philip Coppa, who owned an unimproved parcel of land adjacent to that of his sister, occupied a residence located on Anna's land. In 1954 plaintiff purchased the unimproved parcel from Philip. * * * Around 1965 plaintiff made plans to erect a large building on the land he bought from Philip, and, in 1966, started construction. The plaintiff needed Anna's property because his building encroached on a portion thereof, and he decided to attempt to purchase it. At the time plaintiff did not know where Anna resided in the United States. * * *

In March, 1966, defendant was again visiting in Forio, Italy. * * * At the hearing in the Superior Court plaintiff testified that in March, 1966, defendant went to plaintiff's store in Forio and that a conversation took place between them about the purchase of Anna's land. [T]he conversation between plaintiff and defendant was in substance as follows:

"Plaintiff asked defendant, when he returned to the United States, to try to see Anna Coppa Dimaio and to purchase the property for him at any cost since he had started construction of his building and a portion of the foundation was on that property. Plaintiff further stated that he would send defendant money when requested to make a down payment and later would send defendant a power of attorney so that a deed could be transferred to plaintiff and defendant could act fully on plaintiff's behalf. Plaintiff also stated that if defendant would secure the property for him, he would give defendant the entire top floor of the building on the Anna Coppa Dimaio property in which Philip Coppa was then living. Defendant stated that he had learned where Mrs. Dimaio lived and he would do his best to convince her to sell the property and make a contract with her for plaintiff."

The defendant contacted Anna in New York and in September, 1968, in New York, secured a deed to her property but placed the property in his own name. After the defendant purchased the property, he sent a telegram to his mother in Italy stating that the property had been bought for $22,000 and asking that $3,000 be sent to him. The defendant's mother showed the telegram to plaintiff who, thinking that defendant was purchasing the property for him, sent $3,000 to defendant in North Providence. The trial justice found that no more than $3,000 was paid for the property. The defendant claimed at the trial that the figure $22,000 in the telegram was a mistake by the telegraph company. The trial justice said that this statement was a deliberate fabrication and that it was clear to him that " * * * defendant by sending the telegram, was attempting to set plaintiff up for a $22,000 demand for the property because he knew plaintiff was keeping in touch with the situation through his mother." The defendant's father recorded the deed in Italy on October 22, 1968, the date of the last check sent to defendant by plaintiff. * * * The trial justice said that defendant had worked his scheme to perfection, noting that defendant "not only had record title to the property which he knew plaintiff wanted very desperately, but he also had plaintiff's $3,000.00 in hand and he was out of pocket no money in making the purchase."

* * * At the time this action was commenced against him, defendant was a resident of this state, residing at North Providence. He went back to Italy in August, 1969. * * *

[The trial judge] concluded that defendant had perpetrated a fraud upon plaintiff and, therefore, held the property in question as a constructive trustee for the benefit of plaintiff; that since the constructive trustee had no duties to perform other than conveying the property to the rightful owner, it was appropriate that defendant be ordered to convey the subject property to plaintiff; and that although the property was in Italy the Rhode Island court had jurisdiction over the person of defendant and, thus, had power to order a conveyance of the land, which was situated outside its territorial limits.

The trial justice ordered defendant to convey the property in question "by deed in form appropriate for recording in Italy," but he allowed defendant to reserve to himself a fee simple interest in the top floor of the building located on said premises. He also allowed defendant 60 days within which to make the conveyance and stated that if defendant did not abide by the court's order, plaintiff could apply to the court for the appointment of a commissioner to make the conveyance in the name of defendant. The trial justice continued in effect an injunction enjoining defendant from transferring the property to anyone except plaintiff. * * *

[D]efendant raises the question of whether the courts of this state have jurisdiction to compel an action relating to real property by a person no longer in this state. The defendant concedes that as a general principle of law, a court of equity may, under proper circumstances, order an individual over whom it has personal jurisdiction to execute a deed conveying an interest in real property situated outside the jurisdiction of the court. However, defendant argues that the aforesaid rule is of no effect in the present action because the trial justice found as a fact that "[d]efendant moved back to Italy in August 1969" and such situation having occurred, the Superior Court was without power to effect a conveyance of the land in question by defendant. * * *

We agree with the trial justice's conclusion that the court had jurisdiction over the person of defendant and, therefore, had power to order a conveyance even though the land was situated outside the territorial limits of this state. See *Fall v. Eastin,* 215 U.S. 1 (1909), cited by defendant, where the court said:

> "But this legislation does not affect the doctrine which we have expressed, which rests, as we have said, on the well-recognized principle that when the subject-matter of a suit in a court of equity is within another state or country, but the parties within the jurisdiction of the court, the suit may be maintained and remedies granted which may directly affect and operate upon the person of the defendant, and not upon the subject-matter, although the subject-matter is referred to in the decree, and the defendant is ordered to do or refrain from certain acts toward it, and it is thus ultimately but *indirectly* affected by the relief granted. In such case the decree is not of itself legal title, nor does it transfer the legal title. It must be executed by the party, and obedience is compelled by proceedings in the nature of contempt, attachment or sequestration. On the other hand, where the suit is strictly local, the subject-matter is specific property, and the relief, when granted is such that it *must* act directly upon the subject-matter, and not upon the person of the defendant, the jurisdiction must be exercised in the state where the subject-matter is situated." * * *

[Judgment affirmed.]

Notes

1. What of the defendant who left Rhode Island for Italy? If the defendant leaves the forum state, what practical value has an in personam decree ordering him to execute a deed to land in another state?

2. In Duke v. Andler, 4 D.L.R. 529 (1932), the Supreme Court of Canada dealt with a California decretal transfer of land in British Columbia. Duke, the buyer, had agreed to secure payment of British Columbia land with a mortgage on land in California, but he was unable to perform that agreement because the California land was already encumbered. Duke fraudulently conveyed the British Columbia property to his wife. In an action brought by the seller in California, the court ordered reconveyance of the property and failing compliance, a Clerk's conveyance. The Clerk executed the conveyance.

The British Columbia courts held that the plaintiffs owned the land by reason of the California judgment and conveyance. On appeal, however, the Canadian Supreme Court refused to enforce the California judgment on the ground that the law and the courts of the situs determine rights in land. Neither the Clerk's conveyance nor the judgment could affect the title. Since the California judgment operates in personam, the Canadian courts should not lend it an in rem effect by vesting title in plaintiff.

UNITED STATES v. McNULTY

United States District Court, Northern District of California, 1978.
446 F.Supp. 90.

ZIRPOLI, DISTRICT JUDGE. On or about March 24, 1973, the defendant, Franklin L. McNulty, won the Irish Hospitals Sweepstakes. He collected 50,000 Irish pounds, or $128,410 at the prevailing rate of exchange. Defendant soon learned, however, that he had a silent partner which would claim its share of the prize. That partner was the Internal Revenue Service, whose interest defendant sought to defeat by collecting his winnings in Ireland and depositing them in a secret bank account on the Island of Jersey, which is located between the United Kingdom and France.

In a narrow sense, defendant has been successful in his efforts to avoid sharing his winnings with the government, for the money apparently remains on the Island of Jersey. Defendant himself, however, having been convicted of income tax evasion, remains in federal prison. On January 23, 1978, moreover, the government prevailed in a civil action for collection of taxes, and defendant was found liable in the amount of $67,791, representing taxes, penalty and interest. The government, though successful in its action, is unlikely to collect its money unless defendant transfers his assets from the Island of Jersey, for he has no other known funds with which to satisfy the judgment.

The government has therefore moved for an order directing defendant to repatriate his assets from the Island of Jersey and deposit them with the clerk of the court. Although no memorandum of points and authorities was submitted with the motion, the Assistant United States Attorney indicated in court that 26 U.S.C. section 7402 provides the authority for the issuance of such an order:

"The district courts of the United States at the instance of the United States shall have such jurisdiction to make and issue in civil actions, writs and orders of injunction, and of *ne exeat republica*, orders appointing receivers, and such other orders and processes, and to render such judgments and decrees as may be necessary or appropriate for the enforcement of the internal revenue laws. The remedies hereby provided are in addition to and not exclusive of any and all other remedies of the United States in such courts or otherwise to enforce such laws."

While this court has found no case specifically invoking that section of the Internal Revenue Code for the type of order sought herein, it is relatively well established that this court may issue such an order. In United States v. Ross, 302 F.2d 831 (2d Cir.1962), an action had been brought to subject defendant's property to jeopardy assessments for unpaid income taxes. The district court had issued a series of interlocutory orders, one of which directed defendant to surrender to a receiver stock located in the Bahamas. Defendant contended that such an order was in excess of the court's jurisdiction, but the court of appeals disagreed:

> "The District Court's order to Ross to turn over his stock certificates to the receiver was not in excess of the court's statutory authorization. The court had personal jurisdiction over Ross, acquired by personal service of summons on his authorized agent. Personal jurisdiction gave the court power to order Ross to transfer property whether that property was within or without the limits of the court's territorial jurisdiction."

In United States v. First National City Bank, 379 U.S. 378 (1965), the Commissioner of Internal Revenue had made jeopardy assessments of some $19 million against a Uruguayan corporation. Although the district court lacked personal jurisdiction over the corporation, it did have jurisdiction over the bank in whose Montevideo branch the corporation maintained a deposit. The court issued an injunction under 26 U.S.C. section 7402(a) "freezing" the corporation's account in the foreign branch of the New York bank. The Supreme Court sustained the order. Implying that once personal jurisdiction over the corporation was acquired the district court could order payment of the foreign assets, the Court observed:

> "The temporary injunction issued by the district Court seems to us to be eminently appropriate to prevent further dissipation of assets. [citation] If such relief were beyond the authority of the District Court, foreign taxpayers facing jeopardy assessments might either transfer assets abroad or dissipate those in foreign accounts under control of American institutions before personal service on the foreign taxpayer could be made. * * * [T]here is here property which would be 'the subject of the provisions of any final decree in the cause.' [citation] We conclude that this temporary injunction is 'a reasonable measure to preserve the status quo' [citation] pending service of process on [the corporation] and an adjudication of the merits."

While the Ninth Circuit has not, as far as this court has been able to determine, confronted this particular question in the area of taxes, it would apparently approve such an order. In Securities and Exchange Commission v. Minas De Artemisa, S.A., 150 F.2d 215 (9th Cir.1945), the court ordered a corporation, which was subject to the personal jurisdiction of the court, to produce corporate books located in Mexico in connection with an SEC investigation. As was done in *First National City Bank* and *Ross,* the court observed that such an order must be framed so as not to conflict with the internal law of the foreign state in which the act was to be performed. There has been no indication, however, that the instant order will violate the banking laws of the Island of Jersey.

It is clear, then, that this court, by virtue of its jurisdiction over the defendant, has the power to order him to repatriate the assets located in the foreign bank. Moreover, there appears to be little hesitation on the part of courts to issue such orders. The view was expressed most directly by the district court in *Ross:*

"Only for the most compelling reasons should a court refuse relief to the Government where a citizen of the United States keeps most of his assets in a foreign country and claims that they are immune from application to his income tax liability because of their situs in a foreign country."

Accordingly, plaintiff's motion is granted, and the defendant is ordered to repatriate assets sufficient to satisfy the judgment entered against him by this court from the Island of Jersey and to deposit said assets with the Clerk of this Court within sixty (60) days of the entry of this order.

Notes

1. *Freedom for Frank.* Frank McNulty's criminal conviction failed to produce the money. The government could not itself collect its civil judgment for taxes in the Island of Jersey. In October, 1978, Frank McNulty was found in contempt for failing to obey the preceding order to repatriate the money; he was committed to the custody of the United States Marshall to coerce him to pay. Judges often remind contemnors confined for coercive contempt, "You carry the jailhouse key in your pocket," for the prisoner may comply any time and be released immediately. After five months in custody failed to coerce McNulty to repatriate the funds, however, Judge Zirpoli concluded that "further incarceration would cease to serve the coercive objective of civil contempt and would become punitive." McNulty was discharged on March 16, 1979. He promised to send Judge Zirpoli an Irish Sweepstakes ticket: "If he wins, God bless him, I hope he goes to Ireland and does the same thing I did." (News Item)

2. *Long-distance Contempt.*

(a) *A Long Coercive Confinement Ends.* In early 1998, Odell Sheppard who had been held in Cook County jail for more than ten years for refusing to produce his daughter or reveal her whereabouts was released. After a decade of hoping that jail would make Sheppard talk, the girl's mother, Norell Sanders, died. The news report quoted the judge as saying, "He has not been released because he has convinced us of his assertions. Mrs. Sanders is deceased. She is the petitioner, and that ends the case." The Washington Post, January 30, 1998, at A24. The history of the litigation up to then is in a denial of habeas corpus, Sheppard v. Fairman, 1996 WL 166951 (N.D.Ill.).

(b) *Another Continues.* H. Beatty Chadwick is threatening Odell Sheppard's dubious place in the record books if he hasn't already surpassed it. In early 1995, a Delaware County Pennsylvania judge ordered Chadwick confined until he produced $2.5 million. Although Chadwick claimed that an investment had gone sour taking the money with it, the judge found that he had spirited the funds out of the country. At last report, an internet search in January 2006, Chadwick was still jailed— awaiting a decision from a three-judge panel that had heard a special master testify that his original story of having lost the money was "plausible."

3. How does the maxim "Equity acts in personam" help you to understand the judge's ability to order the defendant's conduct and coerce an uncooperative defendant into obedience? See Doug Rendleman, Disobedience and Coercive Contempt Confinement: The Terminally Stubborn Contemnor, 48 Wash. & Lee L.Rev. 185 (1991).

4. *Other Limits on Extra-territorial Injunctions.*

(a) *International Collection.* A plaintiff class of torture victims of the late Ferdinand Marcos with a judgment of almost $2,000,000,000 to collect obtained an injunction to protect the Estate's assets. The Republic of the Philippines, which had its own collection efforts underway to recover for looted assets, was forbidden, on the theory that it was an "agent, representative, aider or abetter of the Estate," from agreeing with the Estate to transfer assets to the Philippines. The court of appeals, rejecting the plaintiffs' claim that Rule 65(d) outranked the Foreign Sovereign Immunities Act, upheld the Republic's claim to lack of personal jurisdiction and sovereign immunity. The appellate court doubted whether, upon breach, the trial court could punish the Republic for contempt. "A court should not issue an unenforceable injunction." In re Estate of Ferdinand Marcos Human Rights Litigation, 94 F.3d 539, 545 (9th Cir.1996).

(b) *International Child Custody.* Child custody litigation under the Hague Convention of the Civil Aspects of International Child Abduction featured a Swedish finding a divorced couple's daughter resided in Sweden and a Utah court decision she was a resident of that state. The child's father had applied the law of "grab and run" in Sweden, but later he filed for custody there. Her mother had sued in Utah before resorting in turn to the law of "grab and run." The Utah district judge declared her in contempt and ordered her to return the little girl. She moved under Rule 41(a)(2) to voluntarily dismiss the Utah lawsuit, but the Utah district judge denied her motion because she was in contempt of its order. The court of appeals held she could voluntarily dismiss the Utah action, instead of obeying, and overcome, in some fashion, her contempt of the order. Thus the ultimate issue of custody would be decided in the father's proceeding in Sweden. That he had filed in Sweden overcame her contumacy in Utah. Ohlander v. Larson, 114 F.3d 1531 (10th Cir.1997). Did the decision ignore the Utah judge's in personam order and indeed reward the mother's disobedience?

(c) *Violation Via Homepage*? British authorities want Professor Peter D. Junger "to take down a report [posted on his homepage] detailing the alleged abuse of children by social workers in Nottinghamshire, England. Professor Junger, who teaches at Cleveland's Case Western Reserve University Law School, refuses to remove the document.

"The solicitors for Nottinghamshire's County Council claim that by displaying the report, Professor Junger violated the U.K. Copyright, Designs and Patents Act of 1988: 'Neither you nor the owners of the Website have sought permission from the Nottinghamshire County Council as copyright holder to store the Report by electronic means,' a solicitor e-mailed. 'I therefore give you notice that unless the report is removed from the Website forthwith and for the avoidance of doubt within 24 hours of receipt by you of this mail, The Nottinghamshire County Council will issue such Court Proceedings including injunction proceedings or take any action as may be appropriate.'

"Although the stated purpose of removing the report is to protect the juveniles' privacy, Professor Junger says the identities of the children were carefully concealed in the original report. (European privacy laws are generally much stricter than those of the United States.)

"Professor Junger's reply to the solicitor reads, in part, 'I and my Web site are located in Cleveland, Ohio ... a locus where the writs of the courts of the United Kingdom have never run.' "Wendy R. Leibowitz, Lawyers and Technology, The National Law Journal, June 30, 1997, at B7.

Is the solicitors' e-mail empty saber rattling?

2. THE PLAINTIFF'S INADEQUATE LEGAL REMEDY, IRREPARABLE INJURY

If the plaintiff has proved the defendant's substantive liability and wants a preventive injunction, is there any reason for the Chancellor to refuse to grant the injunction? Traditional practice has been that the judge will require the plaintiff to show that her legal remedies will be inadequate or, the equivalent test stated in different words, that she will encounter irreparable injury without an injunction. Why should the court condition the plaintiff's choice?

(a) *The Traditional View.* In 1965, the Harvard Law Review's Note said: "Few legal rubrics can vie in frequency of use with the maxim that equity will not grant specific relief—injunction or specific performance of contracts—when there exists any adequate remedy at law. Under this doctrine, injunctions have been denied on the ground that damages, extraordinary legal remedies, detinue and replevin, criminal sanctions, and statutory civil, criminal, and administrative procedures were adequate to deal with the plaintiff's problem. Using analogous language, courts have referred injunction plaintiffs to the political process, the police or self-help.

"The adequate remedy rule well reflected Chancery's subordinate position as it developed in medieval England against the background of the established courts of law. Equity was a 'gloss' on the law; its sole justification for assuming jurisdiction was that traditional legal remedies and procedures could not offer the plaintiff satisfactory relief. Chancery waxed powerful during the Elizabethan and Stuart periods, and maintained its broadened jurisdiction during the eighteenth and nineteenth centuries notwithstanding improvements in the common law. Yet, held in check by the notion of adequacy, equitable remedies remained essentially supplementary. The adequacy doctrine was carried over to the Colonies, where it was fixed upon the federal courts by the Judiciary Act of 1789, and incorporated into the statutes or decisions of almost every American jurisdiction.

"The adequate remedy test has been expounded in forms that differ as to what burden the plaintiff must meet: it must be shown 'that he has exhausted his remedies at law'; that 'the refusal of a court of equity to interpose would, from the insufficiency of the legal relief, or the imperfection of the legal procedure, work a substantial injustice to the litigant party under all the facts of the case'; or merely that the remedy at law is not 'as practical and as efficient to the ends of justice and its prompt administration, as the remedy in equity.'

"The merger of law and equity, by bringing to a close the long competition between the two courts and committing the choice of remedies to a single set of judges, might be thought to have ended the traditional preference for nonequitable remedies and procedures. But at least in form, the adequacy test remains on the books and appears in the case law." Developments in the Law—Injunctions, 78 Harv.L.Rev. 994, 997–998 (1965).

(b) *The Inadequacy Prerequisite's Obituary.* Professor Douglas Laycock in 1990 used "irreparability" language to "conclude that the irreparable injury rule is dead. It does not describe what the cases do, and it cannot account for the results. Injunctions are routine, and damages are never adequate unless the court wants them to be. Courts can freely turn to the precedents granting injunctions or the precedents denying injunctions, depending on whether they want to hold the legal remedy adequate or inadequate. Whether they want to hold the legal remedy adequate depends on whether they have some other reason to deny the equitable remedy, and it is these other reasons that drive the decisions.

"Instead of one general principle for choosing among remedies—legal remedies are preferred where adequate—we have many narrower rules. There is a rule about fungible goods in orderly markets, a rule about preliminary relief, a rule about undue hardship, and so on. These rules are often stated in the cases. But when courts invoke these rules, they often go on to invoke the irreparable injury rule as well. Sometimes they rely solely or principally on the irreparable injury rule, and leave the application of some more specific rule merely implicit in their statement of the case. Analysis would be both simpler and clearer if we abandoned the rhetoric of irreparable injury and spoke solely and directly of the real reasons for choosing remedies. * * *

"I seek to complete the assimilation of equity, and to eliminate the last remnant of the conception that equity is subordinate, extraordinary, or unusual. Except where a statute or constitution requires it, I would not ask whether a remedy is legal or equitable. Instead, I would ask functional questions: is the remedy specific or substitutionary, is it a personal command or an impersonal judgment, is it preliminary or permanent? On the facts of each case, does plaintiff's preferred remedy impose unnecessary costs, or undermine substantive or procedural policies?" Douglas Laycock, The Death of the Irreparable Injury Rule, 103 Harv.L.Rev. 687, 692–93 (1990). This article was expanded into a book, Douglas Laycock, The Death of the Irreparable Injury Rule (1991).

(c) *Perspective.* Professor Ken York responded to Professor Laycock. "Recently we have been apprised of the death of God, of Contract, and now the Irreparable Injury Requirement for an injunction. Such obits would be more convincing if the designated decedents were to behave in the conventional and appropriate manner of the genuinely dead. Inconveniently they have not. The terminal debility of the rule is not detectable.

"The irreparable injury requirement (demoted to lower case) has been the subject of penetrating and accurate academic criticism. No doubt an immutable 'hierarchy of judicial remedies' is an unacceptable encumbrance to protecting and cleaning up the environment and to ending unconstitutional institutional practices in education, penology, and health care.

"In civil litigation between private parties, our primary concern here, we can criticize courts for applying the irreparable injury loosely and using it to disguise results reached for other reasons.

"Nevertheless, because of habit or conviction, the rule continues to appear in practice as well as print in civil litigation. Recurring scenarios have led to standard treatments that, although incongruous and difficult to harmonize, are unlikely to change much. Breach of contract to sell ordinary goods: damages are an adequate legal remedy. Breach of contract to sell land: specific performance because damages are an inadequate legal remedy. If other remedies are indisputably adequate for any particular dispute, does plaintiff have a real reason to seek an equitable remedy? The burden placed upon a plaintiff to establish the inadequacy of other remedies is not a heavy one.

"Finally, the irreparable injury rule plays a major role in applications for temporary injunctions, probably the numerical bulk of occasions to put the rule into play. This subject will receive attention shortly."

(d) Your editor's efforts to sort out what contemporary judges mean by the phrases inadequate remedy and irreparable injury are: Doug Rendleman, The Inadequate Remedy at Law Prerequisite for an Injunction, 33 U.Fla.L.Rev. 346 (1981), which was written before Professor Laycock's obituary; a review of Professor Laycock's book, Doug Rendleman, Irreparability Irreparably Damaged,

90 Mich.L.Rev. 1642 (1992), which, needless to say, came after; and Doug Rendleman, Irreparability Resurrected? Does a Recalibrated Irreparable Injury Rule Threaten the Warren Court's Establishment Clause Legacy?, 59 Wash. & Lee L.Rev. 1343 (2002).

(e) *Present Status.* Courts continue to state the irreparable injury rule and to cite it as a reason to deny an injunction. For example, the Arkansas court rejected Wal–Mart's prayer for an injunction against a union solicitation campaign at the plaintiff's stores on the ground that Wal–Mart suffered no irreparable injury from the union solicitation (trespass) at Wal–Mart stores. United Food and Commercial Workers International Union v. Wal–Mart Stores, Inc., 353 Ark. 902, 120 S.W.3d 89 (2003).

More precise rules that articulate the real reasons to reject injunctions will emerge from the crucible of the existing doctrine. Readers of this chapter will learn the language of inadequacy-irreparability and the habits of thought it created.

Chancery courts have traditionally granted injunctions, (i), where the plaintiff's rights and interests were "equitable," and, (ii), where plaintiff lacked an adequate remedy at law.

(i) Matters historically within the Chancery Court's "equitable jurisdiction" were typically guardianships, trusts and fiduciary relationships, probate, enforcement of liens, and quiet title. The automatic "equitable" classification derived from law courts' original lack of subject matter jurisdiction not from any inadequacy of plaintiff's legal remedy.

(ii) The inadequacy test operates where matters are subject to either law or equity: contracts, torts, property, and constitutional law. Plaintiff triggers the analysis by seeking an injunction, a constructive trust, specific performance, or some other equitable remedy. Several maxims of equity developed to bar the Chancellor from granting an equitable remedy. From the demise of these maxims and the example of In re Debs, discussed in *Gallo*, below, courts constructed the modern injunction.

3. EQUITY CANNOT PROTECT PERSONAL, POLITICAL, OR RELIGIOUS RIGHTS

Earlier courts often stated that a Chancery court would not protect a plaintiff's personal rights, but only her property rights.

Kenyon v. City of Chicopee remains a leading decision rejecting that maxim. Jehovah's Witnesses sought to enjoin the authorities' harassing criminal prosecutions. The government argued that, while a court would grant an injunction to protect the Jehovah's Witnesses' property rights to conduct a business, the court could not grant an injunction to protect their personal rights to free speech and free exercise of religion. "We are impressed," the court responded, "by the plaintiffs' suggestion that if equity would safeguard their right to sell bananas it ought to be at least equally solicitous of their personal liberties guaranteed by the Constitution." Kenyon v. City of Chicopee, 320 Mass. 528, 533–34, 70 N.E.2d 241, 244 (1946), is also discussed below in *Norcisa*. Today not many courts will disclaim the ability to protect "personal" rights. A court may find other ways to limit injunctive legerdemain.

Another restriction, stated almost in terms of a maxim, was that an equity court would not resolve disputes of a "peculiarly political nature." Colegrove v.

Green, 328 U.S. 549 (1946). Political controversies were to be resolved by legislative or executive action. A judicial resolution was thought to be impractical as well as dangerously infringing upon the separation of powers. The precise question raised by Colegrove v. Green, the apportionment of Congressional districts, was held to be justiciable in Baker v. Carr, 369 U.S. 186 (1962). Since that decision, courts have examined the entire spectrum of possible disputes over the election process.

The word "political" however, has different levels of meanings ranging from "grass roots" politicking, on through the election process up to the realm of national and foreign policy matters. At the retail level, the restriction may still hold. For example, in Porter County Democratic Party Precinct Review Committee v. Spinks, 551 N.E.2d 457, 459 (Ind.App.1990), county precinct committeemen sought an injunction against their removal by the County Central Committee. Denying the injunction the court observed: "Courts of equity have no jurisdiction * * * with respect to matters * * * of a political nature unless civil property rights are involved. * * * A court of equity will not supervise the acts and management of a political party. * * * [A] member of a political party when denied certain rights as such member must look to some other source for redress."

No modern law school casebook is complete without a citation to Bush v. Gore, 531 U.S. 98 (2000). This one is appropriate, because Bush v. Gore was a "Remedies" or, more accurately, a "right without a remedy" decision. Seven justices agreed with the substantive point that the Florida Supreme Court's recount procedure violated the Equal Protection Clause: Justices Scalia, Thomas, O'Connor, Kennedy, Souter, and Breyer, plus Chief Justice Rehnquist. But the substantive majority disintegrated on the question of remedy and, citing the lack of time, five justices halted the recount without a remand to draw up a constitutional recount procedure: Justices Scalia, Thomas, O'Connor, and Kennedy, plus Chief Justice Rehnquist joined the per curiam opinion.

Just as courts traditionally have been loath to enter the "political thicket," so also have religious controversies been beyond the scope of judicial power. For obvious reasons, a court is incapable of resolving an ecclesiastical question or to determine the "true" faith. A court may resolve a dispute about property rights, but only on the basis of "neutral principles of law, developed for use in all property disputes." Presbyterian Church v. Mary Elizabeth Blue Hull Memorial Presbyterian Church, 393 U.S. 440, 449 (1969). See Scotts African Union Methodist Protestant Church v. Conference of African Union First Colored Methodist Protestant Church, 98 F.3d 78 (3d Cir.1996), cert. denied, 519 U.S. 1058 (1997); Parish of the Advent v. Protestant Episcopal Diocese of Massachusetts, 426 Mass. 268, 688 N.E.2d 923 (1997).

In 1999 the South Dakota court held that a judge lacks jurisdiction to grant a restraining order in a religious dispute. Plaintiffs had sued for several torts and for restitution and sought interlocutory injunctive relief and money recovery. Decker ex rel. Decker v. Tschetter Hutterian Brethren, 594 N.W.2d 357 (S.D. 1999).

A court may grant an injunction in the delicate area of church-state relations. To protect students' Constitutional right to be free from an establishment of religion, a trial court granted and an appellate court affirmed a preliminary injunction against student-initiated prayer at public school events.

Ingebretsen v. Jackson Public School District, 88 F.3d 274 (5th Cir.1996), cert. denied, 519 U.S. 965 (1996).

Indeed courts regularly issue injunctions to prevent defendants from interfering with plaintiffs' personal and political constitutional rights. Could any harm be more irreparable and money damages more inadequate than for a plaintiff's constitutional injury? Can a defendant persuade the judge to stand idly aside, to observe passively violations of the Constitution, and, then, to tell the victims to be content with money damages?

While we are on the subject of inter-governmental relations, courts used to say that:

4. EQUITY LACKS JURISDICTION TO ENJOIN A CRIMINAL PROSECUTION

NORCISA v. BOARD OF SELECTMEN

Supreme Judicial Court of Massachusetts, 1975.
368 Mass. 161, 330 N.E.2d 830.

QUIRICO, JUSTICE. This is an appeal by the defendants, the board of selectmen of Provincetown (selectmen) and their agent, from a decree * * * declaring that the plaintiff and her retail clothing business in the town of Provincetown (town) are not within the scope of G.L. c. 101, §§ 1–12, the Transient Vendor Statute, and ordering that the town and its agents, servants, and employees "are hereby restrained and permanently enjoined from enforcing * * * any of the provisions of Mass.G.L. c. 101, §§ 1–12, against the Petitioner or the retail business she operates." * * * Prior to the commencement of this suit in equity, a criminal complaint had issued * * * charging the plaintiff with violating G.L. c. 101, §§ 6, 8. This criminal complaint was still pending when the decree appealed from issued. The obvious purpose and effect of the decree was to enjoin the pending criminal prosecution. We reverse.

 * * * It appears * * * that sometime late in 1973 the plaintiff, who was a resident of Provincetown, opened a retail clothing business in that town under the name of The Town Crier Wearhouse. At the time she opened her business, the plaintiff was informed by the agent for the selectmen "that she would not be able to open and operate her business unless she paid to Provincetown a license fee of two hundred dollars ($200.00), furnish a bond of five hundred dollars ($500.00), to the Commonwealth, and applied for both a state and town Transient Vendor's License, all of the above pursuant to and authorized by G.L. c. 101, § 3."

The plaintiff's position * * * is that she was not a transient vendor at the time the selectmen sought to categorize her as one, that she had not been a transient vendor in the past, and that she would not be a transient vendor in the future. She further asserted that she had performed no acts which could be construed as classifying her as anything except a retailer of clothes, that she intended to conduct her business as a full time retail clothing shop, and that she would take no action inconsistent with these assertions. * * *

At one time, it was common for courts to express the view that an equity court had no "jurisdiction" to enjoin a criminal prosecution. In In re Sawyer, 124 U.S. 200 (1888), the court said, "The office and jurisdiction of a court of equity, unless enlarged by express statute, are limited to the protection of rights of property. It has no jurisdiction over the prosecution, the punishment, or the pardon of crimes or misdemeanors * * *. To assume such a jurisdiction, or to sustain a bill in equity to restrain or relieve against proceedings for the punishment of offenses, * * * is to invade the domain of the courts of common law, or of the executive and administrative department of the government."

In this Commonwealth, however, it was clearly established that courts with general equity powers have the power to restrain criminal prosecutions. In Shuman v. Gilbert, 229 Mass. 225, 118 N.E. 254 (1918), for example, this court recognized the "general rule" that criminal prosecutions are not to be enjoined, but pointed out, "[T]here is an exception to this comprehensive statement. Jurisdiction in equity to restrain the institution of prosecutions under unconstitutional or void statutes or local ordinances has been upheld by this court when property rights would be injured irreparably, and when other elements necessary to support cognizance by equity are present."

As pointed out in the *Shuman* case, the occasions when an equity court may properly enjoin a criminal prosecution remain the exception to the "general rule" of nonintervention. Some of the basic policy reasons underlying the rule of nonintervention were well-expressed by the Supreme Court of Hawaii: "Courts of equity are not constituted to deal with crimes and criminal proceedings. They have no power to punish admitted offenders of a challenged penal statute after holding it to be valid, or to compensate those injured by the violations thereof while the hands of the officers of the law have been stayed by injunction. To that extent such courts are incapable of affording a complete remedy. Equity, therefore, takes no part in the administration of the criminal law. It neither aids, restrains, nor obstructs criminal courts in the exercise of their jurisdiction. Ordinarily a court of equity deals only with civil cases involving property rights where it can afford a complete remedy by injunctive relief. Hence it does not interfere in the enforcement of penal statutes even though invalid unless there be exceptional circumstances and a clear showing that an injunction is urgently necessary to afford adequate protection to rights of property so as to circumvent great and irreparable injury until the validity of the particular penal statute is sustained." Liu v. Farr, 39 Hawaii 23, 35–36 (1950).

Both the *Shuman* and *Liu* cases quoted above indicated that equity would act only to protect "property rights" from irreparable damage by criminal prosecution. In the leading case of Kenyon v. Chicopee, 320 Mass. 528, 70 N.E.2d 241 (1946), however, we largely rejected the personal rights-property rights distinction as a factor in considering whether an injunction should issue. We considered this question and said: "We believe the true rule to be that equity will protect personal rights by injunction upon the same conditions upon which it will protect property rights by injunction. In general, these conditions are, [1] that unless relief is granted a substantial right of the plaintiff will be impaired to a material degree; [2] that the remedy at law is inadequate; and [3] that injunctive relief can be applied with practical success and without imposing an impossible burden on the court or bringing its processes into disrepute." This, then, is the test which the probate judge should have applied in considering the request for an injunction, and it is the test which we now apply to the facts before us. In so doing, we assume without deciding that parts (1) and (3) of the *Kenyon* test are satisfied and concentrate on part (2), that is, whether the remedy at law would be adequate in this case.

The plaintiff variously claims that G.L. c. 101, §§ 1–12, is either unconstitutional on its face or as applied, or that the statute, properly construed, does not apply to her at all. In accordance with these claims, she asserts that she cannot be prosecuted for failure to comply with the statute. If we assume, again without deciding the question, that the plaintiff indeed cannot properly be prosecuted under this statute, the issue resolves itself simply to whether the available defenses to the District Court criminal complaint amount to an adequate remedy at law. In the circumstances of this case, we think they plainly do.

In both the *Shuman* and *Kenyon* cases, the question was considered whether, in the circumstances of those cases, the defense to the criminal prosecution provided an adequate remedy at law. Since the injunction was denied in the former case and granted in the latter, it is instructive to compare them.

In the *Shuman* case, six merchants alleged that the defendant chief of police of Northampton threatened to prosecute them for conducting a business without a license, which they claimed they were not obligated to obtain. The plaintiff's bill sought to make out a case of irreparable damage and inadequacy of legal remedy by alleging, inter alia, that it would take several months to obtain a decision on the case from an appellate court and that in the intervening period the loss of profits and advantageous business relations would cause the plaintiffs great and irreparable damage. To these averments, a demurrer was sustained. This court upheld the sustaining of the demurrer. After noting that in the event of multiple, oppressive, and wrongful prosecutions, an injunction might properly issue, we said: "A possibility that complaints may be lodged against six persons is not enough under these circumstances to make out a case of multiplicity. The allegations as to repeated complaints are not sufficient to warrant the inference that the courts of this commonwealth will countenance continued and oppressive prosecutions when once a genuine test case open to fair question has been presented and is on its way to final decision." We further rejected any notion that our courts of criminal jurisdiction could not protect the rights in question: "[The bill] assumes that one innocent of any infraction of the law will be found guilty by the district court and by the superior court, a presumption which as matter of law cannot be indulged, at least upon such general allegations. The allegations as to property damage are nothing more than the ordinary averments which might be made by anybody engaged in business, undertaking a branch of commercial adventure believed by the officers charged with enforcing the law to be in contravention of some penal statute confessedly valid in itself. Simply that one is in business and may be injured in respect of his business by prosecution for an alleged crime, is no sufficient reason for asking a court of equity to ascertain in advance whether the business as conducted is in violation of a penal statute."

In the *Kenyon* case, by contrast, we reversed interlocutory decrees sustaining demurrers where the bill alleged that members of Jehovah's Witnesses had been repeatedly, on different dates, arrested, prosecuted, and convicted under an unconstitutional ordinance, prohibiting distribution of handbills, that on at least two occasions a defendant judge had convicted some of the plaintiffs despite being shown United States Supreme Court decisions holding such an ordinance unconstitutional, that the defendants well knew that the ordinances were unconstitutional and void, that the plaintiffs' means of paying bail fees and of posting bail and appeal bonds were exhausted, and that the defendants had threatened to and would continue to make false arrests, all to the irreparable damage of the plaintiffs' attempts to exercise their constitutional rights. In these circumstances, we held that an injunction against further prosecutions could properly issue if the allegations were ultimately proved. We observed: "The plaintiffs' rights are of the most fundamental character. According to the bill they have been violated repeatedly. It is plain that the legal remedies by defending against repeated complaints and bringing successive actions for malicious prosecution or false arrest are not adequate."

In the present case, the plaintiff is the subject of a complaint charging a single violation of the statute. She avers that the statute is either unconstitutional on its face or as applied, or that, properly construed, it is inapplicable to her. These averments, of course, would, if established, each constitute a complete defense to the violation charged. We repeat here a passage from a United States Supreme Court case which applies equally to the matter before us: "It is a familiar rule that courts of equity do not ordinarily restrain criminal prosecutions. No person is immune from prosecution in good faith for his alleged criminal acts. Its imminence, even though alleged to be in violation of constitutional guarantees, is not a ground for equity relief since the lawfulness or constitutionality of the statute or ordinance on which the prosecution is based may be determined as readily in the criminal case as in a suit for injunction. * * * It does not appear from the record that petitioners have been threatened with any injury other than that incidental to every criminal proceeding brought lawfully and in good faith, or that a * * * court of equity by withdrawing the determination of guilt from the * * * [criminal] courts could rightly afford petitioners any protection which they could not secure by prompt trial and appeal pursued to this Court." Douglas v. Jeannette, 319 U.S. 157, 163–164 (1943).

In general, we believe the Federal policy of ordinarily refusing to enjoin pending State criminal prosecutions is sound. This policy, based partly on principles of Federal–State comity and partly on the general equitable principles we have summarized in this opinion, Younger v. Harris, 401 U.S. 37, 43–44 (1971), prohibits equitable interference with criminal prosecutions absent "very special circumstances." "Very special circumstances" may be merely a shorthand way of requiring a stricter application of general equitable principles, for example, that no injunction will issue unless the plaintiff will suffer irreparable and immediate injury without it. But however the concept is phrased, the necessity of defending a single criminal prosecution rarely, if ever, justifies issuance of the injunction.

Our decision would not be different if we were considering only those portions of the proceedings below which involved a request for and grant of declaratory relief under G.L. c. 231A, §§ 2. The fundamental jurisprudential considerations underlying the general prohibition against enjoining a pending criminal prosecution apply with full force to support a prohibition against issuing declaratory decrees concerning a pending criminal prosecution. To conclude otherwise would encourage fragmentation and proliferation of litigation and disrupt the orderly administration of the criminal law.

The rule we adopt today in regard to the issuance of declaratory judgments when criminal litigation is pending is merely a logical extension of our rules which generally proscribe the issuance of such a judgment when an appropriate administrative proceeding is in progress, East Chop Tennis Club v. Massachusetts Commn. Against Discrimination, 364 Mass. 444, 305 N.E.2d 507 (1973), or when a civil proceeding in which the same issue is or can be raised is already pending between the parties. Jacoby v. Babcock Artificial Kidney Center, Inc., 364 Mass. 561, 307 N.E.2d 2 (1974). In the latter case we said: "Generally, '[a] court cannot declare rights as to matters involved in a prior pending action.' Anderson, Actions for Declaratory Judgments (2d ed.) § 209 (1951). While declarations of rights may be appropriate in exceptional cases even when other proceedings are in progress, there is an ordinary presumption against such relief. * * * In the *East Chop* case we stated that 'the existence of * * * [a] dispute alone is insufficient reason to disrupt the ordinary administrative process.' * * * This applies a fortiori to pending court proceedings. The declaratory relief procedure was not intended to permit the same claim to be adjudicated in multiple suits." In applying these principles in the criminal prosecution context, we follow the Federal rule, Samuels v. Mackell, 401 U.S. 66, 69–73 (1971); and the rule adopted in most States which have considered the issue. Cases in which declaratory relief was granted where no criminal prosecution was actually pending are, of course, readily distinguishable. Steffel v. Thompson, 415 U.S. 452, 457 (1974). [citations]

For the reasons given above, the injunction and declaratory relief should not have been granted.

Notes

1. *Unconstitutional Statute.* As the court in *Norcisa* suggests, injunctive relief may be granted prohibiting the authorities from enforcing a penal statute found to be unconstitutional. In Andrews v. Waste Control, Inc., 409 So.2d 707 (Miss.1982), the court approved an injunction against enforcement of a void county resolution that regulated the weight loads of trucks on a county road plaintiff used in his business.

2. *Inapplicable Statute.* A court may grant relief because of a valid statute is not applicable to a particular factual situation. See Huntworth v. Tanner, 87 Wash. 670, 152 P. 523 (1915). Plaintiff in *Norcisa* sought unsuccessfully to invoke this line of decisions.

3. *Caution.* Denying an injunction against the confiscation of the plaintiff's poker machines pursuant to a gaming statute, the Ohio Supreme Court said: "A court should exercise great caution regarding the granting of an injunction which would interfere with another branch of government and especially with the ability of the executive branch to enforce the law. * * * Unless the police seek to enforce an unconstitutional or void law, we will not inhibit their efforts to enforce the law." A limited injunction was granted for machines that were picked up despite the absence of any proof they were being used for profit. Garono v. State, 37 Ohio St.3d 171, 173, 524 N.E.2d 496, 499 (1988).

4. *"Our Federalism—United States Court—State Criminal Proceeding.* Younger v. Harris, which the court cites in *Norcisa*, involved the propriety of a federal court enjoining a state criminal prosecution. This question includes consideration of "general equitable principles," as the *Norcisa* court says; but the problem is even more complex because it also involves the relationship between a federal court and a state court. *Younger* held that a federal court should not enjoin a state prosecution except upon a "showing of bad faith, harassment, or any other unusual circumstance that would call for equitable relief." This result was based on the Court's view of "our federalism" which requires accommodation of "the legitimate interests of both State and National Governments." Younger v. Harris, 401 U.S. 37, 44, 54 (1971).

Younger raises potential federal-state conflict in addition to potential judicial-executive conflict. Should the state court have relied on *Younger* so heavily in *Norcisa*, an appeal that raised only the judicial-executive issue?

5. *State Civil Proceeding*. The Supreme Court has not resolved how far *Younger* applies to preclude federal injunctions against state civil lawsuits. The Court has found *Younger* principles applicable to federal suits to enjoin several types of state civil actions: (a) A state court judgment finding a theatre exhibiting obscene films a nuisance. Huffman v. Pursue, Ltd., 420 U.S. 592 (1975). (b) A contempt citation in judgment creditors' supplemental proceedings. Juidice v. Vail, 430 U.S. 327 (1977). (c) An injunction against the utilization of the Illinois procedure to recover welfare overpayment. Trainor v. Hernandez, 431 U.S. 434 (1977). (d) A child custody proceeding. Moore v. Sims, 442 U.S. 415 (1979). (e) A proceeding to discipline an attorney. Middlesex County Ethics Committee v. Garden State Bar Association, 457 U.S. 423 (1982). (f) A state administrative procedure where a religious school argued a First Amendment right to be free from the agency's jurisdiction. Ohio Civil Rights Commission v. Dayton Christian Schools, Inc., 477 U.S. 619 (1986). (g) Collection of the Texas civil judgment in the Texaco–Pennzoil lawsuit, while the appeal was pending. Pennzoil Co. v. Texaco, Inc., 481 U.S. 1 (1987).

Two later Supreme Court decisions define the outer boundaries of *Younger* civil abstention. (h) The Court disapproved abstention when plaintiff sought money damages, holding the abstention doctrines to be available only when the plaintiff requested equitable or otherwise discretionary relief. Quackenbush v. Allstate Insurance Co., 517 U.S. 706 (1996) (i) Dealing mainly with the domestic relations exception to diversity jurisdiction, the Court also barred federal-court abstention when there was no pending state proceeding. Ankenbrandt v. Richards, 504 U.S. 689 (1992).

During the last decade, the Supreme Court has left the basic body of *Younger* doctrine to the lower courts. A representative decision is Pompey v. Broward County: Persons detained for civil contempt in a state "Daddy Roundup" of alleged family support deadbeats sought a federal injunction requiring a better system of appointing an attorneys for an indigents before incarcerating him for contempt. "If the injunction plaintiffs seek were issued, any parent who was held in [state] contempt could and probably would seek relief in the federal district court on the grounds that the state judge had violated the federal injunction." And a disobedient state judge would be eligible in turn for federal contempt. The federal court thought that available state appeals and habeas corpus supplied the a contemnor an adequate and orderly method of raising his Sixth and Fourteenth Amendment contentions. Pompey v. Broward County, 95 F.3d 1543, 1550 (11th Cir.1996). See also, Anthony v. Council, 316 F.3d 412 (3d Cir.2003).

The imprecision and lack of fixed content in terms like "material injury" and "irreparable harm" give a court considerable flexibility and make predictions of success hazardous. Courses in Constitutional Law and Federal Courts explore the difficulty of turning the slogan, "Our Federalism," into rules a lawyer can understand and a judge can administer.

What's next for plaintiff? A potential plaintiff might consider devising a satisfactory federal damages theory or following the *Kenyon* plaintiffs into state court.

6. *Declaratory Judgment.* When the authorities have not begun a criminal prosecution, a potential criminal defendant may file for a declaratory judgment asking the court to determine whether a statute is unconstitutional or whether it is inapplicable to undisputed facts. A declaratory judgment is a freestanding remedy. The judge declares to the litigants what the law is and how it applies to their dispute; in a little more detail, a declaratory judgment is a final judicial determination which

clarifies or settles the parties' controversial legal relations by telling them what their rights and obligations are. A court may grant a declaratory judgment under statute; in addition to the state statute cited in *Norcisa*, see the federal statute, 28 U.S.C. § 2201.

A plaintiff may seek either a declaratory judgment or an injunction prior to actual injury. A declaratory judgment differs from an injunction in that a defendant's violation will not lead to contempt. But a declaratory judgment may be a foundation for an injunction or a damages judgment later in the lawsuit. Or it may resolve the dispute without more because the parties govern themselves accordingly. A declaratory judgment is a useful remedy in insurance coverage and patent validity disputes. A plaintiff may also consider a declaratory judgment when an injunction is potentially abrasive in inter- or intra-governmental relations.

One court, instead of enjoining, granted the plaintiff a declaratory judgment that a Texas prison rule requiring him to remain clean-shaven was inconsistent with his religious practice of wearing a 1/4 inch beard. Lewis v. Scott, 910 F.Supp. 282 (E.D.Tex.1995). Is a declaratory judgment the more civilized remedy? While a declaration lacks an injunction's contempt teeth, does a court in a society committed to the rule of law always need a bite to back up its bark?

7. *Block that Declaratory Judgment!* The Supreme Court ruled that a federal court may grant declaratory relief to determine the validity of a state statute without satisfying the *Younger* tests. Steffel v. Thompson, 415 U.S. 452 (1974). Once the state authorities begin a criminal prosecution, however, federal declaratory relief is less freely available. The court in *Norcisa* agrees. The date the federal declaratory action is commenced does not control; *Younger*'s principles govern if the state begins criminal proceedings "after the federal complaint is filed but before any proceedings of substance have taken place in the federal court." Hicks v. Miranda, 422 U.S. 332, 349 (1975).

5. EQUITY LACKS JURISDICTION TO ENJOIN A CRIME

Introduction. Courts and writers have frequently asserted that equity lacks jurisdiction to enjoin a crime. To Pomeroy in 1883 the doctrine was obvious enough to reduce to a brief footnote: "Injunction never granted to restrain criminal acts." Pomeroy, Equity Jurisprudence § 1347, n.1 (1883).

Where plaintiff's "property" rights are involved, however, the court may grant plaintiff an injunction if the defendant's activity, though criminal, could be classified as a public nuisance. Courts molded this concept to expand the sphere for injunctions.

PEOPLE EX REL. GALLO v. ACUNA

Supreme Court of California, 1997.
14 Cal.4th 1090, 60 Cal.Rptr.2d 277, 929 P.2d 596, certiorari denied, 521 U.S. 1121 (1997).

BROWN, JUSTICE. At the request of the City Attorney of the City of San Jose (hereafter the City), we granted review to resolve an array of challenges to two provisions of a preliminary injunction entered by the superior court against individual members of an alleged "criminal street gang." The underlying action was instituted under the provisions of sections 731 of the Code of Civil Procedure and 3480 of the Civil Code, the operative core of California's civil "public nuisance" statutes.

The 48 declarations submitted by the City in support of its plea for injunctive relief paint a graphic portrait of life in the community of Rocksprings.

Rocksprings is an urban war zone. The four-square-block neighborhood, claimed as the turf of a gang variously known as Varrio Sureno Town, Varrio Sureno Treces (VST), or Varrio Sureno Locos (VSL), is an occupied territory. Gang members, all of whom live elsewhere, congregate on lawns, on sidewalks, and in front of apartment complexes at all hours of the day and night. They display a casual contempt for notions of law, order, and decency—openly drinking, smoking dope, sniffing toluene, and even snorting cocaine laid out in neat lines on the hoods of residents' cars. The people who live in Rocksprings are subjected to loud talk, loud music, vulgarity, profanity, brutality, fistfights and the sound of gunfire echoing in the streets. Gang members take over sidewalks, driveways, carports, apartment parking areas, and impede traffic on the public thoroughfares to conduct their drive-up drug bazaar. Murder, attempted murder, drive-by shootings, assault and battery, vandalism, arson, and theft are commonplace. The community has become a staging area for gang-related violence and a dumping ground for the weapons and instrumentalities of crime once the deed is done. Area residents have had their garages used as urinals; their homes commandeered as escape routes; their walls, fences, garage doors, sidewalks, and even their vehicles turned into a sullen canvas of gang graffiti.

The people of this community are prisoners in their own homes. Violence and the threat of violence are constant. Residents remain indoors, especially at night. They do not allow their children to play outside. Strangers wearing the wrong color clothing are at risk. Relatives and friends refuse to visit. The laundry rooms, the trash dumpsters, the residents' vehicles, and their parking spaces are used to deal and stash drugs. Verbal harassment, physical intimidation, threats of retaliation, and retaliation are the likely fate of anyone who complains of the gang's illegal activities or tells police where drugs may be hidden.

Among other allegations, the City's complaint asserted that the named defendants and others "[f]or more than 12 months precedent to the date of [the] complaint, continuing up to the present time * * * [have] occupied [and] used the area commonly known as 'Rocksprings' * * * in such a manner so as to constitute a public nuisance * * * injurious to the health, indecent or offensive to the senses, [and] an obstruction to the free use of property so as to interfere with the comfortable enjoyment of life or property by those persons living in the * * * neighborhood."

After alleging the usual requisites for equitable relief—the prospect of "great and irreparable injury" and the absence of "a plain, adequate and speedy remedy at law"—the complaint prayed for a broad and comprehensive injunction against defendants' alleged activities in Rocksprings. The superior court granted an ex parte temporary restraining order enjoining all 38 defendants named in the complaint and issued an order to show cause (OSC) why a preliminary injunction should not be entered.

Only five of the named defendants appeared in response to the OSC. Following a hearing, the superior court entered a preliminary injunction against the 33 defendants who had not appeared and continued the matter as to those 5 defendants who opposed entry of a preliminary injunction, leaving the temporary restraining order in force as to them. Eleven of the named defendants * * * moved to vacate the injunctions. After the matter was briefed and argued, the superior court entered a preliminary injunction. The multi-part decree, consisting of some 24 paragraphs, was the subject of an interlocutory appeal by these 11 defendants.

The Court of Appeal disagreed with the superior court, upholding only provisions of the preliminary injunction enjoining acts or conduct defined as crimes under specific provisions of the Penal Code. Although its premise is never clearly articulated, that ruling effectively limits the scope of permissible injunctive relief under California's public nuisance statutes to independently criminal conduct. The Court of Appeal also concluded many of the provisions of the preliminary injunction were void and unenforceable under either the First and Fifth Amendments to the federal Constitution as unconstitutionally vague or overbroad. Altogether, 15 of the 24 provisions of the trial court's preliminary injunction were partially or entirely invalidated. However, the City's petition only sought review of two provisions—paragraphs (a) and (k). We granted the City's petition and now reverse.

We consider first the scope of and conditions precedent to the exercise of the superior court's equitable jurisdiction to enjoin a public nuisance. We then assess defendants' challenges to paragraphs (a) and (k) of the superior court's preliminary injunction, challenges based on restraints inherent in the administration of equitable remedies, and those arising from constitutionally based limitations. Finally, we consider (and reject) defendants' arguments that the "STEP" Act [The "Street Terrorism Enforcement and Prevention Act." Cal. Penal Code, § 186.22.] is the exclusive means of obtaining nuisance-based injunctive relief against a criminal street gang. We will conclude the two challenged provisions fall within the superior court's equitable power to abate a public nuisance and neither runs afoul of rights secured to defendants by the federal Constitution.

I. Equitable Jurisdiction to Enjoin Public Nuisances: A. The Origin and Nature of Actions to Enjoin Public Nuisances. Often the public interest in tranquility, security, and protection is invoked only to be blithely dismissed, subordinated to the paramount right of the individual. In this case, however, the true nature of the trade-off becomes painfully obvious. Liberty unrestrained is an invitation to anarchy. Freedom and responsibility are joined at the hip. * * * There must be an irreducible minimum of reciprocity for civil society to function. * * *

In the public nuisance context, the community's right to security and protection must be reconciled with the individual's right to expressive and associative freedom. Reconciliation begins with the acknowledgment that the interests of the community are not invariably less important than the freedom of individuals. Indeed, the security and protection of the community is the bedrock on which the superstructure of individual liberty rests. From Montesquieu to Locke to Madison, the description of the pivotal compact remains unchanged: by entering society, individuals give up the unrestrained right to act as they think fit; in return, each has a positive right to society's protection. * * * As we explain, a principal office of the centuries old doctrine of the "public nuisance" has been the maintenance of public order—tranquility, security and protection—when the criminal law proves inadequate.

There are few "forms of action" in the history of Anglo–American law with a pedigree older than suits seeking to restrain nuisances, whether public or private. Actions to abate private nuisances by injunction are the oldest of these apparent twins, which have almost nothing in common except the word "nuisance" itself. Unlike the private nuisance—tied to and designed to vindicate individual ownership interests in land—the "common" or public nuisance emerged from distinctly different historical origins. The public nuisance doctrine is aimed at the protection and redress of community interests and, at least in theory, embodies a kind of collective ideal of civil life which the courts have vindicated by equitable remedies since the beginning of the 16th century. * * *

In this country, as in England, civil suits in equity to enjoin public nuisances at the instance of public law officers—typically a state's Attorney General—grew increasingly common during the course of the 19th century, a trend that was not without critics. [citations]

With the publication of the Restatement Second of Torts in 1965, the law of public nuisances had crystallized to such an extent that its features could be clearly delineated. Section 821B of Restatement Second of Torts identifies five general categories of "public rights," the unreasonable interference with which may constitute a public nuisance: "the public health, the public safety, the public peace, the public comfort or the public convenience." A "public right," according to the Restatement Second, "is one common to all members of the general public. It is collective in nature and not like the individual right that everyone has not to be assaulted or defamed or defrauded or negligently injured."

In California, the early common law categories of public nuisance, codified in 1872 and still applicable, define anything that is "injurious to health, or is indecent or offensive to the senses, or an obstruction to the free use of property, so as to interfere with the comfortable enjoyment of life or property, or unlawfully obstructs the free passage or use, in the customary manner, of any navigable lake, or river, bay, stream, canal, or basin, or any public park, square, street, or highway," as a nuisance. (Civ.Code, § 3479.) Civil Code sections 3480 and 3481 divide the class of nuisances into public and private. A public nuisance is one which "affects at the same time an entire community or neighborhood, or any considerable number of persons." (Civ.Code, § 3480.) Rounding out the taxonomy of the Civil Code, section 3491 provides that "the remedies against a public nuisance are: 1. Indictment or information; 2. A civil action; or, 3. Abatement."

Section 370 of the Penal Code mirrors these civil provisions, combining the characteristics of nuisances generally with a distinctly public quality: that a given activity "interfere with the comfortable enjoyment of life or property by an entire community or neighborhood, or by any considerable number of persons." In People ex rel. Busch v. Projection Room Theater (1976) 17 Cal.3d 42, 49, 130 Cal.Rptr. 328, 550 P.2d 600, we parsed these code provisions, remarking on "the substantial identity of definitions appearing in Penal Code section 370 and 371, and Civil Code section 3479 and 3480." After quoting the text of section 370, we observed: "[T]he proscribed act may be anything which alternatively is injurious to health or is indecent, or offensive to the senses; the result of the act must interfere with the comfortable enjoyment of life or property; and those affected by the act may be an entire neighborhood or a considerable number of persons, and as amplified by Penal Code section 371 the extent of the annoyance or damage on the affected individuals may be unequal."

It is this community aspect of the public nuisance, reflected in the civil and criminal counterparts of the California code, that distinguishes it from its private cousin, and makes possible its use, by means of the equitable injunction, to protect the quality of organized social life. Of course, not every interference with collective social interests constitutes a public nuisance. To qualify, and thus be enjoinable, the interference must be both substantial and unreasonable. * * *

The Restatement Second formulates the requirement of substantiality as proof of "significant harm," defined as a "real and appreciable invasion of the plaintiff's interests," one that is "definitely offensive, seriously annoying or intolerable." The measure is an objective one: "If normal persons in that locality would not be substantially annoyed or disturbed by the situation then the invasion is not a significant one." The unreasonableness of a given interference represents a judgment reached by comparing the social utility of an activity against the gravity of the harm it inflicts, taking into account a handful of relevant factors. Here again, the standard is an objective one. * * *

B. Expansion and Contraction of "Criminal Equity." With the legitimacy of equitable relief to control public nuisances well established, American courts began to enlarge the jurisdiction of what has been called by some "criminal equity" and, by others, "government by injunction." The highwater mark of this trend may have been reached in In re Debs (1896) 158 U.S. 564 where a strike by employees at the Pullman car works in Chicago paralyzed much of the nation's rail transportation and, with it, national commerce. The strike was broken by the entry of a public nuisance injunction—the controversial "Pullman injunction." * * *

Justice Brewer's opinion for the court in In re Debs, reads like a primer on the first duty of government by consent—maintenance of the public order—and the utility of the public nuisance injunction in fulfilling that aspect of the social contract. Justice Brewer rested the power of the courts to issue such an injunction on the "obligations which [government] is under to promote the interest of all, and to prevent the wrongdoing of one resulting in injury to the general welfare," a duty which the court's opinion said was "often of itself sufficient to give [the government] standing in court."

An end to this expansive trend, at least as it was reflected in the jurisprudence of this court, came with Chief Justice Gibson's opinion in People v. Lim (1941) 18 Cal.2d 872, 118 P.2d 472. Although we upheld the complaint as sufficient, our opinion in People v. Lim, articulated an important limitation on the scope of the government's power to exploit the public nuisance injunction as an adjunct of general legal policy. * * *

After identifying a division among the authorities "as to whether the expansion of the field of public nuisances in which equity will grant injunctions must be accomplished by an act of the legislature," the Lim court came down firmly on the side of legislative supremacy. "The courts of this state," we wrote, "have refused to sanction the granting of injunctions on behalf of the state merely by a judicial extension of the definition of 'public nuisance.' * * * [They have] refused to grant injunctions on behalf of the state except where the objectionable activity can be brought within the terms of the statutory definition of public nuisance."

Reflected in the light of our holding in People v. Lim, two features of California's public nuisance scheme stand out. First, subject to overriding constitutional limitations, the ultimate legal authority to declare a given act or condition a public nuisance rests with the Legislature; the courts lack power to extend the definition of the wrong or to grant equitable relief against conduct not reasonably within the ambit of the statutory definition of a public nuisance.

This lawmaking supremacy serves as a brake on any tendency in the courts to enjoin conduct and punish it with the contempt power under a standardless notion of what constitutes a "public nuisance." * * *

Second, our opinion in People v. Lim, affirms the equal dignity, at least as far as the protection of equity is concerned, of private, property-based interests and those values that are in essence collective, arising out of a shared ideal of community life and the minimum conditions for a civilized society. * * * In a sense that cannot easily be dismissed, the availability of equitable relief to counter public nuisances is an expression of " 'the interest of the public in the quality of life and the total community environment.' "People ex rel. Busch v. Projection Room Theater.

C.   The Relation Between Crimes And Public Nuisances. As Justice Brewer noted in the *Debs* case: "A chancellor has no criminal jurisdiction. Something more than the threatened commission of an offense against the laws of the land is necessary to call into exercise the injunctive powers of the court. There must be some interference, actual or threatened, with property or rights * * * but when such interferences appear the jurisdiction of a court of equity arises, and is not destroyed by the fact that they are accompanied by or are themselves violations of the criminal law." We made the same point in People v. Lim: * * * "We think the proper rule, therefore, and the one to which this state is committed is expressed in the following language from State v. Ehrlick: 'It is also competent for the Legislature * * * to declare any act criminal and make the repetition or continuance thereof a public nuisance * * * or to vest in courts of equity the power to abate them by injunction.' "

In the *Ehrlick* case itself, the West Virginia high court wrote that "the Attorney General may proceed in equity on behalf of the public to abate the nuisance, if it be one. Whether it be a criminal nuisance or not is wholly immaterial. If it is indictable as a crime, it does not bar the remedy in equity, because the citizen and the general public have an immediate right to the enjoyment of the thing interfered with. A criminal prosecution is inadequate in such case, because it does not prevent the doing of the unlawful act. It may ultimately correct the wrong, but, while the process of correction is going on, the public is deprived of an important and valuable right, wherefore the injury is irreparable. In such cases it is not the criminality of the act that gives jurisdiction in equity, but the deprivation of personal and property rights interfered with, injured, destroyed, or taken away by the unlawful act."

The Court of Appeal was thus partly accurate in reasoning that "a public nuisance is always a criminal offense," for indeed it is. (See Pen.Code, § 372 [maintenance of a public nuisance is a misdemeanor].) It is the corollary to that proposition—that the superior court's injunction was valid only to the extent that it enjoined conduct that is independently proscribed by the Penal Code— that is flawed. Acts or conduct which qualify as public nuisances are enjoinable as civil wrongs or prosecutable as criminal misdemeanors, a characteristic that derives not from their status as independent crimes, but from their inherent tendency to injure or interfere with the community's exercise and enjoyment of rights common to the public. It is precisely this recognition of—and willingness to vindicate—the value of community and the collective interests it furthers rather than to punish criminal acts that lie at the heart of the public nuisance as an equitable doctrine. * * *

II.   Defendants' Constitutional Challenges to Provisions (a) and (k) of the Preliminary Injunction. * * *

B.   First Amendment Challenges. 1. Associational Interests. The Court of Appeal held that paragraph (a) of the preliminary injunction, enjoining defendants from "Standing, sitting, walking, driving, gathering or appearing anywhere in public view with any other defendant * * * or with any other known 'VST' (Varrio Sureno Town or Varrio Sureno Treces) or 'VSL' (Varrio Sureno Locos) member," was invalid on associational grounds; that is, the provision infringed defendants' right to associate with fellow gang members, a right protected by the First Amendment. We disagree. [In a part of the decision shortened for this casebook, the court held that the First Amendment does not "protect the collective public activities of the gang members within the four-block precinct of Rocksprings, activities directed in the main at trafficking in illegal drugs and securing control of the community through systematic acts of intimidation and violence."]

The Court of Appeal also invalidated paragraph (a) of the trial court's preliminary decree on the ground that these provisions were "overbroad," as that term has come to be understood and applied in the context of First Amendment litigation. * * *

[T]he foundation of the overbreadth doctrine is the inhibitory effect a contested statute may exert on the freedom of those who, although possibly subject to its reach, are not before the court. It is out of a generous concern for a statute's effects on the activities of such third persons that the high court has permitted facial challenges on behalf of those who are not parties to the litigation. * * *

Defendants do not attack the public nuisance statute itself, claiming that it suffers from the vice of overbreadth; instead, they attack the terms of the interlocutory decree as being unconstitutionally overbroad. The source of the [United States Supreme Court's] concern in the overbreadth cases, however, and the foundation of the doctrine itself, is the perceived danger to the constitutionally protected interests of those who, because they are not before the court, lack a judicial forum in which to litigate claims * * * .

It is the absent members of this unrepresented class who, "sensitive to the perils posed by * * * indefinite language, avoid the risk * * * by restricting their conduct to that which is unquestionably safe" Baggett v. Bullitt (1964) 377 U.S. 360, 372, for whom the overbreadth doctrine was fashioned.

The high court recently identified a related and constitutionally significant difference between injunctions and statutes in the context of protected speech claims. In Madsen v. Women's Health Center, Inc., 512 U.S. 753 (1994), the court pointed out that the narrow and particularized focus inherent in the nature of the injunction as an equitable remedy is also significant in evaluating the contention that features of a given decree suffer from constitutional overbreadth. Like the injunction in *Madsen*, the trial court's interlocutory decree here does not embody the broad and abstract commands of a statute. Instead, it is the product of a concrete judicial proceeding prompted by particular events— inimical to the well-being of the residents of the community of Rocksprings— that led to a specific request by the City for preventive relief.

As with any injunction, the preliminary decree here is addressed to identifiable parties and to specific circumstances; the enjoined acts are particularly described in the trial court's order. Unlike the pervasive "chill" of an abstract statutory command that may broadly affect the conduct of an absent class and induce self-censorship, the decree here did not issue until after these defendants had had their day in court. * * *

The only individuals subject to the trial court's interlocutory decree in this case, including those features contested as "overbroad," are named parties to this action; their activities allegedly protected by the First Amendment have been and are being aggressively litigated. There is accordingly no basis, legal or factual, for the professed concern that protected speech or communicative conduct by anyone other than defendants might be endangered by the terms of the trial court's injunction. In that sense, defendants' claim of overbreadth, made with respect to paragraph (a) of the preliminary injunction, is not cognizable.

Our conclusion with respect to defendants' "overbreadth" claim does not mean they may not be heard to complain that the provisions of the preliminary injunction—as applied to them and their conduct in Rocksprings—are broader than constitutionally sustainable. Rather, in this case that contention falls under the standard formulated by the court in *Madsen*,—the requirement that the superior court's decree burden no more of defendants' speech than necessary to serve the significant governmental interest at stake. We will consider that distinct claim separately, when we come to evaluate the sufficiency of the injunction under the standard announced by the court in Madsen. * * *

[T]he Court of Appeal was persuaded of the merits of defendants' constitutional challenge to the preliminary decree, ruling that provisions (a) and (k) were unconstitutionally vague and thus unenforceable. * * * [T]he underlying concern is the core due process requirement of adequate notice. "No one may be required at peril of life, liberty or property to speculate as to the meaning of penal statutes. All are entitled to be informed as to what the State commands or forbids." Lanzetta v. New Jersey (1939) 306 U.S. 451, 453. The operative corollary is that "a statute which either forbids or requires the doing of an act in terms so vague that men of common intelligence must necessarily guess at its meaning and differ as to its application, violates the first essential of due process of law." Connally v. General Construction Co. (1926) 269 U.S. 385, 391. * * *

[A] law that is "void for vagueness" not only fails to provide adequate notice to those who must observe its strictures, but also "impermissibly delegates basic policy matters to policemen, judges, and juries for resolution on an ad hoc and subjective basis, with the attendant dangers of arbitrary and discriminatory applications." Grayned v. City of Rockford (1972) 408 U.S. 104, 108–109. * * *

In the Court of Appeal's view, provision (a)'s prohibition against associating with "any other known 'VST' * * * or 'VSL' member" might apply to a circumstance in which a defendant was engaged in one of the prohibited activities with someone known to the police but not known to him to be a gang member. According to the Court of Appeal, such indefiniteness presented "a classic case of vagueness." We agree that in such a hypothetical case, the City would have to establish a defendant's own knowledge of his associate's gang membership to meet its burden of proving conduct in violation of the injunction. Far from being a "classic" instance of constitutional vagueness, however, we think the element of knowledge is fairly implied in the decree. To the extent that it might not be, we are confident that the trial court will, * * * impose such a limiting construction on paragraph (a) by inserting a knowledge requirement should an attempt be made to enforce that paragraph of the injunction. With that minor emendation, the text of provision (a) passes scrutiny under the vagueness doctrine.

The Court of Appeal found paragraph (k), enjoining defendants from "confronting, intimidating, annoying, harassing, threatening, challenging, provoking, assaulting and/or battering any residents or patrons, or visitors to 'Rocksprings' * * * known to have complained about gang activities [,]" impermissibly vague in two respects. First, like paragraph (a), it speaks of persons "known to have complained about gang activities," without indicating how or even whether a defendant is to be charged with this knowledge. The discussion with respect to the knowledge requirement of provision (a) of the decree applies equally to this provision and, so construed, it too passes muster.

Second, according to the Court of Appeal, provision (k) fails to define sufficiently the words "confront," "annoy," "provoke," "challenge," or "harass"; it thus fails to provide a standard of conduct for those whose activities are proscribed. Yet similar words were upheld against claims of vagueness by the Supreme Court in *Madsen*. There, the high court affirmed injunctive relief prohibiting petitioners from engaging in similar—if not more broadly phrased— conduct: " 'intimidating, harassing, touching, pushing, shoving, crowding, or assaulting persons entering or leaving.' "We find nothing in the context of this case, factually similar in many respects to the situation before the court in *Madsen*, that makes the same words, sufficiently definite there, somehow constitutionally infirm here. * * *

Finally, the declarations filed by the City in support of preliminary relief leave little doubt as to what kind of conduct the decree seeks to enjoin. One Rocksprings resident recounted an incident in which gang members had threatened to cut out the tongue of her nine-year-old daughter if she talked to the police; she stated that other residents had been threatened as well. Another resident reported her neighbor's property had been vandalized and the resident threatened after complaining to police that gang members had urinated in her garage. A police officer declared Rocksprings residents had told him gang members confront and threaten them with physical violence when asked to leave residential property. Others refused to furnish declarations, fearing for their lives if any gang member should discover their identities. We conclude neither of the two provisions should have been invalidated by the Court of Appeal on vagueness grounds.

III.   Claim That the STEP Act Is the Exclusive Means of Abating Gang Behavior as a Public Nuisance. Defendants contend that the STEP Act (Pen. Code, § 186.20 et seq.) is the exclusive means of enjoining criminal street gangs and preempts use of the general public nuisance statutes. We disagree. By express provision, the act is not the exclusive remedy for abating gang activity constituting a public nuisance. Under the STEP Act, a building or place used by members of a criminal street gang for specified illegal activities is declared a nuisance per se: "Every building or place used by members of a criminal street gang for the purpose of the commission of [specified] offenses * * * and every building or place wherein or upon which that criminal conduct by gang members takes place, is a nuisance which shall be enjoined, abated, and prevented, and for which damages may be recovered, whether it is a public or private nuisance." The act goes on to provide that "[n]othing in this chapter shall preclude any aggrieved person from seeking any other remedy provided by law." It thus plainly contemplates remedies in addition to the act to abate criminal gang activities, including those made available by the general public nuisance statutes.

In this case, the City expressly sought equitable relief, not under the STEP Act, but under the general public nuisance statutes. Accordingly, we need not determine whether some or all of the conduct enjoined would also fall within the scope of the act or whether any of the defendants could be enjoined under its provisions.

IV. Evaluating the Limits of the Preliminary Injunction. A. Substantive Limits. Having concluded that provisions (a) and (k) of the preliminary injunction are not unconstitutionally vague or overbroad and do not infringe defendants' constitutionally protected associational interests, we must complete our inquiry by considering the limitations on the scope of the interlocutory decree as a matter of both public nuisance and constitutional law. We must ask, in other words, two questions: First, whether the activity enjoined under these two provisions reasonably falls within the statutory definition of a public nuisance as construed in People v. Lim, and second, whether the two provisions comply with the constitutional standard announced by the Supreme Court in *Madsen*, that is, whether they "burden no more speech than necessary to serve a significant governmental interest."

That the conduct enjoined by the trial court meets the statutory definition of a public nuisance is clear from the account of conditions in Rocksprings recited at the outset of this opinion. To constitute a public nuisance under our Civil Code, conduct must be "injurious to health, * * * indecent or offensive to the senses, * * * an obstruction to the free use of property, so as to interfere with the comfortable enjoyment of life or property, or unlawfully obstruct[ ] free passage or use, in the customary manner, of any * * * public park, square, street or highway." In addition, the conduct must affect "an entire community or neighborhood, or any considerable number of persons."

The many declarations filed with the superior court by the City in support of its request for injunctive relief meet these criteria. Gang members not only routinely obstruct Rocksprings residents' use of their own property—by such activities as dealing drugs from apartment houses, lawns, carports, and even residents' automobiles—but habitually obstruct the "free passage or use, in the customary manner," of the public streets of Rocksprings. It is likewise clear from this record that the conduct of gang members qualifies as "indecent or offensive to the senses" of reasonable area residents: the hooligan-like atmosphere that prevails night and day in Rocksprings—the drinking, consumption of illegal drugs, loud talk, loud music, vulgarity, profanity, brutality, fistfights and gunfire—easily meet the statutory standard. Nor is it difficult to see how threats of violence to individual residents and families in Rocksprings, murder, attempted murder, drive-by shootings, assault and battery, vandalism, arson and associated crimes obstruct the free use of property and interfere with the enjoyment of life of an entire community.

Do provisions (a) and (k) of the superior court's preliminary injunction meet the constitutional test formulated by the Supreme Court in *Madsen*, by "burden[ing] no more speech than necessary to serve" an important governmental interest? We conclude both provisions satisfy the constitutional test. As noted, provision (a) effectively forbids gang members from engaging in any form of social intercourse with anyone known to them to be a gang member "anywhere in public view" within the four-block area of Rocksprings. The provision's ban on all forms of association—"standing, sitting, walking, driving, gathering or appearing anywhere in public view"—does not violate the *Madsen* standard merely because of its breadth. The provision seeks to ensure that, within the circumscribed area of Rocksprings, gang members have no opportunity to combine.

It is the threat of collective conduct by gang members loitering in a specific and narrowly described neighborhood that the provision is sensibly intended to forestall. Given that overriding purpose, the prohibitions enumerated in provision (a) are not easily divisible. Permitting two or more gang members to drive together but not sit, or to stand together but not walk, would obviously defeat the core purpose behind the proscription. Moreover, given the factual showing made by the City in support of preliminary relief—the carnival-like atmosphere of collective mayhem described above—we cannot say that the ban on any association between gang members within the neighborhood goes beyond what is required to abate the nuisance.

The effect of provision (a)'s ban on defendants' protected speech is minimal. To judge from the evidence placed before the superior court, the gangs appear to have had no constitutionally protected or even lawful goals within the limited territory of Rocksprings. So far as the record before the trial court shows, the gangs and their members engaged in no expressive or speech-related activities which were not either criminally or civilly unlawful or inextricably intertwined with unlawful conduct. According to the declaration of Officer Niehoff, an eight-year veteran of the San Jose Police Department: "Illegal drug dealing by Sureno gang members, including VSL/VST, is a common practice, and the gang entity provides protection to the individual members, allowing them to establish areas where they can conduct their illegal activities. The protective shield of the gang has allowed individual members to commit crimes such as narcotic trafficking that result in personal gain. These crimes are committed in association with the gang because of the protection offered to the members by virtue of their gang affiliation. In the Rocksprings area, the fact that numerous narcotics transactions occurred is a direct result of the protective shield provided by VSL/VST. Individuals who claimed membership in VSL or VST were at liberty to deal drugs in a veritable 'safe' zone."

Does provision (a)'s prohibition on a gang member associating with even a single fellow gang member within Rocksprings transgress the test of *Madsen*? Could not the restriction be limited to barring associations between, say, three other gang members? Two gang members? On such a highly particular question, we are compelled to defer to the superior knowledge of the trial judge, who is in a better position than we to determine what conditions "on the ground" in Rocksprings will reasonably permit. Outside the perimeter of Rocksprings, the superior court's writ does not run; gang members are subject to no special restrictions that do not affect the general population. Given the limited area within which the superior court's injunction operates, the absence of any showing of constitutionally protected activity by gang members within that area, the aggravated nature of gang misconduct, the fact that even within Rocksprings gang members may associate freely out of public view, and the kind of narrow yet irreducible arbitrariness that inheres in such line-drawing, we conclude that this aspect of provision (a) passes muster as well under the standard of *Madsen*.

We reach a similar resolution with respect to provision (k). That provision forbids those subject to the injunction from confronting, intimidating or similarly challenging—including assaulting and battering—residents of Rocksprings, "or any other persons" whom gang members know have complained about their conduct within the neighborhood. It has long been the rule, of course, that physical violence and the threat of violence are not constitutionally protected. * * *

[The court's decision on "Those Bound By The Preliminary Injunction" is reprinted below with other material on that subject.]

V.   Conclusion. To hold that the liberty of the peaceful, industrious residents of Rocksprings must be forfeited to preserve the illusion of freedom for those whose ill conduct is deleterious to the community as a whole is to ignore half the political promise of the Constitution and the whole of its sense. The freedom to leave one's house and move about at will, and to have a measure of personal security is "implicit in the concept of ordered liberty" enshrined in the history and basic constitutional documents of English-speaking peoples. Wolf v. Colorado (1949) 338 U.S. 25, 27–28. Preserving the peace is the first duty of government, and it is for the protection of the community from the predations of the idle, the contentious, and the brutal that government was invented. * * *

The judgment of the Court of Appeal is reversed insofar as it invalidated paragraphs (a) and (k) of the preliminary injunction and concluded that defendant Blanca Gonzalez was not subject to its terms. Because our grant of review encompassed only those two of the fifteen provisions invalidated by the Court of Appeal, we do not address any other aspect of the preliminary injunction entered by the superior court.

KENNARD, JUSTICE, concurring and dissenting. * * * I do not * * * join the majority in upholding the injunction's paragraph (a), which prohibits the named defendants from being in the company of any other VSL or VST member while "[s]tanding, sitting, walking, driving, gathering or appearing anywhere in public view" in the four-block Rocksprings area. The evidence presented in this case falls far short of establishing that so drastic a restriction on the rights of defendants and other VSL and VST members to peacefully assemble is necessary to abate the public nuisance. * * *

CHIN, JUSTICE, concurring and dissenting. I would hold that the evidence is insufficient to enjoin * * * Blanca Gonzalez.

The legal principle at issue is quite simple. The law requires some link between each defendant who is subject to an injunction and the problem the injunction addresses. The majority argues that in this case gang membership and a one-time presence in Rocksprings is enough to establish this link. The majority reasons the trial court could have enjoined the gangs as a whole, and therefore it could enjoin individual gang members instead. I agree that, in an appropriate case, a court may enjoin individuals based on group membership. Cf. Madsen v. Women's Health Center, Inc. But the requirement of proof is no less rigorous in such a case. "For liability to be imposed by reason of association alone, it is necessary to establish that the group itself possessed unlawful goals and that the individual held a specific intent to further those illegal aims." (NAACP v. Claiborne Hardware Co. (1982) 458 U.S. 886, 920. I do not believe the City of San Jose (the City) has met this standard with respect to * * * Blanca Gonzalez. * * *

The only evidence linking Blanca Gonzalez with the nuisance in Rocksprings is that she was in Rocksprings "wearing a black top and black jeans," which according to police was "consistent with members of Sureno criminal street gangs," and she claimed gang membership. This evidence is not sufficient to prove (even at the preliminary injunction stage) that she "held a specific intent to further [the gangs'] illegal aims," assuming the Sureno gangs have illegal aims. * * *

The gangs in question here are loosely organized associations of individuals with no express common purpose or central leadership. Some people may dress as gang members or claim membership in the gangs because of peer pressure or out of fear; the people primarily responsible for the public nuisance in Rocksprings may be a small minority of gang members. I do not discount the serious threat to community values that criminal street gangs pose. Nevertheless, we cannot turn a blind eye to the necessities of proof. I believe the majority has done so in the case of * * * Blanca Gonzalez.

MOSK, JUSTICE, dissenting. No doubt Montesquieu, Locke, and Madison will turn over in their graves when they learn they are cited in an opinion that does not enhance liberty but deprives a number of simple rights to a group of Latino youths who have not been convicted of a crime. Mindful of the admonition of another great 18th century political philosopher, Benjamin Franklin, that "[t]hey that can give up essential liberty to obtain a little temporary safety deserve neither liberty nor safety," I would, unlike the majority, in large part affirm the judgment of the Court of Appeal. * * *

[T]he City did not challenge the Court of Appeal's determination that the following conduct, inter alia, was improperly enjoined: possession or use in Rocksprings of such everyday items as beepers, pens, spray paint cans, nails, screwdrivers, or any "sharp objects capable of defacing private or public property"; "encouraging" or "participating" in the use or possession of narcotics; "engaging in conversation, or otherwise communicating with the occupants of any vehicle"; using communicative hand signs or signals describing or referring to the gangs; wearing clothing bearing the name or letters associated with the gangs; climbing trees or walls or "passing through" fences. The City impliedly concedes that the Court of Appeal correctly struck these provisions of the injunction as enjoining more conduct than was necessary to abate the nuisance and on constitutional grounds. * * *

I agree with the Court of Appeal that following provisions of the preliminary injunction should be sustained, because they restrict gang-related conduct that the superior court not unreasonably found was likely to be proved on the merits to constitute a public nuisance in the Rocksprings neighborhood: paragraphs (b) (public consumption of alcoholic beverages or drugs); (d) (fighting in the public streets); (f) (spray painting or otherwise applying graffiti to public or private property); (g) (trespassing on or encouraging others to trespass on any private property); (h) (blocking free ingress and egress to the public sidewalks or street or to any driveways leading or appurtenant thereto in Rocksprings); (j) (discharging firearms); (p) (demanding entry into another person's residence); (t) (littering in any public place or place open to public view); and (u) (urinating or defecating in any public place or place open to public view). The record includes allegations and supporting declarations concerning the prevalence of these activities by VSL–VST gang members in Rocksprings. The activities also readily fall within the statutory definition of a "nuisance" as "[a]nything which is injurious to health, * * * or is indecent or offensive to the senses, or an obstruction to the free use of property, so as to interfere with the comfortable enjoyment of life or property, or unlawfully obstructs the free passage or use, in the customary manner, of any * * * public park, square, street, or highway" and as a "public nuisance" as "one which affects at the same time an entire community or neighborhood, or any considerable number of persons. That some or all of these activities may also constitute criminal violations does not limit the superior court's power to grant a preliminary injunction in this case. * * *

Paragraph (a) enjoins "[s]tanding, sitting, walking, driving, gathering or appearing anywhere in public with any other defendant herein, or with any other known 'VST' * * * or 'VSL' * * * member." It applies without any requirement or condition that a defendant or his associate be engaged in any illegal activity or misconduct related to the alleged public nuisance.

The provision is impermissibly vague. Who is a "known" VST or VSL member? And by whom is such membership "known"? * * * In the absence of any specific definition of gang membership, neither police officers nor courts are provided with a consistent standard for determining when a violation of the injunction occurred. * * *

Apart from these fundamental vagueness problems, the prohibitions under paragraph (a) [penalize] much ordinary and lawful activity that does not fall within the statutory definition of a public nuisance. The prohibitions are not only sweeping, but absolute: they apply without regard to the defendant's intent or to the circumstances. In my view, a defendant may not be subject to a contempt sanction for merely walking in, driving through, or "appearing" in the Rocksprings neighborhood in the company of any "known" gang member without causing any disruption. Such everyday conduct is not "injurious to health, * * * or * * * indecent or offensive to the senses, or an obstruction to the free use of property"; nor does it affect "at the same time an entire community or neighborhood." * * *

Activity in Rocksprings that consists of "in any manner confronting, annoying, * * * challenging, [or] provoking" others may include so much ordinary social behavior—and so much that depends on the individual sensibilities of those who might feel annoyed, challenged, or provoked—that it impermissibly invites arbitrary enforcement. * * *

The majority would permit our cities to close off entire neighborhoods to Latino youths who have done nothing more than dress in blue or black clothing or associate with others who do so; they would authorize criminal penalties for ordinary, nondisruptive acts of walking or driving through a residential neighborhood with a relative or friend. In my view, such a blunderbuss approach amounts to both bad law and bad policy. Chief Justice Warren warned in Jay v. Boyd (1956) 351 U.S. 345, 367: "Unfortunately, there are some who think that the way to save freedom in this country is to adopt the techniques of tyranny." The majority here appear to embrace that misguided belief. Accordingly, I dissent.

Notes

1. The New York City authorities used Gallo v. Acuna as a model for a public-nuisance lawsuit seeking an injunction to clean up prostitution in and around Queens Plaza. The City's lawsuit failed ignominiously at the trial; this failure is

recorded in Judge Lonschein's opinion, City of New York v. Andrews, 186 Misc.2d 533, 719 N.Y.S.2d 442 (Sup.Ct.2000).

Judge Lonschein brought experience to *Andrews*: "[A]s the Justice assigned to all nuisance abatement cases in Queens, over the last few years I have directed the closing of dozens of houses of prostitution, pursuant to the provisions of that law, in all parts of Queens. Similarly, I have, pursuant to that law directed the closing of well over a hundred other illegal businesses which created a nuisance in their neighborhoods, such as crack houses, fencing operations, illegal sales of liquor, gambling dens, nude dancing establishments and the like."

Andrews will be cited and quoted below to contrast it with Gallo v. Acuna.

2. *A Personal Criminal Statute.* An injunction is a miniature criminal statute that threatens to subject the defendant to criminal contempt for a violation. A defendant's argument against granting an injunction to forbid crimes, that the plaintiff's remedy of a criminal prosecution is an adequate remedy at law, is, at base, an argument that a defendant is entitled to criminal procedural protections, including a jury and proof beyond a reasonable doubt.

Andrews: "A separate concept is that, as a general matter, the prosecution of criminal matters should be left to the criminal courts, and the remedies found there are generally considered to be sufficient. That such prosecutions have been unsuccessful due to the reluctance of juries to convict is not a reason for equity to intervene.

"Here, the totality of numerous criminal acts has, without doubt, created a nuisance that adversely affects property interests not only of the City itself but of all the legitimate people and businesses in the Queens Plaza area. The mere incantation of the word 'nuisance' does not mean that this situation is best treated by civil injunction, however. I have grave doubts that this nuisance is one which is amenable to equity jurisdiction at all. * * * [T]he court is asked to craft an unprecedented injunction, ad hoc, wholly on the basis of common-law principles. These principles do not compel the issuance of the injunction sought, the proof does not justify it, and I decline the invitation to go so far into uncharted territory.

"The City has made it quite plain that it intends to use this injunction to bypass the Criminal Court, which it sees as providing inadequate relief. As to the male defendants, whom the City alleges are the organized pimps controlling the operation, the argument may fairly be said to come down to this: They know who the bad guys are, but they don't have enough evidence to prove it in Criminal Court, and so they want to use the lesser civil standard of proof to get relief here. * * *

"The City has absolutely failed to prove its scandalous innuendo that the judges of the Criminal Court have been unwilling to enforce the law. The City's attorneys claimed at the hearing that part of their lack of effectiveness in enforcing the prostitution laws in the Queens Plaza area is due to the low priority placed on this offense by the Criminal Court. They claimed to be faced with a classic 'revolving door' situation, where the Court puts the prostitutes back on the streets on the same night they are arrested, in effect allowing them to pay their fines by repeating their offenses. * * * There was no proof whatever that the female defendants have not received appropriate sentences when convicted.

"I emphatically reject the notion that this court may serve as an ad hoc alternative to the Criminal Court. I do not sit in review of the sentencing decisions of the judges of that Court, and will not presume to evaluate those decisions as an element of this action. If the City finds itself aggrieved by a perceived leniency in those sentencing decisions, it can attempt to persuade the judges to be more stringent. If the judges cannot be so persuaded, recourse can be had to the Legislature, in an attempt to mandate stricter sentences.''

How does the court in Gallo v. Acuna respond to the defendants' argument that the government is limited to the criminal statutes to enforce the criminal law?

3. *A Common Law Crime.* A related argument, that a public nuisance injunction can only forbid criminal activity, is grounded on the idea that the legislature defines the criminal law in a criminal statute and that a court ought not create the equivalent of a new crime through granting an injunction.

In Gallo v. Acuna, how does the court deal with the defendants' argument that the law limits a plaintiff's public-nuisance injunction to forbidding the defendants' criminal activity?

4. *Criminal Misconduct Enjoined.* Earlier public nuisance injunctions forbade defendants' criminal activity: prohibition violations, prostitution, illegal gambling, People v. Lim which is cited, and dissemination of obscene material, People ex rel. Busch v. Projection Room Theater which is cited.

The courts found the government's remedy of bringing criminal prosecutions against the defendants' to be ''inadequate'' for several reasons: the defendant's criminal activity may not generate a complaining victim; the criminal sanctions may be too small to deter the defendant's illegal activity; and a criminal jury may not take the defendant's crimes seriously enough, often declining to convict.

5. *Government By Injunction.* The *Gallo* court's injunction against street gangs resembles earlier courts' injunctions against strikes. In 1898, commenting on the *Debs* decision, which the *Gallo* court cites, Mr. Gregory tells us that Mr. Debs's counsel, Clarence Darrow, quoted ''this witticism'' in the Supreme Court brief ''but without naming its author.'' ''The present Chief Justice of the United States, before he became the head of the bench, remarked of a reforming member of the Chicago bar, 'Brother B. would codify all laws in an act of two sections: 1st, All people must be good; 2d, Courts of equity are hereby given full power and authority to enforce the provisions of this act.' '' Charles Noble Gregory, Government By Injunction, 11 Harv. L. Rev. 487, 510 (1898). Congress passed the Norris–La Guardia Act in 1932 to curb the federal courts' injunctions against strikes. 29 U.S.C. §§ 101–07.

6. *The Street Gang Menace.* The authorities have prosecuted street-gang members under the federal R.I.C.O., (Racketeer Influenced Corrupt Organizations) Act, as well as the conspiracy statutes and for specific crimes. The California Street Terrorism Enforcement and Prevention Act, S.T.E.P., which the court discussed, is a specialized and narrower version of federal R.I.C.O. Both have a civil component and provide for an injunction. Why do you suppose the San Jose authorities chose to sue the gang members under the general public nuisance statute instead of the more focused S.T.E.P. statute? *Easy Conviction*

7. *A Criminal Statute.* The city of Chicago designed an anti-loitering ordinance to control street gangs' criminal activities. An officer who observed a criminal street gang member ''loitering in any public place with one or more other persons'' could order ''all such persons to disperse and remove themselves.'' The warned person's failure to obey the officer's order promptly constituted the criminal offence.

The United States Supreme Court invalidated the ordinance on void for vagueness grounds. Chicago v. Morales, 527 U.S. 41 (1999).

How does the injunction in *Gallo* differ from Chicago's anti-loitering ordinance?

In *Andrews*, Judge Lonschein wrote that ''the viability of [Gallo v.] Acuna may fairly be called into question after the holding of the Supreme Court in City of Chicago v. Morales.''

8. *Buffer Zone.* In addition to defendants' criminal activity, the street-gang injunction forbade preparatory, related, and connected activity. The abortion clinic injunction in Madsen v. Women's Health Center, which the *Gallo* court cited, also forbids preparatory, related, and connected activity. In *Madsen* the Supreme Court approved a 36–foot "buffer zone" injunction; it forbids defendants' expressive conduct, otherwise protected speech, which occurs within the buffer zone. An injunction restricting defendants' speech, the Court said, may "burden no more speech than necessary to serve a significant governmental interest." It struck down a 300–foot "no approach" zone open only to invited protestors. Madsen v. Women's Health Center, Inc., 512 U.S. 753, 765 (1994).

In Schenck v. Pro–Choice Network, a later decision, the trial judge had granted an injunction with (a) a fixed 15–foot buffer zone around a clinic's entrances and driveway; (b) a "floating" 15–foot buffer zone around people entering and leaving the clinic; and (c) a "cease and desist" provision allowing a "sidewalk counselor" access to someone in the fixed zone so long as the approached person did not signal that she did not wish to be counseled. (a) The *Schenck* Court followed *Madsen* and approved the fixed buffer zone. (b) But that Court struck down the floating buffer zone. (c) After upholding the "cease and desist" provision for the fixed zone, the Court did not decide the constitutionality of the "cease and desist" provision for the floating zone. Schenck v. Pro–Choice Network, 519 U.S. 357, 359 (1997).

In addition to the state's criminal statutes and common law torts like trespass and assault, the federal Freedom of Access to Clinic Entrances Act is a basis for federal court jurisdiction and an injunction against forbidden forms of obstruction at an abortion clinic. 18 U.S.C. §§ 248(a)–248(e). A successful FACE plaintiff may also recover compensatory damages and punitive damages as well as reasonable attorneys' and expert witnesses' fees. Of course an anti-abortion protest gone awry may also be enjoined as a public nuisance. Town of West Hartford v. Operation Rescue, 726 F.Supp. 371 (D.Conn.1989). However, the Supreme Court rejected an abortion clinic's federal RICO claims against anti-abortion protesters. Scheidler v. National Organization for Women, 126 S.Ct. 1264 (2006).

This book returns to the abortion-clinic injunction when considering remedies to protect the property owner's right to exclude.

9. The original buffer-zone injunction had established a 25–foot floating buffer zone around the late Jacqueline Kennedy Onassis to protect her from the torts of, and harassment by, Galella, a paparazzo. Galella v. Onassis, 487 F.2d 986 (2d Cir.1973).

10. *Preparatory Misconduct.* In addition to banning defendants' crimes, a plaintiff may seek an injunction that forbids defendants' activity that is preparatory, related, and ancillary to the crimes. In Gallo v. Acuna, for example, paragraph (a) forbids gang members from associating with other gang members in the injunction area.

In *Andrews,* Judge Lonschein described the injunction the City sought: "The City seeks, in item 'A,' nothing less than the civil banishment of the named individuals from the Queens Plaza area between the hours of 11:00 p.m. and 7:00 a.m. While the literal terms of the item only prohibit the defendants from appearing 'in public view,' there can be no doubt that the defendants would be completely unable to comply unless they stayed out of the area entirely. If they were to be seen walking on the streets or driving to the Queensboro Bridge, or even taking the subway to Manhattan, they would be subject to a contempt proceeding. This demand is completely unprecedented in my experience, and the City points to no New York precedents even remotely similar to it. * * *

"I must conclude that the injunction sought by the City here intrudes upon the defendants' constitutional freedoms to travel and remain in the Queens Plaza area, far more than is necessary to serve the legitimate governmental interest in suppressing the prostitution trade there. On constitutional grounds, therefore, it may not be granted.

"Aside from constitutional concerns, the injunction sought by the City is not a prudent or proper use of the court's equity powers. I have noted at length [the] view that the civil banishment injunction goes far beyond that which is necessary to address the actual wrong the City claims the defendants are perpetrating. The City argues that the defendants have no legitimate business in Queens Plaza, would not go there at the times referred to in the injunction except to engage in the prostitution business, and so are not burdened by the proposed banishment. This argument misses the point. It is the City's burden to justify the injunction as necessary to meet the wrong actually alleged. To put the matter in the traditional framework, the City has not established that a balancing of the equities favors this injunction."

The Gallo v. Acuna injunction had not flunked constitutional tests. Why might the City of New York have asked for an injunction that was broader than the Gallo v. Acuna injunction?

11. *The Modern Public Nuisance.* When someone uses property to commit a crime or offence, a local jurisdiction's enforcement tools include zoning, building codes, public health enforcement, as well as forfeiture, civil and criminal. Nevertheless, litigants and courts continue to shape the malleable public nuisance concept to deal with contemporary issues.

(a) *Crack.* Some public nuisance abatement of crack houses occurs in connection with criminal prosecutions. One abatement order required the house to remain vacant for one year. United States v. Wade, 992 F.Supp. 6 (D.D.C.1997). Neighboring owners sued in Kellner v. Cappellini, 135 Misc.2d 759, 516 N.Y.S.2d 827 (Civ.Ct. 1986).

(b) *AIDS.* City of New York v. New Saint Mark's Baths, 130 Misc.2d 911, 497 N.Y.S.2d 979 (1986).

(c) *Love Canal and Other Hazardous Waste Sites*: United States v. Occidental Chemical Corp., 965 F.Supp. 408 (W.D.N.Y.1997), is a later decision. United States v. Hooker Chemicals & Plastics Corp., 722 F.Supp. 960 (W.D.N.Y.1989), established the public nuisance.

(d) *Illegal Gambling.* United States v. Santee Sioux Tribe of Nebraska, 135 F.3d 558, 565 (8th Cir.1998).

(e) *Global Warming–Greenhouse Gases.* Eight states and New York City sued six power companies charging that the defendants' plants' fossil-fuel emissions were a public nuisance and seeking an injunction to cap and reduce the defendants' emissions of carbon dioxide. The judge dismissed the complaint on the ground that it presented a non-justiciable political question. State of Connecticut v. American Electric Power Co., 406 F.Supp.2d 265 (S.D.N.Y.2005).

(f) *Digression: Public Nuisance for Damages—Guns and Lead–Based Paint.* The Attorney Generals' lawsuits against the tobacco companies for reimbursement of medical expenses ended in settlements worth $246 billion. This success spurred State and local governments to file public-nuisance reimbursement actions against firms associated with dangerous products. Many state and local governments have brought public-nuisance lawsuits chiefly seeking damages against the manufacturers, distributors, and dealers of both firearms and lead-based paint. In 2004 and 2005, courts in Illinois characterizing these public-nuisance lawsuits as "repackaged" products-liability claims, dismissed two of them. Firearms in City of Chicago v. Beretta U.S.A.

Corp., 213 Ill.2d 351, 821 N.E.2d 1099 (2004) (Garman, J.). Lead-based paint in City of Chicago v. American Cyanamid Co., 355 Ill.App.3d 209, 823 N.E.2d 126 (2005).

On the other hand, in February 2006, a Rhode Island jury found that three lead-paint manufacturers created a public nuisance. Rhode Island v. Lead Industries Association, C.A. No. 99–5226. The "remedies" phase remained. And several other lawsuits are awaiting trial.

12. *Obscenity as a Nuisance.* The *Gallo* court relies on a California obscenity-nuisance decision, People ex rel. Busch v. Projection Room Theater. In fact, the authorities' use of public-nuisance injunctions to control obscenity in books, theatres, and live shows has met with indifferent success and created much confusion. An article on obscenity injunctions singles out *Busch* for criticism. Doug Rendleman, Civilizing Pornography: The Case for an Exclusive Obscenity Nuisance Statute, 44 U.Chi.L.Rev. 509, 522–24 (1977).

The defendants' constitutional right to free expression may prevent the authorities from closing an "adult" business to curtail customers' illegal activity.

The United States Supreme Court held that the federal Constitution's First Amendment did not bar an injunction that closed a bookstore. Arcara v. Cloud Books, Inc., 478 U.S. 697 (1986). But, on remand, the New York Court of Appeals found that the state constitution afforded more breathing space than the "minimal standards" in the federal First Amendment. The authorities had not shown that an injunction closing the store was the narrowest course to accomplish its goals. The authorities were left with criminal prosecutions of the customers and narrower injunctions. People ex rel. Arcara v. Cloud Books, Inc., 68 N.Y.2d 553, 510 N.Y.S.2d 844, 503 N.E.2d 492 (1986).

In People v. Sequoia Books, the only crime defendants had committed was the sale of obscene material. The authorities argued for an injunction closing the bookstore with a provision that the proprietor could post a bond and remain open. The Illinois Supreme Court held the closure and bond provisions unconstitutional:

"Insofar as the remedy of nuisance abatement is intended as simply another weapon in the State's antiobscenity arsenal, it is too blunt an instrument. Under the ordinary penal law relating to obscenity, punishment is fairly well calibrated to the nature and gravity of the crime. Each discrete act of selling obscene material is subject to penal sanction. Someone who sells 100 obscene books is, theoretically at least, subject to more severe punishment than someone who sells only a single volume. Under the nuisance statute, on the other hand, the owner of property from which a single obscene work is sold stands in the same danger of losing, for one year, the entire value of his investment, as does the owner of a property from which are sold obscene works in the hundreds or thousands.

"This blunderbuss approach to the regulation of obscenity is inconsistent with our traditional insistence that the regulation of any form of expression, even of obscenity, be carefully drawn so as not to impact unduly upon protected speech. * * * Moreover, obscenity, unlike the other criminal acts which may trigger a nuisance abatement, is unique—because it is so closely related to, and so hard to distinguish from, protected speech. For this reason, nuisance abatements tend to single out owners of bookstores for harsher treatment than the owners of other kinds of commercial property, and may also be unconstitutional on that ground as well. * * *

"Lastly, we consider the State's interest in controlling the environmental or secondary effects of the sale of obscenity. This interest may be what the State is talking about when it says that 'the property focus of the instant legislation is what distinguishes this case from those which involve the licensing or banning of the communicative activity itself.' However, the State has at its disposal far less draconian, and far more narrowly focused, means of combating pornography's environmental effects. Zoning restrictions, which may either disperse sale of sexually explicit materials to widely separated locations [citation] or confine it to a relatively small, nonresidential zone [citation] have been repeatedly upheld. The State can also abate as nuisances establishments which tolerate or promote sexual and other crimes on their premises. (Arcara v. Cloud Books, Inc., 478 U.S. 697 (1986)). Given the existence of these alternatives, the State has no need to combat obscenity's environmental effects by abating, as nuisances, particular properties upon which obscene works have been sold." People v. Sequoia Books, Inc., 127 Ill.2d 271, 288–91, 537 N.E.2d 302, 310–12 (1989), cert. denied, 493 U.S. 1042 (1990).

13. *The Injunction Triumphant.* The material above reveals the earlier general limits on granting an injunction either defeated or tattered and in full retreat. The injunction has become the major remedy to protect constitutional rights. Environmental interests have joined the constitutional as candidates for injunctive protection. Courts grant injunctions freely to protect trade secrets, copyrights, patents, and trademarks. A court will usually order an employee discharged in violation of civil rights statutes or the constitution to be reinstated. Structural injunctions are injunctions, usually federal, which protect citizens' constitutional interests in state and local government institutions, schools, prisons and jails, mental health, foster children, and public housing.

14. *What's Next?* Paralleling the decline of the irreparable injury rule or inadequacy prerequisite and other limitations, courts will develop more precise rules to govern granting injunctions. The new rules will be tempered by countervailing considerations that militate against granting an injunction. These rules will be based on policies like deference to other courts, protection of litigants' right to a jury, dislike of forcing personal relations, and distaste for complex supervision. The separate rules for temporary restraining orders and preliminary injunctions are examined below.

15. *Where Will It All Lead?*

News Item, The National Law Journal, March 25, 1996, A27, not further reported:

Boy Ordered To Play Nice: Three-year-old Jonathan had better not make little Stacy cry anymore.

Drawing a line in the sandbox, a Boston judge has issued a court order to make the little boy play nice.

"Maybe it's a little emotional, maybe it's overprotective, but you do what you can," said Stacy's mother, Antonina Pevnev, who filed for the restraining order, claiming that Jonathan kicked her daughter in the head.

The incident took place while the 3-year-olds were playing in the Charles River Park playground on the Charles River. Jonathan had bullied Stacy before, Ms. Pevnev said.

Ms. Pevnev went to court, asking that Jonathan-and his mother, Margareth Inge, not even be allowed in the playground while her daughter was there.

On March 4, Superior Court Judge Charles Spurlock decided that the mothers must keep the children supervised and separated while at the playground.

Violators can be held in contempt, fined or even jailed-in theory, at least. But since it would be tough to prove a 3–year-old had knowingly violated a court order, chances are that only the grown-ups would get punished.

6. EQUITY WILL NOT ENJOIN A LIBEL

Even though the plaintiff in Tory v. Cochran seeks to enjoin defendant's defamation, the Traditional Maxim that "Equity Will Not Enjoin a Libel" has mostly been absorbed into the constitutional rule that disfavors a prior restraint. An injunction is a prior restraint if, in advance, it forbids a defendant's speech. Courts think that a prior restraint threatens a defendant's expression more than a subsequent punishment which would take the form of tort damages or a criminal conviction. But the prior restraint rule is not an absolute one: a court will indulge a heavy presumption against the constitutional validity of a prior restraint.

The prior restraint rule differs from the Maxims that we studied earlier. Denying a plaintiff an injunction that forbids a defendant's defamation means that the judge stands aside and lets the defendant's wrong occur instead of taking an active step to prevent it. This passive stance may seem wrong. A correction never catches up with the falsehood. A plaintiff's reputation and emotional distress damages are difficult for a jury to measure. Money can neither replace a plaintiff's reputation nor alleviate his emotional distress. Tort damages after a libel are a less adequate remedy for a plaintiff than an injunction before it. On the usual irreparable injury rule analysis, a plaintiff should have an injunction against libel.

Why does a court disfavor an injunction as a prior restraint? An injunction, it is feared, will suppress the defendant's speech and lead to over-enforcement. Also, since there will be no jury for an injunction, the prior restraint rule is related to the law's preference for a jury trial in a damages action.

TORY v. COCHRAN

Supreme Court of the United States, 2005.
544 U.S. 734.

JUSTICE BREYER delivered the opinion of the Court. Johnnie Cochran brought a state-law defamation action against petitioner Ulysses Tory. The state trial court determined that Tory (with the help of petitioner Ruth Craft and others) had engaged in unlawful defamatory activity. It found, for example, that Tory, while claiming falsely that Cochran owed him money, had complained to the local bar association, had written Cochran threatening letters demanding $10 million, had picketed Cochran's office holding up signs containing various insults and obscenities; and, with a group of associates, had pursued Cochran while chanting similar threats and insults. The court concluded that Tory's claim that Cochran owed him money was without foundation, that Tory engaged in a continuous pattern of libelous and slanderous activity, and that Tory had used false and defamatory speech to "coerce" Cochran into paying "amounts of money to which Tory was not entitled" as a "tribute" or a "premium" for "desisting" from this libelous and slanderous activity.

After noting that Tory had indicated that he would continue to engage in this activity in the absence of a court order, the Superior Court issued a permanent injunction. The injunction, among other things, prohibited Tory, Craft, and their "agents" or "representatives" from "picketing," from "displaying signs, placards or other written or printed material," and from "orally uttering statements" about Johnnie L. Cochran, Jr., and about Cochran's law firm in "any public forum."

Tory and Craft appealed. The California Court of Appeal affirmed. Tory and Craft then filed a petition for a writ of certiorari, raising the following question: "Whether a permanent injunction as a remedy in a defamation action, preventing all future speech about an admitted public figure, violates the First Amendment." We granted the petition.

After oral argument, Cochran's counsel informed the Court of Johnnie Cochran's recent death. Counsel also moved to substitute Johnnie Cochran's widow, Sylvia Dale Mason Cochran, as respondent, and suggested that we dismiss the case as moot. Tory and Craft filed a response agreeing to the substitution of Ms. Cochran. But they denied that the case was moot.

We agree with Tory and Craft that the case is not moot. Despite Johnnie Cochran's death, the injunction remains in effect. Nothing in its language says to the contrary. Cochran's counsel tells us that California law does not recognize a "cause of action for an injury to the memory of a deceased person's reputation," see Kelly v. Johnson Pub. Co., 160 Cal.App.2d 718 (1958), which circumstance, counsel believes, "moots" a *portion* of the injunction (the portion "personal to Cochran"). But counsel adds that "[t]he [i]njunction continues to be necessary, valid and enforceable." The parties have not identified, nor have we found, any source of California law that says the injunction here *automatically* becomes invalid upon Cochran's death, not even the portion personal to Cochran. Counsel also points to the "value of" Cochran's "law practice" and adds that his widow has an interest in enforcing the injunction. And, as we understand California law, a person cannot definitively know whether an injunction is legally void until a court has ruled that it is. See Mason v. United States Fidelity & Guaranty Co., 60 Cal.App.2d 587, 591 (1943) ("[W]here the party served believes" a court order "invalid he should take the proper steps to have it dissolved"); People v. Gonzalez, 12 Cal.4th 804, 818 (1996) ("[A] person subject to a court's injunction may elect whether to challenge the constitutional validity of the injunction when it is issued, or to reserve that claim until a violation of the injunction is charged as a contempt of court"). Given the uncertainty of California law, we take it as a given that the injunction here continues significantly to restrain petitioners' speech, presenting an ongoing federal controversy. [citations] Consequently, we need not, and we do not, dismiss this case as moot. [citation]

At the same time, Johnnie Cochran's death makes it unnecessary, indeed unwarranted, for us to explore [Tory's] basic claims, namely (1) that the First Amendment forbids the issuance of a permanent injunction in a defamation case, at least when the plaintiff is a public figure, and (2) that the injunction (considered prior to Cochran's death) was not properly tailored and consequently violated the First Amendment. Rather, we need only point out that the injunction, as written, has now lost its underlying rationale. Since picketing Cochran and his law offices while engaging in injunction-forbidden speech could no longer achieve the objectives that the trial court had in mind (*i.e.,* coercing Cochran to pay a "tribute" for desisting in this activity), the grounds for the injunction are much diminished, if they have not disappeared altogether. Consequently the injunction, as written, now amounts to an overly broad prior restraint upon speech, lacking plausible justification. See Nebraska Press Assn. v. Stuart, 427 U.S. 539, 559 (1976) ("[P]rior restraints on speech and publication are the most serious and the least tolerable infringement on First Amendment rights"); Pittsburgh Press Co. v. Pittsburgh Comm'n on Human Relations, 413 U.S. 376, 390 (1973) (a prior restraint should not "swee[p]" any "more broadly than necessary"). As such, the Constitution forbids it. See Carroll v. President and Comm'rs of Princess Anne, 393 U.S. 175 (1968) (An "order" issued in "the area of First Amendment rights" must be "precis[e]" and narrowly "tailored" to achieve the "pin-pointed objective" of the "needs of the case"); see also Board of Airport Comm'rs of Los Angeles v. Jews for Jesus, Inc., 482 U.S. 569 (1987) (regulation prohibiting "all 'First Amendment activities'"substantially overbroad).

We consequently grant the motion to substitute Sylvia Dale Mason Cochran for Johnnie Cochran as respondent. We vacate the judgment of the California Court of Appeal, and we remand the case for proceedings not inconsistent with this opinion. If, as the Cochran supplemental brief suggests, injunctive relief may still be warranted, any appropriate party remains free to ask for such relief. We express no view on the constitutional validity of any such new relief, tailored to these changed circumstances, should it be entered.

It is so ordered.

JUSTICE THOMAS, with whom JUSTICE SCALIA joins, dissenting. I would dismiss the writ of certiorari as improvidently granted. * * * Whether or not Johnnie Cochran's death moots this case, it certainly renders the case an inappropriate vehicle for resolving the question presented. * * *

In deciding the threshold mootness issue, a complicated problem in its own right, the Court strains to reach the validity of the injunction after Cochran's death. Whether the injunction remains valid in these changed circumstances is neither the reason we took this case nor an important question, but merely a matter of case-specific error correction. [Defendants] remain free to seek relief on both constitutional and state-law grounds in the California courts. And, if the injunction is invalid, they need not obey it: California does not recognize the "collateral bar" rule, and thus permits collateral challenges to injunctions in contempt proceedings. People v. Gonzalez. The California courts can resolve the matter and, given the new state of affairs, might very well adjudge the case moot or the injunction invalid on state-law grounds rather than the constitutional grounds the Court rushes to embrace. * * *

The Court's decision invites the doubts it seeks to avoid. Its decision is unnecessary and potentially self-defeating. The more prudent course is to dismiss the writ as improvidently granted. I respectfully dissent.

Notes

1. Under California law, could defendants have violated the injunction and argued to defend contempt that the injunction was moot?

2. Would the injunction forbid defendant Tory from having a change of heart and praising Johnnie Cochran as the world's greatest lawyer?

Does the majority accept defendants' second argument—that the injunction was "not properly tailored," in other words that it was too broad? If so, does the Court vacate the injunction because it forbids defendants' nondefamatory expression?

Does the Court implicitly reject defendants' first argument—that a public figure plaintiff cannot enjoin a defendant's defamation?

3. Suppose a former client falsely accuses a lawyer of stealing—"Attorney Cochroch stole money from my settlement." Could the trial judge find that the

specific defamatory statement was libelous and enjoin the defendant from repeating it?

Should the Supreme Court have held that a judge's injunction that forbids the defendant from repeating a specific defamatory statement about the plaintiff is not an improper prior restraint

As this edition is being prepared, a California appeal court has held that a judge's injunction forbidding the defendant's statements that the court had adjudicated to be defamatory is an improper prior restraint. The judge may grant a plaintiff an injunction against expression in support of a statutory policy, but, the court held, not one that forbids a defendant's common-law defamation. The court may grant a plaintiff an injunction to uphold a statutory policy; in particular, it may enjoin defendant's discrimination with an injunction forbidding racial epithets in the workplace. However, a common-law defamation plaintiff's only remedy is damages. Balboa Island Village Inn v. Lemen, 17 Cal.Rptr.3d 352 (Cal.App.2004), review granted, 22 Cal.Rptr.3d 517, 102 P.3d 904 (2004). The California Supreme Court will review that decision; the court had granted review, but it had deferred its decision pending the United States Supreme Court's decision in Tory v. Cochran, above.

4. Would a pin-pointed injunction forbidding the defendant from repeating a specific defamatory statement about the plaintiff be worthless as a practical matter?

5. The prior restraint rule may not apply to a defendant's commercial speech. A judge will grant the plaintiff an injunction against a defendant's speech, for example his false advertising, securities fraud, or commercial disparagement.

B. INJUNCTION PROCEDURE

1. INTERLOCUTORY RELIEF: TRO AND PRELIMINARY INJUNCTION

Because money damages will be inadequate relief, plaintiff requires an injunction promptly to eliminate or to minimize her irreparable loss before the judge's final decision. Plaintiff maintains that unless the judge grants her an injunction—right now—defendant's misconduct is, or soon will be, inflicting irreparable harm. The judge may grant plaintiff's request for a temporary restraining order (TRO) or a preliminary injunction to protect plaintiff's entitlement and to preserve the controversy for a meaningful decision after full trial.

The judge's intractable problem is how to accomplish the plaintiff's worthy goal while protecting the defendant from the severity of a possibly erroneous interlocutory injunction granted after less than a full hearing. If the judge incorrectly denies plaintiff a preliminary injunction, that will harm plaintiff irreparably. However, moving quickly to protect plaintiff's substantive interest from irreparable injury requires the judge to take procedural shortcuts. This lack of full judicial consideration in turn increases the risk of an incorrectly granted preliminary injunction, an error that may injure defendant.

The federal system uses the terms (a) injunction or permanent injunction, (b) preliminary injunction, and (c) temporary restraining order or TRO. A judge may grant an injunction or a permanent injunction only after a full trial. A preliminary injunction follows a hearing and adversary proceeding. See Federal Rule of Civil Procedure 65(a). A judge may issue a temporary restraining order with no adversary hearing at all; such an order is called an ex parte TRO. See Federal Rule of Civil Procedure 65(b).

Some state procedural systems use different terminology. State rules and statutes may refer to interlocutory orders as provisional, pendente lite, or temporary injunctions as you may learn when you examine the appropriate sources in your jurisdiction.

ROE v. CRAWFORD

United States District Court, W.D. of Missouri, 2005.
396 F.Supp.2d 1041.
Stay denied, 126 S.Ct. 477 (2005).

ORDER AND MODIFIED JUDGMENT OF PRELIMINARY INJUNCTION

WHIPPLE, DISTRICT JUDGE. On October 13, 2005, the Court held a telephone conference on the Verified Complaint. Motion and Affidavits filed by Plaintiff. Plaintiff appeared by counsel, Thomas Blumenthal. Defendants appeared by counsel, Michael Pritchett, Missouri Assistant Attorney General. After considering the arguments made by counsel, the Court granted Plaintiff's Motion for a Preliminary Injunction. The Defendants failed to comply with the Court's Order. Pending now before the Court is Defendants' Motion to Stay or Suspend the Preliminary Injunction Pending Appeal and Request for Expedited Ruling.

I. *Motion to Stay.*

Defendants move to stay execution of the Court's Order dated October 13, 2005, granting a preliminary injunction in favor of Plaintiff Roe pending appeal. Fed. R. Civ. P. 62(c). * * *

Defendants' Motion to Stay is merely a recitation of the points in opposition made at the October 13, 2005 Preliminary Injunction Hearing. For the reasons stated in the Court's Order of October 13, 2005, Defendants' Motion is DENIED.

Defendants are hereby ORDERED to carry out the Court's Modified Judgment of Preliminary Injunction set forth below.

II. *Modified Judgment of Preliminary Injunction*

A. *Factual Background.* Plaintiff Roe is a pregnant female over the age of eighteen (18) years who desires to terminate her pregnancy. It appears that when measured from the first day of her last menstrual period Plaintiff is approximately 16–17 weeks pregnant. She is currently incarcerated at Women's Diagnostic and Correctional Center (WERDCC). Medical services to terminate a pregnancy are not offered at the detention facility. The nearest clinic that performs medical services to terminate pregnancy at Plaintiff's stage of pregnancy is Reproductive Health Services of Planned Parenthood of St. Louis (RHS) located at 4251 Forest Park Avenue, St. Louis, MO 63108. A procedure such as the one being sought is only performed on Fridays, and requires one, possibly two days to perform safely, depending on the actual condition of the patient after examination. Defendants' conduct of delaying the procedure creates an increased health risk to Plaintiff as well as an increased cost of the two day procedure.

Defendants have previously provided transportation and security to RHS for detainees seeking such a procedure. Such transportation was the status quo until at least some time in 2004. Defendants in this instance have refused to allow Plaintiff to leave the premises to have this outpatient procedure performed. Plaintiff has made some reasonable effort to obtain the procedure but has been unable to do so.

Plaintiff brings two constitutional claims. First, she alleges that the prison's policy that female prisoners will not be sent out of their institutions for abortions that are not medically necessary deprives her of her Fourteenth Amendment right to reproductive choice. Second, Plaintiff alleges that by forcing her to carry her unwanted pregnancy to term, WERDCC evinces a deliberate indifference to her serious medical needs in violation of the Eighth and Fourteenth Amendments' prescription of cruel and unusual punishment. Plaintiff requests a preliminary injunction requiring the Defendants to transport her to a local health care provider for the purpose of providing medial services to terminate her pregnancy. For the following reasons, Plaintiff's Motion is GRANTED.

B. *Preliminary Injunction.* It is well settled law that a plaintiff's application for preliminary injunctive relief involves the court's examination of the following four factors: (1) the threat of irreparable harm to the movant; (2) the state of the balance between this harm and the injury that granting the injunction will inflict on other parties; (3) the probability that movant will succeed on the merits; and (4) the public interest. [citation] Considering the parties' respective positions in light of these guidelines, and for the following reasons, the Court finds that Plaintiff is entitled to the injunctive relief sought.

1. *Threat of Irreparable Harm to the Movant.* The United States Supreme Court has made clear that the denial of a woman's right to choose to terminate her pregnancy constitutes irreparable injury:

> The detriment that the State would impose upon the pregnant woman by denying this choice altogether is apparent. Specific and direct harm medically diagnosable even in early pregnancy may be involved. Maternity, or additional offspring, may force upon the woman a distressful life and future. Psychological harm may be imminent. Mental and physical health may be taxed by child care. There is also the distress, for all concerned, associated with the unwanted child, and there is the problem of bringing a child into a family already unable, psychologically and otherwise, to care for it.

Roe v. Wade, 410 U.S. 113, 153 (1973).

Further, it is well-accepted that a substantial dely in the decision to abort increases the risks associated with the procedure. [citation] *See also* Williams v. Zbaraz, 442 U.S. 1309, 1314 (Stevens, J., sitting as Circuit Justice) (increased risk of "maternal morbidity and mortality" supports claim of irreparable injury). Defendants' conduct denies Plaintiff the right to choose to terminate her pregnancy and has already delayed Plaintiff's procedure by six weeks. Complaint at ¶ 24. Further delay by Defendants may cause Plaintiff substantial injury, exposing her to increased medical, financial, and psychological risks. Thus, the Court finds that Plaintiff has established the requisite irreparable injury.

2. *Balance of Harm.* Defendants contend that to accommodate Plaintiff's request they will suffer harm outweighing that suffered by Roe. They argue the public risks harm any time a prisoner is removed from a facility and that as accommodation of Plaintiff's request requires official supervision, fewer officers at the facility puts both the officers and the inmates at risk. will substantially increase the risk to the public. As discussed above, further delay of Plaintiff's request will cause Plaintiff irreparable harm. The Court finds that equities balance in the Plaintiff's favor.

3. *Probability of Success on the Merits.* Plaintiff has established the probability of ultimately succeeding on the merits of this case. In determining the constitutionality of prison regulations, the Supreme Court has held "when a prison regulation impinges on inmates' constitutional rights, the regulation is valid if it is reasonably related to legitimate penological interests." Turner v. Safley, 482 U.S. 78 (1987). In Roe v. Wade, the Supreme Court held that "[the] right of privacy * * * is broad enough to encompass a woman's decision whether or not to terminate her pregnancy." A woman's constitutional right to choose an abortion survives incarceration and must be justified by a legitimate penological objective. [citation]

Legitimate penological interests include the deterrence of crime, rehabilitation of prisoners and institutional safety. [citation] Defendants argue that the prison policy not to transport female prisoners out of the institution for abortions that are not medically necessary is reasonably related to the penological interests of security and cost. These interests, however, are not legitimate penological interests. "[A]ll other things being equal, inmates who wish to have an abortion pose no greater security risk than any other inmate who requires outside medical attention." [citation]

Second, Plaintiff contends that Defendants' conduct violates her Eighth Amendment rights, as applied to the States, through the Fourteenth Amendment. The Court agrees that a prison official's deliberate indifference to a serious medical need violates the Eighth Amendment. [citation]

4. *Public Interest.* Finally, granting the preliminary injunction will do no harm to the public interest. Defendant argues that transporting Plaintiff for a nontherapeutic abortion will harm the "state's public policy, reflected by its statutes [citations] to discourage abortions and encourage childbirth." The Eighth Circuit, in agreeing with the State's interpretation of the statute, has held that the statute "does not prevent state employees from arranging for abortion procedures for inmates or from transporting and escorting inmates to abortion facilities." Reproductive Health Serv. v. Webster, 851 F.2d 1071, 1084, *rev'd on other grounds,* 492 U.S. 490 (1989).

Conversely, the public interest demands that an injunction enjoin a policy which impinges on Roe's constitutional rights and privileges.

III. *Conclusion*

Pursuant to the Court's Modified Judgment of Preliminary Injunction, Defendants are directed to transport Plaintiff to Reproductive Health Services of Planned Parenthood of St. Louis (RHS) * * * on Saturday, October 15, 2005 at 9:00 A.M. for the purpose of providing medical services to terminate her pregnancy, including, but not limited to any necessary counseling, education, surgery, and follow-up services, for a period of no more than 48 hours.

Absent a stay granted by the Eighth Circuit Court of Appeals prior to Saturday, October 15, 2005 at 9:00 A.M., an application for a stay of this Modified Order does not authorize Defendants to refuse to carry out its terms. This Court will not tolerate further defiance of its Orders. IT IS SO ORDERED.

Notes

1. *Litigation on a Fast Track.* Pseudonymous prisoner Jane Roe was 16–17 weeks pregnant when she sued the Missouri correction authorities. Willing to pay for

her abortion, Roe needed to be released and transported to a suitable facility. Judge Whipple's original hearing on Roe's complaint and motion for a preliminary injunction was on Thursday the 13th leading to the judge's first preliminary injunction. On Friday the 14th, the judge's principal decision above responded to the defendant's motion for a stay of the first preliminary injunction.

Judge Whipple's decision above with its modified preliminary injunction did not end the litigation. The defendants did not take Roe to St. Louis on Saturday. Instead, the Eighth Circuit Court of Appeals having declined a stay, the defendants sought an emergency temporary stay of the preliminary injunction from United States Supreme Court Justice Thomas, the circuit justice for the eighth circuit. He granted a temporary stay so that the full Court could consider the matter.

On Monday the 17th, the Supreme Court's two-sentence order was: "Application for a stay presented to Justice Thomas and by him referred to the Court denied. Temporary stay entered October 14, 2005, vacated." Crawford v. Roe, 126 S.Ct. 477 (2005). The Supreme Court's order reinstated Judge Whipple's decision and preliminary injunction.

After the order, Roe obtained an abortion.

2. *The Four–Point Test.* The judge decides legal issues in the matrix of the four-point standard for a preliminary injunction. As Judge Whipple's citation of Turner v. Safley indicates, a prison inmate has attenuated rights. For example, the authorities may read a prisoner's mail. But the State had a duty to provide medical care to a prisoner. Although she has a constitutional right to an abortion, the state need not subsidize a woman in obtaining one.

Did the State's refusal to bring Roe to an abortion clinic amount to declining to subsidize the procedure? Or did the State's declining transportation to incarcerated Roe interfere with her constitutional rights to medical care and to an abortion?

How does Judge Whipple deal with the preceding questions under the four-point preliminary injunction test?

3. Roe's situation in light of the legal standard provides a real test of whether a judge can use the preliminary injunction standard to reduce total harm, that is irreparable injury to the plaintiff seeking an interlocutory injunction and harm to the defendant from an incorrect TRO or preliminary injunction granted after procedural shortcuts.

By the way, is Judge Whipple's "preliminary" injunction a preliminary or an effectively final one?

4. *A Disfavored Preliminary Injunction.* The four-point test may be only a starting place. One variation governs in the tenth federal circuit. It turns on the kind of preliminary injunction a plaintiff seeks. It identifies three categories of disfavored preliminary injunctions: (a) one that alters the status quo, as opposed to preserving it; (b) one that is mandatory, as opposed to prohibitory; (c) and one that gives the plaintiff the full relief she seeks at trial. Then the judge should scrutinize a plaintiff's motion for a disfavored preliminary injunction carefully "to assure that the exigencies of the case support the granting of a remedy that is extraordinary even in the normal course." Before granting a disfavored preliminary injunction, the judge will place a heightened burden on the plaintiff by requiring her to make a strong showing of both likelihood of success on the merits and the balance of harms. O Centro Espirita Beneficiente Uniao Do Vegetal v. Ashcroft, 389 F.3d 973 (10th Cir. 2004) (en banc), affirmed without discussing the preliminary injunction standard, Gonzales v. O Centro Espirita Beneficiente Uniao Do Vegetal, 126 S.Ct. 1211 (2006).

Is Roe's preliminary injunction in one or all of the Tenth Circuit's three categories of disfavored preliminary injunctions? If so, does Roe satisfy the "heightened burden" on likelihood of success on the merits and the balance of harms?

5. *A Sliding Scale.* Moreover, a plaintiff seeking a disfavored preliminary injunction may not rely on a "modified-likelihood-of-success-on-the-merits standard." *O Centro.*

The modified or "sliding-scale" standard has two sides. (a) A plaintiff who makes a less strong showing of likelihood of success on the merits must make a strong showing that the balance of irreparable injury favors her. (b) On the other hand, a plaintiff who makes a strong showing that she is likely to succeed on the merits need not make such a strong showing that the balance of harms favors her; however, a plaintiff who shows a small likelihood of irreparable injury must show that success on the merits is almost certain.

The Second Circuit's statement of the sliding-scale test is: "Preliminary injunctive relief in this Circuit calls for a showing of (a) irreparable harm and (b) either (1) likelihood of success on the merits or (2) sufficiently serious questions going to the merits to make them a fair ground for litigation and a balance of hardships tipping decidedly toward the party requesting the preliminary relief." Jackson Dairy, Inc. v. H.P. Hood & Sons, Inc., 596 F.2d 70, 72 (2d Cir. 1979)(per curiam). Quoted and applied in CDC Group PLC v. Cogentrix Energy, Inc., 354 F.Supp.2d 387, 389 (S.D.N.Y. 2005).

6. *Math–Math Avoidance?* (a) *Math.* The *American Hospital Supply* standard for granting a preliminary injunction was stated, cited, and recited for a time.

"A district judge asked to decide whether to grant or deny a preliminary injunction must choose the course of action that will minimize the costs of being mistaken. Because he is forced to act on an incomplete record, the danger of a mistake is substantial. And a mistake can be costly. If the judge grants the preliminary injunction to a plaintiff who it later turns out is not entitled to any judicial relief—whose legal rights have not been violated—the judge commits a mistake whose gravity is measured by the irreparable harm, if any, that the injunction causes to the defendant while it is in effect. If the judge denies the preliminary injunction to a plaintiff who it later turns out is entitled to judicial relief, the judge commits a mistake whose gravity is measured by the irreparable harm, if any, that the denial of the preliminary injunction does to the plaintiff.

"These mistakes can be compared, and the one likely to be less costly can be selected, with the help of a simple formula: grant the preliminary injunction if but only if $P \times H_p > (1—P) \times H_d$, or, in words, only if the harm to the plaintiff if the injunction is denied, multiplied by the probability that the denial would be an error (that the plaintiff, in other words, will win at trial), exceeds the harm to the defendant if the injunction is granted, multiplied by the probability that granting the injunction would be an error. That probability is simply one minus the probability that the plaintiff will win at trial; for if the plaintiff has, say, a 40 percent chance of winning, the defendant must have a 60 percent chance of winning $(1.00 - .40 = .60)$. The left-hand side of the formula is simply the probability of an erroneous denial weighted by the cost of denial to the plaintiff, and the right-hand side simply the probability of an erroneous grant weighted by the cost of grant to the defendant." American Hospital Supply v. Hospital Products, 780 F.2d 589, 593 (7th Cir.1986) (Judge Posner). The formula was influenced by John Leubsdorf, The Standard for Preliminary Injunctions, 91 Harv.L.Rev. 525 (1978).

(b) *Math Avoidance.* Despite its elegance and analytical precision, the *American Hospital Supply* formula appears to have fallen into disuse even in the seventh federal circuit: "To prevail on a motion for a preliminary injunction, [plaintiff] must show that (1) its case has a likelihood of success on the merits; (2) no adequate remedy at law exists; and (3) it will suffer irreparable harm if the injunction is not granted. [citation] If these three conditions are met, the court must balance the harm to [plaintiff] if the injunction is not issued against the harm to [defendants] if it is issued. This balancing involves a sliding scale analysis: the greater [plaintiff's] chances of success on the merits, the less strong a showing it must make that the balance of harm is in its favor." FoodComm International v. Barry, 328 F.3d 300, 303 (7th Cir. 2003).

7.　*The Injunction Bond.* The judge's balancing of harms in the preliminary injunction standard considers plaintiff's irreparable injury without a preliminary injunction. The defendant's harm from a preliminary injunction is on the other side of the judge's fulcrum. Defendant's harm may also be irreparable, but it may be quite reparable. And, if the preliminary injunction turns out to be incorrect, the judge may compel plaintiff to repair defendant's reparable harm.

Fed.R.Civ.P. 65(c): "No restraining order or preliminary injunction shall issue except upon the giving of security by the applicant, in such sum as the court deems proper, for the payment of such costs and damages as may be incurred or suffered by any party who is found to have been wrongfully enjoined or restrained."

If the TRO or preliminary injunction turns out to have been incorrect, plaintiff and its surety are liable to defendant for losses the order caused. Fed.R.Civ.P. 65.1. "A party injured by the issuance of an injunction later determined to be erroneous has no action for damages in the absence of a bond." W.R. Grace and Co. v. Local Union 759, 461 U.S. 757, 770 n.14 (1983) (dicta).

In defendant's action on the injunction bond, defendant may recover losses directly attributable to the erroneous TRO or preliminary injunction. But the amount of the plaintiff's bond limits defendant's recovery.

The plaintiff's cost to post an injunction bond and the possibility of her liability on it have a cautionary effect on plaintiff. But if the plaintiff is indigent or suing to protect a constitutional right, is requiring her to post an injunction bond an intolerable price on justice? Some courts have disregarded Rule 65(c)'s "shall" and dispensed with the bond where plaintiff is indigent or asserts a constitutional right. Hadix v. Caruso, 2005 WL 2671289 (W.D.Mich. 2005). In Roe v. Crawford, Judge Whipple did not mention requiring Roe to bond the preliminary injunction. Should Roe qualify for an unbonded preliminary injunction?

When plaintiff showed an extraordinarily high likelihood of success on the merits another judge waived a bond. Maine Association of Interdependent Neighborhoods v. Petit, 647 F.Supp. 1312, 1319 (D.Me.1986).

Other courts have decided that under Rule 65(c)'s language, an injunction bond is mandatory but that the amount of the bond is within the judge's discretion. Ram Products Co., Inc. v. Chauncey, 967 F.Supp. 1071, 1093 (N.D.Ind.1997). A judge may use equitable discretion to set a nominal bond. Would Roe qualify for a low or nominal bond?

In environmental litigation, an injunction bond large enough to compensate defendants adequately might frustrate a plaintiff-private organization's effort to enforce the statute; one judge required an injunction bond of $100 for a preliminary injunction against a timber sale. Wilderness Society v. Tyrrel, 701 F.Supp. 1473, 1492 (E.D.Cal.1988).

If Judge Whipple had required Roe to post a bond to cover the State's potential costs from a potentially erroneous preliminary injunction what would have been a realistic amount?

8. *Calendar Preference and Appeals.* (a) Although plaintiff's motion for a preliminary injunction will be set down for an early hearing, once the judge grants or denies interlocutory relief, the winner has a diminished sense of urgency for a trial on the merits. Victory or defeat at this stage is also significant because of the trial backlog in many jurisdictions. Parties often settle after a judge's decision on a motion for a preliminary injunction because the judge's decision gives them a forecast of the final decision.

(b) The losing plaintiff or defendant may appeal. In federal procedure, an interlocutory appeal is permitted from orders "granting, continuing, modifying, refusing or dissolving injunctions." 28 U.S.C. § 1292(a)(1). This exception to the final-judgment rule is justified because an incorrect decision to grant or deny a preliminary injunction may injure the parties' important rights irreparably.

2. JURY TRIAL AFTER MERGER

The jury, a crucial force in damages litigation, is absent when a plaintiff seeks an injunction or other equitable remedy. Courts have interpreted the constitutional provisions to divide litigation into "Suits at common law," or damages litigation before a jury, and equitable litigation which is tried by a judge. The inadequacy prerequisite for Chancery relief, which we studied above, requires a plaintiff who seeks an equitable remedy to show that the damages remedy is inadequate; one of its purposes is to protect the constitutional right to a jury trial. Where a constitution or statute calls for a jury trial, the jury's populism, common sense, and community conscience offsets the judge's professionalism, expertise, and elitism. For now, our inquiry is how the Supreme Court distinguishes "Suits at common law" for juries from the more placid domain of equity where the judge presides, alone.

Dairy Queen v. Wood is a proper place to start. Dairy Queen sued McCullough for breach of a licensing agreement covering the trademark "Dairy Queen." Dairy Queen sought injunctive relief and "an accounting for profits" arising out of McCullough's alleged infringement of the "Dairy Queen" trademark. McCullough demanded a jury trial which Dairy Queen opposed. Dairy Queen's "contention that their money claim is 'purely equitable' is based primarily upon the fact that their complaint is cast in terms of an 'accounting,' rather than in terms of an action for 'debt' or 'damages.'" McCullough argued that "insofar as [Dairy Queen's] complaint requests a money judgment it presents a claim which is unquestionably legal."

Justice Black's opinion accepted McCullough's argument. "The most natural construction of [Dairy Queen's] claim for a money judgment would seem to be that it is a claim that they are entitled to recover whatever was owed them under the contract as of the date of its purported termination plus damages for infringement of their trade-mark since that date. * * * As an action on a debt allegedly due under a contract, it would be difficult to conceive of an action of a more traditionally legal character. And as an action for damages based upon a charge of trade-mark infringement, it would be no less subject to cognizance by a court of law.

"[Dairy Queen's] contention that this money claim is 'purely equitable' is based primarily upon the fact that their complaint is cast in terms of an 'accounting,' rather than in terms of an action for 'debt' or 'damages.' But the constitutional right to trial by jury cannot be made to depend upon the choice of words used in the pleadings. The necessary prerequisite to the right to maintain a suit for an equitable accounting, like all other equitable remedies, is * * * the absence of an adequate remedy at law. * * * A jury, under proper instructions from the court, could readily determine the recovery, if any, to be had here, whether the theory finally settled upon is that of breach of contract, that of trademark infringement, or any combination of the two. The legal remedy cannot be characterized as inadequate merely because the measure of damages may necessitate a look into [McCullough's] business records." Dairy Queen v. Wood, 369 U.S. 469, 476–79 (1962).

Justice Black's opinion in *Dairy Queen* shifted the jury trial test from the historical law-equity classification toward a more practical and simpler criterion of whether the plaintiff's claim asks for money.

Eight years after *Dairy Queen*, in a footnote to Ross v. Bernhard, the Supreme Court stated a three-part test. The first part was historical, the status of the cause of action before the merger of law and equity. The second turned on remedy, the relief sought. The third examined a jury's practical ability and limitations in deciding issues. Ross v. Bernhard, 396 U.S. 531, 538 n.10 (1970). A shareholders' derivative suit is "equitable," the Court said; but the Court confirmed the parties' right to a jury trial if the underlying corporate claim was for money.

Parts of *Dairy Queen* read as if substantial complexity might withdraw a trial from the jury's realm and Ross v. Bernard's footnote alluded to "the practical abilities and limitations of juries." For a time, some observers hoped juries could be excluded from complex trials. Although the authority that supports a complexity exception to the Seventh Amendment has not been disapproved definitively, contemporary federal juries hear hideously complicated patent infringement and antitrust trials.

One court responded, "KPL's reasoning for striking the jury demand was that the subject matter would be too confusing for a jury. However, juries are commonly called upon to decide complex cases. We fail to see how the complexity of the subject was particularly prejudicial to KPL and we find no abuse of discretion." Green Construction Co. v. Kansas Power & Light Co., 1 F.3d 1005, 1011 (10th Cir.1993).

The Supreme Court has apparently dropped *Ross*'s third point. "To determine whether a particular action will resolve legal rights, and therefore give rise to a jury trial right, we examine both the nature of the issues involved and the remedy sought. [citations] First we compare the statutory action to 18th-century actions brought in the courts of law and equity. Second, we examine the remedy sought and determine whether it is legal or equitable in nature. [citations]" [internal quotation marks omitted] Wooddell v. International Brotherhood of Electrical Workers, Local 71, 502 U.S. 93, 97 (1991). Maintaining that the second, or remedies, test is the most important and giving greater weight to whether the remedy plaintiff seeks is legal or equitable is Pereira v. Farace, 413 F.3d 330, 337 (2005).

Claims for compensatory money damages are "at common law" and subject to the jury right. Also "at common law," are replevin, ejectment, ownership of real property, and legal restitution. That plaintiff's request for money is not always "at common law," however, complicates analysis under the remedies test. Other forms of money recovery may be equitable and reserved for the trial judge.

When do litigants have a right to jury factfinding for money recovery that is not compensatory? One court dealt with punitive damages, prejudgment interest, and attorney fees. Plaintiff's request for punitive damages is intended to punish a wrongdoer which is a legal, not an equitable, claim; it is subject to the Seventh Amendment right to a jury trial. However plaintiff's prejudgment interest and attorney fees are equitable, not legal, and the Seventh Amendment does not compel a jury right. Younis Brothers & Co. v. Cigna Worldwide Insurance Co., 882 F.Supp. 1468, 1475 (E.D.Pa.1994).

Prejudgment interest was, however, decided by the jury in Pulliam v. Coastal Emergency Services of Richmond, Inc., 257 Va. 1, 509 S.E.2d 307, 310, 320–21 (1999). The court held that prejudgment interest on plaintiff's money judgment was a part of plaintiff's damages and subject to the legislative cap.

The Arkansas court, dealing with that State's newly merged law and chancery courts, distinguished legal restitution, which may lead to a jury right, from equitable restitution, an equitable lien, which does not. First National Bank of DeWitt v. Cruthis, 360 Ark. 528, ___ S.W.3d ___ (2005).

The Re-examination Clause. In Cooper Industries v. Leatherman Tool Group, the Supreme Court held that a federal Court of Appeals should conduct its *Gore-Campbell* review of a jury's punitive damages verdict de novo instead of using the more deferential abuse-of-discretion standard of review an appellate court usually accords to a trial jury's findings of fact. The decision seems to have turned on the word "fact" in the last half of the Seventh Amendment, the Re-examination Clause, which says that "no fact tried by a jury, shall be otherwise re-examined in any Court of the United States, than according to the rules of the common law."

"Unlike the measure of actual damages suffered, which presents a question of historical or predictive fact, [citation] the level of punitive damages is not really a 'fact' 'tried' by the jury." Gasperini v. Center for Humanities, Inc., 518 U.S. 415, 459 (1996) (SCALIA, J., dissenting). Because the jury's award of punitive damages does not constitute a finding of 'fact,' appellate review of the district court's determination that an award is consistent with due process does not implicate the Seventh Amendment concerns raised by respondent and its amicus." Cooper Industries, Inc. v. Leatherman Tool Group, Inc., 532 U.S. 424, 436–41, n.14 (2001).

Remedies Test. There is constant pressure to utilize the remedies test for the parties' right to a jury trial. That test it is more practical and easier to apply. "The second inquiry," whether the remedy sought is legal or equitable in nature, the Court has said is "the more important in our analysis." Wooddell v. International Brotherhood of Electrical Workers, Local 71, 502 U.S. 93, 97 (1991). And Justice Brennan argued for a remedies test in his concurring opinion in Chauffeurs, Teamsters and Helpers, Local 391 v. Terry, 494 U.S. 558, 572–80 (1990).

In 1996, while deciding how to divide functions between the judge and the jury in a patent infringement action at law, the Supreme Court restated the historical test and assigned to the judge the construction of patent claims. Markman v. Westview Instruments, Inc., 517 U.S. 370, 375 (1996). That set the stage for

FELTNER v. COLUMBIA PICTURES TELEVISION

Supreme Court of the United States, 1998.
523 U.S. 340.

JUSTICE THOMAS delivered the opinion of the Court. Section 504(c) of the Copyright Act permits a copyright owner "to recover, instead of actual damages and profits, an award of statutory damages, in a sum of not less than $500 or more than $20,000 as the court considers just." In this case, we consider whether § 504(c) or the Seventh Amendment grants a right to a jury trial when a copyright owner elects to recover statutory damages. We hold that although the statute is silent on the point, the Seventh Amendment provides a right to a jury trial, which includes a right to a jury determination of the amount of statutory damages. * * *

C.   Elvin Feltner owns Krypton International Corporation, which in 1990 acquired three television stations in the southeastern United States. Columbia Pictures Television, Inc., had licensed several television series to these stations, including "Who's the Boss," "Silver Spoons," "Hart to Hart," and "T.J. Hooker." After the stations became delinquent in making their royalty payments to Columbia, Krypton and Columbia entered into negotiations to restructure the stations' debt. These discussions were unavailing, and Columbia terminated the stations' license agreements in October 1991. Despite Columbia's termination, the stations continued broadcasting the programs.

Columbia sued Feltner * * * in federal district court alleging, copyright infringement arising from the stations' unauthorized broadcasting of the programs. Columbia sought various forms of relief under the Copyright Act of 1976 including a permanent injunction, impoundment of all copies of the programs, actual damages or, in the alternative, statutory damages, and costs and attorney's fees. On Columbia's motion, the District Court entered partial summary judgment as to liability for Columbia on its copyright infringement claims. * * *

Columbia exercised the option afforded by § 504(c) of the Copyright Act to recover "Statutory Damages" in lieu of actual damages. In relevant part, § 504(c) provides:

"STATUTORY DAMAGES—

"(1) Except as provided by clause (2) of this subsection, the copyright owner may elect, at any time before final judgment is rendered, to recover, instead of actual damages and profits, an award of statutory damages for all infringements involved in the action, with respect to any one work, * * * in a sum of not less than $500 or more than $20,000 as the court considers just * * * ."

"(2) In a case where the copyright owner sustains the burden of proving, and the court finds, that infringement was committed willfully, the court [in] its discretion may increase the award of statutory damages to a sum of not more than $100,000. In a case where the infringer sustains the burden of proving, and the court finds, that such infringer was not aware and had no reason to believe that his or her acts constituted an infringement of copyright, the court in its discretion may reduce the award of statutory damages to a sum of not less than $200 * * * ."

The District Court denied Feltner's request for a jury trial on statutory damages, ruling instead that such issues would be determined at a bench trial.

After two days of trial, the trial judge held that each episode of each series constituted a separate work and that the airing of the same episode by different stations controlled by Feltner constituted separate violations; accordingly, the trial judge determined that there had been a total of 440 acts of infringement. The trial judge further found that Feltner's infringement was willful and fixed statutory damages at $20,000 per act of infringement. Applying that amount to the number of acts of infringement, the trial judge determined that Columbia was entitled to $8,800,000 in statutory damages, plus costs and attorney's fees.

The Court of Appeals for the Ninth Circuit affirmed in all relevant respects. Most importantly for present purposes, the court rejected Feltner's argument that he was entitled to have a jury determine statutory damages. * * * [T]he Court of Appeals held that § 504(c) does not grant a right to a jury determination of statutory damages. * * * The Court of Appeals further concluded that the "Seventh Amendment does not provide a right to a jury trial on the issue of statutory damages because an award of such damages is equitable in nature." We granted certiorari.

Before inquiring into the applicability of the Seventh Amendment, we must " 'first ascertain whether a construction of the statute is fairly possible by which the [constitutional] question may be avoided.' " Tull v. United States, 481 U.S. 412, 417, n.3, (1987). Such a construction is not possible here, for we cannot discern "any congressional intent to grant * * * the right to a jury trial," on an award of statutory damages.

The language of § 504(c) does not grant a right to have a jury assess statutory damages. Statutory damages are to be assessed in an amount that "the court considers just." Further, in the event that "the court finds" the infringement was willful or innocent, "the court in its discretion" may, within limits, increase or decrease the amount of statutory damages. These phrases, like the entire statutory provision, make no mention of a right to a jury trial or, for that matter, to juries at all.

The word "court" in this context appears to mean judge, not jury. [citation] In fact, the other remedies provisions of the Copyright Act use the term "court" in contexts generally thought to confer authority on a judge, rather than a jury. See, e.g., § 502 ("court * * * may * * * grant temporary and final injunctions"); § 503(a) ("the court may order the impounding * * * of all copies or phonorecords"); § 503(b) ("[a]s part of a final judgment or decree, the court may order the destruction or other reasonable disposition of all copies or phonorecords"); § 505 ("the court in its discretion may allow the recovery of full costs" of litigation and "the court may also award a reasonable attorney's fee"). In contrast, the Copyright Act does not use the term "court" in the subsection addressing awards of actual damages and profits, see § 504(b), which generally are thought to constitute legal relief. [citations] * * *

We thus discern no statutory right to a jury trial when a copyright owner elects to recover statutory damages. Accordingly, we must reach the constitutional question.

The Seventh Amendment provides that "[i]n Suits at common law, where the value in controversy shall exceed twenty dollars, the right of trial by jury shall be preserved * * * ." Since Justice Story's time, the Court has understood "Suits at common law" to refer "not merely [to] suits, which the common law recognized among its old and settled proceedings, but [to] suits in which legal rights were to be ascertained and determined, in contradistinction to those where equitable rights alone were recognized, and equitable remedies were administered." Parsons v. Bedford, 3 Pet. 433, 447 (1830). The Seventh Amendment thus applies not only to common-law causes of action, but also to "actions brought to enforce statutory rights that are analogous to common-law causes of action ordinarily decided in English law courts in the late 18th century, as opposed to those customarily heard by courts of equity or admiralty." Granfinanciera, S.A. v. Nordberg, 492 U.S. 33, 42 (1989). To determine whether a statutory action is more analogous to cases tried in courts of law than to suits tried in courts of equity or admiralty, we examine both the nature of the statutory action and the remedy sought.

Unlike many of our recent Seventh Amendment cases, which have involved modern statutory rights unknown to 18th-century England, see, e.g., Wooddell v. International Brotherhood of Electrical Workers, (alleged violations of union's duties under Labor Management Relations Act, 1947, and Labor–Management Reporting and Disclosure Act of 1959); Granfinanciera v. Nordberg, (action to rescind fraudulent preference under Bankruptcy Act); Tull v. United States, (government's claim for civil penalties under Clean Water Act); Curtis v. Loether, (claim under Title VIII of Civil Rights Act of 1968), in this case there are close analogues to actions seeking statutory damages under § 504(c). Before the adoption of the Seventh Amendment, the common law and statutes in England and this country granted copyright owners causes of action for infringement. More importantly, copyright suits for monetary damages were tried in courts of law, and thus before juries.

By the middle of the 17th century, the common law recognized an author's right to prevent the unauthorized publication of his manuscript. [citation] This protection derived from the principle that the manuscript was the product of intellectual labor and was as much the author's property as the material on which it was written. [citations] Actions seeking damages for infringement of common-law copyright, like actions seeking damages for invasions of other property rights, were tried in courts of law in actions on the case. [citation] Actions on the case, like other actions at law, were tried before juries. [citations]   *history*

In 1710, the first English copyright statute, the Statute of Anne, was enacted to protect published books. Under the Statute of Anne, damages for infringement were set at "one Penny for every Sheet which shall be found in [the infringer's] custody, either printed or printing, published, or exposed to Sale," half ("one Moiety") to go to the Crown and half to the copyright owner, and were "to be recovered * * * by action of Debt, Bill, Plaint, or Information." Like the earlier practice with regard to common-law copyright claims for damages, actions seeking damages under the Statute of Anne were tried in courts of law. [citations]

[The Court summarizes similar state statutes from the period between the revolution and the federal constitution.]

In 1790, Congress passed the first federal copyright statute, the Copyright Act of 1790, which similarly authorized the awarding of damages for copyright infringements. The Copyright Act of 1790 provided that damages for copyright infringement of published works would be "the sum of fifty cents for every sheet which shall be found in [the infringer's] possession, * * * to be recovered by action of debt in any court of record in the United States, wherein the same is cognizable." Like the Statute of Anne, the Copyright Act of 1790 provided that half ("one moiety") of such damages were to go to the copyright owner and half to the United States. For infringement of an unpublished manuscript, the statute entitled a copyright owner to "all damages occasioned by such injury, to be recovered by a special action on the case founded upon this act, in any court having cognizance thereof."

There is no evidence that the Copyright Act of 1790 changed the practice of trying copyright actions for damages in courts of law before juries. As we have noted, actions on the case and actions of debt were actions at law for which a jury was required. Moreover, actions to recover damages under the Copyright Act of 1831—which differed from the Copyright Act of 1790 only in the amount (increased to $1 from 50 cents) authorized to be recovered for certain infringing sheets—were consistently tried to juries. [citations]

Columbia does not dispute this historical evidence. In fact, Columbia makes no attempt to draw an analogy between an action for statutory damages under § 504(c) and any historical cause of action—including those actions for monetary relief that we have characterized as equitable, such as actions for disgorgement of improper profits. [citations] Rather, Columbia merely contends that statutory damages are clearly equitable in nature.

We are not persuaded. We have recognized the "general rule" that monetary relief is legal, [citation] and an award of statutory damages may serve purposes traditionally associated with legal relief, such as compensation and punishment. [citations] Nor, as we have previously stated, is a monetary remedy rendered equitable simply because it is "not fixed or readily calculable from a fixed formula." And there is historical evidence that cases involving discretionary monetary relief were tried before juries. [citation] Accordingly, we must conclude that the Seventh Amendment provides a right to a jury trial where the copyright owner elects to recover statutory damages.

The right to a jury trial includes the right to have a jury determine the amount of statutory damages, if any, awarded to the copyright owner. It has long been recognized that "by the law the jury are judges of the damages." Lord Townshend v. Hughes, 86 Eng. Rep. 994, 994–995 (C.P. 1677). Thus in Dimick v. Schiedt, 293 U.S. 474 (1935), the Court stated that "the common law rule as it existed at the time of the adoption of the Constitution" was that "in cases where the amount of damages was uncertain[,] their assessment was a matter so peculiarly within the province of the jury that the Court should not alter it." And there is overwhelming evidence that the consistent practice at common law was for juries to award damages. [citations]

More specifically, this was the consistent practice in copyright cases. * * * In addition, juries assessed the amount of damages under the Copyright Act of 1831, even though that statute, like the Copyright Act of 1790, fixed damages at a set amount per infringing sheet. [citations] * * *

For the foregoing reasons, we hold that the Seventh Amendment provides a right to a jury trial on all issues pertinent to an award of statutory damages under § 504(c) of the Copyright Act, including the amount itself. The judgment below is reversed, and we remand the case for proceedings consistent with this opinion.

It is so ordered.

JUSTICE SCALIA, concurring in the judgment. It is often enough that we must hold an enactment of Congress to be unconstitutional. I see no reason to do so here-not because I believe that jury trial is not constitutionally required (I do not reach that issue), but because the statute can and therefore should be read to provide jury trial. [The statute's word "court," Justice Scalia maintained, includes "jury."]

Notes

1. *How to Set the Amount of Statutory Damages.* Before *Feltner*, one court wrote, "Among the numerous factors considered by the courts in setting statutory damage amounts are the expenses saved and profits reaped by the infringer; the deterrent effect of the award on a defendant and on third parties; and the infringer's state of mind in committing the infringement." Playboy Enterprises, Inc. v. Webbworld, Inc., 991 F.Supp. 543, 560 (N.D.Tex.1997).

2. *Questions.* What decisions does § 504(c) ask the factfinder to make? Under § 504(c), what purposes are served by taking Feltner's money and giving it to Columbia?

Why do you think Columbia elected statutory damages? Why might Feltner have wanted a jury trial on statutory damages.

3. *The Statute.* Since there is no Seventh Amendment right to a bench trial, Congress can have a jury trial for anything it wants. Do you think Congress intended a jury trial for statutory damages?

4. *The Seventh Amendment.* In rejecting Columbia's argument, "statutory damages are clearly equitable in nature," does the Court apply a "historical" test or a "remedy" test? Chapter 1 has a summary of the common law writs including trespass "on the case" and "debt."

5. *Be Careful What You Wish For.* Columbia's copyright infringement lawsuit against Feltner was tried before a Los Angeles jury in April 1999. Feltner argued that Columbia's shows weren't marketable and that Columbia was not damaged. The jury set Columbia's statutory damages at $70,000 per episode, total $31,680,000. Feltner appealed, but the court of appeals affirmed the jury's verdict in Columbia Pictures Television v. Feltner, 259 F.3d 1186 (9th Cir. 2001), cert. denied, 534 U.S. 1127 (2002).

6. Let's turn to the competition between the historical test and the remedies test in a state court.

C & K ENGINEERING CONTRACTORS
v. AMBER STEEL CO.

Supreme Court of California, 1978.
23 Cal.3d 1, 151 Cal.Rptr. 323, 587 P.2d 1136.

RICHARDSON, JUSTICE. The issue posed by this case is whether or not defendant was improperly denied its constitutional right to a jury trial. (Cal. Const., art. I, § 16.) We will conclude that because plaintiff's suit for damages for breach of contract was based entirely upon the equitable doctrine of promissory estoppel, the gist of the action must be deemed equitable in nature and, under well established principles, neither party was entitled to a jury trial as a matter of right.

Plaintiff, a general contractor, solicited bids from defendant and other subcontractors for the installation of reinforcing steel in the construction of a waste water treatment plant in Fresno County. Plaintiff included defendant's bid in its master bid, which was ultimately accepted by the public sanitation district, the proposed owner of the plant. After defendant refused to perform in accordance with its bid on the subcontract, plaintiff brought the present action to recover $102,660 in damages for defendant's alleged breach of contract. * * *

The allegations of plaintiff's first cause of action may be summarized: defendant submitted a written bid of $139,511 for the work; defendant gave a subsequent "verbal promise" that the work would be performed for the bid price; plaintiff "reasonably relied" on defendant's bid and promise in submitting its master bid; defendant knew or should have known that plaintiff would submit a master bid based upon defendant's bid; defendant refused to perform in accordance with its bid; plaintiff was required to expend $242,171 to perform the reinforcing steel work; as a result plaintiff was damaged in the amount of $102,660; and "Injustice can be avoided only by enforcement of defendant's promise to perform. * * * "

Defendant's answer to the complaint alleged its bid was the result of an "honest mistake" in calculation; plaintiff knew of the mistake but failed to notify defendant or permit it to revise its bid as is customary in the industry; and plaintiff's conduct in this regard should bar it from recovering damages.

Defendant demanded a jury trial. The trial court, deeming the case to be essentially in equity, denied the request but empaneled an advisory jury to consider the sole issue of plaintiff's reasonable reliance on defendant's promise. The jury found that plaintiff reasonably relied to its detriment on defendant's bid. The trial court adopted this finding and entered judgment in plaintiff's favor for $102,610, the approximate amount of its prayer, together with interest and costs. Defendant appeals.

Defendant's primary contention is that it was improperly denied a jury trial of plaintiff's action for damages. In resolving this contention we first review the nature and derivation of the doctrine of promissory estoppel. Thereafter, we discuss certain authorities governing the right to jury trial in this state. As will appear, we have concluded that by reason of the essentially equitable nature of the doctrine and plaintiff's exclusive reliance upon it in the present action, the case was properly triable by the court with an advisory jury. * * *

The elements of the doctrine of promissory estoppel, as described concisely in section 90 of the Restatement of Contracts, are as follows: "A promise which the promisor should reasonably expect to induce action or forbearance of a definite and substantial character on the part of the promisee and which does induce such action or forbearance is binding if injustice can be avoided only by enforcement of the promise." The foregoing rule has been judicially adopted in California and it applies to actions, such as the present case, to enforce a subcontractor's bid. [citations] It is undisputed that plaintiff's complaint in the matter before us relies exclusively upon the doctrine to enforce defendant's alleged promise to perform its bid. In fact, the language of the complaint, summarized above, paraphrases that of section 90 in asserting that "Injustice can be avoided only by enforcement of defendant's promise to perform." * * *

We have recently characterized promissory estoppel as "a doctrine which employs *equitable* principles to satisfy the requirement that consideration must be given in exchange for the promise sought to be enforced. [citations]" * * *

Treatise writers and commentators have confirmed the generally *equitable* nature of promissory estoppel in enforcing a promise which otherwise would be unenforceable. [citations] As expressed by Professor Henderson, "[P]romissory estoppel is a *peculiarly equitable doctrine* designed to deal with situations which, in total impact, necessarily call into play discretionary powers * * *." One distinguished commentator has observed that promissory estoppel derives from both "the decisions of the courts of common law from the very beginnings of the action of assumpsit [as well as] the decrees of courts of equity making a very flexible use of the doctrine of 'estoppel,' * * * " (1A Corbin, Contracts (1963) § 194.)

The equitable character of promissory estoppel is confirmed by a close scrutiny of the purpose of the doctrine, namely, that "*injustice* can be avoided only by enforcement of the promise." (Rest., Contracts § 90, italics added.) As expressed by us in a similar subcontractor bid case, once the prerequisites of the doctrine are met, "* * * *it is only fair* that plaintiff should have at least an opportunity to accept defendant's bid after the general contract has been awarded to him." [citations] * * *

We conclude, accordingly, that the doctrine of promissory estoppel is essentially equitable in nature, developed to provide a remedy (namely, enforcement of a gratuitous promise) which was not generally available in courts of law prior to 1850. We now move to an examination of the authorities on the subject of the right to a jury trial, to determine whether the equitable nature of plaintiff's action precluded a jury trial as a matter of right.

The right to a jury trial is guaranteed by our Constitution. (Cal. Const., art. I, § 16.) We have long acknowledged that the right so guaranteed, however, is the right as it existed at common law in 1850, when the Constitution was first adopted, "and what that right is, is a purely historical question, a fact which is to be ascertained like any other social, political or legal fact." [citations] As a general proposition, "The jury trial is a matter of right in a civil action at law, but not in equity." [citations]

As we stated, "If the action has to deal with ordinary common-law rights cognizable in courts of law, it is to that extent an action at law. In determining whether the action was one triable by a jury at common law, the court is not bound by the form of the action but rather by the nature of the rights involved and the facts of the particular case—the *gist* of the action. A jury trial must be granted where the *gist* of the action is legal, where the action is in reality cognizable at law." On the other hand, if the action is essentially one in equity and the relief sought "depends upon the application of equitable doctrines," the parties are not entitled to a jury trial. (E.g., Hartman v. Burford (1966) 242 Cal.App.2d 268, 270, 51 Cal.Rptr. 309, 311 [enforcement of promise to make a will]; Tibbitts v. Fife (1958) 162 Cal.App.2d 568, 572, 328 P.2d 212 [establishment of constructive trust].) Although we have said that "the legal or equitable nature of a cause of action ordinarily is determined by the mode of relief to be afforded" (Raedeke v. Gibraltar Sav. & Loan Assn., 10 Cal.3d 665, 672, 111 Cal.Rptr. 693, 696, 517 P.2d 1157, 1160), the prayer for relief in a particular case is not conclusive [citations]. Thus, "The fact that damages is one of a full range of possible remedies does not guarantee * * * the right to a jury." [citations]

In the present case, the complaint purports to seek recovery of damages for breach of contract, in form an action at law in which a right to jury trial ordinarily would exist. [citations] As we have seen, however, the complaint seeks relief which was available only in equity, namely, the enforcement of defendant's gratuitous promise to perform its bid through application of the equitable doctrine of promissory estoppel. Although there is no direct authority on point, several cases have held that actions based upon the analogous principle of equitable estoppel may be tried by the court without a jury. (Jaffe v. Albertson Co. (1966)) 243 Cal.App.2d 592, 607–608, 53 Cal.Rptr. 25 [estoppel to bar reliance on statute of frauds]; Moss v. Bluemm (1964) 229 Cal.App.2d 70, 72–73, 40 Cal.Rptr. 50 [estoppel to bar statute of limitations defense]; Richard v. Degen & Brody, Inc. (1960) 181 Cal.App.2d 289, 295, 5 Cal.Rptr. 263 [estoppel as defense to unlawful detainer action]; [citations].

Defendant responds by relying primarily upon certain dictum in *Raedeke,* which also concerned an action based on promissory estoppel. The *Raedeke* complaint alleged *dual* theories of traditional breach of contract and promissory estoppel. We stressed that the "resolution of the instant case did not depend entirely upon the application of equitable principles; the doctrine of promissory estoppel was only one of two alternative theories of recovery." Accordingly, we held in *Raedeke* that plaintiffs were entitled to a jury trial, and that the trial court erred in treating the jury's findings and verdict as advisory only. In a footnote, however, we added the following dictum: "Moreover, even as to plaintiff's reliance upon promissory estoppel, there is some basis for holding that the action remained one at law. 'The fact that equitable principles are applied in the action does not necessarily identify the resultant relief as equitable. [citations] Equitable principles are a guide to courts of law as well as of equity. [citations] Furthermore, the incidental adoption of equitable sounding measures to effect the application of equitable principles in an action at law, such as for damages, does not change the character of that action. [citations]' "

The foregoing general principles do not alter our conclusion that the present action is, essentially, one recognized only in courts of equity and, despite plaintiff's request for damages, is not an "action at law" involving, to use the *Raedeke* language, the "incidental adoption of equitable sounding measures." Defendant before us has argued that because plaintiff sought to recover damages rather than to compel defendant to perform its bid, plaintiff requested relief which is available at common law. Yet, as we have seen, damages at law were unavailable in actions for breach of a gratuitous promise. The only manner in which damages have been recognized in such cases of gratuitous promises is by application of the equitable doctrine of promissory estoppel which renders such promises legally binding. Without the employment of this doctrine, essentially equitable, there was no remedy at all. As illustrated by the express language of section 90 of the Restatement of Contracts, promissory estoppel is used to avoid injustice "by *enforcement* of the promise." (Italics added.)

Furthermore, the addition, in such cases, of a prayer for damages does not convert what is essentially an equitable action into a legal one for which a jury trial would be available. This was demonstrated in a recent case, Southern Pac. Transportation Co. v. Superior Court, 58 Cal.App.3d 433, 129 Cal.Rptr. 912, wherein plaintiff sought damages as a good faith improver of land owned by another person. (See Code Civ.Proc., § 871.1 et seq.) The appellate court rejected the contention that plaintiff's request for damages necessarily identified the action as one at law. The court first noted that since the good faith improver statute had no counterpart in English common law, "classification of the action as either legal or equitable depends upon characterization of the nature of the relief sought."

The *Southern Pac. Transportation* court properly observed that under the statute, the trial court must "effect such an adjustment of the rights, equities, and interests" of the parties as was consistent with substantial justice. (Code Civ.Proc., § 871.5.) Thus, the action was essentially one calling for the exercise of equitable principles. The court added, "The fact that damages is one of a full range of possible remedies does not guarantee real parties the right to a jury," since "there is no possibility of severing the legal from the equitable."

We conclude that the trial court properly treated the action as equitable in nature, to be tried by the court with or without an advisory jury as the court elected. * * *

The judgment is affirmed.

NEWMAN, JUSTICE, dissenting. I dissent. The Chancery Court in England sometimes created rights, sometimes remedies. When California courts decide whether a jury trial should be assured, I believe that they should focus not on rights but on remedies. A plaintiff who seeks damages should be entitled to a jury. One who seeks specific performance or an injunction or quiet title, etc. (plus supplementary damages or "damages in lieu" that would have been allowed in Chancery) is not entitled to a jury.

The majority opinion here discusses "promissory estoppel," "equitable estoppel," "equitable principles," "equitable doctrine," "equitable nature," and even "injustice." To pretend that words like those enable us to isolate "ordinary common-law rights cognizable in courts of law" or that "the *gist* of the action" governs seems to me to be uninstructive fictionalizing. We are told that courts deal with "a purely historical question, a fact which is to be ascertained like any other social, political or legal fact." Yet how often, I wonder, do (or should) California judges instead decide whether the wisdom of a Corbin, in 1963, outweighs comments by Ames, Seavey, Shattuck, and Williston written during the period from 1888 to 1957?

In fact, most rights that are now enforced via a jury were created not by courts but by legislatures. We look at the *remedy* sought, not at the judicial or legislative history of the *right,* to decide whether the trial is to be "legal" or "equitable." There are troubling borderlines, but the basic rule should be that no jury is required when plaintiff seeks equitable relief rather than "legal" damages. That approach requires no complex, historical research regarding when and by whom certain rights were created. It also requires less reliance on the anomalies of England's unique juridical history. Courts thus may focus on a basic policy concern; that is, the typically more continuing and more personalized involvement of the trial judge in specific performance and injunctive decrees than in mere judgments for damages.

The doctrine of promissory estoppel was not, I suggest, "developed to provide a remedy (namely, enforcement of a gratuitous promise)" as the majority here contend. What it really did was to help create a new right (just as statutes help create new rights) that apparently, but only if we reject what seems to have been Corbin's view, was enforced as of 1850 in Chancery but not at common law.

Plaintiff in this case sought damages for an alleged breach of contract. He did not seek equitable relief. Thus defendant should have been granted the jury trial he requested.

Notes

1. *The Historical Test Vindicated.* The California court has adhered to the historical test to determine the right to jury trial. Thus the court held that only a court of equity can pierce the corporate veil. "There is no right to jury trial of the alter ego issue." Wyle v. Alioto, 236 Cal.Rptr. 849, 851 (Cal.Ct.App. 1987).

2. *The Remedies Test.* A Michigan state court agreed with the dissenting opinion that the remedy claimant seeks determines the right to jury trial. While the court agreed that promissory estoppel is a traditional equity doctrine, it nevertheless held a jury trial was required because the remedy sought was money damages rather than traditional equitable relief. ECCO Limited v. Balimoy Manufacturing Co., 179 Mich.App. 748, 446 N.W.2d 546 (1989).

3. *Promissory Estoppel and the Seventh Amendment.* How should a federal court bound by Dairy Queen v. Wood and Feltner v. Columbia Pictures Television decide *C & K Engineering*?

Merex, A.G. v. Fairchild Weston Systems, a decision from before *Feltner*, is helpful. After the trial judge had labeled a jury verdict for Merex for promissory estoppel as advisory and disapproved it, Merex appealed seeking a binding Seventh Amendment jury trial.

The court of appeals rejected Merex's argument. The "protean" doctrine of promissory estoppel, which did not exist when the Seventh Amendment was ratified, "eludes classification as either entirely legal or entirely equitable." The court distinguished between two promissory estoppel plaintiffs: When the first promissory estoppel plaintiff sues for contract damages and asserts reliance as a substitute for consideration, the analogy to law is compelling. A second promissory estoppel plaintiff "seeks to avoid the draconian application of the Statute of Frauds, [where] the pull of equity becomes irresistible." Because "Merex is seeking to use promissory estoppel to circumvent New York's Statute of Frauds * * * the claim is more equitable than promissory in nature." No jury trial.

But if Merex sought expectation damages, weren't they legal relief? An equitable promissory estoppel plaintiff, the court hinted, could only recover restitution and its reliance expense, that is "out-of-pocket expenses," not "expectation damages." Merex A.G. v. Fairchild Weston Systems, Inc., 29 F.3d 821, 823–26 (2d Cir.1994).

Another court applied the *Merex* approach to a plaintiff who did not seek to avoid the Statute of Frauds and found a jury right. Roberts v. Karimi, 204 F.Supp.2d 523, 527 (S.D.N.Y 2002).

4. *Tort Reform and the Right to a Jury Trial.* Litigants have assailed state statutory tort reforms maintaining that the legislation violates the state constitutional right to a jury trial. Courts held the jury's role in assessing punitive damages to be protected against statutes assigning measurement of punitive damages to the judge; the courts emphasized the jury's exclusive province of deciding factual issues, including damages. Others disagreed. pp. 189, 212–13.

5. *Punitive Damages with an Equitable Remedy?* May a juryless Chancery judge add punitive damages to an injunction or other equitable remedy?

The traditional rule denied punitive damages in equity. The argument went like this: The Court of Chancery's relief was in personam, and Chancery only awarded money to supplement its in personam relief, to give plaintiff complete relief. Compensatory damages constitute complete relief for plaintiff. Punishment is foreign to Chancery's equitable principles. Plaintiff has no "right" to recover punitive damages; instead punitive damages are awarded in the jury's discretion. Because Chancery lacks a jury, plaintiff may not recover punitive damages in Chancery.

Some traditional holdouts remain, but the trend is for the Chancery court to augment a plaintiff's equitable relief with punitive damages when punitive damages are appropriate to punish and deter.

(a) *Traditional Holdouts.* Where plaintiff seeks only an equitable remedy, a court may conclude that punitive damages are "incompatible with equitable principles." This may reflect either an idealized view of equity or a concern that a judge's grant of punitive damages contradicts the right to a trial by jury. See, Rexnord, Inc. v. Ferris, 294 Or. 392, 657 P.2d 673 (1983).

The Supreme Court held that the statutory phrase "appropriate equitable relief" that defined a plaintiff's remedies for a defendant's violation of the federal ERISA statute did not include punitive damages because they are not "equitable." Massachusetts Mutual Life Insurance Co. v. Russell, 473 U.S. 134, 144 (1985).

One federal court forbade a trust beneficiary from recovering punitive damages against a fiduciary-trustee bank under Pennsylvania state law; moreover, the bank's misconduct was not egregious enough to justify punitive damages. In support of denying punitive damages to the beneficiary, the court examined a Pennsylvania orphans' court decision that denied a plaintiff's claim for punitive damages against trustees who willfully breached their fiduciary duties, Freedman Estate, 1 Fiduc. Rep. 2d 60, 67 (Pa.Com.Pl.1980), where the court noted that an orphans' court is "a court of equity governed in minute detail." Packard v. Provident Nat'l Bank, 994 F.2d 1039, 1048 (3d Cir.), cert. denied, 510 U.S. 964 (1993).

A second federal court of appeals declined to find a right to a jury trial for investment-fund shareholders' claim to recover excessive fees. "A jury trial is not guaranteed to those seeking relief in equity. [citations] We have held that claims arising under section 36(b) of the Investment Company Act of 1940, * * * for breach of fiduciary duty to recover excessive fees, are equitable in nature. [citations] Thus, a party seeking relief under section 36(b) ordinarily is not entitled to a jury trial. * * * The central issue in this action is whether the fund adviser violated its fiduciary duty to the fund by exacting an exorbitant fee. Any unreasonable portion of the fee must be returned to the fund. This restitutionary relief is clearly equitable in nature regardless of whether it is called damages. As a result, plaintiffs are not entitled to jury trial." Kalish v. Franklin Advisers, Inc., 928 F.2d 590, 591–92 (2d Cir.), cert. denied, 502 U.S. 818 (1991).

Under Dairy Queen v. Wood and Feltner v. Columbia Pictures Television, might the Supreme Court disapprove the federal courts' characterizations of a plaintiff's claim for money as equitable and uphold plaintiffs' right to a jury trial?

In Kohler v. Fletcher, the beneficiary of an express trust sued for breach of the trustees' fiduciary duty. She asked for damages for loss of consortium and punitive damages. The court held that, under the Restatement (Second) of Trusts §§ 197 and 198, the beneficiary's remedies for breach of an express trust were exclusively equitable. The beneficiary could not recover emotional distress damages, lost consortium, or punitive damages. Kohler v. Fletcher, 442 N.W.2d 169 (Minn.App.1989).

(b) *The Modern Trend.* After law and equity are merged, any civil court has the "power" to impose punitive damages.

A leading decision is the New York court's I.H.P. Corp. v. 210 Central Park South Corp. After plaintiff recovered an injunction plus punitive damages for defendants' repeated trespasses, defendants argued on appeal that the trial court could not impose punitive damages as incidental to equitable relief.

"We have," the court responded, "one court of general jurisdiction which administers *all* of New York law, be that law of legal or equitable origin. * * * No amount of authority in other States should persuade us that Judge Cardozo was wrong when he said in Susquehanna S.S. Co. v. Anderson & Co.: 'The whole body of principles, whether of law or of equity, bearing on the case, becomes the reservoir to be drawn upon by the court in enlightening its judgment.' * * * Of course, we are obliged to preserve inviolate 'Trial by jury in all cases in which it has heretofore been guaranteed by constitutional provision' (N.Y. Const., art. I, § 2)." But defendants who had not demanded a jury trial properly had waived their right to one. I.H.P. Corp. v. 210 Central Park South Corp., 12 N.Y.2d 329, 332–33, 239 N.Y.S.2d 547, 189 N.E.2d 812 (1963).

In Mississippi, which retained separate chancery courts, the state supreme court, abandoning a well-established rule to the contrary, confirmed the chancery court's ability to impose punitive damages. "We have here a case where the core charge made by Plaintiff Serio in his complaint is 'collusive, deceitful and fraudulent conduct.' Complete relief, Serio charges, requires temporary and permanent injunctive relief, and accounting, actual and punitive damages. Our chancery courts delight to do complete justice and not by halves. * * * There is no sensible reason why all relief to which he may be entitled should not be afforded by * * * a chancery court." The dissent raised the litigants' right to a jury trial. Tideway Oil Programs, Inc. v. Serio, 431 So.2d 454, 461–62 (Miss.1983).

A modern court may simply add punitive damages to an equitable remedy. Oakley v. Simmons, 799 S.W.2d 669 (Tenn.App.1990). If plaintiff was entitled to an injunction, the court may uphold an award of punitive damages without any compensatory damages. A Wisconsin court followed *I.H.P.* A union member obtained a permanent injunction against the union forbidding the union from calling him a "scab" and finding him in bad standing. The court permitted punitive damages as within the trial judge's discretion: "[P]unitive damages is not a jury issue." White v. Ruditys, 117 Wis.2d 130, 142, 343 N.W.2d 421, 426 (App.1983). If the remedies test is the constitutional standard, isn't that incorrect?

If a state requires a plaintiff to prove "actual damages" as a prerequisite for recovery of punitive damages, is equitable relief "actual damages"? Two decisions deal with the actual-damages prerequisite for punitive damages and approve rescission plus punitive damages. Medasys Acquisition Corp. v. SDMS, P.C., 203 Ariz. 420, 55 P.3d 763 (2002) (rescission plus punitive damages); Madrid v. Marquez, 131 N.M. 132, 33 P.3d 683 (App. 2001) (rescission-reformation plus punitive damages).

3. EQUITABLE CLEANUP

ZIEBARTH v. KALENZE
Supreme Court of North Dakota, 1976.
238 N.W.2d 261.

VOGEL, JUSTICE. * * * The plaintiff-appellee, Silver Ziebarth, a cattle buyer, sought specific performance of a contract for the sale of cattle from the defendant-appellant, Leroy Kalenze, a rancher in the business of selling cattle.

The district court, without a jury, found for Ziebarth. The court awarded damages in the sum of $4,589 plus costs in lieu of specific performance. Kalenze moved at the end of the plaintiff's case, for dismissal of the action on the ground that the pleadings asked for specific performance of the contract, whereas the subject matter of the contract, the cattle, was no longer available, making specific performance impossible. The district court denied the motion.

Kalenze appeals * * * from the order of the district court denying his motion to dismiss, and asserts that he was deprived of a jury trial on the issue of damages because of the denial of the motion. He never filed a demand for a jury in the trial court. * * *

On June 16, 1971, Ziebarth and Kalenze entered into a written contract. Ziebarth agreed to purchase all of the Simmental heifer calves produced from Kalenze's cows which were to be artificially inseminated with Simmental semen furnished by Ziebarth.

* * * Ziebarth claims that Kalenze breached the contract when he sold the calves to another party for $450 per head. * * *

The first issue to be decided in this appeal is whether the trial judge erred in denying the defendant's motion to dismiss when it became apparent that the specific relief prayed for in the plaintiff's complaint was impossible to grant as a remedy.

The plaintiff Ziebarth brought this case in equity, demanding specific performance of the contract at the agreed price pursuant to the remedies available to a buyer under the Uniform Commercial Code (UCC § 2–716). This section provides, in part:

"1. Specific performance may be decreed where the goods are unique or in other proper circumstances.

"2. The decree for specific performance may include such terms and conditions as to payment of the price, *damages,* or other relief as the court may deem just." [Emphasis supplied.]

The Code clearly allows the court to grant damages in an action by a buyer for specific performance, *in the court's decree* for specific performance. It is not clear, however, whether the Code allows damages to be awarded *in lieu of a decree* in equity. This case presents the unusual circumstance of a case brought in equity in which specific performance was not possible: The subject matter of the contract had been sold to a third party prior to commencement of the suit. It is not apparent from the pleadings or the testimony whether the plaintiff in this case knew that specific performance was impossible at the time he pled his case in equity.

Of course, the defendant knew when he was served with process that specific performance was impossible, but he did not mention that fact in his answer. If the plaintiff had known that damages, and not specific performance, was the proper remedy—in fact, the only remedy available in this case—and had made the appropriate motion to amend, then the trial court should have allowed the plaintiff to amend his pleadings to conform to his remedy at law or dismissed the suit in equity. * * *

The case law on the issue of the court's jurisdiction to grant damages in lieu of the equitable relief prayed for is conflicting. Some courts recognize the doctrine of substituted legal relief in equity. Historically, where the ground for equitable relief failed, the bill in equity was dismissed and the parties were left to seek in the common-law courts whatever legal remedies remained. But in 1786, an equity court did not dismiss the bill, but retained jurisdiction for granting legal relief where specific performance failed only because of the defendant's wrongful conduct after the suit was begun. This became the basis for granting substituted legal relief in equity. James, Right to Jury Trial in Civil Actions, 72 Yale L.J. 655, 659 (1962). In order for the doctrine to be applied in a particular case, however, the plaintiff must first establish his right to equitable relief, to which damages might then be incidental or subsidiary. [citation] In Raasch v. Goulet, 57 N.D. 674, 223 N.W. 808 (1929), this court held that the right to recover damages under the doctrine of substituted legal relief (or equity's "clean up" jurisdiction, as it is sometimes referred to) depends on the right to specific performance and is not available until the latter is established.

It is thus the rule in some jurisdictions, and the traditional view, that the court cannot give judgment for damages in an action brought in equity unless the plaintiff first proves his right to equitable relief. [citations] There is language in Raasch v. Goulet to support this rule of "substituted legal relief." But we decline to follow this rule of the common law, and to the extent that *Raasch* indicates acceptance of it, we overrule it. In our view, the fusion of law and equity, which has been the law of North Dakota since Statehood, and the law of the Territory of Dakota from the time of its adoption of the Field Code of Civil Procedure at the first legislative session in 1862, puts the authority to grant equitable or legal relief in courts of general jurisdiction, regardless of technicalities such as the rule of "substituted legal relief." Early judges, trained in common-law pleading, were perhaps unwilling to accept the fusion of law and equity at face value. More recently, however, we have at least followed the "clean up jurisdiction" theory and we have held that the existence of a remedy at law does not prelude equitable relief if the equitable remedy is better adapted to render more perfect and complete justice than the remedy at law. We believe that a legal remedy should be granted where equity fails. It would involve needless waste of time and money to send the case back for repleading and retrial to accomplish the same result we have now before us.

The holding of the two preceding paragraphs, of course, is limited to cases where the rules stated in them do not operate to deprive a litigant of a right to a jury trial. The distinction between law and equity is still of primary importance in determining the right to a jury trial. But a jury trial can be waived by failing to demand it.

In the present case, it is apparent that the defendant knew that specific performance was impossible when the complaint was served on him. He therefore must have known that the only possible remedy, if the plaintiff prevailed, would be damages. If so, he knew he had a right to a jury trial. The right to a jury trial, if demanded under the facts of this case, would be absolute. The defendant could have demanded a jury trial, even though the complaint on its face showed grounds for equitable relief only. [citations] At a hearing on a motion based on the demand for a jury, the defendant could have shown his right to a jury trial and the trial court would have erred if it had refused to order the jury trial. But in the absence of a demand, there was no error. The trial court decides which cases are triable by a jury by examining the complaint. [citations] * * * We hold today that the right to a jury trial is likewise waived if not demanded in a case where the complaint demands equitable relief but the defendant is aware that only legal relief could be granted if the plaintiff should prevail. Or, as Professor James puts it,

"Waiver of jury trial under statute or rule will not be relieved against because of the emergence of legal claims based on facts which were pleaded at the time of the waiver. In the usual case plaintiff claims specific performance of a contract which he claims was breached; defendant denies the contract, or the breach or both and claims specific performance is inappropriate anyhow. In this situation it is perfectly foreseeable to defendant that if the court should agree with his own claim about the inappropriateness of specific performance, the pleaded facts present a legal issue. Armed with this chance for foresight, defendant should not be allowed to withhold his jury claim without waiver." [citations]

[Reversed and remanded on other grounds.]

Notes

1. *The Seventh Amendment and Federal Cleanup.* Does a federal court's equitable cleanup power survive the Supreme Court's line of decisions from *Dairy Queen* to *Feltner*?

2. *Other Law–Equity Differences.* Classification as legal or equitable may have other important effects. (a) The provisional remedy of *attachment* may not be authorized for suits in equity. See Jennings v. McCall Corp., 224 F.Supp. 919 (W.D.Mo.1963). Examine the state's attachment statute carefully to make this determination. (b) *Prejudgment interest* may be affected by an "equitable" labeling. See, e.g., N.Y.Civ.Prac.L. & R. 5001(a), which turns prejudgment interest in equity on the court's discretion. (c) There may be an equity exception to the general rule denying recovery of attorney's fees.

Finally, classification as legal or equitable may be significant in the appellate process. (d) In the federal system, it may determine the *appealability* of interlocutory orders. See Pepper v. Miani, 734 F.2d 1420 (10th Cir.1984); (e) And it may affect the *scope of review.* In some states the appellate court reviews the trial judge's findings of fact in an equity trial de novo; the appellate court is not bound by the trial judge's findings of fact, however it may "give weight" to them. Hyler v. Garner, 548 N.W.2d 864, 870 (Iowa 1996).

3. *Subject Matter Jurisdiction.* Constitutions and statutes often limit a lower court's subject matter jurisdiction to restrict the court to money relief or to exclude equity. How do limits on subject matter jurisdiction affect the court's power to apply an "equitable" substantive doctrine or to grant equitable relief? Courts interpret these limitations on their own power. And their answers vary.

(a) A plaintiff sued in a municipal court of limited jurisdiction which lacked "equitable jurisdiction" to collect a business debt from an individual through the alter ego theory. Disregarding the corporate entity, the court held, is "essentially equitable." "No sound policy reason occurs as to why in a case otherwise within municipal court jurisdiction, equitable principles should not be generally applicable. Such a rule would tend to obviate the frequent and understandable misapprehension of litigants as to just where jurisdiction lies. It would prevent time consuming delays, such as here, which must at times result in denial of justice. But the state Constitution, article VI, section 5, casts the power to make such a determination on the Legislature, not the courts. Confronted with a somewhat similar legislative denial of equitable jurisdiction to the municipal court, the Court of Appeal in Strachan v. American Ins. Co., said: 'While the matter could be well handled by the municipal court, it is not within our power to enlarge the legislative grant of jurisdiction to the municipal court. The respondent must be left to his remedy by independent action in equity in the superior court.' " Castellini v. Municipal Court of San Francisco, 7 Cal.App.3d 174, 176–77 86 Cal.Rptr. 698 (1970).

(b) "Rescission is an equitable remedy," said another court, "and we must keep in mind that courts exercising Tucker Act jurisdiction generally do not have jurisdiction over suits for equitable relief against the United States. The Act authorizes jurisdiction only over actions for money judgments. There nevertheless seems to be a narrow 'exception' to this limitation on Tucker Act jurisdiction, in that '[w]here the relief is monetary, [a court exercising Tucker Act jurisdiction] can call upon such equitable concepts as rescission and reformation to help * * * reach the right result.'" Larionoff v. United States, 533 F.2d 1167, 1181 (D.C. Cir.1976), aff'd, 431 U.S. 864 (1977).

4. *The Right to a Complex Jury Trial in State Court.* We saw above the hint of a complexity exception to the federal Seventh Amendment and its present suspension. Does the complexity exception to jury trial exist in state practice?

Kentucky's Civil Rule 39.01 limited the right to a jury trial when the court "finds that because of the peculiar questions involved, or because the action involves complicated accounts, or a great detail of facts, it is impracticable for a jury intelligently to try the case." In a breach of fiduciary duty action, which the court called tortious, seeking damages, the trial court denied a jury trial. Under the Kentucky Constitution, the state supreme court said, "the fact that a number of items are involved does not convert a legal issue into an equitable one. * * * [T]o deny a jury trial is to speculate on a jury's capabilities. A jury, historically, when used, has operated as a check against the arbitrary action of a trial court." The court declared the rule unconstitutional and "remanded for trial by jury." Steelvest, Inc. v. Scansteel Service Center, Inc., 908 S.W.2d 104, 109 (Ky.1995).

5. *Chancery Procedure: Merged and Forgotten?*

(a) *Interpleader.* To aid someone confronted with conflicting claims to a single asset, Chancery developed the bill of interpleader which permits a debtor to avoid multiple litigation by turning the disputed property over to the court. An interpleader required the competing claimants to litigate among themselves who is entitled to the asset. The classical bill of interpleader, hedged by technical requirements, has been largely superceded by a simplified interpleader procedure. See Fed.R.Civ.P. 22; 28 U.S.C. § 1335.

(b) *The Writs of Assistance, Sequestration, and Ne Exeat.* The writ of assistance directed a sheriff to put plaintiff into possession of property which was the subject of the dispute. Sequestration directed "sequestrators" to take possession of defendant's chattels and the rents and profits of his land, to sell the chattels, and to apply the proceeds and the accrued rents to the satisfaction of a judgment. Modern statutes authorizing the collection and enforcement of judgments have largely supplanted these traditional equitable remedies. The writ of ne exeat forbids the defendant's threatened exit from the jurisdiction; still recognized by the federal courts and some states, it is a sharp tool but one seldom used. And when used, often reversed. For example, Aetna with a civil money judgment against Markarian received a ne exeat requiring him to surrender his passport and forbidding him to leave the state or to remove any of his assets. The court of appeals calling this "essentially a form of equitable bail," vacated. Aetna Casualty and Surety Co. v. Markarian, 114 F.3d 346, 347, 350 (1st Cir. 1997).

6. *"Substantive" Equity.* The merger of law and equity continues apace with revision of civil practice statutes and rules of civil procedure. The Federal Rules of Civil Procedure are an attractive model. Only a diminishing handful of states retain separate courts of law and equity after Arkansas and Virginia joined the ranks of merged systems. The separate Delaware Court of Chancery is not an endangered species, however, so long as it continues to be the nation's premier business and corporate court. Finally, the federal bankruptcy court is a court of equity that applies

the principles and rules of equity jurisprudence. Young v. United States, 535 U.S. 43, 50 (2002).

What differences between law and equity remain? Have any substantive "principles of equity" survived merger?

C. THE MODERN INJUNCTION: DISCRETION AND FLEXIBILITY

The English Chancery Courts left a generous legacy to the United States's judicial systems. Contemporary courts with merged procedure have welcomed Chancery's language and forms, including interpleader, depositions, interrogatories, subpoenas, declaratory relief, injunctions, receivers, appeals, complaints, answers, decrees, petitioners, civil contempt, and more.

On a different level, English Chancery decisions have served as a conduit for two components of practical jurisprudence: (a) a court may need to override a legal rule otherwise irreproachable and necessary; and (b) a mechanism for the court to effect this override without collapsing the structure of rules into an ad hoc or ad hominem vacuum.

Our courts' inherited equitable remedies carry with them certain well-known characteristics. Freed from a prescribed set of legal rules, the court's equitable remedies become discretionary and therefore flexible; this combination has proved an irresistible attraction to judicial activists-social engineers and an anathema to those who think that the judge's function is to decide a discrete dispute. Hence the equitable arena is another one where tactical maneuvering between liberals and conservatives occurs.

1. THE CHANCELLOR'S DISCRETION

NAVAJO ACADEMY. v. NAVAJO UNITED METHODIST MISSION SCHOOL

Supreme Court of New Mexico, 1990.
109 N.M. 324, 785 P.2d 235.

MONTGOMERY, JUSTICE. This appeal challenges the propriety of a district court order which, while it has the effect of terminating a tenancy as to real property, allows the tenant to remain in possession of the property for an extended period after termination. * * * We hold that, given the trial court's findings and the unusual circumstances of this case, the court did not abuse its equitable discretion as a court of equity in permitting the tenant to remain on the property for three years following termination of the lease, and accordingly we affirm.

The Navajo Academy, Inc. (the Academy), is a New Mexico corporation organized by the Navajo Tribe to operate a preparatory school for Navajo college-bound youth. Originally located in Ganado, Arizona, it moved its campus to Farmington, New Mexico, in 1978 at the invitation of the Navajo United Methodist Mission School, Inc. (the Mission School). The Mission School is a New Mexico corporation operated in conjunction with the United Methodist Church to conduct a school in Farmington. Its facilities were deteriorating and its student enrollment declining when it invited the Academy to move to the Farmington campus and commence operations there.

The terms and conditions of this move were not written. There was an understanding, however, between the Academy's headmaster and the Mission School's superintendent that the Academy could occupy as much of the campus, including dormitories, classrooms and support buildings, as it needed to house its program, rent-free. There was a tacit understanding that the Academy could stay on the campus for as long as it provided a quality educational program for Navajo children.

In the 1978–79 school year, the Academy's enrollment was about twenty-five students. Because of the quality of its program and the fact that it charged no tuition, whereas the Mission School did make such a charge, the Academy's enrollment climbed steadily and the Mission School's enrollment declined. Within a few years the Mission School had lost all of its students, who were not enrolled in the Academy, and by the 1986–87 school year the Academy's enrollment had grown to approximately 250 students.

The one hundred-acre Farmington campus is owned by the Women's Division of the Board of Global Ministries of the United Methodist Church (the Women's Division). Over the years, the Women's Division had leased the campus to the Mission School in a series of four-year leases which were continually renewed. By 1982 the Academy had come to occupy virtually the entire campus. The original understanding remained unwritten but became even more clearly understood to encompass a long-term relationship of indefinite duration. At about the same time, it also became clear that something had to be done about the deteriorating condition of the campus. The Academy and the Mission School agreed on a course of action: The Academy would make application to the Bureau of Indian Affairs (BIA) for substantial sums of money to repair and renovate the facilities, and the Mission School would support this application with a commitment that the Academy would have the use of the campus for a long term. Pursuant to this arrangement, the Mission School delivered to the Academy an executed copy of a resolution by the Mission School's board authorizing and directing the development of a long-term lease with an indefinite term of no less than twenty-five years. The trial court found that this resolution constituted a promise to provide a long-term lease so that the BIA would embark on a multi-year program of providing substantial sums to the Academy for facilities repair and renovation.

In the same year, 1982, the parties began entering into what was to be a series of short-term subleases, under which the Academy leased the campus from the Mission School for each succeeding school year from 1982–83 to 1986–87. (In 1983–84 there was a direct lease between the Women's Division and the Academy.) Neither the subleases nor the 1983–84 direct lease required that any rent, other than a token amount, be paid. The only consideration for these leases was performance by the Academy of its commitment to provide a quality educational program for Navajo youth and to carry out ordinary maintenance of the facilities. The trial court found that the sub-leases were not intended to replace the understanding between the Academy and the Mission School relating to the Academy's continued, indefinite occupancy of the campus.

The Mission School's promise to provide a long-term lease was not kept. For one thing, the Women's Division had a strict policy against leasing its property for periods longer than four years, and despite the efforts of the Academy and the Mission School that policy could not be changed. However, according to the trial court's findings, the Women's Division condoned the relationship between the Academy and the Mission School and placed representatives of the Mission School in positions of apparent authority to act for and bind the Women's Division. * * *

In 1987 the relationship between the two organizations began quickly to deteriorate. The Mission School requested that, for the next ensuing school year (1987–88), substantial rent ($220,000.00) be paid by the Academy. The Mission School proposed other changes in the sublease relationship and eventually delivered an ultimatum to the Academy requiring it to vacate the property if the Mission School's new sublease was not signed by a stipulated date. * * * It had become clear that the relationship had broken down and that the Academy's occupancy of the campus would have to end.

The Mission School thereupon brought an action in magistrate court for forcible entry and detainer, seeking to evict the Academy. The Academy responded by bringing this action in the District Court for San Juan County to prohibit the magistrate court from entertaining the eviction action and to obtain various other forms of relief. Among the items of relief sought in the Academy's complaint were a declaration that it was entitled to continued occupancy of the property under a "constructive" long-term lease, damages of $1,800,000 for conversion as a result of its expenditures in improving the campus, declaratory and injunctive relief on behalf of the students and compensatory and punitive damages for interference with contractual relations. After a five-day bench trial, the court entered findings of fact and conclusions of law generally favorable to the Academy but awarding none of the relief requested except for the order permitting the Academy to remain on the campus for three years after the date of the trial court's judgment. * * *

The trial court found that the Mission School promised to give a twenty-five-year lease in exchange for the making of certain expenditures by the Academy. It is undisputed that the Academy did make those expenditures (even though the funds for the expenditures were derived from the BIA), and our review of the evidence convinces us that the Mission School did indeed promise to enter into a long-term lease in exchange for these expenditures. It is similarly undisputed that the Mission School never tendered a long-term lease. Therefore, it breached the agreement which the trial court found, and that breach had nothing to do with the Academy's own disavowal of any future involvement by the Mission School in its educational program. * * *

[D]espite the assumption underlying most or all of the appellants' arguments, the trial court did not specifically enforce the Mission School's promise to give a twenty-five-year lease. Rather, the trial court determined, in effect, that the Academy's leasehold interest had terminated—or was, as appellants argue, "terminable at will"—but nevertheless considered the practical effect of an order evicting the Academy from the premises. The trial court further considered the equities in the case before it and found that the Academy had come before the court with clean hands. Under the circumstances, therefore, the trial court decided that the most equitable remedy, while making clear that the Academy would be required to vacate the premises at the end of three years at most, would be to grant it that long a period in which to locate a new campus and move its 250 students to another location. As indicated previously, we do not believe that the fashioning of this equitable remedy, in a suit invoking the equitable powers of the court, was an abuse of discretion.

At bottom, this suit was originated by the Mission School when it applied to the magistrate for relief from forcible entry and detainer. When the Academy sought to prohibit the magistrate court from entertaining this action, it requested equitable relief in the form of a declaration that it held under a "constructive" long-term lease. Though the original action was to prevent relief by way of forcible entry and detainer, which has its origins at law, and to enforce a long-term lease, it is anything but new for this Court to validate an equitable solution to a problem such as the one before us when a party asks for justice and a "legal" remedy is inadequate; "equity frequently interferes." * * * See also Hilburn v. Brodhead, 79 N.M. 460, 464, 444 P.2d 971, 975 (1968) ("[A] court of equity has power to meet the problem presented, and to fashion a proper remedy to accomplish a just and proper result."); 1 J. Pomeroy, Equity Jurisprudence § 109 (5th ed. 1941):

> "Equitable remedies * * * are distinguished by their flexibility, their unlimited variety, their adaptability to circumstances, and the natural rules which govern their use. There is in fact no limit to their variety and application; the court of equity has the power of devising its remedy and shaping it so as to fit the changing circumstances of every case and the complex relations of all the parties."

In the case at bar, the trial court devised a remedy that permits the Academy to continue functioning as a school as it searches for a new home. * * *

We believe that this remedy did not "exceed the bounds of reason," since, in addition to all the other factors, the numerous and costly improvements the Academy bestowed upon the Mission School campus can be viewed as the equivalent of several years' rent. We conclude that the trial court's order permitting the Academy to remain on the campus for a period of time not to exceed three years from the date of the judgment was not an abuse of discretion, and the judgment is affirmed.

Notes

1. *The Navajo Academy's Missing Substantive Theory.* The Navajo Academy is subject to eviction under summary unlawful detainer procedures, a provisional statutory legal remedy in which "equitable" considerations are barred, usually, anyway. What is the Academy to do? Consider the wide range of possible negotiated solutions.

The court's response would be easier to accept if the Navajo Academy had stated a viable theory of property, contract, tort, or restitution. A tenant's improvement of real property belongs to the landlord. The statute of frauds prevents a tenant's success on an unwritten lease or "promise." Fraud and promissory estoppel might also have been considered. The Navajo Academy's request for restitution for the Mission School's alleged unjust enrichment might encounter the difficulty that the school's enrichment, if any, came from the Bureau of Indian Affairs, not the Navajo Academy. Are there any other legal alternatives? Is the Navajo Academy's legal remedy inadequate? Or just absent?

2. *An "Equitable" Cause of Action?* "There is no 'injunctive' cause of action under New York or federal law. Instead [a plaintiff] must allege some wrongful conduct on the part of [a defendant] for which their requested injunction is an appropriate remedy." Reuben H. Donnelley Corp. v. Mark I Marketing Corp., 893 F.Supp. 285, 293 (S.D.N.Y.1995).

3. Is the Navajo Academy qualified for an equitable remedy? Has the court reversed the "no right without a remedy" formulation and entered a remedy in the absence of a right?

WEINBERGER v. ROMERO–BARCELO

Supreme Court of the United States, 1982.
456 U.S. 305.

WHITE, JUSTICE. The issue in this case is whether the Federal Water Pollution Control Act (FWPCA or the Act) 33 U.S.C. § 1251 et seq., requires a district court to enjoin immediately all discharges of pollutants that do not comply with the Act's permit requirements or whether the district court retains discretion to order other relief to achieve compliance. * * *

For many years, the Navy has used Vieques Island, a small island off the Puerto Rico coast, for weapons training. Currently all Atlantic Fleet vessels assigned to the Mediterranean and the Indian Ocean are required to complete their training at Vie ques because it permits a full range of exercises under conditions similar to combat. During air-to-ground training, however, pilots sometimes miss land-based targets, and ordnance falls into the sea. That is, accidental bombings of the navigable waters and, occasionally, intentional bombings of water targets occur. The District Court found that these discharges have not harmed the quality of the water.

In 1978, respondents, who include the Governor of Puerto Rico and residents of the island, sued to enjoin the Navy's operations on the island. * * *

Under the FWPCA, the "discharge of any pollutant" requires a National Pollutant Discharge Elimination System (NPDES) permit. 33 U.S.C. § 1311(a), § 1323(a) (1976 ed. and Supp. III). * * * As the District Court construed the FWPCA, the release of ordnance from aircraft or from ships into navigable waters is a discharge of pollutants. * * *

Recognizing that violations of the Act "must be cured," the District Court ordered the Navy to apply for a NPDES permit. It refused, however, to enjoin Navy operations pending consideration of the permit application. It explained that the Navy's "technical violations" were not causing any "appreciable harm" to the environment. "Moreover, because of the importance of the island as a training center, the granting of the injunctive relief sought would cause grievous, and perhaps irreparable harm, not only to Defendant Navy, but to the general welfare of this Nation."[1] The District Court concluded that an injunction was not necessary to ensure suitably prompt compliance by the Navy. To support this conclusion, it emphasized an equity court's traditionally broad discretion in deciding appropriate relief and quoted from the classic description of injunctive relief in Hecht v. Bowles, 321 U.S. 321, 329–330 (1944): "The historic injunctive process was designed to deter, not to punish."

The Court of Appeals for the First Circuit vacated the District Court's order and remanded with instructions that the court order the Navy to cease the violation until it obtained a permit. Relying on TVA v. Hill, 437 U.S. 153 (1978), in which this Court held that an imminent violation of the Endangered Species Act required injunctive relief, the Court of Appeals concluded that the District

1. [Footnotes renumbered.] The District Court also took into consideration the delay by plaintiffs asserting their claims. It concluded that although laches should not totally bar the claims, it did strongly militate against the granting of injunctive relief.

Court erred in undertaking a traditional balancing of the parties' competing interests. "Whether or not the Navy's activities in fact harm the coastal waters, it has an absolute statutory obligation to stop any discharges of pollutant until the permit procedure has been followed and the Administrator of the Environmental Protection Agency, upon review of the evidence, has granted a permit." The court suggested that "if the order would interfere significantly with military preparedness, the Navy should request that the President grant it an exemption from the requirements in the interest of national security."[2]

It goes without saying that an injunction is an equitable remedy. It "is not a remedy which issues as of course," Harrisonville v. U.S. Dickey Clay Mfg. Co., 289 U.S. 334, 338 (1933), or "to restrain an act the injurious consequences of which are merely trifling." [citations] The Court has repeatedly held that the basis for injunctive relief in the federal courts has always been irreparable injury and the inadequacy of legal remedies. [citations]

Where plaintiff and defendant present competing claims of injury, the traditional function of equity has been to arrive at a "nice adjustment and reconciliation" between the competing claims, Hecht Co. v. Bowles. In such cases, the court "balances the conveniences of the parties and possible injuries to them according as they may be affected by the granting or withholding of the injunction." Yakus v. United States, 321 U.S. 414, 440 (1944). "The essence of equity has been the power of the chancellor to do equity and to mold each decree to the necessities of the particular case. Flexibility rather than rigidity has distinguished it." Hecht Co. v. Bowles.

In exercising their sound discretion, courts of equity should pay particular regard for the public consequences in employing the extraordinary remedy of injunction. Railroad Comm'n. v. Pullman Co., 312 U.S. 496, 500 (1941). Thus, the Court has noted that "the award of an interlocutory injunction by courts of equity has never been regarded as strictly a matter of right, even though irreparable injury may otherwise result to the plaintiff," and that "where an injunction is asked which will adversely affect a public interest for whose impairment, even temporarily, an injunction bond cannot compensate, the court may in the public interest withhold relief until a final determination of the rights of the parties, though postponement may be burdensome to the plaintiff." Yakus v. United States, (footnote omitted). The grant of jurisdiction to insure compliance with a statute hardly suggests an absolute duty to do so under any and all circumstances, and a federal judge sitting as chancellor is not mechanically obligated to grant an injunction for every violation of law. TVA v. Hill; Hecht Co. v. Bowles.

These commonplace considerations applicable to cases in which injunctions are sought in the federal courts reflect a "practice with a background of several hundred years of history," Hecht Co. v. Bowles, a practice of which Congress is assuredly well aware. Of course, Congress may intervene and guide or control the exercise of the courts' discretion, but we do not lightly assume that Congress has intended to depart from established principles. Hecht Co. v. Bowles. As the Court said in Porter v. Warner Holding Co., 328 U.S. 395, 398 (1946):

2. 33 U.S.C. § 1323(a) (Supp. III 1976) provides, in relevant part:

The President may exempt any effluent source of any department, agency, or instrumentality in the executive branch from compliance with any such a requirement if he determines it to be in the paramount interest of the United States to do so. * * *

"Moreover, the comprehensiveness of this equitable jurisdiction is not to be denied or limited in the absence of a clear and valid legislative command. Unless a statute in as many words, or by a necessary and inescapable inference, restricts the court's jurisdiction in equity, the full scope of that jurisdiction is to be recognized and applied. 'The great principles of the equity, securing complete justice, should not be yielded to light inferences, or doubtful construction.' Brown v. Swann, 10 Pet. 497, 503."

In TVA v. Hill, we held that Congress had foreclosed the exercise of the usual discretion possessed by a court of equity. There, we thought that "one would be hard pressed to find a statutory provision whose terms were any plainer" than that before us. The statute involved, the Endangered Species Act, required the district court to enjoin completion of the Tellico Dam in order to preserve the snail darter, a species of perch. The purpose and language of the statute under consideration in *Hill,* not the bare fact of a statutory violation, compelled that conclusion. Section 1536 of the Act requires federal agencies to "insure that actions authorized, funded, or carried out by them do not jeopardize the continued existence of [any] endangered species * * * or result in the destruction or habitat of such species which is determined * * * to be critical." The statute thus contains a flat ban on the destruction of critical habitats.

It was conceded in *Hill* that completion of the dam would eliminate an endangered species by destroying its critical habitat. Refusal to enjoin the action would have ignored the "explicit provisions of the Endangered Species Act." Congress, it appeared to us, had chosen the snail darter over the dam. The purpose and language of the statute limited the remedies available to the district court; only an injunction could vindicate the objectives of the Act.

That is not the case here. An injunction is not the only means of ensuring compliance. The FWPCA itself, for example, provides for fines and criminal penalties. 33 U.S.C. § 1319(c) and (d). Respondents suggest that failure to enjoin the Navy will undermine the integrity of the permit process by allowing the statutory violation to continue. The integrity of the nation's waters, however, not the permit process, is the purpose of the FWPCA.[3] As Congress explained, the objective of the FWPCA is to "restore and maintain the chemical, physical and biological integrity of the Nation's waters." 33 U.S.C. § 1251(a).

This purpose is to be achieved by compliance with the Act, including compliance with the permit requirements. Here, however, the discharge of ordnance had not polluted the waters, and, although the District Court declined to enjoin the discharges, it neither ignored the statutory violation nor undercut the purpose and function of the permit system. The court ordered the Navy to apply for a permit.[4] It temporarily, not permanently, allowed the Navy to continue its activities without a permit.

3. The objective of this statute is in some respects similar to that sought in nuisance suits, where courts have fully exercised their equitable discretion and ingenuity in ordering remedies. E.g., Spur Ind. Inc. v. Del E. Webb Development Co., 108 Ariz. 178, 494 P.2d 700 (1972); Boomer v. Atlantic Cement Co., 26 N.Y.2d 219, 309 N.Y.S.2d 312, 257 N.E.2d 870 (1970).

4. The Navy applied for an NPDES permit in December, 1979. In May, 1981, the EPA issued a draft NPDES permit and a notice of intent to issue that permit. The FWPCA requires a certification of compliance with state water quality standards before the EPA may issue an NPDES permit. 33 U.S.C. § 134(a). The Environmental Quality Board of the Commonwealth of Puerto Rico denied the Navy a water quality certificate in connection with this application for an NPDES in June, 1981. In February, 1982, the Environmental Quality Board denied the Navy's

Other aspects of the statutory scheme also suggest that Congress did not intend to deny courts the discretion to rely on remedies other than an immediate prohibitory injunction. Although the ultimate objective of the FWPCA is to eliminate all discharges of pollutants into the navigable waters by 1985, the statute sets forth a scheme of phased compliance. As enacted, it called for the achievement of the "best practicable control technology currently available" by July 1, 1977 and the "best available technology economically achievable" by July 1, 1983. 33 U.S.C. § 1311(b) (Supp. IV 1970). This scheme of phased compliance further suggests that this is a statute in which Congress envisioned, rather than curtailed, the exercise of discretion.

The FWPCA directs the Administrator of the EPA to seek an injunction to restrain immediately discharges of pollutants he finds to be presenting "an imminent and substantial endangerment of the health of persons or to the welfare of persons." 33 U.S.C. § 1364(a). This rule of immediate cessation, however, is limited to the indicated class of violations. For other kinds of violations, the FWPCA authorizes the Administrator of the EPA "to commence a civil action for appropriate relief, including a permanent or temporary injunction, for any violation for which he is authorized to issue a compliance order. * * * "33 U.S.C. 1319(b).[5] The provision makes clear that Congress did not anticipate that all discharges would be immediately enjoined. Consistent with this view, the administrative practice has not been to request immediate cessation orders. "Rather, enforcement actions typically result, by consent or otherwise, in a remedial order setting out a detailed schedule of compliance designed to cure the identified violation of the Act." Brief for United States 17. Here, again, the statutory scheme contemplates equitable consideration.

This Court explained in Hecht v. Bowles, that a major departure from the long tradition of equity practice should not be lightly implied. As we did there, we construe the statute at issue "in favor of that interpretation which affords a full opportunity for equity courts to treat enforcement proceedings * * * in accordance with their traditional practices, as conditioned by the necessities of the public interest which Congress has sought to protect." We do not read the FWPCA as foreclosing completely the exercise of the court's discretion. Rather than requiring a District Court to issue an injunction for any and all statutory violations, the FWPCA permits the District Court to order that relief it considers necessary to secure prompt compliance with the Act. That relief can include, but is not limited to, an order of immediate cessation.

The exercise of equitable discretion, which must include the ability to deny as well as grant injunctive relief, can fully protect the range of public interests at issue at this stage in the proceedings. The District Court did not face a situation in which a permit would very likely not issue and the requirements and objective

reconsideration request and announced it was adhering to its original ruling. In a letter dated April 9, 1982, the Solicitor General informed the Clerk of the Court that the Navy has filed an action challenging the denial of the water quality certificate. United States of America v. Commonwealth of Puerto Rico, No. 82–0726 (D.P.R.).

5. The statute at issue in Hecht v. Bowles, contained language very similar to that in § 1319(b). It directed the Administrator to seek "a permanent or temporary injunction, restraining order, or other order" to halt violations. The Court determined that such statutory language

did not require the court to issue an injunction even when the Administrator had sued for injunctive relief. In *Hecht,* the court's equitable discretion overrode that of the Administrator. If a court can properly refuse an injunction in the circumstances of *Hecht,* the exercise of its discretion seems clearly appropriate in a case such as this, where the EPA Administrator was not a party and had not yet expressed his judgment. The action of the district court permitted it to obtain the benefit of the EPA's recommendation before deciding to enjoin the discharge.

of the statute could therefore not be vindicated if discharges were permitted to continue. Should it become clear that no permit will be issued and that compliance with the FWPCA will not be forthcoming, the statutory scheme and purpose would require the court to reconsider the balance it has struck.

Because Congress, in enacting the FWPCA, has not foreclosed the exercise of equitable discretion, the proper standard for appellate review is whether the district court abused its discretion in denying an immediate cessation order while the Navy applied for a permit. We reverse and remand to Court of Appeals for proceedings consistent with this opinion.

It is so ordered.

STEVENS, JUSTICE, dissenting. * * * Our cases concerning equitable remedies have repeatedly identified two critical distinctions that the Court simply ignores today. The first is the distinction between cases in which only private interests are involved and those in which a requested injunction will implicate a public interest. Second, within the category of public interest cases, those cases in which there is no danger that a past violation of law will recur have always been treated differently from those in which an existing violation is certain to continue.

Yakus v. United States, 321 U.S. 414, 441, illustrates the first distinction. The Court there held that Congress constitutionally could preclude a private party from obtaining an injunction against enforcement of federal price control regulations pending an adjudication of their validity. In that case, the public interest, reflected in an act of Congress, was in opposition to the availability of injunctive relief. The Court stated, however, that the public interest factor would have the same special weight if it favored the granting of an injunction. * * *

Hecht Co. v. Bowles, which the Court repeatedly cites, did involve an attempt to obtain an injunction against future violations of a federal statute. That case fell into the category of cases in which a past violation of law had been found and the question was whether an injunction should issue to prevent future violations. [citations] Because the record established that the past violations were inadvertent, that they had been promptly terminated, and that the defendant had taken vigorous and adequate steps to prevent any recurrence, the Court held that the District Court had discretion to deny injunctive relief. But in reaching that conclusion, the Court made it clear that judicial discretion "must be exercised in light of the large objectives of the Act. For the standards of the public interest, not the requirements of private litigation, measure the propriety and need for injunctive relief in these cases." Indeed, the Court emphasized that any exercise of discretion "should reflect an acute awareness of the congressional admonition" in the statute at issue.

In contrast to the decision in *Hecht,* today the Court pays mere lip service to the statutory mandate and attaches no weight to the fact that the Navy's violation of law has not been corrected.[1] The Court cites no precedent for its holding that an ongoing deliberate violation of a federal statute should be treated like any garden-variety private nuisance action in which the chancellor has the widest discretion in fashioning relief.[2] * * *

1. The Navy has been in continuous violation of the statute during the entire decade since its enactment.

2. Indeed, I am unaware of any case in which the Court has permitted a statutory violation to continue.

The Court distinguishes TVA v. Hill, on the ground that the Endangered Species Act contained a "flat ban" on the destruction of critical habitats. But the statute involved in this case also contains a flat ban against discharges of pollutants into coastal waters without a permit. Surely the congressional directive to protect the Nation's waters from gradual but possibly irreversible contamination is no less clear than the command to protect the snail darter. To assume that Congress has placed a greater value on the protection of vanishing forms of animal life than on the protection of our water resources is to ignore the text, the legislative history,[3] and the previously consistent interpretation of this statute.

It is true that in TVA v. Hill there was no room for compromise between the federal project and the statutory objective to preserve an endangered species; either the snail darter or the completion of the Tellico Dam had to be sacrificed. In the FWPCA, the Court tells us, the congressional objective is to protect the integrity of the Nation's waters, not to protect the integrity of the permit process. Therefore, the Court continues, a federal court may compromise the process chosen by Congress to protect our waters as long as the court is content that the waters are not actually being harmed by the particular discharge of pollutants.

On analysis, however, this reasoning does not distinguish the two cases. Courts are in no better position to decide whether the permit process is necessary to achieve the objectives of the FWPCA than they are to decide whether the destruction of the snail darter is an acceptable cost of completing the Tellico Dam. Congress has made both decisions, and there is nothing in the respective statutes or legislative histories to suggest that Congress invited the federal courts to second-guess the former decision any more than the latter. * * *

The Court's sophistry is premised on a gross misunderstanding of the statutory scheme. Naturally, in 1972 Congress did not expect dischargers to end pollution immediately. Rather, it entrusted to expert administrative agencies the task of establishing timetables by which dischargers could reach that ultimate goal. These timetables are determined by the agencies and included in the NPDES permits; the conditions in the permits constitute the terms by which compliance with the statute is measured. Quite obviously, then, the requirement that each discharger subject itself to the permit process is crucial to the operation of the "scheme of phased compliance." By requiring each discharger to obtain a permit *before* continuing its discharges of pollutants, Congress demonstrated an intolerance for delay in compliance with the statute. It is also obvious that the "exercise of discretion and balancing of equities" were tasks delegated by Congress to expert agencies, not to federal courts, yet the Court simply ignores the difference. * * *

The decision in TVA v. Hill did not depend on any peculiar or unique statutory language. Nor did it rest on any special interest in snail darters. The decision reflected a profound respect for the law and the proper allocation of lawmaking responsibilities in our government.[4] There we refused to sit as a

---

3. The Senate Report emphasized that "if the timetables established throughout the Act are to be met, the threat of sanction must be real, and enforcement provisions must be swift and direct." S.Rep. No. 91–414, 92d Cong., 1st Sess., 65 (1971).

4. Our individual appraisal of the wisdom or unwisdom of a particular course consciously selected by the Congress is to be put aside in the process of interpreting a statute. Once the meaning of an enactment is discerned and its consti-

committee of review. Today the Court authorizes free thinking federal judges to do just that. Instead of requiring adherence to carefully integrated statutory procedures that assign to nonjudicial decisionmakers the responsibilities for evaluating potential harm to our water supply as well as potential harm to our national security, the Court unnecessarily and casually substitutes the chancellor's clumsy foot for the rule of law.

I respectfully dissent.

Notes

1. *Unlimited Equitable Discretion?* Is court's claim of "equitable discretion" just a pretty way to say that a judge may ignore a rule he or she disagrees with? Is it contrary to the principals of the rule of law and *stare decisis* which compel a judge to apply a doctrine that he or she disagrees with?

Did the Court ignore the legislative branch of government? Both the majority and the dissent rely heavily on equity tradition. Which is the more "liberal" and which the more "conservative" opinion? If a Court majority feels that Congress has failed to vote sufficient money to protect the environment, does it have the power to increase the appropriation? Can the Congress write and enact a statute that will limit a court's equitable discretion? Does the holding turn on whether the defendant violated the statute or on whether the judge had discretion to excuse defendants' admitted violation? Does the Court merely order defendants to comply as promptly as is feasible? See Zygmuat J.B. Plater, Statutory Violations and Equitable Discretion, 70 Calif.L.Rev. 524 (1982).

2. *When Did the Shooting Stop?* In May, 1997, the EPA, for the first time, suspended military training for environmental reasons. The Massachusetts Military Reservation became so polluted with lead from shells on firing ranges that public health and drinking water were threatened. Shooting practice was banned. The Washington Post, May 19, 1997 at A8.

Viéques? Over decades, in addition to lawsuits and political pressure, thousands of people marched and protested the Navy's target practice on Viéques, including Robert Kennedy, Jr. who spent a month in jail for trespassing during a protest. Errant bombs aimed at targets on Viéques killed a Puerto Rican civilian in 1999. On May 1, 2003, jubilant Puerto Ricans cheered after the president kept his promise and the Navy officially ended its bombing exercises on Viéques. The Department of the Interior will clean up the island after 60 years of Navy bombing. The New York Times, May 2, 2003 at A22.

3. *A Better Way?* Is there a preferable way for a court to decide whether to issue an injunction? Two other approaches follow.

(a) "A modern federal equity judge does not have the limitless discretion of a medieval Lord Chancellor to grant or withhold a remedy. * * * Modern equity has

tutionality determined, the judicial process comes to an end. We do not sit as a committee of review, nor are we vested with the power of veto. The lines ascribed to Sir Thomas More by Robert Bolt are not without relevance here: "The law, Roper, the law. I know what's legal, not what's right. And I'll stick to what's legal. * * * I'm *not* God. The currents and eddies of right and wrong, which you find such plain-sailing, I can't navigate, I'm no voyager. But in the thickets of the law, oh there I'm a forester. * * * What would you do? Cut a great road through the law to get after the Devil? * * * And when the last law was down, and the Devil turned around on you—where would you hide, Roper, the laws all being flat? * * * This country's planted thick with laws from coast to coast—Man's laws, not God's—and if you cut them down * * * d'you really think you could stand upright in the winds that would blow them? * * * Yes, I'd give the Devil benefit of law, for my own safety's sake." R. Bolt, A Man for All Seasons, Act I, p. 147 (Three Plays, Heinemann ed. 1967).

rules and standards, just like law. * * * And although the ratio of rules to standards is lower in equity than in law, in cases where the plaintiff has an established entitlement to an equitable remedy the judge cannot refuse the remedy because it offends his personal sense of justice." Matter of Freligh, 894 F.2d 881, 887 (7th Cir.1989).

(b) Defendant Massey Yardley was found to have discriminated against Delores Paigo on the basis of her age; although back pay was ordered, she declined to be reinstated in her former position. The EEOC appealed after the trial judge denied its motion for an injunction.

"The EEOC contends that the district court abused its discretion in denying its post-verdict motion for injunctive relief. The EEOC asked for an order enjoining Massey Yardley from further age discrimination and requiring company management to undergo EEOC training, the posting of a notice concerning the present matter, and neutral and fair employment references for Paigo. The district court refused this relief without opinion. We review a district court's decision to deny equitable, including injunctive, relief under an abuse of discretion standard. * * * The district court abuses its discretion, inter alia, when it denies injunctive relief in the face of evidence of consistent past discrimination, or when it fails to articulate its reasons for denying the requested relief. [citation]

"Paigo's decision not to seek reinstatement in this case does not prevent the EEOC from pursuing the broader equitable remedies listed above, it being the EEOC, and not the individual claimant, that is suing. [citations] (It should be added that while Paigo did not seek reinstatement, she may desire and believe she needs an injunction ordering the company to provide neutral and fair job references for her as well as desisting from mention of this action.) In E.E.O.C. v. Harris Chernin, Inc., 10 F.3d 1286, 1292 (7th Cir.1993), * * * the Seventh Circuit suggested that the EEOC is normally entitled to injunctive relief where it proves discrimination against one employee and the employer fails to prove that the violation is not likely to recur. The EEOC represents the public interest when litigating claims, and, through injunctive relief, seeks to protect not only the rights of the individual claimant, but those of similarly-situated employees by deterring the employer from future discrimination. * * *

"The discriminatory conduct here was primarily that of Cox and Griffin, both of whom remain in the same supervisory positions at the dealership without, so far as can be ascertained, having been disciplined for their behavior. Indeed no one at the company seems to have admitted to any wrongdoing. (Yardley, the president, testified that he did not believe there was any indication of age discrimination against Paigo, characterizing her claims as 'silly' and 'ridiculous.') And, while a draft anti-harassment policy was proffered along with the second unconditional offer of reinstatement, there was no evidence at trial that the draft was adopted or disseminated. All of this suggests that Massey Yardley failed 'to prove that the violation is unlikely to recur,' * * * and that injunctive relief may be needed 'to eliminate the discriminatory effects of the past as well as bar like discrimination in the future.' Kilgo v. Bowman Transp., Inc., 789 F.2d 859, 880 (11th Cir.1986) * * *

"We conclude that the district court abused its discretion in turning down all equitable relief out of hand while failing to provide any reasons for so doing. Accordingly, we remand the case to the district court so that it can grant the requested relief, or insofar as it finds persuasive reasons to deny particular items of relief, to state its reasons for so doing." U.S. E.E.O.C. v. Massey Yardley Chrysler Plymouth, 117 F.3d 1244, 1253–54, n.10, n. 11 (11th Cir.1997).

4. *Stay Tuned.* As this edition was being prepared for publication, the Supreme Court granted cert to determine whether a federal judge has discretion to deny a

patent owner an injunction against an infringing defendant. The Federal Circuit court had held that the judge had almost no discretion to refuse to grant a successful plaintiff a permanent injunction to protect its invention—a judge may reject an injunction if the plaintiff will not "practice" its patent and the public health is endangered. MercExchange, LLC v. eBay, Inc., 401 F.3d 1323, 1338–39 (Fed.Cir.), cert. granted, 126 S.Ct. 733 (2005). The Supreme Court cited the "equitable discretion" feature of *Weinberger* with approval in eBay, Inc. v. MercExchange, L.L.C., 126 S.Ct. 1837 (2006).

5. *Equitable Discretion and Federal Court Abstention.* A federal court's equitable and discretionary power, for example to grant an injunction or a declaratory judgment, may be abrasive enough to disrupt delicate federal-state relationships. Because the federal court ought to exercise its jurisdiction where it exists "federal courts have the power to dismiss or remand cases based on abstention principles only where the relief being sought is equitable or otherwise discretionary." The district court should not, the Supreme Court held, have remanded an action for money damages. Quackenbush v. Allstate Insurance Co., 517 U.S. 706, 731 (1996).

6. *Discretion Not to Supervise?* One court refused to enjoin the breach of a ten-year mall lease, remarking that it did not want to find itself "in the business of managing a shopping center." New Park Forest Associates II v. Rogers Enterprises, Inc., 195 Ill.App.3d 757, 765, 552 N.E.2d 1215, 1220, appeal denied, 133 Ill.2d 559, 561 N.E.2d 694 (1990).

The structural injunction will be discussed below. A judge uses a structural injunction to protect the constitutional rights of prison inmates, for example. Granting a comprehensive and detailed structural order and supervising its administration over a long term puts the judge "in the business of managing a prison."

Courts appear to be more willing to supervise relief to protect plaintiffs' constitutional rights than when a plaintiff's rights under a contract or lease are threatened.

2. TWO MAXIMS OF EQUITY: CLEAN HANDS AND LACHES

The Maxims of Equity. For a starting maxim we may say that "Equity is Fond of Maxims." Pomeroy's fifth edition Volume II, § 363 of Equity Jurisprudence (1941) lists:

 1. Equity regards as done which ought to be done.
 2. Equity looks to the intent rather than to the form.
 3. He who seeks equity must do equity.
 4. He who comes into equity must come with clean hands.
 5. Equality is equity.
 6. Where there are equal equities, the first in time shall prevail.
 7. Where there is equal equity, the law must prevail.
 8. Equity aids the vigilant, not those who slumber on their rights.
 9. Equity imputes an intention to fulfill an obligation.
 10. Equity will not suffer a wrong without a remedy.
 11. Equity follows the law.

No canonical register of maxims exists; most lists contain between ten and fifteen maxims in diverse orders with various inclusions and exclusions. The maxim "Equity acts in personam" was examined earlier in this chapter. Other maxims are "Equity abhors forfeitures," "He who trusts most loses most,"

"Equity delights in doing justice and not by halves," and perhaps half in jest "Equity does everything by fifths."

How does a modern judge take the maxims into account when deciding a lawsuit? "Equity," is the subject of each maxim; that word lends an aura of distance and mystery to the inquiry. The maxims are not a comprehensive code. Nor do the Medieval Chancellors seem to have deduced them from an overarching concept of equity. The maxims are abstract and generally stated. A judge usually cannot use a vague maxim to decide the issues in a lawsuit. But a judge can decide the case under a narrow rule and quote a maxim to support the result or to express the conclusion. A judge may recite "unclean hands," for example, as a conclusion to restate a more precise reason to refuse relief, like fraud, illegality, or plaintiff's breach. The "common law" has similar rules, including "No man can take advantage of his own wrong," which resembles the unclean hands defense. Are the maxims rules or just pithy aphorisms and mottos?

At least two of the maxims may constrain judges from granting equitable relief: the "clean hands" maxim and that concerning laches, "equity aids the vigilant."

a. Clean Hands

Seller

GREEN v. HIGGINS

Supreme Court of Kansas, 1975.
217 Kan. 217, 535 P.2d 446.

PRAGER, JUSTICE. This is an action for specific performance of a contract for the sale of real estate. The facts are not in dispute and are essentially as follows: On May 7, 1969, the defendants-appellees, Damon W. Higgins and Cleo D. Higgins, sold a tract of land to Robert E. Brown and Mark S. Gilman. At the time of this transaction and as a part of the consideration therefor, the Higgins agreed that Brown and Gilman should have a right of first refusal to purchase adjoining land from the Higgins should they desire to sell it. In addition, as a result of this same sale, a real estate agent, Lienna McCulley, obtained an agreement with the Higgins which gave Miss McCulley the right to handle any subsequent sale of the adjoining tract if the contracting or sale occurred prior to June 1, 1971. In April of 1971 the Higgins desired to sell the adjoining tract of land which was subject to the contractual rights just mentioned. The plaintiffs-appellants, Philip A. Green and Barbara A. Green, desired to purchase the adjoining tract of land from the Higgins at a proposed purchase price of $30,000. A contract for the purchase of the property for the proposed price was executed by the Greens and the Higgins on April 21, 1971. Prior to the time the contract was prepared and executed the Higgins advised the Greens that Lienna McCulley would be entitled to a commission on the sale if the contracting or sale occurred prior to June 1, 1971. The contract was dated June 2, 1971, in order to defeat Lienna McCulley's right to handle the sale of the property and to cheat her out of her real estate commission.

Plaintiff, Philip A. Green, testified in his deposition that after this contract was signed Higgins advised him that the property was subject to the right of first refusal held by Brown and Gilman pursuant to the contract of May 7, 1969. Green and Higgins apparently decided that something had to be done to avoid Higgins's obligation to give the first right of refusal to Brown and Gilman. Green testified in substance that he suggested to Higgins that a fictitious contract be prepared and delivered to Brown and Gilman with a letter giving them the opportunity to enter into a contract for the same price or otherwise the right of first refusal would be waived. The fictitious contract was dictated by Mr. Green and typed by Mrs. Green. In this fictitious contract the purchase price was stated to be $40,000 and the designated purchaser of the property was Medallion Investment Properties, Inc., a corporation of which Mr. Green was the president. It is undisputed that this fictitious contract with an inflated purchase price in the amount of $40,000 was prepared and delivered to Brown and Gilman to discourage them from exercising their right of first refusal, since the indicated purchase price of $40,000 was an excessive price for the property. This gambit was apparently successful since Brown and Gilman did not exercise their right of first refusal to purchase the property under the terms stated in the fictitious contract.

Thereafter the Higgins decided that they did not want to carry out their contract with the Greens and so advised the Greens. At that point the only money which had changed hands was the $100 given to Higgins by Green at the time the contract was executed. The Higgins offered to return this in August or September of 1971. In January of 1972 Green tendered the balance of the purchase price, $29,900 and requested a warranty deed from Higgins which Higgins refused to provide. On March 28, 1972, the Greens filed this action for specific performance of the contract. The Higgins counterclaimed for damages based upon an alleged clouding of their title and further prayed that their title to the land be quieted against the Greens. * * *

In denying relief to both parties the district court found * * * that the conduct of both the plaintiffs Green and the defendants Higgins had been willful, fraudulent, illegal, and unconscionable, that neither party had come into court with clean hands, and thus neither should be granted any relief by the court. The plaintiffs Green have appealed to this court from the judgment of the district court dismissing their petition and denying them specific performance. * * *

In this case the clean hands doctrine had been specifically raised as an affirmative defense in the defendants' answer. That defense was the basis of the defendants' motion to dismiss. * * * The clean hands doctrine in substance provides that no person can obtain affirmative relief in equity with respect to a transaction in which he has, himself, been guilty of inequitable conduct. It is difficult to formulate a general statement as to what will amount to unclean hands other than to state it is conduct which the court regards as inequitable. Like other doctrines of equity, the clean hands maxim is not a binding rule, but is to be applied in the sound discretion of the court. The clean hands doctrine has been recognized in many Kansas cases. The application of the clean hands doctrine is subject to certain limitations. Conduct which will render a party's hands unclean so as to deny him access to a court of equity must be willful conduct which is fraudulent, illegal or unconscionable. Furthermore the objectionable misconduct must bear an immediate relation to the subject-matter of the suit and in some measure affect the equitable relations subsisting between the parties to the litigation and arising out of the transaction. Stated in another way the misconduct which may justify a denial of equitable relief must be _related_ misconduct rather than _collateral_ misconduct arising outside the specific transaction which is the subject-matter of the litigation before the court.

It should also be emphasized that in applying the clean hands maxim, courts are concerned primarily with their own integrity. The doctrine of unclean hands is derived from the unwillingness of a court to give its peculiar relief to a suitor who in the very controversy has so conducted himself as to shock the moral sensibilities of the judge. It has nothing to do with the rights or liabilities of the parties. In applying the unclean hands doctrine, courts act for their own protection, and not as a matter of "defense" to the defendant.

The plaintiffs Green on this appeal argue that a defendant cannot invoke the protection of the clean hands maxim unless he has suffered from the misconduct of the plaintiff. They argue that here the defendants Higgins participated in the claimed misconduct and that any injury suffered would be to third parties and not to the defendants themselves. [citations] In our judgment such an interpretation of the clean hands doctrine does not accord with its principal purpose. A court may refuse its relief to the plaintiff though the defendant himself participated in the misconduct, not because it is a privilege of such a defendant, but because the court refuses to lend its aid to either party to such a transaction. The best-reasoned cases hold that the maxim applies, even though the misconduct of the plaintiff has not injured anyone and even though the defendant himself was a participant in the misconduct. [citations]

With these basic principles in mind we turn now to the undisputed facts in this case to determine whether or not the district court abused its discretion in denying relief to both the plaintiffs and the defendants. Here all parties have conceded that the following facts are true: That the contract entered into between the parties on April 21, 1971 was dated June 2, 1971, in order to deprive Lienna McCulley of her right to a sales commission which she had previously obtained through contract; that a fictitious contract was prepared by which it appeared the Higgins agreed to sell the real estate to Medallion Investment Properties, Inc. for $40,000; that the fraudulent contract was prepared at the suggestion of the plaintiff, Philip A. Green, and was submitted by Higgins to Brown and Gilman in order to deprive them of their right of first refusal to purchase the property at a proposed price. It simply cannot be denied that the plaintiffs Green actively and willfully participated in fraudulent and unconscionable activities to obtain title to the land and to defeat various legal rights held by third parties. The misconduct involved here was directly related to the subject-matter of the litigation and must be classified as related misconduct, not collateral misconduct. Under all the facts and circumstances we cannot say that the trial court abused its discretion in denying relief to both the plaintiffs and defendants by reason of the clean hands doctrine.

The judgment of the trial court is affirmed.

Notes

1. *Questions.* If the tract was worth $35,000, should the court allow Higgins, who had contracted to sell it to the Greens for $30,000, to sell it to someone else for $35,000?

To avoid splitting a cause of action, a plaintiff should sue a defendant for all available relief in one action. Federal Rules 8 and 18 and state equivalents allow a claimant to ask for alternative remedies. Should the Greens have sought specific performance and, in the alternative, expectancy damages?

What rights might the broker and the holders of the right of first refusal have after this decision?

2. *Scope of Unclean Hands.* A defendant may interpose unclean hands when plaintiff seeks an injunction, specific performance, a constructive trust, or any other equitable remedy. Substantive areas and types of claims where unclean hands comes up include violation of a constitutional right, covenant not to compete, quiet title, cancellation, partition, and copyright or trademark infringement. The contract-restitution doctrines of fraud, unconscionability, and illegality-in pari delicto are related to unclean hands.

An aura of moral superiority surrounds the unclean hands maxim. The maxim may focus the judge's attention on a quest for ethical superiority and distract his or her attention from the whole dispute and the consequences of the decision.

A judge's view of what is unethical or inequitable may be idiosyncratic. A judge may hinge granting or denying an equitable remedy on something outside the defined rules of law. The unclean hands doctrine is also free-floating procedurally, for the judge can raise it sua sponte.

The doctrine of unclean hands has a shapeless, amorphous, and open-ended quality which leads courts to the following principles of confinement: (a) The plaintiff's misconduct cited as unclean hands must have been related to the dispute plaintiff sues on or to the relief the plaintiff seeks. (b) Unclean hands is discretionary with the trial judge. (c) Public policy may override the unclean hands defense.

One consequence of a decision barring a plaintiff from relief because of unclean hands is that a defendant who has breached a contract or committed a violation of legal rights evades the plaintiff's request for an equitable remedy. And perhaps for any remedy. Although technically unclean hands may not bar plaintiff's second action to seek a legal remedy after an unclean hands dismissal, plaintiff may nevertheless be barred by res judicata-claim preclusion for splitting a cause of action, by the statute of limitations, or by a related affirmative defense like fraud or illegality.

A doctrine which is stated as sweepingly as unclean hands, which has an area of operation defined as variably as unclean hands, and which has exceptions articulated as generally as unclean hands is an unstable and unpredictable doctrine. One question is whether courts could formulate more specific rules.

3. *Judge Posner on Unclean Hands.* "The maxim that 'he who comes into equity must come with clean hands,' although comparatively recent as equity maxims go, [citations] captures very nicely the moralistic, rule-less, natural-law character of the equity jurisprudence created by the Lord Chancellors of England when the office was filled by clerics. The moralistic language in which the principles of equity continue to be couched is a legacy of the time when a common lawyer could, without sounding too silly, denounce equity as 'a Roguish thing' because 'Equity is according to the Conscience of him that is Chancellor, and as that is larger or narrower, so is equity.' The Table–Talk of John Selden 64 (Singer ed. 1847 [1689]). But the time itself is long past, and the proposition that equitable relief is 'discretionary' cannot be maintained today without careful qualification. A modern judge, English or American, state or federal, bears very little resemblance to a Becket or a Wolsey or a More, but instead administers a system of rules which bind him whether they have their origin in law or in equity and whether they are enforced by damages or by injunctions. To tell a plaintiff that although his legally protected rights have been invaded and he has no adequate remedy at law (i.e., damages) the judge has decided to withhold equitable relief as a matter of discretion just would not wash today. Even when the plaintiff is asking for the extraordinary remedy of a preliminary injunction—extraordinary because it is often a very costly remedy to the defendant, yet is ordered on the basis of only a summary inquiry into the merits of

the plaintiff's suit—the request is evaluated according to definite standards, rather than committed to a free-wheeling ethical discretion.

"Today, 'unclean hands' really just means that in equity as in law the plaintiff's fault, like the defendant's, may be relevant to the question of what if any remedy the plaintiff is entitled to. An obviously sensible application of this principle is to withhold an equitable remedy that would encourage, or reward (and thereby encourage), illegal activity, as where the injunction would aid in consummating a crime." Shondel v. McDermott, 775 F.2d 859, 867–68 (7th Cir.1985).

Judge Posner gave further evidence of his skepticism about relying on undefined ethical considerations in applying the clean hands maxim. He stated that the doctrine "functionally rather than moralistically conceived, gives recognition to the fact that equitable decrees may have effects on third parties—persons who are not parties to a lawsuit, including taxpayers and members of the law-abiding public—and so should not be entered without consideration of those effects." Byron v. Clay, 867 F.2d 1049, 1051 (7th Cir.1989)

4. *Unclean Hands in Damage Actions at Law?* When law and equity were merged, many equitable defenses became available in actions at law. Could a defendant in a damages action bar the plaintiff's recovery because of the plaintiff's unclean hands? Usually not, because, even after merger, the unclean hands defense is usually confined to equity alone, and it is typically not available in actions at law. "The unclean hands defense is not available in an action at law." observed one court. RIV VIL, Inc. v. Tucker, 979 F.Supp. 645, 659 (N.D.Ill.1997).

Merger, a court held, was a procedural reform which did not affect substantive doctrines like unclean hands. The clean hands maxim is not an equitable defense that was merged with law in the sense that it is available to the defendant in a negligence action for damages. McKinley v. Weidner, 73 Or.App. 396, 698 P.2d 983 (1985). The legal affirmative defense of *in pari delicto*, or illegality, however, covers much of the same misconduct; illegality is a defense to an action on a contract.

"But," Judge Posner explained, "with the merger of law and equity, it is difficult to see why equitable defenses should be limited to equitable suits any more; and of course many are not so limited [citation], and perhaps unclean hands should be one of these. Even before the merger there was a counterpart legal doctrine to unclean hands—*in pari delicto*—which forbade a plaintiff to recover damages if his fault was equal to the defendant's. [citation] We need not worry about the precise scope of the doctrine. [citation] It is enough to observe that a highwayman who decided to sue his partner for common law damages as well as for an equitable accounting for profits would surely have gotten no further with his 'legal' claim than with his 'equitable' one." Byron v. Clay, 867 F.2d 1049, 1052 (7th Cir.1989).

With the near demise of contributory negligence and its application only in negligence anyway, tort doctrine lacks an all-purpose defense based on plaintiff's misconduct. A court may employ the clean hands maxim to fill the vacuum. For example after being advised by defense counsel to lie at a deposition and being found out, a doctor sued counsel for legal malpractice in giving the advice. The court thought the plaintiff's misconduct-unclean hands barred the malpractice claim he alleged. Blain v. The Doctor's Company, 222 Cal.App.3d 1048, 272 Cal.Rptr. 250 (1990).

Similarly a court may misclassify a legal claim as an equitable claim and wield unclean hands to bar a damages judgment in the action at law. One court mischaracterized the torts of fraud and intentional infliction of mental suffering as "equitable" and barred by a litigant's unclean hands. Al–Ibrahim v. Edde, 897 F.Supp. 620, 625–26 (D.D.C.1995).

What happens when plaintiff seeks both equitable and legal relief? "The doctrine of unclean hands applies only to bar equitable remedies and does not bar legal remedies. * * * [citations] In the copyright context, unclean hands may bar injunctive relief but would not bar recovery of statutory damages." Olan Mills, Inc. v. Linn Photo Co., 795 F.Supp. 1423, 1430 (N.D.Iowa 1991).

5. *The Parties' Unclean Hands and the Public Interest.* Ralston made a false advertising claim about its Puppy Chow; Alpo also advertised its puppy food falsely. In the lawsuit that followed, each claimed the other had violated § 43(a) of the federal Lanham Act and both sought injunctions. If defendant's false advertising deceives the public, a competitor is entitled to an injunction. The district judge said:

"[B]oth parties have made false, deceptive, and misleading claims which are actionable. * * * [B]oth parties are entitled to relief * * *." The unclean hands defense is available against Lanham Act remedies. To be unclean hands, the misconduct must relate to the matter in controversy. Both parties had misbehaved concerning the same product, puppy food. Each claimed the other's hands are unclean, and each argued against any injunction:

"[T]he court must take into account the public and the competitors' interests in preventing the proliferation of false and deceptive advertising. [citations] The [unclean hands] defenses may be rejected where, as is the case here, failure to grant an injunction would only increase the damage inflicted on the buying public. Given that the worst effects of Alpo's and Ralston's conduct have been visited on the buying public, this court believes that the equitable defenses raised cannot bar relief which is necessary and in the public interest." Alpo Petfoods, Inc. v. Ralston Purina Co., 720 F.Supp. 194, 197, 214 (D.D.C.1989).

The Ralston vs. Alpo dog-food fight continued in the appellate court, but neither party appealed the trial judge's decision to reject both parties' unclean hands defenses. Alpo Petfoods, Inc. v. Ralston Purina Co., aff'd in part, rev'd in part, 913 F.2d 958, 970 (D.C. Cir.1990).

b. *Laches*

STONE v. WILLIAMS, (STONE I)

United States Court of Appeals, Second Circuit, 1989.
873 F.2d 620.

CARDAMONE, CIRCUIT JUDGE. Cathy Yvonne Stone brought this action * * * for her purported share of copyright renewal rights to songs composed by Hank Williams, Sr., her natural father. The defendants in this action are Hank Williams, Jr., the son of Hank Williams and stepson of Billie Jean Williams Berlin, who was married to Hank Williams at the time of his death, and a number of music companies * * *. The sole issue presented is whether the district court abused its discretion when it granted defendants' motion for summary judgment and dismissed appellant's complaint on the grounds of laches. Even granting to Ms. Stone's situation the fullest stretch of sympathy, her own delay and procrastination in the end bars her suit. The district court's judgment, therefore, is affirmed.

The dispute arises over copyright renewal proceeds for 60 published and copyrighted songs written or performed by country and western singer Hank Williams (Williams, Sr.) who died intestate on January 1, 1953 at the age of 29. During his lifetime the well-known singer and composer wrote such popular hits as "Your Cheatin' Heart" and "Hey Good Lookin'." We set forth the facts briefly in chronological order.

Appellant Stone was born on January 6, 1953 in Alabama, five days after Williams, Sr. died. While Ms. Stone's biological mother, Bobbie Jett, was pregnant with her in October of 1952, she and Williams, Sr. executed an agreement under which he acknowledged that he might be the father of appellant, but specifically did not admit paternity. The agreement further provided that Williams, Sr. pay Bobbie Jett for Ms. Stone's support, and placed the infant's custody until age 2 in Lillian Williams Stone, mother of Williams, Sr., who was present at the drafting and the execution of the agreement together with the two principals. Pursuant to its terms, Lillian Stone adopted plaintiff, and Bobbie Jett left for California. Until her death in 1955 Mrs. Stone cared for appellant. At that point, Williams, Sr.'s sister, Irene Smith, reneged on her promise to care for Cathy Stone if anything happened to Lillian Stone. As a result, appellant became a ward of the State of Alabama, and at age three in 1956 a foster child of the Deupree family. The Deuprees adopted her in 1959.

Williams, Sr. had a son, Hank Williams, Jr. The assignment of Hank Williams, Jr.'s copyright interests in his father's music generated litigation in 1967 and 1968 in the Circuit Court of Montgomery County, Alabama. That court appointed a guardian *ad litem,* attorney Drayton Hamilton, to ascertain any unknown potential heirs to the Williams' estate and to represent their interests. After investigating, Hamilton concluded that the only such person was appellant Stone. Unbeknownst to Ms. Stone, her adoptive family, the Deuprees, had asked Hamilton to leave her out of the 1967 proceedings, because they thought it unlikely that she would win and were worried that their then 14–year–old daughter would be subjected to embarrassing publicity because of her status as the illegitimate child of a famous country western singer. Nonetheless, Hamilton zealously litigated Ms. Stone's interests, but to no avail. The Alabama court determined that Hank Williams, Jr. was the sole heir of his father, and further held that appellant, as a natural child who had been adopted by another family, had no rights in any proceeds from the Williams, Sr.'s songs or their renewal rights. * * *

After the disruptive first few years of her life, Ms. Stone appears to have enjoyed an ordinary childhood, and developed a closely bonded relationship with the Deuprees, with no knowledge of her natural parents. Then, in late 1973, shortly before appellant's 21st birthday, Mrs. Deupree told her of the rumors regarding the identity of her natural father, but added that everything had been decided against her. This disclosure was necessary because, upon turning age 21, Ms. Stone was entitled to a small inheritance from Williams, Sr.'s mother, Lillian Stone. The Deuprees were concerned that appellant might encounter reporters while claiming the inheritance and wanted to arm her with knowledge. After picking up the inheritance check (about $3,800) at the Mobile County Courthouse, Ms. Stone went to a library and read a biography on Williams, Sr., entitled *Sing a Sad Song,* written by Roger Williams. This book mentioned the possibility that Williams, Sr. had fathered an illegitimate daughter, and the author speculated on the child's entitlement to a renewal interest in his songs. Ms. Stone surmised that she might be that daughter.

In the following years, appellant asked the Deuprees about her background and talked to some attorney acquaintances, but did little else to ascertain her connection to Williams. She recalls that the Deuprees told her that there was nothing more to do. In 1979, she met with personnel from the state agency responsible for adoptions—the Alabama Department of Pensions and Securities—but states that she no longer remembers the substance of the conversation.

The record, including appellant's deposition, suggests that her feelings about Williams' parentage were ambivalent.

Her attitude crystallized in 1980 when she received a telephone call from her adoptive father, George Deupree. Evidently alluding to his decision not to pursue Ms. Stone's rights in the 1967–68 lawsuits, Deupree told her that he had undergone a change of heart after seeing Hank Williams, Jr. on a television show. Deupree has since died, but appellant related the conversation in her deposition: "I want to ask you if you would like to find out if Hank Williams is your father. He said think about it. And he said I will help you in any way that I can. And he said I think I was wrong in withholding information from you and not discussing it. And I will do everything I can to help you."

Following this call, Ms. Stone stepped up her efforts to learn about her relationship to Williams, Sr. She looked up newspaper articles about him, and sought out his relatives and those of her natural mother, Bobbie Jett, who had also since died. She met with attorney Hamilton, her former guardian *ad litem,* and discussed with him the 1952 custody and support agreement between Bobbie Jett and Williams, Sr., and obtained the records from the 1967 and 1968 Circuit Court proceedings. But Ms. Stone did not examine those documents until after she met attorney Keith Adkinson (who later became her husband) in 1984.

Appellant filed the original declaratory judgment complaint in this action on September 12, 1985 which, as amended to include all of the above-named defendants, contains two claims. The first claim against all the defendants arises under the Copyright Acts of 1909 and 1976 and seeks a number of declarations, including that Ms. Stone is the natural daughter of Williams, Sr., and as such is entitled to a proportionate share of the renewal rights from his songs. The second claim alleges that certain of the defendants committed a conspiracy to defraud her.

In addition to this federal action, Hank Williams, Jr. and Ms. Stone sued each other in Alabama state court in 1985, each seeking a declaratory judgment on appellant's status vis-à-vis Hank Williams, Sr. That court held that even though Ms. Stone was the natural child of Williams, Sr., she was not his heir under Alabama law. Thus, it gave preclusive effect to the prior 1967 and 1968 Alabama Circuit Court state ruling.

* * * The district court, in granting defendants' motion for summary judgment and dismissing her complaint, relied on the doctrine of laches and did not reach the other issues.

Historically laches developed as an equitable defense based on the Latin maxim *vigilantibus non dormientibus aequitas subvenit* (equity aids the vigilant, not those who sleep on their rights). [citation] In contrast to a statute of limitations that provides a time bar within which suit must be instituted, laches asks whether the plaintiff in asserting her rights was guilty of unreasonable delay that prejudiced the defendants. [citations] The answers to these questions are to be drawn from the equitable circumstances peculiar to each case.

A ruling on the applicability of laches is overturned only when it can be said to constitute an abuse of discretion. * * *

Although laches promotes many of the same goals as a statute of limitations, the doctrine is more flexible and requires an assessment of the facts of each case—it is the reasonableness of the delay rather than the number of years that elapse which is the focus of inquiry. [citations] In holding that Ms. Stone unreasonably delayed in bringing this action to have her rights declared, the district court focused on the years 1974–85, beginning with Mrs. Deupree's conversation with appellant regarding the inheritance, and ending with the filing of the complaint that initiated the instant case.

In our view, the delay for the period from 1974 to 1980 may well have been entirely excusable under the circumstances. First, her relationship with the Deuprees is by all indications the paradigm of a successful adoption. Thus, it is not surprising that loyalty and gratitude to Mr. and Mrs. Deupree, whom she considered her real parents, gave her pause at doing anything that might hurt their feelings. For this reason, George Deupree's telephone call to Ms. Stone is significant. Only after he called in 1980 could appellant be sure that investigating her natural parentage would not damage the only family bonds she knew. Second, Ms. Stone's embarrassment at asserting her relationship to Williams, Sr. is also understandable, because his notoriety would have made publicity almost impossible for her to avoid. This is substantiated by the extensive press coverage of the 1967 and 1968 court proceedings.

Third, only in recent years have courts and the general public come to recognize that children born of unmarried parents should not be penalized by being accorded a status for which they are not to blame. In the 1967 and 1968 proceedings, attorney Hamilton argued on Ms. Stone's behalf that discriminating against illegitimate children violated the Federal Constitution. Unfortunately for appellant, Hamilton was before his time; the case that would remove much of the stigma associated with illegitimacy was then pending before the Supreme Court, but not decided until after appellant's rights had been adjudicated. See Levy v. Louisiana, 391 U.S. 68 (1968) (holding unconstitutional state statute that discriminated against illegitimates to discourage births out of wedlock).

But even though Ms. Stone might arguably be excused for the reasons just stated from filing suit until 1980, there is simply no plausible explanation for delay in filing the instant complaint until September 1985, after five more years had passed. Appellant's filial loyalty is admirable, and one can sympathize with her feelings of embarrassment and trepidation attendant upon widespread personal publicity. But these reasons for delay cannot last forever for purposes of laches. A point arrives when a plaintiff must either assert her rights or lose them. Here Ms. Stone's procrastination and delay, which silently allowed time to slip away, remain as the only reason for her failure to bring suit earlier.

Where plaintiff has not slept on her rights, but has been prevented from asserting them based, for example, on justified ignorance of the facts constituting a cause of action, personal disability, or because of ongoing settlement negotiations, the delay is reasonable and the equitable defense of laches will not bar an action. There is no such reasonable excuse, or any issue of fact presented in the instant case that would permit a jury to excuse appellant's delay for the five years beginning in 1980 and ending in September 1985.

Laches is not imposed as a bar to suit simply because a plaintiff's delay is found unexcused; it must also be determined whether the defendants have been prejudiced as a result of that delay. [citation] Although an evaluation of prejudice is another subject of focus in laches analysis, it is integrally related to the inquiry regarding delay. Where there is no excuse for delay, as here, defendants need show little prejudice; a weak excuse for delay may, on the other hand, suffice to defeat a laches defense if no prejudice has been shown. [citation] Defendants may be prejudiced in several different ways. [citation] One form of prejudice is the decreased ability of the defendants to vindicate themselves that results from the death of witnesses or on account of fading memories or stale evidence. Another type of prejudice operates on the principle that it would be inequitable in light of some change in defendant's position to permit plaintiff's claim to be enforced. Defendants here were prejudiced in both ways.

As the district court noted, some of the key people having knowledge of the events preceding Ms. Stone's birth have died since 1974—George Deupree, Bobbie Jett and Audrey Mae Williams. All of their deaths are not equally prejudicial. For example, Bobbie Jett died in 1974, so absence of her testimony cannot be found to prejudice defendants because she would not have been alive to testify even if appellant had filed suit immediately. Nevertheless, the circumstances giving rise to this appeal have already spanned over two decades and the additional five years of Ms. Stone's unexcused delay doubtless would hamper the defense further—appellant's deposition reveals that even her memory has faded significantly in the interim. We conclude that the defendants were prejudiced to some degree by evidence that was lost by death or weakened during the delay. Because the defendants were injured in other ways by the delay, we need not hold that a finding of this kind of prejudice is alone sufficient to support the laches defense.

Prejudice may also be found if, during the period of delay, the circumstances or relationships between the parties have changed so that it would be unfair to let the suit go forward. The defendants have entered into numerous transactions involving Williams, Sr.'s songs. Ms. Stone responds that these transactions need not be unraveled—she could simply share in the profits. But that argument ignores the fact that the transactions were premised on the apparent certainty of the ownership of the songs' renewal rights—attributable to appellant's delay. This procrastination prejudiced defendants by lulling them into a false sense of security that the renewal rights were as they appeared and that she would not contest the 1967 and 1968 court rulings. [citations]

We cannot be sure that defendants would have struck the bargains they did had they anticipated the diminution in their profits that Ms. Stone seeks. This result is logically not altered by whether the defendants made actual expenditures or whether they simply incurred the opportunity costs implicated in foregoing other ventures. As Judge Learned Hand wrote as a district court judge in a copyright case in which the plaintiff delayed for 16 years before filing suit, it would be unfair for a plaintiff "to stand inactive while the proposed infringer spends large sums of money in its exploitation, and to intervene only when his speculation has proved a success. Delay under such circumstances allows the owner to speculate without risk with the other's money, he cannot possibly lose, and he may win." Haas v. Leo Feist, Inc., 234 F. 105, 108 (S.D.N.Y.1916). We therefore agree with the district court that the change in relationships and circumstances that occurred while Ms. Stone delayed would prejudice the defendants if the case were allowed to proceed at this late date.

Finally, we note that the underlying value of the laches doctrine, as with statutes of limitations, is that of repose. Even assuming that appellant's claims are meritorious, the availability of the laches defense represents a conclusion that the societal interest in a correct decision can be outweighed by the disruption its tardy filing would cause. Thus, courts, parties and witnesses "ought to be relieved of the burden of trying stale claims when a plaintiff has slept on his rights." See Burnett v. New York Central R.R. Co., 380 U.S. 424, 428 (1965).

[Affirmed.]

STONE v. WILLIAMS, (STONE II)

United States Court of Appeals, Second Circuit, 1989.
891 F.2d 401.

[Plaintiff Stone filed a petition for rehearing. The court granted the petition and reversed the preceding opinion, Judge Cardamone again writing for the court.

[After the preceding opinion was argued but before it was decided, the Alabama Supreme Court had decided Stone's appeal in separate litigation where she was seeking to reopen her father's estate and to obtain her share of the estate. The Alabama court "reversed the trial court's award of summary judgment to defendants finding that they had intentionally, willfully and fraudulently concealed plaintiff's identity, existence, claim and rights as a natural child of Hank Williams, Sr." Because of fraud and errors of law, the Alabama court had also set aside the Montgomery Circuit Court decrees that Stone was not an heir to the estate. The Alabama court also held that laches did not bar plaintiff's claim because her delay was excusable. Although the parties and applicable law differed, the court of appeals reconsidered on two related theories.]

However, recited evidence in the Alabama court makes clear that the present defendants were aware of plaintiff's rights to the copyright renewals long before plaintiff. Irene Smith, who was instrumental in concealing from plaintiff evidence of who her father was, acted as Hank Williams, Jr.'s guardian during the 1967–68 proceedings. Similarly, Smith, as administratrix, and Stewart, as attorney, of Hank Williams' estate, conspired to conceal from Cathy Stone her potential rights, and took pains to cut off those rights. These actions of his guardian benefitted Hank Williams, Jr. Hank Williams, Jr.'s counsel was further advised by Stewart that a portion of the estate income was being withheld for appellant. Williams, Jr. never disavowed Stewart's actions, or mentioned any of these facts in prior court proceedings in Alabama in 1985 or in the district court proceeding we earlier reviewed and to which he and plaintiff were parties.

The prejudice to defendants we identified in our prior opinion, would not have existed but for the failure of the present defendants to reveal the facts of which they had knowledge. Defendants could have sought a court declaration of their rights vis-a-vis plaintiff. Instead they chose to remain silent. They should not now be allowed to claim that they are prejudiced by plaintiff's present assertion of her rights when they were aware of them all along.

Consequently, in reassessing the equitable circumstances peculiar to this case, the equities fall on plaintiff's side. The present litigation is a contest, after all, between Hank Williams' heirs over copyright renewal rights. To allow defendants to bar plaintiff from claiming her rights when the availability of the laches defense was obtained by them in such an unworthy manner would not only grant defendants a windfall in this suit to which they are not entitled, but would also encourage a party to deliberately mislead a court. Courts of equity exist to relieve a party from the defense of laches under such circumstances. [citation]

Consequently, the evidence of fraud, which the Alabama Supreme Court found persuasive, makes summary judgment dismissing plaintiff's claim on the grounds of laches inappropriate. The figure representing justice is blindfolded so that the scales are held even, but justice is not blind to reality."

Notes

1. *Her Cheated Heart, Continued.* On remand from *Stone* II's decision that Cathy Stone was not barred by laches, the trial judge took up defendants' remaining arguments for summary judgment. Stone's cause of action for a declaration of her rights under the Copyright Act accrued in 1979, the district judge held, when she learned of her possible identity; so the Copyright Act's three-year statute of limitations walled Stone out of recovery. Another appeal ensued.

In *Stone* III, Judge Cardamone didn't think so. Stone's cause of action accrued in 1979. But each of defendants' alleged infringements was a separate cause of action, so Stone could recover for each time the defendants' infringed and withheld royalties in the three-year statutory period preceding the date her suit was filed. "Stone's suit is timely insofar as relief [which was an accounting or a constructive trust, both equitable remedies] is sought for defendants' failure to remit to her a proportionate share of royalties received within three years of suit."

What about the rule that the statute of limitations on the substantive right plaintiff asserts applies when she is seeking the equitable remedy of a constructive trust? "The analogous legal remedy for Stone's attempt to impose a constructive trust is an action for accounting [sic] and/or damages. The basis for such an action is her claimed entitlement to a share of the copyright renewals. The nature of the right is such that a new claim for relief arises each time the right is invaded by defendants' failure to remit to plaintiff her due share of renewals. Hence if Stone is entitled to a share of renewals, a constructive trust may be imposed upon income derived from it within three years of suit." More on this point below.

Defendants furthermore were bound by the Alabama court's adjudication of Williams Sr.'s paternity of Stone and she was entitled to at least some share of the copyright renewals. Once again the court of appeals remanded to the trial judge. Stone v. Williams, 970 F.2d 1043, 1051–52 (2d Cir. 1992), *Stone* III.

Explanation of editor's brash [sic]: An "accounting" is usually considered, at least initially, to be equitable. George Palmer, The Law of Restitution § 1.5(c) (1978). See Dairy Queen v. Wood, 369 U.S. 469, 478 (1962) pp. 278–79.

It's All Over Now. In 1993 "the bitter litigation arising from plaintiff's belated discovery that she is the daughter of the late famous country and western singer Hank Williams, Sr." was settled. After a fight worthy of one of the country ballads she sings, Cathy Stone, known professionally as Jett Williams, will have a share. Is Jett set? By then the renewals and royalties were reportedly in the millions. Washington Post, June 25, 1993 at C3.

2. *Laches and the Statute of Limitations.* We learn from the series of opinions in the Stone v. Williams litigation that laches and the statute of limitations may coexist in the same dispute, indeed the same lawsuit. A court may diminish laches by looking to the nearest statute of limitations and saying "Equity follows the law." as it holds the statute of limitations either to govern or to define the plaintiff's delay period for laches. There are other approaches:

(a) "The answer short and simple is that laches is a defense only to actions in equity, and is not a defense to an action at law. The relevant statute of limitations provides the only barrier to stale actions at law. Reviewing the complaint, it is apparent that this is an action for breach of contract and that no equitable relief is sought. Accordingly, this defense is not available to defendant." M. Lowenstein & Sons v. Austin, 430 F.Supp. 844, 846 (S.D.N.Y.1977).

(b) "In applying the doctrine of laches, an important consideration is the appropriate role of an analogous statute of limitation. * * *

"The lower federal courts have ascribed varying degrees of importance to analogous statutes of limitation. Some courts have held that the running of an analogous statute of limitation creates a rebuttable presumption of unreasonable delay and prejudice flowing therefrom. [citation] Other courts have completely disregarded statutes of limitation in considering a defense of laches, [citations], or treated them as merely one element in the congeries of factors to be considered in determining whether the length of delay was unreasonable and whether the potential for prejudice was great. [citations] We find that the last approach accords most favorably with the purpose of the doctrine of laches and congressional intent regarding the doctrine's application to claims * * * to protect veteran's reemployment rights." Goodman v. McDonnell Douglas Corp., 606 F.2d 800, 804–805 (8th Cir.1979), cert. denied, 446 U.S. 913 (1980)

(c) When an original owner sued "good faith purchasers" to recover a work of art a thief had stolen 20 years before, the defendants raised both laches and the three-year statute of limitations on the plaintiff's legal cause of action for replevin. The New York Court of Appeals rejected a discovery-reasonable diligence approach to accruing an owner's cause of action for replevin. The owner's replevin cause of action, the New York court maintained, does not accrue and the statutory period does not begin to run until the owner demands the property and the purchaser refuses. Thus the owner controls when the replevin cause of action against a purchaser accrues. This decision might extend the owner's time to sue almost indefinitely.

Enter laches: If, however, the owner's lack of reasonable diligence in pursuing the art and its delay in suing were excessive and if this delay prejudices the purchaser, the court said that the purchaser may claim laches. So an owner who sues a defendant for replevin within the applicable statute of limitations period may nevertheless be barred by laches.

A thief in possession of stolen art for 20 years could have asserted the statute of limitations successfully, because an owner's cause of action against a thief accrues on the date of the theft, "even if the property owner was unaware of the theft at the time it occurred." Solomon R. Guggenheim Foundation v. Lubell, 77 N.Y.2d 311, 318, 567 N.Y.S.2d 623, 626, 569 N.E.2d 426, 429 (1991).

3. *Equity No; Damages Yes.* If the plaintiffs seek legal and equitable remedies, either together or in the alternative, laches may bar them from equitable relief, but leave them free to pursue a legal remedy. For example, a judge denied plaintiffs specific performance because of laches but nevertheless awarded them expectancy damages. Estate of Younge v. Huysmans, 127 N.H. 461, 506 A.2d 282 (1985).

4. *Equitable Discretion—Legal Rigidity.* The abstract contrast between laches with its focus on plaintiff's unreasonable delay plus defendant's prejudice and the statute of limitations with its focus on plaintiff's delay alone is striking. The choice between laches and a statute of limitations can be viewed as an example of a choice between flexible equitable discretion and rigid legal rules. In reality, however, the contrast is less marked.

Statutes of limitations are under pressure from the belief that a victim with a valid cause of action ought not be barred by a technicality. The disputes where this strain is most acute involve asbestos, childhood sexual abuse, and stolen art. Courts have developed and expanded "discovery" rules to delay the date the plaintiff's legal cause of action accrues and the statutory period begins to run.

Remedies students may recall from Property [Georgia] O'Keeffe v. Snyder, 83 N.J. 478, 491, 416 A.2d 862, 869 (1980). The New Jersey court said its discovery-due diligence rule was "a principle of equity, the purpose of which is to mitigate the unjust results that otherwise might flow from strict adherence to a rule of law." A discovery rule ameliorates the statute of limitations into something more discretionary and more like laches.

Perhaps the lesson of Guggenheim v. Lubell, above, is that when a statute of limitations becomes *too* flexible, there will be no time limit at all. Where the statute of limitations seemed perpetual, the uncertainty led the court to import laches analysis into the disputes. But what corrects the imbalance when laches becomes too flexible?

5. *Longest Wait*? Native titles and early treaties generate litigation about ancient wrongs that lead to laches defenses. An example is City of Sherrill v. Oneida Nation.

In 1807, an Oneida deeded some Indian reservation land in New York to a non-Indian. The transaction violated the federal Nonintercourse Act which bars the sale of tribal land without United States permission.

After the Supreme Court held in 1985 that the Oneida Indian Nation (OIN) could sue for damages for violation of their property rights, in 1997 and 1998 the OIN acquired part of the former tribal lands that were transferred in 1807. OIN claimed that the purchase unified the tribal aboriginal title with the fee simple title and revived OIN sovereignty. Thus the land was exempt from Sherrill's taxes.

OIN sued the city in United States court for an injunction that would bar the imposition of any property tax. Reversing the lower courts' decisions for the OIN, the Supreme Court held that OIN's laches barred the OIN "from rekindling embers of sovereignty that long ago grew cold."

"The principle that the passage of time can preclude relief has deep roots in our law, and this Court has recognized this prescription in various guises. It is well established that laches, a doctrine focused on one side's inaction and the other's legitimate reliance, may bar long-dormant claims for equitable relief. * * *

"The appropriateness of the relief OIN here seeks must be evaluated in light of the long history of state sovereign control over the territory. From the early 1800's into the 1970's, the United States largely accepted, or was indifferent to, New York's governance of the land in question and the validity *vel non* of the Oneidas' sales to the State. In fact, the United States' policy and practice through much of the early 19th century was designed to dislodge east coast lands from Indian possession. Moreover, the properties here involved have greatly increased in value since the Oneidas sold them 200 years ago. Notably, it was not until lately that the Oneidas sought to regain ancient sovereignty over land converted from wilderness to become part of cities like Sherrill. * * *

"[T]he question of damages for the Tribe's ancient dispossession is not at issue in this case, and we therefore do not disturb our holding in Oneida II [that the OEN could recover damages]. However, the distance from 1805 to the present day, the Oneidas' long delay in seeking equitable relief against New York or its local units, and developments in the city of Sherrill spanning several generations, evoke the doctrines of laches, acquiescence, and impossibility, and render inequitable the piecemeal shift in governance this suit seeks unilaterally to initiate." City of Sherrill, New York v. Oneida Nation of New York, 544 U.S. 197 (2005).

While barring a claim this old might not surprise a student, two features of the Supreme Court's *Oneida* decision are notable. First, the Court states the second "element" of laches not as the defendant's "prejudice" from the plaintiff's delay but as the defendant's "legitimate reliance." Whether that alters the test in federal cases outside ancient Native claims is unknown at this writing, as is whether a change from "prejudice" to "reliance" makes a difference.

Second, in contrast to most laches decisions, the *Oneida Nation* Court held that plaintiff's legal claim for damages is not time-barred, but that their equitable claim for an injunction is. Three months later in a similar lawsuit involving the Cayuga Nation's claims in central New York, the federal Court of Appeals gave *Oneida Nation* a broad reading. Because of the Cayuga's dispossession nearly 200 years ago in violation of the Nonintercourse Act, the trial judge had awarded them $248 million in damages and prejudgment interest. The tribe had sued within the applicable statute of limitations. However, the majority, emphasizing the disruptiveness of the remedy, held that the equitable doctrine of laches also applied to the tribe's legal claim which it characterized as ejectment; moreover, the tribe's lack of success in ejectment barred its trespass claim for damages. Cayuga Indian Nation of New York v. Pataki, 413 F.3d 266, 273–74, 278 (2d Cir.2005). The dissent insisted that the tribe's laches barred it from ejectment for a possessory remedy that resembled an equitable injunction, but that its delay did not bar it from the other ejectment remedy, mesne profits or damages. The Cayuga Nation's petition for certiorari was denied by the Supreme Court in May, 2006. 126 S.Ct. 2021, 2022 (2006).

6. *Scope of Laches.* Various types of remedies, claims and issues trigger defendants' laches defenses: breach of trust, constructive trust, equitable lien, tracing, equitable redemption from a mortgage foreclosure, adverse possession, quiet title, reformation of a deed, a restrictive covenant, an option to repurchase real property, specific performance, public employee contracts, a claim that a contract is illusory and void, unconscionable or lacking mutuality, revocation of acceptance, rescission, correction of a military discharge, patent infringement, copyright renewal, and an injunction against copyright infringement.

D. CONTEMPT

Just as a damages action does not end with a money judgment, a chancery suit does not end with an injunction. The defendant must still pay the judgment or obey the injunction. Plaintiff enforces an injunction against an obstreperous defendant with contempt. Orderly analysis of this complicated procedure will be advanced if certain distinctions are explained at the outset. A firm grasp of the differences in classification between direct and indirect, civil and criminal, and prospective and retrospective contempt will assist your understanding of a technical subject.

The first distinction, between direct and indirect contempt, turns on geography. Direct contempt is recalcitrant or unseemly conduct that occurs in the courtroom; an overly zealous lawyer or an obstreperous litigant are the usual examples. Our primary concern here is with indirect contempt which consists of a defendant's disobedience of an injunction outside the courtroom. The major consequence of the direct-indirect classification is procedural. A judge may punish the direct contemnor on the spot. On the other hand, a defendant charged with indirect contempt is entitled to at least notice and a hearing.

The second, more significant, classification is between criminal contempt and civil contempt. That distinction turns on the remedy the judge imposes. The judge's purpose with a criminal contempt sanction is a public one, to punish and deter. In contrast, a judge uses civil contempt to secure for the private plaintiff the benefits of the injunction. Civil contempt has two distinct branches. In most states and in federal court, civil contempt may take the form of compensatory contempt, requiring the contemnor to pay the plaintiff for any loss caused by the violation. Doug Rendleman, Compensatory Contempt: Plaintiff's Remedy When Defendant Violates an Injunction, 1980 U.Ill.L.Rev. 971. Civil contempt may also be coercive contempt with the goal of securing for the plaintiff the benefits awarded by the injunction. A judge's coercive contempt order is a revocable, indeterminate threat to imprison or fine the defendant for continued disobedience; it resembles a second injunction with the penalty for breach specified. If the defendant complies with the judge's order, coercive contempt is never in fact applied at all. Thus Judge Zirpoli told Frank McNulty, "you have the key to the jail door yourself."

Because their purpose is to benefit the plaintiff, compensatory contempt and coercive contempt are classified as civil contempt. The procedure employed is therefore civil with two refinements: there is no jury and usually the burden of proof requires clear and convincing evidence. A criminal contemnor, on the other hand, may claim almost complete criminal procedural protections. The rule that a judge may not impose a criminal contempt sanction without following criminal procedure has been a fertile source of trial court error and appellate reversal beginning with Gompers v. Buck's Stove & Range Co., 221 U.S. 418 (1911).

A third and final way to classify contempt is retrospective-prospective. Retrospective contempt confesses failure; defendant breached the injunction and the judge no longer can secure for plaintiff the conduct to which she is entitled. The judge must therefore substitute compensatory contempt, money compensation, or criminal contempt, punishment of the wrongdoer. Since the defendant's conduct that the injunction mandated cannot be attained, compensatory contempt includes an additional incongruity: the judge must employ the backward-looking money remedy notwithstanding the prior decision that money is an inadequate remedy to protect the plaintiff's interest.

Coercive contempt, on the other hand, is prospective, devised by the judge to compel defendant's future conduct. The measures the judge normally employs are threats to fine or imprison the defendant. As we have already learned, coercive contempt sometimes misfires. Coercive imprisonment of Frank McNulty only stiffened his resistance; Judge Zirpoli released McNulty after five months. p. 236. When judges' coercive confinement orders failed to coerce defendants to make deeds ordered as specific performance of land sale contracts, legislatures provided for decretal transfers to give plaintiffs marketable title. See pp. 230–31.

The foregoing is based on Doug Rendleman, How to Enforce an Injunction, 10 Litig. 23 (Fall, 1983).

1. WHAT ORDERS SUPPORT CONTEMPT?

H.K. PORTER CO. v. NATIONAL FRICTION PRODUCTS

United States Court of Appeals, Seventh Circuit, 1977.
568 F.2d 24.

WYZANSKI, SENIOR DISTRICT JUDGE. Plaintiff appeals from the March 4, 1977 order of the District Court for the Northern District of Indiana, South Bend

Division, dismissing plaintiff's August 28, 1975 "Motion for issuance of order to show cause and for contempt judgment." * * *

October 3, 1967 plaintiff filed a complaint alleging that the corporate and individual defendants infringed plaintiff's rights in trade secrets and confidential information. March 25, 1968 plaintiff and defendants entered into a four-page Settlement Agreement. Paragraph 2 provided:

"That National and Figert agree that they will not sell any of said two compounds previously submitted by National to Frigidaire Division of General Motors Corporation for use in making of an air conditioner pulley in competition with the molding compound presently supplied by Porter to said Frigidaire Division of General Motors Corporation and, particularly, that National will not submit any compound to Frigidaire Division of General Motors Corporation for use in making an air conditioner pulley in which the formula of such compound is taken directly from plaintiff's formula and Compound No. 7580–1C, as contained in plaintiff's deposition exhibits one (1) through four (4) inclusive, as aforesaid."

April 15, 1968, in response to a motion made by all the parties, the district court entered an order which included the following: * * *

The Court further orders * * * that the said Settlement Agreement is hereby adopted and made a part of the decree by reference as the judgment herein.

August 28, 1975 plaintiff filed its "Motion for issuance of order to show cause and for contempt judgment." Therein it was alleged:

4. National Friction Products Corporation and its President and General Manager, Edward J. Sydor, individually, have failed and refused to comply with and have disobeyed and disregarded the provisions of said court order and consent decree. * * *

Plaintiff prayed that the corporate defendant and its president (who is not a defendant) should be adjudged in contempt of the district court for having violated the terms of the April 15, 1968 court order and that the court order the corporate defendant and its president to "purge themselves of said contempt by payment to the plaintiff of the sum of Three Hundred Thousand and No/100 dollars ($300,000.00) in compensatory damages and One Million and No/100 dollars ($1,000,000.00) in punitive damages, together with all costs of this proceeding, including reasonable attorneys' fees." * * *

Our view is that contempt proceedings were improper because the April 15, 1968 order of the District Court failed to comply with Fed.Civ.Proc. Rule 65(d).

We begin by noting that we are dealing exclusively with the power of the district court with respect to civil contempts. * * *

What we are faced with is plaintiff's prayer for both compensatory and coercive remedies for a civil contempt; [citation] $300,000 is sought to reimburse plaintiff for $200,000 in already-sustained losses in expected profits and defined additional losses and expenses incurred because the corporate defendant and its president, allegedly, did not comply with the Settlement Agreement "made part of the [April 15, 1968] decree [of the district court] by reference." A further $1,000,000 is sought to coerce the corporate defendant and its president into compliance.

Before either the compensatory or coercive aspects of a court's civil contempt power can be brought into play first, there must have been disobedience of "an operative command capable of 'enforcement.' " International Longshoremen's Association, Local 1291 v. Philadelphia Marine Trade Assoc., 389 U.S. 64, 74 (1967), and second, that command, if it is in substance an injunction, must comply with Rule 65(d) of the Federal Rules of Civil Procedure.

We turn to the question whether the district court's April 15, 1968 order met the first of these conditions precedent. Of course, a party may incur a legal duty by entering into a settlement agreement, and a court may, pursuant to that agreement, incorporate the terms of the party's obligation in its judgment; but to furnish support for a contempt order the judgment must set forth in specific detail an unequivocal command. Here the district court on April 15, 1968 did not go beyond entering a judgment approving of the obligations incurred under the Settlement Agreement. Its judgment did not use language which turned a contractual duty into an obligation to obey an operative command. This case thus resembles one where a court issues a declaratory judgment as to obligations under a contract. In that situation, a party who departed from the judgment so declared would not be in contempt of court because there was no command, although there was a judgment of specific obligation.

Even if we could construe the April 15, 1968 order of the district court as embodying an operative command, it would be unenforceable by contempt proceedings because it would then have to be regarded as an injunctive order required to conform to Fed.Rule of Civ.Proc. 65(d).

It is beyond cavil that when it merely incorporated by reference the Settlement Agreement, the April 15, 1968 order ignored that rule's mandatory requirement that an injunction "shall describe in reasonable detail, and not by reference to the complaint or other document, the act or acts sought to be restrained." The error in the April 15, 1968 order was "serious and decisive" and precluded the plaintiff from successfully invoking the district court's contempt powers.

Rule 65(d) is no mere extract from a manual of procedural practice. It is a page from the book of liberty.

Equitable decrees, unlike mere money judgments issuing from a common law court, do not depend upon execution by the sheriff but are direct orders to a party. They trace their historical origin to the royal command addressed to a defeated litigant, directing him, under peril of imprisonment, to obey the chancellor's direction. [citation] Because of the risks of contempt proceedings, civil or criminal, paramount interests of liberty and due process make it indispensable for the chancellor or his surrogate to speak clearly, explicitly, and specifically if violation of his direction is to subject a litigant—(not to mention, as in the case at bar, a third person who is not a party of record but merely an officer of a party)—to coercive or penal measures, as well as to payment of damages.

The failure of the equity court to spell out in a decree's text the specific obligations resting upon the defeated litigant is fatal to any contempt proceeding unless we are to disregard the teachings of the masters of our law (see Swift and Co. v. United States, 196 U.S. 375, 401 (1905), where Justice Holmes, in oft-quoted language, said that "The defendants ought to be informed as accurately as the case permits what they are forbidden to do,") and the political struggles to limit the powers of the federal judiciary.

When the question of contempt is raised, just as it is inadequate if the decree has merely referred to a statute, even though the statute clearly created the legal obligation which warranted the decree, so it is not enough for enforcement by contempt proceedings if the decree merely referred to a contract, even though the contract clearly created the legal obligation which warranted the decree.

Judgment is affirmed.

Notes

1. *A Differing View*: "The Union argues that the incorporation by the district court of sections of the SFFD General Order into its 1988 injunction violated Rule 65(d) and was an abuse of discretion which requires reversal.

"The law of this circuit is that '[o]rdinarily, an injunction should not incorporate by reference another document.' [citation] The Union cites language in the opinions of other circuits which appears to read the incorporation requirement very strictly. [citation to *H.K. Porter*] * * *

"The primary purpose of Rule 65(d) is to assure adequate notice to parties faced with the possibility of contempt. [citations] Here, the document incorporated into the 1988 injunction consisted of fire department rules already binding upon the officers of the SFFD. It is unlikely the officers could argue they were unaware of these rules.

"We conclude that the district court's failure to cause a copy of the SFFD General Order to be stapled to the 1988 injunction does not require reversal of the court's grant of the injunction." Davis v. City and County of San Francisco, 890 F.2d 1438, 1450 (9th Cir.1989), cert. denied, 498 U.S. 897 (1990).

In a later decision, the court repeated its approval of incorporating an order into an injunction. "[T]he district court acted consistently with the rationale of Rule 65(d). The defendants were aware of the order because it was physically attached to the injunction itself. Thus the defendants received adequate notice that they could face contempt if they violated the order. Under these circumstances, the district court did not err by attaching the order to the injunction." State of California v. Campbell, 138 F.3d 772, 783 (9th Cir.1998).

Do you prefer the *H.K. Porter* court's technical reading of Rule 65(d)?

2. Judge Wyzanski's remark about "the political struggles to limit the powers of the federal judiciary" refers to the Norris–LaGuardia Act which Congress passed in 1932 to curb federal courts' injunctions against strikes.

2. WHAT IS A VIOLATION?

PLAYBOY ENTERPRISES v. CHUCKLEBERRY PUBLISHING

United States District Court, Southern District of New York, 1996.
939 F.Supp. 1032.

SCHEINDLIN, DISTRICT JUDGE: Plaintiff, Playboy Enterprises, Inc. ("PEI"), has moved for a finding of contempt against Defendant, Tattilo Editrice, S.p.A. ("Tattilo"). PEI alleges that by operating an Internet site from Italy under the PLAYMEN label, Tattilo has violated a judgment dated June 26, 1981, enjoining it from publishing, printing, distributing or selling in the United States an English language male sophisticate magazine under the name "PLAYMEN" ("Injunction"). * * *

In 1967, Tattilo began publishing a male sophisticate magazine in Italy under the name PLAYMEN. Although the magazine carried an English title, it was written entirely in Italian. In July 1979, Tattilo announced plans to publish an English language version of PLAYMEN in the United States. Shortly thereafter, PEI brought suit against Tattilo to enjoin Tattilo's use of the name PLAYMEN in connection with a male sophisticate magazine and related products. PEI has published the well-known male entertainment magazine "PLAYBOY" since 1953, which is sold throughout the world in a multitude of foreign languages. Plaintiff's suit for injunctive relief alleged trademark infringement, false designation of origin, unfair competition based on infringement of Plaintiff's common law trademark rights, and violations of the New York Anti–Dilution Statute.

A permanent injunction was awarded on April 1, 1981, and a judgment subsequently entered on June 26, 1981. * * *

PEI was similarly successful in enjoining the use of the PLAYMEN name in the courts of England, France and West Germany. However, the Italian courts ruled that "lexically" PLAYBOY was a weak mark and not entitled to protection in that country. The publication of PLAYMEN in Italy continues to the present day.

On approximately January 22, 1996, PEI discovered that Tattilo had created an Internet site featuring the PLAYMEN name. This Internet site makes available images of the cover of the Italian magazine, as well as its "Women of the Month" feature and several other sexually explicit photographic images. Users of the Internet site also receive "special discounts" on other Tattilo products, such as CD ROMs and Photo CDs. Tattilo created this site by uploading these images onto a World Wide Web server located in Italy. * * *

Two distinct services are available on the PLAYMEN Internet site. "PLAYMEN Lite" is available without a paid subscription, allowing users of the Internet to view moderately explicit images via computer. It appears that the main (if not sole) purpose of the PLAYMEN Lite service is to allow prospective users to experience a less explicit version of the PLAYMEN product before committing to purchasing a subscription. In addition, the PLAYMEN Internet site offers the more sexually explicit service called "PLAYMEN Pro." PLAYMEN Pro is available only to users who have paid the subscription price.

In order to access the Lite version of the PLAYMEN Internet service, the prospective user must first contact Tattilo. The user will then receive a temporary user name and password via e-mail. To subscribe to PLAYMEN Pro, the prospective user must fill out a form and send it via fax to Tattilo. Within 24 hours, the user receives by e-mail a unique password and login name that enable the user to browse the PLAYMEN Pro service.

The PLAYMEN Internet site is widely available to patrons living in the United States. More to the point, anyone in the United States with access to the Internet has the capacity to browse the PLAYMEN Internet site, review, and obtain print and electronic copies of sexually explicit pages of PLAYMEN magazine. All that is required to establish the account is the brief contact with Tattilo outlined above.

The Standard for Holding a Party in Contempt. * * * An order of contempt "is a potent weapon, to which courts should not resort where there is a fair ground of doubt as to the wrongfulness of the defendant's conduct." King v.

Allied Vision, Ltd., 65 F.3d 1051, 1058 (2d Cir.1995) (citations omitted). A contempt order is warranted only where the moving party establishes by clear and convincing evidence that the alleged contemnor violated the district court's edict.

Generally, the purpose of holding a party in civil contempt is "to enforce compliance with an order of the court or to compensate for losses or damages." Powell v. Ward, 643 F.2d 924, 931 (2d Cir.1981) (citation omitted). A court has the power to hold a party in civil contempt when (1) there is a "clear and unambiguous" court order; (2) there is clear and convincing proof of noncompliance; and (3) the party has not attempted to comply in a reasonably diligent manner. New York State Nat'l Org. for Women v. Terry, 886 F.2d 1339, 1351 (2d Cir.1989), cert. denied, 495 U.S. 947 (1990). A "clear and unambiguous" order is one "specific and definite enough to apprise those within its scope of the conduct that is being proscribed." *Terry.* * * * Finally, failure to comply with the court order need not be willful. [citation]

The primary issue before the Court is whether the Defendant distributed or sold the PLAYMEN magazine in the United States when it established an Internet site containing pictorial images under the PLAYMEN name.

[The court held it had personal jurisdiction over Tattilo which does not sell, distribute, publish or advertise for its text-based Italian PLAYMEN magazine in the United States because "this Court retained jurisdiction over Defendant for the purposes of enforcing the 1981 Injunction."]

Whether the Injunction Could Have Been Violated. As an initial matter, the question arises whether a fifteen-year-old injunction prohibiting certain traditional publishing activities should be applied to the recent development of cyberspace and the Internet. If the dissemination of information over the Internet, in any form, cannot constitute a violation of the Injunction, then the inquiry is over. * * * The purpose behind the Injunction was to restrict the ability of Defendant to distribute its product in the United States, where it has been found to infringe upon the trademark of Playboy. Allowing the Defendant to contravene the clear intent of the Injunction by permitting it to distribute its pictorial images over the Internet would emasculate the Injunction. The Injunction's failure to refer to the Internet by name does not limit its applicability to this new medium. Injunctions entered before the recent explosion of computer technology must continue to have meaning. * * *

Whether the Injunction Was Violated. Subsection 1(c) of the Injunction permanently enjoined Tattilo from:

> using "PLAYBOY," "PLAYMEN" or any other word confusingly similar with either such word in or as part of any trademark, service mark, brand name, trade name or other business or commercial designation, in connection with the sale, offering for sale or distributing in the United States, importing into or exporting from the United States, English language publications and related products.

Three conditions must be met to support a finding of a violation of this provision. First, the word PLAYMEN must have been used as part of any trademark, service mark, brand name, trade name or other business or commercial designation. Second, such use must have been in connection with an English language publication or related product. Third, such use must have been made in connection with a sale or distribution within the United States.

There is ample evidence that the word PLAYMEN has been used as a trade name or business or commercial designation of the Internet site. * * * The site's URL, which typically remains displayed on the computer screen once the site is accessed, is "playmen.it." Moreover, the word PLAYMEN prominently appears (along with the PLAYMEN logo) in oversized font on the site's "home page," the electronic equivalent of a magazine cover and table of contents. The PLAYMEN name and logo appear in this same form at the top of each "page" accessed on the site. The site's address, and the prominence of the PLAYMEN name, demonstrate an association between the PLAYMEN name and the Internet site.

Similarly, the PLAYMEN name has been used in connection with an English language publication or related product. First, although there is an intriguing question as to whether an Internet site consisting of uploaded pictorial images constitutes a "publication," there is no doubt that the "related product" clause is satisfied by this use. Second, this product appears in the English language. Although a portion of the text is written in Italian, enough sections appear in English to allow an English-speaking user to navigate the site with ease. Paramount among these is the PLAYMEN page purportedly answering frequently asked questions about the Internet site, such as the price of a subscription ("$30 U.S., or 50000 [sic] Italian lire for 6 months, payable by all major credit cards"), benefits of a subscription ("You get a unique password, that can be used only by one person at a time, to browse on Playmen Pro, where you can find about 500 xxx rated pictures always updated, mpeg movies, photo cd images, and many other things"), and a description of the PLAYMEN magazine itself ("The 'Playmen' magazine is written in Italian, and is sold in Italy and all the major countries in Europe"). Therefore, the English language publication/related product requirement has been met.

The final condition—for a distribution or sale to have taken place within the United States—is analytically more difficult. * * *

Defendant does more than simply provide access to the Internet. It also provides its own services, PLAYMEN Lite and PLAYMEN Pro, and supplies the content for these services. Moreover * * * these pictorial images can be downloaded to and stored upon the computers of subscribers to the service. In fact, Defendant actively invites such use: the Internet site allows the user to decide between viewing and downloading the images. Thus this use of Defendant's Internet site constitutes a distribution.

In order to violate the Injunction, however, Defendant must distribute the pictorial images within the United States. Defendant argues that it is merely posting pictorial images on a computer server in Italy, rather than distributing those images to anyone within the United States. A computer operator wishing to view these images must, in effect, transport himself to Italy to view Tattilo's pictorial displays. The use of the Internet is akin to boarding a plane, landing in Italy, and purchasing a copy of PLAYMEN magazine, an activity permitted under Italian law. Thus Defendant argues that its publication of pictorial images over the Internet cannot be barred by the Injunction despite the fact that computer operators can view these pictorial images in the United States.

Once more, I disagree. Defendant has actively solicited United States customers to its Internet site, and in doing so has distributed its product within the United States. When a potential subscriber faxes the required form to Tattilo, he receives back via e-mail a password and user name. By this process, Tattilo distributes its product within the United States.

Defendant's analogy of "flying to Italy" to purchase a copy of the PLAY-MEN magazine is inapposite. Tattilo may of course maintain its Italian Internet site. The Internet is a world-wide phenomenon, accessible from every corner of the globe. Tattilo cannot be prohibited from operating its Internet site merely because the site is accessible from within one country in which its product is banned. To hold otherwise "would be tantamount to a declaration that this Court, and every other court throughout the world, may assert jurisdiction over all information providers on the global World Wide Web." Such a holding would have a devastating impact on those who use this global service. The Internet deserves special protection as a place where public discourse may be conducted without regard to nationality, religion, sex, age, or to monitors of community standards of decency. [citation]

However, this special protection does not extend to ignoring court orders and injunctions. If it did, injunctions would cease to have meaning and intellectual property would no longer be adequately protected. In the absence of enforcement, intellectual property laws could be easily circumvented through the creation of Internet sites that permit the very distribution that has been enjoined. Our long-standing system of intellectual property protections has encouraged creative minds to be productive. Diluting those protections may discourage that creativity.

While this Court has neither the jurisdiction nor the desire to prohibit the creation of Internet sites around the globe, it may prohibit access to those sites in this country. Therefore, while Tattilo may continue to operate its Internet site, it must refrain from accepting subscriptions from customers living in the United States. In accord with this holding, an Italian customer who subsequently moves to the United States may maintain his or her subscription to the Internet site.

I therefore conclude that Tattilo has violated subsection 1(c) of the Injunction by using its PLAYMEN Internet site to distribute its products in the United States. The clear intent of the Injunction was to prohibit Tattilo from selling its PLAYMEN magazine and related products to United States customers. Tattilo has knowingly attempted to circumvent the Injunction by selling its products over the Internet. Cyberspace is not a "safe haven" from which Tattilo may flout the Court's Injunction.

[The sanctions are reproduced at the end of the decision.]

For the foregoing reasons, the motion for a finding of contempt is granted. SO ORDERED.

OPINION AND ORDER ON RECONSIDERATION. Defendant now requests that the Court amend its Order. * * * Defendant submits that the Court misconstrued the process by which a user of the Internet site accesses PLAYMEN Lite, resulting in the incorrect determination that the PLAYMEN Lite service violated the Injunction. Defendant argues that the continued availability of PLAYMEN Lite within the United States would not violate the Injunction. * * *

PEI requests that Tattilo be ordered to refrain from "publishing, promoting and selling in the English language PLAYMEN publications and related products." * * *

While the Opinion held that deliberate and intentional contact with the United States was established based on the requirement that prospective customers fax subscription forms to Italy, and that user names and IDs are sent to United States customers from Italy, this is not the only basis for finding that a distribution occurred within the United States. The PLAYMEN Lite service allows (indeed invites) a user to download Tattilo's pictorial images onto his or her home computer. PLAYMEN Lite can thus be viewed as an "advertisement" by which Tattilo distributes its pictorial images throughout the United States. That the local user "pulls" these images from Tattilo's computer in Italy, as opposed to Tattilo "sending" them to this country, is irrelevant. By inviting United States users to download these images, Tattilo is causing and contributing to their distribution within the United States.

Moreover, the availability of PLAYMEN Lite within the United States violates the Injunction even if the user could not download the images. PLAYMEN Lite is nearly identical to PLAYMEN Pro. Both reveal many of the same images; both allow the user to download these images; both services purport to sell products such as movies and CD–Roms to their users. Most notably, as demonstrated at the hearing, the two services utilize many of the same screens and links.

This implies that PLAYMEN Lite and PLAYMEN Pro are not two separate and distinct services as Defendant has argued, but are actually one service—the "PLAYMEN Internet Service"—part of which requires a password and part of which does not. In other words, PLAYMEN Lite is nothing more than an "advertisement" or "coming attractions" for the money-making PLAYMEN Pro service. * * * When a PLAYMEN Lite user is considering purchasing a subscription to PLAYMEN Pro, but would like to sample the product first, Tattilo will provide a temporary password that will allow the user to access the pages of PLAYMEN Pro through PLAYMEN Lite.

As such, PLAYMEN Lite represents a free distribution of Tattilo's product, a product which has been banned in this country since the 1981 Injunction. I decline to hold that Tattilo may maintain some portion of its service but shut down other portions of its Internet site. Because PLAYMEN Lite and PLAYMEN Pro are essentially one entity, they must be treated as such.

Therefore, the PLAYMEN Lite service violates the Injunction. * * *

PEI has also failed to set forth any ground for reconsideration. As previously stated, this Court has no power to restrict Tattilo from providing its PLAYMEN Internet service outside the United States. There are many English speaking countries throughout the world. This Court has no jurisdiction to control Tattilo's activities in those countries. As a result, PEI's motion for an order prohibiting Tattilo from using English on its Internet site is denied.

Sanctions. Sanctions for "indirect" civil contempt-contempt resulting from actions occurring outside the courtroom-are designed specifically to compel future compliance with a court order and are avoidable through compliance. [citations]

[The civil contempt sanction is] Tattilo is required, within two weeks of the date of this Order, to: (1) either shut down its Internet site completely or refrain from accepting any new subscriptions from customers residing in the United States; (2) invalidate the user names and passwords to the Internet site previously purchased by United States customers; (3) refund to its United States customers the remaining unused portions of their subscriptions; (4) remit to PEI all gross profits earned from subscriptions to its PLAYMEN Pro Internet service by customers in the United States; (5) remit to PEI all gross profits earned from the sale of goods and services advertised on its PLAYMEN Internet service to customers in the United States; (6) revise its Internet site to indicate that all subscription requests from potential United States customers will be denied; and (7) remit to PEI its costs and attorney's fees incurred in making this application. If these conditions have not been met within the stated two-week period, Tattilo shall pay to PEI a fine of $1,000 per day until it complies with this Order.

Notes

1. *Classifying the Court's Sanctions.* The sanctions combine first, in (1), (2), (3) and (6), a new injunction or a modified original injunction; second, in (4), (5) and (7), compensatory contempt; and finally, an ostensibly coercive contempt fine, which the Tattilo can avoid by compliance, but which is payable upon breach to PEI, perhaps as compensation.

2. *Back to the Maxim: Equity Acts In Personam.* To review PEI's potential difficulties enforcing an injunction from a court in the United States against a defendant like Tattilo in Italy, see pp. 231–34.

3. THE PUZZLE OF CRIMINAL CONTEMPT—COERCIVE CONTEMPT

INTERNATIONAL UNION, UNITED MINE WORKERS OF AMERICA v. BAGWELL

Supreme Court of the United States, 1994.
512 U.S. 821.

JUSTICE BLACKMUN delivered the opinion of the Court. We are called upon once again to consider the distinction between civil and criminal contempt. Specifically, we address whether contempt fines levied against a union for violations of a labor injunction are coercive civil fines, or are criminal fines that constitutionally could be imposed only through a jury trial. We conclude that the fines are criminal and, accordingly, we reverse the judgment of the Supreme Court of Virginia.

Petitioners, the International Union, United Mine Workers of America and United Mine Workers of America, District 28 (collectively, the union) engaged in a protracted labor dispute with the Clinchfield Coal Company and Sea "B" Mining Company (collectively, the companies) over alleged unfair labor practices. In April 1989, the companies filed suit in the Circuit Court of Russell County, Virginia, to enjoin the union from conducting unlawful strike-related activities. The trial court entered an injunction which, as later amended, prohibited the union and its members from, among other things, obstructing ingress and egress to company facilities, throwing objects at and physically threatening company employees, placing tire-damaging "jackrocks" on roads used by company vehicles, and picketing with more than a specified number of people at designated sites. The court additionally ordered the union to take all steps necessary to ensure compliance with the injunction, to place supervisors at picket sites, and to report all violations to the court.

On May 16, 1989, the trial court held a contempt hearing and found that petitioners had committed 72 violations of the injunction. After fining the union $642,000 for its disobedience, the court announced that it would fine the union $100,000 for any future violent breach of the injunction and $20,000 for any future nonviolent infraction, "such as exceeding picket numbers, [or] blocking entrances or exits." The Court early stated that its purpose was to "impos[e] prospective civil fines[,] the payment of which would only be required if it were shown the defendants disobeyed the Court's orders."

In seven subsequent contempt hearings held between June and December 1989, the court found the union in contempt for more than 400 separate violations of the injunction, many of them violent. Based on the court's stated "intention that these fines are civil and coercive," each contempt hearing was conducted as a civil proceeding before the trial judge, in which the parties conducted discovery, introduced evidence, and called and cross-examined witnesses. The trial court required that contumacious acts be proved beyond a reasonable doubt, but did not afford the union a right to jury trial.

As a result of these contempt proceedings, the court levied over $64,000,000 in fines against the union, approximately $12,000,000 of which was ordered payable to the companies. Because the union objected to payment of any fines to the companies and in light of the law enforcement burdens posed by the strike, the court ordered that the remaining roughly $52,000,000 in fines be paid to the Commonwealth of Virginia and Russell and Dickenson Counties, "the two counties most heavily affected by the unlawful activity."

While appeals from the contempt orders were pending, the union and the companies settled the underlying labor dispute, agreed to vacate the contempt fines, and jointly moved to dismiss the case. A special mediator representing the Secretary of Labor, and the governments of Russell and Dickenson Counties, supported the parties' motion to vacate the outstanding fines. The trial court granted the motion to dismiss, dissolved the injunction, and vacated the $12,000,000 in fines payable to the companies. After reiterating its belief that the remaining $52,000,000 owed to the counties and the Commonwealth were coercive, civil fines, the trial court refused to vacate these fines, concluding they were "payable in effect to the public."

The companies withdrew as parties in light of the settlement and declined to seek further enforcement of the outstanding contempt fines. Because the Commonwealth Attorneys of Russell and Dickenson Counties also had asked to be disqualified from the case, the court appointed respondent John L. Bagwell to act as Special Commissioner to collect the unpaid contempt fines on behalf of the counties and the Commonwealth.

The Court of Appeals of Virginia reversed and ordered that the contempt fines be vacated pursuant to the settlement agreement. Assuming for the purposes of argument that the fines were civil, the court concluded "that civil contempt fines imposed during or as a part of a civil proceeding between private parties are settled when the underlying litigation is settled by the parties and the court is without discretion to refuse to vacate such fines."

On consolidated appeals, the Supreme Court of Virginia reversed. The court held that whether coercive, civil contempt sanctions could be settled by private parties was a question of state law, and that Virginia public policy disfavored such a rule, "if the dignity of the law and public respect for the judiciary are to be maintained." The court also rejected petitioners' contention that the outstanding fines were criminal and could not be imposed absent a criminal trial. Because the trial court's prospective fine schedule was intended to coerce compliance with the injunction and the union could avoid the fines through obedience, the court reasoned, the fines were civil and coercive and properly imposed in civil proceedings:

"When a court orders a defendant to perform an affirmative act and provides that the defendant shall be fined a fixed amount for each day he refuses to comply, the defendant has control of his own destiny. The same is true with respect to the court's orders in the present case. A prospective fine schedule was established solely for the purpose of coercing the Union to refrain from engaging in certain conduct. Consequently, the Union controlled its own fate."

This Court granted certiorari.

"Criminal contempt is a crime in the ordinary sense," Bloom v. Illinois, 391 U.S. 194, 201 (1968), and "criminal penalties may not be imposed on someone who has not been afforded the protections that the Constitution requires of such criminal proceedings." Hicks v. Feiock, 485 U.S. 624, 632 (1988). See In re Bradley, 318 U.S. 50 (1943) (double jeopardy); Cooke v. United States, 267 U.S. 517, 537 (1925) (rights to notice of charges, assistance of counsel, summary process, and to present a defense); Gompers v. Buck's Stove & Range Co., 221 U.S. 418, 444 (1911) (privilege against self-incrimination, right to proof beyond a reasonable doubt). For "serious" criminal contempts involving imprisonment of more than six months, these protections include the right to jury trial. Bloom, see also Taylor v. Hayes, 418 U.S. 488, 495 (1974). In contrast, civil contempt sanctions, or those penalties designed to compel future compliance with a court order, are considered to be coercive and avoidable through obedience, and thus may be imposed in an ordinary civil proceeding upon notice and an opportunity to be heard. Neither a jury trial nor proof beyond a reasonable doubt is required.

Although the procedural contours of the two forms of contempt are well established, the distinguishing characteristics of civil versus criminal contempts are somewhat less clear. In the leading early case addressing this issue in the context of imprisonment, Gompers v. Bucks Stove & Range Co., the Court emphasized that whether a contempt is civil or criminal turns on the "character and purpose" of the sanction involved. Thus, a contempt sanction is considered civil if it "is remedial, and for the benefit of the complainant. But if it is for criminal contempt the sentence is punitive, to vindicate the authority of the court."

As Gompers recognized, however, the stated purposes of a contempt sanction alone cannot be determinative. "[W]hen a court imposes fines and punishments on a contemnor, it is not only vindicating its legal authority to enter the initial court order, but it also is seeking to give effect to the law's purpose of modifying the contemnor's behavior to conform to the terms required in the order." Hicks. Most contempt sanctions, like most criminal punishments, to some extent punish a prior offense as well as coerce an offender's future obedience. The Hicks Court accordingly held that conclusions about the civil or criminal nature of a contempt sanction are properly drawn, not from "the subjective intent of a State's laws and its courts," but "from an examination of the character of the relief itself."

The paradigmatic coercive, civil contempt sanction, as set forth in Gompers, involves confining a contemnor indefinitely until he complies with an affirmative command. * * * In these circumstances, the contemnor is able to purge the contempt and obtain his release by committing an affirmative act, and thus "carries the keys of his prison in his own pocket." Gompers, quoting In re Nevitt, 117 Fed. 448, 451 (1902).

By contrast, a fixed sentence of imprisonment is punitive and criminal if it is imposed retrospectively for a "completed act of disobedience," *Gompers*, such that the contemnor cannot avoid or abbreviate the confinement through later compliance. Thus, the *Gompers* Court concluded that a 12–month sentence imposed on Samuel Gompers for violating an anti-boycott injunction was criminal. When a contempt involves the prior conduct of an isolated, prohibited act, the resulting sanction has no coercive effect. "[T]he defendant is furnished no key, and he cannot shorten the term by promising not to repeat the offense."

This dichotomy between coercive and punitive imprisonment has been extended to the fine context. A contempt fine accordingly is considered civil and remedial if it either "coerce[s] the defendant into compliance with the court's order, [or] * * * compensate[s] the complainant for losses sustained." United States v. United Mine Workers of America, 330 U.S. 258, 303–304 (1947). Where a fine is not compensatory, it is civil only if the contemnor is afforded an opportunity to purge. See Penfield Co. v. SEC, 330 U.S. 585, 590 (1947). Thus, a "flat, unconditional fine" totaling even as little as $50 announced after a finding of contempt is criminal if the contemnor has no subsequent opportunity to reduce or avoid the fine through compliance.

A close analogy to coercive imprisonment is a per diem fine imposed for each day a contemnor fails to comply with an affirmative court order. Like civil imprisonment, such fines exert a constant coercive pressure, and once the jural command is obeyed, the future, indefinite, daily fines are purged. Less comfortable is the analogy between coercive imprisonment and suspended, determinate fines. In this Court's sole prior decision squarely addressing the judicial power to impose coercive civil contempt fines, *United Mine Workers*, it held that fixed fines also may be considered purgable and civil when imposed and suspended pending future compliance. * * *

This Court has not revisited the issue of coercive civil contempt fines addressed in *United Mine Workers*. Since that decision, the Court has erected substantial procedural protections in other areas of contempt law, such as criminal contempts, [citations] Lower federal courts and state courts such as the trial court here nevertheless have relied on *United Mine Workers* to authorize a relatively unlimited judicial power to impose noncompensatory civil contempt fines.

Underlying the somewhat elusive distinction between civil and criminal contempt fines, and the ultimate question posed in this case, is what procedural protections are due before any particular contempt penalty may be imposed. Because civil contempt sanctions are viewed as nonpunitive and avoidable, fewer procedural protections for such sanctions have been required. To the extent that such contempts take on a punitive character, however, and are not justified by other considerations central to the contempt power, criminal procedural protections may be in order.

The traditional justification for the relative breadth of the contempt power has been necessity: Courts independently must be vested with "power to impose silence, respect, and decorum, in their presence, and submission to their lawful mandates, and * * * to preserve themselves and their officers from the approach and insults of pollution." Anderson v. Dunn, 6 Wheat. 204, 227 (1821). Courts thus have embraced an inherent contempt authority, see *Gompers*. [citations] as a power "necessary to the exercise of all others." United States v. Hudson, 7 Cranch 32, 34 (1812).

But the contempt power also uniquely is "liable to abuse." *Bloom.* Unlike most areas of law, where a legislature defines both the sanctionable conduct and the penalty to be imposed, civil contempt proceedings leave the offended judge solely responsible for identifying, prosecuting, adjudicating, and sanctioning the contumacious conduct. Contumacy "often strikes at the most vulnerable and human qualities of a judge's temperament," *Bloom,* and its fusion of legislative, executive, and judicial powers "summons forth * * * the prospect of 'the most tyrannical licentiousness.'" Young v. United States ex rel. Vuitton, 481 U.S. 787, 822 (1987) (SCALIA, J., concurring in judgment). Accordingly, "in [criminal] contempt cases an even more compelling argument can be made [than in ordinary criminal cases] for providing a right to jury trial as a protection against the arbitrary exercise of official power." *Bloom.*

Our jurisprudence in the contempt area has attempted to balance the competing concerns of necessity and potential arbitrariness by allowing a relatively unencumbered contempt power when its exercise is most essential, and requiring progressively greater procedural protections when other considerations come into play.

Still further procedural protections are afforded for contempts occurring out of court, where the considerations justifying expedited procedures do not pertain. Summary adjudication of indirect contempts is prohibited, e.g., Cooke v. United States, and criminal contempt sanctions are entitled to full criminal process. E.g., *Hicks.* * * *

For a discrete category of indirect contempts, however, civil procedural protections may be insufficient. Contempts involving out-of-court disobedience to complex injunctions often require elaborate and reliable factfinding. * * * Such contempts do not obstruct the court's ability to adjudicate the proceedings before it, and the risk of erroneous deprivation from the lack of a neutral factfinder may be substantial. Under these circumstances, criminal procedural protections such as the rights to counsel and proof beyond a reasonable doubt are both necessary and appropriate to protect the due process rights of parties and prevent the arbitrary exercise of judicial power.

In the instant case, neither any party nor any court of the Commonwealth has suggested that the challenged fines are compensatory. At no point did the trial court attempt to calibrate the fines to damages caused by the union's contumacious activities or indicate that the fines were "to compensate the complainant for losses sustained." *United Mine Workers.* The nonparty governments, in turn, never requested any compensation or presented any evidence regarding their injuries, never moved to intervene in the suit, and never actively defended the fines imposed. The issue before us accordingly is limited to whether these fines, despite their noncompensatory character, are coercive civil or criminal sanctions.

The parties propose two independent tests for determining whether the fines are civil or criminal. Petitioners argue that because the injunction primarily prohibited certain conduct rather than mandated affirmative acts, the sanctions are criminal. Respondent in turn urges that because the trial court established a prospective fine schedule that the union could avoid through compliance, the fines are civil in character.

Neither theory satisfactorily identifies those contempt fines that are criminal and thus must be imposed through the criminal process. Petitioners correctly note that *Gompers* suggests a possible dichotomy "between refusing to do an act commanded,—remedied by imprisonment until the party performs the required act; and doing an act forbidden,—punished by imprisonment for a definite term." The distinction between mandatory and prohibitory orders is easily applied in the classic contempt scenario, where contempt sanctions are used to enforce orders compelling or forbidding a single, discrete act. In such cases, orders commanding an affirmative act simply designate those actions that are capable of being coerced.

But the distinction between coercion of affirmative acts and punishment of prohibited conduct is difficult to apply when conduct that can recur is involved, or when an injunction contains both mandatory and prohibitory provisions. Moreover, in borderline cases injunctive provisions containing essentially the same command can be phrased either in mandatory or prohibitory terms. Under a literal application of petitioners' theory, an injunction ordering the union: "Do not strike," would appear to be prohibitory and criminal, while an injunction ordering the union: "Continue working," would be mandatory and civil. Dobbs, Contempt of Court: A Survey, 56 Cornell L.Rev. 183, 239 (1971). In enforcing the present injunction, the trial court imposed fines without regard to the mandatory or prohibitory nature of the clause violated. Accordingly, even though a parsing of the injunction's various provisions might support the classification of contempts such as rock-throwing and placing tire-damaging "jackrocks" on roads as criminal and the refusal to place supervisors at picket sites as civil, the parties have not asked us to review the order in that manner. In a case like this involving an injunction that prescribes a detailed code of conduct, it is more appropriate to identify the character of the entire decree.

Despite respondent's urging, we also are not persuaded that dispositive significance should be accorded to the fact that the trial court prospectively announced the sanctions it would impose. Had the trial court simply levied the fines after finding the union guilty of contempt, the resulting "determinate and unconditional" fines would be considered "solely and exclusively punitive." *Hicks*. Respondent nevertheless contends that the trial court's announcement of a prospective fine schedule allowed the union to "avoid paying the fine[s] simply by performing the * * * act required by the court's order," *Hicks*, and thus transformed these fines into coercive, civil ones. Respondent maintains here, as the Virginia Supreme Court held below, that the trial court could have imposed a daily civil fine to coerce the union into compliance, and that a prospective fine schedule is indistinguishable from such a sanction.

Respondent's argument highlights the difficulties encountered in parsing coercive civil and criminal contempt fines. The fines imposed here concededly are difficult to distinguish either from determinate, punitive fines or from initially suspended, civil fines. Ultimately, however, the fact that the trial court announced the fines before the contumacy, rather than after the fact, does not in itself justify respondent's conclusion that the fines are civil or meaningfully distinguish these penalties from the ordinary criminal law. Due process traditionally requires that criminal laws provide prior notice both of the conduct to be prohibited and of the sanction to be imposed. The trial court here simply announced the penalty—determinate fines of $20,000 or $100,000 per violation—that would be imposed for future contempts. The union's ability to avoid the contempt fines was indistinguishable from the ability of any ordinary citizen to avoid a criminal sanction by conforming his behavior to the law. The fines are not coercive day fines, or even suspended fines, but are more closely analogous to fixed, determinate, retrospective criminal fines which petitioners had no opportunity to purge once imposed. We therefore decline to conclude that the mere fact that the sanctions were announced in advance rendered them coercive and civil as a matter of constitutional law.

Other considerations convince us that the fines challenged here are criminal. The union's sanctionable conduct did not occur in the court's presence or otherwise implicate the court's ability to maintain order and adjudicate the proceedings before it. Nor did the union's contumacy involve simple, affirmative acts, such as the paradigmatic civil contempts examined in *Gompers*. Instead, the Virginia trial court levied contempt fines for widespread, ongoing, out-of-court violations of a complex injunction. In so doing, the court effectively policed petitioners' compliance with an entire code of conduct that the court itself had imposed. The union's contumacy lasted many months and spanned a substantial portion of the State. The fines assessed were serious, totaling over $52,000,000. Under such circumstances, disinterested factfinding and even-handed adjudication were essential, and petitioners were entitled to a criminal jury trial.

Our decision concededly imposes some procedural burdens on courts' ability to sanction widespread, indirect contempts of complex injunctions through noncompensatory fines. Our holding, however, leaves unaltered the longstanding authority of judges to adjudicate direct contempts summarily, and to enter broad compensatory awards for all contempts through civil proceedings. See, e.g., Sheet Metal Workers v. Equal Employment Opportunity Comm'n, 478 U.S. 421 (1986). Because the right to trial by jury applies only to serious criminal sanctions, courts still may impose noncompensatory, petty fines for contempts such as the present ones without conducting a jury trial. We also do not disturb a court's ability to levy, albeit through the criminal contempt process, serious fines like those in this case.

Ultimately, whatever slight burden our holding may impose on the judicial contempt power cannot be controlling. The Court recognized more than a quarter-century ago:

"We cannot say that the need to further respect for judges and courts is entitled to more consideration than the interest of the individual not be subjected to serious criminal punishment without the benefit of all the procedural protections worked out carefully over the years and deemed fundamental to our system of justice. Genuine respect, which alone can lend true dignity to our judicial establishment, will be engendered, not by the fear of unlimited authority, but by the firm administration of the law through those institutionalized procedures which have been worked out over the centuries." *Bloom*.

Where, as here, "a serious contempt is at issue, considerations of efficiency must give way to the more fundamental interest of ensuring the even-handed exercise of judicial power."

The judgment of the Supreme Court of Virginia is reversed. It is so ordered.

JUSTICE SCALIA, concurring.

I join the Court's opinion classifying the $52,000,000 in contempt fines levied against petitioners as criminal. As the Court's opinion demonstrates, our cases have employed a variety of not easily reconcilable tests for differentiating between civil and criminal contempts. Since all of those tests would yield the same result here, there is no need to decide which is the correct one—and a case so extreme on its facts is not the best case in which to make that decision. I wish to suggest, however, that when we come to making it, a careful examination of historical practice will ultimately yield the answer.

That one and the same person should be able to make the rule, to adjudicate its violation, and to assess its penalty is out of accord with our usual notions of fairness and separation of powers. [citations] And it is worse still for that person to conduct the adjudication without affording the protections usually given in criminal trials. Only the clearest of historical practice could establish that such a departure from the procedures that the Constitution normally requires is not a denial of due process of law. * * *

Even equitable decrees that were prohibitory rather than mandatory were, in earlier times, much less sweeping than their modern counterparts. Prior to the labor injunctions of the late 1800's, injunctions were issued primarily in relatively narrow disputes over property. [citations]

Contemporary courts have abandoned these earlier limitations upon the scope of their mandatory and injunctive decrees. [citations] They routinely issue complex decrees which involve them in extended disputes and place them in continuing supervisory roles over parties and institutions. See, e.g., Missouri v. Jenkins, 495 U.S. 33, 56–58 (1990); Swann v. Charlotte–Mecklenburg Bd. of Ed., 402 U.S. 1, 16 (1971). * * *

The order at issue here provides a relatively tame example of the modern, complex decree. The amended injunction prohibited, inter alia, rock-throwing, the puncturing of tires, threatening, following or interfering with respondents' employees, placing pickets in other than specified locations, and roving picketing; and it required, inter alia, that petitioners provide a list of names of designated supervisors. * * *

As the scope of injunctions has expanded, they have lost some of the distinctive features that made enforcement through civil process acceptable. It is not that the times, or our perceptions of fairness, have changed (that is in my view no basis for either tightening or relaxing the traditional demands of due process); but rather that the modern judicial order is in its relevant essentials not the same device that in former times could always be enforced by civil contempt. So adjustments will have to be made. We will have to decide at some point which modern injunctions sufficiently resemble their historical namesakes to warrant the same extraordinary means of enforcement. We need not draw that line in the present case, and so I am content to join the opinion of the Court.

Justice Ginsburg, with whom The Chief Justice joins, concurring in part and concurring in the judgment. * * *

Two considerations persuade me that the contempt proceedings in this case should be classified as "criminal" rather than "civil." First, were we to accept the logic of Bagwell's argument that the fines here were civil, because "conditional" and "coercive," no fine would elude that categorization. * * *

Second, the Virginia courts' refusal to vacate the fines, despite the parties' settlement and joint motion, is characteristic of criminal, not civil proceedings. In explaining why the fines outlived the underlying civil dispute, the Supreme Court of Virginia stated: "Courts of the Commonwealth must have the authority to enforce their orders by employing coercive, civil sanctions if the dignity of the law and public respect for the judiciary are to be maintained." The Virginia court's references to upholding public authority and maintaining "the dignity of the law" reflect the very purposes *Gompers* ranked on the criminal contempt side. Moreover, with the private complainant gone from the scene, and an official appointed by the Commonwealth to collect the fines for the Commonwealth's coffers, it is implausible to invoke the justification of benefitting the civil complainant. The Commonwealth here pursues the fines on its own account, not as the agent of a private party, and without tying the exactions exclusively to a claim for compensation. * * * If, as the trial court declared, the proceedings were indeed civil from the outset, then the court should have granted the parties' motions to vacate the fines.

Notes

1. The label "criminal" on a defendant's contempt should remove the matter, for most purposes, from civil remedies. The private plaintiff ostensibly takes only vicarious enjoyment from a criminal contempt brought against the defendant. Realistically, however, any threat of criminal contempt increases the possibility that defendant will obey the injunction.

In the federal system and in many states, a defendant's criminal contempt prosecution will be maintained by an official prosecutor or another "disinterested" official appointed to act for the government against the defendant. Young v. United States ex rel. Vuitton et Fils S.A., 481 U.S. 787 (1987). Arguing that the plaintiff, whose interest is at stake, ought to be allowed to prosecute many defendants for criminal contempt is Joan Meier, The "Right" to a Disinterested Prosecutor of Criminal Contempt: Unpacking Public and Private Interests, 70 Wash.U.L.Q. 85 (1992).

2. *Procedural Considerations.* Defendant's violation of an injunction poses the possibility of criminal contempt, compensatory contempt, coercive contempt or a combination. To avoid reversal, heed *Gompers*'s lesson: the Constitution requires criminal procedural protection to impose a criminal contempt sanction on a defendant.

The Supreme Court had summarized these requirements before *Bagwell*: "[T]his Court has found that defendants in criminal contempt proceedings must be presumed innocent, proved guilty beyond a reasonable doubt, and accorded the right to refuse to testify against themselves; must be advised of charges, have a reasonable opportunity to respond to them, and be permitted the assistance of counsel and the right to call witnesses; must be given a public trial before an unbiased judge; and must be afforded a jury trial for serious contempts." Young v. United States ex rel. Vuitton et Fils S.A., 481 U.S. 787, 798–99 (1987).

Do you think a potential criminal contemnor ought to be entitled to *Miranda* warnings? Should the judge exclude illegally seized evidence?

3. *Willfulness Required for Criminal Contempt.* The authorities charged two contemnors with criminal contempt for violating an injunction by obstructing access to an abortion clinic. The judge described the breach as "an elderly bishop and a young monk quietly praying with rosary beads in the Clinic's driveway." Applying a definition of willfulness as "deliberate conduct done with a bad purpose either to disobey or to disregard the law," the judge found "as a matter of fact that Lynch's and Moscinski's sincere, genuine, objectively based and, indeed, conscience-driven religious belief precludes a finding of willfulness." Even if the contemnors' breach had been willful, the judge would acquit them, exercising "the prerogative of leniency which a fact-finder has to refuse to convict a defendant, even if the circumstances would otherwise be sufficient to convict." United States v. Lynch, 952 F.Supp. 167, 170–71 (S.D.N.Y.1997). Despite the idea that the government cannot

appeal an acquittal, the government appealed this one, to its ultimate chagrin. Appeal dismissed: United States v. Lynch, 162 F.3d 732 (2d Cir 1998), rehearing denied, 181 F.3d 330 (2d Cir 1999).

4. Occasionally the judge embeds a suspended determinate jail sentence in the original injunction decree, to be activated if the injunction is violated. Jencks v. Goforth, 57 N.M. 627, 261 P.2d 655 (1953). It is argued that this is a coercive device and the defendant may avoid confinement by the simple expedient of compliance. The New Mexico Supreme Court later repeated its approval with a half-hearted apology that "we did not intend to indicate that this was the best method of handling a civil contempt." Local 890 v. New Jersey Zinc Co., 58 N.M. 416, 419, 272 P.2d 322, 324 (1954). Suppose the defendant violates an injunction with an embedded but suspended determinate jail sentence. After the Supreme Court's *Bagwell* decision, would imposing the jail sentence be a criminal contempt and require criminal procedure?

An injunction which forbade defendants from obstructing access to New York abortion clinics contained a scale of escalating noncompensatory fines. Defendants had violated it. The judge had imposed the "civil contempt" fines without criminal procedure. Were the noncompensatory fines payable to the court really criminal contempt requiring criminal procedure? The court interpreted *Bagwell* to mean that the fines "could have been properly imposed as civil had contemnors been afforded a subsequent opportunity to purge." Which the judge supplied: "Defendants can avoid payment of the fines by agreeing to obey the Permanent Injunction in the future." New York State National Organization for Women v. Terry, 952 F.Supp. 1033, 1043 (S.D.N.Y. 1997).

5. Does the *Bagwell* Court change the inquiry from the purpose of the sanction to (a) the complexity of the litigation or (b) the conduct sanctioned?

6. *Criminal Procedure.* One way for a plaintiff to avoid reversal of the defendant's coercive contempt as embodying penal elements is to observe all criminal contempt procedural requirements. United States v. United Mine Workers, 330 U.S. 258, 298–99 (1947).

The private plaintiff may be concerned if criminal procedural protections impede enforcement of private rights. For example in a criminal contempt prosecution, the contemnor may claim freedom from self incrimination to prevent discovery and to avoid testifying at trial.

4. CONFINEMENT, CONTEMPT, AND CASH MONEY: ABILITY TO COMPLY

Constitutional and statutory prohibitions that forbid imprisoning a debtor to collect a civil debt prevent a creditor from confining a contemnor to collect a money debt. That, however, is only the beginning of the story of the courts' quest to achieve plaintiffs' substantive rights through injunctions and contempt.

Statutes authorize a judgment creditor with a money judgment to institute collection proceedings in aid of execution. These statutes permit a creditor to conduct discovery proceedings to find the judgment debtor's assets, to set aside the debtor's fraudulent conveyances, and to reach the debtor's assets not subject to execution. Since the judge enters an order only after a hearing to determine the debtor's and his transferee's ability to perform, the judge may enforce the order with contempt even though it requires the defendant to pay money. The defendant's failure to comply is regarded as contumacious conduct. Thomas, Head and Greisen Employees Trust v. Buster, 95 F.3d 1449 (9th Cir.1996), is a complex modern application of the New York court's leading decision in Reeves v. Crownshield, 274 N.Y. 74, 8 N.E.2d 283 (1937).

Compensatory contempt is a money substitute; the judge orders a disobedient injunction defendant to pay plaintiff. A plaintiff usually employs the techniques available to other judgment creditors to collect a compensatory contempt judgment, but stiffer measures, even confinement, may be available. Doug Rendleman, Compensatory Contempt: Plaintiff's Remedy When Defendant Violates an Injunction, 1980 U.Ill.L.Rev. 971, 1003–07.

Some obligations to pay money are not constitutional "debts." Most courts construe the constitutional word "debt" to mean a contractual or tort obligation; they hold that a decree which requires someone to pay family support is not within the prohibition. Thus family support debtors in default are often imprisoned for contempt. Stepp v. Stepp, 955 P.2d 722, 726 (Okl. 1998). Earlier in this chapter we encountered family support debtors unsuccessfully seeking a federal injunction to increase their procedural protections before being confined. Note 5 p. 247.

"You can't get any blood out of a turnip," runs the old adage. A judge will not order a defendant to do the impossible. "[T]he justification for coercive imprisonment as applied to civil contempt depends upon the ability of the contemnor to comply with the court's order." Shillitani v. United States, 384 U.S. 364, 371 (1966). Contemnor may assert the defense of inability to comply or to pay money to prevent being held in contempt.

A "deadbeat dad" was six years behind on his child support payments. The trial judge incarcerated him to force him to pay about 2/3 of the arrearage. Two months later at a hearing on his petition for release, he proved he had no money or property. After the trial judge found that his continued incarceration was warranted because he "had allowed his support obligation to accrue for six years," the Georgia supreme court ordered him released: "Incarceration for an indefinite period until the performance of a specified act" is coercive civil contempt which cannot continue if the contemnor is unable to comply and "lacks the ability to purge himself." Hughes v. Georgia Department of Human Resources, 269 Ga. 587, 502 S.E.2d 233, 234 (1998).

The allocation of the burden of proving the contemnor's inability to comply may depend upon the classification of the contempt as civil contempt or criminal contempt. In Hicks v. Feiock, a father had been served with an order to show cause why he should not be held in contempt for failure to make court-ordered child support payments. He was adjudged in contempt and sentenced to five days in jail on a total of five counts; but his jail sentence was suspended and he was placed on probation for three years; one condition of his probation was payment of the accumulated arrearage. On appeal, he contended that a state statute making proof of nonpayment prima facie evidence of contempt violated his constitutional right to due process by shifting the burden of proof of inability to pay to him. The California Court of Appeals annulled the contempt order.

The United States Supreme Court held that if the statutory presumption were applied to a criminal contempt, "such a statute would violate the Due Process Clause because it would undercut the State's burden to prove guilt beyond a reasonable doubt. If applied in a civil proceeding, however, this particular statute would be constitutionally valid." The case was remanded for the state court to determine whether the father's payment of arrearage would purge him of past violation. If so, the contempt was classified as civil contempt and the statutory presumption would not violate due process. Hicks v. Feiock, 485 U.S. 624, 637–38 (1988).

Another defendant was imprisoned for refusing to bring his son to a dependency hearing. The court ruled that in a civil contempt, "the law presumes that one is capable of performing those actions required by the court. Thus, inability to comply is an affirmative defense. A contemnor has both the burden of production of inability to comply, as well as the burden of persuasion." King v. Department of Social and Health Services, 110 Wash.2d 793, 756 P.2d 1303, 1310 (1988).

MOSS v. SUPERIOR COURT, ORTIZ, REAL PARTY IN INTEREST

Supreme Court of California, 1998.
17 Cal.4th 396, 71 Cal.Rptr.2d 215, 950 P.2d 59.

BAXTER, JUSTICE. May a parent whose inability to pay court-ordered child support results from a willful failure to seek and obtain employment be adjudged in contempt of court and punished for violation of the order? * * * [T]he Court of Appeal reluctantly held that to impose a contempt sanction in those circumstances is beyond the power of the court. It therefore annulled the judgment of contempt in issue in this proceeding. * * *

We conclude that there is no constitutional impediment to imposition of contempt sanctions on a parent for violation of a judicial child support order when the parent's financial inability to comply with the order is the result of the parent's willful failure to seek and accept available employment that is commensurate with his or her skills and ability. * * * We also address the burden of proof in these contempt proceedings and conclude that inability to comply with a child support order is an affirmative defense. The alleged contemnor must prove inability to comply by a preponderance of the evidence which was not done here.

We shall affirm the judgment of the Court of Appeal however. We must do so because, in light of the past understanding, * * * our holding that a willfully unemployed, nonsupporting parent is subject to contempt sanctions if the parent fails to comply with a child support order might be deemed an unanticipated change in the law, and Tamara Ortiz, the custodial parent, did not carry her burden of proof under the existing law by showing that Brent Moss, the alleged contemnor, had the actual financial ability to comply with the order.

The "Declaration for Contempt" in this matter, executed by Tamara S. Ortiz on June 22, 1995, alleged that a judgment of dissolution filed March 17, 1992, ordered Brent N. Moss to pay * * * a total of $483 a month support for the two children of the marriage, [which was later reduced]. The declaration alleged that Brent had knowledge of the order and was able to comply with each order when it was disobeyed. No payments were made from July 1, 1994, through June 15, 1995. A total of $5,012 was due and unpaid.

Brent was unemployed when the support order was made. The amount to be paid was based on his ability to earn $1,671 gross income per month. * * *

The superior court issued an order to show cause on June 17, 1995, directing Brent to appear and show cause why he should not be found guilty of contempt for willful disobedience of the support order.

At the November 7, 1995, hearing on the order to show cause, Tamara testified that she and Brent, her then husband, were present when the support order was made and that he had not paid any support at all since July 1, 1994.

Brent's counsel assumed that Tamara bore the burden of proof on ability to pay support. On cross-examination Tamara testified that Brent did not have a car and at times had no food in his house. She was not aware of him having a job in the past four years, and did not know if he had any money or any ability to pay.

Betty Lou Moss, Brent's mother, testified that she provided Brent with a home. She paid the utilities expenses most times, but on other times he did so. He worked at odd jobs, and she did not know how much he earned from them. Brent often ate at her home. She did not know if he purchased food on his own. When the children were with him, they slept at his house, but he brought them to Betty Moss's home to eat. Betty Moss did not know if Brent ever fed them at his house. She did not remember how long it had been since Brent had a job. He did not discuss jobs with her. He did odd jobs like lawn mowing once in a while, but she did not know how much he earned. When she asked him about getting a job he said he was trying. He did not tell her what he was trying, however.

No other evidence was presented.

Counsel for Brent did not dispute the existence of a valid order for support, his client's knowledge of that order, and possible "willfulness," but argued that there had been no evidence of ability to comply with the support order. He also argued that in a contempt proceeding to enforce a child support order, the citee need only raise the question of ability to comply, at which point the party seeking the contempt sanction had the burden of proving ability to comply beyond a reasonable doubt. In his view, inability to comply had been adequately raised by the evidence and compelling Brent to work under threat of punishment would constitute involuntary servitude.

Tamara's counsel argued that Brent had the burden of proving inability to comply with the order as an affirmative defense and that ability to comply did not require ability to pay the full amount of support ordered.

The court agreed that the burden of proving inability to comply lay with Brent and observed that there had been no evidence whatsoever that Brent was not able to work. The court found that Brent did have the ability to pay something in child support as the evidence permitted an inference that he was receiving money from some source other than his mother. In partial explanation of that conclusion, the court stated that Brent was well dressed and had to be doing something to buy his own clothes and feed himself when he did not eat at his mother's home. The court also stated that Brent was "a person who could get a job flipping hamburgers at MacDonald's * * *. I don't know why he couldn't get a job at minimum wage. He's, in my mind, chosen not to." Brent's attorney then conceded that Brent had the ability to work. When asked later if there was a finding of ability to work, however, the court said only that Brent had "the ability to get money. Now, whether you want to say it's the ability to work, which here is no evidence that he can't, or the ability to get money from his mother, which he apparently freely does as he needs to * * * I am left with the inference that he has money from another source." The court also expressed the view that permitting a parent who had the ability to work and support the parent's children, but failed to do so would make a "mockery" of the contempt power.

The court found Brent guilty of * * * contempt, but delayed imposition of sentence to permit Brent to seek appellate review. The only factual finding set forth in the minute order of November 7, 1995, was that "Respondent has the ability to pay the court ordered support." * * *

On March 5, 1996, the superior court imposed a sentence of five days in jail for each of six counts of contempt, ordered Brent to perform ten hours of community servitude for each of the six counts. Execution of sentence was stayed to permit Brent to purge himself of contempt by making specified payments, and he was placed on three years informal probation. * * *

Brent's petition [to the Court of Appeal] for writ of mandate sought to set aside the contempt judgment on the ground that, although he raised the issue of inability to pay, Tamara presented no evidence that he had any resources with which to pay child support and therefore had the ability to comply with the order. [Brent] also claimed that, while the amount of support fixed by a child support order may be based on ability to earn, a finding of contempt may not be based on ability to earn. The Court of Appeal set aside the contempt judgment, holding that the evidence was not sufficient to prove that Brent had the ability to pay, and * * * the Court of Appeal reluctantly concluded that he could not be adjudged in contempt based only on ability to earn. * * * [Tamara appealed.]

The duty of a parent to support the parent's child or children is a fundamental parental obligation. We are satisfied that there is no constitutional impediment to use of the contempt power to punish a parent who, otherwise lacking monetary ability to pay child support, willfully fails and refuses to seek and accept available employment commensurate with the parent's skills and abilities.

[Earlier California decisions were] based on the constitutional proscriptions of involuntary servitude or imprisonment for debt. We consider each in turn, examining first the circumstances which may constitute involuntary servitude within the meaning of the Thirteenth Amendment of the federal Constitution and the California Constitution.

Section 1 of the Thirteenth Amendment of the federal Constitution provides: "Neither slavery nor involuntary servitude, except as a punishment for crime whereof the party shall have been duly convicted, shall exist within the United States, or any place subject to their jurisdiction."

The Thirteenth Amendment, unlike the Fourteenth Amendment, prohibits conduct by private persons as well as governmental entities. It has been construed and applied primarily to circumstances in which one individual sought to compel work by another. In its decisions applying the Thirteenth Amendment, the United States Supreme Court has recognized that many fundamental societal obligations involving compelled labor do not violate the proscription of involuntary servitude. It has never held that employment undertaken to comply with a judicially imposed requirement that a party seek and accept employment when necessary to meet a parent's fundamental obligation to support a child is involuntary servitude.

In those decisions in which a Thirteenth Amendment violation has been found on the basis of involuntary servitude, the court has equated the employment condition to peonage under which a person is bound to the service of a particular employer or master until an obligation to that person is satisfied. A court order that a parent support a child, compliance with which may require that the parent seek and accept employment, does not bind the parent to any particular employer or form of employment or otherwise affect the freedom of the parent. The parent is free to elect the type of employment and the employer, subject only to an expectation that to the extent necessary to meet the familial support obligation, the employment will be commensurate with the education, training, and abilities of the parent. * * *

The obligation of a parent to support a child, and to become employed if that is necessary to meet the obligation, is in no way comparable or akin to peonage or slavery. It is among the most fundamental obligations recognized by modern society. The duty is not simply one imposed by statute, but "rests on fundamental natural laws and has always been recognized by the courts in the absence of any statute declaring it." (Lewis v. Lewis (1917) 174 Cal. 336, 339, 163 P. 42.) It is an obligation that existed under common law [citation] and has long been recognized in a majority of American jurisdictions as not only a moral obligation, but one that is legally enforceable. [citation] The state's interest in and public policy mandating parental support of children is so strong that jurisdictions faced with the question hold that it extends even to juvenile fathers who were the victims of statutory rape by adult women. [citations] * * *

A parent's obligation to support a minor child is a social obligation that is no less important than compulsory military service, road building, jury service and other constitutionally permissible enforced labor. Even if the necessity of accepting employment in order to meet this obligation were somehow analogous to those forms of compelled labor, we have no doubt that this form of labor would be recognized as an exception to the ban on involuntary servitude found in the Thirteenth Amendment. It is clear to us, however, that employment undertaken to meet a child support obligation is not analogous to government-controlled labor and does not otherwise create a condition of peonage or slavery. Unlike those recognized exceptions to the Thirteenth Amendment in which labor is compulsory, undertaking employment because an income is necessary to enable a parent to comply with a valid court order to support a child does not impose on the parent any government control over the type of employment, the employer for whom the parent's labor will be performed, or any other aspect of the parent's individual freedom that might be associated with peonage or slavery. * * *

The court has also reaffirmed its understanding that the Thirteenth Amendment was not intended to apply to "exceptional cases" in which the right to labor was recognized at common law when the amendment was adopted. Examples given were the right of parents to the custody of children, whose labor could be compelled by the parent, and laws which prevent persons who have contracted to work aboard a ship from deserting the ship. Other forms of "coerced" service which courts have held do not violate the Thirteenth Amendment include providing equal access to public accommodations (Heart of Atlanta Motel Inc. v. United States (1964) 379 U.S. 241 [codification of common law duty of innkeeper]); community service requirement for high school graduation (Immediato v. Rye Neck School Dist. (2d Cir.1996) 73 F.3d 454; Steirer by Steirer v. Bethlehem Area School Dist. (1993) 987 F.2d 989 [no analogy to slavery]); provision of free legal service as condition of practicing law (United States v. 30.64 Acres of Land (9th Cir.1986) 795 F.2d 796); performance of medical services after acceptance of scholarship money to complete degree (United States v. Redovan [damages alternative available]). [Note 2, pp. 710–12 below] * * *

While the court also cautioned that it drew no conclusions from its historical survey about the potential scope of the Thirteenth Amendment, and used broad language regarding physical or legal coercion, to date the only types of compelled labor it has characterized as involuntary servitude have been ones "akin to peonage." This understanding of the Thirteenth Amendment underlies the concern expressed in our decisions declining specific enforcement of contracts for personal services that such enforcement might constitute impermissible involuntary servitude. (See, e.g., Beverly Glen Music, Inc. v. Warner Communications, Inc., [p. 688 below]). * * *

As the authorities reviewed above demonstrate, the court's approach in cases of alleged involuntary servitude has been contextual. No single definition of the term has evolved and each situation must be examined to determine if it bears the indices of peonage or slavery. To date however, neither the Supreme Court nor any state court that has enforced a child support order has suggested that undertaking gainful employment in order to avoid sanctions for violation of a valid child support order is analogous to the peonage or involuntary servitude prohibited by the Thirteenth Amendment. Employment chosen by the employee which the employee is free to leave either in favor of another employer or if the working conditions are objectively intolerable, is simply not "akin to peonage." It does not become so because a person would prefer not to work but must do so in order to comply with a legal duty to support the person's children. * * *

[The California Constitution, the court held] affords Brent no greater rights than does the Thirteenth Amendment to the federal Constitution. * * *

Tamara also contends that the prohibition of imprisonment for debt found in article I, section 10 of the California Constitution does not support application of [an earlier decision] to child support obligations. We agree.

Article I, section 10 of the California Constitution, states in pertinent part: "A person may not be imprisoned in a civil action for debt or tort, or in peacetime for a militia fine."

It has long been settled that this provision does not apply to imprisonment for crime. * * *

Family support obligations are not ordinary debts subject to the constitutional prohibition of imprisonment for debt. [citations] * * *

Even were the obligation considered a debt, however, * * * children are dependent on their parents for the necessities of life and it is essential to the public welfare that parents provide support with which to care for their needs. * * * [A] parent who knows that support is due, has the ability to earn money to pay that support, and still willfully refuses to seek and accept available employment to enable the parent to meet the support obligation acts against fundamental societal norms and fair dealing, and necessarily intentionally does an act which prejudices the rights of his children. This conduct would fall within the fraud exception to the constitutional prohibition of imprisonment for debt. * * *

We also reject Brent's claim that express legislative authorization should be required before a contempt sanction is permitted in these circumstances. This claim needs little discussion. Express statutory authorization for both contempt sanctions and criminal penalties already exists for any willful violation of a court order. [citations] Inasmuch as the Legislature has expressly authorized the court to consider earning capacity in making a child support order if doing so is in the best interests of the child [citation] there can be no question but that the Legislature intends that that parental ability to work in order to support a child be considered in any enforcement action. We will not presume that the Legislature intended to leave the courts powerless to enforce orders expressly authorized by [the] Family Code. Rather, the presumption is that the Legislature is aware that violation of a court order is punishable as a contempt and intended that violation of an order * * * be punished in the same manner as any other contempt based on violation of a court order. * * *

As noted earlier, Tamara took the position, and the trial court agreed, that inability to comply with a support order is an affirmative defense. The trial court based its contempt judgment on evidence that the support order had been made, Brent had notice of the order, an inference that Brent must have had some income to meet those needs not met by his mother, and its observation that Brent had the ability to earn money to pay something toward his support obligation. Brent had argued that he needed only to raise the question of ability to comply in order to shift to Tamara the burden of presenting evidence sufficient to prove beyond a reasonable doubt that he had the present financial ability to comply with the order.

Brent's argument reflects a basic misunderstanding of the allocation of burden in support proceedings. Ability to comply with a support order is not an element of the contempt which must be proven beyond a reasonable doubt by the petitioner. It is an affirmative defense which must be proven by a preponderance of the evidence by the alleged contemnor. * * *

The Supreme Court has confirmed that whether ability to comply is to be an element of the contempt or an affirmative defense, and whether Code of Civil Procedure section 1209.5 shifts the burden of persuasion or simply imposes a burden of producing some evidence showing inability to comply are questions of state law. (Hicks v. Feiock (1988) 485 U.S. 624, 629.)

[The court quoted the California Court of Appeal:] "The contemnor is the person in the best position to know whether inability to pay is even a consideration in the proceeding and also has the best access to evidence on the issue, particularly in cases of self-employment." * * *

[T]he elements of this contempt are only a valid court order, the alleged contemnor's knowledge of the order, and noncompliance. If the petitioner proves those elements beyond a reasonable doubt the violation is established. He or she need go no farther. To prevail on the affirmative defense of inability to comply with the support, order, the contemnor must prove such inability by a preponderance of the evidence. * * *

We see no constitutional impediment to the Legislature's creation of a contempt offense for failure to support a child in which ability to pay is not an element. The ability of the parent to pay the amount of support ordered has been determined by the court which made the order. [citation] The nonsupporting parent has been given the opportunity to offer evidence on the question and to challenge the order in the appellate court. He or she is also afforded the opportunity to seek modification of the order if circumstances change making compliance difficult or impossible. [citation] The contempt penalty for failure to comply with the support order is limited to five days in jail and a $1,000 fine for each monthly payment that is not made in full. [citation] The offense is comparable to a "strict liability" regulatory or "public welfare" offense in this regard [citation], but unlike some regulatory offenses, the contemnor may escape liability by establishing an affirmative defense. Under these circumstances the omission of an element of willfulness does not offend due process. [citation]

DISPOSITION. Nonetheless, the judgment of the Court of Appeal must be affirmed. Our disapproval [of earlier decisions] * * * may reasonably be seen as both an unanticipated expansion of the law of contempt in the child support context and a change in the evidentiary burden of which Brent had no notice at the time of trial. Neither rule may be retroactively applied therefore. * * *

JUSTICE KENNARD, dissenting. [A]pplying this statutory scheme to Brent does not violate the due process fair warning requirement. I would apply it. * * *

I would reverse the judgment of the Court of Appeal and direct that court to affirm the trial court's judgment imposing contempt sanctions.

Notes

1. A Maryland family support debtor created inability to comply, that is to pay, by ending her employment and relying on the charity of others. The trial judge, aware she lacked cash or assets, nevertheless "sentenced her to 20 days in the detention center, but ordered that she could purge herself of the contempt by paying $500."

The Maryland Court of Appeals thought not: "Whether a defendant has failed to pay court ordered support when he or she had the ability to do so and whether that defendant has, in bad faith, caused his or her own present inability to comply, with the intent of frustrating the court order, are material, and, indeed, necessary, considerations bearing on whether a defendant should be punished. Those considerations do not address whether the defendant is in civil contempt, the object of which is remedial—to force compliance. Even if the present inability to comply is the product of the defendant's bad faith, compliance still cannot be coerced by civil contempt. Thus, to the extent that this record reflects that the [support debtor] failed to pay the court-ordered support when able and quit her job in bad faith, for the purpose of avoiding the responsibility and, in the process frustrated the court order, the petitioner-[support creditor] could have, and should have, initiated criminal contempt proceedings, for the purpose of punishing the [support debtor] for those acts. That would, of course, have required the termination of the civil contempt proceedings." Lynch v. Lynch, 342 Md. 509, 528–29, 677 A.2d 584, 594 (1996).

The voluntarily impoverished support debtor is uncoercable, resembling Frank McNulty and other terminally stubborn contemnors. pp. 236. The Maryland court encourages the plaintiff to convert coercive contempt to criminal contempt. Will the risk of a fixed, unpurgable criminal contempt sentence discourage a defendant from self-imposed inability to pay and other acts of terminal stubbornness?

2. Was the trial judge's order to Brent civil-coercive contempt or criminal contempt? At trial the distinction between civil contempt and criminal contempt affects both the burden of proof and the plaintiff's ability to call the contemnor as a witness. If an unemployed family support contemnor were in jail, would he have a subsequent opportunity to reduce or avoid the confinement through compliance?

5. THE COLLATERAL BAR

EX PARTE PURVIS

Supreme Court Of Alabama, 1980.
382 So.2d 512.

EMBRY, JUSTICE. This petition for writ of habeas corpus arises out of a strike against The Water Works Board of the City of Birmingham by hourly employees of that Board. The petition was filed on behalf of James R. Purvis after he was incarcerated under a sentence of criminal contempt by the Circuit Court of Jefferson County. The contempt sentence was based on Purvis' violation of a temporary restraining order enjoining the strike and all picketing activities against the Board. Purvis was sentenced to an aggregate of fifteen days in jail for three separate instances of contempt. This court granted a stay of execution of the sentence after Purvis had served eight days of the sentence.

We deny the petition.

The dispositive issue in this proceeding is whether Purvis can challenge, by petition for the writ of habeas corpus, the constitutional validity of the trial court's temporary restraining order when Purvis failed to try to have the order dissolved or modified before violating it?

In July of 1979, Purvis requested the Board to recognize his union as the exclusive bargaining representative for the hourly-paid employees of the Board. * * * On 31 July 1979 Purvis advised the Board its employees would commence a strike against it and all of its facilities unless the union's demands were met. Upon the Board's refusal, the strike and picketing of the Board's facilities were commenced at approximately 6:00 a.m. on Thursday, 2 August 1979. That same morning the Board petitioned the Jefferson County Circuit Court for a temporary restraining order alleging, *inter alia,* the strike was illegal, striking employees were harassing and interfering with customers entering and leaving its buildings and property, and it, and the City of Birmingham would suffer irreparable injury if the order was not issued before notice could be served on the defendants.

At 1:40 on Thursday, 2 August 1979, a temporary restraining order was issued which contained, among other things, the following:

"A. The defendants, separately and severally, their officers, agents, and members, and all persons acting in concert or combination with them, who have actual notice of this temporary restraining order by personal service or otherwise be and they are hereby restrained, pending the final determination of this action, from:

"1. causing, inducing, engaging in or encouraging a strike, work stoppage, or concerted refusal to work at The Board or any of its facilities for the purpose of requiring The Board to agree to defendants' demands that the plaintiff recognize, bargain with or enter into agreements with the defendant Union. * * * "

At 4:08 p.m. on Thursday, 2 August 1979, Purvis was served with a copy of the temporary restraining order by a deputy sheriff. The evidence at the contempt hearing discloses that Purvis told the deputy "he would stay out, even if he had to go to jail." Consistent with this declaration Purvis continued to picket the Board's Shades Mountain facility the rest of Thursday afternoon and the morning of Friday, 3 August 1979. The evidence further discloses that Purvis ignored and violated the order by threatening a supervisor that drove through the picket line.

On Friday, 3 August 1979, the Board filed a petition to show cause why Purvis should not be held in contempt of court. Purvis was served that same day at 1:55 p.m. Purvis then filed a motion to dissolve or modify the temporary restraining order. The court ordered Purvis to appear before the court on Monday morning, 6 August 1979, to show cause why he should not be held in contempt and, further, denied Purvis' motion to dissolve or modify the temporary restraining order.

On Saturday morning, 4 August 1979, the Board amended its petition to show cause. On Monday, 6 August 1979, after a hearing, the trial court found Purvis had violated the temporary restraining order after having received proper notice by: (1) continuing to picket Thursday afternoon; (2) threatening to assault a supervisor; and (3) his picketing activities on Friday morning. Three separate judgments of criminal contempt were entered against Purvis and he was sentenced to three consecutive five day sentences for each offense as well as being fined $100 for each offense. Thereafter, this petition was filed.

Purvis contends the trial court's temporary restraining order was transparently invalid, unconstitutional and required the irretrievable surrender of his important constitutional rights; therefore, there can be no valid finding of contempt because adequate and effective appellate procedures did not exist to challenge the order's validity. We cannot agree with this contention.

It has long been the rule of law that an order issued by a court with jurisdiction over the subject matter must be obeyed by the parties subject to the order until it is reversed by orderly and proper proceedings even though the order may be constitutionally defective or invalid. Walker v. City of Birmingham, 279 Ala. 53, 181 So.2d 493 (1965), aff'd, 388 U.S. 307 (1967); United States v. United Mine Workers of America, 330 U.S. 258 (1947). Purvis acknowledges this established principle of law but asserts the order had such a chilling effect on his First Amendment rights that the order was void on its face, therefore, he was entitled to disregard the order because there was insufficient time to appeal from it. We cannot agree that the order was transparently invalid or that such exigent circumstances existed as to allow Purvis to disregard it.

We recognize that court orders may be disregarded in certain rare cases where compliance with the court order would cause irreparable injury and appellate vindication would not have its ordinary consequences of totally repairing the error. However, such cases generally involve orders issued during criminal trials. We further recognize that if an injunction is transparently invalid, or only has a frivolous pretense to validity, its validity may be challenged in a contempt proceeding. Walker v. City of Birmingham. In this case, however, Purvis was not justified in refusing to obey the temporary restraining order. See United States v. United Mine Workers of America, supra.

The United States Supreme Court has consistently recognized that the state has a strong interest in regulating the use of its streets and other public places; and when protest takes the form of mass demonstration, parades, or picketing on public streets and sidewalks, the state has a legitimate concern in preventing public disorder and violence and promoting the free passage of traffic. *Walker.* Moreover, the First and Fourteenth Amendments to the United States Constitution, although they do protect, do not afford the same kind of freedom to those who communicate ideas by conduct, such as picketing on streets and highways, as the amendments afford those who communicate ideas by mere speech. Shuttlesworth v. City of Birmingham, 394 U.S. 147 (1969); *Walker*. Since violence erupted during the strike and picketing, and the City of Birmingham's water service was in danger of being shut down, the trial court's temporary restraining order was not transparently invalid or frivolous. Also, a hearing was scheduled within five days, and Purvis could easily have sought modification or dissolution of the order before disobeying it.

In reaching our decision we must emphasize that we are not encouraging the issuance of temporary restraining orders against peaceful picketing. It is very clear that peaceful picketing is protected by the First Amendment. *Shuttlesworth; Thornhill v. State of Alabama*, 310 U.S. 88 (1940). First Amendment rights should only be enjoined in extreme situations. Temporary restraining orders should only be issued without a prior hearing when it is clear from specific facts alleged by affidavit or by verified complaint that immediate and irreparable injury, loss, or damage, will result if the temporary restraining order is not issued prior to allowing the opposing party an opportunity to be heard. *Rule 65(b)(1), ARCP. When a temporary restraining order is to be issued without hearing, curtailing First Amendment rights, even closer scrutiny of the existing circumstances under which it is sought should be exercised by the trial court.*

The sole basis for our decision in this case is the need to maintain the integrity of court orders. In reaching this decision we make no finding respecting the constitutional validity of the temporary restraining order. It is clear in this case that Purvis was fully cognizant that he risked jail confinement if he deliberately defied the court order; yet he chose to do so. We fully agree with the statement of Justice Stewart in Walker v. City of Birmingham:

> "The rule of law that Alabama followed in this case reflects a belief that in the fair administration of justice no man can be judge in his own case, however exalted his station, however righteous his motives, and irrespective of his race, color, politics, or religion. This Court cannot hold that the petitioners were constitutionally free to ignore all the procedures of the law and carry their battle to the streets. One may sympathize with the petitioners' impatient commitment to their cause. But respect for judicial process is a small price to pay for the civilizing hand of law, which alone can give abiding meaning to constitutional freedom." * * *

[T]he petition for writ of habeas corpus is denied and the stay of execution of the remainder of the sentences vacated.

Notes

1. *Lowering the Collateral Bar*: *Transparent Invalidity.*

(a) At the instance of Sacramento County, California, a court granted a TRO ex parte to prohibit a threatened strike by the Social Workers' Union. Defendants did not attempt to modify the decree; fully aware of its existence, they deliberately disobeyed it. The defendants were charged, not under the contempt provision of the Code of Civil Procedure, but instead under a provision of the Penal Code (§ 166 subsection 4) that makes certain conduct in contempt of court a misdemeanor. A writ of habeas corpus, a collateral attack on the decree, was sought. The California Supreme Court held that the order was too vague to pass the constitutional standards required to constrain defendants' First–Amendment rights. Their willful disobedience was therefore not punishable by criminal contempt. The court referred to Walker v. Birmingham:

"The County herein relies heavily upon the *Walker* case in an effort to sustain its position that petitioners must be precluded from raising constitutional objections to the subject order because they did not seek its modification or vacation prior to their willful disobedience of it. It is apparent, however, that the *holding* of the *Walker* case, as distinguished from its language, is only that the rule of law followed by the State of Alabama did not, in the particular circumstances of that case, constitute an intrusion upon First Amendment freedoms. In California, * * * the rule followed is considerably more consistent with the exercise of First Amendment freedoms than that adopted in Alabama, and it is therefore difficult to perceive how the *Walker* decision is of relevance herein. Further, it is notable that the majority in *Walker* indicated that the Alabama rule might be constitutionally impermissible in a case wherein the order or ordinance involved was unconstitutional on its face, or was 'transparently invalid or had only a frivolous pretense to validity.' Thus it appears that the *Walker* decision is consistent with the California rule that an order void upon its face cannot support a contempt judgment." In re Berry, 68 Cal.2d 137, 150, 65 Cal.Rptr. 273, 282, 436 P.2d 273, 282 (1968). The California court reaffirmed its position in People v. Gonzalez, 12 Cal.4th 804, 50 Cal.Rptr.2d 74, 910 P.2d 1366 (1996).

(b) Free press-fair trial disputes present "an apparent conflict between two fundamental legal principles: the hallowed First Amendment principle that the press shall not be subjected to prior restraints; the other, the sine qua non of orderly government, that, until modified or vacated, a court order must be obeyed." The trial judge granted a TRO forbidding the Journal from publishing material about a deceased man who was reputed to have been involved with organized crime; but the Journal published the material two days later. The trial judge imposed criminal contempt sanctions on the Journal and its editor.

The court of appeals panel decision thought the TRO was a prior restraint of speech and reversed the contempt under the "exception to the collateral bar rule for transparently invalid court orders. Requiring a party subject to such an order to obey or face contempt would give the courts powers far in excess of any authorized by the Constitution or Congress. Recognizing an exception to the collateral bar rule for transparently invalid orders does not violate the principle that 'no man can be judge in his own case' anymore than does recognizing such an exception for jurisdictional defects. The key to both exceptions is the notion that although a court order—even an arguably incorrect court order—demands respect, so does the right of the citizen to be free of clearly improper exercises of judicial authority.

"Although an exception to the collateral bar rule is appropriate for transparently void orders, it is inappropriate for arguably proper orders. This distinction is necessary both to protect the authority of the courts when they address close questions and to create a strong incentive for parties to follow the orderly process of law. No such protection or incentive is needed when the order is transparently invalid because in that instance the court is acting so far in excess of its authority that it has no right to expect compliance and no interest is protected by requiring compliance.

"The line between a transparently invalid order and one that is merely invalid is, of course, not always distinct. As a general rule, if the court reviewing the order finds the order to have had any pretense to validity at the time it was issued, the reviewing court should enforce the collateral bar rule. Such a heavy presumption in favor of validity is necessary to protect the rightful power of the courts. Nonetheless, there are instances where an order will be so patently unconstitutional that it will be excepted from the collateral bar rule."

The panel opinion and the whole court of appeals, en banc, differed on the other exception to the collateral bar rule.

The panel: "When, as here, the court order is a transparently invalid prior restraint on pure speech, the delay and expense of an appeal is unnecessary. Indeed, the delay caused by an appellate review requirement could, in the case of a prior restraint involving news concerning an imminent event, cause the restrained information to lose its value. The absence of such a requirement will not, however, lead to wide-spread disregard of court orders. Rarely will a party be subject to a transparently invalid court order. Prior restraints on pure speech represent an unusual class of orders because they are presumptively unconstitutional. And even when a party believes it is subject to a transparently invalid order, seeking review in an appellate court is a far safer means of testing the order. For if the party chooses to violate the order and the order turns out not to be transparently invalid, the party must suffer the consequences of a contempt citation."

Five months later the whole court issued an en banc opinion "as an addendum to, and modification of, said panel opinion."

"Nevertheless it seems to us that some finer tuning is available to minimize the disharmony between respect for court orders and respect for free speech.

"It is not asking much, beyond some additional expense and time, to require a publisher, even when it thinks it is the subject of a transparently unconstitutional order of prior restraint, to make a good faith effort to seek emergency relief from the appellate court. If timely access to the appellate court is not available or if timely decision is not forthcoming, the publisher may then proceed to publish and challenge the constitutionality of the order in the contempt proceedings. In such event whatever added expense and time are involved, such a price does not seem disproportionate to the respect owing court processes; and there is no prolongation of any prior restraint. On the other hand, should the appellate court grant the requested relief, the conflict between principles has been resolved and the expense and time involved have vastly been offset by aborting any contempt proceedings.

"We realize that our ruling means that a publisher seeking to challenge an order it deems transparently unconstitutional must concern itself with establishing a record of its good faith effort. But that is a price we should pay for the preference of court over party determination of invalidity. * * * [We] would deem it unfair to subject the publisher to the very substantial sanctions imposed by the district court because of its failure to follow the procedure we have just announced. We recognize that our announcement is technically dictum, but are confident that its stature as a deliberate position taken by us in this en banc consideration will serve its purpose." In re Providence Journal Co., 820 F.2d 1342, 1344, 1347–48, 1352–53 (1st Cir.1986), modified, 820 F.2d 1354–55 (1st Cir.1987).

The Supreme Court granted certiorari; but it later dismissed for lack of jurisdiction, giving as a reason that the special prosecutor lacked authority to represent the United States. United States v. Providence Journal Co., 485 U.S. 693 (1988).

2. *Rejecting the Collateral Bar.* The media's attention when Michael Irvin was charged in Texas state court with possession of cocaine led the trial judge to enter a "gag" order limiting pretrial publicity. Dennis Pedini, who had been admonished in court, "was interviewed by the television program Hard Copy. [Pedini] also provided a hidden-camera videotape which purportedly shows Michael Irvin purchasing cocaine and talking about his drug habits." After being convicted of contempt, Pedini filed federal habeas corpus contesting the constitutionality of the gag order.

The defendant, the federal court wrote, "questions whether [Pedini] can challenge the validity of the 'gag' order in an application for writ of habeas corpus. He argues that the order should have been attacked in a separate proceeding before it was violated. This 'collateral bar rule' was approved by the United States Supreme Court in Walker v. City of Birmingham. In *Walker*, the Supreme Court upheld an Alabama procedural rule that prohibits a party from challenging a court order on collateral review. However, a state is not required to adopt the collateral bar rule as a matter of federal law. [citation] Texas has expressly rejected such a rule in cases where a person has been confined for disregarding an unconstitutional restriction on protected speech. [citations] Therefore, this Court can address the merits of [Pedini's] claim."

The federal court examined the merits, held the order neither overly broad nor contrary to the First Amendment, and denied Pedini relief. Pedini v. Bowles, 940 F.Supp. 1020, 1022, 1024 (N.D.Tex.1996).

In a bankruptcy decision in 1995, the United States Supreme Court adhered to the collateral bar rule: obligors to an injunction who correctly think it is wrong should appeal or move to modify; they may not collaterally attack the injunction by violating it. Celotex v. Edwards, 514 U.S. 300 (1995).

Is the Texas approach of reviewing the merits without the collateral bar rule the better practice? As Justice Doggett wrote, "I cannot see how justice is served by leaving imprisoned those found to have violated an order shown to be unconstitutional." Ex parte Tucci, 859 S.W.2d 1, 2 n.4 (Tex. 1993).

6. WHO MUST OBEY?

Quite a bit of injunction litigation involves a plaintiff with perishable rights and a need for haste suing an unwieldy group of defendants and potential defendants.

The issue of who must obey an injunction is a distinctive feature of injunction litigation. To advance the policy of protecting plaintiff's substantive entitlement, an injunction must reach beyond named defendant to prevent defendant from violating the injunction through a straw.

The countervailing considerations are due process and separation of powers. Procedural due process means that a person who must obey a court order should have received notice of the lawsuit and an opportunity to be heard and participate in court. The named defendant's agents and agent surrogates are bound because the court assumes that the employer or principal represented their interests.

Separation of powers distinguishes legislative from judicial power. A legal rule that creates a general public duty to obey comes from the legislature; we call this rule a statute. A judge cannot grant an injunction that creates a criminal statute that everyone must obey. Doug Rendleman, Beyond Contempt: Obligors to Injunctions, 53 Tex.L.Rev. 873 (1975).

An initial issue is whether the person charged with contempt received adequate notice of the order he is charged with violating. Due process forbids a contempt conviction when the person charged did not know of the court order. Walker v. City of Birmingham, 279 Ala. 53, 63–64, 181 So.2d 493, 503–04 (1965), affirmed 388 U.S. 307 (1967).

Where someone who was not formally served with the injunction is charged, that contemnor's knowledge of the order may be proved by its publication in a newspaper or broadcast on the radio or television. More informal notice may suffice. Evidence that an announcement was made by bullhorn or that notice was in general circulation in the affected group may be adequate to establish actual knowledge. Megantz v. Ash, 412 F.2d 804 (1st Cir.1969); United Packing House Workers v. Boynton, 240 Iowa 212, 35 N.W.2d 881 (1949).

E-mail Service. "One does not think of the tradition-bound British judiciary as avatars of the cutting edge. Big white wigs, yes. Wired, not.

"Yet this spring, a Queen's Bench judge allowed a pair of London lawyers to serve an injunction via e-mail. It apparently was the first time an English court has literally extended its jurisdiction into cyberspace. * * *

Given that an unknown individual allegedly had sent harassing e-mail messages to Lambeth and Croad's (unnamed) rock-star client, "the only practical way to bring the order to the notice of our defendant was via the Internet into his PC," the lawyers wrote.

"This from a court, they noted, where orders are still 'entered into leather-bound ledgers in copper-plate handwriting.' " Todd Woody, 'Net Gain, Legal Times, July 1, 1996 at 27.

Consider, (a) whether the court obtained personal jurisdiction over defendants; and (b) whether defendants will respond if "served" with an e-mail "show-cause" order to defend a charge of contempt.

People ex rel. Gallo v. Acuna, Revisited. Here we return to the San Jose city authorities' public nuisance action against street gang members. The trial judge had granted the city a comprehensive preliminary injunction; the named defendants were individual members of an alleged "criminal street gang." Defendants appealed from the preliminary injunction. Two substantive paragraphs were before the California Supreme Court: one forbids defendants from associating with other defendants or other gang members within the designated nuisance area, the other enjoins defendants from "confronting"—plus several near synonyms—residents who have complained about the gangs. The parts of the decision dealing with the public nuisance issues are above. p. 248.

In the part of the decision below, the court distinguishes defendants' liability for damages from their obligation to obey an injunction:

"Defendants contend that they may not be bound by the [preliminary] injunction except on proof that each possessed 'a specific intent to further an unlawful aim embraced by [the gang].' The quoted language is the test formulated by the United States Supreme Court in NAACP v. Claiborne Hardware Co., 458 U.S. 886, 925 (1982) as being required to sustain damages liability against individual members of a group. *Claiborne Hardware* is distinguishable on its facts. Defendants there were members of a local chapter of a national civil rights organization. Each was held liable in state court proceedings for business losses suffered by the plaintiff merchants over the seven-year duration of a civil rights boycott sponsored by the organization. Although the boycott was for the most part peaceable and law abiding, there were sporadic incidents of violence by some members, resulting in economic losses to the plaintiffs.

"Vacating the state court damages award, the high court held that 'mere association with [the] group—absent a specific intent to further an unlawful aim embraced by that group—is an insufficient predicate for liability.' The state courts, the Supreme Court reasoned, had 'relied on isolated acts of violence during a limited period to uphold [plaintiffs'] recovery of all business losses sustained over a 7–year span.' * * * The court's judgment 'screens reality' and cannot stand. Unlike the record in *Claiborne Hardware*, the evidence submitted by the City in support of the preliminary injunction here presents a portrait of gang affiliated youths whose collective activities, within the four-block area of Rocksprings, create and sustain the 'urban war zone' described at the outset of this opinion. The precedents that control the reach of injunctive relief in such circumstances are Milk Wagon Drivers v. Meadowmoor Dairies, 312 U.S. 287 (1941) and Madsen v. Women's Health Center, Inc., 512 U.S. 753 (1994).

"In *Milk Wagon Drivers* the trial court issued a preliminary injunction 'restraining all union conduct, violent and peaceful,' arising out of a labor dispute. The union protested, arguing the decree violated the First Amendment rights of its members by enjoining acts of peaceful picketing. The Illinois Supreme Court affirmed the broad scope of the interlocutory decree and directed that a permanent injunction, restraining peaceful as well as violent acts by union members, be entered as well. The United States Supreme Court upheld the injunction, framing the case as one where 'the question * * * is whether a state can choose to authorize its courts to enjoin acts of picketing in themselves peaceful when they are enmeshed with contemporaneously violent conduct which is concededly outlawed.'

"As in *Milk Wagon Drivers*, here 'the injunction is confined,' encompassing conduct occurring within a narrow, four-block residential neighborhood. As in *Milk Wagon Drivers*, it 'deals with this narrow area precisely because the coercive conduct affected it. An injunction so adjusted to a particular situation is in accord with the settled practice of equity * * * [and] * * * must be read in the context of its circumstances.' As in *Milk Wagon Drivers*, the high court in *Madsen*, upheld an injunction directed against 'congregating, picketing, patrolling, demonstrating or entering' within 36 feet of a health clinic in which therapeutic abortions were performed. That provision of the decree, along with another setting restrictions on noise, was directed not only at the anti-abortion organizations themselves, but at allied organizations and 'their officers, agents, members, employees and servants, and * * * all persons acting in concert or participation with them, or on their behalf.'

"Both *Milk Wagon Drivers*, and *Madsen*, thus stand for the proposition that, in a proper case, an organization and its individual members are enjoinable without meeting the 'specific intent to further unlawful group aims' standard applied in *Claiborne Hardware*. Certainly that proposition comprehends paragraphs (a) and (k) of the preliminary injunction, the only two provisions now before us. For we have already concluded that the conduct proscribed by those two provisions—appearing publicly in Rocksprings with others known to a defendant to be gang members, and harassing area residents known to a defendant to have complained to public authorities about gang activities in Rocksprings—are activities integral to the public nuisance that afflicts Rocksprings and do not implicate protected First Amendment conduct.

"That being the case, the interim relief entered by the superior court is indistinguishable from time-honored equitable practice applicable to labor unions, abortion protesters or other identifiable groups. Because such groups can act only through the medium of their membership, 'it has been a common practice to make the injunction run also to classes of persons through whom the enjoined person may act, such as agents, servants, employees, aiders [and] abettors.' Berger v. Superior Court, 175 Cal. 719, 721, 167 P. 143, 144 (1917). cf. Fed.Rules Civ.Proc., Rule 65(d), an injunction 'is binding only upon the parties to the action, their officers, agents, servants, employees, and attorneys, and upon those persons in active concert or participation with them who receive actual notice of the order by personal service or otherwise.'

"We see nothing in this case—where instead of naming the gang organizations themselves as parties, the City named as individual defendants all 38 gang members it was able to identify—that removes it from the usual rule. * * * The City's evidence in support of preliminary equitable relief demonstrated that it was the gang itself, acting through its membership, that was responsible for creating and maintaining the public nuisance in Rocksprings. Because the City could have named the gangs themselves as defendants and proceeded against them, its decision to name individual gang members instead does not take the case out of the familiar rule that both the organization and the members through which it acts are subject to injunctive relief.

"For present purposes, it is enough to observe that there was sufficient evidence before the superior court to support the conclusions that the gang and its members present in Rocksprings were responsible for the public nuisance, that each of the individual defendants either admitted gang membership or was identified as a gang member, and that each was observed by police officials in the Rocksprings neighborhood. Although all but three of the eleven defendants who chose to contest entry of the preliminary injunction—Miguel Moreno, Rafael Ruiz, and Blanca Gonzalez—were shown to have committed acts, primarily drug related, comprising specific elements of the public nuisance, such individualized proof is not a condition to the entry of preliminary relief based on a showing that it is the gang, acting through its individual members, that is responsible for the conditions prevailing in Rocksprings. Additional proceedings will be required to enforce the specific terms of the preliminary injunction. Should contempt proceedings ensue, each individual defendant will have an opportunity to contest any claim by the City that he or she has violated specific terms of the preliminary injunction." People ex rel. Gallo v. Acuna, 14 Cal.4th 1090, 1121–24, 60 Cal.Rptr.2d 277, 297–99, 929 P.2d 596, 616–18 (1997).

Were you surprised to learn that the California court defines the group that can be incarcerated for contempt more expansively than the group that can be required to pay damages? Most litigation about who is obligated to obey an injunction occurs after someone violates one and is charged with criminal contempt.

PEOPLE v. CONRAD

California Court of Appeal, 1997.
55 Cal.App.4th 896, 64 Cal.Rptr.2d 248.

WALKER, ASSOCIATE JUSTICE. Cheryl Conrad, Sandra Evans, Bryan Kemper, Ruben Obregon, Michael Ross, Johnny Schwab, Joanne Holden, Alice Gambino, and Jeffrey White appeal their misdemeanor convictions for disobedience of a lawful court order. (Pen.Code, § 166, subd. (a)(4).) Appellants are abortion protesters who were arrested for picketing in front of the Planned Parenthood clinic in Vallejo. The clinic has a valid court order enjoining the similar activity of Christine Williams, Solano Citizens for Life, "and their agents, representatives, employees and members, and each of them, and each and every person acting at the direction of or in combination or in concert with defendants." Our Supreme Court has upheld this injunction (see Planned Parenthood Shasta-

Diablo, Inc. v. Williams (1995) 10 Cal.4th 1009 (*Williams II*), and the United States Supreme Court has denied certiorari (see Williams v. Planned Parenthood Shasta–Diablo, Inc. (1997) 117 S.Ct. 1285.

Appellants claim, first, that the trial judge applied the wrong legal standard to find that they acted "in concert" with the enjoined parties so as to make them liable for violating the injunction and, second, that, measured by the correct standard, the evidence was insufficient to sustain their convictions. We agree.

Facts: The Planned Parenthood clinic in Vallejo is situated at 990 Broadway, a "busy avenue, with light commercial establishments on either side of" the clinic. A parking lot surrounds the premises, and two driveways cross the public sidewalk that borders the lot, providing access from Broadway to the clinic and other businesses. The injunction we construe here was issued on August 1, 1991, after the enjoined parties had repeatedly obstructed the clinic entrances, interfered with traffic on the driveways, and harassed and intimidated clinic patients and staff. The injunction forbids specific harassing conduct and banishes the enjoined parties' "picketing, demonstrating [and] counseling" activity to the sidewalk opposite the clinic on the other side of Broadway.

Uncontradicted evidence adduced at a bench trial showed that on June 10, 1994, appellants White and Schwab, among others, picketed the clinic from the sidewalk that borders the parking lot. The clinic director, Lynde Ann Rouche, tried to hand them copies of the injunction, but they refused to take them, insisting that "it didn't apply to them." Rouche spoke to White, who, she knew from photographs, had an "important role with Operation Rescue of California." White told her the protesters were there to "test the injunction" by "getting arrested." Eventually, White and Schwab "chose to be arrested." After they were cited and released, everyone left. Norman Reece, an enjoined party who pickets the Vallejo clinic "between one [and] five times a week," observed the demonstration from his van, which was parked across the street.

On July 11, 1994, appellants again picketed Planned Parenthood on the clinic side of Broadway. Again, Rouche tried to hand them copies of the injunction, and, again, they insisted it did not apply to them. Again, Reece drove up in his van, but when he slowed down, appellant Ross waved him away. Rouche testified, "Mr. Ross was frantically motioning [Reece] to continue on, indicating * * * 'Go away.' " When Ross gestured, Reece drove away. Eventually, the Vallejo police arrested the protesters who refused to cross Broadway in accordance with the injunction.

Kathleen Nolan, the executive associate for Planned Parenthood, testified that the clinic had a written policy, devised with legal counsel, outlining, among other things, the scope of the injunction. According to Nolan, "It stated that anybody who was doing the same things that those specific people had been enjoined against were acting in concert with those people." In other words, she said, "the injunction covered anybody committing the same acts as the specific [enjoined] people made." Rouche testified that she had the same understanding, and that she had served the injunction on pro-choice demonstrators as well as on appellants.

After the prosecution rested, appellants made a motion for acquittal, which the court denied. Appellants' testimony was all to the same effect: they were not members of Solano Citizens for Life, and did not know any of the enjoined parties. Most had traveled from other parts of California with a pro-life caravan of sorts, Operation Rescue's "Summer of Missions," a four-week camping trip and anti-abortion campaign with planned stops throughout the state. They had stopped in Vallejo expressly to test the limits of the injunction, which the California Supreme Court had recently upheld for the first time. A flyer distributed by Operation Rescue of California, advertising the Summer of Missions, mentioned the Vallejo injunction specifically.

The text of the flyer reads as follows: "Summer of Missions activities to ignore injunctions that violate first amendment rights. Vallejo ruling won't affect planned activities. This summer pro-life activists plan to travel up and down the California Coast in a national event called the Summer of Missions. The Summer of Missions is a four week combined vacation and pro-life event. This summer vacation is sponsored by Operation Rescue National, Operation Rescue of California, California Missionaries to the Pre-born, and Youth for America National. Injunctions that violate first amendment rights to free speech and freedom of assembly will simply be ignored. No one will *unknowingly* violate any injunction or law (the Freedom of Access to Clinic Entrances law). Everyone who does, will understand that they are violating an injunction or law.

Planned events include No Place To Hide Campaigns (protesting at doctors' homes and offices), protests, prayer vigils, and other forms of protest protected by the First Amendment."

When he took the stand, Ross explained why he had motioned for Reece to leave: "[White] mentioned to me that there was another pro-lifer across the street that was named in the injunction and he, [White], * * * asked me to wave him off." Ross denied knowing Reece, but he conceded that it was probably White's intention to minimize contact with any enjoined party because "if that person was named on the injunction, it wouldn't look good for us to have that person there."

The prosecutor made her closing argument, incorporating the statements she had made against appellants' motion for acquittal: "[A] group of anti-abortion protesters doing the very things that are enjoined in the permanent injunction with knowledge of the injunction are in a sense standing in the shoes of the named litigants." "[Appellants say they are acting independently.] That's playing games; that is the shell game. That is just semantics. It's clearly an intentional ploy to challenge the order and that's exactly what they did and that's why we're here."

The trial judge found the appellants guilty, presumably on the legal theory he articulated before he denied their motion for acquittal: "First of all, I don't think the concept of acting 'in concert' is so narrowly interpreted that it would allow a group to escape the restrictions of an injunction or injunctive order by the expediency of simply saying they belong to an organization with a different name, despite the fact that they share a mutuality of purpose and that they are participating in the same prohibit[ed] activity."

1.   The Injunction's Scope: Appellants argue that acting "in concert" with enjoined parties requires more than simply knowing of the injunction and acting in ways the parties are enjoined from acting. We agree. * * *

Injunctions are not effective against the world at large. (Regal Knitwear Co. v. N.L.R.B. (1945) 324 U.S. 9, 13 (*Regal Knitwear*); and see *Williams I,* ["[a] restriction that enjoined all picketers in addition to petitioners would clearly have been overbroad"].) * * * [I]njunctions are fashioned and enforced without the safeguards that attend the passage and govern the enforcement of more general prohibitions. "Injunctions * * * carry greater risks of censorship and discriminatory application than do general ordinances. '[T]here is no more effective practical guaranty against arbitrary and unreasonable government than to require that the principles of law which officials would impose upon a minority must be imposed generally.' " Madsen v. Women's Health Center, Inc. (1994) 512 U.S. 753.

On the other hand, as the trial court recognized, enjoined parties may not play jurisdictional "shell games." They may not nullify an injunctive decree by carrying out prohibited acts with or through nonparties to the original proceeding. (*Regal Knitwear*) * * * Any such nonparty who knowingly violates the terms of an injunction is subject to the contempt powers of the court.

It is clear from this language that, in addition to knowledge of the injunction, some actual relationship with an enjoined party is required to bring a nonparty actor within the injunction's scope. An enjoined party, in other words, has to be demonstrably implicated in the nonparty's activity. Mere "mutuality of purpose" is not enough. Here, it must be appellants' actual relationship to an enjoined party, and not their convictions about abortion, that make them contemners. In sum, we conclude that a nonparty to an injunction is subject to the contempt power of the court when, with knowledge of the injunction, the nonparty violates its terms *with or for* those who are restrained.

Here, the prosecutor argued, and the trial court appeared to accept, that knowing of the injunction and doing what it forbade, without more, placed appellants "in concert" with the enjoined parties and, therefore, in contempt of the injunction. As we have explained, while knowledge is required, it is not alone enough to make a contemnor of an independent actor. We must determine, therefore, whether the evidence linking the enjoined parties to the appellants was sufficient to prove that appellants acted with or for them.

2. Sufficiency of the Evidence: "The test on appeal is whether substantial evidence supports the conclusion of the trier of fact, not whether the evidence proves guilt beyond a reasonable doubt." (People v. Reilly (1970) 3 Cal.3d 421, 425.) "[T]his inquiry does not require a court to 'ask itself whether *it* believes that the evidence at the trial established guilt beyond a reasonable doubt.' Instead the relevant question is whether, after viewing the evidence in the light most favorable to the prosecution, *any* rational trier of fact could have found the essential elements of the crime beyond a reasonable doubt." (Jackson v. Virginia (1979) 443 U.S. 307, 318–319.) Still, "we must resolve the issue in the light of the *whole record* * * * and may not limit our appraisal to isolated bits of evidence selected by the respondent." (People v. Johnson (1980) 26 Cal.3d 557, 577.)

Here, the evidence showed that appellants knew the provisions of the injunction, and had come to Vallejo specifically to do what the enjoined parties could not. It did not show, however, appellants' membership in, or affiliation with, any enjoined organization or person; it did not show a connection between Operation Rescue, or any of the groups that sponsored appellants' journey to Vallejo, and any enjoined organization or person; and it did not show that appellants were playing the "shell games" with which the court was properly concerned. Instead, it showed a single interaction between appellants and an enjoined party, Ross's motioning to Reece to leave the vicinity of the demonstration. This, we conclude, is too insubstantial, in the light of the whole record, to support the conclusion that appellants acted "in concert" with Reece. We, therefore, reverse appellants' convictions.

Notes

1. When may a person who is not served with process and who did not participate in the lawsuit be held in contempt? Holding a nonparty in contempt of an order issued in a lawsuit presents a serious due process issue. Thus a non-party, acting independently of defendant, is free to ignore an injunction. Independent Federation of Flight Attendants v. Cooper, 134 F.3d 917 (8th Cir.1998).

Judge Learned Hand stated the underlying proposition forcefully: "[N]o court can make a decree which will bind anyone but a party; a court of equity is as much limited as a court of law; it cannot lawfully enjoin the world at large, no matter how broadly it words its decree. If it assumes to do so, the decree is pro tanto brutum fulmen, and the persons enjoined are free to ignore it." Alemite Manufacturing Corp. v. Staff, 42 F.2d 832, 832 (2d Cir.1930).

The practical lesson for an injunction plaintiff to learn from Judge Learned Hand is to sue people because entities often disappear after being enjoined. That not every plaintiff has learned the judge's lesson is evident from Saga International, Inc. v. John D. Brush & Co. In almost a duplicate of *Alemite*, a consent injunction enjoined the corporation and "officers." The corporation's sometime president, now flying a different flag, when charged with violating the injunction, successfully argued that "an officer is bound by an injunction against his corporation *only in his capacity as an officer*." Saga International, Inc. v. John D. Brush & Co., Inc., 984 F.Supp. 1283, 1286 (C.D.Cal.1997).

3. *Active Concert.* Concepts of agency and membership in an organization may not help an abortion-clinic plaintiff deal with demonstrators who are united by opposition to the plaintiff but little else.

The plaintiff cannot evade this issue by drafting an injunction which names large groups of nonparties, like "all persons who are residents of Colquitt County, Georgia." Harrington v. Colquitt County Board of Education, 449 F.2d 161, 161 (5th Cir.1971). Or by charging the defendant as the "John Doe" or "unknown party" described in the decree. State v. Gross, 117 N.H. 853, 379 A.2d 804 (1977). Three examples follow.

(a) *Campus Protest.* An injunction prohibited students "and all other persons" from acting within or adjacent to plaintiff's buildings in "such unlawful manner as to disrupt or interfere with plaintiff's lawful and normal operations." Faculty members, not parties, but sympathetic with the students, entered the President's office and refused to leave. The court ruled that the faculty members had acted independently of, and not in concert with, the students who had obeyed the injunction. Evidence that the faculty members agreed with the general purpose of the strike was not sufficient to establish that their conduct was in concert with named defendants. State University v. Denton, 35 A.D.2d 176, 316 N.Y.S.2d 297, 299 (1970).

(b) *School Desegregation.* The trial court dealt with racial unrest in paired high schools by an injunction providing that "no person shall enter" the school premises other than teachers and students. In violation of that order, Hall, a nonparty, went on the school grounds where he was arrested. Hall was subsequently convicted of contempt. In rejecting the argument that Hall was a nonparty who acted in pursuance of his independent interests, the court ruled that Hall had "imperiled the court's fundamental power to make a binding adjudication between the parties properly before it." The judge had inherent power to punish Hall for contempt in order to protect the court's ability to render judgment. United States v. Hall, 472

F.2d 261, 265 (5th Cir.1972). The decision is criticized in Doug Rendleman, Beyond Contempt: Obligors to Injunctions, 53 Tex.L.Rev. 873, 916–24 (1975).

(c) *Another Abortion Clinic Protest.* An injunction that regulated anti-abortion protest at a Planned Parenthood clinic in Ohio ran against a defendant class of "all persons picketing" that location. The court found several contemnors in active concert with named defendants. While declining to disapprove the defendant class, the court noted "it is difficult to see, as a practical matter, how the decision to certify a defendant class added to the reach of the trial court's powers under Civ.R. 65(D)." Planned Parenthood Association of Cincinnati, Inc. v. Project Jericho, 52 Ohio St.3d 56, 66 n.9, 556 N.E.2d 157, 168 n.9., reh'g denied, 53 Ohio St.3d 706, 558 N.E.2d 61 (1990).

The Ohio court did not consider the possibility that pro-abortion protestors in dissonance instead of in concert with named defendants might act contrary to the injunction.

(d) *Back to the San Jose Street Gang Injunction.* What advice would you give to a person who was a "friend" of a named defendant but neither a gang member nor a named defendant?

4. *Questions About People v. Conrad.* Federal Rule 65(d) defines the obligor group as other persons in "active concert or participation" with "actual notice" of the injunction. In addition, someone who is prosecuted for violating a federal injunction is usually charged with criminal contempt instead of with violating a criminal statute like California's. Having said that, despite the differences in the language and the charge, a court's analysis would be about the same under either the federal or the California court of appeal's approach in People v. Conrad.

(a) If there had been no injunction, the First Amendment would protect abortion-clinic protesters' peaceful and orderly picketing on a public sidewalk. The injunction, in effect, extends the property owner's right to exclude a trespasser into the public sidewalk in front of the clinic. The intensity of abortion-clinic protest requires an extraordinary injunction.

(b) The Operation Rescue protestors' conduct is on the fault line between protected and punishable. The result turns on the meaning of "in concert." Was the *Conrad* court's interpretation of "in concert" informed by the policies of due process and separation of powers?

"The issue of who was acting 'in concert' with the named defendants was a matter to be taken up in individual cases, and not to be decided on the basis of protestors' viewpoints." Justice Souter concurring in Madsen v. Women's Health Center, 512 U.S. 753, 776–77 (1994).

(c) Was Planned Parenthood's lawyer's advice to the clinic staff about how to administer the injunction merely based on an inaccurate prediction?

(d) The *Conrad* court is careful to distinguish an injunction from a statute. The Colorado legislature passed a criminal statute establishing a 100–foot zone around an abortion clinic; inside of that zone, an eight-foot buffer zone protects a person from a protestor's unwanted speech. The United States Supreme Court held that the statute did not violate potential protestors' First Amendment rights. Hill v. Colorado, 530 U.S. 703 (2000).

5. *Misconduct Outside the Injunction Court's Jurisdiction.* "Nonparties who reside outside the territorial jurisdiction of a district court may be subject to that court's jurisdiction if, with actual notice of the court's order, they actively aid and abet a party in violating that order. This is so despite the absence of other contacts

with the forum." Waffenschmidt v. MacKay, 763 F.2d 711, 714, rehearing denied, 770 F.2d 1081 (5th Cir.1985), cert. denied, 474 U.S. 1056 (1986).

E. THE ENFORCEMENT OF CONSTITUTIONAL AND PUBLIC LAW THROUGH STRUCTURAL INJUNCTIONS

Although this book focuses on courts' remedial solutions in civil lawsuits between private parties, the vast body of law dealing with injunctions to enforce plaintiffs' constitutional and public rights is important enough to summarize. In addition, we will use structural injunctions to summarize modifying and dissolving an injunction and to provide a transition to Injunction Reform.

Beginning, in particular, with school desegregation in the 1950s, federal, and some state, judges have granted injunctions to protect plaintiffs' constitutional rights. Doug Rendleman, Brown II's "All Deliberate Speed" at Fifty: Golden Anniversary or Mid–Life Crisis for the Constitutional Injunction as a School Desegregation Remedy?, 41 San Diego L.Rev. 1575 (2004).

Indeed, a damage verdict for the victims of officially sanctioned school segregation has not even been seriously suggested. Almost without discussion, the injunction became the plaintiffs' remedy of choice to protect their constitutional rights. Elrod v. Burns, 427 U.S. 347, 373 (1976); Doug Rendleman, Irreparability Resurrected?: Does A Recalibrated Irreparable Injury Rule Threaten the Warren Court's Establishment Clause Legacy, 59 Wash. & Lee L.Rev. 1343, 1380–88 (2002).

The courts expanded structural injunctions to states' residential institutions, particularly to jails and prisons. Judges discovered that prisoners possess important constitutional rights that could be protected from infringement by injunctions. As a result, at one time, jails and prisons in about forty states operated under judges' watchful eyes. Judicial regulation has been expanded so that in addition to schools, jails and prisons, it now includes mental health institutions and even police departments.

Because the judicially mandated orders protect plaintiffs' constitutional rights by "restructuring" governmental bureaucracies, they were named "structural injunctions" by Professor Owen Fiss. The judge grants a structural injunction both to prohibit specific acts and, more importantly, to direct and manage the entire administrative operation of the affected institution.

A structural injunction uniquely strains the legal process. The rules of procedure were designed for two-party litigation aimed at resolving defined issues about past events. Structural litigation, usually a plaintiff class action, is unfocused, amorphous, and oriented toward the future. Precisely how to draft an order to effectuate plaintiffs' constitutional rights will vary from judge to judge. Precedent may not be of much assistance. Further complications result from the protracted nature of structural litigation. Decades may pass, since fundamental change takes time. Vast administrative details are to be managed, necessitating masters and monitors.

Finally structural litigation raises two kinds of questions about the legitimacy of judicial supervision, separation of powers and federalism. Underlying the question of legitimacy is the issue of whether the federal judges in their eagerness to secure a more just society have usurped legislative, executive and state functions. Given federalism's parameters, should a federal judge tell state and local officials how to run their institution? Arguing "No" is Professor John Choon Yoo in Who Measures the Chancellor's Foot? The Inherent Remedial Authority of the Federal Courts, 84 Cal.L.Rev. 1121 (1996). If remedy is defined as what a court does on behalf of winning plaintiffs, Professor Yoo would put the court's remedial enterprise out of business. The federal courts' remedial exercises have, he asserts, arrogated states' executive and legislative power; after finding that the defendants violated the federal constitution, the judge, he maintains, ought to withdraw from the field, leaving the plaintiffs' remedy to the other branches.

Even someone who accepts the structural injunction as a legitimate exercise of judicial authority agrees that drafting and administering one may raise separation of powers and federalism problems. Change is expensive. Can a judge insist on increasing expenditures to maintain public institutions? "[A] court order directing a local government body to levy its own taxes is plainly a judicial act within the power of a federal court," said the Supreme Court in Missouri v. Jenkins, 495 U.S. 33, 55 (1990).

The Chancery Court had appointed masters, sometimes called commissioners in chancery, to make equitable decrees effective; masters continue in modern practice, now governed by rule or statute. See Fed.R.Civ.P. 53. A master may be particularly useful in administering a structural injunction. In the structural litigation over the Texas prison system, the document defining the master's power covers more than five pages of the report. See Ruiz v. Estelle, 679 F.2d 1115, 1168–1172 (5th Cir.1982). A master comes at a price; for unlike the judge, who is supported by the taxpayers, the parties themselves compensate the master. See New York State Association for Retarded Children v. Carey, 631 F.2d 162 (2d Cir.1980).

The dynamic of taxpayer reluctance, bureaucratic inertia, negotiated consent decrees, and reliance on masters and ancillary personnel leads to detailed structural injunctions. Justice Scalia's opinion in Lewis v. Casey, 518 U.S. 343, 349, 362 (1996), revealed a critical attitude. An Arizona federal judge had implemented prison inmates' "right of access to the courts" by requiring a more adequate law library. Concerned to protect illiterate inmates and others who did not speak English, the judge entered a 25–page injunction that specified library hours, check-out procedure, librarians' qualifications, inmates' access to stacks, a video-taped course in legal research, the permissible noise level, and legal assistants including bilingual legal assistants.

Justice Scalia stated, among other reasons to reverse, an "inordinately—indeed, wildly—intrusive" system-wide injunction. His decision also addressed separation of powers and federalism issues; the opinion's observations about separation of powers were part of its discussion of "standing" and system-wide relief. "It is for the courts to remedy past or imminent official interference with individual inmates' presentation of claims to the courts; it is for the political branches of the State and Federal Governments to manage prisons in such fashion that official interference with [inmates] presentation of claims [to courts] will not occur." Turning to the role of the parties in shaping the trial court's order, the process of shaping the order, the decision says, "failed to give adequate consideration to the views of the state prison authorities." The opinion may change the balance between, on the one hand, stressing the importance of vindicating the plaintiffs' constitutional rights with a structural injunction and, on the other, an increased emphasis on separation of powers and federalism that militates against active judicial solutions.

How can a judge enforce a structural order? A good place to begin thinking about administration of a structural injunction is Dixon v. Barry, 967 F.Supp. 535 (D.D.C.1997). When plaintiffs filed their class action in 1974, the District of Columbia's mental health system was mostly based at a residential institution, St. Elizabeth's Hospital. Plaintiffs, a class of eight to ten thousand mentally ill members with illnesses not severe enough to require hospital treatment, prevailed in 1975 and established their substantive right under statute to "community-based treatment in the least restrictive means."

This left only the appropriate remedy. For a score of years the parties negotiated successive consent decrees and submitted plans and reports as well as numerous targets. Expert technical assistants and special masters were appointed.

Following an April 1997 hearing, Judge Aubrey E. Robinson, Jr., still presiding, but by now a Senior District Judge, upheld the plaintiffs' contention that the "District has fallen woefully short of its obligations." Far from improving plaintiffs' lot under the aegis of the court orders, in general "very little has changed" and conditions of homeless class members had deteriorated. "[T]he court finds that the repeated failure of the District to comply with the court's orders eliminates any basis for judicial restraint when remedying noncompliance. Several courts have noted that when the local authority repeatedly fails to comply with the court's orders, there is no basis for judicial respect or restraint when the facts justify a receiver."

Fresh out of patience, Judge Robinson did just that. A receiver was established to "oversee, supervise, and direct all financial, contractual legal, and administrative, and personnel functions of the [Commission on Mental Health Services] and to restructure the CMHS into an organization that is oriented toward" providing "all class members with timely and accessible care and shall serve class members in the least restrictive setting commensurate with their individual needs." Having lost most of their power to an appointed judge, the elected executive and legislative authorities were reduced to paying the judge's appointed receiver.

In 2002, after changes in way the District of Columbia was governed, the D.C. government finally regained full control of its mental health facilities.

Contempt in Administering a Structural Injunction. The courts' experience with structural contempt is mixed, at best. Defendants' bureaucratic inertia, pleas for more time, and cries of poverty are more common responses to a structural injunction than their outright defiance. Defendants resort to the defense of inability to comply. State and local government officials, ostensibly conscientious professionals, and civil servants who "just work here" are poor candidates to be incarcerated for contempt. Stiff measures tend to undermine long-term relationships anyway. Even a judge's patience may wear thin, however, and reveal weariness and frustration.

After the city department of corrections failed to comply with an order regulating the housing of inmates, the judge imposed a sanction: a "fine" to be paid to each individual confined in a non-housing area. Benjamin v. Sielaff, 752 F.Supp. 140 (S.D.N.Y.1990).

Judge Robinson's experience with contempt in Dixon v. Barry was that "use of the Court's contempt power has resulted only in action by the District sufficient to end the threat of contempt, and has not resulted in advancing the District closer to compliance."

The Supreme Court contributed to structural contempt in Spallone v. United States, 493 U.S. 265, 280 (1990). To combat discrimination in public housing, a federal judge, out of patience, imposed coercive fines on individual defendants who were city council members. Under the doctrine of using the least possible contempt power to achieve obedience, the Supreme Court said that the judge "should have proceeded with such contempt sanctions first against the city alone in order to secure compliance."

Modifying or Dissolving an Injunction: Where Does It All End? An injunction is a continuous remedy effective against anyone obligated to obey it, as Tattilo learned in Playboy Enterprises v. Chuckleberry Publishing, p. 328. That injunction circumscribed defendant's conduct tomorrow, the day after, and 15 years later. Implicit in an injunction is the judge's prediction that its prohibitions will continue to be necessary. Predictions of the future, even a judge's, are notoriously enigmatic.

Just as it protects an incorrect injunction in contempt, the collateral bar rule insulates an obsolete one. A defendant's request to interpret, to modify, or to dissolve an injunction is a safer course of action than conduct that may be contemptuous.

Suppose the defendant wonders what exactly the injunction means. A "person subject to an injunction always has the right to ask the court that is administering it whether it applies to conduct in which the person proposes to engage. If this looks like a request for an 'advisory opinion,' it is one that even a federal court can grant, in order to prevent unwitting contempts." Matter of Hendrix, 986 F.2d 195, 200 (7th Cir.1993). In retrospect, this is advice that Tattilo might have heeded before it launched its wares into cyberspace.

Suppose things change? If the defendant is required to continue to obey it after the law or the facts change, an injunction will burden the defendant, treat it inconsistently with others similarly or identically situated, and embarrass the court. The finality, preclusion, and res judicata principles that militate against reopening a final judgment for money damages are less pronounced for an injunction. In recent years, courts administering injunctions have focused less on finality and more on pragmatic and flexible adjustments to legal and factual change. Rufo v. Inmates of the Suffolk County Jail, 502 U.S. 367 (1992); Freeman v. Pitts, 503 U.S. 467 (1992); Board of Education v. Dowell, 498 U.S. 237 (1991).

When should a judge change or vacate an injunction? Under the procedural rule, the judge may grant relief from an injunction when its prospective application is "no longer equitable." Fed.R.Civ.P. 60(b)(5). What exactly does that mean?

In evaluating defendant's requests to modify or vacate an injunction, the judge must examine the defendant's original violation and the injunction. Then the judge will determine (a) whether either the legal or the factual circumstances have changed significantly; and (b) whether the proposed modification or dissolution is appropriate to address the change. The test to determine whether a judge should terminate a structural school-desegregation injunction has two elements: (a) whether the defendant is complying in good faith with the constitution and injunction; and (b) whether vestiges of defendants' violations like segregation have been eliminated "to the extent practicable." Board of Education v. Dowell, 498 U.S. 237, 248 (1991). See also, Rufo v. Inmates of the Suffolk County Jail, 502 U.S. 367 (1992).

A judge grants an injunction to protect plaintiff's constitutional, statutory, or common-law rights. Changes occur over time. An amended statute, for example, may entitle the defendant to be free from an injunction. If the legislature amends a statute to authorize conduct that was formerly forbidden, the judge should modify or dissolve an injunction that was based on the superseded law. Protectoseal Co. v. Barancik, 23 F.3d 1184 (7th Cir.1994).

A judicial decision may also change the law. After a mother and grandparents entered into a stipulated order in 2001 allowing grandparent visitation, in 2003 the court held in another case that the state grandparent–visitation statute violated due process. The mother moved to vacate the visitation order. The Iowa supreme court held that the earlier decision was a change of legal circumstances that justified the judge in vacating the visitation order. Spiker v. Spiker, 708 N.W.2d 347 (Iowa 2006). However, the Arkansas court had held that a parent who had failed to appeal a grandparent-visitation order was barred by res judicata from upsetting the order even though a recent decision had invalidated the statute the order was based on. Hunt v. Perry, 355 Ark. 303, 138 S.W.3d 656 (2003), cert. denied, 541 U.S. 1074 (2004). Which decision is correct? Under the principle of similar treatment for those similarly situated, should the court hold that one person is bound by an obsolete doctrine while others live by the current law?

If the facts change, the judge may ask whether the present state of facts would warrant granting the original injunction; if not, the judge should modify or dissolve the decree. In re Detroit Auto Dealers Association, Inc., 84 F.3d 787, 790 (6th Cir.1996). If a business's trademark becomes a "generic" part of the language, like cellophane, aspirin or cola, then the judge ought to dissolve an injunction based on the former trademark status.

Official defendants seek to be liberated from a structural injunction that they consider burdensome, expensive, and intrusive. A structural injunction is perforce provisional since the judge's ongoing supervision is integral to its administration. During the administrative phase of institutional reform litigation, the judge and the parties continue to shape the injunction to remove whatever conditions threatened or continue to threaten constitutional values. Termination and modification standards have departed from pure remedy and become somewhat of a branch of the complex legal and factual law of school desegregation and prison reform litigation.

Federalism policies have been brought to bear on dissolving a structural injunction. "Our nation's concept of federalism" one court observed, "does not contemplate a perpetual role of a federal court as overseer of state functions." Lynch v. Sessions, 942 F.Supp. 1419, 1427 (M.D.Ala.1996).

Many structural injunctions emerged from a crucible of negotiation conducted under the shadow of what the parties expected from the judge. A consent judgment-decree with an injunction has a contractual quality; traditionally a court would modify a consent decree only after "a clear showing of grievous wrong evoked by new and unforeseen circumstances." United States v. Swift & Co., 286 U.S. 106, 119 (1932). For a structural consent injunction at least, no "grievous wrong" is required; the standard to modify or vacate is the flexible standard summarized above. Rufo v. Inmates of the Suffolk County Jail, 502 U.S. 367, 368 (1992).

What does the future hold? The Supreme Court's approach to drafting and administering a structural injunction will continue to shape the doctrine for modifying and dissolving all injunctions. As suggested above, the hostility to structural injunctions in Justice Scalia's opinion in Lewis v. Casey, 518 U.S. 343 (1996), might signal to a trial judge a new balance between using a structural injunction to vindicate plaintiffs' constitutional rights and emphasizing separation of powers—federalism. If so, a judge may release defendants under either the *Dowell-Rufo* standard, above, or a new standard. For some legislative developments, read on.

F. INJUNCTION REFORM

The Equity–Injunctions Chapter closes with the injunction equivalent to the subject of "Tort Reform" which ended the Damages Chapter.

Our society's most controversial legal issues become the subjects of judges' injunctions. During the last 100 years, striking workers, demonstrating civil rights advocates, and protestors at abortion clinics have regularly litigated contested issues of injunctions and contempt. Since Brown v. Board of Education and school desegregation, particularly since the rise of the structural injunction in state prison and hospital facilities, federal judges' injunctions affecting state and local government defendants have also been controversial.

The strong medicine of an injunction wielded by an activist judge circumscribes their freedom in ways defendants deem unnecessarily intrusive. Injunction defendants have both followed and led tort defendants into legislatures to seek and sometimes to secure statutory redress for their litigation grievances. Two examples of injunction reform legislation follow: limitations on strike injunctions and injunctions which affect unconstitutional prison conditions, with an interlude between them.

(a) *The Strike Injunction.* In re Debs, 158 U.S. 564 (1895), which the California Supreme Court in People ex rel. Gallo v. Acuna, above p. 248, cites and relies on, began an era of federal judges' injunctions against strikes. Critics thought strike injunctions disturbed delicate state-federal and judicial-legislative-executive balances in addition to interfering abusively with the power alignment between labor and management. Cries of opposition began immediately after the Court's *Debs* decision with the Government By Injunction article which is cited after Gallo v. Acuna. The Democratic Party's national platform called for banning the federal strike injunction. Felix Frankfurter and Nathan Greene's *The Labor Injunction* in 1930 was a detailed study documenting the authors' view that United States judges misused strike injunctions to thwart organized labor.

Congress dealt with the federal strike injunction in 1932 with the Norris–LaGuardia Act. Its principal section provides that, "No court of the United States shall have jurisdiction to issue any restraining order or temporary or permanent injunction in any case involving or growing out of any labor dispute." 29 U.S.C. § 104. State legislatures passed similar statutes stripping their courts of jurisdiction.

The Norris–LaGuardia Act, the National Labor Relations Act, and the change in the political-legal climate attenuated federal judges' injunctions against strikes. The Supreme Court declined to hold that the Norris–LaGuardia Act was unconstitutional. "There can be no question of the power of Congress to define and limit the jurisdiction of the inferior courts of the United States." Lauf v. E.G. Shinner & Co., 303 U.S. 323, 330 (1938).

(b) *Interlude.* Legislator-critics of the Supreme Court's school prayer, abortion, and busing decisions have introduced numerous Injunction Reform bills; this proposed legislation is often called "jurisdiction-stripping" or "court-stripping." Proponents base the bills on Article III section 1 and section 5 of the Fourteenth Amendment; they maintain that the proposed legislation merely circumscribes the lower federal courts' remedial power and does not limit either jurisdiction or the Supreme Court's power.

There are two types of proposed legislation: One would eliminate federal jurisdiction over the controversial subject. The other would eliminate or circumscribe a federal court's ability to order a particular type of injunction, for example a busing decree to remedy school segregation.

Congress possesses "plenary control over the jurisdiction of the federal courts." Brotherhood of R. R. Trainmen v. Toledo P. & W. R.R., 321 U.S. 50, 63–64 (1944). Even so, there are arguments against reformers' proposals to deny an injunction to a plaintiffs who seeks to enforce individual and civil rights. A powerful attack on the suggested legislation was Professor Lawrence Sager's, Foreword: Constitutional Limitations on Congress' Authority to Regulate the Jurisdiction of the Federal Courts, 95 Harv. L. Rev. 17 (1981).

Under the United States constitutional system, the federal court protects unpopular minorities, the rule of law, and the balance of power between the branches of government. The courts grant injunctions to advance all these goals. A legislature's power to limit a court's jurisdiction or available remedies may itself be subject to constitutional limitations. These arguments fall under the headings of separation of powers and equal protection. Congress, it may be argued, cannot exercise its admitted power to limit the federal court's jurisdiction in a way that destroys another constitutional right. Congress's power over federal courts' jurisdiction is limited by the general provisions elsewhere in the Constitution that limit legislative power.

In *Swann,* the Court reaffirmed the federal court's constitutional obligation "to eliminate from the public schools all vestiges of state-imposed segregation." Swann v. Charlotte–Mecklenburg Board of Education, 402 U.S. 1, 15 (1971). In *Green* the Court told federal judges to "take whatever steps might be necessary to convert [a segregated school system] to a unitary system." Green v. County School Board, 391 U.S. 430, 437–38 (1968). "[Q]uite apart from the guarantee of equal protection, if a law impinges upon a fundamental right explicitly or implicitly secured by the Constitution [it] is presumptively unconstitutional." Harris v. McRae, 448 U.S. 297, 312 (1980). If a plaintiff's constitutional rights have been violated and if legislation leaves the court with attenuated remedial authority to order satisfactory relief, then the legislation may be unconstitutional. Thus to single out one group of constitutional plaintiffs and to deny them access to federal jurisdiction or to a particular federal remedy may violate the Fourteenth Amendment's Equal Protection Clause.

c) *Unconstitutional Prison Conditions.* The last generation has hardly been a liberal epoch; in 1985, a knowledgeable observer might have predicted twilight for the structural injunction. However, the structural injunction became the traditional way of doing quite a bit of public business.

Politicians, reluctant to vote money for incarcerated convicts, nevertheless supported get-tough criminal law enforcement and longer criminal sentences. Inmates, formed into plaintiff classes, found their way into courtrooms. By others' default and because of their duty to protect plaintiffs' constitutional rights, the courts became overseers of jails and prisons. Prison and jail conditions, judges held, could be inhumane enough to constitute cruel and unusual punishment.

Many jurisdictions have been injunction defendants in jail and prison litigation for a quarter of a century. A tendency to micromanage has been apparent all along in structural litigation, and excesses were inevitable. Inmates litigate food, recreation, health care, and the temperature of water in showers. In 1996, the Supreme Court reversed a detailed prison library injunction. Quoted above was Lewis v. Casey, 518 U.S. 343 (1996). Judicial injunction reform?

In addition to outlays to raise conditions to minimum constitutional levels, structural litigation has cost state and local authorities money for attorney fees, theirs and the plaintiffs', for contempt fines for noncompliance, and for expenses for masters, monitors and other outside experts. Defendants' motions to dissolve and modify prison-conditions structural injunctions have been the vehicles for the Supreme Court to develop more "flexible" standards. Those decisions are summarized above.

The same arguments found their way into legislative halls. Chafing under judges' supervision, defendants and their political allies sought to dismantle extensive structural injunctions. The time has come, they maintained, to get the judges off our backs. Contrary to principles of separation of powers, judges have arrogated the political branches' functions. Federalism principles, they concluded, militate against federal judges' intrusions in state and local institutions.

The specter of Norris–LaGuardia, which had haunted structural injunctions, reappeared in 1996 when Congress passed and the President signed the Prison Litigation Reform Act, (PLRA). 18 U.S.C. § 3626.

The PLRA recognized the violations of inmates' constitutional rights which the prison injunctions seek to vindicate; unlike the Norris–LaGuardia Act it did not strip the federal court of jurisdiction.

The PLRA affects inmates' litigation about prison conditions, not litigation about "the fact or duration of confinement." Its goals are (a) to make it more difficult for inmates to challenge the conditions of their confinement; and (b) to curtail the relief that a federal judge can order. A summary of some of the provisions which circumscribe a court's injunctive powers follows.

A conditions injunction must be drawn narrowly, extending "no further than necessary to correct the violation." The order must be the least intrusive way to overcome the violation.

Only three-judge panels may enter "a prisoner release order." That court must make explicit findings: overcrowding created a constitutional violation; a previous, less-intrusive order, did not overcome the violation; and release is the only solution.

The breadth of a consent decree that parties can voluntarily enter is restricted. If administrators want, certain consent decrees may be eliminated immediately.

A federal judge must rule promptly on a defendant's motion to modify-dissolve a prison-conditions injunction; if the judge does not rule expeditiously, an injunction will be stayed according to a schedule.

A conditions injunction may be dissolved on defendants' motion after two years unless the plaintiffs prove that defendants' violations continue to exist. An injunction expires after two years unless the record supports and the judge finds that the relief is necessary to correct a violation and that the injunction "is narrowly drawn and the least intrusive means to correct the violation."

Special masters are limited in several ways. The federal judiciary will pay special masters; the defendants will not pay these charges.

Congress has power to enact statutes that govern procedure. In Miller v. French, the Supreme Court upheld the PLRA provision that automatically stayed a prison-conditions injunction unless the judge ruled within the 30 days after the defendant's motion to terminate it. The prohibition against legislation that reopens a final court judgment does not, the Court held, apply to a prospective prison-conditions injunction. Miller v. French, 530 U.S. 327 (2000).

Although Miller v. French appears to have stanched litigation about whether the PLRA violates separation of powers, prison-conditions litigation continues in the shadow of the injunction-reform legislation. See, Hadix v. Caruso, 2005 WL 2671289 (W.D.Mich. 2005), the 87th reported decision about this particular prison-conditions injunction. The 88th is the judge's refusal to reconsider the 87th.

Injunction Reform: The Next Wave. Frew ex rel. Frew v. Hawkins, below, has the earmarks of contemporary structural injunction litigation. A plaintiff class of more than one million people sued state officials to implement their rights under a federal statute. The district judge certified the class action. There was no finding that the state had violated the statute. The plaintiffs and the defendants negotiated and entered into a detailed consent decree.

When the plaintiffs complained that the state was out of compliance with the consent decree, the state sought relief from their duties under the decree by invoking a doctrine that had not been argued in a structural injunction or consent decree—sovereign immunity exists under the Eleventh Amendment because the State is complying with the federal statute.

The decision finds its way into our Injunction Reform material because it may be judicial injunction reform and because it spurred Senator Lamar Alexander to introduce the Injunction Reform bill that follows it.

FREW EX REL. FREW v. HAWKINS

Supreme Court of the United States, 2004.
540 U.S. 431.

KENNEDY, J. * * * In this case we consider whether the Eleventh Amendment bars enforcement of a federal consent decree entered into by state officials.

Medicaid is a cooperative federal-state program that provides federal funding for state medical services to the poor. [citation] State participation is oluntary; but once a State elects to join the program, it must administer a state plan that meets federal requirements. One requirement is that every participating State must have an Early and Periodic Screening, Diagnosis, and Treatment (EPSDT) program. [citation] EPSDT programs provide health care services to children to reduce lifelong vulnerability to illness or disease. The EPSDT provisions of the Medicaid statute require participating States to provide various medical services to eligible children, and to provide notice of the services.

The [plaintiffs] here are mothers of children eligible for EPSDT services in Texas. In 1993 they filed a civil action pursuant to 42 U.S.C. § 1983, seeking injunctive relief against * * * various officials at [state] agencies charged with implementing the Texas EPSDT program. The named officials included the Commissioners of the two agencies, the Texas State Medicaid Director, and certain employees at the Texas Department of Health. The individuals were sued in their official capacities and were represented throughout the litigation by the office of the Texas attorney general.

The [plaintiffs] alleged that the Texas program did not satisfy the requirements of federal law. They asserted that the Texas program did not ensure eligible children would receive health, dental, vision, and hearing screens; failed to meet annual participation goals; and gave eligible recipients inadequate notice of available services. The [plaintiffs] also claimed the program lacked proper case management and corrective procedures and did not provide uniform services throughout Texas. * * *

[T]he District Court certified a class consisting of children in Texas entitled to EPSDT services, a class of more than 1 million persons. Following extensive settlement negotiations, the [plaintiffs] and the state officials agreed to resolve the suit by entering into a consent decree. The District Court conducted a fairness hearing, approved the consent decree, and entered it in 1996.

Judicial enforcement of the 1996 consent decree is the subject of the present dispute. The decree is a detailed document about 80 pages long that orders a comprehensive plan for implementing the federal statute. In contrast with the brief and general mandate in the statute itself, the consent decree requires the state officials to implement many specific procedures. An example illustrates the nature of the difference. The EPSDT statute requires States to "provid[e] or arrang[e] for the provision of * * * screening services in all cases where they are requested," and also to arrange for "corrective treatment" in such cases. [citation] The consent decree implements the provision in part by directing the Texas Department of Health to staff and maintain toll-free telephone numbers for eligible recipients who seek assistance in scheduling and arranging appointments. According to the decree, the advisors at the toll-free numbers must furnish the name, address, and telephone numbers of one or more health care providers in the appropriate specialty in a convenient location, and they also must assist with transportation arrangements to and from appointments. The advisers must inform recipients enrolled in managed care health plans that they are free to choose a primary care physician upon enrollment.

Two years after the consent decree was entered, the [plaintiffs] filed a motion to enforce it in the District Court. The state officials, it was alleged, had not complied with the decree in various respects. The officials denied the allegations and maintained that the Eleventh Amendment rendered the decree unenforceable even if they were in noncompliance. After an evidentiary hearing, the District Court issued a detailed opinion concluding that certain provisions of the consent decree had been violated. The District Court rejected the [defendants'] Eleventh Amendment argument and directed the parties to submit proposals outlining possible remedies for the violations.

The state officials filed an interlocutory appeal, and the Court of Appeals for the Fifth Circuit reversed. The Court of Appeals held that the Eleventh Amendment prevented enforcement of the decree unless the violation of the consent decree was also a statutory violation of the Medicaid Act that imposed a clear and binding obligation on the State. The Court of Appeals assessed the violations identified by the District Court and concluded that none provided a valid basis for enforcement. Regardless of whether the EPSDT program complied with the detailed consent decree, the Court of Appeals reasoned, the program was good enough to comply with the general mandates of federal law. The Court of Appeals concluded that because the [plaintiffs] had not established a violation of federal law, the District Court lacked jurisdiction to remedy the consent decree violations. * * *

The [plaintiffs argue that] the consent decree can be enforced without violating the Eleventh Amendment. * * * [T]hey contend that enforcement is permitted under the principles of Ex parte Young, 209 U.S. 123 (1908). We agree that the decree is enforceable under Ex parte Young. * * *

This case involves the intersection of two areas of federal law: the reach of the Eleventh Amendment and the rules governing consent decrees. The Eleventh Amendment confirms the sovereign status of the States by shielding them from suits by individuals absent their consent. Seminole Tribe of Fla. v. Florida, 517 U.S. 44, 54 (1996). To ensure the enforcement of federal law, however, the Eleventh Amendment permits suits for prospective injunctive relief against state officials acting in violation of federal law. Ex parte Young. This standard allows courts to order prospective relief see Edelman v. Jordan, 415 U.S. 651 (1974); Milliken v. Bradley, 433 U.S. 267 (1977), as well as measures ancillary to appropriate prospective relief, Green v. Mansour, 474 U.S. 64, 71–73 (1985). Federal courts may not award retrospective relief, for instance money damages or its equivalent, if the State invokes its immunity. *Edelman.*

Consent decrees have elements of both contracts and judicial decrees. Firefighters v. Cleveland, 478 U.S. 501, 519 (1986). A consent decree "embodies an agreement of the parties" and is also "an agreement that the parties desire and expect will be reflected in, and be enforceable as, a judicial decree that is subject to the rules generally applicable to other judgments and decrees." Rufo v. Inmates of Suffolk County Jail. Consent decrees entered in federal court must be directed to protecting federal interests. In *Firefighters,* we observed that a federal consent decree must spring from, and serve to resolve, a dispute within the court's subject-matter jurisdiction; must come within the general scope of the case made by the pleadings; and must further the objectives of the law upon which the complaint was based.

This brings us to the intersection of the principles governing consent decrees and the Eleventh Amendment. As we understand their argument, the state officials do not contend that the terms of the decree were impermissible under Ex parte Young. Nor do they contend that the consent decree failed to comply with *Firefighters.* The officials challenge only the enforcement of the decree, not its entry. They argue that the Eleventh Amendment narrows the circumstances in which courts can enforce federal consent decrees involving state officials.

The theory advanced by the state officials is similar to the one accepted by the Court of Appeals. The officials reason that Ex parte Young creates a narrow exception to the general rule of Eleventh Amendment immunity from suit. Consent decrees involving state representatives threaten to broaden this exception, they contend, because decrees allow state officials to bind state governments to significantly more commitments than what federal law requires. Permitting the enforcement of a broad consent decree would give courts jurisdiction over not just federal law, but also everything else that officials agreed to when they entered into the consent decree. A State in full compliance with federal law could remain subject to federal court oversight through a course of judicial proceedings brought to enforce the consent decree. To avoid circumventing Eleventh Amendment protections, the officials argue, a federal court should not enforce a consent decree arising from an Ex parte Young suit unless the court first identifies, at the enforcement stage, a violation of federal law such as the EPSDT statute itself.

We disagree with this view of the Eleventh Amendment. The decree is a federal court order that springs from a federal dispute and furthers the objectives of federal law. See *Firefighters*. The decree states that it creates "a mandatory, enforceable obligation." In light of the State's assertion of its Eleventh Amendment immunity, the state officials lacked the authority to agree to remedies beyond the scope of Ex parte Young absent a waiver, as the [plaintiffs] concede. We can assume, moreover, that the state officials could not enter into a consent decree failing to satisfy the general requirements of consent decrees outlined in *Firefighters*. The [plaintiffs'] motion to enforce, however, sought enforcement of a remedy consistent with Ex parte Young and *Firefighters*, a remedy the state officials themselves had accepted when they asked the District Court to approve the decree. Enforcing the agreement does not violate the Eleventh Amendment. * * *

Here * * * the order to be enforced is a federal decree entered to implement a federal statute. The decree does implement the Medicaid statute in a highly detailed way, requiring the state officials to take some steps that the statute does not specifically require. The same could be said, however, of any effort to implement the general EPSDT statute in a particular way. The decree reflects a choice among various ways that a State could implement the Medicaid Act. As a result, enforcing the decree vindicates an agreement that the state officials reached to comply with federal law.

Hutto v. Finney, 437 U.S. 678 (1978), is instructive on this point. In *Finney,* the Court upheld a District Court's award of attorney's fees designed to encourage state compliance with an existing court order. State prisoners had sued state prison officials claiming that the conditions of their confinement violated the Eighth Amendment, and the District Court had ordered the officials to improve prison conditions. When the officials refused to comply in good faith with the order, the District Court awarded attorney's fees to the prisoners' lawyers to be paid from the state treasury. The state officials objected, arguing that the relief was not valid under the Eleventh Amendment because it exceeded the scope of *Ex parte Young.* The Court rejected this argument:

"In exercising their prospective powers under Ex parte Young and Edelman v. Jordan, federal courts are not reduced to issuing injunctions against state officers and hoping for compliance. Once issued, an injunction may be enforced * * *. If a state agency refuses to adhere to a court order, a financial penalty may be the most effective means of insuring compliance. The principles of federalism that inform Eleventh Amendment doctrine surely do not require federal courts to enforce their decrees only by sending high state officials to jail. The less intrusive power to impose a fine is properly treated as ancillary to the federal court's power to impose injunctive relief.''

The award of attorney's fees ''vindicated the District Court's authority over a recalcitrant litigant,'' the Court continued. ''We see no reason to distinguish this award from any other penalty imposed to enforce a prospective injunction.''

While *Finney* is somewhat different from the present case in that it involved the scope of remedies for violation of a prior order rather than the antecedent question whether remedies are permitted in the first instance, a similar principle applies. Federal courts are not reduced to approving consent decrees and hoping for compliance. Once entered, a consent decree may be enforced.

The state officials warn that enforcement of consent decrees can undermine the sovereign interests and accountability of state governments. The attorneys general of 19 States assert similar arguments as *amici curiae.* The concerns they express are legitimate ones. If not limited to reasonable and necessary implementations of federal law, remedies outlined in consent decrees involving state officeholders may improperly deprive future officials of their designated legislative and executive powers. They may also lead to federal court oversight of state programs for long periods of time even absent an ongoing violation of federal law.

When a federal court has entered a consent decree under Ex parte Young, the law's primary response to these concerns has its source not in the Eleventh Amendment but in the court's equitable powers and the direction given by the Federal Rules of Civil Procedure. In particular, Rule 60(b)(5) allows a party to move for relief if ''it is no longer equitable that the judgment should have prospective application.'' The Rule encompasses the traditional power of a court of equity to modify its decree in light of changed circumstances. In Rufo v. Inmates of Suffolk County Jail, the Court explored the application of the Rule to consent decrees involving institutional reform. The Court noted that district courts should apply a ''flexible standard'' to the modification of consent decrees when a significant change in facts or law warrants their amendment.

Rufo rejected the idea that the institutional concerns of government officials were ''only marginally relevant'' when officials moved to amend a consent decree, and noted that ''principles of federalism and simple common sense require the [district] court to give significant weight'' to the views of government officials. When a suit under Ex parte Young requires a detailed order to ensure compliance with a decree for prospective relief, and the decree in effect mandates the State, through its named officials, to administer a significant federal program, principles of federalism require that state officials with frontline responsibility for administering the program be given latitude and substantial discretion.

The federal court must exercise its equitable powers to ensure that when the objects of the decree have been attained, responsibility for discharging the State's obligations is returned promptly to the State and its officials. As public servants, the officials of the State must be presumed to have a high degree of competence in deciding how best to discharge their governmental responsibilities. A State, in the ordinary course, depends upon successor officials, both appointed and elected, to bring new insights and solutions to problems of allocating revenues and resources. The basic obligations of federal law may remain the same, but the precise manner of their discharge may not. If the State establishes reason to modify the decree, the court should make the necessary changes; where it has not done so, however, the decree should be enforced according to its terms.

The judgment of the Court of Appeals is reversed * * * .

Notes

1. *Who Won?* A deal's a deal? If plaintiffs sue a State official for violating a federal statute, may the official agree to a consent decree that requires more than the federal statute? How should a federal judge respond when asked to approve a class-action consent decree that is deeper or wider than the federal statute? Does judicial approval-entry of a class action consent decree differ from the judicial enforcement the plaintiffs sought in *Frew*?

2. *Local Control.* The Court encourages a federal trial judge to respect defendants, state and local officials. The pedigree for the Court's deference to defendants runs back to Brown v. Board of Education's remedial decision, *Brown II*. "Full implementation of these constitutional principles may require solution of varied local school problems. School authorities have the primary responsibility for elucidating, assessing, and solving these problems; courts will have to consider whether the action of school authorities constitutes good faith implementation of the governing constitutional principles." Brown v. Board of Education, 349 U.S. 294, 299 (1955).

Is the *Frew* Court too trusting? May the Court's emphasis on the defendants encourage a trial judge to leave the plaintiffs' federal constitutional or statutory rights inadequately protected? Is it more fitting for Congress to deal with this issue through legislation like the PLRA?

3. Senator Alexander proposed a Federal Consent Decree Fairness Act, S 11, 109th Congress, 1st Session. The Senate Judiciary Committee held hearings in July 2005. The following is a Discussion Draft from the fall of 2005 that incorporates modifications from the Senate hearings:

A BILL

To amend chapter 111 of title 28, United States Code, to limit the duration of Federal consent decrees to which State and local governments are a party, and for other purposes.

Be it enacted by the Senate and House of Representatives of the United States of America in Congress assembled.

SECTION 1. SHORT TITLE.

This Act may be cited as the "Federal Consent Decree Fairness Act."

SECTION 2. FINDINGS.

Congress finds that:

(1) Consent decrees are for remedying violations of requirements of Federal law, and they should not be used to advance any policy extraneous to that purpose.

(2) Consent decrees are also for protecting the party or class facing injury and should not be expanded to apply to parties not involved in the litigation.

(3) In structuring consent decrees, courts should take into account the interests of State and local governments in managing their own affairs.

(4) Consent decrees should be structured and administered to give due deference to the policy judgments of State and local officials and their successors as to how to obey the law.

(5) Whenever possible, courts should not impose consent decrees that require technically complex and evolving policy choices, especially in the absence of judicially discoverable and manageable standards.

(6) Consent decrees should not be unlimited, but should contain an explicit and realistic strategy for ending court supervision.

SECTION 3. LIMITATION ON CONSENT DECREES.

(a) In General.—Chapter 111 of title 28, United States Code, is amended by adding at the end of the following:

"Sec. 1660. Consent Decrees.

(a) Definitions.—In this section the term 'consent decree'—

> (1) means any order imposing injunctive relief against a State or local government or a State of local official sued in their official capacity entered by a court of the United States that is based in whole or in part upon the consent or acquiescence of the parties;

> (2) does not include—

>> "(A) private settlements:

>> "(B) any order entered by a court of the United States to implement a plan to end segregation of students or faculty on the basis of race, color, or national origin in elementary schools, secondary school, or institutions of higher education; and

>> "(C) any order entered in any action—

>>> "(I) filed by the Department of Justice; or

>>> "(ii) in which 1 State is an adverse party to another State.

(b) Limitation on Duration.—

> "(1) In general.—A State or local government or a State or local official, or their successor, sued in their official capacity may file a motion under this section with the court that entered a consent decree to modify or vacate the consent decree upon the earlier of—

>> "(A) 4 years after a consent decree is originally entered by a court of the United States, regardless if the consent decree has been modified or reentered during that period; or

>> "(B) in the case of a civil action in which—

>>> "(i) a State is a party, the expiration of the term of office of the highest elected State official who authorized the consent of the State in the consent decree;

>>> "(ii) a local government is a party, the expiration of the term of office of the highest elected local government official who authorized the consent of the local government to the consent decree; or

"(iii) consent to the decree was authorized by an appointed State or local official, upon the expiration of the term of office of the elected official who appointed that State or local official.

"(2) BURDEN OF PROOF.—With respect to any motion filed under paragraph (1), the burden of proof shall be on the party who originally filed the civil action to demonstrate that the denial of the motion to vacate or modify a consent decree or any part of a consent decree is necessary to prevent the violation of a requirement of Federal law that—

"(A) was actionable by such party; and

"(B) was addressed in the original consent decree.

"(3) RULING ON MOTION.—Not later than 30 days after the filing of a motion under this subsection, the court shall enter a scheduling order that—

"(A) limits the time of the parties to—

"(I) file motions; and

"(ii) complete any required discovery; and

"(B) sets the date or dates of any hearings determined necessary."

(b) TECHNICAL AND CONFORMING AMENDMENT.—

The table of sections for chapter 111 of title 28, United States Code, is amended by adding at the end the following:

"1660. Consent decrees".

SECTION 4. DEPARTMENT OF JUSTICE REPORT.

(a) IN GENERAL.—Not later than October 1 of each year, and annually thereafter, the Attorney General shall submit a report to Congress on all active consent decrees in which the Department of Justice is a party.

(b) CONTENT OF REPORTS.—The Report required under subsection (a) shall include a written statement by the Attorney General explaining why each consent decree listed in the report requires continued court supervision.

(c) PREPARATION OF REPORT.—In preparing the report required under subsection (a), the Attorney General shall solicit, and include in the report, statements relating to each consent decree from State and local officials who—

(1) support continued court supervision; and

(2) oppose continued court supervision.

SECTION 5. GENERAL PRINCIPLES.

(a) NO EFFECT ON OTHER LAWS RELATING TO MODIFYING OR VACATING CONSENT DECREES.—Nothing in the amendment made by section 3 shall be construed to preempt or modify any other provision of law providing for the modification or vacating of a consent decree.

(b) FURTHER PROCEEDINGS NOT REQUIRED.—Nothing in the amendments made by section 3 shall be construed to affect or require further judicial proceedings relating to prior adjudications of liability or class certifications.

SECTION 6. EFFECTIVE DATE.

The amendments made by this Act shall take effect on the date of enactment of this Act and apply to all consent decrees regardless of—

(1) the date on which the order of a consent decree is entered; or

(2) whether any relief has been obtained under a consent decree before the date of enactment of this Act.

Notes

1. Less drastic injunction reform than the Norris–LaGuardia Act and the PLRA, the Federal Consent Decree Fairness Act does not affect the federal court's "jurisdiction." What would the bill add to *Frew*? In light of *Frew*, is new legislation needed?

2. *Consent*? The State and local government defendants, presumably after complete and deliberate consideration, have agreed to a consent decree. Do the officials need a federal judge's oversight to protect them from being overreached?

3. Why might Congress tie the Act's timetable for a defendant to move to modify or dissolve a federal consent decree to the State's election cycle? Would this timetable give a consent decree enough time to work? Would the timetable prevent an outgoing or lame-duck State official from locking his successor into an onerous program the successor opposes?

4. *Motion to Modify*. Under present law, including *Frew*, if there is no ongoing violation of federal law, could a consent-decree defendant move to modify or dissolve the decree because of changed factual and legal circumstances? Does present law require a consent-decree defendant to prove the "negative" that the decree is unnecessary?

5. Would the Act let a State or local government defendant repudiate a consent decree that has turned out to be unpopular, expensive, or burdensome? Could the defendant move to modify or terminate a consent decree without offering any proof? Could this Bill be renamed "An Act to Put the Foxes in Charge of the Henhouse"?

6. Consider how the Act might affect future litigation. Will the judge's guidelines to approve a consent decree interfere with the parties' bargaining give and take necessary to reach agreement?

Will future class-action plaintiffs be less willing to negotiate an amicable settlement and enter into a consent decree? Will future plaintiffs be more likely to litigate to final judgment? If so, would the Act undermine the policy of encouraging the parties to settle lawsuits to avoid the cost, delay, and uncertainty of litigation?

7. In advancing federalism policies, would the Bill erode the public's rights under federal statutory and constitutional law and the federal court's authority to protect those rights?

Chapter 4

UNJUST ENRICHMENT—RESTITUTION

A defendant's civil liability to a plaintiff for restitution based on the defendant's unjust enrichment is a substantive branch of the common law like property, contract, and tort. The plaintiff may seek restitution as a freestanding remedy based on the defendant's unjust enrichment alone; the defendant's breach of contract, tort, or violation of plaintiff's property rights is not a prerequisite.

Freestanding restitution, restitution in the absence of the defendant's tort or breach of contract, is this chapter's principal subject. The chapter will also introduce you to the distinct vocabulary of restitution, the differences between legal restitution and equitable restitution, and to how to measure restitution.

A plaintiff's mistaken transfer to a defendant is an example of freestanding restitution. If a misaimed First Bank computer fires money into Sarah's checking account, no gift to Sarah was intended, no contract between the two was breached, no conversion or other tort occurred, and no property right was infringed. But the money unjustly enriches Sarah, and surprise!, surprise!, she cannot keep it.

Also, in a substantive area like contract, tort or property, the plaintiff may show that the defendant violated her rights and seek restitution as an alternative remedy to compensatory damages or an injunction. The defendant's "wrong," breach of contract or tort, satisfies the need to show "unjustness." A potential plaintiff should examine possible restitution claims as alternatives to compensatory damages or an injunction. Where a choice exists, for example where the defendant's gain exceeds the plaintiff's loss, the plaintiff ought to seek the more beneficial. Later chapters examine the plaintiff's choice between restitution and other remedies.

Restitution based on the defendant's unjust enrichment is a Remedies topic as important as compensatory damages and injunctions. This Chapter is short compared to the subject's length and importance; indeed, the late Professor George Palmer's treatise on Restitution fills four formidable volumes.

A. UNJUST? ENRICHMENT?

This Chapter's main topic, stated metaphorically, that you cannot reap what another has sowed, is a powerful one, as is illustrated, literally, by:

KISTLER v. STODDARD

Court of Appeals of Arkansas, 1985.
15 Ark.App. 8, 688 S.W.2d 746.

[Stoddard was a tenant farmer who for more than 20 years had rented crop land on yearly leases based on a farm year beginning on January 1. He planted his fall wheat crop in November, 1980. The farm owner, Barrett, having died, the heirs sold the land. Shannon, the buyer, did not renew Stoddard's lease for the year beginning in January 1981. Stoddard sought restitution from Shannon.]

The chancellor found that: Shannon was aware that the wheat crop was planted at the time of the purchase; the value of the wheat crop did not enter into the price negotiations for the plantation; Shannon did not elect to plow the wheat under but chose to reap the benefit of Stoddard's labor; Stoddard was unaware, at the time he planted the wheat, of the proposed sale to Shannon; and that Stoddard was justified, considering the past practices of the parties (Stoddard and Barrett and the executor of Barrett's estate), in planting the wheat crop with the expectation of being able to harvest it the next spring.

[T]he chancellor awarded Stoddard $5,711.93, finding that to do otherwise would result in Shannon's being unjustly enriched by that amount. [Shannon appealed.]

[Defendants argued on appeal] that Stoddard should not be allowed to recover because he planted wheat only a few months before his lease term was to expire, knowing that the wheat would not mature during the period of his lease. Further, [defendants] argue that the wheat crop was part of the realty and that, when Shannon bought the land, the crop went with the realty. They correctly argue that Stoddard had no right to enter onto the land for the purpose of harvesting the wheat once his lease expired on December 31, 1981. However, Stoddard made no claim to any such right. He only claimed a right to the cost of his efforts, the benefit of which inured to enrich Shannon. We agree that Stoddard's efforts were undertaken in good faith, since he reasonably could have relied on past practices and was unaware of the impending sale to Shannon until well after planting time.

The question remaining is whether, on the facts of this case, the chancellor correctly decided that the doctrine of unjust enrichment required that Shannon reimburse Stoddard for his costs in planting the wheat. We agree with the chancellor.

The doctrine of unjust enrichment is an equitable one, providing that one party should not be allowed to benefit at the expense of another because of an innocent mistake or unintentional error. [citations] Here the chancellor correctly determined that, absent restitution being paid to Stoddard, Shannon would without justification reap the benefits of Stoddard's labor and expense. It is true that Shannon, once the purchase was finalized, owned the wheat crop and that Stoddard had no legal or equitable claim to the crop itself. But resolution of that issue does not mean that Shannon is entitled to be unjustly enriched in the amount [Stoddard] expended to plant the crop. * * *

Affirmed.

Notes

1.   *Unjust Enrichment*: *Kistler v. Stoddard Reconsidered*. Here follows a series of questions to help focus your judgment on the critical issues in Kistler v. Stoddard and later restitution decisions. While answering the questions will not steer everyone to the same solution, the various answers should focus our collective judgment and lead to a beneficial discussion.

The two words at restitution's core, unjust and enrichment are essential, but we are wiser to discuss them in reverse order.

Before being held liable for restitution, the defendant must have received a "benefit." What will qualify as a benefit, although often clear, may be an issue for debate and judgment. Was defendant Shannon enriched?

Was Shannon's enrichment, if any, at plaintiff Stoddard's expense?

Was Shannon's enrichment unjust?

2.   Many plaintiffs' restitution claims occur in the shadow of someone else's property or contract right. If the court grants Stoddard restitution, will that interfere seriously with a property, contract, tort or other substantive policy? See, Doug Rendleman, When is Enrichment Unjust?: Restitution Visits an Onyx Bathroom, 36 Loy. L.A. L.Rev. 991 (2003).

Under well-established property law, when Shannon purchased the farm, the growing crops came with it. The tenant, Stoddard, could have been aware of property rights and could have negotiated a provision to control his lease-renewal rights. Instead Stoddard planted wheat in November assuming a lease to come. Before planting a crop to be harvested in a later lease-year, should Stoddard have put something in the lease? Should he have relied on a future lease with his landlord?

3.   *Emblemets*. A related property doctrine is emblements. At common law, a tenant for an uncertain term may, after termination, enter, harvest, and remove an annual crop that he planted.

Whether a tenant for a certain term from year to year has a right to emblements is not clear. In some states, the doctrine of emblements will permit a terminated agricultural tenant to re-enter the formerly leased land and harvest a previously planted crop. AKC, Inc. v. Joel Opatut Family Trust, 337 N.J.Super. 381, 766 A.2d 1235 (Ch.Div.2000). A treatise says that "the trend of recent decisions has been * * * to award the year-to-year tenant the crops planted before he has notice of the termination of his tenancy, but deny to him crops planted after such notice." Walter Raushenbush, Brown on Personal Property § 17.2 (3d ed. 1975).

Arkansas has no emblements statute; although its courts have dealt with common law emblements several times in other contexts, there are no Arkansas decisions on emblements between landlord and tenant. The court agreed with the defendants "that Stoddard had no right to enter onto the land for the purpose of harvesting the wheat once his lease expired." Should the court have, in effect, granted Stoddard a right to emblements that doesn't exist in the state's statutory or common law jurisprudence? Or does the doctrine of emblements elsewhere mean that the Arkansas court's decision to grant Stoddard restitution is a moderate and incremental step?

4.   A restitution dispute is difficult. When a court should grant a plaintiff restitution and how to measure restitution without eroding related property, contract, and tort doctrines which rebuff the plaintiff's claims is a major challenge.

Finally, how much unjust enrichment occurred? How should the court measure Stoddard's restitution? The court's measurement options include: (a) Stoddard's cost of putting the crop in; (b) the crop's value in the ground when Shannon purchased the land; and (c) the crop's value when harvested minus Shannon's expenditures to harvest it.

5. *Important Distinctions.* Restitution is a complex and unruly topic with many subdivisions but with neither a uniform vocabulary nor a universal theoretical base. General ideas, while helpful, usually do not cover the whole subject. No overarching principle exists from which all restitution rules may be drawn. History and slippery words require us to attend to several distinctions at the outset.

(a) *Restoration and Restitution.* The distinction between restitution in money and specific or in specie restitution is a distinction between (i) granting the plaintiff a money judgment measured by the defendant's unjust enrichment as in Kistler v. Stoddard; and (ii) forcing the defendant to return or restore a specific thing to the plaintiff. Replevin, ejectment, and many constructive trusts are specific restitution or restoration-restitution. Replevin and ejectment will not concern us in this chapter, and restoration of specific property will come up in later chapters as an alternative to other solutions. A court will often grant a plaintiff replevin or ejectment to vindicate her pre-existing ownership rights under property law, and these remedies can usually be distinguished from freestanding restitution based on the defendant's unjust enrichment.

In popular speech, "restitution" means "restore," "return," or "give back." These definitions are too narrow to describe a court's analysis of restitution based on a defendant's unjust enrichment. Suppose the defendant diverted a benefit which would otherwise have gone to the plaintiff. The court may simply ignore the supposed requirement that the defendant's enrichment must be at the plaintiff's expense. Or the court may find the intercepting defendant unjustly enriched "at the expense of" the plaintiff and order the defendant's "restitution" of something the plaintiff never had.

(b) *Law and Equity.* The distinction between legal restitution, usually quasi-contract, and equitable restitution, usually a constructive trust, is confusing and nonfunctional because of two anachronisms. The first anachronism is an obsolete and mostly forgotten set of concepts, the common law forms of action. The second is an institution almost abandoned, the dual courts of Common Law and Chancery, which we remember today because of the litigants' constitutional right to a jury trial at "Common Law" but not in an "Equitable or Chancery" dispute. Nevertheless, the distinction between legal restitution and equitable restitution has enough momentum to preserve it in the organization of this chapter.

(c) *Rescission and Restitution.* Rescission-restitution for the parties' transaction that has gone awry comes up in the chapters on contract remedies below. One point about restitution analysis is important here. Although a court almost always says that it is grounding restitution on the defendant's unjust enrichment, sometimes there is a better description for what is happening: a court that follows rescission of the parties' contract with what it names restitution intends more to restore the parties to their pre-contractual status quo than to prevent the defendant's unjust enrichment.

(d) *Injunction-Specific Performance and Restitution.* How does an injunction differ from restitution? An injunction is an order to the defendant to do something or to refrain from doing something. Specific performance is a specialized order to a defendant to do, that is to fulfill his contract. Restitution is usually a money remedy like damages; however, the court's specific restitution judgment, replevin, ejectment and sometimes a constructive trust, often operates like an injunction to let the plaintiff have something in fact.

(e) *Compensation and Restitution.* Compensatory damages are money recovery that the court measures by the plaintiff's loss. But a court measures the plaintiff's restitution in money to thwart the defendant's improper gains from unjust enrichment; the court's restitution to prevent or reverse the defendant's unjust enrichment implements a different policy than damages to compensate the plaintiff's loss. A lawyer or a judge may use the word "damages" in a general sense to include all of a plaintiff's money recovery, including restitution. In this book's vocabulary of remedies, however, "restitutionary damages" or "damages measured by restitution" are oxymorons.

When the defendant is liable for restitution measured by his gains, the plaintiff may recover more as restitution than she lost and would be able to recover as compensatory damages. Why might the court countenance letting the plaintiff's recovery of restitution exceeds her losses? First, the prospect of a large recovery may spur the plaintiff's activity to carry out the substantive law. Second, when the defendant pays the plaintiff restitution which exceeds compensation, that deters the particular defendant and others from the improper activity that led to the defendant's enrichment.

(f) *Criminal Restitution.* Finally, be sure to distinguish criminal restitution from the present subject, civil restitution based on the defendant's unjust enrichment. Criminal restitution is money a criminal court orders a convicted criminal to pay to the victim; it is usually compensation for the victim. In short, the word "restitution" simply means something different in the criminal context.

6. *Introduction to Boudier.* Three-party cases are more difficult than a two-party case like Kistler v. Stoddard. The Cour de Cassation is a French appellate court. France has a Civil Code. A French court's decision or order, called a *jugement*, is usually more concise than a typical common-law court opinion. In the *jugement* that follows, I have added explanations and translations in brackets.

PATUREAU-MIRAN C. BOUDIER*

Cass. Req., 15 June 1892 [S.1893.1.28.]

Facts: Patureau–Miran, owner of a property at Miran (Indre), let it to Garnier–Godard on 5 March 1886 at a rent of 5,500 francs (fr.) p.a. The tenant not having fulfilled his obligations, the lease was terminated on 22 December 1888, when the tenant owed the sum of 15,000 fr. to the landlord for rent and equipment. In part settlement the tenant relinquished to the landlord the standing crop. After a valuation the tenant's debt was assessed at 5,376 fr. It was on these terms that Patureau–Miran resumed possession. Later Boudier, father and son, merchants of manure, presented to Patureau–Miran a bill for 324 fr. for manure sold and delivered to Garnier–Godard before the termination of the lease.

Held. The trial court gave judgment for Boudier. Among the grounds of the appeal [the defendant landowner's points] were: violation of art. 1165 Code Civil (The principle of privity of contract) and misapplication of the principles of the action de in rem verso [action for restitution based on the defendant's unjust enrichment]. The Cour de cassation rejected these arguments.

* Translation of the decision and M. Labbe's note from Jack Beatson & Eltjo Schrange, Un- justified Enrichment 39–42 (2003) and Professor Mark Drumbl.

Jugement: [On the defendant's first ground the Court held:] Considering that it is a matter of principle that agreements have effect only between the contracting parties and do not affect third parties, it is certain that this principle has not been disregarded by the *jugement* [or decision below] attacked; that indeed the *jugement* did not, as the *pourvoi* claims, assert that the defendant could be liable to the plaintiff because of the supply of manure by the plaintiff to a third party, but only because of the profit derived by the defendant from the use of the manure on his land; from which it follows that the ground fails because of the fact on which it is based.

[On the defendant's second ground:] Considering that the action de in rem verso, derives from the principle of equity which forbids one to enrich oneself at the expense of another and has been regulated by no text of our laws, its exercise is subject to no fixed condition; that it is sufficient that the plaintiff alleges and offers to establish the existence of an advantage which, by a sacrifice or an act, he has conferred on the other party; and since the plaintiff had proved by witnesses that the manure supplied on the date indicated in the *jugement* had indeed been used on the land of the defendant for the crops from which the defendant has profited, the *jugement* has done no more than make an exact application of the principles in this matter.

Notes

1. *A Broad and Spacious Doctrine*? What does the *Boudier* court's statement of a plaintiff's restitution cause of action require the plaintiff to show to recover? Could a court apply this standard to a defendant's successful competition with the plaintiff in business or to a merchant's retail sale to a buyer when the merchant has marked up the merchandise?

2. *Moses v, Macferlan*. In England in 1760, Lord Mansfield explaining general assumpsit, the doctrine we would call restitution today, wrote that "the gist of this kind of action is, that the defendant, upon the circumstances of the case, is obliged by the ties of natural justice and equity to refund the money." Moses v, Macferlan, 2 Burr. 1005, 1012, 97 Eng.Rep. 676, 681 (K.B. 1760). Is Lord Mansfield's restitution formula broader or narrower than the *Boudier* court's?

3. *Restatement, Section 1*. In 1937, section one of the first Restatement of Restitution read simply that "A person who has been unjustly enriched at the expense of another is required to make restitution to the other."

This section has the virtue of basing restitution on the defendant's unjust enrichment, but the vice of leaving all the definitions at large. By the way, since a new restitution restatement is in the making, this chapter will often cite to its sections which are in tentative drafts

4. *The Search for Limiting Principles*.

(a) *The Code*. French lawyers and courts find the premises and foundations for legal arguments and decisions in the Civil Code; a code citation is set out before each decision. The Civil Code has a chapter on quasi-contracts with sections on mistake and management of another's affairs, but nothing touching the general principle of preventing unjust enrichment.

Although judge-made law is not typical in France, in *Boudier*, the court based its decision on the broad and undefined principle of "equity." A present-day French court will not premise its restitution decision on "equity," but instead on "the principles of unjustified enrichment" located in Civil Code Article 1371, "Quasi-contracts are purely voluntary human facts from which there results an obligation of some kind to a third party and sometimes a reciprocal obligation between the two parties."

(b) *Clarification.* M. Labbé, a famous writer of notes to decisions thought that the court's opinion in *Boudier* needed to be clarified.

"Unless one examines the matter closely, the affinity between art. 1165 [the privity of contract article] and art. 2102 [on the priority of creditors] is considerable enough to make the acceptance of the action de in rem verso [restitution] seem at first to violate the principles of these two articles. We think that it is worth trying to clarify this affinity, which may easily give rise to confusion.

"If, when manure has been supplied to a tenant farmer and has been used to improve the land, one says that the owner of the land is liable for the price, one appears to ignore the principle embodied in the maxim 'res inter alios acta aliis neque nocet neque prodest' [one is neither advantaged nor disadvantaged by what takes place between others]. For it seems that from one cause (the agreement between the tenant and the seller of the manure) one is deriving two actions, one against the tenant and the other against the owner of the land, the first being in conformity with the contract and in agreement with the maxim, and the other ... being in conflict with the maxim. The confusion will be complete, or at least less easy to avoid, if the debt of the tenant and the debt of the owner are both for the same sum, namely the price agreed for the manure.

"If one looks closely, however, one can easily distinguish two effects which are parallel but not identical, one deriving from the contract, with its corollary embodied in the maxim, and the other deriving from an enrichment which has nothing to do with the contract. The contract for the sale of the manure creates a right for the seller and a debt for the tenant—no other parties are involved. Whether the manure has been used or lost its irrelevant. But the fact that the manure has been spread on the land and that the fertility of the land has in consequence been increased adds a value to the land from which the owner unjustly derives a benefit without having spent a penny. This new fact creates a different obligation—in favor of the supplier of the manure and against the owner of the land. The object of this obligation is not a sum fixed in advance, but a figure to be settled, a figure which may be higher or lower than the contract price. However the difficulty of arriving at this figure will commonly lead to the contract price being taken as representing the amount which has been 'in rem versum.'

"There are thus two debts, one owed by the tenant and the other by the owner. They have a common purpose, the satisfaction of the seller of the manure. But once one debt has been paid, the other will disappear, save that if it is the action de in rem verso which is concluded first and the amount payable by the landowner is less than the contract price, the liability of the tenant will survive to the extent of the difference.

"In the present *jugement* any confusion would have been avoided by the inclusion of a phrase on the following lines: the sum payable will be the same as the contractual price, because there is nothing to show that the increase in value resulting from the use of the manure, which is the true measure of the amount owing, is not the equivalent of the market price of the manure needed to produce this increased value ...

"If neither art. 1165 nor art. 2102 Code Civil has been violated, have the conditions of the action de in rem verso been satisfied? There are two doctrines as to these conditions. One, which is the more precise and narrow, assimilates the action de in rem verso to [an action resembling suing a principal on an agent's contract.]

"One thus turns to the other doctrine, that of the action de in rem verso. This doctrine is more vague. It says that no-one should enrich himself at the expense of another without just cause; for equity does not permit it. This is the only foundation of the action de in rem verso. See Aubry and Rau, vol. 6, pp. 246, 247 § 578. Our *jugement* gives its authority to this supple and elastic doctrine.

"The advocate who argued for the *pourvoi* seemed to derive inspiration from the ideas of Aubry and Rau: 'The action de in rem verso should be allowed generally as a sanction for the rule of equity that one should not enrich oneself at the expense of another, whenever the patrimony of one person is enriched, without just cause, at the expense of another and there is not available to that other, to obtain what belongs to him or is owed to him, any action deriving from a contract, a quasi-contract or a quasi-delict.' The advocate therefore subjected the action de in rem verso to two principal conditions: first, that the person enriched did not have a *just cause* for retaining the enrichment, secondly, that he did not have a *legitimate cause of action* against another person. These conditions were not satisfied in the present case, he argued. First, the tenant had expressly undertaken as a term in the lease to manure the land and to take all proper steps to make it more fertile. The landlord therefore had a just ground for profiting from this term in the lease. Secondly, the supplier of the manure had contracted with the tenant, against whom he therefore had a contractual right. He had an action; he did not have the action de in rem verso.

"What reply did the Court give to these arguments? It simply invoked the principle of equity ... If one relies only on the text of the *jugement*, there could be nothing more vague or less precise. In order therefore better to understand how the Court thought to refute the arguments in the *pourvoi* we now add two points which we find in the *rapport* of [trial] Judge Loubers. First, when experts drew up an account on the termination of the tenant's occupation of the land, the value which they put on the crop was calculated after deduction of the value of the manure. They therefore assumed that the landlord would only have the value of the crop if he paid for the value of the manure. Secondly, the tenant was insolvent and the supplier of the manure was therefore at risk of losing its value. These two facts are not without importance in determining on what conditions the action de in rem verso was given and in helping to establish a theory of this action. We think that the true principle from which one must not depart is that no-one should enrich himself at the expense of another *without just cause*. We regret that the words which we have emphasized were not reproduced in the Court's formula." D.1892.1.596.

5. *Back in the U.S.A.* Two restitution plaintiffs will be disqualified from the outset, for a court will not consider their defendants' enrichment to be "unjust."

(a) *Donor.* A person may not bestow a benefit as a gift and then claim restitution from the recipient. In lay English, a "volunteer" is a person who serves the community, not someone working for pay. A court will deny the "Good Samaritan" restitution because she acted deliberately and because a court will not ascribe crass commercial purposes to diminish her altruism.

One plaintiff sought to recover restitution quantum meruit for services she rendered on behalf of the Unification Church. The court denied her restitution observing that she performed the services "without expecting any reward other than the creation of a better world." Turner v. Unification Church, 473 F.Supp. 367, 378 (D.R.I. 1978), affirmed, 602 F.2d 458 (1st Cir 1979).

The court may also deny restitution to a plaintiff who, acting out of family duty, performed services for a closely related person.

(b) *Intermeddler Volunteer*. The first Restatement of Restitution limited the plaintiff's restitution for an unsolicited benefit in section two. "A person who officiously confers a benefit upon another is not entitled to restitution therefor."

A court, refusing to require a defendant who received a benefit to pay the plaintiff restitution, may label the plaintiff who conferred the benefit a "volunteer" or an "intermeddler," sometimes even an "officious intermeddler." Giving content to this jargon, while difficult, is crucial.

A person may not confer an unsolicited benefit on another and ask a court, through the magic of restitution, to declare the recipient her debtor. For unless something overcomes the recipient's right to choose, the court should allow him to decide how to spend his money and afford him an opportunity to reject the benefit.

A judge should hesitate before using restitution to intervene in someone's choice of how to spend his money. First, restitution may interfere with the defendant's autonomy to select from an assortment of alternatives. Second, the parties' bargained contractual exchange allocates their resources more efficiently than a court decision.

One example will illustrate both reasons. Suppose Paula, a painter, decides that a vacationing homeowner's house needs painting and slaps a coat on it. How might Don, the returning homeowner, respond if Paula the painter could recover restitution for the value of her services? The coat of paint is a benefit Don did not desire, did not contract for, and may be unable to afford. Restitution, even if based on an actual benefit to homeowner-Don, would force him to pay someone he did not select for paint he did not want in a color he did not pick.

6. *More Manure?* Buyer and Seller formed an ineffective contract to convey Seller's land to Buyer; before learning that the contract was ineffective, Buyer spread manure on the land, changing "pasture to crop bearing soil" and increasing its value. After the agreement failed, Buyer sought restitution for the improvements. Although Seller was "satisfied with the previous tilth," the court granted Buyer restitution. Estok v. Heguy, (1963), 40 D.L.R.(2d) 88, 44 W.W.R. 167 (B.C.S.C.).

Did the court tell Seller to pay Buyer for a benefit that he had not asked for and that he did not want?

7. In Bailey v. West, a driver named Kelly had dropped a lame race horse named "Bascom's Folly" at plaintiff Bailey's horse farm without making a contract for boarding the horse. Although Bailey did not know about it then, defendant West, who had agreed to buy "Bascom's Folly" from Strauss, was disputing with Strauss which one of them owned the lame horse. During the about 50 months Bailey kept the horse, he sent bills to both West and Strauss; but West returned Bailey's bills unpaid, denying both ownership of the horse and a contract with Bailey to board it. After the state supreme court decided that West owned "Bascom's Folly," Bailey sold the horse to "a third party" and sued West "for the reasonable value of his services rendered in connection with the feeding, care and maintenance of a certain race horse named Bascom's Folly" for 50 months. The trial judge decided that Bailey should recover for the first five months of boarding.

After the Supreme Court of Rhode Island rejected Bailey's argument for recovery under an express contract, it turned to restitution:

"The key question raised by this appeal with respect to the establishment of a quasi-contract is whether or not plaintiff was acting as a 'volunteer' at the time he accepted the horse for boarding at his farm. There is a long line of authority which has clearly enunciated the general rule that * * * 'if a performance is rendered by one person without any request by another, it is very unlikely that this person will be under a legal duty to pay compensation.' 1 A Corbin, Contracts § 234.

"The Restatement of Restitution, § 2 (1937) provides: 'A person who officiously confers a benefit upon another is not entitled to restitution therefor.' Comment *a* in the above-mentioned section states in part as follows: 'Policy ordinarily requires that a person who has conferred a benefit * * * by way of giving another services * * * should not be permitted to require the other to pay therefor, unless the one conferring the benefit had a valid reason for so doing. A person is not required to deal with another unless he so desires and, ordinarily, a person should not be required to become an obligor unless he so desires.'

"Applying those principles to the facts in the case at bar it is clear that plaintiff cannot recover. * * * The defendant's attorney asked plaintiff if he had any conversation with Kelly at that time, and plaintiff answered in substance that he had noticed that the horse was very lame and that Kelly had told him: 'That's why they wouldn't accept him at Belmont Track.' The plaintiff also testified that he had inquired of Kelly as to the ownership of 'Bascom's Folly,' and had been told that 'Dr. Strauss made a deal and that's all I know.' It further appears from the record that plaintiff acknowledged receipt of the horse by signing a uniform livestock bill of lading, which clearly indicated on its face that the horse in question had been consigned by defendant's trainer not to plaintiff, but to Dr. Strauss's trainer at Belmont Park. Knowing at the time he accepted the horse for boarding that a controversy surrounded its ownership, plaintiff could not reasonably expect remuneration from defendant, nor can it be said that defendant acquiesced in the conferment of a benefit upon him. * * *

"It is our judgment that the plaintiff was a mere volunteer who boarded and maintained 'Bascom's Folly' at his own risk and with full knowledge that he might not be reimbursed for expenses he incurred incident thereto." Bailey v. West, 105 R.I. 61, 67–68 249 A.2d 414, 417–18 (1969).

7. *Rescuer.* For policy reasons arising from a court's sensible concern to preserve life and health, a rescuer may recover restitution for professional services reasonably necessary to protect a person's life or health in an emergency. Restatement (Third) of Restitution and Unjust Enrichment § 20 (Tent. Draft No. 2, (2002)); Restatement of Restitution § 114, 116 (1937).

One court rejected a long-standing admiralty rule that saving lives at sea ("pure life salvage") merited moral approval, but no pecuniary recovery. The owner of a vessel that altered its course to aid a stricken seaman aboard another ship without a medical staff recovered restitution. The rescuer's claim was against the other ship's owner, not the seaman who fortunately survived. What was the defendant's actual benefit? The court concluded that the reasonable value of the services, measured by the expense of changing course to effect the rescue, was proper regardless of the actual benefit conferred. Peninsular & Oriental Steam Navigation Co. v. Overseas Oil Carriers, 553 F.2d 830 (2d Cir.1977).

A plaintiff may under certain circumstances recover restitution for services and expenditures in caring for another's property. Restatement (Third) of Restitution and Unjust Enrichment § 21 (Tent. Draft No. 2, 2002). The plaintiff must believe that the owner will accept the benefit. Did Bailey's agistor's claim against West for the care of "Bascom's Folly" falter at this stage?

8. *Introduction to Kossian.* Kossian v. American National Insurance Company features plaintiff Kossian's debris removal after a fire at the Bakersfield Inn.

The ill-starred Bakersfield Inn had already sparked one restitution decision before the fire. In 1959, while the hotel was in probate, the probate court approved the administrator's sale to the Nelson–Smith Hotel Company. An escrow was opened, conditioned upon performance by Nelson–Smith. Shortly thereafter Nelson entered into possession of the inn and contracted with Griffith, later the plaintiff, to repave the driveways and parking lots. Plaintiff performed. Nelson–Smith defaulted against both the plaintiff and the administrator who had sold the hotel; the probate court set aside the decree of confirmation; and the estate had to retake possession of the Inn. Plaintiff sued the administrator:

"The only theory upon which the [plaintiff's] recovery is sought to be sustained is [the administrator's] unjust enrichment. * * *

"It is contended that the defendant acquiesced to, and had knowledge of, and accepted the benefit of, the services, and it is therefore claimed that he should be compelled to pay for them, whether they were authorized or whether he wanted them or not. We do not think this proposition is sound. The work, itself, was done after Nelson took possession of the inn on August 17, 1959. It was done by his authority. Nelson was in as purchaser and defendant could not then reasonably foresee that the total purchase price would not be paid and he would be compelled to regain possession. He was therefore not in a position to forbid the work going on. He was not called upon to forbid or otherwise restrain it. * * *

"We are of the opinion that plaintiff does not have a cause of action against this defendant. It saw fit to accept employment from the Nelson–Smith Hotel Company, which was admittedly without authority from this defendant. It dealt with Smith, Nelson's representative, without ascertaining his authority to bind the owners of the inn, and it is fundamental that one so dealing does so at his peril. He is bound to inquire and to know if the authority exists. This the plaintiff failed to do. * * * It went ahead with the work relying on an express written contract with Nelson–Smith Hotel Company, expecting that its services would be paid for by that company. It must now look to that company for payment.

"Under the circumstances here, plaintiff may not recover from this defendant, and the judgment must, therefore, be reversed.

"Although our conclusion may seem harsh to this plaintiff, it must be remembered that one situated as was the plaintiff in this case is amply protected by the law. It has its remedy against the Nelson–Smith Hotel Company." Griffith Co. v. Hofues, 201 Cal.App.2d 502, 506–08, 19 Cal.Rptr. 900, 903–04 (1962).

KOSSIAN v. AMERICAN NATIONAL INSURANCE CO.

Court of Appeal of California, 1967.
254 Cal.App.2d 647, 62 Cal.Rptr. 225.

STONE, ASSOCIATE JUSTICE. On February 19, 1964, fire destroyed a portion of the Bakersfield Inn, owned by one Reichert. At the time, the property was subject to a first deed of trust in which defendant was the beneficiary. Pursuant to the requirements of the deed of trust, defendant's interest in the property was protected by policies of fire insurance. On March 16, 1964, Reichert, as owner in possession, entered into a written contract with plaintiff whereby plaintiff agreed to clean up and remove the debris from the fire damaged portion of the Inn for the sum of $18,900. Defendant had no knowledge of the execution of the agreement between plaintiff and Reichert.

Plaintiff commenced work in the middle of March 1964, and completed it in early April. During the entire time work was in progress Reichert was in possession of the premises as owner, although defendant caused a notice of Reichert's default under the deed of trust to be filed four days after the contract for demolition was entered into between plaintiff and Reichert. The record does not reflect that plaintiff had actual knowledge of the notice of default until after the work was completed.

Some time after plaintiff had fully performed the contract, Reichert filed a petition in bankruptcy. The trustee in bankruptcy abandoned the premises comprising the Bakersfield Inn, together with any interest in the four fire insurance policies up to the amount of $424,000. Each policy contained a provision insuring against the cost of cleaning up and removing debris caused by fire damage.

Following abandonment of the policies by the trustee in bankruptcy, Reichert and his wife assigned their interest in them to defendant in accordance with the terms of the deed of trust. Defendant submitted proofs of loss, claiming a total of $160,000, including the sum of $18,000 as the estimated cost for recovering and cleaning up debris. These claims were rejected by the carriers; negotiations followed; the compromise figure of $135,620 was agreed upon and this amount paid to defendant. We do not have an itemization of the adjusted claims of loss upon which the compromised loss settlement was made, so that the record is not clear as to what part of the $18,900 cost of debris removal defendant received. It is clear, however, that the insurance payment included at least a part of the cost of debris removal and demolition.

[The trial judge granted defendant's motion for summary judgment. Plaintiff appealed.]

Defendant demonstrates, by a careful analysis of the facts, that there was no direct relationship between plaintiff and defendant in regard to either the work performed on the property after the fire or in relation to the fire insurance policies. The contract for debris removal was between plaintiff and Reichert, and defendant did not induce plaintiff, directly or indirectly, to enter into that contract. Plaintiff had no lien against the property resulting from his work, and if he had such a lien it would have been wiped out by defendant's foreclosure of its first deed of trust.

Had the circumstances been simply that defendant, by foreclosure, took the property improved by plaintiff's debris removal, there would be a benefit conferred upon defendant by plaintiff, but no unjust enrichment. It is the additional fact that defendant made a claim to the insurance carriers for the value of work done by plaintiff that is the nub of the case.

Defendant argues that plaintiff was not a party to the insurance contracts, while defendant had a contract right to collect indemnity for losses resulting from the fire, including the debris removal cost. This contract right was embodied in the insurance policies. Defendant relies upon Russell v. Williams, 58 Cal.2d 487, 490, where it is said:

"It is a principle of long standing that a policy of fire insurance does not insure the property covered thereby, but is a personal contract indemnifying the insured against loss resulting from the destruction of or damage to his interest in that property. [citations] This principle gives rise to the supplemental rule that, in the absence of a special contract, the proceeds of a fire insurance policy are not a substitute for the property the loss of which is the subject of indemnity."

Defendant says it made no agreement, express or implied, with plaintiff that it would pay for the debris removal or that any part of the insurance proceeds would be applied for that purpose. Therefore, concludes defendant, there being no privity of relationship between it and plaintiff, and no fraud or deceit alleged or proved, defendant has the right to the property benefitted by plaintiff's work and labor expended in removing the debris and to the insurance payments as well.

Plaintiff makes no claim to the insurance "fund" upon the ground he relied thereon similar to the reliance of a mechanic or materialman that forms the basis of an equitable claim to a building fund. He relies upon the basic premise that defendant should not be allowed to have the fruits of plaintiff's labor and also the money value of that labor. This, of course, is a simplified pronouncement of the doctrine of unjust enrichment, a theory which can, in some instances, have validity without privity of relationship. The most prevalent implied-in-fact contract recognized under the doctrine of unjust enrichment is predicated upon a relationship between the parties from which the court infers an intent. However, the doctrine also recognizes an obligation *imposed* by law regardless of the intent of the parties. In these instances there need be no relationship that gives substance to an implied intent basic to the "contract" concept, rather the obligation is imposed because good conscience dictates that under the circumstances the person benefitted should make reimbursement. * * *

Plaintiff's claim does not rest upon a quasi-contract implied in fact, but upon an equitable obligation imposed by law. It is true that defendant's right to the insurance payment was a contract right embodied in the policies of insurance; nevertheless the indemnity payment was based in part upon a claim of loss that did not exist because plaintiff had already remedied the loss by his work for which he was not paid.

We are cited no California cases that are close aboard, and independent research reveals none. Lack of precedent applicable to the facts peculiar to this case is not surprising, however, as the authors of the Restatement recognize that the essential nature of equity cases concerned with problems of restitution makes definitive precedent unlikely. We are guided by the "Underlying Principles" delineated in the Restatement on Restitution:

> "The rules stated in the Restatement of this Subject depend for their validity upon certain basic assumptions in regard to what is required by justice in the various situations. In this Topic, these are stated in the form of principles. They cannot be stated as rules since either they are too indefinite to be of value in a specific case or, for historical or other reasons, they are not universally applied. They are distinguished from rules in that they are intended only as general guides for the conduct of the courts."

The governing principle is expressed in the opening sentence of the Restatement on Restitution, as follows:

> "The Restatement of this Subject deals with situations in which one person is accountable to another on the ground that otherwise he would unjustly benefit or the other would unjustly suffer loss."

The question, simply stated, is whether in a jurisdiction that recognizes the equitable doctrine of unjust enrichment one party should be indemnified twice for the same loss, once in labor and materials and again in money, to the detriment (forfeiture) of the party who furnished the labor and materials. We conclude that the doctrine of unjust enrichment is applicable to the facts of this case, and that plaintiff is entitled to reimbursement out of the insurance proceeds paid defendant for work done by plaintiff. * * *

[I]t is clear that defendant, in addition to taking over the property which plaintiff cleared of debris, also received indemnity insurance payments covering at least part of the cost for clearing that property of debris. The amount can be made certain by a trial on the merits, and if it develops that defendant recovered only a part of the cost for debris removal, this fact does not preclude a partial recovery by plaintiff. We learn from the Restatement.

> "Where a person is entitled to restitution from another because the other, without tortious conduct, has received a benefit, the measure of recovery for the benefit thus received is the value of what was received * * *."

Thus, to the extent defendant received insurance for debris removal performed by plaintiff, plaintiff should recover. If defendant received less than the value of plaintiff's work, as defendant seems to contend, then plaintiff should recover *pro tanto*.

The judgment is reversed.

Note

1. *Origin of Benefit.* The plaintiff's loss may be the defendant's benefit. Sometimes, however, the defendant's benefit originates with a third party. When this happens restitution decisions diverge. One approach tends to insist that the defendant's "benefit" have been acquired directly "at the plaintiff's expense." Another approach concentrates primarily on the defendant's "enrichment" and de-emphasizes the idea that the defendant's enrichment must have originated with the plaintiff. If the defendant "diverts" a benefit from a third party which would have otherwise gone to plaintiff, the court may characterize this enrichment as at the plaintiff's expense.

2. Consider the events in *Kossian*. The defendant-American's enrichment appears to be fire insurance proceeds. Did American divert the insurance proceeds from plaintiff-Kossian? Could the fire insurance company argue that American was "enriched" at *its* expense since the insured had already been made whole by Kossian?

3. *Introduction to Knaus v. Dennler—Restitution of Benefits Conferred Incidentally.* When a homeowner remodels her home, she increases the market value of her neighbors' houses. A mineowner may drain its flooded mineshafts, lowering the water level in another company's adjacent mines. Neither the homeowner not the mineowner may have had a charitable motive in conferring the benefits. May either recover restitution?

KNAUS v. DENNLER

Appellate Court of Illinois, 1988.
170 Ill.App.3d 746, 525 N.E.2d 207.

JUSTICE WELCH delivered the opinion of the court. Plaintiffs appeal from a judgment of the circuit court of St. Clair County dismissing their complaint seeking proportionate sharing of expenses between owners of adjoining lakefront properties for the repair of the dam which retains the lake around which the properties are situated.

In March 1982, plaintiffs purchased real property known as Lot 1 of the Fifth Addition to Lakewood Place. The lot purchased by plaintiffs abutted a lake, and included approximately one-half to two-thirds of the earthen dam which retained the lake. The remaining portion of the dam was situated on the lakefront property adjoining plaintiffs' property immediately to the south.

In June 1982, plaintiffs discovered one or two small holes developing in the portion of the dam situated on their property. Plaintiffs were aware at the time of purchase that their lot included a portion of the earthen dam, but, according to the record, plaintiffs made no inquiry as to the condition of the dam; nor did the previous owner disclose at any time prior to the closing of the sale that the dam had required repairs for leakage during the seller's ownership.

Prompted by interest in repairing the leaking dam, plaintiffs contacted the United States Department of Agricultural Soil Conservation and an independent excavating contractor. At plaintiffs' request, the excavating contractor visited plaintiffs' property in July 1982 and inspected the dam. Later in July or early in August of 1982, a heavy rain resulted in an enlarging of the holes in the dam. Again the excavating contractor inspected the dam at plaintiffs' request. On August 9 or 12, 1982, plaintiffs arranged a meeting with other owners of property abutting the lake so that a decision could be made as to what procedures should be taken to repair the dam. Although the record is replete with conflicting testimony pertaining to what transpired at the meeting and whether a unanimous decision among lakefront property owners was attained, repairs began at plaintiffs' request on August 18, 1982. A second property owners meeting followed on August 19, 1982, at which, according to the record, differences of opinion resulted in the meeting becoming "heated."

At the second meeting, the excavator recommended that the entire dam be reconstructed so as to comply with the accepted standards for dam construction and maintenance. The Smedleys, owners of the portion of the dam not owned by the Knauses, objected to their portion of the dam being reconstructed, and advised the excavator to stay off their property. The excavating work, reconstructing only the portion of the dam situated on the Knaus' property, was completed on September 11, 1982. The total cost for the excavating was $11,920.51. An additional $1,360 was expended for landscaping and repairs necessary to cosmetically finish the reconstructed portion of the dam and restore the asphalt driveway and surrounding area which had suffered superficial damages resulting from the traverse of large trucks transporting excavating equipment to and from the job site.

The underlying law suit was filed originally on June 6, 1983, seeking to recover from the named defendants proportionate shares of the expenses incurred in reconstructing the dam. While some lakefront property owners had contributed money to help cover the costs, the defendants had refused to do so. * * * On April 11, 1985, the court dismissed counts one, two, and three of plaintiffs' second amended complaint, and entered judgment in favor of defendants. * * *

Counts two and three of plaintiffs' complaint claim that the defendants breached an implied contract. In count two, the alleged implied contract arose out of the common law riparian rights of property owners. Under common law, riparian rights of property owners abutting the same body of water are equal, and no such property owner may exercise its riparian rights in such a manner so as to prevent the exercise of the same rights by other similarly situated property owners. Therefore, according to plaintiffs, there existed an implied contract in law between the plaintiffs and defendants to maintain the lake, including the dam, so that all lakefront property owners could continue exercising their riparian rights.

Count three alleged that an implied contract arose out of language contained in the plat depicting the lakefront property situated around the lake here in issue. The plat states, *inter alia,* "[t]hat the purchaser of any lot in this subdivision shall acquire the fee simple title to the entire area of the lot. However, the right to use that part of the area of said lot comprising the lake area (*i.e.* within the "Water Line"), shall be reserved for the joint use of all the present or future owners of lots in this subdivision." Therefore, according to plaintiffs, there existed an implied contract between plaintiffs and defendants to maintain the dam of the lake and be mutually responsible for costs incurred for any necessary repairs. We find neither count two nor count three sufficient to state a cause of action, and therefore the trial court's dismissal of these counts was proper.

Illinois courts recognize an action derived from the doctrine referred to as quasi contract, contract implied in law, or *quantum meruit,* the obligations of which may be enforced independent of any agreement between the parties or of their personal intentions. An implied contract is one which reason and justice dictate, and is founded on the equitable doctrine of unjust enrichment. Recovery under an unjust enrichment theory requires a showing that the defendant has voluntarily accepted a benefit which it would be inequitable for him to retain without payment since the law implies a promise to pay compensation when value of services are knowingly accepted. [citation]

In the present case, the record indicates that plaintiffs attempted to enter into a written agreement with the defendants binding defendants to pay a portion of the cost of repairing the dam. Defendants refused to enter such an agreement, and trial testimony indicates that defendants Smedley informed plaintiffs prior to the initiation of repairs that defendants Smedley did not consider themselves responsible for the cost of repairs performed on plaintiffs' property. Defendants Dennler refused to sign any agreement proposed by the plaintiffs, and became upset with the extensiveness of repairs once undertaken. Defendant Woolard did not express objection to the repairs, but did not sign the agreement offered by plaintiffs, and stated that she was not in a position financially to contribute to the cost of repairs.

Because plaintiffs instructed that repairs be commenced notwithstanding defendants' opposition and lack of willingness to enter the agreement proposed by plaintiffs, we are unable to find that defendants voluntarily accepted a benefit, as required to establish unjust enrichment under Premier Electrical Construction Company v. LaSalle National Bank (1984), 132 Ill.App.3d 485. Instead, because the benefit was conferred in the face of opposition and disinterest, it appears to fall into the category of "officiously" or "gratuitously" conferred benefit for which quasi-contractual relief is not available in Illinois.
* * *

Finally, plaintiffs contend that the trial court's judgment in favor of defendants Smedley in the amount of $130 against the plaintiffs for trespass was against the manifest weight of the evidence. Trespass is the invasion of exclusive possession and physical condition of land. [citation] In the present case, plaintiffs hired the excavator to repair the dam, and in repairing the dam the excavator's machinery invaded the physical condition of defendants Smedley's property. Plaintiffs' defense based on consent is of no merit as plaintiff Diane Knaus testified that shortly after the excavation began defendant Frank Smedley stated that he did not want the excavator on the Smedley property. * * * Therefore, we find that the trial court's finding in favor of defendants Smedley on their counterclaim for trespass damages is not against the manifest weight of the evidence and will stand.

For the foregoing reasons, the judgment of the circuit court of St. Clair County is hereby affirmed.

Affirmed.

Notes

1. *Questions.* Does fronting on a lake give an owner's lot a higher value? How can several lake front owners plan in advance to maximize the value and share the expense of the dam that benefits all of them? Would ownership of the dam as tenants in common have been a wise choice? The Knauses unsuccessfully put forward several property theories, riparian rights, rights created by the plat, and concurrent ownership. A neighborhood association established through covenants and financed through assessments is a familiar technique several owners may use to manage common resources. Government ownership of a park maintained by tax funds is another possibility.

Were the Knauses' repairs necessary to preserve the dam? Was there an emergency that required the Knauses' immediate action? Did the Knauses intend to make a gift to their neighbors?

One name for a person who uses resources without paying for them is "free rider." Are the Knauses' neighbors free riders? Did the Knauses' repair benefit the neighbors? Were the neighbors benefitted at the Knauses' expense? Did the neighbors accept the benefit? Could they reject or return the benefit? Is their refusal to share the Knauses' repair expense a sufficient reason to withhold restitution? Is the ability to improve property and assess the cost against the benefitted group ultimately a governmental power?

2. If the Knauses had sued their seller for failure to disclose the leaky dam and if they had prevailed, their remedy would probably have been limited to rescission of the sales contract and restitution of their payments.

3. By the way, would Kossian have recovered restitution under the rule the Illinois court states and applies?

4. *The Common Fund.* Reconsider the common fund theory of attorney fee recovery pp. 162–63.

5. *Beyond Common Fund.* Bell retained Attorney Blatt under a contingency fee contract to recover a $56,830 medical claim which Bell's insurer, HMA, had declined to pay. While Bell's lawsuit against HMA was pending, Sparks Regional Medical Center, the hospital, "filed a claim with Medicare and received partial payment in the amount of $11,155.00. By accepting this Medicare payment, Sparks evidently waived any action it might otherwise have had against Bell for the balance of the bill."

Just before trial, Bell and HMA settled for $56,830, the "precise amount" Bell sought; but, in an interpleader action, the court held the money to be "insurance proceeds" which Bell had assigned to Sparks and Holt–Krock, another medical creditor.

So Blatt sued Sparks and Holt–Krock for restitution on the ground that the defendants had "knowingly accepted the benefits" of his "legal services, which were solely responsible for producing the recovery." The trial judge, concluding that Sparks and Holt–Krock had been unjustly enriched, ordered them to pay pro rata amounts of a $15,225 fee to Blatt.

If Blatt's services had enriched the defendants, the appellate court held, the enrichment was not unjust. Blatt and Bell had a contingency fee contract. The settlement, which made no allowance for attorney fees, succeeded in relieving Bell of the $56,000 debt. "For purposes of the fee agreement between the attorney and his client, there was no amount 'recovered' by the client. As a result of the interpleader action, the settlement money flowed straight to the" defendants. "As creditors, the [defendants] were entitled to their recovery and they were not, in some equitable sense or otherwise, bound to restore it. There was no operative act, intent, or situation on the [defendants'] part * * * to make the enrichment unjust."

"Courts should be hesitant to employ a quasi-contractual theory of recovery where an underlying express contract already exists and fairly distributes the risks among the parties involved. * * * [Blatt] obtained a good result—indeed, the best result—for his client. Because the case was settled, it cannot be said the attorney, who must have been somewhat skilled in negotiations of this kind, was somehow unfairly denied a fee. He simply failed to protect his own interest in obtaining a fee while he was also protecting his client's interest. * * * We believe the application of rules from common-fund cases stretches the analogy too far. * * * [O]ur conclusion in this case is in accord with the well-settled American rule that attorney's fees are not allowed except when expressly provided for by statute." Sparks Regional Medical Center v. Blatt, 55 Ark.App. 311, 314, 318–19, 935 S.W.2d 304, 306–07 (1996).

Did attorney Blatt have a duty to client Bell to accept the settlement offer which provided nothing for attorney fees? See Evans v. Jeff D., Note 6, p. 177.

Should Sparks Regional Medical Center keep both the Medicaid payment and the insurance proceeds? *Kossian*, p. 393.

B. LEGAL RESTITUTION: QUASI–CONTRACTS

After unjust enrichment and volunteer-intermeddler, we return to the vocabulary of restitution, which, the introduction to this Chapter promised, can be confusing. To begin with, restitution divides into a legal restitution branch, the present subject, and an equitable restitution branch, which is taken up below.

Legal restitution, in turn, has two branches: (a) Money or value restitution, which we are studying, occurs when the successful plaintiff recovers a money judgment measured by the defendant's unjust enrichment. (b) Specific or in specie restitution includes replevin and ejectment; it usually occurs, as will be studied in the Property Chapter, where the defendant returns the plaintiff's exact chattel or real property respectively.

The language of the law expresses the substance of legal restitution for money through the vocabulary of contract. In medieval England, long before the merger of law and equity, the common law courts first invented and later developed legal restitution under the assumpsit form of action, more particularly under general assumpsit or indebitatus assumpsit. The profession has never brushed the anachronisms off.

Since assumpsit was a contract form of action, another term for legal restitution is quasi-contract, which is the word this book usually employs.

Quasi-contract had several parts, the "common counts," which are now neither common nor commonly known. The common counts that courts use today are: (a) money had and received; (b) goods sold and delivered or quantum valebant; and (c) quantum meruit. A short explanation of each follows: (a) Money had and received. The plaintiff alleges that the defendant has money which in good conscience belongs to the plaintiff because of duress, fraud, mistake, or another reason. Money had and received includes a transfer to the defendant from either the plaintiff or a third person. The plaintiff's federal form complaint for money had and received is below. (b) Quantum valebant. The plaintiff's recovery is for goods "sold and delivered" to the defendant. (c) Quantum meruit. The plaintiff has performed services which will enrich the defendant unjustly unless the defendant pays him. In *Kossian*, p. 393, although the court grounds its decision on the bedrock unjust enrichment principle, plaintiff Kossian's theory might be classified as quantum meruit to recover for the value of the cleanup and removal services that Kossian furnished to defendant-American without any exchange of promises.

Although the 1937 Restitution Restatement, which is quoted below, retains its vocabulary, common law pleading has long ago passed from the professional scene. Few contemporary lawyers and judges grasp "assumpsit" firmly; fewer still demarcate general assumpsit and indebitatus assumpsit. If the terms are not obsolete, they are confusing because they yoke restitution based on unjust enrichment with breach of a true contract. The terms general assumpsit, special assumpsit, and indebitatus assumpsit could profitably be scuttled.

Confusion increases when someone says that a quasi-contract is based on a "promise implied in law." The early English courts established quasi-contract in assumpsit for convenience and because it was close at hand. The courts developed quasi-contracts, a/k/a contracts implied in *law,* from the *general* assumpsit form of action. They developed *express* contracts from the *special* assumpsit form of action. A contract implied in fact is an express contract the parties created without verbal conduct. The verbal similarity of "contract implied in law" and "contract implied in fact" leads people to the unsound conclusion that the subjects are more alike than they really are.

The "implied" component of the designation "contract implied in law" is a signal that the "contract" label is a legal fiction. Medieval courts devised the legal fiction that the law "implied" a contract; their purpose was to use general assumpsit to avert the defendant's unjust enrichment. A defendant who improperly retains a benefit will be unjustly enriched; so that defendant, the court "implies," made a fictional promise to restore the benefit to the plaintiff. Even though assumpsit was also the home base for the parties' genuine contract, neither an express contract nor a contract implied in fact is essential for a quasi-contract. Stripping off the fiction and conclusion leaves the essential kernel: the defendant's unjust enrichment activates the plaintiff's quasi-contract restitution.

Articulating "implied contracts" as a topic divided into "contracts implied in law" and "contracts implied in fact" is also confusing. For it combines and then divides two dissimilar subjects, restitution quasi-contract variety and a genuine contract formed through the parties' nonverbal conduct, under one analytical head. Freestanding restitution differs fundamentally from contract breach; saying that a court will base restitution on an obligation imposed on the defendant by law while a court will base breach of contract in an obligation the parties voluntarily assumed also presents analytically distinct subjects in confusingly similarly ways. "Contracts implied in law" should be dropped from the language of restitution.

Nevertheless a student will find statutes of limitations and attachment statutes that deal with legal restitution, quasi-contract variety, under the heading of contract. Legal digests, encyclopedias, and indexes may also classify quasi-contract under contracts. Forms of action survive in the 1937 Restatement.

Quasi-contract may be a freestanding form of recovery in restitution. A court may, like the courts in *Kistler* and *Kossian*, base a plaintiff's quasi-contract restitution on the defendant's unjust enrichment standing alone; the court need not find a tort, breach of contract, or violation of property right.

This is a good place to summarize legal restitution's vocabulary surplus. Essentially the same analytical work is performed by five synonyms: legal restitution, general assumpsit, indebitatus assumpsit, contract implied in law, and quasi-contract. Money had and received and quantum meruit are near synonyms, a little more specialized, but equally susceptible to being confused. Every one of the synonyms is spongy enough to absorb unnecessary meaning from similar sounding, but unrelated, doctrines, particularly from offer-acceptance contracts.

A student has another vocabulary puzzle to tussle with.

Courts and commentators frequently join the courts in our principal cases above in referring to a plaintiff's quasi-contractual restitution as "equitable." The word "equity" has multiple meanings. What is meant by "equitable" in the quasi-contract context is fairness and correcting injustice. Stirring the word "equity" or "equitable" into the quasi-contract mix risks extending its customary meaning, fairness, to the technical distinction between legal remedies and equitable remedies. In Remedies, I try to refer to the technical meanings of "equity" or "equitable" as the Court of Chancery, the business of Chancery, or the equitable remedies of injunction, specific performance or constructive trust. None of these subjects is invoked in quasi-contract. A plaintiff's quasi-contract restitution is an action at law; it is subject to the constitutional right to a jury trial; and if the plaintiff prevails, it ends with a money judgment.

This work attempts to limit its terminology to the terms quasi-contracts and the common counts, money had and received and quantum meruit. Courts' language has been retained.

What if restitution's analysis and vocabulary had a fresh start? First, a better term than quasi-contract would be developed; money had and received and quantum meruit would perish as well. Lawyers, law students, and judges ought to be able to deal with the difficult issues of restitution, enrichment and unjustness, with more attention to the real issues. In short, the defendant's unjust enrichment is the substantive breach; restitution is the plaintiff's remedy.

Second, the distinction between equitable restitution and legal restitution would be downgraded. To divide restitution into legal and equitable branches is artificial and not functional. The practical issue is what form the plaintiff's remedy for restitution should take. The legal-equitable distinction cannot be eliminated because the constitutional issue, whether the right to a jury trial exists, will continue to depend on historical and technical equitable-legal distinctions; fortunately jury trials have not been a significant restitution issue.

Warning—reform of the legal vocabulary is not for the impatient. Be alert for broad, imprecise, and inaccurate terminology in restitution.

The preceding will introduce you to three intellectual missteps that a lawyer or a court may take in restitution analysis. Citations are omitted below to protect the guilty.

The first misstep, called the "contract fallacy," occurs within legal restitution. A lawyer or judge may use the names "implied contract" or "contract implied in law" when talking about legal restitution.

The lawyer or judge may commit the contract fallacy by reasoning as follows: Legal restitution is an implied contract; therefore legal restitution has the other attributes of a contract. The court may decide that because restitution is an implied contract, the time bar for restitution is determined by the contract statute of limitations instead of the tort statute of limitations. That use of a contract characterization for restitution is comparatively benign—a court has to bar a dawdling plaintiff's restitution claim under some statute of limitations. The full-fledged contract fallacy consists of reifying the implied contract fiction: if a valid contract could not have been formed, the court will not imply one in law.

Consider examples of reifying the contract in restitution: (a) Restitution is an implied contract. If this plaintiff's transfer to this defendant had been pursuant to a contract, such a contract would be ultra vires (outside its legal power) for this defendant; therefore, this defendant cannot be responsible for restitution. (b) Restitution is an implied contract. If this plaintiff's payment to this defendant had been under a supposed contract, the contract would have failed because the defendant is a minor; since a minor is not responsible for his contract, the court will not imply one to make the minor responsible for restitution. (c) Restitution is an implied contract. Plaintiff performed services for the defendant under an agreement the Statute of Frauds requires to be in writing; because no enforceable contract existed, the court will not recognize an implied contract in the form of restitution-quantum meruit. All three of these examples of bad reasoning could lead a court to refuse to grant a plaintiff's restitution claim that it should recognize as valid.

Legal restitution came to modern law through the contract doctrine of assumpsit; but as Lord Atkin put it, implying a "debt" and a "promise to repay" are legal fictions that should have dropped out of our legal vocabulary when the forms of actions were abolished. "These fantastic resemblances of contracts invented in order to meet requirements of the law as to forms of action which have now disappeared should not in these days be allowed to affect actual rights. When these ghosts of the past stand in the path of justice clanking their mediaeval chains the proper course of the judges is to pass through them undeterred." United Australia v. Barclays Bank, A.C. 1, 28–29 (H.L. 1941).

A modern court ought to concentrate on the defendant's alleged unjust enrichment instead of borrowing fictions from contract. As part of trimming restitution's vocabulary surplus, the legal profession should reject the "implied contract" terminology in favor of a unifying concept of unjust enrichment.

Second is the "equity fallacy." The courts in our decisions have used the words "equity" and "equitable" to describe restitution. These courts are using "equity" in the nontechnical sense to mean "fairness."

A lawyer or court commits the "equity fallacy" by supposing that the word "equity" referring to restitution as fairness means an equitable remedy in the sense that an injunction or specific performance is an equitable remedy.

The equity fallacy occurs in the examples that follow. (a) Restitution is equitable. Equitable litigants have no constitutional right to a jury trial. This restitution litigant has no right to a jury trial. (b) Restitution is equitable. A litigant with an adequate legal remedy cannot receive an equitable remedy. This plaintiff who is seeking restitution, having not shown that her legal remedy is inadequate, cannot recover restitution. (c) Restitution is equitable. This plaintiff's restitution claim will be time-barred under the equitable doctrine of laches rather than the statute of limitations.

As we have seen, restitution is divided into legal and equitable branches for purposes of jury trial, qualification for remedy, and time bar. A court that commits the equity fallacy might (a) deprive a legal restitution plaintiff like Campbell of his right to a jury trial, (b) as a prerequisite for recovery of quantum meruit, require a legal-restitution plaintiff like Campbell to show that compensatory damages are inadequate, or (c) allow a plaintiff's legal restitution claim that was time-barred by the passage of the statute of limitations period to proceed.

The "tort fallacy" is the third misstep. Many lawyers and professors dealing with the state attorneys generals' recoupment suits against the tobacco companies leading to settlements worth $246 billions have written that the lawsuits were "torts," even "mass torts." However, many plaintiff's tort suits against the tobacco companies had failed; the attorneys generals' recoupment lawsuits were based on other substantive theories, principally restitution. The "tort-fallacy" mis-statements have not caused much harm so far, except to the authors' credibility. Their analytical mistake is fundamental, however, for the notion that "restitution is a tort" belies restitution's status as a body of the common law separate from contract, property, and tort. If restitution were a tort, we could omit this chapter and the American Law Institute could scuttle its Restatement (Third) of Restitution and Unjust Enrichment.

Detour Back to Arkansas. Our first restitution decision, Kistler v. Stoddard, seems to have been legal restitution filed as equity perhaps because it arose in equitable probate proceedings or perhaps because of an error. The separate courts of law and equity that existed then in Arkansas are now merged, and the state's Supreme Court has distinguished equitable restitution and legal restitution and held that a jury trial is appropriate for legal restitution. First National Bank of DeWitt v. Cruthis, 360 Ark. 528, ___ S.W.3d ___ (2005).

The Supremes. Is there anybody else out there who is confused? We discussed the Supreme Court's ERISA decisions in the last chapter in the context of Law vs. Equity. Here we can revisit them and focus on restitution. In Mertens v. Hewitt Associates, the Court foreshadowed its confusion by observing that "Petitioners * * * do not * * * seek a remedy traditionally viewed as 'equitable' such as injunction or restitution." The Court's boner under the "equity fallacy" consisted of saying later that " 'equitable relief' can also refer to those categories of relief that were *typically* available in equity (such as injunction, mandamus, and restitution, but not compensatory damages)." Mertens v. Hewitt Associates, 508 U.S. 248, 255, 256 (1993).

As we have learned, restitution is sometimes equitable, sometimes at common law. Was the Court simply ignorant of the major areas of legal restitution like quantum meruit and quasi-contract?

Mertens was a hopelessly technical Employee Retirement Income Security Act (ERISA) case, where a badly drafted statute and narrow, technical issues were exacerbated by underwhelming briefs. Justice Scalia, the decision's author, did partially rehabilitate himself in a later ERISA opinion where he correctly distinguished legal restitution as separate from equitable restitution. In the process, however, he wrote that "The restitution sought here by Great–West is * * * a freestanding claim for money damages." Great–West Life & Annuity Insurance Co. v. Knudson, 534 U.S. 204, 212–17, 218 n.4 (2002). The latter misstatement is broader than the equity fallacy, for it stirs the unjust enrichment base for restitution into the compensatory base for damages, combining the separate remedies' discrete policy bases.

The Supreme Court decided Sereboff v. Mid Atlantic Medical Services, Inc., 126 S.Ct. 1869 (2006). An ERISA fiduciary sued its insureds, the Sereboffs, to recover the medical-expenses part of the insured's tort settlement that the fiduciary had already paid. The fiduciary's subrogation claim against its insureds was "equitable" restitution, the Court held, because the fiduciary "sought its recovery through a constructive trust or equitable lien on a specifically identifiable fund, not from the Sereboffs' assets generally, as would be the case with a contract action at law."

Pleading quasi-contract claims. Two examples from the 1930s show the traditional approach to pleading quasi-contract.

Restatement, Restitution (1937)[†] § 5. Forms of Action: "The appropriate proceeding in an action at law for the payment of money by way of restitution is: (a) in States retaining common law forms of action, an action of general assumpsit; (b) in States distinguishing actions of contract from actions of tort, an action of contract; (c) in States which have statutes providing for the abolition of the distinctions between forms of action, an action in which the facts entitling the plaintiff to restitution are set forth."

Expect the new restitution restatement to move beyond the forms of action and code pleading.

Federal Rules of Civil Procedure, Rule 84. Forms. The forms contained in the Appendix of Forms are sufficient under the rules and are intended to indicate the simplicity and brevity of statement which the rules contemplate.

Form 8. *Complaint for Money Had and Received*

1. Allegation of jurisdiction.

2. Defendant owes plaintiff ____ dollars for money had and received from one G.H. on June 1, 1936, to be paid by defendant to plaintiff.

Wherefore (etc.).

1. MEASURING THE DEFENDANT'S BENEFIT—SERVICES

Frequently a person, later the plaintiff, will assume that a contract exists and will confer a benefit on another, later the defendant. The plaintiff's assumption may be erroneous for a variety of reasons. For example, the contract may fail because of a misunderstanding or the bargain may exist but be unenforceable because of the statute of frauds.

Or the plaintiff may believe erroneously that he was dealing with an authorized agent, whose "principal" winds up with the benefit. Restitution is the plaintiff's sole remedy because no contract exists and no tort occurred. Difficult questions arise: whether the recipient (equally mixed up) should be liable at all; and if so, how to calculate its "enrichment."

Consider the plight of an artisan who has performed services for someone under the mistaken belief that a contract exists. Although curbside "equity" suggests splitting the difference between the innocent parties, the rules of restitution may cast the entire loss on the unhappy artisan. This may be harsh, but as the Restatement of Restitution observes, "it would be still more harsh to require a recipient to pay for services which he did not want or for which he could not afford to pay although he may have been glad to have them." § 41 *comment a.* A court may be tempted to blame, however slightly, the recipient and to shift the entire burden on to it, an obvious solution if the artisan performed in reliance on an unenforceable bargain, since the recipient has at least broken its word.

Your answers to the following questions may influence your decision whether to allow restitution for services a plaintiff conferred in misreliance upon a supposed contract: (a) Did the recipient expect someone to pay for the services? (b) Although perhaps the recipient did not expect to pay, did he request the services? (c) Was the recipient aware that services were being rendered?

If your answers justify telling the recipient to pay for the services, the next issue is how much. Where the recipient's benefit is tangibles or money capable of specific restitution, a court will be able to measure it. Restatement of Restitution § 39 (1937). But when the plaintiff's mistaken performance improves the recipient's property or consists of services, questions arise about how to value the benefit. Keep the following points in mind as you read on

(a) Should the court measure the value from the standpoint of the plaintiff or the defendant? Literal application of unjust enrichment doctrine might limit the plaintiff's recovery to the defendant's actual benefit; this may be slight, even less than nothing. On the other hand, awarding the plaintiff the benefit's market value may resemble contract damages in the guise of restitution. The plaintiff may recover the same amount for a quasi-contract as he would for a true contract, an anomaly which also increases confusion between the two.

(b) No contract may exist because of the parties' misunderstanding, but the recipient may have mentioned a rate of pay. Or the parties' oral agreement at an explicit rate of compensation may be unenforceable under the statute of frauds. Should the stipulated compensation measure the defendant's actual benefit? Will this award the plaintiff contract "expectancy" damages in the guise of restitution?

CAMPBELL v. TENNESSEE VALLEY AUTHORITY

United States Court of Appeals, Fifth Circuit, 1969.
421 F.2d 293.

LEWIS R. MORGAN, CIRCUIT JUDGE. This is an action in *quantum meruit* brought by Raymond Campbell against the Tennessee Valley Authority (hereafter TVA) to recover $30,240 for the microfilming of certain technical trade journals which were a part of TVA's technical library located at Muscle Shoals, Alabama. The District Court entered a judgment upon a verdict for Campbell in the amount of $30,240. We affirm.

Campbell entered into an oral agreement with Earl Daniel, Director of the TVA Technical Library, to reproduce 13 sets of technical trade journals on 16 mm. microfilm at a price of $90 per roll. Mr. Daniel had no authority to make such a purchase for TVA and entered into the agreement with Campbell without the knowledge of his superiors. Campbell photographed, developed and processed 336 rolls of 16 mm. film containing the journals in question, placed the film in cartridges and delivered them to the TVA Technical Library at Muscle Shoals. Under the terms of the oral agreement, the charge for this work was to have been $30,240. The cartridges were placed on the shelves of the library and were available to its patrons for approximately two months. There is evidence in the record that in this two-month period three of the cartridges were each used once. The microfilm cartridges were then returned to Campbell by registered mail along with a letter from Daniel stating that there was no contract for their reproduction, that he had no authority to enter into such a contract, and that the price of the film was excessive. Campbell refused to accept the film and it was returned to the library, where it has since been stored. TVA has refused to pay for the film. The journals reproduced by Campbell were destroyed upon instruction by Daniel.

Campbell's original complaint relied on an express contract with TVA. TVA's motion for summary judgment on the ground that there could be no express contract since its employee Daniel had no authority to enter such a contract was granted. Campbell then amended his complaint to set out a claim for recovery based on *quantum meruit* or a contract implied in law. * * *

The principal contention made by appellant TVA is that the District Court committed error in instructing the jury that the measure of damages in this case was "the fair market value of the microfilm that benefitted TVA."

The portions of the District Court's instructions to the jury dealing with the question of the measure of damages are as follows:

"Another authority has said 'The obligee shall be compensated, not for any loss or damage suffered by him, but for the benefit which he has conferred upon the obligor.' * * *

"In valuing the benefits or loss to TVA, you must use fair market value. In other words, you must use the values that the same or similar microfilm and the journals would sell for on the open market.

" * * * If the TVA had agreed to purchase, we will say, a typewriter—they used the expression bulldozer—and they used the typewriter and sent it back, under the authorities the plaintiff would be entitled to recover only the value of the use of the typewriter, because the typewriter could be sold to somebody else. * * * There would be a market value for the typewriter. * * * But if something is designed for a person to use for a particular thing, and they accept it, and it has no market value other than that particular use, you could see that it would be a complete loss. Those are the two extremes that you might visualize. You have here certain microfilm that were (sic) made. What would be the value of these microfilm if they could be sold to somebody else?"

It is TVA's contention that it "is obligated to pay not for the film itself, but only for the 'benefit,' or unjust enrichment, if any, which it received by reason of the *use* it made of the film while it was in the library." The first question thus presented to this Court is whether a person who is entitled to recover from an agency of the federal government under a theory of *quantum meruit* is entitled to the reasonable, or fair market, value of the goods or services so provided, or to the reasonable value of the benefit so realized by the Government. In other words, is the measure of recovery to be determined by the amount of money that would be necessary to acquire on the open market the goods or services from which the benefit is derived, or is the measure of recovery how much the benefit has been worth to the person upon whom it was conferred? * * *

In re Moyer, W.D. Virginia 1960, 190 F.Supp. 867, 873, held that "the measure of recovery * * * on the principle of *quantum meruit* * * * is the reasonable value of the work performed, less the amount of compensation, whether in money or otherwise, already received." Evans v. Mason, 82 Ariz. 40, 308 P.2d 245 (1957), an action in *quantum meruit* to recover for services rendered to decedent pursuant to a parol contract barred by the Statute of Frauds held that the measure of damages is the actual value of the services rendered to the decedent. On the other hand, Hill v. Waxberg (9 Cir.1956) 237 F.2d 936, 16 Alaska 477, an action by a contractor to recover for services and expenditures made in contemplation of a proposed building contract, held the "restitution is properly limited to the value of the benefit which was acquired."

This confusion in the cases is clarified by a statement made in a footnote of the court's decision in Martin v. Campanaro (2 Cir., 1946), 156 F.2d 127, 130 n. 5, cert. den. 329 U.S. 759:

> "The claimants are entitled to recover on a quantum meruit basis. But 'quantum meruit' is ambiguous; it may mean (1) that there is a contract 'implied in fact' to pay the reasonable value of the services, or (2) that, to prevent unjust enrichment, the claimant may recover on a quasi-contract (an 'as if' contract) for that reasonable value. It has been suggested that the latter is a rule-of-thumb measure of damages adopted in quasi contract cases where the actual unjust enrichment or benefit to the defendant is too difficult to prove."

In the present situation the District Court was correct in using the "rule of thumb" measure of damages and in instructing the jury that the measure of damages was "the fair market value of the microfilm that benefitted TVA," instead of instructing that the measure of damages was the reasonable value of the benefit realized by TVA from the microfilm, since the actual benefit to TVA would not have been susceptible of proof. The value realized by a library in having a particular reference work available to its patrons cannot be adequately expressed in dollars and cents. The real benefit is realized, not so much by the library itself, as by those who depend upon the library in their research activities, and the benefit is not so much that the books, technical journals and other research sources are actually *used*, on a regular basis, but that they are conveniently *available for use.* If use, rather than availability, were the only test of the benefit conferred by a book in a library, a good university library could be many times smaller than the present day standard and still retain its effectiveness as a center for research.

The journals which had been reproduced had been destroyed, making the microfilm copies the only ones available. Moreover, there was evidence that the journals in question were a necessary part of a technical library. Likewise, it does not appear the microfilm copies had value to anyone other than to the library.

Furthermore, in view of the fact that the microfilmed technical journals furnished by Campbell had no readily marketable value to anyone except the TVA because of their unique character and the special circumstances of this case, the District Court properly instructed the jury that the measure of recovery was the fair market value, even though the microfilm was available on the library's shelves for only two months. * * *

TVA argues that if the jury could find that the "fair market value of the microfilm that benefitted TVA" could be the contract price between the parties, it could not exceed the lowest contract price that would have been obtainable had competitive bidding taken place on the microfilming under 16 U.S.C.A. § 831h(b)(1964), and that the evidence is uncontradicted that University Microfilming, a division of Xerox Corporation, would have done the microfilming for $10,000. Thus, TVA contends that Campbell could recover no more than $10,000 and that his recovery of $30,240 was contrary to the law and the evidence.

While there is authority for the proposition that the upper limit of recovery in an action of this nature is the amount agreed to by the parties in the unenforceable contract, Hill v. Waxberg, 237 F.2d at 940, n. 6, the testimony of Holladay, the representative from the University Microfilm division of Xerox, that his company would have done the microfilming here in question for $10,000 did not constitute a bid under 16 U.S.C.A. § 831h(b), and thus can in no way be considered an upper limit on Campbell's recovery. It is also hornbook law that the jury is in no way bound by the testimony of experts. * * *

The judgment of the District Court is Affirmed.

RIVES, CIRCUIT JUDGE (dissenting). With deference, I submit that the district judge inadvertently imported into the claimed quasi contract, "implied in law," too much of the actual agreement between the appellee Campbell and Daniel, the *unauthorized* agent of TVA. Campbell concedes, as he must, that only a quasi contract is now involved. * * *

This litigation began with the filing of a complaint which alleged that Earl Daniel, as agent of the TVA, acting within the line and scope of his authority, agreed with Campbell for him to produce and deliver microfilm of certain trade journals for which Campbell was to be paid $90.00 per roll; that TVA ordered 336 rolls, all of which were delivered; but that TVA refused to pay to Campbell the agreed amount of the contract, $30,240.00. The district court granted TVA's motion for summary judgment as to that claim.

Campbell then amended his complaint by filing counts in general assumpsit seeking to recover a quantum meruit.

"Amendment: Comes now the plaintiff in the above captioned cause and amends his complaint by adding the following:

"Second Cause of Action, Count 2: The Plaintiff expressly adopts the allegations of Paragraph 1 of Count 1. The plaintiff claims of the defendant $30,240.00 due from it for merchandise, goods and chattel sold by the plaintiff to the defendant from the first day of January, 1967 through the 13th day of February, 1967, which sum of money with the interest thereon is still unpaid.

"Count 3: The Plaintiff claims of the defendant $30,240.00 due from it for work and labor done for the defendant by the plaintiff from the first day of January, 1967 through the 13th day of February, 1967, which sum of money with the interest thereon is still unpaid. Plaintiff expressly adopts the allegations of paragraph 1 of Count 1 of the bill of complaint."

While the amended complaint is broad enough to sustain recovery on a contract implied *in fact,* as well as on one implied *in law,* I repeat that the sole claim is on a contract implied *in law.* Judge Grooms correctly so charged the jury:

"Members of the jury, this case began as a contract case, but it was determined at the outset that Mr. Earl Daniel had no authority to make a contract; the contract was void for that reason, and the contract aspect went out and then the complaint was amended to claim for work and labor and for goods and chattels, merchandise, goods, and chattels sold to the defendant, T.V.A. on the theory of what we know as a quantum meruit. That is an old form of action, and it literally means as much as he deserves. Quantum means quantity, merit [sic], as much as he deserves. The case has proceeded since then on the theory of quantum meruit. * * *

"As I stated to you the words quantum meruit, liberally [sic] translated, means as much as he deserves. The basis of a recovery under a quantum meruit is that the defendant has received a benefit from the plaintiff which it is unjust for him to retain without paying for it. Quantum meruit is a devise [sic] to prevent unjust enrichment by requiring a recipient of work or services to pay the party furnishing such work and services as much as he reasonably deserves for this work."

The jury verdict of $30,240.00 is in the exact amount the plaintiff Campbell claimed that Daniel promised for TVA to pay for the film (336 rolls at $90.00 per roll). A reading of the record makes obvious, I submit, that the unauthorized express contract has simply been enforced under the guise of a quasi contract or quantum meruit. * * *

[W]hen goods or services are furnished to the federal government pursuant to an unenforceable or invalid contract, the courts will, in certain limited fact situations, grant relief of a quasi-contractual nature. Such relief is appropriate only when it serves to prevent the government from being unjustly enriched at the expense of another. * * *

[In] Crocker v. United States, 240 U.S. 74, 81–82, Mr. Justice Van Devanter, speaking for the Court, said:

"It [the corrupt arrangement] was made by Lorenz and Crawford while endeavoring to secure the contract for the company and was a means to that end. They were the company's agents and were securing the contract at its request. It accepted the fruits of their efforts and thereby sanctioned what they did, and made their knowledge its own. * * *

"It results that no recovery could be had upon the contract with the Postmaster General, because it was tainted with fraud and rescinded by him on that ground. But this was not an obstacle to a recovery upon a *quantum valebat.*"

* * * Continuing, the Court held that no recovery could be had upon a quantum valebat because there was lacking the requisite proof of the value of the letter carriers' satchels so furnished and retained. The claimant's insistence in *Crock-*

er, was remarkably similar to that of Campbell in the present case. As stated by Mr. Justice Van Devanter for the court:

> "He [the claimant] insists, however, that the findings show the price at which the government contracted to take the satchels with the shoulder straps, and also what it cost the government to supply the straps, and that the difference should be regarded, in the absence of other evidence, as representing the value of the satchels as furnished,—that is, without the straps. The insistence proceeds upon the theory that the contract price was in the nature of an admission by the government of the value of the satchels with the straps. However this might be in other circumstances, it is wholly inadmissible here, for the fraud with which the contract was tainted completely discredited the contract price, and prevented it from being treated as an admission of the value by the government. It therefore was incumbent upon the claimant to show the value by other evidence, and, as this was not done, no recovery could be had upon a *quantum valebat.*"

Thus, it would seem that the *possible* basis for recovery considered in *Crocker* was a contract implied *in fact,* rather than *in law,* because the Government actually accepted and permanently retained the satchels and, hence, was contractually liable for their value. In the present case, as has been shown, no TVA employee with proper authority accepted the microfilm, and TVA made every reasonable effort to return the rolls to Campbell. Upon Campbell's refusal to accept delivery of the film, it was stored and its use forbidden.

In forbidding use of the film, TVA may have gone further than law and equity required in view of the fact that Campbell had destroyed TVA's original journals. It should be noted that in *Crocker* the contract price of the satchels was inadmissible to prove value because the contract was tainted with fraud. While there was no fraud in the present case, there was a complete absence of competitive bidding necessary to establish a valid contract price. Let me divert to express my opinion that the price agreed on between Daniel and Campbell is wholly inadmissible to prove the value of the film.

In Prestex, Inc. v. United States, 1963, 320 F.2d 367, the government contracting officer advertised for bids on white duck cloth of certain specifications to be used in making summer uniforms for the cadets of the United States Military Academy. Prestex submitted its bid with an attached sample which appeared to meet the specifications, but which, as a later laboratory test showed, was in material variance. Prestex was awarded the contract and had the 25,000 yards of cloth manufactured. The government, after testing a sample of the finished cloth, refused to accept delivery. The Court of Claims held that the award was illegal and granted the government's motion for summary judgment. Clearly, that decision does not support the majority ruling. The opinion does, however, contain an admirable statement of the principles of equity and justice which call for "relief of a quasi-contractual nature * * * *in certain limited fact situations.*" (Emphasis supplied.)

> "Even though a contract be unenforceable against the Government, because not properly advertised, not authorized, or for some other reason, it is only fair and just that the Government pay for goods delivered or services rendered and accepted under it. In certain limited fact situations, therefore, the courts will grant relief of a quasi-contractual nature when the Government elects to rescind an invalid contract. No one would deny that ordinary principles of equity and justice preclude the United States from retaining

the services, materials, and benefits and at the same time refusing to pay for them on the ground that the contracting officer's promise was unauthorized, or unenforceable for some other reason. However, the basic fact of legal significance charging the Government with liability in these situations is its retention of benefits in the form of goods or services." (Footnotes omitted.)

In Williams v. United States, 1955, 127 F.Supp. 617, it was held that the contracting officer had ratified the agreement in question and that the government had received the benefits of its performance. The *Williams* case involved a contract implied *in fact*. Indeed it has been held that the Court of Claims has no jurisdiction of an action against the United States in those cases where, if the transaction were between private parties, recovery could be had upon a contract implied *in law*.

The underlying principle is that of forbidding unjust enrichment. "A person who has been unjustly enriched at the expense of another is required to make restitution to the other." A.L.I. Restatement, Restitution § 1, p. 12.

Chapter 2 of that text "states the conditions under which there is a right to restitution because of a mistake in the conferring of a benefit." A.L.I. Restatement, Restitution Introductory Note, p. 26. Such a right may arise in the case of a person who has paid money (Id. § 16) or transferred property (Id. § 39), or rendered services (Id. § 40) to another which have inured to the latter's benefit, in the mistaken belief that he is performing a valid contract with the other, although the contract is later avoided. A right to restitution, however, does not arise in such cases unless the recipient of the property or services is *unjustly enriched*.

> "Even where a person has received a benefit from another, he is liable to pay therefor only if the circumstances of its receipt or retention are such that, as between the two persons, it is unjust for him to retain it. The mere fact that a person benefits another is not of itself sufficient to require the other to make restitution therefore."

A.L.I. Restatement, Restitution p. 13.

Under the facts and circumstances of this case, it is doubtful whether TVA was *enriched* or *harmed* by Campbell's services when consideration is given to the fact that Campbell destroyed TVA's original journals.

Assuming arguendo that TVA was benefitted by Campbell's services, it was not *unjustly* enriched: It has been demonstrated that no authorized agent of TVA accepted delivery of the rolls of microfilm; that TVA has not wrongfully retained the microfilm, but has made every reasonable effort to return it to Campbell, and that upon Campbell's refusal to accept the film, TVA has stored it and forbidden its use. The only possible benefit retained by TVA is in the two-month period that the microfilm remained in its Technical Library. In that two months, three of the rolls were each used once. There was no evidence that the person making such limited use of the film knew or had reason to know that he was using film which did not belong to TVA or that he was in any way obligating TVA to pay for the film. Such knowledge is, I submit, necessary for this limited user to impose upon TVA a duty of restitution. See A.L.I. Restatement, Restitution §§ 40 and 41. Further, a precedent should not be laid for the public policy requirement of competitive bidding to be frustrated by the application of some principle of restitution or quasi contract. For all of the foregoing reasons, I am firmly of the opinion that TVA is not liable to Campbell in any amount.

[Even] *If* Liable, What Is the Extent of TVA's Liability.

It is incomprehensible to me that Campbell should be rewarded for *his* destruction of TVA's original trade journals. Perhaps the best precedent is the classic case of the son who murdered his father and mother, but was granted mercy because he was an orphan.

The majority holding measures the extent of TVA's liability by Campbell's loss. That overlooks the fundamental reason for granting restitution or quantum meruit relief, *viz.*, to avoid unjust enrichment. Ordinarily in such cases the benefit to the one and the loss to the other are co-extensive. However, when the benefit is less than the loss, the recovery is limited to the benefit. * * *

I respectfully dissent.

Notes

1. *Quantum Meruit, Three Approaches.* (a) *Texas Style.* "To recover under quantum meruit a claimant must prove that: 1. valuable services were rendered or materials furnished; 2. for the person sought to be charged; 3. which services and materials were accepted by the person sought to be charged, used and enjoyed by him; 4. under such circumstances as reasonably notified the person sought to be charged that the plaintiff in performing such services was expecting to be paid by the person sought to be charged." Vortt Exploration Co. v. Chevron U.S.A., Inc., 787 S.W.2d 942, 944 (Tex.1990).

(b) *Free Acceptance.* Free acceptance occurs and the defendant benefitted from and freely accepted the plaintiff's services if the defendant in fact or as a reasonable person should have know that the plaintiff who was rendering the services expected to be paid and yet the defendant did not reject the services. A court cannot impose contract liability on a defendant who was entirely passive; but this defendant did choose—he chose to accept the benefit from the plaintiff.

(c) *Professor Kovacic.* A court should analyze quantum meruit by asking whether the defendant received and retained a benefit from the plaintiff's work and whether it is unjust for the defendant to retain the benefit without paying the plaintiff for it. Requiring the defendant to "accept" a benefit is unnecessary when the defendant cannot stop or return it. Candace Kovacic, A Proposal to Simplify Quantum Meruit Litigation, 35 Am.U.L.Rev. 547, 638–39 (1986).

2. *Questions.* Start with the idea that Campbell had no contract with TVA under the agency doctrines of actual authority or apparent authority. To recover, Campbell must qualify for quantum meruit restitution. Is Campbell's recovery of restitution justified because someone who worked for TVA knew that Campbell expected to be paid? What evidence of its "actual benefit" should TVA have presented?

When the court measures a plaintiff's restitution for services to the defendant, a large difference may exist between (a) a benefit that adds to the defendant's economic wealth; and (b) a benefit measured by the value of the plaintiff's performance under an agreement that failed as a contract. George Palmer, The Law of Restitution § 4.2 (1978).

If Campbell, the plaintiff, may recover restitution from TVA measured by the performance he bargained for, several questions emerge. May this way of measuring Campbell's restitution validate a noncontract as a contract? Does it lead restitution away from preventing defendant TVA's unjust enrichment? Does it award Campbell contractual expectation damages disguised as restitution? Does this measurement of restitution undermine the reason to deny Campbell's contract recovery? Is the "contract" price evidence of the amount of "benefit" Campbell conferred on TVA? Does Campbell's recovery of the "contract" price undermine the statutory policy of requiring competitive bids? Dan B. Dobbs, Remedies § 4.5 (2d ed. 1993).

3. *An Anecdote.* Judge Richard Rives, the dissenter, had only one year of college; his legal education consisted of clerking and reading law in an office in Montgomery, Alabama. After he was nominated for the United States Circuit Court of Appeals, he spoke to Supreme Court Justice Hugo Black.

> "I just wonder," Rives inquired, "if I am competent to fill this job and really ought to accept or ought to stay in my law practice. I'd really like to have your advice."

> "Well, I will be glad to give it to you, Dick," said Black, a twinkle in his eye. "When the cases reach the Supreme Court, and it's almost true when they reach the Circuit Court of Appeals, they are so extremely close they could be decided either way."

> Black paused, then added, "You can't do any real harm." Jack Bass, Taming the Storm 115 (1993).

Did it require a law school education for Judge Rives to propose the wisest solution here?

4. *The Turkish Bathhouse.* A crooked architect substituted documents for a homeowner and a contractor. Defendant, the homeowner, believed he was to pay $23,200 for a Turkish bathhouse; plaintiff, the contractor, thought he was to be paid $33,721 to build it. Each believed, incorrectly, that he had a contract with the other. The contractor's actual cost to build the bathhouse was $32,950; but the structure increased the property's market value only $22,000. The homeowner refused to pay more than $23,200, the contract price the architect had represented to him. The contractor sued seeking additional compensation for labor and materials. Vickery v. Ritchie, 202 Mass. 247, 88 N.E. 835 (1909).

Should the contractor in addition to the $23,200 recover $10,521? $9,750? Nothing? The court said the homeowner should pay the contractor a total of $33,500, the appraised value of the contractor's work and materials.

Instead should the parties split the difference between $23,200 and $33,721? See Warren A. Seavey, Embezzlement by Agents of Two Principals: Contribution?, 64 Harv.L.Rev. 431 (1951).

The most recent word is Professor Kull's "$23,200." "Judged by the unjust enrichment axiom, the [$33,500] decision is indefensible." Andrew Kull, Rationalizing Restitution, 83 Cal.L.Rev. 1191, 1211 (1995).

5. *Rights of Cohabitants.* Before Marvin v. Marvin, which a law student may read in first-year Property or Family Law, courts emphasized that a contract to supply sexual relations in return for valuable consideration was an illegal contract of prostitution. Thus a court granted no remedies to a cohabitant. The *Marvin* court, however, changed that forever by saying that a cohabitant plaintiff might recover unless sexual relations were the explicit consideration. Marvin v. Marvin, 18 Cal.3d 660, 134 Cal.Rptr. 815, 557 P.2d 106 (1976). For the traditional, *Marvin* raises the paradox of conferring the benefits of marriage on the consciously unmarried.

From *Marvin* on, many courts have found that the cohabitants' sexual relations were outside the scope of their agreement. This may lead the court either to find a contract to divide property or to grant restitution of one form or another. A contract implied from the parties' conduct and restitution-quantum meruit variety are closely related, as the *Maglica* court below declines to explain.

MAGLICA v. MAGLICA

California Court of Appeal, Review Denied, 1998.
66 Cal.App.4th 442, 78 Cal.Rptr.2d 101.

SILLS, PRESIDING JUSTICE. This case forces us to confront the legal doctrine known as "quantum meruit" in the context of a case about an unmarried couple who lived together and worked in a business solely owned by one of them. Quantum meruit is a Latin phrase, meaning "as much as he deserves," and is based on the idea that someone should get paid for beneficial goods or services which he or she bestows on another. See, e.g., Earhart v. William Low Co. (1979) 25 Cal.3d 503, 518, ("Where one person renders services at the request of another and the latter obtains benefits from the services, the law ordinarily implies a promise to pay for the services."); Palmer v. Gregg (1967) 65 Cal.2d 657, 660, ("The measure of recovery in quantum meruit is the reasonable value of the services rendered, provided they were of direct benefit to the defendant.")

The trial judge instructed the jury that the reasonable value of the plaintiff's services was either the value of what it would have cost the defendant to obtain those services from someone else or the "value by which" he had "benefitted [sic] as a result" of those services. The instruction allowed the jury to reach a whopping number in favor of the plaintiff—$84 million—because of the tremendous growth in the value of the business over the years.

As we explain later, the finding that the couple had no contract in the first place is itself somewhat suspect because certain jury instructions did not accurately convey the law concerning implied-in-fact contracts. However, assuming that there was indeed no contract, the quantum meruit award cannot stand. The legal test for recovery in quantum meruit is not the value of the benefit, but value of the services (assuming, of course, that the services were beneficial to the recipient in the first place). In this case the failure to appreciate that fine distinction meant a big difference. People who work for businesses for a period of years and then walk away with $84 million do so because they have acquired some equity in the business, not because $84 million dollars is the going rate for the services of even the most workaholic manager. In substance, the court was allowing the jury to value the plaintiff's services as if she had made a sweetheart stock option deal—yet such a deal was precisely what the jury found she did not make. So the $84 million judgment cannot stand.

On the other hand, plaintiff was hindered in her ability to prove the existence of an implied-in-fact contract by a series of jury instructions which may have misled the jury about certain of the factors which bear on such contracts. The instructions were insufficiently qualified. They told the jury flat out that such facts as a couple's living together or holding themselves out as husband and wife or sharing a common surname did not mean that they had any agreement to share assets. That is not exactly correct. Such factors can, indeed, when taken together with other facts and in context, show the existence of an implied-in-fact contract. At most the jury instructions should have said that such factors do not by themselves necessarily show an implied-in-fact contract. Accordingly, when the case is retried, the plaintiff will have another chance to prove that she indeed had a deal for a share of equity in the defendant's business.

The important facts in this case may be briefly stated. Anthony Maglica, a Croatian immigrant, founded his own machine shop business, Mag Instrument, in 1955. He got divorced in 1971 and kept the business. That year he met Claire Halasz, an interior designer. They got on famously, and lived together, holding themselves out as man and wife—hence Claire began using the name Claire Maglica—but never actually got married. And, while Claire worked side by side building the business, Anthony never agreed—or at least the jury found Anthony never agreed—to give Claire a share of the business. When the business was incorporated in 1974 all shares went into Anthony's name. Anthony was the president and Claire was the secretary. They were paid equal salaries from the business after incorporation. In 1978 the business began manufacturing flash-lights, and, thanks in part to some great ideas and hard work on Claire's part (for example, coming out with a purse-sized flashlight in colors), the business boomed. Mag Instrument is now worth hundreds of millions of dollars.

In 1992 Claire discovered that Anthony was trying to transfer stock to his children but not her, and the couple split up in October. In June 1993 Claire sued Anthony for, among other things, breach of contract, breach of partnership agreement, fraud, breach of fiduciary duty and quantum meruit. The case came to trial in the spring of 1994. The jury awarded $84 million for the breach of fiduciary duty and quantum meruit causes of action, finding that $84 million was the reasonable value of Claire's services.

The Jury's Finding That There Was No Agreement To Hold Property for One Another Meant There Was No Breach of Fiduciary Duty. Preliminarily we must deal with the problem of fiduciary duty, as it was an alternative basis for the jury's award. We cannot, however, affirm the judgment on this basis because it is at odds with the jury's factual finding that Anthony never agreed to give Claire a share of his business. Having found factually that there was no contract, the jury could not legally conclude that Anthony breached a fiduciary duty.

The reason is that fiduciary duties are either imposed by law or are undertaken by agreement, and neither way of establishing the existence of a fiduciary duty applies here. As to the former, the fact that Claire and Anthony remained unmarried during their relationship is dispositive. California specifically abolished the idea of a "common law marriage" in 1895 (see Elden v. Sheldon (1988) 46 Cal.3d 267, 275, 250) and that, if it is not too harsh to say it, was clearly the substance of Claire and Anthony's relationship. They had a common law marriage.

As our Supreme Court said in *Elden*, "[f]ormally married couples are granted significant rights and bear important responsibilities toward one another which are not shared by those who cohabit without marriage." The court noted, in that context, that a variety of statutes impose rights and obligations on married people. One set of such imposed rights and obligations, for example, is Family Code sections 1100 through 1103, which both establish a fiduciary duty between spouses with regard to the management and control of community assets and provide for remedies for a breach of that duty.

It would be contrary to what our Supreme Court said in *Elden* and to the evident policy of the law to promote formal (as distinct from common law) marriage to impose fiduciary duties based on a common law marriage. * * *

That leaves contract, and the jury found there was no contract. Claire, despite the closeness of their relationship, never entrusted her property to Anthony; she only rendered services. And without entrustment of property, or an oral agreement to purchase property together, there can be no fiduciary relationship no matter how "confidential" a relationship between an unmarried, cohabiting couple. * * *

Quantum Meruit Allows Recovery For the Value of Beneficial Services, Not the Value By Which Someone Benefits From Those Services. The absence of a contract between Claire and Anthony, however, would not preclude her recovery in quantum meruit: As every first year law student knows or should know, recovery in quantum meruit does not require a contract.

The classic formulation concerning the measure of recovery in quantum meruit is found in Palmer v. Gregg. Justice Mosk, writing for the court, said: "The measure of recovery in quantum meruit is the reasonable value of the services rendered provided they were of direct benefit to the defendant."

The underlying idea behind quantum meruit is the law's distaste for unjust enrichment. If one has received a benefit which one may not justly retain, one should "restore the aggrieved party to his [or her] former position by return of the thing or its equivalent in money." [citation]

The idea that one must be benefitted by the goods and services bestowed is thus integral to recovery in quantum meruit; hence courts have always required that the plaintiff have bestowed some benefit on the defendant as a prerequisite to recovery. [citation]

But the threshold requirement that there be a benefit from the services can lead to confusion, as it did in the case before us. It is one thing to require that the defendant be benefitted by services, it is quite another to measure the reasonable value of those services by the value by which the defendant was "benefitted" as a result of them. Contract price and the reasonable value of services rendered are two separate things; sometimes the reasonable value of services exceeds a contract price. [citation] And sometimes it does not.

Here is the exact language of the plaintiff's jury instruction at issue:

"Plaintiff may be compensated for the reasonable value of services rendered to Defendant and Mag Instrument, Inc. either by awarding Plaintiff: 1. The reasonable value of what it would have cost Defendant to obtain the services Plaintiff provided from another person; or 2. The value by which Defendant has benefitted as a result of the services rendered by Plaintiff."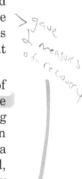

At root, allowing quantum meruit recovery based on "resulting benefit" of services rather than the reasonable value of beneficial services affords the plaintiff the best of both contractual and quasi-contractual recovery. Resulting benefit is an open-ended standard, which, as we have mentioned earlier, can result in the plaintiff obtaining recovery amounting to de facto ownership in a business all out of reasonable relation to the value of services rendered. After all, a particular service timely rendered can have, as Androcles was once pleasantly surprised to discover in the case of a particular lion, disproportionate value to what it would cost on the open market. * * *

The jury instruction given here allows the value of services to depend on their impact on a defendant's business rather than their reasonable value. True, the services must be of benefit if there is to be any recovery at all; even so, the benefit is not necessarily related to the reasonable value of a particular set of services. Sometimes luck, sometimes the impact of others makes the difference. Some enterprises are successful; others less so. Allowing recovery based on resulting benefit would mean the law imposes an exchange of equity for services, and that can result in a windfall—as in the present case—or a serious shortfall in others. Equity-for-service compensation packages are extraordinary in the labor market, and always the result of specific bargaining. To impose such a measure of recovery would make a deal for the parties that they did not make themselves. If courts cannot use quantum meruit to change the terms of a contract which the parties did make, [citation] it follows that neither can they use quantum meruit to impose a highly generous and extraordinary contract that the parties did not make.

Telling the jury that it could measure the value of Claire's services by "[t]he value by which Defendant has benefitted as a result of [her] services" was error. It allowed the jury to value Claire's services as having bought her a de facto ownership interest in a business whose owner never agreed to give her an interest. On remand, that part of the jury instruction must be dropped.

Claire's Quantum Meruit Claim Is Not Barred by the Statute of Limitations. * * * [is omitted].

Certain Jury Instructions May Have Misled the Jury Into Finding There Was No Implied Contract When In Fact There Was One. As we have shown, the quantum meruit damage award cannot stand in the wake of the jury's finding that Claire and Anthony had no agreement to share the equity in Anthony's business. But the validity of that very finding itself is challenged in Claire's protective cross-appeal, where she attacks a series of five jury instructions, specially drafted and proffered by Anthony. We are aware of no standard jury instructions dealing directly with implied contracts arising out of cohabitation between unmarried people.

Here are the five:

1. NO CONTRACT RESULTS FROM PARTIES HOLDING THEMSELVES OUT AS HUSBAND AND WIFE. You cannot find an agreement to share property or form a partnership from the fact that the parties held themselves out as husband and wife. The fact that unmarried persons live together as husband and wife and share a surname does not mean that they have any agreement to share earnings or assets.

2. NO IMPLIED CONTRACT FROM LIVING TOGETHER. You cannot find an implied contract to share property or form a partnership simply from the fact that the parties lived together[.]

3. CREATION OF AN IMPLIED CONTRACT. The fact the parties are living together does not change any of the requirements for finding an express or implied contract between the parties.

4. COMPANIONSHIP DOES NOT CONSTITUTE CONSIDERATION. Providing services such as a constant companion and confidant does not constitute the consideration required by law to support a contract to share property, does not support any right of recovery and such services are not otherwise compensable.

5. OBLIGATIONS IMPOSED BY LEGAL MARRIAGE. In California, there are various obligations imposed upon parties who become legally and formally married. These obligations do not arise under the law merely by living together without a formal and legal marriage.

We agree with Claire that it was error for the trial court to give three of these five instructions. The three instructions are so infelicitously worded that they might have misled the jury into concluding that evidence which can indeed support a finding of an implied contract could not.

The third and fifth instructions are simple truisms. The problem with the [other] three instructions is this: They isolate three uncontested facts about the case: (1) living together, (2) holding out to others as husband and wife, (3) providing services "such as" being a constant companion and confidant—and, seriatim, tell the jury that these facts definitely do not mean there was an implied contract. The first instruction says "does not" mean there is an agreement, the second says the jury "cannot find" an "implied" agreement, and the fourth says "does not support any right." True, none of these facts by themselves and alone necessarily compel the conclusion that there was an implied contract. But that does not mean that these facts cannot, in conjunction with all the facts and circumstances of the case, establish an implied contract. In point of fact, they can.

Unlike the "quasi-contractual" quantum meruit theory which operates without an actual agreement of the parties, an implied-in-fact contract entails an actual contract, but one manifested in conduct rather than expressed in words. * * * Because an implied-in-fact contract can be found where there is no expression of agreement in words, the line between an implied-in-fact contract and recovery in quantum meruit—where there may be no actual agreement at all—is fuzzy indeed. We will not attempt, in dicta, to clear up that fuzziness here. Suffice to say that because quantum meruit is a theory which implies a promise to pay for services as a matter of law for reasons of justice, [citation] while implied-in-fact contracts are predicated on actual agreements, albeit not ones expressed in words [citations] recovery in quantum meruit is necessarily a different theory than recovery on an implied-in-fact contract. Neither do we address the quantum of proof necessary to support recovery on a quantum meruit theory or attempt to divine the dividing line between services which may be so gratuitously volunteered under circumstances in which there can be no reasonable expectation of payment and services which do qualify for recovery in quantum meruit. These matters have not been briefed and may be left for another day.

In Alderson v. Alderson (1986) 180 Cal.App.3d 450, 461, the court observed that a number of factors—including direct testimony of an agreement; holding out socially as husband and wife; the woman and her children taking the man's surname; pooling of finances to purchase a number of joint rental properties; joint decision-making in rental property purchases; rendering bookkeeping services for, paying the bills on, and collecting the rents of, those joint rental properties; and the nature of title taken in those rental properties—could all support a finding there was an implied agreement to share the rental property acquisitions equally.

We certainly do not say that living together, holding out as husband and wife, and being a companion and confidant, even taken together, are sufficient in and of themselves to show an implied agreement to divide the equity in a business owned by one of the couple. However, Alderson clearly shows that such facts, together with others bearing more directly on the business and the way the parties treated the equity and proceeds of the business, can be part of a series of facts which do show such an agreement. The vice of the three instructions here is that they affirmatively suggested that living together, holding out, and companionship could not, as a matter of law, even be part of the support for a finding of an implied agreement. That meant the jury could have completely omitted these facts when considering the other factors which might also have borne on whether there was an implied contract.

On remand, the three instructions should not be given. The jury should be told, rather, that while the facts that a couple live together, hold themselves out as married, and act as companions and confidants toward each other do not, by themselves, show an implied agreement to share property, those facts, when taken together and in conjunction with other facts bearing more directly on the alleged arrangement to share property, can show an implied agreement to share property.

DISPOSITION: The judgment is reversed. The case is remanded for a new trial. At the new trial the jury instructions identified in this opinion as erroneous shall not be given. * * *

Notes

1. *Fiduciary Duty.* Why did the court reject Claire's contention that Anthony breached a fiduciary duty to her? The two ways for a fiduciary duty to arise are by agreement or imposed by law. The jury had found no agreement. That leaves a duty implied by law—from marriage. Married couples have fiduciary duties to each other concerning community assets, but Claire and Anthony were not formally married. California's uniform policy beginning in 1895 with legislation is to deny legal effect to a "common-law" marriage, to promote formal marriage.

2. *Restitution.* The court considers whether to grant Claire quantum-meruit restitution. Did Claire incorrectly believe that a marriage contract existed? Did Claire expect Anthony to share? Was Anthony aware of Claire's thought and expectation? Did Claire render valuable services to Anthony? Do the circumstances negate a gift from Claire to Anthony? Did Anthony know of Claire's services and circumstances and accept the benefit from Claire?

Do your answers match the elements of quantum meruit? California's "elements" of quantum meruit are in the quotation from *Earhart*. See also the Texas court's narrower statement of quantum meruit in *Vortt*, Note 1, p. 413.

3. How should the jury measure Claire's quantum meruit restitution? The court's quotation from Palmer v. Gregg directs the jury to measure plaintiff's quantum meruit by the "reasonable value" of plaintiff's services, "provided they were of direct benefit to the defendant."

The trial judge's restitution-measurement instruction really had two theories of measurement, (a) the cost from someone else and (b) the value of Anthony's benefit. The jury apparently followed the second, leading its $84 million verdict for Claire.

Measurement of restitution should reflect two goals. The first goal is the substantive purpose that called for restitution. Is preventing Anthony's unjust enrichment that purpose? The second is to avoid undermining the contract policy that led to refusing Claire a contract recovery. This turns out to be tricky because while we know for sure that Claire and Anthony are not formally married, we do not know for sure that there was no express contract between them.

Consider the following analogy to the previous decision, Campbell v. TVA. In his dissent in *Campbell*, Judge Rives urged the court to avoid granting or measuring restitution in a way that undermined the purpose of the competitive bidding statute. The parallel to the competitive bidding statute in *Maglica* is California's ban on according legal effect to common law marriage. The restitution court should not grant or measure restitution in a way that, in effect, gives the Claire–Anthony relationship the essence of a marriage. When a relationship breaks up, the major benefit of a formal marriage is "equitable division," each gets half of the property acquired during the marriage. That would be too much.

What are Claire's and Anthony's theories of value?

At the threshold, defendant must "benefit" from plaintiff's services. Apparently defendant's "benefit" establishes one of the elements of quantum meruit. But defendant's "benefit" is not the measurement rule. Which is? "Reasonable value of services [plaintiff] rendered" to defendant.

If the court accepts Claire's theory of measurement, would it validate their cohabiting relationship as a marriage? Would this result be contrary to the California statute that forbids giving legal effect as a marriage to cohabitation?

What reasons does the court give to accept Anthony's theory of measurement?

Does the court's measurement of restitution frustrate the substantive purpose of preventing unjust enrichment? Will it leave Anthony's unjust enrichment incompletely corrected? Does it undervalue Claire's entrepreneurship? Restitution ought to be measured by the defendant's gain. But isn't the court's measure really a damages measure, not a restitution measure?

Should the court have allowed Claire to recover the amount Anthony benefitted from her services? A traditional woman's role is to be a person behind the scenes; but here Claire lacked the protection of formal marriage or ownership. Was the court influenced too much by traditional family law and property arrangements and not enough by unjust enrichment principles?

4. *Contract, Implied in Fact.* Claire had sought to recover for an actual contract, one manifested in conduct, not words. Why were the trial judge's jury instructions on a Claire–Anthony implied-in-fact contract defective?

5. *Broken Bootstrap.* Does the court use the jury's possibly incorrect finding of no-contract as the strained basis for its (arguably incorrect) fiduciary duty and quantum meruit holdings?

6. *Settlement?* The court holds that Claire is entitled to a second trial. What is the settlement value of Claire's case after this decision?

C. EQUITABLE RESTITUTION

1. THE CONSTRUCTIVE TRUST

While the English common law courts were fabricating noncontractual "implied contracts," the Court of Chancery was raising "constructive trusts." If the defendant's fiduciary breach or fraud deprived the plaintiff of property, the Chancellor reasoned that a defendant who was enriched unjustly is constructively a "trustee" for plaintiff, the "beneficiary." The Chancellors' invention of a legal fiction to establish a "constructive trust" beside an express trust is as creative as the common law courts' development of a fictional or quasi-contract within the "true" contract's form of action. Each innovation prevents defendants' unjust enrichment; each expands the meaning of legal language; each contains the seeds of potential confusion.

What features does this constructive trust have? The defendant has been enriched unjustly. "Tracing" is a distinctive technique for a constructive trust. The plaintiff identifies her asset which effected the defendant's enrichment; in technical terms, she will "trace" her asset into the defendant's ownership and identify it or its product as the constructive trust "res." The plaintiff traces or identifies the asset as belonging in "good conscience" to her even though the defendant holds title to it. The Chancellor, assuming that the defendant owns the "title" of the asset, decrees the defendant to be trustee, constructively, of the asset for the benefit of the plaintiff. The feature of formal trust doctrine necessary for the constructive trust is the separation of the defendant's legal title from the plaintiff's equitable title. The Chancellor's order to the defendant-constructive trustee is to "execute" the constructive trust, to convey the asset to the plaintiff; this personal order illustrates the maxim, Equity acts in personam. The Chancellor thus averts the defendant's unjust enrichment by labeling him a constructive trustee and ordering him to convey the property to the plaintiff.

The plaintiff's ability to trace her asset has four important consequences, which we examine in more detail below. In short, they are: (a) If the defendant invested the plaintiff's asset, the trust res, in property that gained value, tracing lets the plaintiff capture the appreciation. So the constructive trust with tracing may reveal a restitution plaintiff recovering more than her losses; this advances the policies of preventing the defendant's unjust enrichment and deterring the misconduct that led to it. (b) If the defendant used the plaintiff's asset for a homestead which under state law is exempt from a creditor's collection process, the plaintiff may nevertheless trace and recover "her" asset even though the defendant's other creditors could not touch it. (c) If the defendant's debts exceed his assets, the plaintiff may nevertheless trace and recover "her" asset, or its product, even though the defendant's other creditors will recover a percentage, perhaps a small one, of their debts. (d) If the plaintiff's asset is an heirloom, tracing lets the plaintiff recover it, not a money substitute; a constructive trust operates like replevin or specific restitution. Tracing arms the constructive trust plaintiff with a formidable weapon to combat the defendant's unjust enrichment.

The plaintiff must trace. Even though the defendant has been unjustly enriched, if the plaintiff cannot trace her asset, the Chancellor lacks a constructive trust res; the plaintiff may have a restitution claim, but she is a general creditor. If tracing gives the plaintiff enhanced rights in an asset, then as a prerequisite to tracing, the plaintiff must show that the asset is associated with the defendant's wrong to the plaintiff. How strictly a court will insist on tracing is the subject of the following decision.

SIMONDS v. SIMONDS
Court of Appeals of New York, 1978.
45 N.Y.2d 233, 380 N.E.2d 189, 408 N.Y.S.2d 359.

BREITEL, CHIEF JUDGE. Plaintiff Mary Simonds, decedent's first wife, seeks to impress a constructive trust on proceeds of insurance policies on decedent's life. The proceeds had been paid to the named beneficiaries, defendants Reva Simonds, decedent's second wife, and their daughter Gayle. Plaintiff, however, asserts as superior an equitable interest arising out of a provision in her separation agreement with decedent. Special Term granted partial summary judgment to plaintiff and impressed a constructive trust to the extent of $7,000 plus interest against proceeds of a policy naming the second wife as beneficiary, and the Appellate Division affirmed. Special Term dismissed the cause of action against defendant Gayle Simonds. No appeal of that dismissal was taken to the Appellate Division. Defendant Reva Simonds, the second wife, appeals.

The separation agreement required the husband to maintain in effect, with the wife as beneficiary to the extent of $7,000, existing life insurance policies or, if the policies were to be canceled or to lapse, insurance policies of equal value. The issue is whether that provision entitles the first wife to impress a constructive trust on proceeds of insurance policies subsequently issued, despite the husband's failure to name her as the beneficiary on any substitute policies once the original life insurance policies had lapsed.

There should be an affirmance. The separation agreement vested in the first wife an equitable right in the then existing policies. Decedent's substitution of policies could not deprive the first wife of her equitable interest, which was then transferred to the new policies. Since the proceeds of the substituted policies have been paid to decedent's second wife, whose interest in the policies is subordinate to plaintiff's, a constructive trust may be imposed.

On March 9, 1960, decedent Frederick Simonds and his wife of 14 years, plaintiff Mary Simonds, entered into a separation agreement which, on March 31, 1960, was incorporated into an Illinois divorce decree granted to plaintiff on grounds of desertion. The agreement provided, somewhat inartfully: "The husband agrees that he will keep all of the policies of Insurance now in full force and effect on his life. Said policies now being in the sum of $21,000.00 and the Husband further agrees that the Wife shall be the beneficiary of said policies in an amount not less than $7,000.00 and the Husband further agrees that he shall pay any and all premiums necessary to maintain such policies of Insurance and if for any reason any of them now existing the policies shall be cancelled or be caused to lapse. He shall procure additional insurance in an amount equal to the face value of the policies having been cancelled or caused to lapse." Thus, the husband was to maintain, somehow, at least $7,000 of life insurance for the benefit of his first wife as a named beneficiary.

On May 26, 1960, less than two months after the divorce, decedent husband married defendant Reva Simonds. Defendant Gayle Simonds was born to the couple shortly thereafter.

Sometime after the separation agreement was signed, the then existing insurance policies were apparently canceled or permitted to lapse. It does not appear from the record why, how, or when this happened, but the policies were not extant at the time of decedent husband's death on August 1, 1971. In the interim, however, decedent has acquired three other life insurance policies, totaling over $55,000, none of which named plaintiff as a beneficiary. * * * The first two policies named Reva Simonds, decedent's second wife, as beneficiary, and the third policy named their daughter. Hence, at the time of decedent's death he had continuously violated the separation agreement by maintaining no life insurance naming the first wife as a beneficiary. * * *

[T]he first wife brought this action against both the second wife and the daughter, seeking to impose a constructive trust on the insurance proceeds to the extent of $7,000. * * * Special Term granted partial summary judgment to the first wife and imposed a constructive trust on the proceeds in the hands of the second wife. A unanimous Appellate Division affirmed. * * *

There is no question that decedent breached his obligation to maintain life insurance with his first wife as beneficiary. Consequently, the first wife would of course be entitled to maintain an action for breach against the estate. The estate's insolvency, however, would make such an action fruitless. Thus, the controversy revolves around plaintiff's right, in equity, to recover $7,000 of the insurance proceeds. * * *

Whatever the legal rights between insurer and insured, the separation agreement vested in the first wife an equitable interest in the insurance policies then in force. An agreement for sufficient consideration, including a separation agreement, to maintain a claimant as a beneficiary of a life insurance policy vests in the claimant an equitable interest in the policies designated. [citations] This interest is superior to that of a named beneficiary who has given no consideration, notwithstanding policy provisions permitting the insured to change the designated beneficiary freely.

This is not to say that an insurance company may not rely on the insured's designation of a beneficiary. None of this opinion bears on the rights or responsibilities of the insurer in law or in equity.

Obviously, the policies now at issue are not the same policies in existence at the time of the separation agreement. But it has been held that mere substitution of policies, or even substitution of insurance companies, does not defeat the equitable interest of one who has given sufficient consideration for a promise to be maintained as beneficiary under an insurance policy. [citations] The persistence of the promisee's equitable interest is all the more evident where the agreement expressly provides for a change in policies, and in effect provides further that the promisee's right shall attach to the new policies.

For a certainty, the first wife's equitable interest would be easier to trace if the new policies were quid pro quo replacements for the original policies. The record does not reveal whether this was so. But inability to trace plaintiff's equitable rights precisely should not require that they not be recognized, much as in the instance of damages difficult to prove. [citations] The separation agreement provides nexus between plaintiff's rights and the later acquired policies. The later policies were expressly contemplated by the parties, and it was agreed that plaintiff would have an interest in them. No reason in equity appears for denying plaintiff that interest, so long as no one who has given value for the policies or otherwise suffered a detriment is involved. The second wife's innocence does not offset the wrong by the now deceased husband.

The conclusion is an application of the general rule that equity regards as done that which should have been done. [citations] Thus, if an insured, upon lapse or cancellation of insurance, followed by replacement with new insurance, has a contractual obligation to designate a particular person as beneficiary, equity will consider the obligee as a beneficiary.

In this case, then, the first wife's interest in the original policies extended as well to the later acquired policies. The husband, upon lapse or cancellation of the earlier policies, had by virtue of the separation agreement an obligation to name her as beneficiary on the later policies, an obligation enforceable in equity despite the husband's failure to comply with the terms of the separation agreement. Due to the husband's failure to do what he should have done, the first wife acquired not only a right at law to sue his estate for breach of contract, a right now worthless, but also an equitable right in the policies, a right which, upon the husband's death, attached to the proceeds. [citations]

And, since the first wife was entitled to $7,000 of the insurance proceeds at the time of the husband's death, she is no less entitled because the proceeds have already been converted by being paid, erroneously, to the named beneficiaries. [citations] Her remedy is imposition of a constructive trust.

In the words of Judge Cardozo, "(a) constructive trust is the formula through which the conscience of equity finds expression. When property has been acquired in such circumstances that the holder of the legal title may not in good conscience retain the beneficial interest, equity converts him into a trustee" (Beatty v. Guggenheim Exploration Co., 225 N.Y. 380, 386, 122 N.E. 378, 380). Thus, a constructive trust is an equitable remedy. It is perhaps more different from an express trust than it is similar (5 Scott, Trusts (3d ed.), s 461). As put so well by Scott and restated at the Appellate Division, "(the constructive trustee) is not compelled to convey the property because he is a constructive trustee; it is because he can be compelled to convey it that he is a constructive trustee."

More precise definitions of a constructive trust have been termed inadequate because of the failure to recognize the broad scope of constructive trust doctrine. As another leading scholar has said of constructive trusts, "(t)he Court does not restrict itself by describing all the specific forms of inequitable holding which will move it to grant relief, but rather reserves freedom to apply this remedy to whatever knavery human ingenuity can invent" (Bogert, Trusts and Trustees (2d ed. rev., 1978), s 471, at p. 29). * * *

For a single example, one who wrongfully prevents a testator from executing a new will eliminating him as beneficiary will be held as a constructive trustee even in the absence of a confidential or fiduciary relation, a promise by the "trustee," and a transfer in reliance by the testator (see, e. g., Latham v. Father Divine, 299 N.Y. 22, 26–27, 85 N.E.2d 168, 169–170). As then Judge Desmond said in response to the argument that a breach of a promise to the testator was necessary for imposition of a constructive trust "(a) constructive trust will be erected whenever necessary to satisfy the demands of justice. * * * (I)ts applicability is limited only by the inventiveness of men who find new ways to enrich themselves unjustly by grasping what should not belong to them." * * *

It is agreed that the purpose of the constructive trust is prevention of unjust enrichment. [citations] Unjust enrichment, however, does not require the performance of any wrongful act by the one enriched. [citations] Innocent parties may frequently be unjustly enriched. What is required, generally, is that a party hold property "under such circumstances that in equity and good conscience he ought not to retain it" Miller v. Schloss, 218 N.Y. 400, 407, 113 N.E. 337, 339. A bona fide purchaser of property upon which a constructive trust would otherwise be imposed takes free of the constructive trust, but a gratuitous donee, however innocent, does not. [citations]

The unjust enrichment in this case is manifest. At a time when decedent was, certainly, anxious to remarry, he entered into a separation agreement with his wife of 14 years. As part of the agreement, he promised to maintain $7,000 in life insurance with the first wife as beneficiary. Later he broke his promise, and died with insurance policies naming only the second wife and daughter as beneficiaries. They have collected the proceeds, amounting to more than $55,000, while the first wife has collected nothing. Had the husband kept his promise, the beneficiaries would have collected $7,000 less in proceeds. To that extent, the beneficiaries have been unjustly enriched, and the proceeds should be subjected to a constructive trust. * * *

The issues in this case should not generate significant controversy. The action is in equity, and the equities are clear. True, some courts have decided the issues differently. [citations] Those cases, however, rely heavily on formalisms and too little on basic equitable principles, long established in Anglo–American law and in this State and especially relevant when family transactions are involved. "A court of equity in decreeing a constructive trust is bound by no unyielding formula. The equity of the transaction must shape the measure of relief" (Beatty v. Guggenheim Exploration Co., (Cardozo, J.). * * *

Order affirmed.

Notes

1.   *Questions.* Life insurance proceeds paid to an insured's named beneficiary are exempt from the claims of the insured decedent's creditors. Did the court shift plaintiff Mary Simonds's loss to another innocent person? Was it fair to Reva, the decedent's widow, to take an exempt asset to pay the deceased's contract debt to his ex-wife? Kelvin Dickinson, Divorce and Life Insurance: Post Mortem Remedies for Breach of a Duty to Maintain a Policy for a Designated Beneficiary, 61 Mo.L.Rev. 533 (1996).

2.   *Relaxed Tracing: Contract, Promise, or Equitable Interest?* In a later New York decision, the decedent and his first wife had "entered into a separation agreement which provided for the continuation of decedent's life insurance policy as follows: 'ninth: The Husband promises and agrees to continue in full force and effect his present [Grumann–Travelers] life insurance policy in the face amount of approximately $15,000.00 with the wife and children as NAMED EQUAL irrevocable beneficiaries.' His Grumann–Travelers group policy lapsed in 1970. In 1976 he took out another $15,000.00 policy, the Technical Data Services–Phoenix policy, which designated his second wife as beneficiary. When he died in 1980, his first wife sought to impress a constructive trust on the proceeds.

"Defendant Rogers, [widow and designated beneficiary] argues that *Simonds* is distinguishable because the separation agreement there obligated the husband to procure additional insurance in the event of lapse—an obligation not explicitly set forth in the agreement here. But the existence of such a provision was not the articulated basis of the *Simonds* decision. The 'additional insurance' language in the agreement in *Simonds* did not and could not identify a specific *res* as subject to the first wife's superior right. It simply made the persistence of the equitable interest 'all the more evident.' [citation] The survival of the equitable interest is also evident here. No less than in *Simonds,* what was certainly the contemplation of the parties, embodied in paragraph ninth of their separation agreement, was the promise that decedent would maintain or replace a $15,000 life insurance policy, and not a promise that would persist only so long as he remained an employee of Grumman. Both life insurance policies were obtained by virtue of decedent's employment, both were in the amount of $15,000, and there is no indication that decedent maintained any other life insurance during the respective terms of the policies. He maintained one $15,000 life insurance policy while an employee of Grumman and, after that had lapsed, maintained a later $15,000 life insurance policy while an employee of Technical Data Services. Thus, despite the time period between the lapse of the Travelers policy and the issuance of the Phoenix policy, the latter may properly be considered a fulfillment of decedent's implied promise to replace the former. To find that decedent had escaped the obligation imposed upon him by the separation agreement simply because of the absence from the agreement of words specifically addressing the cancellation of the first policy, when the intendment is plain, would be to erect a legal formalism and defeat an essential purpose of equity." Rogers v. Rogers, 63 N.Y.2d 582, 584–85, 587–88, 483 N.Y.S.2d 976, 473 N.E.2d 226 (1984).

Were the insurance proceeds sufficiently connected to the decedent's wrong to warrant the tracing the court approved?

3. *Estoppel By Deed.* Can you justify the constructive trusts in *Simonds* and *Rogers* on the ground that the insurance policies are the "products" of the earlier policies? A draft of the third restatement suggests that estoppel by deed may be a better analogy than tracing. Restatement (Third) of Restitution and Unjust Enrichment § 48, Comment and Reporter's Note (d)(4), (Preliminary Draft No. 7 (2005).

Property Review: when X, who doesn't own Redacre, gives Y a deed to Redacre, Y owns nothing because X had no interest in Redacre; when X later acquires Redacre, the court will "estop" him from denying that Y owns it. Apply the analogy as follows: when the ex-husband acquires an insurance policy that comes within the terms of his broken promise to his ex-wife, the court will estop him from denying ex-wife's right as a beneficiary of that policy.

Is the restatement's estoppel-by-deed analogy more persuasive than the New York courts' "relaxed" tracing?

4. The Massachussets Supreme Judicial Court joined the ranks of the courts the *Simonds* court mentions in its last paragraph that "have decided the issues differently." The decedent had changed the beneficiary of one policy from her first to her second spouse; the court approved granting the second spouse and their children rights in that policy. After remarrying, the decedent had purchased a second policy which was paid to her second spouse. Emphasizing that the decedent's second spouse had done nothing improper, the Massachussets court refused to impose a constructive trust on the proceeds of that second insurance policy. "Although the deceased was in breach of her obligation to name Foster [her first spouse] as beneficiary of policies totaling $200,000 at the time she purchased the Prudential policy, that breach has no bearing on her right to purchase a life insurance policy naming her new husband as beneficiary or to confer on him any other gift or benefit (regardless of consideration) not specifically barred by a provision in the separation agreement." Foster v. Hurley, 444 Mass. 157, 826 N.E.2d 719, 728–29 (2005).

Is the *Simonds* court right in observing that the courts which disagree with it "rely heavily on formalisms and too little on basic equitable principles, long established in Anglo–American law * * * and especially relevant when family transactions are involved"?

5. *Equitable Restitution.* The constructive trust is the major equitable restitution remedy. Others are resulting trust, equitable lien, accounting, and subrogation. Other equitable remedies which are related to restitution are reformation and equitable rescission-cancellation which may lead to restitution.

Equitable restitution is not subject to the right to a jury trial. The plaintiff's legal remedy, compensatory damages or legal restitution-quasi-contract, must be inadequate. The plaintiff's inadequacy prerequisite is satisfied if the defendant is a fiduciary under exclusive equity jurisdiction, if the defendant owns title to the property and a personal order to reconvey is needed, or if the plaintiff must trace her asset to avert the defendant's unjust enrichment.

6. *Misconduct Threshold.* Is the threshold for a constructive trust the defendant's unjust enrichment alone or is it unjust enrichment plus? Answers vary.

(a) In Simonds v. Simonds, the New York court said "[T]he purpose of the constructive trust is prevention of unjust enrichment."

(b) A narrower view in Wisconsin. "[I]n defining the elements necessary to invoke [a] constructive trust this court has consistently said that unjust enrichment alone is not sufficient. * * * Additional factors suggested have included actual or constructive fraud, duress, abuse of confidential relationship. mistake, commission of a wrong or any form of unconscionable conduct." Prince v. Bryant, 87 Wis.2d 662, 667, 275 N.W.2d 676, 678 (Wis. 1979).

(c) Harris v. Sentry Title involved the imposition of a constructive trust on proceeds from a complicated land acquisition scheme. Summarizing Texas law, Judge Williams found two "general prerequisites" for a constructive trust: "The first is a prior, unrelated history of close and trusted dealings of the same general nature or scope as the subject transactions. The second is a finding that unjust enrichment would result if the remedy of constructive trust were not imposed." Harris v. Sentry Title Co., 715 F.2d 941, 947 (5th Cir.1983), cert. denied, 469 U.S. 1037 (1984). The court, in a subsequent proceeding in the case, reemphasized the necessity of a confidential relationship in the absence of fraud. 727 F.2d 1368 (5th Cir.1984).

(d) Compare the Reporter's Note in the tentative draft of the "second" Restatement of Restitution. "Sometimes it is said that a constructive trust can be predicated only on a fiduciary relationship or actual fraud. [citation] Such expressions are to be rejected as stating the grounds for the remedy too narrowly." Restatement (Second) of Restitution § 30, Reporter's Note on Comments b and c at p. 23 (Tentative Draft No. 2, 1984).

7. *Mobile Assets? Preliminary Injunctions and Lis Pendens.* What if the assets the plaintiff seeks for the constructive trust "res" may grow wings and fly to another jurisdiction?

(a) The Republic of the Philippines sought to recover money it alleged was wrongfully taken by ex-President Marcos. The court granted a preliminary injunction to prevent the defendant's transfer of property that the plaintiff claimed was held under a constructive trust. Republic of Philippines v. Marcos, 806 F.2d 344 (2d Cir.1986), cert. dismissed, 480 U.S. 942, cert. denied, 481 U.S. 1048 (1987).

(b) A plaintiff may file lis pendens to prevent the defendant from transferring to another if the alleged constructive trust res is realty. MDO Development Corp. v. Kelly, 726 F.Supp. 79, 86–87 (S.D.N.Y.1989), amendment denied, 735 F.Supp. 591 (S.D.N.Y.1990).

(c) The forum Chancellor with in personam jurisdiction over the defendant may order him to convey an asset in another state or nation to the plaintiff. Matarese v. Calise, p. 231.

2. TRACING

Tracing Described. "Where a person by the consciously wrongful disposition of the property of another acquires other property, the person whose property is so used is * * * entitled * * * to the property so acquired. If the property so acquired is or becomes more valuable than the property used in acquiring it, the profit thus made by the wrongdoer cannot be retained by him; the person whose property was used in making the profit is entitled to it. The result, it is true, is that the claimant obtains more than the amount of which he was deprived, more than restitution for his loss; he is put in a better position than that in which he would have been if no wrong had been done to him. Nevertheless, since the profit is made from his property, it is just that he should have the profit rather than that the wrongdoer should keep it. * * * Accordingly, the person whose property is wrongfully used in acquiring other property can by a proceeding in equity reach the other property and compel the wrongdoer to convey it to him. The wrongdoer holds the property so acquired upon a constructive trust for the claimant." Restatement of Restitution § 202, comment c (1937).

Suppose the federal government proves that: a tax debtor, seeking to secrete his assets, gave his daughter some money; his daughter exchanged the money for a racehorse named Devil His Due; Devil His Due finished second in a handicap and earned a $77,000 purse. Could the court (a) find that the debtor's daughter is a constructive trustee of the money and later the horse for her father, (b) trace the father's money from the horse into the purse, and (c) grant the government a constructive trust and recovery against the father's beneficial interest in the purse? "If so, a constructive trust may be deemed imposed upon such funds, which trust would accordingly follow the 'beneficial interest' of ownership in the true asset." LiButti v. United States, 107 F.3d 110, 125 (2d Cir.1997).

Limits on Tracing: Creditors, Life Insurance Proceeds, and Homestead. Should the court impress a constructive trust on plaintiff's assets as far as plaintiff can trace them? One court traced with a broad brush, observing "when legitimate assets are co-mingled with illegitimate ones such that the assets cannot be separated out, a constructive trust may extend over the entire asset pool." S.E.C. v. The Better Life Club, 995 F.Supp. 167, 181 (D.D.C.1998). But should the court trace only as far as the policy of tracing dictates?

1. *Creditors.* To put a simplified example, suppose Grifter defrauded numerous investors: through the time-honored device of a Ponzi scheme, he secured gullible victims' investments for a bogus enterprise while using later "investors" money to repay earlier patsies. When found out, Grifter had one asset, $100,000, in an account in National Bank. Ten fraud victims had each lost $100,000. One victim, Pureheart, the fraudster's last victim was able to trace her $100,000 loss into Grifter's National Bank account. If Pureheart is able to claim a constructive trust and trace, she will recover all of her $100,000; but none of the other nine victims will recover anything. On the other hand, if all ten of Grifter's victimized creditors recover pro rata, each, including Pureheart, will receive 10% or $10,000. In support of pro rata distribution, one court reasoned that "it seemed inequitable to allow [Pureheart] to benefit merely because the defendants spent the other victims' money first. [Pureheart] would obtain a preferred claim over funds if the court were to impose the constructive trust. * * * [A]ll the fraud victims were in equal positions and should be treated as such." United States v. Durham, 86 F.3d 70, 73 (5th Cir.1996). See also, S.E.C. v. Drucker, 318 F.Supp.2d 1205 (N.D.Ga. 2004); United States v. Real Property, Blaine County, Idaho, 89 F.3d 551 (9th Cir.1996). Cunningham v. Brown, 265 U.S. 1 (1924), which the courts follow and quote, involved the original Ponzi; "equality is equity," opined the Court.

2. *Life Insurance Proceeds.* Thompson, a crooked accountant, embezzled $75,000 from his employer. He used $250 of the stolen money to insure his life for $100,000. He died suddenly leaving nothing in his estate for his creditors and family. The policy proceeds were claimed both by his spouse who was named beneficiary and by his former employer who traced its money into the policy and asserted a constructive trust.

The spouse argued that a named beneficiary takes insurance proceeds free of the decedent's creditors. Note 1, p. 426. Moreover the social function of life insurance is to provide support for the decedent's family.

Thompson's employer, the embezzlement victim, argued for a constructive trust equal to the percentage of premiums the embezzler paid for with its money, here 100%. It claimed to own the proceeds in equity because they were traceable to the money Thompson embezzled from it. The insurance proceeds, a product of the embezzled money, are a substituted constructive trust res. The named beneficiary, although innocent of any wrong, may, like Reva Simonds, be a constructive trustee.

The court had several options: (a) Decline the constructive trust and tracing altogether so that the named beneficiary takes all the proceeds. (b) Let the embezzlement victim trace its money into the proceeds and impose an equitable lien on $250. (c) Impose a constructive trust for the $75,000 the employer lost. (d) Impose a constructive trust on all the proceeds.

Of the proposed solution (d), granting the victim restitution of policy proceeds which exceed its losses, Professor Palmer observed, "We are cursed with a lawyer's logic that reaches an undesirable result as the logical deduction from a fixed premise. There are several forms of cure: the use of common sense; the recognition that there are few if any universals in the law; or an examination of the premise. In this case the premise is false." George Palmer, The Law of Restitution § 2.15 (1978).

One court adopted two of the options. "Where the wrongdoer mingles wrongfully and rightfully acquired funds, owner of wrongfully acquired funds is entitled to share proportionately in acquired property to the extent of his involuntary contributions. This principle is specifically applicable to life insurance proceeds where a portion of the premiums were paid with wrongfully acquired money. * * * However, [the embezzler's employer] has sought no more than the embezzled monies, interest and costs. Further, the surviving wife is an innocent beneficiary. * * * We hold [that the employer] is entitled to * * * insurance proceeds, but not to exceed the total amount of embezzled monies, interest and costs." G & M Motor Co. v. Thompson, 567 P.2d 80, 83–84 (Okl. 1977).

3. *Homestead.* Charlie Crook uses embezzled money to buy a homestead which is exempt from creditors' claims under state law. May the victim of his theft trace her assets into Crook's homestead property? A court may impose a constructive trust on property the defendant purchased with the plaintiff's money even though the property is exempt from the defendant's other creditors under the homestead exemption. Maki v. Chong, 119 Nev. 390, 75 P.3d 376 (2003); Cox v. Waudby, 433 N.W.2d 716 (Iowa 1988).

4. *Tracing Questions.* Do you think a plaintiff should be able to trace as far as she can identify her "title" in the asset? Have courts used policy sensibly to determine how far to trace and when to stop tracing? Or does tracing favor one person over others so blatantly that you think it should be abolished?

D. DEFENSES TO RESTITUTION

A restitution defendant may use the usual defenses that apply to a lawsuit, like issue preclusion and claim preclusion. In addition, the defendant may use several affirmative defenses that are unique to restitution or have important features in restitution. The following material discusses the restitution slant on the defendant's affirmative defenses.

We need to identify the "elements" of a plaintiff's cause of action for restitution before we can identify the defendant's affirmative defenses. At a minimum, the restitution plaintiff must plead and prove the defendant's enrichment and the unjustness of retaining it; some courts would also insist on plaintiff's minus to balance the defendant's plus, that the defendant's enrichment be "at the expense of" the plaintiff.

When the plaintiff sues, the defendant may negate one of the elements of the plaintiff's cause of action, enrichment or unjustness. For example, suppose the defendant shows that his benefit was a valid gift from the plaintiff under property law.

The defendant's affirmative defense differs from negating an element of the plaintiff's cause of action. An affirmative defense consists of new factual material that the defendant brings in, not to challenge the truth of the plaintiff's facts, but, nevertheless, to defeat the plaintiff's right to recover. For example, the defendant shows that the statute of limitations has run on the plaintiff's cause of action. The defendant bears the burden of pleading an affirmative defense and must prove it also.

Court decisions ostensibly refusing a plaintiff restitution because of her "volunteer" or "intermeddler" status usually involve a plaintiff's attempt to recover for her unsolicited benefits to the defendant. Some writers about restitution refer to the plaintiff's "volunteer" or "intermeddler" status as a defense to restitution. But pinning the volunteer-intermeddler tag on the plaintiff is almost always a court's way of negating either the defendant's enrichment or the transfer's unjustness.

Affirmative defenses a restitution defendant may interpose include (a) time bar, (b) estoppel-change of position, (c) bona fide purchase, and (d) discharge for value.

(a) Time bar. The time bar of a plaintiff's restitution claim merits our separate attention because it will differ depending on whether the claim is legal restitution or equitable restitution. The plaintiff's legal restitution under the name of assumpsit, quasi-contract, contract implied in law, quantum meruit, or money had and received will be time-barred under the state's statute of limitations; because legal restitution began in assumpsit, a contract form of action, the restitution statute of limitations will usually be the jurisdiction's contract statute of limitations.

Equitable restitution, labeled constructive trust, resulting trust, equitable lien, subrogation or accounting, will be barred under the Chancery court's equitable doctrine of laches. The casebook has examined a constructive-trust plaintiff's alleged laches in Stone v. Williams, p. 315, where the plaintiff sued for equitable restitution remedies, an accounting or a constructive trust.

(b) Change of position-estoppel. Suppose the bank's computer erroneously gives Dan Defendant $500. When the bank sues Dan, he no longer has the money. Suppose Mugger de-enriched Dan on the way home from the bank, changing his position. Beyond that obvious example, a lot depends on circumstances.

Dan's defense of change of position will succeed if making restitution would be "inequitable." On the one hand, if Dan had expected someone to deposit money in his account as a gift and if he disbursed it to pay his creditors, then he will sustain the defense. On the other hand, if Dan counts the money, learns it was a mistake, and, nevertheless, goes on a spending spree, then he will not sustain the defense.

The court ought to accept the defendant's change of position defense in both legal restitution and equitable restitution. Change of position will primarily be a defendant's defense to the plaintiff's transfer by mistake, but a defendant may raise change of position against any reason the plaintiff alleges for restitution. The court may disqualify the defendant from the defense because he was in bad faith.

If someone receives a Social Security overpayment, then that is a payment by mistake; if the recipient disburses the money, then that may be a change of position. The following is quoted from the Code of Federal Regulations:

> Against equity and good conscience; defined. (a) Recovery of an overpayment is "against equity and good conscience" (under title II and title XVIII) if an individual—

> (1) Changed his or her position for the worse (Example 1) or relinquished a valuable right (Example 2) because of reliance upon a notice that a payment would be made or because of the overpayment itself; * * *

> (b) The individual's financial circumstances are not material to a finding of "against equity and good conscience."

> Example 1. A widow, having been awarded benefits for herself and daughter, entered her daughter in private school because the monthly benefits made this possible. After the widow and her daughter received payments for almost a year, the deceased worker was found to be not insured and all payments to the widow and child were incorrect. The widow has no other funds with which to pay the daughter's private school expenses. Having entered the daughter in private school and thus incurred a financial obligation toward which the benefits had been applied, she was in a worse position financially than if she and her daughter had never been entitled to benefits. In this situation, the recovery of the payments would be "against equity and good conscience."

> Example 2. After being awarded old-age insurance benefits, an individual resigned from employment on the assumption he would receive regular monthly benefit payments. It was discovered 3 years later that (due to a Social Security Administration error) his award was erroneous because he did not have the required insured status. Due to his age, the individual was unable to get his job back and could not get any other employment. In this situation, recovery of the overpayments would be "against equity and good conscience" because the individual gave up a valuable right. 20 C.F.R., § 404.509 (2005).

Estoppel may also be a defendant's successful defense to restitution. Suppose Dan looks at his records and asks a bank officer whether the records are right; the officer assures Dan that "the money's yours." Then Dan changes his position; he spends the money, pays a creditor, or invests in stock which goes south. The plaintiff represented a fact which let the defendant treat the money as if it were his own. But, standing alone, the bank's mistaken payment to Dan is not a representation that creates an estoppel.

Estoppel is a narrower defense than change of position; for in order to succeed, the estoppel defendant must establish that he relied on the plaintiff's representation. But, while the defendant's change of position may be only a partial defense, the plaintiff's estoppel is a total defense to the plaintiff's restitution claim.

(c) Bona fide purchase. If Dan had used the bank's mistaken payment of $500 to pay the debt he owed to Bob and the bank had sued Bob, then Bob would have a successful affirmative defense of bona fide purchase. Bob lacked notice that the money wasn't Dan's. Bob was a "purchaser" because he gave up Dan's debt to him in return for the $500 Dan gave him.

(d) Discharge for value. We will illustrate this defense with an example taken from a case. Spedley, who maintained an account with Security Pacific Bank, ordered Security Pacific to transfer $2,000,000 to Banque Worms to pay part of Spedley's debt to Banque Worms. Then Spedley ordered Security Pacific to stop payment and to pay X Bank instead. However, Security Pacific in spite of Spedley's stop order, mistakenly completed an electronic transfer to Banque Worms. Bank Worms applied the payment to Spedley's debt to it. Spedley was broke. When Security Pacific sought to recover its mistaken payment to Banque Worms, Banque Worms resisted, citing discharge for value. Banque Worms had applied Security Pacific's mistaken electronic transfer to discharge Spedley's debt; having given up its debt, Banque Worms was a bona fide purchaser of the money. The courts approved Banque Worms's defense. Banque Worms v. BankAmerica International, 77 N.Y.2d 362, 568 N.Y.S.2d 541, 570 N.E.2d 189 (1991)(responding to federal court's certified question); 928 F.2d 538 (2d Cir. 1991)(applying the New York court's response).

The defendant's bona fide purchase and discharge for value defenses advance two important commercial policies: First, they foster transactional certainty and stability, more particularly transactional finality; and second they encourage the free flow of cash and cash equivalents.

E.   RESTITUTION REFORM?

The Damages Chapter ended with a discussion of Tort Reform, the Injunctions—Equity Chapter with one on Injunction Reform. Is there a similar hue and cry to reform restitution comparable to "tort reform" and legislation to curb injunctions?

The danger to restitution is less that courts' excessive enthusiasm for restitution will offend powerful political forces than that the legal profession will forget restitution's basic doctrines. Misunderstanding and misapplication endanger restitution.

The doctrine of restitution, beginning with its vocabulary, is confusing and inadequate to allow judges and juries to focus critical judgment on the issues involved. The profession's use of terminology borrowed in the Medieval period from contracts and trusts has distracted lawyers' and judges' attention from the difficult issues of judgment. The questions of enrichment-benefit and unjustness are difficult enough without the diversions.

"Confusion over the content of restitution carries significant adverse consequences. To put it bluntly, American lawyers today (judges and law professors included) do not know what restitution is. * * * The technical competence of published opinions in straightforward restitution cases has noticeably declined; judges and lawyers sometimes fail to grasp the rudiments of the doctrine even when they know where to find it." Andrew Kull, Rationalizing Restitution, 83 Cal.L.Rev. 1191, 1195 (1995).

Strong language that. But witness the Supreme Court's mistakes under the equity fallacy, pp. 404–05. The solution, Restitution Reform if you will, is not legislation to curb judges' and juries' exuberance for restitution. The reform agenda is the steady work of education, developing accessible and rational standards and disseminating them through the profession.

Like contracts, torts and property, restitution is a common law subject. Courts created restitution; they have developed it as they applied it. The 1937 Restatement of Restitution is couched in the language of the forms of action and the dual courts of the common law and Chancery. Although restitution may never be as prominent or well known as contracts, torts and property, the public and the profession deserve an accessible body of restitution doctrine which is more prominent and better known.

Far from fearing that juries and judges are overusing restitution, disrupting transactions and the legal system generally and putting at risk the nation's competitiveness, federalism and the public peace, the Restatement people, the wise heads at the American Law Institute, have taken up the task of restitution. A second restatement, which was cited above, was started in the 1980s, but not completed. A Restatement of the Law, Third, Restitution and Unjust Enrichment is underway. Like a hotel skipping a 13th floor, the ALI is omitting a completed second restatement to put restitution in step with other restatements, now in their third manifestations.

The Restatement Third's reporter is Professor Andrew Kull who was quoted above. Professor Kull favors a restitution that is small but tough. The project's advisory committee includes your editor plus several eminent judges, practitioners, and professors. Discussion and drafting are in train; Tentative Drafts have been approved at ALI meetings; expect a completed restatement in several more years.

Restitution reform begins with students and teachers in law school; it will continue as lawyers interview clients, draft pleadings, conduct discovery, negotiate settlements, try lawsuits, and argue appeals. Do well by doing good. Learn the basics of restitution and apply them on behalf of the clients you deal with. This will both serve your clients and keep the flame of restitution learning flickering, perhaps burning, through the dark age before the renaissance of restitution reform.

Chapter 5

RESTITUTION IN TRANSACTIONS

Welcome to the Borderland Between Restitution and Contract. In this chapter, we examine the plaintiff's restitution remedy when a transaction fails as a contract or when a court rescinds a contract and considers granting restitution.

Election of remedies and lack of injury are a defendant's specialized defenses against a plaintiff's rescission-restitution. Although these two defenses ought to have faded faster than they have, both still retain enough vitality to warrant casebook status to warn the unwary of their presence.

The other doctrines in this chapter are the statute of frauds, lack of capacity, duress, undue influence, unconscionability, mistake, and illegality-violation of public policy. All are both shields and swords. Each doctrine is available to a defendant as a shield, an affirmative defenses to bar a plaintiff's successful contract suit. And each doctrine has enough positive force to allow a plaintiff to employ it as a sword for rescission and perhaps restitution. This Chapter examines the sword features. Many of the doctrines are spongy and difficult to keep separate, especially during litigation's early stages. Alternative pleading and perhaps alternative submission to the factfinder may be wise.

A. DISQUALIFYING THE PLAINTIFF FOR RESCISSION—RESTITUTION

1. ELECTION OF ANOTHER REMEDY

When a seller breaches a contract, the buyer has a choice. First, the buyer may stand upon the transaction and seek a remedy compatible with that "election"—specific performance, tort damages for deceit, or contract remedies for breach. The buyer's second choice is to rescind the contract, to avoid the transaction altogether, and, if the contract has been partially executed or performed, to seek restitution, return of her consideration.

Modern procedural and substantive law have altered the starkness of the buyer's "election" without, however, eliminating it. A plaintiff's complaint may seek alternative, even inconsistent, remedies, for example compensatory damages as well as rescission-restitution. A plaintiff may also amend her complaint freely, adding and subtracting remedies. Fed.R.Civ.P. 15. Finally, the federal rules tell a judge to "grant the relief to which the [successful plaintiff] is entitled, even if the party has not demanded such relief in the party's pleadings." Fed.R.Civ.P. 54(c).

[handwritten margin notes: may elect -stand upon trans - void trans]

The Uniform Commercial Code rejects the doctrine of election of remedies, resting instead on the idea that remedies are "essentially cumulative." Nevertheless "whether the [plaintiff's] pursuit of one remedy bars another depends entirely on the facts of the individual case." Section 2–703, Comment 1.

A court should prevent a plaintiff from receiving a duplicative combination of remedies, for example both specific performance and expectancy damages. More to the point, a court ought to avoid combining a remedy affirming with one disaffirming the transaction, for example expectancy damages plus restitution.

A court may attempt to avoid duplication by requiring the plaintiff to make an "election." "The doctrine of election of remedies is an 'application of the doctrine of estoppel' * * *. The purpose of the doctrine is to prevent duplicative recovery for the same wrong by requiring a party to elect between legally coexistent and inconsistent remedies." Wynfield Inns v. Edward LeRoux Group, Inc., 896 F.2d 483, 488 (11th Cir.1990).

An example: Williams sued her former employer; she pleaded alternatively breach of a handbook provision and breach of the implied covenant of covenant of good faith and fair dealing. The jury was instructed on both and apparently returned full verdicts for damages for both. How did the court prevent Williams's double dip? The reason to require plaintiff to elect is to prevent double recovery. When plaintiff has alternative theories of recovery for one violation of her rights, she may plead and prove both, but she may not recover on both. Williams, the appellate court held, must elect between the handbook and the implied covenant, probably taking the larger verdict. The court allowed plaintiff to maintain her alternative substantive theories of recovery; yet it prevented her from recovering double damages; it preserved her flexibility by waiting until after the jury verdict to require her to elect between verdicts. Williams v. Riedman, 339 S.C. 251, 529 S.E.2d 28 (App. 2000).

After a full opportunity to develop the whole case, the plaintiff will be barred by a final judgment from suing the defendant again to pursue a remedy she did not seek in the first action. Restatement (Second) of Judgments §§ 24–26 (1982).

Sometimes a plaintiff cannot escape the decision because indecision itself is a decision.

GANNETT CO. v. REGISTER PUBLISHING CO.

United States District Court, District of Connecticut, 1977.
428 F.Supp. 818.

Newman, District Judge. On October 20, 1976, the Hartford Times ceased publication. Its obituary notice stated that the paper had been "strangled by litigation." The controversy has not ended with its demise. The issue now pending concerns whether Gannett Co., Inc. ("Gannett") or The Register Publishing Company ("the Register") owns what remains of the paper. In lawyer's language, the question is whether the Register is entitled to rescind the contract by which it agreed to purchase from Gannett more than 99% of the shares of The Hartford Times, Inc.

* * * After negotiations culminating in a closing on October 10, 1973, Gannett entered into a Purchase Agreement [which] provided that Gannett would sell its shares of the common stock of The Hartford Times, Inc. together

with all outstanding stock of Community Offset, Inc. to the Register for an aggregate purchase price of $7,000,000, with appropriate adjustments in the purchase price to be made based on the difference between current assets and liabilities as reflected on the consolidated balance sheet to be prepared for the Times.

Shortly after the closing the Register became aware of discrepancies in the circulation statistics and financial statements of the Times as provided by Gannett. It learned of overvaluation of assets and of a series of devices that had been used for several years to conceal the reporting of inflated circulation figures. Consequently the Register decided not to pay Gannett the amount due under the net current asset adjustment provisions of the Purchase Agreement. Audits conducted over the next several weeks confirmed the Register's suspicions that the information supplied to it by Gannett prior to the execution of the Purchase Agreement had been false and misleading in many respects. When [settlement negotiations] fell through, Gannett filed this federal court action against the Register on April 15, 1974, for failure to pay the amount due under the net current asset adjustment provision. On June 12, 1974, the Register filed its counterclaim, alleging breach of contract, common law fraud, and securities law violations. In its counterclaim the Register sought compensatory and exemplary damages, or in the alternative, rescission of the Purchase Agreement and restitution of all benefits conferred by it on Gannett.

* * * After full and careful consideration, it is the conclusion of the Court that rescission is unavailable.

New York law, like the law of most states, gives an injured party the option to rescind a contract induced by fraud. But the right does not persist indefinitely. New York law is very clear, that the right to rescind for fraud must be exercised within a reasonable time after the injured party learns of the wrong. If the injured party neglects to notify the other party promptly of his intention to rescind, or if he accepts benefits under the contract and thereby affirms it, he loses his right to rescind. * * * In determining whether the injured party has lost the power to avoid the contract by delaying unreasonably in manifesting to the other party his intention to avoid the transaction, the speculative character of the contract is an influential factor. Restatement, Contracts, § 483. Comment (a) to this section of the Restatement states:

> "But the injured party delays giving information of his intention at his peril. He cannot lie by and delay choosing whether avoidance or affirmance will be more profitable, especially if the contract relates to a speculative transaction."

It is somewhat misleading to think of the choice an injured party has to make between avoiding and affirming a contract in "election of remedies" terms. The Register argues that under Rule 8 of the Federal Rules of Civil Procedure it is permitted to use alternative pleadings, and that there is nothing improper about its prayer in the alternative for damages or rescission in the counterclaim.[1] As a matter of pleading, this is true. But the real issue is not one of pleading but of substantive contract law. Professor Moore has distinguished "election of inconsistent remedies" from "instances where a choice, afforded by substantive law, terminated rights upon which the remedy invoked was dependent":

1. See also N.Y.C.P.L.R. § 3002(e), and Uniform Commercial Code, § 2–721, providing that claims for damages and rescission are not inconsistent.

"One fraudulently induced into a contract, for instance, may, as a matter of substantive law, either affirm or disaffirm the agreement. An election of the substantive right to affirm extinguishes the substantive right to disaffirm. And so an attempt to invoke the remedy of rescission after an action on the contract may fail, not because of election of inconsistent remedies, but because the plaintiff no longer has the substantive right to disaffirm." [Emphasis added].

1B Moore's Federal Practice ¶ 0.405[7]. It is the substantive law of contracts that extinguishes the right, and not any doctrine of pleading.

Similarly, the use of "waiver" terminology only obscures whether affirmance or avoidance has taken place. The Register argues that unless it "waived" its rescission remedy in writing, rescission is available as a matter of law by virtue of § 15(d) of the Purchase Agreement, which reads:

"No waiver of any provision of this Agreement shall be effective unless in writing and similarly signed, nor shall any failure of any party to enforce any right or remedy hereunder be deemed a waiver of such right or remedy for the future in the same or any situation."

But if the Register affirmed the contract, then its right to rescind terminated by operation of law, regardless of whether it "waived" the right in writing.[2]

"The right to terminate in the face of a breach is only an option to declare the contract at an end; if the contract is continued, the party doing so has not, strictly speaking, 'waived' his right but has executed it in favor of continued contractual relations."

Apex Pool Equipment Corp. v. Lee, 419 F.2d 556, 562 (2d Cir.1969).

For similar reasons the "laches" language used by the parties tends to obscure the real issue. When the Register argues that the doctrine of laches is inapplicable because the action is one at law rather than in equity, its attack on the use of a technical word may be abstractly correct; but when it implies that the remedy of rescission continues to be available as long as suit is filed within the statute of limitations, it is simply in error.[3] The right itself, and not just the remedy, is extinguished unless the injured party perfects the right by promptly taking the affirmative steps required by the law of contracts. In the language of § 480 of the Restatement of Contracts, the power to avoid the transaction is *conditional* on an offer made promptly after acquiring knowledge of the fraud. Sections 483 and 484 provide that *the power of avoidance is lost* if the injured party unreasonably delays manifesting his intention to avoid to the other party, or if he manifests an intention to affirm, or if he exercises dominion over the object of the contract. The emphasized words are substantive and not procedural concepts.

---

2. Perhaps if the facts showed that the Register did promptly and unequivocally notify Gannett, thereby demonstrably preserving its rescission remedy, then the waiver provision of the Agreement might come into play if Gannett tried to claim that some offhand remark short of a written waiver and not constituting an affirmance of the contract was a relinquishment of the remedy.

3. In many cases one and two-month periods have been held to constitute excessive delay. See, e.g., Sy–Jo Luncheonette, Inc. v. Marsav Distrib-

utors, Inc., 279 A.D. 715, 108 N.Y.S.2d 349 (1st Dept.1951).

While Comment a to § 490 of the Restatement of Contracts states that the power of avoidance continues "indefinitely" and may be set up as a defense if the injured party waits to be sued, it adds the important qualification "unless he affirms the transaction, *or fails to give information of his intention to exercise his power of avoidance* when the circumstances are such as to require information." [emphasis added].

Exercise of acts of ownership over the subject matter of the contract will validate the transaction and terminate the power of avoidance, regardless of whether the other party has suffered any prejudice. Restatement, Contracts, §§ 482, 484. The injured party must offer to restore the *status quo ante* by tendering what he has received in substantially as good condition as when it was transferred to him. Restatement, Contracts §§ 349, 480. But the *status quo ante* requirement is not inflexible. Mere depreciation in market value will not prevent rescission, and other factors may make the equitable remedy of rescission available even though the property cannot be returned in the same condition. Restatement, Contracts, § 349, comment (b). If the wrongful acts of the defrauding party are what make restoration of the *status quo* impossible, rescission is not foreclosed. Restatement, Contracts, § 349(2)(b).

Of course, the factual issues in determining whether an injured party has exercised acts of ownership over the property and whether changes in the property render rescission inequitable are substantially more difficult where the property is a multi-million dollar business rather than a car or a cow or a country estate. The newspaper business poses particularly intractable problems since someone—whether plaintiff or defendant—must make daily decisions to keep the paper running in order to preserve subscription and advertising revenues which are highly sensitive to a variety of circumstances. The cases that have dealt with rescission of a contract for the sale of a business have evolved a rule that the injured party need not ignore the business and allow it to fail if the other party refuses to take it back upon a timely demand for rescission.[4] Rather, as long as the injured party's actions can be fairly viewed as necessary steps to preserve the value of the business for the one ultimately determined to be the owner, rescission is still available.

A few cases illustrate the foregoing principles, in the context of relatively clearcut factual situations. In Caruso v. Moy, 164 Neb. 68, 81 N.W.2d 826 (1957), the plaintiff bought a prosperous Chinese–American restaurant, changed the bill of fare to Italian–American, and tried to rescind the contract of sale on the ground of fraud when business fell off. The court found that he had continued to operate the business for too long a period of time after learning of the fraud before seeking rescission and that he had thereby made the business his own. He changed the restaurant substantially so that business fell off to less than half what it had been previously, possibly due in part to his own mismanagement.[5] On these facts, he was not entitled to rescission.

In Sy–Jo Luncheonette, Inc. v. Marsav Distributors, Inc., 279 A.D. 715, 108 N.Y.S.2d 349 (1st Dept.1951), the plaintiffs discovered the alleged fraud within the first week after the purchase of the business. Yet they continued to operate the business for more than two months before sending a notice of election to rescind. Further, they inaugurated new pricing policies and changed the method of operating the business, causing a decline in gross receipts. Rescission was held to be unavailable.

But other cases have granted rescission even though the injured party has continued to operate the business. Especially where the property may depreciate materially if abandoned, as where a large part of its value stems from the fact

---

4. However, he may close the business upon proper notification to the other party. [citation]

5. Even the best management will not preserve the rescission right, however, where the

pattern of facts shows an intent to affirm the contract.

that it is a going concern, the injured party may take such steps as are reasonably necessary to conserve the value of the business for the one ultimately determined to be the owner. The duty of care of a defrauded party who continues to operate a business for the benefit of the other party after sending a timely rescission notice and tendering the property back is that of a gratuitous bailee. * * *

In light of the foregoing legal standards, the pertinent factual inquiries are the following:

1. When did the Register discover the fraud?

2. Did the Register promptly notify Gannett of its intention to rescind and offer to return the property?

3. Did the Register affirm the contract after knowledge of the fraud by exercising acts of ownership over the Times? Or did its conduct in continuing to operate the Times constitute a justifiable attempt by a gratuitous bailee to conserve the property for the benefit of the ultimate owner?

4. If the Register has otherwise preserved its rights, is rescission nonetheless inequitable due to changed conditions and inability to restore the *status quo ante?*

The Register was on notice of the possibility of fraud on October 11, 1973, the day after the closing. On that day Raymond Dumont, the Controller of the Times, talked with Richard Harris, Vice President and Director of the Register and new Assistant Publisher of the Times, and told him that there were discrepancies in the circulation statistics of the Times. In meetings over the next few days Dumont disclosed the possible overvaluation of certain assets on the balance sheets of the Times as appended to the Purchase Agreement, and described a series of devices used for several years at the Times to conceal the reporting of inflated circulation figures to both Gannett and the Audit Bureau of Circulations, a nationally recognized organization that collects and publishes the circulation statistics of member newspapers.

A number of cases have held that the reasonable time period within which rescission must be demanded starts the moment the injured party is on notice of the fraud. Whether notice means actual knowledge or only facts reasonably prompting further inquiry need not be resolved here, since in this case actual knowledge followed closely on the heels of the date the Register was put on notice of the possibility of fraud. * * * Exhibits introduced by Gannett document that during the months of October and November most of the frauds came to light.

Further, the Register took a number of actions in the months of October and November indicating its awareness of the frauds and its apprehension that the frauds were of sufficient materiality to have breached the contract. On the advice of Curtiss Thompson, counsel to the Register, the payments due to Gannett under the net current asset adjustment provision of the Purchase Agreement were withheld. This action was confirmed by a resolution of the Register's Board of Directors on October 25, 1973. * * * As of that date, John Fassett, who was a lawyer on the Register's board of directors, and possibly Thompson as well, were of the opinion that the Register had the option of rescinding the contract. * * *

I find, therefore, that full knowledge of the fraud may well have occurred at some point between October 11, 1973, and November 30, 1973, but that the very latest date for charging the Register with the responsibility of notifying Gannett within a reasonable time of its intention to rescind was November 30, 1973. * * *

The Register filed its counterclaim with a prayer for rescission on June 12, 1974. That date is therefore the latest date that the necessary rescission notice or demand took place. Whether any of the Register's earlier actions constituted notice of intent to rescind or otherwise preserved the right to rescind is the principal factual dispute between the parties. The difficulty in resolving this dispute stems in large part from the fact that during virtually the entire period between November 30, 1973, and June 12, 1974, the parties were engaged in serious settlement discussions. * * *

One claim is that the pendency of the settlement negotiations tolled the running of the promptness clock and that the Register was under no obligation to notify Gannett of intent to rescind until the negotiations had irrevocably fallen through. This approach, which would tend to further the general policy of the law to encourage settlement of disputes short of litigation, finds some support in the case law of rescission. As one court has stated of delay in seeking rescission:

> "Time alone is of slight significance, and, when it appears, as it does here, that the delay was occasioned by efforts to reach an amicable adjustment with offers and counter offers, the time so taken and the efforts so made cannot be counted as a time of sleeping on rights or an intention to forego remedy."

Plate v. Detroit Fidelity & Surety Co., 229 Mich. 482, 201 N.W. 457, 458 (1924). The appeal of this approach is that it favors the innocent party who has been trying in good faith to resolve the controversy amicably and puts the risk of uncertainty on the perpetrator of the fraud.

For several reasons, however, I am unwilling to accept an approach that would totally preclude any inquiry into what happened during the period of settlement negotiations. If the settlement period continues for any significant length of time, the buyer has the opportunity to indulge in just the sort of speculation the promptness rule was designed to prevent. Two sorts of essentially speculative delay could unreasonably prolong the period of settlement negotiations: delay for the purpose of speculation on the value of the property involved, and delay for the purpose of negotiating a favorable monetary settlement of the dispute. The latter is, in essence, speculation on the value of a potential lawsuit. While the amount of damages that might be acceptable in a settlement is not the item courts usually have in mind when they deny a rescinding buyer the right to "speculate," this amount bears a close relationship to the current value of the property being sold. The relationship is nonetheless close for being inverse: the buyer who sees the value of the property he bought declining will normally increase his damage demand so that an acceptable damage figure is inevitably a function of the subsequent value of the property. To let a rescinding buyer extend the time period in which he must demand rescission until the possibility of a monetary settlement has been pursued to an unsuccessful conclusion would have the undesirable feature of permitting the buyer to keep one eye on the fluctuating value of the property while he adjusts his negotiating demands. A complete tolling of the running of the reasonable time period during settlement negotiations could thus allow a buyer to prolong his opportunity for speculation, at least until the seller decided to call a halt by breaking off the discussions or by making his own unequivocal rescission offer, refusal of which would waive the buyer's rescission option or estop him from later asserting it. Furthermore, a party that wants rescission, even though the victim of a fraud, is not being disadvantaged at all by being required to make up his mind within a reasonable period after knowledge of the fraud and to give notice that he wants to return the property. At least with respect to functioning businesses, such an obligation promotes needed certainty in the marketplace. Moreover, it is a principle easily understood by parties seeking rescission and easily followed. Further, any inquiry into whether the period was prolonged for *bona fide* settlement purposes rather than with a speculative motive would require some examination of the reasonableness of the terms and figures demanded by the rescinder, in direct conflict with the settlement privilege and the policies behind it.

Counting the settlement period either entirely "in" or entirely "out" in determining the reasonable promptness of a rescission demand would each have undesirable risk allocation consequences. The first puts all the risk on the innocent buyer and deters the amicable resolution of disputes. The second places the entire risk of speculation on the seller, who may not even know until the unsuccessful end of damage negotiations that rescission has been in the buyer's mind all along.

The better approach, appropriate to a remedy as drastic as rescission, takes into account all the facts and circumstances that bear on reasonableness, with due regard for the sensitive nature of settlement negotiations and the policy reasons for protecting them. Though discussions may continue over months or even years, the acts and omissions of the parties must retain their normal legal significance. Exercise of acts of ownership over the property evidencing an intent to affirm the contract, will extinguish the right to disaffirm regardless of the pendency of negotiations, as will disposal of the property with knowledge of the fraud or any other act or omission that is clearly inconsistent with a later claim for rescission. Time no more stands still during settlement negotiations culminating with a rescission demand than it does when the statute of limitations runs during settlement. The fact that the parties agree, as they apparently did at the commencement of negotiations in this case, that settlement talks will be "without prejudice" and understand that participation in the negotiations will not *of itself* lessen their substantive rights does not always relieve the would-be rescinder of his duty to take the steps the law requires to preserve his rescission remedy. Legally significant acts and omissions can operate of their own force to terminate the right to rescission. The pendency of settlement discussions is simply one circumstance, albeit an important one, in determining the reasonableness of what the rescinding party did or failed to do.

There may well be situations in which the absence of a rescission demand would be reasonable under all the circumstances, as where the value and condition of the property remained constant during the negotiations so that no element of prejudice to the seller came into play, or where the seller's assurances of a favorable monetary settlement dissuaded the buyer from making an early demand. Or a slight delay in making a rescission demand, which would not preserve the remedy in the absence of settlement efforts, might well be reasonably timely if made unequivocally early in such discussions. Similarly if a buyer, once alerted to his right to rescind, promptly demands rescission, he should not lose the remedy because he negotiates with the seller, even for an extended time, to see if the rescission can be handled amicably without resort to litigation. I do not hold that the passage of time precludes rescission regardless of the circumstances. Rather I find that under the circumstances of this particular case rescission is unavailable. The absence of a rescission demand takes on special significance in this case, where the evidence is persuasive that even apart from the Register's omissions, its acts evidenced an intent to affirm the contract.

At no time during the relevant period did the Register's Board of Directors resolve to present a rescission offer to Gannett, although the subject of rescission was discussed at several board meetings. At the meeting on October 25, 1973, the possibility of rescission was discussed, but the operating officers of the Times reaffirmed their view that the purchase was desirable.

* * * It was not until February 25, 1975, that the Board of Directors specifically approved a rescission proposal to be submitted to Gannett. * * *

Several aspects of the testimony show convincingly that the Register wished to affirm the purchase contract and keep the Times rather than rescind. The first is Lionel Jackson's testimony in Court. The statements of Jackson, as Publisher and Chief Executive Officer of the Register and member of the negotiating committee appointed by the Board of Directors, are probably the most probative evidence of the corporate opinion of the Register during the time period in question. In response to questioning by the Court, Jackson testified:

> "I can say, your Honor, that the rest of the board—I can't speak for, I can only say for myself—that it was very, very distasteful for me to have to think about rescission because, after all, we didn't get into all this thing. We hoped to have a very successful joint newspaper situation in Hartford and New Haven, and we bought it with a purpose in mind, and it was—it certainly didn't help our reputation to have The Hartford Times turn out to be what it was, and rescission would have made it even worse."

Further, the Register had been engaged in defending the purchase of the Times in a lawsuit in the state court. The majority of the outstanding shares of the Register Publishing Company are owned by the John Day Jackson trust. When Jackson and Henry J. Conland, two of the three trustees of that trust, announced their intention to cause the Register to acquire the Times from Gannett, several beneficiaries of the trust instituted an action in the Superior Court in New Haven County in May of 1973 to enjoin the purchase. After injunctive relief was denied and the purchase consummated, the plaintiffs filed a substituted complaint alleging breach of fiduciary duty and seeking, *inter alia,* rescission of the sale. During the entire period in question the Register was defending the purchase of the Times in state court as a prudent investment. A decision to rescind the contract might well have been an admission that the beneficiaries were right. In a highly significant letter dated June 5, 1974, and sent by Lionel Jackson and Henry Conland to Rose Sheppard, Jackson's sister and a plaintiff in the state court action, Jackson and Conland stated:

> "We don't know where you got the impression that The Register Publishing Company is seeking rescission, but it is obviously the result of misconstrued information which has caused the destruction of the family relationship."

This passage drastically undercuts the Register's claim that it was actively seeking to preserve the rescission remedy. * * *

On the basis of all the evidence I find that no notification of intent to rescind was given to Gannett within a reasonable time after the Register had discovered the frauds.

Wholly apart from the reasonableness of the delay in demanding rescission, the Register's conduct clearly evidences an intent to affirm the contract for the purchase of the Times. The evidence is persuasive that during the period after discovery of the frauds the Register exercised dominion over the Times by treating it as its own property and did not operate it as a gratuitous bailee for the benefit of the ultimate owner. * * *

If the Register had truly intended to hold the Times for Gannett's benefit in the event rescission was ultimately effected, one would have expected at least some sort of notice to Gannett of major changes to be made in the management of the Times to allow Gannett an opportunity to agree to voluntary rescission before irrevocable steps were taken. Probably the most important action taken was the decision to go to cold type from hot metal, a step that apparently most newspapers around the country are gradually taking, but one that requires substantial capital outlays. The testimony showed that the conversion to cold type was estimated to require an investment in the neighborhood of $500,000 to result in substantial savings over the long run after an initial period of increased expense during the transition period. I am willing to agree with the Register that the decision to go to cold type was a prudent one that would result in long-range savings. But this kind of major investment without consultation with or even notification to Gannett is inconsistent with the theory that the Register considered itself the bailee rather than the owner of the Times. * * *

Other substantial changes include a price increase of the Sunday paper from 15 cents to 25 cents and of the daily and Saturday papers from 10 cents to 15 cents, which had the effect of causing a significant drop in circulation not all of which could have been recouped even by a later price reduction after rescission; the cessation of distribution in outlying geographical areas; the discontinuation of 16 syndicated features and the addition of 48 others; and a shift in editorial policy. This catalogue is not exhaustive but illustrative. In short, many of the characteristics that give a newspaper its identity—editorial policy, features, price, and market, among others—were all significantly changed by the Register either before the rescission demand was made or while the claim was pending. The point is not that it would be impossible to reverse the changes, but rather that the pattern of the changes indicates the Register's intention to treat the Times as its own.

Equally supportive of the conclusion that the Register fully considered the Times to be its own property is the highly significant pattern of steps to integrate the operation of the Times with the operation of the New Haven Register and the New Haven Journal–Courier, the two New Haven papers published by the Register. Gannett has extensively catalogued the integration moves, and again not all of them need be discussed. Illustrative are the tying in of the cold type printing system to the Register's computer system in New Haven, the removal of a Univac Computer from the Times to New Haven to render computer services for the Times in New Haven, performance of bookkeeping functions for the Times by Register personnel in New Haven, the elimination of personnel from the Times staff and the absorption of their functions by Register staff, and others. I accept the Register's explanation that these moves were made to effect economies by eliminating duplication of equipment and personnel.[6] But as these steps were taken, it inevitably became

---

6. The Register supports its "gratuitous bailee" characterization of its actions by pointing out that all the changes made were either necessary or desirable cost-cutting measures. This

more and more difficult to view the Times as a separate entity. After these changes neither Gannett nor any potential owner other than the Register would have been able to step in and operate the paper without substantial outlays and hiring to fill in for the functions then being performed in New Haven.

Under these circumstances, the Register must be deemed to have affirmed the contract and lost its right to rescission.

* * * Furthermore, to force return of the shares of The Hartford Times, Inc. upon Gannett at this stage would clearly be inequitable. The Times is no longer a going concern. Its value lies primarily in the tangible assets plus whatever highly speculative good will is still in existence that would to some extent help to reestablish circulation if publication were resumed.

While I have ruled against the Register on the availability of rescission, nothing in this memorandum should be taken as reflecting any view on the amount of damages that could eventually be awarded. This is entirely an open question at this point, and if the frauds as alleged and the damages as claimed can be proven, a substantial recovery of compensatory and exemplary damages may be possible.

Notes

1. *Questions.* Is election of remedies, as the court applies it, a specialized doctrine of estoppel? Does the court require a plaintiff to elect to prevent duplicative relief? Is there a better way to prevent duplication?

What goal does the court seek to achieve? Are the rules of election of remedies too blunt to achieve the court's goals?

2. *Election by Delay–Specialized Laches.* Applying a statute which requires a rescission plaintiff to proceed promptly, the South Dakota court held that two and a half years was too long for the buyers to wait to sue the sellers to rescind for mistake, apparently because of difficulty the trial judge would have restoring the pre-contract status quo. The buyers had dropped their damages action during trial. Knudsen v. Jensen, 521 N.W.2d 415 (S.D. 1994).

3. *Election-Ratification by Failure to Tender–Return Benefits.* As part of ending her employment with Entergy, Delores Oubre signed a release of all claims. After receiving the last installment of her severance pay, she charged Entergy with age discrimination under the federal statute.

Oubre's release did not conform to the statutory requirements to release age discrimination claims. But Entergy argued that because she retained the money, she had ratified the irregular release and disqualified herself from rescinding it: "The employer maintains, however, that before the innocent party can elect avoidance, she

may well be true, but the fact that a significant change effects economies does not prove that rescission is still available. If the Register's argument were accepted, the rule of law requiring a rescinding party to refrain from acts of ownership over the property would shrink in scope to cover mismanagement or wastefulness only. The cases dealing with rescission of a going concern have never permitted substantive changes in the nature of the business, regardless of the effect on costs. See Gargotto v. Sherman, 297 Ky. 597, 180 S.W.2d 565 (1944) (removal of amusement machines and victrola from restaurant); Fryer v. Campbell, 48 Wyo. 122, 43 P.2d 994 (1935) (con-

tinued operation of motion picture theater causing deterioration in machinery and furniture); Meyers v. Hoops, 140 N.E.2d 65 (Ct.App.Ohio 1955) (changes in personnel equipment, and stock); Caruso v. Moy, 164 Neb. 68, 81 N.W.2d 826 (1957) (change in bill of fare of restaurant from Chinese–American to Italian–American); Sy–Jo Luncheonette, Inc. v. Marsav Distributors, Inc., 279 A.D. 715, 108 N.Y.S.2d 349 (1st Dept. 1951) (new pricing policies). Charges of mismanagement were made in the latter two cases, but the rule of law on acts of ownership applies even where the rescinder's management is beyond reproach.

must first tender back any benefits received under the contract. If she fails to do so within a reasonable time after learning of her rights, the employer maintains, she ratifies the contract and so makes it binding."

"The statute," the Supreme Court decided, "governs the effect of the [plaintiff's] release on [Age Discrimination in Employment Act] claims, and the employer cannot invoke the employee's failure to tender back as a way of excusing its own failure to comply." Oubre's severance pay may come up later, since the employer may have "claims for restitution, recoupment, or setoff against the employee." Oubre v. Entergy Operations, Inc., 522 U.S. 422 (1998).

4. *Rescission the Sole Remedy.* The relationship between the buyers' damages and rescission-restitution actions is complex. For example, after finding that violations of state and federal wetlands standards created a mutual mistake in a land sale, the trial judge let the seller "elect" either payment of the buyer's diminution damages or rescission-restitution. After the seller elected damages, the buyer appealed. The Vermont supreme court reversed on the ground that rescission was the only available remedy. The trial judge had allowed the seller to remit the buyer to recovering damages; the supreme court said that this solution substitutes "for the contract actually made by the parties a different one, which the court feels they would have made if they had known the correct quantities involved." Rancourt v. Verba, 165 Vt. 225, 678 A.2d 886, 888 (1996).

Suppose the trial judge had let the *buyer* decide whether (a) to keep the tract and recover diminution damages, or (b) to rescind and recover the price. After the buyer chooses damages, should an appellate court force her to relinquish the land in return for a refund?

2. LACK OF INJURY

EARL v. SAKS & CO.

Supreme Court of California, 1951.
36 Cal.2d 602, 226 P.2d 340.

SCHAUER, J. A.K. Barbee appeals from judgments in consolidated actions hereinafter described, that respondent Mrs. Richard Earl is the owner of a certain mink coat and that Barbee owes respondent Saks and Company $3,981.25. He contends that an asserted sale of the coat to him by Saks, and an asserted gift of the coat by him to Mrs. Earl, were voidable, and were rescinded by him, because his consent thereto was induced by fraud of Mrs. Earl and Saks. We have concluded that these contentions are tenable.

On April 4, 1947, Barbee and Mrs. Earl went to the fur salon of Saks. A representative of Saks showed them a mink coat and told them its price was $5,000. Barbee told Saks that he would like to buy the coat for Mrs. Earl but that he would pay no more than $4,000 for it. Saks rejected repeated offers of Barbee to purchase the coat for $4,000. Unknown to Barbee, Mrs. Earl then asked Saks to pretend to sell the coat to him for $4,000, and stated that she would pay the difference between $4,000 and the price of the coat. Saks agreed to this. It told Barbee that it would sell the coat to him for $3,981.25, made out a sales slip for that amount, and Barbee signed it in the belief that was the full price of the coat. Saks then delivered the coat to Barbee; he in turn delivered it to Mrs. Earl and said that he gave it to her. Mrs. Earl, wearing the coat, left the store with Barbee.

The next day, April 5, Mrs. Earl returned the coat to Saks to be monogrammed and paid Saks the balance of its price, $916.30. Later the same day

Barbee told Saks that he had revoked the gift to Mrs. Earl, that he was the owner of the coat (which he thought he had purchased for $3,981.25), that he would pay the agreed price ($3,981.25) only if Saks would deliver the coat to him, and that it was not to deliver the coat to Mrs. Earl. Thereafter Mrs. Earl demanded that Saks deliver the coat to her; Saks refused and attempted to return her $918.30; but she refused to accept the money; Saks retained (and still retains) possession of the coat.

Mrs. Earl then sued Saks, alleging conversion of the coat. Saks answered, denying the conversion, and at the same time filed a pleading which it denominated "Cross–Complaint in Interpleader," which, however, not only named Mrs. Earl and Barbee as asserted interpleader cross-defendants but also implicitly and necessarily, in the light of the circumstances, required, if Saks was to prevail, the granting of affirmative adversary relief against Barbee or Mrs. Earl or both of them. Saks alleged that it sold the coat to Barbee for $3,981.25; that Mrs. Earl, "as additional consideration * * * to induce" Saks to make the sale to Barbee, agreed to pay Saks $916.30 and later paid Saks that sum; that Saks is indifferent between the claims of the cross-defendants and is willing to deliver the coat to either cross-defendant as the court may direct (but, it is implicit from Saks' several pleadings read together, only upon condition that it recover from Barbee or from Mrs. Earl or from both of them the full price of the coat); it asked that the cross-defendants be required to "litigate between themselves their claims to said mink coat"; it did not offer to relinquish its asserted claim for any part of the full price of approximately $4,900. Mrs. Earl's answer to the cross-complaint admitted that she paid Saks $916.30 and alleged that at that time title to the coat "was transferred to her as is more fully alleged in her complaint." The complaint, however, contains no allegations as to transfer of title. Barbee in answer to the cross-complaint admitted that he told Saks he would pay the price discussed between Saks and Barbee if and only if Saks "would sell and deliver the coat to him at and for [such] price," and alleged that Mrs. Earl's agreement to pay Saks $916.30 was fraudulently concealed from him by Saks and Mrs. Earl; that they represented to him that the full price of the coat was $3,981.25; and that if he had known of the secret agreement he would not have agreed to buy the coat. No pleadings joining issues between Barbee and Mrs. Earl were filed. Saks also brought a separate action against Barbee, alleging that he owed Saks $3,981.25 for goods sold and delivered. Barbee in answer made allegations of fraud substantially similar to those in his answer to Saks' cross-complaint. The two actions were consolidated for trial.

From what has been stated it appears that Saks, because of its duplicitous compact with Mrs. Earl, finds itself in this position: It knowingly and purposefully caused Barbee to believe that it was selling him—and him only—a certain fur coat for the full price of $3,981.25. It wants to collect the $3,981.25 from Barbee but it cannot (or will not) deliver the coat to him—fully paid, for $3,981.25 or otherwise—because, although it has possession of the coat, it has already collected $916.30 for the same coat from Mrs. Earl, and she claims to own the coat and refuses to release her claim to it (or for damages for its alleged conversion) as against either Saks or Barbee. Mrs. Earl further claims the coat as against both Saks and Barbee on the theory of an asserted gift from Barbee. But the gift is, necessarily, dependent upon Barbee's having purchased the coat from Saks and that purchase, it is obvious, was induced by the joint fraud of Mrs. Earl and Saks. Saks and Mrs. Earl—both guilty of express fraud—are seeking the aid of the court to recover that which they are entitled to, if at all, only because of their fraud.

While, as indicated above, the pleadings do not specifically allege, or suggest the theory of, the origin of Mrs. Earl's claim of title to the coat, the trial proceeded on the theory that the issues were whether there was a sale by Saks to Barbee and a gift by Barbee to Mrs. Earl, and whether the two transactions were voidable by Barbee because of the secret agreement and misrepresentation. Barbee testified that he would not have bought the coat if he had known that the price was more than $4,000. Every element of the transaction and all the circumstances shown appear to support this position; no evidence is inconsistent with it. At the trial Barbee's counsel restated the position which Barbee had announced to Saks before the actions were instituted: "we are perfectly willing to accept the coat and pay * * * the price that we agreed to pay for it [$3,981.25] * * * but we certainly are under the circumstances disclosed here already in this evidence [the secret agreement] * * * not willing to let this coat be handed over to this young lady." Counsel for Barbee also offered to prove that the gift was made in reliance on Mrs. Earl's representations that she would "reciprocate his affection and would give up running around with other men" and that Barbee rescinded the gift when he learned that those representations were false. The offered proof on the latter theory was properly rejected, for no such issue was raised by the pleadings.

The trial court gave judgment against Mrs. Earl on her complaint for conversion and in favor of Saks on its complaint against Barbee for goods sold and delivered. On Saks' "Cross–Complaint in Interpleader" it gave judgment that Mrs. Earl is the owner and entitled to possession of the coat. We are satisfied that the judgment in neither action is tenable insofar as it is adverse to the defendant and cross-defendant Barbee. * * *

Rescission of Gift. The trial court was not entitled to disbelieve Barbee's uncontradicted testimony (supported by the circumstances shown and by the undisputed evidence of all parties that he repeatedly insisted he would not pay more than $4,000) that he would not have bought the coat if he had known of the secret agreement between Saks and Mrs. Earl. Although Barbee did not expressly allege or testify that he would not have given the coat to Mrs. Earl if he had known of the secret agreement, it is apparent that the case was tried as if this were in issue and that in fact he would not have made the gift had he known of the secret agreement. Obviously Barbee's belief that the full price of the coat was $3,981.25 underlay and was a material element in, and inducing cause of, the gift as well as the immediately preceding purchase. As previously indicated, he could not have made the gift unless he made the purchase, and it is indisputably established that the purchase was induced by the express fraud of both Mrs. Earl and Saks. The facts that Barbee at the trial, by correctly rejected offers of proof, sought to show another fraudulent representation which also was an inducement to his making the gift, and that he announced rescission before he learned of the secret agreement, do not prevent him from now basing his defense on such secret agreement. "One may justify an asserted rescission by proving that at the time there was an adequate cause although it did not become known to him until later. One cannot waive or acquiesce in a wrong while ignorant thereof."

A gift can be rescinded if it was induced by fraud or material misrepresentation (whether of the donee or a third person) or by mistake as to a "basic fact."

(Rest., Restitution, §§ 26, 39); see Murdock v. Murdock (1920), 49 Cal.App. 775, 783–785 [194 P. 762] [fraud of donee].

"A failure by the donee to reveal material facts when he knows that the donor is mistaken as to them is fraudulent nondisclosure." (Rest., Restitution, § 26, comment c.)

"A mistake which entails the substantial frustration of the donor's purpose entitles him to restitution. No more definite general statement can be made as to what constitutes a basic mistake in the making of a gift. The donor is entitled to restitution if he was mistaken as to the * * * identity or essential characteristics of the gift." (Rest., Restitution, § 26, comment c.)

Since Barbee was not merely mistaken but was actively misled as to a material element in the purchase and as to an essential characteristic of the gift—he believed that the coat was purchased entirely by him so that it could be given in its entirety as a gift—he was entitled to, as he did, rescind the gift.

Rescission of Contract. It appears from the findings of probative facts that Saks did more than merely fail to disclose its agreement with Mrs. Earl. In the circumstances, implicit in the finding that Barbee "was informed by Saks and Company's representatives that they would sell said mink coat to him for the sum of $3,981.25" is a finding that Saks actively misrepresented that the price had been reduced and that $3,981.25 was the full price. It is completely unreasonable to deny that a representation by a clerk in a reputable store that an article has a certain price, followed by the clerk's preparation and the customer's signing of a sales check showing purchase of the article for that price, amounts to a representation by the store that the *total* price and the *entire* sales transaction are as represented. This misrepresentation, it appears from the undisputed evidence, was made by Saks with knowledge that Barbee insisted on a reduction in price; from this it follows that such misrepresentation must have been made with intent to deceive Barbee and to induce him to buy the coat. * * *

Saks relies on California cases which say that "fraud which has produced and will produce no injury will not justify a rescission." [citations] It asserts that a person is not injured by being induced to buy a $5,000 coat for $4,000. But the coat was neither sold nor bought for $4,000. Saks was selling the coat for the full price, and a person other than seller Saks and buyer Barbee paid a substantial part—approximately one fifth—of the full price. Furthermore, this "no injury, no rescission" formula is not very helpful, because of disagreement in the authorities as to what is meant by "injury." In a sense, anyone who is fraudulently induced to enter into a contract is "injured"; his "interest in making a free choice and in exercising his own best judgment in making decisions with respect to economic transactions and enterprises has been interfered with." (See McCleary, Damage as a Requisite to Rescission for Misrepresentation, 36 Mich.L.Rev. 1, 227, 245.)

Also relied on by Saks is a definition of "injury" which has sometimes appeared in some California cases: "it may be conceded that it must be shown that [one who would rescind] * * * by reason of fraud, suffered an injury of a pecuniary nature, that is, an injury to his property rights, as distinguished from a mere injury to his feelings, but it will be sufficient if the facts alleged show that material injury will necessarily ensue from the fraud, although the amount of pecuniary loss is not stated." (Spreckels v. Gorrill (1907), supra, 152 Cal. 383, 388.) The "concession" or implication that in every case there must be "pecuniary loss" is incorrect. (See Hefferan v. Freebairn (1950), 34 Cal.2d 715, 721 [214 P.2d 386].) And the definition does not take account of the cases which allow rescission of a transaction induced by an agent's misrepresentation of his principal's identity, even though there was no economic reason for the unwillingness to deal with the principal. [citations]

The McCleary article suggests the following classification of the cases which have considered rescission for fraud:

1. The representee can rescind where he obtains the very thing that he expected but it is worth less than he was led reasonably to expect. In most cases where rescission is sought the representee has received something of less economic value than he expected.

2. The representee can rescind where he obtains something substantially different from that which he was led to expect. If one is induced to buy a certain lot of land by misrepresentation that it contains a vineyard, he need not keep it when he learns that it contains instead an apple orchard; even though the lot of land is the identical lot of land and although the orchard may be more valuable than the vineyard which he expected to get, it is obviously unfair to require him to keep what he did not bargain for and did not want. The undisputed evidence describing the present sale would put it in this class. The coat bargained for between Barbee and Saks, within the knowledge and belief of Barbee, as was known to Saks, was a coat fully paid for by Barbee, which Saks knew was to be used as a gift, but Saks intended to and did deliver something substantially different; i.e., a coat on which Barbee was charged only with a down payment and for which his intended donee had secretly agreed to pay in a substantial part. The seller was to receive approximately 25 per cent more for the coat than the buyer was paying and the element of a complete gift was being destroyed.

3. Where the representee obtains exactly that which he expects, although there was misrepresentation, the social interest in the stability of transactions may or may not outweigh the social interest in not having one intentionally take advantage of another. Saks attempts to describe the present sale so as to put it in this class. It says that Barbee bargained for and expected to get a certain coat for a cost to him of not more than $4,000, and this is what he got. In the present situation, however, where the motives of Barbee were clearly noneconomic, the general social interest in stability of transactions is overridden by the interest in not having a seller make intentional misrepresentations which mislead a would-be donor into the erroneous belief that he alone is purchasing and that his donee is to receive from him a fully paid for gift, when the seller is fully aware of the effect which the misrepresentations may have and intends that they should have that effect. Again, it is important, the element of a complete gift by donor to donee is being destroyed through the misrepresentation and concealment.

Saks contends that Barbee has not rescinded, and cannot rescind, the sale because he has stated that he was willing to carry out the objectively manifested bargain to purchase the coat for $3,981.25. But at no time since Barbee's announced willingness to stand on the transaction which he believed he had entered into with Saks, did Saks offer to comply with the transaction and give Barbee what he bargained for: a coat for which he was paying in full, without Mrs. Earl, a stranger to the Saks–Barbee transaction, paying a portion of the price. Indeed, Saks, at the time of the rescission and mentioned offer by Barbee, was apparently unable to sell Barbee the coat in question as a fully paid for coat for $3,981.25 because Mrs. Earl refused to take back the $916.30 which she paid for the coat and which Saks had previously accepted. Barbee's counsel, at the trial, made clear his position; after the secret agreement, misrepresentation and payment of $916.30 were in evidence he said, "under the circumstances of this case we shouldn't be required to pay Saks and company anything. * * * [He] would do anything that could be done to repudiate that transaction and say it never was a real transaction." We are satisfied that the contract of purchase and the gift were voidable and were properly rescinded.

For the reasons above stated, the judgments are reversed.

TRAYNOR, J. [dissenting]. Barbee received what he bargained for. * * * The mink coat that he examined and agreed to pay $3,981.25 for, was the one he received and gave to Mrs. Earl. He concedes that the fair value of the coat was $5,000. It was not unreasonable for the trial court to conclude that, since the coat Barbee received was actually worth more than he agreed to pay, he would not have rejected it because Mrs. Earl arranged to pay the difference. * * * It was under no compulsion to believe his statement that he would have rejected it. * * *

It was for the trial court to determine whether Barbee was a man of such temperament that he would have preferred having Mrs. Earl get along without the fur coat to accepting her contribution toward its purchase. He declared his love for her, expressing the sentiment several times that he wanted to give her a fur coat. She was "very much in love with the coat and wanted it badly." It was important to him that the woman he loved possess the coat; it was important to her to possess it. Her contribution enabled him to fulfill his wish and hers at a price he was willing to pay. Since they were both fur-coat-minded, it is a reasonable inference that he would not have risked disturbing the relationship between them by depriving her of the coat because she was willing to contribute toward its purchase.

Counsel at the trial made it clear that Barbee sought rescission of the sale because Mrs. Earl failed to live up to his expectations. This failure can in no way be attributed to Saks and Company. Its coat was of sound quality and came up to Mrs. Earl's expectations. The court properly rejected Barbee's offer of proof of his expectations and disappointment. Not only were they no concern of Saks and Company, but no issue was raised in the pleadings regarding his arrangements with Mrs. Earl. I would therefore affirm the judgments.

HARPER v. ADAMETZ

Supreme Court of Errors of Connecticut, 1955.
142 Conn. 218, 113 A.2d 136.

BALDWIN, ASSOCIATE JUSTICE. * * * Joseph B. Tesar was conservator of the estate of his father, William Tesar, an incompetent, who owned eighty acres of land and the buildings thereon in the town of Haddam. The defendant Jere Adametz, a real estate agent, hereinafter referred to as Jere, was acting as agent for the sale of Tesar's property. Jere advertised a portion of it, consisting of five acres and an old colonial house, for $6200, and the advertisement, in a New Haven newspaper, came to the attention of the plaintiff. On December 6, 1948, the plaintiff wrote to Jere expressing an interest in the property advertised. Jere acknowledged this letter on December 8. On December 12, Jere showed the plaintiff the eighty-acre farm and told him that the seller was asking $8500 for it but that the buildings and a smaller acreage could be bought for less. The plaintiff made no offer but showed an interest in purchasing the smaller acreage. On the following day, December 13, Jere wrote to Joseph Tesar, the conservator, stating that he had a client who had offered $6500 cash for the farm (meaning eighty acres) and asked for an immediate reply. On December 15, the attorney for Tesar wrote to Jere stating that Tesar would accept the offer for the entire farm subject to the approval of the Probate Court and asking that a written offer with at least a 10 per cent deposit be sent to him.

The plaintiff visited the property on December 19 and 26, and on one of those dates he made an offer to Jere of $7000 for the entire farm. Jere promised to convey this offer to Tesar, but he did not do so. Instead, he sent his own check for $500 to Tesar on December 29 as a deposit on the purported offer of $6500.

Jere told Fred Mazanek, a relative of the Tesars, that the plaintiff wanted to purchase only a small portion of the acreage and that he, Jere, would like to obtain the rest for his son but that he did not want to lose his commission. He prevailed upon Mazanek and John Hibbard, a friend of the family, to act as a medium for the passing of title to the farm. On or about January 2, 1949, Jere told the plaintiff that his offer had been rejected because Tesar desired to keep a major portion of the farm in the family and that certain relatives of the Tesars wished to buy most of the acreage, but that he, Jere, could arrange for the plaintiff to buy the buildings and part of the land. The plaintiff then made an offer of $6000 for seventeen acres, including the buildings, and Jere accepted the offer. The plaintiff was satisfied with his purchase.

On January 4, Joseph Tesar signed a contract to sell the entire farm of eighty acres to Mazanek and Hibbard for $6500. The sale was approved by the Probate Court, and a conservator's deed dated January 26 was delivered on February 8 to Mazanek and Hibbard. At the same time, on February 8, they executed and delivered a deed for seventeen acres, including the buildings, to the plaintiff, who paid $6000. On March 11, Mazanek and Hibbard conveyed sixty-three acres, the balance of the farm, to the defendant Walter Adametz, Jere's son. Mazanek and Hibbard were mere "go betweens" who paid nothing when they "bought" the farm and received nothing when they "sold" it to the plaintiff and Walter. Walter paid nothing for the sixty-three acres he acquired. Tesar did not know of the plaintiff's offer of $7000 for the entire farm, and the plaintiff did not know that this offer had not been transmitted to Tesar. The representation by Jere to Tesar on December 13 that he had a $6500 offer for the farm was false. At the time he sent his own check for $500 to Tesar on the purported offer of $6500, the only offer he had was the plaintiff's offer of $7000. Jere engineered the transactions herein related to obtain sixty-three acres of the farm for himself and Walter at the price of $500 and at the same time collect a commission of $325 for the sale.

On these facts, the court concluded that Jere was the agent for Tesar and not for the plaintiff, that there was no contract between Tesar and the plaintiff for the purchase of any property other than the buildings and seventeen acres of land, that the plaintiff sustained no loss by reason of any misrepresentation made by Jere, and that therefore the plaintiff had failed to prove actionable fraud.

It is the general rule that in an action at law for fraud the plaintiff, to recover, must prove that he has been injured. * * * In the ordinary case, this means that the plaintiff must sustain a substantial pecuniary loss. [citations] The plaintiff in this action did receive what he paid for. * * * He did not, however, because of Jere's fraud, obtain what he was seeking. While acting as an agent for Tesar but with the intent of making a secret profit for himself, Jere told his principal that he had a cash offer of $6500 for the entire farm. This statement was false, and in making it Jere violated his trust. His conduct was a fraud upon Tesar. * * *

Jere was not the agent of the plaintiff. Nevertheless, he could not deliberately deceive him. It was Jere's advertisement in the newspaper which had aroused the interest of the plaintiff in the property and had brought him to Haddam to inspect it. Jere told the plaintiff at that time that the entire farm was for sale for $8500. When the plaintiff later made an offer of $7000 for it, Jere said nothing about having submitted a bogus offer of $6500, and he promised to submit the plaintiff's offer to Tesar. He failed to do so and later lied to the plaintiff by telling him that Tesar had rejected it. It was not until after this that the plaintiff offered $6000 for seventeen acres and the buildings. It can be claimed that when the plaintiff made his $7000 offer Tesar had already signified his willingness to accept the purported offer of $6500 made by Jere in behalf of a fictitious client and that the plaintiff's offer came too late. But the $6500 offer was a fraud and Tesar was not bound to accept it. He could have revoked Jere's authority. * * * Thereafter, he could have sold the property to the plaintiff. Jere's false statements, his concealment of the facts, his promise to submit the plaintiff's offer to Tesar when everything indicates that he had no intention of doing so, worked a fraud upon the plaintiff. * * * As a result, the plaintiff has been denied the right to have his bona fide offer of $7000 submitted to Tesar. In short, the plaintiff has been deprived of his bargain. Jere and Walter, by their fraud, have acquired sixty-three acres of land for $175.

This is an action in equity as well as at law. Equity is a system of positive jurisprudence founded upon established principles which can be adapted to new circumstances where a court of law is powerless to give relief. [citations] In equity as in law, misrepresentation, to constitute fraud, must be material. [citations] That is to say, the representation must prejudice the party relying upon it. He must suffer some injury or pecuniary loss. Some courts have held that the pecuniary loss need be only slight. [citations] Others have held that mere lack of pecuniary injury or loss does not prevent the granting of relief by way of rescission and restitution. [citations] In Brett v. Cooney, 75 Conn. 338, 53 A. 729, the plaintiffs were induced by a series of false statements to sell their property to a person who in turn conveyed to another whom the plaintiffs had previously rejected as an undesirable purchaser. The plaintiffs suffered no financial loss. However, after citing Barnes v. Starr, 64 Conn. 136, 150, 28 A. 980, which states that proof of injury is a prerequisite to recovery for fraud, the court said: "But in measuring injury equity does not concern itself merely with money losses. If it finds that a clear right has been invaded, and that redress can be secured by putting the parties back in their original position, it will seldom refuse its aid because the plaintiff can show no substantial damage to his pecuniary interests." * * *

The plaintiff had a clear right to have his offer for the farm transmitted to Tesar. Having been invited by Jere's advertisement to bid for the property, he had a right to assume that Jere would deal honestly with him and be faithful to his principal. Instead, Jere withheld the offer, later lied to the plaintiff about it and, by using the plaintiff's willingness to accept seventeen acres, acquired the farm for himself for less than the plaintiff had offered for it. He induced the plaintiff to make an offer and then used that offer, and the plaintiff's money to make a secret profit. By his fraudulent misrepresentations, he deprived the plaintiff of his bargain and obtained for himself some of the land which the plaintiff had offered to buy. "If one acquires property by means of a fraudulent misrepresentation of a material fact, equity will assist the defrauded person by fastening a constructive trust on the property." It is true that this rule is most often applied in situations where the relationship between the plaintiff and the defendant is one which equity clearly recognizes as fiduciary. But equity has carefully refrained from defining a fiduciary relationship in precise detail and in such a manner as to exclude new situations. It has left the bars down for situations in which there is a justifiable trust confided on one side and a resulting superiority and influence on the other. * * *

Equity will not permit these defendants to keep a benefit which came to them by reason of Jere's fraudulent conduct. It is true that Tesar has not acted to right the wrong done to him. Had he done so, it is probable that the plaintiff could have had the farm. This should not prevent the plaintiff, in his own right, from having a remedy for the wrong done to him. The plaintiff has proffered $1000, which represents the balance of the amount of his original offer over and above the purchase price he paid for the seventeen acres. Upon the payment of this sum into court, to await further order, an order should enter directing the defendant Walter to convey the sixty-three acres to the plaintiff.

There is error, the judgment is set aside and the case is remanded to the Superior Court for proceedings in accordance with this opinion.

O'SULLIVAN, ASSOCIATE JUSTICE (dissenting). The case suggests two possible theories for claiming actionable fraud on the part of Jere Adametz, hereinafter called the defendant. The first is based on his failure to disclose to the plaintiff that he had bought the Tesar farm, and the second on certain fraudulent representations made by him to the plaintiff. In other words, the one rests on his silence, the other on what he said. Neither theory, it seems to me has any merit.

As indicated, the first theory is based on the fact that, while holding himself out as Tesar's agent, the defendant purchased the farm and thereafter sold to the plaintiff, through two dummies, seventeen of the eighty acres without revealing to the plaintiff the true nature of the entire transaction and the furtive steps which he, the defendant, had taken in acquiring the land for his son. Our law is clear that, under the circumstances found by the court to have prevailed, no duty was imposed upon the defendant to refrain from buying the farm himself or to disclose that he had done so, as long as he was not acting at the time as agent for, or did not occupy a confidential relationship towards, the plaintiff. Kurtz v. Farrington, 104 Conn. 257, 265, 132 A. 540, 48 A.L.R. 259. Since the plaintiff concedes that the defendant was not his agent and since the facts do not admit of the existence of any confidential relationship between the parties, neither the defendant's conduct nor his silence about it presents an instance of actionable fraud.

The second theory is grounded on certain representations, fraudulently made by the defendant, to the effect that he had submitted to Tesar the plaintiff's offer to pay $7,000 for the entire farm and that Tesar, while rejecting that offer, had authorized the defendant to sell to the plaintiff for $6,000 the seventeen acres upon which stood the house and the other buildings. To recover on the basis of these obviously false representations, the plaintiff had to establish (1) that they were made as statements of fact, (2) that they were untrue and known by the defendant to be untrue, (3) that they were made for the purpose of inducing the plaintiff to act upon them, (4) that the plaintiff was in fact induced to act upon them and (5) that in so acting he was legally injured. * * * All the foregoing essentials must be proven, and the absence of any one of them is fatal to recovery. * * *

It is to be noted that the plaintiff, as a result of the representations, took no positive act respecting the remaining sixty-three acres. It is, of course, true that fraudulent representations may be actionable even in the absence of a positive act, since fraud inducing inaction can be as culpable as fraud which prompts action. * * * Thus, recovery was permitted where the representations caused the plaintiff to refrain from perfecting an inchoate lien, or from rescinding a contract, or from selling his property, or from putting his merchandise on the market. Cases such as those cited, however, give no comfort to the plaintiff since his failure to act did not affect any property interest owned by him. The law does not appear to subject a defendant to legal culpability for fraudulent representations in those instances where the person, induced to inaction, sustains no damage to his property interests or rights. Such instances would be those of injuria absque damno. * * *

But even if the law were otherwise, the plaintiff would not be advantaged. * * * Since the finding does not disclose that the sixty-three acres are worth over $1,000, the plaintiff has failed to establish any pecuniary loss whatsoever.

For the reasons stated above, I must disagree with my colleagues.

Note

Reported decisions with *Harper*'s pattern, called double-escrowing, recur frequently. An observer may to draw some foreboding conclusions about "agency costs," not to mention human nature. Ehlen v. Lewis, 984 F.Supp. 5 (D.D.C. 1997); Nguyen v. Scott, 206 Cal.App.3d 725, 253 Cal.Rptr. 800 (Cal.App. 1988); Ward v. Taggart, 51 Cal.2d 736, 336 P.2d 534 (1959).

In Ehlen v. Lewis, Judge Sporkin added attorney fees to plaintiff's recovery "because of the knowingly malicious nature of Defendants' actions." In Ward v. Taggart, the court approved the plaintiff's punitive damages in addition to restitution; punitive damages, the court said, would deter similar misconduct.

B. FROM DEFECTIVE NEGOTIATIONS TO PLAIN OVERREACHING

1. SELLER'S FAILURE TO DISCLOSE

REED v. KING

Court of Appeal of California, Third District, 1983.
145 Cal.App.3d 261, 193 Cal.Rptr. 130.

BLEASE, ASSOCIATE JUSTICE. In the sale of a house, must the seller disclose it was the site of a multiple murder? Dorris Reed purchased a house from Robert King. Neither King nor his real estate agents (the other named defendants) told Reed that a woman and her four children were murdered there ten years earlier. However, it seems "truth will come to light; murder cannot be hid long." (Shakespeare, Merchant of Venice, Act II, Scene II.) Reed learned of the gruesome episode from a neighbor after the sale. She sues seeking rescission and damages. King and the real estate agent defendants successfully demurred to her first amended complaint for failure to state a cause of action. Reed appeals the ensuing judgment of dismissal. We will reverse the judgment.

We take all issuable facts pled in Reed's complaint as true. King and his real estate agent knew about the murders and knew the event materially affected the market value of the house when they listed it for sale. They represented to Reed the premises were in good condition and fit for an "elderly lady" living alone. They did not disclose the fact of the murders. At some point King asked a neighbor not to inform Reed of that event. Nonetheless, after Reed moved in neighbors informed her no one was interested in purchasing the house because of the stigma. Reed paid $76,000, but the house is only worth $65,000 because of its past. * * *

Does Reed's pleading state a cause of action? Concealed within this question is the nettlesome problem of the duty of disclosure of blemishes on real property which are not physical defects or legal impairments to use.

Reed seeks to state a cause of action sounding in contract, i.e. rescission, or in tort, i.e. deceit. In either event her allegations must reveal a fraud. * * *

The trial court perceived the defect in Reed's complaint to be a failure to allege concealment of a material fact. "Concealment" and "material" are legal conclusions concerning the effect of the issuable facts pled. As appears, the analytic pathways to these conclusions are intertwined.

Concealment is a term of art which includes mere non-disclosure when a party has a duty to disclose. See e.g. Lingsch v. Savage. Reed's complaint reveals only non-disclosure despite the allegation King asked a neighbor to hold his peace. There is no allegation the attempt at suppression was a cause in fact of Reed's ignorance.[1] (See Rest.2d Contracts, §§ 160, 162–164; Rest.2d Torts, § 550; Rest.Restitution, § 9.) Accordingly, the critical question is: does the seller have duty to disclose here? Resolution of this question depends on the materiality of the fact of the murders.

In general, a seller of real property has a duty to disclose: "where the seller knows of facts *materially* affecting the value or desirability of the property which are known or accessible only to him and also knows that such facts are not known to, or within the reach of the diligent attention and observation of the buyer, the seller is under a duty to disclose them to the buyer."[2] (Lingsch v. Savage, supra.)

Whether information "is of sufficient materiality to affect the value or desirability of the property * * * depends on the facts of the particular case." Materiality "is a question of law, and is part of the concept of right to rely or justifiable reliance." Accordingly, the term is essentially a label affixed to a normative conclusion.[3] Three considerations bear on this legal conclusion: the

---

1. [Footnotes renumbered.] Reed elsewhere in the complaint asserts defendants "actively concealed" the fact of the murders and this in part misled her. However, no connection is made or apparent between the legal conclusion of active concealment and any issuable fact pled by Reed. Accordingly, the assertion is insufficient. Similarly we do not view the statement the house was fit for Reed to inhabit as transmuting her case from one of non-disclosure to one of false representation. To view the representation as patently false is to find "elderly ladies" uni-formly susceptible to squeamishness. We decline to indulge this stereotypical assumption. To view the representation as misleading because it conflicts with a duty to disclose is to beg that question.

2. The real estate agent or broker representing the seller is under the same duty of disclosure. (Lingsch v. Savage, supra.)

3. This often subsumes a policy analysis of the effect of permitting rescission on the stability of contracts. "In the case law of fraud, the

gravity of the harm inflicted by non-disclosure; the fairness of imposing a duty of discovery on the buyer as an alternative to compelling disclosure; and its impact on the stability of contracts if rescission is permitted.

Numerous cases have found non-disclosure of physical defects and legal impediments to use of real property are material. However, to our knowledge, no prior real estate sale case has faced an issue of non-disclosure of the kind presented here. (Compare Earl v. Saks & Co.) Should this variety of ill-repute be required to be disclosed? Is this a circumstance where "non-disclosure of the fact amounts to a failure to act in good faith and in accordance with reasonable standards of fair dealing." (Rest.2d Contracts, § 161, subd. (b).)

The paramount argument against an affirmative conclusion is it permits the camel's nose of unrestrained irrationality admission to the tent. If such an "irrational" consideration is permitted as a basis of rescission the stability of all conveyances will be seriously undermined. Any fact that might disquiet the enjoyment of some segment of the buying public may be seized upon by a disgruntled purchaser to void a bargain. In our view, keeping this genie in the bottle is not as difficult a task as these arguments assume. We do not view a decision allowing Reed to survive a demurrer in these unusual circumstances as endorsing the materiality of facts predicating peripheral, insubstantial, or fancied harms.

The murder of innocents is highly unusual in its potential for so disturbing buyers they may be unable to reside in a home where it has occurred. This fact may foreseeably deprive a buyer of the intended use of the purchase. Murder is not such a common occurrence that *buyers* should be charged with anticipating and discovering this disquieting possibility. Accordingly, the fact is not one for which a duty of inquiry and discovery can sensibly be imposed upon the buyer.

Reed alleges the fact of the murders has a quantifiable effect on the market value of the premises. We cannot say this allegation is inherently wrong and, in the pleading posture of the case, we assume it to be true. If information known or accessible only to the seller has a significant and measurable effect on market value and, as is alleged here, the seller is aware of this effect, we see no principled basis for making the duty to disclose turn upon the character of the information. Physical usefulness is not and never has been the sole criterion of valuation. Stamp collections and gold speculation would be insane activities if utilitarian considerations were the sole measure of value.

Reputation and history can have a significant effect on the value of realty. "George Washington slept here" is worth something, however physically inconsequential that consideration may be. Ill-repute or "bad will" conversely may depress the value of property. Failure to disclose such a negative fact where it will have a foreseeably depressing effect on income expected to be generated by a business is tortious. (See Rest.2d Torts, § 551, illus. 11.) Some cases have held that *unreasonable* fears of the potential buying public that a gas or oil pipeline may rupture may depress the market value of land and entitle the owner to incremental compensation in eminent domain. (See Annot., Eminent Domain:

word 'material' has become a sort of talisman. It is suggested that it has no meaning when undefined other than to the user since the word actually means no more than that the fraud is the sort which will justify rescission or damages in deceit. However, courts continue to use mate-

riality as a test without explanatory reference to the varying standards of reliance, damage, etc. they are following." (Note, Rescission: Fraud as Ground: Contracts (1951) 39 Cal.L.Rev. 309, 310–311, fn. 4.)

Elements and measure of compensation for oil or gas pipeline through private property (1954) 38 A.L.R.2d 788, 801–804.)

Whether Reed will be able to prove her allegation the decade-old multiple murder has a significant effect on market value we cannot determine. If she is able to do so by competent evidence she is entitled to a favorable ruling on the issues of materiality and duty to disclose.[4] Her demonstration of objective tangible harm would still the concern that permitting her to go forward will open the floodgates to rescission on subjective and idiosyncratic grounds.

A more troublesome question would arise if a buyer in similar circumstances were unable to plead or establish a significant and quantifiable effect on market value. However, this question is not presented in the posture of this case. Reed has not alleged the fact of the murders has rendered the premises useless to her as a residence. As currently pled, the gravamen of her case is pecuniary harm. We decline to speculate on the abstract alternative.

The judgment is reversed.

Notes

1.   *The Home Buyer's Right to Know.* The movement in home sales from caveat emptor to seller-tell-all stems from Reed v. King, Lingsch v. Savage, which the *Reed* court cites, and similar decisions. Concerned about liability exposure, organized groups of realtors lobbied state legislatures to pass disclosure statutes—complete with forms. Today two-thirds of the states have statutes that expand the residential seller's duty to disclose. A modern buyer usually also hires an independent inspector.

Most nondisclosure disputes involve zoning, leaky roofs, foundations, wet basements, termites, sewers, wells, and septic tanks. One grew out of a neighborhood noise nuisance. Shapiro v. Sutherland, 70 Cal.Rptr.2d 548 (Ct.App.1998).

Environmental hazards that, undisclosed, may trigger a buyer's challenge include asbestos, radon, lead, mercury, flood plain locations, seismic hazards, fire-risk zones, and possible landslides. What about offsite hazards? Although the state had no real-estate disclosure statute, the New Jersey court found sellers and brokers had breached a duty to disclose a nearby potentially toxic landfill to 195 buyers of new homes. Strawn v. Canuso, 140 N.J. 43, 657 A.2d 420 (1995). The buyers' lawsuit settled before trial for $3,000,000.

The common law governs in a state without a disclosure statute. And a court in a state with a disclosure statute may say that common law supplements the statute; in other words, a disclosure statute may not list everything a seller must disclose. In states without disclosure statutes, many brokers use property-condition disclosure forms.

2.   *Stigma.* Important disclosure disputes stem from "stigmatized property." Remember the undisclosed poltergeist from first-year Property? Stambovsky v. Ackley, 169 A.D.2d 254, 572 N.Y.S.2d 672 (1991).

---

4. The ruling of the trial court requiring the additional element of notoriety, i.e. widespread public knowledge, is unpersuasive. Lack of notoriety may facilitate resale to yet another unsuspecting buyer at the "market price" of a house with no ill-repute. However, it appears the buyer will learn of the possibly unsettling history of the house soon after moving in. Those who suf- fer no discomfort from the specter of residing in such quarters per se, will nonetheless be discomforted by the prospect they have bought a house that may be difficult to sell to less hardy souls. Non-disclosure must be evaluated as fair or unfair regardless of the ease with which a buyer may escape this discomfort by foisting it upon another.

A fraud-negligence-warranty lawsuit in Maryland arose from the paranormal. The Carvens who bought a lot in a former farm alleged that the developer who had harvested the tombstones on a family graveyard that became their house lot had, however, left the graves' contents underground. Ms. Carven disinterred bones and a casket handle about a foot under the surface. The trial judge dismissed the Carven's lawsuit on the ground that a Maryland statute of repose barred litigation more than 20 years after an "improvement" on land. But the appellate court concluded that a developer's desecration of a graveyard and his subsequent concealment of its existence to facilitate its sale as a residential lot did not comprise an immune "improvement." The court remanded the Carven's lawsuit to the circuit court for a trial. Hickman, ex rel. Hickman v. Carven, 366 Md. 362, 784 A.2d 31 (2001).

Perhaps responding to Reed v. King and other controversies, the New York "stigma" statute shields a seller who does not disclose a former occupant's death from AIDS, suicide, or murder. N.Y. Real Property Law § 443–a. Is that "shield" too narrow?

Houses where notorious murders occurred are frequently bargains; some are demolished because the stigma reduces their market value.

3.   Cultural and offsite disclosure issues persist. Should a seller disclose a nearby domestic violence shelter? In the absence of a statute, should a seller disclose a multiple murder?

Megan's Laws require sex offenders to register with local police. These registrations are usually available at the nearest computer connected to the Internet. Must the seller or the broker inquire and disclose a registered sex offender in the vicinity?

4.   *Beyond Restitution.* A buyer's recovery may exceed mere rescission-restitution, particularly if the buyer succeeds on a common-law tort like fraud or negligent misrepresentation.

The law of seller's disclosure is developing rapidly, and it varies from state to state. Check codes, pocket parts, and advance sheets.

5.   *Buyer's Identity.* Many earlier rescission decisions that turned on a concealed buyer involved segregated housing. A prospective buyer of the "wrong" persuasion would have a straw buyer with the "right" persuasion purchase the property and transfer it promptly to the buyer. The original owner would sue to rescind. Today civil rights statutes forbid an owner from discriminating in the sale of property based on a buyer's race, color, religion, sex, national origin, disability, children, and, in some states and cities, sexual orientation. The Mississippi court refers to these statutes below.

(a) Gray sold a tract to the Church; the Church sold half of it to Roussel. Gray sued to rescind for fraud. "Gray maintains that he would not have sold any of his remaining property to Roussel under any circumstances and that he had no idea that Roussel had any connection with the sale he was negotiating with Baker. * * * Gray says this was according to a prearranged scheme."

"The identity of one's visible vendee," observed the Mississippi supreme court, "is a material matter. Where a vendor would not have made a conveyance of land had he known of a prior agreement by the vendee to convey to another the vendor found objectionable, that vendor is entitled to a judicial rescission of the instrument of conveyance. It matters not that the advent of the obnoxious ultimate purchaser may cause the vendor no pecuniary loss. The vendor's rights in his property extend to the right to refuse to sell to such third party for good reason, for bad reason or for no reason at all—so long as he does not act for some legally impermissible reason (a caveat not applicable in today's factual setting)."

"On the other hand, and for purposes of clarification of the rule under which Gray proceeds, if a purchaser is acting in good faith at the time of sale—that is, if the ostensible purchaser has no deal with any third party that is not disclosed to the seller—that purchaser may the day after the closing himself sell to a third party. Absent deception practiced on the seller, one who by purchase acquires fee simple title to a parcel of real property has an unrestricted right in his next breath to convey to a third party. That such a third party may be offensive to the original seller, that the third party may be one the original seller would never have sold to in the first instance, in no way operates to vitiate the original sale. What may render that sale voidable is the original purchaser's act of deceit, his failure to disclose to the original seller plans that the property or part thereof will be ultimately conveyed to the obnoxious third party." Gray v. Baker, 485 So.2d 306 (Miss.1986).

(b) An undisclosed acquisition agent for a power company's hydroelectric project lied to a prospective land seller about the way the tract would be used. The South Carolina court did not disapprove: Seller did not allege a cause of action for rescission. No fiduciary relationship existed. No confidence was reposed in vendee. No duty required a buyer to disclose facts that increase value. Misrepresentation of an intended use must be material. Finley v. Dalton, 251 S.C. 586, 164 S.E.2d 763 (1968).

2. UNDUE INFLUENCE

An undue influence and duress defendant has disclosed too much. And the wrong things. The California court's *Odorizzi* decision, which follows, is a product of its times and shares those stereotypes; but the court's expansive discussion of several defenses remains instructive.

ODORIZZI v. BLOOMFIELD SCHOOL DISTRICT

California Court of Appeal, 1966.
246 Cal.App.2d 123, 54 Cal.Rptr. 533.

FLEMING, JUSTICE. Plaintiff Donald Odorizzi was employed during 1964 as an elementary school teacher by defendant Bloomfield School District and was under contract with the District to continue to teach school the following year as a permanent employee. On June 10 he was arrested on criminal charge of homosexual activity, and on June 11 he signed and delivered to his superiors his written resignation as a teacher, a resignation which the District accepted on June 13. In July the criminal charges against Odorizzi were dismissed under Penal Code, section 995, and in September he sought to resume his employment with the District. On the District's refusal to reinstate him he filed suit for declaratory and other relief.

Odorizzi's amended complaint asserts his resignation was invalid because obtained through duress, fraud, mistake, and undue influence and given at a time when he lacked capacity to make a valid contract. Specifically, Odorizzi declares he was under such severe mental and emotional strain at the time he signed his resignation, having just completed the process of arrest, questioning by the police, booking, and release on bail, and having gone for forty hours without sleep, that he was incapable of rational thought or action. While he was in this condition and unable to think clearly, the superintendent of the District and the principal of his school came to his apartment. They said they were trying to help him and had his best interests at heart, that he should take their advice and immediately resign his position with the District, that there was no time to consult an attorney, that if he did not resign immediately the District would suspend and dismiss him from his position and publicize the proceedings, his "aforedescribed arrest" and cause him "to suffer extreme embarrassment and humiliation"; but that if he resigned at once the incident would not be publicized and would not jeopardize his chances of securing employment as a teacher elsewhere. Odorizzi pleads that because of his faith and confidence in their representations they were able to substitute their will and judgment in place of his own and thus obtain his signature to his purported resignation. A demurrer to his amended complaint was sustained without leave to amend. P

By his complaint plaintiff in effect seeks to rescind his resignation pursuant to Civil Code, section 1689, on the ground that his consent had not been real or free within the meaning of Civil Code, section 1567, but had been obtained through duress, menace, fraud, undue influence, or mistake. A pleading under these sections is sufficient if, stripped of its conclusions, it sets forth sufficient facts to justify legal relief. * * * In our view the facts in the amended complaint are insufficient to state a cause of action for duress, menace, fraud, or mistake, C but they do set out sufficient elements to justify rescission of a consent because of undue influence. We summarize our conclusions on each of these points.

1. No duress or menace has been pleaded. Duress consists in unlawful confinement of another's person, or relatives or property, which causes him to consent to a transaction through fear. * * * Duress is often used interchangeably with menace [citation] but in California menace is technically a threat of duress or a threat of injury to the person, property, or character of another. (Civ.Code, § 1570.) We agree with respondent's contention that neither duress nor menace was involved in this case, because the action or threat in duress or menace must be unlawful, and a threat to take legal action is not unlawful unless the party making the threat knows the falsity of his claim. * * * The amended complaint shows in substance that the school representatives announced their intention to initiate suspension and dismissal proceedings under Education Code, sections 13403, 13408 et seq. at a time when the filing of such proceedings was not only their legal right but their positive duty as school officials. Although the filing of such proceedings might be extremely damaging to plaintiff's reputation, the injury would remain incidental so long as the school officials acted in good faith in the performance of their duties. * * * Neither duress nor menace was present as a ground for rescission.

2. Nor do we find a cause of action for fraud, either actual or constructive. (Civ.Code, §§ 1571 to 1574.) Actual fraud involves conscious misrepresentation, or concealment, or non-disclosure of a material fact which induces the innocent party to enter the contract. * * * A complaint for fraud must plead misrepresentation, knowledge of falsity, intent to induce reliance, justifiable reliance, and resulting damage. * * * While the amended complaint charged misrepresentation, it failed to assert the elements of knowledge of falsity, intent to induce reliance, and justifiable reliance. A cause of action for actual fraud was therefore not stated. * * * Constructive fraud arises on a breach of duty by one in a confidential or fiduciary relationship to another which induces justifiable reliance by the latter to his prejudice. (Civ.Code, § 1573.) Plaintiff has attempted to bring himself within this category, for the amended complaint asserts the existence of a confidential relationship between the school superintendent and principal as agents of the defendant, and the plaintiff. Such a confidential relationship may exist whenever a person with justification places trust and confidence in the integrity and fidelity of another. * * * Plaintiff, however, sets forth no facts to support his conclusion of a confidential relationship between

the representatives of the school district and himself, other than that the parties bore the relationship of employer and employee to each other. Under prevailing judicial opinion no presumption of a confidential relationship arises from the bare fact that parties to a contract are employer and employee; rather, additional ties must be brought out in order to create the presumption of a confidential relationship between the two. The absence of a confidential relationship between employer and employee is especially apparent where, as here, the parties were negotiating to bring about a termination of their relationship. In such a situation each party is expected to look after his own interests, and a lack of confidentiality is implicit in the subject matter of their dealings. We think the allegations of constructive fraud were inadequate.

3. As to mistake, the amended complaint fails to disclose any facts which would suggest that consent had been obtained through a mistake of fact or of law. The material facts of the transaction were known to both parties. Neither party was laboring under any misapprehension of law of which the other took advantage. * * *

4. However, the pleading does set out a claim that plaintiff's consent to the transaction had been obtained through the use of undue influence.

Undue influence, in the sense we are concerned with here, is a shorthand legal phrase used to describe persuasion which tends to be coercive in nature, persuasion which overcomes the will without convincing the judgment. The hallmark of such persuasion is high pressure, a pressure which works on mental, moral, or emotional weakness to such an extent that it approaches the boundaries of coercion. In this sense, undue influence has been called over persuasion. [citation] Misrepresentations of law or fact are not essential to the charge, for a person's will may be overborne without misrepresentation. By statutory definition undue influence includes "taking an unfair advantage of another's weakness of mind; or * * * taking a grossly oppressive and unfair advantage of another's necessities or distress." (Civ.Code § 1575.) While most reported cases of undue influence involve persons who bear a confidential relationship to one another, a confidential or authoritative relationship between the parties need not be present when the undue influence involves unfair advantage taken of another's weakness or distress. [citations] * * *

In essence undue influence involves the use of excessive pressure to persuade one vulnerable to such pressure, pressure applied by a dominant subject to a servient object. In combination, the elements of undue susceptibility in the servient person and excessive pressure by the dominating person make the latter's influence undue, for it results in the apparent will of the servient person being in fact the will of the dominant person.

Undue susceptibility may consist of total weakness of mind which leaves a person entirely without understanding (Civ.Code § 38); or, a lesser weakness which destroys the capacity of a person to make a contract even though he is not totally incapacitated. (Civ.Code, § 39); * * * or, the first element in our equation, a still lesser weakness which provides sufficient grounds to rescind a contract for undue influence. (Civ.Code, § 1575).

Such lesser weakness need not be longlasting nor wholly incapacitating, but may be merely a lack of full vigor due to age * * * physical condition * * * emotional anguish * * * or a combination of such factors. The reported cases have usually involved elderly, sick, senile persons alleged to have executed wills or deeds under pressure. (Malone v. Malone, 155 Cal.App.2d 161, 317 P.2d 65 [constant importuning of a senile husband]; Stewart v. Marvin, 139 Cal.App.2d 769, 294 P.2d 114 [persistent nagging of elderly spouse].) In some of its aspects this lesser weakness could perhaps be called weakness of spirit. But whatever name we give it, this first element of undue influence resolves itself into a lessened capacity of the object to make a free contract.

In the present case plaintiff has pleaded that such weakness at the time he signed his resignation prevented him from freely and competently applying his judgment to the problem before him. Plaintiff declares he was under severe mental and emotional strain at the time because he had just completed the process of arrest, questioning, booking, and release on bail and had been without sleep for forty hours. It is possible that exhaustion and emotional turmoil may wholly incapacitate a person from exercising his judgment. As an abstract question of pleading, plaintiff has pleaded that possibility and sufficient allegations to state a case for rescission.

Undue influence in its second aspect involves an application of excessive strength by a dominant subject against a servient object. Judicial consideration of this second element in undue influence has been relatively rare, for there are few cases denying persons who persuade but do not misrepresent the benefit of their bargain. Yet logically, the same legal consequences should apply to the results of excessive strength as to the results of undue weakness. Whether from weakness on one side, or strength on the other, or a combination of the two, undue influence occurs whenever there results "that kind of influence or supremacy of one mind over another by which that other is prevented from acting according to his own wish or judgment." Undue influence involves a type of mismatch which our statute calls unfair advantage. (Civ.Code, § 1575.) Whether a person of subnormal capacities has been subjected to ordinary force or a person of normal capacities subjected to extraordinary force, the match is equally out of balance. If will has been overcome against judgment, consent may be rescinded.

The difficulty, of course, lies in determining when the forces of persuasion have overflowed their normal banks and become oppressive flood waters. There are second thoughts to every bargain, and hindsight is still better than foresight. Undue influence cannot be used as a pretext to avoid bad bargains or escape from bargains which refuse to come up to expectations. A woman who buys a dress on impulse, which on critical inspection by her best friend turns out to be less fashionable than she had thought, is not legally entitled to set aside the sale on the ground that the saleswoman used all her wiles to close the sale. A man who buys a tract of desert land in the expectation that it is in the immediate path of the city's growth and will become another Palm Springs, an expectation cultivated in glowing terms by the seller, cannot rescind his bargain when things turn out differently. If we are temporarily persuaded against our better judgment to do something about which we later have second thoughts, we must abide the consequences of the risks inherent in managing our own affairs. * * *

However, over persuasion is generally accompanied by certain characteristics which tend to create a pattern. The pattern usually involves several of the following elements: (1) discussion of the transaction at an unusual or inappropriate time, (2) consummation of the transaction in an unusual place, (3) insistent demand that the business be finished at once, (4) extreme emphasis on untoward consequences of delay, (5) the use of multiple persuaders by the dominant side against a single servient party, (6) absence of third-party advisers to the servient party, (7) statements that there is no time to consult financial advisers or attorneys. If a number of these elements are simultaneously present, the persuasion may be characterized as excessive. * * *

The difference between legitimate persuasion and excessive pressure, like the difference between seduction and rape, rests to a considerable extent in the manner in which the parties go about their business. For example, if a day or two after Odorizzi's release on bail the superintendent of the school district had called him into his office during business hours and directed his attention to those provisions of the Education Code compelling his leave of absence and authorizing his suspension, on the filing of written charges, had told him that the District contemplated filing written charges against him, had pointed out the alternative of resignation available to him, had informed him he was free to consult counsel or any adviser he wished and to consider the matter overnight and return with his decision the next day, it is extremely unlikely that any complaint about the use of excessive pressure could ever have been made against the school district. * * *

But, according to the allegations of the complaint, this is not the way it happened, and if it had happened that way, plaintiff would never have resigned. * * *

Plaintiff has thus pleaded both subjective and objective elements entering the undue influence equation and stated sufficient facts to put in issue the question whether his free will had been overborne by defendant's agents at a time when he was unable to function in a normal manner. * * * The question cannot be resolved by an analysis of pleading but requires a finding of fact.

We express no opinion on the merits of plaintiff's case * * *.

The judgment is reversed.

Notes

1. *Over persuasion.* Undue influence involves (a) a "trusting" person under the influence of a "dominant" person through a confidential or dominance relationship; and (b) the dominant person's excessive persuasion or coercion that overcomes the trusting person's free will, often leading to the dominant person's gain and the trusting person's detriment.

While the dominant person's failure to disclose fully may be one way to exercise undue influence, undue influence may exist even though all facts are accurately revealed. Nor does undue influence require the defendant to misrepresent the facts or to tamper with the plaintiff's comprehension of the facts. Tampering with the plaintiff's judgment is enough. Unlike duress, undue influence does not involve the defendant's overcoming the plaintiff's will; it does involve the defendant's use of improper persuasion or coercion to misguide the plaintiff's will. What persuasion or coercion is improper enough to comprise undue influence cannot be reduced to a formula but must be determined in context. The two points to examine are (a) the dominant defendant's behavior, and (b) the plaintiff's impaired consent.

(a) *Dominance Relationship.* Odorizzi alleged "domination" undue influence. The court emphasizes defendants' dominating conduct. Did the superintendent and principal have a confidential relationship with Odorizzi? Was the relationship during the crucial period one of their dominance coupled with his subservience? Does the court's list of the earmarks of undue influence convince you that the defendants allegedly abused their power to over persuade Odorizzi or to coerce him to resign?

(b) *Odorizzi's Vulnerability*. Undue influence also stems from the trusting plaintiff's susceptibility, his capacity to understand and decide. These concepts are related to mistake and lack of capacity, in other words, to Odorizzi's diminished competence to resign.

Odorizzi may or may not have been gay. Although he was arrested, the authorities dropped the charges. He alleged that he was under a great deal of stress. The court evaluated his mental state from his perspective at the time he "resigned." Whether Odorizzi was gay or not, in a dismissal proceeding, he would have been identified as gay. Could he stand up to the defendants' pressure on him to resign quickly and quietly? How do you assess his later decision to file this public lawsuit to rescind his resignation?

The defendants' threat that Odorizzi's formal dismissal for homosexuality would end his teaching career may have been correct then. How do you assess the defendant's promise of secrecy if Odorizzi resigned quietly? Five years after this decision, the California court held that a teacher's homosexuality, standing alone, was an insufficient reason to revoke his teaching certificate. Morrison v. State Board of Education, 1 Cal.3d 214, 82 Cal.Rptr. 175, 461 P.2d 375 (1969).

(c) Did Odorizzi's supervisors threaten him with an involuntary outing? Should he have resisted their importunations?

(d) Do the judge's gender-stereotyped analogies undermine the decision's persuasive force?

2. *A Jury?* Undue influence originated in chancery courts where it developed parallel to the common-law courts' duress. The judge determines the issue of undue influence without a jury. Is a jury capable of assessing the nuances of medicine and psychology that bear on an undue influence plaintiff's vulnerability? But will a judge do better job of evaluating Odorizzi's allegations?

3. *Effect of Undue Influence on "Business Compulsion."* If undue influence *does* include a person who took advantage of another's necessity and distress and if undue influence is a ground for rescinding an executed contract, then its effect on business transactions could be marked. Actually courts have applied the doctrine cautiously. Rarely does a person's "unfair taking advantage of another's necessities or distress" stand alone as the ground to avoid their commercial transaction. But arguments adduced for so-called "business compulsion" must be attributed to these chancery notions as well as to the recent prominence given to the doctrine of "unconscionability" in commercial transactions.

3.　DURESS—BUSINESS COMPULSION

"California courts have recognized the economic duress doctrine in private sector cases for at least 50 years. The doctrine is equitably based and represents 'but an expansion by courts of equity of the old common-law doctrine of duress.' As it has evolved to the present day, the economic duress doctrine is not limited by early statutory and judicial expressions requiring an unlawful act in the nature of a tort or a crime. Instead, the doctrine now may come into play upon the doing of a wrongful act which is sufficiently coercive to cause a reasonably prudent person faced with no reasonable alternative to succumb to the perpetrator's pressure. The assertion of a claim known to be false or a bad faith threat to breach a contract or to withhold a payment may constitute a wrongful act for purposes of the economic duress doctrine. [citations]." Rich & Whillock v. Ashton Development, 157 Cal.App.3d 1154, 1158–59, 204 Cal.Rptr. 86, 89 (1984).

Economic Duress

SELMER CO. v. BLAKESLEE–MIDWEST CO.

United States Court of Appeals, Seventh Circuit, 1983.
704 F.2d 924.

POSNER, CIRCUIT JUDGE. This appeal by the plaintiff from summary judgment for the defendants in a diversity case requires us to consider the meaning, under Wisconsin contract law, of "economic duress" as a defense to a settlement of a contract dispute.

On this appeal, we must take as true the following facts. The plaintiff, Selmer, agreed to act as a subcontractor on a construction project for which the defendant Blakeslee–Midwest Prestressed Concrete Company was the general contractor. Under the contract between Blakeslee–Midwest and Selmer, Selmer was to receive $210,000 for erecting prestressed concrete materials supplied to it by Blakeslee–Midwest. Blakeslee–Midwest failed to fulfill its contractual obligations; among other things, it was tardy in supplying Selmer with the prestressed concrete materials. Selmer could have terminated the contract without penalty but instead agreed orally with Blakeslee–Midwest to complete its work, provided Blakeslee–Midwest would pay Selmer for the extra costs of completion due to Blakeslee–Midwest's defaults. When the job was completed, Selmer demanded payment of $120,000. Blakeslee–Midwest offered $67,000 and refused to budge from this offer. Selmer, because it was in desperate financial straits, accepted the offer.

Two and a half years later Selmer brought this suit against Blakeslee–Midwest claiming that its extra costs had amounted to $150,000 ($120,000 being merely a settlement offer), and asking for that amount minus the $67,000 it had received, plus consequential and punitive damages. Although Selmer, presumably in order to be able to claim such damages, describes this as a tort rather than a contract action, it seems really to be a suit on Blakeslee–Midwest's alleged oral promise to reimburse Selmer in full for the extra costs of completing the original contract after Blakeslee–Midwest defaulted. But the characterization is unimportant. Selmer concedes that, whatever its suit is, it is barred by the settlement agreement if, as the district court held, that agreement is valid. The only question is whether there is a triable issue as to whether the settlement agreement is invalid because procured by "economic duress."

If you extract a promise by means of a threat, the promise is unenforceable. This is not, as so often stated, see, e.g., Totem Marine Tug & Barge, Inc. v. Alyeska Pipeline Serv. Co., 584 P.2d 15, 22 (Alaska 1978), because such a promise is involuntary, unless "involuntary" is a conclusion rather than the description of a mental state. If the threat is ferocious ("your money or your life") and believed, the victim may be desperately eager to fend it off with a promise. Such promises are made unenforceable in order to discourage threats by making them less profitable. The fundamental issue in a duress case is therefore not the victim's state of mind but whether the statement that induced the promise is the kind of offer to deal that we want to discourage, and hence that we call a "threat." Selmer argues that Blakeslee–Midwest said to it in effect, "give up $53,000 of your claim for extras [$120,000 minus $67,000], or you will get nothing." This has the verbal form of a threat but is easily recast as a promise innocuous on its face—"I promise to pay you $67,000 for a release of your claim." There is a practical argument against treating such a statement as a threat: it will make an inference of duress inescapable in any negotiation where one party makes an offer from which it refuses to budge, for the other party will always be able to argue that he settled only because there was a (figurative) gun at his head. It would not matter whether the party refusing to budge was the payor like Blakeslee–Midwest or the promisor like Selmer. If Selmer had refused to complete the job without being paid exorbitantly for the extras and Blakeslee–Midwest had complied with this demand because financial catastrophe would have loomed if Selmer had walked off the job, we would have the same case. A vast number of contract settlements would be subject to being ripped open upon an allegation of duress if Selmer's argument was accepted.

Sensitive—maybe oversensitive—to this danger, the older cases held that a threat not to honor a contract could not be considered duress. [citations] But the principle was not absolute, as is shown by Alaska Packers' Ass'n v. Domenico, 117 Fed. 99 (9th Cir.1902). Sailors and fishermen (the libelants) "agreed in writing, for a certain stated compensation, to render their services to the appellant in remote waters where the season for conducting fishing operations is extremely short, and in which enterprise the appellant had a large amount of money invested; and, after having entered upon the discharge of their contract, and at a time when it was impossible for the appellant to secure other men in their places, the libelants, without any valid cause, absolutely refused to continue the services they were under contract to perform unless the appellant would consent to pay them more money." The appellant agreed, but later reneged, and the libelants sued. They lost; the court refused to enforce the new agreement. Although the technical ground of decision was the absence of fresh consideration for the modified agreement, it seems apparent both from the quoted language and from a reference on the same page to coercion that the court's underlying concern was that the modified agreement had been procured by duress in the form of the threat to break the original contract.

Alaska Packers' Ass'n shows that because the legal remedies for breach of contract are not always adequate, a refusal to honor a contract may force the other party to the contract to surrender his rights—in *Alaska Packers' Ass'n*, the appellant's right to the libelants' labor at the agreed wage. It undermines the institution of contract to allow a contract party to use the threat of breach to get the contract modified in his favor not because anything has happened to require modification in the mutual interest of the parties but simply because the other party, unless he knuckles under to the threat, will incur costs for which he will have no adequate legal remedy. If contractual protections are illusory, people will be reluctant to make contracts. Allowing contract modifications to be avoided in circumstances such as those in *Alaska Packers' Ass'n* assures prospective contract parties that signing a contract is not stepping into a trap, and by thus encouraging people to make contracts promotes the efficient allocation of resources.

Capps v. Georgia Pac. Corp., 253 Or. 248, 453 P.2d 935 (1969), illustrates the principle of *Alaska Packers' Ass'n* in the context of settling contract disputes. The defendant promised to give the plaintiff, as a commission for finding a suitable lessee for a piece of real estate, 5 percent of the total rental plus one half of the first month's rent. The plaintiff found a suitable lessee and the lease was signed. Under the terms of the commission arrangement the defendant owed the plaintiff $157,000, but he paid only $5,000, and got a release from the plaintiff of the rest. The plaintiff later sued for the balance of the $157,000, alleging that when requesting payment of the agreed-upon commission he had "informed Defendant that due to Plaintiff's adverse financial condition, he was in danger of immediately losing other personal property through repossession and foreclosure unless funds from Defendant were immediately made available for the purpose of paying these creditors.''

But "Defendant, through its agent * * * advised Plaintiff that though he was entitled to the sums demanded in Plaintiff's Complaint, unless he signed the purported release set forth in Defendant's Answer, Plaintiff would receive no part thereof, inasmuch as Defendant had extensive resources and powerful and brilliant attorneys who would and could prevent Plaintiff in any subsequent legal proceeding from obtaining payment of all or any portion of said sums." We can disregard the reference to the defendant's "powerful and brilliant attorneys" yet agree with the Oregon Supreme Court that the confluence of the plaintiff's necessitous financial condition, the defendant's acknowledged indebtedness for the full $157,000, and the settlement of the indebtedness for less than 3 cents on the dollar—with no suggestion that the defendant did not have the money to pay the debt in full—showed duress. The case did not involve the settlement of a genuine dispute, but, as in *Alaska Packers' Ass'n,* an attempt to exploit the contract promisee's lack of an adequate legal remedy.

Although *Capps* is not a Wisconsin case, we have no reason to think that Wisconsin courts would reach a different result. But the only feature that the present case shares with *Capps* is that the plaintiff was in financial difficulties. Since Blakeslee–Midwest did not acknowledge that it owed Selmer $120,000, and since the settlement exceeded 50 percent of Selmer's demand, the terms of the settlement are not unreasonable on their face, as in *Capps.* Thus the question is starkly posed whether financial difficulty can by itself justify setting aside a settlement on grounds of duress. It cannot. "The mere stress of business conditions will not constitute duress where the defendant was not responsible for the conditions." Johnson, Drake & Piper, Inc. v. United States, 531 F.2d 1037, 1042 (Ct.Cl.1976) (per curiam). The adverse effect on the finality of settlements and hence on the willingness of parties to settle their contract disputes without litigation would be great if the cash needs of one party were alone enough to entitle him to a trial on the validity of the settlement. In particular, people who desperately wanted to settle for cash—who simply could not afford to litigate—would be unable to settle, because they could not enter into a *binding* settlement; being desperate, they could always get it set aside later on grounds of duress. It is a detriment, not a benefit, to one's long-run interests not to be able to make a binding commitment.

Matters stand differently when the complaining party's financial distress is due to the other party's conduct. Although Selmer claims that it was the extra expense caused by Blakeslee–Midwest's breaches of the original contract that put it in a financial vise, it could have walked away from the contract without loss or penalty when Blakeslee–Midwest broke the contract. Selmer was not forced by its contract to remain on the job, and was not prevented by circumstances from walking away from the contract, as the appellant in *Alaska Packers' Ass'n* had been; it stayed on the job for extra pay. We do not know why Selmer was unable to weather the crisis that arose when Blakeslee–Midwest refused to pay $120,000 for Selmer's extra expenses—whether Selmer was under-capitalized or overborrowed or what—but Blakeslee–Midwest cannot be held responsible for whatever it was that made Selmer so necessitous, when, as we have said, Selmer need not have embarked on the extended contract. * * *

Affirmed.

Note

Promptness of Rescission for Economic Duress. The court rejected the Gruvers' claim that they had signed a franchise termination agreement under economic duress, but added this footnote: "Midas' argument that [the Gruvers] may not rely on economic duress because they have not promptly disaffirmed their termination agreements and returned all the benefits they received from these agreements lacks merit. While the law is clear that a court will not rescind a contract unless the party seeking rescission promptly disaffirms the contract, [citations] no Oregon court has applied this to invalidate a claim of economic duress in signing an agreement containing a release of claims. The whole point of an economic duress claim is that plaintiff had no reasonable choice but to enter into the contract. * * * [W]hen a plaintiff has no reasonable choice but to enter into a contract, the plaintiff cannot reasonably be expected immediately to return the benefit. * * * It would thus, be at odds with the purpose of the economic duress rule to bar claims of economic duress for failure to disaffirm the transaction. [citations] Traditional set-off rules, reducing a successful plaintiff's damages by the value of any benefit he has already received are sufficient to protect a defendant's interest." Gruver v. Midas International Corp., 925 F.2d 280, 283 n. 1 (9th Cir.1991).

4. UNCONSCIONABILITY

The "Chancellor's Conscience" was the benchmark of Chancery jurisdiction. "Unconscionability" is thus an avatar of inequity itself—descriptive rather than definitive. The unconscionability concept continues in contemporary law. Both the Restatement of Contracts and the Uniform Commercial Code condemn unconscionability. Restatement (Second) Contracts § 208 (1981); U.C.C. § 2–302. Right now two versions of the U.C.C. are at large, Original and Revised; you will learn why by jumping ahead to the "Digression" at the beginning of Chapter 7. For now, the unconscionability concept lives on in the Revised U.C.C.'s § 2–302.

Notably, however, the tentative drafts of the third Restatement of Restitution and Unjust Enrichment, which includes black-letter rules for mistake, fraud, duress, undue influence, incapacity and illegality, lack a section on unconscionability. Restatement (Third) of Restitution and Unjust Enrichment (Tent. Draft No. 1 (2001)).

The U.C.C.'s Sales Unconscionability: "If the court as a matter of law finds the contract or any clause of the contract to have been unconscionable at the time it was made the court may refuse to enforce the contract, or it may enforce the remainder of the contract without the unconscionable clause, or it may so limit the application of any unconscionable clause as to avoid any unconscionable result." U.C.C. § 2–302(1).

Right to Jury Trial. Is the judge's conscience consulted or the community's?

"Plaintiff's argument that its right to a jury trial on the issue of unconscionability is guaranteed by the seventh amendment of the Constitution hardly merits consideration. In 1791, when the amendment was adopted, the discretionary power to grant equitable relief according to the 'conscience' of the chancellor was so unmistakably a matter for the equity side rather than the law side of the court no further discussion of the constitutional ground is warranted." County Asphalt, Inc. v. Lewis Welding and Engineering Corp., 444 F.2d 372, 379 (2d Cir.), cert. denied, 404 U.S. 939 (1971).

The Revised U.C.C.'s Preliminary Official Comment 3 for § 2–302 reads, "This section is addressed to the court, and the decision is to be made by it. The commercial evidence * * * is for the court's consideration, not the jury's. Only the agreement which results from the court's action is to be submitted to the general trier of the facts."

Why not let a jury examine the community's conscience and decide the issue of unconscionability?

Procedural, Substantive, and Remedial Unconscionability. Professor Arthur Leff suggested the subsets of "procedural unconscionability" and "substantive unconscionability" to facilitate orderly analysis and appropriate decisions. Arthur Leff, Unconscionability and the Code—The Emperor's New Clause, 115 U.Pa.L.Rev. 485 (1967). See D. Dobbs, Remedies § 10.7 (2d ed. 1993).

The procedural-substantive unconscionability distinction is between (a) defendant's unconscionable or overreaching conduct before the parties form the contract, that is defendant's misconduct extrinsic to but inducing the plaintiff to assent to the contract, thus "procedural"; and (b) a contract itself unconscionable, either because of its intrinsic unfairness or internally unfair terms, thus "substantive." We supplement the foregoing categories to accommodate a Remedies course: with appropriate deference, we divide substantive unconscionability further into substantive and "remedial" unconscionability.

Procedural Unconscionability: Procedural unconscionability consists of defendant's practices that resemble deceit, misrepresentation, non-disclosure, duress, undue influence, sharp practice, fiduciary breaches, contract breaches, etc. Oppression means unequal bargaining power, prolix, unintelligible terms, and lack of real negotiation or a meaningful choice. The plaintiff was induced, pressured, or duped into a transaction.

Remedial Unconscionability: Some unfair contract clauses like confession of judgment, restricted remedies for breach of warranty, forfeiture clauses, and acceleration clauses are invocable only upon default. These may be classified under the heading of "remedial unconscionability." If the parties' bargain itself is fair or not unfair enough, then the judge should let it stand, deleting clauses that impose unnecessarily harsh consequences for default or unfair remedial advantages.

This leaves as pure substantive unconscionability only the truly lousy deal, not tainted by the defendant's "procedural" misconduct or by dramatically one-sided remedial provisions.

Substantive Unconscionability: This category includes intrinsically harsh, lop-sided bargains. One question about substantive unconscionability is whether it should exist at all.

Professor Richard Epstein rejects "substantive unconscionability," commenting: "One of the major conceptual tools used by courts in their assault upon private agreements has been the doctrine of unconscionability. That doctrine has a place in contract law, but it is not the one usually assigned it by its advocates. The doctrine should not, in my view, allow courts to act as roving commissions to set aside those agreements whose substantive terms they find objectionable. Instead, it should be used only to allow courts to police the process whereby private agreements are formed, and in that connection, only to facilitate the setting aside of agreements that are as a matter of probabilities likely to be vitiated by the classical defenses of duress, fraud, or incompetence. * * *"

"Ideally, the unconscionability doctrine protects against fraud, duress and incompetence, without demanding specific proof of any of them. Instead of looking to a writing requirement to control against these abuses, it looks both to the subject matter of the agreements and to the social positions of the persons who enter into them. The difficult question with unconscionability is not whether it works towards a legitimate end, but whether its application comes at too great a price." Richard Epstein, Unconscionability: A Critical Reappraisal, 18 J. Law & Econ. 293, 294–95, 302–03 (1975) © 1975, University of Chicago.

In *Discover Bank* below, the California court seems to require the plaintiff to show both procedural unconscionability and substantive unconscionability.

The Judge's Response to Unconscionability? Suppose the judge finds that a merchant's sale to a consumer buyer is unconscionable. What should the buyer's remedy or remedies be? (a) Rescission and restitution, a return and a refund to the buyer. (b) Force the seller to disgorge its profits, as distinguished from an individual refund. (c) Rewrite the contract, "equitably" limiting the seller's claim. (d) Deny the seller's recovery of the purchase price. (e) Grant an injunction that forbids the seller from using or enforcing the offensive provision in the future. (f) Some other "equitable" remedy?

~ *Out in the Cold.* One plaintiff, a freezer buyer, had paid $619.88 of a total contract price of $1,234.80 (including time charges, tax and insurance). The court found the maximum value of the freezer was $300. "[I]t is apparent," the court wrote, "that defendant has already been amply compensated. In accordance with [U.C.C. § 2–302(1)], the application of the payment provision should be limited to amounts already paid by the plaintiffs and the contract be reformed and amended by changing the payment called for therein to equal the amount of payments actually so paid by plaintiffs." Jones v. Star Credit Corp., 59 Misc.2d 189, 298 N.Y.S.2d 264, 268 (Sup.Ct. 1969).

Statutory Alternatives. State Unfair Trade Practice and Consumer Protection Acts allow an individual to sue. A state's attorney general may bring a class action on behalf of aggrieved consumers. See for example Kugler v. Romain, 58 N.J. 522, 279 A.2d 640 (1971).

Another legislative technique to protect a consumer from a seller's high-pressure tactics is to create a statutory "cooling-off" period within which the customer may choose to exit. The prototype of these statutes applies to door-to-door home sales, usually installment sales.

Where Have You Gone, U.C.C. Unconscionability? Despite the emphasis on unconscionability in law school, recent appellate decisions finding sales contracts or remedies limitations to be unconscionable are rare. Several factors seem to be involved. Judges often recoil from the amorphous and open-ended "substantive" standard of unconscionability. Consumers' claims are usually small. Many consumers "lump it," grin and bear raw deals. Consumer's claims do not attract lawyers because of the difficulty of recovering punitive damages or attorney fees.

The Future. There is neither much evidence that our society has entered a Golden Age of conscionable contracting nor much reason to think that it ever will. Discernable trends are toward more seller disclosure before contracting and more alternative dispute resolution when differences arise.

U.C.C. unconscionability was part of a legal transition to improved consumer protection. The next stage was for legislatures to enact more specific state and federal consumer-protection statutes. Unconscionability will remain in place as a fallback where consumer protection legislation is weak or to fill gaps in it.

A New Frontier. Businesses have added arbitration clauses and clauses banning class actions to their contracts with consumers. A consumer who assails one of these clauses often alleges its unconscionability along with its violation of a consumer-protection statute.

DISCOVER BANK v. SUPERIOR COURT

Supreme Court of California, 2005.
36 Cal.4th 148, 30 Cal.Rptr.3d 76, 113 P.3d 1100.

MORENO, J. This case concerns the validity of a provision in an arbitration agreement between Discover Bank and a credit cardholder forbidding classwide arbitration. The credit cardholder, a California resident, alleges that Discover Bank had a practice of representing to cardholders that late payment fees would not be assessed if payment was received by a certain date, whereas in actuality they were assessed if payment was received after 1:00 p.m. on that date, thereby leading to damages that were small as to individual consumers but large in the aggregate. Plaintiff filed a complaint claiming damages for this alleged deceptive practice, and Discover Bank successfully moved to compel arbitration pursuant to its arbitration agreement with plaintiff.

Plaintiff now seeks to pursue a classwide arbitration, which is well accepted under California law. [citations] But plaintiff's arbitration agreement with Discover Bank has a clause forbidding classwide arbitration. * * * The trial court ruled that the class arbitration waiver was unconscionable and enforced the arbitration agreement with the proviso that plaintiff could seek classwide arbitration. The Court of Appeal, without disputing that such class arbitration waivers may be unconscionable under California law * * * held that the Federal Arbitration Act (FAA) preempts the state law rule that class arbitration waivers are unconscionable.

As explained below, we conclude that, at least under some circumstances, the law in California is that class action waivers in consumer contracts of adhesion are unenforceable, whether the consumer is being asked to waive the right to class action litigation or the right to classwide arbitration. We further conclude that the Court of Appeal is incorrect that the FAA preempts California law in this respect. Finally, we will remand to the Court of Appeal to decide the choice-of-law issue.

I. FACTUAL AND PROCEDURAL BACKGROUND. The following undisputed facts are largely drawn from the Court of Appeal opinion. Plaintiff Christopher Boehr obtained a credit card from defendant Discover Bank in April 1986. * * *

When plaintiff's credit card was issued, the agreement did not contain an arbitration clause. Discover Bank subsequently added the arbitration clause in July 1999, pursuant to a change-of-terms provision in the agreement. Relying on the change-of-terms provision, Discover Bank added the arbitration clause by sending to its existing cardholders (including plaintiff) a notice that stated in relevant part: "NOTICE OF AMENDMENT * * * WE ARE ADDING A NEW ARBITRATION SECTION WHICH PROVIDES THAT IN THE EVENT YOU OR WE ELECT TO RESOLVE ANY CLAIM OR DISPUTE BETWEEN US BY ARBITRATION, NEITHER YOU NOR WE SHALL HAVE THE RIGHT TO

LITIGATE THAT CLAIM IN COURT OR TO HAVE A JURY TRIAL ON THAT CLAIM.''

In addition, the arbitration clause precluded both sides from participating in classwide arbitration, consolidating claims, or arbitrating claims as a representative or in a private attorney general capacity: ''NEITHER YOU NOR WE SHALL BE ENTITLED TO JOIN OR CONSOLIDATE CLAIMS IN ARBITRATION BY OR AGAINST OTHER CARDMEMBERS WITH RESPECT TO OTHER ACCOUNTS, OR ARBITRATE ANY CLAIM AS A REPRESENTATIVE OR MEMBER OF A CLASS OR IN A PRIVATE ATTORNEY GENERAL CAPACITY.''

The arbitration agreement also stated that the FAA would govern the agreement. * * * Existing cardholders were notified that if they did not wish to accept the new arbitration clause, they must notify Discover Bank of their objections and cease using their accounts. Their continued use of an account would be deemed to constitute acceptance of the new terms. Plaintiff did not notify Discover Bank of any objection to the arbitration clause or cease using his account before the stated deadline.

On August 15, 2001, Boehr filed a putative class action complaint in superior court against Discover Bank. Plaintiff alleged two causes of action—breach of contract and violation of the Delaware Consumer Fraud Act. The latter act in part prohibits misrepresentations ''of any material fact with intent that others rely upon such concealment, suppression or omission in connection with the sale, lease or advertisement of any merchandise.'' He alleged that Discover Bank breached its cardholder agreement by imposing a late fee of approximately $29 on payments that were received on the payment due date, but after Discover Bank's undisclosed 1:00 p.m. ''cut-off time.'' * * * The complaint acknowledged that the contract with Discover Bank provided that the contract was ''governed by federal law and the law of Delaware.'' Plaintiff alleged, however, that ''this choice of law provision applies only to plaintiff's substantive claims and not to other issues related to the contract, which plaintiff contends are governed by California or other applicable law.''

Discover Bank moved to compel arbitration of plaintiff's claim on an individual basis and to dismiss the class action pursuant to the arbitration agreement's class action waiver.

Plaintiff opposed the motion, contending among other things that the class action waiver was unconscionable and unenforceable under California law. Discover Bank, on the other hand, argued that the FAA requires the enforcement of the express provisions of an arbitration clause, including class action waivers. * * *

The trial court initially granted Discover Bank's motion in its entirety under Delaware law. After Discover Bank's motion to compel arbitration was granted, the Fourth District Court of Appeal decided Szetela v. Discover Bank (2002) 97 Cal.App.4th 1094 (*Szetela*), which held, for reasons explained below, that a virtually identical class action waiver was unconscionable. Plaintiff, citing *Szetela,* moved for reconsideration of that portion of the order enforcing the class action waiver.

The lower court found *Szetela* constituted new and controlling authority for the proposition that, under California law, an arbitration class action waiver is unconscionable and, thus, unenforceable. * * * Upon determining it would be proper to sever the class action waiver clause from the rest of the arbitration agreement, the trial court struck the class action waiver clause from the agreement, ordered plaintiff to arbitrate his claims individually, and left open the possibility that plaintiff may succeed in certifying an arbitration class under California law.

After the lower court granted plaintiff's motion for reconsideration, Discover Bank filed a writ petition seeking reinstatement of the lower court's original order enforcing the arbitration clause in its entirety by compelling plaintiff to arbitrate on an individual basis and precluding him from participating in class litigation or class arbitration. The Court of Appeal issued an order to show cause.

The Court of Appeal granted Discover Bank's writ. It did not take issue with the premise that class action waivers are unenforceable, at least under some circumstances, under California law * * * . But the Court of Appeal held, for reasons elaborated below, that any California rule prohibiting class action waivers was preempted by the FAA, and that *Szetela* had failed to adequately analyze the federal preemption issue. It therefore upheld the Discover Bank class action waiver. We granted review.

II.   DISCUSSION. A. Class Action Law Suits and Class Action Arbitration. Before addressing the questions at issue in this case, we first consider the justifications for class action lawsuits. These justifications were set forth in Justice Mosk's oft-quoted majority opinion in Vasquez v. Superior Court (1971) 4 Cal.3d 800: "Frequently numerous consumers are exposed to the same dubious practice by the same seller so that proof of the prevalence of the practice as to one consumer would provide proof for all. Individual actions by each of the defrauded consumers is [sic] often impracticable because the amount of individual recovery would be insufficient to justify bringing a separate action; thus an unscrupulous seller retains the benefits of its wrongful conduct. A class action by consumers produces several salutary by-products, including a therapeutic effect upon those sellers who indulge in fraudulent practices, aid to legitimate business enterprises by curtailing illegitimate competition, and avoidance to the judicial process of the burden of multiple litigation involving identical claims. The benefit to the parties and the courts would, in many circumstances, be substantial." * * *

These same concerns were acknowledged by the United States Supreme Court: " 'The policy at the very core of the class action mechanism is to overcome the problem that small recoveries do not provide the incentive for any individual to bring a solo action prosecuting his or her rights. A class action solves this problem by aggregating the relatively paltry potential recoveries into something worth someone's (usually an attorney's) labor.' " (Amchem Products, Inc. v. Windsor (1997) 521 U.S. 591, 617).

It is this important role of class action remedies in California law that led this court to devise the hybrid procedure of classwide arbitration in Keating v. Superior Court (1982) 31 Cal.3d 584. In that case, plaintiff 7–Eleven franchisors sought to invalidate an arbitration agreement between them and Southland Corporation and proceed with class action litigation to redress Southland's alleged systemic misconduct. This court held that the arbitration agreement was enforceable for most of the claims. In considering the impact that enforcement of the arbitration agreement would have on class action claims, the *Keating* court stated: "This court has repeatedly emphasized the importance of the class action device for vindicating rights asserted by large groups of persons. We have observed that the class suit 'both eliminates the possibility of repetitious litigation and provides small claimants with a method of obtaining redress for claims which would otherwise be too small to warrant individual litigation. [Citation.]' [Citation.] Denial of a class action in cases where it is appropriate may have the effect of allowing an unscrupulous wrongdoer to 'retain[ ] the benefits of its wrongful conduct.' [Citation.] [Moreover,] '[c]ontroversies involving widely used contracts of adhesion present ideal cases for class adjudication; the contracts are uniform, the same principles of interpretation apply to each contract, and all members of the class will share a common interest in the interpretation of an agreement to which each is a party.' "

The *Keating* court recognized that "[w]ithout doubt a judicially ordered classwide arbitration would entail a greater degree of judicial involvement than is normally associated with arbitration, ideally 'a complete proceeding, without resort to court facilities.' [Citation.] The court would have to make initial determinations regarding certification and notice to the class, and if classwide arbitration proceeds it may be called upon to exercise a measure of external supervision in order to safeguard the rights of absent class members to adequate representation and in the event of dismissal or settlement. A good deal of care, and ingenuity, would be required to avoid judicial intrusion upon the merits of the dispute, or upon the conduct of the proceedings themselves and to minimize complexity, costs, or delay. [Citation.] An adhesion contract is not a normal arbitration setting, however, and what is at stake is not some abstract institutional interest but the interests of the affected parties." * * *

B. The Enforceability of Class Action Waivers. *Keating* judicially authorized classwide arbitration in a case in which the arbitration agreement at issue was silent on the matter. It did not answer directly the question whether a class action waiver may be unenforceable as contrary to public policy or unconscionable. Recent cases have addressed that question. First, the Court of Appeal discussed the validity of a contractual class action waiver outside the arbitration context in America Online, Inc. v. Superior Court (2001) 90 Cal.App.4th 1 (*AOL*). Several former AOL subscribers alleged that AOL had continued to debit their credit cards for monthly service fees after their subscriptions had been canceled. The plaintiffs filed a class action lawsuit alleging violation of the Consumers Legal Remedies Act (CLRA), the Unfair Business Practices Act and several common law causes of action. The subscription contracts contained Virginia forum selection and choice-of-law provisions. Because Virginia law did not permit consumer class action lawsuits, those provisions were the "functional equivalent" of a waiver of class action lawsuits.

The *AOL* court held the forum selection and choice-of-law provisions to be unenforceable. * * * The *AOL* court found in the CLRA a statute that * * * contained an antiwaiver provision, Civil Code section 1751, which states: "Any waiver by a consumer of the provisions of this title is contrary to public policy and shall be unenforceable and void." The court reasoned that following Virginia law would result in a waiver of the CLRA in light of the fact that the equivalent Virginia consumer protection statute, the Virginia Consumer Protection Act of 1977 was significantly weaker. Among the most important differences between the two statutes was the lack of a provision permitting class action relief in the Virginia statute. After quoting the passage in *Vasquez*, regarding the importance of class actions in vindicating consumer rights quoted above, the court stated: "That this view has endured over the last 30 years is of little surprise given the importance class action consumer litigation has come to play in this state. In light of that history, we cannot accept AOL's assertion that the elimination of class actions for consumer remedies * * * is a matter of insubstantial moment. The unavailability of class action relief in this context is sufficient in and by itself to preclude enforcement of the * * * forum selection clause."

In *Szetela,* the court considered a class arbitration waiver. Plaintiff was a member of a class of credit cardholders seeking action against Discover Bank for improperly charging fees for exceeding their credit limits and imposing other penalties. He sued for breach of contract, breach of the covenant of good faith and fair dealing, fraudulent or negligent misrepresentation, and deceptive business practices. The arbitration clause and class arbitration waiver were very similar to those at issue in the present case. The trial court granted Discover Bank's motion for arbitration. Plaintiff recovered $29 in an individual arbitration and then appealed the trial court order compelling arbitration.

The court held that the class arbitration waiver was unenforceable. It first recognized that unconscionability was one reason to refuse to enforce an arbitration waiver. It found procedural unconscionability in the adhesive nature of the contract. The court also found substantive unconscionability in the imposition of a one-sided and oppressive class action waiver provision. "This provision is clearly meant to prevent customers, such as Szetela and those he seeks to represent, from seeking redress for relatively small amounts of money, such as the $29 sought by Szetela. Fully aware that few customers will go to the time and trouble of suing in small claims court, Discover has instead sought to create for itself virtual immunity from class or representative actions despite their potential merit, while suffering no similar detriment to its own rights. * * * The clause is not only harsh and unfair to Discover customers who might be owed a relatively small sum of money, but it also serves as a disincentive for Discover to avoid the type of conduct that might lead to class action litigation in the first place. By imposing this clause on its customers, Discover has essentially granted itself a license to push the boundaries of good business practices to their furthest limits, fully aware that relatively few, if any, customers will seek legal remedies, and that any remedies obtained will only pertain to that single customer without collateral estoppel effect. The potential for millions of customers to be overcharged small amounts without an effective method of redress cannot be ignored. Therefore, the provision violates fundamental notions of fairness. * * * This is not only substantively unconscionable, it violates public policy by granting Discover a 'get out of jail free' card while compromising important consumer rights." * * *

[P]laintiff contends that class action or arbitration waivers in consumer contracts, and in this particular contract, should be invalidated as unconscionable under California law.

"To briefly recapitulate the principles of unconscionability, the doctrine has 'both a "procedural" and a "substantive" element,' the former focusing on 'oppression' or 'surprise' due to unequal bargaining power, the latter on 'overly harsh' or 'one-sided' results." [Citation.] The procedural element of an unconscionable contract generally takes the form of a contract of adhesion, 'which, imposed and drafted by the party of superior bargaining strength, relegates to the subscribing party only the opportunity to adhere to the contract or reject it. " * * * Substantively unconscionable terms may take various forms, but may generally be described as unfairly one-sided." (Little v. Auto Stiegler, Inc. (2003)

29 Cal.4th 1064, 1071 (*Little*), cert. den. *sub nom. Auto Stiegler, Inc. v. Little* (2003) 540 U.S. 818).

We agree that at least some class action waivers in consumer contracts are unconscionable under California law. First, when, a consumer is given an amendment to its cardholder agreement in the form of a "bill stuffer" that he would be deemed to accept if he did not close his account, an element of procedural unconscionability is present. [citation] Moreover, although adhesive contracts are generally enforced [citation], class action waivers found in such contracts may also be substantively unconscionable inasmuch as they may operate effectively as exculpatory contract clauses that are contrary to public policy. As stated in Civil Code section 1668: "All contracts which have for their object, directly or indirectly, to exempt anyone from responsibility for his own fraud, or willful injury to the person or property of another, or violation of law, whether willful or negligent, are against the policy of the law."

Class action and arbitration waivers are not, in the abstract, exculpatory clauses. But because, as discussed above, damages in consumer cases are often small and because "[a] company which wrongfully exacts a dollar from each of millions of customers will reap a handsome profit," (*Linder*) "the class action is often the only effective way to halt and redress such exploitation." Moreover, such class action or arbitration waivers are indisputably one-sided. "Although styled as a mutual prohibition on representative or class actions, it is difficult to envision the circumstances under which the provision might negatively impact Discover [Bank], because credit card companies typically do not sue their customers in class-action lawsuits." (*Szetela*). Such one-sided, exculpatory contracts in a contract of adhesion, at least to the extent they operate to insulate a party from liability that otherwise would be imposed under California law, are generally unconscionable.

We acknowledge that other courts disagree. Some courts have viewed class actions or arbitrations as a merely procedural right, the waiver of which is not unconscionable. (See, e.g., [citations]; but see [citations]). But as the above cited cases of this court have continually affirmed, class actions and arbitrations are, particularly in the consumer context, often inextricably linked to the vindication of substantive rights. Affixing the "procedural" label on such devices understates their importance and is not helpful in resolving the unconscionability issue. * * *

Nor are we persuaded by the rationale stated by some courts that the potential availability of attorney fees to the prevailing party in arbitration or litigation ameliorates the problem posed by such class action waivers. [citations] There is no indication other than these courts' unsupported assertions that, in the case of small individual recovery, attorney fees are an adequate substitute for the class action or arbitration mechanism. Nor do we agree with the concurring and dissenting opinion that small claims litigation, government prosecution, or informal resolution are adequate substitutes.

We do not hold that all class action waivers are necessarily unconscionable. But when the waiver is found in a consumer contract of adhesion in a setting in which disputes between the contracting parties predictably involve small amounts of damages, and when it is alleged that the party with the superior bargaining power has carried out a scheme to deliberately cheat large numbers of consumers out of individually small sums of money, then, at least to the extent the obligation at issue is governed by California law, the waiver becomes in practice the exemption of the party "from responsibility for [its] own fraud, or willful injury to the person or property of another." (Civ.Code, § 1668.) Under these circumstances, such waivers are unconscionable under California law and should not be enforced.

C. Federal Arbitration Act Preemption of California Rules Against Class Action Waivers. [Editor: Most of the court's discussion has been omitted.] We reiterate what this court said over 20 years ago in *Keating:* "Classwide arbitration, as Sir Winston Churchill said of democracy, must be evaluated, not in relation to some ideal but in relation to its alternatives." We continue to believe that the alternatives—either not enforcing arbitration agreements and requiring class action litigation, or allowing arbitration agreements to be used as a means of completely inoculating parties against class liability—are unacceptable. Nothing in the FAA * * * requires us to reconsider that assessment.

D. Choice-of-Law Issue. * * * As reviewed above, in *AOL* the court concluded that a Virginia choice-of-law provision that would have compelled waiver of plaintiff's right to bring a class action lawsuit under the CLRA would not be enforced against a California resident, concluding that the CLRA class action remedy furthered a "strong public policy of the state." The present case differs from *AOL* in that plaintiff is not invoking the anti-waiver provision of the CLRA, nor is he seeking to enforce an obligation imposed by the CLRA or any other California statute. Instead, he has brought this action under the Delaware Consumer Fraud Act and Delaware contract law, but seeks to enforce those Delaware laws in a California court with a California unconscionability rule against class action waivers that arguably is not found under Delaware law. Whether he may do so remains to be determined on remand. Also to be addressed is plaintiffs' argument that class arbitration rules are procedural rules that California courts are to apply even when the substantive law dictated by contract is from another state [citation], as well as any other choice-of-law arguments appropriately raised.

III. DISPOSITION. The judgment of the Court of Appeal is reversed, and the cause is remanded for proceedings consistent with this opinion.

Concurring and Dissenting Opinion by BAXTER, J. I concur in part and dissent in part. I agree with the majority that *federal* law does not *compel* enforcement of contractual class action waivers simply because they are contained in arbitration agreements. But I lament the majority's determination to use this case as a vehicle to resolve the issue of *California's* policy on class action waivers. * * *

[T]he majority exaggerates the difficulty of pursuing modest claims where class treatment is unavailable and overlooks the many other means by which Discover Bank could be called to account for the mischarges plaintiff alleges. For example:

(1) The cardholder may contact the bank and attempt to resolve the matter informally. Discover Bank's cardholder agreement specifically provides a 60–day period in which to contact the company with billing questions and disputes. Plaintiff's complaint does not state that he pursued this avenue. (Indeed, though the complaint asserts widespread improper billing practices by Discover Bank, it does not allege that the bank has ever mischarged plaintiff himself. Plaintiff admitted in his deposition that he does not know whether Discover Bank has ever done so.)

(2) Pursuant to the agreement, the cardholder may pursue one-on-one arbitration of Delaware state law claims, including those under the Delaware Consumer Fraud Act. The agreement includes several provisions designed to make the individual arbitration process fair and accessible. Under the agreement's terms, Discover Bank will arbitrate in the federal judicial district where the cardholder resides. * * *

(3) For claims under $5,000, the cardholder may proceed in small claims court. [citation] In the cardholder agreement, Discover Bank promises that it "will not invoke [its] right to arbitrate an individual claim," involving less than $5,000, which is pending only in a small claims court. The only mandatory expense of a small claims action is a modest filing fee plus the actual cost of any mail service by the court clerk. [citation] The claim is pled by filling out a standard form. [citation] No formal discovery is permitted, and neither party may be represented by a lawyer, though free advisory assistance is available to the claimant [citation].

(4) The cardholder may arbitrate, pursuant to the terms of the cardholder agreement, his rights under such federal statutes as [the Truth in Lending Act] (TILA). [citation] [F]ederal circuits addressing the issue have uniformly held that claimants must arbitrate TILA claims pursuant to agreement, that arbitration precludes class relief under TILA, that arbitration agreements containing express waivers of class treatment, even for small individual amounts in dispute, are not unconscionable with respect to TILA claims, and that, although TILA contemplates class actions, it includes no "unwaivable" right to class relief. [citations] This statute imposes mandatory disclosure requirements for consumer credit transactions, including those arising on credit card accounts. As to the latter, the statute provides for detailed disclosure of the terms on which credit is being extended, including annual percentage rates, methods of computing outstanding balances, finance charges, grace periods, and late fees. [citation] The cardholder, if he or she prevails, may recover actual damages, twice the finance charge imposed in connection with each violative transaction, and attorney fees and costs. [citation]

(5) If Discover Bank's conduct violates California's unfair competition statutes [citation], which broadly prohibit "any unlawful, unfair or fraudulent business act or practice" [citation], the Attorney General and designated local law enforcement officials (who are not bound by the cardholder agreement) may sue on the People's behalf for injunctive relief and for mandatory civil penalties of up to $2,500 for each violation [citations].

(6) Finally, in the highly regulated banking and credit industry, other means of sanctioning and remediating illegal conduct are available at the behest of both federal and Delaware law. [The] Federal Deposit Insurance Corporation may issue cease-and-desist orders and order corrective measures including restitution; [both the Delaware State Banking Commissioner and the Delaware Attorney General have investigative and enforcement powers.]

Under these circumstances, it cannot be said that, by upholding cardholders' contractual waiver of a class remedy under Delaware law, we would effectively absolve Discover Bank of its objectionable conduct. Thus, there is no basis to conclude that enforcement of the class waiver * * * would contravene a fundamental California statutory policy against exculpatory agreements.

Finally, even if the application of Delaware law permitting class waivers would violate fundamental California public policy, I conclude that California has no materially greater interest in applying its own policy to this controversy than does Delaware. * * *

Indeed, California, its courts, and its judicial resources will be *negatively* impacted if, by invoking its own liberal antiwaiver rule in derogation of contrary law chosen by the parties, this state attracts nationwide consumer class litigation of the sort plaintiff seeks to maintain. * * *

I would hold the parties to their agreement, * * * which calls for individual arbitration of disputes arising between Discover Bank and its cardholders. Accordingly, I would affirm the judgment of the Court of Appeal, which directed the issuance of a petition for mandate requiring the trial court to (1) compel arbitration of plaintiff's complaint and (2) reinstate the waiver of class treatment.

Notes

1. Exactly what clause does plaintiff argue is unconscionable under California law? Apply this casebook's division of unconscionability into procedural and substantive-remedial subsets. Which subset does the offensive clause fit into?

2. Does the court require an unconscionability plaintiff to show both procedural unconscionability and substantive unconscionability to prevail? Why does the plaintiff succeed?

Should an unconscionability plaintiff who shows either procedural unconscionability or substantive unconscionability succeed? Is the California court's burden too heavy?

3. *Arbitration.* Why isn't the clause that requires plaintiff to arbitrate unconscionable?

4. *The Class Action.* A class action enables a private lawyer to aggregate numerous small claims into a large enough unit to make litigation worthwhile and thereby to enforce a public policy. What public policy does this plaintiff seek to vindicate with this action? What part of the law does the plaintiff's contract violate? Consider the alternatives available to enforce that particular public policy. Was the court correct to allow the plaintiff and his lawyer to maintain this class action?

C. NO ENFORCEABLE CONTRACT

The parties' agreement may fail as an enforceable contract for a number of reasons, a statute of frauds defense, a party's lack of capacity, failure of consideration, the parties' mistake, and illegality. What if one party has conferred value on the other? Since the parties do not have an enforceable contract, a plaintiff cannot recover expectancy damages or receive specific performance. That is what the defenses mean. But, if plaintiff has conferred value on the other party, unjustly enriching him, then may she recover restitution? The courts' answers will vary. One affirmative defense that will not support restitution is the statute of limitations; if the debtor holds her creditor off for the statutory period, she is liberated. But many plaintiffs' restitution claims succeed.

1. REQUIRED WRITING MISSING

The Statute of Frauds. The most common statute of frauds requires a writing for a land sale, but the U.C.C. also requires a writing for a sale of goods

§ 2–201. Inflation alert: the Revised U.C.C. raises the threshold value from $500 to "$5,000 or more."

Other contracts that many states require to be written include a lawyer's contract with a client for a contingent fee and a brokerage contract to sell or lease real estate.

Unjust Enrichment. Suppose that because of computer and Fax confusion, a broker's agreement with a landowner to find a tenant fails to satisfy the statute. But in lassoing a tenant, the broker has performed a valuable service; the landlord has accepted the broker's service; and both parties expect or expected payment of compensation. Typically if a listing agreement fails under the statute of frauds, the broker may nevertheless recover restitution-quantum meruit to prevent the owner's unjust enrichment. Coldwell Banker Commercial/Feist & Feist Realty Corp. v. Blancke P.W. L.L.C, 368 N.J.Super. 382, 846 A.2d 633 (2004).

Suppose Ben makes an oral contact with Sarah to buy Redacre from her for $2,000. Ben gives Sarah $200 earnest money. If Sarah, interposing the statute of frauds, decides not to sell Redacre to Ben, isn't she unjustly enriched unless she returns $200 to Ben?

SCHWEITER v. HALSEY

Supreme Court of Washington, 1961.
57 Wash.2d 707, 359 P.2d 821.

DONWORTH, JUDGE. Halsey and wife (appellants) owned a large farm in Asotin county (partly tillable land and partly pasture land) subject to a mortgage. They listed this land for sale with Mason & Teague (brokers) of Lewiston, Idaho.

These brokers showed the property to Schweiter brothers (respondents), who were desirous of purchasing the tillable land only. Appellants were agreeable to selling that portion of the land but had no legal description thereof.

Respondents needed not less than fifty thousand dollars to finance the deal. The mortgagee was willing to increase the amount of the mortgage to fifty thousand dollars at six percent interest. Respondents were so advised by the brokers, who also suggested that a loan might be obtained from a life insurance company at a lower rate.

On October 23, 1956, the parties executed an earnest-money receipt. Although the earnest-money receipt indicated that the legal description of the property to be sold was attached, there was, in fact, no legal description attached at the time the receipt was executed. The brokers had a legal description of the entire property, and respondents instructed them to retain respondents' copy of the receipt. Several weeks later, upon completion of a survey, the legal description of the tillable land was attached thereto by the brokers, and respondents were notified of this fact.

On December 1, 1956, respondents, together with one of the brokers, went to Spokane with a legal description of all the land to be covered by the mortgage and made a formal application for a loan. Ten days later, the brokers were notified by the insurance company that the loan had been approved. They promptly notified respondents of this fact. Respondents asked that the closing of the transaction be delayed until after January first for tax reasons.

Meanwhile, the insurance company asked for a preliminary title report and a copy of the proposed deed from appellants to respondents. These were furnished, and later a proposed note and mortgage to be signed by respondents were furnished by the insurance company.

Appellants executed the deed and the brokers requested respondents to execute the note and mortgage. Respondent J.E. Schweiter went to the brokers' office and stated that his wife had refused to sign the papers. On January 11, 1957, respondents gave notice of rescission of the transaction and appellants promptly tendered performance, which was refused by respondents.

On April 26, 1957, respondents instituted this action for the purpose of obtaining a declaration of the rights and duties of the parties under the earnest-money agreement. Shortly thereafter, appellants sold the tillable land to a third party for seven thousand dollars less than respondents had agreed to pay for it.

Appellants filed an answer containing a cross-complaint in which they sought to recover the seven-thousand-dollar loss on the sale, plus other special damages.

The trial court rendered a memorandum decision holding that the earnest-money agreement was void because it contained no legal description of the real estate involved in the transaction. * * *

Appellants assign error to the entry of conclusions of law Nos. 1 and 2, reading as follows:

"I. That the earnest money [sic] executed by plaintiffs on October 23, 1956 * * * is void as being in violation of the Statute of Frauds;"

"II. That plaintiffs shall have judgment against defendants in the sum of $5,000.00;"

We shall dispose of the assignments in the order in which they are raised.

Conclusion of Law No. 1 is in accord with the law of this state. We have consistently held that an earnest-money agreement containing an inadequate legal description of the property to be conveyed is void as being in violation of the statute of frauds. * * *

Conclusion of Law No. 2 does not follow from Conclusion of Law No. 1 and is, therefore, erroneous. Although the earnest-money agreement was unenforceable and could not be made the subject of reformation, this does not entitle respondents to a return of their earnest money. At no time did appellants repudiate the contract. On the contrary, they tendered performance and did not otherwise dispose of the property until after respondents commenced this action. Under these facts, the case falls directly within the rule of Dubke v. Kassa, 1947, 29 Wash.2d 486, 187 P.2d 611 wherein we said:

'The applicable rule is that a vendee under an agreement for the sale and purchase of property which does not satisfy the statute of frauds, * * * cannot recover payments made upon the purchase price if the vendor has not repudiated the contract but is ready, willing, and able to perform in accordance therewith, even though the contract is not enforceable against the vendee either at law or in equity. [citations]'

Further in the opinion we also said:

"It does not seem to be, nor can it be, seriously urged that appellants sacrificed their right to retain the payment received, because they sold the property to a third person after the respondent had commenced this action."

Unfortunately, neither party called the trial court's attention to the *Dubke* case.

Thus it appears that this court, in accord with the great weight of authority, has consistently denied recovery of earnest money paid under a void or unenforceable agreement to convey real estate where the buyer has defaulted and the seller was at all times ready, able and willing to consummate the transaction. * * *

The judgment of the trial court, in so far as it awards the return of the five thousand dollars earnest money to respondents, is reversed with directions to dismiss the action. In all other respects, the judgment is affirmed.

FINLEY, CHIEF JUSTICE (dissenting). Frankly, I question the validity of the *Dubke ratio decidendi* and the assumption underlying the majority opinion. If the purported contract in the instant case is absolutely void—rather than being voidable or simply creative of a right as to which no remedy is available for enforcement—then there is simply and absolutely no consideration to support the payment made by the vendee, and he ought to recover it. Reedy v. Ebsen, 1932, 60 S.D. 1, 242 N.W. 592. Actually, it seems to me incongruous and a bit on the ridiculous side to say the writing is void or even unenforceable (which is the equivalent of saying that it created no legal relations between the parties), and then to say that for some unarticulated, vague or mysterious reason, the legal or other relationships of the parties were altered sufficiently to be judicially cognizable and to give the vendor a legal right to keep the vendees' down payment.

Our statute of frauds, RCW 64.04.010, provides:

"Every conveyance of real estate, or any interest therein, and every contract creating or evidencing any encumbrance upon real estate, shall be by deed:"

By way of comparison, note:

(1) RCW 19.36.010: "In the following cases, specified in this section, any agreement, contract and promise *shall be void,* unless such agreement, contract or promise, or some note or memorandum thereof, be in writing, and signed by the party to be charged there-with, or by some person thereunto by him lawfully authorized, that is to say: [Specified situations omitted.]" (Emphasis supplied.)

(2) English Statute of Frauds: " * * * no action shall be brought upon any contract or sale of lands, tenements or hereditaments, or any interest in or concerning them" unless in writing.

RCW 19.36.010 is clearly illustrative of the type of statute under which an attempt to contract, failing to meet the statutory requisites, is absolutely void. The English statute, on the other hand, lends itself readily to the construction that an oral contract for the sale of land is valid, but there is simply no remedy available for its enforcement. RCW 64.04.010, governing contracts for the sale of land in Washington does not fall neatly into either category. As is noted in the majority opinion, we have from time to time spoken of contracts not meeting the requirements of this statute, rather loosely, as being both void and unenforceable. In most cases it makes little difference. In the instant case, however, it makes a great deal of difference. The words *void* and *unenforceable* are terms of art and are mutually exclusive. Before this case can be decided, we must determine which of those terms is made appropriate by RCW 64.04.010. As a matter of legal logic, it cannot be both.

In Reedy v. Ebsen, the South Dakota court set forth the following quotation from Brandeis v. Neustadtl, 1860, 13 Wis. 142, 158, explaining the difference as follows:

> 'The parol contract, being void, furnished no consideration for the payment. A consideration, to be sufficient, must be either a benefit to one party or a damage to the other. The purchaser can derive no benefit from the supposed contract. Nothing passes to him by virtue of it; he obtains no interest in the land, and no promise or agreement on the part of the seller to convey him any; and he can never derive any advantage from what has transpired, except it be as a matter of favor on the seller's part. * * * The reason given for not allowing the purchaser under the English statute, and those like it, to repudiate the agreement and recover back what he has paid, so long as the seller is in no default, is very obvious. But it cannot be given here. It is that the agreement is not void but voidable, or, to speak more correctly, not actionable. * * * The repeal of the statute in such case would at once enable the purchaser to maintain his action upon the agreement. With us it is otherwise. Its repeal would leave him in no better situation than formerly. There is in that case a valid living contract between the parties, and though the remedy be suspended, it binds the conscience, and, until it has been broken, constitutes a sufficient consideration for the payment of the money. There being thus a good consideration, if the purchaser chooses to rely upon the honor of the seller for the performance of his contract, instead of putting it in such form that the courts can enforce it, it is no injustice to say to him that he shall not ignore it, at least until that honor has been violated. * * * Under our statute there is no contract; nothing which can be the foundation of any legal or equitable obligation; and how can the court create one? * * * *It finds one party in the unexplained possession of the money of another, which he knowingly received without any legal equivalent, and not as a gift, and which he has no legal or equitable right to retain; and why should he not refund? * * *'* (Emphasis supplied.) [60 S.D. 1, 242 N.W. 592.]

[A]ssuming again that the legal description is defective, it seems to me that the language of RCW 64.04.010 most strongly supports a conclusion that the earnest-money agreement in the instant case is not merely unenforceable, but is void. Thus, I cannot agree with the reasoning of the majority.

Note

Question: Suppose that the purchaser has now changed his mind and desires to reform the earnest money receipt to insert an accurate legal description. What legal argument could the seller raise against the reformation remedy?

ABRAMS v. UNITY MUTUAL LIFE INSURANCE CO.

United States Court of Appeals, Seventh Circuit, 2001.
237 F.3d 862.

DIANE P. WOOD, CIRCUIT JUDGE. In the funeral business, the term "preneed" insurance refers to a product that a person may buy to provide in advance for funeral and burial expenses. Richard Abrams, who owned a number of funeral businesses, had some expertise in this kind of preneed life insurance. Unity Mutual Life Insurance (Unity) was interested in moving into the preneed market and decided to use Abrams as its general agent. Although the parties never entered into a written contract, Abrams provided several services to Unity in connection with various pre-need products. The relationship soured, however, in 1997, over a dispute relating to Unity's compensation for Abrams's services. Abrams eventually sued Unity under several contract theories, but the district court granted summary judgment in Unity's favor on all of his claims. Abrams now appeals only the grant of summary judgment on his unjust enrichment claim. We affirm.

In 1991, Abrams and Unity began discussing the possibility of a business arrangement in which Abrams would become a general agent for Unity, helping Unity develop and market its first preneed insurance program. In return, Abrams was to receive commission payments in an amount equal to a percentage of preneed products ultimately sold. The parties' discussions led to a series of six draft agreements, but no formal agreement was ever signed. Nevertheless, Abrams kept working for Unity, based on a "handshake" agreement and an oral promise from Unity employee Shirley Cruickshank that, although the contract negotiations were "getting cumbersome," Abrams would receive commission payments for his services.

Abrams claims that between 1991 and 1997, he developed and marketed preneed insurance products for Unity and also trained Unity's employees and agents on selling the products. These efforts were significant in scope. Abrams asserted that he introduced Unity's product to about 12,000 funeral homes by including a reference to Unity in a newsletter he regularly sent out. He also mentioned Unity a few times in a regular column he wrote in a trade publication. Notwithstanding these efforts, however, sales of Unity's preneed insurance products were not as high as anticipated, and Unity terminated its relationship with Abrams in 1997.

Abrams then brought this lawsuit * * * alleging that Unity owed him commissions for the sales of all insurance polices resulting from his efforts under the putative oral agreement. He relied upon theories of breach of contract, promissory estoppel, and unjust enrichment and sought damages in excess of $75,000. * * *

Unity responded by taking Abrams's deposition and promptly thereafter moving for summary judgment. The court * * * granted summary judgment on all counts, finding that there was no signed written agreement and that any oral agreement violated New York's Statute of Frauds. * * * The promissory estoppel claim failed because Abrams could show neither a clear and unambiguous promise by Unity nor unconscionable injury resulting from Unity's actions. * * * The district court concluded that the unjust enrichment claim was based on an unenforceable underlying contract and thus was an impermissible attempt to circumvent New York's Statute of Frauds. Abrams * * * challenges only the district court's dismissal of the unjust enrichment claim.

The existence of an enforceable contract is not a prerequisite for a claim for unjust enrichment when a plaintiff is seeking payment for services that he has provided to the defendant. [citations] Nevertheless, such a claim may be barred if it is based on the same promise and seeks the same relief as an otherwise barred contract claim. [citations]

For our purposes, the relevant question is whether Abrams's unjust enrichment claim is sufficiently distinct from the underlying contract claims to permit him to go forward with it * * * . Abrams's case might have been stronger if he had detailed the particulars of the services he claimed to have provided to Unity, including the number of hours and the reasonable value of the services, because this would have clarified both the difference between the basis of the unjust enrichment claim and the basis of the contract claims and the difference between the recovery for the unjust enrichment claim and a contract recovery. But Abrams offered no such particulars * * * , even after Unity complained that the unjust enrichment claim was an effort to evade the Statute of Frauds. Abrams only provided a vague list of services that he performed for Unity, including training Unity employees on selling preneed insurance, introducing Unity to several insurance agents and brokers, visiting funeral homes on Unity's behalf, preparing a newsletter sent to funeral homes, and developing a marketing and distribution system. He does not tell us how many hours he spent working for Unity. He does not tell us the reasonable value of those services; nor does he point to any document in the record from which a court could glean such facts.

Instead, Abrams relied on the commissions structure discussed by the parties as a basis for determining the reasonable value of his services. Herein lies the fatal flaw in his claim. By asking us to look to the alleged contract to demonstrate the value of his services, he depends on proof of either an unenforceable oral contract or unenforceable written draft agreements. (We presume he is suggesting that he receive commissions on the sales Unity entered into over the years he was providing services, but not even this is clear; he may be asserting a claim to commissions on all sales of preneed contracts to funeral homes Unity learned about through his efforts—perhaps for all eternity—and it is hard if not impossible to distinguish this claim from his contract claim.) If we were to give him the relief he seeks, *i.e.*, the commissions, we would be enforcing the oral agreement and circumventing the Statute of Frauds. Such a result is clearly barred by New York law. [citation] Abrams's unjust enrichment claim is, in effect, indistinguishable from his claim for breach of contract. Sadly enough for Abrams, the parties never entered an enforceable agreement regarding the commissions, and the Statute of Frauds makes "handshake" agreements of the kind he had worthless. On the facts presented here, Abrams cannot recover the commissions either through a breach of contract claim or as an indirect way of proving the value of his services for an unjust enrichment claim. * * *

Finally, even if New York would recognize this kind of unjust enrichment claim in principle, Abrams would still lose because he failed to meet his burden to establish one of the key elements of the claim—the reasonable value of his services. [citations] Once Unity moved for summary judgment, the burden shifted to Abrams to establish that there was "sufficient evidence favoring the nonmoving party for a jury to return a verdict for that party." Anderson v.

Liberty Lobby, Inc., 477 U.S. 242, 249 (1986). * * * [A] nonmoving party cannot survive summary judgment without pointing to evidence that, if believed by the trier of fact, would support a verdict in its favor. Even though the question whether a defendant has been enriched, and how much, is usually a question of fact, Abrams simply has not provided any information regarding the services he provided and their value. This amounts to a failure to meet his summary judgment burden on a critical element of his claim, and thus independently supports the district court's decision. * * *

Because Abrams's unjust enrichment claim depends on proof of an unenforceable contract, it is barred by the Statute of Frauds. Furthermore, Abrams did not produce the evidence necessary to create a genuine issue of fact on the question of the value of his services for unjust enrichment purposes. For both of these reasons, we AFFIRM the judgment of the district court.

Questions

1. *Restitution.* Did Abrams's services benefit Unity Mutual? If Unity Mutual was enriched, was its enrichment unjust? ✓

In developing his opposition to Unity Mutual's motion for summary judgment, had Arbams overlooked the different elements of a contract and a restitution cause of action? ✓

2. *Measurement.* Why didn't Abrams's proof of the agreed rate of payment satisfy the court? Why should a court forbid a restitution plaintiff from recovering the contract rate? What element of his restitution cause of action did Abrams fail to support?

Does the court educate the plaintiff about how he should have developed his opposition to the defendant's motion for summary judgment? What affidavits should Abrams have developed and submitted to keep his restitution claim alive? Amendment.

In Campbell v. T.V.A., p. 406, the court of appeals affirmed a jury verdict for Campbell for restitution measured by the payment rate in the invalid contract. How does Abrams v. Unity Mutual differ?

In deciding whether to grant restitution and how to measure it, the court should consider why the plaintiff cannot recover under related bodies of law, here contract law. The court says that allowing Abrams to recover restitution measured by the contract rate would circumvent the Statute of Frauds, that is plaintiff's recovery measured by the contract rate would resurrect a bargain that the statute of frauds dooms. In recovering restitution under a failed agreement for services, the plaintiff should receive the reasonable value of his services, not what the defendant promised in exchange; for the latter measure of restitution would undermine the purpose of the statute of frauds. Thus a plaintiff suing a defendant for restitution-quantum meruit to recover value he conferred on the defendant under an oral agreement barred by the statute of frauds must prove the reasonable value of his services separately from the compensation arrangement in the failed contract.

Judge Wood never says that Abrams could not recover restitution-quantum meruit. Abrams's opposition to Unity Mutual's motion for summary judgment lacked proof of "reasonable value," the final element of his restitution-quantum meruit cause of action. A quantum meruit plaintiff's recovery of the reasonable value of his services, which would usually be less than the agreed rate, would prevent the defendant's unjust enrichment. Judge Wood's education project begins "Abrams's case might have been stronger if" and continues for the rest of the paragraph.

The *Campbell* court decided before Anderson v. Liberty Lobby or "modern" summary judgment doctrine. In *Campbell*, the defendant had proved reasonable value, but the jury ignored it. The defendant appealed from the jury verdict for the agreed rate. Finally, the majority may be incorrect because Campbell's recovery of the agreed rate undermined the competitive bidding statute, as the dissent argued.

2. LACK OF CAPACITY TO CONTRACT

HALBMAN v. LEMKE

Supreme Court of Wisconsin, 1980.
99 Wis.2d 241, 298 N.W.2d 562.

CALLOW, JUSTICE. * * * On or about July 13, 1973, James Halbman, Jr. (Halbman), a minor, entered into an agreement with Michael Lemke (Lemke) whereby Lemke agreed to sell Halbman a 1968 Oldsmobile for the sum of $1,250. Lemke was the manager of L & M Standard Station in Greenfield, Wisconsin, and Halbman was an employee at L & M. At the time the agreement was made Halbman paid Lemke $1,000 cash and took possession of the car. Arrangements were made for Halbman to pay $25 per week until the balance was paid, at which time title would be transferred. About five weeks after the purchase agreement, and after Halbman had paid a total of $1,100 of the purchase price, a connecting rod on the vehicle's engine broke. Lemke, while denying any obligation, offered to assist Halbman in installing a used engine in the vehicle if Halbman, at his expense, could secure one. Halbman declined the offer and in September took the vehicle to a garage where it was repaired at a cost of $637.40. Halbman did not pay the repair bill.

In October of 1973 Lemke endorsed the vehicle's title over to Halbman, although the full purchase price had not been paid by Halbman, in an effort to avoid any liability for the operation, maintenance, or use of the vehicle. On October 15, 1973, Halbman returned the title to Lemke by letter which disaffirmed the purchase contract and demanded the return of all money theretofore paid by Halbman. Lemke did not return the money paid by Halbman.

The repair bill remained unpaid, and the vehicle remained in the garage where the repairs had been made. In the spring of 1974, in satisfaction of a garageman's lien for the outstanding amount, the garage elected to remove the vehicle's engine and transmission and then towed the vehicle to the residence of James Halbman, Sr., the father of the plaintiff minor. Lemke was asked several times to remove the vehicle from the senior Halbman's home, but he declined to do so, claiming he was under no legal obligation to remove it. During the period when the vehicle was at the garage and then subsequently at the home of the plaintiff's father, it was subjected to vandalism, making it unsalvageable.

Halbman initiated this action seeking the return of the $1,100 he had paid toward the purchase of the vehicle, and Lemke counterclaimed for $150, the amount still owing on the contract. Based upon the uncontroverted facts, the trial court granted judgment in favor of Halbman, concluding that when a minor disaffirms a contract for the purchase of an item, he need only offer to return the property remaining in his hands without making restitution for any use or depreciation.

[Lemke appeals.]

Neither party challenges the absolute right of a minor to disaffirm a contract for the purchase of items which are not necessities. That right, variously known as the doctrine of incapacity or the "infancy doctrine," is one of the oldest and most venerable of our common law traditions. * * * Thus it is settled law in this state that a contract of a minor for items which are not necessities is void or voidable at the minor's option. [citations]

Once there has been a disaffirmance, however, as in this case between a minor vendee and an adult vendor, unresolved problems arise regarding the rights and responsibilities of the parties relative to the disposition of the consideration exchanged on the contract. As a general rule a minor who disaffirms a contract is entitled to recover all consideration he has conferred incident to the transaction. In return the minor is expected to restore as much of the consideration as, at the time of disaffirmance, remains in the minor's possession. [citations] The minor's right to disaffirm is not contingent upon the return of the property, however, as disaffirmance is permitted even where such return cannot be made. Olson v. Veum, 197 Wis. 342, 345, 222 N.W. 233 (1928). [citations]

The return of property remaining in the hands of the minor is not the issue presented here. In this case we have a situation where the property cannot be returned to the vendor in its entirety because it has been damaged and therefore diminished in value, and the vendor seeks to recover the depreciation. * * *

The law regarding the rights and responsibilities of the parties relative to the consideration exchanged on a disaffirmed contract is characterized by confusion, inconsistency, and a general lack of uniformity as jurisdictions attempt to reach a fair application of the infancy doctrine in today's marketplace. [citations] That both parties rely on this court's decision in Olson v. Veum is symptomatic of the problem.

In *Olson* a minor, with his brother, an adult, purchased farm implements and materials, paying by signing notes payable at a future date. Prior to the maturity of the first note, the brothers ceased their joint farming business, and the minor abandoned his interest in the material purchased by leaving it with his brother. The vendor initiated an action against the minor to recover on the note, and the minor (who had by then reached majority) disaffirmed. The trial court ordered judgment for the plaintiff on the note, finding there had been insufficient disaffirmance to sustain the plea of infancy. This court reversed, holding that the contract of a minor for the purchase of items which are not necessities may be disaffirmed even when the minor cannot make restitution. Lemke calls our attention to the following language in that decision:

> "To sustain the judgment below is to overlook the substantial distinction between a mere denial by an infant of contract liability where the other party is seeking to enforce it and those cases where he who was the minor not only disaffirms such contract but seeks the aid of the court to restore to him that with which he has parted at the making of the contract. In the one case he is using his infancy merely as a shield, in the other also as a sword."

From this Lemke infers that when a minor, as a plaintiff, seeks to disaffirm a contract and recover his consideration, different rules should apply than if the minor is defending against an action on the contract by the other party. This theory is not without some support among scholars. See: Calamari and Perillo, The Law of Contracts, sec. 126, 207–09 (Hornbook Series 1970), treating separately the obligations of the infant as a plaintiff and the infant as a defendant.

Additionally, Lemke advances the thesis in the dissenting opinion by court of appeals Judge Cannon, arguing that a disaffirming minor's obligation to make restitution turns upon his ability to do so. For this proposition, the following language in Olson v. Veum is cited: "The authorities are clear that when it is shown, as it is here, that the infant cannot make restitution, then his absolute right to disaffirm is not to be questioned."

In this case Lemke argues that the *Olson* language excuses the minor only when restitution is not possible. Here Lemke holds Halbman's $1,100, and accordingly there is no question as to Halbman's ability to make restitution.

Halbman argues in response that, while the "sword—shield" dichotomy may apply where the minor has misrepresented his age to induce the contract, that did not occur here and he may avoid the contract without making restitution notwithstanding his ability to do so.

The principal problem is the use of the word "restitution" in *Olson*. A minor, as we have stated, is under an enforceable duty to return to the vendor, upon disaffirmance, as much of the consideration as remains in his possession. When the contract is disaffirmed, title to that part of the purchased property which is retained by the minor revests in the vendor; it no longer belongs to the minor. [citation] The rationale for the rule is plain: a minor who disaffirms a purchase and recovers his purchase price should not also be permitted to profit by retaining the property purchased. The infancy doctrine is designed to protect the minor, sometimes at the expense of an innocent vendor, but it is not to be used to bilk merchants out of property as well as proceeds of the sale. Consequently, it is clear that, when the minor no longer possesses the property which was the subject matter of the contract, the rule requiring the return of property does not apply.[1] The minor will not be required to give up what he does not have. We conclude that *Olson* does no more than set forth the foregoing rationale and that the word "restitution" as it is used in that opinion is limited to the return of the property to the vendor. We do not agree with Lemke and the court of appeals' dissent that *Olson* requires a minor to make restitution for loss or damage to the property if he is capable of doing so.

Here Lemke seeks restitution of the value of the depreciation by virtue of the damage to the vehicle prior to disaffirmance. Such a recovery would require Halbman to return more than that remaining in his possession. It seeks compensatory value for that which he cannot return. Where there is misrepresentation by a minor or willful destruction of property, the vendor may be able to recover damages in tort. [citations] But absent these factors, as in the present case, we believe that to require a disaffirming minor to make restitution for

---

1. Although we are not presented with the question here, we recognize there is considerable disagreement among the authorities on whether a minor who disposes of the property should be made to restore the vendor with something in its stead. The general rule appears to limit the minor's responsibility for restoration to specie only. [citation] But see: Boyce v. Doyle, 113 N.J.Super. 240, 273 A.2d 408 (1971), adopting a "status quo" theory which requires the minor to restore the precontract status quo, even if it means returning proceeds or other value. Fisher v. Taylor Motor Co., 249 N.C. 617, 107 S.E.2d 94 (1959), requiring the minor to restore only the property remaining in the hands of the minor, " 'or account for so much of its value as may have been invested in other property which he has in hand or owns and controls.' " Finally, some attention is given to the "New Hampshire Rule" or benefits theory which requires the disaffirming minor to pay for the contract to the extent he benefitted from it. [citation]

diminished value is, in effect, to bind the minor to a part of the obligation which by law he is privileged to avoid. [citations]

The cases upon which the petitioner relies for the proposition that a disaffirming minor must make restitution for loss and depreciation serve to illustrate some of the ways other jurisdictions have approached this problem of balancing the needs of minors against the rights of innocent merchants. In Barber v. Gross, 74 S.D. 254, 51 N.W.2d 696 (1952), the South Dakota Supreme Court held that a minor could disaffirm a contract as a defense to an action by the merchant to enforce the contract but that the minor was obligated by a South Dakota statute, upon sufficient proof of loss by the plaintiff, to make restitution for depreciation. Cain v. Coleman, 396 S.W.2d 251 (Tex.Civ.App. 1965), involved a minor seeking to disaffirm a contract for the purchase of a used car where the dealer claimed the minor had misrepresented his age. In reversing summary judgment granted in favor of the minor, the court recognized the minor's obligation to make restitution for the depreciation of the vehicle. The Texas court has also ruled, in a case where there was no issue of misrepresentation, that upon disaffirmance and tender by a minor the vendor is obligated to take the property "as is," Rutherford v. Hughes, 228 S.W.2d 909, 912 (Tex.Civ.App.1950). Scalone v. Talley Motors, Inc., 158 N.Y.S.2d 615, 3 App.Div.2d 674 (1957), and Rose v. Sheehan Buick, Inc., 204 So.2d 903 (Fla.App. 1967), represent the proposition that a disaffirming minor must do equity in the form of restitution for loss or depreciation of the property returned. Because these cases would at some point force the minor to bear the cost of the very improvidence from which the infancy doctrine is supposed to protect him, we cannot follow them.

As we noted in *Kiefer,* modifications of the rules governing the capacity of infants to contract are best left to the legislature. Until such changes are forthcoming, however, we hold that, absent misrepresentation or tortious damage to the property, a minor who disaffirms a contract for the purchase of an item which is not a necessity may recover his purchase price without liability for use, depreciation, damage, or other diminution in value.

The decision of the court of appeals is affirmed.

Notes

1. The tentative draft of the Restatement (Third) of Restitution and Unjust Enrichment allows a minor to rescind an unratified contract:

"Buyer, age 16, purchases a used car from Dealer, paying $5000 cash. Buyer makes no misrepresentation of age. Dealer is acting in good faith, and the terms of the transaction are fair and reasonable. Several months later the car develops mechanical problems; when Buyer continues to drive the car without obtaining the necessary repairs, the car becomes inoperable. Buyer then repudiates the purchase. Buyer is entitled to rescind the transaction on the ground of incapacity. Upon rescission, Buyer is entitled to recover $5000, plus interest; Dealer is entitled to recover the car, plus an amount equal to its depreciation in value while in Buyer's possession. Dealer's claim for depreciation may be applied in set-off against Dealer's liability to refund the purchase price." Section 16, Illustration 13.

In Illustration 13, is the restitution following rescission contrary to *Halbman*? If so, which best advances the protective policy of denying contractual capacity to a minor? Which reduces a minor's opportunities to take advantage of others without regard to the consequences to them? Which protects someone who has dealt in good faith with a minor? Which do you think is the better view?

2. *Internet Transaction.* Should a .com merchant dealing with a possibly underage buyer ask the buyer to affirm majority age? The courts are divided about whether a seller can invoke estoppel against a minor who has misrepresented his age. Since a court is likely to hold that a minor is liable for a tort, a seller may consider a deceit action or counterclaim.

D.   GROUND FOR RESTITUTION

1.   DEFICIENT CONSIDERATION

JOHNSON v. GENERAL MOTORS CORP. CHEVROLET MOTOR DIVISION

Supreme Court of Kansas, 1983.
233 Kan. 1044, 668 P.2d 139.

LOCKETT, JUSTICE. This action involves revocation of acceptance pursuant to K.S.A. 2–608. The issues raised in this appeal focus on the appropriate measure of damages for a buyer's use of goods after revocation of acceptance.

John and Joan Johnson, the appellants, purchased a new 1981 Chevrolet Silverado half-ton diesel pickup truck from Ed Roberts Chevrolet in Bonner Springs, Kansas, on October 7, 1980. The Johnsons traded in a 1979 Chevrolet pickup and paid $4,202.10 in cash in exchange for the new pickup. The total cost of the new truck was $11,119.65. The Johnsons received a limited warranty for the truck from the General Motors Corporation (GMC).

Problems with the new truck appeared immediately. On the trip home from the dealership, the truck's accelerator stuck in a wide open position while the truck was in traffic. Also, a substantial amount of oil leaked from the truck. The pickup was brought to the dealer for repairs but the problems continued. * * * Repairs were attempted under GMC's warranty agreement but the Johnsons had lost confidence in the truck. On November 30, 1980, the Johnsons, through their attorney, sought to revoke their acceptance of the truck and to return it for a refund of the purchase price. Their offer to return the truck was refused by GMC and the Johnsons continued to use the truck after a lawsuit was filed. Some repairs were performed under the warranty agreement during the time period after revocation and prior to trial.

On March 2, 1981, the Johnsons filed this action against GMC. The case was tried to the court April 2, 1982, and it was decided that the Johnsons' revocation was justified. GMC does not appeal this ruling. The court held a second hearing on June 18, 1982, to determine what setoff amount should be awarded to GMC because of the appellants' continued use of the truck after revocation. The trial court awarded a setoff of $4,702.94. The Johnsons would be refunded the remainder of the purchase price.

The principal issue is whether the trial court erred in allowing a setoff from the purchase price of the truck for the buyers' continued use of the truck after the buyers' revocation of acceptance. The buyers continued to drive the truck an additional 14,619 miles after notifying GMC of the revocation of acceptance. * * *

Under proper rejection or revocation of acceptance, the buyer is freed from his obligation to pay the purchase price. A buyer has a right to recover that portion of the purchase price already paid when rejection or revocation of acceptance is proper.

A buyer that has accepted a truck and sues for breach of warranty will recover only for the injury that resulted from defects in the truck at the time of the sale. A buyer that properly rejects or revokes after acceptance is first made whole from the injuries resulting from the seller's failure to perform his part of the agreement, escapes the bargain, and forces any loss resulting from depreciation of the goods back on the seller.

The basic policy for revocation of acceptance is contained in 2–608 which states in part:

"(1) The buyer may revoke his acceptance of a lot or commercial unit whose nonconformity substantially impairs its value to him if he has accepted it. * * *"

"(b) without discovery of such nonconformity if his acceptance was reasonably induced either by the difficulty of discovery before acceptance or by the seller's assurances."

"(2) Revocation of acceptance must occur within a reasonable time after the buyer discovers or should have discovered the ground for it and before any substantial change in condition of the goods which is not caused by their own defects. It is not effective until the buyer notifies the seller of it."

"(3) A buyer who so revokes has the same rights and duties with regard to the goods involved as if he had rejected them."

The truck was purchased October 7, 1980. On November 30, 1980, through their attorney, the buyers notified the seller of their revocation of acceptance of the truck and requested a refund of the purchase price. GMC refused to accept the return of the truck but continued its offer to cure the defects under the warranty agreement given by GMC at the time of the sale. At the trial the court determined that the buyers' revocation of acceptance was proper and occurred within a reasonable time after buyers discovered the defects.

Since the buyers had taken possession of the goods, they had a security interest in the goods for the purchase price paid and any expenses reasonably incurred for the care and custody of the truck. Vesting the revoking buyer with a security interest for payments made and expenses incurred is pursuant to 2–711, which states in part:

'(1) Where the seller fails to make delivery or repudiates or the buyer rightfully rejects or justifiably revokes acceptance then with respect to any goods involved, and with respect to the whole if the breach goes to the whole contract (section 2–612), the buyer may cancel and whether or not he has done so may in addition to recovering so much of the price as has been paid'

'(a) "cover" * * * or

'(b) recover damages * * *

'(3) On rightful rejection or justifiable revocation of acceptance a buyer has a security interest in goods in his possession or control for any payments made on their price and any expenses reasonably incurred in their inspection, receipt, transportation, care and custody and may hold such goods and resell them in like manner as an aggrieved seller (section 2–706).'

A buyer who revokes has the same rights and duties with regard to the goods involved as if he had rejected them. 2–608(3). This places the revoking buyer in the same position with one who rejects prior to acceptance thus eliminating the need for different sets of standards for resolving commercial disputes. The manner and effect of rejection and revocation are contained in the U.C.C.

After notification of rejection or revocation to the seller, a merchant buyer is obligated to follow any reasonable instructions received from the seller. If no instructions are received from the seller, a merchant buyer or buyer may choose any of the options available to him under the U.C.C. The goods may be returned, stored for the seller, or sold for the seller's account with reimbursement to the buyer for reasonable expenses incurred caring for and expenses incurred in the sale of the goods. K.S.A. 2–603 and K.S.A. 2–604. A buyer is not permitted to retain such funds as he might believe adequate for his damages if he resells the goods. The proceeds are to be held by the selling buyer until his damages are properly determined.

Here buyers exercised none of the options available to them under the U.C.C. Instead, buyers, after revocation of acceptance, continued to use the truck. The U.C.C. states after rejection any exercise of ownership by the buyer with respect to any commercial unit is wrongful as against the seller. K.S.A. 2–602(2)(a). A buyer's continued use of the goods after revocation of acceptance can constitute an acceptance of ownership and invalidate a cancellation of a sale. Here buyers were placed in a position where if they stored the truck or properly sold the truck, they would not have a vehicle for transportation until the trial of the issues or would be required to lease or purchase an additional vehicle. The buyers' continued use of the vehicle under these circumstances was not an act of continued use which constituted an acceptance of ownership after revocation. With little or no low-cost public transportation available to the public, private transportation has changed from a luxury to a necessity.

The buyers suggest that a revoking purchaser may use the goods after revocation without penalty or cost in limited circumstances where use of the goods is required even after notice of revocation of acceptance. This issue has not been settled by earlier Kansas decisions construing K.S.A. 2–608. * * * Precode decisions avoided the question altogether because the common law required purchasers to elect between "rescission" and recovery of damages. Prompt return of unsatisfactory goods was a condition precedent to an action for rescission. * * * The question of cancellation in the absence of immediate return of the goods did not arise until enactment of the Code.

There is much support for the proposition of awarding a setoff for continued use of goods after revocation of acceptance. Many courts have awarded setoffs in circumstances similar to the present case. [citations]

The Colorado Court of Appeals in Stroh v. Am. Rec., 35 Colo.App. at 201–03, 530 P.2d 989, used this reasoning to justify a setoff:

'Having determined that plaintiffs' revocation of acceptance was effective, we must determine whether their acts thereafter entitled them to an award for the entire purchase price. A buyer who asserts a right to revoke acceptance has the same duties and obligations as a buyer who asserts a right to reject the goods before acceptance. C.R.S. 2–608(3). After rejection of goods, any exercise of dominion and ownership rights is considered wrongful as against the seller. C.R.S. 2–602(2)(a). The purpose of this requirement is to insure that the seller may regain possession of the goods in order to resell the goods or utilize them in order to minimize his loss. Accordingly, notice of revocation of acceptance is necessarily a recognition by the buyer that the property belongs to the seller. Here, after revocation of acceptance on October 15, 1970, plaintiffs retained only a security interest for return of their purchase price. C.R.S. 2–711(3). However, they continued to occupy the mobile home as their residence until they purchased a house in March of 1972 and thereupon vacated the mobile home. Even though defendants did not give instructions with respect to the home after they received notice of revocation of acceptance, plaintiffs' remedies under C.R.S. 2–711, do not include the right to beneficial use of the home. See C.R.S. 2–603. Therefore, we hold that plaintiffs' continued occupancy of the mobile home after the reasonable time at which plaintiffs should have acted under C.R.S. 2–604, was wrongful and defendants are entitled to an award of damages.'

'There is no specific provision in the Uniform Commercial Code for an offset award of damages for wrongful use by the buyer. However, C.R.S. 1–103, provides that:'

'Unless displaced by the particular provisions of this chapter, the principles of law and equity, including the law merchant and the law relative to capacity to contract, principal and agent, estoppel, fraud, misrepresentation, duress, coercion, mistake, bankruptcy, or other validating or invalidating cause shall supplement its provisions.'

'We recognize that the general rule is that where a buyer is entitled to rescind the sale and elects to do so, the buyer shall thereafter be deemed to hold the goods as a bailee for the seller. [citations] Thus, if the buyer uses the goods while he holds them as a bailee, he becomes liable for the value of that use.'

'Since the evidence showed that plaintiffs used the mobile home for a considerable length of time after they should have acted under C.R.S. 2–604, it follows that this use reduced the value of the home. Accordingly, defendants are entitled to an offset of a fair and reasonable use value of the mobile home for this period.' * * *"

The weight of authority supports the granting of a setoff for use after revocation. We agree that a seller is entitled to a setoff for the buyers' continued use of the truck after their revocation of acceptance. * * *

The purpose of allowing revocation after acceptance is to restore the buyer to the economic position the buyer would have been in if the goods were never delivered. After revocation of acceptance any significant use by the buyer should allow the seller to recover from the buyers restitution for the fair value of any benefit obtained resulting from such use. The seller could avoid depreciation of the goods by accepting the buyers' revocation.

GMC contends the established rate of leased vehicle depreciation provides a simple and uniform method for calculating the value of the buyers' post-revocation use. The calculation would have been the same whether or not the buyer drove 10 or 14,619 miles after revocation of acceptance. The only variable is the cost per mile.

The buyers had attempted revocation of acceptance two months after purchase. It was GMC's failure to accept the vehicle's return by the buyers that necessitated a law suit. Sixteen plus months after the buyers' notice of revocation of acceptance the court tried the case and determined that the buyers' revocation was proper. GMC's pure depreciation method using the lease vehicle's monthly depreciation rate was not the proper method of determining the offset due to the buyers' use of the vehicle after revocation. This method allows the seller to recover a setoff based upon a period of time from the seller's refusal to accept back defective goods until there is a judicial determination that the seller was wrong not to accept the buyers' revocation of acceptance. The proper setoff is the value of use of the goods received by the buyer after his revocation of acceptance.

At the trial, over buyers' objection, GMC introduced into evidence the Federal Highway Administration booklet entitled "Cost of Owning and Operating Automobiles and Vans 1982." The booklet was authenticated by the government's resident administrator in compliance with K.S.A. 60–465. The trial court did not abuse its discretion when it overruled the buyers' objection to the introduction of the booklet into evidence. The Federal Highway Administration booklet stated the cost of owning and operating a similar vehicle to the truck purchased by the buyers is calculated at 33.2 cents per mile. After deduction of maintenance, gas and oil, parking and tolls, insurance and state and federal taxes, expenses the buyers have already paid, the booklet concluded the original vehicle cost to operate is 10.7 cents per mile. Since buyers drove the vehicle 14,619 miles at 10.7 cents per mile after revocation, the setoff would be $1,564.23. From the evidence presented in this case, GMC is entitled to the sum of $1,564.23 as a setoff for the buyers' use of the truck after revocation of acceptance.

The buyers claim the trial court erred in failing to award them prejudgment interest from the date of revocation of acceptance. K.S.A. 16–201 provides:

"Creditors shall be allowed to receive interest at the rate of ten percent per annum, when no other rate of interest is agreed upon, for any money after it becomes due; for money lent or money due on settlement of account, from the day of liquidating the account and ascertaining the balance; for money received for the use of another and retained without the owner's knowledge of the receipt; for money due and withheld by an unreasonable and vexatious delay of payment or settlement of accounts; for all other money due and to become due for the forbearance of payment whereof an express promise to pay interest has been made; and for money due from corporations and individuals to their daily or monthly employees, from and after the end of each month, unless paid within fifteen days thereafter."
* * *

The price buyers paid for the truck is not disputed ($11,119.65). For prejudgment interest to be awarded, the amount owed must be a liquidated sum. A setoff or counterclaim does not alter the fact a liquidated sum is owed as of a certain date. However, the setoff is credited against the liquidated claim as of the date the claim was due. * * *

A party justifiably revoking acceptance pursuant to 2–608 is entitled to prejudgment interest from the date revocation is attempted. Any setoff due the seller because of a buyer's continued use of the goods after an attempt to revoke should be deducted from the total judgment which includes prejudgment interest. The setoff arises only after a seller refuses to accept return of the defective goods, and no setoff is due the seller on the revocation date.

Here there was no setoff at the date the claim was due. The setoff occurred after the due date because of seller's refusal to accept return of the defective vehicle. Prejudgment interest on the purchase price would commence to accumulate from November 30, 1980, until the date of judgment. * * *

The awarding of a setoff to GMC is affirmed, but from the evidence presented in this case, the setoff should be $1,564.23. The decision not to grant the plaintiffs prejudgment interest is reversed. The interest should be calculated upon the entire purchase price from the date revocation was attempted until the date of judgment at the rate of ten percent. The case is affirmed in part, reversed in part and remanded to enter judgment in accordance with this opinion.

Notes

1. *Label.* Revocation of acceptance by another name is rescission-restitution.

2. *Breach Plus?* A buyer may revoke his acceptance when the goods' "nonconformity substantially impairs its value to him." Does the U.C.C. require more than a simple breach?

3. *Lost Confidence.* The Johnsons had "lost confidence in the truck." What difference ought the buyers' missing trust make? Section 2–608(1) says "The buyer may revoke his acceptance of a lot or commercial unit whose nonconformity substantially impairs its value *to him* if he has accepted it."

Aside from many "her" or "it" buyers, does § 2–608's "to him" language lend a subjective or personal quality to "substantially impairs"?

U.C.C.'s Politically Incorrect Gender Usage Rehabilitated: Remember the Revised U.C.C? Section 2–608(1) in the Revised U.C.C. is rewritten as sexually neutral, but it retains the subjective quality with "the buyer."

4. *Confusion.* Referring to "damages for breach of warranty" under the benefit of bargain rule, one court said that a contract for a painting was rescinded, found the buyer entitled to damages equal to the purchase price, and concluded, "Plaintiff must return the Painting to the Defendant in order to avoid duplicative recovery." Rogath v. Siebenmann, 941 F.Supp. 416, 424–25 (S.D.N.Y.1996).

Had the court sorted out the differences between a buyer's revocation of an acceptance and his suit for breach of warranty?

5. *Keeping the Truck.* Does letting the Johnsons revoke by notifying the seller without returning the truck make it difficult to distinguish a buyer's revocation of acceptance from his claim for breach of warranty? If the Johnsons really wanted out of the deal, why didn't they return the truck? Why didn't driving the truck over 14,000 miles rescind the Johnsons' revocation?

The common-law test for whether a buyer's continued use of the goods defeated his right to revoke acceptance appears to be whether the buyer's use is reasonable under the circumstances. CPC International, Inc. v. Techni–Chem, Inc., 660 F.Supp. 1509 (N.D.Ill.1987) (continued use may minimize economic waste); Aubrey's R.V. Center, Inc. v. Tandy Corp., 46 Wash.App. 595, 731 P.2d 1124 (1987). But where a buyer continued to use chattels for three years after discovery of the alleged defects, made no offer to return them, and rejected an offer to replace them, the court thought that an attempted revocation was ineffective. Sobiech v. International Staple & Machine Co., 867 F.2d 778 (2d Cir.1989).

Revised U.C.C.'s Section 2–608(4) deals with the buyer who revokes acceptance but continues to use the goods. If a buyer's use is "unreasonable," the seller can treat it as an acceptance. If a buyer's use is "reasonable," it isn't an acceptance, but "in an appropriate case," the buyer must compensate the seller for the value of his use. Would that addition have helped the court decide whether the Johnsons could revoke their acceptance?

6. *Restitution After Revocation.* The court's goal with rescission-restitution is to put the buyer and seller back where they were before they formed the contract.

(a) Both the buyer and the seller restore the other's consideration, the Johnsons return the pickup, GM refunds the money.

(b) To accommodate to the time the revoked contract was in effect, each pays the other for using the other's consideration. How does the court justify requiring Johnsons to pay GM for using the truck? Should the court determine the Johnsons' use value from depreciation tables and averages or from the Johnsons' actual experience with the particular defective truck?

Is anything more than deeming GM to be a "borrower" of the Johnsons' purchase price necessary to charge it with interest? For restitution to a buyer following revocation, was the *Johnson* court's test of whether the sum was "liquidated" out of place?

7. *Restitution Plus Additional Recovery.* In addition to restitution of benefits conferred on the seller, a buyer who justifiably revokes an acceptance may recover any additional costs incurred in reliance on the contract. Thus a court held that a buyer who revoked acceptance of a contract to purchase a computer was entitled to recover not only the price but also financing charges. Aubrey's R.V. Center, Inc. v. Tandy Corp., 46 Wash.App. 595, 731 P.2d 1124 (1987).

A truck buyer revoked a contract for breach of warranty. He claimed that a Toyota dealer's failure to repair his truck caused him to default on a note. The default impaired his credit rating. This in turn increased his costs of doing business. Buyer recovered these costs as consequential damages. City National Bank v. Wells, 181 W.Va. 763, 384 S.E.2d 374 (1989).

8. *Buyer's Security Interest.* As the *Johnson* court indicates, the buyer who revokes his acceptance has a security interest in the chattel to secure return of the purchase price. Without this right, the buyer would be required to return the chattel and could end up with neither the price nor the chattel. See Ford Motor Credit Co. v. Caiazzo, 387 Pa.Super. 561, 564 A.2d 931 (1989).

9. *Detour: A Survey of an Automobile Buyer's Remedies.* Ms. Consumer purchased a new Chariot automobile from Dealer. She concludes that the Chariot is a lemon because Dealer is unable to keep it running satisfactorily. Dealer asserts that it can fix the vehicle. What are a frustrated consumer's remedies?

Under the U.C.C., Consumer has two "goods oriented" remedies: she may reject nonconforming goods and she may revoke her acceptance of substantially nonconforming goods she has already "accepted." U.C.C. §§ 2–508, 2–608. These remedies are essentially rescission; she should be entitled to receive her consideration back. See Seekings v. Jimmy GMC of Tucson, Inc., 130 Ariz. 596, 638 P.2d 210 (1981); Johnson v. General Motors Corp., Chevrolet Motor Division, supra. As could be expected, automobile manufacturers and dealers have traditionally resisted this remedy when consumers wish to return "lemons." Despite a dealer's repeated inability repair a car, it may continue to assert that the car can be fixed.

Where the buyer has accepted and retained defective goods, § 2–714(2) measures her damages for breach of warranty as the value the goods should have had less the goods' actual value. In addition, §§ 2–714(3) and 2–715 allow her to recover for reliance expenses, personal injury, and property damage.

Sellers use standard form contracts to reduce their potential liability by disclaiming or excluding implied warranties of quality, merchantability and fitness for a particular purpose, and by limiting buyer's remedies, U.C.C. §§ 2–316, 2–719. Since several states' legislatures have adopted local versions of the U.C.C. that alter a seller's ability to exclude a buyer's warranties, a lawyer should examine local law.

Congress enacted the Magnuson–Moss Warranty Act. 15 U.S.C. §§ 2301–2312. That Act sets minimum standards for a written warranty and makes it worthwhile for a lawyer to sue a dealer and manufacturer by allowing Consumer to recover her attorney fees.

Magnuson–Moss which applies to all consumer items is used for a wide variety of products. States have general unfair/deceptive trade practices statutes for consumer protection; these statutes establish for a consumer buyer a stripped-down and simplified cause of action instead of common-law fraud.

State "lemon laws" apply only to automobiles. A lemon statute may force the manufacturer to refund the price or replace an automobile (minus "a reasonable allowance for use") if the car is out of service for more than 30 days in its first year or if a defect remains after four trips to the shop. Lemon statutes usually also provide for attorney fees. Check your state code.

If the seller's practice is uniform and widespread, a consumer lawyer might expand an individual's lemon suit to a class action. Fifty different laws in the 50 states make a nationwide plaintiff class problematic.

Consumer, or her lawyer, may find information about her state's consumer protection law and process through her state's Attorney General's website.

Both Magnuson–Moss and many state lemon laws provide for arbitration where the manufacturer has a procedure that meets Federal Trade Commission regulations. Arbitration binds the manufacturer, but if the consumer remains dissatisfied, she may sue. The results of the arbitration are admissible in court.

Consumer may also pursue her common-law tort remedies for fraud and fraudulent misrepresentation. Jurors may be sympathetic to a plaintiff whose new Chariot give her nothing but grief. Fraud measures the buyer's damages more generously than warranty and may lead to punitive damages. Remember that Dr. Gore took advantage of this generosity, but bear in mind that he did not get to keep all the money the jury awarded him. Consider also the special damages that Ms. Consumer may incur if, for example, her Chariot breaks down far from home on a business trip or vacation.

2. MISTAKE

In my dentist's chair, my least favorite word is "Oops." If you make a careless mistake and injure another you may be labeled a tortfeasor and forced to pay for the damages the mistake caused. However, if you make a mistaken agreement or transfer, then you may, under some circumstances, appeal, not from the trial judge, but from yourself. You may even convince the court to reverse your mistake. Identifying just what those circumstances or mistakes are has been a legal puzzle.

RENNER v. KEHL

Supreme Court of Arizona, En Banc, 1986.
150 Ariz. 94, 722 P.2d 262.

GORDON, VICE CHIEF JUSTICE. * * * In 1981 the petitioners, defendants below, acquired from the State of Arizona agricultural development leases covering

2,262 acres of unimproved desert land near Yuma. The petitioners made no attempt to develop the property themselves, but instead decided to sell their interest in the land. The respondents, plaintiffs below, were residents of the state of Washington interested in the large scale commercial cultivation of jojoba. The respondents and their agent, who was familiar with commercial jojoba development, were shown the petitioners' property and became interested in purchasing it. The property appeared to be ideal for the respondents' purposes; the soil and climate were good and both parties were of the opinion that sufficient water was available beneath the land to sustain jojoba production. The respondents made it clear that they were interested in the property only for jojoba production and required adequate water supplies.

The respondents decided to buy the leases and on June 5, 1981, executed a Real Estate Purchase Contract to that effect. Respondents agreed to pay $222,200 for the leases, and paid petitioners $80,200 as a down payment, the remainder to be paid in annual installments. In November of 1981 respondents began development of the property for jojoba production. As part of the development process the respondents had five test wells drilled, none of which produced water of sufficient quantity or quality for commercial jojoba cultivation. After spending approximately $229,000 developing the land respondents determined that the aquifer underlying the property was inadequate for commercial development of jojoba. At this point the project was abandoned and the respondents sued to rescind the purchase contract. The petitioners counterclaimed for the balance of payments due under the contract. * * * The court found that the respondents were entitled to rescission based on mutual mistake of fact and failure of consideration, and ordered the respondents to reassign the lease to the petitioners. The petitioners were ordered to pay the respondents $309,849.84 ($80,200 representing the down payment and $229,649.48 representing the cost of developing the property) together with costs and attorney's fees.

The petitioners appealed to the court of appeals, which affirmed. The petitioners raise the same arguments before this Court, *viz.,* that rescission was not justified, or if rescission was appropriate petitioners are not liable for consequential damages.

Mutual mistake of fact is an accepted basis for rescission. [citations] * * * The trial court found that the sole purpose of the contract was to enable respondents to grow jojoba, which depends upon an adequate water supply. The trial court specifically found that "There would have been no sale if both sellers and buyers had not believed it was possible to grow jojoba commercially on the leased acres" and that "[b]ased upon the factual data available, all parties were of the opinion that there would be sufficient good quality water for commercial jojoba production, and that it would be close enough to the surface that it would be economically feasible to pump it for irrigation of large acreages." Consequently, the trial court concluded that "[p]laintiffs are entitled to rescind the purchase agreement because of the mutual mistake of fact and because there was a total failure of consideration."

The belief of the parties that adequate water supplies existed beneath the property was "a basic assumption on which both parties made the contract," Restatement (Second) of Contracts § 152 comment b, and their mutual mistake "ha[d] such a material effect on the agreed exchange of performances as to upset the very bases of the contract." Id. comment a. The contract was therefore voidable and the respondents were entitled to rescission.

The trial court also ordered that petitioners pay the respondents $309,849.84 together with costs and attorney's fees. Of the $309,849.84 awarded to the respondents, $229,649.84 represents reimbursement of the costs borne by the respondents in developing the property for jojoba production. The petitioners challenge the $229,649.84 awarded as an improper grant of "consequential damages."[1]

The court of appeals upheld the full award '[b]ecause the plaintiffs have not received a double recovery in the award of rescission and consequential damages.' * * * The appeals court relied upon Fousel v. Ted Walker Mobile Homes, Inc., 124 Ariz. 126, 602 P.2d 507 (App.1979), for the proposition that rescission can support an award of consequential damages.

In *Fousel* the plaintiffs purchased a mobile home from the defendants, who engaged in a series of misrepresentations which cost the plaintiffs considerable inconvenience and expense. The plaintiffs prevailed upon their claim for fraud and breach of contract and were awarded $2,705.26 in consequential damages and $10,000 in punitive damages. The sole issue on appeal was whether any damages could be awarded where the plaintiffs elected to sue for rescission. The court of appeals held that the doctrine of election of remedies does not necessarily bar an award of consequential or punitive damages, only "benefit of the bargain" damages. However, *Fousel* was predicated upon proof of breach of contract for fraud. The court stated that a party who has rescinded a contract may recover "any incidental or consequential damages resulting from *a breach of the contract*" (emphasis added). The court quoted from Jennings v. Lee, supra, wherein we stated that "[t]here is ample authority that a *defrauded* party may not only receive back the consideration he gave, but also may recover any sums that are necessary to restore him to his position prior to the making of the contract."

In this case there was no breach of contract for fraud. We are dealing with a rescission based upon mutual mistake, which implies freedom from fault on the part of both parties. See Restatement (Second) of Contracts § 152. There was no determination that fraud or misrepresentation occurred; indeed, the trial court concluded that "[t]here was no fraud or misrepresentation on the part of the defendants or their agents." The reliance of the court of appeals upon *Fousel* was misplaced; we hold that absent proof of breach for fraud or misrepresentation a party who rescinds a contract may not recover consequential damages. Accordingly, we reverse that portion of the trial court's order awarding consequential damages and vacate that portion of the court of appeals' decision which affirms the award of consequential damages.

This does not mean, however, that the respondents are entitled only to recover their down payment. When a party rescinds a contract on the ground of mutual mistake he is entitled to restitution for any benefit that he has conferred on the other party by way of part performance or reliance. Restatement (Second) of Contracts § 376. Restitutionary recoveries are not designed to be compensatory; their justification lies in the avoidance of unjust enrichment on the part of the defendant. Thus the defendant is generally liable for restitution of a benefit that would be unjust for him to keep, even though he gained it honestly. Id.;

---

1. [Footnote renumbered.] Consequential or "incidental" damages represent a plaintiff's expenses incurred in reliance upon the contract. See Fousel v. Ted Walker Mobile Homes, Inc., 124 Ariz. 126, 602 P.2d 507 (App.1979). In *Fous-* *el* these expenses included the cost of custom-made awnings, skirting and steps purchased for their mobile home, *see* discussion, *infra;* in this case they would represent the cost of developing the land for jojoba production.

Restatement (Second) of Contracts § 376 comment a. The issue we must now address is the proper measure of the restitutionary interest.

The first step determining the proper measure of restitution requires that the rescinding party return or offer to return, conditional on restitution, any interest in property that he has received in the bargain. Restatement (Second) of Contracts § 384(1)(a). In Arizona this includes reimbursement for the fair market value of the use of the property. With respect to land contracts we have noted that "[i]t is of course essential to justify the rescinding of a contract that the rescinding party offer to place the other in status quo, and this includes the offer to credit the vendors with a reasonable rental value for the time during which the land was occupied." Mortensen v. Berzell Investment Company, 102 Ariz. at 351, 429 P.2d at 948. Earlier we stated that "[t]he offer to surrender possession of property received under the contract need not be unqualified, but may be made conditional upon the vendor's restitution of amounts paid on the contract, less proper allowances in respect of vendee's use of the premises." Mahurin v. Schmeck, 95 Ariz. 333, 341, 390 P.2d 576, 581 (1964). Thus the respondents were obliged to return the land to the petitioners in exchange for their down payment, and in addition to pay the petitioners the fair rental value of the land for the duration of their occupancy.

However, to avoid unjust enrichment the petitioners must pay the respondents a sum equal to the amount by which their property has been enhanced in value by the respondents' efforts. The Restatement (Second) of Contracts § 376 provides that "[i]f [a party] has received and must return land * * * he may have made improvements on the land in reliance on the contract and he is entitled to recover the reasonable value of those improvements. * * * The rule stated in this section applies to avoidance on any ground, including * * * mistake." comment a. The reasonable value of any improvements is measured by "the extent to which the other party's property has been increased in value or his other interests advanced." Restatement (Second) of Contracts § 371(b). Thus the petitioners must pay to the respondents that amount of money which represents the enhanced value of the land due to the respondents' development efforts. In short, the respondents are entitled to their down payment, plus the amount by which their efforts increased the value of the petitioners' property, minus an amount which represents the fair rental value of the land during their occupancy. They are not entitled to the $229,648.84 expended upon development, because that would shift the entire risk of mistake onto the petitioners, which is incompatible with equitable rescission.

Notes

1. *What's a Mistake? What Should the Court Do?* The new Restatement of Restitution helps:

(1) A transfer induced by mistake is subject to rescission at the instance of the transferor * * *. Rescission under this section includes a claim to the recovery of benefits conferred.

(2) The mistake that will serve as the basis for rescission and restitution, * * * is a misapprehension of fact or law on the part of the transferor, where

   (a) but for the mistake the transfer would not have taken place; and

   (b) the transferor does not bear the risk of the mistake.

(3) A transferor bears the risk of a mistake when

(a) the risk in question is assigned to the transferor as a matter of law;

(b) the risk has been allocated to the transferor by agreement of the parties, express or implied; or

(c) the transferor has assumed the risk by deciding to act in conscious ignorance of relevant circumstances. Restatement (Third) of Restitution and Unjust Enrichment § 5 (Tentative Draft No. 1 (2001)).

2. What part of the restatement section in the Note above contains the rule that the *Renner* court applied? Should the *Renner* court have followed a "procedural" plus "substantive" analysis of mistake and required the buyers to show a "procedural" flaw like inequality or imbalance in the parties' negotiation that preceded the contract? Is the flaw "substantive" only, the buyers' hardship in being unable to use the ranch for their intended purpose?

3. *Restitution Following Rescission, Continued.* The court in *Johnson*, p. 492, above, dealt with two kinds of post-rescission restitution: (a) each party returns the other party's consideration; and (b) each party pays the other party the value of using the other party's consideration, rent and interest. The *Renner* court adds (c) the court may order the seller to pay for any improvements the buyer made.

Although the *Renner* court does not mention it, rescinding buyers may recover the price they paid plus interest from the date of the payment. See Brunner v. LaCasse, 234 Mont. 368, 763 P.2d 662 (1988), aff'd, 241 Mont. 102, 785 P.2d 210 (1990); Miller v. Sears, 636 P.2d 1183 (Alaska 1981). The court in Wall v. Foster Petroleum Corp., 791 P.2d 1148 (Colo.App.1989), allowed the buyers to recover prejudgment interest from the date their complaint was filed. The court offset the buyer's claim for interest on the price against the seller's claim for the reasonable value of the buyers' using the premises in Dugan v. Jones, 724 P.2d 955 (Utah 1986).

If the rescinding buyer's improvement does not benefit the seller, the buyer cannot recover the amount expended. See Carter v. Matthews, 288 Ark. 37, 701 S.W.2d 374 (1986). Where the buyer rescinded because of the seller's breach, however, the buyer recovered the reasonable market value of the work done, not limited to the enhanced value of the property if that would be less. See Whitson v. Lende, 442 N.W.2d 267 (S.D.1989); MCC Investments v. Crystal Properties, 451 N.W.2d 243 (Minn.App. 1990).

When a seller rescinds a land sale contract because of buyer's fraud, the seller may recover the premises and may also claim the rental value of the land while the buyer was in possession plus out-of-pocket expenses. Which of these are restitution and which damages? The confusing use of these terms continues. Head & Seemann, Inc. v. Gregg, 107 Wis.2d 126, 318 N.W.2d 381 (1982).

4. *The Vendee's Lien.* Upon rescission, a land buyer's restitution claim may be secured by a "vendee's lien" on the land. Mihranian v. Padula, 134 N.J.Super. 557, 563–64, 342 A.2d 523, 526–27 (1975), judgment aff'd, 70 N.J. 252, 359 A.2d 473 (1976).

5. *Mistaken Insurance Settlement.* If an insurer mistakenly pays an insured's claim upon demand and without investigation, unhampered by any doubts an inquiry might raise, the insurer may recover that payment, as made under mistake. If the insurer investigates thoroughly and resolves latent doubts because it discovers nothing amiss, the payment is also under mistake. But if the insurer pays off despite unresolved doubts created by investigation, it may not recover. Is a little doubt a dangerous thing? What is the practical lesson? Read on.

TERRA NOVA INSURANCE CO. v. ASSOCIATES COMMERCIAL CORP.

United States District Court, Eastern District of Wisconsin, 1988.
697 F.Supp. 1048.

TERENCE T. EVANS, DISTRICT JUDGE. It all began in February, 1982. Brian Scharbarth's truck started tormenting him with mechanical troubles on a run from Wisconsin to California. Lesser truckers might have gotten their vehicles repaired, but Scharbarth arranged to have his stolen. Right there at a truck stop in Sparks, Nevada. Sierra Sid's, to be exact. He did it for the insurance money. And before you could say "chop shop," the truck was in one in Albuquerque, New Mexico, where it was quickly stripped and dismantled. Scharbarth, just as quickly, made a claim for his "loss" with his insurers, the plaintiffs in this suit.

Suspecting fraud, the insurers put a gumshoe on the case. Investigator Heinz A. Rost came back with a blunt report. "My feeling about this claim," he told his superiors, "is about the same as someone trying to make me swallow a 3 lb. fish. First of all, I dislike fish, second, I surely wouldn't try to swallow it whole, especially when it offends my sense of smell the way this claim does."

That was April 1982. But the next month, the insurance companies coughed up anyway. They sent a check for $62,210 to Scharbarth and the payee on his policy, Associates Commercial Corporation, which held a security interest in the truck. The companies paid up because they were worried about their duty to act in good faith in their dealings with Scharbarth. In counsel's words, they "did not want to unduly delay the settlement of his claim." Call the payment lunkheaded, or call it bright. I call it a business decision.

Associates knew nothing about Scharbarth's fraud. It kept the amount that Scharbarth owed on the truck, $49,647.51, and it conveyed its interest in the vehicle to the plaintiffs. Another $11,500 went for a replacement tractor unit. Scharbarth personally netted only $1,057.49 of the $62,210, reminding us, yet again, that crime doesn't pay.[1]

Enter the G-men. Like Rost (no ichthyophagist he), the FBI had also been sniffing into the incident at Sierra Sid's. The Bureau's legwork eventually paid off: In October 1985, a grand jury indicted Scharbarth for mail fraud. He pleaded guilty, and I sentenced him to two years in the big house on February 10, 1986.

On April 16, 1986, the plaintiffs' lawyer wrote to Associates looking for the return of $62,210. Until it received that letter, Associates had remained in the dark regarding Scharbarth's ugly machinations. Even after learning the dark truth, though, Associates wouldn't part with a dime. So the plaintiffs sued in October 1987. Where lesser litigants might have settled, Associates and the plaintiffs have now moved for summary judgment.

In the circumstances of this dispute—where an innocent party received payment from insurers on a claim that the insurers strongly suspected was fraudulent four years earlier—I will grant summary judgment in favor of Associates. At the same time, however, I will grant the plaintiffs summary judgment against Scharbarth, who admitted his fraud in his answer to the complaint. My reasons follow. * * *

---

1. [Footnotes renumbered.] The remaining five dollars are not important to this story, or so it seems.

According to the plaintiffs' lawyer, "Only after he was convicted in February 1986 did the plaintiffs have the proof that Mr. Scharbarth was involved in the alleged theft and, therefore, that there was no coverage for the loss of the truck." But this statement is somewhat misleading. Only after the conviction did the plaintiffs have proof *beyond a reasonable doubt* that Scharbarth had defrauded them in February 1982. Weeks before they paid his claim, however, they strongly suspected that Scharbarth had arranged for the theft.

The plaintiffs' affairs in this matter were handled by Casualty Underwriters, Inc., which in turn delegated responsibility to Floyd Johnson of Commercial Equipment Adjustors, Inc. Mr. Johnson testified at a deposition that his firm checked out Scharbarth's claim and that he hired three outside investigators as well—Gar Riddle, Don Kluxdal, and Mr. Rost. Mr. Riddle reported to Mr. Johnson that "[w]hile this may be a legitimate theft report, there are several discrepancies [in Scharbarth's story] which stand out." Mr. Riddle found it suspicious, for example, that Scharbarth never told any employee at Sierra Sid's about the theft.

Mr. Kluxdal's initial report did not contain any smoking guns, though he did see fit to interview Scharbarth's passenger and ask him whether the two of them had anything to do with the theft. (The answer was "no.") In a later report to Mr. Johnson, Mr. Kluxdal wrote, "I guess I probably will never feel satisfied your insured wasn't involved, simply because he is not accustomed to telling the truth." Mr. Kluxdal's recommendation was this:

> "To sum it all up if we were to deny the claim on what information we have, we wouldn't win. We can't prove anything beyond a reasonable doubt that your insured was involved. Since this can't be done and after considerable length of time, we can see no alternative but to settle."

Mr. Rost's report raised a red flag, as suggested by the colorful quotation at the beginning of this opinion. "All verifiable evidence indicates the insured is not telling the truth," Mr. Rost also said. He recommended to Mr. Johnson that "this claim not be paid without clarification by the insured to the satisfaction of Mr. F.A. Johnson and this investigator." Mr. Johnson discussed the findings of his investigators with Casualty Underwriters.

The claim was paid on May 4, 1982. A single check was made out to Scharbarth and Associates. In settlement of the claim, Scharbarth and Associates gave the plaintiffs all rights to the truck.

On May 28, 1982, the indefatigable Mr. Rost contacted Mr. Johnson to say that an informer had linked Scharbarth to the theft. However, the plaintiffs did not attempt to recover their money at that time and never notified Associates about the problem until April 1986.

Two final facts may be important: First, the plaintiffs attempt to pay theft claims within sixty days, but they waited almost ninety days to pay Scharbarth and Associates. Second, neither Scharbarth nor Associates had threatened or initiated legal action against the plaintiffs to receive payment on the claim, although Scharbarth expressed a desire to receive a prompt payment.

The facts that I have related are not disputed. Instead, the plaintiffs and Associates disagree as to what legal theory ought to govern the case. The plaintiffs argue that Associates should make restitution under a theory of unjust enrichment. Associates counters that the plaintiffs are really asserting a claim that payment was made under a mistake of fact, *i.e.* that the plaintiffs assumed the "loss" was bona fide but later learned otherwise. Associates says the law of mistake of fact does not sustain the plaintiffs' claim (because the plaintiffs were conscious of the possibility that the claim may have been fraudulent). In addition, Associates asserts that the plaintiffs' claim is estopped and barred by laches (because Associates abandoned any effort to mitigate its loss in reliance on the plaintiffs' check). These issues are legal questions appropriate for summary judgment.

Rather than deciding which theory is *the* right one, I will analyze this dispute with general principles in mind. At the outset, it is indisputable that neither Associates nor Scharbarth was entitled to payment by the plaintiffs in the first instance. Once payment was made, however, Associates may have obtained some rights to the money.

A leading treatise says the following under the heading "Right of Insurer to Recover Payments:"

'As a general rule, if the insurer pays a loss, being induced so to do by fraud, or by mistake as to facts which, if it had had knowledge thereof, would have been a sufficient defense in an action by the insured upon the policy, the money so paid may be recovered. * * *'

'An insurer is not entitled to recover a payment made by it under a mistake of law. * * *'

'The insurer is not entitled to recover an improper payment unless it can show that it was not aware of the true facts at the time of paying the loss, and could not have learned of them by reasonable diligence.'

18 Couch, Anderson & Rhodes, Couch on Insurance 2d (Rev. ed.) §§ 74:191–205 (1983).

As for the theory of restitution,

"If an obligation procured by fraud is paid voluntarily with a full knowledge of the facts, the amount so paid cannot be recovered. * * *

"[W]here one who makes a payment upon a controverted claim or demand is conscious of a want of knowledge of the material facts, or is uncertain, doubtful, or speculative concerning them, particularly where they have been in dispute and their status is specially brought to his attention, such payment is not made under a mistake of fact justifying recovery thereof."

66 Am.Jur.2d §§ 116 & 122 (Restitution and Implied Contracts) (1973).

Applying these principles to the case at hand, one conclusion is immediately apparent. The plaintiffs are not entitled to get their money back just because they paid the claim to avoid charges of bad faith. That was a mistake of law, and restitution is inappropriate.[2]

Mistake of fact is a tougher call. The Couch formulation would seem to favor the plaintiffs, who exercised "reasonable diligence" in attempting to ascertain the true facts, or who should at least be afforded a trial on that question. The *American Jurisprudence* rule, on the other hand, would seem to favor Associates

2. The plaintiffs probably would have incurred no extra liability if they had withheld payment pending further investigation or pending the outcome of the FBI inquiry, of which they were aware. This is so because anyone suing the insurers would have had to show the absence of a reasonable basis for their denial of benefits. [citation] But these insurers had a reasonable basis for delay, even if they did not have proof of Scharbarth's fraud beyond a reasonable doubt.

because the plaintiffs knew they were not sure of Scharbarth's veracity. Fortunately, an old Wisconsin case has clarified the approach taken in this state. It is closer to the *American Jurisprudence* rule.

In Meeme Mutual Home Protective Fire Insurance Co. v. Lorfeld, the Wisconsin Supreme Court refused to order restitution to an insurance company that paid a loss payee for fire damages even though the insured later confessed to having torched the insured property. 194 Wis. 322, 216 N.W. 507 (1927). The trial court had found that the insurance company *and* the third-party payee "had suspicions on that subject but lacked proof." The state Supreme Court held:

> "[W]here one waives an investigation after his attention has been called to the possibility of the existence of the fact, he is not acting under a mistake of fact in the legal sense. Here the attention of the plaintiff was called to the fact that the fire might be of incendiary origin. It had the benefit of investigation by the state fire marshal as well as such investigation as it had made or could make on its own account; and with full knowledge of all the facts, conscious of the fact that the fire might be of incendiary origin, it nevertheless paid. Under such circumstances, it cannot be said that the plaintiff acted under a mistake of fact in the legal sense."

In the instant case, the plaintiffs did not waive an investigation. To the contrary, they set three investigators on Scharbarth's trail. Still, the plaintiffs were conscious of the fact that Scharbarth's claim might have been fraudulent, and they nevertheless paid him and an innocent mortgagee. This is what I meant when I called the plaintiffs' payment a business decision. They made a calculated choice that payment of a dubious claim was a better risk than defending against a suit by Scharbarth and/or Associates. See Grand Trunk Western Railroad Co. v. Lahiff, 218 Wis. 457, 463, 261 N.W. 11 (1935) (insurance company in *Meeme* "must be taken to have elected to discount the possibilities of an incendiary fire"). Under Wisconsin law, then, the plaintiffs cannot recover from Associates for what turns out to have been their mistake of fact in the factual but not legal sense.

I think, too, that the plaintiffs are barred from recouping their money from Associates under restitutionary principles which Associates labels as estoppel. In reliance on the insurance settlement, Associates changed its position to its detriment, and restitution is therefore inappropriate. Myers v. Fidelity & Casualty Company of New York, 759 F.2d 1542, 1548 (11th Cir.1985) (insurer could not recover payment from innocent mortgagee under principles of restitution) (quoting 13 S. Williston & W. Jaeger, A Treatise on the Law of Contracts, § 1595 (1970)). Although Associates could not have recovered the truck itself—because the truck was quickly chopped into parts by the thieves—Associates gave up any effort to make up its loss in other ways. For example, it might have pursued Scharbarth (before he went to prison) or his coconspirators (when they could have been located) to return what was left of the truck.

The equities do not fall the same way when it comes to the plaintiffs' case against Scharbarth. He has been unjustly enriched. More fundamentally, he willfully defrauded the plaintiffs. The plaintiffs are entitled to summary judgment against him. The only question is, How much may the plaintiffs recover?

In his answer to the complaint, Scharbarth, appearing *pro se,* stated that the plaintiffs failed to mitigate their damages. In addition, he contended that if the plaintiffs were entitled to recover, his own liability would be limited to the amount he personally netted in the fraud—$1,057.49. These are weak arguments, but I will give Scharbarth an opportunity to flesh them out if he so desires. Accordingly, if Scharbarth wants to limit his liability, he will have thirty days from the date of this order to submit reasons why he should not be held responsible for the entire $62,210 plus prejudgment interest at the rate of 5 percent. He should label his response a "Brief on Award of Damages." * * *

If Scharbarth does not file such a document, I will enter judgment against him for the entire amount paid by the plaintiffs plus interest and court costs.

Notes

1. *Analysis of Mistake.* Even though two of the judge's statements turn out to be extraneous, we will not let them pass without comment. First, that the parties disagree about the governing "legal theory": one side argues that it is a claim for restitution and the other that it is to recover money paid under a mistake of fact. Is there any difference?

Second, is the judge's comment that plaintiff cannot get its money back because it paid under a mistake of law. The insurer did not pay because it mistakenly believed that a rule of law required it to pay; it paid to avoid being hit with a bad faith law lawsuit. This enduring risk in the insurance business is unrelated to any illusions about what the law is.

3. (a) *Assumption of the Risk.* What part of the Restatement of Restitution's § 5, p. 502, does the judge apply?

4. *Another Explanation?* Professor Kull wrote that, in the interest of finality, if a defendant-creditor has in good faith received satisfaction of a genuine debt, it has a defense to the payor's restitution claim. He deals with *Terra Nova* in a footnote. "[A] truck driver arranged for his rig to be stolen, then filed a fraudulent theft claim with his insurers. Insurers paid the loss to driver's secured lender. Following discovery of the fraud, insurers tried to recover the payment from lender. Restitution was properly denied, since a secured creditor/payee who surrenders his security on receipt of payment has an obvious affirmative defense. The court's entertaining opinion fails to mention the true explanation of the result." Andrew Kull, Defenses to Restitution: The Bona Fide Creditor, 81 Boston U. L.Rev 919, 940, n.61 (2001).

5. *Miracle Cure?* Kase, an insured under a disability policy suffered an eye injury that caused his total loss of sight which an ophthalmologist declared to be "irrecoverable." Based on this opinion, his insurer paid him the lump sum the policy provided for loss of eyes. Three years later Kase, as though by miracle, recovered his sight. Was the insurance company's payment made to him under a mistake of fact and recoverable? See Metropolitan Life Insurance Co. v. Kase, 718 F.2d 306 (9th Cir.), reh'g denied, 720 F.2d 1081 (9th Cir.1983).

LENAWEE COUNTY BOARD OF HEALTH v. MESSERLY

Supreme Court of Michigan, 1982.
417 Mich. 17, 331 N.W.2d 203.

RYAN, JUSTICE. * * * The facts of the case are not seriously in dispute. In 1971, the Messerlys acquired approximately one acre plus 600 square feet of land. A three-unit apartment building was situated upon the 600–square–foot portion. The trial court found that, prior to this transfer, the Messerlys' predecessor in title, Mr. Bloom, had installed a septic tank on the property without a permit and in violation of the applicable health code. The Messerlys used the building as an income investment property until 1973 when they sold it, upon land contract, to James Barnes who likewise used it primarily as an income-producing investment.

Mr. and Mrs. Barnes, with the permission of the Messerlys, sold approximately one acre of the property in 1976, and the remaining 600 square feet and building were offered for sale soon thereafter when Mr. and Mrs. Barnes defaulted on their land contract. Mr. and Mrs. Pickles evidenced an interest in the property, but were dissatisfied with the terms of the Barnes–Messerly land contract. Consequently, to accommodate the Pickleses' preference to enter into a land contract directly with the Messerlys, Mr. and Mrs. Barnes executed a quit-claim deed which conveyed their interest in the property back to the Messerlys. After inspecting the property, Mr. and Mrs. Pickles executed a new land contract with the Messerlys on March 21, 1977. It provided for a purchase price of $25,500. A clause was added to the end of the land contract form which provides:

> "17. Purchaser Has Examined This Property and Agrees to Accept Same in Its Present Condition. There Are No Other or Additional Written or Oral Understandings."

Five or six days later, when the Pickleses went to introduce themselves to the tenants, they discovered raw sewage seeping out of the ground. * * * The Lenawee County Board of Health subsequently condemned the property and initiated this lawsuit in the Lenawee Circuit Court * * * to obtain a permanent injunction proscribing human habitation of the premises until the property was brought into conformance with the Lenawee County sanitation code. The injunction was granted, and the Lenawee County Board of Health was permitted to withdraw from the lawsuit by stipulation of the parties.

When no payments were made on the land contract, the Messerlys filed a cross-complaint against the Pickleses seeking foreclosure, sale of the property, and a deficiency judgment. Mr. and Mrs. Pickles then counterclaimed for rescission. * * *

After a bench trial, the court concluded that the Pickleses had no cause of action * * *

Mr. and Mrs. Pickles appealed from the adverse judgment. The Court of Appeals * * * in a two-to-one decision, reversed the finding of no cause of action on the Pickleses' claims against the Messerlys. It concluded that the mutual mistake between the Messerlys and the Pickleses went to a basic, as opposed to a collateral, element of the contract, and that the parties intended to transfer income-producing rental property but, in actuality, the vendees paid $25,500 for an asset without value.[1]

We granted the Messerlys' application for leave to appeal. * * *

An examination of the record reveals that the septic system was defective prior to the date on which the land contract was executed. The Messerly's grantor installed a nonconforming septic system without a permit prior to the transfer of the property to the Messerlys in 1971. Moreover, virtually undisputed

---

1. [Footnotes renumbered.] The trial court found that the only way that the property could be put to residential use would be to pump and haul the sewage, a method which is economically unfeasible, as the cost of such a disposal system amounts to double the income generated by the property. There was speculation by the trial court that the adjoining land might be utilized to make the property suitable for residential use, but, in the absence of testimony directed at the point, the court refused to draw any conclusions. The trial court and the Court of Appeals both found that the property was valueless, or had a negative value.

testimony indicates that, assuming ideal soil conditions, 2,500 square feet of property is necessary to support a sewage system adequate to serve a three-family dwelling. Likewise, 750 square feet is mandated for a one-family home. Thus, the division of the parcel and sale of one acre of the property by Mr. and Mrs. Barnes in 1976 made it impossible to remedy the already illegal septic system within the confines of the 600–square–foot parcel. * * *

Appellants argue that the parties' mistake relates only to the quality or value of the real estate transferred, and that such mistakes are collateral to the agreement and do not justify rescission, citing A & M Land Development Co. v. Miller, 354 Mich. 681, 94 N.W.2d 197 (1959).

In that case, the plaintiff was the purchaser of 91 lots of real property. It sought partial rescission of the land contract when it was frustrated in its attempts to develop 42 of the lots because it could not obtain permits from the county health department to install septic tanks on these lots. This Court refused to allow rescission because the mistake, whether mutual or unilateral, related only to the value of the property. * * *

Appellees contend, on the other hand, that in this case the parties were mistaken as to the very nature of the character of the consideration and claim that the pervasive and essential quality of this mistake renders rescission appropriate. They cite in support of that view Sherwood v. Walker, 66 Mich. 568, 33 N.W. 919 (1887), the famous "barren cow" case. In that case, the parties agreed to the sale and purchase of a cow which was thought to be barren, but which was, in reality, with calf. When the seller discovered the fertile condition of his cow, he refused to deliver her. * * *

As the parties suggest, the foregoing precedent arguably distinguishes mistakes affecting the essence of the consideration from those which go to its quality or value, affording relief on a per se basis for the former but not the latter.

However, the distinctions which may be drawn from *Sherwood* and *A & M Land Development Co.* do not provide a satisfactory analysis of the nature of a mistake sufficient to invalidate a contract. Often, a mistake relates to an underlying factual assumption which, when discovered, directly affects value, but simultaneously and materially affects the essence of the contractual consideration. It is disingenuous to label such a mistake collateral.

Appellant and appellee both mistakenly believed that the property which was the subject of their land contract would generate income as rental property. The fact that it could not be used for human habitation deprived the property of its income-earning potential and rendered it less valuable. However, this mistake, while directly and dramatically affecting the property's value, cannot accurately be characterized as collateral because it also affects the very essence of the consideration. "The thing sold and bought [income generating rental property] had in fact no existence." Sherwood v. Walker.

We find that the inexact and confusing distinction between contractual mistakes running to value and those touching the substance of the consideration serves only as an impediment to a clear and helpful analysis for the equitable resolution of cases in which mistake is alleged and proven. Accordingly, the holdings of *A & M Land Development Co.* and *Sherwood* with respect to the material or collateral nature of a mistake are limited to the facts of those cases.

Instead, we think the better-reasoned approach is a case-by-case analysis whereby rescission is indicated when the mistaken belief relates to a basic assumption of the parties upon which the contract is made, and which materially affects the agreed performances of the parties. Restatement Contracts, 2d, § 152, pp. 385–386.[2] Rescission is not available, however, to relieve a party who has assumed the risk of loss in connection with the mistake. Restatement Contracts, 2d, §§ 152, 154, pp. 385–386, 402–406.[3]

All of the parties to this contract erroneously assumed that the property transferred by the vendors to the vendees was suitable for human habitation and could be utilized to generate rental income. The fundamental nature of these assumptions is indicated by the fact that their invalidity changed the character of the property transferred, thereby frustrating, indeed precluding, Mr. and Mrs. Pickles' intended use of the real estate. Although the Pickleses are disadvantaged by enforcement of the contract, performance is advantageous to the Messerlys, as the property at issue is less valuable absent its income-earning potential. Nothing short of rescission can remedy the mistake. Thus, the parties' mistake as to a basic assumption materially affects the agreed performances of the parties.

Despite the significance of the mistake made by the parties, we reverse the Court of Appeals * * *

In cases of mistake by two equally innocent parties, we are required, in the exercise of our equitable powers, to determine which blameless party should assume the loss resulting from the misapprehension they shared.[4] * * *

Equity suggests that, in this case, the risk should be allocated to the purchasers. We are guided to that conclusion, in part, by the standards announced in § 154 of the Restatement of Contracts 2d, for determining when a party bears the risk of mistake. Section 154(a) suggests that the court should look first to whether the parties have agreed to the allocation of the risk between themselves. While there is no express assumption in the contract by either party of the risk of the property becoming uninhabitable, there was indeed some agreed allocation of the risk to the vendees by the incorporation of an "as is" clause into the contract which, we repeat, provided:

2. Section 152 delineates the legal significance of a mistake.

"§ 152. When Mistake of Both Parties Makes a Contract Voidable

"(1) Where a mistake of both parties at the time a contract was made as to a basic assumption on which the contract was made has a material effect on the agreed exchange of performances, the contract is voidable by the adversely affected party unless he bears the risk of the mistake under the rule stated in § 154.

"(2) In determining whether the mistake has a material effect on the agreed exchange of performances, account is taken of any relief by way of reformation, restitution, or otherwise."

3. "§ 154. When a Party Bears the Risk of a Mistake

"A party bears the risk of a mistake when

"(a) the risk is allocated to him by agreement of the parties, or

"(b) he is aware, at the time the contract is made, that he has only limited knowledge with respect to the facts to which the mistake relates but treats his limited knowledge as sufficient, or

"(c) the risk is allocated to him by the court on the ground that it is reasonable in the circumstances to do so."

4. This risk-of-loss analysis is absent in both *A & M Land Development Co.* and *Sherwood,* and this omission helps to explain, in part, the disparate treatment in the two cases. Had such an inquiry been undertaken in *Sherwood,* we believe that the result might have been different. Moreover, a determination as to which party assumed the risk in *A & M Land Development Co.* would have alleviated the need to characterize the mistake as collateral so as to justify the result denying rescission. Despite the absence of any inquiry as to the assumption of risk in those two leading cases, we find that there exists sufficient precedent to warrant such an analysis in future cases of mistake.

"Purchaser has examined this property and agrees to accept same in its present condition. There are no other or additional written or oral understandings."

That is a persuasive indication that the parties considered that, as between them, such risk as related to the "present condition" of the property should lie with the purchaser. If the "as is" clause is to have any meaning at all, it must be interpreted to refer to those defects which were unknown at the time that the contract was executed.[5] Thus, the parties themselves assigned the risk of loss to Mr. and Mrs. Pickles.[6]

We conclude that Mr. and Mrs. Pickles are not entitled to the equitable remedy of rescission and, accordingly, reverse the decision of the Court of Appeals.

Notes

1. The Restatement of Restitution's mistake formula is quoted above, p. 502. That test is an elaboration of the Contracts Restatement's test that the Michigan court adopts. Under these modern rules, must the subject bought and sold be a different thing? Must the buyer and seller have intended to form a different contract? Will the modern tests lead courts to reverse more agreements and transfers?

2. *Products Liability "As Is."* A product that a buyer purchased "as is" malfunctioned, injuring the buyer's employee. In the employee's products liability lawsuit, the seller argued that the "as is" clause relieved it from potential liability to the plaintiff. The court distinguished *Lenawee*, above, and let the employee's suit for negligence and implied warranty continue. Inman v. Heidelberg Eastern, Inc., 917 F.Supp. 1154, 1162 (E.D.Mich. 1996).

A court will be more likely to give effect to an "as is" clause in products liability litigation if: (a) the actual buyer sues the seller; (b) the plaintiff sues the seller for property damage, not for personal injury; or (c) the product was used when the buyer bought it. Restatement of Torts: Products Liability § 18, Comments (1998).

MUTUAL OF OMAHA INSURANCE CO. v. RUSSELL

United States Court of Appeals, Tenth Circuit, 1968.
402 F.2d 339, cert. denied, 394 U.S. 973 (1969).

JOHN R. BROWN, CIRCUIT JUDGE. * * * Rev. and Mrs. Russell were residents of Kansas City, Kansas. On Thursday, January 24, 1963, upon receiving word that one of her brothers had died in Lubbock, Texas, Mrs. Russell decided to fly to Lubbock for the funeral. Reservations were made for a flight the next day, Friday, but the return flight was left open because the funeral date had not been set. On Friday Rev. and Mrs. Russell and their son went to the airport in Kansas City, Missouri, picked up their tickets at the Continental Airlines counter, and proceeded toward the awaiting plane.

5. An "as is" clause waives those implied warranties which accompany the sale of a new home. [citation] or the sale of goods. [citation] Since implied warranties protect against latent defects, an "as is" clause will impose upon the purchaser the assumption of the risk of latent defects, such as an inadequate sanitation system, even when there are no implied warranties.

6. An "as is" clause does not preclude a purchaser from alleging fraud or misrepresentation as a basis for rescission. However, Mr. and Mrs. Pickles did not appeal the trial court's finding that there was no fraud or misrepresentation, so we are bound thereby.

As the Russells passed one of Insurer's vending machines for dispensing flight insurance, Rev. Russell decided that Mrs. Russell should have insurance to cover her during the trip. This machine dispensed Insurer's policy T–20. In many ways the T–20 affords severely limited coverage in that it provides protection only for accidents while aboard an airplane or in established limousines going to or coming from the airport. On the other hand, the T–20's coverage expressly remains in effect for the duration of the round trip or for twelve months, whichever occurs first. Similarly, since events and covered occurrences were more restrictive, the face amount of insurance per premium dollar was larger than other policies. Had a T–20 been machine-issued the Assured's death would have been covered. But no one had the proper change to operate the machine, so the Russells stepped just south of the machine to one of Insurer's staffed insurance booths. The booth had signs overhead reading "Flight Insurance" and was attended by a Miss Fletcher.

Rev. Russell asked either for flight insurance or insurance to cover his wife on her round trip to Lubbock. Miss Fletcher then asked "How much?", meaning what amount of insurance coverage. Mrs. Russell asked for the least amount and $20,000 was the amount agreed upon. Without then explaining various policies available, Miss Fletcher took out an application form and began to fill it out. She then asked either how long would Mrs. Russell be gone or when would she be returning. Mrs. Russell turned to her husband and asked "Three days?" Rev. Russell said she should allow herself more than that—at least four days. Miss Fletcher completed the form and turned it around for Mrs. Russell's signature. Mrs. Russell signed and paid the $2.25 premium. Miss Fletcher stapled the policy together and handed it to Rev. Russell.

The policy purchased was not, however, the T–20; rather it was the T–18, a significantly different policy. The T–18 is a general accident policy that covers almost all risks—whether air related or not—during the life of the policy. The term is stated in terms of twenty-four hour periods on a daily basis up to thirty-one days. The premium is higher on the T–18 for the same dollar amount of insurance and the T–18 is not sold in vending machines. As the Schedule signed by Mrs. Russell shows, the T–18 was issued for only four days, and expired at 11:00 a.m., Tuesday, January 29, 1963, about twelve hours prior to the Assured's death.

The District Court credited Rev. Russell's testimony that Miss Fletcher never mentioned any other available policies,[1] did not explain the T–18, and did not warn plaintiff that the policy would expire at 11:00 a.m. on Tuesday, January 29, 1963. The Judge also found that the Assured intended to buy insurance that would cover Mrs. Russell's round trip, which both she and her husband thought would occur within four days.

After buying the insurance, Mrs. Russell boarded her plane and arrived safely in Lubbock, Texas. There the funeral was delayed because a son of the deceased had not arrived from England. The funeral was finally held on Tuesday, January 29, and Mrs. Russell was fatally injured when her airplane crashed that night at 10:45 p.m. while attempting to land at the Kansas City, Missouri, airport. The insurance policy had expired by its own terms about twelve hours earlier. The Insurer denied liability.

---

1. [Footnotes renumbered.] Insurer sold eleven different types of insurance policies at its sales booth.

* * * The District Judge held that the contract was clear and unambiguous and as written did not cover the accident. But now of direct importance he held that as a matter of equity the policy should be reformed to cover the accident. Judgment for $20,000 was entered for the Assured. Insurer appealed contending that it is not liable since the policy had expired and the company was not guilty of any inequitable conduct that would give rise to the remedy of reformation. The Assured cross-appealed contending that the judgment should have been for $90,000, the amount of straight flight insurance (T–20) that $2.25 would have bought, but the Assured did not appeal the decision that the policy could not be construed to cover the accident. * * * Neither party disagrees about the general principles of equity applicable here.[2] The rub comes in the proper application of those principles to the facts of this case. Reformation is an ancient remedy used to reframe written contracts to reflect accurately the real agreement between contracting parties when, either through mutual mistake or unilateral mistake coupled with actual or equitable fraud by the other party, the writing does not embody the contract as actually made.

But reformation is an extraordinary remedy, and courts exercise it with great caution. * * * Even in situations where obvious mistakes have been made, courts will not rewrite the contract between the parties, but will only enforce the legal obligations of the parties according to their original agreement. * * * Here, of course, the Assured does not contend that mutual mistake occurred and it is well that he does not do so for obviously the Insurer intended to sell the exact policy with the exact coverage that it did. Rather, the Assured's theory rests on another accepted reformation doctrine—mistake by one party coupled with constructive or equitable fraud by the other.

Thus the whole case boils down in reality to one question: Did Insurer have a duty to tell the Assured that several insurance policies were available and to explain fully the provisions and limitations of those policies? * * *

As in nearly all cases, an inquiry of this type involves consideration of the competing interests. On the one hand we have the right of the public to be free of fraud and oppression wrought by those in a superior bargaining position. But on the other hand we are confronted with the realities of doing business, the enforcement of contracts, and instability which flows from opening up written contracts to oral accretions.

The Assured urges, and the District Court declared, that an explanation was owing. By whom was it to be given? In what form was it to be offered? Orally or in writing? If orally, how would an insurer conscious of its duty of fair dealing toward a peripatetic public in a hurry assure that an adequate, reliable statement was made? The "explanation" would vary as work shifts changed and sales personnel rotated. They would be expansive or restrictive as the loquacious or taciturn quality of the employee predominated. If the insurer turned to a written statement, how or in what manner would it assure itself that the impatient prospect would pay any more heed to it than the terms of the policy contract? And what happens when, out of an abundance of good faith, an effort is made to explain (in non-legalese) what a legal document prescribes? And as to either method or a mixture of both, what are the significant distinctions to be pointed out? Which ones to emphasize? To minimize? To omit? How many policies need to be explained? Just the two most common—T–20 and T–18? Or all eleven? In the meantime what is happening to time—that precious irreplaceable which

2. And neither party disagrees that this is a case of first impression.

accounts for the traveler's pressure at the airport facing either dispensing machine or an attractive sales person who may well try harder but without benefit of a legal education? The flight would either be missed or the "offer" of flight insurance withdrawn for want of adequate time for equity's mandated "explanation."[3] Hardship, or what seems to be hardship, may sometimes occur if the law adheres to its long-held notions of the non-variability of written contracts. But a too-quick relaxation in the contrails of the jet age might well be worse, not better.[4]

We think that imposing a duty to offer such explanations under circumstances of this kind—requiring as it does an effort by lay persons to interpret the legal meaning of the proposed contract as well as others available—would be fraught with great danger to the stability of contracts. * * *

The printed contract controls. There it ends.

Reversed.

Notes

1. *News Item.* Raymond George collected $6,745 at Hollywood Park Saturday, cashing in $50 worth of win tickets he desperately tried to unload before the fifth race.

George asked for five $10 win tickets on No. 9, Astor Place. By mistake, he was sold tickets on No. 10, Partner's Hope. When the mutual clerk failed to sell the "wrong" tickets before the race, George was stuck with them. Partner's Hope won and paid $269.80 for $2.

To say he was unhappy about the situation—Partner's Hope was a 99–1 shot on the toteboard—when the error occurred, is an understatement.

"He was really hot about it," said E.G. Anderson, a track security officer. "He was demanding his money back, and I took him to the information window to have him fill out the proper forms. About then one of his friends came running up to tell him the horse had won."

Question: did the racetrack have the remedy of reformation?

2. *Reformation or Rescission?* Subtle considerations may bear on whether to request reformation or rescission. Consider the late Seavers, co-owners of an airplane. Mr. Seaver took out a liability policy in his name; he represented that he was the sole and unconditional owner. If he had listed Mrs. Seaver properly as co-owner, she would have been excluded from coverage if her husband was negligent. The Seavers were killed when the plane crashed. When her estate sued his estate, the insurance company was tendered the defense. The insurer requested reformation and won. Under the reformed policy with Mrs. Seaver a co-owner, the policy remained in

---

3. Of course, if in answer to an inquiry by a prospect or by an affirmative statement made by the insurer's agent to the prospect it was indicated that the policy would cover the round trip, then the insurer would certainly have to give some explanatory warning before issuing a T–18 policy which is for a fixed period of time, and not written in terms of round trip.

4. Consider, for example, the T–18 policy which Rev. Russell bought. Although it is a short-term policy, the coverage provisions are much broader and more inclusive than a straight flight insurance policy (the T–20). For example, if Mrs. Russell had been killed in a taxi smashup while riding to the Lubbock airport for her return flight or had she been killed in a hotel fire while there, she would have been covered under the T–18 but not under the T–20. Would the machine-sale of a T–20 be defective for want of a warning recording that at the nearby counter, better or different coverage was available?

force (figuratively speaking); but, because of the exclusion, the policy did not cover the claim. Why might the insurer not rescind for the misrepresentation? If so, the premiums should be returned. See Monarch Insurance Co. v. Lankard, 715 F.Supp. 304 (D.Kan. 1989).

3. ILLEGALITY—VIOLATION OF PUBLIC POLICY

A court will decline to award a plaintiff contract remedies for breach of a contract for illegal consideration or a contract that violates public policy. Indeed if evidence of illegality appears, the judge may, sua sponte, deny both parties any relief even though neither party raises the defense.

What does the illegality-public policy defense include? Not many plaintiffs file lawsuits for breaches of defendants' contracts to sell illegal drugs; for the parties to a drug transaction typically find another venue for their particular form of alternative dispute resolution. In disputes that people actually litigate, less obviously "illegal" transactions fall under the headings of illegality and violation of public policy—Sunday contracts, unlicensed contractors, bribes and kickbacks, gambling debts and agreements, and restraints on alienation. The two difficult decisions which follow examine whether transactions violate public policy.

The court, it is often said, will refuse all relief on an illegal contract; the court will leave the parties where it found them. If that rubric means that the judge will refuse to countenance granting the contract remedies, either specific performance or expectancy damages for breach, then we will not argue.

But what about restitution to prevent one party's unjust enrichment? If the a court grants one party restitution, does that differ from granting the "contract" remedies of expectancy damages and specific performance? Are the reasons to ban specific performance and expectancy damages persuasive enough to prevent the judge from granting restitution to prevent one party's unjust enrichment? In other words, does refusing a plaintiff relief on an illegal contract also mean that the judge will leave another party unjustly enriched?

Typically, a buyer of land under an oral contract may recover her down payment if the seller repudiates the agreement. If a statute says that parties may not form a contract on Sunday, may a land purchaser under an "illegal" Sunday contract recover restitution of her down payment? Where the contract was contrary to the Free State's Blue Laws when made, but the statute had been amended prospectively, the Maryland court ordered the seller to make restitution to a buyer who had repudiated the "illegal" contract. Woel v. Griffith, 253 Md. 451, 253 A.2d 353 (1969).

The sweeping statement that forbids a court from aiding either party to an illegal transaction is too broad. After finding that a contract is illegal or violates public policy, the court ought to ask in addition: (a) was one party unjustly enriched? and (b) will ordering restitution to prevent that unjust enrichment conflict with those policies? Professor Palmer suggested that the court should consider "the seriousness of the illegality, the nature of the plaintiff's participation, the injustice of the specific enrichment, and whether a judgment depriving the defendant of that enrichment will subvert the policy underlying the rule of law that makes the transaction illegal." George Palmer, The Law of Restitution § 8.1 at 174 (1978).

BOVARD v. AMERICAN HORSE ENTERPRISES, INC.

California Court of Appeal, 1988.
201 Cal.App.3d 832, 247 Cal.Rptr. 340.

PUGLIA, PRESIDING JUSTICE. * * * [P]laintiff Bovard separately sued defendants Ralph and American Horse Enterprises, Inc. a corporation, * * * to recover on promissory notes executed by defendants in connection with Ralph's purchase of the corporation in 1978 [from Bovard]. * * *

On the third day of trial, Bovard testified as to the nature of the business conducted by American Horse Enterprises, Inc., at the time the corporation was sold to Ralph. Bovard explained the corporation made jewelry and drug paraphernalia, which consisted of "roach clips" and "bongs" used to smoke marijuana and tobacco. At that point the trial court excused the jury and asked counsel to prepare arguments on the question whether the contract for sale of the corporation was illegal and void.

The following day, after considering the arguments of counsel, the trial court dismissed the * * * complaint. The court found that the corporation predominantly produced paraphernalia used to smoke marijuana and was not engaged significantly in jewelry production, and that Bovard had recovered the corporate machinery through self-help. The parties do not challenge these findings. The court acknowledged that the manufacture of drug paraphernalia was not itself illegal in 1978 when Bovard and Ralph contracted for the sale of American Horse Enterprises, Inc. However, the court concluded a public policy against the manufacture of drug paraphernalia was implicit in the statute making the possession, use and transfer of marijuana unlawful.[1] The trial court held the consideration for the contract was contrary to the policy of express law, and the contract was therefore illegal and void. Finally, the court found the parties were in pari delicto and thus with respect to their contractual dispute should be left as the court found them.

"The consideration of a contract must be lawful within the meaning of section sixteen hundred and sixty-seven." (Civ.Code, § 1607.) "That is not lawful which is: 1. Contrary to an express provision of law; 2. Contrary to the policy of express law, though not expressly prohibited; or, 3. Otherwise contrary to good morals." (Civ.Code, § 1667.) "If any part of a single consideration for one or more objects, or of several considerations for a single object, is unlawful, the entire contract is void." (Civ.Code, § 1608.)

The trial court concluded the consideration for the contract was contrary to the policy of the law as expressed in the statute prohibiting the possession, use and transfer of marijuana. Whether a contract is contrary to public policy is a question of law to be determined from the circumstances of the particular case. [citations] Here, the critical facts are not in dispute. Whenever a court becomes aware that a contract is illegal, it has a duty to refrain from entertaining an action to enforce the contract. [citations] Furthermore the court will not permit the parties to maintain an action to settle or compromise a claim based on an illegal contract. [citations]

The question whether a contract violates public policy necessarily involves a degree of subjectivity. Therefore, " * * * courts have been cautious in blithely

---

1. [Footnotes renumbered.] The manufacture of drug paraphernalia, including bongs and roach clips, was made criminal effective January 1, 1983.

applying public policy reasons to nullify otherwise enforceable contracts. This concern has been graphically articulated by the California Supreme Court as follows: 'It has been well said that public policy is an unruly horse, astride of which you are carried into unknown and uncertain paths. * * * While contracts opposed to morality or law should not be allowed to show themselves in courts of justice, yet public policy requires and encourages the making of contracts by competent parties upon all valid and lawful considerations, and courts so recognizing have allowed parties the widest latitude in this regard; and, unless it is entirely plain that a contract is violative of sound public policy, a court will never so declare. 'The power of the courts to declare a contract void for being in contravention of sound public policy is a very delicate and undefined power, and, like the power to declare a statute unconstitutional, should be exercised only in cases free from doubt.' [citation] * * * " No court ought to refuse its aid to enforce a contract on doubtful and uncertain grounds. The burden is on the defendant to show that its enforcement would be in violation of the settled public policy of this state, or injurious to the morals of its people. [citation] Moran v. Harris (1982) 131 Cal.App.3d 913, 919–920, 182 Cal.Rptr. 519, quoting Stephens v. Southern Pacific Co. (1895) 109 Cal. 86, 89–90, 41 P. 783.)

Bovard places great reliance on Moran v. Harris to support his argument the trial court erred in finding the contract violative of public policy. In *Moran,* two lawyers entered into a fee splitting agreement relative to a case referred by one to the other. The agreement was made in 1972, ten months before the adoption of a rule of professional conduct prohibiting such agreements. In 1975, the attorney to whom the case had been referred settled the case, but then refused to split the attorney's fees with the referring attorney. The trial court held the fee splitting contract violated public policy. The appellate court reversed, noting the rule of professional conduct had been amended effective January 1, 1979, to permit fee splitting agreements; thus there was no statute or rule prohibiting fee splitting agreements either at the time the attorneys' contract was formed or after January 1, 1979, during the pendency of the action to enforce the fee splitting contract. Therefore, the court held there was no basis for a finding that the contract violated public policy.

Here, in contrast to *Moran,* there is positive law on which to premise a finding of public policy, although the trial court did not find the manufacture of marijuana paraphernalia against public policy on the basis of the later enacted ordinance or statute prohibiting such manufacture. Rather, the court's finding was based on a statute prohibiting the possession, use and transfer of marijuana which long antedated the parties' contract.[2]

Moran suggests factors to consider in analyzing whether a contract violates public policy: "Before labeling a contract as being contrary to public policy, courts must carefully inquire into the nature of the conduct, the extent of public harm which may be involved, and the moral quality of the conduct of the parties in light of the prevailing standards of the community. [citations]"

These factors are more comprehensively set out in the Restatement Second of Contracts section 178:

"(1) A promise or other term of an agreement is unenforceable on grounds of public policy if legislation provides that it is unenforceable or the

---

2. "In determining whether the subject of a given contract violates public policy, courts must rely on the state of the law as it existed at the time the contract was made. [citations]" (Moran v. Harris.)

interest in its enforcement is clearly outweighed in the circumstances by a public policy against the enforcement of such terms.

"(2) In weighing the interest in the enforcement of a term, account is taken of

"(a) the parties' justified expectations,

"(b) any forfeiture that would result if enforcement were denied, and

"(c) any special public interest in the enforcement of the particular term.

"(3) In weighing a public policy against enforcement of a term, account is taken of

"(a) the strength of that policy as manifested by legislation or judicial decisions,

"(b) the likelihood that a refusal to enforce the term will further that policy,

"(c) the seriousness of any misconduct involved and the extent to which it was deliberate, and

"(d) the directness of the connection between that misconduct and the term."

Applying the Restatement test to the present circumstances, we conclude the interest in enforcing this contract is very tenuous. Neither party was reasonably justified in expecting the government would not eventually act to geld American Horse Enterprises, a business harnessed to the production of paraphernalia used to facilitate the use of an illegal drug. Moreover, although voidance of the contract imposed a forfeiture on Bovard, he did recover the corporate machinery, the only assets of the business which could be used for lawful purposes, i.e., to manufacture jewelry. Thus, the forfeiture was significantly mitigated if not negligible. Finally, there is no special public interest in the enforcement of this contract, only the general interest in preventing a party to a contract from avoiding a debt.

On the other hand, the Restatement factors favoring a public policy against enforcement of this contract are very strong. As we have explained, the public policy against manufacturing paraphernalia to facilitate the use of marijuana is strongly implied in the statutory prohibition against the possession, use, etc., of marijuana, a prohibition which dates back at least to 1929. Obviously, refusal to enforce the instant contract will further that public policy not only in the present circumstances but by serving notice on manufacturers of drug paraphernalia that they may not resort to the judicial system to protect or advance their business interests. Moreover, it is immaterial that the business conducted by American Horse Enterprises was not expressly prohibited by law when Bovard and Ralph made their agreement since both parties knew that the corporation's products would be used primarily for purposes which were expressly illegal. We conclude the trial court correctly declared the contract contrary to the policy of express law and therefore illegal and void. * * *

[Affirmed.]

Questions

1. Should the court treat the parties' credit transaction the same way it would treat their agreement for the illegal drug itself?

2.   Does the court allow a buyer to keep, without paying, assets that the buyer and others can use for illegal conduct? Does that result really advance the policy that led the legislature to forbid the conduct?

3.   Would it make any difference if a cancer patient used some of the marijuana "paraphernalia" for medicinal purposes legal under state law? Although nine states' laws allowed people to grow and use it for therapeutic purposes, in 2005, the Supreme Court held that Congress could prohibit people from growing and using marijuana for medicinal purposes. Gonzales v. Raich, 545 U.S. 1 (2005).

R.R. v. M.H. & ANOTHER, D.H., THE HUSBAND OF M.H.

Supreme Judicial Court of Massachusetts, 1998.
426 Mass. 501, 689 N.E.2d 790.

WILKINS, CHIEF JUSTICE. On a report by a judge in the Probate and Family Court, we are concerned with the validity of a surrogacy parenting agreement between the plaintiff (father) and the defendant (mother). Both the mother and the father are married but not to each other. A child was conceived through artificial insemination of the mother with the father's sperm, after the mother and father had executed the surrogate parenting agreement. The agreement provided that the father would have custody of the child. During the sixth month of her pregnancy and after she had received funds from the father pursuant to the surrogacy agreement, the mother changed her mind and decided that she wanted to keep the child.

The father thereupon brought this action and obtained a preliminary order awarding him temporary custody of the child. The mother's appeal from that order is moot because the parties have since agreed on custody and visitation and the judge has approved that agreement. We, therefore, do not discuss the circumstances of the temporary custody order, and nothing we say in this opinion should be understood to suggest that the subjects of custody or visitation need be reconsidered. The judge's order granting the preliminary injunction is before us on her report of the propriety of that order which was based in part on her conclusion that the father was likely to prevail on his assertion that the surrogacy agreement is enforceable. * * * The question of the enforceability of the surrogacy agreement is before us. * * * This court has not previously dealt with the enforceability of a surrogacy agreement.

The baby girl who is the subject of this action was born on August 15, 1997, in Leominster. The defendant mother and the plaintiff father are her biological parents. The father and his wife, who live in Rhode Island, were married in June, 1989. The wife is infertile. Sometime in 1994, she and the father learned of an egg donor program but did not pursue it because the procedure was not covered by insurance and had a relatively low success rate. Because of their ages (they were both in their forties), they concluded that pursuing adoption was not feasible. In April, 1996, responding to a newspaper advertisement for surrogacy services, they consulted a Rhode Island attorney who had drafted surrogacy contracts for both surrogates and couples seeking surrogacy services. On the attorney's advice, the father and his wife consulted the New England Surrogate Parenting Advisors (NESPA), a for-profit corporation that helps infertile couples find women willing to act as surrogate mothers. They entered into a contract with NESPA in September, 1996, and paid a fee of $6,000.

Meanwhile, in the spring of 1996, the mother, who was married and had two children, responded to a NESPA advertisement. She reported to NESPA that her family was complete and that she desired to allow others less fortunate than herself to have children. The mother submitted a surrogacy application to NESPA. The judge found that the mother was motivated to apply to NESPA by a desire to be pregnant, in order to earn money, and to help an infertile couple.

In October, Dr. Angela Figueroa of NESPA brought the mother together with the father and his wife. They had a seemingly informative exchange of information and views. The mother was advised to seek an attorney's advice concerning the surrogacy agreement. Shortly thereafter, the mother, the father, and his wife met again to discuss the surrogacy and other matters. The mother also met with a clinical psychologist as part of NESPA's evaluation of her suitability to act as a surrogate. The psychologist, who also evaluated the father and his wife, advised the mother to consult legal counsel, to give her husband a chance to air his concerns, to discuss arrangements for contact with the child, to consider and discuss her expectations concerning termination of the pregnancy, and to arrange a meeting between her husband and the father and his wife. Her husband had had a vasectomy in 1994 and did not have sexual relations with the mother after October, 1996. The psychologist concluded that the mother was solid, thoughtful, and well grounded, that she would have no problem giving the child to the father, and that she was happy to act as a surrogate. The mother told the psychologist that she was not motivated by money, although she did plan to use the funds received for her children's education. The mother's husband told the psychologist by telephone that he supported his wife's decision.

The mother signed the surrogate parenting agreement and her signature was notarized on November 1. The father signed on November 18. The agreement stated that the parties intended that the "Surrogate shall be inseminated with the semen of Natural Father" and "that, on the birth of the child or children so conceived, Natural Father, as the Natural Father, will have the full legal parental rights of a father, and surrogate will permit Natural Father to take the child or children home from the hospital to live with he [sic] and his wife." The agreement acknowledged that the mother's parental rights would not terminate if she permitted the father to take the child home and have custody, that the mother could at any time seek to enforce her parental rights by court order, but that, if she attempted to obtain custody or visitation rights, she would forfeit her rights under the agreement and would be obligated to reimburse the father for all fees and expenses paid to her under it. The agreement provided that its interpretation would be governed by Rhode Island law. [But the court held Massachusetts law governed.]

The agreement provided for compensation to the mother in the amount of $10,000 "for services rendered in conceiving, carrying and giving birth to the Child." Payment of the $10,000 was to be made as follows: $500 on verification of the pregnancy; $2,500 at the end of the third month; $3,500 at the end of the sixth month; and $3,500 at the time of birth "and when delivery of child occurs." The agreement stated that no payment was made in connection with adoption of the child, the termination of parental rights, or consent to surrender the child for adoption. The father acknowledged the mother's right to determine whether to carry the pregnancy to term, but the mother agreed to refund all payments if, without the father's consent, she had an abortion that was not necessary for her physical health. The father assumed various expenses of the pregnancy, including tests, and had the right to name the child. The mother would be obliged, however, to repay all expenses and fees for services if tests showed that the father was not the biological father of the child, or if the mother refused to permit the father to take the child home from the hospital. The agreement also provided that the mother would maintain some contact with the child after the birth.

The judge found that the mother entered into the agreement on her own volition after consulting legal counsel. There was no evidence of undue influence, coercion, or duress. The mother fully understood that she was contracting to give custody of the baby to the father. She sought to inseminate herself on November 30 and December 1, 1996. The attempt at conception was successful.

The lawyer for the father sent the mother a check for $500 in December, 1996, and another for $2,500 in February. In May, the father's lawyer sent the mother a check for $3,500. She told the lawyer that she had changed her mind and wanted to keep the child. She returned the check uncashed in the middle of June. The mother has made no attempt to refund the amounts that the father paid her, including $550 that he paid for pregnancy-related expenses.

Approximately two weeks after the mother changed her mind and returned the check for $3,500, and before the child was born, the father commenced this action against the mother seeking to establish his paternity, alleging breach of contract, and requesting a declaration of his rights under the surrogacy agreement. Subsequently, the wife's husband was added as a defendant. The judge appointed a guardian ad litem to represent the interests of the unborn child. Proceedings were held on aspects of the preliminary injunction request (now resolved) and on the mother's motion to determine whether surrogacy contracts are enforceable in Massachusetts.

On August 4, 1997, the judge entered an order directing the mother to give the child to the father when it was discharged from the hospital and granting the father temporary physical custody of the child. She did so based on her determination that the father's custody claim was likely to prevail on the merits of the contract claim, and, if not on that claim, then on the basis of the best interests of the child. The mother was granted the right to frequent visits.

On August 13, 1997, the judge reported the propriety of her August 1 order which, as we have said, was based in part on her conclusion that the surrogacy contract was enforceable. She * * * set forth the [following] questions:

> 1. Is a surrogacy contract enforceable, wherein a woman, the egg donor, provides child bearing services to a man, the semen donor, and delivers to him physical custody of their child in exchange for monetary consideration, and which further provides that she retains her constitutional rights to abortion during pregnancy and to parental rights after the birth of the child, but conditions and limits the exercise of those rights, unless she forgoes the benefits of the contract and/or makes restitution of benefits already received? If the answer to the question on contract enforceability is affirmative, secondary questions that derive from the primary question are: 2. If the surrogate mother has received payment for her services, is specific performance an appropriate remedy for her breach, as to the provision that she relinquish physical custody of the child when born? 3. Under what circumstances would such a contract be unconscionable? * * *

A significant minority of States have legislation addressing surrogacy agreements. Some simply deny enforcement of all such agreements. [Citing statutes in Arizona, the District of Columbia, Indiana, Michigan, New York, North Dakota, and Utah.] Others expressly deny enforcement only if the surrogate is to be compensated. [Citing statutes in Kentucky, Louisiana, Nebraska, and Washington.] Some States have simply exempted surrogacy agreements from provisions making it a crime to sell babies. [Citing statutes in Alabama, Iowa, and West Virginia.] A few States have explicitly made unpaid surrogacy agreements lawful. [Citing statutes in Florida, Nevada, New Hampshire, and Virginia.] Florida, New Hampshire, and Virginia require that the intended mother be infertile. [citations] New Hampshire and Virginia place restrictions on who may act as a surrogate and require advance judicial approval of the agreement. [citations] New Hampshire permits the surrogate to opt out of the agreement to surrender custody at any time up to seventy-two hours after birth. [citation] Virginia allows a surrogate who is the child's genetic mother to terminate the agreement within 180 days of the last assisted conception. [citation] Last Arkansas raises a presumption that a child born to a surrogate mother is the child of the intended parents and not the surrogate. [citation]

There are few appellate court opinions on the enforceability of traditional surrogacy agreements. The Kentucky Legislature * * * has provided that a compensated surrogacy agreement is unenforceable, thus changing the rule that the Supreme Court of Kentucky announced [citation]. In In re Marriage of Moschetta, 25 Cal.App.4th 1218, 30 Cal.Rptr.2d 893 (1994), the court declined to enforce a traditional surrogacy agreement because it was incompatible with California parentage and adoption statutes. The surrogate, who was to be paid $10,000, had agreed that (a) the father could obtain sole custody of any resulting child, (b) she would agree to terminate her parental rights, and (c) she would aid the father's wife in adopting the child. The court sent the case back to the trial court for a determination whether the father should be awarded primary physical custody.

The best known opinion is that of the Supreme Court of New Jersey in Matter of Baby M., 109 N.J. 396, 537 A.2d 1227 (1988), where the court invalidated a compensated surrogacy contract because it conflicted with the law and public policy of the State. The *Baby M* surrogacy agreement involved broader concessions from the mother than the agreement before us because it provided that the mother would surrender her parental rights and would allow the father's wife to adopt the child. The agreement, therefore, directly conflicted with a statute prohibiting the payment of money to obtain an adoption and a statute barring enforcement of an agreement to adoption made prior to the birth of the child. The court acknowledged that an award of custody to the father was in the best interests of the child, but struck down orders terminating the mother's parental rights and authorizing the adoption of the child by the husband's wife. The court added that it found no "legal prohibition against surrogacy when the surrogate mother volunteers, without any payment, to act as a surrogate and is given the right to change her mind and to assert her parental rights." * * *

The case before us concerns traditional surrogacy, in which the fertile member of an infertile couple is one of the child's biological parents. Surrogate fatherhood, the insemination of the fertile wife with sperm of a donor, often an anonymous donor, is a recognized and accepted procedure. In Adoption of Galen, 425 Mass. 201, 680 N.E.2d 70 (1997), and in Adoption of Tammy, 416 Mass. 205, 619 N.E.2d 315 (1993), each involving the surrogate fatherhood of a child, we upheld the right of a woman to adopt the child of a woman with whom she had a committed relationship.

If the mother's husband consents to the procedure, the resulting child is considered the legitimate child of the mother and her husband. General Laws c. 46, § 4B. Section 4B does not comment on the rights and obligations, if any, of the biological father, although inferentially he has none. In the case before us, the infertile spouse is the wife. No statute decrees the consequences of the artificial insemination of a surrogate with the sperm of a fertile husband. This situation presents different considerations from surrogate fatherhood because surrogate motherhood is never anonymous and her commitment and contribution is unavoidably much greater than that of a sperm donor.

We must face the possible application of G.L. c. 46, § 4B, to this case. Section 4B tells us that a husband who consents to the artificial insemination of his wife with the sperm of another is considered to be the father of any resulting child. In the case before us, the birth mother was married at the time of her artificial insemination. Despite what he told the psychologist, her husband was not supportive of her desire to become a surrogate parent but acknowledged that it was her decision and her body. The husband, who filed a complaint for divorce on August 8, 1997, may have simply been indifferent because he knew that the marriage was falling apart. The judge found that he was not the biological father of the child. His interest might have been vastly greater if he had been informed that § 4B literally says that any child produced by the artificial insemination of his wife with his consent would be his legitimate child whom he would have a duty to support. It is doubtful, however, that the Legislature intended § 4B to apply to the child of a married surrogate mother. Section 4B seems to concern the status of a child born to a fertile mother whose husband, presumably infertile, consented to her artificial insemination with the sperm of another man so that the couple could have a child biologically related to the mother.

Adoption statutes. Policies underlying our adoption legislation suggest that a surrogate parenting agreement should be given no effect if the mother's agreement was obtained prior to a reasonable time after the child's birth or if her agreement was induced by the payment of money. Adoption legislation is, of course, not applicable to child custody, but it does provide us with some guidance. Although the agreement makes no reference to adoption and does not concern the termination of parental rights or the adoption of the child by the father's wife, the normal expectation in the case of a surrogacy agreement seems to be that the father's wife will adopt the child with the consent of the mother (and the father). Under G.L. c. 210, § 2, adoption requires the written consent of the father and the mother but, in these circumstances, not the mother's husband. Any such consent, written, witnessed, and notarized, is not to be executed "sooner than the fourth calendar day after the date of birth of the child to be adopted." That statutory standard should be interpreted as providing that no mother may effectively agree to surrender her child for adoption earlier than the fourth day after its birth, by which time she better knows the strength of her bond with her child. Although a consent to surrender custody has less permanency than a consent to adoption, the legislative judgment that a mother should have time after a child's birth to reflect on her wishes concerning the child weighs heavily in our consideration whether to give effect to a prenatal custody agreement. No private agreement concerning adoption or custody can be conclusive in any event because a judge, passing on custody of a child, must decide what is in the best interests of the child.

Adoptive parents may pay expenses of a birth parent but may make no direct payment to her. [citations] Even though the agreement seeks to attribute that payment of $10,000, not to custody or adoption, but solely to the mother's services in carrying the child, the father ostensibly was promised more than those services because, as a practical matter, the mother agreed to surrender custody of the child. She could assert custody rights, according to the agreement, only if she repaid the father all amounts that she had received and also reimbursed him for all expenses he had incurred. The statutory prohibition of payment for receiving a child through adoption suggests that, as a matter of policy, a mother's agreement to surrender custody in exchange for money (beyond pregnancy-related expenses) should be given no effect in deciding the custody of the child.

Conclusion. The mother's purported consent to custody in the agreement is ineffective because no such consent should be recognized unless given on or after the fourth day following the child's birth. In reaching this conclusion, we apply to consent to custody the same principle which underlies the statutory restriction on when a mother's consent to adoption may be effectively given. Moreover, the payment of money to influence the mother's custody decision makes the agreement as to custody void. Eliminating any financial reward to a surrogate mother is the only way to assure that no economic pressure will cause a woman, who may well be a member of an economically vulnerable class, to act as a surrogate. It is true that a surrogate enters into the agreement before she becomes pregnant and thus is not presented with the desperation that a poor unwed pregnant woman may confront. However, compensated surrogacy arrangements raise the concern that, under financial pressure, a woman will permit her body to be used and her child to be given away.

There is no doubt that compensation was a factor in inducing the mother to enter into the surrogacy agreement and to cede custody to the father. If the payment of $10,000 was really only compensation for the mother's services in carrying the child and giving birth and was unrelated to custody of the child, the agreement would not have provided that the mother must refund all compensation paid (and expenses paid) if she should challenge the father's right to custody. Nor would the agreement have provided that final payment be made only when the child is delivered to the father. We simply decline, on public policy grounds, to apply to a surrogacy agreement of the type involved here the general principle that an agreement between informed, mature adults should be enforced absent proof of duress, fraud, or undue influence.

We recognize that there is nothing inherently unlawful in an arrangement by which an informed woman agrees to attempt to conceive artificially and give birth to a child whose father would be the husband of an infertile wife. We suspect that many such arrangements are made and carried out without disagreement.

If no compensation is paid beyond pregnancy-related expenses and if the mother is not bound by her consent to the father's custody of the child unless she consents after a suitable period has passed following the child's birth, the objections we have identified in this opinion to the enforceability of a surrogate's consent to custody would be overcome. Other conditions might be important in deciding the enforceability of a surrogacy agreement, such as a requirement that (a) the mother's husband give his informed consent to the agreement in advance; (b) the mother be an adult and have had at least one successful pregnancy; (c) the mother, her husband, and the intended parents have been evaluated for the soundness of their judgment and for their capacity to carry out the agreement;

(d) the father's wife be incapable of bearing a child without endangering her health; (e) the intended parents be suitable persons to assume custody of the child; and (f) all parties have the advice of counsel. The mother and father may not, however, make a binding best-interests-of-the-child determination by private agreement. Any custody agreement is subject to a judicial determination of custody based on the best interests of the child.

The conditions that we describe are not likely to be satisfactory to an intended father because, following the birth of the child, the mother can refuse to consent to the father's custody even though the father has incurred substantial pregnancy-related expenses. A surrogacy agreement judicially approved before conception may be a better procedure, as is permitted by statutes in Virginia and New Hampshire. A Massachusetts statute concerning surrogacy agreements, pro or con, would provide guidance to judges, lawyers, infertile couples interested in surrogate parenthood, and prospective surrogate mothers.

The National Conference of Commissioners on Uniform State Laws has approved alternative proposals concerning surrogacy agreements. One alternative simply states that "[a]n agreement in which a woman agrees to become a surrogate or to relinquish her rights and duties as parent of a child thereafter conceived through assisted conception is void." The other alternative provides for judicial approval of an agreement before conception if various conditions are met and allows the payment of compensation. [citation]

We do not reach but comment briefly on the mother's argument that the agreement was unconscionable. She actively sought to become a surrogate and entered into the surrogacy agreement voluntarily, advised by counsel, not under duress, and fully informed. Unconscionability is not apparent on this record.

A declaration shall be entered that the surrogacy agreement is not enforceable. Such further orders as may be appropriate, consistent with this opinion, may be entered in the Probate and Family Court.

So ordered.

Notes

1. *Sale?, Services?* R.R.'s consideration was money; he is analogous to a buyer or employer. What did M.H. promise in return for R.R.'s money? Did she agree to sell a baby or to furnish gestation services?

2. *Substitute?* What does "surrogate" mean in the context of the parties' agreement? From M.H.'s perspective after she has changed her mind, in what sense was she a "substitute"?

3. *A Contrast.* In re Marriage of Buzzanca concerned, not the validity, but the consequences, of a surrogacy agreement.

Jaycee was conceived after John and Luanne Buzzacana paid $10,000 to a gestational surrogate mother and used anonymous egg and sperm. John, who filed for divorce before Jaycee was born, sought to avoid paying Luanne child support.

The trial court decided that, without a formal adoption, it lacked jurisdiction to award child support between two people who were biologically unrelated to the child. In effect, Jaycee lacked legal parents. The judge's conclusion did not survive on appeal.

The appellate court found, first, that Luanne was Jaycee's "legal" mother who did not need to adopt her. "[T]here is absolutely no dispute that Luanne caused

Jaycee's conception and birth by initiating the surrogacy arrangement whereby an embryo was implanted into a woman who agreed to carry the baby to term on Luanne's behalf."

Second, the court found that John was Jaycee's legal father. "[F]or all practical purposes John caused Jaycee's conception every bit as much as if things had been done the old fashioned way." [Editor: not quite.]

Third, more to the point, the court held that John is obligated to pay Luanne child support. In re Marriage of Buzzanca, 61 Cal.App.4th 1410, 1425, 72 Cal.Rptr.2d 280, 291 (1998).

Questions About R.R. v. M.H. Did the parties' intent triumph over biology? Is the parties' intent a more satisfactory basis for a judicial decision than the "unruly horse" of public policy? If the Massachusetts court had subscribed to an intent-to-parent standard, would it have decided R.R. v. M.H. differently? Remember two things about the R.R.-M.H. surrogacy agreement: how it created a disincentive for the biological mother to challenge child custody; and how it apparently required the mother's husband to pay child support.

4. *The Process or the Substance?* (a) *The Process.* One the one hand, the court in R.R. v. M.H. emphasizes the idea that the process leading up to the parties' agreement was unsatisfactory because a woman cannot make a binding commitment to relinquish a baby before the end of the "cooling off" period when the baby is four days old. The traditional "procedural" defenses are lack of capacity, duress, undue influence, and fraud. Are you satisfied that none of them exist? What about "procedural unconscionability"?

How many agreements are preceded by as much consultation, advice, and deliberation as this one was? Given all the groundwork, should the court have barred the birth mother from agreeing to relinquish custody until after the baby is four days old?

(b) *The Substance.* On the other hand, the court does imply that some types of agreements are intrinsically too unfair to one party to be recognized as contracts. Does the court really consider "substantive" unconscionability?

Why might a court upset parties' agreement on public policy grounds? One reason is to protect the "weaker" party, for example to prevent an employee from working for an employer for less than the minimum wage. Another reason is that the court disapproves of the subject matter of one side of the exchange, for example illegal drugs. Is either reason involved in R.R. v. M.H.?

5. *Source of Public Policy.* How do the state's adoption statutes affect the court's common-law role of determining whether the parties' agreement violated public policy?

The state's adoption statutes do not apply to an agreement to surrender custody. The state has a statute approving surrogate fatherhood. If a male can be compensated as a sperm donor, why should a court disapprove someone who compensates a female who serves as a womb donor? Why not extend the policy of the surrogate-fatherhood statute to approve surrogate motherhood?

Why does the court instead extend the policies of the adoption statutes? Does the court think that, in effect, the custody agreement is really one for adoption? Are the policies of the adoption statutes to prevent "baby-selling," to protect birth mothers, and to preserve the court's role in adoption and child custody? Do those policies control here?

If the Uniform Laws commissioners cannot make up their minds about a surrogacy statute, should the court expect the state legislature to enact one?

The "public" policy must come from the government. Here does it really come from judges, rather than the legislature?

Does the court subordinate the public policy of protecting the parties' bargained expectations?

6. *Approval of Surrogacy.* Regarding the decision a difficult one, the court sets out circumstances which would support approval of surrogacy. Why might the court think it appropriate to be an uncompensated surrogate but inappropriate to carry a baby for money?

Does the court vacillate between approving altruism and setting moral boundaries on market activity? Should the court move beyond altruism and approve payment? Does the court depart from contract principles of autonomy, bargaining, and consent? Where the government, through its legislature, has expressed itself ambiguously, should judges let the parties' bargained expectations govern? Would more of a market-based approach open opportunities for both childless couples and low-income women?

Or is the court's message to go ahead with a surrogacy arrangement, but to provide for payment to coincide with performance?

7. *Restitution When an Agreement Violates Public Policy.* When a court finds that the parties' agreement is contrary to public policy, it should reject specific performance and expectancy damages. The controversy is about whether the court ought to refuse restitution as well. Many decisions say the court will leave both parties to an illegal contract where it finds them; other courts grant restitution under limited circumstances to avoid one party's unjust enrichment.

Suppose M.H. had cashed the $3,500 check instead of returning it. If she had received $6,500 before changing her mind, should the court require her to refund it? Does your answer depend on something we don't know for sure, who has custody of the child?

Suppose that although the agreement called for the mother to be paid $10,000, the father somehow has custody of the baby but had paid the mother nothing. If the mother sues the father, what should the court do? Invalidate the agreement and aid neither party to it? Give the mother custody? Award the mother a judgment for $10,000?

The father and his spouse had paid NESPA $6,000 before the court negated most of NESPA's expertise and assistance. Does a contract to facilitate an agreement contrary to public policy itself violate public policy? See Bovard v. American Horse, above. Under what circumstances should a court require NESPA to refund a fee?

8. *Remedies for Breach of a Valid Surrogacy Contract.* If the court were to hold that a surrogacy contract did not violate public policy, it would next consider remedies for breach.

(a) Suppose, as in R.R. v. M.H., that the mother repudiates the agreement.

In Ohio, surrogate parents, not genetically related to the triplets, nevertheless decided to keep them as well as the $24,000 the genetic father had paid them. Reversing the trial judge, the appellate court held that the contract did not violate Ohio public policy. J.F. v. D.B., 165 Ohio App.3d 791, 848 N.E.2d 873 (2006).

Should the court order specific performance, commanding a mother to hand over her baby? In J.F. v. D.B., the "mother" was not genetically related to the triplets.

What contract damages would follow breach? What kind of expectancy damages might a plaintiff-"father" recover? Could the father recover contract damages for mental anguish-mental suffering? Would his mental anguish damages have been within the parties' contemplation when they formed the contract?

If the judge were to order rescission-restitution, what restitution would each party make to restore the other party's status quo ante?

In J.F. v. D.B., the father sued for a refund under a clause in the contract. The appellate court approved this contractual remedy.

(b) Now suppose that the "father" breaches by declining to accept "delivery." Specific performance? Contract damages? Restitution?

Chapter 6

CONTORT AND REMEDIES

A. TORT AND CONTRACT DAMAGES

This chapter is about the differences between tort and contract remedies in lawsuits that grow out of transactions.

Tort law expresses public policy developed by official decisionmakers in courts and legislatures. Contract law focuses on the bargain the parties set for themselves. Tort doctrines in contractual settings lead to important tactical decisions for litigants and difficult choices between public policy and bargained expectations for the courts. The policies of compensation and deterrence may fade in the plaintiff's quest to recover more, the defendant's quest to pay less, and the court's search for administrable limits.

The plaintiff's lawyer should choose from remedial alternatives carefully because the substantive and remedial rules a court will apply to an agreement gone awry are complex and subtle.

A buyer may label a seller's conduct either a broken promise about the goods, a misstatement of fact, or simply a mistake. The labels lead to differing legal conclusions and remedies. (a) A seller's breached warranty leads to a buyer's contract action yielding contract remedies. (b) A seller's misrepresentation, fraud or deceit, opens the door to the buyer's tort action and tort remedies. (c) Mistake usually leads to rescission-restitution, one subject in the previous chapter, which, while usually less desirable than either tort or contract, is superior to no remedy at all.

Alternative pleading rules let the buyer pursue contract, tort, and mistake, at least during the early stages of a lawsuit. At the pleading stage it is exceedingly difficult for a judge or anyone else to tell the difference between a breached warranty, a misrepresentation, or a mistake. As we studied in the prior chapter, the wild card of election of remedies may force the plaintiff to decide promptly between rescission-restitution and recovery of damages.

Suppose the plaintiff prefers damages. A damages plaintiff with a choice between being a tort plaintiff and being a contract plaintiff will usually prefer the tort. If the trial court had limited Dr. Gore to contract-warranty recovery for his repainted BMW, he would not have become famous, or notorious. p. 133, The possibility that either BMW or the BMW seller had committed the tort of fraud made Dr. Gore's lawsuit interesting because the tort characterization opened the door to the possibility that he might recover punitive damages. Larger special damages also make the misrepresentation torts more desirable for a plaintiff; for example, a fraud plaintiff may recover for mental-suffering damages while a contract plaintiff usually cannot. As we will learn, however, a court may use the "economic loss rule" to nullify the pull of tort and to channel transactional litigation into contract.

BYROM, DO DAMAGES DEPEND ON THE SAME PRINCIPLES THROUGHOUT THE LAW OF TORT AND CONTRACT?

6 U.Queensland L.J. 118, 120–122 (1968).

In both tort and contract, the wrongdoer is to be held responsible for the consequences of his wrongful acts, but as Fleming says,[1] "As a matter of practical politics, some limitation must be placed upon legal responsibility, because the consequences of an act theoretically stretch to infinity. * * * Legal policy and accepted value judgments must be the final arbiter of what balance to strike between the claim to full reparation for the loss suffered by an innocent victim of another's culpable activity and the grievous burden that would be imposed on human activity if a wrongdoer were held to answer for all the consequences of his default." * * *

Thus far the policies in tort and contract are the same. They differ in the formulation of the claim of the wrongdoer not to be held responsible for all the consequences of his default, no matter how widespread or bizarre those consequences may be.

In tort, the duty is imposed by law. The person under that tortious duty has no choice as to whether he will shoulder it or not. So his claim to relief cannot be formulated in terms of what he can expect at the time when he undertakes his duty. Rather it is relevant to consider the time at which he commits the act which is alleged to be the breach of duty. It is here that the limits are imposed. * * *

In contract, on the other hand, the limits are employed at a different stage. The contractual duty is accepted voluntarily, presumably after an assessment of how onerous the duty will be, compared with the value of the consideration to be furnished in return. Once the duty is accepted, i.e., once the contract is made, the duty is strict. No amount of care will excuse a breach of that duty.

The limits are not invoked by enquiring as to the consequences which ought to be guarded against at the time when the purported breach occurs. The answer to any such enquiry would be simply that a party to a contract must guard against everything he has expressly or impliedly promised to guard against. We are taken back in time to the formation of the contract. We must ask how onerous the duty was which the party alleged to be in breach undertook. The exact limits of that duty may be expressly prescribed in the contract. The provision of a genuine estimate of liquidated damages or of a valid exclusion clause covering the alleged breach are examples of this. In such cases there is no need for other limits, and none are introduced. On the other hand, in the great majority of cases, no such express limits to the duty will be found in the contract. Then the extent of the duty must be gleaned from the surrounding circumstances when the duty was accepted. As in tort the limits to the duty are employed to protect the wrongdoer at the expense of the injured party, but in contract, unlike tort, the law makes demands of the injured party, and if those

---

1. Fleming, The Law of Torts 176 (3rd ed. 1965).

demands are not met, his interests will then be ignored with far more freedom then is ever possible in tort.

As has been said, the contractual duty is undertaken after a comparison of the value of the consideration and of how onerous the duty will prove. This latter factor has three facets, the difficulty of discharging the duty, the likelihood of failing to discharge the duty, and the consequences of that failure which will amount to the quantum of the compensation he will have to pay. Only if he thinks the value of the consideration outweighs this threefold combination will a party undertake the contractual duty. The first two facets are things of which he must judge alone, but the final one, the consequences of a breach of duty, may well be beyond his knowledge, and yet within the knowledge of the other party. Here it is that the law makes its demand of the injured party. If he knows of factors which may take the consequences of breach of contract beyond what is to be expected and hence make the quantum of compensation greater than normal, the law demands that he disclose those factors to the other party in time for that party to consider them as he assesses whether or not it is worth his while to undertake the duty. The price of non-disclosure is that recovery will be limited. This then is a policy for establishing additional limits to recovery for breaches of contract which has no analogy in the policies underlying the rules of tort. * * *

As has been stated, the principles upon which damages depend, in both tort and contract, are aimed at striking a balance between the claim to full reparation by the innocent party on the one hand and the need to limit the wrongdoer's obligation to compensate for consequences which are unacceptably widespread or bizarre. * * *

Of course, only those consequences which were directly caused by the default can possibly be the subjects of compensation. It is not suggested that the principles of causation are in any way different in tort and contract, nor could it be expected that they would be, in view of the fact that the policy of attempting full reparation is identical in both fields.

When it comes to the problem of applying limits to full reparation, however, just as there are differences in the policies underlying tort and contract, so there are differences in the principles by which damages are to be determined. * * *

In tort there is no doubt that, in general, if the consequences of a default can be reasonably foreseen, damages are recoverable. Conversely, if no injury is foreseeable, no damages are recoverable. * * *

[I]t has never been suggested that it would be in the slightest degree relevant to enquire if the amount of compensation which will have to be paid is greater or less than the amount which can reasonably be foreseen. * * * The cases of the eggshell skull in personal injury and of Lord Justice Scrutton's "shabby millionaire" in the field of pecuniary loss resulting from personal injury are too well known to allow such an argument. They are representative, as Fleming says,[2] "of the truism that a tortfeasor cannot invoke the plea that he had no reason to expect his casualty to be so expensive." In tort, then, damages are recoverable in full or not at all. Recovery is not limited by reference to reasonable quantum.

In contract, no one doubts that Hadley v. Baxendale is the source of the general rule for computing damages. No court would entertain any suggested

2. Fleming, The Law of Torts 188 (3rd ed. 1965).

formulation which ran contrary to the famous test formulated by Alderson B. in that case.

It has been asserted there are two differences between the rules discussed as applicable to tort and this rule. They will be examined in turn.

The first difference is in the degree of foresight demanded if liability is to follow. In contract, following Baron Alderson's test, the consequence must either be reasonably considered as following naturally from the breach, or be within the reasonable contemplation of the parties as the probable result of the breach. How unusual may a consequence be without falling outside the ambit of compensation? Could there be a consequence which is "reasonably foreseeable," as that is understood in tort, and yet which is not "within the reasonable contemplation of the parties as the probable result of the breach," as that is understood in contract? If so, this clearly points to a difference between the rules of contract and tort.

The second alleged difference between the rules of tort and contract is that in tort the rule of foresight is applied to the kind of damage, not its quantum, whereas in contract the main use of the contemplation rule is to limit quantum. As has been said, in tort, for each separate item, damages are recovered in full or not at all. A consideration of the policy discussed above leads one to expect a different result in contract. In tort, the way the default occurs may be all important, but in contract, it is the extent of the duty shouldered at the time of contract which is vital. The extent of this duty is measured at least as much by the amount to be paid in compensation as by the way in which the compensation becomes payable. * * *

At this stage it is proposed to examine the results of these differences as the rules of contract and tort are applied to various hypothetical fact situations in each of which an injured party claims compensation for loss of earnings resulting from a personal injury.

If an average man is injured through careless driving and as a result must spend ten days off work, it is clear he can recover from the driver any loss of earnings he may suffer during those ten days.

If an average man engages a surgeon to perform a minor operation, but due to the surgeon's admitted carelessness, he has to spend ten days longer off work than would normally be the case, it is reasonably clear that he too can recover his loss of earnings, if he brought his action upon his contract with the surgeon. That is a consequence which the surgeon should contemplate as a not unlikely result of his breach of contract in failing to take proper care in the conduct of the operation.

If a pop-singer with a gigantic earning power were injured as a result of careless driving and was unable to appear for ten days, he too could recover his actual loss of earnings from the driver. The fact that the quantum of loss is unforeseeable is irrelevant.

Suppose such a pop-singer were to engage a surgeon as in the earlier example. If he uses his real name, rather than his stage name, and does not disclose his true identity to the surgeon, how much will he recover from the surgeon if he brings his claim in contract? The surgeon could not reasonably contemplate the actual loss of earnings, although he ought to contemplate some lesser amount. It is submitted that the singer would recover no more than the maximum loss of earnings which could normally be expected to result from ten days' incapacity, however such figure may be assessed.

If the singer brought an action against the surgeon in tort, how could the position be distinguished from the similar action against the driver in the earlier example? In tort, it is submitted, he would recover the full extent of his loss.

Here is a serious anomaly. That two different amounts should be recovered in contract and tort is unfortunate.

Questions

Given the divergent policies that contract and tort advance, do you think that it is really "unfortunate" that the court's damages measures do vary? If, however, you think that the "anomaly" is to be resolved, an important question remains: (a) should the court lower plaintiff's tort damages to contract levels; or (b) should it raise her contract damages to tort levels? One answer comes in

EVRA CORP. v. SWISS BANK CORP.

United States Court of Appeals, Seventh Circuit, 1982.
673 F.2d 951, cert. denied, 459 U.S. 1017 (1982).

[Hyman–Michaels, a scrap metal dealer, lost a valuable charter contract with Pandora Shipping because Swiss Bank failed to effect a telex deposit in Pandora's Paris account. Hyman–Michaels sued Swiss Bank to recover the expenses of an arbitration with the other party to the charter contract and the profits it lost because of the cancellation of the charter.

The trial judge awarded Hyman–Michaels $2.1 million, $16,000 for the arbitration, the rest lost profit. The parts of the opinion that deal with the remoteness issue are reproduced.]

POSNER, CIRCUIT JUDGE. * * * When a bank fails to make a requested transfer of funds, this can cause two kinds of loss. First, the funds themselves or interest on them may be lost, and of course the fee paid for the transfer, having bought nothing, becomes a loss item. These are "direct" (sometimes called "general") damages. Hyman–Michaels is not seeking any direct damages in this case and apparently sustained none. It did not lose any part of the $27,000; although its account with Continental Bank was debited by this amount prematurely, it was not an interest-bearing account so Hyman–Michaels lost no interest; and Hyman–Michaels paid no fee either to Continental or to Swiss Bank for the aborted transfer. A second type of loss, which either the payor or the payee may suffer, is a dislocation in one's business triggered by the failure to pay. Swiss Bank's failure to transfer funds to the Banque de Paris when requested to do so by Continental Bank set off a chain reaction which resulted in an arbitration proceeding that was costly to Hyman–Michaels and in the cancellation of a highly profitable contract. It is those costs and lost profits—"consequential" or, as they are sometimes called, "special" damages—that Hyman–Michaels seeks in this lawsuit, and recovered below. It is conceded that if Hyman–Michaels was entitled to consequential damages, the district court measured them correctly. The only issue is whether it was entitled to consequential damages. * * *

The rule of Hadley v. Baxendale—that consequential damages will not be awarded unless the defendant was put on notice of the special circumstances giving rise to them—has been applied in many Illinois cases, and *Hadley* cited approvingly. In *Siegel* [v. Western Union Tel. Co., 312 Ill.App. 86, 37 N.E.2d 868 (1941)], the plaintiff had delivered $200 to Western Union with instructions to transmit it to a friend of the plaintiff's. The money was to be bet (legally) on a horse, but this was not disclosed in the instructions. Western Union misdirected the money order and it did not reach the friend until several hours after the race had taken place. The horse that the plaintiff had intended to bet on won and would have paid $1650 on the plaintiff's $200 bet if the bet had been placed. He sued Western Union for his $1450 lost profit, but the court held that under the rule of Hadley v. Baxendale Western Union was not liable, because it "had no notice or knowledge of the purpose for which the money was being transmitted."

The present case is similar, though Swiss Bank knew more than Western Union knew in *Siegel;* it knew or should have known, from Continental Bank's previous telexes, that Hyman–Michaels was paying the Pandora Shipping Company for the hire of a motor vessel named *Pandora*. But it did not know when payment was due, what the terms of the charter were, or that they had turned out to be extremely favorable to Hyman–Michaels. And it did not know that Hyman–Michaels knew the *Pandora's* owner would try to cancel the charter, and probably would succeed, if Hyman–Michaels was ever again late in making payment, or that despite this peril Hyman–Michaels would not try to pay until the last possible moment and in the event of a delay in transmission would not do everything in its power to minimize the consequences of the delay. Electronic funds transfers are not so unusual as to automatically place a bank on notice of extraordinary consequences if such a transfer goes awry. Swiss Bank did not have enough information to infer that if it lost a $27,000 payment order it would face a liability in excess of $2 million.

It is true that in both *Hadley* and *Siegel* there was a contract between the parties and here there was none. * * * We must therefore ask what difference it should make whether the parties are or are not bound to each other by a contract. On the one hand, it seems odd that the absence of a contract would enlarge rather than limit the extent of liability. After all, under Swiss law the absence of a contract would be devastating to Hyman–Michaels' claim. Privity is not a wholly artificial concept. It is one thing to imply a duty to one with whom one has a contract and another to imply it to the entire world.

On the other hand, contract liability is strict. A breach of contract does not connote wrongdoing; it may have been caused by circumstances beyond the promisor's control—a strike, a fire, the failure of a supplier to deliver an essential input. And while such contract doctrines as impossibility, impracticability, and frustration relieve promisors from liability for some failures to perform that are beyond their control, many other such failures are actionable although they could not have been prevented by the exercise of due care. The district judge found that Swiss Bank had been negligent in losing Continental Bank's telex message and it can be argued that Swiss Bank should therefore be liable for a broader set of consequences than if it had only broken a contract. But *Siegel* implicitly rejects this distinction. Western Union had not merely broken its contract to deliver the plaintiff's money order; it had "negligently misdirected" the money order. "The company's negligence is conceded." Yet it was not liable for the consequences.

Siegel, we conclude, is authority for holding that Swiss Bank is not liable for the consequences of negligently failing to transfer Hyman–Michaels' funds to Banque de Paris; reason for such a holding is found in the animating principle of

Hadley v. Baxendale, which is that the costs of the untoward consequence of a course of dealings should be borne by that party who was able to avert the consequence at least cost and failed to do so. In *Hadley* the untoward consequence was the shutting down of the mill. The carrier could have avoided it by delivering the engine shaft on time. But the mill owners, as the court noted, could have avoided it simply by having a spare shaft. Prudence required that they have a spare shaft anyway, since a replacement could not be obtained at once even if there was no undue delay in carting the broken shaft to and the replacement shaft from the manufacturer. The court refused to imply a duty on the part of the carrier to guarantee the mill owners against the consequences of their own lack of prudence, though of course if the parties had stipulated for such a guarantee the court would have enforced it. The notice requirement of Hadley v. Baxendale is designed to assure that such an improbable guarantee really is intended.

This case is much the same, though it arises in a tort rather than a contract setting. Hyman–Michaels showed a lack of prudence throughout. It was imprudent for it to mail in Chicago a letter that unless received the next day in Geneva would put Hyman–Michaels in breach of a contract that was very profitable to it and that the other party to the contract had every interest in canceling. It was imprudent thereafter for Hyman–Michaels, having narrowly avoided cancellation and having (in the words of its appeal brief in this court) been "put * * * on notice that the payment provision of the Charter would be strictly enforced thereafter," to wait till arguably the last day before payment was due to instruct its bank to transfer the necessary funds overseas. And it was imprudent in the last degree for Hyman–Michaels, when it received notice of cancellation on the last possible day payment was due, to fail to pull out all the stops to get payment to the Banque de Paris on that day * * *.

This is not to condone the sloppy handling of incoming telex messages in Swiss Bank's foreign department. But Hyman–Michaels is a sophisticated business enterprise. It knew or should have known that even the Swiss are not infallible.

We are not the first to remark the affinity between the rule of Hadley v. Baxendale and the doctrine, which is one of tort as well as contract law and is a settled part of the common law of Illinois, of avoidable consequences. [citation] If you are hurt in an automobile accident and unreasonably fail to seek medical treatment, the injurer, even if negligent, will not be held liable for the aggravation of the injury due to your own unreasonable behavior after the accident. If in addition you failed to fasten your seat belt, you may be barred from collecting the tort damages that would have been prevented if you had done so. [citation] Hyman–Michaels' behavior in steering close to the wind prior to April 27 was like not fastening one's seat belt; its failure on April 27 to wire a duplicate payment immediately after disaster struck was like refusing to seek medical attention after a serious accident. The seat-belt cases show that the doctrine of avoidable consequences applies whether the tort victim acts imprudently before or after the tort is committed. Hyman–Michaels did both.

The rule of Hadley v. Baxendale links up with tort concepts in another way. The rule is sometimes stated in the form that only foreseeable damages are recoverable in a breach of contract action. E.g., Restatement (Second) of Contracts § 351 (1979). So expressed, it corresponds to the tort principle that limits liability to the foreseeable consequence of the defendant's carelessness. [citation]

The amount of care that a person ought to take is a function of the probability and magnitude of the harm that may occur if he does not take care. See, e.g., United States v. Carroll Towing Co., 159 F.2d 169, 173 (2d Cir.1947). If he does not know what that probability and magnitude are, he cannot determine how much care to take. That would be Swiss Bank's dilemma if it were liable for consequential damages from failing to carry out payment orders in timely fashion. To estimate the extent of its probable liability in order to know how many and how elaborate fail-safe features to install in its telex rooms or how much insurance to buy against the inevitable failures, Swiss Bank would have to collect reams of information about firms that are not even its regular customers. It had no banking relationship with Hyman–Michaels. It did not know or have reason to know how at once precious and fragile Hyman–Michaels' contract with the *Pandora's* owner was. These were circumstances too remote from Swiss Bank's practical range of knowledge to have affected its decisions as to who should man the telex machines in the foreign department or whether it should have more intelligent machines or should install more machines in the cable department, any more than the falling of a platform scale because a conductor jostled a passenger who was carrying fireworks was a prospect that could have influenced the amount of care taken by the Long Island Railroad. See Palsgraf v. Long Island R.R., 248 N.Y. 339, 162 N.E. 99 (1928).

In short, Swiss Bank was not required in the absence of a contractual undertaking to take precautions or insure against a harm that it could not measure but that was known with precision to Hyman–Michaels, which could by the exercise of common prudence have averted it completely. As Chief Judge Cardozo (the author of *Palsgraf*) remarked in discussing the application of Hadley v. Baxendale to the liability of telegraph companies for errors in transmission, "The sender can protect himself by insurance in one form or another if the risk of non-delivery or error appears to be too great. * * * The company, if it takes out insurance for itself, can do no more than guess at the loss to be avoided." Kerr S.S. Co. v. Radio Corp. of America, 245 N.Y. 284, 291–92, 157 N.E. 140, 142 (1927). * * *

The undisputed facts, recited in this opinion, show as a matter of law that Hyman–Michaels is not entitled to recover consequential damages from Swiss Bank.

Notes

1. *Questions.* Could Hyman–Michaels have recovered its lost profits under the approach Professor Byrom suggested in his article? What reasons does the court give for applying a contract remoteness test to the defendant's negligence tort? Is the court's decision limited to torts in a commercial setting?

2. *General Damages—Special Damages.* The court discusses the distinction between "direct" or what this book calls general damages and "consequential" or what this book calls special damages. General damages and special damages have similar meanings in breach of contract and property damages cases. In the most sweeping sense, a court will refer to a plaintiff's general damages as the typical consequences of a defendant's breach, the harm any victim would encounter, as "following naturally from the breach." More precisely, plaintiff's general damages are a calculation based on value. For a seller's breach of contract, the buyer recovers the item's market value less its contract price. For property damages, the owner recovers diminished value, the property's value before the harm less its value after. Gavcus v. Potts, p. 17.

Special damages are harms that are peculiar to a particular plaintiff; plaintiff's harms that would not occur regularly to others. Examples of the distinction between plaintiffs' general damages and their special damages are in Cohn v. J.C. Penney Co., Inc., 537 P.2d 306, 306 (Utah 1975). Observe that in stating general damages the court equates the cost to rebuild the dam with diminution in its value. "Plaintiff sues defendant for blowing up his dam in the river and claims damages in the amount of $5,000. His proof shows the cost of repairs to the dam to be $1,000. He offers evidence to the effect that he had a water mill which had to be shut down for two months during the rebuilding of the dam and that he lost profits in the amount of $4,000 as a result thereof. The rebuilding of the dam is an item of general damages, but the loss of profits due to inoperation of the mill is an item of special damage because it is peculiar to his case. Another man might have his dam blown up and might not even own a mill, or it might not be operative. Still another man might have special damages because he could not irrigate his farm as a result of the destruction of the dam which he owned and the lowering of the water below the bottom of his lateral ditch."

In *EVRA* the plaintiff's lost business profit is special damages. This book returns a contract-breach plaintiff's recovery of its lost business profits in the next chapter.

Courts distinguish between general damages and special damages in four ways that limit special damages and make them more difficult to recover. (a) Pleading. In procedural systems like the Federal Rules of Civil Procedure, a plaintiff must plead special damages specifically. Fed.R.Civ.P. 9(g). Most definitions of special damages and general damages come from courts' pleading decisions. (b) Proof. A plaintiff must prove special damages with reasonable certainty, as accurately as is reasonably possible. This prerequisite comes up over and over in Remedies. (c) Remoteness. Plaintiff may not recover special damages that are too remote, even if they were realized, pleaded, and proved. The mysterious doctrines of proximate cause in torts and Hadley v. Baxendale's contemplation test in contracts are what this book calls remoteness tests. Does the *EVRA* court think that plaintiff's recovery of its lost business profit is barred because it is too remote? Would plaintiff's lost profit have been too remote under the tort test? (d) Waiver. A plaintiff's opportunity to recover special-consequential damages is subject to bargaining. In contracts covered by the Uniform Commercial Code's § 2–719(3), "Consequential damages may be limited or excluded unless the limitation or exclusion is unconscionable." And are you surprised that most sellers' form contracts limit or exclude the buyer's special damages.

In the crucible of the adversary system, while plaintiffs seek characterization as "general damages," defendants argue for "special damages." The overarching reasons to place barriers in the path of a plaintiff seeking to recover special damages are clear: in contract and property, a plaintiff's special damages are difficult for the potential defendant to predict in advance and potentially open-ended leading to uncertainty and the risk of a crushing verdict. Do these reasons conflict with the court's goal of providing full compensation for an injured victim?

The terms general damages and special damages have specialized meanings in personal injury damages where general damages are plaintiff's pain and suffering damages, and special damages are plaintiff's pecuniary losses, in particular lost earnings and medical expense. In personal injury cases, plaintiff's pain and suffering, general damages, generates the risks of uncertainty and openendedness.

Why use the same words to express different, perhaps contradictory, concepts? Frustrating lapses in communication are inevitable. We are stuck with the vocabulary that we inherited to express the ideas of damages, even though an ideal lawgiver who was writing new rules to implement the policies of damages would develop a more refined vocabulary.

For now, when you read or hear "general damages" or "special damages" be careful about two kinds of context. (a) The type of damages. The vernacular meanings of "general damages" and "special damages" in personal injuries differ from breach of contract and property. (b) The reason for the distinction. Each of the four reasons to distinguish between general damages and special damages has a different purpose and may lead to different results.

B. WHERE DO TORT DAMAGES END?
THE ECONOMIC LOSS RULE

Although the announced goal of tort damages is to compensate the plaintiff, cutoffs are inevitable. Proximate causes eventually become too attenuated to justify plaintiff's recovery. A more definite cutoff affects the following plaintiffs' recovery of their "economic loss" for defendants' negligence.

LOCAL JOINT EXECUTIVE BOARD, CULINARY WORKERS UNION, LOCAL NO. 226 v. STERN

Supreme Court of Nevada, 1982.
98 Nev. 409, 651 P.2d 637.

PER CURIAM. This lawsuit arises from the November 1980 fire at the MGM Grand Hotel in Las Vegas, Nevada. The individual appellants were employees at the time of the fire, and brought this class action to recover lost salaries and employment benefits for the period they were unemployed as a result of the fire. The unions also sued to recover union dues lost because of the fire. Respondents were involved in the design or construction of the hotel. Appellants sought recovery under both negligence and strict liability theories. The district court granted respondents' motions to dismiss, on the ground that appellants had not stated a cause of action to recover economic loss. This appeal followed.

The well established common law rule is that absent privity of contract or an injury to person or property, a plaintiff may not recover in negligence for economic loss. Robins Dry Dock & Repair Co. v. Flint, 275 U.S. 303 (1927). Purely economic loss is recoverable in actions for tortious interference with contractual relations or prospective economic advantage, but the interference must be intentional. [citations] The primary purpose of the rule is to shield a defendant from unlimited liability for all of the economic consequences of a negligent act, particularly in a commercial or professional setting, and thus to keep the risk of liability reasonably calculable.

A small minority of jurisdictions do permit recovery for negligent interference with economic expectancies under certain limited circumstances. See, e.g., J'Aire Corp. v. Gregory, 24 Cal.3d 799, 157 Cal.Rptr. 407, 598 P.2d 60 (1979). However, we believe the tests that have been developed to determine who should recover for negligent interference with contract or prospective economic advantage are presently inadequate to guide trial courts to consistent, predictable, and fair results. The foreseeability of economic loss, even when modified by other factors, is a standard that sweeps too broadly in a professional or commercial context, portending liability that is socially harmful in its potential scope and uncertainty. We therefore decline to adopt the minority view allowing such recovery.

Notes

1. The court rejects the recovery of economic losses by employees whose persons or property have not been touched by the tortfeasors' negligence, even though their pocketbooks were nicked. The doctrine is customarily traced through maritime cases back to the *Stern* court's lead citation, *Robins Dry Dock*, where Justice Holmes said "The law does not spread its protection so far."

2. *The Exxon Valdez's Oil Spill.* The maritime economic loss rule remains strong. Four representative Alaska business and property owners claimed damages from the 1989 EXXON VALDEZ oil spill in Prince William Sound; they sued under the Trans–Alaska Pipeline Liability Fund. "Kodiak Electric Cooperative, an electric utility, claims to have lost its largest customers when seafood processing companies closed or operated at low levels because of the shortage of fish for processing; Killer Whale Café, a restaurant, claims to have lost much of its patronage when the oil spill idled commercial fishermen for a season; Michael T. Tuhy d/b/a 2 E Fish Company and Alaska Sport Angling Photography (ASAP), two tourist-oriented businesses, claim cancellations and loss of customers due to cancellation of a part of the fishing season; and Marine Welding, Inc., a boat repair company, claims a decline of business because of the decrease in fishing operations after the spill."

The Fund and the trial court said the owners' losses were not proximately caused by the oil spill. The court of appeals agreed:

"Under the Act, the Fund is 'strictly liable without regard to fault * * * for all damages * * * sustained by any person or entity * * * as the result of discharge of oil from [a vessel loaded with oil transported through the pipeline and loaded at the pipeline terminal facilities].' 43 U.S.C. § 1653(c)(1) In applying this provision, the Fund relied on the district court's earlier order in which it had instructed the Fund that '[I]n assessing causation, the Fund may consider remoteness of whatever dimension. Time, place, and like factors are all proper considerations, leading to a decision that economic damages were or were not the result of the Exxon Valdez oil spill.' * * *"

"The Fund also relied on this court's decision in Benefiel v. Exxon Corp., 959 F.2d 805 (9th Cir.1992), holding that recovery under the Act is properly denied for damage not caused directly by the oil spill but flowing from a series of intervening events triggered by the spill.

"The determinations complained of fall into two groups. One comprises claims of businesses who suffered losses because the impact of the oil spill on their customers caused patronage to decline. Thus, Kodiak Electric Cooperative lost business because its largest customers, seafood processing companies, agreed to reduce the amount of fish processed; the Killer Whale Café had to close because of a decline of business; tourist businesses suffered losses from cancellations of bookings. Those claims were denied as too remote because of the presence of intervening causes, such as diversion of labor to clean-up activities, the independent decisions of prospective customers, or a general decline of business due to the disruption of fishing. Another group comprises claims deemed geographically remote; both Marine Welding and ASAP were located outside of the geographic limits of the oil spill.

"Because the Fund's determinations of whether damage was 'the result of discharge of oil' are predominantly factual, judicial review is deferential. [citations] The Fund's determinations were consistent with our interpretation of the Act's purpose in *Benefiel* that 'Congress envisioned damages arising out of the physical effects of oil discharges * * * [not] remote and derivative damages * * * outside the zone of dangers against which Congress intended to protect when it passed [the

Act].' It was incumbent on the Fund to draw a line at some point along the chain of causation dividing the claims it would entertain from those that were too remote. Because they were not lacking a factual basis and have not been shown to be clearly erroneous, the district court was correct when it affirmed the Fund's determinations." Adkins v. Trans–Alaska Pipeline, 101 F.3d 86, 88–89 (9th Cir.1996).

3. *Examples*. The tort branch of the economic loss rule includes other kinds of cases. (a) When an employer requests lost income after an important employee is put out of action by a negligent tortfeasor, courts decline. Snow v. West, 250 Or. 114, 440 P.2d 864 (1968); Phoenix Professional Hockey Club, Inc. v. Hirmer, 108 Ariz. 482, 502 P.2d 164 (1972). (b) Where a contractor negligently built a bridge that had to be closed for repairs, the court held that the affected hotel operators and local businesses could not recover their economic losses. Nebraska Innkeepers, Inc. v. Pittsburgh–Des Moines Corp., 345 N.W.2d 124 (Iowa 1984).

The tort branch of the economic loss rule excludes plaintiffs from recovering some forms of economic loss even when they lack any contractual remedy; for these plaintiffs, there is no tomorrow. The economic loss rule also has a contract branch: Although a buyer may not recover for its economic loss under tort doctrines of products liability, it may recover them in contract. However, a contract plaintiff is subject to contract statutes of limitations, privity requirements, disclaimers of remedies and damages, and, more important for our purposes here, the *Hadley* or contemplation limitation on special damages. The contract economic loss rule will come up again in the next chapter.

4. *Why Limit Plaintiff's Recovery of Economic Damages?* The issue has been stated: "While it may seem that there should be a remedy for every wrong, this is an ideal limited perforce by the realities of this world. Every injury has ramifying consequences like the ripplings of the waters without end. The problem for the law is to limit the legal consequences of wrongs to a controllable degree." Tobin v. Grossman, 24 N.Y.2d 609, 619, 301 N.Y.S.2d 554, 561, 249 N.E.2d 419, 424 (1969). Many explanations have been attempted—ranging from the assertion that there is no substantive tort at all, to the idea that a simple remedies problem concerns the certainty rather than the existence of damages.

(a) *"Non proximately caused—too remote and speculative."* In the words of Judge Kaufman "we conclude that recovery was properly denied because the injuries to [plaintiffs] were too 'remote' or 'indirect' a consequence of defendant's negligence." *In re Kinsman Transit Co.*, 388 F.2d 821, 823 (2d Cir.1968), cert. denied, 380 U.S. 944 (1965)

Defendant, the courts assume, has committed a tort, but the plaintiff may not recover damages which are too remote. Common experience makes this explanation, by itself, unsatisfactory. Any lawyer who is losing billable time while tied up in a traffic jam caused after negligent drivers have collided in the highway ahead will readily understand. Are these lost billings significantly more remote than the economic losses of the owner of one of the *directly* involved vehicles?

(b) *"Economic damages in these circumstances are not foreseeable."* The word "foreseeable" here is confusing. A court may use "foreseeability" to determine whether plaintiff may recover special damages for breach of contract. "Foreseeability" of plaintiff's injury is necessary to render defendant's conduct negligent, as a matter of the substantive law of torts rather than damages. If plaintiff establishes defendant's "negligence," then the tort defendant is, we are told, liable for all damages proximately caused. Surely it should not be necessary to run through a *Palsgraf* routine (if a citation is required, the student should stop reading here and reapply for admission) on the issue of existence of a duty, and again on the issue of the quantum of damages. As Judge Friendly more elegantly summarized it:

"The oft-encountered argument that failure to limit liability to foreseeable consequences may subject the defendant to a loss wholly out of proportion to his fault seems scarcely consistent with the universally accepted rule that the defendant takes the plaintiff as he finds him and will be responsible for the full extent of the injury even though a latent susceptibility of the plaintiff renders this far more serious than could reasonably have been anticipated. * * *

"The weight of authority in this country rejects the limitation of damages to consequences foreseeable at the time of the negligent conduct, when the consequences are 'direct' and the damages, although other and greater than expectable, is of the same general sort as was risked." In re Kinsman Transit Co., 338 F.2d 708, 724 (2d Cir.1964), cert. denied, 380 U.S. 944 (1965).

Nevertheless it is admittedly difficult to disassociate "foreseeability" from the calculation of damages for the tort of negligence. After all, the *existence* of plaintiff's damages is a necessary substantive component of the negligence tort, unlike intentional torts like trespass. And even the quote from Judge Friendly, above, does not close the door.

(c) *A plaintiff suffering purely economic damages from defendant's negligence is outside the circle of those defendant owes a duty.* This "rationale" is abrupt: no tort, no damages. Here is admittedly a defendant's wrong proximately causing plaintiff's nonspeculative damages; but plaintiff has no remedy. See, for example, Phoenix Professional Hockey Club, Inc. v. Hirmer, supra Note 3. The hockey club sought damages for the cost of a substitute goalie while their regular one was incapacitated by an auto accident defendant negligently caused. The court conceded that the plaintiff's claim was not speculative; but it denied recovery because a victim's employer is outside the "class of people" to whom the tortfeasor owes a duty.

The current trend has been for courts to expand defendants' tort duty of care to groups of indirectly affected individuals previously excluded. Courts have expanded consortium recovery to wives and minor children. Giuliani v. Guiler, 951 S.W.2d 318 (Ky.1997). Courts extend emotional distress recovery to parents and even nonrelatives who are emotionally shocked and psychologically, but not physically, injured when they witness negligent physical harm. Kately v. Wilkinson, 148 Cal.App.3d 576, 195 Cal.Rptr. 902 (1983). Expanding this trend, enlarging the scope of defendants' "duty," would remove the barrier to recovery of damages leaving only the question of uncertainty.

(d) *A policy approach—Pandora's Box, floodgate, slippery slopes, etc.* In a worker's unsuccessful claim for wages much like *Stern,* the court elaborated: "While the reason usually given for the refusal to permit recovery in this class of cases is that the damages are 'indirect' or are 'too remote' it is our opinion that the principal reason that has motivated the courts in denying recovery in this class of cases is that to permit recovery of damages in such cases would open the door to a mass of litigation which might very well overwhelm the courts so that in the long run while injustice might result in special cases, the ends of justice are conserved by laying down and enforcing the general rule as is so well stated by Mr. Justice Holmes in Robins Dry Dock & Repair Co. v. Flint.

"If one who by his negligence is legally responsible for an explosion or a conflagration should be required to respond in damages not only to those who have sustained personal injuries or physical property damage but also to every one who has suffered an economic loss, by reason of the explosion or conflagration, we might well be appalled by the results that would follow. * * *

"Cases might well occur where a manufacturer would be obliged to close down his factory because of the inability of his supplier due to a fire loss to make prompt deliveries; the power company with a contract to supply a factory with electricity would be deprived of the profit which it would have made if the operation of the factory had not been interrupted by reason of fire damage; a man who had a contract to paint a building may not be able to proceed with his work; a salesman who would have sold the products of the factory may be deprived of his commissions; the neighborhood restaurant which relies on the trade of the factory employees may suffer a substantial loss. The claims of workmen for loss of wages who were employed in such a factory and cannot continue to work there because of a fire, represent only a small fraction of the claims which would arise if recovery is allowed in this class of cases.

"It is our opinion that the courts generally have reached a wise result in limiting claims for damages in this class of cases to who may have sustained personal injuries or physical property damage and in refusing to open their doors in such cases to claims of loss of wages and other economic loss based on contract." Stevenson v. East Ohio Gas Co., 73 N.E.2d 200, 203–04 (Ohio App.1946).

Is the rule excluding plaintiffs' economic loss from defendants' negligence recovery a wise one? If so, which is the most satisfactory explanation for it?

5. Even though a tort plaintiff's damages are limited by the economic loss rule and remoteness tests like proximate cause, she will usually recover more in tort than in contract. A plaintiff in litigation related to a transaction will often search for a related tort.

C. FROM CONTRACT, A TORT?

J'AIRE CORP. v. GREGORY

Supreme Court of California, 1979.
24 Cal.3d 799, 157 Cal.Rptr. 407, 598 P.2d 60.

BIRD, CHIEF JUSTICE. * * * Appellant, J'Aire Corporation, operates a restaurant at the Sonoma County Airport in premises leased from the County of Sonoma. Under the terms of the lease the county was to provide heat and air conditioning. In 1975 the county entered into a contract with respondent for improvements to the restaurant premises, including renovation of the heating and air conditioning systems and installation of insulation.

* * * The work was not completed within a reasonable time. Because the restaurant could not operate during part of the construction and was without heat and air conditioning for a longer period, appellant suffered loss of business and resulting loss of profits.

* * * The second cause of action sounded in tort and was based upon negligence in not completing the work within a reasonable time. Damages of $50,000 were claimed.

* * * On appeal the sustaining of the demurrer to the cause of action is challenged. * * *

This court has held that a plaintiff's interest in prospective economic advantage may be protected against injury occasioned by negligent as well as intentional conduct. For example, economic losses such as lost earnings or profits are recoverable as part of general damages in a suit for personal injury based on negligence. [citations] Where negligent conduct causes injury to real or personal property, the plaintiff may recover damages for profits lost during the time necessary to repair or replace the property.

Even when only injury to prospective economic advantage is claimed, recovery is not foreclosed. Where a special relationship exists between the parties, a plaintiff may recover for loss of expected economic advantage through the negligent performance of a contract although the parties were not in contractual privity.[1]

It is evident that a duty was owed by respondent to appellant in the present case. (1) The contract entered into between respondent and the county was for the renovation of the premises in which appellant maintained its business. The contract could not have been performed without impinging on that business. Thus respondent's performance was intended to, and did, directly affect appellant. (2) Accordingly, it was clearly foreseeable that any significant delay in completing the construction would adversely affect appellant's business beyond the normal disruption associated with such construction. Appellant alleges this fact was repeatedly drawn to respondent's attention. (3) Further, appellant's complaint leaves no doubt that appellant suffered harm since it was unable to operate its business for one month and suffered additional loss of business while the premises were without heat and air conditioning. (4) Appellant has also alleged that delays occasioned by the respondent's conduct were closely connected to, indeed directly caused its injury. (5) In addition, respondent's lack of diligence in the present case was particularly blameworthy since it continued after the probability of damage was drawn directly to respondent's attention. (6) Finally, public policy supports finding a duty of care in the present case. The wilful failure or refusal of a contractor to prosecute a construction project with diligence, where another is injured as a result, has been made grounds for disciplining a licensed contractor. * * *

As appellant points out, injury to a tenant's business can often result in greater hardship than damage to a tenant's person or property. Where the risk of harm is foreseeable, as it was in the present case, an injury to the plaintiff's economic interests should not go uncompensated merely because it was unaccompanied by any injury to his person or property.

To hold under these facts that a cause of action has been stated for negligent interference with prospective economic advantage is consistent with the recent trend in tort cases. This court has repeatedly eschewed overly rigid common law formulations of duty in favor of allowing compensation for foreseeable injuries caused by a defendant's want of ordinary care. [citations] Rather than traditional notions of duty, this court has focused on foreseeability as the key component necessary to establish liability: * * * Respondent is liable if his lack of ordinary care caused foreseeable injury to the economic interests of appellant. * * *

Respondent cites Fifield Manor v. Finston (1960) 54 Cal.2d 632, 7 Cal.Rptr. 377, 354 P.2d 1073 for the proposition that recovery may not be had for negligent loss of prospective economic advantage. *Fifield* concerned the parallel tort of interference with contractual relations. There a non-profit retirement home that had contracted with Ross to provide him with lifetime medical care

---

1. Countervailing public policies may preclude recovery for injury to prospective economic advantage in some cases, such as the strong public policy favoring organized activity by workers. Accordingly, interference with the prospective economic advantage of an employer or business has traditionally not been considered tortious when it results from union activity, including picketing, striking, primary and secondary boycotts or similar activity, that is otherwise lawful and reasonably related to labor conditions. The present case does not alter this principle.

sued a driver who negligently struck and killed Ross. The plaintiff argued it had become liable under the contract for Ross' medical bills and sought recovery from the driver, on both a theory of direct liability and one of subrogation. Recovery was denied.

The critical factor of foreseeability distinguishes *Fifield* from the present case. Although it was reasonably foreseeable that defendant's negligence might cause injury to Ross, it was less foreseeable that it would injure the retirement home's economic interest. Defendant had not entered into any relationship or undertaken any activity where negligence on his part was reasonably likely to affect plaintiff adversely. * * *

Respondent also relies on Adams v. Southern Pac. Transportation Co. (1975) 50 Cal.App.3d 37, 123 Cal.Rptr. 216. In *Adams* plaintiff employees were held unable to sue the railroad whose cargo of bombs exploded, destroying the factory where they worked. It should be noted that the Court of Appeal in *Adams* clearly believed that plaintiffs should be permitted to maintain an action for negligent interference with prospective economic interests. It reluctantly held they could not only under the belief that *Fifield* precluded such recovery. Adhering to the *Fifield* rule, the Court of Appeal in *Adams* did not determine whether the railroad owed plaintiffs a duty of care. In the present case, plaintiff's injury stemmed directly from conduct intended to affect plaintiff and was more readily foreseeable than the damage to the employer's property in *Adams*. To the extent that *Adams* holds that there can be no recovery for negligent interference with prospective economic advantage, it is disapproved.

The chief dangers which have been cited [above] in allowing recovery for negligent interference with prospective economic advantage are the possibility of excessive liability, the creation of an undue burden on freedom of action, the possibility of fraudulent or collusive claims and the often speculative nature of damages. * * * Central to these fears is the possibility that liability will be imposed for remote consequences, out of proportion to the magnitude of the defendant's wrongful conduct.

However, the factors enumerated * * * [above] place a limit on recovery by focusing judicial attention on the foreseeability of the injury and the nexus between the defendant's conduct and the plaintiff's injury. These factors and ordinary principles of tort law such as proximate cause are fully adequate to limit recovery without the drastic consequence of an absolute rule which bars recovery in all such cases. (See Dillon v. Legg, supra, 68 Cal.2d at p. 746, 69 Cal.Rptr. 72, 441 P.2d 912.) Following these principles, recovery for negligent interference with prospective economic advantage will be limited to instances where the risk of harm is foreseeable and is closely connected with the defendant's conduct, where damages are not wholly speculative and the injury is not part of the plaintiff's ordinary business risk. * * *

The judgment of dismissal is reversed.

Question

Is the *J'Aire* court's confidence in "foreseeability" misplaced? See the next-to-the-last sentence in *Stern*, p. 539.

RARDIN v. T & D MACHINE HANDLING, INC.

United States Court of Appeals, Seventh Circuit, 1989.
890 F.2d 24.

POSNER, CIRCUIT JUDGE. Jack Rardin, the plaintiff, bought for use in his printing business a used printing press from Whitacre–Sunbelt, Inc. for $47,700. The price included an allowance of $1,200 to cover the cost of dismantling the press for shipment and loading it on a truck at Whitacre's premises in Georgia for transportation to Rardin in Illinois. The contract of sale provided that the press was to be "Sold As Is, Where Is," that payment was to be made before the removal of the press from Whitacre's premises, and that Whitacre was to be responsible only for such damage to the press as might be "incurred by reason of the fault or negligence of [Whitacre's] employees, agents, contractors or representatives." To dismantle and load the press, Whitacre hired T & D Machine Handling, Inc., which performed these tasks carelessly; as a result the press was damaged. Not only did Rardin incur costs to repair the press; he also lost profits in his printing business during the time it took to put the press into operating order. He brought this suit against Whitacre, T & D, and others; settled with Whitacre; dismissed all the other defendants except T & D; and now appeals from the dismissal of his case against T & D for failure to state a claim. (The facts we recited are all taken from the complaint.) The only issue is whether Rardin stated a claim against T & D under Illinois law, which the parties agree controls this diversity suit.

The contract indemnified Rardin against physical damage to the press caused by the negligence of Whitacre's contractor, T & D, and the settlement with Whitacre extinguished Rardin's claim for the cost of repairing the damage. The damages that Rardin seeks from T & D are the profits that he lost as a result of the delay in putting the press into operation in his business, a delay caused by T & D's negligence in damaging the press. Rardin could not have sought these damages from Whitacre under the warranty, because consequential damages (of which a loss of profits that is due to delay is the classic example) are not recoverable in a breach of contract suit, with exceptions not applicable here. Rardin had no contract with T & D, and his claim against T & D is a tort claim; consequential damages are the norm in tort law.

We agree with the district judge that Illinois law does not provide a tort remedy in a case such as this. We may put a simpler version of the case, as follows: A takes his watch to a retail store, B, for repair. B sends it out to a watchmaker, C. Through negligence, C damages the watch, and when it is returned to A via B it does not tell time accurately. As a result, A misses an important meeting with his creditors. They petition him into bankruptcy. He loses everything. Can he obtain damages from C, the watchmaker, for the consequences of C's negligence? There is no issue of causation in our hypothetical case; there is none in Rardin's. We may assume that but for C's negligence A would have made the meeting and averted the bankruptcy, just as but for T & D's negligence the press would have arrived in working condition. The issue is not causation; it is duty.

The basic reason why no court (we believe) would impose liability on C in a suit by A is that C could not estimate the consequences of his carelessness, ignorant as he was of the circumstances of A, who is B's customer. In principle, it is true, merely to conclude that C was negligent is to affirm that the costs of care to him were less than the costs of his carelessness to all who might be hurt by it; that, essentially, is what negligence means, in Illinois as elsewhere. [citation] So in a perfect world of rational actors and complete information, and with damages set equal to the plaintiff's injury, there would be no negligence: the costs of negligence would be greater to the defendant than the costs of care and therefore it would never pay to be negligent. And if there were no negligence, the scope of liability for negligence would have no practical significance. But all this is a matter of abstract principle, and it is not realistic to assume that *every* responsible citizen can and will avoid *ever* being negligent. In fact, all that taking care does is make it less likely that one will commit a careless act. In deciding how much effort to expend on being careful—and therefore how far to reduce the probability of a careless accident—the potential injurer must have at least a rough idea of the extent of liability. C in our example could not form such an idea. He does not know the circumstances of the myriad owners of watches sent him to repair. He cannot know what costs he will impose if through momentary inattention he negligently damages one of the watches in his charge.

Two further points argue against liability. The first is that A could by his contract with B have protected himself against the consequences of C's negligence. He could have insisted that B guarantee him against all untoward consequences, however remote or difficult to foresee, of a failure to redeliver the watch in working order. The fact that B would in all likelihood refuse to give such a guaranty for a consideration acceptable to A is evidence that liability for all the consequences of every negligent act is not in fact optimal. Second, A could have protected himself not through guarantees but simply by reducing his dependence on his watch. Knowing how important the meeting was he could have left himself a margin for error or consulted another timepiece. Why impose liability for a harm that the victim could easily have prevented himself?

The present case is essentially the same as our hypothetical example. T & D is in the business of dismantling and loading printing presses. It is not privy to the circumstances of the owners of those presses. It did not deal directly with the owner, that is, with Rardin. It knew nothing about his business and could not without an inquiry that Rardin would have considered intrusive (indeed bizarre) have determined the financial consequences to Rardin if the press arrived in damaged condition.

The spirit of Hadley v. Baxendale, 9 Ex. 341, 156 Eng.Rep. 145 (1854), still the leading case on the nonrecoverability of consequential damages in breach of contract suits, broods over this case although not cited by either party or by the district court and although the present case is a tort case rather than a contract case. The plaintiffs in Hadley v. Baxendale owned a mill, and the defendants were in business as a common carrier. The defendants agreed to carry the plaintiffs' broken mill shaft to its original manufacturer, who was to make a new shaft using the broken one as a model. The defendants failed to deliver the broken shaft within the time required by the contract. Meanwhile, the plaintiffs, having no spare shaft, had been forced to shut down the mill. The plaintiffs sued the defendants for the profits lost during the additional period the mill remained closed as a result of the defendants' delay in delivering the shaft to the manufacturer. The plaintiffs lost the case. The defendants were not privy to the mill's finances and hence could not form an accurate estimate of how costly delay would be and therefore how much care to take to prevent it. The plaintiffs, however, as the court noted, could have protected themselves from the consequences of a delay by keeping a spare shaft on hand. Indeed, simple prudence dictated such a precaution, both because a replacement shaft could not be obtained immediately in any event (it had to be manufactured), and because conditions beyond the defendants' control could easily cause delay in the delivery of a broken shaft to the manufacturer should the shaft ever break. See also EVRA Corp. v. Swiss Bank Corp. Rardin, too, could have taken measures to protect himself against the financial consequences of unexpected delay. He could have arranged in advance to contract out some of his printing work, he could have bought business insurance, or he could have negotiated for a liquidated-damages clause in his contract with Whitacre that would have compensated him for delay in putting the press into working condition after it arrived.

As we noted in EVRA Corp. v. Swiss Bank Corp., Illinois follows Hadley v. Baxendale. So if this were a contract case, Rardin would lose—and this regardless of whether the breach of contract were involuntary or, as he alleges, due to the promisor's negligence. It is a tort case, but so was *EVRA*, where, applying Illinois law, we concluded that the plaintiff could not recover consequential damages. * * * This case differs from both *Hadley* and *EVRA* in that there is no suggestion that Rardin was imprudent in failing to take precautions against damage or delay. But as in those cases the defendant was not in a position to assess the consequences of its negligence. In this respect the present case and *EVRA* are actually stronger for defendants even though these are tort rather than contract cases since neither case involves a defendant who is dealing face-to-face with the plaintiff. While it is generally true that consequential damages are recoverable in tort law although not in contract law, *EVRA* shows that the classification of a case as a tort case or a contract case is not decisive on this question. * * *

[C]onsistent with the analysis in *EVRA*, * * * contractual-type limitations on liability may make sense in many tort cases that are not contract cases only because there is no privity of contract between the parties. The contractual linkage between Rardin and T & D was indirect but unmistakable, and Rardin could as we have said have protected himself through his contractual arrangements with Whitacre, while there was little that T & D could do to shield itself from liability to Whitacre's customer except be more careful—and we have explained why a finding of negligence alone should not expose a defendant to unlimited liability. * * *

Admittedly these doctrines are in tension with other doctrines of tort law that appear to expose the tortfeasor to unlimited liability. One is the principle that allows recovery of full tort damages in a personal-injury suit for injury resulting from a defective or unreasonably dangerous product—a form of legal action that arises in a contractual setting and indeed originated in suits for breach of warranty. Another is the principle, also of personal-injury law, that the injurer takes his victim as he finds him and is therefore liable for the full extent of the injury even if unforeseeable—even if the person he runs down is Henry Ford and sustains a huge earnings loss, or because of a preexisting injury sustains a much greater loss than the average victim would have done. Both are doctrines of personal-injury law, however, and there are at least three differences between the personal-injury case and the economic-loss case, whether in a stranger or in a contractual setting. The first difference is that the potential variance in liability is larger when the victim of a tort is a business, because businesses vary in their financial magnitude more than individuals do; more precisely, physical capital is more variable than human capital. The second is that many business losses are offset elsewhere in the system: Rardin's competitors undoubtedly picked up much or all of the business he lost as a result of the delay in putting the press into operation, so that his loss overstates the social loss caused by T & D's negligence. Third, tort law is a field largely shaped by the special considerations involved in personal-injury cases, as contract law is not. Tort doctrines are, therefore, prima facie more suitable for the governance of such cases than contract doctrines are. * * *

Although cases barring the recovery, whether under tort or contract law, of consequential damages in contractual settings ordinarily involve smaller potential losses than pure stranger cases do, this is not always so. In our watch hypothetical, in *EVRA,* and for all we know in *Hadley* and in the present case, the financial consequences of a seemingly trivial slip might be enormous. And it is in contractual settings that the potential victim ordinarily is best able to work out alternative protective arrangements and need not rely on tort law. Our conclusion that there is no tort liability in this case does not, therefore, leave buyers in the plaintiff's position remediless. Rardin could have sought guarantees from Whitacre (at a price, of course), but what he could not do was require the tort system to compensate him for business losses occasioned by negligent damage to his property.

A final example will nail the point down. The defendant in H.R. Moch Co. v. Rensselaer Water Co., 247 N.Y. 160, 159 N.E. 896 (1928), had agreed to supply the City of Rensselaer with water of specified pressure for the city's mains. There was a fire, the company was notified but failed to keep up the pressure, and as a result the fire department could not extinguish the fire, which destroyed the plaintiff's building. In a famous opinion denying liability, Chief Judge Cardozo stated that even if the failure of pressure was due to negligence on the defendant's part, the plaintiff could not obtain damages. The city was acting as the agent of its residents in negotiating with the water company, and the water company was entitled to assume that, if it was to be the fire insurer for the city's property, the city would compensate it accordingly. Similarly, in dealing with T & D, Whitacre was acting in effect as Rardin's agent, and T & D was entitled to assume that, if it was to be an insurer of Rardin's business losses, Whitacre on behalf of Rardin would compensate it accordingly. Rardin in short could protect itself against T & D's negligence by negotiating appropriate terms with Whitacre.

The protracted analysis that we have thought necessary to address the parties' contentions underscores the desirability—perhaps urgency—of harmonizing the entire complex and confusing pattern of liability and nonliability for tortious conduct in contractual settings. But that is a task for the Supreme Court of Illinois rather than for us in this diversity case governed by Illinois law. It is enough for us that Illinois law does not permit a tort suit for profits lost as the result of the failure to complete a commercial undertaking.

Affirmed.

Notes

1. *Questions.* Are the following statements from the *Rardin* opinion consistent with your understanding of Hadley v. Baxendale? "[C]onsequential damages (of which a loss of profits that is due to delay is the classic example) are not recoverable in a breach of contract suit with exceptions not applicable here." "[I]t is generally

true that consequential damages are recoverable in tort law although not in contract law."

Do you think Rardin's printing press is "essentially the same" as the court's watch hypothetical? Are his lost profits more to be anticipated from a damaged printing press than bankruptcy from a bungled watch repair?

2. *One Picture is Worth*? A professional photographer who deals with a shop which sends the film to a lab for processing does resemble the watch hypothetical. Valenti, a professional photographer, took film to Colonial, which sent it to Qualex to be developed in its labs. The Qualex labs processed Valenti's film improperly. The lab's letters offering Valenti replacement film recognized his professional status. Valenti, whose contract was with Colonial, not the labs, sued Qualex for negligent damage to 43 rolls of film, 1610 images, and sought damages of $2,415,000, or $1,500 per transparency.

The trial judge granted and the court of appeals approved summary judgment for the labs on Valenti's negligence claim: "When only economic loss is incurred, the plaintiff may only raise contract theories even if the defendant's alleged conduct constituted a tort as well as a breach of contract. * * * Plaintiffs sought the benefit of their damaged transparencies, which was the lost revenues they had expected. These are economic damages arising in a commercial setting," and plaintiff cannot recover them in negligence.

"[T]his circuit's *Rardin* decision [Editor: The principal case.] is quite relevant to our analysis. Like the *Rardin* defendant, Qualex did not deal directly with plaintiffs, owed no duty directly to plaintiffs, and is not liable to plaintiffs under Illinois tort law. Like the *Rardin* plaintiff, the Valentis could have protected themselves against the consequences of Qualex's negligence (perhaps by dealing directly with Qualex and making an agreement with the processor on the value of their film, or perhaps by insisting on a guarantee from Colonial against unforeseen consequences), but did not do so. * * * [T]hey cannot now 'require the tort system to compensate [them] for business losses occasioned by negligent damage to [their] property.' "Valenti v. Qualex, Inc., 970 F.2d 363 (7th Cir.1992).

The court did not discuss whether Qualex could have contemplated or foreseen the magnitude of the photographer's losses.

D. HOW REMEDIES AFFECT THE PLAINTIFF'S CHOICE OF SUBSTANTIVE THEORY

Despite Judge Posner's plea for the "desirability—perhaps urgency—of harmonizing the entire complex and confusing pattern of liability and nonliability for tortious conduct in contractual settings," the precise dividing line between tort and contract is neither clear in any one jurisdiction nor uniform among the various jurisdictions.

Pressure on the conceptual boundary between tort and contract is first recorded in 1348 in the Humber Ferry case. S.F.C. Milsom, Historical Foundations of the Common Law 316–19 (2d ed. 1981). If lawyers arguing their clients' causes ever stop testing the boundaries between substantive areas, a lot of common law legal development will halt. Presenting novel ways to view problems, called characterization, occurs because changing the nomenclature changes the ideas, indeed it may improve plaintiff's remedies. "The life of the common law." Milsom wrote, "has been in the abuse of its elementary ideas. If the rules of property give what seems an unjust answer, try obligation; and equity has proved that from the materials of obligation you can counterfeit the phenomena of property. If the rules of contract give what now seems an unjust answer, try tort. Your counterfeit will look odd to one brought up on categories of Roman origin; but it will work. If the rules of one tort, say deceit, give what now seems an unjust answer, try another, try negligence. And so the legal world goes round." (p. 6).

Modern alternative pleading systems enable a plaintiff to allege multiple substantive theories. A defendant's tortious conduct in a contractual setting potentially involves the torts of fraud, deceit, misrepresentation, conversion, tortious interference with contract and prospective advantage, products liability-especially implied warranty, abusive discharge of an employee, and professional malpractice.

Examples. (a) The question of whether "bad faith" breach of a contract is a tort is a contemporary example of characterization at work. Courts have struggled with the tort meaning of a defendant's breach of the covenant of good faith and fair dealing implied in a contract. See Restatement (Second) of Contracts § 205 (1981). A "bad faith" tort cause of action originated in insurance cases where the insurance company improperly failed to settle its insured's liability within the policy limits. Crisci v. Security Insurance Co., 66 Cal.2d 425, 58 Cal.Rptr. 13, 426 P.2d 173 (1967). The tort spread into plaintiff's first-party insurance claims against their own insurance carriers, initially in refusal to pay medical disability claims and later to property damage and title insurance claims. Remember that State Farm v. Campbell, p. 145, the Supreme Court's punitive damages decision, grew out of insureds' bad faith dispute with their own insurance company.

Courts have resisted plaintiffs' pressure to extend the "bad faith" tort to commercial transactions, probably because the domain of contracts would be diminished if the trend continued unabated. In Freeman & Mills v. Belcher Oil, the California court traced its expansion of the bad faith tort and, overruling a prior decision, attempted to confine it. The majority states "a general rule precluding tort recovery for noninsurance contract breach, at least in the absence of violation of 'an independent duty arising from principles of tort law' [citation] other than the bad faith denial of the existence of, or liability under, the breached contract." Justice Mosk, concurring and dissenting, "would permit an action for tortious breach of contract in a commercial setting when a party intentionally breaches a contractual obligation with neither probable cause nor belief that the obligation does not exist and when the party intends or knows that the breach will result in severe consequential damages to the other party that are not readily subject to mitigation, and such harm in fact occurs." Freeman & Mills, Inc. v. Belcher Oil Co., 11 Cal.4th 85, 102, 116, 44 Cal.Rptr.2d 420, 430–31, 900 P.2d 669, 679–80 (1995),

(b) Similarly Judge Robert Keeton, in declining to find a tort theory to support Vanessa Redgrave's claim that the Boston Symphony Orchestra terminated a contract for a series of concerts because of her political views, stated: "Rights are not to be determined by playing a game of labels. If the relationship of the parties is such as to support a cause of action in tort that cause of action is not to be denied because the parties happen also to have made a contract. Conversely, a breach of contract is not, standing alone, a tort as well. And it cannot be converted into a tort merely by attaching to the contract, or to the breach, new labels that sound in tort. Calling a 'breach of contract' a 'tortious repudiation of contract' is no more helpful in identifying a ground of tort liability than would be an argument that every breach of contract—or perhaps every willful breach—is a tort." Redgrave v. Boston Symphony Orchestra, Inc., 557 F.Supp. 230, 238 (D.Mass.1983), Redgrave v. Boston Symphony Orchestra, Inc., 855 F.2d 888 (1st Cir.1988), cert. denied, 488 U.S. 1043 (1989), affirmed plaintiff's damages verdict for breach of contract.

However the potential rewards to a plaintiff for a successful sally along the tort-contract frontier assure that plaintiffs' probes will continue. A legal wrong which a plaintiff may assert as either a contract or a tort presents the plaintiff with both remedial and procedural opportunities. For a successful tort plaintiff may receive damages measures not generally available to a contract plaintiff; these measures include punitive damages, special damages liberated from Hadley v. Baxendale's contemplation test, as well as emotional distress and mental suffering damages. In a real and practical sense, when an opportunity arises, remedial and procedural considerations dictate the substantive theories the plaintiff will pursue. The lawyer's job is to characterize creatively and persuasively in a client's behalf; the judge's job is to characterize in a principled way that responds to the policies of the substantive areas.

A list of remedial and procedural considerations may explain litigants' otherwise puzzling choices of substantive law throughout this book:

1. *Compensatory Damages*. The differing amounts of compensatory damages for torts and contract breaches were discussed above.

2. *Punitive Damages*. The possibility of recovering punitive damages is a potent incentive for a plaintiff to allege a tort.

3. *Prejudgment Interest*. Consideration of prejudgment interest may, however, militate against a tort approach.

4. *Statutes of Limitations*. The length of the respective statutes of limitations affects many plaintiffs' choices. Tort statutes of limitations tend to be shorter than those for breach of contract. In medical malpractice, for example, too much delay may leave the plaintiff with only a breach of contract possibility.

5. *The Statute of Frauds*. The lack of a writing may bar a plaintiff's breach of contract action, but not in tort for fraud or restitution of defendant's unjust enrichment.

6. *Comparative or Contributory Negligence*. The defendant's possible defense of contributory or comparative negligence is an obvious reason for a plaintiff to incline toward breach of contract.

7. *Governmental Immunity*. Sovereign immunity from breach of contract actions has yielded; to a large extent the same is true of tort liability under the Federal Tort Claims Act and state equivalents. But some exceptions and holdouts may exist.

8. *Prejudgment Attachment*. The attachment statute may not permit plaintiff's prejudgment attachment of defendant's property in a tort case. Cal.Civ. Proc.Code § 483.010.

9. *Assignability and Survivability*. The assignability or survivability of the cause of action may militate against a tort approach, but the differences have been modified.

10. *Discharge in Bankruptcy.* A defendant's contract liability is more likely to be discharged in his bankruptcy than a tort judgment, particularly for an intentional tort or punitive damages.

11. *Attorney fees.* In addition to a contract that provides for attorney fees, a lawyer must check the statutes and common-law exceptions to the American Rule.

12. *Insurance Coverage.* The defendant's liability insurance is likely to cover its negligent torts, but not its intentional torts or contracts.

Are there others?

End Week 5

Chapter 7

BREACHED SALES AGREEMENTS

When someone breaches a contract, the nonbreaching party's first choice is whether to involve a court at all. People in business often prefer to avoid the expense and delay associated with a lawsuit. Most contracts that go awry do not end up in court, and the parties settle most contract lawsuits before a court's final decision on the plaintiff's remedy.

The plaintiff's lawyer should approach remedial alternatives under the headings of client preferences and tactical advantages. A lawyer who settles a dispute or lawsuit should know the client's alternatives to a negotiated agreement, that is the fallback remedies and damages measures available, if it comes to that, in a court. And the contract disputes that parties do litigate to remedy become crucial precedents because those court decisions create and maintain the structure of rules within which others negotiate settlements.

Contract disputes the parties do litigate to remedy usually have one or more of three characteristics. (a) The contract was a dismal deal for one of the parties, either when the contract was formed or in retrospect. (b) The deal unraveled in a way that caused the future plaintiff a lot of loss, personal injury, lost business profits, or other special damages. (c) One or both of the parties lacks the interest in a long-term relationship that would lead to a mutually acceptable compromise without extended conflict.

Digression on the Uniform Commercial Code[s]. In breached sales contracts for "goods," the decisions and Notes below cite and quote the U.C.C., but a student ought to keep a complete copy of the Code close at hand to consult while studying this material. After all, the U.C.C. is a Code, not just a collection of sections.

The U.C.C.'s sales article, Article 2, has been and remains somewhat of a moving target. A Study Group, a Drafting Committee, the Permanent Editorial Board, the National Conference of Commissioners on Uniform State Laws, (NCCUSL), and the American Law Institute, (ALI), worked on a new Article 2 through most of the 1990s. But in 1999, NCCUSL suspended its dealings with a substantially revised 1999 draft because of concern that industry opposition would prevent uniform enactment by state legislatures.

A new drafting committee was selected with a new chair and a new reporter. The next draft of proposed amendments to Article 2, was a less substantial revision, even retaining the original Article 2's numbering and structure. This

2003 Revised Article 2 will be submitted to the state legislatures for adoption; if enacted, it will be statutory law; this book refers to it as the Revised U.C.C.

The decisions in this chapter quote and apply the Original U.C.C, the state U.C.C. statutes that were the positive law in effect when the courts decided our casebook's cases. This casebook refers to it as the Original U.C.C.

Some of the Revised U.C.C.'s changes in remedies have been controversial. Where we think it will be helpful, we quote the Revised U.C.C.'s changes in the Notes. The Revised U.C.C. version consulted and cited is American Law Institute, Amendments to U.C.C. Article 2–Sales, Proposed Final Draft, approved by ALI members, May 13, 2003.

Back to remedies. The plaintiff's remedial goal in a breached sales contract is usually to obtain the breaching party's performance or its money equivalent. The buyer's two principal contract remedies are (a) specific performance, and (b) expectancy (or general) damages, usually based on a market value—contract price differential. The buyer's standard recovery for a seller's breach of warranty is "the difference * * * between the value of the goods accepted and the value they would have had if they had been as warranted." Original U.C.C. § 2–714(2).

Within breach of contract, the successful contract plaintiff will select between receiving specific performance and recovering expectancy damages. The judge's test to decide between "equitable" specific performance and common-law damages remedies is whether the damages remedy is "inadequate" for plaintiff because the defendant's consideration is "unique," a standard which may, but should not, skew the judge's choice towards damages.

The contract remedies have a two-sided social function. For the nonbreaching plaintiff, the court will strive to fulfill contractual expectations. For the breaching defendant, the court's purpose is to respond in a way that will encourage it (and others) to perform contracts, even losing ones. The idea, actual or by example, that even if you breach a contract, you will perform or pay, ought, in the future, to deter parties from breaching contracts.

The plaintiff's next decision involves the addition of special, often called consequential, damages. This work includes plaintiff's reliance recovery in special damages. A buyer's recovery for the seller's breach of contract may be, or may include, restitution, recovery measured by the defendant's unjust enrichment.

Another of the plaintiff's choices is between, on the one hand, specific performance and expectancy damages, the actual or cash money consummation of the failed deal, or, on the other, rescission-restitution which returns the parties to the world before the deal was struck. Restitution make take one of two forms. (a) If a contract was formed, rescission-restitution. (b) If the parties' agreement did not end in a contract, freestanding restitution based on defendant's unjust enrichment; many freestanding restitution doctrines are in Chapter 5 above.

I. BUYER'S REMEDIES

A. SPECIFIC PERFORMANCE

Prerequisites for Specific Performance.

A Contract. The buyer and seller must have formed a valid contract based on offer, acceptance and consideration.

A land transaction proceeds in two stages. The buyer and seller first agree to a binder contract, under various names. In a sale of land, the parties' valid binder contract triggers "equitable conversion," or eligibility for specific performance, of which more below. The transaction's second stage occurs at the settlement or closing, where the buyer receives the seller's deed.

Statute of Frauds. Under the statute of frauds, a "contract for the sale of lands" must be "in writing and signed by the party to be charged therewith." Mass. Gen. Laws Ann. ch. 259, § 1. A contract to sell goods for $500 "or more" must be written. Original U.C.C. § 2–201. The Revised U.C.C. ups that to $5000.

The Chancellor may insist on a more detailed contract for specific performance than he would require to award the buyer damages; the Chancellor must ascertain that the contract's terms are precise enough to enter an appropriate specific performance decree, to supervise that performance, and perhaps to punish the seller's disobedience with contempt. Restatement (Second) of Contracts § 362 (1979).

Breach. The seller must have breached the contract. A real estate binder contract often includes "contingencies," time-limited conditions precedent, like a satisfactory inspection, due diligence, a loan commitment, and even the sale of the purchaser's home. If a contingency does not pan out, the buyer will not have breached it; instead the contract is voided and seller returns the buyer's earnest money. When the contingencies are removed, the parties should settle on the closing date specified in the binder contract. Failure to perform is a breach.

If the seller breaches, the buyer will weigh alternative remedies, particularly specific performance and damages. And the buyer must qualify for specific performance.

Sales of land and sales of goods present slightly different specific-performance profiles. In McCarthy v. Tobin, this chapter's first decision, a seller's breach of a land contract raises the issue of what are the minimum terms for a binding contract.

Equity. Specific performance is an equitable remedy. Normally a plaintiff seeking an equitable remedy must show that her legal remedy, usually damages, is inadequate, that unless the judge grants her the equitable remedy, she will be irreparably injured. The judge's test for specific performance is whether the property is "unique." There will be no jury. The chancellor will enforce specific performance with a personal order to the defendant-seller to perform the contract. The chancellor has a fallback method of enforcement, a decretal transfer. Rule 70, Fed. and Mass. R. Civ. P. 70.

Tender. In order to qualify for specific performance of a land sale contract, the plaintiff must "tender" to the defendant whatever is required by the contract. The ready, willing, and able buyer must tender the amount due.

Time is of the Essence. If the contract contains a "time-is-of-the-essence" clause, as most form binder contracts do, a buyer's failure to tender performance on that date liberates the seller from contractual obligations. Wilson v. Klein, 715 S.W.2d 814 (Tex.App.1986). Time is not of the essence, however, unless either express language in the contract makes it so or it can be implied from the circumstances of the transaction. Limpus v. Armstrong, 3 Mass.App.Ct. 19, 322 N.E.2d 187 (1975). Some delay in performance may not be a substantial breach of the contract. In Cook v. Rezek, 89 S.D. 667, 237 N.W.2d 18 (1975), the court considered the buyer's seventeen-day delay in making a $500 down payment immaterial and granted him specific performance. If the binder contract does not include a time-is-of-the-essence clause, then time is not of the essence; but the chancellor will, nevertheless, imply a reasonable time. Bryan v. Moore, 863 A.2d 258 (Del.Ch. 2004).

Equitable Defenses. If the defendant seller proves one of the affirmative defenses to any contract, for example, mistake or illegality, then the buyer's contract claim fails. The seller may raise an *equitable* defense, for example, laches, unclean hands or extreme hardship, to defeat the buyer's equitable remedy of specific performance. A defendant's equitable defense is a defense to the plaintiff's equitable remedy, specific performance, not to the plaintiff's substantive contract claim. If the seller's equitable defense succeeds, the chancellor will refuse to grant the buyer specific performance, but he will leave her to her legal remedy, damages.

McCARTHY v. TOBIN

Supreme Judicial Court of Massachusetts, 1999.
429 Mass. 84, 706 N.E.2d 629.

ABRAMS, J. On August 9, 1995, McCarthy executed an offer to purchase real estate on a pre-printed form generated by the Greater Boston Real Estate Board. The [Offer to Purchase] OTP contained, among other provisions, a description of the property, the price to be paid, deposit requirements, limited title requirements, and the time and place for closing. The OTP also included several provisions that are the basis of this dispute. The OTP required that the parties "shall, on or before 5 P.M. August 16, 1995, execute the applicable Standard Form Purchase and Sale Agreement recommended by the Greater Boston Real Estate Board * * * which, when executed, shall be the agreement between the parties hereto." In the section containing additional terms and conditions, a typewritten insertion states, "Subject to a Purchase and Sale Agreement satisfactory to Buyer and Seller." The OTP provided, "Time is of the essence hereof." Finally, an unnumbered paragraph immediately above the signature line states: "NOTICE: This is a legal document that creates binding obligations. If not understood, consult an attorney." Tobin signed the OTP on August 11, 1995.

On August 16, 1995, sometime after 5 P.M., Tobin's lawyer sent a first draft of the purchase and sale agreement by facsimile transmission to McCarthy's lawyer. On August 21, McCarthy's lawyer sent a letter by facsimile transmission containing his comments and proposing several changes to Tobin's lawyer. The changes laid out the requirements for good title; imposed on Tobin the risk of casualty to the premises before sale; solicited indemnification, for title insurance purposes, regarding mechanics' liens, parties in possession, and hazardous materials; and sought an acknowledgment that the premises' systems were operational. The next day, the two lawyers discussed the proposed revisions. They did not discuss an extension of the deadline for signing the purchase and sale agreement, and Tobin's lawyer did not object to the fact that the deadline had already passed. On August 23, Tobin's lawyer sent a second draft of the agreement to McCarthy's lawyer. On August 25, a Friday, McCarthy's lawyer informed Tobin's lawyer that the agreement was acceptable, McCarthy would sign it, and it would be delivered the following Monday. On Saturday, August 26, McCarthy signed the purchase and sale agreement. On the same day, Tobin accepted the DiMinicos' offer to purchase the property.

On August 28, McCarthy delivered the executed agreement and a deposit to Tobin's broker. The next day, Tobin's lawyer told McCarthy's lawyer that the agreement was late and that Tobin had already accepted the DiMinicos' offer. In September, 1995, Tobin and the DiMinicos executed a purchase and sale agreement. Before the deal closed, McCarthy filed this action for specific performance and damages.

The plaintiff, John J. McCarthy, Jr., claims that the defendant, Ann G. Tobin, agreed to sell * * * [the] real estate to him. He asserts that they created a binding agreement when they signed a standard Offer to Purchase form. The DiMinicos intervened because they later agreed to purchase the property in question from Tobin. McCarthy and Tobin each moved for summary judgment and the DiMinicos for partial summary judgment. The motion judge allowed Tobin's and the DiMinicos' motions, declaring that Tobin had no obligation to sell to McCarthy and therefore McCarthy had no right to the specific performance of the real estate agreement. The Appeals Court vacated the judgment in favor of Tobin and the DiMinicos and remanded for entry of judgment in favor of McCarthy. The Appeals Court reasoned that the OTP was a firm offer that became a contract binding on the parties when it was accepted. We granted the interveners' application for further appellate review following the Appeals Court's opinion concluding that the plaintiff was entitled to specific performance. * * *

Firm offer. The primary issue is whether the OTP executed by McCarthy and Tobin was a binding contract. Tobin and the DiMinicos argue that it was not because of the provision requiring the execution of a purchase and sale agreement. McCarthy urges that he and Tobin intended to be bound by the OTP and that execution of the purchase and sale agreement was merely a formality.

McCarthy argues that the OTP adequately described the property to be sold and the price to be paid. The remaining terms covered by the purchase and sale agreement were subsidiary matters which did not preclude the formation of a binding contract. [citation] We agree.

The controlling fact is the intention of the parties. [citation]

Tobin argues that language contemplating the execution of a final written agreement gives rise to a strong inference that she and McCarthy have not agreed to all material aspects of a transaction and thus that they do not intend to be bound. [citations] [The court disagrees] See Coan v. Holbrook, 327 Mass. 221, 224, 97 N.E.2d 649 (1951) ("Mutual manifestations of assent that are in themselves sufficient to make a contract will not be prevented from so operating by the mere fact that the parties also manifest an intention to prepare and adopt a written memorial thereof.")

The interveners argue that McCarthy departed from the customary resolution of any open issues, and therefore manifested his intent not to be bound, by requesting several additions to the purchase and sale agreement. We agree with the Appeals Court, however, that McCarthy's revisions were "ministerial and nonessential terms of the bargain."

The inference that the OTP was binding is bolstered by the notice printed on the form. McCarthy and Tobin were alerted to the fact that the OTP "create[d] binding obligations." The question is what those obligations were. The DiMinicos argue that the OTP merely obligated the parties to negotiate the purchase and sale agreement in good faith. We disagree. The OTP employs familiar contractual language. It states that McCarthy "hereby offer[s] to buy" the property, and Tobin's signature indicates that "[t]his Offer is hereby accepted." The OTP also details the amount to be paid and when, describes the property bought, and specifies for how long the offer was open. This was a firm offer, the acceptance of which bound Tobin to sell and McCarthy to buy the subject property. We conclude that the OTP reflects the parties' intention to be bound. * * * The form may be redrafted if it does not reflect the intention of the parties.

Waiver. Even though the purchase and sale agreement was not necessary to bind the parties, its execution was required by the OTP. The agreement is unambiguous in this regard and thus must be enforced. [citation]

The typewritten addition subjecting the OTP to a purchase and sale agreement satisfactory to both parties may be contradictory, but it is not ambiguous. Whether we construe the preprinted language or the addition as controlling, there was a waiver.

Courts hold parties to deadlines they have imposed on themselves when they agree that time is of the essence. [citation] The DiMinicos argue that McCarthy violated his obligations by failing to execute the purchase and sale agreement by the August 16 deadline.

The August 16 date is a condition subsequent. Without an executed purchase and sale agreement by that date, the OTP provides that the parties' obligations to each other are extinguished. [citation] Conditions, however, may be waived. [citation]

We are persuaded that Tobin waived the August 16 deadline. The issue of waiver is ordinarily one for the fact finder. If the facts are undisputed, however, waiver is a question of law. Tobin's lawyer, acting as her agent, voluntarily undertook the task of drafting the purchase and sale agreement. He did not produce the first draft until it was impossible for McCarthy to sign it before the deadline. He also did not object to the passage of the deadline in the telephone calls and facsimile transmissions that followed. Instead, he continued to deal with McCarthy's lawyer in an effort to craft a mutually satisfactory agreement. In the only express communication concerning the execution of the agreement, Tobin's lawyer implied that a date later than August 16 was satisfactory. Words and conduct attributable to Tobin signified her waiver of the August 16 deadline. [citation] Once there was a waiver, time was no longer of the essence. McCarthy's subsequent tender of the signed agreement and a deposit was timely and within reason. We conclude that there is no issue of material fact and that McCarthy was entitled to a judgment as a matter of law. See Mass.R.Civ.P. 56(c).

Specific performance. On remand, the issue of the appropriate remedy will arise. A judge generally has considerable discretion with respect to granting specific performance, but it is usually granted in disputes involving the conveyance of land. [citation] "It is well-settled law in this Commonwealth that real property is unique and that money damages will often be inadequate to redress a deprivation of an interest in land." Greenfield Country Estates Tenants Ass'n, Inc. v. Deep, 423 Mass. 81, 88, 666 N.E.2d 988 (1996). It is therefore proper to allow McCarthy specific relief.

McCarthy's right to specific performance is unaltered by Tobin's execution of a purchase and sale agreement with the DiMinicos. McCarthy filed this action prior to the execution of that agreement. The DiMinicos had actual notice of McCarthy's claim to the property and assumed the risk of a result favorable to McCarthy. The DiMinicos closed on the property. They hold legal title, subject to the equitable obligation to convey the property to McCarthy on payment of the purchase price set by Tobin and McCarthy. [citation]

The judgment is vacated. The case is remanded to the Superior Court for the entry of a judgment in favor of McCarthy's claim for specific performance.

Notes

1. *The Buyer's Specific Performance.* A land buyer's right to specific performance is well established enough to be routine in the United States. Although the chancellor of equity is famous, or notorious, for his wide discretion, a trial judge lacks discretion to deny a qualified buyer specific performance. A court will assume that each parcel of land is "unique." Without discussion, the court will accept the inadequacy of the buyer's damages remedy at law, damages. See Cal.Civ.Code § 3387.

In Canada, however, a land buyer seeking specific performance must show factually that the land is unique usually with proof related to the attributes of the buyer or the particular property.

2. Enforcing a specific performance order in a land sale is straightforward. The seller's duty is to make a recordable deed. If a seller refuses, the judge may provide for a deed from the clerk under Rule 70, Federal Rules of Civil Procedure, or the state equivalent. The procedure may not require the defendant-seller to co-operate.

3. *Specific Performance of an Affirmative Promise, the Chancellor's Discretion, and the Buyer's Quality of Life.* When plaintiff-Petry purchased her lot, it abutted unconstructed, but promised, Lake Briarwood. After the developer was reorganized in bankruptcy, a group of lot owners settled litigation with the developer, agreeing to substitute a recreational area for the lake.

Plaintiff sued the developer seeking damages, specific performance of the agreement to construct the lake, and an injunction forbidding performance of the settlement agreement. The Pennsylvania Supreme Court affirmed the trial judge's order transferring the case to law because damages were an adequate remedy for plaintiff.

"Those factors which outweigh [plaintiff's] interest in the uniqueness or special value of having Lake Briarwood built include: the ability to calculate or ascertain [plaintiff's] money damages; the fact that enforcing an affirmative covenant or contract imposes a supervisory burden on the trial court; the fact that purchasing in reliance on an affirmative undertaking involves greater risk than purchasing in reliance on a negative covenant or promise; and the fact that granting [plaintiff] specific performance would adversely affect the rights of numerous other lot owners and the Community Association at large.

"This Court has repeatedly held that a decree of specific performance is a matter of grace and not of right, [citations] and that the exercise of the power to grant specific performance is discretionary [citation]. Based on a balancing of the equities set forth above, we find that no abuse of discretion occurred here in transferring this matter to the law side of the trial court based on the pleadings and oral argument." Petry v. Tanglwood Lakes, Inc., 514 Pa. 51, 60, 522 A.2d 1053, 1057 (1987).

Justice Larsen dissented: "This case is not about the value of a piece of property as it currently exists and the value of that same property if Briarwood Lake had been constructed. The questions raised here are much broader. They deal with life style values not cash values. The majority's acceptance of the theory that the failure to build the lake merely involves a diminution in the value of [plaintiff's] property fails to give due consideration to the very unique quality of the property as a lake front lot. Indeed, this unique feature is what attracts prospective owners and sells the lots." Petry v. Tanglwood Lakes, Inc., 514 Pa. 51, 61, 522 A.2d 1053, 1058 (1987).

4. *Reselling Buyer*. An occasional seller has argued successfully that the buyer's damages remedy is adequate because the buyer has entered into a contract of resale. See Hazelton v. Miller, 25 App.D.C. 337 (1905), aff'd on other grounds, sub nom. Hazelton v. Sheckels, 202 U.S. 71 (1906). But most courts have rejected this contention. See Justus v. Clelland, 133 Ariz. 381, 651 P.2d 1206 (App. 1982).

5. Scholars maintain that specific performance is a better remedy than money damages. Professor Douglas Laycock rejects the idea of a hierarchy of remedies with the judge favoring money damages unless the plaintiff shows that damages are inadequate. "[T]he real ground for specific performance is irreplaceability, and * * * uniqueness is not the only cause of irreplaceability. Damages are inadequate unless they can be used to replace the specific thing that was lost, however ordinary that thing is." Douglas Laycock, The Death of the Irreparable Injury Rule, 103 Harv. L.Rev. 687, 707 (1990). See also, Robert E. Scott & George Triantis, Embedded Options and the Case Against Compensation in Contract Law, 104 Colum. L.Rev. 1428, 1486–87 (2004); Alan Schwartz, The Case for Specific Performance, 89 Yale L.J. 271 (1979); Peter Linzer, On the Amorality of Contract Remedies—Efficiency, Equity and the Second Restatement, 81 Colum.L.Rev. 111 (1981)

In McCarthy v. Tobin, the court hedges buyer-McCarthy's right to specific performance when it observes "that real property is unique and that money damages will often be inadequate to redress a deprivation of an interest in land." The court might have omitted the "often."

6. *Procedure—Tactics. (a) Lis Pendens*. If the buyer-plaintiff files a lis pendens notice with a specific performance lawsuit, the seller will be effectively prevented from selling the land to another buyer, because that second buyer will take the land subject to the result in the plaintiff-buyer's lawsuit.

Massachusetts has a lis pendens statute. Mass. Gen. Laws Ann. ch. 184, § 15. But McCarthy did not file a lis pendens with his specific performance action, perhaps because Tobin had already accepted the DiMinicos' offer when McCarthy's lawyer delivered his final agreement to Tobin's lawyer.

(b) *Parties—Let's All Join In*. A court will treat the lawyer's decisions as if they were the client's choices. Tobin's lawyer delayed which, in retrospect, waived the condition subsequent and the time-is-of-the-essence clause. McCarthy sued Tobin, his seller, for specific performance and damages; but Tobin had already formed another contract to transfer the property to the DiMinicos. Apparently after McCarthy sued Tobin, she deeded the land to the DiMinicos; the court says "they hold legal title."

(c) *Joinder*. Could McCarthy have joined the DiMinicos as defendants? Most of the Massachusetts state-court procedure rules are the same as the federal rules, including the numbering. According to Rule 19(a), a plaintiff may join as a defendant someone who "claims an interest relating to the subject matter of the action and is so situated that the disposition of the action in the person's absence may (I) as a practical matter impair or impede the person's ability to protect that interest." Mass. R. Civ. P. 19(a). When he sued, should McCarthy have joined the DiMinicos as defendants?

(d) *Intervention*. The DiMinicos solved McCarthy's joinder problem when they intervened. Did the DiMinicos qualify for intervention to protect the interest they claimed in the land? Rule 24(a)(2)'s test for intervention follows Rule 19's test for joinder, but it adds "unless the applicant's interest is adequately represented by existing parties." Mass. R. Civ. P. 24(a)(2). An intervenor becomes a defendant and has a right to defend.

But should the DiMinicos have intervened? An intervenor will reap the success of victory or suffer the hazard of defeat.

7. *Remedy*. What is McCarthy's remedy? The court says "specific performance." Before you accept that read on.

Although the court doesn't use the words "constructive trust," it uses the language of constructive trust. When a breaching seller resells to a third person, a court might hold that the seller possesses the proceeds in a constructive trust for the original buyer. George Palmer, The Law of Restitution § 4.9(b) (1978).

McCarthy's relief is not against his seller Tobin, but against the DiMinicos who had no contract to perform with McCarthy, specifically or otherwise. McCarthy might have sued the DiMinicos for damages for the tort of inducing Tobin to breach his contract with them. But he sued Tobin for breach of contract and the DiMinicos intervened.

The court may decide that the DiMinicos are constructive trustees for McCarthy: the DiMinicos, the court says, "hold legal title, subject to the equitable obligation to convey the property to McCarthy on payment of the purchase price set by Tobin and McCarthy." Is McCarthy's remedy a constructive trust that the court misnamed specific performance?

Both specific performance and a constructive trust are equitable remedies, so substituting one phrase for the other may not prejudice the DiMinicos if they had advance warning. See Rule 54(c): "every final judgment shall grant the relief to which the party in whose favor it is rendered is entitled, even if the party has not demanded such relief in the party's pleading." Mass. R. Civ. P. 54(c). But read on.

8. *Defense of Hardship*? Might the DiMinicos, who were strangers to the McCarthy–Tobin contract and nonparties to McCarthy's original lawsuit, have argued a hardship equitable defense to McCarthy's "specific performance" remedy? The DiMinicos' hardship defense would fail unless the buyers were bona fide purchasers without notice of the McCarthy contract. If the DiMinicos' hardship defense had succeeded, they would have kept the property and McCarthy would have been remitted to his remedy at law, recovering damages from Tobin. That isn't what happened.

If the DiMinicos hadn't intervened, would McCarthy have had to invite them in?

9. *Sorting It Out or "Follow the Money."* According to the court, doesn't McCarthy pay the DiMinicos the amount his contract with Tobin specified? Since the opinion doesn't have the prices in the two contracts, we can speculate about two possibilities.

(a) Suppose that McCarthy's contract with Tobin was for a higher price, $10, than the DiMinicos', $5. If the DiMinicos have already paid Tobin $5 when McCarthy pays them $10, may they keep the whole $10? If, on the other hand, the DiMinicos must pay Tobin $5, does this give Tobin the profit she would have made from her contract with McCarthy that she breached?

(b) Or, as is more likely, suppose that the DiMinicos' contract with Tobin was for a higher price, $10, than McCarthy's, $5. After McCarthy pays them $5, are the DiMinicos simply out $5? If Tobin's deed to them was a warranty deed, the DiMinicos should be able to recover $5 from Tobin on her breached covenant of title.

10. *Specific Performance Plus Damages*. McCarthy also sued Tobin for "damages." Although "damages" appear to have fallen out of this appeal, a land buyer

seeking specific performance has two possible kinds of money recovery, if you like, damages:

(a) The buyer's specific performance may fail, perhaps because of a seller's equitable defense like unclean hands or laches. Or specific performance may turn out to be impossible; for example in a case like McCarthy v. Tobin, the seller may convey the property to a bona fide purchaser. See Ziebarth v. Kalenze in Chapter 3. If so, the buyer ought to be entitled as a fallback remedy to recover expectancy damages from the breaching seller; either the buyer could amend her complaint, Rule 15, to seek damages in the alternative, Rules 8(e)(2), 18(a), or the judge could grant damages under Rule 54(c)'s "every final judgment shall grant the relief to which the party in whose favor it is rendered is entitled, even if the party has not demanded such relief in the party's pleading." We will study the buyer's measure of damages later.

(b) Lawsuits take time. If the judge grants the buyer late specific performance, she may be entitled to recover delay damages, measured by rental value or lost use.

11. *Difficulty of Supervision.* Another objection to specific performance is that the unruly parties, who have been unable to co-operate up to now, will continue to squabble; thus the judge will be drawn into the parties' imbroglio with bad consequences on all sides. Is the objection to specific performance when it will require cooperation and a continuing series of acts really grounded in judicial misgivings about difficulty of supervision? When both the buyer and the seller are large business corporations, should the judge be concerned about compelling "personal" relations? Should a judge who may use an injunction to manage a school or a prison dread to order a corporation to ship photocopy toner? Copylease Corp. v. Memorex Corp., 408 F.Supp. 758 (S.D.N.Y.1976). Are the specific performance orders that are most important to plaintiffs among the most difficult for judges to supervise?

Slow Boat to China? The buyer Falk, a purchasing agent for a locomotive works in China, purchased from Axiam a "fully automated piston skirt size gauge with diameter measurement," which included the agreement the seller unjustifiably breached, "an obligation on the part of Axiam to travel to China to install the gauge, test the gauge, and train others to correctly use the gauge." Because the "unique" gauge "was a specialized device which required the technical and specialized knowledge of Axiam engineers," the court granted Falk specific performance. "While courts will generally not order specific performance of personal service obligations, * * * the type of obligation at issue in this case is a corporate obligation, not a 'personal' one." Falk v. Axiam Inc., 944 F.Supp. 542, 544, 552, n. 3 (S.D.Tex.1996).

12. *Equitable Conversion.* A court will use the equitable-conversion doctrine to determine when the land buyer's and seller's rights to secure specific performance begins. A land transaction usually occurs in two stages: the first stage is a written binder contract based on the buyer's earnest money where the buyer and seller agree; the second stage is the "closing" where the seller exchanges a deed to the land for the rest of the buyer's money.

Equitable conversion rules may govern the way a court will treat the buyer's and the seller's interests during the period between the binder contract and the deed. When a buyer and a seller enter into a binding executory land contract, equity (a) "converts" the buyer's contractual interest from personal property into real property, and (b) "converts" the seller's contractual interest from real property into personal property. The buyer becomes the seller's debtor for the purchase money, and the seller owns the right to receive the buyer's purchase money.

Before the seller accepted the buyer's offer, the buyer had money and the seller had land; after seller accepts but before the deed, the buyer and seller still "have" the money and land respectively; but, because "equity" which "regards as done what ought to be done" has converted the buyer's and seller's interests. The chancellor will treat the buyer's money as if it were land and the seller's land as if it were money.

The equitable-conversion doctrine anticipates specific performance; because, after equitable conversion occurs, the chancellor will order the seller to convey the land. The fiction of conversion tells the judge to treat that anticipation as the buyer's equitable ownership of the real property. From the time of equitable conversion, a court will say that the buyer has equitable title, the right to secure specific performance.

The equitable conversion fiction is amiable so long as it is restricted to telling the chancellor when the parties' rights to specific performance begin; but once the fiction of conversion begins to control relationships outside that sphere, it can create serious consequences.

A court may need to determine the legal effect of other events between the binder contract and the closing.

(a) What if the seller's judgment creditor dockets a judgment which creates a judgment lien on the seller's "real property?" Lach v. Deseret Bank, 746 P.2d 802 (Utah Ct.App. 1987).

b) What if the seller dies and her will leaves her real property to X, her personal property to Y? In re Estate of Sweet, 254 So.2d 562 (Fla.Dist.Ct.App.1971).

(c) Suppose the buildings and other improvements on the property are destroyed. Does the buyer have to accept the seller's deed? Paine v. Meller, 31 Eng.Rep. 1088 (Ch. 1801).

A court may reason deductively from the idea that the binder contract converted the buyer's interest from personal to real property and the seller's interest from real to personal property. Thus:

(a) The judgment debtor's property was personal and the seller's creditor's judgment lien does not attach to it. Lach v. Deseret Bank, 746 P.2d 802 (Utah Ct.App.1987).

(b) The seller died with personal property, which Y receives. In re Estate of Sweet, 254 So.2d 562 (Fla.App.1971).

(c) The buyer bore the risk of loss of "her" realty; she pays the seller the full contract price for the land without the buildings and improvements. Paine v. Meller, 31 Eng.Rep. 1088 (Ch. 1801).

A court's "logical" extension of equitable conversion from specific performance to govern these other issues may mask a choice between equitable conversion and another body of doctrine. (a) For the judgment lien, the debtor-creditor and recording act doctrines. (b) For the death of the seller, the wills and estates policies, including the testator's intent. And (c) for the destruction of the buildings and improvements, contractual policies of risk bearing and contract interpretation.

If a court extends equitable conversion to other realms where the difference between realty and personalty matters, it may decide disputes in ways that erode other rules more related to the dispute. This in turns leads to confusion, capricious and unsound decisions, and conflicting lines of authority. Would the law be clearer and more predictable if courts restricted equitable conversion to explaining specific performance? Or should the fiction of equitable conversion be deleted completely from the legal vocabulary, leaving only the idea that after the seller accepts the binder contract, if one party breaches, the other may usually secure specific performance?

13. *Other Interests in Land.* Usually a court will ignore the technical categories of common-law estates and, for example, find damages an inadequate remedy for the parties' agreement to transfer a leasehold or an easement.

A New York decision differed. The buyer of the lessor's interest breached a contract to lease advertising space on the exterior wall of a building. The lessee sought specific performance. Ruling that specific performance of real property leases is not granted as a matter of course and that physical uniqueness is insufficient to establish the inadequacy of damages, the court held that the proper test was whether the lessee's damages were susceptible of calculation with reasonable certainty. It denied specific performance because it found that they were. Van Wagner Advertising Corp. v. S & M Enterprises, 67 N.Y.2d 186, 501 N.Y.S.2d 628, 492 N.E.2d 756 (1986).

14. *Dispensing with Specific Performance.* May the buyer and seller agree to exclude specific performance as a remedy for breach of a land sale contract? The court upheld the restriction in Greenstein v. Greenbrook, Ltd., 413 So.2d 842 (Fla.App. 1982).

15. *Governing Law.* While the applicable law governing a land deal is the court-made common law with some statutes, a transaction for "goods" falls under the Uniform Commercial Code.

16. *Specific Performance for Seller's Breach of a "Goods" Contract.* There is one significant difference between specific performance of a contract to sell land and one to sell "goods." In the parties' contract for goods, the court will take the uniqueness prerequisite more seriously before granting a buyer specific performance.

For land sales, the "uniqueness" test does not lead the court to discerning analysis; specific performance is routine. The Original U.C.C. says "specific performance may be decreed where the goods are unique or in other proper circumstances." § 2–716(1). The Revision preserves the test. Although each parcel of land *is* unique, the goods buyer who seeks specific performance must demonstrate that the particular goods are unique.

Should legislatures and courts treat a buyer's request for specific performance differently depending on whether the contract is for real property or personal property? In the age of the tract house and the identical condo unit, is the idea that each parcel of "land" is unique obsolete? Or, should legislatures and courts relax the uniqueness test for specific performance of a contract to sell goods to be comparable with a land contract? In other words, should the Revised U.C.C.'s specific performance section, § 2–716, have dispensed with the prerequisite "unique or in other proper circumstances?"

This chapter closes with a decision on specific performance of a seller's breach of a contract to sell an automobile, a complicated decision which will serve as a recap of many of the tactics and choices involved in sales remedies.

17. *Preventing the Goods Seller's Transfer.* As mentioned above, a buyer who sues for specific performance of a land contract may file a lis pendens notice and effectively prevent the seller from transferring the land while the lawsuit is pending. Although the buyer of goods lacks a similar specialized legal-latin technique, the buyer's timely temporary restraining order or preliminary injunction forbidding the defendant's transfer will bar a seller from frustrating specific performance.

B. BUYER'S DAMAGES FOR SELLER'S BREACH

1. TORT v. CONTRACT

Common Law Deceit. The court stated the elements of a plaintiff's fraud action for damages: "1. There must be a representation; 2. That representation must be false; 3. It must have to do with a past or present fact; 4. That fact must be material; 5. It must be susceptible of knowledge; 6. The representer must know it to be false, or in the alternative, must assert it as of his own knowledge without knowing whether it is true or false; 7. The representer must intend to have the other person induced to act, or justified in acting upon it; 8. That person must be so induced to act or so justified in acting; 9. That person's action must be in reliance upon the representation; 10. That person must suffer damage; 11. That damage must be attributable to the misrepresentation, that is, the statement must be the proximate cause of the injury. These elements must be affirmatively proved; they are not to be presumed." Hanson v. Ford Motor Co., 278 F.2d 586, 591 (8th Cir.1960).

SELMAN v. SHIRLEY

Supreme Court of Oregon, 1939.
161 Or. 582, 91 P.2d 312.

On July 1, 1933, S.W. Selman and his wife Nona entered into a written contract to purchase for $2,000 a 160–acre ranch in Benton county, Oregon, from H.E. Shirley and his wife. Payments were to be made in the following manner: $500 upon execution of the contract; $200 on or before October 1, 1934, and a like sum of $200 on or before the 1st day of October annually thereafter until the full purchase price was paid. Selman and his wife paid $550 upon execution of the contract, took possession of the premises and have retained the same ever since. $200 was paid on October 1, 1934, but the Selmans failed to make the annual payment due on October 1, 1935. On October 22, 1935, the Shirleys commenced an action in ejectment.

Soon after the action in ejectment was commenced, the Selmans instituted the instant suit * * * to recover damages for fraud and deceit alleged to have been practiced upon them in the transaction. * * *

Plaintiffs, in their amended complaint, charge that they were induced to buy the 160–acre tract of land on account of the following representations:

(1) "that said premises had growing thereon at least Four Thousand (4000) cords of merchantable fire wood;

(2) "that there was sufficient water in the stream running through said premises to irrigate at least ten acres of land thereon in the driest season of the year; * * * and,"

(3) "that there was available, adjacent to the road leading to said premises from the Philomath–Alsea Highway, sufficient gravel to gravel said road and that said gravel could be had for the hauling, that said gravel belonged to Benton County, Oregon."

Plaintiffs allege that the above representations were false and fraudulent in that:

(1) "in truth and in fact there was no merchantable fire wood growing upon said premises;

(2) "that there was not sufficient water to irrigate ten acres or any other amount in excess of One–Eighth of an acre; and * * *,

(3) "that the gravel * * * was privately owned and was not available for graveling said road."

Plaintiffs inspected the premises before entering into the contract of purchase, but assert that they were strangers in Benton county and "had no knowledge or experience in judging timber or timber lands" and that they relied wholly upon the representations made to them. On trial they testified that on account of rain and the muddy ground they were unable to inspect the timber.

The trial court entered findings of fact: * * *

"IV. That the defendant H.E. Shirley knowingly and falsely represented to plaintiff that there was at least four thousand cords of wood on said premises; that said representation was false and was made by defendant H.E. Shirley with the intention of inducing plaintiffs to purchase said premises; that the plaintiffs in purchasing said premises relied upon said representation.

"V. That said premises so purchased by plaintiffs from defendants H.E. Shirley and Ruth Shirley were of the fair market value of $2000.00 at the time said contract was entered into, to-wit, July 1, 1933; that plaintiffs have suffered no damage, having agreed to pay $2000.00 for said premises."

The decree * * * dismissed the suit against the defendants based on the charge of fraud. From this decree, the plaintiffs appealed.

[Editors' Note: The statement of facts is from the dissenting opinion of Belt, J. The majority opinion held that plaintiffs were entitled to recover damages based on the benefit of the bargain rule.]

ROSSMAN, JUSTICE. [On Rehearing.] The brief accompanying the respondents' (defendants') petition for a rehearing contends that we erred when we applied in this suit the benefit-of-the-bargain rule. * * *

We are likely to become so engrossed in efforts to formulate a rule of damages capable of precise application in all future cases and incapable of misapplication in any, that we may lose sight of our real duty in the present case * * *. [T]he ascertainment of what, if any, damages were the proximate result of the wrong is the only problem before us.

Regardless of whether the out-of-pocket-loss rule or the benefit-of-the-bargain rule is the correct one, the fundamental rule, universally employed, is the one just indicated: The victims of fraud are entitled to compensation for every wrong which was the natural and proximate result of the fraud. * * *

In order to indicate the manner in which one writer, at least, has applied this simple formula in instances like the present we quote the following statement made in Sutherland on Damages, 4th ed., § 1171: "The party guilty of the fraud is to be charged with such damages as have naturally and proximately resulted therefrom. He is to make good his representations as though he had given a warranty to that effect. He is to make compensation for the difference between the real state of the case and what it was represented to be. Thus, in cases involving sales, leases or other like contracts, where it appears that there is a fraudulently false representation of quantity, quality, price, or title the measure of damages is the difference in value between that which is actual and that which was represented to exist."

To facilitate its application the proximate result rule is often subdivided into four auxiliary rules: (1) A defrauded party is entitled to all out-of-pocket losses; (2) he is entitled to the benefit of his bargain; (3) if the property was falsely represented as improved with or containing some items which are not there, he is entitled to the cost of installing them; and (4) he is entitled to all consequential damages. These are merely subdivisions of the main rule, and are employed by the courts according to the facts and demands of the various cases. * * *

This place was not a farm; it was not a wood lot; it was merely a tract of logged-off land no different in kind from thousands of other tracts in the Coast Range. But the plaintiffs had no thought of buying a piece of logged-off land. Logged-off land was never mentioned in the negotiations. The plaintiffs wanted a wood lot where they could cut wood and sell it. * * * It is evident that they wanted not only land, but also standing timber capable of being cut into cordwood. In fact, they depended upon the wood and a truckman indebted to them who had promised to cut the trees into cordwood as a means of paying for their purchase. The defendants, in order to make the deal more alluring, represented that the land contained an irrigating stream and that a gravel bed nearby would yield sufficient material, free of cost to make the road leading into this place passable. As a matter of fact, all of the representations were false, and the plaintiffs found themselves with a piece of logged-off land not substantially different from innumerable other tracts in this state which the owners permitted to revert to the tax-levying bodies after the removal of the timber. * * *

We shall now review a few facts concerning value. Selman testified that he would not have accepted the place even as a gift had he not been deceived into the belief that timber was growing upon it and that an irrigating stream flowed through it. Charles Franklin, a farmer who had lived in the vicinity of this property for sixty-five years, and who had logged it off, swore concerning it: "Not much value in any of it now. The principal value was in the timber, but the condition it is in now, it is run down so, that it would take a heck of a lot to get it in a prosperous condition again." * * * This tract is a mile off the main highway and the road leading to it is impassable most of the year. * * * The tract, according to one witness, is "hill land, ferns, fern land mostly." Two of the corners are covered with second-growth fir which has sprung up among the stumps. The first-growth fir, amounting to 200 cords, is unmerchantable. In one small area the Selmans found an abandoned strawberry patch which has proved to be non-productive. Another patch consisting of several acres was at one time planted in oats. Upon two sides of the property is a dilapidated fence. The improvements consist of a four-room house, twenty years old, which Franklin, who built it, described as "just a common box house, very common. * * * We just built it as cheap as we possibly could." Selman testified that the roof leaked like a sieve, and Blakely said, "It isn't a house I would care to live in." The barn, 30 by 50 feet in size, was built forty-six years ago. It was never painted and has a leaky roof. Shirley acquired the property in 1927 and during his ownership never lived upon it, although in the season of 1931–1932 he permitted it to be occupied by an individual named Hofstetter who sowed several acres in rye grass and planted the strawberry patch; otherwise the property remained unoccupied during Shirley's six-year ownership. * * *

The fact that the defendants represented that the property was served by a good irrigating stream and held a growth of timber capable of yielding 4000 cords worth 50 cents per cord, when they asked $2,000 for the property, is an admission that the bare ground, studded with stumps and without a supply of water, was not worth $2,000. The opinion evidence was insufficient to overcome the effect of this admission.

This is an instance, therefore, in which the proof of fraud is clear; in fact, virtually admitted. But, disregarding value for the time being, we shall consider for a moment the results which will follow if the plaintiffs are entitled to nothing, and if judgment must be entered against them for costs. To make the matter entirely clear, let us assume that the land is worth $2,000 and that we are committed to the out-of-pocket-loss rule which assumes that the proximate result of the vendor's fraud is his receipt of something worth more than that with which he parted. That rule does not concern itself with the fact that the fraudulent statements induced the innocent vendee to expect something which he did not receive. It views proximate result from the contemplations of the cozening vendor at the time he induced the vendee to make the purchase, and in this manner restricts recovery to the out-of-pocket-loss. Therefore, assuming that the land was worth $2,000, (1) the plaintiffs would not be entitled to judgment; (2) the action of ejectment would not be stayed; and (3) the plaintiffs would be evicted from the land. If that result occurs the fraudulent representations will have cost Shirley nothing, and upon regaining possession of the property he will be in a position to repeat the fraudulent representations to another prospective buyer, knowing beforehand that if the truth is discovered the worst that can happen to him is that he will again possess the property. But, in the event that the defrauded buyer pays the purchase price, Shirley will receive $2,000 for the land alone although his representations will have induced the buyer to expect not only land, but also timber, a stream and gravel. Thus, the benefit-of-the-bargain principle will operate, but it will operate in reverse— the fraudulent vendor, and not the innocent victim, will get the benefit of the bargain. Next, if the plaintiffs are awarded no damages we will have virtually remade the contract between the parties, for it is now admitted that for the purchase money the plaintiffs were entitled not merely to the land, but also to the wood, etc. Hence, if the law of damages leaves the plaintiffs empty handed, and they are compelled to pay $2,000 for the land in order to save themselves from eviction, they will receive only a fraction of that which the defendants' written words told them they would receive. Finally, if the contract had followed the preceding negotiations, as it should have done, it would have made some mention of the timber, and in that event the plaintiffs could have maintained an action for breach of contract. * * * In other words, the plaintiffs would have been entitled to damages for the Shirleys' failure to provide the timber. Are they now to fare worse because they were deceived into a belief that they would receive the timber as well as the land, and therefore neglected to see to it that the contract contained a warranty concerning the timber? If that is true, the defendants have improved their own condition by multiplying their misdeeds, and we have the paradox that it is less culpable—and cheaper too—to commit fraud (always legally and morally wrong) than merely to breach a contract which, although legally wrong, may in instances be morally excusable. But why should more be obtainable in one form of action than in the other? We abolished the forms of action in order to obviate that absurdity and to make it possible to award adequate relief to the victim of the wrong regardless of the form of the action. Generally, more is obtainable in tort actions than in those based upon a contract because in the former the damages include everything which was the proximate result of the wrong, including compensation for all injuries which were in the contemplation of the parties at the time the contract was effected, while in the latter the damages are limited to those which were in contemplation when the contract was entered into. * * *

The defendants, in seeking to ward off the plaintiffs' claim for damages, rely largely upon the reasoning set forth in Smith v. Bolles, 132 U.S. 125, and Sigafus v. Porter, 179 U.S. 116. In the former, the plaintiff, who claimed that he had been deceived by the defendant into the purchase of some shares of stock in a gold mining corporation, sought the recovery of damages under the benefit-of-the-bargain rule. In the second case the circumstances were the same except that the subject matter of the false representation was a gold mine. In each instance, the federal supreme court held that the damages were out-of-pocket losses. Concerning the first of these two decisions, Professor McCormick, in his treatise on Damages, states in a footnote on page 450: "Court bases result on view that wrongdoer is liable only for consequences which he might reasonably have contemplated—a proposition dubious in its soundness and in its application." We concur in that criticism. Because the out-of-pocket-loss rule determines the proximate result from the expectations of the fraudulent vendor rather than those of the innocent vendee, the vast majority of the jurisdictions have refused to embrace that rule; and apparently for the same reason Texas, in 1919, by legislative enactment (Art. 4004, Tex.Rev.Civ.Stat. 1925; 4 Tex.Law Rev. 386) substituted for it the benefit-of-the-bargain rule. The second decision, from which two of the judges dissented, was based largely upon the first. At the times when those two decisions were written the federal courts refused to employ the rule of damages embraced by local practice * * * the so-called federal common law has disappeared and the federal courts now employ the common law as locally interpreted. * * *

Thus it is almost certain that neither of these cases would employ the out-of-pocket-loss rule were they to be decided by the same court today unless the court believed that the speculative losses which the plaintiffs sought were too conjectural to be recoverable. Therefore, the federal rule which has been the backbone of the out-of-pocket-loss rule is gone.

* * * Lichtenthaler v. Clow, 109 Or. 381, 220 P. 567, Purdy v. Underwood, 87 Or. 56, 169 P. 536, and Cawston v. Sturgis, 29 Or. 331, 43 P. 656, all of which are reviewed in our previous decision, likewise arose out of the purchase of real property for money. In each of those cases the buyer, in determining whether to make the purchase, contemplated the property, not in the abstract, but as a tract of a given size; and the seller, knowing that fact, represented that it contained the desired area. In each instance when it developed that the representation was false, the vendor was held liable for damages equal to the value of the missing area. In other words, the buyer was entitled, not merely to a part, but to all that he paid for, regardless of whether or not the amount he actually received was worth the sum he paid. * * * The rule is thus stated in Purdy v. Underwood: "When, however, as in the case at bar, a specified sum of money is paid for each integral part of property expected to be received, a failure to transfer a portion thereof at such ratable price, constitutes the measure of damages sustained." The situation is the same in the present case. Shirley represented that 4000 cords of timber, worth 50 cents per cord, stood upon the property. As a matter of fact, only 200 cords were there. Standing trees are, of course, deemed part and parcel of the land. Had he represented that 170 acres were in the tract when actually it consisted of only 160, all would agree that he would be compelled to respond in damages. In the absence of homogeneity of value we would have divided the purchase price by the number of acres and in this manner have ascertained the value per acre. We would then have multiplied the value per acre by the number of missing acres and thus have arrived at the damages. We know

that Shirley represented that the stumpage value of the timber was 50 cents per cord, and we also know that he represented that the property held 4000 cords. * * *

Suppose the defendants had conveyed to the plaintiffs the timber only, all would agree that damages equal in amount to the value of the land would be recoverable. The reverse must be true, and since the plaintiffs received only the land they must be entitled to damages equal to the value of the timber.

We shall now show by the decisions of the other courts that the mere fact that the missing item is not land but is something else, does not deny relief to the plaintiffs. In Nunn v. Howard, 216 Ky. 685, 288 S.W. 678, 679, the plaintiff had sold to the defendant a house and lot, falsely representing in so doing that an unfailing well was upon the premises. The defendant spent $158 in providing a well of the represented kind. The decision, after stating these facts, continued: "that being true, it follows that appellee is liable in damages for the representations so made, and that in the circumstances the most accurate measure of damages is the reasonable cost of drilling the new well. It follows that the item of $158 should have been allowed." In Okoomian v. Brandt, 101 Conn. 427, 126 A. 332, the defendant, who had sold the plaintiff an improved lot under a false representation that the three tenants were each paying $35 per month rental, was held liable in the amount of $325.50 damages, that being the sum which the plaintiff expended in the installation of permanent electrical equipment in order to bring the income of the property up to the represented amount. In Shane v. Jacobson, 136 Minn. 386, 162 N.W. 472, 473, the plaintiff had been induced to buy a farm under a false representation that 80 acres of it was tiled. The Minnesota court adheres to the out-of-pocket-loss rule. * * * In measuring the plaintiff's damages under that rule, the court held that the plaintiff was entitled to recover the cost of installing the tiling, together with the rental value of the land while the work was in progress. We quote from the decision the following: "In other words, the damages in contemplation of the parties as naturally flowing from a misrepresentation in respect to this tiling would be the cost thereof, to which, perhaps, should be added the depreciation of rental value of the land affected while the tiling was being done. The rule is that a defrauded party is entitled to such damages as naturally and proximately result from the fraud. * * * Suppose, in this case, that plaintiff had bought the farm when he met defendant in Iowa, without seeing it, upon defendant's representations as to soil, lay of the land, and improvements, and all the representations had been true, except that a granary of certain dimensions and material, represented to be one of the buildings, was not there, a structure which could be erected for say $200; could it be justly claimed that the natural and proximate loss to plaintiff for this one false representation could then have been more than the cost of placing such a granary as represented upon the farm? * * * Therefore the actual cost of placing tiling thereon, and the extent to which such improvement would increase the value of the farm was proper and very material evidence bearing upon the amount of recovery, and without which an intelligent answer could not be given as to the natural and proximate loss to plaintiff."

From all of the above it is seen, not only that the plaintiffs were damaged, for convincing evidence shows that the property is worth less than $2,000, but that we have an approved means of measuring the damages, which are the proximate result of the false statements made by the defendants. If the latter had represented that there was upon the property a pile of wood containing 4000 cords, the damages to which the plaintiffs would have been entitled would have been the value of that amount of wood. The same result ought to follow when, as in this case, the defendant represented that there was standing timber upon the property capable of yielding 4000 cords worth 50 cents per cord upon the stump. * * *

Of course, if one adheres rigorously to the out-of-pocket-loss rule or to the benefit-of-the-bargain rule certainty will be achieved, but it will be achieved in many instances at the expense of justice.

In our previous decision we cited authorities indicating that neither rule has been uniformly applied, and in preceding paragraphs of this decision have amplified them. We know of no difficulty which has resulted from flexibility. An examination of the decisions in the states employing flexibility discloses that they are not large in number, nor do they afford any indication that flexibility has created uncertainty. It is inevitable that ordinarily only out-of-pocket losses will be recoverable, for ordinarily that is the only loss which is incurred or which can be proved with sufficient certainty. Consequential damages are universally recoverable. If the representation can be made good by the expenditure of a sum less than that which is the difference between the actual value and the represented value, the cost of the installation is the sum which is recoverable. Professor McCormick recommends that the loss-of-the-bargain rule should also be employed where a false representation was made with moral culpability, as distinguished from one made by a person who is ignorant of the facts. But since punitive damages are recoverable in this state, there exists no occasion for a departure from the out-of-pocket-loss rule in cases of that kind. * * *

Since the petition for a rehearing has disclosed no error in our previous decision, we adhere to that opinion. * * *

BELT, JUSTICE (dissenting). On original hearing the court held, with the writer dissenting, that plaintiffs had been defrauded and were entitled to damages "upon the basis of 50 cents per cord for the difference between the represented 4,000 cords and the actual 200 cords," which amounted to $1,900. There was a balance of $1,250, together with interest due, on the purchase price, as $750 had been paid thereon. Therefore, this court's decree enabled plaintiffs to acquire this 160–acre ranch for $100. In reaching this conclusion, the majority of the court held that plaintiffs were entitled to the "benefit of the bargain" rule asserted by defendants. Had the "benefit of the bargain" rule been also applied so as to compensate plaintiffs for the failure of water to irrigate the 10–acre tract and the loss of gravel, we would have the anomalous situation of the vendors being deprived of their property without compensation and being mulcted in damages besides.

In the lower court, evidence was received on behalf of the defendant vendors that, at the time the contract was entered into, the land had a market value of $2,000. Since the contract price, or $2,000, was the market value of the land, the defendants contend that no damages are recoverable in an action of this kind. Plaintiffs introduced no evidence concerning the market value of the land. It was their contention that the "out of pocket" rule had no application to the facts and they relied on the benefit of their bargain in the assessment of damages.

It should be borne in mind that there was no misrepresentation concerning the quantity of land or the boundaries thereof. It is not a case of shortage in acreage as in Lichtenthaler v. Clow, 109 Or. 381, 220 P. 567. * * * The issue on this appeal is clearly and definitely defined. What is the proper measure of damages to be applied to the facts in this case? Are plaintiffs entitled to the benefit of their bargain, namely, the difference between the value of 4000 cords of wood and 200 cords of wood? Or is the proper measure the difference between the contract price of the land and its market value? * * *

What is the proper measure of damages in tort actions wherein fraud has induced the sale or exchange of property? This has long been a controversial question among judges, lawyers, professors, and text writers. As stated in a well-considered article entitled "The Measure of Damages in Tort for Deceit," 18 Boston U.L.Rev. 681: "Upon this subject American courts are divided; text-writers present a broken front; a left wing wars with a right; academicians cannot agree; the Law Institute advisers dissent from the reporters; precedent neutralizes precedent; abstract reasoning carries no persuasion; arguments have no other effect than to engender counter-arguments; one practical consideration clashes with another practical consideration; nothing is settled as the just law or general rule." * * *

No well-considered case holds that a hard and fast rule should be applied in all cases. Objections have been made to both rules. However, the American Law Institute, after a thorough consideration of the subject, reached the conclusion that the better-reasoned cases support the "out-of-pocket" rule. Hence, we find in the Restatement of the Law on Torts, § 549: "The measure of damages which the recipient of a fraudulent misrepresentation is entitled to recover from its maker as damages under the rule stated in § 525 is the pecuniary loss which results from the falsity of the matter represented, including * * *." The "comment" in reference to the above clause is so clear-cut and pertinent to the facts in this case that we quote it in full: "Under the rule stated in this Clause the recipient of a fraudulent misrepresentation is entitled to recover from its maker only the actual loss which because of its falsity he sustains by his action or inaction in reliance upon it. If notwithstanding the falsity of the representation the thing which a vendee acquires is of equal or greater value than the price paid and he has suffered no harm through using it in reliance upon its being as represented, he has suffered no loss and can recover nothing. The fact that he would have made a profit if the representation had been true does not entitle him to recover for his disappointment in not receiving the gain which he was led to expect. Thus where A induces B to purchase a parcel of farm land by falsely representing that it contains valuable mineral deposits, B is not entitled to recover anything if the land as farming land is worth as much as the price paid although had it contained the minerals represented it would have been worth much more. If the fraudulent misrepresentation is so made as to constitute a warranty, the person acting in reliance upon it may of course waive the fraud and bring an action on the warranty, in which case the measure of damages is that appropriate to a warranty, namely, the difference between the value of the article as it is and the value which it would have had had the fact warranted been true." * * *

Whatever may be the rule in other jurisdictions, it has long been settled in this state that, in tort actions for fraud inducing the sale or exchange of real property, the measure of damages is the difference between the value of the property parted with and the actual value of the property received. This court has never endeavored to treat a tort action as being equivalent to a breach of contract. It has adhered to the fundamental principles of tort. The party defrauded is entitled to be made whole—i.e., he is not to be out of pocket. * * *

Plaintiffs had their opportunity to introduce evidence relative to the market value of the land purchased, but they failed to do so. What they really sought was damages arising from breach of contract. The fallacy of such contention lies in the fact that the vendors did not contract to sell, nor did the plaintiffs agree to buy, 4000 cords of wood. Plaintiffs, under the terms of the contract, agreed to buy a 160–acre farm. Applying the "benefit of the bargain" rule to the facts in the instant case leads to absurdity for it amounts to the vendees' acquiring the land for practically nothing. * * *

What has been said thus far is on the assumption that the misrepresentations were made as alleged and that plaintiffs relied thereon, although it is difficult to understand how anyone, after inspection, could have been deceived about logged-off land. It would seem that the black stumps would speak for themselves. It is also difficult to understand why the Selmans continued to make payments after learning, in August 1933, of the shortage of wood and their alleged consequent damages. * * *

The equities of the case are not entirely with the plaintiffs. They have been in possession of 160 acres of land since August, 1933, and it has been their home, however humble it may be. They have paid $750, together with interest, on the purchase price. This farm or hill ranch had, according to Shirley, a rental value of $150 per year. It is utterly unreasonable to state that it is worth only $100. Yet that is what this court must say if we adhere to the decision on original hearing. Can it be that the testimony of all witnesses on market value is to be ignored? Mr. Dollarhide, a disinterested and fair witness, testified without contradiction that he offered Shirley $2,000 in cash for the ranch, but learned that it had just been sold to the plaintiffs. Dollarhide thereupon went out to see Mrs. Selman, "to see if she would sell it," but she would not do so. Dollarhide and three other witnesses testified that the market value of the 160–acre ranch was $2,000. Otherwise stated, that it was worth $12.50 per acre.

This farm is not all logged-off land, 40 acres are assessed as tillable land. It is a typical hill ranch, valuable mostly for pasturage purposes. Blakely, a witness friendly to plaintiffs, said that, at the time of inspecting the ranch, nothing was said about wood or timber. The plaintiffs, according to this witness, wanted a place off the main highway and out of traffic.

However, let it be understood that this opinion is bottomed on the legal proposition that the "benefit of the bargain" rule does not apply to the facts in this case. We have adverted to these features of the case only to refute the idea of a gross miscarriage of justice. * * *

The decree of the lower court should, therefore, be affirmed.

Notes

1. *Alternative Measures of General–Expectancy Damages.* The second restatement of torts also lets plaintiff choose between benefit of the bargain and out of pocket. Restatement (Second) of Torts § 549, Comment h.; Reporter's Note (1976). "A plaintiff should have the opportunity to use either measure, providing the measure selected accomplishes substantial justice." Turnbull v. LaRose, 702 P.2d 1331, 1336 (Alaska 1985).

2. Dura Pharmaceuticals v. Broudo in Chapter 2, p. 20, also involved a defendant's alleged misrepresentation. Plaintiffs sued defendant under the securities statutes. The Supreme Court's decision turned on whether the plaintiffs had alleged

a loss caused by defendant's alleged misconduct. How does the *Dura* Court's approach to the timing and valuation of plaintiffs' loss compare to the Selman v. Shirley court's?

3. *Emotional Distress as Special Damages.* In many jurisdictions, a fraud plaintiff may not recover any emotional distress damages. Arguing against this exclusion on the ground that fraud is a dignitary, not a commercial, tort is Andrew Merritt, Damages for Emotional Distress in Fraud Litigation: Dignitary Torts in a Commercial Society, 42 Vand.L.Rev. 1 (1989).

A plaintiff's damages for the related torts of negligent misrepresentation and negligent failure to disclose will not, one court held, include emotional distress. Osbourne v. Capital City Mortgage Corp., 667 A.2d 1321 (D.C. 1995). Controversy surrounds whether a plaintiff may recover emotional distress damages for the related theories of recovery: breach of fiduciary duty and violation of consumer protection statutes.

4. *Punitive Damages.* Under the majority rule, a court will bar a plaintiff from recovering punitive damages for a defendant's breach of contract unless the defendant committed an "independent tort." The Commercial Code which subscribes to the "compensation principle" does not provide for punitive damages. Original U.C.C. § 1–106(1). Caution: Revised U.C.C. Article 1 puts the Original U.C.C.'s § 1–106 "compensation principle" in § 1–305(a).

The plaintiff must show that the breaching defendant also committed a tort such as fraud, conversion, breach of fiduciary duty, or intentional infliction of mental distress.

A plaintiff's recovery of punitive damages for the defendant's breach of contract would be inconsistent with facilitating a seller's efficient breach. Professor Dodge argued that the theory of efficient breach is unsound; he maintained that a court should let a contract plaintiff recover punitive damages for a defendant's willful breach of contract; he reasoned that the threat of punitive damages will encourage a potential breaching contract party to negotiate a release. William Dodge, The Case for Punitive Damages in Contracts, 48 Duke L.J. 629 (1999). This chapter returns to efficient breach below.

Most courts will accept the defendant's fraud as a foundation for the plaintiff's recovery of punitive damages.

In 1961, the New York Court of Appeals ruled that punitive damages are permissible only where the plaintiff proves that defendants were engaged in a "virtually larcenous scheme to trap generally the unwary." The majority opinion justified the plaintiff's recovery of punitive damages where "a high degree of moral culpability" is found:

"Exemplary damages are more likely to serve their desired purpose of deterring similar conduct in a fraud case, such as that before us, than in any other area of tort. One who acts out of anger or hate, for instance, in committing assault or libel, is not likely to be deterred by the fear of punitive damages. On the other hand, those who deliberately and coolly engage in a far-flung fraudulent scheme, systematically conducted for profit, are very much more likely to pause and consider the consequences if they have to pay more than the actual loss suffered by an individual plaintiff. An occasional award of compensatory damages against such parties would have little deterrent effect. A judgment simply for compensatory damages would require the offender to do no more than return the money which he had taken from the plaintiff. In the calculation of his expected profits, the wrongdoer is likely to allow for a certain amount of money which will have to be returned to those victims who object too vigorously, and he will be perfectly content to bear the additional cost of litigation as the price for continuing his illicit business." Walker v. Sheldon, 10 N.Y.2d 401, 404–406, 223 N.Y.S.2d 488, 490, 492, 179 N.E.2d 497, 498–500 (1961).

The New York courts continue to say that a fraud victim may recover punitive damages where the defendant's fraud is gross, wanton or willful and a pattern of similar conduct is directed at the public. New York University v. Continental Ins. Co., 87 N.Y.2d 308, 639 N.Y.S.2d 283, 662 N.E.2d 763, 767 (1995); Rocanova v. Equitable Life Assurance Soc'y of U.S., 83 N.Y.2d 603, 612 N.Y.S.2d 339, 634 N.E.2d 940, 944 (1994).

5. *Punitive Damages Without Compensatory Damages?* May a fraud victim who hasn't proved any compensatory damages, nevertheless, recover punitive damages? Two approaches exist.

(a) Yes. "Because of the fortuitous circumstance that an injured plaintiff failed to prove compensatory damages, the defendant should not be freed of responsibility for aggravated misconduct. People should not be able with impunity to trench willfully upon a right. Moreover, it is especially fitting to allow punitive damage for actions such as legal fraud, since intent rather than mere negligence is the requisite state of mind. The punitive award is not required to have a fixed proportional relationship to the amount of compensatory damages." Nappe v. Anschelewitz, Barr, Ansell & Bonello, 97 N.J. 37, 50, 477 A.2d 1224, 1231 (1984).

(b) No. After the trial judge had added punitive damages to rescission and $1 nominal damages, the appellate court took the punitive damages back, holding the record must support actual damages as a basis for punitive damages. Maxwell v. Gallagher, 709 A.2d 100 (D.C.Ct.App.1998).

6. *Discharge in Bankruptcy.* (a) *Fraud.* If a fraudster files for bankruptcy to discharge the plaintiff's judgment, the victim may bar discharge if a judgment is one for "actual fraud." Cohen v. de la Cruz, 523 U.S. 213 (1998).

The plaintiff's damages in Cohen v. de la Cruz had been trebled under the state consumer protection statute; the Court also barred the fraudster from discharging the multiplied part. Even though Cohen v. de la Cruz does not deal specifically with punitive damages, its reasoning appears to include them within the category of nondischargeable.

(b) *Breach of Contract.* A defendant who files bankruptcy should, however, be able to shake off most judgments for debts to plaintiffs based on his breaches of contract. A judgment for "constructive" fraud or negligent misrepresentation may not fall under the heading of "actual fraud," and may be dischargeable.

2. EXPECTANCY DAMAGES v. RESCISSION–RESTITUTION

HORTON v. O'ROURKE
Florida District Court of Appeal, 1975.
321 So.2d 612.

McNULTY, CHIEF JUDGE. * * * The operative facts are simply stated. Between March 3, 1972 and May 3, 1972, the four appellee families executed written contracts with H & H Construction Company to purchase homes being constructed on land owned by appellee Overlord Investments, Inc. Upon completion of the homes in the summer of 1972, the families took possession without closing, under rental agreements ranging from $90 to $135 per month. Closing was conditioned upon clearance of all outstanding title defects.

Upon taking possession, the purchasers-lessees received a notice of the existence of a Federal Tax Lien encumbering the property in excess of $94,000.

After receiving several assurances that the lien would soon be removed, they made improvements and continued the rental agreement for 22 months. But on March 15, 1974, appellant notified the purchasers in writing that clearance of the defect was impossible. Appellant offered either to return the earnest money deposits or enter into new rental agreements at a higher rate.

Thereafter, on April 15, 1974, appellee Overlord Investments, Inc., record title holder of the land, brought suit to oust each purchaser. After answering, the purchasers-appellees filed individual suits for specific performance against both Overlord Investments and appellant, alleging a principal-agent relationship, which resulted in this appeal.

Following a non-jury trial on the four consolidated cases, a final judgment was rendered denying specific performance, exonerating Overlord from any obligation to purchasers-appellees and awarding the purchasers pecuniary damages against appellant. In arriving at the amount of such damages, the court applied the standard measure of contract damages whereby a purchaser ordinarily receives the benefit of his bargain, measured by the court in this case by the difference between the value of the land when it should have been conveyed less the contract price as yet unpaid.

In the one meritorious point on appeal, appellant contends that application of this standard measure of damages giving purchasers *in a land sale contract* the benefit of their bargain is error in the absence of a showing of bad faith. We agree.

In Florida and many other jurisdictions the courts follow the English rule announced in Flureau v. Thornhill whereby in the absence of bad faith the damages recoverable for breach by the vendor of an executory contract to convey title to real estate are the purchase money paid by the purchaser together with interest and expenses of investigating title. Lest there be unjust enrichment, under the facts in this case, we would add to that here the cost of improvements made by purchasers in contemplation of the conveyance, with the express or implied approval of the vendor, which inure to the benefit of the vendor.

Appellees' reliance on A.J. Richey Corp. v. Garvey as authority to the contrary is misplaced in that, in that case, there was clearly a lack of good faith. Here, there is no suggestion of bad faith on appellant's part. Indeed, the record reveals that he dealt above board, made every effort and went to considerable expense to clear the title defect and to consummate ultimately the contract to convey. * * *

Accordingly, the judgment appealed from should be, and it is hereby, reversed.

Notes

1. *Market Economics.* Economic analysis of contract remedies often has an uncanny affinity for the outcomes courts had already reached through common law analysis. But not always.

Contract law in a market economy structures the process of exchange. Each resource should be owned and used by the person who values it the most; this will assure that society as a whole employs available resources in the most productive fashion. Economic theory assumes that people seek to maximize their utility through exchanges. People use contracts to exchange goods with others. Each person or firm expects to improve its position from performance of a contract because each values the consideration it receives more highly than the consideration it surrenders. If the contract moves both exchanged assets to more highly valued uses, both parties benefit.

One of the functions of a contract is to allocate risk during the time the contract is executory. A seller who concludes that performance will be unprofitable may be tempted to withdraw, to not complete delivery under the contract. The economic function of contract remedies is to provide a nonbreaching buyer with some equivalent to performance when the seller exits in breach from an executory contract.

Suppose the seller's goods' market value rises. The existence of a potential remedy for the nonbreaching buyer will encourage the seller, who may be tempted to breach, nevertheless to perform the unprofitable contract. A seller who knows that the buyer's action for specific performance will be in the offing has a reduced incentive to decline to deliver.

Although specific performance may be the buyer's favored remedy, circumstances or preferences may eliminate it and limit the buyer to recovering money damages. The way a court measures the buyer's recovery of money damages may determine whether and when a seller who is tempted to breach actually will breach. Contract damages are intended to place the nonbreaching buyer in a financial position that compares favorably to the seller's performance. That normally calls for expectation damages, the buyer's profit potential under the breached contract: where the seller reneges, the buyer should receive the difference between the value of the asset the seller promised to deliver and its contract price.

People who subscribe to market-economic analysis consider expectancy damages, properly measured, to be economically efficient. For that measure encourages a seller to complete performance unless performance would consume resources inefficiently. Where the seller's performance would be inefficient, the market economist's expectancy measure allows the seller to breach and pay the buyer's damages. We return to the "efficient breach" concept below.

The expectancy measure also allows the nonbreaching buyer to minimize her loss by cover or otherwise. But by the same analysis, a court should not award the nonbreaching buyer less than her expected profit. Awarding the buyer her expectancy will encourage all contract sellers to perform contracts that increase social utility by moving assets from people who value them less to those who value them more.

2. In *Horton*, the Florida court applying the rule of Flureau v. Thornhill refuses to award the buyers their expectancy damages; instead the court remits the buyers to a recovery measured by restitution and reliance. Restitution prevents a breaching seller from being unjustly enriched at the buyer's expense. Allowing the buyers to recover their reliance expense discourages the seller from carelessly encouraging people to think that a contract exists and spending money in confidence.

Nevertheless the *Flureau* rule is a puzzling anomaly. The way to assure that a seller will breach only to promote efficiency is to award the nonbreaching buyer lost profit. Generally also, measuring the nonbreaching buyer's loss by expectancy approximates the cost of breach to society better than the reliance measure. This occurs because the restitution-reliance measure excludes from recovery the nonbreaching buyer's shrewdness, luck, skill and opportunity costs.

Question. Why does the anomalous *Flureau* rule survive?

3. *Exceptions.* (a) The Florida court admits the usual exception, long adopted in England, that *Flureau* does not apply when the seller lacked good faith.

(b) The Corbin Contracts treatise states another exception: "If the seller knows that he has not the title and expects to get it in time to keep his promise to convey, he must pay damages on his failure; and it makes no difference how reasonable may have been his expectation that he could procure title in himself." 11 Arthur Lipton Corbin, Contracts § 1098 (Interim ed. & Supp. 2005).

4. *Rejecting Flureau.* In Donovan v. Bachstadt, the New Jersey court began, "New Jersey follows the English rule, which generally limits a buyer's recovery to the return of his deposit unless the seller wilfully refuses to convey or is guilty of fraud or deceit. The traditional formulation of the English rule has been expressed by T. Cyprian Williams, an English barrister, as follows:

> 'Where the breach of contract is occasioned by the vendor's inability, without his own fault, to show a good title, the purchaser is entitled to recover as damages his deposit, if any, with interest, and his expenses incurred in connection with the agreement, but not more than nominal damages for the loss of his bargain.' [T.C. Williams, The Contract of Sale of Land 128 (1930)]

'We are satisfied that the American rule is preferable. The English principle developed because of the uncertainties of title due to the complexity of the rules governing title to land during the eighteenth and nineteenth centuries. At that time the only evidence of title was contained in deeds which were in a phrase attributed to Lord Westbury, "difficult to read, disgusting to touch, and impossible to understand." The reason for the English principle that creates an exception to the law governing damages for breaches of executory contracts for the sale of property is no longer valid, and the exception should be eliminated.'

'There is no sound basis why benefit of the bargain damages should not be awarded whether the subject matter of the contract is realty or personalty. Serious losses should not be borne by the vendee of real estate to the benefit of the defaulting vendor. * * *'

'The innocent purchaser should be permitted to recover benefit of the bargain damages irrespective of the good or bad faith of the seller. Contract culpability depends on the breach of the contractual promise. Where, as here, the seller agreed that title would be marketable, the seller's liability should depend upon his breach of that promise.'

'The English rule is consistent with the limitation on recovery in suits on a covenant for breach of warranty. The damages for a buyer, who has taken title and is ousted because the [seller's] title is defective, are limited to the consideration paid and interest thereon. There appears to be no real difference between that situation and one where the vendor who does not have good title refuses to convey. In both cases the buyer loses the property because of a defect in the title. The fact that one sues for breach of a warranty covenant does not justify depriving a buyer of compensatory damages to which he is justly entitled when the seller breaches the contract of sale. Professor Corbin has suggested that any inconsistency in this respect should be resolved by awarding full compensatory damages when the action is for breach of warranty. (Arthur Corbin, Corbin on Contracts § 1098). Moreover, an anomaly already exists, for our courts have acknowledged that a buyer may recover such damages upon a showing of the seller's bad faith. [citations]

'We are satisfied that a buyer should be permitted to recover benefit of the bargain damages when the seller breaches an executory contract to convey real property. Here the defendant agreed to convey marketable title. He made that bargained-for promise and breached it and is responsible to the plaintiff for the damages occasioned thereby." Donovan v. Bachstadt, 91 N.J. 434, 453 A.2d 160 (1982).

Another court adopted the American damages rule because it is more "equitable." The court observed that, under the English rule, a seller is strongly tempted to avoid the contract when inflation causes the price of real estate to rise. Burgess v. Arita, 5 Haw.App. 581, 590, 704 P.2d 930, 937, reh'g denied, 5 Haw.App. 682, 753 P.2d 253 (1985).

About half the jurisdictions in the United States subscribe to the American Rule. Should the other half join them?

5. *Deed Covenants.* A land transaction is "closed" when the grantor delivers a warranty deed with covenants and the buyer pays. If, sometime later, the grantor's deed covenants are breached, for example because the "true" owner shows up and the grantor's title fails, then, as the *Donovan* court indicates, the buyer-grantee, who has lost the property, recovers only a refund of the price she paid to the grantor for the land; in short she recovers restitution.

In three situations, a buyer-grantee's recovery or restitution for breach of her seller-grantor's deed covenants under-compensates the buyer-grantee: (a) When the buyer had made a profitable contract because the land was worth more than the contract price. (b) When the land value has risen. And (c) when the buyer has improved the property.

Courts have largely ignored Corbin's advice to increase the grantee's recovery. A contrary rule would allow the buyer-grantee to recover based on the land's value as warranted either at the time the contract was formed or when "true" owner with a paramount title evicts her.

But, it is argued, measuring the grantee's recovery at the date she is evicted by the paramount owner "opens the grantor to liability for an amount which may be many times the price [he] received and which may extend, especially under the 'future' covenants, for many decades into the future. Given the wide availability of title insurance as an alternative form of protection for the grantee which can, in theory, be increased in dollar coverage whenever he or she desires, it is very doubtful that the law should place such a vast and uncertain potential burden on the grantor in the absence of fraud or a very clear promise to undertake it." William B. Stoebuck & Dale A. Whitman, *The Law of Property* 913–14 (3d ed. 2000). A careful title search before accepting the seller's deed also protects the buyer.

Nevertheless, isn't the Corbin treatise right to favor increasing the buyer's recovery for the seller's breach of deed covenants to the buyer's expectancy?

3. MEASURING THE BUYER'S EXPECTANCY

WILSON v. HAYS

Court of Civil Appeals of Texas, 1976.
544 S.W.2d 833.

JAMES, JUSTICE. This is a suit by the buyer against the seller for breach of an oral contract to sell and deliver used bricks. Trial was had to a jury, which rendered a verdict favorable to the Plaintiff buyer, pursuant to which verdict the trial court entered judgment. * * *

Plaintiff–Appellee W.D. Hays was in the business of buying and selling used building materials. Defendant–Appellant Bobby Wilson doing business as Wilson Salvage Co. was in the business of wrecking or demolishing buildings. * * * Hays and Wilson entered into an oral agreement whereby Wilson agreed to sell and deliver 600,000 used uncleaned bricks to Hays at a price of one cent per brick, and Hays agreed to buy said bricks at said price. Hays paid Wilson $6,000.00 in advance. Wilson delivered the uncleaned brick to a designated area where Hays had people hired to clean and stack the brick. Wilson delivered a lesser number of brick than 600,000, thereby precipitating this suit.

Plaintiff–Appellee Hays brought this suit for the return of the proportionate part of the purchase price paid for the bricks he did not get, plus damages. In answer to special issues the jury found: * * *

(6) That Bobby Wilson did not deliver 600,000 uncleaned bricks to Hays (but)

(6A) delivered only 400,000 bricks to Hays;

(7) The market value of used bricks in Midland, Texas in April 1972, was five cents per brick; * * *

Pursuant to the jury verdict, the trial court entered judgment in favor of Plaintiff Hays against Defendant Bobby Wilson in the amount of $[10,000], plus accrued interest. * * * From this judgment, Defendant Wilson appeals. * * *

Plaintiff–Appellee Hays's remedies and measures of damages as a buyer of goods in the case at bar are governed by Sections 2.711, 2.712, [and] 2.713 * * * of the Texas Business and Commerce Code. We herewith quote the portions of said sections that bear upon the case at bar:

'Section 2.711. Buyer's Remedies in General; * * *

(a) Where the seller fails to make delivery or repudiates * * * the buyer may cancel and whether or not he has done so may in addition to recovering so much of the price as has been paid

(1) 'cover' and have damages under the next section as to all the goods affected whether or not they have been identified to the contract; or

(2) recover damages for non-delivery as provided in this chapter (Section 2.713)." * * *

'Section 2.712. "Cover" Buyer's Procurement of Substitute Goods

'(a) After a breach within the preceding section the buyer may "cover" by making in good faith and without unreasonable delay any reasonable purchase of or contract to purchase goods in substitution for those due from the seller.

'(b) The buyer may recover from the seller as damages the difference between the cost of cover and the contract price together with any incidental or consequential damages as hereinafter defined (Section 2.715), but less expenses saved in consequence of the seller's breach.

'(c) Failure of the buyer to effect cover within the section does not bar him from any other remedy.'

'Section 2.713. Buyer's Damages for Non–Delivery or Repudiation

"(a) * * * the measure of damages for non-delivery or repudiation by the seller is the difference between the market price at the time when the buyer learned of the breach and the contract price together with any incidental and consequential damages provided in this chapter (Sec. 2.715), but less expenses saved in consequence of the seller's breach." * * *

Let us analyze the verdict and judgment in the light of the foregoing statutory provisions. In the first place, it is established that Plaintiff Hays paid

$6000.00 for 600,000 used brick at the rate of one cent per brick, whereas he received only 400,000. Therefore he paid $2000 for 200,000 brick that he never got, and he is thereby entitled to recover $2000.00 under Section 2.711 for "recovering so much of the price as has been paid."

Next, under Section 2.713, he is entitled to damages for "non-delivery or repudiation," and here his measure of damages is the difference between the market price and the contract price. The contract price of the 200,000 brick not delivered is established at $2000.00. The market price at the appropriate time and place of the undelivered brick was five cents per brick or $10,000.00. This jury finding of market value (five cents per brick) although challenged by Appellant for legal and factual insufficiency, is amply supported by the evidence and is well within the range of probative testimony. Therefore under Section 2.713 and appropriate jury findings, Plaintiff is entitled to $8000.00 damages (or $10,000.00 market price less $2000.00 contract price) for non-delivery. * * *

As stated before, the judgment is proper and should be affirmed for the amount of $10,000.00, same being composed of $2000.00 paid by Plaintiff for which he received no bricks plus $8000.00 damages for non-delivery.

Notes

1. Was the brick contract favorable for the buyer? Do the damages put the buyer where seller's full performance would have? If, after the seller breached, the buyer had bought substitute used bricks, "covered," at the market price, would the buyer have recovered the same amount under § 2–712?

2. *Buyer's Resale Contract.* What if buyer-Hayes had been under contract to resell the bricks to Delgado for two cents each? Read on.

Problem. Under a contract for 1997 vintage wine, Wine–Producer shipped 1000 bottles of 2005 wine mislabeled as 1997 to Wine–Merchant. The mislabeled wine breached Producer's express warranty of 1997 vintage. Merchant sold the wine to her retail customers; no customer complained about the wine's quality. After learning about the mislabeled wine, Merchant seeks to recover damages from Producer for breach of warranty. Under U.C.C. § 2–714, a buyer's damages for breach of warranty are value as expressly warranted, $16 per bottle for 1000 bottles, minus actual value, $10 per bottle, equals $6,000 damages. Producer argues that, having sold the mislabeled wine at her full markup price without any liability to any buyer, Merchant has no loss and may recover no damages.

TEXPAR ENERGY, INC. v. MURPHY OIL USA, INC.

United States Court of Appeals, Seventh Circuit, 1995.
45 F.3d 1111.

[On May 29, 1992, TexPar contracted to purchase 15,000 tons of asphalt from Murphy at an average price of $53 per ton. On the same day, TexPar contracted to sell the 15,000 tons to Starry Construction Company at an average price of $56 per ton. TexPar stood to profit by $45,000 if both contracts were performed.]

REAVLEY, CIRCUIT JUDGE. During the first half of 1992, the price of asphalt varied widely. Evidence was presented of prices ranging from $40 to $100 per ton. The wide range of prices reflected volatile market forces. From the supply standpoint, asphalt is one of the end products of petroleum refining, and must be sold or stockpiled to accommodate the production of more valuable petroleum products. Demand depends in large measure on the availability of government funding for highway construction. Weather also affects asphalt supply and demand. The price rose rapidly in June of 1992, and consequently, the sale price of $53 per ton lost its attractiveness to Murphy.

In May and early June TexPar took delivery of 690 tons of asphalt; but, on June 5, Murphy stopped its deliveries and notified TexPar that its sales manager lacked authority to make the contract. By then, the price of asphalt had risen to $80 per ton. Starry insisted that TexPar deliver the full 15,000 tons at $56 per ton as TexPar and Starry had agreed. Ultimately, with TexPar's approval, Starry and Murphy negotiated directly and agreed on a price of $68.50 per ton. This arrangement was reached several weeks after the repudiation by Murphy. By this time the market price had dropped, according to TexPar. TexPar agreed to pay Starry the $12.50 difference between the new price of $68.50 per ton and the original $56 per ton price. TexPar therefore paid Starry approximately $191,000, [$12.50 per ton plus Starry's incidental costs] to cover the price difference.

[The trial judge had instructed the jury under UCC § 2–713.] The jury found that the difference between the market price ($80) and the contract price ($53) of the undelivered asphalt (14,310 tons) on the date of repudiation (June 5), amounted to $386,370. The court entered judgment for this amount.

[U.C.C. § 2–713] provides a measure of the buyer's damages for nondelivery or repudiation: * * * "the measure of damages for nondelivery or repudiation by the seller is the difference between the market price at the time when the buyer learned of the breach and the contract price * * * ."

Murphy does not dispute that if this provision is applied, the damages awarded are proper, since Murphy does not dispute the quantity of goods, the market price or the date of notice of repudiation used by the jury to calculate damages. Instead, Murphy argues that the general measure of damages in a breach of contract case is the amount needed to place the plaintiff in as good a position as he would have been if the contract had been performed. Murphy argues that since TexPar's award—$386,370—far exceeds its out-of-pocket expenses ($191,000) and lost profits ($45,000) occasioned by the repudiation, the court erred in instructing the jury merely to find the difference in market price and entering judgment in that amount.

We cannot quarrel with Murphy that the general measure of damages in contract cases is the expectancy or "benefit of the bargain" measure. The UCC itself embraces such a measure in § 1–106, providing that the UCC remedies "shall be liberally administered to the end that the aggrieved party may be put in as good a position as if the other party had fully performed."

Nevertheless, we do not believe that the district court erred in awarding damages based on a straightforward application of § 2–713. That provision is found in the article on the sale of goods, and specifies a remedy for the circumstances presented here—the seller's nondelivery of goods for which there is a market price at the time of repudiation.

We can see no sound reason for looking to an alternative measure of damages. Murphy argues that TexPar shouldn't be awarded a "windfall" amount in excess of its out-of-pocket damages. Since it depends on the market price on a date after the making of the contract, the remedy under § 2–713 necessarily does not correspond to the buyer's actual losses, barring a coincidence. Our problem with Murphy's suggested measure of damages is that limiting the buyer's damages in cases such as this one to the buyer's out-of-pocket losses could, depending on the market, create a windfall for the seller. If the price of asphalt had fallen back to $56 per ton by the time Starry and Murphy had arranged for replacement asphalt, TexPar's damages would have been zero by this measure, * * * and Murphy could have reaped a windfall by selling at the market price of $80 in early June instead of the $53 price negotiated with TexPar.

Murphy argues that it did not in fact realize a windfall, since its cost of production was $70 per ton and it eventually agreed to sell to Starry for $68.50. We find this argument unpersuasive. Applying the market value measure of damages under UCC § 2–713, as the district court did, is expressly allowed under the Code. Since § 2–713 addresses the circumstances of a seller's nondelivery of goods with a market price, we see no error in applying this specific provision over the more general remedies provision found at § 1–106. * * * The UCC § 2–713 remedy serves the purpose of discouraging sellers from repudiating their contracts as the market rises, if the buyer should resell as did TexPar, or gambling that the buyer's damages will be small should the market drop. It also has the advantage of promoting uniformity and predictability in commercial transactions, by fixing damages on the date of the breach, rather than allowing the vicissitudes of the market in the future to determine damages. * * *

Affirmed.

Notes

1. *A Contrast, H–W–H Cattle Co. v. Schroeder.* "HWH was an order-buying cattle company which purchased cattle on commission for feedlots. As an order-buyer, HWH did not own any feedlots itself. * * * On September 13, 1978, HWH entered into a contract with Clayton Schroeder to purchase 2,000 steers for $67.00 per hundredweight ($0.67 per pound). The contract specified that the cattle would be delivered between March 1, and May 31, 1979, in Artesia, New Mexico. HWH gave Schroeder a $50,000 down payment for the cattle. HWH in turn had a contract with its customer, Western Trio Cattle Co. (Western Trio), to sell it 2,000 head of cattle of the same description for $67.35 per hundredweight. Western Trio had given HWH a $50,000 down payment which it had used to pay Schroeder.

"Schroeder was only able to deliver 1,397 cattle to HWH, leaving it 603 head short of fulfilling its contract. As a result, HWH filed an action for breach of contract against Schroeder. * * * The district court found that Schroeder breached its contract with HWH by failing to deliver 603 head of cattle. The court awarded to HWH * * * $1,371.83 in damages for HWH's lost commission on the 603 cattle not delivered. HWH now brings this appeal.

"The parties agree that the dispute is governed by the Uniform Commercial Code as adopted in Iowa, and that the only issue before the Court is the proper measure of damages. Section 2–711(1) provides that a buyer has two options when the seller fails to deliver; the buyer may [cover under § 2–712 or recover under § 2–713.]

"HWH contends that it is entitled to damages under the second option, § 2–713, which provides: * * * 'the measure of damages for nondelivery or repudiation by the seller is the difference between the market price at the time when the buyer learned of the breach and the contract price.'

"HWH contended before the district court, as it does here, that it is entitled to damages based upon the market price of cattle meeting the contract description in Artesia, New Mexico on June 1, 1979, the day after the last day of delivery under the contract. The district court rejected this argument because it concluded that it would result in an undeserved windfall to HWH, as HWH had already voluntarily limited its 'market price' by agreeing to sell these cattle to Western Trio for $0.35 per hundredweight more than it paid for the cattle. The district court also found that the parties modified the time for delivery, in that HWH indicated it would have accepted delivery through the summer of 1979. During this time, the price of cattle fell back to around $67.00 per hundredweight.

"We conclude that the district court did not err in so holding. To adopt HWH's position in this case would result in granting it a windfall, and thus violate the general principle concerning remedies underlying Article Two of the Uniform Commercial Code in Iowa Code Ann. § 1–106, which provides:

(1) The remedies provided by this Chapter shall be liberally administered to the end that the aggrieved party may be put in as good a position as if the other party had fully performed but neither consequential nor special nor penal damages may be had except as specifically provided in this chapter or by other rule of law.

"We read this admonition from the Code to suggest that a court should look through the form of a transaction to its substance when necessary to fulfill the parties' expectations expressed in the contract. This is precisely what the district court did in this case, by limiting the damage award to HWH to its expectancy interest and thereby avoiding a windfall of some $62,000.

"It is clear from McGlaun's testimony that HWH only purchased cattle to meet a specific customer's needs. As an order-buyer, it thus never expected to receive more than its $0.35 commission on any transaction, including its order purchase for Western Trio. HWH argues that it should receive market-price damages because it is liable to Western Trio for its failure to deliver the 603 cattle, and that Western Trio's damages would be measured by the difference between the market price on June 1, 1979, and the contract price. The district court properly rejected this contention, noting that Western Trio had made no demand on HWH to fulfill the remainder of the contract. The evidence at trial indicated that Western Trio would have, at best, only broken even on the resale of cattle delivered under the contract due to the fallen cattle market in the autumn of 1979. Moreover, McGlaun testified that Western Trio is managed by the Hitch family, which also owns HWH. We thus view Western Trio's failure to sue HWH as an equitable consideration in support of the district court's judgment." H–W–H Cattle Co. v. Schroeder, 767 F.2d 437, 438–40 (8th Cir.1985).

2. *Questions.* To compare *TexPar Energy* with *H–W–H*, answer the following questions about *H–W–H*.

(a) On June 1, 1979, cattle were selling for $88 per hundredweight. Each cow or steer would weigh about 500 pounds. Is the court correct that H–W–H's damages under § 2–713 for 603 undelivered cattle would be $62,000?

(b) If H–W–H had covered the breached contract on June 1 by buying 603 500–pound steers at the market price, how much might it have recovered under § 2–712? Would market less contract under § 2–713 have led to the same amount?

(c) Where did the court find the damage measure, buyer's resale contract less contract price? Section 1–106(1) isn't even in the U.C.C.'s Sales Article 2. Editor's Caution: § 1–106 in the Revised U.C.C.'s Article 1 deals with singular-plural and gender; Revised Article 1 has the Original U.C.C.'s § 1–106 "compensation principle" in § 1–305(a).

(d) Would measuring H–W–H's damages under § 2–713 really create a "windfall"?

3. *Take Me Back to TexPar Energy.* Does the *TexPar Energy* court deal with the argument that measuring the buyer's damages under § 2–713 will lead to a "windfall"? Was the court correct that *not* measuring the buyer's damages under § 2–713 would create a "windfall" for the breaching seller? By the way, what does "windfall" mean?

4. *Timing the Expectancy.* One issue between the *TexPar Energy* and *H-W-H* courts is what date to use to set expectancy or lost profits. Does measuring the buyer's expectancy on the date the contract was formed respect the way the parties allocated the risk of market fluctuation?

5 *The Resale Contracts.* A second issue between the *TexPar Energy* and *H-W-H* courts is whether to broaden the inquiry to the buyer's resale contract. Does considering the buyer's resale contract undermine the goals of § 2–713? Which court sends the right signal to a seller in a rising market?

6. *Market-Contract.* Awarding a buyer expectancy damages under § 2–713 based on market price less contract price has at least three effects: (a) It isolates the breached transaction. (b) It charges the breaching seller with the economic cost of its breach, viewed from before the breach. (c) It may be easier to administer than some other systems. Critics argue that expectancy damages are inaccurate, at best, and may even over-compensate the buyer.

7. *A Critic.* One critic of the § 2–713 market-contract solution is Professor Roy Ryden Anderson:

"One final failure of the [Revised Article 2, which Professor Anderson names the] Current Revision regarding Section 2–713 deserves mention. A recurring situation under current Article 2 has involved a buyer acting as a middleman, who purchases from the seller at one price and then immediately resells to its customer at a higher price, thereby guaranteeing itself a profit on the differential and hedging its buy contract against market fluctuation. Subsequently, the market price of the goods rises dramatically, and the seller breaches. Unable to find substitute goods, the buyer secures from its customer a release or settles its contract with the customer for a nominal amount.

"The buyer then sues the seller, seeking damages under Section 2–713. The issue posed is whether the buyer can recover windfall damages based on the market formula or whether the buyer is limited to compensatory damages measured by the profit the buyer would have made on its contract with its customer. * * * To date, four reported decisions have addressed the issue in applying Article 2. The first two cases to do so denied the buyer recovery of damages based on market price and, citing the Code's compensation principle in Section 1–106, held that recovery would be limited to the buyer's actual loss measured by the lost profit on its resale contract. [Professor Anderson cites H–W–H–Co. v. Schroeder and another decision.]

"However, two more recent cases reached the opposite result by allowing the buyer to recover damages based on market price, even though both courts candidly acknowledged that the recovery was in excess of the buyer's actual loss. [Professor Anderson cites TexPar Energy, Inc. v. Murphy Oil USA, Inc. and another decision.] Both cases justified ignoring the Code's compensation principle by misapplying the basic principle of statutory construction that a specific provision should govern a general one. The courts reasoned that the compensation principle in [Editor: Original U.C.C.] Section 1–106 should yield to the specific provision of Section 2–713 that allows the buyer a recovery of market damages without limitation. The reasoning of these courts borders on the absurd. The 'specific over general' principle of statutory construction does not apply to situations where it is clear that the intent of the statute is to the contrary. The Code provision in [Original U.C.C.] Section 1–106, mandating that the courts liberally administer remedies by limiting recovery to actual loss, is clearly intended to govern each and every Code remedy provision including the market formula in Section 2–713. Otherwise, the provision has no meaning. These two decisions would simply read [Original U.C.C.] Section 1–106 out of the Code because, under their analysis, there could never be a situation to which [Original U.C.C.] Section 1–106 would apply."

Professor Anderson discusses the 1999 Article 2 revision (which he favors) but which was withdrawn. The 1999 revision, he continued, "both codified the principle of mitigation of damages and restated the compensation principle from [Original U.C.C.] Section 1–106."

Professor Anderson turned to the Revised Article 2, which he calls the Current Revision and criticizes. "Once again, as is its wont, the Current Revision ignores positive gains made by the Original [1999] Revision despite firm assurances to the contrary by the Conference on Commissioners. The Current Revision also ignores the recommendations of the Study Group and the ABA Task Force. Once again, the reason is apparent and consistent with the unspoken agenda in the Current Revision of restructuring Article 2 remedies so as to give primacy to supracompensatory damages based on market price in contravention of both the compensation and the mitigation principles." Roy Ryden Anderson, Of Hidden Agendas, Naked Emperors, and a Few Good Soldiers: The Conference's Breach of Promise . . . Regarding Article 2 Damage Remedies, 54 SMU L. Rev. 795, 833 n.206 (2001).

We will be hearing more from Professor Anderson later.

8. *Question.* Two competing solutions are exemplified by *TexPar* and *H-W-H*. Which do you favor?

9. The buyer's resale contract affected recovery in another way in the next case.

WOLF v. COHEN

United States Court of Appeals, District of Columbia Circuit, 1967.
379 F.2d 477.

BASTIAN, SENIOR CIRCUIT JUDGE. On August 31, 1962, Parkwood, Inc., the owner of a parcel of land in the District of Columbia, entered into a contract to sell the property to one Butler for $1,000,000. Thereafter, Parkwood, Inc., conveyed the property to the Cohens, subject to Butler's rights under his contract of purchase. Butler, in turn, assigned his rights under the contract to one Lovitz. It is clear that Lovitz was the straw party for the real parties in interest, Messrs. Wolf, Wolf, and Dreyfuss. * * *

On December 4, 1962, the date for the settlement of the contract, the Cohens and Parkwood, Inc. defaulted. Cross motions were filed in the District Court and, on December 13, 1963, judgment was entered * * * decreeing specific performance against the Cohens and Parkwood, Inc. Appeal was taken from this judgment and, on December 14, 1964, we affirmed the judgment of the District Court, with costs.

On January 25, 1965, an amendment of the original judgment of the District Court was entered by that court, directing the specific performance of the written agreement of purchase and providing that all rents, taxes, water, rent, insurance, interest on existing encumbrances, operating charges and other apportionable items should be adjusted to the date of the actual transfer of the property. The case was set for trial for determination of the damages, if any, to which Messrs. Wolf, Wolf, and Dreyfuss, et al., were entitled under the counter-claim as a result of the breach of contract by the Cohens and Parkwood, Inc. On February 5, 1965, the property was, pursuant to the decree of the District Court, conveyed to Messrs. Wolf, Wolf, and Dreyfuss.

From now on herein Messrs. Wolf, Wolf, and Dreyfuss, et al., will be denominated plaintiffs or appellants, and the Cohens and Parkwood, Inc., defendants or appellees.

After the filing of affidavits the case came on for hearing on the issue of damages on cross motions for summary judgment. It was claimed by plaintiffs that they were entitled to damages in the amount of $355,000, based on the following:

Under the contract of sale, the purchase price of the property was $1,000,000. Plaintiffs claimed that, prior to the original settlement date, they contracted to resell the property for $1,800,000 but, because of delay of perform-ance, the prospective purchaser had withdrawn, as he had a right to do under his contract. Thus, plaintiffs claimed, they were deprived of a profit of $800,000. It appears without contradiction that the market value of the property was $1,000,000 on the date the contract of August 31, 1962, should have been settled, and that the market value on February 5, 1965, when the sale was finally completed, was $1,445,000. Thus plaintiffs claimed that the difference between this latter amount and $1,800,000, the price at which they claimed they could have sold the property on the originally scheduled date of conveyance, left them damaged in the sum of $355,000. Interest thereon from December 4, 1962, was claimed * * * .

The District Court, after argument on the cross motions for summary judgment, filed its opinion on June 9, 1966, holding that plaintiffs were not entitled to receive damages for the delay in settlement * * *. On June 30 formal judgment was entered and this appeal followed.

When the contract was breached, the case went forward as to the vendees' right to performance, and the claim for damages was severed. Thereafter the vendees filed their statement of undisputed material facts pursuant to the District Court's Rule 9(h). They specifically alleged: "The fair market value of the real estate on the actual date of settlement, February 5, 1965 was $1,445,000."

Despite the value as thus represented, in amount of $445,000 greater than the original price, the vendees contend that the District Court erred in denying their additional claim for what they alleged they might have received had there been timely settlement in the first place.

We do not agree. No matter what the rule in other jurisdictions may be, it has long been settled in this jurisdiction that the measure of damages for breach of a contract of sale is the difference between the contract price and the fair market value of the property. Here, as appears above, the *undisputed* evidence is that the value of the property was $1,000,000 at the time of the original settlement date, and that the value of the property as of February 5, 1965, the date the property was actually conveyed to appellants, was $1,445,000.

In Quick v. Pointer, 88 U.S.App.D.C. 47, 186 F.2d 355 (1950), we had before us an appeal from a judgment of the District Court for breach of a contract to sell real estate. The contract price was $16,000. Some ten days after the contract was made, and before the settlement date, the purchaser made a contract for resale at $19,500. Because the original vendor did not have proper title, he was unable to conclude the sale and the vendee filed suit for damages. The District Court gave judgment for $3,500, the difference between the prices in the two contracts. In reversing, we held that the measure of damages for such a breach is the difference between the contract price and the fair market value of the property and, as there was before the court no evidence of the fair market value of the property, we reversed. * * *

In connection with its consideration of *Quick,* the District Court, in the judgment appealed from and in its opinion, used this language: "No reason appears discernible for applying a different principle where damages are sought in addition to specific performance than where action is brought solely to recover damages."

Nor do we see any such discernible reason. If appellants had sued for damages they would not, under *Quick,* have been entitled to damages as the evidence is that the sale price was exactly the same as the value put on the property by the expert who testified and whose testimony is accepted by both sides. *Quick* would have been on all fours with the present case. The fact that appellants elected to take the property is to our minds *a fortiori.*

Accordingly, we deny plaintiffs' claim for damages for the delay in settlement. * * *

Affirmed.

Notes

1. *How Buyer's Resale Contract Affects Specific Performance.* Where the buyer plans to resell, should the court deny specific performance because recovering expectancy damages will be an adequate remedy? See Note 4, p. 561.

2. *Hardly Hadley.* In Gilmore v. Cohen, the court denied the buyer lost profits for lack of proof of reasonable certainty. The resale contract may establish the buyer's lost profit. Gilmore v. Cohen, 95 Ariz. 34, 386 P.2d 81 (1963).

But should the court invoke Hadley v. Baxendale to deny the buyer's recovery of lost resale profit? Edward Yorio, Contract Enforcement: Specific Performance and Injunctions §§ 9.6.6.5, 10.2.2.1, 10.2.2.2 (1989).

3. *Dating Expectancy Damages.* If the court uses the market-contract damage formula, should the date for calculating market value be the date of breach or the date of judgment? Edward Yorio, Contract Enforcement: Specific Performance and Injunctions § 10.2.7 (1989).

4. *Tort Preferred.* The New Hampshire court found that the Bank had breached a contract to sell a lot to the Huysmanses. Specific performance was denied because of the buyers' laches. The court turned to the buyers' damages:

"The Bank appeals the master's award of $15,000 in damages to the Huysmanses for aggravation and harassment sustained by them as a consequence of the Bank's conduct. We reverse and remand. * * * [N]o evidence exists to support the amount of damages awarded by the master.

"Damages for aggravation and harassment are damages for emotional distress. '[R]ecovery of damages for mental suffering and emotional distress is not generally permitted in actions arising out of breach of contract.' Crowley v. Global Realty, Inc.,

124 N.H. 814, 817, 474 A.2d 1056, 1057 (1984). [citation]. Liberal compensatory damages, which include damages for mental suffering, will be awarded in tort actions, however, when the acts complained of were wanton, malicious, or oppressive. In *Crowley*, this court held that damages for family distress are permissible in a claim of intentional misrepresentation of fact in connection with the sale of a family home. The Huysmanses, however, did not bring an action in tort or allege and prove any wanton or malicious conduct in the Bank's breach of the contract, and are not entitled to damages for emotional distress.

"The Huysmanses nevertheless may be entitled to damages based upon the lost benefit of the bargain. 'In breach of contract cases, the purpose of awarding damages is not merely to restore the plaintiff to his former position, but to give him the benefit of his bargain—to put him in the position he would have been in if the contract had been fulfilled.' M.W. Goodell Construction Co. v. Monadnock Skating Club, Inc., 121 N.H. 320, 322, 429 A.2d 329, 330 (1981). A liquidated damages clause was not a part of the contract between the Huysmanses and the Bank and, therefore, the master could have properly calculated a damage award based upon the benefit of the bargain." Estate of Younge v. Huysmans, 127 N.H. 461, 467–68, 506 A.2d 282, 285–86 (1985).

5. *Prevue.* One way to describe the issue in the *Hourihan* decisions below is cost vs. value: Should the buyers recover (a) the cost to repair the house, or (b) its diminished value? The dispute generated two published decisions: the Florida district court of appeal's opinion is followed by the Florida Supreme Court's last word.

HOURIHAN v. GROSSMAN HOLDINGS LTD.
GROSSMAN HOLDINGS LTD. V. HOURIHAN

District Court of Appeal of Florida, 1981.
396 So.2d 753.
Supreme Court of Florida, 1982.
414 So.2d 1037.

NESBITT, JUDGE. [Writing for the District Court of Appeal] Appellants entered into a sale contract to purchase a house to be built by appellees on a particular lot. The contract provided that appellees would construct a dwelling on the lot "which is substantially the same as either the plans and specifications therefor on file at Seller's office, or, if constructed, the model therefor located in Seller's model area." Prior to the commencement of the construction, the buyers learned of and remonstrated against the contractors' plan to build the house as a "mirror image" of the plans and model shown to the buyers when they entered into the contract. Their desire that the house be constructed in accordance with the plans was so that they could obtain the optimal benefit of the prevailing winds which would minimize the need for air conditioning as well as for esthetic reasons.[1] Nonetheless, the contractors erected a mirror image of the dwelling. The buyers then commenced this action for breach of contract. At the conclusion of the bench trial, the trial court found the builders had breached their contract by building the mirror image but denied all money damages to the buyers on the ground that the award of money damages under the circumstances would constitute economic waste and because the value of the house as constructed had enhanced substantially over the contract price.

---

1. [Footnote renumbered.] Buyers were shown plans whereby the master bedroom, the "Great" room, and the living room would have a southeastern exposure thereby enabling them to take advantage of the tradewinds. The mirror image faced north and allegedly blocked off the winds. Additionally, the buyers would have had a view of the residential area. Instead, they now could view the "scenic" traffic of a major artery.

We agree with the appellants' contention that the trial court applied the wrong measure of damages.

In Edgar v. Hosea, 210 So.2d 233 (Fla. 3d DCA 1968), this court aligned itself with what is now complained of as being the minority view as follows:

> "[D]amages for a contractor's breach of a contract to construct a dwelling, where it is not constructed in accordance with the plans and specifications, are the amount required to reconstruct it to make it conform to such plans and specifications, rather than the difference in loan or market value on the finished dwelling, since unlike a commercial structure, a dwelling has an esthetic value and must be constructed as the owner wants it, even though the finished dwelling may be just as good."

The appellees insist that: (a) application of the foregoing rule violates the fundamental concept that compensatory damages are not awardable where to do so would constitute economic waste; and (b) the application of Edgar v. Hosea, would require a whole or partial dismantling or reassembling of a useable building. In this case, the rule against economic waste has no application for at least two reasons. First, as is made plain by Section 346 of the Restatement of Contracts, the rule is applicable only to instances for *unavoidable* harm that the builder had reason to foresee." [emphasis supplied] Secondly, it is clear that the rule for economic waste is applicable to commercial buildings rather than residential dwellings.

Moreover, in this case it is clear that the appellees/contractors may not proclaim that they substantially complied with the contract, because there was a willful and intentional failure to perform in accordance with the plans and specifications over the buyers' protests.

The rule in Edgar v. Hosea, to which we re-adhere, has not had the pernicious effect complained of by the building industry. We take judicial notice of the burgeoning construction of residences, notwithstanding that holding pronounced over twelve years ago. Indeed, it is our view that any other rule would be contrary to the pride of ownership that average homeowners expect when entering into what probably is the largest investment they will ever undertake—one which they may live with the greater portion of their lives.

The appellees also contend that the buyers were not damaged because the house had increased in value so as to offset the damages resulting from the breach. Whether the increase is illusory, because it is purely a result of inflation, or real, because of a general increase in the value of the home, this argument cannot aid the appellees. Upon entering into the contract to purchase the home, any increase in value (or decrease, for that matter) rightfully belongs to the buyers. Had the appellees constructed the house as contracted for, the buyers would have reaped the benefit of the increase in value of that home. Likewise, had the value of the home decreased, due to market conditions, the buyers would suffer the loss. Surely, the appellees do not suggest the buyers' damages would be increased due to a drop in value. Consequently, the trial court improperly applied the increase in the value of the home to offset the damages. * * *

[Grossman took the case to the Florida Supreme Court.]

McDonald, Justice. [Writing for the Florida Supreme Court.] We * * * disapprove the measure of damages applied by the third district [court of appeals] in the instant case. * * *

Grossman claims that subsection 346(1)(a) of the Restatement (First) of Contracts (1932) supports the diminution of value theory and urges this Court to adopt the Restatement as this state's law regarding damages for breach of a construction contract.

Subsection 346(1)(a)[1] of the Restatement provides as follows:

"(1) For a breach by one who has contracted to construct a specified product, the other party can get judgment for compensatory damages for all unavoidable harm that the builder had reason to foresee when the contract was made, less such part of the contract price as has not been paid and is not still payable, determined as follows:

(a) For defective or unfinished construction he can get judgment for either

(I) the reasonable cost of construction and completion in accordance with the contract, if this is possible and does not involve unreasonable economic waste; or

(ii) the difference between the value that the product contracted for would have had and the value of the performance that has been received by the plaintiff, if construction and completion in accordance with the contract would involve unreasonable economic waste."

The comment on subsection 346(1)(a) states:

"The purpose of money damages is to put the injured party in as good a position as that in which full performance would have put him; but this does not mean that he is to be put in the same specific physical position. Satisfaction for his harm is made either by giving him a sum of money sufficient to produce the physical product contracted for or by giving him the exchange value that product would have had if it had been constructed. In very many cases it makes little difference whether the measure of recovery is based upon the value of the promised product as a whole or upon the cost of procuring and constructing it piecemeal. There are numerous cases, however, in which the value of the finished product is much less than the cost of producing it after the breach has occurred. Sometimes defects in a complete structure cannot be physically remedied without tearing down and rebuilding, at a cost that would be imprudent and unreasonable. The law does not require damages to be measured by a method requiring such economic waste. If no such waste is involved, the cost of remedying the defect is the amount awarded as compensation for failure to render the promised performance."

Subsection 346(1)(a), therefore, is designed to restore the injured party to the condition he would have been in if the contract had been performed. This aim corresponds with general Florida law. [citations] We adopt subsection 346(1)(a) as the law in Florida regarding breaches of construction contracts.

Applying subsection 346(1)(a) to the instant case, we find that the district court reached an incorrect conclusion. The subsection itself makes no distinction between residential and nonresidential construction. Indeed, the illustrations contained in the Restatement deal with both types of buildings. We disagree with the district court's conclusion that the rule as enunciated in subsection 346(1)(a)(ii) is applicable only to commercial buildings.

---

1. [Footnote renumbered.] Similar provisions are contained in Restatement (Second) of Con- tracts § 348(2) (1981), but we prefer the lan- guage in Restatement (First).

Grossman also complains that the district court's ruling awards damages that are punitive in nature. Punitive damages are not recoverable for breach of contract, but where the acts constituting the breach also amount to a cause of action in tort, punitive damages may be recovered. [citations] The Hourihans, however, presented only the breach of contract issue to the district court. The amount of compensatory damages flowing from a breach of contract is not affected by the manner of the breach.

Turning to the trial court's judgment, we agree in part and disagree in part with its findings. The record supports the trial court's finding that reconstructing the house would result in economic waste, and we will not disturb this finding. On the other hand, we find the trial court's refusal to consider awarding damages because of the then-current value of the house to be incorrect.

Damages for a breach of contract should be measured as of the date of the breach. [citations] Fluctuations in value after the breach do not affect the nonbreaching party's recovery. Here, it may be possible to demonstrate a difference in value as of the date of delivery between the house the Hourihans contracted for and the house that Grossman built. If such difference exists, the Hourihans should have the opportunity to prove it on remand and recover that amount as damages.

We therefore disapprove the measure of damages applied by the district court, but we agree that the case should be remanded for a new trial on damages.

Notes

1. *What Next for the Hourihans*? In 1982, the Hourihans' house was worth $85,000, $35,000 more than when it was built; but they were living in Miami and renting it to tenants. They still preferred to charge the builder with the cost of tearing the house down and building it "right." National Law Journal, May 10, 1982.

2. *Questions*. May the Hourihans recover special damages for the increased expense of air conditioning the house? What about the loss of the view? May they pocket the damages and sell the house for $85,000?

How can the judge or jury as factfinder be sure that the buyers' claim of aesthetic loss is not a late-blooming desire to exploit a small deviation to secure a cheaper house? Should the buyers or the contractor bear the burden of persuading/dissuading the factfinder of the buyers' aesthetic or subjective loss? Should the court ask whether the buyers are consumers purchasing a home to occupy?

Could the builder anticipate that its breach would cause the buyers' subjective loss? Can the factfinder measure the extent of the buyers' subjective loss? Should the court consider whether the builders' cost to complete grossly exceeds the buyers' subjective loss?

If the court awards the buyers specific performance or a cost of rebuilding that exceeds their subjective loss, will bargaining between the buyers and the seller result in a settlement somewhere between cost and subjective value?

3. *An Issue for the Jury*? The court awarded the owner the cost of repair of a home even though that exceeded the original contract price:

"It is true that in a case where the cost of repair exceeds the damages under the value formula, an award under the cost of repair measure may place the owner in a better economic position than if the contract had been fully performed, since he could pocket the award and then sell the defective structure. On the other hand, it is possible that the owner will use the damage award for its intended purpose and turn the structure into the one originally envisioned. He may do this for a number of reasons, including personal esthetics or a hope for increased value in the future. If he does this his economic position will equal the one he would have been in had the contractor fully performed. The fact finder is the one in the best position to determine whether the owner will actually complete performance, or whether he is only interested in obtaining the best immediate economic position he can. In some cases, such as where the property is held solely for investment, the court may conclude as a matter of law that the damage award cannot exceed the diminution in value. Where, however, the property has special significance to the owner and repair seems likely, the cost of repair may be appropriate even if it exceeds the diminution in value." Advanced, Inc. v. Wilks, 711 P.2d 524, 527 (Alaska 1985).

4. *Preventive Law*. How can the buyers protect their interest in cooling breezes and a pleasant view? (a) Insert a liquidated damages provision into the binder contract? (b) Sue the developer for specific performance? (c) Seek damages measured by cost of conforming the property to the contract?

5. *Variation*. Suppose the builder breached its contract in a way that saved it money but built a structure that was equal in value to the structure promised. May the owner recover the expense the builder saved by breach? Would that measure lead to a windfall for the owner? Discourage parties from breaching uneconomical contracts?

Remember the famous Contracts decision, Groves v. John Wunder Co., 205 Minn. 163, 286 N.W. 235 (1939), where the court awarded the $60,000 cost of performance even though performance would have only added $12,000 value. The majority of courts, however, award only diminished value. Peevyhouse v. Garland Coal & Mining Co., 382 P.2d 109 (Ok. 1962).

6. *Bad Faith*. Professor Pat Marschall suggests the following solution:

"In choosing the measure of damages, the willfulness factor should be considered first and should be deemed crucial. If willfulness is found, the court should automatically choose cost of repair damages because this higher measure tends to deter breach and more fully compensates the plaintiff's lost expectations. If the defendant's breach was inadvertent, and therefore unknowing, or if it was intended to benefit the plaintiff, the breach would be labeled nonwillful. Since deterrence of an unknowing breach cannot be achieved by automatically awarding the higher cost damages, the court should decide which of the two measures, cost or value, is the more reasonable under the circumstances of the particular case. To do this, the court should adopt an open-ended balancing approach in which the remaining factors are assigned weights and balanced against each other. Aesthetic preferences of the owner which are expressed through contract terms or specifications should be weighed more heavily than the economic factors of waste and disproportionality because remedies for breach of contract should focus most heavily on giving the plaintiff his precise expectations created at the time of the bargain. These expectations include not only any expected increase in the market value of plaintiff's house or land, but other more personal economic and noneconomic benefits as well.

"Assuming that a defendant has been found to be a nonwillful breacher, and the open-ended balancing approach is being used to determine which measure of damages is more reasonable, it has been suggested that any relevant factors should be considered. However, some factors should not be deemed relevant. One irrelevant factor is how the plaintiff may spend his damage award. The court's job is to determine a reasonable monetary substitute for what plaintiff bargained for but did not get due to the defendant's breach. Once this is done, the plaintiff is free to spend that award as he wishes. If the court awards cost of repair damages and the plaintiff then takes a trip to Europe instead of replacing his defective roof or leveling his land, the court should wish him bon voyage without any second thought about the propriety of the award." Marschall, Willfulness: A Crucial Factor in Choosing Remedies for Breach of Contract, 24 Ariz.L.Rev. 733, 757–758 (1982)(citations deleted).

7. *Cost to Reconstruct—Reliance Recovery.* As an alternative to benefit of the bargain damages represented by the two measures above, a buyer may opt instead to recover out of pocket expenditures made in reliance on the contract. In Herbert W. Jaeger & Associates v. Slovak American Charitable Association, 156 Ill.App.3d 106, 507 N.E.2d 863 (1987), the owner sought to recover payments made to the contractor and subcontractors plus the cost of demolishing the structure. The court ruled that this was an acceptable alternative measure of damages where the usual method was too speculative. We will return to reliance recovery below.

<h1 style="text-align:center">OLOFFSON v. COOMER</h1>

Appellate Court of Illinois, Third District, 1973.
11 Ill.App.3d 918, 296 N.E.2d 871.

ALLOY, PRESIDING JUSTICE. * * * Oloffson was a grain dealer. Coomer was a farmer. Oloffson was in the business of merchandising grain. Consequently, he was a "merchant" within the meaning of section 2–104 of the Uniform Commercial Code. Coomer, however, was simply in the business of growing rather than merchandising grain. He, therefore, was not a "merchant" with respect to the merchandising of grain.

On April 16, 1970, Coomer agreed to sell to Oloffson, for delivery in October and December of 1970, 40,000 bushels of corn. Oloffson testified at the trial that the entire agreement was embodied in two separate contracts, each covering 20,000 bushels and that the first 20,000 bushels were to be delivered on or before October 30 at a price of $1.12¾ per bushel and the second 20,000 bushels were to be delivered on or before December 15, at a price of $1.12¼ per bushel. Coomer, in his testimony, agreed that the 40,000 bushels were to be delivered but stated that he was to deliver all he could by October 30 and the balance by December 15.

On June 3, 1970, Coomer informed Oloffson that he was not going to plant corn because the season had been too wet. He told Oloffson to arrange elsewhere to obtain the corn if Oloffson had obligated himself to deliver to any third party. The price for a bushel of corn on June 3, 1970, for future delivery, was $1.16. In September of 1970, Oloffson asked Coomer about delivery of the corn and Coomer repeated that he would not be able to deliver. Oloffson, however, persisted. He mailed Coomer confirmations of the April 16 agreement. Coomer ignored these. Oloffson's attorney then requested that Coomer perform. Coomer ignored this request likewise. The scheduled delivery dates referred to passed with no corn delivered. Oloffson then covered his obligation to his own vendee by purchasing 20,000 bushels at $1.35 per bushel and 20,000 bushels at $1.49 per bushel. The judgment from which Oloffson appeals awarded Oloffson as damages, the difference between the contract and the market prices on June 3, 1970, the day upon which Coomer first advised Oloffson he would not deliver.

Oloffson argues on this appeal that the proper measure of his damages was the difference between the contract price and the market price on the dates the corn should have been delivered in accordance with the April 16 agreement. Plaintiff does not seek any other damages. The trial court prior to entry of judgment, in an opinion finding the facts and reviewing the law, found that plaintiff was entitled to recover judgment only for the sum of $1,500 plus costs as we have indicated which is equal to the amount of the difference between the minimum contract price and the price on June 3, 1970, of $1.16 per bushel (taking the greatest differential from $1.12¼ per bushel multiplied by 40,000 bushels). We believe the findings and the judgment of the trial court were proper and should be affirmed.

It is clear that on June 3, 1970, Coomer repudiated the contract "with respect to performance not yet due." Under the terms of the Uniform Commercial Code the loss would impair the value of the contract to the remaining party in the amount as indicated. As a consequence on June 3, 1970, Oloffson, as the "aggrieved party," could then:

"(a) for a commercially reasonable time await performance by the repudiating party; or

"(b) resort to any remedy for breach (Section 2–703 or Section 2–711), even though he has notified the repudiating party that he would await the latter's performance and has urged retraction;"

If Oloffson chose to proceed under subparagraph (a) referred to, he could have awaited Coomer's performance for a "commercially reasonable time." As we indicate in the course of this opinion, that "commercially reasonable time" expired on June 3, 1970. The Uniform Commercial Code made a change in existing Illinois law in this respect, in that, prior to the adoption of the Code, a buyer in a position as Oloffson was privileged to await a seller's performance until the date that, according to the agreement, such performance was scheduled. To the extent that a "commercially reasonable time" is less than such date of performance, the Code now conditions the buyer's right to await performance.

If, alternatively, Oloffson had proceeded under subparagraph (b) by treating the repudiation as a breach, the remedies to which he would have been entitled were set forth in section 2–711 which is the only applicable section to which section 2–610(b) refers, according to the relevant portion of 2–711:

"(1) Where the seller fails to make delivery or repudiates or the buyer rightfully rejects or justifiably revokes acceptance then with respect to any goods involved, and with respect to the whole if the breach goes to the whole contract (Section 2–612), the buyer may cancel and whether or not he has done so may in addition to recovering so much of the price as has been paid

"(a) 'cover' and have damages under the next section as to all the goods affected whether or not they have been identified to the contract; or

"(b) recover damages from non-delivery as provided in this Article (Section 2–713)."

Plaintiff, therefore, was privileged under section 2–610 of the Uniform Commercial Code to proceed either under subparagraph (a) or under subparagraph (b). At the expiration of the "commercially reasonable time" specified in subparagraph (a), he in effect would have a duty to proceed under subparagraph (b) since subparagraph (b) directs reference to remedies generally available to a buyer upon a seller's breach.

Oloffson's right to await Coomer's performance under section 2–610(a) was conditioned upon his:

(i) waiting no longer than a "commercially reasonable time"; and

(ii) dealing with Coomer in good faith.

Since Coomer's statement to Oloffson on June 3, 1970, was unequivocal and since "cover" easily and immediately was available to Oloffson in the well-organized and easily accessible market for purchases of grain to be delivered in the future, it would be unreasonable for Oloffson on June 3, 1970, to have awaited Coomer's performance rather than to have proceeded under section 2–610(b) and, thereunder, to elect then to treat the repudiation as a breach. Therefore, if Oloffson were relying on this right to effect cover under section 2–711(1)(a), June 3, 1970, might for the foregoing reason alone have been the day on which he acquired cover.

Additionally, however, the record and the finding of the trial court indicates that Oloffson adhered to a usage of trade that permitted his customers to cancel the contract for a future delivery of grain by making known to him a desire to cancel and paying to him the difference between the contract and market price on the day of cancellation. There is no indication whatever that Coomer was aware of this usage of trade. The trial court specifically found, as a fact, that, in the context in which Oloffson's failure to disclose this information occurred, Oloffson failed to act in good faith. According to Oloffson, he didn't ask for this information: "I'm no information sender. If he had asked I would have told him exactly what to do. * * * I didn't feel my responsibility. I thought it his to ask, in which case I would tell him exactly what to do." We feel that the words "for a commercially reasonable time" as set forth in Section 2–610(a) must be read relatively to the obligation of good faith that is defined in Section 2–103(1)(b) and imposed expressly in Section 1–203.

The Uniform Commercial Code imposes upon the parties the obligation to deal with each other in good faith regardless of whether they are merchants. The Sales Article of the Code specifically defines good faith, "in the case of a merchant * * * [as] honesty in fact and the observance of reasonable commercial standards of fair dealing in the trade." For the foregoing reasons and likewise because Oloffson's failure to disclose in good faith might itself have been responsible for Coomer's failure to comply with the usage of trade which we must assume was known only to Oloffson, we conclude that a commercially reasonable time under the facts before us expired on June 3, 1970.

Imputing to Oloffson the consequences of Coomer's having acted upon the information that Oloffson in good faith should have transmitted to him, Oloffson knew or should have known on June 3, 1970, the limit of damages he probably could recover. If he were obligated to deliver grain to a third party, he knew or should have known that unless he covered on June 3, 1970, his own capital would be at risk with respect to his obligation to his own vendee. Therefore, on June 3, 1970, Oloffson, in effect, had a duty to proceed under subparagraph (b) of section 2–610 and under subparagraphs (a) and (b) of subparagraph 1 of section 2–711. If Oloffson had so proceeded under subparagraph (a) of section 2–711, he should have effected cover and would have been entitled to recover damages all as provided in section 2–712, which requires that he would have had to cover in good faith without unreasonable delay. Since he would have had to effect cover on June 3, 1970, according to section 2–712(2), he would have been entitled to exactly the damages which the trial court awarded him in this cause.

Assuming that Oloffson had proceeded under subparagraph (b) of section 2–711, he would have been entitled to recover from Coomer under section 2–713 and section 2–723 of the Commercial Code, the difference between the contract price and the market price on June 3, 1970, which is the date upon which he learned of the breach. This would produce precisely the same amount of damages which the trial court awarded him. * * *

Affirmed.

Notes

1. *Section 2–713 and the Buyer's Expectancy Damages.* Was the court correct to conclude that the grain buyer must cover on the same day the seller repudiates? Did trade usage limit the buyer's damages provisions of the contract and Article 2?

The court doesn't quote Original U.C.C. § 2–713: the buyer's measure of expectancy damages "is the difference between the market price at the time the buyer learned of the breach and the contract price."

Revised U.C.C. § 2–713(1)(a) would amend the buyer's expectancy damages measure in two ways. The first changes the basic rule's timing: the buyer's measure of expectancy damages "is the difference between the market *price at the time for tender under the contract* and the contract price." (italics added).

Although the new timing rule appears to affect the result in *Oloffson*, the second change, a new subsection, may implement that court's analysis: when the seller repudiates, the buyer may recover "the difference between the market price at the expiration of a commercially reasonable time after the buyer learned of the repudiation, but no later than [the contract's time for tender] and the contract price." Revised U.C.C. § 2–713(1)(b).

2. *Market-contract vs. Cover-contract.* Assume the grain dealer did what the court said he should have: after the farmer-seller's breach, he bought corn from another seller on June 3. Assume also that the dealer paid the other seller $1.12 ½, the price in the farmer's breached contract which was a good deal for the dealer because it was below the market price of $1.16. Could the dealer then recover under § 2–713 from the breaching farmer the difference between the market price, $1.16, and the contract price, $1.12½?

Whether, after a seller's breach, the buyer may make a substitute purchase and yet recover market-contract damages has been controversial. This is because of § 2–712's "cover" damages. Section 2–712 uses the buyer's substitute contract, which it calls "cover," instead of market value to measure the buyer's damages. The buyer's § 2–712 cover damages are the buyer's cost of cover minus the contract price. Under § 2–712, if the dealer's second contract is "cover," then cost of cover, $1.12 ½ minus contract price, $1.12 ½ equals zero expectancy damages.

Cover-contract is a desirable formula for a buyer who, after a seller breaches, makes a substitute purchase *above* the market price. In our example, if the dealer properly covers the farmer's breached contract at $1.20, he may recover damages based on the larger amount, $1.20 minus $1.12½. To qualify for cover-contract recovery, the buyer must purchase a substitute "in good faith and without unreasonable delay," prerequisites that prevent sweetheart deals and excessive recoveries.

After a seller's breach, a buyer who does not purchase anything may recover market-contract damages; in other words, cover is not mandatory. But a buyer's cover-contract damages measure under § 2–712 competes with his market-contract measure, § 2–713, if, as in the example that begins this Note, the buyer makes a second contract at or below the market price and seeks to relinquish or waive cover-contract recovery to choose instead market-contract damages.

Supporting this buyer's ability to select market-contract damages is the plaintiff's freedom to choose the damages measure he prefers. This is the position then-Professor Ellen Peters took in her influential "Roadmap" article, Ellen A. Peters, Remedies for Breach of Contracts Relating to the Sale of Goods Under the Uniform Commercial Code: A Roadmap for Article Two, 73 Yale L.J. 199, 260–61 (1963).

However, two policies militate against allowing the "covering" buyer an option to recover market-contract damages. First, the principle of <u>avoidable consequences</u> tells the buyer, a future plaintiff, to take reasonable steps to reduce his losses—and the future defendant's damages. Second, a buyer's recovery of higher damages based on market-contract may yield a sum that exceeds the amount required to compensate him, a "windfall," critics argue.

Kay

The statutory language in U.C.C. §§ 2–712 and 2–713 are woolly in both the Original and Revised codes. The Revised U.C.C.'s amendments to Article 2's § 2–713, Comment 7. favors cover-contract:

"7. A buyer that has covered under § 2–712 may not recover the contract price[-] market price difference under [§ 2–713], but instead must base the damages on those provided in Section 2–712. To award an additional amount because the buyer could show the market price was higher than the contract price would put the buyer in a better position than performance would have. Of course, the seller would bear the burden of proving that cover had the economic effect of limiting the buyer's actual loss to an amount less than the contract market difference.

"An apparent cover, which does not in fact replace the goods contracted for, should not foreclose the [buyer's] use of the contract price[-]market price measure of damages. If the breaching seller cannot prove that the new purchase is in fact a replacement for the one not delivered under the contract, the 'cover' purchase should not foreclose the buyer's recovery under 2–713 of the market[-]contract difference."

A skeptic might ask several questions about the Revised U.C.C.'s Comment: Is the buyer likely to volunteer information about a second contract? Will the seller find out about the buyer's second contract only by suing and taking expensive discovery? How does the court decide which of buyer's substitute contracts are "cover"? Is it advisable and expedient to have a rule to force the buyer to make an early election of remedies? Ellen A. Peters, Remedies for Breach of Contracts Relating to the Sale of Goods Under the Uniform Commercial Code: A Roadmap for Article Two, 73 Yale L.J. 199, 260–61 (1963).

The wiser course of action is to regard the issue as open. What do you think?

3. *Efficient-Opportunistic Breach.* Under *Oloffson,* could a farmer behave as follows? In May, Farmer sells her fall crop to Grain Dealer for $1.13. In June, Farmer concludes that the market will rise, breaches the $1.13 contract, and pays Grain Dealer $1500. In December, Farmer sells her harvested crop to someone else for $1.50.

Is the answer under *Oloffson*—yes? Is that because of the trade usage and because the court dates the buyer's damages at the date of the seller's breach? Is Farmer's tack a canny assessment to maximize profit or a sharp practice that should be condemned?

4. *The Argument for Efficient Breach.* "[I]n some cases a party is tempted to break his contract simply because his profit from breach would exceed his profit from completion of the contract. If it would also exceed the expected profit to the other party from completion of the contract, and if damages are limited to the loss of that profit, there will be an incentive to commit a breach. But there should be; it is an efficient breach. Suppose I sign a contract to deliver 100,000 custom-ground widgets at 10 [cents] apiece to A for use in his boiler factory. After I have delivered 10,000, B

comes to me, explains that he desperately needs 25,000 custom-ground widgets at once since otherwise he will be forced to close his pianola factory at great cost, and offers me 15 [cents] apiece for them. I sell him the widgets and as a result do not complete timely delivery to A, causing him to lose $1,000 in profits. Having obtained an additional profit of $1,250 on the sale to B, I am better off even after reimbursing A for his loss, and B is also better off. The breach is Pareto superior. True, if I had refused to sell to B, he could have gone to A and negotiated an assignment to him of part of A's contract with me. But this would have introduced an additional step, with additional transaction costs-and high ones, because it would be a bilateral-monopoly negotiation. On the other hand litigation costs would be reduced." Richard Posner, Economic Analysis of Law § 4.9, at 120 (6th ed. 2003). Judge Posner wrote about a seller's efficient breach in Northern Indiana Public Service Co. v. Carbon County Coal Co., 799 F.2d 265, 279–80 (7th Cir. 1986).

Whenever there are shortages, price increases or inflation of performance costs, a seller may be tempted to breach an executory contract. A seller who breaches his contract with B to sell to X for a higher price is a good example of an "efficient breach." In McCarthy v. Tobin, p. 557, we don't know the prices in Tobin's contracts with McCarthy and the DiMinicos, but, if the price in the second contract was higher than the first, that lawsuit could have stemmed from a seller's "efficient breach." We don't know, in fact, how often sellers' efficient breaches occur because the sellers aren't telling. A buyer may not find out about its seller's second sale; it may not sue the seller; if it sues, it may not conduct discovery to learn about the seller's (re)sale; and its lawyer may not understand the efficient breach arguments we are about to review.

Let's use the following hypothetical to explain the economic theory: Remember that assets are worth different things to different people depending on their ability to exploit them and their opportunity cost. Please accept the figures for now. S, a farmer, contracts to sell Redacre to B, a developer, for 100. Redacre's value to S as a farm is 80; its market value is 105. Given their respective assumptions about Redacre's value, this contract is profitable for both S and B. While the S–B contract is fully executory, X, a shopping-center magnate, offers S 110.

After the seller breaches, the buyer has an incentive to sue the seller for breach of the contract. B's expectancy damages will be market value, 105, less contract price, 100, equals 5.

The following summary of economic theory builds on Note 1 after Horton v. O'Rourke, p. 577.

A buyer's contract damages should equal the buyer's expectancy; that damages measure facilitates the seller's choice between performing the contract and breaching it plus paying the buyer's damages. Awarding the buyer its expected profit creates an incentive for the seller to perform the S–B contract unless performance would be inefficient. Recovering expectancy damages makes the buyer indifferent to the fact that the seller did not perform the contract.

The seller should not pay the buyer damages that exceed the buyer's expectancy. The expectancy damages measure will create an incentive for the seller to breach and pay buyer damages when performance of S–B is wasteful, that is when the seller's profit from breach (minus the damages the seller pays to the buyer) would exceed the seller's profit from delivery to buyer under S–B.

While the S–B contract was executory, X comes along and offers S 110 for Redacre. S breaches S–B and sells Redacre to X for 110. As damages, S pays B the expected profit, 5, and keeps 5. B is indifferent, having achieved the expected profit. S is better off having collected an extra 5.

Society is better off. Pareto is happy. If X is willing to pay S 110, Redacre is worth 110 to X. This transfers Redacre to a more valuable use because it has been moved to X, a person who values it more than S or B. Based on X's willingness and ability to pay, X will exploit Redacre most efficiently.

5. *Questioning Efficient Breach.* The critiques of efficient breach theory which follow are transaction costs, ethics, reputation, specific performance, damages, and restitution.

(a) *Transaction Costs.* Applying the efficient breach theory stated in the widget example favors S → X over S → B; B → X, because S → X eliminates expensive transaction costs. But could a seller's efficient breach increase total transaction costs? Perhaps the seller's breach will lead to two transactions: if S breaches the contract with B, then S's transaction with X may be followed by a dispute between S and B over B's damages. The efficient-breach solution may not reduce transaction costs because the seller still has to settle with the buyer: S → X; S–B. A remedy for B that would deter or prevent S's breach and sale to X might reduce the number of transactions. After X comes along, S should negotiate with B about cancelling S–B. Daniel Friedmann, The Efficient Breach Fallacy, 18 J. Legal Stud. 1, 6–7 (1989).

(b) *Ethics.* Professor Marschall argues that people ought to keep their promises. Accordingly a seller who breaches a contract, here S–B, intending to take advantage of another opportunity, here to sell to X, should pay the buyer enhanced damages. The seller has a duty to keep the promise to buyer in fact, not a choice between performing it and paying damages to the buyer. Pat Marschall, Willfulness: A Crucial Factor in Choosing Remedies for Breach of Contract, 24 Ariz.L.Rev. 733 (1982).

(c) *Reputation.* A seller's efficient breach may be an imprudent tactic. As a matter of practical business strategy, it may be argued, a seller with an onerous contract should avoid an efficient, opportunistic, or any other breach. For the seller's breach of contract will harm its reputation; its bad reputation will affect others' willingness to deal with it in the future. One opportunistic breach, perhaps advantageous to the seller in the short run, may be a self-inflicted commercial wound because, in the long run, a seller's reputation as an unpredictable contract partner will erode its ability to form beneficial executory contracts with many other buyers.

(d) *Remedial Arguments Against Efficient Breach.* a buyer has three possible remedies to deter or prevent the seller's efficient breach: specific performance, damages that exceed expectancy, and restitution.

(i) *Specific Performance.* Should the court grant a buyer specific performance when the seller repudiates before time to deliver? Efficient breach theory is aligned with the rule that the buyer's usual remedy for a seller's breach of contract is money damages.

A court will routinely grant a buyer specific performance of a seller's breached contract to sell land, as Tobin and the DiMinicos learned in McCarthy v. Tobin. When the market value of land under contract begins to rapidly escalate, spurring the seller to wiggle and look around for an exit, the court will routinely grant the buyer's request for specific performance. Kalinowski v. Yeh, 9 Haw.App. 473, 847 P.2d 673, 678 (1993) In the land deal in the hypothetical, buyer-B can force the seller to perform S–B. If the judge grants B specific performance of S–B, then Buyer, if so inclined, can sell Redacre to X for 110.

Judge Posner in *Carbon County*, cited above, and the court in *General Textile*, cited below, reject specific performance. Each plaintiff's damages can be calculated accurately, so both plaintiffs' damages remedies are adequate.

In *Carbon County*, Judge Posner adds that specific performance would, if granted, have two unfortunate consequences: (a) If specific performance actually led to performance, it would be a wasteful performance; and (b) a specific performance order would create incentives for a plaintiff to coerce an unbalanced settlement.

Should a court routinely grant a "goods" buyer specific performance of a seller's breached contract? Under U.C.C. § 2–716, a judge will not automatically grant a buyer specific performance because the section requires the buyer to show either that the goods are "unique" or that other "proper circumstances" exist.

Professor Douglas Laycock maintains that, for a goods buyer, money damages are inadequate unless the buyer can take the money damages and replace the seller's item. For Laycock, a grain futures contract, like the Coomer–Oloffson contract, which the seller repudiates several months before the date for the seller's delivery may be one where the buyer can take the seller's damages money and buy more corn. Laycock's reading of the courts' decisions, however, is that a court will almost always grant specific performance to a buyer who wants it.

Granting specific performance freely, in addition to its remedial impact, has an ethical dimension. The seller should keep his promise. If the buyer has a right to the promised item, a court will order the seller's specific performance. The seller does not have a choice either to deliver to the buyer or to breach the contract and pay the buyer damages.

For a buyer, money damages are a means to an end. "Courts do not limit [specific performance] so that promised resources can be reallocated to their most valued use, and courts do not recognize a [seller's] general right to breach and pay [the buyer] damages. Whenever anything important depends on the choice of remedy, courts protect plaintiff's entitlement to the specific thing he was promised. Efficient breach theory is an academic theory of what the law might be, or what some people think the law should be. But it is not the law." Douglas Laycock, The Death of the Irreparable Injury Rule 260 (1991).

Irreparable Injury and Efficient Breach. A judge's specific performance order to a seller is a specialized injunction that orders the seller to fulfill its contractual duties. A buyer seeking specific performance may move for a TRO and a preliminary injunction to prevent a seller's breach.

Consider General Textile Printing v. Expromtorg International, 862 F.Supp. 1070, 1072, 1075 (S.D.N.Y. 1994). After the price rose from .55 to .70 cents per yard, the defendant-seller breached a contract to sell the plaintiff-buyer 1.4 million yards of greige fabric; the plaintiff, which had purchased over 1 million yards of fabric on the open market to "cover" the breached contract, sued the seller asking the court to grant a preliminary injunction ordering the defendant "to immediately comply with the requirements of the underlying agreement."

Because of the plaintiff's ability to prove its money damages, the court declined to grant the plaintiff-buyer a preliminary injunction forbidding the defendant-seller from selling the fabric to others at the higher price and requiring the defendant to sell it to the plaintiff. The court quoted an earlier decision, "While the Court has the discretion to permit injunctive relief for breach of contract, the classic remedy for breach of contract is an action at law for damages. If the injury complained of may be compensated by an award of monetary damages, then an adequate remedy at law exists and no irreparable harm may be found as a matter of law."

General Textile Printing is inconsistent with Professor Laycock's approach to specific performance. Perhaps the court in *General Textile* denied the plaintiff-buyer a preliminary injunction to facilitate the defendant-seller's efficient breach. The plaintiff had "covered" by purchasing substitute fabric. "Furthermore," the court observed, "even if the market for greige goods proves to be in such short supply that plaintiff cannot purchase cover, and thus cannot calculate cover damages, plaintiff may be entitled to lost profits. * * * Since plaintiff is a middleman, its lost profits could be calculated as the difference between the contract price, and the downstream market price." See Original U.C.C. §§ 2–712, 2–713.

After the quoted decision, the litigants' greige-goods dispute went into arbitration, General Textile Printing v. Expromtorg International, 891 F.Supp. 949 (S.D.N.Y. 1995), and is not further reported.

(ii) *Damages.* Its proponents premise efficient breach on an assumption of "perfect" compensation, which they often leave unstated. One of the assumptions that Judge Posner states in both the widgets example, quoted above and in *Carbon County*, is that a court will measure a contract plaintiff's expectancy damages by that plaintiff's actual profit.

However, more typically a court will measure a buyer's expectancy damages measure for a seller's breach by market-contract; U.C.C. § 2–713, for example, bases a buyer's expectancy damages on market price or value less contract price.

A critic of efficient breach theory may disagree with the market economics proponent's idea that contract damages compensate a buyer satisfactorily. A critic may make several points. After a seller's breach, the buyer's special damages are limited. A contract plaintiff usually cannot recover her subjective and idiosyncratic values, for example, emotional distress. *Hadley*'s contemplation cutoff will often eliminate a buyer's lost-business profit. The buyer may not be able to recover for the cost and delay of searching for another seller. Under the usual approaches a buyer-plaintiff cannot recover its cost of recovering the damages, its attorney's fee, and its interest recovery is limited. Unless the defendant committed an independent tort, a breach-of-contract plaintiff cannot recover punitive damages at all. Dan Farber, Reassessing the Economic Efficiency of Compensatory Damages for Breach of Contract, 66 Va.L.Rev. 1443 (1980). Alan Schwartz, The Case for Specific Performance, 89 Yale L.J. 271, 276 (1979).

What do you think? Are a buyer's contract damages under-compensatory? If so, does this refute the argument for efficient breach?

A court might change the buyer's market-contract damages measure. Suppose that the S–X contract is completed at 110 before B sues S, and it is too late for the court to grant B specific performance or an injunction. B's expectancy damages, market-contract, yield 5. There are two ways for the court to strip S of the 10.

(iii) *Augmented Damages.* The court, first, could measure Buyer's damages by Seller's resale contract to X, 110, less the price in the breached S–B contract, 100, to yield Buyer's recovery of 10 damages. There is not much precedent for this measure. Under a later case in this book, Roth v. Speck, the court may measure an employer's damages using the breaching employee's higher second contract.

(iv) *Restitution.* Granting the buyer restitution is a second way for the court to increase the buyer's money recovery. After Seller breaches S–B and sells to X for 110, Buyer may argue for restitution of 10 to capture the Seller's improper gain from S → X. Buyer's recovery of 10 from Seller is conceptually restitution based on Seller's unjust enrichment from its wrongful act, breach of S–B. Granting Buyer restitution based on Seller's unjust enrichment is appropriate even if we assume that Buyer could have only resold Redacre for market value, 105, and would not have been able to sell Redacre to X for 110.

Someone who supports granting restitution to Buyer will emphasize Seller's conscious wrong, breaching S–B, and Seller's improper decision to bypass negotiation with Buyer to release S–B before conveying Redacre to X. Deterrence is the basic reason for Buyer to recover restitution from Seller. The prospect of only paying the buyer's expectancy damages, here 5, will not deter an opportunistic seller enough, because paying the first buyer expectancy damages will leave a breaching seller with some profit, here 5. Only the fear of restitution which will strip a breaching seller of all of its benefit from the breach and second sale will deter future sellers' breaches of contract. In our hypothetical, Seller will be less inclined to breach S–B and sell to X if it anticipates that a court will force it to pay Buyer 10 restitution.

An opponent of restitution will disagree with the preceding argument that Seller ought to be "punished" for intentionally breaching S–B. The opponent will maintain that Seller ought to be rewarded for searching out X and making the beneficial contract with X. Finally the opponent will maintain that Buyer should not receive more restitution than its actual compensatory damages would have been.

The tentative draft of the new Restatement of Restitution approves restitution for a buyer when the seller's breach is "both material and opportunistic." The buyer could choose restitution, measured by the seller's "disgorgement" of profits, as an alternative to expectancy damages. Damages would be appropriate if the buyer could purchase "a full equivalent to the [seller's] promised performance in a substitute transaction." Restatement (Third) of Restitution and Unjust Enrichment §§ 39(1), 39(2)(c)(i) (Tent. Draft No. 4, 2005).

Efficient breach or restitution, which is the better argument? James M. Fischer, Understanding Remedies 667–68 (1999). Andrew Kull, Restitution and the Noncontractual Transfer, 11 J. Contract L. 93, 104 (1997).

12. *Conclusion.* A fan of efficient breach will be hostile to granting Buyer specific performance, to awarding Buyer damages that exceed market-contract, and to granting Buyer restitution. Would the efficient-breach fan also be skeptical of a penalty-type liquidated damages clause, a plaintiff's recovery of punitive damages for a defendant's willful breach of contract, and allowing a tort of bad faith breach of contract? William Dodge, The Case for Punitive Damages in Contracts, 48 Duke L.J. 629 (1999).

Efficient breach is micro-economics based in rational-choice theory. Rational-choice theory posits a world where people struggle with others for strategic advantage. People make "rational" choices to maximize their self-interest, capital of some kind, usually in the form of wealth.

In the end, someone who favors efficient breach approves of Seller breaking its promise to sell to Buyer so long as Seller is willing to pay Buyer damages. It posits that Seller can substitute money for Buyer's contractual right to Redacre.

Is Seller's wealth maximization an adequate explanation? A complete explanation? Should a person behave like that? Do people have different commitments? Does a person's ethical makeup affect intentional contract breach and other opportunistic behavior?

4. BUYER'S SPECIAL DAMAGES: LOST BUSINESS PROFITS

AM/PM FRANCHISE ASSOCIATION v. ATLANTIC RICHFIELD COMPANY

Supreme Court of Pennsylvania, 1990.
526 Pa. 110, 584 A.2d 915.

CAPPY, JUSTICE. * * * The Plaintiffs claim to represent a class of over 150 franchisees of ARCO that operated AM/PM Mini Markets in Pennsylvania and New York during a three and one-half year period.

ARCO entered into franchise agreements with the plaintiffs which were comprised of a premises lease, a lessee dealer gasoline agreement, and an

AM/PM mini-market agreement. The products agreement mandated that the franchisees sell only ARCO petroleum products.

The complaint sets forth the following facts: ARCO began experimenting with its formula for unleaded gasoline and provided its franchisees with an unleaded gasoline blended with oxinol, * * * from early 1982 through September 30, 1985.

During this three and a half year period, the franchisees were required to sell the oxinol blend to their clients who desired unleaded gasoline. The franchisees were given no opportunity to buy regular unleaded gasoline from ARCO during that period.

Plaintiffs claim that numerous purchasers of the oxinol blend gasoline experienced poor engine performance and physical damage to fuel system components. Specifically, plaintiffs claim that the oxinol gasoline permitted an excess accumulation of alcohol and/or water which interfered with the efficiency of gasoline engines. * * * The plaintiffs claim that the gasoline did not conform to ARCO's warranties about the product.

As the problems with the oxinol blend became known, the plaintiffs claim to have suffered a precipitous drop in the volume of their business and an attendant loss of profits. Specifically, plaintiffs point to the rise in sales from 1973 until 1982, when sales began to fall dramatically; allegedly due to defective oxinol blend gasoline.

In their complaint, plaintiffs allege three counts of Breach of Warranty, Breach of Implied Duty, Misrepresentation, and Exemplary Damages. They request damages for "lost profits, consequential and incidental damages." [The trial court dismissed plaintiffs' action and they appealed.]

The point at which we start our inquiry is the Uniform Commercial Code Section 2714, entitled "Damages of buyer for breach in regard to accepted goods" is one of the governing provisions in the case before us,[1] and provides, in pertinent part:

"(b) measure of damages for breach of warranty.—The measure of damages for breach of warranty is the difference at the time and place of acceptance between the value of the goods accepted and the value they would have had if they had been as warranted, unless special circumstances show proximate damages of a different amount.

"(c) Incidental and consequential damages.—In a proper case any incidental and consequential damages under section 2715 (relating to incidental and consequential damages of buyer) may also be recovered."

Section 2–715 is entitled "Incidental and Consequential Damages of Buyer" and provides, in pertinent part:

"(a) Incidental damages.—Incidental damages resulting from the breach of the seller include:

(3) any other reasonable expenses incident to the delay or other breach.[2]

---

1. [Footnotes renumbered.] The plaintiffs claim they have accepted gasoline which allegedly does not conform to the warranty. Thus, we believe § 2714 is one of the governing provisions.

2. The incidental damage provision is aimed at reimbursing the buyer for expenses incurred in rightfully rejecting goods, or in connection with effecting cover. We have not quoted all the sections included in the subtitle of Incidental

"(B) Consequential damages.—Consequential damages resulting from the breach of the seller include:

> (1) any loss resulting from general or particular requirements and needs of which the seller at the time of contracting had reason to know and which could not reasonably be prevented by cover or otherwise."

Pursuant to the provisions of the [Editor: Original] U.C.C., plaintiffs are entitled to seek "general" damages, so-called, under section 2–714(b), and consequential damages as provided by section 2–714(c).

There has been substantial confusion in the courts and among litigants about what consequential damages actually are and what types of consequential damages are available in a breach of warranty case. Where a buyer in the business of reselling goods can prove that a breach by the seller has caused him to lose profitable resales, the buyer's lost profits constitute a form of consequential damages. We now hold that in addition to general damages, there are three types of lost profit recoverable as consequential damages that may flow from a breach of warranty: (1) loss of primary profits; (2) loss of secondary profits; and (3) a loss of good will damages (or prospective damages, as they are sometimes termed).

In order to alleviate the confusion that has developed concerning the various damages, we use an example to help illustrate the different types.

General damages in the case of accepted goods (such as occurred here) are the actual difference in value between the goods as promised and the goods as received. Thus, suppose a buyer bought five hundred tires from a wholesaler that were to be delivered in good condition, and in that condition would be worth $2,500. The tires were delivered with holes in them which rendered them worthless. The buyer would be entitled to $2,500 from the seller—the difference between the value of the tires as warranted and the value of the tires as received; those would be the general damages.

Consequential damages are generally understood to be other damages which naturally and proximately flow from the breach and include three types of lost profit damages: (1) lost primary profits; (2) lost secondary profits; and (3) loss of prospective profits, also commonly referred to as good will damages.

Lost primary profits are the difference between what the buyer would have earned from reselling the goods in question had there been no breach and what was earned after the breach occurred. Thus, if the buyer of the tires proved that he would have resold the tires for $5,000, he would be able to claim an additional $2,500 for loss of tire profits; the difference between what he would have earned from the sale of the tires and what he actually did earn from the sale (or lack of sales) from the tires.

If the buyer of the tires also sold, for example, hubcaps with every set of tires, he would also suffer a loss of hubcap profits. These types of damages are what we term "loss of secondary profits."

If the buyer's regular customers were so disgruntled about the defective tires that they no longer frequented the buyer's business and began to patronize a competitor's business, the buyer would have suffered a "loss of good will"

Damages. The courts below have not addressed
the claim for incidental damages, nor have the
parties to the litigation.

beyond the direct loss of profits from the nonconforming goods; his future business would be adversely affected as a result of the defective tires. Thus, good will damages refer to profits lost on future sales rather than on sales of the defective goods themselves.

While this example provides a simple framework to understand the different types of possible damages in a breach of warranty case, it does not encompass the myriad of circumstances in which a claim for damages can arise, nor does it specify which of these different damages have been allowed in Pennsylvania.

In addition to recognizing general damages under § 2–714 of the Code, Pennsylvania allows consequential damages in the form of lost profits to be recovered. [citations]

Pennsylvania has, however, disallowed good will damages; finding them to be too speculative to permit recovery. In the cases disallowing good will damages, part of the reason we found them too speculative is that the damages were not contemplated by the parties at the time the contract was made.

In 1977, this court had occasion to re-examine sections 2714 and 2715 of the Uniform Commercial Code in the case of R.I. Lampus Co. v. Neville Cement Products Corp., 474 Pa. 199, 378 A.2d 288 (1977). Before the *Lampus* case, we required the party seeking consequential damages in the form of lost profits to show that there were "special circumstances" indicating that such damages were actually contemplated by the parties at the time they entered into the agreement. This rule, termed the "tacit-agreement" test, "permit[ted] the plaintiff to recover damages arising from special circumstances only if 'the defendant fairly may be supposed to have assumed consciously, or to have warranted the plaintiff reasonably to suppose that it assumed, [such liability] when the contract was made.' "

In *Lampus,* we overruled the restrictive "tacit-agreement" test and replaced it with the "reason to know" test; which requires that "[i]f a seller knows of a buyer's general or particular requirements and needs, that seller is liable for *the resulting consequential damages* whether or not that seller contemplated or agreed to such damages." (emphasis supplied). Thus, in order to obtain consequential damages, the plaintiff need only prove that the damages were reasonably foreseeable at the time the agreement was entered into.

Turning to the case at hand, we must determine whether the plaintiffs have alleged sufficient facts to permit them to proceed with a claim for consequential damages. * * *

The first claim the plaintiff makes for damages is for the profits lost from the sales of gasoline. The plaintiffs claim that the breach of warranty by the defendant concerning the gasoline caused the plaintiffs to lose sales during a three and one half year period while they received nonconforming gasoline from ARCO. In the case of Kassab v. Central Soya, 432 Pa. 217, 246 A.2d 848 (1968), we permitted lost profits for cattle sales when the plaintiff showed that the defective feed caused harm to their cattle, causing the public to stop buying their cattle. The allegation here is similar. When the gasoline buying public discovered that the gasoline was defective, many stopped purchasing ARCO gasoline.

Employing the reasoning of *Kassab* and taking it one step further, we believe that the plaintiffs here are entitled to show that the gasoline buying community did not buy their gasoline from 1982 through 1985 because of the reasonable belief that the gasoline was defective and would harm their engines.

The lost gasoline sales are comparable to the lost cattle sales in *Kassab*. The distinction between the two cases is that the Kassabs had bought the feed all at one time and thus all their livestock was affected. The instant plaintiffs bought their gasoline in regular intervals and could only earn a profit on what they could sell per month. The defendant's argument—that the plaintiffs sold all the gasoline they bought—misses the point. While they may have sold every gallon, they sold significantly fewer gallons during the period that ARCO allegedly delivered nonconforming gasoline. Thus, during this period, the plaintiffs' lost sales were just as directly attributable to the defective gasoline as the lost profits were attributable to the defective tires in the example we used previously.[3]

Thus, if prior to the manufacture of defective gasoline the plaintiffs sold 100,000 gallons per month every month and then as a result of the defective gasoline, they sold only 60,000 gallons per month every month until ARCO discontinued that gasoline, then the plaintiffs have lost the profits they would have received on 40,000 gallons per month for the three year claimed period. Lost profits are, in fact, the difference between what the plaintiff actually earned and what they would have earned had the defendant not committed the breach. Because the gasoline was allegedly not in conformance with the warranties, the plaintiffs may be entitled to lost profits for the gasoline on a breach of warranty theory. The lost gasoline sales are what we have termed "loss of primary profits," and they are recoverable pursuant to § 2–715 of the U.C.C. upon proper proof.

We note, furthermore, that the remedy of cover was unavailable to the plaintiffs. * * *

[T]hey were contractually required to purchase all their gasoline from ARCO. In effect, they had to accept the allegedly nonconforming gasoline and had no possible way to avoid the attendant loss of profits. Thus, since they could not cover, the only remedy that was available to them was to file suit. * * *

The plaintiffs allege that in addition to a loss of profits for sales of gasoline, they had a concomitant loss of sales for other items that they sold in their mini-marts during the period of time that ARCO supplied nonconforming gasoline. Their rationale is that when the number of customers buying gasoline decreased, so did the number of customers buying items at the mini-mart. In other words, related facets of their business suffered as a result of the defective gasoline. This type of injury is what we characterize as "loss of secondary profits"; meaning that the sales of other products suffered as a result of the breach of warranty. This court has not had an opportunity to address whether these types of damages are recoverable.

In the case before us, the essence of plaintiffs' allegations is that customers frequent the mini-marts because it is convenient to do so at the time they purchase gasoline. Customers of the mini-mart are foremost gasoline buying patrons; gasoline is their primary purchase and sundries are their incidental purchases. Here, the plaintiffs claim that the *primary product* sales so affected the incidental sales as to create a loss in other aspects of their business. It is

---

3. The current case, unlike the tire example, involves a requirements contract rather than a fixed quantity agreement. In a requirement contract, profits lost during the period of time in which the seller supplies nonconforming goods constitute lost primary profits. The Code does not require that the buyer prove he would have purchased the same amount as usually required, for § 2715 permits the buyer to mitigate his damages by "cover or otherwise." Thus the buyer need not buy his usual amount of goods and then be unable to sell them before he can claim a loss of profits.

reasonable to assume that if the gasoline sales dropped dramatically, there was a ripple effect on the mini-mart sales. Additionally, when a primary product does not conform to the warranty, we believe that it is foreseeable that there will be a loss of secondary profits. Thus, permitting these damages would correspond with the requirement of foreseeability as set forth in *Lampus,* and the Code. It is much less foreseeable to assume there will be a loss of secondary profits when the nonconforming products are not the primary ones. We believe that unless it is a primary product that does not conform to the warranty, the causal relationship between the breach and the loss is too attenuated to permit damages for the loss of secondary profits. * * *

We find that the present case presents compelling reasons for permitting damages for loss of secondary profits. Henceforth, in a breach of warranty case, when a primary product of the plaintiff is alleged to be nonconforming and the plaintiff is unable to cover by purchasing substitute goods, we hold that upon proper proof, the plaintiff should be entitled to sue for loss of secondary profits.[4]

Historically, Pennsylvania has disallowed recovery for loss of good will damages or prospective profits in breach of warranty cases. The cases generally relied upon for this proposition are Michelin Tire Co. v. Schulz, 295 Pa. 140, 145 A. 67 (1929); Harry Rubin & Sons, Inc. v. Consolidated Pipe Co. of America, 396 Pa. 506, 153 A.2d 472 (1959); and Kassab v. Central Soya, 432 Pa. 217, 246 A.2d 848 (1968).

The defendant and the lower courts rely on these cases for the proposition that the plaintiffs claims are for "good will damages" and thus too speculative as a matter of law to permit recovery. While this analysis is seductive in its simplicity, it ignores the nuances of each of these cases and the effect R.I. Lampus Co. v. Neville Cement Products Corp., has had on this area of law.

In fact, in the case of *Rubin & Sons,* the court remarked "[i]ndeed if such were the holding [permitting good will damages], damages which the parties never contemplated would seem to be involved in every contract of sale."

With the advent of the *Lampus* "reason-to-know" test—which is a test of foreseeability—the holdings under each of these cases have much less precedential effect, since the *Lampus* test is much less restrictive than the tacit-agreement test.

Although the plaintiffs do not style their claim as one for good will damages, the Superior Court, the trial court, and the defendant have all characterized the claim for lost profits in this case as good will damages. What actually constitutes good will damages has caused much consternation to the courts and litigants. We in fact have serious doubts that the plaintiffs are even seeking good will damages. However, in order to determine that issue in the case before us, we must first discuss what good will damages are and whether they are allowable.

As one commentator aptly noted, "[l]oss of good will is a mercurial concept and, as such, is difficult to define. In a broad sense, it refers to a loss of future profits."[5] Other jurisdictions have considered loss of good will to be a loss of profits and reputation among customers. [citation] Generally, good will refers to the reputation that businesses have built over the course of time that is reflected

---

4. What constitutes a "primary product" will be dependent on the facts of each case. However, we would define a "primary product" as an item upon which the aggrieved party relies for a substantial amount of its revenue. The plaintiff must show that without that product, his business would be severely incapacitated.

5. Anderson, Incidental and Consequential Damages, 7 J.L. & Com. 327, 420 (1987).

by the return of customers to purchase goods and the attendant profits that accompanies such sales. Thus the phrase "good will damages" is coextensive with prospective profits and loss of business reputation.

Secondly, we must decide when good will damages arise in a breach of warranty situation. Essentially, damage to good will in a case in which the seller supplies a quantity dictated by the buyer's requirements arises only *after* the seller has ceased providing nonconforming goods—or the buyer has purchased substitute goods. Damage to good will in this case would refer to the loss of business sales that occurred after the buyer was able to provide acceptable goods to his customers; it does not refer to the period of time during which he is forced to sell the nonconforming goods.

Thirdly, we must address whether good will damages are too speculative to permit recovery, as we held in *Michelin, Rubin & Sons,* and *Kassab.* Although we disallowed good will damages in those cases, they are not recent. They were written in a time when business was conducted on a more simple basis, where market studies and economic forecasting were unexplored sciences.

We are now in an era in which computers, economic forecasting, sophisticated marketing studies and demographic studies are widely used and accepted. As such, we believe that the rationale for precluding prospective profits under the rubric of "too speculative" ignores the realities of the marketplace and the science of modern economics. We believe that claims for prospective profits should not be barred *ab initio.* Rather, plaintiffs should be given an opportunity to set forth and attempt to prove their damages.

Twenty years ago, the Third Circuit Court of Appeals noted in a case disallowing claims for prospective profits that damages once considered speculative may not be in the future:

"This is not to say we approve the Pennsylvania view or believe it will be the Pennsylvania position in the future [prohibiting good will damages]. Considering the advances made in techniques of market analysis and the use of highly sophisticated computers it may be that lost profits of this nature are no more speculative than lost profits from the destruction of a factory or hotel, and perhaps Pennsylvania will reconsider the reason for its rule in a future case."

Neville Chemical Co. v. Union Carbide Corp., 422 F.2d 1205, 1227 (1970).

We believe the time has come to reconsider that rule. In doing so, we find our position on recovery for good will damages (or prospective profits) to be out of step with modern day business practices and techniques, as well as the law of other jurisdictions. [citations] As noted by Professor Anderson in his well-crafted article on incidental and consequential damages,

"[T]o date, only the Pennsylvania courts have categorically denied recovery for loss of goodwill under any circumstances, an issue which has been oft-litigated in Pennsylvania. If one removes the Pennsylvania cases from the court, a significant majority of the cases have allowed for the recovery of lost goodwill in proper circumstances."

Furthermore, our rule has been repeatedly criticized by other courts and commentators. [citations] In reviewing our case law on the issue of prospective profits, we have not had a significant case come before us since *Kassab* was decided in 1968. Since that time, astronauts have walked on the moon, engineers have developed computers capable of amazing feats and biomedical engineers and physicians have made enormous strides in organ transplantation and replacement. It is evident that the world of 1990 is not the same world as it was in 1929 when the *Michelin* case was decided, nor even the same world as it was in 1968 when *Kassab* was decided. While these rapid technological developments have not been without their concomitant problems, they have made possible many things that were not possible before; including the calculation of prospective profits. For these reasons, we overrule *Michelin, Rubin & Sons, Inc.,* and *Kassab,* to the extent they prohibit a plaintiff from alleging a claim for damage to good will as a matter of law. * * *

[W]e now hold that plaintiffs should be entitled to try to prove good will damages; provided they are able to introduce sufficient evidence (1) to establish that the such profits were causally related to a breach of warranty and (2) to provide the trier of fact with a reasonable basis from which to calculate damages.[6]

Turning to the facts of this case, we note that the plaintiffs have made no claim for good will damages, since none was incurred; ARCO having cured the breach by stopping the supply of the nonconforming gasoline. The damages claimed are only for the period of time that the plaintiffs were forced to purchase the gasoline with oxinol. Thus, we reverse the decision of the lower courts in holding that the plaintiffs' claim was for good will damages. * * *

We now hold that there are three types of lost profits recoverable as consequential damages available under § 2714 and § 2715 of the Uniform Commercial Code: (1) loss of primary profits; (2) loss of secondary profits; and (3) good will damages, defined as a loss of prospective profits or business reputation. While this categorization of damages represents a new direction for the court, we believe that it is the better direction.

As a final note, we do not find that this case should be decided on tort principles, but on warranty principles. The relationship between the parties is of a contractual nature and should be decided on contractual principles. For that reason, we uphold the decision of the court below dismissing the tort claims. Additionally, we do not believe that our case law or the Uniform Commercial Code authorizes a legitimate claim for exemplary damages and thus affirm the lower court's dismissal of such claim. * * *

It is so ordered.

Notes

1. The tacit-agreement test survives, though the plaintiff proved the tacit agreement and recovered lost-business-profit consequential damages. Bank of America v. C.D. Smith Motor Co., 106 S.W.3d 425, 430–31 (Ark. 2003).

2. *Efficiency.* Mr. Richard Danzig asked whether the U.C.C.'s version of Hadley v. Baxendale is economically efficient:

"Resting the seller's liability on whether the type of damages incurred was 'normal' (or, in the U.C.C.'s words, whether it was a type of damage of which the seller has 'reason to know'), seems undesirable because it lets an all-or-nothing

---

6. There are a number of different ways that damages may be removed from the realm of speculation and be submitted to the jury with a rational basis from which the amount can be inferred. As long as the method of proof provides the jury with "a reasonable basis" for calculating damages, the issue should be submitted to the trier of fact. This is the approach taken by most jurisdictions. [citations]

decision ride on an indicator about which many sellers cannot, at the time of breach, speculate with confidence. Further, if the recoverability of a type of damages is established, a seller may often have no reasonable basis for determining the magnitude of the damages involved. On this dimension—obviously critical to any calculus of the care warranted to avoid breach—the rule has nothing to say. Lastly, if the rule were truly finely geared to optimizing the allocation of resources, it would place its emphasis on the damage known to the seller at the time of breach, rather than at the time of contract, at least where the breach was voluntary. When the rule was framed stress had to be placed on communication at the time of the making of a contract because that was the only occasion on which information exchange could be coerced without fear of imposing enormous transaction costs. Now the telephone and vastly improved telegraphic facilities make it possible to mandate discussion at the time of breach. Would it be desirable to move the focus of the rule to this point? On this question, some empirical evidence would be desirable. Do the average transaction costs associated with information exchange at the time of the contract multiplied by the number of instances in which such information is exchanged exceed the average transaction costs of information exchange at the time of voluntary breach multiplied by the number of occasions when breach is seriously considered? If so, there is much to be said for a revision in the rule." Richard Danzig, Hadley v. Baxendale: A Study in the Industrialization of the Law, 4 J. Legal Stud. 249, 282–283 (1975).

Since Mr. Danzig's article was published, fax, e-mail, instant messaging, and overnight delivery services have become familiar features of business and law practice. Do these developments strengthen his arguments?

3. *Avoidable Consequences.* The court may limit a buyer's special-consequential damages because of the buyer's failure to take reasonable measures to avoid the consequences of the seller's breach. In Carnation Co. v. Olivet Egg Ranch, 189 Cal.App.3d 809, 229 Cal.Rptr. 261 (1986), the court allocated to the buyer the burden of proving the loss, but placed on the seller the burden of proving the inadequacy of buyer's efforts to avoid consequential damages.

4. *Buyer's Lost Resale Profit.* "When the aggrieved buyer is in the business of reselling the breaching seller's goods, the buyer may recover the lost profits as consequential damages." The buyer established seller's "reason to know" by proving that the seller was aware the buyer was a broker-buyer that would resell. Canusa v. A & R Lobosco, Inc., 986 F.Supp. 723, 731–33 (E.D.N.Y. 1997).

Could the buyer recover damages under § 2–713, "the difference between the market price * * * and the contract price" plus lost resale profits?

5. *Problem.* You represent AirSnack, a company that sells snack items to airlines. AirSnack is suing, North Eastern, an airline, for a contract to supply snacks that the airline breached in 1999. AirSnack is seeking to recover its lost profits between North Eastern's 1999 breach and July 1, 2006. You are preparing an economist as an expert witness to project AirSnack's lost profits. The terrorist bombing on September 11, 2001 wreaked havoc on the airline business with disastrous fallout for its snack-food suppliers. Do you view AirSnack's projected lost profits stream from the perspective of the date of North Eastern's breach, which ignores 9/11, or the date of trial which takes 9/11 into account?

5. THE NEW BUSINESS "RULE"

MINDGAMES, INC. v. WESTERN PUBLISHING COMPANY, INC.

United States Court of Appeals, Seventh Circuit, 2000.
218 F.3d 652.

POSNER, CHIEF JUDGE. This is a diversity suit for breach of contract, governed by Arkansas law because of a choice of law provision in the contract. The plaintiff, MindGames, was formed in March of 1988 by Larry Blackwell to manufacture and sell an adult board game, "Clever Endeavor," that he had invented. The first games were shipped in the fall of 1989 and by the end of the year, 75 days later, 30,000 had been sold. In March of 1990, MindGames licensed the game to the defendant, Western, a major marketer of games. Western had marketed the very successful adult board games "Trivial Pursuit" and "Pictionary" and thought "Clever Endeavor" might be as successful. The license contract, on which this suit is premised, required Western to pay MindGames a 15 percent royalty on all games sold. The contract was by its terms to remain in effect until the end of January of 1993, or for another year if before then Western paid MindGames at least $1.5 million in the form of royalties due under the contract or otherwise, and for subsequent years as well if Western paid an annual renewal fee of $300,000.

During the first year of the contract, Western sold 165,000 copies of "Clever Endeavor" and paid MindGames $600,000 in royalties. After that, sales fell precipitously (though we're not told by how much) but the parties continued under the contract through January 31, 1994, though Western did not pay the $900,000 ($1.5 million minus $600,000) that the contract would have required it to pay in order to be entitled to extend the contract for a year after its expiration. In February of 1994 the parties finally parted. Later that year MindGames brought this suit, which seeks $900,000, plus lost royalties of some $40 million that MindGames claims it would have earned had not Western failed to carry out the promotional obligations that the contract imposed on it, plus $300,000 on the theory that Western renewed the contract for a third year, beginning in February of 1994; Western sold off its remaining inventory of "Clever Endeavor" in that year.

The district court granted summary judgment for Western, holding that the contract did not entitle MindGames to a renewal fee and that Arkansas's "new business" rule barred any recovery of lost profits. * * *

The rejection of MindGames' claim to the renewal fee for the second year (and *a fortiori* the third) was clearly correct. * * *

The more difficult issue is MindGames' right to recover lost profits for Western's alleged breach of its duty to promote "Clever Endeavor." A minority of states have or purport to have a rule barring a new business, as distinct from an established one, from obtaining damages for lost profits as a result of a tort or a breach of contract. [citations] The rule of Hadley v. Baxendale often prevents the victim of a breach of contract from obtaining lost profits, but that rule is not invoked here. Neither the "new business" rule nor the rule of Hadley v. Baxendale stands for the *general* proposition that lost profits are never a recoverable item of damages in a tort or breach of contract case.

Arkansas is said to be one of the "new business" rule states on the strength of a case decided by the state's supreme court many years ago. The appellants in Marvell Light & Ice Co. v. General Electric Co., 162 Ark. 467, 259 S.W. 741 (1924), sought to recover the profits that they claimed to have lost as a result of a five and a half month delay in the delivery of icemaking machinery; the delay, the appellants claimed, had forced them to delay putting their ice factory into operation. The court concluded, however, that because there was no indication "that the manufacture and sale of ice by appellants was an established business so that proof of the amount lost on account of the delay * * * might be made with reasonable certainty," "the anticipated profits of the new business are too remote, speculative, and uncertain to support a judgment for their loss." It quoted an earlier decision in which another court had said that "he who is prevented from embarking in [*sic*—must mean 'on'] a new business can recover no profits, because there are no provable data of past business from which the fact that anticipated profits would have been realized can be legally deduced." Central Coal & Coke Co. v. Hartman, 111 Fed. 96, 99 (8th Cir.1901). That quotation is taken to have made Arkansas a "new business" state, although the rest of the *Marvell* opinion indicates that the court was concerned that the anticipated profits of the *particular* new business at issue, rather than of every new business, were too speculative to support an award of damages. On its facts, moreover, *Marvell* was a classic Hadley v. Baxendale type of case—in fact virtually a rerun of *Hadley*, except that the appellants alleged that they had notified the seller of the icemaking machinery of the damages that they would suffer if delivery was delayed, and the seller had agreed to be liable for those damages. The decision is puzzling in light of that allegation; it is doubly puzzling because, assuming that by the time of the trial the ice factory was up and running, it should not have been difficult to compute the damages that the appellants had lost by virtue of the five and a half month delay in placing the factory in operation. Presumably it would have had five and a half months of additional profits.

Marvell has never been overruled; [but the court predicted that it would not be binding law in Arkansas]. * * *

That is the best prediction in this case. *Marvell* was decided more than three quarters of a century ago, and the "new business" rule which it has been thought to have announced has not been mentioned in a published Arkansas case since. The opinion doesn't make a lot of sense on its facts, as we have seen, and the Eighth Circuit case on which it relied has long been superseded in that circuit. [Citation] The Arkansas cases decided since *Marvell* that deal with damages issues exhibit a liberal approach to the estimation of damages that is inconsistent with a flat rule denying damages for lost profits to all businesses that are not well established. [Citations] Ozark Gas Transmission Systems v. Barclay, 10 Ark.App. 152, 662 S.W.2d 188, 192 (1983). The *Ozark* decision, for example, allowed an orchard farmer to recover for the damages to a *new* orchard. The "new business" rule has, moreover, been abandoned in most states that once followed it, [citations] and it seems to retain little vitality even in states * * * which purport to employ the hard-core per se approach. [Citations]

Western tries to distinguish *Ozark* by pointing to the fact that the plaintiff there was an established orchard farmer, albeit the particular orchard represented a new venture for him. This effort to distinguish that case brings into view the primary objection to the "new business" rule, an objection of such force as to explain its decline and make it unlikely that Arkansas would follow it if the occasion for its supreme court to choose arose. The objection has to do with the difference between *rule* and *standard* as methods of legal governance. A rule singles out one or a few facts and makes it or them conclusive of legal liability; a standard permits consideration of all or at least most facts that are relevant to the standard's rationale. A speed limit is a rule; negligence is a standard. Rules have the advantage of being definite and of limiting factual inquiry but the disadvantage of being inflexible, even arbitrary, and thus overinclusive, or of being underinclusive and thus opening up loopholes (or of being *both* over- and under-inclusive!). Standards are flexible, but vague and open-ended; they make business planning difficult, invite the sometimes unpredictable exercise of judicial discretion, and are more costly to adjudicate—and yet when based on lay intuition they may actually be more intelligible, and thus in a sense clearer and more precise, to the persons whose behavior they seek to guide than rules would be. No sensible person supposes that rules are always superior to standards, or vice versa, though some judges are drawn to the definiteness of rules and others to the flexibility of standards. But that is psychology; the important point is that some activities are better governed by rules, others by standards. States that have rejected the "new business" rule are content to control the award of damages for lost profits by means of a standard—damages may not be awarded on the basis of wild conjecture, they must be proved to a reasonable certainty. [citations] The "new business" rule is an attempt now widely regarded as failed to control the award of such damages by means of a rule.

The rule doesn't work because it manages to be at once vague and arbitrary. One reason is that the facts that it makes determinative, "new," "business," and "profits," are not facts, but rather are the conclusions of a reasoning process that is based on the rationale for the rule and that as a result turns the rule into an implicit standard. What, for example, is a "new" business? What, for that matter, is a "business"? And are royalties what the rule means by "profits"? MindGames was formed more than a year before it signed the license agreement with Western, and it sold 30,000 games in the six months between the first sales and the signing of the contract. MindGames' only "business," moreover, was the licensing of intellectual property. An author who signs a contract with a publisher for the publication of his book would not ordinarily be regarded as being engaged in a "business," or his royalties or advance described as "profits." Suppose a first-time author sued a publisher for an accounting, and the only issue was how many copies the publisher had sold. Under the "new business" rule as construed by Western, the author could not recover his lost royalties even though there was no uncertainty about what he had lost. So construed and applied, the rule would have no relation to its rationale, which is to prevent the award of speculative damages.

Western goes even further, arguing that even if it, Western, a well-established firm, were the plaintiff, it could not recover its lost profits because the sale of "Clever Endeavor" was a new business. On this construal of the rule, "business" does not mean the enterprise; it means any business activity. So Western's sale of a new game is a new business, yet we know from the *Ozark* decision that an orchard farmer's operation of a new orchard is an old business.

The rule could be made sensible by appropriate definition of its terms, but we find it hard to see what would be gained, given the existence of the serviceable and familiar standard of excessive speculativeness. The rule may have made sense at one time; the reduction in decision costs and uncertainty brought about by avoiding a speculative mire may have swamped the increased social costs resulting from the systematically inadequate damages that a "new business" rule decrees. But today the courts have become sufficiently sophisticated in analyzing lost-earnings claims, and have accumulated sufficient precedent on the standard of undue speculativeness in damages awards, to make the balance of costs and benefits tip against the rule. In any event we are far in this case, in logic as well as time, from the ice factory whose opening was delayed by the General Electric Company. We greatly doubt that there is a "new business" rule in the common law of Arkansas today, but if there is it surely does not extend so far beyond the facts of the only case in which the rule was ever invoked to justify its invocation here. There is no authority for, and no common sense appeal to, such an extension.

But that leaves us with the question of undue speculation in estimating damages. Abrogation of the "new business" rule does not produce a free-for-all. What makes MindGames' claim of lost royalties indeed dubious is not any "new business" rule but the fact that the success of a board game, like that of a book or movie, is so uncertain. Here newness enters into judicial consideration of the damages claim not as a rule but as a factor in applying the standard. Just as a start-up company should not be permitted to obtain pie-in-the-sky damages upon allegations that it was snuffed out before it could begin to operate (unlike the ice factory in *Marvell,* which did begin production, albeit a little later than planned), capitalizing fantasized earnings into a huge present value sought as damages, so a novice writer should not be permitted to obtain damages from his publisher on the premise that but for the latter's laxity he would have had a bestseller, when only a tiny fraction of new books achieve that success. Damages must be proved, and not just dreamed, though "some degree of speculation is permissible in computing damages, because reasonable doubts as to remedy ought to be resolved against the wrongdoer." Jones Motor Co. v. Holtkamp, Liese, Beckemeier & Childress, P.C., 197 F.3d 1190, 1194 (7th Cir.1999).

This is not to suggest that damages for lost earnings on intellectual property can never be recovered; that "entertainment damages" are not recoverable in breach of contract cases. That would just be a variant of the discredited "new business" rule. What is important is that Blackwell had no track record when he created "Clever Endeavor." He could not point to other games that he had invented and that had sold well. He was not in the position of the bestselling author who can prove from his past success that his new book, which the defendant failed to promote, would have been likely—not certain, of course—to have enjoyed a success comparable to that of the average of his previous books if only it had been promoted as promised. That would be like a case of a new business launched by an entrepreneur with a proven track record.

In the precontract sales period and the first year of the contract a total of 195,000 copies of "Clever Endeavor" were sold; then sales fizzled. The public is fickle. It is possible that if Western had marketed the game more vigorously, more would have been sold, but an equally if not more plausible possibility is that the reason that Western didn't market the game more vigorously was that it correctly sensed that demand had dried up.

Even if that alternative is rejected, we do not see how the number of copies that would have been sold but for the alleged breach could be determined given the evidence presented in the summary judgment proceedings (a potentially important qualification, of course); and so MindGames' proof of damages is indeed excessively speculative. [Citations] Those proceedings were completed with no evidence having been presented from which a rational trier of fact could conclude *on this record* that some specific quantity, or for that matter some broad but bounded range of alternative estimates, of copies of "Clever Endeavor" would have been sold had Western honored the contract. MindGames obtained $600,000 in royalties on sales of 165,000 copies of the game, implying that Western would have had to sell more than 10 million copies to generate the $40 million in lost royalties that MindGames seeks to recover.

When the breach occurred, MindGames should have terminated the contract and sought distribution by other means. The fact that it did not do so—that so far as appears it has made no effort to market "Clever Endeavor" since the market for the game collapsed in 1991—is telling evidence of a lack of commercial promise unrelated to Western's conduct. * * *

MindGames * * * pointed to no evidence from which lost royalties could be calculated to even a rough approximation. We find its silence eloquent and Western's argument compelling, and so the judgment in favor of Western is AFFIRMED.

FAIRCHILD, CIRCUIT JUDGE, dissenting in part. * * * [I] respectfully disagree with the conclusion that, as a matter of law, [Mindgames's lost royalties] claim is too speculative to support an award of damages.

This was never a claim in which MindGames sought to recover lost profits from the operation of a business. The damages sought would be measured by the royalties which Western would have been obliged to pay on sales which did not occur because of Western's alleged failure to perform its contract. Western's obligation to pay royalties arose from the sales of games manufactured, promoted and sold by it, and whether MindGames showed a profit, as well as Mind-Games' lack of history, was wholly irrelevant. The ultimate questions would be whether there was a breach by Western and whether the breach caused a loss of sales.

Sales did not meet expectations. In the period from March 30, 1990 to January 31,1991, 165,000 games were sold; in the year ending January 31, 1992, 58,113; in the year ending January 31, 1993, 26,394; and in the year after the initial term, 7,438. The sales in the initial term totaled approximately $4,000,000 and royalties $600,000. Soon after January 31, 1993, Western was sufficiently interested in continuing as licensee to agree to pay a minimum royalty of $27,500 for the coming year. MindGames' complaint alleged that a substantial number of games produced by Western failed to meet quality standards; Western failed to promote and make reasonable efforts to sell; and its efforts did not meet standards under the agreement or those recognized in the industry. It is MindGames' position that these failures caused loss of sales.

Western's motion for partial summary judgment was premised on the new business rule which Western perceived as announced in *Marvell,* and the district court granted the motion on that basis. If, as we all agree, *Marvell* does not control this case, then the applicable Arkansas doctrine is that MindGames is entitled to recover any royalties on sales which MindGames can prove to a reasonable certainty would have been made had Western carried out the contract. The rule that damages which are uncertain cannot be recovered does not apply to uncertainty as to the value of the benefits to be derived, but to uncertainty as to whether any benefit would be derived at all. [Citations] In my opinion we cannot say on this record, as a matter of law, that MindGames can not prove to a reasonable certainty that Western's failures to perform, if proved, caused a loss of sales. * * * I would remand for further proceedings on this part of MindGames' complaint.

Notes

1. Would MindGames be able to prove missing royalties from unmade sales under the *AM/PM* court's approach to lost actual profit?

2. Are the *MindGames* court's reasons to dispense with the new business rule persuasive? Why does the court think that standards will work better than a per se rule for lost business profits?

The new business rule, observed the South Carolina court, is now "a rule of evidentiary sufficiency rather than an automatic bar." Drews Co. v. Ledwith–Wolfe Assocs., 296 S.C. 207, 371 S.E.2d 532, 534 (1988).

3. The *Mindgames* court's standards approach to a plaintiff's lost business profit assumes that the plaintiff's recovery of lost profits depends on whether it proves income projections, facts, and context to provide the judge or jury a basis to ascertain its lost profits with a reasonable degree of certainty and exactness. A typical business plaintiff would retain an expert witness to develop its lost world of business profit.

Factors that the Texas court said militate against a plaintiff's recovery of lost profit include a new business enterprise, the lack of a history of profits, changing market conditions, chancy business opportunities, an untested product, and an unknown market. The factfinder will consider the evidence on these factors. Not even the absence of a history of profits will be independently dispositive. That the plaintiff had not been able to make a working unit of the product it intended to sell, however, undermined its ability to recover lost profits on unmade sales. Texas Instruments v. Teletron Energy Management, 877 S.W.2d 276, 278–80 (Tex.1994).

Why does the majority think MindGames' claim is too speculative? How do you think MindGames would fare under the Texas court's "factors"?

A hard row to hoe? Although not finding a per se rule, a New York federal judge observed "we have found no case from a New York state court permitting a recovery of lost profits to a 'new business.'" Coastal Aviation, Inc. v. Commander Aircraft Co., 937 F.Supp. 1051, 1065 (S.D.N.Y. 1996), affirmed, unpublished opinion, 108 F.3d 1369, 1997 WL 138112 (2d Cir.1997).

Mindgames is a breach of contract dispute. Should a court be more tolerant of the "reasonable certainty" of a plaintiff's evidence of lost business profit in a legal malpractice or antitrust lawsuit where the defendant is more blameworthy and the court seeks to protect the public?

4. "To my mind," wrote Justice Ellen Peters in a dissenting opinion that argued in favor of awarding the plaintiff future lost profits, "it is not surprising that start-up companies, in the first years of their operation, would have a difficult time making ends meet. It is not farfetched to assume that Steve Jobs, when he started Apple Computers, might have had difficulty in obtaining financing for so untested an idea as a personal computer. At that time, how could he have projected profits with analytic precision?" Beverly Hills Concepts, Inc. v. Schatz and Schatz, Ribicoff & Kotkin, 247 Conn. 48, 717 A.2d 724, 744 (1998).

5. Applying the new-business standard to plaintiff's income projections is factual and contextual and requires a flexible approach. The *MindGames* majority grants the defendant summary judgment, meaning that there is no jury question. Does applying the new-business standards resemble the determination of negligence in a tort case? Is it a task better reserved for a jury's community conscience? Do you

think that a jury would do a better job of applying the new-business standards than a judge?

6. EMOTIONAL DISTRESS AND A TORT–CONTRACT INTERLUDE

ERLICH v. MENEZES

Supreme Court of California, 1999.
21 Cal.4th 543, 87 Cal.Rptr.2d 886, 981 P.2d 978.

BROWN, J. We granted review in this case to determine whether emotional distress damages are recoverable for the negligent breach of a contract to construct a house. A jury awarded the homeowners the full cost necessary to repair their home as well as damages for emotional distress caused by the contractor's negligent performance. Since the contractor's negligence directly caused only economic injury and property damage, and breached no duty independent of the contract, we conclude the homeowners may not recover damages for emotional distress based upon breach of a contract to build a house.

I. FACTUAL AND PROCEDURAL BACKGROUND. * * * Barry and Sandra Erlich contracted with John Menezes, a licensed general contractor, to build a "dreamhouse" on their ocean-view lot. The Erlichs moved into their house in December 1990. In February 1991, the rains came. "[T]he house leaked from every conceivable location. Walls were saturated in [an upstairs bedroom], two bedrooms downstairs, and the pool room. Nearly every window in the house leaked. The living room filled with three inches of standing water. In several locations water 'poured in * * * streams' from the ceilings and walls. The ceiling in the garage became so saturated * * * [that] the plaster liquefied and fell in chunks to the floor."

Menezes's attempts to stop the leaks proved ineffectual. Caulking placed around the windows melted, " 'ran down [the] windows and stained them and ran across the driveway and ran down the house [until it] * * * looked like someone threw balloons with paint in them at the house.' " Despite several repair efforts, which included using sledgehammers and jackhammers to cut holes in the exterior walls and ceilings, application of new waterproofing materials on portions of the roof and exterior walls, and more caulk, the house continued to leak—from the windows, from the roofs, and water seeped between the floors. Fluorescent light fixtures in the garage filled with water and had to be removed.

"The Erlichs eventually had their home inspected by another general contractor and a structural engineer. In addition to confirming defects in the roof, exterior stucco, windows and waterproofing, the inspection revealed serious errors in the construction of the home's structural components. None of the 20 shear, or load-bearing walls specified in the plans were properly installed. The three turrets on the roof were inadequately connected to the roof beams and, as a result, had begun to collapse. Other connections in the roof framing were also improperly constructed. Three decks were in danger of 'catastrophic collapse' because they had been finished with mortar and ceramic tile, rather than with the light-weight roofing material originally specified. Finally, the foundation of the main beam for the two-story living room was poured by digging a shallow hole, dumping in 'two sacks of dry concrete mix, putting some water in the hole and mixing it up with a shovel.' " This foundation, required to carry a load of

12,000 pounds, could only support about 2,000. The beam is settling and the surrounding concrete is cracking.

According to the Erlichs' expert, problems were major and pervasive, concerning everything "related to a window or waterproofing, everywhere that there was something related to framing," stucco, or the walking deck.

Both of the Erlichs testified that they suffered emotional distress as a result of the defective condition of the house and Menezes's invasive and unsuccessful repair attempts. Barry Erlich testified he felt "absolutely sick" and had to be "carted away in an ambulance" when he learned the full extent of the structural problems. He has a permanent heart condition, known as superventricular tachyarrhythmia, attributable, in part, to excessive stress. Although the condition can be controlled with medication, it has forced him to resign his positions as athletic director, department head and track coach.

Sandra Erlich feared the house would collapse in an earthquake and feared for her daughter's safety. Stickers were placed on her bedroom windows, and alarms and emergency lights installed so rescue crews would find her room first in an emergency.

Plaintiffs sought recovery on several theories, including breach of contract, fraud, negligent misrepresentation, and negligent construction. Both the breach of contract claim and the negligence claim alleged numerous construction defects.

Menezes prevailed on the fraud and negligent misrepresentation claims. The jury found he breached his contract with the Erlichs by negligently constructing their home and awarded $406,700 as the cost of repairs. Each spouse was awarded $50,000 for emotional distress, and Barry Erlich received an additional $50,000 for physical pain and suffering and $15,000 for lost earnings.

By a two-to-one majority, the Court of Appeal affirmed the judgment, including the emotional distress award. The majority noted the breach of a contractual duty may support an action in tort. The jury found Menezes was negligent. Since his negligence exposed the Erlichs to "intolerable living conditions and a constant, justifiable fear about the safety of their home," the majority decided the Erlichs were properly compensated for their emotional distress.

The dissent pointed out that no reported California case has upheld an award of emotional distress damages based upon simple breach of a contract to build a house. Since Menezes's negligence directly caused only economic injury and property damage, the Erlichs were not entitled to recover damages for their emotional distress.

We granted review to resolve the question.

II. DISCUSSION. A. In an action for breach of contract, the measure of damages is "the amount which will compensate the party aggrieved for all the detriment proximately caused thereby, or which, in the ordinary course of things, would be likely to result therefrom" (Civ.Code, § 3300), provided the damages are "clearly ascertainable in both their nature and origin" (Civ.Code, § 3301). In an action not arising from contract, the measure of damages is "the amount which will compensate for all the detriment proximately caused thereby, whether it could have been anticipated or not" (Civ.Code, § 3333).

"Contract damages are generally limited to those within the contemplation of the parties when the contract was entered into or at least reasonably foreseeable by them at that time; consequential damages beyond the expectation of the parties are not recoverable. This limitation on available damages serves to encourage contractual relations and commercial activity by enabling parties to estimate in advance the financial risks of their enterprise." "In contrast, tort damages are awarded to [fully] compensate the victim for [all] injury suffered." (Applied Equipment Corp. v. Litton Saudi Arabia Ltd. (1994) 7 Cal.4th 503, 515, 28 Cal.Rptr.2d 475, 869 P.2d 454.

" '[T]he distinction between tort and contract is well grounded in common law, and divergent objectives underlie the remedies created in the two areas. Whereas contract actions are created to enforce the intentions of the parties to the agreement, tort law is primarily designed to vindicate "social policy." (Hunter v. Up–Right, Inc. (1993) 6 Cal.4th 1174, 1180, 26 Cal.Rptr.2d 8, 864 P.2d 88, quoting Foley v. Interactive Data Corp., p. 732.) While the purposes behind contract and tort law are distinct, the boundary line between them is not and the distinction between the remedies for each is not "found ready made." (Freeman & Mills, Inc. v. Belcher Oil Co. (1995) 11 Cal.4th 85, 106, 44 Cal.Rptr.2d 420, 900 P.2d 669 (conc. and dis. opn. of Mosk, J.) (quoting Holmes, The Common Law (1881)) These uncertain boundaries and the apparent breadth of the recovery available for tort actions create pressure to obliterate the distinction between contracts and torts—an expansion of tort law at the expense of contract principles which Grant Gilmore aptly dubbed "contorts." ' In this case we consider whether a negligent breach of a contract will support an award of damages for emotional distress—either as tort damages for negligence or as consequential or special contract damages."

B. In concluding emotional distress damages were properly awarded, the Court of Appeal correctly observed that "the same wrongful act may constitute both a breach of contract and an invasion of an interest protected by the law of torts." Here, the court permitted plaintiffs to recover both full repair costs as normal contract damages and emotional distress damages as a tort remedy. The Court of Appeal also noted that "[a] contractual obligation may create a legal duty and the breach of that duty may support an action in tort." This is true; however, conduct amounting to a breach of contract becomes tortious only when it also violates a duty independent of the contract arising from principles of tort law. * * *

Tort damages have been permitted in contract cases where a breach of duty directly causes physical injury [citation]; for breach of the covenant of good faith and fair dealing in insurance contracts [citation]; for wrongful discharge in violation of fundamental public policy [citation]; or where the contract was fraudulently induced. [citation] In each of these cases, the duty that gives rise to tort liability is either completely independent of the contract or arises from conduct which is both intentional and intended to harm. [citation]

Plaintiff's theory of tort recovery is that mental distress is a foreseeable consequence of negligent breaches of standard commercial contracts. However, foreseeability alone is not sufficient to create an independent tort duty. " 'Whether a defendant owes a duty of care is a question of law. Its existence depends upon the foreseeability of the risk and a weighing of policy considerations for and against imposition of liability.' " (Burgess v. Superior Court (1992) 2 Cal.4th 1064, 1072, 9 Cal.Rptr.2d 615, 831 P.2d 1197.) Because the consequences of a negligent act must be limited to avoid an intolerable burden on society the determination of duty "recognizes that policy considerations may dictate a cause of action should not be sanctioned no matter how foreseeable the risk." "[T]here are clear judicial days on which a court can foresee forever and thus determine liability but none on which that foresight alone provides a socially and judicially acceptable limit on recovery of damages for [an] injury." (Thing v. La Chusa (1989) 48 Cal.3d 644, 668, 257 Cal.Rptr. 865, 771 P.2d 814.) In short, foreseeability is not synonymous with duty; nor is it a substitute.

The question thus remains: is the mere negligent breach of a contract sufficient? The answer is no. It may admittedly be difficult to categorize the cases, but to state the rule succinctly: "[C]ourts will generally enforce the breach of a contractual promise through contract law, except when the actions that constitute the breach violate a social policy that merits the imposition of tort remedies." (*Freeman & Mills*) The familiar paradigm of tortious breach of contract in this state is the insurance contract. There we relied on the covenant of good faith and fair dealing, implied in every contract, to justify tort liability. (*Foley*) In holding that a tort action is available for breach of the covenant in an insurance contract, we have "emphasized the 'special relationship' between insurer and insured, characterized by elements of public interest, adhesion, and fiduciary responsibility." (*Freeman & Mills*)

The special relationship test, which has been criticized as illusory and not sufficiently precise [citation], has little relevance to the question before us. Menezes is in the business of building single-family homes. He is one among thousands of contractors who provide the same service, and the Erlichs could take their choice among any contractors willing to accept work in the area where their home would be constructed. Although they undoubtedly relied on his claimed expertise, they were in a position to view, inspect, and criticize his work, or to hire someone who could. Most significantly, there is no indication Menezes sought to frustrate the Erlichs' enjoyment of contracted-for benefits. He did build a house. His ineptitude led to numerous problems which he attempted to correct. And he remains ultimately responsible for reimbursing the cost of doing the job properly.

Moreover, since, as *Foley* noted, the insurance cases represented "a major departure from traditional principles of contract law," any claim for automatic extension of that exceptional approach whenever "certain hallmarks and similarities can be adduced in another contract setting" should be carefully considered.

Our previous decisions detail the reasons for denying tort recovery in contract breach cases: the different objectives underlying tort and contract breach; the importance of predictability in assuring commercial stability in contractual dealings; the potential for converting every contract breach into a tort, with accompanying punitive damage recovery; and the preference for legislative action in affording appropriate remedies. (*Freeman & Mills*) The same concerns support a cautious approach here. Restrictions on contract remedies serve to protect the " 'freedom to bargain over special risks and [to] promote contract formation by limiting liability to the value of the promise.' "

Generally, outside the insurance context, "a tortious breach of contract * * * may be found when (1) the breach is accompanied by a traditional common law tort, such as fraud or conversion; (2) the means used to breach the contract are tortious, involving deceit or undue coercion or; (3) one party intentionally breaches the contract intending or knowing that such a breach will cause severe, unmitigable harm in the form of mental anguish, personal hardship, or substantial consequential damages." (*Freeman & Mills*) Focusing on intentional conduct gives substance to the proposition that a breach of contract is tortious only when some independent duty arising from tort law is violated. [citation] If every negligent breach of a contract gives rise to tort damages the limitation would be meaningless, as would the statutory distinction between tort and contract remedies.

In this case, the jury concluded Menezes did not act intentionally; nor was he guilty of fraud or misrepresentation. This is a claim for negligent breach of a contract, which is not sufficient to support tortious damages for violation of an independent tort duty.

It may ultimately be more useful, in attempting to develop a common law of tortious breach, to affirmatively identify specific practices utilized by contracting parties that merit the imposition of tort remedies instead of comparing each new claim to a template for exceptions. In the interim, however, it is sufficient to note that more than mere negligence has been involved in each case where tort damages have been permitted. The benefits of broad compensation must be balanced against the burdens on commercial stability. "[C]ourts should be careful to apply tort remedies only when the conduct in question is so clear in its deviation from socially useful business practices that the effect of enforcing such tort duties will be * * * to aid rather than discourage commerce." (*Freeman & Mills*)

C. Even assuming Menezes's negligence constituted a sufficient independent duty to the Erlichs, such a finding would not entitle them to emotional distress damages on these facts.

[The court held that a plaintiff cannot recover emotional distress damages for the defendant's negligence that causes only economic injury.]

[T]he Erlichs could have avoided the threatened injury by moving out of the house until necessary repairs had been completed. If they had, relocation expenses would have been part of their damages. In any event, the general measure of damages where injury to property is capable of being repaired is the reasonable cost of repair together with the value of lost use during the period of injury. [citation] * * * The Erlichs seek recovery for emotional distress engendered by an injury to their property. * * * Although the Erlichs feared physical injury, Menezes's negligent breach of contract resulted in only damage to their property, and they could have avoided any threat of harm. * * *

Here, the breach—the negligent construction of the Erlichs' house—did not cause physical injury. No one was hit by a falling beam. Although the Erlichs state they feared the house was structurally unsafe and might collapse in an earthquake, they lived in it for five years. The only physical injury alleged is Barry Erlich's heart disease, which flowed from the emotional distress and not directly from the negligent construction.

The Erlichs may have hoped to build their dream home and live happily ever after, but there is a reason that tag line belongs only in fairy tales. Building a house may turn out to be a stress-free project; it is much more likely to be the stuff of urban legends—the cause of bankruptcy, marital dissolution, hypertension and fleeting fantasies ranging from homicide to suicide. As Justice Yegan noted below, "No reasonable homeowner can embark on a building project with certainty that the project will be completed to perfection. Indeed, errors are so likely to occur that few if any homeowners would be justified in resting their peace of mind on [its] timely or correct completion." * * *

D. Having concluded tort damages are not available, we finally consider whether damages for emotional distress should be included as consequential or special damages in a contract claim. "Contract damages are generally limited to those within the contemplation of the parties when the contract was entered into or at least reasonably foreseeable by them at the time; consequential damages beyond the expectations of the parties are not recoverable. This limitation on available damages serves to encourage contractual relations and commercial activity by enabling parties to estimate in advance the financial risks of their enterprise." (*Applied Equipment*)

" '[W]hen two parties make a contract, they agree upon the rules and regulations which will govern their relationship; the risks inherent in the agreement and the likelihood of its breach. The parties to the contract in essence create a mini-universe for themselves, in which each voluntarily chooses his contracting partner, each trusts the other's willingness to keep his word and honor his commitments, and in which they define their respective obligations, rewards and risks. Under such a scenario, it is appropriate to enforce only such obligations as each party voluntarily assumed, and to give him only such benefits as he expected to receive; this is the function of contract law.' " (*Applied Equipment*)

Accordingly, damages for mental suffering and emotional distress are generally not recoverable in an action for breach of an ordinary commercial contract in California. [citation] "Recovery for emotional disturbance will be excluded unless the breach also caused bodily harm or the contract or the breach is of such a kind that serious emotional disturbance was a particularly likely result." (Rest.2d Contracts, § 353.) The Restatement specifically notes the breach of a contract to build a home is not "particularly likely" to result in "serious emotional disturbance."

Cases permitting recovery for emotional distress typically involve mental anguish stemming from more personal undertakings the traumatic results of which were unavoidable. [The court cites cases that involve an infant injured during childbirth, a misdiagnosed venereal disease and subsequent failure of marriage, a fatal waterskiing accident, and a failure to adequately preserve a corpse.]

Thus, when the express object of the contract is the mental and emotional well-being of one of the contracting parties, the breach of the contract may give rise to damages for mental suffering or emotional distress. [The court cites cases that involve an agreement of two gambling clubs to exclude a husband's gambling-addicted wife from clubs and not to cash her checks, a cemetery's agreement to keep burial service private and to protect a grave from vandalism, and a bailment for heirloom jewelry where the jewelry's great sentimental value was made known to bailee.]

Cases from other jurisdictions have formulated a similar rule, barring recovery of emotional distress damages for breach of contract except in cases involving contracts in which emotional concerns are the essence of the contract. [The court cites cases to support the point that "contracts pertaining to one's dwelling are not among those contracts which, if breached, are particularly likely to result in serious emotional disturbance."] Typical damages for breach of house construction contracts can appropriately be calculated in terms of monetary loss. McMeakin v. Roofing & Sheet Metal Supply (Okla.Ct.App. 1990) 807 P.2d 288 [affirming order granting summary judgment in favor of defendant roofing company after it negligently stacked too many brick tiles on roof, causing roof to collapse and completely destroy home, leading to plaintiff's heart attack one month later]. [citations]

Plaintiffs argue strenuously that a broader notion of damages is appropriate when the contract is for the construction of a home. Amici curiae urge us to permit emotional distress damages in cases of negligent construction of a personal residence when the negligent construction causes gross interference with the normal use and habitability of the residence.

Such a rule would make the financial risks of construction agreements difficult to predict. Contract damages must be clearly ascertainable in both nature and origin. (Civ.Code, § 3301). A contracting party cannot be required to assume limitless responsibility for all consequences of a breach and must be advised of any special harm that might result in order to determine whether or not to accept the risk of contracting.

Moreover, adding an emotional distress component to recovery for construction defects could increase the already prohibitively high cost of housing in California, affect the availability of insurance for builders, and greatly diminish the supply of affordable housing. The potential for such broad-ranging economic consequences—costs likely to be paid by the public generally—means the task of fashioning appropriate limits on the availability of emotional distress claims should be left to the Legislature. (See Tex. Prop.Code Ann. § 27.001 et seq. (1999); Hawaii Rev. Stat. § 663–8.9 (1998).

Permitting damages for emotional distress on the theory that certain contracts carry a lot of emotional freight provides no useful guidance. Courts have carved out a narrow range of exceptions to the general rule of exclusion where emotional tranquillity is the contract's essence. Refusal to broaden the bases for recovery reflects a fundamental policy choice. A rule which focuses not on the risks contracting parties voluntarily assume but on one party's reaction to inadequate performance, cannot provide any principled limit on liability.

The discussion in *Kwan,* a case dealing with the breach of a sales contract for the purchase of a car, is instructive. "[A] contract for [the] sale of an automobile is not essentially tied to the buyer's mental or emotional well-being. Personal as the choice of a car may be, the central reason for buying one is usually transportation * * * . In spite of America's much-discussed 'love affair with the automobile,' disruption of an owner's relationship with his or her car is not, in the normal case, comparable to the loss or mistreatment of a family member's remains [citation], an invasion of one's privacy [citation], or the loss of one's spouse to a gambling addiction [citation]. In the latter situations, the contract exists primarily to further or protect emotional interests; the direct and foreseeable injuries resulting from a breach are also primarily emotional. In contrast, the undeniable aggravation, irritation and anxiety that may result from [the] breach of an automobile warranty are secondary effects deriving from the decreased usefulness of the car and the frequently frustrating process of having an automobile repaired. While [the] purchase of an automobile may sometimes lead to severe emotional distress, such a result is not ordinarily foreseeable from the nature of the contract." Kwan v. Mercedes–Benz of North America, Inc. (1994) 23 Cal.App.4th 174, 188, 28 Cal.Rptr.2d 371.

Most other jurisdictions have reached the same conclusion. (See Sanders v. Zeagler (La.1997)) 686 So.2d 819, 822–823 [principal object of a contract for the construction of a house was to obtain a place to live and emotional distress damages were not recoverable]. [citations]

We agree. The available damages for defective construction are limited to the cost of repairing the home, including lost use or relocation expenses, or the diminution in value. (Orndorff v. Christiana Community Builders, p. 786.) The Erlichs received more than $400,000 in traditional contract damages to correct the defects in their home. While their distress was undoubtedly real and serious, we conclude the balance of policy considerations—the potential for significant increases in liability in amounts disproportionate to culpability, the court's inability to formulate appropriate limits on the availability of claims, and the magnitude of the impact on stability and predictability in commercial affairs—counsel against expanding contract damages to include mental distress claims in negligent construction cases.

DISPOSITION. The judgment of the Court of Appeal is reversed and the matter is remanded for further proceedings consistent with this opinion.

Notes

1. *Questions About the Erlichs' Quest for Emotional Distress Damages.* (a) *Fraud.* The stakes in the tort-contract characterization are high. If the jury had found for the Erlichs on their fraud count, that may have opened the door to emotional distress recovery and to punitive damages. Why is the *Erlich* court's distinction between tort and contract so murky? Jahn v. Brickey, 168 Cal.App.3d 399, 214 Cal.Rptr. 119. 123 (1985)? See Notes 3 and 4 after Selman v. Shirley, pp. 578–79; Younge v. Huysmans, p. 589.

(b) *Bad Faith.* As the *Erlich* court indicates, courts in California, and elsewhere, have generally confined the tort of "bad faith contract breach" to insurance contracts. Does a homeowner's agreement with a contractor resemble an insured's relationship with her insurance company?

(c) *Foreseeability.* The California Supreme Court says that "foreseeability alone is not sufficient to create an independent tort duty." Is that statement consistent with that court's earlier decision in *J'Aire*, p. 543?

Do you think that the contractor breached the agreement inadvertently, that is negligently, or on purpose, that is intentionally?

The court quotes the contemplation-foreseeability limitation on a contract plaintiff's recovery of special damages. Given the relationship of trust between the homeowner and the contractor, the circumstances of the contract and the magnitude of the contractor's breaches, should the contractor have been able to predict (contemplate) the homeowners' emotional distress? If you think that the contemplation test should have allowed the homeowners to recover for their emotional distress, is the court's exclusion of those damages a separate rule cutting back most contract plaintiffs' ability to recover special damages?

(d) *Undercompensation?* Do the homeowners receive less than full compensation for the contractor's breach? If so, what reasons does the court give for undercompensating them? Were the homeowners' reactions to the contractor's breaches unreasonable or out of proportion to their plight? Does barring homeowners from recovery for their emotional distress encourage potential plaintiffs to take measures to help themselves? What does the court mean by saying that the plaintiffs' recovery for their emotional distress will put an "intolerable burden on society"?

(e) *Attorney Fee.* An unstated reason for a court to let a plaintiff recover damages for emotional distress is to finance litigation—to provide a fund for the plaintiff's attorney fee. Suppose a plaintiff who made a contingency fee contract with her lawyer recovers only her out-of-pocket losses. After she pays her lawyer, will she be left under-compensated?

2. *Contracts Limiting Buyer's Remedies and Damages.* Contracts may circumscribe a buyer's warranties, recovery of consequential damages, and remedies including recovery of lost profits. The important statutes are U.C.C. § 2–719(2) and (3), § 2–316, as well as state and federal consumer legislation. Behind these statutes is a policy thicket.

One approach tells a court to inquire into an agreements that limits a buyer's remedies in light of public policy goals like loss avoidance, loss spreading, and ameliorating the effect of unequal bargaining power. Another approach focuses the court on the transactional nexus between the buyer and the seller and informs the court to favor free bargaining, market economics, and party autonomy; it tells the court to view a sale with a warranty as a product plus an insurance policy that the buyer may not want to pay for and may have agreed not to pay for.

A buyer who reads a seller's form that accompanies a sale is likely to read language like the following in a contract drafted by the seller, PIC, to sell breeding stock to Delmarva, a hog producer:

CREDITS AND PROCEDURES: In case of complaint, purchaser shall call or write to PIC.... If the pig identified is determined to have been incapable of breeding after isolation and acclimatization, PIC will authorize slaughter following notification. A credit for the invoiced cost of the pig, less slaughter value, will be issued. * * *

LIMITATION OF LIABILITY: PIC shall have no liability for risk of loss of pigs delivered under the terms of this agreement after delivery, which shall be deemed complete immediately upon the arrival of the shipment at the purchaser's premises. Except for the credit provision provided for above, PIC shall have no liability for losses resulting from communicable diseases or for losses resulting or claimed to have resulted from advice and information given by PIC, whether in oral or written form. PIC'S liability shall be limited by the above terms, and PIC shall not be liable for any consequential losses, any veterinarian's fees, or any other costs incurred in any manner whatsoever after pigs are in purchaser's possession. * * *

EXCLUSIVE REMEDIES: Purchaser's remedies provided herein are exclusive remedies, and all other remedies, statutory or otherwise, are expressly waived by purchaser. The purchaser is aware of the risks of swine production and therefore, waiver is neither unreasonable nor unconscionable.

DISCLAIMER: These conditions of sale contain all warranties made by PIC to purchaser. NO OTHER WARRANTIES, EXPRESSED OR IMPLIED OTHER THAN THOSE SET FORTH HEREIN, ARE GIVEN. ALL PIGS SOLD HEREIN ARE SOLD "AS IS," AND PIC SPECIFICALLY DISCLAIMS ANY WARRANTY OF MERCHANTABILITY AND ANY WARRANTY OF FITNESS FOR ANY PARTICULAR PURPOSE. THERE ARE NO WARRANTIES WHICH EXTEND BEYOND THE DESCRIPTION OF THE FACE HEREOF.

Pig Improvement Co., Inc. v. Middle States Holding Co., 943 F.Supp. 392, 397–98 (D.Del.1996). The material that follows is based on this language.

The buyer, hog producer Delmarva, claimed seller-PIC's breeding pigs introduced a disease into its herd which led to lost profit. What effect did the court give the contractual language above?

Section 2–719(1)(a): The contract may add or substitute remedies; it may "alter the measure of damages" a buyer may recover. The Code gives two examples of limited or substituted remedies: return for a refund and repair-replace. How did PIC's form language limit Delmarva's remedy?

Section 2–719(2) and (3) determine whether limited remedies are appropriate. Section 2–719 (2): If an exclusive or limited remedy fails "of its essential purpose," the buyer's remedies are those "provided in this" code. Section 2–719(3). If a contract excludes consequential damages, as the breeding stock contract does, the court is to avoid the exclusion if "the limitation or exclusion is unconscionable." The official comments after (3) refer the reader to the sales article's unconscionability section, § 2–302; courts use § 2–302 unconscionability analysis for exclusions of consequential damages. It is prima facie unconscionable for a seller to limit a buyer's consequential damages for personal injury by consumer goods.

What does § 2–719(2) mean by saying a limited remedy may fail of its essential purpose? Courts have developed at least two approaches to § 2–719(2).

Under the first, the judge reads unconscionability into § 2–719(2) and broadens the inquiry to fairness. 943 F.Supp. 392, 402. The Delaware federal judge read § 2–719(2) to incorporate unconscionability. PIC's limitation of Delmarva's remedies to the credit procedure and its exclusion of consequential damages were not, the court held, unconscionable. 943 F.Supp. 392, 403.

A second way to determine whether a buyer's circumscribed remedy flunks is to ask whether the exclusive remedy fails to achieve "its" purpose. This analysis focuses on the seller's purpose and the limiting language; it disregards "the essential purpose of the U.C.C., contract law, or of equity." 943 F.Supp. 392, 402, n. 14. If a court follows this second approach, a limited remedy would seldom "fail." "It" would accomplish the seller's "purpose": a clause that limits damages serves "its" purpose of limiting buyer's damages.

Delmarva might also have argued that, in addition to the tests in § 2–719(2) and (3), language limiting buyer's remedies must also pass Original U.C.C. § 1–304's test, "Every contract * * * imposes an obligation of good faith on its * * * enforcement." If PIC had acted in "bad faith," it was deprived the benefit of the limited remedy.

Section 2–316 tells sellers how to disclaim implied warranties. Under § 2–316(2), but subject to (3), which follows, to exclude merchantability, the contract must use the word "merchantability." Under § 2–316(3)(a), "notwithstanding" (2), to exclude "all implied warranties," the contract may use "language which in common understanding calls the buyer's attention to the exclusion of warranties and makes plain that there is no implied warranty," for example the words "as is." Which method did PIC's form use? Was that overkill? Suppose PIC's form had said "This warranty is in lieu of all other warranties express or implied." Would this be plain and common enough to exclude the warranty of merchantability without repeating the word?

A seller's form, one court held, may waive "merchantability" either (a) expressly by using the word, § 2–316(2), or (b) by using other plain language to exclude all implied warranties, § 2–316(3)(a). Lefebvre Intergraphics, Inc. v. Sanden Machine Ltd., 946 F.Supp. 1358, 1362–63 (N.D.Ill.1996).

In analyzing PIC's form, the judge thought a contract which negates all implied warranties is effective only between merchants and then only if it mentions "merchantability" conspicuously. Did PIC's language in the breeding stock contract disclaim implied warranties successfully? 943 F.Supp. 392, 405.

Section 2–316 does not cite § 2–302, the sales article's unconscionability provision. Some courts nevertheless find § 2–302 unconscionability applicable to limit a seller's warranty disclaimer. What do you think?

Although the U.C.C. governs a seller's commercial sales to a business buyer, state consumer protection legislation may augment the U.C.C. for an eligible buyer. State consumer protection acts create a cause of action for a seller's unfair or deceptive trade practices in providing a consumer with goods or services for personal, household or family purposes. While "deceptive" may parallel "misrepresented," the court may read the language expansively to include omissions and to create a broader standard for a consumer's recovery than the tort of misrepresentation would have. Moreover, the word "unfair" appears to create an even broader and more desirable standard for an eligible buyer. A buyer's damages under a state consumer protection statute may be tort damages.

In response to Delmarva's argument that PIC, the seller, had engaged in "unfair or deceptive trade practices" under the Maryland Consumer Protection Act, the court remitted Delmarva to the U.C.C. because "the Act was not designed to extend its protection to the commercial setting at bar." 943 F.Supp. 392, 407–08.

Examine the CREDITS AND PROCEDURES paragraph in PIC's form above. Do you think it contains an express warranty of fitness for breeding? In Delmarva's suit, the court held that an express warranty of fitness for breeding survived the seller's motion for summary judgment. Without implied warranties and consequential damages and limited to the credit procedure for a remedy, Delmarva's prospects were dimmed.

3. *What's Consequential?* An equipment lessee sued for breach of warranty. The lessor interposed the contract's exclusion of liability for "indirect or consequential damages." The court discussed what the exclusionary clause meant:

"Although the Michigan Supreme Court has on at least one occasion enforced a contract provision similar to paragraph 8, neither in Michigan nor elsewhere does the term 'consequential damages' have a clearly established meaning."

"In the absence of a settled rule, it is not surprising that the parties urge widely divergent construction of the term. Burroughs maintains that in this action 'direct' (and therefore recoverable) damages are measured by the difference between the value of the data-processing equipment had it been as warranted, and its value as actually delivered, and that all damages that followed the breach are consequential. ADP agrees that consequential damages follow or flow from a breach, but, relying on cases decided under the Uniform Commercial Code, suggests that only those post-breach damages whose valuation is somewhat speculative, such as lost profits, are properly called 'consequential.' * * *"

"The only firm starting point to be derived from the case law is that the commercial context in which a contract is made is of substantial importance in determining whether particular damages flowing from its breach are direct or consequential. It may also be said at the outset that no rule limits direct damages to the difference between the value of the equipment as warranted and its value as delivered."

"In Ruggles v. Buffalo Foundry, 27 F.2d 234 (6th Cir.1928) the Court explained the distinction between 'general' and 'special' damages while construing a clause that prohibited recovery of 'any special, indirect, or consequential damages * * *.' That Court appears to have equated consequential and special damages, an equation * * * to which this Court will adhere."

"The distinction between general and special damages is not that one is and the other is not the direct and proximate consequence of the breach complained of, but that general damages are such as naturally and ordinarily follow the breach, whereas special damages are those that ensue, not necessarily or ordinarily, but because of special circumstances."

"The Court's first task in the present case is thus to decide whether the damages claimed by ADP on the contract counts (in excess of the reliance damages) were, in an objective sense, foreseeable. The Court must then inquire, with regard to those damages found to be foreseeable, whether they are in that category because such damages ordinarily follow the breach of a contract such as the lease agreement entered into by ADP and Burroughs, or only because Burroughs had knowledge of special circumstances. Those damages in the latter class are not recoverable because of the consequential damages exclusion clause of the lease." Applied Data Processing, Inc. v. Burroughs Corp., 394 F.Supp. 504, 508–10 (D.Conn.1975).

If a buyer's "general" damages are value warranted less value delivered, § 2–714(2), would a court be wise to say that all other damages are consequential?

"In essence," observed another court interpreting a warranty exclusion, "consequential damages are economic losses, such as lost profits." Moreover while plaintiff's increased costs because of the breach are consequential damages, its pre-breach "reliance" expenditures are direct damages. Roneker v. Kenworth Truck Company, 977 F.Supp. 237, 240 (W.D.N.Y.1997).

Are the courts' distinctions sustainable?

4. *Personal Injury.* U.C.C. § 2–719(3): "Limitation of consequential damages for injury to the person in the case of consumer goods is prima facie unconscionable but limitation of damages where the loss is commercial is not."

The Products Liability Restatement's blackletter rule is similar: "Disclaimers and limitations of remedies by product sellers or other distributors, waivers by products purchasers, and other similar contractual exculpations, oral or written, do not bar or reduce otherwise valid product liability claims against sellers or other distributors for harm to persons."

"It is," the Restatement's Comment explains, "presumed that the [buyer] lacks sufficient information and bargaining power to execute a fair contractual limitation of rights to recover." Restatement of Torts: Products Liability § 18, and Comment a. (1998).

7. THE ECONOMIC LOSS RULE REVISITED: CONTRACTS BRANCH

Product failure does not enter a lawyer's office with the disappointed buyer wearing any substantive label; breach of warranty is but one possible label opened for a plaintiff's alternative pleading of substantive theories and remedies. A tort label, products liability, has several advantages: it avoids the waivers and exclusions examined in the prior Notes; it liberates the plaintiff from Hadley v. Baxendale's contemplation limit on special damages; and it unlocks the plaintiff's access to recovery for mental suffering and to possible punitive damages. Courts developed products liability duties, including strict product liability in tort, because tort doctrines protected buyers and their families from danger more satisfactorily than contract and warranty law. Along with the products-liability tort came the need to draw the line between products liability and contract-warranty doctrines. The *AM/PM* court's final paragraph reveals a court struggling to define the boundary between tort and warranty.

Courts developed two competing tests to define the border. First, a defendant has no tort-product liability duty when a defective product causes [a buyer-plaintiff] purely monetary harm. Seely v. White Motor Co., 63 Cal.2d 9, 45 Cal.Rptr. 17, 403 P.2d 145 (1965). Following what developed into the "economic loss rule," suppose a business owner buys a defective plant lamp for her reception area. If the lamp shorts, explodes, and burns her, she can recover for the personal injury under products liability. If the defective lamp starts a fire in her offices, she may recover for injury to "other property" under products liability. If the lamp simply self-destructs, that is economic loss and the economic loss rule limits the buyer to her contract action for breach of warranty. If her business's lighting fixtures self-destruct and the business is closed to replace them, she may recover her lost business and profits, an economic loss, only in warranty.

The second test was from Santor v. A and M Karagheusian, Inc. The New Jersey court said that the manufacturer's products liability or tort duty to a buyer to make a nondefective product includes a defective product that injures itself. An unreasonable risk of harm to the buyer's person or to her other property is not a prerequisite to her ability to sue the manufacturer for products liability. The distinction between the buyer's personal injury and injury to other property, on the one hand, and injury to the product itself and lost profits, on the other, is, the court maintained, an arbitrary one. A buyer may recover in products liability for all her damages proximately caused by the seller's breach of duty. Following the policy of loss spreading, a manufacturer can predict and insure against product failure, thus ameliorating the fear of unlimited liability. Santor v. A and M Karagheusian, Inc., 44 N.J. 52, 207 A.2d 305, 312–13 (1965).

The *Santor* test, always a minority, seems to have passed from the scene. The New Jersey court's last word is that "a tort cause of action for economic loss duplicating the one provided by the U.C.C. is superfluous and counterproductive." Alloway v. General Marine Industries, L.P., 149 N.J. 620, 641, 695 A.2d 264, 275 (1997).

The dominant *Seely* test, received a boost from the Supreme Court in 1986 in East River Steamship Corp. v. Transamerica Delaval. Ship charterers sued a turbine manufacturer-seller in admiralty. The charterers sued for tort after the contract statute of limitations had apparently run. The charterers' products-liability torts were strict liability and negligence in designing and manufacturing the turbines, one of which "had been installed backwards." The charterers sought to recover damages for the cost to repair the turbines and for their lost profit. East River Steamship Corp. v. Transamerica Delaval, Inc., 476 U.S. 858, 861 (1986).

The charterers' claims, the seller, Delaval, contended, "were not cognizable in tort." The Supreme Court agreed: We "hold that a manufacturer in a commercial relationship has no duty under either a negligence or strict products-liability theory to prevent a product from injuring itself."

"The distinction that the law has drawn between tort recovery for physical injuries and warranty recovery for economic loss is not arbitrary and does not rest on the 'luck' of one plaintiff in having an accident causing physical injury. The distinction rests, rather, on an understanding of the nature of the responsibility a manufacturer must undertake in distributing his products." Seely v. White Motor Co. When a product injures only itself the reasons for imposing a tort duty are weak and those for leaving the party to its contractual remedies are strong.

"The tort concern with safety is reduced when an injury is only to the product itself. When a person is injured, the 'cost of an injury and the loss of time or health may be an overwhelming misfortune,' and one the person is not prepared to meet. Escola v. Coca Cola Bottling Co. of Fresno, 24 Cal.2d 453, 462, 150 P.2d 436, 441 (1944) (concurring opinion). In contrast, when a product injures itself, the commercial user stands to lose the value of the product, risks the displeasure of its customers who find that the product does not meet their needs, or, as in this case, experiences increased costs in performing a service. Losses like these can be insured. [citations] Society need not presume that a customer needs special protection. The increased cost to the public that would result from holding a manufacturer liable in tort for injury to the product itself is not justified." Cf. United States v. Carroll Towing Co., 159 F.2d 169, 173 (C.A.2 1947).

"Damage to a product itself is most naturally understood as a warranty claim. Such damage means simply that the product has not met the customer's expectations. * * * The maintenance of product value and quality is precisely the purpose of express and implied warranties. See § 2–313 (express warranty), § 2–314 (implied warranty of merchantability), and § 2–315 (warranty of fitness for a particular purpose). Therefore, a claim of a nonworking product can be brought as a breach-of-warranty action. Or, if the customer prefers, it can reject the product or revoke its acceptance and sue for breach of contract. See U.C.C. §§ 2–601, 2–608, 2–612."

"Contract law, and the law of warranty in particular, is well suited to commercial controversies of the sort involved in this case because the parties may set the terms of their own agreements. The manufacturer can restrict its liability, within limits, by disclaiming warranties or limiting remedies. See U.C.C. §§ 2–316, 2–719. In exchange, the purchaser pays less for the product. Since a commercial situation generally does not involve large disparities in bargaining power, cf. Henningsen v. Bloomfield Motors, Inc., 32 N.J. 358, 161 A.2d 69 (1960), we see no reason to intrude into the parties' allocation of the risk."

"While giving recognition to the manufacturer's bargain, warranty law sufficiently protects the purchaser by allowing it to obtain the benefit of its bargain. The expectation damages available in warranty for purely economic loss give a plaintiff the full benefit of its bargain by compensating for forgone business opportunities. Recovery on a warranty theory would give the charterers their repair costs and lost profits, and would place them in the position they would have been in had the turbines functioned properly. In contrast, tort damages generally compensate the plaintiff for loss and return him to the position he occupied before the injury. [citations] Tort damages are analogous to reliance damages, which are awarded in contract when there is particular difficulty in measuring the expectation interest. [citation] See Hawkins v. McGee, 84 N.H. 114, 146 A. 641 (1929). Thus, both the nature of the injury and the resulting damages indicate it is more natural to think of injury to a product itself in terms of warranty."

"A warranty action also has a built-in limitation on liability, whereas a tort action could subject the manufacturer to damages of an indefinite amount. The limitation in a contract action comes from the agreement of the parties and the requirement that consequential damages, such as lost profits, be a foreseeable result of the breach. See Hadley v. Baxendale. In a warranty action where the loss is purely economic, the limitation derives from the requirements of foreseeability and of privity, which is still generally enforced for such claims in a commercial setting. See U.C.C. § 2–715.''

''In products-liability law, where there is a duty to the public generally, foreseeability is an inadequate brake. [citations] Permitting recovery for all foreseeable claims for purely economic loss could make a manufacturer liable for vast sums. It would be difficult for a manufacturer to take into account the expectations of persons downstream who may encounter its product. In this case, for example, if the charterers—already one step removed from the transaction—were permitted to recover their economic losses, then the companies that subchartered the ships might claim their economic losses from the delays, and the charterers' customers also might claim their economic losses, and so on. 'The law does not spread its protection so far.' Robins Dry Dock & Repair Co. v. Flint, 275 U.S. 303, 309 (1927).''

Even if the statute of limitations had not run on the charterers' warranty claim, there were formidable barriers to their success in warranty. Some charterers had settled and ''could not have asserted the warranty claims.'' Also the parties' agreements said ''the charterers took the ships 'as is' after inspection.''

The economic loss rule received another boost when the American Law Institute adopted it in the Products Liability Restatement. Restatement of Torts: Products Liability § 21 (1998).

A Wisconsin decision illustrates the ''elusive'' ''other property'' exception to the economic loss rule. A seller's ''milk replacer'' fed to buyer's calves damaged the animals, some of which died. The majority held that the Wisconsin version of the economic loss rule barred the buyer's products-liability torts against the seller and manufacturer. Because the buyer was disappointed with the seller's contractual performance, the ''other property'' exception to the economic loss rule was not implicated. ''Like the ever-expanding, all-consuming alien life form portrayed in the 1958 B-movie classic *The Blob,* the economic loss doctrine seems to be a swelling globule on the legal landscape of this state.'' observed Justice Abrahamson dissenting. Grams v. Milk Products, Inc., 283 Wis.2d 511, 699 N.W.2d 167, 180 (2005).

The economic loss rule has another life in pure tort which is treated above. p. 539.

Fraud–Misrepresentation, Economic Loss, and Warranty. A disappointed buyer may characterize the seller's broken promise as either a misrepresentation or a breach of warranty. The buyer's misrepresentation tort is more desirable than breach of warranty because, for, in addition to avoiding disclaimers and exclusions, a successful misrepresentation plaintiff may recover broader special damages and, like Dr. Gore, is eligible for punitive damages. p. 133. Earlier, the requirement that a buyer prove the seller's conscious intent to deceive to establish a misrepresentation kept the theories apart; but recently courts have qualified the intent prerequisite and expanded both seller's duty to disclose and the tort of negligent misrepresentation. Misrepresentation is often difficult to distinguish from a breach of contract, particularly at the pleading and pre-trial stages.

The first question is whether the seller's conduct equals misrepresentation. The Delaware federal judge responded to Delmarva's arguments that PIC had committed a misrepresentation by concluding that "the instant case does not present circumstances in which the law creates an extra-contractual tort duty to exercise due care to avoid negligence or to exercise reasonable care in making representations." "There is simply no evidence of misrepresentations made by PIC for a fraudulent purpose or of an extra-contractual duty to disclose which was breached." 943 F.Supp. 392, 406–07.

Courts have related fraud-misrepresentation to the economic loss rule. As a court usually articulates it, the economic loss rule does not bar a buyer's intentional tort. A seller's breach of warranty is a broken promise. Perhaps the seller knew the promise to the buyer was incorrect. Or perhaps the seller had a fiduciary duty to furnish the buyer only accurate information. Perhaps instead of knowing that his promise to buyer was false, the seller was negligent and should have known that it was incorrect.

If a seller intentionally lies to the buyer, the tricked buyer may sue the seller for fraud in the inducement claiming to be free from the economic loss rule. For example, the Florida Supreme Court held that the economic loss rule does not bar a plaintiff-buyer's fraudulent-inducement tort. The tort standard is based on the seller's untrue representation. This tort is not derived from the parties' contract; instead the plaintiff proves it through facts, the defendant's acts of fraud, which occurred prior to the contract; these facts differ from the facts of the seller's breach of contract. The seller's mistruths leading the plaintiff to agree to a contract are unrelated to the events which constitute the seller's breach of contract. HTP, Ltd. v. Lineas Aereas Costarricenses, 685 So.2d 1238 (Fla.1996). Future Tech International, Inc. v. Tae Il Media, Ltd., 944 F.Supp. 1538, 1568 (S.D.Fla.1996). See also, Kaloti Enterprises v. Kellog Sales Co., 283 Wis.2d 555, 699 N.W.2d 205, 219–20 (2005).

Liberated from the economic loss rule by the seller's misrepresentation, the deceived buyer may recover the punitive damages that are barred in breach of contract. Robinson Helicopter Co., Inc. v. Dana Corp., 34 Cal.4th 979, 991, 22 Cal.Rptr.3d 352, 102 P.3d 268 (2004) ($6 million punitive damages).

In a further refinement of the Florida economic loss rule, an aircraft owner sued the company that had earlier serviced the plane for the owner's seller. The servicing company, Florida's supreme court held, could not take advantage of the products liability branch of the economic loss rule. The court's explanation cleared up some confusion about the breadth of the economic loss rule. The economic loss rule governs in products liability and related areas where a contractual relationship exists. It does not hold sway in fraudulent inducement, negligent misrepresentation, professional malpractice, negligent performance of services, or intentional torts. Indemnity Insurance Company of North America v. American Aviation, Inc., 891 S.2d 532 (Fla. 2004), implemented by, 399 F.3d 1275 (11th Cir.2005).

On the other hand, in the absence of definitive state precedent, the federal Third Circuit Court of Appeals predicted that a Pennsylvania state court would wield the economic loss rule to cut off a buyer's negligent misrepresentation claim. Several factors led the federal court to confine the buyer's recovery for seller's negligent misrepresentation to contract: litigants who were business entities, a commercial contract, economic loss to the product or lost profit, a bargained contract which dealt with the issue, and the negligence which consisted of a misrepresentation. Duquesne Light Co. v. Westinghouse Electric Corp., 66 F.3d 604, 618–20 (3d Cir.1995).

Still lacking binding guidance from the Pennsylvania courts seven years later, the same federal court held that an automobile buyer-individual consumer's claim for fraudulent concealment was barred by the economic loss rule. Werwinski v. Ford Motor co., 286 F.3d 661, 676 (3d Cir.2002).

When a seller allegedly misrepresented the quality of goods it sold to a buyer, another federal court held that the economic loss rule barred the buyer's tort of innocent misrepresentation and confined the buyer to recovering from the seller for breach of contract. Lake & Piepkow Farms v. Purina Mills, Inc., 955 F.Supp. 791, 795 (W.D.Mich.1997).

Related economic-loss-rule refinements involving a defendant with a fiduciary duty, for example a lawyer, a consumer suing a merchant under an unfair-trade practices or consumer-protection statute, or the sale of a personal residence have also generated parallel lines of conflicting authority and confusion. See, rejecting the economic loss rule in a fiduciary relationship, Ploog v. HomeSide Lending, 209 F.Supp.2d 863, 875 (N.D.Ill. 2002).

Harmony or Disarray? Judge Posner emphasized the "desirability—perhaps urgency—of harmonizing the entire complex and confusing pattern of liability and nonliability for tortious conduct in contractual settings." Rardin v. T & D Machine Handling, Inc., p. ___. Is this task simply hopeless?

Look Ma, No Profits. Contract law makes it difficult for a plaintiff to recover its lost profits; the economic loss rule may bar its recovery of lost profit altogether.

Let's turn to a plaintiff who cannot recover lost profits because there are none or because they are speculative. This plaintiff may fall back on "reliance" recovery as a surrogate or a substitute.

8. RELIANCE RECOVERY

WARTZMAN v. HIGHTOWER PRODUCTIONS, LTD.

Court of Special Appeals of Maryland, 1983.
53 Md.App. 656, 456 A.2d 82.

JAMES S. GETTY, JUDGE. (Specially Assigned). Woody Hightower did not succeed in breaking the Guinness World Record for flagpole sitting; his failure to accomplish this seemingly nebulous feat, however, did generate protracted litigation. We are concerned here with whether Judge Robert L. Karwacki, presiding in the Superior Court of Baltimore City, correctly permitted a jury to consider the issue of "reliance damages" sustained by the appellees. * * *

Hightower Productions, Ltd. came into being in 1974 as a promotional venture conceived by Ira Adler, Frank Billitz and J. Daniel Quinn. The principals intended to employ a singer-entertainer who would live in a specially constructed mobile flagpole perch from April 1, 1975, until New Year's Eve at which time he would descend in Times Square in New York before a nationwide television audience, having established a new world record for flagpole sitting.

The young man selected to perform this feat was to be known as "Woody Hightower." The venture was to be publicized by radio and television exposure, by adopting a theme song and by having the uncrowned champion make appearances from his perch throughout the country at concerts, state fairs and shopping centers.

In November, 1974, the three principals approached Michael Kaminkow of the law firm of Wartzman, Rombro, Rudd and Omansky, P.A., for the specific purpose of incorporating their venture. Mr. Kaminkow, a trial attorney, referred them to his partner, Paul Wartzman.

The three principals met with Mr. Wartzman at his home and reviewed the promotional scheme with him. They indicated that they needed to sell stock to the public in order to raise the $250,000 necessary to finance the project. Shortly thereafter, the law firm prepared and filed the articles of incorporation and Hightower Productions, Ltd. came into existence on November 6, 1974. The Articles of Incorporation authorized the issuance of one million shares of stock of the par value of $10 per share, or a total of $100,000.00.

Following incorporation, the three principals began developing the project. With an initial investment of $20,000, they opened a corporate account at Maryland National Bank and an office in the Pikesville Plaza Building. Then began the search for "Woody Hightower." After numerous interviews, twenty-three year old John Jordan emerged as "Woody Hightower."

After selecting the flagpole tenant, the corporation then sought and obtained a company to construct the premises to house him. This consisted of a seven foot wide perch that was to include a bed, toilet, water, refrigerator and heat. The accommodations were atop an hydraulic lift system mounted upon a flat bed tractor trailer.

Hightower employed two public relations specialists to coordinate press and public relations efforts and to obtain major corporate backers. "Woody" received a proclamation from the Mayor and City Council of Baltimore and after a press breakfast at the Hilton Hotel on "All Fools Day" ascended to his home in the sky.

Within ten days, Hightower obtained a live appearance for "Woody" on the Mike Douglas Show, and a commitment for an appearance on the Wonderama television program. The principals anticipated a "snow-balling" effect from commercial enterprises as the project progressed with no substantial monetary commitments for approximately six months.

Hightower raised $43,000.00 by selling stock in the corporation. Within two weeks of "Woody's" ascension, another stockholders' meeting was scheduled, because the corporation was low on funds. At that time, Mr. Wartzman informed the principals that no further stock could be sold, because the corporation was "structured wrong," and it would be necessary to obtain the services of a securities attorney to correct the problem. Mr. Wartzman had acquired this information in a casual conversation with a friend who recommended that the corporation should consult with a securities specialist.

The problem was that the law firm had failed to prepare an offering memorandum and failed to assure that the corporation had made the required disclosures to prospective investors in accordance with the provisions of the Maryland Securities Act. Mr. Wartzman advised Hightower that the cost of the specialist would be between $10,000.00 and $15,000.00. Hightower asked the firm to pay for the required services and the request was rejected.

Hightower then employed substitute counsel and scheduled a shareholders' meeting on April 28, 1975. At that meeting, the stockholders were advised that

Hightower was not in compliance with the securities laws; that $43,000.00, the amount investors had paid for issued stock, had to be covered by the promoters and placed in escrow; that the fee of a securities specialist would be $10,000.00 to $15,000.00 and that the additional work would require between six and eight weeks. In the interim, additional stock could not be sold, nor could "Woody" be exhibited across state lines. Faced with these problems, the shareholders decided to discontinue the entire project.

On October 8, 1975, Hightower filed suit alleging breach of contract and negligence for the law firm's failure to have created a corporation authorized to raise the capital necessary to fund the venture. At the trial, Hightower introduced into evidence its obligations and expenditures incurred in reliance on the defendant law firm's creation of a corporation authorized to raise the $250,000.00 necessary to fund the project. The development costs incurred included corporate obligations amounting to $155,339 including: initial investments by Adler and Billitz, $20,000; shareholders, excluding the three promoters, $43,010; outstanding liabilities exclusive of salaries, $58,929; liability to talent consultants, $25,000; and accrued salaries to employees, $8,400.

* * * The only claim submitted for the jury's consideration was the claim of the corporation, Hightower, against the defendant law firm.

The jury returned a verdict in favor of Hightower in the amount of $170,508.43. Wartzman, Rombro, Rudd, and Omansky, P.A., appealed to this Court. * * *

The appellants raise [these] issues for our consideration:

1. The trial court erred in permitting Hightower to recover "reliance damages" or "development costs."

2. If "reliance damages" were recoverable, the trial court failed to properly instruct the jury on the law concerning their recovery.

3. The trial court erred in refusing to instruct the jury on the duty to mitigate damages. * * *

The appellants first contend that the jury verdict included all of Hightower's expenditures and obligations incurred during its existence resulting in the law firm being absolute surety for all costs incurred in a highly speculative venture. While they do not suggest the analogy, the appellants would no doubt equate the verdict as tantamount to holding the blacksmith liable for the value of the kingdom where the smith left out a nail in shoeing the king's horse, because of which the shoe was lost, the horse was lost, the king was lost and the kingdom was lost. Appellants contend that there is a lack of nexus or causation between the alleged failure of Mr. Wartzman to discharge his duties as an attorney and the loss claimed by Hightower. Stated differently, an unjust result will obtain where a person performing a collateral service for a new venture will, upon failure to fully perform the service, be liable as full guarantor for all costs incurred by the enterprise.

Ordinarily, profits lost due to a breach of contract are recoverable. Where anticipated profits are too speculative to be determined, monies spent in part performance, in preparation for or in reliance on the contract are recoverable. Dialist Co. v. Pulford, 42 Md.App. 173, 399 A.2d 1374 (1979).

In *Dialist,* a distributor, Pulford, brought suit for breach of an exclusive contract that he had with Dialist. Pulford paid $2500.00 for the distributorship, terminated his employment with another company and expended funds in order to begin developing the area where the product was to be sold. When Pulford learned that another distributor was also given part of his territory he terminated his services.

This Court upheld the award of development costs to Pulford which included out of pocket expenses, telephone installation, office furniture, two months of forfeited salary and the value of medical insurance lost. The Court determined that the expenditures were not in preparation for or part performance of a contract, but in reliance upon it. "Such expenditures are not brought about by reason of the breach. They are induced by reliance on the contract itself and rendered worthless by its breach."

Recovery based upon reliance interest is not without limitation. If it can be shown that full performance would have resulted in a net loss, the plaintiff cannot escape the consequences of a bad bargain by falling back on his reliance interest. Where the breach has prevented an anticipated gain and made proof of loss difficult to ascertain, the injured party has a right to damages based upon his reliance interest, including expenditures made in preparation for performance, or in performance, less any loss that the party in breach can prove with reasonable certainty the injured party would have suffered had the contract been performed. Restatement, Second, Contracts, Sec. 349.

The appellants' contention that permitting the jury to consider reliance damages in this case rendered the appellants insurers of the venture is without merit. Section 349 of the Restatement, cited above, expressly authorizes the breaching party to prove any loss that the injured party would have suffered had the contract been performed. Such proof would avoid making the breaching party a guarantor of the success of the venture. * * *

In the present case the appellants knew, or should have known, that the success of the venture rested upon the ability of Hightower to sell stock and secure advertising as public interest in the adventure accelerated. Appellant's contention that their failure to properly incorporate Hightower was collateral and lacked the necessary nexus to permit consideration of reliance damages is not persuasive. The very life blood of the project depended on the corporation's ability to sell stock to fund the promotion. This is the reason for the employment of the appellants. In reliance thereon, Hightower sold stock and incurred substantial obligations. When it could no longer sell its stock, the entire project failed. No greater nexus need be established. Aside from questioning the expertise of the promoters based upon their previous employment, the appellants were unable to establish that the stunt was doomed to fail. The inability to establish that financial chaos was inevitable does not make the appellants insurers and does not preclude Hightower from recovering reliance damages. The issue was properly submitted to the jury.

Appellants contend that the appellees should be limited to the recovery of damages under traditional contract and negligence concepts * * * that a contracting party is expected to take account of only those risks that are foreseeable at the time he makes the contract and is not liable in the event of breach for loss that he did not at the time of contracting have reason to foresee as a probable result of such a breach. This limitation is set forth in Restatement, Contracts, (2d), Sec. 351.

Exceptional perception is not relevant to the test of foreseeability when applied to an attorney who is relied upon by a layman to protect his investment from pitfalls which are not readily apparent to those in foreign fields of endeavor. * * *

The appellants are aggrieved by the amount of the verdict which they consider to be excessive. According to the docket entries, the appellants did not seek any modification of the verdict. * * * We note that in answer to interrogatories filed in October, 1981, corporate damages were stated to be $155,339.00. This figure included shareholders' investments and accrued salaries amounting to $51,410. The court's instructions precluded inclusion of these items as recoverable damages. It would appear, therefore, that the verdict may well have exceeded the guidelines set forth by the trial court. That issue is not before us, however. * * *

The Court instructed the jury that in order to find liability that the plaintiff must prove three things:

"First, the employment of the defendants in behalf of the Plaintiff and the extent of the duties for which the Defendants were employed; secondly, that the Defendants neglected the duties undertaken in the employment and, thirdly, that such negligence resulted in and was the proximate cause of loss by the Plaintiff, that is that the Plaintiff was deprived of any right or parted with anything of value in reliance upon the negligence of the defendants."

The instruction given fairly apprised the jury of the Plaintiffs' burden and adequately covered the reliance damage concept. Additionally, the court instructed the jury that they could not consider unpaid salaries due its officers or employees or amounts invested by stockholders as recoverable damages. * * *

We find no error in the instructions.

Appellants further except to the trial court's refusal to grant any instruction on the issue of Hightower's obligation to mitigate its damages. The instruction offered by appellants is a correct statement of the law. Correctness alone, however, is insufficient to require the court to grant the prayer; there must be evidence to support the proposition to which it relates.

The evidence in this case establishes that Hightower did not have the $43,000.00 to place in escrow covering stock sold, did not have the $10,000.00 or $15,000.00 to employ a securities specialist and could not continue stock sales or exhibitions to obtain the necessary funds. Mr. Wartzman's offer to set up an appointment for Hightower with an expert in security transactions at Hightower's expense can hardly be construed as a mitigating device that Hightower was obligated to accept. The party who is in default may not mitigate his damages by showing that the other party could have reduced those damages by expending large amounts of money or incurring substantial obligations. Since such risks arose because of the breach, they are to be borne by the defaulting party.

The doctrine of avoidable consequences, moreover, does not apply where both parties have an equal opportunity to mitigate damages. Appellants had the same opportunity to employ and pay a securities specialist as they contend Hightower should have done. They refused. Having rejected Hightower's request to assume the costs of an additional attorney, they are estopped from asserting a failure by Hightower to reduce its loss.

There is no evidence in this case that the additional funds necessary to continue the operation pending a restructuring of the corporation were within the financial capabilities of Hightower. The Court properly declined to instruct the jury on the issue of mitigation. * * *

Judgment Affirmed.

Notes

1. *Specific Performance?* The Hightower group had a new law firm in April, 1975. Why didn't they sue the defendants for specific performance right away?

2. *Negligence.* Almost all legal malpractice lawsuits stem from a contract between the lawyer and the client which has gone awry. But a former client suing her lawyer for malpractice usually alleges the tort of negligence because her tort damages will be larger and because the lawyer-defendant's insurance coverage against negligence facilitates payment of any settlement or judgment.

The principal opinion analyzes "reliance" damages for breach of contract; but the court-approved jury instruction mentions only the negligence tort. Are plaintiff's contract "reliance" damages the same as those proximately caused by defendants' negligence? Do we ever rely upon someone else's negligence to our injury?

3. *Reliance Recovery.* The plaintiff's judgment is larger than the reliance damages it claimed. Moreover the court approved instructions to the jury to exclude from damages the amounts the shareholders invested and the unpaid salaries due the officers and employees. Why aren't these items reliance damages?

4. *Under the Winstar, Reliance Includes Special Damages.* Under contracts with a government agency, banks took over failed thrift institutions; but, because of later legislation, the banks were unable to continue the relaxed-reserve requirements that the agency promised to them. The federal government was found liable to the banks. United States v. Winstar Corp., 518 U.S. 839 (1996). The issues of the banks' recovery from the government on *Winstar* claims are vexatious because of the high stakes from the large losses in over a hundred similar claims.

The bank in the lead damages litigation, The Glendale Federal Bank, based its recovery on the Fuller–Perdue trinity: expectation, restitution, and reliance. The bank could not, the Federal Circuit Court of Appeals said, recover its "expectation," in the form of its lost business profits because they were "too speculative." There could be no restitution: the court declined to grant the bank "restitution based on an assumption that the [bank] is entitled to the supposed gains received by the [government], when those gains are both speculative and indeterminate." Glendale Federal Bank v. United States, 239 F.3d 1374, 1382 (Fed.Cir.2001).

The court approved Glendale Federal's $381 million post-breach "reliance" damages. This recovery was comprised of extra interest and other expenses the bank had to pay after it lost the promised relaxed reserve. Glendale Federal Bank v. United States, 378 F.3d 1308, 1310 (Fed.Cir. 2004).

This recovery, as described by the court, is difficult to fit into definitions of reliance; it is neither the plaintiff's out-of-pocket expenses to prepare for the defendant's promised performance nor the plaintiff's lost opportunities because of the defendant's breach. The bank's "reliance" recovery seems to be ordinary special damages, the plaintiff's extra expenses incurred because of the defendant's breach. Indeed, in the earlier appeal, the court had defined reliance damages as "damages for any loss [the plaintiff] actually sustained as a result of the [defendant's] breach." Glendale Federal Bank v. United States, 239 F.3d 1374, 1382 (Fed.Cir. 2001). It would probably be a lot wiser and far less confusing to call the *Winstar* plaintiffs' "reliance" recovery either special damages or the more specific and accurate name the court uses—"wounded-bank damages."

II. SELLER'S REMEDIES

If the buyer breaches, the seller will consider three basic remedies: specific performance, keeping the buyer's earnest money as liquidated damages, and money recovery which can include expectancy damages, special damages, and restitution.

A. SPECIFIC PERFORMANCE

CENTEX HOMES CORP. v. BOAG

Superior Court of New Jersey, Chancery Division, 1974.
128 N.J.Super. 385, 320 A.2d 194.

GELMAN, J.S.C., Temporarily Assigned. Plaintiff Centex Homes Corporation (Centex) is engaged in the development and construction of a luxury high-rise condominium project in the Boroughs of Cliffside Park and Fort Lee. The project when completed will consist of six 31–story buildings containing in excess of 3600 condominium apartment units, together with recreational buildings and facilities, parking garages and other common elements associated with this form of residential development. As sponsor of the project Centex offers the condominium apartment units for sale to the public. * * *

On September 13, 1972 defendants Mr. & Mrs. Eugene Boag executed a contract for the purchase of apartment unit No. 2019 in the building under construction and known as "Winston Towers 200." The contract purchase price was $73,700, and prior to signing the contract defendants had given Centex a deposit in the amount of $525. At or shortly after signing the contract defendants delivered to Centex a check in the amount of $6,870 which, together with the deposit, represented approximately 10% of the total purchase of the apartment unit. Shortly thereafter Boag was notified by his employer that he was to be transferred to the Chicago, Illinois, area. Under date of September 27, 1972 he advised Centex that he "would be unable to complete the purchase" agreement and stopped payment on the $6,870, check. * * * On August 8, 1973 Centex instituted this action in Chancery Division for specific performance of the purchase agreement or, in the alternative, for liquidated damages in the amount of $6,870. The matter is presently before this court on the motion of Centex for summary judgment.

Both parties acknowledge, and our research has confirmed, that no court in this State or in the United States has determined in any reported decision whether the equitable remedy of specific performance will lie for the enforcement of a contract for the sale of a condominium apartment. The closest decision on point is Silverman v. Alcoa Plaza Associates, 37 A.D.2d 166, 323 N.Y.S.2d 39 (App.Div.1971), which involved a default by a contract-purchaser of shares of stock and a proprietary lease in a cooperative apartment building. The seller, who was also the sponsor of the project, retained the deposit and sold the stock and the lease to a third party for the same purchase price. The original purchaser thereafter brought suit to recover his deposit, and on appeal the court held that the sale of shares of stock in a cooperative apartment building, even though associated with a proprietary lease, was a sale of personalty and not of an interest in real estate. Hence, the seller was not entitled to retain the contract deposit as liquidated damages. Under New York law, if the contract was deemed to be for the sale of realty, the seller could retain the deposit in lieu of damages.

As distinguished from a cooperative plan of ownership such as involved in *Silverman*, under a condominium housing scheme each condominium apartment unit constitutes a separate parcel of real property which may be dealt with in the same manner as any real estate. Upon closing of title the apartment unit owner receives a recordable deed which confers upon him the same rights and subjects him to the same obligations as in the case of traditional forms of real estate ownership, the only difference being that the condominium owner receives in addition an undivided interest in the common elements associated with the building and assigned to each unit. [citations]

Centex urges that since the subject matter of the contract is the transfer of a fee interest in real estate, the remedy of specific performance is available to enforce the agreement under principles of equity which are well-settled in this state. [citations]

The principle underlying the specific performance remedy is equity's jurisdiction to grant relief where the damage remedy at law is inadequate. The text writers generally agree that at the time this branch of equity jurisdiction was evolving in England, the presumed uniqueness of land as well as its importance to the social order of that era led to the conclusion that damages at law could never be adequate to compensate for the breach of a contract to transfer an interest in land. Hence specific performance became a fixed remedy in this class of transactions. * * *

While the inadequacy of the damage remedy suffices to explain the origin of the vendee's right to obtain specific performance in equity, it does not provide a rationale for the availability of the remedy at the instance of the vendor of real estate. Except upon a showing of unusual circumstances or a change in the vendor's position, such as where the vendee has entered into possession, the vendor's damages are usually measurable, his remedy at law is adequate and there is no jurisdictional basis for equitable relief.

But see Restatement, Contracts § 360, comment c. The Restatement's reasoning amounts to the inconsistent propositions that (1) because the vendor may not have sustained any damage which is actionable at law, specific performance should be granted, and (2) he would otherwise sustain damage equal to the loss of interest on the proceeds of the sale. Yet loss of interest is readily measurable and can be recovered in an action at law, and to the extent that the vendor has sustained no economic injury, there is no compelling reason for equity to grant to him the otherwise extraordinary remedy of specific performance. At the end of the comment, the author suggests that the vendor is entitled to specific performance because that remedy should be mutual, a concept which is substantially rejected as a decisional basis in §§ 372 and 373 of the Restatement.

The early English precedents suggest that the availability of the remedy in a suit by a vendor was an outgrowth of the equitable concept of mutuality, I.e., that equity would not specifically enforce an agreement unless the remedy was available to both parties. [citations]

So far as can be determined from our decisional law, the mutuality of remedy concept has been the prop which has supported equitable jurisdiction to grant specific performance in actions by vendors of real estate. Another theory has been suggested as a basis for equity's jurisdiction to grant specific performance to a vendor: the vendee's breach constitutes an "equitable conversion" of the purchase price of which the vendee is deemed to be a trustee. [citations] This view has never been suggested in any reported decision in New Jersey, although it has been alluded to in another context. [citation] * * *

The first reported discussion of the question occurs in Hopper v. Hopper, 16 N.J.Eq. 147 (Ch.1863), which was an action by a vendor to compel specific performance of a contract for the sale of land. In answer to the contention that equity lacked jurisdiction because the vendor had an adequate legal remedy, Chancellor Green said:

"It constitutes no objection to the relief prayed for, that the application is made by the vendor to enforce the payment of the purchase money, and not by the vendee to compel a delivery of the title. The vendor has not a complete remedy at law. Pecuniary damages for the breach of the contract is not what the complainant asks, or is entitled to receive at the hands of a court of equity. He asks to receive the price stipulated to be paid in lieu of the land. The doctrine is well established that the remedy is mutual, and that the vendor may maintain his bill in all cases where the purchaser could sue for a specific performance of the agreement."

No other rationale has been offered by our decisions subsequent to *Hopper*, and specific performance has been routinely granted to vendors without further discussion of the underlying jurisdictional issue. [citations]

Our present Supreme Court has squarely held, however, that mutuality of remedy is not an appropriate basis for granting or denying specific performance. Fleischer v. James Drug Stores, 1 N.J. 138, 62 A.2d 383 (1948). The test is whether the obligations of the contract are mutual and not whether each is entitled to precisely the same remedy in the event of a breach. In *Fleischer* plaintiff sought specific performance against a cooperative buying and selling association although his membership contract was terminable by him on 60 days' notice. Justice Heher said:

And the requisite mutuality is not wanting. The contention contra rests upon the premise that, although the corporation 'an terminate the contract only in certain restricted and unusual circumstances, any "member" may withdraw at any time by merely giving notice.'

Clearly, there is mutuality of obligation, for until his withdrawal complainant is under a continuing obligation of performance in the event of performance by the corporation. It is not essential that the remedy of specific performance be mutual. * * * The modern view is that the rule of mutuality of remedy is satisfied if the decree of specific performance operates effectively against both parties and gives to each the benefit of a mutual obligation. * * *

The fact that the remedy of specific enforcement is available to one party to a contract is not in itself a sufficient reason for making the remedy available to the other; but it may be decisive when the adequacy of damages is difficult to determine and there is no other reason for refusing specific enforcement. It is not necessary, to serve the ends of equal justice, that the parties shall have identical remedies in case of breach.

The disappearance of the mutuality of remedy doctrine from our law dictates the conclusion that specific performance relief should no longer be automatically available to a vendor of real estate, but should be confined to those special instances where a vendor will otherwise suffer an economic injury for which his damage remedy at law will not be adequate, or where other equitable considerations require that the relief be granted. * * *

Here the subject matter of the real estate transaction—a condominium apartment unit—has no unique quality but is one of hundreds of virtually identical units being offered by a developer for sale to the public. The units are sold by means of sample, in this case model apartments, in much the same manner as items of personal property are sold in the market place. The sales prices for the units are fixed in accordance with schedule filed by Centex as part of its offering plan, and the only variance as between apartments having the same floor plan (of which six plans are available) is the floor level or the building location within the project. In actuality, the condominium apartment units, regardless of their realty label, share the same characteristics as personal property.

From the foregoing one must conclude that the damages sustained by a condominium sponsor resulting from the breach of the sales agreement are readily measurable and the damage remedy at law is wholly adequate. No compelling reasons have been shown by Centex for the granting of specific performance relief and its complaint is therefore dismissed as to the first count.

Centex also seeks money damages pursuant to a liquidated damage clause in its contract with the defendants. It is sufficient to note only that under the language of that clause (which was authored by Centex) liquidated damages are limited to such moneys as were paid by defendant at the time the default occurred. Since the default here consisted of the defendant's stopping payment of his check for the balance of the down-payment, Centex's liquidated damages are limited to the retention of the "moneys paid" prior to that date, or the initial $525 deposit. Accordingly, the second court of the complaint for damage relief will also be dismissed.

Notes

1. *Riding Down Condo Canyon.* Does the "uniqueness" test falter when the buyer and seller contract for a condominium unit? Condo buyers suing sellers for specific performance have successfully resisted sellers' arguments that condominium units cannot be "unique." Courts have specifically enforced buyers' contracts, although it is helpful if the buyer can show some particular quality of uniqueness. For example, after the contract, the unit's price "rapidly escalated" in Kalinowski v. Yeh, 9 Haw.App. 473, 847 P.2d 673, 678 (1993). Also, the buyers occupied and improved the unit in Schwinder v. Austin Bank of Chicago, 348 Ill.App.3d 461, 809 N.E.2d 180, 196–97 (2004). See Giannini v. First National Bank, 136 Ill.App.3d 971, 483 N.E.2d 924 (1985); Pruitt v. Graziano, 215 N.J.Super. 330, 521 A.2d 1313 (1987).

2. *Specific Performance for the Seller.* Should the result differ where the seller sues the buyer for specific performance? An Illinois court declined a seller's request for specific performance on the ground that expectation damages were an adequate remedy. Lakshman v. Vecchione, 102 Ill.App.3d 629, 430 N.E.2d 199 (1981).

Is a seller's specific performance suit against the buyer really one for money, usually the purchase price? If the seller sued the buyer explicitly for money damages, the buyer could demand a jury trial. Does the *Centex* court allow a future condo buyer to summon a jury to pass community judgment on the dispute?

If the court had granted Centex specific performance, do you think the Boags would have paid Centex the price and taken title? Would Centex probably have been willing to settle a specific performance decree in return for the Boags' paying it a sum of money? Which is better situated to sell the condo to another buyer, Centex or the Boags?

Professor Edward Yorio said that,"the existing rules governing specific performance are more efficient on balance than a regime in which specific performance became the routine remedy for breach of contract. * * * [T]he case for giving the seller an automatic right to specific performance is weak. Since the seller has decided to part with the property in dispute, personal or subjective motives do not complicate the measurement of damages. Assuming that the property can be resold at the market price, an award of damages measured by the difference between the contract and market price fully compensates the seller for the loss caused by the breach. Specific performance may be proper in certain circumstances, such as when valuing or reselling the property in dispute is difficult or when the seller has an immediate need for liquidity, but none of these factors supports a universal rule entitling the seller to specific relief." Edward Yorio, Contract Enforcement: Specific Performance and Injunctions §§ 1.4.4, 10.3.1 (1989) (citations omitted).

3. *Goods.* The caption to Revised U.C.C.'s § 2–716 reads "Specific Performance; Buyer's Right of Replevin." Preliminary Official Comment 1: "The caption has been amended to make it clear that either party may be entitled to specific performance."

Should a seller of goods be entitled to specific performance on the same terms as a buyer? Is a seller's action to recover money damages measured by "the price," U.C.C. § 2–709, the seller's equivalent to the buyer's specific performance? Would giving the seller an equitable action for specific performance in addition to its action for the price frustrate the buyer's right to jury trial in the seller's action for money damages?

Should the U.C.C. forbid a merchant seller from suing a consumer buyer for specific performance? Indeed many retail sellers let a consumer buyer return unwanted goods for a full refund for as long as a year. Of course the consumer buyer pays part of the price for her unilateral option to rescind. Robert E. Scott & George Triantis, Embedded Options and the Case Against Compensation in Contract Law, 104 Colum. L.Rev. 1428, 1488 (2004).

4. *Justification?* A court will usually approve a seller's request for specific performance; but, as the *Centex* decision shows, the court's justification is not entirely persuasive. A court may maintain that the seller's legal remedy of damages is inadequate because "any award of money damages would be speculative at best and, in all probability, would not provide adequate compensation." Derwell Co. v. Apic, Inc., 278 A.2d 338, 343 (Del.Ch.1971). Another court granted specific performance to a seller who planned to use the cash realized from the sale of a residence to further his business interests. Shuptrine v. Quinn, 597 S.W.2d 728 (Tenn.1979). And the Restatement (Second) of Contracts § 360 comment e (1981), retains the rule allowing specific performance to the seller.

B. SELLER'S DAMAGES

1. Seller's Expectancy (and Other) Damages

When the buyer breaches a contract, the seller's basic expectancy damages measure is: contract price less market price.

For a land contract, the court will determine the market price at the date set for conveyance; for "goods," under the U.C.C., the "market price at the time and place for tender" governs. U.C.C. § 2–708(1).

Other damages measures for a land seller are (a) to recover the price, which, as discussed above, resembles specific performance, and (b) to forfeit as liquidated damages the buyer's earnest money.

Other Commercial Code goods seller's damages measures are: (a) the contract price less the seller's resale price, § 2–706; (b) the price, § 2–709; and (c) the seller's "lost profit," § 2–708(2).

A land seller may recover proved special damages subject to *Hadley*'s contemplation test. Examples include carrying charges like interest and reselling expenses.

The Original U.C.C. limits the seller's special damages to "incidental" damages, the expense of dealing with the goods after the buyer breaches. The seller may not recover "consequential" damages, that is garden-variety special damages. U.C.C. § 2–710.

The Revised U.C.C. adds "incidental or consequential damages" to the seller's expectancy damages sections and defines consequential damages to "include any loss resulting from general or particular requirements and needs of which the buyer at the time of contracting had reason to know and which could not reasonably be prevented by resale or otherwise." Revised U.C.C. § 2–710(2). However, a breaching consumer buyer does not have to pay the seller's consequential damages. Revised U.C.C. § 2–710(3).

A goods seller may also recover liquidated damages from the breaching buyer. U.C.C § 2–718.

JAGGER BROTHERS v. TECHNICAL TEXTILE CO.

Superior Court of Pennsylvania, 1964.
202 Pa.Super. 639, 198 A.2d 888.

MONTGOMERY, JUDGE. This appeal concerns the measure of damages in an action of assumpsit based on a written contract under which appellant agreed to purchase, at $2.15 per pound, 20,000 pounds of yarn to be manufactured by appellee. Appellee manufactured 3,723 pounds of the yarn and delivered it to appellant, who accepted and paid for it. The remaining 16,277 pounds were never manufactured because appellant advised appellee by letter, dated August 12, 1960, that it repudiated the contract and would refuse any future delivery of yarn.

Appellee was awarded $4,069.25 in a nonjury trial, which award was based on testimony offered by appellee that the market price of the yarn was $1.90 per pound on August 12, 1960. The award represents 16,277 times the difference between the contract price and the market price ($.25 per pound). No evidence was offered as to the cost of manufacturing the yarn.

Appellant contends that the proper measure of damages in such cases is the difference between the cost of manufacturing and the contract price; and, therefore, since appellee did not prove its cost of manufacture, it is entitled only to nominal damages.

Appellee contends that it has properly proved its damages under section 2–708 of the Uniform Commercial Code, which reads as follows:

"Seller's Damages for Non–Acceptance or Repudiation—(1) Subject to subsection (2) and to the provisions of this Article with respect to proof of market price (Section 2–723) the measure of damages for non-acceptance or repudiation by the buyer is the difference between the market price at the time and place for tender and the unpaid contract price together with any incidental damage provided in this Article (Section 2–710), but less expenses saved in consequence of the buyer's breach."

Prior to the Uniform Commercial Code the law was the same [citation]. [F]or a breach of contract for the sale of personal chattels, yet to be manufactured, the vendor is entitled to recover the difference between the selling price and the market value at the time and place of delivery. * * *

Judgment affirmed.

Notes

1. *Questions.* Was the contract a favorable one for the buyer? Does any U.C.C. section support the damages measure the buyer argued for? The next Note quotes § 2–708(2). Would it apply? Might the contract have been an unfavorable one for the seller? Might the buyer's breach have been an "efficient" one? In deciding how to measure damages, should the court focus on the market-contract differential or on this seller's actual losses under this particular breached contract? Compare TexPar Energy, Inc. v. Murphy Oil USA, Inc., and, in the Note following, H–W–H Cattle Co. v. Schroeder, pp. 582–87.

2. *U.C.C. § 2–708(2):* "If the measure of damages provided in subsection (1) or in Section 2–706 is inadequate to put the seller in as good a position as performance would have done, the measure of damages is the profit (including reasonable overhead) that the seller would have made from full performance by the buyer * * *."

3. *Seller Recovers the Price.* The seller sued the buyer for the contract price of some made-to-order air conditioning ductwork or air cabinets which it had delivered to the buyer. The buyer, who could not use the air cabinets because of an error in the construction plans, had shipped them back to the seller.

Section 2–709 Action for the Price

    (1) When the buyer fails to pay the price as it becomes due the seller may recover, together with any incidental damages under section 2–710, the price

        (a) of goods accepted * * *; and

        (b) of goods identified to the contract if the seller is unable after reasonable effort to resell them at a reasonable price or the circumstances reasonably indicate that such effort will be unavailing.

The defendant-buyer argued "that the [jury] instruction, which submits [the seller's] action for the price, fails to require [in the terms of § 2–709] that the goods were accepted or that plaintiff was unable after reasonable effort to resell the goods or that the circumstances reasonably indicated that such effort would be unavailing."

The court thought that an "action for the price accrues to the seller when the goods have been accepted by the buyer, in which event, the requirements of subsection (b) that the seller make an effort to resell the goods—which relate to goods that have been neither delivered, tendered, nor otherwise accepted—do not become operative. * * * When, as here, the goods conform to the contract, the buyer has a positive duty to accept and the legal obligation to pay according to the contract terms as established. * * * Nor may defendant's return of the air cabinets be construed as a rightful rejection of goods under § 2–602. A delivery or tender by the seller of goods which in all respects conform to the contract gives rise to a positive duty on the buyer to accept and his failure to do so constitutes a wrongful rejection which gives the seller immediate remedies for breach." R.R. Waites Co. v. E.H. Thrift Air Conditioning, Inc., 510 S.W.2d 759 (Mo.App.1974).

Original U.C.C. § 2–709(2) continues: "Where the seller sues for the price he must hold for the buyer any goods which have been identified to the contract and are still in his control except that if resale becomes possible he may resell them at any time prior to the collection of the judgment. The net proceeds of any such resale must be credited to the buyer and payment of the judgment entitles him to any goods not resold."

If you represented the buyer, would you tell your client to pay the judgment? Does § 2–709(2) advance the policies of § 2–709(1)?

McMILLAN v. MEUSER MATERIAL AND EQUIPMENT CO.

Supreme Court of Arkansas, 1976.
260 Ark. 422, 541 S.W.2d 911.

HOLT, JUSTICE. The trial court, sitting as a jury, found appellant McMillan breached a contract to buy a bulldozer from appellee Meuser and assessed $2,700 as appellee's damages ($2,595 actual and $105 incidental). From that judgment comes this appeal.

On December 13, 1973, the parties entered into their agreement. The purchase price, including a bellhousing, was $9,825, f.o.b. Springdale. Meuser arranged transportation of the bulldozer to Greeley, Colorado, the residence of appellant. On December 24, 1973, McMillan stopped payment on his check asserting that since the agreed delivery date was December 21, the delivery was past due. Appellee's version is that the delivery date was January 1, 1974. After unsuccessful negotiations between the parties or about two months after the appellant purchaser stopped payment on his check, appellee brought this action. On March 5, 1975, or about fourteen months following the alleged breach of the purchase contract, appellee sold the bulldozer for $7,230 at a private sale. During this fourteen month interval, the equipment remained unsheltered, although regularly serviced, on an Arkansas farm, which was its situs when the sale contract was made. * * *

We turn now to appellant's contention that the resale by appellee Meuser was not in accordance with the requirements of § 2–706. The statute provides in pertinent part:

'(1) Under the conditions stated in Section 2–703 on seller's remedies, the seller may resell the goods concerned [f]or the undelivered balance thereof. Where the resale is made in good faith and in a commercially reasonable manner the seller may recover the difference between the resale price and the contract price together with any incidental damages allowed under the provisions of this article (section 2–710) but less expenses saved in consequence of the buyer's breach.'

(2) Except as otherwise provided in subsection (3) or unless otherwise agreed resale may be at public or private sale including sale by way of one or more contracts to sell or of identification to an existing contract of the seller. Sale may be as a unit or in parcels and at any time and place and on any terms but every aspect of the sale including the method, manner, time, place, and terms must be commercially reasonable." * * *

The purpose of the resale provisions is discussed in Anderson, Uniform Commercial Code 2d, § 2–706:19, at p. 385, where it is stated:

'The object of the resale is simply to determine exactly the seller's damages. These damages are the difference between the contract price and the market price at the time and place when performance should have been made by the buyer. The object of the resale in such a case is to determine what the market price in fact was. Unless the resale is made at about the time when performance was due it will be of slight probative value, especially if the goods are of a kind which fluctuate rapidly in value, to show what the market price actually was at the only time which is legally important.'

In Comment 5 following § 2–706, the writers make it clear that "what is such a reasonable time depends upon the nature of the goods, the conditions of the market and the other circumstances of the case."

In Bache & Co., Inc. v. International Controls Corp., D.C., 339 F.Supp. 341 (1972), it was held, at least as to the sale of securities, that the resale must be as soon as practicable following notice of the buyer's refusal to accept tender of the goods. There a delay in excess of a month before resale was held unreasonable. In Uganski v. Little Giant Crane & Shovel, Inc., 35 Mich.App. 88, 192 N.W.2d 580 (1971), Uganski, the buyer, after his revocation of acceptance, resold heavy equipment, a crane, some two years and two months from the date of his notice of revocation of acceptance. There the court held his two year delay in reselling the crane was commercially unreasonable.

Here, even though we accord a liberal interpretation to the [Original] U.C.C., § 1–106, which mandates that remedies be so administered, we are of the view that the resale of the bulldozer, in excess of fourteen months after the alleged breach, will be of "slight probative value" as an indication of the market price at the time of the breach. Appellee Meuser is in the construction business and "deal[s] in bulldozers." Meuser himself testified that he was "aware of the state of the economy in the bulldozer market" and since the time of the alleged breach in December, 1973, the market for bulldozers had declined due to a recession in the construction industry and high fuel prices. As indicated, he testified he made no effort to resell the goods for in excess of a year. * * *

The court's award of $105 for incidental expenses incurred by appellee in servicing the bulldozer during the fourteen months from appellant's breach of the contract until appellee sold the equipment is supported by substantial evidence. In fact, appellee's testimony as to the necessity and the beneficial results of the servicing and maintenance of the equipment appears undisputed. As to the resale of the bulldozer, the appellee, admittedly, is in the construction business, sells bulldozer and was aware of the declining market. As previously indicated, as a matter of law, the long delay in the resale of the bulldozer by the appellee is commercially unreasonable. Consequently, the judgment is affirmed upon the condition that the award of $2,595 for actual damages is offered as a remittitur within the next seventeen days. Otherwise, the judgment is reversed and remanded.

Affirmed upon condition of remittitur.

Notes

1. *Policy of Resale.* Another court stated a second possible rationale for the U.C.C.'s resale damages measure: "This rule is based on the principle of avoidable consequences. The defaulting buyer should be credited with the price actually obtained or obtainable for these goods by a new sale." Coos Lumber Co. v. Builders Lumber & Supply Corp., 104 N.H. 404, 406, 188 A.2d 330, 332 (1963)

Is the resale price a substitute for the market value, conclusive of the market value, or evidence of the market value?

2. *May Seller Waive Resale Recovery?* (a) *Waiver After an Actual Resale.* What if the seller resold the bulldozer to B-three in a "commercially reasonable" resale for $9,000 even though its "market value" was $8,000. May the seller recover contract, $9,825, less market value, $8,000, instead of contract, $9,825, less resale, $9000?

What effect would limiting the seller's recovery to contract less resale have? Would it discourage the seller's prompt resale? Would it encourage seller's resale without notice to the buyer? See Sprague v. Sumitomo Forestry Company, Ltd., just below.

(b) *Waiver After Rejecting Resale.* Sam Seller owned a piece of specialized construction equipment that was a duplicate because of a merger. The equipment's market value was $900,000. Sam made a contract to sell the equipment to Ben Byer for $1,000,000. Ben Byer breached.

Beezel offered Sam $1,000,000 for the equipment. Sam, thinking he would be able to sell the equipment to yet another buyer for more than $1,000,000, rejected Beezel's offer. Unfortunately, however, Sam was unable to find another buyer who would pay more than $900,000. Sam still owns the equipment.

Sam sued Beyer arguing that he can still freely elect expectancy damages of $100,000 from Byer under § 2–708(1). In other words, his selection is not affected by § 2–706(1) or any other section or rule of law.

Byer maintains that the court must consider: (a) the policy of resale, § 2–706(1); (b) the policy of avoidable consequences; (c) and the policy of Original § 1–106's language, "that the aggrieved party may be put in as good a position as if the other party had fully performed." Under these policies Sam's recovery would be zero.

3. *Resale Exceeds Contract Price.* What if the seller had resold the bulldozer to B-two for $11,000? Should the buyer, who may be liable for resale below the contract price, receive the benefit of seller's resale that exceeds the contract price? Section 2–706(6) settles this quickly: "The seller is not accountable to the buyer for any profit made on resale."

4. *Home Seller's Resale.* The buyer breached a contract to buy the plaintiff's home for $205,000. Within a few days after the breach, the plaintiff entered into a new contract to sell the property for $215,000. The plaintiff incurred various expenses to maintain the home during the two months preceding the conveyance to the new buyer; the plaintiff sought to recover expenditures of $2648 as damages for the buyer's breach. Ruling that the seller should not be permitted a "windfall," the court held that the buyer may credit the higher price of the rapid resale against the damages. Smith v. Mady, 146 Cal.App.3d 129, 194 Cal.Rptr. 42 (1983).

The court will measure the seller's damages by comparing the cash value of the contract to the cash fair market value at the time of the breach. If, however, the land increases in value before trial and if the seller resells it for more than the contract price, that seller no longer has any expectancy damages. As a corollary, courts have insisted that the seller ought to "mitigate" damages by diligently and promptly seeking to resell the property. Spurgeon v. Drumheller, 174 Cal.App.3d 659, 220 Cal.Rptr. 195 (1985); Nielsen v. Farrington, 223 Cal.App.3d 1582, 273 Cal.Rptr. 312 (1990).

If, however, the breaching buyer sues and files a lis pendens that renders the property unmarketable, the court may determine fair market value at the time of trial. An actual resale of the property is not required to trigger the offset rule. Askari v. R & R Land Co., 179 Cal.App.3d 1101, 225 Cal.Rptr. 285 (1986).

If the seller resells the property at a loss, the resale price is evidence of the market value at the time of the buyer's breach. Roesch v. Bray, 46 Ohio App.3d 49, 545 N.E.2d 1301 (1988); American Mechanical Corp. v. Union Mach. Co., 21 Mass.App.Ct. 97, 485 N.E.2d 680 (1985).

5. *Bulldozer Seller's Special–Consequential–Incidental Damages.* If the bulldozer seller had conducted a "commercially reasonable" sale and sold to B-four for $11,000, then could he recover from the breaching buyer the $105 he spent to service the bulldozer? Section 2–710.

6. *Delayed Resale.* "Even though there was a three-year delay between breach and resale here, we cannot say that the jury was required to find the resale was commercially unreasonable." There was no market for the machines when the buyer breached; each machine cost over $30,000; and the seller "made a continuing good faith effort to locate other purchasers." Firwood Manufacturing Co., Inc. v. General Tire, Inc., 96 F.3d 163, 169 (6th Cir.1996).

How might the lack of a market value to calculate the seller's damages under § 2–708(1) affect whether a court is willing to accept a seller's delayed or otherwise "suboptimal" resale?

SPRAGUE v. SUMITOMO FORESTRY COMPANY, LIMITED

Supreme Court of Washington, En Banc, 1985.
104 Wash.2d 751, 709 P.2d 1200.

DORE, JUSTICE. [Sprague, a logger, entered into a contract with Sumitomo for the sale of logs. Because of difficulties with its sawmill, Sumitomo canceled the contract.]

Subsequent to receiving Sumitomo's unequivocal cancellation of the log purchase contract, Sprague promptly filed a complaint against Sumitomo for breach of contract. Sumitomo served its answer alleging that Sprague had an affirmative duty to mitigate damages.

After receiving Sumitomo's answer, Sprague mitigated his damages by reselling the timber to five different purchasers at private sales.

At trial Sprague sought to recover the difference between the contract price and resale price of the timber, together with incidental damages arising from Sumitomo's unequivocal cancellation. Sumitomo claimed mutual rescission and asserted affirmative defenses, including that Sprague "failed to proceed as required by 2–702 et seq." * * *

Via a special verdict form, the jury found * * * that the contract price was $197,204 and the resale price was $144,924 with net contractual damages of $52,280; (4) that Sprague sustained incidental damages of $216,498 for the following items: (a) cost of refinancing, $39,674; (b) extra transportation cost, $5,612; (c) loss of revenue on Flip Blowdown not covered by contract, $9,121; (d) loss of logging time, 11 weeks, $171,200; and (e) cost of moving tower, $2,115.

The major thrust of Sumitomo's appellate argument here is that Sprague did not give the requisite notice of intention to resell the canceled goods as required by 2–706(3) and, therefore, Sprague is not entitled to recover the difference between the contract price and the resale price.

The catalogue of a seller's remedies in a breach of contract case governed by the sale of goods provisions of the Uniform Commercial Code is found in 2–703.

In the present case, the catalogue of available remedies can quickly be reduced to two; these are:

(1) resale and recovery under 2–706, or

(2) recovery of the difference between the contract price and the market price under 2–708(1).

At trial Sprague apparently proceeded, pursuant to 2–706, to recover as damages the difference between the resale price and contract price. 2–706(1) provides that if the seller acts in good faith and in a commercially reasonable manner, he may recover the difference between the resale price and the contract price, together with any incidental damages allowed under 2–710, less expenses saved.

Section 2–706(2) goes on to permit resale at public or private sale. Of critical importance here is the requirement of 2–706(3) which provides that where an aggrieved seller resells goods which are the subject of a breach at a private sale, he must give the buyer "reasonable notification of his intention to resell."

In response to his failure to give specific notice of intention to resell, and in support of his judgment, Sprague argues: that the lack of notice was an affirmative defense which the buyer failed to plead, or that the buyer, from all the surrounding facts and circumstances, knew or should have known that the seller was going to resell the logs. * * *

To recover under 2–706, Sprague was required to give notice of intent to resell. This is an element of the seller's right to invoke the remedies of 2–706. Therefore, the buyer need not plead as an affirmative defense those elements which seller must prove.

Next, can the notice requirement be satisfied by the fact that the buyer knew or should have known that the seller intended to resell? From the plain language of 2–706, the giving by the seller of notice of intention to resell is a specific requirement to entitle seller to claim as damages the difference between resale price and the contract price. The words of subsection (3) are precise: "the seller *must* give the buyer reasonable notification of his intention to resell." (Italics ours.) 2–706(3). * * *

It is a general rule of appellate practice that the judgment of the trial court will not be reversed when it can be sustained on any theory, although different from that indicated in the decision of the trial judge. Although the jury verdict cannot be upheld under the resale method of determining damages, we find that the record supports the verdict under the alternate method of establishing damages, computed by measuring the difference between the market price and the contract price as provided in 2–708. * * *

It is fundamental under 2–703 and the sections that follow that an aggrieved seller is not required to elect between damages under 2–706 and 2–708. 2–703 cumulatively sets forth the remedies available to a seller upon the buyer's breach. The pertinent commentary thereto indicates specifically that the remedies provided are cumulative and not exclusive and that as a fundamental policy Article 2 of the U.C.C. rejects any doctrine of election of remedy.

The seller has the burden of proof with respect to market price or market value. A seller cannot avail himself of the benefit of 2–708 when he has not presented evidence of market price or market value. However, the resale price of goods may be considered as appropriate evidence of the market value at the time of tender in determining damages pursuant to 2–708.

While, admittedly, Sprague's resale came after the time for tender, it can still be utilized as a market price. 2–723(2) states:

> "(2) If evidence of a price prevailing at the times or places described in this Article is not readily available the price prevailing within any reasonable time before *or after* the time described or at any other place which in commercial judgment or under usage of trade would serve as a reasonable substitute for the one described may be used, * * * "

(Italics ours.)

The court is granted a "reasonable leeway" (Official Comments to 2–723) in measuring market price. During the trial of this action, not only was there testimony to the effect that in an effort to mitigate damages, respondent Sprague sold the Flip Blowdown logs to five purchasers at private sales in 1981 and 1982, there was also testimony that the market price remained at the same level as at the time and place of tender in late 1980.

The net contractual damages of $52,280 ($197,204 contract price—$144,924 resale price) which was awarded respondent under the jury verdict thus equaled the measure of damages available under 2–708(1). We affirm this award.

Sprague is entitled also to incidental damages. 2–708 provides that the seller is entitled to the difference between the market price and contract price "together with any incidental damages provided in this Article (2–710), but less expenses saved in consequence of the buyer's breach." Incidental damages are defined in 2–710 as follows:

> "Incidental damages to an aggrieved seller include any commercially reasonable charges, expenses or commissions incurred in stopping delivery, in the transportation, care and custody of goods after the buyer's breach, in connection with return or resale of the goods or otherwise resulting from the breach."

At trial, the jury found that respondent sustained incidental damages of $216,498 for the following items: (a) cost of refinancing, $39,674; (b) extra transportation cost, $5,612; © loss of revenue on Flip Blowdown not covered by contract, $9,121; (d) loss of logging time, 11 weeks, $171,200; and (e) cost of moving tower, $2,115.

Sumitomo contends that some of these items are not incidental damages but more properly classified as consequential. Consequential damages are *not* allowed except as specifically provided in RCW Title 62A or by other rule of law. [Original U.C.C. §] 1–106. Washington Comment to section 2–710 indicates that consequential damages are denied to sellers under the Uniform Commercial Code. 2–710.

The distinction between consequential and incidental damages was made in Petroleo Brasileiro, S.A., Petrobras v. Ameropan Oil Corp., 372 F.Supp. 503, 508 (E.D.N.Y.1974).

> "While the distinction between the two is not an obvious one, the Code makes plain that incidental damages are normally incurred when a buyer (or seller) repudiates the contract or wrongfully rejects the goods, causing the other to incur such expenses as transporting, storing, or reselling the goods. On the other hand, *consequential damages* do not arise within the

scope of the immediate buyer-seller transaction, but rather *stem from losses incurred by the non-breaching party in its dealings, often with third parties,* which were a proximate result of the breach, and which were reasonably foreseeable by the breaching party at the time of contracting."

(Citations omitted. Italics ours.)

We find that the loss of logging time is an inappropriate item of incidental damages. Sprague's damage claim for loss of logging time is essentially a claim for lost profits on a contract with Mt. Baker Plywood. In *Petroleo Brasileiro,* the court stated that "consequential damages do not arise within the scope of the immediate buyer-seller transaction [as do incidental damages], but rather stem from losses incurred by the non-breaching party in its dealings, often with third parties." *Petroleo Brasileiro.* Applying this test to Sprague's claim for loss of logging time, Sprague's loss clearly did not arise within the scope of his contract with Sumitomo; instead, Sprague incurred this loss as a consequence of his delay in performing his contract with Mt. Baker Plywood, a third party. The fact that Sumitomo's conduct proximately caused Sprague's loss is irrelevant to this analysis. The focus is upon losses arising within the scope of the immediate contract. Accordingly, Sprague's loss can only be characterized as consequential. Therefore, the judgment awarded Sprague is reduced by $171,200.

The remaining costs are not seriously contested by appellant and appear to be appropriate items of incidental damages. * * *

The judgment is reduced by $171,200 to eliminate an improper element of damages. As modified, the judgment is affirmed.

Questions

Does the court construe "resale" more technically than necessary? Was the court too willing to default to contract-market? Does the court's definition limit seller's special damages?

2. THE PUZZLE OF SELLER'S PROFITS

The seller's damages measures we have already examined may not always be satisfactory, as a lawsuit about a breached contract for centennial-commemorative coins illustrates. "In conjunction with the statewide celebration of the one hundredth anniversary of the purchase of Alaska from Russia, the Anchorage Centennial Commission contracted with Van Wormer & Rodrigues, Inc. to buy 50,000 gold-colored metal coins. After Van Wormer had partially completed the order, the commission notified Van Wormer that it was terminating the contract."

At trial Van Wormer recovered the price of the 29,000 centennial coins that it had already manufactured. The seller's appeal dealt with its ability to recover its profit for 21,000 unmanufactured coins. (a) What about § 2–708(1), contract less market? (b) Is § 2–706, contract less resale, feasible? (c) Should the seller recover the price under § 2–709? (d) Section 2–708(2) to the rescue?

"Examination of the record in this cause fails to reveal any basis for the trial court's conclusion that Van Wormer was not entitled to recover its loss of profits in regard to the 21,000 coins which had been ordered by the commission, but had not been manufactured at the time of the commission's repudiation of the contract. * * *"

"In the case at bar we are in accord with Van Wormer's argument to the effect that since there is no market for these made-to-order coins the proper measure of damages is governed by [2–708(2)] which provides:"

'If the measure of damages provided in [1] [the difference between contract and market] is inadequate to put the seller in as good a position as performance would have done, then the measure of damages is the profit * * * which the seller would have made from full performance by the buyer.' * * *

"We, therefore, conclude that the judgment entered below should be modified to include an award to Van Wormer for its loss of profits on the remaining 21,000 coins under the contract." Anchorage Centennial Development Co. v. Van Wormer & Rodrigues, Inc., 443 P.2d 596, 597, 599 (Alaska 1968).

Following the court's calculation under § 2–708(2), contract price less its cost to manufacture, the seller recovered 3 cents for each unmanufactured coin.

The seller's recovery of lost profit gets complicated in a "lost-volume seller" case.

R.E. DAVIS CHEMICAL CORP. v. DIASONICS, INC.

United States Court of Appeals, Seventh Circuit, 1987.
826 F.2d 678.

CUDAHY, CIRCUIT JUDGE. Diasonics is a California corporation engaged in the business of manufacturing and selling medical diagnostic equipment. Davis is an Illinois corporation that contracted to purchase a piece of medical diagnostic equipment from Diasonics. On or about February 23, 1984, Davis and Diasonics entered into a written contract under which Davis agreed to purchase the equipment. Pursuant to this agreement, Davis paid Diasonics a $300,000 deposit on February 29, 1984. * * * Davis then breached its contract with Diasonics; it refused to take delivery of the equipment or to pay the balance due under the agreement. Diasonics later resold the equipment to a third party for the same price at which it was to be sold to Davis.

Davis sued Diasonics, asking for restitution of its $300,000 down payment under section 2–718(2) of the Uniform Commercial Code (the "U.C.C." or the "Code").[1] Diasonics counterclaimed. Diasonics did not deny that Davis was entitled to recover its $300,000 deposit less $500 as provided in section 2–718(2)(b). However, Diasonics claimed that it was entitled to an offset under section 2–718(3). Diasonics alleged that it was a "lost volume seller," and, as such, it lost the profit from one sale when Davis breached its contract. Diasonics'

---

1. [Footnotes renumbered.] The pertinent portion of section 2–718 provides: § 2–718. Liquidation or Limitation of Damages; Deposits * * *

(2) Where the seller justifiably withholds delivery of goods because of the buyer's breach, the buyer is entitled to restitution of any amount by which the sum of his payments exceeds

(a) the amount to which the seller is entitled by virtue of terms liquidating the seller's damages in accordance with subsection (1), or

(b) in the absence of such terms, 20% of the value of the total performance for which the buyer is obligated under the contract or $500, whichever is smaller.

(3) The buyer's right to restitution under subsection (2) is subject to offset to the extent that the seller establishes

(a) a right to recover damages under the provisions of this Article other than subsection (1), and

(b) the amount or value of any benefits received by the buyer directly or indirectly by reason of the contract.

position was that, in order to be put in as good a position as it would have been in had Davis performed, it was entitled to recover its lost profit on its contract with Davis under section 2–708(2) of the U.C.C. Section 2–708 provides:

§ 2–708. Seller's Damages for Nonacceptance or Repudiation

"(1) Subject to subsection (2) and to Section 2–723:"

(a) the measure of damages for nonacceptance by the buyer is the difference between the contract price and the market price at the time and place for tender together with any incidental or consequential damages provided in Section 2–710, but less expenses saved in consequence of the buyer's breach; and

(b) the measure of damages for repudiation by the buyer is the difference between the contract price and the market price at the place for tender at the expiration of a commercially reasonable time after the seller learned of the repudiation, but no later than the time stated in paragraph (a), together with any incidental or consequential damages provided in Section 2–710, less expenses saved in consequence of the buyer's breach.

"(2) If the measure of damages provided in subsection (1) is inadequate to put the seller in as good a position as performance would have done then the measure of damages is the profit (including reasonable overhead) which the seller would have made from full performance by the buyer, together with any incidental damages provided in this Article (Section 2–710), due allowance for costs reasonably incurred and due credit for payments or proceeds of resale."

The [district] court entered summary judgment for Davis. The court held that lost volume sellers were not entitled to recover damages under 2–708(2) but rather were limited to recovering the difference between the resale price and the contract price along with incidental damages under section 2–706(1). Section 2–706(1) provides:

§ 2–706. Seller's Resale Including Contract for Resale

"(1) Under the conditions stated in Section 2–703 on seller's remedies, the seller may resell the goods concerned or the undelivered balance thereof. Where the resale is made in good faith and in a commercially reasonable manner the seller may recover the difference between the resale price and the contract price together with any incidental damages allowed under the provisions of this Article (Section 2–710), but less expenses saved in consequence of the buyer's breach."

Davis was awarded $322,656, which represented Davis' down payment plus prejudgment interest less Diasonics' incidental damages. Diasonics appeals the district court's decision respecting its measure of damages * * *.

We consider first Diasonics' claim that the district court erred in holding that Diasonics was limited to the measure of damages provided in 2–706 and could not recover lost profits as a lost volume seller under 2–708(2). * * * Courts applying the laws of other states have unanimously adopted the position that a lost volume seller can recover its lost profits under 2–708(2). [citations] Contrary to the result reached by the district court, we conclude that the Illinois Supreme Court would follow these other cases and would allow a lost volume seller to recover its lost profit under 2–708(2).

We begin our analysis with 2–718(2) and (3). Under 2–718(2)(b), Davis is entitled to the return of its down payment less $500. Davis' right to restitution, however, is qualified under 2–718(3)(a) to the extent that Diasonics can establish a right to recover damages under any other provision of Article 2 of the U.C.C .. Article 2 contains four provisions that concern the recovery of a seller's general damages (as opposed to its incidental or consequential damages): 2–706 (contract price less resale price); 2–708(1) (contract price less market price); 2–708(2) (profit); and 2–709 (price). The problem we face here is determining whether Diasonics' damages should be measured under 2–706 or 2–708(2).[2] To answer this question, we need to engage in a detailed look at the language and structure of these various damage provisions.

The Code does not provide a great deal of guidance as to when a particular damage remedy is appropriate. The damage remedies provided under the Code are catalogued in section 2–703, but this section does not indicate that there is any hierarchy among the remedies.[3] One method of approaching the damage sections is to conclude that 2–708 is relegated to a role inferior to that of 2–706 and 2–709 and that one can turn to 2–708 only after one has concluded that neither 2–706 nor 2–709 is applicable.[4] Under this interpretation of the relationship between 2–706 and 2–708, if the goods have been resold, the seller can sue to recover damages measured by the difference between the contract price and the resale price under 2–706. The seller can turn to 2–708 only if it resells in a commercially unreasonable manner or if it cannot resell but an action for the price is inappropriate under 2–709. The district court adopted this reading of the Code's damage remedies and, accordingly, limited Diasonics to the measure of damages provided in 2–706 because it resold the equipment in a commercially reasonable manner.

The district court's interpretation of 2–706 and 2–708, however, creates its own problems of statutory construction. There is some suggestion in the Code that the "fact that plaintiff resold the goods [in a commercially reasonable

2. An action for the price, provided for under 2–709, is not an option in this case because Diasonics resold the equipment that it had intended to sell to Davis.

3. Section 2–703 provides: § 2–703. Seller's Remedies in General. Where the buyer wrongfully rejects or revokes acceptance of goods or fails to make a payment due on or before delivery or repudiates with respect to a part or the whole, then with respect to any goods directly affected and, if the breach is of the whole contract (Section 2–612), then also with respect to the whole undelivered balance, the aggrieved seller may

(a) withhold delivery of such goods;

(b) stop delivery by any bailee as hereafter provided (Section 2–705);

© proceed under the next section respecting goods still unidentified to the contract;

(d) resell and recover damages as hereafter provided (Section 2–706);

(e) recover damages for non-acceptance (Section 2–708) or in a proper case the price (Section 2–709);

(f) cancel.

4. Evidence to support this approach can be found in the language of the various damage sections and of the official comments to the UCC. See § 2–709(3) ("a seller who is held not entitled to the price under this Section shall nevertheless be awarded damages for non-acceptance under the preceding section [§ 2–708]"); UCC comment 7 to § 2–709 ("[i]f the action for the price fails, the seller may nonetheless have proved a case entitling him to damages for non-acceptance [under § 2–708]"); UCC comment 2 to § 2–706 ("[f]ailure to act properly under this section deprives the seller of the measure of damages here provided and relegates him to that provided in Section 2–708"); UCC comment 1 to § 2–704 (describes § 2–706 as the "primary remedy" available to a seller upon breach by the buyer).

As one commentator has noted, 2–706

"is the Code section drafted specifically to define the damage rights of aggrieved reselling sellers, and there is no suggestion within it that the profit formula of section 2–708(2) is in any way intended to qualify or be superior to it."

Shanker, The Case for a Literal Reading of UCC Section 2–708(2) (One Profit for the Reseller), 24 Case W.Res. 697, 699 (1973).

manner] does *not* compel him to use the resale remedy of § 2–706 rather than the damage remedy of § 2–708." Harris, A Radical Restatement of the Law of Seller's Damages: Sales Act and Commercial Code Results Compared, 18 Stan. L.Rev. 66, 101 n. 174 (1965) (emphasis in original). Official comment 1 to 2–703, which catalogues the remedies available to a seller, states that these "remedies are essentially cumulative in nature" and that "[w]hether the pursuit of one remedy bars another depends entirely on the facts of the individual case."[5]

Those courts that found that a lost volume seller can recover its lost profits under 2–708(2) implicitly rejected the position adopted by the district court; those courts started with the assumption that 2–708 applied to a lost volume seller without considering whether the seller was limited to the remedy provided under 2–706. None of those courts even suggested that a seller who resold goods in a commercially reasonable manner was limited to the damage formula provided under 2–706. We conclude that the Illinois Supreme Court, if presented with this question, would adopt the position of these other jurisdictions and would conclude that a reselling seller, such as Diasonics, is free to reject the damage formula prescribed in 2–706 and choose to proceed under 2–708.

Concluding that Diasonics is entitled to seek damages under 2–708, however, does not automatically result in Diasonics being awarded its lost profit. Two different measures of damages are provided in 2–708. Subsection 2–708(1) provides for a measure of damages calculated by subtracting the market price at the time and place for tender from the contract price.[6] The profit measure of damages, for which Diasonics is asking, is contained in 2–708(2). However, one applies 2–708(2) only if "the measure of damages provided in subsection (1) is inadequate to put the seller in as good a position as performance would have done." Diasonics claims that 2–708(1) does not provide an adequate measure of damages when the seller is a lost volume seller.[7] To understand Diasonics' argument, we need to define the concept of the lost volume seller. Those cases that have addressed this issue have defined a lost volume seller as one that has a predictable and finite number of customers and that has the capacity either to sell to all new buyers [citations] or to make the one additional sale represented by the resale after the breach. [citations] According to a number of courts and commentators, if the seller would have made the sale represented by the resale

---

5. UCC comment 2 to 2–708(2) also suggests that 2–708 has broader applicability than suggested by the district court. UCC comment 2 provides:

"This section permits the recovery of lost profits in all appropriate cases, which would include all standard priced goods. The normal measure there would be list price less cost to the dealer or list price less manufacturing cost to the manufacturer."

The district court's restrictive interpretation of 2–708(2) was based in part on UCC comment 1 to 2–704 which describes 2–706 as the aggrieved seller's primary remedy. The district court concluded that, if a lost volume seller could recover its lost profit under 2–708(2), every seller would attempt to recover damages under 2–708(2) and 2–706 would become the aggrieved seller's residuary remedy. This argument ignores the fact that to recover under 2–708(2), a seller must first establish its status as a lost volume seller. The district court also concluded that a lost volume seller cannot recover its lost profit under

2–708(2) because such a result would negate a seller's duty to mitigate damages. This position fails to recognize the fact that, by definition, a lost volume seller cannot mitigate damages through resale. Resale does not reduce a lost volume seller's damages because the breach has still resulted in its losing one sale and a corresponding profit.

6. There is some debate in the commentaries about whether a seller who has resold the goods may ignore the measure of damages provided in 2–706 and elect to proceed under 2–708(1). Under some circumstances the contract-market price differential will result in overcompensating such a seller. [citation] We need not struggle with this question here because Diasonics has not sought to recover damages under 2–708(1).

7. This is also the position adopted by those courts that have held that a lost volume seller can recover its lost profits under 2–708(2).

whether or not the breach occurred, damages measured by the difference between the contract price and market price cannot put the lost volume seller in as good a position as it would have been in had the buyer performed.[8] The breach effectively cost the seller a "profit," and the seller can only be made whole by awarding it damages in the amount of its "lost profit" under 2–708(2).

We agree with Diasonics' position that, under some circumstances, the measure of damages provided under 2–708(1) will not put a reselling seller in as good a position as it would have been in had the buyer performed because the breach resulted in the seller losing sales volume. However, we disagree with the definition of "lost volume seller" adopted by other courts. Courts awarding lost profits to a lost volume seller have focused on whether the seller had the capacity to supply the breached units in addition to what it actually sold. In reality, however, the relevant questions include, not only whether the seller could have produced the breached units in addition to its actual volume, but also whether it would have been profitable for the seller to produce both units. As one commentator has noted, under

> "the economic law of diminishing returns or increasing marginal costs[,] * * * as a seller's volume increases, then a point will inevitably be reached where the cost of selling each additional item diminishes the incremental return to the seller and eventually makes it entirely unprofitable to conclude the next sale."

Shanker, at 705. Thus, under some conditions, awarding a lost volume seller its presumed lost profit will result in overcompensating the seller, and 2–708(2) would not take effect because the damage formula provided in 2–708(1) does place the seller in as good a position as if the buyer had performed. Therefore, on remand, Diasonics must establish, not only that it had the capacity to produce the breached unit in addition to the unit resold, but also that it would have been profitable for it to have produced and sold both. Diasonics carries the burden of establishing these facts because the burden of proof is generally on the party claiming injury to establish the amount of its damages; especially in a case such as this, the plaintiff has easiest access to the relevant data. [citations]

One final problem with awarding a lost volume seller its lost profits was raised by the district court. This problem stems from the formulation of the measure of damages provided under 2–708(2) which is "the profit (including reasonable overhead) which the seller would have made from full performance by the buyer, together with any incidental damages provided in this Article (Section 2–710), due allowance for costs reasonably incurred and due credit for payments or *proceeds of resale.*" The literal language of 2–708(2) requires that the proceeds from resale be credited against the amount of damages awarded which, in most cases, would result in the seller recovering nominal damages. In those cases in which the lost volume seller was awarded its lost profit as damages, the courts have circumvented this problem by concluding that this language only applies to proceeds realized from the resale of uncompleted goods for scrap. [citations]. Although neither the text of 2–708(2) nor the official comments limit its application to resale of goods for scrap, there is evidence that

8. According to one commentator, "Resale results in loss of volume only if three conditions are met: (1) the person who bought the resold entity would have been solicited by plaintiff had there been no breach and resale; (2) the solicitation would have been successful; and (3) the plaintiff could have performed that additional contract."

Harris, (footnotes omitted).

the drafters of 2–708 seemed to have had this more limited application in mind when they proposed amending 2–708 to include the phrase "due credit for payments or proceeds of resale." [citations] We conclude that the Illinois Supreme Court would adopt this more restrictive interpretation of this phrase rendering it inapplicable to this case.

We therefore reverse the grant of summary judgment in favor of Davis and remand with instructions that the district court calculate Diasonics' damages under 2–708(2) if Diasonics can establish, not only that it had the capacity to make the sale to Davis as well as the sale to the resale buyer, but also that it would have been profitable for it to make both sales. Of course, Diasonics, in addition, must show that it probably would have made the second sale absent the breach.

Notes

1. *Qualifying for Lost–Volume Seller Status.* What does a seller have to prove to establish lost-volume status? A Notewriter commenting on the principal decision suggested only two questions to confine lost-volume status to the needs that gave rise to the damages measure. (a) Whether the seller has capacity to make both sales. (b) Whether the sales are wholly independent events so that the second sale would have occurred without the breach. Jerald B. Holisky, Finding the "Lost Volume Seller": Two Independent Sales Deserve Two Profits Under Illinois Law, 22 John Marshall L.Rev. 363 (1988).

Another court held that, where supply exceeds demand, the seller need not prove a market to recover "lost volume" profits. Islamic Republic of Iran v. Boeing Co., 771 F.2d 1279 (9th Cir. 1985).

In a later appeal of the principal case, the court rejected the argument that the seller "must precisely identify the resale buyer" to qualify for lost volume status. But the court of appeals remanded to the trial judge for additional "fact-intensive inquiry" on the amount of damages. R.E. Davis Chemical Corp. v. Diasonics, Inc., 924 F.2d 709, 711 (7th Cir. 1991).

2. In its next-to-last paragraph, the court simply ignores the "due-allowance, due-credit" clause at the end of § 2–708(2). Revised U.C.C.'s § 2–708(2) eliminates the court's "problem" by deleting that clause.

C. LIQUIDATED DAMAGES

Reducing Uncertainty by Agreement: "Liquidated damage provisions have had a checkered history. While the freedom of parties to structure their agreement is universally acknowledged to be at the heart of the law of contract, the limited enforcement of clauses where parties have agreed to specified measures of damages is a judicial check on the freedom of contract based on public policy notions of the courts of equity. [citation] As a general test, if a contested clause providing for definite preagreed damages is intended by the parties to operate in lieu of performance, it will be deemed a liquidated damages clause and may be enforced by the courts. If such a clause is intended to operate as a means to compel performance, it will be deemed a penalty and will not be enforced. [citation] * * * Where the court has sustained a liquidated damages clause the measure of damages for a breach will be the sum in the clause, no more, no less. If the clause is rejected as being a penalty, the recovery is limited to actual damages proven.

"New York law permits the use of liquidated damages clauses in contracts. See, e.g., N.Y.U.C.C. § 2–718. A party seeking to enforce a liquidated damages clause must meet two tests. First, at the time the contract was entered into, the anticipated damages in the event of a breach must be incapable of, or very difficult of, accurate estimation. Second, the amount of the damages specified in the liquidated damages clause must not be disproportionate to the damage reasonably anticipated for the breach as of the time the contract was made." Brecher v. Laikin, 430 F.Supp. 103, 106 (S.D.N.Y.1977). Liquidated vs. penalty is a question of law for the judge.

We will call the *Brecher* court's approach the penalty rule because that court states a test to distinguish a valid liquidated damages clause from an improper penalty clause: contract parties may stipulate damages only when the loss is difficult to prove, and their effort was a good-faith estimate. The material below presents competing rules. First is a market-economics example to illustrate the argument against the penalty rule.

Economic Analysis of Liquidated Damages. Assume, that Owner retains Cleaner to restore his oil portrait of his late lamented cat Puff. Although his portrait may be worth about $5 on the garage-sale market, Owner thinks it is priceless. Owner seeks a stipulated damage clause of $10,000 to assure that Cleaner restores and returns his portrait; Cleaner after agreeing raises her regular $25 fee to $50. Is $10,000 an invalid penalty?

Will the $10,000 clause encourage Cleaner to be careful and to perform as promised? If Cleaner fails to perform, the stipulated damage clause advances the compensation goal by covering Owner's unprovable, impalpable, and otherwise unforeseeable damages even though Owner's loss is idiosyncratic and subjective. If the risk of paying $10,000 to Owner worries Cleaner, she may use the extra $25 consideration to buy insurance. Cleaner is probably a more efficient insurer than Owner because Cleaner can assess the probability of loss and take steps to avoid loss at less cost than Owner.

Striking down a "penalty" clause means that the court is not protecting Owner's idiosyncratic values. Owner knows her own utility better than a judge. The court's approval of the clause would respect the autonomy of both Owner and Cleaner. Moreover, a court's disapproval would induce people like Owner to insure even though it is cheaper and more efficient for Cleaner to insure. And disapproval would increases litigation costs since the penalty rule means that every clause is subject to attack on the ground that it may be improper. For a cogent argument that the penalty rule is "anachronistic," which was published about the same time the *Brecher* case was decided, see Charles Goetz and Robert Scott, Liquidated Damages, Penalties and the Just Compensation Principle, 77 Colum.L.Rev. 544 (1977).

The next decision illustrates the New York rule for earnest money in a land contract. Ask yourself whether the market economics view above has been the law all along for New York land deals.

UZAN v. 845 UN LIMITED PARTNERSHIP

Supreme Court, Appellate Division, New York, 2004.
10 A.D.3d 230, 778 N.Y.S.2d 171.

MAZZARELLI, J. This appeal presents the issue of whether plaintiffs, who defaulted on the purchase of four luxury condominium units, have forfeited their

25% down payments as a matter of law. * * * [W]e hold that upon their default and failure to cure, plaintiffs forfeited all rights to their deposits pursuant to the rule set forth in Maxton Builders, Inc. v. Lo Galbo, 68 N.Y.2d 373 (1986).

Facts. In October 1998, Defendant 845 UN Limited Partnership (sponsor or 845 UN) began to sell apartments at The Trump World Tower (Trump World), a luxury condominium building to be constructed at 845 United Nations Plaza. Donald Trump is the managing general partner of the sponsor. Plaintiffs Cem Uzan and Hakan Uzan, two brothers, are Turkish billionaires who sought to purchase multiple units in the building.

In April 1999, plaintiffs and an associate executed seven purchase agreements for apartments in Trump World. Only four of those units (the penthouse units) are the subject of this lawsuit and appeal. As relevant, Cem Uzan defaulted on contracts to buy two penthouse units on the 90th floor of the building, and Hakan defaulted on contracts to purchase two other penthouse units on the 89th floor.

The building had not been constructed when plaintiffs executed their purchase agreements. In paragraph 17.4 of those contracts, the sponsor projected that the first closing in the building would occur on or about April 1, 2001, nearly two years after the signing of the agreements.

The condominium offering plan included a section titled "Special Risks to be Considered by Purchasers," which stated:

> Purchasers will be required to make a down payment upon execution of a Purchase Agreement in an amount equal to 10% of the purchase price, and within 180 days after receipt of the executed Purchase Agreement from Sponsor or 15 days after Purchaser receives a written notice or amendment to the Plan declaring the Plan effective, whichever is earlier, an additional down payment equal to 15% of the purchase price. * * *

Once construction was completed, the building's offering plan was amended to require a 15% down payment. Notably, both the original and the amended offering plans prominently disclosed the sponsor's right to retain the *entire down payment* should there be an uncured default.

Negotiations Preceding Execution of the Purchase Agreements. Plaintiffs were represented by experienced local counsel during the two-month-long negotiation for the purchase of the apartments. There were numerous telephone conversations between counsel, and at least four extensively marked-up copies of draft purchase agreements were exchanged. In consideration for plaintiffs' purchase of multiple units, the sponsor reduced the aggregate purchase price of the penthouse units by more than $7 million from the list price in the offering plan for a total cost of approximately $32 million. Plaintiffs also negotiated a number of revisions to the standard purchase agreement, including extensions of time for payment of the down payment. As amended, each purchase agreement obligated plaintiffs to make a 25% down payment: 10% at contract, an additional 7½% down payment twelve months later, and a final 7½% down payment 18 months after the execution of the contract. At no time did plaintiffs object to the total amount required as a non-refundable down payment.

There were other significant amendments to the standard purchase agreement which benefitted plaintiffs. These included: (1) rights to terminate the contracts if the closing had not occurred by December 31, 2003; (2) rights to advertise the units for resale prior to closing; (3) conditional rights to assign the purchase agreements to a third party; and (4) the right of each brother to terminate his contracts if the sponsor terminated the purchase agreements for the other brother's units. It is noted that according to counsel for the sponsor, the right to assign the purchase contracts prior to closing had not been granted to any other purchaser of a unit at Trump World. Also, at plaintiffs' urging, the sponsor added language to the purchase agreements agreeing not to install machinery on the roof that would cause noise or vibration in the apartments.

The executed purchase agreements provide, at paragraph 12(b), that:

> [u]pon the occurrence of an Event of Default * * * [i]f Sponsor elects to cancel * * * [and i]f the default is not cured within * * * thirty (30) days, then this Agreement shall be deemed canceled, and Sponsor shall have the right to retain, as and for liquidated damages, the Down payment and any interest earned on the Down payment.

Plaintiffs paid the first 10% down payment installment for the penthouse units on April 26, 1999 when they signed the purchase agreements. They paid the second 7½% installment in April 2000, and the third 7½% installment in October 2000. The total 25% down payment of approximately $8 million was placed in an escrow account.

Default, Failure to Cure, and this Action. On September 11, 2001, terrorists attacked New York City by flying two planes into the World Trade Center, the city's two tallest buildings, murdering thousands of people. Plaintiffs, asserting concerns of future terrorist attacks, failed to appear at the October 19, 2001 closing, resulting in their default. By letter dated October 19, 2001, plaintiffs' counsel stated:

> [W]e believe that our clients are entitled to rescind their Purchase Agreements in view of the terrorist attack which occurred on September 11 and has not abated. In particular, our clients are concerned that the top floors in a "trophy" building, described as the tallest residential building in the world, will be an attractive terrorist target. The situation is further aggravated by the fact that the building bears the name of Donald Trump, perhaps the most widely known symbol of American capitalism. Finally, the United Nations complex brings even more attention to this location.

That day 845 UN sent plaintiffs default letters, notifying them that they had 30 days to cure. On November 19, 2001, upon expiration of the cure period, the sponsor terminated the four purchase agreements.

Plaintiffs then brought this action. * * * [Plaintiffs' third cause of action] sought a declaratory judgment that the down payment was an "unconscionable, illegal and unenforceable penalty." * * *

Motions for Summary Judgment. After exchanging discovery and conducting various depositions, plaintiffs moved for summary judgment on their third cause of action, arguing that forfeiture of the down payments was an unenforceable penalty. * * *

Defendant opposed the motion and cross-moved for summary judgment, asserting that defaulting vendees on real estate contracts may not recover their down payments. Defendant submitted the affidavits of Donald Trump, [as well as Weitzman's and Martin's].

Defendant also included the offering plan, the purchase agreements, Cem Uzan's 2000 purchase agreement for an apartment at 515 Park Avenue (with a

25% down payment provision), various correspondence between the parties, excerpts from the deposition testimony of Hakan Uzan, Jeffrey M. Diamond and Donald Trump, studies regarding the Manhattan real estate market, and an estimation of the sponsor's damages as of March 31, 2003. Defendant's submissions contain substantial evidence of the common usage of a 20–25% down payment in the pre-construction luxury condominium market.

The Role of the 25% Down Payment. In his affidavit in support of the cross motion, Donald Trump stated that he sought 25% down payments from pre-construction purchasers at the Trump World Tower because of the substantial length of time between contract signing and closing, during which period the sponsor had to keep the units off the market, and because of the obvious associated risks. Trump also affirmed that down payments in the range of 20% to 25% are standard practice in the new construction luxury condominium submarket in New York City. He cited three projects where he was the developer, The Trump Palace, 610 Park Avenue and Trump International Hotel and Tower, all of which had similar down payment provisions. Trump also noted that,

> [i]n new construction condominium projects, purchasers often speculate on the market by putting down initial down payments of 10% and 15% and watching how the market moves. If the market value increases, they will then make the second down payment. If the market prices drop, they may then walk away from their down payment.

Weitzman's affirmation echoed Trump's opinion that 20% to 25% down payments are customary in New York City for new construction condominium apartments, because of the volatility of the market. Weitzman also discussed other risk factors specific to developers of newly constructed luxury condominium projects. She concluded that from the sponsor's perspective, future competition is largely unknown, requiring an educated guess by the developer of the appropriate level of services and amenities to be provided at the building. Weitzman also noted that the demographic profile for potential purchasers in the luxury condominium submarket includes many foreign nationals, who are inherently high risk purchasers because their incomes and assets are often difficult to measure, and to reach. Both Weitzman and Martin stated, based upon research detailed in their affidavits, that the volatility of individual real estate transactions increases with the size of the unit involved, and that price swings for three-and four-bedroom units, such as the penthouse units plaintiffs sought to purchase here, were greater than for smaller apartments. * * *

The Order Appealed. * * * [T]he IAS court granted defendant partial summary judgment, finding that plaintiffs forfeited the portion of their down payment amounting to 10% of the purchase price, pursuant to Maxton Builders, Inc. v. Lo Galbo. The court held that the remainder of the down payment was subject to a liquidated damages analysis to determine whether it bore a reasonable relation to the sponsor's actual or probable loss. Defendant appeals from that portion of the order which denied it full relief.

Discussion. More than a century ago, the Court of Appeals, in Lawrence v. Miller, 86 N.Y. 131 [1881], held that a vendee who defaults on a real estate contract without lawful excuse cannot recover his or her down payment. It reaffirmed this holding in *Maxton* again in 1986. The facts of *Lawrence* are common to real estate transactions, and parallel those presented here. In that case, plaintiff made a $2000 down payment on the purchase of certain real estate, and then defaulted. The seller refused to extend plaintiff's time to perform the contract, retained the down payment, and ultimately sold the property to another purchaser. In plaintiff's subsequent action for a refund of the down payment, the Court of Appeals affirmed a judgment dismissing the complaint, stating:

> To allow a recovery of this money would be to sustain an action by a party on his own breach of his own contract, which the law does not allow. When we once declare in this case that the vendor has done all that the law asks of him, we also declare that the vendee has not so done on his part. And then to maintain this action would be to declare that a party may violate his agreement, and make an infraction of it by himself a cause of action. That would be ill doctrine.

For over a century, courts have consistently upheld what was called the *Lawrence* rule and recognized a distinction between real estate deposits and general liquidated damages clauses. Liquidated damages clauses have traditionally been subject to judicial oversight to confirm that the stipulated damages bear a reasonable proportion to the probable loss caused by the breach. By contrast, real estate down payments have been subject to limited supervision. They have only been refunded upon a showing of disparity of bargaining power between the parties, duress, fraud, illegality or mutual mistake. [citations]

In *Maxton,* plaintiff had contracted to sell defendants a house, and accepted a check for a 10% down payment. When defendants canceled the contract and placed a stop payment on the check, plaintiff sued for the down payment, citing the *Lawrence* rule. Defendants argued that plaintiff's recovery should be limited to its actual damages. In ruling for the vendor, the Court of Appeals identified two legal principles as flowing from *Lawrence.* First, that the vendor was entitled to retain the down payment in a real estate contract, without reference to his actual damages. Second, the "parent" rule, upon which the first rule was based, that one who breaches a contract may not recover the value of his part performance.

The Court noted that the parent rule had been substantially undermined in the 100 years since *Lawrence.* Many courts had rejected the parent rule because of criticism that it produced a forfeiture "and the amount of the forfeiture increases as performance proceeds, so that the penalty grows larger as the breach grows smaller."

The Court also noted that since *Lawrence,* the rule of allowing recovery of down payments of not more than 10% in real estate contracts continues to be followed by a "majority of jurisdictions," including in New York. Thereafter, the court noted the long and widespread reliance on the *Lawrence* rule in real estate transactions, and it concluded that, based upon notions of efficiency and avoiding unnecessary litigation, the rule should remain in effect.

After acknowledging that "[R]eal estate contracts are probably the best examples of arms length transactions," the Court broadly concluded:

> Except in cases where there is a real risk of overreaching, there should be no need for the courts to relieve the parties of the consequences of their contract. *If the parties are dissatisfied with the rule of [Lawrence], the time to say so is at the bargaining table.* [emphasis supplied].

The *Maxton/Lawrence* rule has since been followed by this Court as well as the other departments to deny a refund of a down payment when a default has occurred. [citations] Further, other departments have specifically applied the *Maxton/Lawrence* rule, where, as here, a real estate down payment of greater than 10% of the purchase price is at issue. [citations include a 50% down payment and a 23% down payment].

In [one] case, the Third Department upheld the forfeiture, on default, of payments approximating 50% of the purchase price for certain real estate. Here, plaintiffs and the IAS court try to distinguish that case by asserting that the holding there was based on the fact that plaintiffs' payments were made in consideration for extensions of time to perform the contract. The Third Department did not rest its holding on that fact; rather it wrote:

> defendant is entitled to retain all monies it received from plaintiff, whether viewed as consideration for the extensions of time granted by defendant to complete performance of the contract or additional deposits made on the contract as a matter of law (see Maxton Bldrs. v. Lo Galbo; Lawrence v. Miller). * * *

[I]t is clear that plaintiffs are not entitled to a return of any portion of their down payment. Here the 25% down payment was a specifically negotiated element of the contracts. There is no question that this was an arm's length transaction. The parties were sophisticated business people, represented by counsel, who spent two months at the bargaining table before executing the amended purchase agreements.

Further, the record evidences that it is customary in the pre-construction luxury condominium industry for parties to price the risk of default at 25% of the purchase price. The purchase agreements included a detailed non-refundable down payment clause to which plaintiffs' counsel had negotiated a specific amendment. That amendment allowed for the payment of 25% of the purchase price in three installments: 10% at contract, an additional 7½% twelve months later, and a final 7½% eighteen months later. Clearly, plaintiffs were fully aware of and accepted the requirement of a non-refundable 25% down payment for these luxury pre-construction condominiums. In fact, Cem Uzan has purchased two other condominiums, one in the same building, with similar down payment provisions.

Plaintiffs negotiated the payment of the 25% down payments in installments to spread their risk over time. In the event of a severe economic downturn, plaintiffs were free to cancel the deal, capping their losses at the amount paid as of the date of their default. For the sponsor, the 25% deposit served to cover its risk for keeping the apartments off the market should the purchaser default.

Finally, there was no evidence of a disparity of bargaining power, or of duress, fraud, illegality or mutual mistake by the parties in drafting the down payment clause of the purchase agreements. The detailed provision concerning the non-refundable deposit was integral to the transaction. If plaintiffs were dissatisfied with the 25% non-refundable down payment provision in the purchase agreements, the time to have voiced objection was at the bargaining table (*see Maxton*). Because they chose to accept it, they are committed to its terms. Thus, upon plaintiffs' default and failure to cure, defendant was entitled to retain the full 25% down payments. * * *

The Clerk is directed to enter judgment in favor of defendant-appellant dismissing the complaint as against it. * * *

All concur.

Note

1. *"You're Forfeited!"* Does the New York rule for a buyer's breach of a land contract follow the penalty rule? Does it implement the economic analysis summarized before the decision? Would it be accurate to say that the buyers paid for an option to complete the deal at the price negotiated and set in the contract? Robert E. Scott & George Triantis, Embedded Options and the Case Against Compensation in Contract Law, 104 Colum. L.Rev. 1428, 1435, 1481 (2004).

2. Does the *Uzan* court succeed in distinguishing land contracts from other contracts?

3. *Specific Performance.* If the units' value had appreciated, the buyers might have completed their contracts and resold the units to other buyers. Supposing that the units' values declined, if the seller-developer had sought specific performance, should the court have granted it?

4. *The Legislature's Role.* Since 1881, the New York Court of Appeals has adhered to the rule that a purchaser who defaults on a real estate contract without lawful excuse cannot recover a down payment. When the Court of Appeals reaffirmed the rule in Maxton Builders v. Lo Galbo, it observed that the legislature had failed to adopt proposals to change the rule. Was the court correct to punt this issue to the legislature?

5. *Where Are the Condos Now?* The Uzans were accused of being fraudsters on a gargantuan scale. For litigation involving a $2 billion judgment, RICO, fraud, a constructive trust and a turnover order, contempt, punitive damages, piercing 130 corporate veils, and injunctions in three nations, see Motorola Credit Corp. v. Uzan, 388 F.3d 39 (2d Cir. 2004). Finally, with the Uzan brothers absent, "on the lam," their Trump World Tower condos were auctioned off by creditors, Motorola and Nokia, to collect a judgment for nearly $3 billion for defaulted loans. The Washington Post, November 11, 2004 at C1.

6. *No Second Look.* The next case takes up the choice between two approaches to the penalty rule which we will call the "second look" rule and the "single look" rule.

KELLY v. MARX

Supreme Judicial Court of Massachusetts, 1999.
428 Mass. 877, 705 N.E.2d 1114.

IRELAND, J. John E. and Pamela B. Kelly (plaintiffs) commenced this action in the Superior Court in November, 1994, seeking to recover funds that they had paid to Steven A. and Merrill S. Marx (defendants) as a deposit for the purchase of the defendants' property. Both parties filed cross motions for summary judgment. The Superior Court judge granted the motion of the defendants after concluding they were entitled to the deposit because the liquidated damages clause in their agreement was enforceable.

The Appeals Court, in a two-to-one decision, reversed the judgment and ordered the deposit returned to the plaintiffs. Under the "second look" doctrine, contained in Shapiro v. Grinspoon, 27 Mass.App.Ct. 596, 604, 541 N.E.2d 359 (1989), the court reached this conclusion by examining both the circumstances at the time of contract formation *and* the actual damages suffered by the parties when the breach occurred. The court concluded that the defendants were not entitled to keep the deposit because they suffered no actual damages, and, therefore, liquidated damages would serve as a penalty and not as compensation for a loss. We granted the defendants' application for further appellate review, and now affirm the Superior Court judgment.

Facts. On March 18, 1994, the plaintiffs signed an offer to purchase residential real estate in Worcester for $355,000 from the defendants. The defendants accepted the offer, and the plaintiffs gave $1,000 to the defendants as a partial deposit. By early May, 1994, the parties executed a purchase and sale agreement (agreement). Clause eighteen of the agreement read: "If the BUYER shall fail to fulfill the BUYER'S agreements herein, all deposits made hereunder by the BUYER shall be retained by the SELLER as liquidated damages." The plaintiffs provided a deposit of $16,750 to the defendants once the agreement was signed, bringing their total deposit to $17,750, five per cent of the purchase price. The offer set September 1, 1994, as the closing date.

The plaintiffs never purchased the property. On August 9, 1994, they notified the defendants in writing to put the house back on the market because they were unable to sell their current home. On August 24, 1994, the defendants accepted the offer of other prospective buyers to purchase, and then signed a purchase and sale agreement with them on September 8, 1994. The new buyers purchased the property for $360,000 on September 20, 1994.

Discussion. We affirm the decision of the Superior Court because we reject the "second look" approach, and conclude that a liquidated damages clause in a purchase and sale agreement will be enforced where, at the time the agreement was made, potential damages were difficult to determine and the clause was a reasonable forecast of damages expected to occur in the event of a breach.

The Appeals Court, in deciding whether to allow liquidated damages, relied on the three-step analysis described in the *Shapiro* case. "[T]he judge should first determine whether the actual damages to the [sellers] are difficult to ascertain. If they are, in view of the reasonableness of the forecast of those damages, the liquidated damages provision should be enforced. If not, he should consider whether [the amount designated as liquidated damages] is so 'unreasonably and grossly disproportionate' to, or is 'unconscionably excessive' of, the actual damages caused by the breach so as to make the liquidated damages a penalty. Finally, if the judge determines that the liquidated damages provision is unenforceable, and that the [sellers'] losses exceed the difference between the contract price and the saleable value of the property at the time of breach, he should award to the defendants the amount of actual damages." Kelly v. Marx, quoting Shapiro v. Grinspoon.

First, the Appeals Court noted that potential damages were "within the ordinary range for a real estate purchase and sale agreement," and "difficult to predict at the time of contracting." Next, however, the court examined the agreement in light of the actual damages at the time of the breach, and concluded that liquidated damages were inappropriate because they would punish the plaintiffs, not compensate the defendants, who suffered no loss from the plaintiffs' breach.

Liquidated damages clauses which provide for the seller of real estate to retain the buyer's deposit are recognized in Massachusetts, [citation], and, as both parties concede here and the Appeals Court concluded, they are a common real estate practice. The question before us is whether enforceability of a liquidated damages clause is to be tested by analyzing the circumstances at contract formation, the prospective or "single look" approach, or when the breach occurs, the retrospective or "second look" approach.

This question has created confusion in our courts, and originates from ambiguous language in the leading, most recent case of this court on liquidated damages in the context of the purchase and sale of real property, A-Z Servicenter, Inc. v. Segall, 334 Mass. 672, 675, 138 N.E.2d 266 (1956). Many decisions, following *A-Z Servicenter,* have concluded that liquidated damages should be measured, first, by assessing the reasonableness of the liquidated damages in light of the parties' ability to anticipate damages at contract formation, and, second, against the actual damages resulting from the breach. This was evident, most notably, in the *Shapiro* case, on which the Appeals Court relied and which contained a three-step analysis based on the *Shapiro* court's interpretation of the *A-Z Servicenter* opinion.

The *Shapiro* court found support for its conclusion from the Restatement (Second) of Contracts § 356 comment b, illustration 4 (1981). The Appeals Court noted that the illustration demonstrates liquidated damages could be unenforceable if the nonbreaching party does not suffer a loss. "Illustration 4 describes a situation in which a contractor's delay in constructing a race track grandstand caused no loss because the owner was not permitted to operate during the period of delay. It states: 'Since the actual loss to [the owner] is not difficult to prove, [the contractor's promise to pay $1,000 for each day of delay] is a term providing for a penalty and is unenforceable on grounds of public policy.'" Kelly v. Marx. We disagree with the Restatement's illustration. It contradicts the express language of § 356(1), which permits liquidated damages where the agreement is "reasonable in light of the anticipated *or* actual loss" (emphasis added). In the illustration, the liquidated damages were reasonable in light of the owners' anticipated or potential loss, and, therefore, should have been enforced.

We agree with the dissenting Justice and the decisions of many other States, [citation] that a judge, in determining the enforceability of a liquidated damages clause, should examine only the circumstances at contract formation. Kelly v. Marx, (Spina, J., dissenting). Our position is that "[w]here actual damages are difficult to ascertain and where the sum agreed upon by the parties at the time of the execution of the contract represents a reasonable estimate of the actual damages, such a contract will be enforced." A-Z Servicenter, Inc. v. Segall. Liquidated damages will not be enforced if the sum is "grossly disproportionate to a reasonable estimate of actual damages" made at the time of contract formation. Lynch v. Andrew, 20 Mass.App.Ct. 623, 627, 628 481 N.E.2d 1383 (1985).

This approach most accurately matches the expectations of the parties, who negotiated a liquidated damage amount that was fair to each side based on their unique concerns and circumstances surrounding the agreement, and their individual estimate of damages in event of a breach. We agree with the reasoning of the dissenting Justice, who pointed out that the "'second look' reveals nothing that the parties had not contemplated" when they entered their contract. Kelly v. Marx, (Spina, J., dissenting).

In addition to meeting the parties' expectations, the "single look" approach helps resolve disputes efficiently by making it unnecessary to wait until actual damages from a breach are proved. By reducing challenges to a liquidated damages clause, the "single look" approach eliminates uncertainty and tends to prevent costly future litigation. The "second look," by contrast, undermines the "peace of mind and certainty of result," the parties sought when they contracted for liquidated damages. It increases the potential for litigation by inviting the aggrieved party to attempt to show evidence of damage when the contract is breached, or, more accurately, evidence of damage flowing from the breach but occurring sometime afterward. * * *

The plaintiffs argue that application of a "second look" approach would allow the court to guard against undue windfalls, such as the one the defendants would receive here if they were to keep the deposit, because the defendants suffered no loss from the breach of the sale. We disagree. In essence, the plaintiffs want to undo the agreement between the parties, who expect to receive stipulated damages, not damages resolved by a court examining postbreach circumstances. The parties agreed to the extent of their damages when they agreed on a liquidated damages clause. "[T]he proper course is to enforce contracts according to their plain meaning and not to undertake to be wiser than the parties, and therefore that in general when parties say that a sum is payable as liquidated damages they will be taken to mean what they say and will be held to their word." Guerin v. Stacey, 175 Mass. 595, 597, 56 N.E. 892 (1900) (Holmes, C.J.).

Turning to the present case, we conclude the plaintiffs are not entitled to the return of the deposit they paid to the defendants. The potential damages were difficult to predict when the agreement was made. * * *

Viewing the facts at the time of contract formation, the liquidated damages were a reasonable estimate of the damage to the defendants. The deposit, five per cent of the purchase price, was a reasonable forecast of the defendants' losses that would result if the buyers were to breach the agreement. These costs could arise from a host of issues relating to finding another buyer and waiting for an uncertain period of time before selling their property, and in light of the risk of an undeterminable loss that is dependant on many factors (primarily the shape of the real estate market at the time of the breach). The sum is not grossly disproportionate to the expected damages arising from a breach of the sale agreement, nor is it "unconscionably excessive" so as to be defeated as a matter of public policy. See A-Z Servicenter, Inc. v. Segall.

Cf. Security Safety Corp. v. Kuznicki, 350 Mass. 157, 213 N.E.2d 866 (1966) (liquidated damages providing for penalty of one-third of contract price unreasonable and unenforceable as a matter of law). We reiterate our view that "[a] term fixing unreasonably large liquidated damages is unenforceable on grounds of public policy as a penalty." Restatement (Second) of Contracts, § 356(1).

As the Appeals Court conceded, "Were our inquiry limited to the circumstances obtaining at the time the parties entered into their agreement, we would permit the sellers to retain the deposit, amounting to five percent of the purchase price." Kelly v. Marx.

Judgment of the Superior Court affirmed.

Note

1. Both § 356 of the second Restatement of Contracts and U.C.C. § 2–718(1) follow the "second-look" doctrine.

2. *The Choice.* The 1993 edition of a leading treatise on property, Roger Cunningham, William Stoebuck, & Dale Whitman, The Law of Property § 10.4 (2d ed. 1993), discussed the choice between the single look and the second look rules:

> The traditional view called for testing the reasonableness of the liquidated damages clause as of the time the contract was formed. Courts have often felt

uncomfortable with this approach in cases in which the property's market value has risen sharply after contracting and before breach, so that the seller has little actual damages or none at all; an estimate of damages which was reasonable when made may sometimes turn out to be a gross exaggeration. More recent cases display a willingness to take this factor into account, and to refuse enforcement of the forfeiture if it would result in a large windfall to the vendor in fact. Note that the very fact that issues of reasonableness of amount, difficulty of estimation, and the like are pertinent and litigable in itself destroys much of the supposed advantage of liquidated damages clauses—their extra-judicial operation. With respect to the question of how great a gap the courts will tolerate between actual damages and the liquidated amount, the cases are much too variable to generalize, but unusually large earnest money deposits are commonly recoverable by purchasers. The ironic result is that the vendor who was piggish may end up with only actual damages, and only after being put to the trouble of proving them in court.

The later edition of the treatise adds a half sentence that endorses the single-look doctrine: "others, more logically, hold that a deposit that was reasonable when made can be retained even if the vendor has no damages at all." The treatise's footnote cites Kelly v. Marx and observes that "the cases are about evenly divided." William Stoebuck & Dale Whitman, Property § 10.4 and 735, n.9 (3d ed. 2000).

If the courts are split and scholarly treatise writers change their minds between editions, can't we say something for both sides. Add *Uzan*, which may stand for no look at all. No look, single-look, second-look, which is best?

3. *Uzan v. 845 UN* and *Kelly v. Marx* could be in the buyer's remedies part of this chapter because the buyers are suing the sellers to recover their earnest money deposits. The decisions are with seller's remedies because of the question, whether, after buyer's breach, the seller can enforce the liquidated damages clauses.

Since the buyers have breached their contracts, they cannot sue the sellers for a contract remedy. The court mentions almost in passing, but does not emphasize, that the buyers had breached the contract. Remember the New York courts' approach in *Uzan?* Should the courts have examined whether a decision to grant affirmative relief to a buyer who has breached a contract encourages other buyers to breach their contracts?

4. *Restitution.* Does the court in *Kelly v. Marx* use the word "restitution"? By one way of looking at it, the buyers are suing the seller for restitution—to prevent the seller's unjust enrichment that would result if she kept their deposit. The court mentions this under the buyers' argument against the seller's "windfall." Should the court have asked whether the seller's unjust enrichment would follow if the seller retained the buyer's down payment? Under the court's approach, a seller would be unjustly enriched only if enforcing a liquidated damages clause would result in a "penalty."

5. *Life After a Second Look.* Justice Ellen Peters's opinion in *Vines v. Orchard Hills* is quoted below. How does *Vines* differ from *Kelly v. Marx?* Which approach is better?

"When the purchasers contracted to buy their condominium in July, 1973, they paid $7880, a sum which the contract of sale designated as liquidated damages. The purchasers decided not to take title to the condominium because Euel D. Vines was transferred by his employer to New Jersey; the Vines so informed the seller by a letter dated January 4, 1974. There has never been any claim that the seller has failed, in any respect, to conform to his obligations under the contract, nor does the complaint allege that the purchasers are legally excused from their performance under the contract. In short, it is the purchasers and not the seller whose breach precipitated the present cause of action.

"In the proceedings below, the purchasers established that the value of the condominium that they had agreed to buy for $78,800 in 1973 had, by the time of the trial in 1979, a fair market value of $160,000. The trial court relied on this figure to conclude that, because the seller had gained what it characterized as a windfall of approximately $80,000, the purchasers were entitled to recover their down payment of $7880. Neither the purchasers nor the seller proffered any evidence at the trial to show the market value of the condominium at the time of the purchasers' breach of their contract or the damages sustained by the seller as a result of that breach.

"The ultimate issue on this appeal is the enforceability of a liquidated damages clause as a defense to a claim of restitution by purchasers in default on a land sale contract. [The court rejected the seller's argument that buyers who had breached were disqualified for restitution.] * * *

"We therefore conclude that a purchaser whose breach is not willful has a restitutionary claim to recover moneys paid that unjustly enrich his seller. In this case, no one has alleged that the purchasers' breach, arising out of a transfer to a more distant place of employment, should be deemed to have been willful. * * *

"The purchaser's right to recover in restitution requires the purchaser to establish that the seller has been unjustly enriched. The purchaser must show more than that the contract has come to an end and that the seller retains moneys paid pursuant to the contract. To prove unjust enrichment, in the ordinary case, the purchaser, because he is the party in breach, must prove that the damages suffered by his seller are less than the moneys received from the purchaser. It may not be easy for the purchaser to prove the extent of the seller's damages, it may even be strategically advantageous for the seller to come forward with relevant evidence of the losses he has incurred and may expect to incur on account of the buyer's breach. Nonetheless, only if the breaching party satisfies his burden of proof that the innocent party has sustained a net gain may a claim for unjust enrichment be sustained.

"In the case before us, the parties themselves stipulated in the contract of sale that the purchasers' down payment of 10 percent of the purchase price represents the damages that would be likely to flow from the purchasers' breach. The question then becomes whether the purchasers have demonstrated the seller's unjust enrichment in the face of the liquidated damages clause to which they agreed. * * *"

"Most of the litigation concerning liquidated damages clauses arises in the context of an affirmative action by the party injured by breach to enforce the clause in order to recover the amount therein stipulated. In such cases, the burden of persuasion about the enforceability of the clause naturally rests with its proponent. [citations] In the case before us, by contrast, where the plaintiffs are themselves in default, the plaintiffs bear the burden of showing that the clause is invalid and unenforceable. [citations] It is not unreasonable in these circumstances to presume that a liquidated damages clause that is appropriately limited in amount bears a reasonable relationship to the damages that the seller has actually suffered. [citations] The seller's damages, as Professor Palmer points out, include not only his expectation damages suffered through loss of his bargain, and his incidental damages such as broker's commissions, but also less quantifiable costs arising out of retention of real property beyond the time of the originally contemplated sale. 1 Palmer, Restitution §§ 5.4, 5.8 (1978). [citations] A liquidated damages clause allowing the seller to retain 10 percent of the contract price as earnest money is presumptively a reasonable allocation of the risks associated with default."

"The presumption of validity that attaches to a clause liquidating the seller's damages at 10 percent of the contract price in the event of the purchaser's unexcused nonperformance is, like most of the presumptions, rebuttable. The purchaser, despite his default, is free to prove that the contract, or any part thereof, was the product of fraud or mistake or unconscionability. In the alternative, the purchaser is free to offer evidence that this breach in fact caused the seller no damages or damages substantially less than the amount stipulated as liquidated damages. * * *"

"The relevant time at which to measure the seller's damages is the time of breach. [citations] Benefits to the seller that are attributable to a rising market subsequent to breach rightfully accrue to the seller. There was no evidence before the court to demonstrate that the seller was not injured at the time of the purchasers' breach by their failure then to consummate the contract. Neither the seller's status as a developer of a condominium project nor the absence of willfulness on the part of the purchasers furnishes a justification for disregarding the liquidated damages clause, although these factors may play some role in the ultimate determination of whether the seller was in fact unjustly enriched by the down payment he retained."

"Because the availability of, and the limits on, restitutionary claims by a plaintiff in default have not previously been clearly spelled out in our cases, it is appropriate to afford to the purchasers herein another opportunity to proffer evidence to substantiate their claim. What showing the purchasers must make cannot be spelled out with specificity in view of the sparsity of the present record. The purchasers may be able to demonstrate that the condominium could, at the time of their breach, have been resold at a price sufficiently higher than their contract price to obviate any loss of profits and to compensate the seller for any incidental and consequential damages. Alternatively, the purchasers may be able to present evidence of unconscionability or of excuse, to avoid the applicability of the liquidated damages clause altogether. The plaintiffs' burden of proof is not an easy one to sustain, but they are entitled to their day in court." Vines v. Orchard Hills, Inc., 181 Conn. 501, 435 A.2d 1022, 1025–1029 (1980).

D. SELLER'S RESTITUTION

WELLSTON COAL CO. v. FRANKLIN PAPER CO.

Supreme Court of Ohio, 1897.
57 Ohio St. 182, 48 N.E. 888.

MINSHALL, J. * * * On August 7, 1890, plaintiff and defendant made a written contract, by which defendant, for the term of one year, agreed to take its entire supply of coal from plaintiff at the rate of $1.90 per ton of 2,000 pounds, on the cars at Franklin, Ohio, which, after deducting freight, would net the plaintiff $1 per ton. The demand for such coal was greater during the late fall and winter months of each year, when plaintiff's business would be active, and less during the spring and summer months, at which times its business would be dull. The sum of $1 per ton for the coal was the market price, outside of freight charges, for coal of the kind mentioned in the contract, during the summer of 1890, and at the time the contract was made. Plaintiff and defendant were familiar with the ups and downs of the coal trade, and knew that the market price of such coal would be higher during the fall and winter months; and they both understood that defendant would require, for its manufacturing operations during the entire period covered by the contract, a large amount of such coal, which, taken by defendant during all the year covered by the contract, would give plaintiff an assured sale for this amount of coal during the dull season. Such contracts for the year's supply of coal were usually made by manufacturers with coal shippers during the summer, and were advantageous to both parties.

These facts were known to both plaintiff and defendant, who contracted with reference to them; and plaintiff would not have made the contract whereby it agreed to supply coal during the fall and winter months at the contract price, which would be less than the then market prices, except for the fact that it would supply the defendant coal at the same price for the balance of the year, when the price would be about the same as the contract price, and, the demand then being small, it would not otherwise be able to sell the coal. During the month of September, 1890, the market price of this coal, outside of freight charges, was $1.05 per ton; and from October 1, 1890, to February 1, 1891, such market price was $1.15 per ton. After February, during the rest of the year covered by the contract, the market price was the same as the contract price. During the period of time from August 1, 1890, to May 13, 1891, when the contract was broken by the defendant, plaintiff furnished defendant, during September and October, 1890, in all, 2,562½ tons of coal, for which it was paid the contract price; while, if the same coal had been sold at the market prices when delivered, plaintiff would have received $333 more for it. About May 13, 1891, defendant wrongfully broke the contract, and refused to take any more coal from plaintiff. The contract did not bind the defendant to take any specified quantity of coal per month, but the average number of tons per month taken before the contract was broken, was 434¼ tons; and, if it had continued to take coal under the contract at the same average number of tons for the balance of May and the months June and July, the plaintiff would have made a total profit for that time, under the contract, of $304.22.

The question is as to the measure of damages to which the plaintiff is entitled in a case like this. It, as before stated, is not on the contract, but for the value of the coal delivered at the market price, before the contract was wrongfully terminated by the defendant, less what had been paid therefor; i.e., the contract price. The plaintiff requested the court to charge the jury that it was entitled to recover, for the coal delivered prior to the repudiation of the contract by the defendant, its market value when the deliveries were made, and is not limited to the price specified in the contract. This the court refused to do, and directed the jury to find a verdict for the plaintiff for nominal damages only. The general rule is that, when full performance of a contract has been prevented by the wrongful act of the defendant, the plaintiff has the right either to sue for damages, or he may disregard the contract, and sue as upon a quantum meruit for what he has performed. The plaintiff has pursued the latter course; and it seems well settled, both in reason and authority, that he had the right to do so. * * *

But it is claimed, on the authority of Doolittle v. McCullough, 12 Ohio St. 360, that the contract price must still be the measure of the plaintiff's recovery. There are many expressions in the opinion in that case that seem to support this view, and much of the reasoning is to the same effect. But all that is there said must be taken as said with reference to the facts of that case. The rule there stated may be regarded as a proper one in a case where, as in that case, it appears from the claim of the plaintiff that the breach of the contract by the defendant worked no loss, but a benefit to him, on the ground, as appears that, had he been required to complete the work, he would have suffered a much greater loss; for, if the least inexpensive part of the work could not have been done without loss, it follows that the doing of the remaining part, under the contract, would have resulted in a still greater loss. The action upon a quantum meruit is of equitable origin, and is still governed by considerations of natural justice. Hence, when one has performed labor or furnished material under a contract that is wrongfully terminated by the other party before completion, the question arises whether the party not in fault should be confined to the contract for what he did, or to a quantum meruit; and this must depend upon whether the act of the other party in terminating the contract works a loss or not to him, regard being had to the contract. If it works no loss, but is in fact a benefit, as in the case of Doolittle v. McCullough, there are no considerations of justice requiring that he should be compensated in a greater sum for what he did than is stipulated in the contract. These considerations exercised a controlling influence in the case just referred to. The plaintiff had a contract with the defendant for the making of certain excavations in the construction of a railroad. He was to receive for the entire work 11 cents per cubic yard. He had performed the least inexpensive part of the work when the contract was wrongfully terminated by the defendant; and on this part, by his own showing, he had suffered a loss. The proof showed that the performance of the remainder, being hardpan, would have cost him a great deal more. It was then evident, as the court observed, that he had sustained no loss, but a benefit, from the termination of the contract by the defendant. But in the case before us the facts are very different. They are in fact just the reverse. The contract was for the delivery of coal at a price generally received during the dullest season of the whole year. The defendant received the coal during the season when the market was above the contract price. He had the benefit of the difference between the market and the contract price; but when the dull season arrived, and the advantages of the contract would accrue to the plaintiff, the defendant repudiated it. The difference between the two cases is thus apparent. In the case before us, justice and fair dealing require that the defendant, having repudiated the contract, should pay the market price for the coal at the time it was delivered. In the former case, as the repudiation of the contract by the defendant did not enrich him to the loss of the plaintiff, there were no considerations of justice on which the plaintiff could claim more than the contract price for what he had done under the contract. The object in allowing a recovery of this kind is not to better the condition of the plaintiff under the contract, were it performed, but to save him from a loss resulting from its wrongful termination by the defendant, or, in more general words, to prevent the defendant from enriching himself at the expense of the plaintiff by his own wrongful act. The real test in all cases of a plaintiff's right to recover as upon a quantum meruit for part performance of a contract, wrongfully terminated by the defendant, depends upon the consideration whether the defendant is thereby enriched at the loss and expense of the plaintiff. If so, then the law adds a legal to the moral obligation, and enforces it. And, while the action is not on the contract itself, yet it is so far kept in view as to preclude a recovery by the plaintiff where he would necessarily have lost more by performing the contract, for the consideration agreed upon, than he did by being prevented from doing so. In this view, the case of Doolittle v. McCullough was rightly decided, and, when limited to its facts, may well stand as authority in all similar cases. Judgment of the circuit court and that of the common pleas reversed, and cause remanded for a new trial.

Notes

1. *Full Performance Rule.* If the buyer breaches after the seller has delivered, that is performed in full, and the buyer's only remaining performance is to pay, then a court will decline to grant restitution to the seller. The seller's action to recover the price from the breaching buyer protects the seller's expectancy fully. U.C.C. § 2–709; Restatement (Second) of Contracts § 373(a) (1981).

But when the buyer breaches after part performance, the seller may seek restitution.

2. *Restitution Under the Uniform Commercial Code?* Do the U.C.C.'s comprehensive remedial provisions for the seller omit the seller's remedy of rescinding the contract followed by recovering money restitution based on the buyer's unjust enrichment? Does a seller need rescission-restitution? Original U.C.C. § 2–703: "Where the buyer * * * repudiates with respect to a part, * * * the aggrieved seller may * * * (f) cancel." In dealing with deeds, many courts have used "cancel" and "cancellation" as synonyms for "rescind" and "rescission." If, in the U.C.C., "cancel" means rescind, then does restitution follow?

3. *Seller's Options?* Assuming restitution is available to the seller, to determine whether a seller needs rescission-restitution, ask whether the seller's other U.C.C. remedies are responsive to Wellston Coal's needs. See §§ 2–709, 2–706, and 2–708(1). Although § 2–708(2) was as yet unborn in 1897, if § 2–708(2) had been available to Wellston Coal, would it have provided the coal seller with a satisfactory recovery?

4. The court states an exception: when the seller would have lost from the unperformed part of the breached contract, its restitution is limited to the contract price. Why not, if the buyer breaches, allow a seller to measure its restitution by market value even when market value exceeds the contract price?

The court in *Algernon Blair*, a decision in the next chapter, refuses to let the breaching defendant use the price in the contract it repudiated to cap the plaintiff's recovery of restitution; under that approach, a seller could recover higher restitution based on market value than the price set in the contract.

5. *The Language of Restitution.* Historically, a plaintiff filed quantum meruit to recover for services; plaintiffs used another common count, quantum valebant, to recover for goods "sold and delivered." But in *Wellston Coal*, the court refers the seller's remedy as quantum meruit. Do you now agree that quantum meruit is an extraordinarily protean remedy? So too the constructive trust. Witness the following constructive trust decision where the plaintiff is a grantee that the court treats like a seller.

goto
686

DIETZ v. DIETZ

Supreme Court of Minnesota, 1955.
244 Minn. 330, 70 N.W.2d 281.

DELL, CHIEF JUSTICE. Action for an accounting and to recover real estate conveyed to plaintiff and defendant Donald Dietz in joint tenancy in consideration for an oral agreement to support. Said defendant appeals from an order denying his motion for a new trial.

Plaintiff, 69 years old at the time of trial is the mother of the defendant Donald Dietz (hereinafter referred to as the defendant). The trial court found, among others, the following facts: After the death of plaintiff's husband in 1942, the defendant, who had considerable business experience, took charge of plaintiff's assets and acted as her financial advisor. In May 1944 the defendant, who was then unmarried, entered into an oral agreement with the plaintiff to the effect that he would support her for the remainder of her life if she would purchase a certain duplex and have title conveyed to him and plaintiff as joint tenants. In reliance upon this promise, the plaintiff purchased the property and caused it to be conveyed to herself and the defendant as joint tenants. Plaintiff paid $5,200 for the property from her own funds, the balance of the purchase price consisting of a mortgage in the amount of $4,800.

The defendant categorically denied making an oral promise to support the plaintiff and testified that the money used to purchase the property in question was his. Plaintiff and defendant occupied the lower duplex of this property until his marriage to the defendant Virginia Dietz in March 1946. After the marriage the defendant and Virginia made their home with the plaintiff in the lower duplex. A strained relationship developed between plaintiff and Virginia and, according to plaintiff, on one occasion Virginia attempted to strike her with a scrub cloth. The disharmony between the parties was evidenced by several other incidents, including periods of time when plaintiff and Virginia did not speak to each other. Finally plaintiff testified that in March 1950 she asked defendant whether she might have her breakfast and was told that she could not have anything to eat in the house "now or at any time" and further that there was no need for her to stay there to protect her rights and that defendant wanted her to get out. * * * Plaintiff left the house that day and went to live with her sister. Neither the defendant nor his wife made any attempt to stop her nor thereafter made any inquiries as to her welfare or provisions for her support.

On the basis of the above evidence the court found that the defendant had breached his oral promise to support the plaintiff. An accounting of the equities of the parties, which is not disputed here, was made taking into consideration, among other things, the rents collected by the defendants, the reasonable value of his use of the premises, expenditures incurred by him, and the reasonable value of his services. Judgment was ordered in favor of the plaintiff for $1,651.48 with interest and awarding her possession and title of the premises free of any claim or interest by the defendants. * * *

The remainder of defendant's arguments are to the general effect that plaintiff is not entitled to recover since parol evidence cannot be used to establish an express trust, create a condition subsequent or otherwise vary the terms of a deed. It is clear, as defendant suggests, that, under the provisions of our statute, a purchase-money resulting trust could not arise in favor of the plaintiff. It is equally well settled that, as a general rule, an express trust in land must be in writing in order to be enforceable. The plaintiff, however, does not contend that she is entitled to relief on either of these theories. Nor is the plaintiff attempting to vary the terms of the deed by creating a condition subsequent. A condition subsequent, as opposed to a conditional limitation or a mere covenant is sometimes found to have been created where a deed, given in consideration for a promise to support, contains language evidencing the obligation. There is no such language in the deed here. A few courts notably those of Wisconsin, have treated the agreement to support, whether oral or in writing, as an "equitable condition subsequent," and have implied the condition in the conveyance even though the deed is absolute in form. [citations] In such a case the grantor may, upon breach of the condition, exercise his right of reentry or rescind and have the conveyance cancelled as if the condition had been incorporated in the deed. In Bruer v. Bruer, 109 Minn. 260, 123 N.W. 813, we approved of the general result reached by the Wisconsin court but held that in the absence of express language in the deed, a condition subsequent could not be implied.[1]

The plaintiff's right of recovery, however, is not dependent upon an implied condition subsequent. As the trial court indicated in its memorandum, recovery was allowed on the theory of an "implied or constructive trust." Apparently defendant has misconceived the nature and character of a constructive trust. It is an equitable remedy imposed to prevent unjust enrichment and is completely dissimilar to an express or resulting trust. Because it arises by operation of law rather than being dependent upon the intention of the parties, it is expressly exempted from the statute of fraud.

* * * We have held that a constructive trust may be imposed where the plaintiff shows "the existence of a fiduciary relation and the abuse by defendant of confidence and trust bestowed under it to plaintiff's harm." It is clear, however, that a fiduciary relationship in a strict sense is not a prerequisite, and any relationship giving rise to justifiable reliance or confidence is sufficient. Not only were the parties here parent and child but the evidence amply supports the conclusion that plaintiff relied upon her son for business advice and counsel. We have previously held that such a relationship is of a confidential nature and fiduciary character. It is equally clear that the defendant was unjustly enriched as a result of his abuse of this confidential relationship.

[Discussion of the Statute of Frauds issue is omitted.]

It is well settled in this state that rescission and cancellation may be decreed in actions brought by the grantor where the grantee fails to furnish the support as agreed in consideration for the conveyance. The instant case, however, appears to be novel in this state in that the relief sought is not by a grantor but by a grantee who supplied the purchase money and caused the property to be placed in joint tenancy. * * * The equities of the instant case are * * * apparent. Under the circumstances the trial court was amply justified in restoring the property to the plaintiff and awarding her judgment for the amount due her under the accounting.

Affirmed.

III. REVIEW—BUYER'S SPECIFIC PERFORMANCE REVISITED

BANDER v. GROSSMAN

New York Supreme Court, 1994.
161 Misc.2d 119, 611 N.Y.S.2d 985.

DIANE A. LEBEDEFF, JUSTICE. Following a jury trial on a claim that the defendant, a sports car dealer, repudiated plaintiff's contract to purchase a rare Astin–Martin automobile, plaintiff moves for judgment on its alternative request for monetary specific performance in the form of a judgment approximately ten times greater than the breach of contract damages awarded by the jury. In

---

1. [Footnote renumbered.] The Wisconsin theory has not generally been followed elsewhere. [citations] Since right of re-entry for breach of condition subsequent can be reserved only to the grantor, Fraser, Future Interests, Uses and Trusts in Minnesota, 28 M.S.A. pp. 53,

58, the question arises whether even under the broad Wisconsin view the plaintiff, as a grantee, could assert the fiction of a constructive condition subsequent and thereby affect the quality of the estate conveyed.

opposition, defendant moves to set aside the breach of contract jury verdict in favor of plaintiff. Both motions are consolidated for purposes of this decision.

Because the complaint presented a mixture of legal and equitable claims, a single trial was held with jury consideration limited to issues related to the legal claim. [citations] On one factual issue relevant to the equitable claim, the uniqueness of the vehicle, the jury was instructed on the applicable law and issued an advisory verdict. The jury found, on the facts, that the automobile was unique.

The attack on the verdict requires an amplification of the underlying facts. In the summer of 1987, plaintiff looked for a sports car to purchase for interim personal use and to sell when the price rose (a practice in which he had previously engaged). The defendant had in his inventory the subject 1965 DB5 Astin–Martin convertible with left hand drive. Plaintiff learned this particular model was one of only twenty in existence, with only forty having been made, although those twenty cars seem to turn over with more frequency than their number might suggest. Plaintiff testified he thought the car was undervalued, based upon his knowledge of sports car prices, and anticipated a price rise. A contract of sale was reached with a purchase price of $40,000, with plaintiff depositing $5,000.

The commercial agreement proceeded to unwind thereafter. The dealer could not obtain the title documents from the wholesaler from whom he had agreed to purchase the vehicle; the deposition testimony of the out-of-state wholesaler was read into evidence and confirmed that the title had been misplaced. The defendant did not transmit this explanation to plaintiff, but instead told a story about problems of getting title from a different individual. In August of 1987, the defendant attempted to return the deposit, but advised that he would continue to try to resolve the title problems. Plaintiff pursued the purchase until, ultimately, in December of 1987, plaintiff's lawyer wrote defendant that the contract had been breached and plaintiff would commence litigation. However, no further action was taken by plaintiff until this case was commenced in 1989, four months after defendant sold the car.

There was no dispute that the contract had been canceled. It was agreed that contract damages were to be given to the jury under the standard of U.C.C. § 2–713, applicable to a buyer who does not cover, the difference between the market price when the buyer learned of the breach and the contract price. * * *

The jury fixed plaintiff's knowledge of the breach as the time his attorney announced it, and did not accept plaintiff's insistence that the contract remained in effect thereafter. * * *

The jury concluded that the market price had increased $20,000 by December, which defendant urges is unsupported. The jury was presented with evidence that the price remained basically flat at $40,000 throughout 1987, and by January of 1988 was in a range from $70,000 to $100,000. The jury clearly rejected the proposition that there was no upward curve in value toward the end of 1987. Accordingly, as of December of 1987, $60,000 was a fair and logical assessment of the value of the car and the jury, as it was instructed to do, deducted from the value the purchase price of the car, to reach an award of $20,000. * * *

It cannot be ignored that the evidence before the jury fully portrayed an intimate community of Astin–Martin enthusiasts, linked by membership in an

Astin–Martin club and supported by an Astin–Martin specialty dealer located in New Jersey. The jury's verdict is soundly premised on the conclusion that, had plaintiff attempted to offer to purchase a comparable Astin–Martin within this community, one would have surfaced with a price of $60,000. After all, the same seller who sold a vehicle in January would only have to be lured into the market a month earlier, somewhat before the market price ascent. [The court rejected the seller's attack on the jury's verdict.] * * *

The request for specific performance raises a novel issue under the Uniform Commercial Code concerning entitlement to specific performance of a contract for the sale of unique goods with a fluctuating price. Section 2–716(1) of the Uniform Commercial Code, which is controlling, provides that "specific performance may be decreed where the goods are unique or in other proper circumstances." The jury's advisory determined that the Astin–Martin car at issue was unique.

As noted above, the car was sold prior to the commencement of this litigation for a price of $185,000 more than the $40,000 contract price, and plaintiff requests that he be granted specific performance in the form of a constructive trust impressed upon the proceeds of sale, plus interest from the date of sale. As it developed, the defendant had not sold at the "top of the market," which peaked in July of 1989, approximately two years after the original contract, when the car had a value of $335,000, which was $295,000 over the contract price. Thereafter, collectible automobile values slumped and the sale price of a comparable Astin–Martin vehicle by January of 1990 was $225,000 and, by the time of trial, was $80,000.

Clearly, plaintiff's request for an award of specific performance monetary damages is legally cognizable, for every object has a price and even rare goods are subject to economic interchangeability. Van Wagner Advertising Corp. v. S & M Enterprises, 67 N.Y.2d 186, 195 (1986); compare, no other opportunity, Triple–A Baseball Club Associates v. Northeastern Baseball, Inc., 832 F.2d 214 (1st Cir.1987). Plaintiff urges that specific performance is particularly appropriate here for U.C.C. § 2–716 has been viewed as a statute enacted to liberalize the availability of specific performance of contracts of sale as a buyers' remedy. [citations] Nonetheless, this change does not lessen the U.C.C.'s "emphasis on the commercial feasibility of replacement" as the most desirable approach (Comment 2, U.C.C. § 2–716), nor does it mean that typical equitable principles are inapplicable to consideration of the remedy.

However, both on the facts and the law, the court determines that, if equitable monetary damages are to be awarded here, that award must be based upon value at the time of trial, rather than on an earlier valuation. Traditionally, equity "give[s] relief adapted to the situation at the time of the decree" Union Bag & Paper Co. v. Allen Bros. Co., 107 App.Div. 529, 539, 95 N.Y.S. 214 [3rd Dept.1905]. This position is consistent with the explicit goal of the Uniform Commercial Code that its remedies are to "be liberally administered to the end that the aggrieved party may be put in as good a position as if the other party had fully performed" ([Original] U.C.C. § 1–106 [1]), which, in the case of specific performance, has led to confining the remedy to restoration of the equivalent of the subject goods to a plaintiff's possession. [citation] Here, if plaintiff were to be awarded enough to be able to acquire another Astin–Martin at current prices, he would achieve the requisite equivalent.

Plaintiff has fervently, but ultimately unconvincingly, argued that the larger amount is his due. While every litigant wishes to gain a maximum economic benefit, a court of equity should not grant an award which would be "disproportionate in its harm to defendant and its assistance to plaintiff." Van Wagner Advertising Corp. v. S & M Enterprises. On the plaintiff's side of this equation, a higher award would give plaintiff more than the current equivalent of the automobile. On the defendant's side, the court found credible the dealer's testimony that he put the funds derived from the sale into his stock, which then decreased in value in the same measure as the car in question, so that a higher award would cause a disproportionate harm. This testimony was uncontroverted by plaintiff and it was undisputed that neither party saw a rise in price of the dimensions present here. The court rejects the request for monetary specific performance to the extent that more than the current market price is sought.

This conclusion limits the debate to the current price of the automobile, which is approximately $40,000 more than the contract price. As to interest in an equitable matter, generally, where damages are fixed as of the date of trial, interest is to commence as of the date judgment is entered, although the court must consider the facts of the case in determining the calculation of interest. [citations] There is a certain factual irony in that, by reason of market factors, the contract remedy plus interest would result in a specific performance monetary damages award only somewhat short of the current price.

The issue of monetary specific performance remains, despite this conclusion, because such an award would be somewhat higher than the contract measure of damages. Plaintiff's position that specific performance must follow a determination that an object is "unique" misperceives the law.

First, specific performance rests upon the discretion of the trial court, reviewable under an abuse of discretion standard. Van Wagner Advertising Corp. v. S & M Enterprises. The use of a permissive "may" in the text of U.C.C. § 2–716 does not modify that standard in any way or change the accepted concept, as set forth in Da Silva v. Musso, 53 N.Y.2d 543, 547 (1981), that specific performance may be declined if it is concluded such relief "would be a 'drastic' or harsh remedy." It should be noted in relation to price fluctuations that even an extreme rise in price is an insufficient reason, as a matter of law, to decline to consider this equitable remedy, [citation] but, on the other hand, neither does a mere "increase in the cost of a replacement … merit the remedy." Klein v. PepsiCo, Inc., 845 F.2d 76, 80 (4th Cir.1988).

Second, a factual determination that an object is "unique," as the jury determined here in an advisory verdict, is an ingredient which has the greatest significance when an action for specific performance is commenced immediately after the breach, and is more complex when other factors or delays are present. In cases concerning the sale of goods promptly commenced after the breach, specific performance is frequently granted and turns primarily upon uniqueness. [citations of decisions concerning a "unique" Rolls–Royce Corniche; a "unique" new "Indy 500 Pace Car" Corvette; "unique" photocopy toner chemicals; "nonunique" airplanes; a "nonunique" 1962 Corvette; and a "nonunique" mobile home.]

Once beyond this simple factual threshold, under New York law, "uniqueness" must be considered as it bears upon the adequacy of the legal remedy. Van Wagner Advertising Corp. v. S & M Enterprises. It is noted that not all jurisdictions take this view. [citations]

With the passage of time, specific performance becomes disfavored. For example, because goods are subject to a rapid change in condition, or the cost of maintenance of the goods is important, time may be found to have been of the essence. * * * Even absent such special circumstances, with a greater delay, where a defendant has changed position or taken any economic risk, the court may conclude that "the plaintiff will lose nothing but an uncontemplated opportunity to gather a windfall". Concert Radio, Inc. v. GAF Corp., 108 A.D.2d 273, 278, 488 N.Y.S.2d 696 [1st Dept.1985], aff'd 73 N.Y.2d 766, 536 N.Y.S.2d 52, 532 N.E.2d 1280 [1988]. Particularly where some other transactions are available, it has been held that a "customer [for resale] may not . . . refuse to cover . . . and thereby speculate on the market entirely at the risk of the [defendant]." Saboundjian v. Bank Audi [USA], 157 A.D.2d 278, 284, 556 N.Y.S.2d 258 [1st Dept.1990], referring in part to [Original] U.C.C. § 1–106 which limits damages under U.C.C. § 2–713 to a buyer's expected profit where the purchase is for resale.

Turning to the facts in the instant case, the plaintiff did not sue in December of 1987, when it is likely a request for specific performance would have been granted. At that point, the defendant had disclaimed the contract and plaintiff was aware of his rights. The plaintiff was not protected by a continued firm assurance that defendant definitely would perfect the car's title. * * * The court does not accept plaintiff's protest that he believed the commercial relationship was intact; the parties had already had a heated discussion and were communicating through attorneys. A more likely explanation of plaintiff's inaction is that he proceeded to complete the purchase in April of 1988 of a Ferrari Testarrosa for $128,000 and a Lamborghini for $40,000 in 1989.

In short, the plaintiff abandoned any active claim of contract enforcement by late spring of 1988. Moreover, to the extent that his two sports cars constituted "cover," he did not present any evidence as to his treatment of those cars such that the court could evaluate damages or quantify what profits he expected to make on the Astin–Martin which he regarded, in significant part, as a business transaction. [citations] Finally, the court determines, as a matter of credibility, that plaintiff would not have pursued this matter had the price fallen below the contract price.

On this point, it is helpful to note that the initial burden of proving the proper remedy remains on the buyer, U.C.C. § 2–715, Official Comment 4. In this instance, plaintiff's very attempt to prove qualifiable specific performance damages has also proved: (a) the value of the disputed automobile was readily established by expert sources; (b) the adequacy of legal contract damages; and (c) the availability of "a substitute transaction [which] is generally a more efficient way to prevent injury than is a suit for specific performance . . . [and gives] a sound economic basis for limiting the injured party to damages" (see, comment c, Restatement [Second] of Contracts § 360).

In closing, the court does not fault plaintiff for his valiant attempt to reach for a higher level of damages. * * * If only in the interest of commercial certainty, there is great wisdom in a rule of thumb that "uniqueness continues to cover one-of-a-kind goods and items of special sentimental value, [and] goods that have particular market significance, such as goods covered by an output contract or which are being specially manufactured." 3A William D. Hawkland and Frederick Moreno, Uniform Commercial Code Series § 2A–521:03 [Clark Boardman Callaghan 1993].

After full consideration of these factors, the court is satisfied that it would be inequitable and improper to grant specific performance in the form of a constructive trust upon the proceeds of sale.

Accordingly, the motion to fix the specific performance damages and the motion to vacate the jury verdict are denied.

Notes

1. *Buyer's Tactics.* Why might the buyer have sought "monetary specific performance?"

Toward the end of the opinion, the court, citing U.C.C. § 2–715, Official Comment 4, says that "the initial burden of proving the proper remedy remains on the buyer." Actually, the comment referring to consequential damages says that the burden on the buyer is to prove "the extent of the loss." Is the court confusing the choice of remedy and the way of measuring the remedy, once it chosen? Does the "proper remedy" always equal the "extent of the loss"?

2. *Unique?* To achieve "specific performance" the buyer must satisfy the test of § 2–716. Does "unique" in § 2–716 have its dictionary meaning? The Astin–Martin was one of twenty. Does it fit within the uniqueness test stated in the court's quotation from Hawkland and Moreno? Is that test of uniqueness too narrow?

3. *Cover.* Section 2–716 also allows a buyer specific performance "in other proper circumstances." Buyer's "inability to cover," the Official Comment explains, "is strong evidence of 'other proper circumstances.' " Cover is "goods in substitution for those due from the seller." § 2–712(1). Did the buyer's purchase of the Ferrari and Lamborghini "cover" the breached Astin–Martin contract? If so, how could the court calculate the buyer's cover damages under § 2–712(2)?

4. *Specific Performance Impossible.* (a) If the seller does not have the item at the time of trial because he sold it to a bona fide purchaser, should the judge, without more, deny the buyer specific performance because that remedy is impossible? Or does impossibility convert the buyer's request for "true" specific performance into one for "an award of specific performance monetary damages"?

(b) *Equitable Cleanup and the Right to a Jury Trial.* Ziebarth v. Kalenze, p. 292, takes up the right to a jury trial when a buyer's specific performance turns out to be impossible. Under *Ziebarth*, would the seller in *Bander* have been entitled to demand a binding jury verdict?

Might the Astin–Martin buyer have sought the "equitable" remedy of "monetary specific performance" to avoid a jury? If so, the tactic did not completely succeed—the jury submission was complex.

5. *Buyer's Remedy?* In the end which remedy does Judge Lebedeff grant to the buyer (a) specific performance monetary damages under § 2–716, or (b) the market-contract differential under § 2–713? What are the judge's reasons for rejecting recovery based on the seller's resale price?

6. *A Constructive Trust?* The buyer's claim for specific performance monetary damages through imposing a constructive trust on the seller's resale proceeds may seem far-fetched. For a constructive trust, a plaintiff identifies ownership of a constructive trust "res," and traces it; the plaintiff claims the defendant "owns" legal title of the plaintiff's property upon which, to prevent the defendant's unjust enrichment, the judge should impose a constructive trust. Under U.C.C. 2–401(2), a buyer usually does not obtain "title" to personal property until the seller delivers it. So the Astin–Martin buyer had no constructive trust property interest to trace.

007. *Restitution?* A buyer's recovery of restitution measured by the breaching seller's resale profit is, however, not so far-fetched. George Palmer, The Law of Restitution § 4.9 (1978).

8. *Equitable Conversion.* When a seller breaches a contract to sell land, a court may use the language of equitable conversion to describe or explain the buyer's restitution of the seller's resale profits.

When the buyer and seller form a binding land contract, appropriate for specific performance, "equity" converts the buyer's interest into real property, the land, and the seller's into personal property, the purchase price. If the buyer thus becomes the land's "equitable" owner, the court may hold that the seller who sold the buyer's land to another is accountable to the buyer for the profit. Alternatively, the seller is, in equity, the trustee of the land for the buyer's benefit. So if this contract had been for land instead of an Astin–Martin, the seller would have sold the buyer's property, and the buyer's constructive trust theory would not have been so far-fetched.

9. *Rescission-Restitution.* Usually a buyer seeking restitution from a breaching seller asks the court to rescind the contract and seeks to recover as restitution values he has transferred to the seller. There is both a plus and a minus, the seller's plus is the buyer's minus, and restitution restores the status quo. So under § 2–711(1), the Astin–Martin buyer, if he had not already received it, is entitled to restitution of his $5,000 deposit from the breaching seller.

10. *"Restitution" of Buyer's Benefit that Seller Diverted.* Here the seller has breached his contract to sell an Astin–Martin to the buyer. The seller has obtained a benefit from a third party, the second buyer, an amount in excess of the price he had agreed to sell it to the buyer for. Perhaps the seller diverted a benefit away from the buyer and captured it for himself. Is the seller unjustly enriched in a way that ought to trigger restitution? Did the seller deprive the buyer of the opportunity to form a beneficial contract with the second buyer?

The remedial parts of the U.C.C. omit this form of restitution, but restitution may be available to the buyer under Original U.C.C. § 1–103, as a supplementary principle, not displaced by the Code.

11. *Capturing the Seller's Resale Profit.* In theory, the buyer has two ways to use the seller's resale to calculate his recovery: either (a) figure the buyer's damages by subtracting from the seller's resale price the contract price, or (b) grant the buyer restitution of the seller's profit from the breaching sale. The court would measure the buyer's restitution by the seller's resale price less the unpaid contract price.

May the buyer use the seller's resale price to calculate his damages? The U.C.C. lets a buyer of personal property recover damages based on the difference between the contract price and either (a) an appropriate covering purchase under § 2–712, or (b) the item's value "at the time after the buyer learned of the breach" under § 2–713.

The Revised U.C.C. § 2–713 would change the timing rules. For seller's failure to deliver or buyer's rejection or rescission, the court will calculate the market value-contract price differential "at the time for tender under the contract." Revised U.C.C. § 2–713(1)(a). For seller's repudiation, the differential will be calculated "at the expiration of a commercially reasonable time after the buyer learned of the repudiation, but no later than [the contractual time for tender]." Revised U.C.C. § 2–713(1)(b).

One possibility under the contract price-market value formula is for the buyer to use the seller's resale price as evidence of market value. Here, however, stronger evidence set the Astin–Martin's value in late 1987; the buyer could not use the automobile's highest value or its value at the time of trial.

So if the buyer is to recover the seller's resale profit, it must be through restitution. Restitution of the seller's profit liberates the buyer from proving market value. Restitution is more desirable to a buyer when the property's value has risen before the seller's resale then dropped before the buyer learned of the breach.

12. *Back to the Beginning.* Should the judge have limited the Astin–Martin buyer's recovery to the U.C.C.'s damages sections?

Chapter 8

BREACH OF EMPLOYMENT
AGREEMENTS

We turn to remedies under a breached employment contract. The employment relationship is extensively regulated, usually by statutes with a social-welfare purpose of protecting an employee. Most law schools have entire courses on employment discrimination and labor law. Although we focus the following material on the remedies a common-law court will grant for a breach of a private employment contract, we will observe the same social purposes limiting the employer's and the employee's range of private bargaining and influencing the way a court will treat the bargain and its remedies after someone violates it.

Employment litigation has several important features. Both sides takes an employment dispute personally and seek vindication through victory. Thus a lawyer will find that an employment lawsuit is difficult to settle; even so, the parties often do settle to prevent the consequences of conflict and to avoid the uncertainty, delay, and expense of litigation.

Breaches of contract and intentional torts are difficult for an employer to insure against. Although insurance is now being written to cover some forms of an employer's employment exposure, many employers are not insured. An employee's judgment may come out of the employer's bottom line.

An employment lawsuit bristles with procedural and substantive complexity. Discovery can be extensive—and ugly. The plaintiff's battle for the jury is serious because jurors tend to identify with a former employee and to show it with a jumbo verdict. A judge's post-verdict review of the jury's decision may lead to reduction or reversal.

The unique United States default rule of an "at will" employment contract is our substantive-remedial starting place: If the parties' employment agreement lacks a specified duration, then either the employer or the employee may terminate it "at will," at any time, for any reason.

The at-will doctrine, which reflects the comparatively open labor markets in the United States, has real meaning where it applies. In addition to being unable to maintain an action for breach of contract, a plaintiff cannot "rely" on an offer of, or employment under, an at-will arrangement. Thus, in addition, she cannot maintain the ancillary and related substantive theories of intentional fraud, negligent fraud, promissory estoppel, restitution-unjust enrichment, and prima facie tort. Marion v. Oakwood Care Center, 5 A.D.3d 740, 774 N.Y.S.2d 562

(2004); Arias v. Women in Need, 274 A.D.2d 353, 712 N.Y.S.2d 103 (2000); Dalton v. Union Bank of Switzerland, 134 A.D.2d 174, 520 N.Y.S.2d 764 (1987).

But stating the at-will rule introduces numerous exceptions. Many upper-echelon employees work under term contracts. Other employees have tenure and rights because of civil service or collective bargaining contracts. An employee handbook may have contractual status. Under state and federal civil rights statutes, an employer cannot terminate an employee for a forbidden reason like race, gender, religion, age, and, often, sexual orientation. Finally, a judge may recoil from the unfairness of an employer firing an employee for a bad reason, like reporting its illegal hazardous waste dump to the environmental authorities.

An employee-plaintiff will seek a tort or statutory remedy to open the door for possible reinstatement or an injunction, punitive damages, emotional distress damages, and attorney fees.

Contrast a sales contract with an employment contract. An employer who parts with money, in the form of wages, resembles a buyer; an employee who receives money resembles a seller. How far does the sale-employment analogy go? Let's start with the employer-buyer's remedies.

A.   EMPLOYER'S REMEDIES

Problem. Janet Janus, a third-year law student who has accepted a position with a middle-sized firm in her home town, receives an unexpected offer from a large metropolitan firm where she had interviewed. The large firm offers Janus a $12,000 higher salary, which is important because of her student loans, better professional support, and specialized work. She calls the home-town partner who tells her that they expect her to start work after the bar exam.

Janus, preferring metropolitan life, consults you.

Professional Responsibility. Should an attorney advise Janus to ignore her contract with the home-town law firm? Breaching a contract may subject a lawyer's client to damages if the other party sues her.

What does the Restatement say? "[A] lawyer may not counsel or assist a client in conduct that the lawyer knows to be criminal or fraudulent or in violation of a court order." says the blackletter to Restatement (Third) of The Law Governing Lawyers § 94(2)(2000). However "a lawyer may ordinarily, without civil liability, advise a client not to enter a contract or to breach an existing contract." Restatement (Third) of The Law Governing Lawyers § 57, comment g. (2000). Does it make sense to distinguish crime, fraud, and violation of a court order from breach of a contract?

Finally, "In counseling a client, a lawyer may address nonlegal aspects of a proposed course of conduct, including moral, reputational, economic, social, political and business aspects." Restatement (Third) of The Law Governing Lawyers § 94(3)(2000).

Legal Duty. Your analysis of Janus's duty may fall under at least three possible headings: (a) You have a moral duty to perform your contract, to not break your promise. (b) If you do breach, the law firm may sue you. A judge will not grant them specific performance forcing you to work for them, but damages are possible. (c) For an employee, an employment contract creates merely a theoretical duty. If you take the better job, almost certainly nothing will happen.

Does your advice depend on whether Janus's contract with the home-town firm is for a fixed term or at will?

Take Your Job And. In support of (c), "Culturally, Americans have come to think of the employment contract as binding only the employer. Many Americans think employees are free to leave at any time if they find a better or more lucrative job, but that it would be outrageous for employers to discharge employees just because they found better or cheaper workers. These expectations do not seem much affected by whether the contract is for life tenure, a fixed term, or employment at will. No legal doctrine makes employment contracts so one-sided, but courts and employers respond to the prevailing ethos. My impression is that employers rarely seek damages for breach of the promise to work, and that they get a hostile reception when they do." Douglas Laycock, The Death of the Irreparable Injury Rule 169–70 (1991).

Roth v. Speck, below with Employer's Damages, contradicts Professor Laycock's "impression."

1. EMPLOYER'S INJUNCTIVE RELIEF: A QUIET STORM

BEVERLY GLEN MUSIC, INC. v. WARNER COMMUNICATIONS, INC.

California Court of Appeal, 1986.
178 Cal.App.3d 1142, 224 Cal.Rptr. 260.

Kingsley, Acting Presiding Justice. The plaintiff appeals from an order denying a preliminary injunction against the defendant, Warner Communications, Inc. We affirm.

In 1982, plaintiff Beverly Glen Music, Inc. signed to a contract a then-unknown singer, Anita Baker. Ms. Baker recorded an album for Beverly Glen which was moderately successful, grossing over one million dollars. In 1984, however, Ms. Baker was offered a considerably better deal by defendant Warner Communications. As she was having some difficulties with Beverly Glen, she accepted Warner's offer and notified plaintiff that she was no longer willing to perform under the contract. Beverly Glen then sued Ms. Baker and sought to have her enjoined from performing for any other recording studio. The injunction was denied, however, as, under Civil Code section 3423, subdivision Fifth, California courts will not enjoin the breach of a personal service contract unless the service is unique in nature and the performer is guaranteed annual compensation of at least $6,000, which Ms. Baker was not.

Following this ruling, the plaintiff voluntarily dismissed the action against Ms. Baker. Plaintiff, however, then sued Warner Communications for inducing Ms. Baker to breach her contract and moved the court for an injunction against Warner to prevent it from employing her. This injunction, too, was denied, the trial court reasoning that what one was forbidden by statute to do directly, one could not accomplish through the back door. It is from this ruling that the plaintiff appeals.

From what we can tell, this is a case of first impression in California. While there are numerous cases on the general inability of an employer to enjoin his former employee from performing services somewhere else, apparently no one has previously thought of enjoining the new employer from accepting the services of the breaching employee. While we commend the plaintiff for its resourcefulness in this regard, we concur in the trial court's interpretation of the maneuver.

"It is a familiar rule that a contract to render personal services cannot be specifically enforced." [citation] An unwilling employee cannot be compelled to continue to provide services to his employer either by ordering specific performance of his contract, or by injunction. To do so runs afoul of the Thirteenth Amendment's prohibition against involuntary servitude. [citation] However, beginning with the English case of Lumley v. Wagner (1852) 42 Eng.Rep. 687, courts have recognized that, while they cannot directly enforce an affirmative promise (in the *Lumley* case, Miss Wagner's promise to perform at the plaintiff's opera house), they can enforce the negative promise implied therein (that the defendant would not perform for someone else that evening). Thus, while it is not possible to compel a defendant to perform his duties under a personal service contract, it is possible to prevent him from employing his talents anywhere else. The net effect is to pressure the defendant to return voluntarily to his employer by denying him the means of earning a living. Indeed, this is its only purpose, for, unless the defendant relents and honors the contract, the plaintiff gains nothing from having brought the injunction.

The California Legislature, however, did not adopt this principle when in 1872 it enacted Civil Code section 3423, subdivision Fifth, and Code of Civil Procedure section 526, subdivision 5. These sections both provided that an injunction could not be granted: "To prevent the breach of a contract the performance of which would not be specifically enforced." In 1919, however, these sections were amended, creating an exception for: "a contract in writing for the rendition or furnishing of personal services from one to another where the minimum compensation for such service is at the rate of not less than six thousand dollars per annum and where the promised service is of a special, unique, unusual, extraordinary or intellectual character."

The plaintiff has already unsuccessfully argued before the trial court that Ms. Baker falls within this exception. It has chosen not to appeal that judgment, and is therefore barred from questioning that determination now. The sole issue before us then is whether plaintiff—although prohibited from enjoining Ms. Baker from performing herself—can seek to enjoin all those who might employ her and prevent them from doing so, thus achieving the same effect.

We rule that plaintiff cannot. Whether plaintiff proceeds against Ms. Baker directly or against those who might employ her, the intent is the same: to deprive Ms. Baker of her livelihood and thereby pressure her to return to plaintiff's employ. Plaintiff contends that this is not an action against Ms. Baker but merely an equitable claim against Warner to deprive it of the wrongful benefits it gained when it "stole" Ms. Baker away. Thus, plaintiff contends, the equities lie not between the plaintiff and Ms. Baker, but between plaintiff and the predatory Warner Communications Company. Yet if Warner's behavior has actually been predatory, plaintiff has an adequate remedy by way of damages. An injunction adds nothing to plaintiff's recovery from Warner except to coerce Ms. Baker to honor her contract. Denying someone his livelihood is a harsh remedy. The Legislature has forbidden it but for one exception. To expand this remedy so that it could be used in virtually all breaches of a personal service contract is to ignore over one hundred years of common law on this issue. We therefore decline to reverse the order.

The order is affirmed.

McClosky and Arguelles, JJ., concur.

Notes

1. *An Affirmative Injunction?* A California statute codifies the rule that a judge will refuse to enforce a personal service contract specifically. Cal.Civ.Code § 3390.

The Contracts Restatement explains the reasons: "The refusal is based in part upon the undesirability of compelling the continuance of personal association after disputes have arisen and confidence and loyalty are gone and, in some instances, of imposing what might seem like involuntary servitude." Restatement (Second) of Contracts. Comment (a) to § 367 (1981).

Is the "injunction against breach" permitted by Cal.Civ.Code § 3423 a decree specifically enforcing the affirmative portion of the employment contract? The California legislature has amended § 3423 to raise the threshold amount and add a graduated scale.

2. *A Negative Injunction?* An employee promises (a) to work for the employer, and (b) not to work for others, not to compete with the employer. The employer's remedies include enforcing the negative covenant; a judge may enjoin the breaching employee to enforce the negative covenant. So the court may forbid the employee with unique talents from working for another employer during the contract's exclusive term. The court may also enjoin the other employer from encouraging the employee to breach as the tort of inducing-breach-of-contract. Central New York Basketball, Inc. v. Barnett, 19 Ohio Op.2d 130, 181 N.E.2d 506 (1961).

Suppose a court grants an employer an injunction that forbids a former employee from taking a specified employment opportunity. Does that injunction ignore the reasoning that led the court in the principal case to deny Beverly Glen Music an injunction?

3. *Noncompetition Covenants.* An employee's covenant not to compete is typical in many employment contracts. A court will distinguish a business seller's covenant not to compete with the buyer from an employee's covenant not to compete with a former employer after employment terminates. The judge will view the seller's covenant with more favor than the employee's since the employee's covenant may deprive her of her livelihood by prohibiting the use of skill and knowledge she acquired during the employment period. Alexander & Alexander, Inc. v. Danahy, 488 N.E.2d 22, 21 Mass.App.Ct. 488 (1986); Family Affair Haircutters, Inc. v. Detling, 488 N.Y.S.2d 204, 110 A.D.2d 745 (App.Div. 1985).

BDO SEIDMAN v. HIRSHBERG

Court of Appeals of New York, 1999.
93 N.Y.2d 382, 690 N.Y.S.2d 854, 712 N.E.2d 1220.

LEVINE, J. BDO SEIDMAN (BDO), a general partnership of certified public accountants, appeals from the affirmance of an order of Supreme Court granting summary judgment dismissing its complaint against defendant, who was formerly employed as an accountant with the firm. The central issue before us is whether the "reimbursement clause" in an agreement between the parties, requiring defendant to compensate BDO for serving any client of the firm's Buffalo office within 18 months after the termination of his employment, is an invalid and unenforceable restrictive covenant. The courts below so held.

FACTS AND PROCEDURAL HISTORY

BDO is a national accounting firm having 40 offices throughout the United States, including four in New York State. Defendant began employment in

BDO's Buffalo office in 1984, when the accounting firm he had been working for was merged into BDO, its partners becoming BDO partners. In 1989, defendant was promoted to the position of manager, apparently a step immediately below attaining partner status. As a condition of receiving the promotion, defendant was required to sign a "Manager's Agreement," the provisions of which are at issue. In paragraph "SIXTH" defendant expressly acknowledged that a fiduciary relationship existed between him and the firm by reason of his having received various disclosures which would give him an advantage in attracting BDO clients. Based upon that stated premise, defendant agreed that if, within 18 months following the termination of his employment, he served any former client of BDO's Buffalo office, he would compensate BDO "for the loss and damages suffered" in an amount equal to 1½ times the fees BDO had charged that client over the last fiscal year of the client's patronage. Defendant was to pay such amount in five annual installments.

Defendant resigned from BDO in October 1993. This action was commenced in January 1995. During pretrial discovery, BDO submitted a list of 100 former clients of its Buffalo office, allegedly lost to defendant, who were billed a total of $138,000 in the year defendant left the firm's practice. Defendant denied serving some of the clients, averred that a substantial number of them were personal clients he had brought to the firm through his own outside contacts, and also claimed that with respect to some clients, he had not been the primary BDO representative servicing the account.

Following discovery, the parties exchanged motions for summary judgment. BDO's submissions on the motion did not contain any evidence that defendant actually solicited former clients, and did not rely in any way on claims that defendant used confidential information in acquiring BDO clients. Supreme Court granted summary judgment to defendant, concluding that the reimbursement clause was an overbroad and unenforceable anti-competitive agreement. The Appellate Division agreed, holding that the entire agreement was invalid.

DISCUSSION

Concededly, the Manager's Agreement defendant signed does not prevent him from competing for new clients, nor does it expressly bar him from serving BDO clients. Instead, it requires him to pay "for the loss and damages" sustained by BDO in losing any of its clients to defendant within 18 months after his departure, an amount equivalent to 1½ times the last annual billing for any such client who became the client of defendant. Nonetheless, it is not seriously disputed that the agreement, in its purpose and effect, is a form of ancillary employee anti-competitive agreement that will be carefully scrutinized by the courts. [citation] Reported cases adjudicating the validity of post-employment restrictive covenants go back almost 300 years. (see, Blake, Employee Agreements Not To Compete, 73 Harv. L. Rev. 625, 629.) In the 19th century, a standard of reasonableness for judging the validity of such agreements developed in case law here and in England, balancing the need of fair protection for the benefit of the employer against the opposing interests of the former employee and the public.

The modern, prevailing common-law standard of reasonableness for employee agreements not to compete applies a three-pronged test. A restraint is reasonable only if it: (1) is *no greater* than is required for the protection of the *legitimate interest* of the employer, (2) does not impose undue hardship on the employee, and (3) is not injurious to the public (*see, e.g., Technical Aid Corp. v. Allen,* 591 A.2d 262, 265–266; Restatement [Second] of Contracts § 188). A violation of any prong renders the covenant invalid.

New York has adopted this prevailing standard of reasonableness in determining the validity of employee agreements not to compete. "In this context a restrictive covenant will only be subject to specific enforcement to the extent that it is reasonable in time and area, necessary to protect the employer's legitimate interests, not harmful to the general public and not unreasonably burdensome to the employee" (Reed, Roberts Assocs. v. Strauman, 40 N.Y.2d 303, 307, 386 N.Y.S.2d 677, 353 N.E.2d 590).

In general, we have strictly applied the rule to limit enforcement of broad restraints on competition. Thus, in *Reed, Roberts,* we limited the cognizable employer interests under the first prong of the common-law rule to the protection against misappropriation of the employer's trade secrets or of confidential customer lists, or protection from competition by a former employee whose services are unique or extraordinary.

With agreements not to compete between professionals, however, we have given greater weight to the interests of the employer in restricting competition within a confined geographical area. In Gelder Med. Group v. Webber, 41 N.Y.2d 680, and *Karpinski v. Ingrasci,* 28 N.Y.2d 45, we enforced total restraints on competition, in limited rural locales, permanently in *Karpinski* and for five years in *Gelder.* The rationale for the differential application of the common-law rule of reasonableness expressed in our decisions was that professionals are deemed to provide "unique or extraordinary" services. (*see, Reed, Roberts)*

BDO urges that accountancy is entitled to the status of a learned profession and, as such, the *Karpinski* and *Gelder Medical Group* precedents militate in favor of the validity of the restrictive covenant here. We agree that accountancy has all the earmarks of a learned profession. CPAs are required to have extensive formal training and education [citation]; they must pass a written examination [citation]; and they are subject to mandatory continuing education requirements [citation]. Their professional conduct is regulated by the Board of Regents under statutory disciplinary procedures [citation]. Moreover, there is a national code of professional conduct for certified public accountants which provides that "[m]embers should accept the obligation to act in a way that will serve the public interest, honor the public trust, and demonstrate commitment to professionalism" (American Institute of Certified Public Accountants Code of Professional Conduct § 53, art. II). The foregoing factors closely correspond to the criteria for a learned profession. * * *

Law firm partnership agreements represent an exception to the liberality with which we have previously treated restraints on competition in the learned professions [citations]. Our decisions invalidating anti-competitive clauses in such agreements were not based on application of the common-law rule, but upon enforcement of the public policy reflected in DR 2–108(A) of the Code of Professional Responsibility. There is no counterpart to DR 2–108(A) in the rules regulating the ethical conduct of accountants. * * *

Nonetheless, *Gelder Medical Group* and *Karpinski* do not dictate the result here. As we noted in *Karpinski,* the application of the test of reasonableness of employee restrictive covenants focuses on the particular facts and circumstances giving context to the agreement. This Court's rationale for giving wider latitude to covenants between members of a learned profession because their services are unique or extraordinary does not realistically apply to the actual context of the anti-competitive agreement here. In the instant case, BDO is a national accounting firm seeking to enforce the agreement within a market consisting of the entirety of a major metropolitan area. Moreover, defendant's unchallenged averments indicate that his status in the firm was not based upon the uniqueness or extraordinary nature of the accounting services he generally performed on behalf of the firm, but in major part on his ability to attract a corporate clientele. Nor was there any proof that defendant possessed any unique or extraordinary ability as an accountant that would give him a competitive advantage over BDO. Moreover, the contexts of the agreements not to compete in *Karpinski* and *Gelder Medical Group* were entirely different. In each case, the former associate would have been in direct competition with the promisee-practitioner for referrals from a narrow group of primary health providers in a rural geographical market for their medical or dental practice specialty.

Thus, our learned profession precedents do not obviate the need for independent scrutiny of the anti-competitive provisions of the Manager's Agreement under the tripartite common-law standard. Close analysis of paragraph SIXTH of the agreement under the first prong of the common-law rule, to identify the legitimate interest of BDO and determine whether the covenant is no more restrictive than is necessary to protect that interest, leads us to conclude that the covenant as written is overbroad in some respects. BDO claims that the legitimate interest it is entitled to protect is its entire client base, which it asserts a modern, large accounting firm expends considerable time and money building and maintaining. However, the only justification for imposing an employee agreement not to compete is to forestall unfair competition. [citation] It seems self-evident that a former employee may be capable of fairly competing for an employer's clients by refraining from use of unfair means to compete. If the employee abstains from unfair means in competing for those clients, the employer's interest in preserving its client base against the competition of the former employer is no more legitimate and worthy of contractual protection than when it vies with unrelated competitors for those clients.

Legal scholars and courts have more circumspectly identified the employer's legitimate interest in employee anti-competitive agreements than that of preservation of the employer's entire client base where, as here, there is no evidence that the employee obtained a competitive advantage by using confidential information. Professor Blake, in his seminal article in the Harvard Law Review, explains that the legitimate purpose of an employer in connection with employee restraints is "to prevent competitive use, for a time, of *information* or *relationships* which pertain peculiarly to the employer and which the *employee acquired* in the course of the employment" [emphasis supplied]. Protection of customer relationships the employee *acquired* in the course of employment may indeed be a legitimate interest. "The risk to the employer reaches a maximum in situations in which the employee must work closely with the client or customer over a long period of time, especially when his services are a significant part of the total transaction." Then, the employee has been enabled to share in the goodwill of a client or customer which the employer's over-all efforts and expenditures created. The employer has a legitimate interest in preventing former employees from exploiting or appropriating the goodwill of a client or customer, which had been created and maintained at the employer's expense, to the employer's competitive detriment. [citation]

It follows from the foregoing that BDO's legitimate interest here is protection against defendant's competitive use of client relationships which BDO enabled him to acquire through his performance of accounting services for the firm's clientele during the course of his employment. Extending the anticompetitive covenant to BDO's clients with whom a relationship with defendant did not develop through assignments to perform direct, substantive accounting services would, therefore, violate the first prong of the common-law rule: it would constitute a restraint "greater than is needed to protect" these legitimate interests (Restatement [Second] of Contracts § 188[1][a]). A different result might obtain had BDO submitted any proof that defendant had used confidential firm information to attract BDO clients with whom he had not had a relationship while employed there.

The foregoing overbreadth was the basis upon which a number of State courts have invalidated restrictive covenant agreements prohibiting employees from providing post-employment accounting services to any client of the employer without regard to whether the employee served the client during the course of employment. [citations] Although other courts have enforced employee restrictive covenants extending to an accounting firm's entire client base, they have either failed adequately to identify the employer's legitimate interest [citations] or having properly identified the interest, did not engage in analysis as to whether the restriction was greater than necessary to protect it. [citation]

To the extent, then, that paragraph SIXTH of the Manager's Agreement requires defendant to compensate BDO for lost patronage of clients with whom he never acquired a relationship through the direct provision of substantive accounting services during his employment, the covenant is invalid and unenforceable. By a parity of reasoning, it would be unreasonable to extend the covenant to personal clients of defendant who came to the firm solely to avail themselves of his services and only as a result of his own independent recruitment efforts, which BDO neither subsidized nor otherwise financially supported as part of a program of client development. Because the goodwill of those clients was not acquired through the expenditure of BDO's resources, the firm has no legitimate interest in preventing defendant from competing for their patronage. Indeed, enforcement of the restrictive covenant as to defendant's personal clients would permit BDO to appropriate goodwill created and maintained through defendant's efforts, essentially turning on its head the principal justification to uphold any employee agreement not to compete based on protection of customer or client relationships.

Except for the overbreadth in the foregoing two respects, the restrictions in paragraph SIXTH do not violate the tripartite common-law test for reasonableness. The restraint on serving BDO clients is limited to 18 months, and to clients of BDO's Buffalo office. The time constraint appears to represent a reasonably brief interlude to enable the firm to replace the client relationship and goodwill defendant was permitted to acquire with some of its clients. Defendant is free to compete immediately for new business in any market and, if the overbroad provisions of the covenant are struck, to retain his personal clients and those clients of BDO's that he had not served to any significant extent while employed at the firm. He has averred that BDO's list of lost accounts contains a number of clients in both categories. Thus, there is scant evidence suggesting that the covenant, if cured of overbreadth, would work an undue hardship on defendant.

Moreover, given the likely broad array of accounting services available in the greater Buffalo area, and the limited remaining class of BDO clientele affected by the covenant, it cannot be said that the restraint, as narrowed, would seriously impinge on the availability of accounting services in the Buffalo area from which the public may draw, or cause any significant dislocation in the market or create a monopoly in accounting services in that locale. These factors militate against a conclusion that a reformed paragraph SIXTH would violate the third prong of the common-law test, injury to the public interest. [citation]

Severance or Partial Enforcement

We conclude that the Appellate Division erred in holding that the entire covenant must be invalidated, and in declining partially to enforce the covenant to the extent necessary to protect BDO's legitimate interest. The Appellate Division rejected partial enforcement or severance of the invalid part of the covenant, because "the court would thereby be required to rewrite the entire covenant." In Karpinski v. Ingrasci, this Court expressly recognized and applied the judicial power to sever and grant partial enforcement for an overbroad employee restrictive covenant. The Court refused to give effect to the portion of the covenant which barred the practice of general dentistry, but enforced it respecting the practice of oral surgery, that being the employer's actual, specialized dental practice.

The issue of whether a court should cure the unreasonable aspect of an overbroad employee restrictive covenant through the means of partial enforcement or severance has been the subject of some debate among courts and commentators. [citations] A legitimate consideration against the exercise of this power is the fear that employers will use their superior bargaining position to impose unreasonable anti-competitive restrictions, uninhibited by the risk that a court will void the entire agreement, leaving the employee free of any restraint. The prevailing, modern view rejects a per se rule that invalidates entirely any overbroad employee agreement not to compete. Instead, when, as here, the unenforceable portion is not an essential part of the agreed exchange, a court should conduct a case specific analysis, focusing on the conduct of the employer in imposing the terms of the agreement. Under this approach, if the employer demonstrates an absence of overreaching, coercive use of dominant bargaining power, or other anti-competitive misconduct, but has in good faith sought to protect a legitimate business interest, consistent with reasonable standards of fair dealing, partial enforcement may be justified. [citation] We essentially adopted this more flexible position in *Karpinski*.

Here, the undisputed facts and circumstances militate in favor of partial enforcement. The covenant was not imposed as a condition of defendant's initial employment, or even his continued employment, but in connection with promotion to a position of responsibility and trust just one step below admittance to the partnership. There is no evidence of coercion or that the Manager's Agreement was part of some general plan to forestall competition. Moreover, no proof was submitted that BDO imposed the covenant in bad faith, knowing full well that it was overbroad. Indeed, as already discussed, the existence of our "learned profession" precedents, and decisions in other States upholding the full terms of this type of agreement, support the contrary conclusion. Therefore, partial enforcement of paragraph SIXTH is warranted.

The Appellate Division's fear that partial enforcement will require rewriting the parties' agreement is unfounded. No additional substantive terms are required. The time and geographical limitations on the covenant remain intact. The only change is to narrow the class of BDO clients to which the covenant applies. [citation] Moreover, to reject partial enforcement based solely on the extent of necessary revision of the contract resembles the now-discredited doctrine that invalidation of an entire restrictive covenant is required unless the invalid portion was so divisible that it could be mechanically severed, as with a "judicial blue pencil." The Restatement (Second) of Contracts rejected that rigid requirement of strict divisibility before a covenant could be partially enforced (*see,* Reporter's Note, Restatement [Second] of Contracts § 184, at 32). Thus, we conclude that severance is appropriate, rendering the restrictive covenant partially enforceable.

DAMAGES

Since defendant does not dispute that at least some BDO clients to which the restrictive covenant validly applies were served by him during the contractual duration of the restraint, plaintiff is entitled to partial summary judgment on the issue of liability. Remittal is required in order to establish plaintiff's damages, including resolution of any contested issue as to which of BDO's former clients served by defendant the restrictive covenant validly covers. * * *

Accordingly, the order of the Appellate Division, insofar as appealed from, should be modified, * * * declaring the restrictive covenant enforceable as here provided, and remitting to Supreme Court for further proceedings in accordance with this opinion and, as so modified, affirmed.

CHIEF JUDGE KAYE and JUDGES BELLACOSA, SMITH, CIPARICK, WESLEY and Rosenblatt concur. * * *

Notes

1. *Contract Law Alert*: The BDO–Hirshberg contract's noncompetition covenant coincided with Hirshberg's promotion to "manager." That meant there was consideration for the covenant. BDO promoted Hirshberg; Hirshberg promised not to compete after employment ended. A former employee may argue that a noncompetition covenant an employer imposed unilaterally in a "new" contract or handbook is not supported by consideration and must fail on contract-law grounds.

2. *You're Unique!* Should an employee be wary when his employer begins to label him as "unique or extraordinary"? Does that mean the employer is dusting off its injunction? Be ready to argue that, flattering as the label is, you are really just another joe or jane.

3. *Accounting.* If accounting qualifies as a "learned profession" why doesn't the court apply that line of decisions to BDO's covenant?

4. *Lawyers' Alert.* A law firm cannot use a post-employment non-competition covenant with a lawyer. A law firm agreement cannot restrict a lawyer's right to practice law—because the public interest requires that the lawyer's actual and potential clients must be free to select their lawyer. This has been controversial.

Doctors too? Although authority is split on whether a physician's post-employment noncompete covenant is valid, the Tennessee court held that a physician's noncompete violates public policy. The court reasoned that a prohibition interferes improperly with a patient's right to choose a suitable professional. Murfreesboro Medical Clinic v. Udom, 166 S.W.3d 674 (Tenn. 2005).

5.   Why doesn't the court give effect to the covenant's "any" and protect BDO's "entire client base" from Hirshberg's post-employment competition?

6.   Suppose three of BDO's clients followed Hirshberg to his new position: C–1 was BDO's client, but Hirshberg serviced the C–1 account; C–2 was BDO's client, but was never serviced by Hirshberg; and Hirshberg brought C–3 to the BDO firm when his old firm merged with BDO. May Hirshberg serve any or all of the three?

7.   *Revision.* If an employee's noncompetition covenant is too broad, will the court invalidate it or narrow it to match the employer's legitimate protectable interest? The lower courts had refused to sever or narrow the covenant; instead they have invalidated the whole covenant on the ground that they cannot "rewrite" it. Why?

Why does BDO's covenant with Hirshberg qualify for narrowing?

8.   *BDO's Remedy.* Eighteen months has long since past, in any event BDO is not seeking an injunction. The covenant calls for liquidated damages—1 ½ times one-year's billings of the rustled clients. Hirshberg has served some BDO clients during the 18–month period. What *protected* clients did Hirshberg serve in the covered period? The answer to that question seems to depend on the new definition of BDO's protectable interest.

9.   *Remedies.* An employer's usual remedy for a violation of a valid covenant is an injunction prohibiting the offending conduct and an accounting of profits. Presto–X–Company v. Ewing, 442 N.W.2d 85 (Iowa 1989); Robert S. Weiss & Associates v. Wiederlight, 208 Conn. 525, 546 A.2d 216 (1988).

10.   The Minnesota court considered partial enforcement of a covenant unreasonably restraining trade. The seller of a small trucking company had made an unlimited covenant not to compete. The court rewrote it to apply only within the city for five years. Rejecting the view that unlimited covenants are completely void, the court accepted the minority version of the "blue pencil" doctrine, stating: "Although the 'blue pencil' doctrine, requiring that the reasonable and unreasonable restraints be severable, still commands a slight majority of jurisdictions, a substantial minority of courts modify unreasonable restraints of trade, whether formally divisible or not, and enforce them to the extent reasonable in the circumstances." Bess v. Bothman, 257 N.W.2d 791, 794 (Minn.1977).

The partial-enforcement doctrine that the court applied in Bess v. Bothman is generally available only where the employer was not guilty of bad faith or over-reaching. Durapin, Inc. v. American Products, Inc., 559 A.2d 1051 (R.I.1989); Ellis v. James V. Hurson Associates, 565 A.2d 615 (D.C.App.1989). Where the restrictive covenant evidences a deliberate intent by the employer to place unreasonable and oppressive restraints on the employee, the court will not modify the covenant, but will strike it down as void, regardless of whether the clauses are severable. Dryvit System, Inc. v. Rushing, 132 Ill.App.3d 9, 477 N.E.2d 35 (1985); Holloway v. Faw, Casson & Co., 78 Md.App. 205, 552 A.2d 1311 (1989), aff'd in part, rev'd in part, 319 Md. 324, 572 A.2d 510 (Md.1990).

Although Maryland is a blue-pencil state, a judge limited blue penciling to erasing the improper parts of the covenant and refused to interpolate new limitations. Deutsche Postal Global Mail, Ltd. v. Conrad, 292 F.Supp.2d 748 (D.Md. 2003).

11.   *Penciling In Damages.* Does a judge's ability to rewrite a restrictive covenant as a basis for an injunction extend to using the rewritten covenant as a

basis for damages? Answering yes is A.N. Deringer, Inc. v. Strough, 103 F.3d 243 (2d Cir.1996).

12. *Quick, Quick Litigation.* The contract itself limits the employer's period of freedom from a former employee's competition. Once a former employee divulges a trade secret or otherwise breaches a confidence, the former employer's harm has occurred. Accordingly, a judge's effective decision and remedy is often granted on the employer-plaintiff's motion for a temporary restraining order or preliminary injunction.

When an ex-employer sues its former employee on a covenant that limits post-employment competition and seeks a TRO or preliminary injunction, the plaintiff's irreparable injury may be in doubt because the judge may hold that it can recover the pecuniary loss as damages. Merrill Lynch, Pierce, Fenner & Smith Inc. v. Callahan, 265 F.Supp.2d 440 (D.Vt. 2003).

13. *Soiled Hands?* The *Merrill Lynch* court in the Note above also declined to grant Merrill Lynch a preliminary injunction because of its unclean hands. The plaintiff's hands were soiled by its practice of expecting new agents to do the same things it was suing its former employees to prevent, that is, utilizing their books of business from their former positions. Other courts have held that an employer-plaintiff cannot breach an employment contract and then sue its former employee on a restrictive covenant. "He who seeks equity must do equity." Williams v. Riedman, 339 S.C. 251, 529 S.E.2d 28, 40–42 (App. 2000) reh'g denied (2000); Associated Spring Corp. v. Roy F. Wilson & Avnet, Inc., 410 F.Supp. 967 (D.S.C. 1976).

2. EMPLOYER'S DAMAGES

ROTH v. SPECK

Municipal Court of Appeals, District of Columbia, 1956.
126 A.2d 153.

QUINN, ASSOC. J. This suit was brought by plaintiff (employer) against defendant (employee) for breach of a written contract of employment. Trial by the court resulted in a finding and judgment for plaintiff for one dollar. Plaintiff appeals.

Plaintiff testified that he was the owner of a beauty salon in Silver Spring, Maryland; that his business was seasonal; and that on April 15, 1955, by a written contract he agreed to employ defendant as a hairdresser for one year. Defendant's salary was to be $75 a week or a commission of fifty percent on the gross receipts from his work, whichever sum was greater. Defendant remained in his employ for approximately six and one-half months and then left. Plaintiff testified that from the beginning defendant earned his salary, needed no special training, and soon built up and maintained a following because of his exceptional skill and talent.

Plaintiff also testified that his net profit was seven percent of the gross receipts per hairdresser. To substantiate this he introduced defendant's statement of earnings, which reflected gross receipts and salary paid to him. Plaintiff testified that in an effort to mitigate his damages he employed another person "to whom he paid $350, which was a complete loss and he had to let this employee go." He then hired still another operator who even at the date of trial was not earning his salary, and was thus employed at a loss to plaintiff. A witness for plaintiff testified that he had been the owner of a beauty salon for many years; that defendant had been in his employ since November 1, 1955, at a weekly salary of $100; and that defendant was a very good operator.

Defendant testified that he left because conditions in plaintiff's shop were unbearable; that he complained to plaintiff on numerous occasions; that he had asked for more money but that salary was not the main reason for his leaving; and that he was presently earning $100 per week.

The sole question presented is what damages plaintiff was entitled to under these circumstances. Plaintiff argues that the trial court did not consider the value of defendant's services or the profits lost by plaintiff and therefore erroneously limited the award to nominal damages. It is established law that where a plaintiff proves a breach of a contractual duty he is entitled to damages; however, when he offers no proof of actual damages or the proof is vague and speculative, he is entitled to no more than nominal damages. While the facts warrant application of this principle to plaintiff's claim concerning lost profits, we think there was proof of actual damage and that the evidence with regard to the value of defendant's services provided an accurate measure of such damage.

The measure of damages for breach of an employment contract by an employee is the cost of obtaining other service equivalent to that promised and not performed. Compensation for additional consequential injury may be recovered if at the time the contract was made the employee had reason to foresee that such injury would result from his breach. However, we need not concern ourselves with the foreseeability of lost profits resulting from defendant's breach since plaintiff's proof on this point was at most conjectural and speculative. * * * It can be seen that defendant's gross receipts, and hence plaintiff's seven percent profit, depended on a number of contingencies—the seasonal fluctuations of business, defendant's skill and industry, and the judgment of the employee who assigned the operators. There was no criterion by which the trial court could have estimated plaintiff's profits with the degree of certainty necessary to allow their recovery; therefore they were not within the range of recoverable damages.

There remains the question as to the value of defendant's services. Defendant was evidently a hairdresser of exceptional talent. This is demonstrated not only by the fact that he experienced no difficulty in securing and retaining another position at a higher salary, but also by plaintiff's own testimony that he was unable to hire a satisfactory substitute. Defendant did not claim that he was required to render services other than those in his original contract with plaintiff in order to obtain a higher salary from his new employer, nor did plaintiff prove by expert testimony how much such services would bring in the market. But plaintiff did prove the amount defendant actually received. Under such circumstances, there was some evidence of the value of defendant's services and therefore of the cost of replacement. As was said in Triangle Waist Co. v. Todd, 223 N.Y. 27, 119 N.E. 85, 86:

> "If one agrees to sell something to another, and then, the next day, sells it to someone else at an advance, the new transaction is not to be ignored in estimating the buyer's loss. * * * The rule is not different when one sells one's labor. The price received upon a genuine sale either of property or of service is some evidence of value."

Twenty-four weeks yet remained when defendant abandoned his contract and obtained employment elsewhere at a higher salary. Until this new compensation is disproved as the value of his services, it may be presumed to be the fair value. That it was the fair value of defendant's services was partially supported by plaintiff's unsuccessful efforts to obtain a comparable replacement. Seemingly, plaintiff would have had to pay $100 a week in order to obtain an equally talented hairdresser, if one could have been found. If this be so, plaintiff having contracted for defendant's services at a guaranteed wage of $75 per week, would be entitled to the difference between the two salaries for the remainder of the contract period. * * *

The judgment will be reversed with instructions to grant a new trial, limited to the issue of damages.

Reversed with instructions.

Notes

1. *Questions About the Court's Damages Measure.* Does the Roth v. Speck court's damages measure give the employer the profit potential of the breached contract? Is the court's damages measure (a) damages to compensate the employer, or (b) restitution to take the benefit of the second transaction from the breaching employee? Does the damages measure reduce an employee's incentive to improve his employment opportunities? Does the measure forbid an employee from an efficient breach? Should Speck differ from the farmer-seller in Notes, pp. 599–604, who breached a grain contract, paid the buyer's damages, and sold later to another buyer for a higher price?

2. *The Employer's Lost Actual Profit.* A professional basketball team sued Sharman, a former coach, and the Lakers, his new team, for damages for breach of contract. In reversing a judgment for the plaintiff and ordering a new trial, the court stated:

"The potential of a new trial impels us to discuss one matter in which the parties are in disagreement. The problem is the measure of damages and the instructions relating thereto. The defendants say that they are not liable for lost profits and that the measure of damages is either the increased replacement expense or, if the employee is unique or irreplaceable, the increased remuneration which the employee would receive in the open market. Defendants point out that Sharman's replacements were obtained at lower salaries than that paid Sharman and that the Los Angeles Lakers paid Sharman basically what he received from the Utah Stars."

"Lost profits may be recovered in an employee breach of contract case if the employer can show that the parties had reason to believe that losses would result from the breach. We are aware of only one California case which addresses the issue." Steelduct Co. v. Henger–Seltzer Co., 26 Cal.2d 634, 160 P.2d 804, 812 (1945) says:

'[T]he elements of the plaintiff's [employer's] damages are two: the reasonably necessary expense to which plaintiff was put in procuring a new agent, and the loss of profits (if any profits were lost) caused by defendants' breach.'

"Consequential damages such as lost profits may be recovered in an appropriate case for breach of an employment contract. In the case here, they can be justified only on a finding that Sharman, as a coach, was unique or irreplaceable. The evidence in this regard was conflicting. The jury should have been told that the plaintiff could not recover damages for lost profits or diminished franchise value without a finding that Sharman was irreplaceable as a coach." Eckles v. Sharman, 548 F.2d 905, 910 (10th Cir. 1977).

3. EMPLOYER'S RESTITUTION

SNEPP v. UNITED STATES

Supreme Court of the United States, 1980.
444 U.S. 507.

PER CURIAM. * * * Based on his experiences as a CIA agent, Snepp published a book about certain CIA activities in South Vietnam. Snepp published the account without submitting it to the Agency for prepublication review. As an express condition of his employment with the CIA in 1968, however, Snepp had executed an agreement promising that he would "not * * * publish * * * any information or material relating to the Agency, its activities or intelligence activities generally, either during or after the term of [his] employment * * * without specific prior approval by the Agency." The promise was an integral part of Snepp's concurrent undertaking "not to disclose any classified information relating to the Agency without proper authorization." Thus, Snepp had pledged not to divulge *classified* information and not to publish *any* information without prepublication clearance. The Government brought this suit to enforce Snepp's agreement. It sought a declaration that Snepp had breached the contract, an injunction requiring Snepp to submit future writings for prepublication review, and an order imposing a constructive trust for the Government's benefit on all profits that Snepp might earn from publishing the book in violation of his fiduciary obligations to the Agency.[1]

The District Court found that Snepp had "willfully, deliberately and surreptitiously breached his position of trust with the CIA and the [1968] secrecy agreement" by publishing his book without submitting it for prepublication review. * * * Finally, the court determined as a fact that publication of the book had "caused the United States irreparable harm and loss." The District Court therefore enjoined future breaches of Snepp's agreement and imposed a constructive trust on Snepp's profits.

The Court of Appeals accepted the findings of the District Court and agreed that Snepp had breached a valid contract. * * * The court, however, concluded that the record did not support imposition of a constructive trust. The conclusion rested on the court's perception that Snepp had a First Amendment right to publish unclassified information and the Government's concession—for the purposes of this litigation—that Snepp's book divulged no classified intelligence. In other words, the court thought that Snepp's fiduciary obligation extended only to preserving the confidentiality of classified material. It therefore limited recovery to nominal damages and to the possibility of punitive damages if the Government—in a jury trial—could prove tortious conduct. * * *

Snepp's employment with the CIA involved an extremely high degree of trust. In the opening sentence of the agreement that he signed, Snepp explicitly recognized that he was entering a trust relationship. The trust agreement specifically imposed the obligation not to publish *any* information relating to the Agency without submitting the information for clearance. Snepp stipulated at trial that—after undertaking this obligation—he had been "assigned to various positions of trust" and that he had been granted "frequent access to classified

---

1. [Footnote renumbered.] At the time of suit, Snepp already had received about $60,000 in advance payments. His contract with his pub- lisher provides for royalties and other potential profits.

information, including information regarding intelligence sources and methods." Snepp published his book about CIA activities on the basis of this background and exposure. He deliberately and surreptitiously violated his obligation to submit all material for prepublication review. Thus, he exposed the classified information with which he had been entrusted to the risk of disclosure.

Whether Snepp violated his trust does not depend upon whether his book actually contained classified information. The Government does not deny—as a general principle—Snepp's right to publish unclassified information. Nor does it contend—at this stage of the litigation—that Snepp's book contains classified material. * * *

Both the District Court and the Court of Appeals found that a former intelligence agent's publication of unreviewed material relating to intelligence activities can be detrimental to vital national interests even if the published information is unclassified. When a former agent relies on his own judgment about what information is detrimental, he may reveal information that the CIA—with its broader understanding of what may expose classified information and confidential sources—could have identified as harmful. In addition to receiving intelligence from domestically based or controlled sources, the CIA obtains information from the intelligence services of friendly nations and from agents operating in foreign countries. The continued availability of these foreign sources depends upon the CIA's ability to guarantee the security of information that might compromise them and even endanger the personal safety of foreign agents. * * *

The decision of the Court of Appeals denies the Government the most appropriate remedy for Snepp's acknowledged wrong. Indeed, as a practical matter, the decision may well leave the Government with no reliable deterrent against similar breaches of security. No one disputes that the actual damages attributable to a publication such as Snepp's generally are unquantifiable. Nominal damages are a hollow alternative, certain to deter no one. The punitive damages recoverable after a jury trial are speculative and unusual. Even if recovered, they may bear no relation to either the Government's irreparable loss or Snepp's unjust gain.

The Government could not pursue the only remedy that the Court of Appeals left it without losing the benefit of the bargain it seeks to enforce. Proof of the tortious conduct necessary to sustain an award of punitive damages might force the Government to disclose some of the very confidences that Snepp promised to protect. * * * When the Government cannot secure its remedy without unacceptable risks, it has no remedy at all.

A constructive trust, on the other hand, protects both the Government and the former agent from unwarranted risks. This remedy is the natural and customary consequence of a breach of trust. It deals fairly with both parties by conforming relief to the dimensions of the wrong. If the agent secures prepublication clearance, he can publish with no fear of liability. If the agent publishes unreviewed material in violation of his fiduciary and contractual obligation, the trust remedy simply requires him to disgorge the benefits of his faithlessness. Since the remedy is swift and sure, it is tailored to deter those who would place sensitive information at risk. And since the remedy reaches only funds attributable to the breach, it cannot saddle the former agent with exemplary damages out of all proportion to his gain. * * * We therefore reverse the judgment of the Court of Appeals insofar as it refused to impose a constructive trust on Snepp's profits, and we remand the cases to the Court of Appeals for reinstatement of the full judgment of the District Court.

So ordered.

JUSTICE STEVENS, with whom JUSTICE BRENNAN and JUSTICE MARSHALL join dissenting. * * * Plainly this is not a typical trust situation in which a settlor has conveyed legal title to certain assets to a trustee for the use and benefit of designated beneficiaries. Rather, it is an employment relationship in which the employee possesses fiduciary obligations arising out of his duty of loyalty to his employer. One of those obligations long recognized by the common law even in the absence of a written employment agreement, is the duty to protect confidential or "classified" information. If Snepp had breached that obligation, the common law would support the implication of a constructive trust upon the benefits derived from his misuse of confidential information.

But Snepp did not breach his duty to protect confidential information. Rather, he breached a contractual duty, imposed in aid of the basic duty to maintain confidentiality, to obtain prepublication clearance. In order to justify the imposition of a constructive trust, the majority attempts to equate this contractual duty with Snepp's duty not to disclose, labeling them both as "fiduciary." I find nothing in the common law to support such an approach.

The Court has not persuaded me that a rule of reason analysis should not be applied to Snepp's covenant to submit to prepublication review. * * * When the Government seeks to enforce a harsh restriction on the employee's freedom, despite its admission that the interest the agreement was designed to protect—the confidentiality of classified information—has not been compromised, an equity court might well be persuaded that the case is not one in which the covenant should be enforced.

But even assuming that Snepp's covenant to submit to prepublication review should be enforced, the constructive trust imposed by the Court is not an appropriate remedy. If an employee has used his employer's confidential information for his own personal profit, a constructive trust over those profits is obviously an appropriate remedy because the profits are the direct result of the breach. But Snepp admittedly did not use confidential information in his book; nor were the profits from his book in any sense a product of his failure to submit the book for prepublication review. For, even if Snepp had submitted the book to the Agency for prepublication review, the Government's censorship authority would surely have been limited to the excision of classified material. In this case, then, it would have been obliged to clear the book for publication in precisely the same form as it now stands. Thus, Snepp has not gained any profits as a result of his breach; the Government, rather than Snepp, will be unjustly enriched if he is required to disgorge profits attributable entirely to his own legitimate activity.

Despite the fact that Snepp has not caused the Government the type of harm that would ordinarily be remedied by the imposition of a constructive trust, the Court attempts to justify a constructive trust remedy on the ground that the Government has suffered *some* harm. The Court states that publication of "unreviewed material" by a former CIA agent "can be detrimental to vital national interests even if the published information is unclassified." It then seems to suggest that the injury in such cases stems from the Agency's inability to catch "harmful" but unclassified information before it is published. * * *

[I]t is difficult to believe that the publication of a book like Snepp's, which does not reveal classified information, has significantly weakened the Agency's position. Nor does it explain whether the unidentified foreign agencies who have stopped cooperating with the CIA have done so because of a legitimate fear that secrets will be revealed or because they merely disagree with our Government's classification policies.

In any event, to the extent that the Government seeks to punish Snepp for the generalized harm he has caused by failing to submit to prepublication review and to deter others from following in his footsteps, punitive damages is, as the Court of Appeals held, clearly the preferable remedy "since a constructive trust depends on the concept of unjust enrichment rather than deterrence and punishment." * * *

The uninhibited character of today's exercise in lawmaking is highlighted by the Court's disregard of two venerable principles that favor a more conservative approach to this case.

First, for centuries the English-speaking judiciary refused to grant equitable relief unless the plaintiff could show that his remedy at law was inadequate. Without waiting for an opportunity to appraise the adequacy of the punitive damages remedy in this case, the Court has jumped to the conclusion that equitable relief is necessary.

Second, and of greater importance, the Court seems unaware of the fact that its drastic new remedy has been fashioned to enforce a species of prior restraint on a citizen's right to criticize his government. Inherent in this prior restraint is the risk that the reviewing agency will misuse its authority to delay the publication of a critical work or to persuade an author to modify the contents of his work beyond the demands of secrecy. * * *

I respectfully dissent.

Notes

1. *Characterization.* Snepp breached his legal duty; thus the CIA's restitution, the constructive trust the Court imposed on his gains, was not freestanding restitution; but it stemmed from his breach. The dissent and the majority maintain that Snepp breached different duties, contract and fiduciary respectively.

The contract-fiduciary characterization matters. In a breach of contract action for damages, the defendant is entitled to demand a jury trial and a successful plaintiff would recover compensatory damages, measured by its loss. The government's pecuniary loss from Snepp's book was zero. A contract plaintiff cannot recover punitive damages unless the defendant committed an independent tort.

When the majority labeled Snepp's misconduct a breach of fiduciary duty, that characterization opened the door for the CIA to recover all of Snepp's gains from the book.

Should the characterization matter? (a) If Snepp's misconduct had only been a breach of his contract with the CIA, should the CIA nevertheless have recovered restitution measured by Snepp's gains? Would it be more satisfactory if the Court had held that Snepp's breach of a fiduciary duty was not a prerequisite for disgorgement, but that his opportunistic breach of contract was enough to trigger restitution?

(b) On the other hand, even if Snepp's publication had breached a fiduciary duty, should the government have been limited to recovering compensatory damages?

2. *Fiduciary.* "Fiduciary" is a slippery term. A court will recognize that a lawyer, a corporate officer or director, the trustee of an express trust, an executor, or a guardian is a fiduciary because of the fiduciary's relationship of expertise, trust, and confidence with another person and the need for the fiduciary's loyalty to that person. Since Snepp was not managing an asset in a beneficiary's best interest, his employment-based relationship was not, as the dissent points out, a core case for a fiduciary duty.

3. *Enrichment?* A court will base restitution on the defendant's unjust enrichment. Was Snepp enriched? If he had submitted his manuscript for the CIA's authorities to review, they would have cleared it for publication and Snepp would have gained the royalty income. Was Snepp's enrichment because of his breach, his failure to submit his manuscript in advance? If Snepp did not disclose any secrets in breach of his duty of loyalty, did he gain anything from his breach? Did Snepp appropriate a beneficiary's asset or its value?

Snepp breached his contractual duty to submit the manuscript for review; but his breach did not compromise the CIA's secret information and sources. The reason for the contractual duty to submit was to prevent the harm; Snepp's breach of that duty was not the harm itself. If a CIA employee's duty to submit manuscript for pre-publication review is preventive, so also are a fiduciary's duties to avoid conflicts of interest and comingling funds. The majority emphasizes that the policy of deterrence supports stripping Snepp of his gains, the royalties. The CIA trusted Snepp with information, secrets that he would not have learned except for his promise. Is the CIA's ability to entrust an employee with secrets a sufficient basis for a fiduciary duty and restitution? Will allowing the government to recover restitution from Snepp, as the Court does, create an intolerable damper on CIA agents' free speech?

4. *Fiduciary Breach—Beyond Restitution.* An employee's breach of fiduciary duty to employer may be a tort which qualifies the employer to recover punitive damages. In Hensley v. Tri–QSI Denver Corp., the employer-plaintiff recovered for breach of contract, which was large, and breach of fiduciary duty, which was small; but the plaintiff was entitled to punitive damages under the Colorado statute based only on the fiduciary tort. Hensley v. Tri–QSI Denver Corp., 98 P.3d 965 (Colo. Ct. App. 2004).

In Maryland, however, the Court of Appeals held that "there is no universal or omnibus tort for the redress of breach of fiduciary duty by any and all fiduciaries." The decision affects the litigants' right to a jury trial and the winner's opportunity to recover punitive damages. Kann v. Kann, 344 Md. 689, 690 A.2d 509 (1997).

5. *Employer's Remedies When an Employee is Bribed.* Sam Sailer "gives" Ben Beyer's purchasing agent, Alice Aggie, a sound system worth $8,000; Beyer's "gratuity" facilitates Aggie's decision to buy Sailer's speakers to sell in Beyer's SoundStores.

Even if Aggie purchased speakers that Beyer wanted from Sailer at a competitive price, when an agent-employee accepts such a "gift," undisclosed commission or bribe, she deprives her principal of her disinterested advice. Her conflict of interest is obvious.

A court will use the language of fiduciary responsibility: a fiduciary who breaches a trust relationship and benefits may not retain the benefit. Observe the shifting focus on compensation and deterrence below as courts examine the remedies that flow from bribes.

(a) *Employer Sues the Employee.* (i) An employee of the Department of Agriculture accepted two automobiles and a deep freeze as gifts from one De Angelis, a participant in programs the department administered. Despite the employee's claims that Mr. De Angelis was just a friend and "a kind and generous man," the court entered judgment for these benefits in favor of the government. United States v. Drisko, 303 F.Supp. 858 (E.D.Va.1969).

(ii) In a notable English case, the House of Lords granted the government restitution from a soldier who, in an occupied country, had accepted bribes to accompany smugglers' trucks through checkpoints. Reading v. Attorney General, [1951] A.C. 507 (H.L.).

Beyer's recovery of $8,000, the amount of her unjust gain, from a disloyal employee like Aggie seems pretty straightforward.

(iii) An employer sued an embezzling employee under the federal Racketeer Influenced Corrupt Organizations Act, (RICO). The court imposed a constructive trust on a house defendant had purchased with the bezzle. It trebled the RICO damage judgment. Finally, "Mr. Kelly's claims for back salary and expense reimbursement are dismissed as not recoverable because of his disloyalty to his employer during the period for which he is making those claims." MDO Development Corp. v. Kelly, 726 F.Supp. 79, 86 (S.D.N.Y. 1989).

(iv) There is an analogy to *Snepp*. Aggie's enrichment came from Sailer. Was Aggie unjustly enriched *at the expense* of Beyer? Beyer can respond that the bribe Aggie received from Sailer was a discount that he was entitled to receive.

In a complex English dispute about whether an owner-principal could recover bribes that contractors had paid to the owner's agent, the chancellor said "the price [that the owner paid the contractors] was actually increased by the amount of the bribe" that the contractors had paid to faithless agent. Daraydan Holdings Ltd. v. Sollard International Ltd., [2004] EWHC 662, para. 87 (Ch).

The source of the agent's enrichment may be crucial when, as in *Snepp*, the principal seeks a constructive trust. For a court may require a constructive trust plaintiff to trace his asset into the defendant's hands.

Snepp's enrichment came from the book buyers and the publisher, not the CIA; Snepp was not unjustly enriched *at the expense of* the CIA. The argument in the purchasing-agent case is that the seller's bribe was built back into the price the principal paid the seller; that argument fails completely in Snepp v. United States.

Suppose a defendant, Snupp, who owes $400,000 to another creditor, Crayon, but has only one asset, $100,000 of improper royalties from a book published in breach of a contract with the CIA. If the court declares Snupp a constructive trustee for the CIA, then the CIA will recover in full—and Crayon will recover nothing. On the other hand, if the CIA recovers a money judgment (for restitution—money had and received), then, in theory, the CIA and Crayon share Snupp's $100,000 asset pro rata, 20% and 80%, $20,000 and $80,000 respectively.

Back to *Snepp*: If Snepp had had other creditors, were the royalties sufficiently identified with the CIA or the wrong to qualify for constructive trust status?

"There are powerful policy reasons," wrote the chancellor in *Daraydan Holdings*, "for ensuring that a fiduciary does not retain gains acquired in violation of fiduciary duty, and I do not consider that it should make any difference whether the fiduciary is insolvent. There is no injustice to the [fiduciary's] creditors in their not sharing in an asset for which the fiduciary has not given value, and which the fiduciary should not have had." Daraydan Holdings Ltd. v. Sollard International Ltd., [2004] EWHC 662, para. 86 (Ch.).

What supports the Court's decision to give the CIA special priority rights in Snepp's royalties? In answering, remember that, unlike the agent in *Daraydan Holdings*, Snepp was not the kind of agent-fiduciary who manages property or conducts business for a principal and that the CIA cannot argue that Snepp diverted the royalties which would have otherwise accrued to it.

(b) *Employer Sues the Briber.* Sailer has facilitated Aggie's violation of her fiduciary duty to Beyer and probably committed the tort of inducing Aggie to breach her contract with Beyer.

(i) *Damages.* The Court of Claims held that the government had a common-law action against a company whose former president had bribed federal employees to obtain mortgage insurance business with the government. The government was unable to prove any specific pecuniary damages since it must be assumed that the company performed the contracts well and for the same consideration the government would have had to pay anyway:

"It is an old maxim of the law that, where the fact of injury is adequately shown, the court should not cavil at the absence of specific or detailed proof of the damages. Here, the plaintiffs engaged in wrongful conduct that clearly hurt the Government. Significant elements of that harm, such as the injury to the impartial administration of governmental programs, are not susceptible to an accurate monetary gauge. We should not deny the Government relief because Sirote managed to cause injury not readily traceable or measurable. Similarly, the Government's inability to attach an exact and provable dollar figure to the harm it sustained should not result in the effective exculpation of the plaintiffs. * * * As between the briber and the bribee's employer, the risks of damage determination should fall on the former."

"On this premise the amount of the bribe provides a reasonable measure of damage, in the absence of a more precise yardstick. That is, after all, the value the plaintiffs placed on their corruption of the defendant's employees; the other side of the coin is that the plaintiffs hoped and expected to benefit by more than the sum of the bribes. It is therefore fair to use that total as the measure of an injury which is probable in its impact but uncertain in its mathematical calculation. [citations] Of course, the Government cannot recover the bribes twice—once from the briber and again from the corrupted employee. But it is entitled to one such recovery." Continental Management, Inc. v. United States, 527 F.2d 613, 619 (Ct.Cl.1975).

Questions: Considering the reasons to compel a bribe-taker to disgorge, why should the court limit the government to one recovery? Did the court's view of the plaintiff's remedy as compensatory damages obscure the possibility of restitution?

(ii) *Unjust Enrichment, Restitution and Disgorgement.* The defendant-Bank's employee had bribed a public official to obtain the plaintiff-County's bond business. The dispute had been through criminal prosecutions and the SEC before the County's civil action against the Bank was tried. Although the Bank had already paid the County the amount of the kickbacks, $206,809.22, the County was suing the Bank for unjust enrichment seeking disgorgement of the Bank's "underwriter's discount." After a complex submission including several other substantive theories, the jury's verdict for the County was for unjust enrichment-disgorgement.

The New Jersey Supreme Court hinged its decision on restitution: the Bank's disgorgement is "not related to whether the County suffered damages." Measurement: the County could recover the Bank's gross profits, the "total fees received [and retained] by the bank." Finally, prejudgment interest ran from the date of the transaction, not the date of the complaint.

County of Essex v. First Union National Bank, 186 N.J. 46, 891 A.2d 600 (2006).

Should a court award Beyer restitution from Sailer measured by the amount of the bribe? The amount of Sailor's gross profit on the speakers? Both?

(c) *Employer Sues Both the Briber and the Employee*. In litigation involving an employer's claims against a bribing seller and an employee who had received kickbacks, the trial judge entered judgment against the seller for procuring breach of contract and measured the employer's recovery by the amount of the employee's salary "during the period of his duplicitous conduct." "The trial court also rendered a judgment against both [the bribing seller and the corrupt employee] for the amount of secret commissions." The seller appealed.

The Tennessee supreme court thought the salary was an appropriate recovery against the employee, but "an inappropriate element of damage to charge against the procurer of the breach." The secret kickbacks the seller paid the employee were the employer's proper damages. "[H]ad [the bribing seller] not paid this money to [plaintiff's employee], it may be presumed that these funds would have inured to the benefit of [the employer] in the form of lower prices or greater commissions." Recovery was trebled under a Tennessee statute.

The Tennessee court quoted the Restatement of Torts: "any damages in fact paid by the third person will reduce the damages actually recoverable" for interference with contract. Restatement (Second) of Torts § 774A(2)(1979), in Dorsett Carpet Mills, Inc. v. Whitt Tile and Marble Distributing Co., 734 S.W.2d 322, 323–26 (Tenn.1987).

The question of whether the employer could collect judgments from both the seller and the employee without receiving duplicated recovery was not, however, raised.

If Beyer seeks to recover a damages judgment from Sailer and restitution from Aggie, he will find authority on both sides. What are the arguments?

Trebling. Kewaunee, the former employer, sued both its former purchasing agent and several sellers who had bribed the purchasing agent. The court accepted the plaintiff's argument "that they should not have to prove out of pocket loss due to the transaction." "Commercial bribery," the court said, "harms an employer as a matter of law, and the proper measure of damages suffered must include at a minimum the amount of the commercial bribes the third party paid." Moreover defendants' bribery qualifies plaintiff for treble "damages" because it is misconduct under the North Carolina unfair and deceptive trade practices act. Kewaunee Scientific Corp. v. Pegram, 130 N.C.App. 576, 503 S.E.2d 417 (1998).

(d) *Suppose the Briber Sues the Employer*? Denial of recovery to a bribe-payer is straightforward in government work. All the bribe-paying plaintiff's claims on the contract are forfeited, because the bribe is "fraud" which triggers "nonenforcement" on public policy grounds. Supermex, Inc. v. United States, 35 Fed.Cl. 29, 40–42 (1996).

The New York Court of Appeals went a little farther. When the firm that had bribed a city employee sued the city for the balance "due," the court turned the tables and held that the City could recover all amounts that it had paid the briber under the bribe-induced contract. S.T. Grand, Inc. v. City of New York, 32 N.Y.2d 300, 344 N.Y.S.2d 938, 298 N.E.2d 105 (1973).

Questions. Suppose Sailer sues Beyer for the price of the speakers it has delivered to Beyer. Should the court deny Sailer recovery on the ground that the "agreement" was tainted by the bribe and illegal in violation of public policy? Should the court let Beyer keep the speakers without paying anything for them? If Beyer counterclaims, should the court, in addition, force Sailer to refund Beyer's earlier payments for speakers?

(e) *The United States Charges the Briber With Mail and Wire Fraud*. Personal injury lawyers who paid indirect kickbacks to insurance adjusters to secure favorable treatment of their clients' claims were convicted of federal mail/wire fraud. United States v. Rybicki, 287 F.3d 257 (2d Cir. 2002), aff'd en banc, 354 F.3d 124 (2d Cir. 2003), cert. denied, 543 U.S. 809 (2004).

(f) *Fiduciary's Employer, Second–Best Plaintiff.* Two officers of a corporation unloaded their personal holdings on the open market after learning inside information which would cause the corporation stock to fall in value; they saved themselves several hundred thousand dollars because the market declined when the information became public. The unfortunate buyers were the losers. However, the New York court allowed the *corporation* to recover the officers' savings. Diamond v. Oreamuno, 24 N.Y.2d 494, 301 N.Y.S.2d 78, 248 N.E.2d 910 (1969).

Attempts by *corporations* to recover "benefits" accruing to persons using "inside information" to trade in the corporation's stock on the open market beyond the limits of *Oreamuno* have not been successful—e.g., attempts to recover profits made by tippees from genuine insiders. Frigitemp Corp. v. Financial Dynamics Fund, 524 F.2d 275 (2d Cir.1975) emphasizes that *Oreamuno* is based on a breach of fiduciary duty.

Courts have found that the *Oreamuno* court went too far. Freeman v. Decio, 584 F.2d 186, 188–96 (7th Cir 1978); Schein v. Chasen, 313 So.2d 739 (Fla.1975).

A federal court in New Jersey thought parallel developments had supplanted *Oreamuno*: "The purpose of the common law claim recognized in the [*Oreamuno*] case was to deter the abuse of corporate office at a time when federal remedies had not yet proven effective. The court, acknowledging the possibility of double liability in theory, stated that in practice it was unlikely that public shareholders would bring a successful federal claim. In any event, the court reasoned, 'the mere possibility of such a suit is not a defense, nor does it render the complaint insufficient.'"

"In the years since the [*Oreamuno*] decision the class action suit under Rule 10b–5 has developed into an effective remedy for insider trading. In addition, under Section 16(b) of the Exchange Act, a corporation may recover 'short-swing profits' realized by insiders trading in the corporation's stock. Under these circumstances a common law claim to recover profits from insiders presents an actual, and needless, risk of double liability. * * *

"[T]he court concludes that the New Jersey courts would not recognize a duplicative claim under common law for recovery of profits from insiders." Frankel v. Slotkin, 795 F.Supp. 76, 81 (E.D.N.Y.1992).

What does the future hold for the *Oreamuno* remedy? Our crystal ball is cloudy. The Supreme Court clarified and expanded the federal *criminal* law of trading on information in breach of a fiduciary duty. United States v. O'Hagan, 521 U.S. 642 (1997). On the other hand in 1995, Congress enacted "tort reform" legislation to curb investor class actions in federal courts. Private Securities Litigation Reform Act of 1995. Corporate officers' misconduct and corruption in the 1990s, exposed when the tech bubble burst, led to new federal responsibilities for officers under the Sarbanes–Oxley Act as well as to numerous criminal prosecutions, state and federal, and shareholder derivative actions. Lifestyle icon Martha Stewart's criminal conviction stemmed from misconduct related to insider trading. In the post-Enron era of increased corporate regulation, including new rights for both shareholders and the corporate entity, we can expect litigation about corporate officers' and directors' liability to dissipate some of the clouds. Stay tuned.

4. EMPLOYER'S LIQUIDATED DAMAGES

Student Loan Alert. Under the National Health Service Corps Scholarship Program eligible students received "scholarships" and agreed to serve in a designated health manpower shortage area. The agreements provided that if the scholar defaulted on the promise to serve, he or she will be liable for liquidated damages of three times the scholarship plus interest.

Dr. Conway. With trebling and interest, the liquidated damages can add up. Dr. Marianne Conway received three years of scholarships, totaling $79,567.09. After a deferment, a breach, several years of thrust and parry, and a lawsuit, the judge said, "Due to the default of the NHSC Scholarship contract, Dr. Conway owes to the United States of America the sum of $520,993.86 through May 25, 1988 with interest accruing thereafter at the rate of 17.395 percent per annum or $113.76 per day." United States v. Conway, 686 F.Supp. 571 (E.D.La.1988), affirmed, 868 F.2d 1269 (5th Cir.1989). Even allowing for a math error, won't Dr. Conway have to run pretty fast just to pay the interest as it accrues?

Consider the argument that, in addition to being a penalty, the NHSC trebling created improper incentives to perform an employment contract.

Dr. Redovan. Another NHSC scholarship recipient, Dr. Redovan, declined an assignment to the Indian Health Service. The government sued him:

Redovan contends "that the treble damage provision contained in the statute and his agreement with NHSC is void and unenforceable because it is a penalty. The United States takes the position that the clause is a valid stipulation of liquidated damages. All cases addressing the enforceability of this provision of which I am aware have agreed that the clause is indeed enforceable. United States v. Bills, 639 F.Supp. 825 (D.N.J.1986); United States v. Hayes, 633 F.Supp. 1183 (M.D.N.C.1986); United States v. Swanson, 618 F.Supp. 1231 (D.Mich.1985). I have made my own independent assessment of the question in light of the facts before me and the cases reported and conclude that the provision is an enforceable damage provision. * * *"

"I conclude that the damage provision contained in the contract and the statute is a valid and enforceable provision, because I simply am unable to find that it is disproportionate to the injury inflicted on the United States by Redovan's failure to perform. First and most obviously, the government has lost and must recover the money provided to Redovan for his education, costs and living expenses. That aspect of damage is simple to ascertain. However, the other costs imposed on the United States are decidedly less easy to measure."

"By defaulting on his service obligation, Redovan has deprived the United States of the services of a physician in a critically underserved location. As Judge Thompson observed in *Bills,* 'One cannot readily estimate the damages occasioned by the * * * loss of a doctor's services in an area determined to be medically underserved.'"

'A physician * * * is not a fungible handyman.' *Swanson.*

"Redovan's selfish conduct results in additional burdens on those already overburdened doctors providing medical care in the health manpower shortage area to which he was assigned. It requires citizens in that area to continue to suffer for the lack of adequate numbers of trained medical professionals. And in addition, his refusal to live up to his obligation subverts the laudatory goal of curing the maldistribution of medical care in the nation. For all of these reasons, I am unable to conclude that the liquidated damage provision is unreasonable or disproportionate to the harm suffered because of Redovan's breach."

"Further, I should also consider the likely expense of hiring a similarly trained physician to serve for three years in the location to which Redovan was assigned. Viewed in that light, I find the liquidated damages provision to be a reasonable estimate of the harm caused by defendant's breach."

"Defendant contends that the damage provision is intended to ensure performance and not to compensate reasonably for the harm caused. Because I conclude that
the damage provision is indeed a reasonable prior estimate of harm caused, the fact
that it also encourages performance of the service obligation does not defeat the
provision."

"Defendant's final contention in opposing the suit is that the damage provision
of the NHSC statute and contract violates the thirteenth amendment's prohibition of
involuntary servitude. Section one of the Thirteenth Amendment provides as follows":

> 'Section 1. Neither slavery nor involuntary servitude, except as a punish-
> ment for crime whereof the party shall have been duly convicted, shall exist
> within the United States, or any place subject to their jurisdiction.'

"Subsequent federal legislation enacted to enforce the Thirteenth Amendment
prohibited the practice of 'peonage,' which is defined as 'compulsory service in
payment of a debt. A peon is one who is compelled to work for his creditor until his
debt is paid.' " Bailey v. Alabama, 219 U.S. 219, 242 (1911). As the Supreme Court
observed in Clyatt v. United States, 197 U.S. 207, 215–16 (1905):

> 'A clear distinction exists between peonage and voluntary performance of
> labor or rendering of services in payment of a debt. In the latter case the debtor,
> though contracting to pay his indebtedness by labor or service, and subject, like
> any other contractor, to an action for breach of that contract, can elect at any
> time to break it, and no law or force compels performance or a continuance of
> the service.'

'In the case before me, it is abundantly clear that Redovan has not been
compelled to perform or continue any service whatever. Instead, he has chosen not to
perform any service whatever. He has remained in Philadelphia and not reported to
his assigned place of service. Because the Government has not sought to compel
service—and Redovan may choose to have a civil money judgment entered against
him in lieu of service—the enforcement of the government's rights in this lawsuit
does not constitute peonage or some other form of involuntary servitude.'

'Indeed, the rights the government seeks to enforce in this action are for a
money judgment. Peonage, or the coerced service of labor in payment of a debt, is not
implicated. Rather, this case presents the converse, that of payment of a debt in the
place of an agreed upon service obligation.'

'The peonage cases cited by the defendant are readily distinguishable. From
Clyatt v. United States in 1905, and Bailey v. Alabama, in 1911, to United States v.
Mussry, 726 F.2d 1448 (9th Cir.1984), the touchstone of involuntary servitude has
been "law or force compel[ling] * * * service." Bailey and the line of similar cases
involve the use of criminal sanctions which employ presumptions to convert breach
of a contract into a criminal offense, with the purpose of compelling labor. * * * All
of the cases cited by the defendant involved unfortunate individuals, some of whom
were illiterate and even unable to communicate in English, who were ill equipped to
understand the scope of the obligation they entered into until the die was cast.
Redovan can hardly claim to be in a similar position. He understood the nature of
the obligation before he entered into it as an educated professional.'

"Further, as I concluded earlier, the damage provision is a reasonable estimation
of the harm caused by defendant's default. Because defendant is required to make
recompense for the harm, and he is unable financially to do so, he claims that the
damage provision coerces his involuntary servitude. It is clear, however, that in
assessing damages for breach of a contract, the court is not required to consider the
breaching party's ability to pay, in order to stay within constitutional bounds. The

fact that the consequences of a large money judgment may encourage Redovan to perform a service obligation does not convert him into a peon."

"For all of these reasons, the defense of involuntary servitude fails, and judgment will be entered for the United States." United States v. Redovan, 656 F.Supp. 121, 127–29 (E.D.Pa.1986).

Observations. The *Conway* and *Redovan* courts "apply principles of general federal contract law." Other NHSC courts followed the standards of review of the Administrative Procedure Act. Both groups of courts have treated scholars' defenses about the same.

There is a new formula to calculate the government's recovery: (a) The amount paid; (b) plus the number of uncompleted months times $7500; (c) plus interest at the maximum legal rate. There is no statute of limitations on the government's filing suit or collecting a judgment. A scholar's bankruptcy discharge will be excruciatingly difficult; none for seven years from when payment is required and then only if the bankruptcy court finds that not discharging the defendant's debt would be "unconscionable." 42 U.S.C. § 254o(c)(1).

Double Jeopardy? Are liquidated damages imposed by a government plaintiff punishment that activates the protection of the Double Jeopardy Clause to preclude a later criminal prosecution for the same conduct? No, because the contractual clauses "are reasonably designed to make the government whole." United States v. Drake, 934 F.Supp. 953, 960 (N.D.Ill.1996).

Redovan is our casebook's second defendant to interpose, unsuccessfully, the Thirteenth Amendment. Remember that Brent Moss argued involuntary servitude as a defense to contempt maintained to "encourage" him, a family support debtor, to secure employment. Moss v. Superior Court, p. 345.

VANDERBILT UNIVERSITY. v. DiNARDO

United States Court of Appeals, Sixth Circuit, 1999.
174 F.3d 751.

GIBSON, CIRCUIT JUDGE. Gerry DiNardo resigned as Vanderbilt's head football coach to become the head football coach for Louisiana State University. As a result, Vanderbilt University brought this breach of contract action. The district court entered summary judgment for Vanderbilt, awarding $281,886.43 pursuant to a damage provision in DiNardo's employment contract with Vanderbilt. DiNardo appeals, arguing that the district court erred in concluding that the contract provision was an enforceable liquidated damage provision and not an unlawful penalty under Tennessee law * * * . We affirm the district court's ruling that the employment contract contained an enforceable liquidated damage provision and the award of liquidated damages under the original contract. * * *

On December 3, 1990, Vanderbilt and DiNardo executed an employment contract hiring DiNardo to be Vanderbilt's head football coach. Section one of the contract provided:

> The University hereby agrees to hire Mr. DiNardo for a period of five (5) years from the date hereof with Mr. DiNardo's assurance that he will serve the entire term of this Contract, a long-term commitment by Mr. DiNardo being important to the University's desire for a stable intercollegiate football program. * * *

The contract also contained reciprocal liquidated damage provisions. Vanderbilt agreed to pay DiNardo his remaining salary should Vanderbilt replace him as football coach, and DiNardo agreed to reimburse Vanderbilt should he leave before his contract expired. Section eight of the contract stated:

> Mr. DiNardo recognizes that his promise to work for the University for the entire term of this 5–year Contract is of the essence of this Contract to the University. Mr. DiNardo also recognizes that the University is making a highly valuable investment in his continued employment by entering into this Contract and its investment would be lost were he to resign or otherwise terminate his employment as Head Football Coach with the University prior to the expiration of this Contract. Accordingly, Mr. DiNardo agrees that in the event he resigns or otherwise terminates his employment as Head Football Coach (as opposed to his resignation or termination from another position at the University to which he may have been reassigned), prior to the expiration of this Contract, and is employed or performing services for a person or institution other than the University, he will pay to the University as liquidated damages an amount equal to his Base Salary, less amounts that would otherwise be deducted or withheld from his Base Salary for income and social security tax purposes, multiplied by the number of years (or portion(s) thereof) remaining on the Contract.

During contract negotiations, section eight was modified at DiNardo's request so that damages would be calculated based on net, rather than gross, salary.

Vanderbilt initially set DiNardo's salary at $100,000 per year. DiNardo received salary increases in 1992, 1993, and 1994. * * *

In November 1994, Louisiana State University contacted Vanderbilt in hopes of speaking with DiNardo about becoming the head football coach for L.S.U. Hoolahan gave DiNardo permission to speak to L.S.U. about the position. On December 12, 1994, DiNardo announced that he was accepting the L.S.U. position.

Vanderbilt sent a demand letter to DiNardo seeking payment of liquidated damages under section eight of the contract. * * * DiNardo did not respond to Vanderbilt's demand for payment.

Vanderbilt brought this action against DiNardo for breach of contract. * * * The district court held that section eight was an enforceable liquidated damages provision, not an unlawful penalty, and that the damages provided under section eight were reasonable. * * * The court entered judgment against DiNardo for $281,886.43. DiNardo appeals.

DiNardo first claims that section eight of the contract is an unenforceable penalty under Tennessee law. DiNardo argues that the provision is not a liquidated damage provision but a "thinly disguised, overly broad non-compete provision," unenforceable under Tennessee law. * * *

Contracting parties may agree to the payment of liquidated damages in the event of a breach. See Beasley v. Horrell, 864 S.W.2d 45, 48 (Tenn.Ct.App.1993). The term "liquidated damages" refers to an amount determined by the parties to be just compensation for damages should a breach occur. Courts will not enforce such a provision, however, if the stipulated amount constitutes a penalty. A penalty is designed to coerce performance by punishing default. In Tennessee, a provision will be considered one for liquidated damages, rather than a penalty, if it is reasonable in relation to the anticipated damages for breach, measured prospectively at the time the contract was entered into, and not grossly disproportionate to the actual damages. When these conditions are met, particularly the first, the parties probably intended the provision to be for liquidated damages. However, any doubt as to the character of the contract provision will be resolved in favor of finding it a penalty.

The district court held that the use of a formula based on DiNardo's salary to calculate liquidated damages was reasonable "given the nature of the unquantifiable damages in the case." The court held that parties to a contract may include consequential damages and even damages not usually awarded by law in a liquidated damage provision provided that they were contemplated by the parties. The court explained:

> The potential damage to [Vanderbilt] extends far beyond the cost of merely hiring a new head football coach. It is this uncertain potentiality that the parties sought to address by providing for a sum certain to apply towards anticipated expenses and losses. It is impossible to estimate how the loss of a head football coach will affect alumni relations, public support, football ticket sales, contributions, etc. * * * As such, to require a precise formula for calculating damages resulting from the breach of contract by a college head football coach would be tantamount to barring the parties from stipulating to liquidated damages evidence in advance.

DiNardo contends that there is no evidence that the parties contemplated that the potential damage from DiNardo's resignation would go beyond the cost of hiring a replacement coach. He argues that his salary has no relationship to Vanderbilt's damages and that the liquidated damage amount is unreasonable and shows that the parties did not intend the provision to be for liquidated damages.

DiNardo's theory of the parties' intent, however, does not square with the record. The contract language establishes that Vanderbilt wanted the five-year contract because "a long-term commitment" by DiNardo was "important to the University's desire for a stable intercollegiate football program," and that this commitment was of "essence" to the contract. * * * Thus, undisputed evidence, and reasonable inferences therefrom, establish that both parties understood and agreed that DiNardo's resignation would result in Vanderbilt suffering damage beyond the cost of hiring a replacement coach.

This evidence also refutes DiNardo's argument that the district court erred in presuming that DiNardo's resignation would necessarily cause damage to the University. That the University may actually benefit from a coaching change (as DiNardo suggests) matters little, as we measure the reasonableness of the liquidated damage provision at the time the parties entered the contract, not when the breach occurred, [citation], and we hardly think the parties entered the contract anticipating that DiNardo's resignation would benefit Vanderbilt.

The stipulated damage amount is reasonable in relation to the amount of damages that could be expected to result from the breach. As we stated, the parties understood that Vanderbilt would suffer damage should DiNardo prematurely terminate his contract, and that these actual damages would be difficult to measure. [citation] * * *

Vanderbilt hired DiNardo for a unique and specialized position, and the parties understood that the amount of damages could not be easily ascertained should a breach occur. Contrary to DiNardo's suggestion, Vanderbilt did not need to undertake an analysis to determine actual damages, and using the number of years left on the contract multiplied by the salary per year was a reasonable way to calculate damages considering the difficulty of ascertaining damages with certainty. [citation] The fact that liquidated damages declined each year DiNardo remained under contract, is directly tied to the parties' express understanding of the importance of a long-term commitment from DiNardo. Furthermore, the liquidated damages provision was reciprocal and the result of negotiations between two parties, each of whom was represented by counsel.

We also reject DiNardo's argument that a question of fact remains as to whether the parties intended section eight to be a "reasonable estimate" of damages. The liquidated damages are in line with Vanderbilt's estimate of its actual damages. Vanderbilt presented evidence that it incurred expenses associated with recruiting a new head coach of $27,000.00; moving expenses for the new coaching staff of $86,840; and a compensation difference between the coaching staffs of $184,311. The stipulated damages clause is reasonable under the circumstances, and we affirm the district court's conclusion that the liquidated damages clause is enforceable under Tennessee law. * * *

DiNardo claims that the [two-year extension in a contract] Addendum did not become a binding contract, and therefore, he is only liable for the one year remaining on the original contract, not the three years held by the district court. [Editor: This part of the court's opinion is omitted.]

[W]e are convinced that there is a disputed question of material fact as to whether the Addendum is enforceable. * * *

Accordingly, we affirm the district court's judgment that the contract contained an enforceable liquidated damage provision, and we affirm the portion of the judgment reflecting damages calculated under the original five-year contract. We reverse the district court's judgment concluding that the [two-year] Addendum was enforceable as a matter of law. We remand for a resolution of the factual issues * * *.

We affirm in part, reverse in part, and remand the case to the district court for further proceedings consistent with this opinion.

DAVID A. NELSON, CIRCUIT JUDGE, concurring in part and dissenting in part.

If section eight of the contract was designed primarily to quantify, in an objectively reasonable way, damages that the university could be expected to suffer in the event of a breach, such damages being difficult to measure in the absence of an agreed formula, the provision is enforceable as a legitimate liquidated damages clause. If section eight was designed primarily to punish Coach DiNardo for taking a job elsewhere, however, the provision is a penalty unenforceable under Tennessee law. My colleagues on the panel and I * * * disagree * * * as to section eight's primary function.

It seems to me that the provision was designed to function as a penalty, not as a liquidation of the university's damages. Insofar as the court holds otherwise, I am constrained to dissent. * * *

My principal reasons for viewing section eight as a penalty are these: (1) although the damages flowing from a premature resignation would normally be the same whether or not Coach DiNardo took a job elsewhere, section eight does not purport to impose liability for liquidated damages unless the coach accepts another job; (2) the section eight formula incorporates other variables that bear little or no relation to any reasonable approximation of anticipated damages; and

(3) there is no evidence that the parties were attempting, in section eight, to come up with a reasonable estimate of the university's probable loss if the coach left. I shall offer a few words of explanation on each of these points.

Section eight does not make Coach DiNardo liable for any liquidated damages at all, interestingly enough, unless, during the unexpired term of his contract, he "is employed or performing services for a person or institution other than the University. * * * " But how the coach spends his post-resignation time could not reasonably be expected to affect the university's damages; should the coach choose to quit in order to lie on a beach somewhere, the university would presumably suffer the same damages that it would suffer if he quit to coach for another school. The logical inference, therefore, would seem to be that section eight was intended to penalize the coach for taking another job, and was not intended to make the university whole by liquidating any damages suffered as a result of being left in the lurch.

This inference is strengthened, as I see it, by a couple of other anomalies in the stipulated damages formula. First, I am aware of no reason to believe that damages arising from the need to replace a prematurely departing coach could reasonably be expected to vary in direct proportion to the number of years left on the coach's contract. Section eight, however, provides that for every additional year remaining on the contract, the stipulated damages will go up by the full amount of the annual take-home pay contemplated under the contract. Like the "other employment" proviso, this makes the formula look more like a penalty than anything else.

Second, the use of a "take-home pay" measuring stick suggests that the function of the stick was to rap the coach's knuckles and not to measure the university's loss. Such factors as the number of tax exemptions claimed by the coach, or the percentage of his pay that he might elect to shelter in a 401(k) plan, would obviously bear no relation at all to the university's anticipated damages.

Finally, the record before us contains no evidence that the contracting parties gave any serious thought to attempting to measure the actual effect that a premature departure could be expected to have on the university's bottom line. On the contrary, the record affirmatively shows that the university did not attempt to determine whether the section eight formula would yield a result reasonably approximating anticipated damages. The record shows that the university could not explain how its anticipated damages might be affected by the coach's obtaining employment elsewhere, this being a subject that the draftsman of the contract testified he had never thought about. And the record shows that the question of why the number of years remaining on the contract would have any bearing on the amount of the university's damages was never analyzed either.

In truth and in fact, in my opinion, any correspondence between the result produced by the section eight formula and a reasonable approximation of anticipated damages would be purely coincidental. What section eight prescribes is a penalty, pure and simple, and a penalty may not be enforced under Tennessee law. On remand, therefore, * * * I would instruct the court to determine the extent of any actual damages suffered by the university as a result of Coach DiNardo's breach of his contract. Whether more than the section eight figure or less, I believe, the university's actual damages should be the measure of its recovery.

Notes

1. *Future Developments*. The case is not further reported, so we do not learn whether the University's recovery was based on one or three years' of DiNardo's salary.

Gerry DiNardo's LSU teams won three straight bowl games in his five years there. He moved to Indiana University, but, after three losing seasons, he was fired in December 2004.

2. *Take Another Look*. Does the Tennessee law that the *DiNardo* court cites follow the "second-look" doctrine that the Kelly v. Marx court rejected? p. 667.

3. *Comparing Harms*. In deciding whether the stipulated sum is a penalty, what harms to Vanderbilt should the court compare to the stipulated sum?

In a part of the trial judge's decision that the court of appeals did not quote, the judge mentioned the "potentially extensive other damages to Vanderbilt which may result in having to suddenly replace a head football coach. Such damages are difficult to quantify, but may include damage to reputation and public relations, lost profits from reduced football ticket sales, lost talents of resigning assistant coaches, broken promises and relationships with players, lost recruits and future recruiting opportunities, reduced membership in athletic clubs and alumni support, decline in donations to the athletic program, redesigning publicity, media guides, logos and uniforms, etc." Vanderbilt University v. DiNardo, 974 F.Supp. 638, 642 (M.D.Tenn. 1997).

A contract plaintiff cannot recover special damages that are beyond the parties' contemplation when they formed the contract. And a contract plaintiff must prove lost future business profits to a reasonable certainty. Would you expect a court to bar Vanderbilt as a contract plaintiff from recovering for some of the injuries that the trial judge and the court of appeals mentioned?

When the court measures Vanderbilt's "anticipated damages," does it include injury that could not have been compensated because of the rules of contemplation and certainty? Should the court have limited Vanderbilt's "anticipated damages" to losses that it could have recovered in court?

4. In Wassenaar v. Panos, the Wisconsin court shed some helpful light on the questions above. *Wassenaar* involved an employer's breach of an employment contract that liquidated the employee's damages, allowing the former employee to recover his full salary for the unexpired term of the contract. Improperly discharged with 21 months left to run, the former employee found a new position after six weeks of unemployment. In setting stipulated damages in a contract, the court said that the parties can anticipate types of loss not recoverable under the damages rules. The special damages a wrongfully-discharged employee recovers may not measure his actual harm, injury to his professional reputation and career development, and his emotional stress. Since "anticipated loss" in a stipulated damages clause can include harm not usually awarded in court as damages, the court held that the clause called for the wrongfully-discharged employee to receive his full salary for the unexpired term of the contract. Moreover, because the liquidated-damages clause is valid, the employee had no duty to avoid the consequences of the employer's breach by finding substitute employment; accordingly the employee's wages from new employment were not subtracted from his recovery of 21 months of salary from the defendant. The plaintiff's recovery that his former employer labeled a "windfall" the court approved maintaining that the plaintiff's full salary measured or was a proxy for an

employee's actual loss including unrecoverable special damages. Wassenar v. Panos, 111 Wis.2d 518, 331 N.W.2d 357, 365–66 (1983).

5. Could Vanderbilt have proved its damages by subtracting DiNardo's Vanderbilt salary from his LSU salary? Roth v. Speck, p. 698.

6. *Employees' Noncompetition Covenants with Liquidated Damages.* (a) An accounting firm partnership agreement included a post-employment covenant that a departing partner would not service any of the firm's clients for five years; the contract set the firm's liquidated damages for breach of the covenant at double the firm's time charges for the year preceding the client's loss to the firm. Several clients took their business to an expelled partner. The firm sued. After a complex trial and appeal, the appellate court remanded for judgment for the firm for the amount the liquidated damages clause called for, which, under the evidence at the first trial, might be nearly $1,000,000. Weber, Lipshie & Co. v. Christian, 52 Cal.App.4th 645, 60 Cal.Rptr.2d 677 (1997).

(b) Another accountant's covenant not to solicit a former client liquidated the firm's damages at 150% of the client's billing in the prior year—even if the client did not leave the firm. "Under this scenario, even though [the firm] would have experienced no actual damages, it would be entitled to the liquidated damages. The entire provision is an unenforceable penalty," said the court. Habif, Arogeti & Wynne, P.C. v. Baggett, 231 Ga.App. 289, 498 S.E.2d 346, 355 (1998).

7. *Other Multiples and Fractions as Penalties.* (a) "[T]he agreement to pay double for a bounced check operates as a penalty and therefore cannot be enforced." Lawyers Title Insurance Corp. v. Dearborn Title Corp., 939 F.Supp. 611, 616 (N.D.Ill.1996).

(b) Retailer-tenant's promise in a mall lease to operate continuously but which doubled the tenant's minimum rent if the outlet closed was a valid liquidated damages clause. Landover Mall Ltd. Partnership v. Kinney Shoe Corp., 944 F.Supp. 443, 445 (D.Md.1996).

(c) A provision that assessed a 50% collection charge on delinquent freight charges created an invalid penalty under general federal contract law. Robins Motor Transportation, Inc. v. Associated Rigging & Hauling Corp., 944 F.Supp. 409, 412 (E.D.Pa. 1996).

B. EMPLOYEE'S REMEDIES

1. SPECIFIC PERFORMANCE—REINSTATEMENT?

A court order to an employer to reinstate an employee wrongfully discharged in breach of contract will fulfill the plaintiff's entitlement under the contract; in addition, the plaintiff's reinstatement eliminates the uncertainty of calculating her future pay under the lump sum rule. However, remember

The Common Law Rule. When an employer breaches an employment or personal-service contract, a court will refuse to order specific performance to enforce the contract. Redgrave v. Boston Symphony Orchestra, Inc., 557 F.Supp. 230, 234–35 (D.Mass. 1983) apparent final appeal, 855 F.2d 888 (1st Cir.1988), cert. denied, 488 U.S. 1043 (1989).

The common law rule may be unstable. Are an employee's arguments for reinstatement more persuasive than an employer's arguments for specific performance?

Thurston. In Archie Thurston's successful breach of employment contract action against Box Elder County, Utah, the trial judge had rejected Thurston's request to be reinstated, citing the common law rule above. Instead the trial judge gave Thurston future damages from his improper termination until he began full-time employment. On appeal, Thurston argued for reinstatement with back pay. The Utah court reconsidered the common law rule:

"Thurston's argument is twofold. First, he asserts that reinstatement with back pay should be an available remedy for a breach of employment contract action. Second, he argues that reinstatement with back pay is the only appropriate remedy in this case because it is the only remedy which will make Thurston whole from his wrongful discharge. * * *"

"Reinstatement, a type of specific performance, is an equitable remedy. The right to an equitable remedy is an exceptional one, and absent statutory mandate, equitable relief should be granted only when a court determines that damages are inadequate and that equitable relief will result in more perfect and complete justice. [citations] However, that an equitable remedy will not be appropriate in many, if not most, actions brought for wrongful termination based upon breach of an employment contract is no reason to refuse to grant reinstatement in every case. For the reasons discussed below, we hold that reinstatement may be considered as a remedy by a trial court when fashioning a remedy for breach of an employment contract. When a trial court determines that under the circumstances of a particular case, an award of damages would be so inadequate as to warrant equitable relief, a court may consider reinstatement as a remedy. Accordingly, we hold that the trial court erred when it concluded as a matter of law that reinstatement is not a permissible remedy in a breach of employment contract action."

"Traditionally, reinstatement has been denied as a remedy for breach of an employment contract under the generally accepted rule that contracts for personal services should not be specifically enforced. [citations] Several reasons underlie this rule. One is the difficulty of enforcing the decree and of measuring the quality of the parties' performance. [citations] Another is a strong prejudice against involuntary personal servitude and the theory that under mutuality of remedies, if an employer may not seek specific performance an employee should not be entitled to it. [citations] A third reason is the undesirability of compelling continued personal associations after disputes have arisen or confidences and loyalty have been destroyed. [citations]"

"These reasons are susceptible to closer scrutiny in light of contemporary employment relationships and the need to protect at-will employees from wrongful termination of their employment. First, we are unpersuaded that a court would have difficulty enforcing an order for reinstatement in a breach of contract action. Reinstatement is an available remedy under state and federal statutory schemes which provide relief for wrongfully discharged employees. [citations of state and federal employment discrimination statutes] In fact, federal courts have considered reinstatement a 'preferred remedy' because it involves the least amount of uncertainty and can most effectively make a wronged employee 'whole.' See Blim v. Western Elec. Co., 731 F.2d 1473, 1479 (10th Cir.1984), cert. denied, 469 U.S. 874 (1984). There is no reason to believe that reinstatement is necessarily more difficult to administer and enforce as a contract remedy than it would be as a statutory remedy."

"Second, reliance on the mutuality of remedies rule to deny equitable relief is unpersuasive, because the rule has long been considered to be without any force. [citations] While it may sound fair on its face, operation of the rule works inequity. In the reinstatement context, it denies a wrongfully terminated employee continued employment and rewards an employer whose wrongful conduct is motivated by nonmonetary concerns.

"Finally, we agree that it is undesirable to compel personal associations in the face of hostilities or lack of confidence and loyalty. Reinstatement would not be an appropriate remedy when hostilities exist between the parties or when the employment relationship has been irreparably damaged by the dispute over the discharge or by lack of confidence and loyalty. The circumstances of a particular case may also make reinstatement an inappropriate remedy, and ordinarily, it should be left to the trial court's careful discrimination to determine its application in each case."

"With the foregoing in mind, we address Thurston's contention that reinstatement with back pay is the only appropriate remedy for the wrongful termination of his employment. The spectrum of remedies available in a breach of contract action is not as narrow at Thurston asserts. A trial court is accorded considerable latitude and discretion in applying and formulating an equitable remedy. [citations] We review the trial court's determination of a remedy in this case under a standard that acknowledges considerable discretion in the trial court, and we will not upset the court's ruling unless it constituted an abuse of discretion. * * *"

"Thurston argues that * * * reinstatement with back pay is always the remedy unless there is evidence of hostility or unless the employee does not want to return to his former employment. Thus, Thurston argues, reinstatement with back pay should be granted in his situation because there is no evidence of hostility and he desires to return to his employment with the County."

"Thurston's argument is unpersuasive. [The court distinguished the authorities Thurston cited.] Thurston's action is not based upon any statutory violation for which reinstatement is a prescribed remedy. Accordingly, the cases based upon statutory violations which Thurston cites are not persuasive on the appropriate remedy for his breach of contract action. * * * As stated above, an order for reinstatement is permissible in a breach of employment contract action as an equitable remedy when damages are inadequate or unascertainable."

"Thurston has failed to show that damages are inadequate or unascertainable in this case. In addition, Thurston's employment was terminated during a reduction in force action. His position was not filled after the RIF, and his duties have been absorbed by other workers. Another employee would have to be laid off to accommodate a reinstatement order, and it is even possible that Thurston could be reached for further layoff if the County properly applied its reduction in force criteria. In light of these facts, it was not an abuse of discretion for the trial court to deny equitable relief." Thurston v. Box Elder County, 892 P.2d 1034, 1039–42 (Utah 1995).

Another judge recognized the court's ability to reinstate a successful plaintiff suing a former employer for breach of an employment contract; but the judge opted for front pay instead. Stafford v. Electronic Data Systems Corp., 749 F.Supp. 781, 784 (E.D.Mich. 1990).

Reinstatement Following Defendant's Constitutional or Statutory Violation. An employee's contractual remedies are influenced by the remedies available to a plaintiff in a constitutional or statutory case.

When plaintiff's discharge violates the constitution or a statute, a court will typically reinstate the employee. Allen v. Autauga County Board of Education, 685 F.2d 1302 (11th Cir.1982). Under Title VII, the employment discrimination provisions in the federal Civil Rights Act, plaintiffs who had been passed over were "instated," including bumping the incumbents who had been hired and assuming the employment grade the incumbents had reached. Allen v. Barram, 215 F.Supp.2d 184(D.D.C. 2002) (decision on remedy); Allen v. Perry, 279 F.Supp.2d 36 (D.D.C. 2003)(decision rejecting defendant's post-trial motions). Under the National Labor Relations Act, the Labor Board's remedies for a wrongfully terminated employee include reinstatement, with or without back pay, although the board may consider how burdensome the remedy is for the employer. Regal Cinemas, Inc. v. National Labor Relations Board, 317 F.3d 300, 314–15 (D.C.Cir. 2003).

One court reinstated a professor and ordered a grant of tenure. "[O]nce a university has been found to have impermissibly discriminated [on the basis of sex] in making a tenure decision, as here, the University's prerogative to make tenure decisions must be subordinated to the goals embodied in Title VII." Brown v. Trustees of Boston University, 891 F.2d 337, 358, 361 (1st Cir.1989), cert. denied, 496 U.S. 937 (1990).

After another court found the defendant had denied plaintiff partnership because of sexual stereotyping, it ordered her reinstated as a partner. Hopkins v. Price Waterhouse, 920 F.2d 967, 980 (D.C. Cir.1990).

In plaintiff Squires's action to redress a discharge in violation of his First Amendment rights, the trial judge declined reinstatement. In addition to constitutional decisions, the court of appeals cited sex, race, and age discrimination cases and ordered him reinstated. "[W]hile the availability of money damages may have significance in the district court's consideration of remedy, reinstatement is the preferred remedy in the absence of special circumstances militating against it." A trial judge must articulate the reasons for refusing to reinstate. Squires v. Bonser, 54 F.3d 168, 173 (3d Cir.1995).

How does the *Squires* court's standard for reinstatement differ from the *Thurston* court's?

Does a plaintiff who was discharged in violation of the constitution or an anti-discrimination statute have a stronger argument for reinstatement than someone discharged in breach of a private contract?

A Sale Compared. How does your analysis of whether the judge should reinstate an employee-plaintiff after his employer breaches an employment contract differ from your analysis of whether the judge should grant a seller specific performance when a buyer breaches a contract to sell land or a chattel?

Courts still disagree about whether a wrongfully discharged employee's opportunity to recover damages is an adequate remedy at law.

(a) *Damages Are Inadequate.* "When a person loses his job, it is at best disingenuous to say that money damages can suffice to make that person whole. The psychological benefits of work are intangible, yet they are real and cannot be ignored." Bullen v. Chaffinch, 336 F.Supp.2d 357, 362 (D.Del. 2004).

"When a person loses his job, it is at best disingenuous to say that money damages can suffice to make that person whole. The psychological benefits of work are intangible, yet they are real and cannot be ignored. * * * [R]einstatement is an effective deterrent in preventing employer retaliation against employees who exercise their constitutional rights. If an employer's best efforts to remove an employee for unconstitutional reasons are presumptively unlikely to succeed, there is, of course, less incentive to use employment decisions to chill the exercise of constitutional rights." Allen v. Autauga County Board of Education, 685 F.2d 1302, 1306 (11th Cir.1982).

(b) *Damages Are Adequate.* A discharged superintendent sought a preliminary injunction of reinstatement, to forbid the school district from filling the vacancy; but the court held that a plaintiff's loss of a job is compensable in money. Manila School District No. 15 v. Wagner, 356 Ark. 149, 148 S.W.3d 244 (2004).

Plaintiff's reinstatement is one of several remedies. If the court takes several years to decide an employment lawsuit, the plaintiff's life may have moved on. Reinstating a former employee may not be propitious or workable where there is bad blood between the parties, for example in a hostile environment sexual harassment case. Moreover, a former employee's reinstatement might not take place because the successful plaintiff may use the leverage of a reinstatement order to pry a magnanimous settlement from her former employer.

The employee's remedy may be a package that combines reinstatement with money for past mistreatment. Thus the judge's decision on a Title VII plaintiff's motion for an injunction will often follow a jury's decision for the plaintiff. Bullen v. Chaffinch, 336 F.Supp.2d 357 (D.Del. 2004); Allen v. Barram, 215 F.Supp.2d 184(D.D.C. 2002)(decision on remedy); Allen v. Perry, 279 F.Supp.2d 36 (D.D.C. 2003)(decision rejecting defendant's post-trial motions).

This leads to:

2. EMPLOYEE'S DAMAGES

DIXIE GLASS CO. v. POLLAK

Court of Civil Appeals of Texas, 1960.
341 S.W.2d 530.

BELL, CH. J. The appellee was employed by written contract of January 1, 1953 as comptroller of appellant for a period of five years and was given an option to renew the contract for three additional five-year terms, the option to be exercised six months prior to the end of each term. The contract provided for a weekly salary of $200 and an annual bonus of 10% of the net profits before deduction for income taxes. The contract was authorized by the unanimous vote of all officers, directors and stockholders in a joint meeting held January 2, 1953. On October 19, 1955, the appellant discharged appellee.

Appellee sued appellant for breach of this contract, contending his discharge was without good cause, and sought recovery of his damages, alleging them to be the value if paid now of the amounts, salary and bonus, that he would have earned under the contract for the full term including the terms for which he was given an option, less any amounts that he should be able to earn during said term from other employment or business which he should be able to obtain by the exercise of reasonable diligence.

Trial was to a jury, which found the discharge was without good cause. The jury found the damages up to the time of trial to be $20,277. It also found appellee would earn $156,000 as salary under the contract up to its termination from the time of trial. It allowed no bonus after the time of trial. It also found appellee's earnings in the future, above all necessary expenses, should be $78,000. The court rendered judgment for appellee for $3,116.24, which was the bonus stipulated to be due appellee as of the date of his discharge on October 19, 1955, together with interest from February 1, 1956, and for $98,277, the amount found by the jury, together with interest from the date of judgment. Execution was stayed as to the $78,000 found to be appellee's damages from the date of trial to the end of the contract.

* * * The trial court submitted damage issues in a manner so as to separate damages up to the time of trial from damages beyond the date of trial. Appellant takes the position there can be no recovery beyond the date of the trial because it cannot be known with reasonable certainty whether the appellee will be damaged and if so how much. * * *

We find there is a conflict in the authorities in the United States. The majority rule is that recovery of damages may be had for the full term, regardless of when the trial occurs. The minority view is that anticipatory damages may not be recovered but recovery is limited to damages suffered to the date of trial. [citations]

We are of the view there is no Texas case authoritatively deciding the question. * * *

We, therefore, hold that where an employer wrongfully breaches a contract of employment prior to the time it has been completely performed, a cause of action for damages for breach of contract immediately arises in favor of the employee and he is entitled, if he elects, to recover his damages for the full term for which he was employed and he is not limited to damages proven only to the date of trial where trial is before the expiration of the term of employment.

Of course his suit is not for wages but is for damages. The measure of damages is the present cash value of the contract to him, if it had not been breached, less any amounts that he should in the exercise of reasonable diligence be able to earn through other employment. The duty is on the employee to use reasonable diligence to obtain other employment and thus minimize his damage. The maximum recovery would be the present value of the contract if it should be fully performed and in the exercise of reasonable diligence the employee could not obtain other employment. * * *

In the case of Granow v. Adler, 24 Ariz. 53, 57–58, 206 P. 590, 592 (1922), the Supreme Court of Arizona held damages recoverable for the full term of the contract though trial occurred prior to the end of the term. The court said:

"To limit recovery to the damages accrued to the time of trial, the contractual term not having elapsed, and then to hold the employee barred by such an award from any further recovery, seems to us to be at war with the general principle which imposes liability upon the party who breaches a contract, to respond to the other party for all damages which arise naturally from the breach, or such as may reasonably be supposed to have been within the contemplation of the parties at the time of making the contract, as a probable result of the breach. If the employee would have all his damages assessed and thereby realize the fruits of his contract, he is, under [this approach], offered the alternative of deferring the bringing of his suit or the trial of the cause until after the expiration of the term of employment. In many cases—more especially in the event of a long term contract—the acceptance of this alternative might deprive the employee of all redress for his injury. The uncertainty involved in the computation of the damages to accrue after trial is not introduced by the act of the employee, but arises from the fault and wrong of the employer, and it appears to us constitutes no just reason for depriving the employee of his right to recover all the damages he has sustained, if he makes the best proof of which the case is susceptible." * * *

The Texas cases hold that on breach of the contract, only one cause of action for damages for breach of contract arises. The employee may not split his cause of action. If, as in many cases he has, an employee sues for damages for less than the full contract period, he waives the balance of his damages. * * * Too, the cause of action arises immediately on breach so that the statute of limitation commences to run so that, at least as to damages that have accrued beyond the particular period of limitation before the filing of suit, recovery is barred. * * *

The result of adopting the minority rule would certainly in the case of a long term contract effectively deprive an employee of the fruits of his contract. He must sue within the period of limitation or lose the part of his damages barred by limitation. If he sues within the period of limitation and is required by the trial court to try the case before the end of the term, he must lose a part of his damages. Even if he is allowed to wait until the end of the term before going to trial he loses in the interim the enjoyment of the fruits of a valid contract that he has been willing to perform but which the employer has wrongfully breached.

We see no more uncertainty in allowing recovery of anticipatory damages in a breach of employment contract case than there is in the case of allowing recovery for diminished earning capacity in a personal injury case.

* * * Many factors, just as in a personal injury case, will have to be considered. Some factors are: age, probable life expectancy, education, experience, past earning capacity, and probable span of employability.

In the case before us there can be little doubt that appellee suffered and will suffer damage. He was at the time of the breach of the contract 58 years of age and he had a contract paying him $10,400 per year. Can there be any reasonable doubt that in the light of human experience appellee will in probability not be able to get any such remunerative employment during the balance of his life? It is a matter of common knowledge that a person of this age cannot well compete in the labor mart. Of course, it cannot be determined with mathematical exactness what his earnings will be. Mathematical exactness is not required. The evidence shows that between discharge and trial, a period of some two years, appellee had tried diligently to obtain work and had obtained some work which paid very little. We mention the facts of this case to demonstrate that in some cases of breach of employment contracts the evidence will show, with probability, resulting damage and the extent of damage. This demonstrates that the minority rule, which says that since it is a breach of employment contract you cannot recover anticipatory damages because they are too uncertain, is not sound. * * *

In view of another trial it should be noted that on retrial the trial court should discount any future amounts recovered as salary to their present worth. Here the jury found appellee would have earned under his contract $156,000 and could earn from other employment $78,000. Judgment was given for $78,000. This should have been discounted to its present worth, based on the unexpired term of the contract at the date of judgment at the rate of 6% per annum. * * *

Notes

1. *Age Discrimination?* If plaintiff Pollak were suing today, his complaint would be likely to include a count for violation of a statute forbidding age discrimination. A successful federal Age Discrimination in Employment Act plaintiff may recover double damages and attorney fees. The problems of measuring his future damages, prediction and uncertainty, would remain the same.

2. *Prediction and Uncertainty.* Vocabulary note: "Back pay" is a plaintiff's prejudgment lost income. "Front pay" is his post-judgment lost future income; front pay compensates the plaintiff either from judgment to his reinstatement or instead of reinstatement. Plaintiff's back pay and front pay until reinstatement are less speculative and lack the predictive difficulty of front pay; if front pay is not ended by the plaintiff's reinstatement, it may continue for an indefinite period. Do you think the jury guessed in reducing Pollak's damages for his lost future earnings?

After plaintiff collects a damages judgment, the "lump sum" is his. He may, as the *Dixie Glass* court seems to fear, retire early on "full pay"; he may take another, perhaps better, position. Other vicissitudes of life that affect a court's prediction of an ex-employee's lost future income include his possible illness and death, changes in broad economic trends, inflation, and interest rate fluctuations. How should a court respond to the uncertainty?

(a) *No Future Damages.* In Illinois, the court will limit plaintiff's damages for an employer's breach of an employment contract to the damages plaintiff may have accrued up to the date of trial. The court will reject the plaintiff's damages after trial because of their speculative and uncertain nature. Pokora v. Warehouse Direct, Inc., 322 Ill.App.3d 870, 751 N.E.2d 1204, 1213–15 (2001).

"Comment: The rationale behind decisions which limit or disallow damages beyond the date of trial conflicts with and seems to disregard the rule in tort actions for personal injury and wrongful death damages, where future lost earnings and impairment of earning capacity are determined routinely. Although such damages may not be susceptible of precise determination, they can be ascertained with reasonable specificity. There is no reason to reward the wrongdoer or contract breaker, due to the inability to calculate damages with precision, once the wrong has been established." Howard Specter & Matthew Finkin, Individual Employment Law and Litigation § 15.04 (1989).

(b) *Future Damages.* Rejecting the trial judge's statement that a plaintiff's recovery of front pay is equitable and a substitute for reinstatement, Justice Ellen Peters wrote for the court that the plaintiff may recover future lost wages based on the same standards as another plaintiff's recovery of future lost business profits. Plaintiff may recover his future lost wages for a "reasonable time." Torosyan v. Boehringer Ingelheim Pharmaceuticals, 234 Conn. 1, 662 A.2d 89, 106 (1995).

(c) *Wait and See.* The defendant sought to assure accurate computation of the plaintiff's compensation in an uncertain future by making a series of 30 years of annual salary payments, each offset by plaintiff's earnings and each following plaintiff's showing of reasonable efforts to "mitigate." The appellate court agreed with plaintiff that periodic hearings and payments would "involve the court in a judicial quagmire of gargantuan proportions." Ritchie v. Michigan Consolidated Gas Co., 163 Mich.App. 358, 374, 413 N.W.2d 796, 804 (1987).

Another judge with more patience retained jurisdiction to monitor whether plaintiff continued to be entitled to front pay. Stafford v. Electronic Data Systems Corp., 749 F.Supp. 781, 792–93 (E.D.Mich. 1990).

(d) *Discretion*. Another possibility is for the court to consider a successful plaintiff to be presumptively entitled to recover past wages, back pay. But the plaintiff's future damages or front pay is an "equitable" remedy, and within the judge's "equitable discretion." Lussier v. Runyon, 50 F.3d 1103 (1st Cir.1995), cert. denied, 516 U.S. 815 (1995).

This is the approach that Connecticut's Justice Peters rejected in Torosyan v. Boehringer Ingelheim Pharmaceuticals, above. In Minnesota, a plaintiff's employment discrimination front pay is legal damages subject to being multiplied under the Minnesota statute. Ray v. Miller Meester Advertising, 684 N.W.2d 404, 407 (Minn. 2004).

The factors another court considered before rejecting plaintiff's reinstatement in favor of awarding him front pay were "(1) whether reinstatement would be a feasible remedy; (2) what the employee's prospects are for other employment, and (3) how many years remain before the employee would be faced with mandatory retirement." Stafford v. Electronic Data Systems Corp., 749 F.Supp. 781, 785 (E.D.Mich. 1990). The certainty of a cutoff the court sought with its third factor was lost when mandatory retirement for most employees ended.

In Wisconsin, when an employer wrongfully discharges an employee contrary to public policy, the jury sets the employee's back pay. Then the trial judge determines whether reinstatement is feasible; if it is not, the judge will calculate the plaintiff's front pay. Kempfer v. Automated Finishing, Inc., 211 Wis.2d 100, 564 N.W.2d 692 (1997).

3. *Emotional Distress, Punitive Damages*. Employment discrimination is more like a statutory tort than a contract action.

In 1991, Congress expanded a successful Title VII employment-discrimination plaintiff's remedies. Before the amendments, a judge could instate or reinstate a plaintiff and award back pay and front pay. But a successful Title VII plaintiff could recover neither emotional distress damages nor punitive damages. Congress dealt with both in 1991 with complicated statutes.

Congress's 1991 amendments to Title VII allow a successful employment-discrimination plaintiff to recover compensatory damages and punitive damages, but it caps both of them, the caps varying according to a sliding scale based on the defendant's size.

Under the 1991 amendments, plaintiff's front pay is not capped because it is neither "compensatory damages," nor "pecuniary damages." Front pay is a reinstatement surrogate. Pollard v. E.I. du Pont de Nemours & Co., 532 U.S. 843 (2001). This may lead an unwary judge to the erroneous decision that plaintiff's front pay is "equitable" in the sense that the parties will not have a Seventh Amendment right to a jury trial on that issue.

An example. Where the court does not order the plaintiff reinstated, her recovery of front pay is discretionary; the court declined to award front pay in part because plaintiff recovered emotional distress and punitive damages. Rodriguez–Torres v. Caribbean Forms Manufacturer, Inc., 399 F.3d 52 (1st Cir. 2005). Other reasons for a court to decline to award a plaintiff front pay include feeble avoidable consequences efforts, punitive damages, multiplied damages.

The *Kolstad* Court dealt with the 1991 punitive-damages amendments. The defendant's misconduct threshold for punitive damages, the Court held, was the typical malice-recklessness standard, not the egregious-conduct prerequisite that the defendant advocated. The Court, however, went on to say that an employer that demonstrates its good faith with an anti-discrimination program for its employees would escape vicarious liability for an agent's discriminatory misconduct. Kolstad v. American Dental Association, 527 U.S. 526 (1999).

4. *Tax Notes.* Plaintiff's recovery for lost wages is taxable income. Wages are received for tax purposes when paid. So an employment plaintiff's large lump-sum settlement or judgment triggers large taxes. Plaintiff pays taxes on punitive damages. However, plaintiff's personal injury damages, including those for emotional distress, escape tax. IRC § 104(a)(2).

Settlements of employment litigation including attorney fees under contingent fee contracts reached the Supreme Court in March, 2005. The Court held that the contingent fee portion of a settlement is taxable to the client, even though it goes to the lawyer, CIR v. Banks, CIR v. Banaitis, 543 U.S. 426 (2005). The Court sidestepped fee awards under federal fee-shifting statutes. However, in the fall of 2004, Congress amended the IRC to liberate the client in whistleblower, discrimination, and civil rights dispute from tax on attorney fee and costs. Under the *Banks* decision, in a judgment or settlement before October 2004, the lawyer's fee under contingency fee contracts is taxable income to the plaintiff.

5. *Reputation Damages.* May a wrongfully discharged employee recover special damages for harm to her professional reputation caused by the discharge? Vanessa Redgrave claimed she had lost professional opportunities because the Boston Symphony Orchestra improperly cancelled her contract with them. The court first noted that courts frequently disallowed contract claims for damage to reputation either because the plaintiff's loss was speculative or because the damages were not within the parties' contemplation when they contracted. Redgrave proved that specific job offers were cancelled because of the discharge; these losses could be found to have been within the contemplation of the parties. Redgrave's recovery for damages to her reputation was justified. Redgrave v. Boston Symphony Orchestra, Inc., 855 F.2d 888 (1st Cir.1988), cert. denied, 488 U.S. 1043 (1989).

3. EMPLOYEE'S AVOIDABLE CONSEQUENCES

PARKER v. TWENTIETH CENTURY–FOX FILM CORP.

Supreme Court of California, 1970.
3 Cal.3d 176, 89 Cal.Rptr. 737, 474 P.2d 689.

BURKE, JUSTICE. * * * Plaintiff [Shirley MacLaine] is well known as an actress, and in the contract between plaintiff and defendant is sometimes referred to as the "Artist." Under the contract, dated August 6, 1965, plaintiff was to play the female lead in defendant's contemplated production of a motion picture entitled "Bloomer Girl." The contract provided that defendant would pay plaintiff a minimum "guaranteed compensation" of $53,571.42 per week for 14 weeks commencing May 23, 1966, for a total of $750,000. Prior to May 1966 defendant decided not to produce the picture and by a letter dated April 4, 1966, it notified plaintiff of that decision and that it would not "comply with our obligations to you under" the written contract.

By the same letter and with the professed purpose "to avoid any damage to you," defendant instead offered to employ plaintiff as the leading actress in another film tentatively entitled "Big Country, Big Man" (hereinafter, "Big Country"). The compensation offered was identical, as were 31 of the 34 numbered provisions or articles of the original contract. Unlike "Bloomer Girl," however, which was to have been a musical production, "Big Country" was a dramatic "western type" movie. "Bloomer Girl" was to have been filmed in

California; "Big Country" was to be produced in Australia. Also, certain terms in the proffered contract varied from those of the original. Plaintiff was given one week within which to accept; she did not and the offer lapsed. Plaintiff then commenced this action seeking recovery of the agreed guaranteed compensation. * * * [S]ummary judgment for $750,000 plus interest was entered in plaintiff's favor. This appeal by defendant followed. * * *

The general rule is that the measure of recovery by a wrongfully discharged employee is the amount of salary agreed upon for the period of service, less the amount which the employer affirmatively proves the employee has earned or with reasonable effort might have earned from other employment. * * * However, before projected earnings from other employment opportunities not sought or accepted by the discharged employee can be applied in mitigation, the employer must show that the other employment was comparable, or substantially similar, to that of which the employee has been deprived; the employee's rejection of or failure to seek other available employment of a different or inferior kind may not be resorted to in order to mitigate damages. * * *

In the present case defendant has raised no issue of *reasonableness of efforts* by plaintiff to obtain other employment; the sole issue is whether plaintiff's refusal of defendant's substitute offer of "Big Country" may be used in mitigation. Nor, if the "Big Country" offer was of employment different or inferior when compared with the original "Bloomer Girl" employment, is there an issue as to whether or not plaintiff acted reasonably in refusing the substitute offer. Despite defendant's arguments to the contrary, no case cited or which our research has discovered holds or suggests that reasonableness is an element of a wrongfully discharged employee's option to reject, or fail to seek, different or inferior employment lest the possible earnings therefrom be charged against him in mitigation of damages.[1]

Applying the foregoing rules to the record in the present case, with all intendments in favor of the party opposing the summary judgment motion— here, defendant—it is clear that the trial court correctly ruled that plaintiff's failure to accept defendant's tendered substitute employment could not be applied in mitigation of damages because the offer of the "Big Country" lead was of employment both different and inferior, and that no factual dispute was presented on that issue. The mere circumstance that "Bloomer Girl" was to be a musical review calling upon plaintiff's talents as a dancer as well as an actress, and was to be produced in the City of Los Angeles, where "Big Country" was a straight dramatic role in a "western type" story taking place in an opal mine in

1. [Footnotes renumbered.] Instead, in each case the reasonableness referred to was that of the *efforts* of the employee to obtain other employment that was not different or inferior; his right to reject the latter was declared as an unqualified rule of law. Thus, Gonzales v. Internat. Assn. of Machinists, 213 Cal.App.2d 817, 823–824, 29 Cal.Rptr. 190, 194, holds that the trial court correctly instructed the jury that plaintiff union member, a machinist, was required to make "such efforts as the average [member of his union] desiring employment would make at that particular time and place" (italics added); but, further, that the court *properly rejected* defendant's *offer of proof of the availability of other kinds of employment* at the same or higher pay than plaintiff usually received and all outside the jurisdiction of his union, as plaintiff could not be required to accept different employment or a nonunion job.

In Harris v. Nat. Union of Marine Cooks and Stewards, 116 Cal.App.2d 759, 761, 254 P.2d 673, 676, the issues were stated to be, inter alia, whether comparable employment was open to each plaintiff employee, and if so whether each plaintiff made a *reasonable effort* to secure such employment. It was held that the trial court *properly sustained an objection to an offer to prove a custom of accepting a job in a lower rank* when work in the higher rank was not available, as "The duty of mitigation of damages * * * does not require the plaintiff 'to seek or to accept other employment of a different or inferior kind.' " * * *

Australia, demonstrates the difference in kind between the two employments; the female lead as a dramatic actress in a western style motion picture can by no stretch of imagination be considered the equivalent of or substantially similar to the lead in a song-and-dance production.

Additionally, the substitute "Big Country" offer proposed to eliminate or impair the director and screenplay approvals accorded to plaintiff under the original "Bloomer Girl" contract, and thus constituted an offer of inferior employment. No expertise or judicial notice is required in order to hold that the deprivation or infringement of an employee's rights held under an original employment contract converts the available "other employment" relied upon by the employer to mitigate damages, into inferior employment which the employee need not seek or accept. * * *

[Affirmed]

SULLIVAN, ACTING CHIEF JUSTICE (dissenting). The familiar rule requiring a plaintiff in a tort or contract action to mitigate damages embodies notions of fairness and socially responsible behavior which are fundamental to our jurisprudence. Most broadly stated, it precludes the recovery of damages which, through the exercise of due diligence, could have been avoided. Thus, in essence, it is a rule requiring reasonable conduct in commercial affairs. This general principle governs the obligations of an employee after his employer has wrongfully repudiated or terminated the employment contract. Rather than permitting the employee simply to remain idle during the balance of the contract period, the law requires him to make a reasonable effort to secure other employment.[1] He is not obliged, however, to seek or accept any and all types of work which may be available. Only work which is in the same field and which is of the same quality need be accepted.

Over the years the courts have employed various phrases to define the type of employment which the employee, upon his wrongful discharge, is under an obligation to accept. Thus in California alone it has been held that he must accept employment which is "substantially similar" * * *; "comparable employment" * * *; employment "in the same general line of the first employment" * * *; "equivalent to his prior position" * * *; "employment in a similar capacity" * * *; employment which is "not * * * of a different or inferior kind." [citations]

For reasons which are unexplained, the majority cite several of these cases yet select from among the various judicial formulations which contain one particular phrase, "Not of a different or inferior kind," with which to analyze this case. I have discovered no historical or theoretical reason to adopt this phrase, which is simply a negative restatement of the affirmative standards set out in the above cases, as the exclusive standard. Indeed, its emergence is an example of the dubious phenomenon of the law responding not to rational judicial choice or changing social conditions, but to unrecognized changes in the

1. [Footnotes renumbered.] The issue is generally discussed in terms of a duty on the part of the employee to minimize loss. The practice is long-established and there is little reason to change despite Judge Cardozo's observation of its subtle inaccuracy. "The servant is free to accept employment or reject it according to his uncensored pleasure. What is meant by the supposed duty is merely this: That if he unreason- ably reject, he will not be heard to say that the loss of wages from then on shall be deemed the jural consequence of the earlier discharge. He has broken the chain of causation, and loss resulting to him thereafter is suffered through his own act." (McClelland v. Climax Hosiery Mills (1930) 252 N.Y. 347, 359, 169 N.E. 605, 609, concurring opinion.)

language of opinions or legal treatises. However, the phrase is a serviceable one and my concern is not with its use as the standard but rather with what I consider its distortion. * * * It has never been the law that the mere existence of *differences between two jobs in the same field* is sufficient, as a matter of law, to excuse an employee wrongfully discharged from one from accepting the other in order to mitigate damages. Such an approach would effectively eliminate any obligation of an employee to attempt to minimize damage arising from a wrongful discharge. The only alternative job offer an employee would be required to accept would be an offer of his former job by his former employer.

I believe that the approach taken by the majority (a superficial listing of differences with no attempt to assess their significance) may subvert a valuable legal doctrine.[2] The inquiry in cases such as this should not be whether differences between the two jobs exist (there will always be differences) but whether the differences which are present are substantial enough to constitute differences in the *kind* of employment or, alternatively, whether they render the substitute work employment of an *inferior kind*.

* * * This necessitates a weighing of the evidence, and it is precisely this undertaking which is forbidden on summary judgment.

Notes

1. *Analogy to a Sale of Goods*. If the former employee's lawsuit resembles a seller's, the plaintiff-employee's proof of the amount due her under the breached contract resembles the goods seller's suit for the price. See U.C.C. § 2–709. The plaintiff-employee who takes a replacement position resembles a seller who, after buyer breaches, resells the goods. U.C.C. § 2–706. At this point, the former employee has avoided damages; her measure of recovery is her contractual wages less her replacement earnings equals her damages. Torosyan v. Boehringer Ingelheim Pharmaceuticals, 234 Conn. 1, 662 A.2d 89 (1995).

Is a "reseller" of personal services more interested in the second buyer's personal qualities than a reseller of bricks, grain, or timber? Is a former employee who takes replacement employment, in effect, working for her breaching employer?

2. *Might Have Been*. Real controversy emerges when a discharged employee does not diligently seek substitute employment. Then the court must speculate about what the world of her diligence would have been like. Her former employer carries the burden of proof in this murky world of "might have been." A judge's avoidable consequences reduction for plaintiff's lack of diligence in seeking substitute employment may resemble a shot in the dark. Betterman v. Fleming Companies, Inc., 271 Wis.2d 193, 677 N.W.2d 673, 682 (App. 2004).

3. *"Some people take, some people get took."* Fran Kubelik (Shirley MacLaine) in *"The Apartment"* (1960), or The Plaintiff's Leisure Windfall. A discharged employee who rejects other employment chooses inactivity plus the chance of recovering damages from her former employer. The common-law rule defines a wrongfully discharged employee's acceptable substitute employment narrowly; but, if she takes an inferior job, the rule prevents her from recovering her lost future wages in addition to retaining the income she earned in this nonsubstitute employment.

---

2. The values of the doctrine of mitigation of damages in this context are that it minimizes the unnecessary personal and social (e.g., nonproductive use of labor, litigation) costs of contractual failure. If a wrongfully discharged employee can, through his own actions and without suffering financial or psychological loss in the process, reduce the damages accruing from the breach of contract, the most sensible policy is to require him to do so. I fear the majority opinion will encourage precisely opposite conduct.

What kind of incentives does this combination create for the discharged employee? Does the rule produce a "leisure windfall" for her? Is a risk-aversive discharged employee more likely to accept nonsubstitute employment?

Should a court expand the former employee's duty to minimize her damages by broadening the way it defines acceptable substitute employment? Should a court give the employee a reasonable time to find comparable employment, then insist that the employee find other employment that she is "fitted" for? How long should it take for the employee to lower her sights? On the other hand, would this approach shift too many risks to the nonbreaching former employee and encourage employers to breach employment contracts?

Does the avoidable consequences rule with the burden of proof on the former employer discourage an employer from terminating an inefficient and uneconomical employment contract? Can a court value an employee's expectancy at less than the full contract rate?

Does the *Parker* court establish a mixed objective-subjective standard as follows: a breached-against employee has an objective duty to look for substitute employment, to conduct a reasonable search. But she has only a subjective or good-faith duty to accept a replacement position? If so, will a plaintiff who prefers to loaf abuse a mixed standard by falsely denying that a substitute job is appropriate? Professor Eisenberg thinks not on the ground that plaintiff's economic, psychological, and social needs will prevail. Mel Eisenberg, The Responsive Model of Contract Law, 36 Stan. L. Rev. 1107, 1147–55 (1984).

4. *Summary Judgment*? Is assessing an actor's career's trajectory and determining whether the studio's substitute offer was a suitable vehicle for that trajectory an issue the judges should let jurors evaluate in light of their collective community judgment?

5. *Collateral Source Rule*. May the defendant-employer reduce a wrongfully discharged employee's lost income damages by the unemployment compensation or other payments that the plaintiff collected?

(a) *Yes*. Some courts, maintaining that the plaintiff's unemployment compensation is not from a collateral source since the employer pays into the fund, allow the employer a deduction to prevent the ex-employee's double recovery. Stevens v. Ravenna Aluminum Industries, Inc., 114 Ohio App.3d 472, 683 N.E.2d 403, 408 (1996); Mers v. Dispatch Printing Co., 39 Ohio App.3d 99, 529 N.E.2d 958 (1988).

(b) *No.* Other courts disallow a reduction, ruling that an employer should not benefit because an employee worked long enough to qualify for unemployment compensation. Sam Teague v. Hawai'i Civil Rights Commission, 89 Hawai'i 269, 971 P.2d 1104, 1115 (1999); Hayes v. Trulock, 51 Wash.App. 795, 755 P.2d 830 (1988).

In Betterman v. Fleming Companies, the court did not reduce plaintiff's lost wages by disability insurance payments. Even though the defendant paid the premiums, the disability insurance was part of plaintiff's compensation. Betterman v. Fleming Companies, Inc., 271 Wis.2d 193, 677 N.W.2d 673, 682 (App. 2004).

(c) *Maybe—The Judge's Discretion*. Whether to deduct unemployment compensation from a plaintiff's back pay is within the trial judge's discretion, but deduction should not occur often, and not here, because deduction dilutes deterrence. The plaintiff's unemployment compensation is from a collateral source. But plaintiff's income from the former employer's "subfund" is a direct benefit and would duplicate back pay, so it should be deducted. Barnes v. Goodyear Tire and Rubber Co., 2001 WL 568033 (Tenn.App.).

(d) The federal circuits are divided, some deducting unemployment compensation, some declining to deduct it, and some granting the judge discretion to deduct it or not. Lussier v. Runyon, 50 F.3d 1103 (1st Cir.1995), cert. denied, 516 U.S. 815 (1995).

6. *Employer Later Discovers Adverse Evidence.* What if plaintiff has been discharged in violation of a statute, but the employer later learns she had committed misconduct which would have justified the earlier discharge? In McKennon v. Nashville Banner Publishing, the Supreme Court dealt with an age-discrimination plaintiff. The defendant argued that plaintiff had come into Chancery with "unclean hands" and was not eligible for equitable relief. The Court rejected that argument; the Chancellor ought to decline to accept a defendant's unclean hands defense where the defendant has violated a statute that advances an important public policy like suppressing discrimination. The employer's newly discovered evidence, the Court held, cannot eliminate plaintiff's remedies altogether, for leaving the wrongfully discharged plaintiff without a remedy would undermine the statutory purpose of deterring an employer's age discrimination. The plaintiff might recover back pay during a loss period beginning with the improper firing, ending with the employer's discovery of a proper reason to fire her. However, plaintiff's reinstatement and front pay would be, the Court asserted, pointless. McKennon v. Nashville Banner Publishing Co., 513 U.S. 352 (1995).

754

4. CONTRACT v. TORT: EXCEPTIONS TO THE AT–WILL DOCTRINE

FOLEY v. INTERACTIVE DATA CORPORATION

Supreme Court of California, In Bank, 1988.
47 Cal.3d 654, 254 Cal.Rptr. 211, 765 P.2d 373.

LUCAS, CHIEF JUSTICE. After Interactive Data Corporation (defendant) fired plaintiff Daniel D. Foley, an executive employee, he filed this action seeking compensatory and punitive damages for wrongful discharge. In his second amended complaint, plaintiff asserted three distinct theories: (1) a tort cause of action alleging a discharge in violation of public policy (Tameny v. Atlantic Richfield Co. (1980) 27 Cal.3d 167, 164 Cal.Rptr. 839, 610 P.2d 1330), (2) a contract cause of action for breach of an implied-in-fact promise to discharge for good cause only (e.g., Pugh v. See's Candies, Inc. (1981) 116 Cal.App.3d 311, 171 Cal.Rptr. 917 [all references are to this case rather than the 1988 post-trial decision appearing at 203 Cal.App.3d 743, 250 Cal.Rptr. 195]), and (3) a cause of action alleging a tortious breach of the implied covenant of good faith and fair dealing (e.g., Cleary v. American Airlines, Inc. (1980) 111 Cal.App.3d 443, 168 Cal.Rptr. 722).

According to the complaint, plaintiff is a former employee of defendant, a wholly owned subsidiary of Chase Manhattan Bank that markets computer-based decision-support services. Defendant hired plaintiff in June 1976 as an assistant product manager at a starting salary of $18,500.

Over the next six years and nine months, plaintiff received a steady series of salary increases, promotions, bonuses, awards and superior performance evaluations. * * * He alleges defendant's officers made repeated oral assurances of job security so long as his performance remained adequate.

Plaintiff also alleged that during his employment, defendant maintained written "Termination Guidelines" that set forth express grounds for discharge and a mandatory seven-step pretermination procedure. Plaintiff understood that these guidelines applied not only to employees under plaintiff's supervision, but to him as well. On the basis of these representations, plaintiff alleged that he reasonably believed defendant would not discharge him except for good cause, and therefore he refrained from accepting or pursuing other job opportunities.

The event that led to plaintiff's discharge was a private conversation in January 1983 with his former supervisor, vice president Richard Earnest. During the previous year defendant had hired Robert Kuhne and subsequently named Kuhne to replace Earnest as plaintiff's immediate supervisor. Plaintiff learned that Kuhne was currently under investigation by the Federal Bureau of Investigation for embezzlement from his former employer, Bank of America. Plaintiff reported what he knew about Kuhne to Earnest, because he was "worried about working for Kuhne and having him in a supervisory position, * * * in view of Kuhne's suspected criminal conduct." Plaintiff asserted he "made this disclosure in the interest and for the benefit of his employer," allegedly because he believed that because defendant and its parent do business with the financial community on a confidential basis, the company would have a legitimate interest in knowing about a high executive's alleged prior criminal conduct.

In response, Earnest allegedly told plaintiff not to discuss "rumors" and to "forget what he heard" about Kuhne's past. In early March, Kuhne informed plaintiff that defendant had decided to replace him for "performance reasons" and that he could transfer to a position in another division in Waltham, Massachusetts. [Plaintiff was discharged shortly thereafter.]

Defendant demurred to all three causes of action. After plaintiff filed two amended pleadings, the trial court sustained defendant's demurrer without leave to amend and dismissed all three causes of action. The Court of Appeal affirmed the dismissal as to all three counts. We will explore each claim in turn.

We turn first to plaintiff's cause of action alleging he was discharged in violation of public policy. Labor Code section 2922 provides in relevant part, "An employment, having no specified term, may be terminated at the will of either party on notice to the other." This presumption may be superseded by a contract, express or implied, limiting the employer's right to discharge the employee. Absent any contract, however, the employment is "at will," and the employee can be fired with or without good cause. But the employer's right to discharge an "at will" employee is still subject to limits imposed by public policy, since otherwise the threat of discharge could be used to coerce employees into committing crimes, concealing wrongdoing, or taking other action harmful to the public weal.

* * * Tameny v. Atlantic Richfield Co., declared that a tort action for wrongful discharge may lie if the employer "condition[s] employment upon required participation in unlawful conduct by the employee." In Tameny, the plaintiff alleged he was fired for refusing to engage in price fixing in violation of the Cartwright Act and the Sherman Antitrust Act. We held the trial court erred in sustaining Atlantic Richfield's demurrer to plaintiff's tort action for wrongful discharge. Writing for the majority, Justice Tobriner concluded that "an employer's authority over its employee does not include the right to demand that the employee commit a criminal act to further its interests. * * * An employer engaging in such conduct violates a basic duty imposed by law upon all employers, and thus an employee who has suffered damages as a result of such discharge may maintain a tort action for wrongful discharge against the employ-

er." As we explained, "an employer's obligation to refrain from discharging an employee who refuses to commit a criminal act does not depend upon any express or implied "'promise[s] set forth in the [employment] contract" '[citation], but rather reflects a duty imposed by law upon all employers in order to implement the fundamental public policies embodied in the state's penal statutes. As such, a wrongful discharge suit exhibits the classic elements of a tort cause of action."

In the present case, plaintiff alleges that defendant discharged him in "sharp derogation" of a substantial public policy that imposes a legal duty on employees to report relevant business information to management. An employee is an agent, and as such "is required to disclose to [his] principal all information he has relevant to the subject matter of the agency." Thus, plaintiff asserts, if he discovered information that might lead his employer to conclude that an employee was an embezzler, and should not be retained, plaintiff had a duty to communicate that information to his principal.

Whether or not there is a statutory duty requiring an employee to report information relevant to his employer's interest, we do not find a substantial public policy prohibiting an employer from discharging an employee for performing that duty. Past decisions recognizing a tort action for discharge in violation of public policy seek to protect the public, by protecting the employee who refuses to commit a crime. No equivalent public interest bars the discharge of the present plaintiff. When the duty of an employee to disclose information to his employer serves only the private interest of the employer, the rationale underlying the *Tameny* cause of action is not implicated.

We conclude that the Court of Appeal properly upheld the trial court's ruling sustaining the demurrer without leave to amend to plaintiff's first cause of action.

Plaintiff's second cause of action alleged that over the course of his nearly seven years of employment with defendant, the company's own conduct and personnel policies gave rise to an "oral contract" not to fire him without good cause. [The court ruled that the claim was not barred by the Statute of Frauds.]

Although plaintiff describes his cause of action as one for breach of an oral contract, he does not allege explicit words by which the parties agreed that he would not be terminated without good cause. Instead he alleges that a course of conduct, including various oral representations, created a reasonable expectation to that effect. Thus, his cause of action is more properly described as one for breach of an implied-in-fact contract.

Before this court, defendant urges that we disapprove precedent permitting a cause of action for wrongful discharge founded on an implied-in-fact contract and require instead an express contract provision requiring good cause for termination, supported by independent consideration. Alternatively, defendant requests that we distinguish *Pugh* and its progeny from the present case. We conclude, however, that *Pugh* correctly applied basic contract principles in the employment context, and that these principles are applicable to plaintiff's agreement with defendant.

The plaintiff in *Pugh* had been employed by the defendant for 32 years, during which time he worked his way up the corporate ladder from dishwasher to vice president. When hired, he had been assured that "if you are loyal * * * and do a good job, your future is secure." During his long employment, the plaintiff received numerous commendations and promotions, and no significant criticism of his work. Throughout this period the company maintained a practice of not terminating administrative personnel without good cause. On this evidence, the Court of Appeal concluded that the jury could determine the existence of an implied promise that the employer would not arbitrarily terminate the plaintiff's employment.

A review of other jurisdictions also reveals a strong trend in favor of recognizing implied contract terms that modify the power of an employer to discharge an employee at will. [citations]

We begin by acknowledging the fundamental principle of freedom of contract: employer and employee are free to agree to a contract terminable at will or subject to limitations. Their agreement will be enforced so long as it does not violate legal strictures external to the contract, such as laws affecting union membership and activity, prohibitions on indentured servitude, or the many other legal restrictions already described which place certain restraints on the employment arrangement. As we have discussed, Labor Code section 2922 establishes a presumption of at-will employment if the parties have made no express oral or written agreement specifying the length of employment or the grounds for termination. This presumption may, however, be overcome by evidence that despite the absence of a specified term, the parties agreed that the employer's power to terminate would be limited in some way, e.g., by a requirement that termination be based only on "good cause."

Defendant contends that courts should not enforce employment security agreements in the absence of evidence of independent consideration and an express manifestation of mutual assent. Although, as explained below, there may be some historical basis for imposing such limitations, any such basis has been eroded by the development of modern contract law and, accordingly, we conclude that defendant's suggested limitations are inappropriate in the modern employment context. We discern no basis for departing from otherwise applicable general contract principles.

The limitations on employment security terms on which defendant relies were developed during a period when courts were generally reluctant to look beyond explicit promises of the parties to a contract. "The court-imposed presumption that the employment contract is terminable at will relies upon the formalistic approach to contract interpretation predominant in late nineteenth century legal thought: manifestations of assent must be evidenced by definite, express terms if promises are to be enforceable." (Note, Protecting At Will Employees, 93 Harv.L.Rev. at p. 1825, fns. omitted.) In the intervening decades, however, courts increasingly demonstrated their willingness to examine the entire relationship of the parties to commercial contracts to ascertain their actual intent, and this trend has been reflected in the body of law guiding contract interpretation. (See, Goetz & Scott, The Limits of Expanded Choice: An Analysis of the Interactions Between Express and Implied Contract Terms (1985)) 73 Cal.L.Rev. 261, 273–276.

Similarly, 20 years ago, Professor Blumrosen observed that during the decades preceding his analysis, courts had demonstrated an increasing willingness to "consider the entire relationship of the parties, and to find that facts and circumstances establish a contract which cannot be terminated by the employer without cause." (Blumrosen, Settlement of Disputes Concerning the Exercise of Employer Disciplinary Power: United States Report, 18 Rutgers L.Rev. at p. 432, fn. omitted.) "This approach has been recognized as consistent with customary interpretation techniques of commercial contracts permitting 'gap filling' by implication of reasonable terms." Miller & Estes, Recent Judicial Limitations on the Right to Discharge: A California Trilogy (1982) 16 U.C.Davis L.Rev. 65, 101, fn. omitted.

Finally, we do not agree with the Court of Appeal that employment security agreements are so inherently harmful or unfair to employers, who do not receive equivalent guarantees of continued service, as to merit treatment different from that accorded other contracts. On the contrary, employers may benefit from the increased loyalty and productivity that such agreements may inspire. Permitting proof of and reliance on implied-in-fact contract terms does not nullify the at-will rule, it merely treats such contracts in a manner in keeping with general contract law.

Defendant's remaining argument is that even if a promise to discharge "for good cause only" could be implied in fact, the evidentiary factors outlined in *Pugh,* and relied on by plaintiff, are inadequate as a matter of law. This contention fails on several grounds.

First, defendant overemphasizes the fact that plaintiff was employed for "only" six years and nine months. Length of employment is a relevant consideration but six years and nine months is sufficient time for conduct to occur on which a trier of fact could find the existence of an implied contract. Plaintiff here alleged repeated oral assurances of job security and consistent promotions, salary increases and bonuses during the term of his employment contributing to his reasonable expectation that he would not be discharged except for good cause.

Second, an allegation of breach of written "Termination Guidelines" implying self-imposed limitations on the employer's power to discharge at will may be sufficient to state a cause of action for breach of an employment contract. *Pugh* is not alone in holding that the trier of fact can infer an agreement to limit the grounds for termination based on the employee's reasonable reliance on the company's personnel manual or policies. [citations]

Finally, unlike the employee in *Pugh,* plaintiff alleges that he supplied the company valuable and separate consideration by signing an agreement whereby he promised not to compete or conceal any computer-related information from defendant for one year after termination. The noncompetition agreement and its attendant "Disclosure and Assignment of Proprietary Information, Inventions, etc." may be probative evidence that "it is more probable that the parties intended a continuing relationship, with limitations upon the employer's dismissal authority [because the] employee has provided some benefit to the employer, or suffers some detriment, beyond the usual rendition of service."

In sum, plaintiff has pleaded facts which, if proved, may be sufficient for a jury to find an implied-in-fact contract limiting defendant's right to discharge him arbitrarily—facts sufficient to overcome the presumption of Labor Code section 2922. On demurrer, we must assume these facts to be true. In other words, plaintiff has pleaded an implied-in-fact contract and its breach, and is entitled to his opportunity to prove those allegations.

We turn now to plaintiff's cause of action for tortious breach of the implied covenant of good faith and fair dealing.

The distinction between tort and contract is well grounded in common law, and divergent objectives underlie the remedies created in the two areas. Whereas contract actions are created to enforce the intentions of the parties to the agreement, tort law is primarily designed to vindicate "social policy." [citation] The covenant of good faith and fair dealing was developed in the contract arena and is aimed at making effective the agreement's promises. Plaintiff asks that we find that the breach of the implied covenant in employment contracts also gives rise to an action seeking an award of tort damages.

In this instance, where an extension of tort remedies is sought for a duty whose breach previously has been compensable by contractual remedies, it is helpful to consider certain principles relevant to contract law. First, predictability about the cost of contractual relationships plays an important role in our commercial system (Putz & Klippen, Commercial Bad Faith: Attorney Fees—Not Tort Liability—Is the Remedy for "Stonewalling" (1987) 21 U.S.F.L.Rev. 419, 432). Moreover, "Courts traditionally have awarded damages for breach of contract to compensate the aggrieved party rather than to punish the breaching party." Note, "Contort": Tortious Breach of the Implied Covenant of Good Faith and Fair Dealing in Noninsurance, Commercial Contracts—Its Existence and Desirability (1985) 60 Notre Dame L.Rev. 510, 526, & fn. 94. With these concepts in mind, we turn to analyze the role of the implied covenant of good faith and fair dealing and the propriety of the extension of remedies urged by plaintiff.

"Every contract imposes upon each party a duty of good faith and fair dealing in its performance and its enforcement." (Rest.2d Contracts, § 205.) This duty has been recognized in the majority of American jurisdictions, the Restatement, and the Uniform Commercial Code. (Burton, Breach of Contract and the Common Law Duty to Perform in Good Faith (1980) 94 Harv.L.Rev. 369.) Because the covenant is a contract term, however, compensation for its breach has almost always been limited to contract rather than tort remedies. * * * Initially, the concept of a duty of good faith developed in contract law as "a kind of 'safety valve' to which judges may turn to fill gaps and qualify or limit rights and duties otherwise arising under rules of law and specific contract language." (Summers, The General Duty of Good Faith—Its Recognition and Conceptualization (1982) 67 Cornell L.Rev. 810, 812.) As a contract concept, breach of the duty led to imposition of contract damages determined by the nature of the breach and standard contract principles.

An exception to this general rule has developed in the context of insurance contracts where, for a variety of policy reasons, courts have held that breach of the implied covenant will provide the basis for an action in tort. California has a well-developed judicial history addressing this exception. In Comunale v. Traders & General Ins. Co. (1958) 50 Cal.2d 654, 658, 328 P.2d 198, we stated, "There is an implied covenant of good faith and fair dealing in every contract that neither party will do anything which will injure the right of the other to receive the benefits of the agreement." Thereafter, in Crisci v. Security Ins. Co. (1967) 66 Cal.2d 425, 58 Cal.Rptr. 13, 426 P.2d 173, for the first time we permitted an insured to recover in tort for emotional damages caused by the insurer's breach of the implied covenant. * * *

The first California appellate case to permit tort recovery in the employment context was *Cleary*. To support its holding that tort as well as contract damages were appropriate to compensate for a breach of the implied covenant, the *Cleary* court relied on insurance cases without engaging in comparative analysis of insurance and employment relationships and without inquiring into whether the insurance cases' departure from established principles of contract law should generally be subject to expansion.

* * * When a court enforces the implied covenant it is in essence acting to protect "the interest in having promises performed" (Prosser, Law of Torts (4th ed. 1971) p. 613)—the traditional realm of a contract action—rather than to protect some general duty to society which the law places on an employer without regard to the substance of its contractual obligations to its employee. Thus, in *Tameny,* as we have explained, the court was careful to draw a distinction between "ex delicto" and "ex contractu" obligations. An allegation of breach of the implied covenant of good faith and fair dealing is an allegation of breach of an "ex contractu" obligation, namely one arising out of the contract itself. The covenant of good faith is read into contracts in order to protect the express covenants or promises of the contract, not to protect some general public policy interest not directly tied to the contract's purposes. The insurance cases thus were a major departure from traditional principles of contract law. We must, therefore, consider with great care claims that extension of the exceptional approach taken in those cases is automatically appropriate if certain hallmarks and similarities can be adduced in another contract setting. With this emphasis on the historical purposes of the covenant of good faith and fair dealing in mind, we turn to consider the bases upon which extension of the insurance model to the employment sphere has been urged.

The "special relationship" test gleaned from the insurance context has been suggested as a model for determining the appropriateness of permitting tort remedies for breach of the implied covenant of the employment context. * * *

After review of the various commentators, and independent consideration of the similarities between the two areas, we are not convinced that a "special relationship" analogous to that between insurer and insured should be deemed to exist in the usual employment relationship which would warrant recognition of a tort action for breach of the implied covenant. Even if we were to assume that the special relationship model is an appropriate one to follow in determining whether to expand tort recovery, a breach in the employment context does not place the employee in the same economic dilemma that an insured faces when an insurer in bad faith refuses to pay a claim or to accept a settlement offer within policy limits. When an insurer takes such actions, the insured cannot turn to the marketplace to find another insurance company willing to pay for the loss already incurred. The wrongfully terminated employee, on the other hand, can (and must, in order to mitigate damages [see Parker v. Twentieth Century–Fox Film Corp.]) make reasonable efforts to seek alternative employment. Moreover, the role of the employer differs from that of the "quasi-public" insurance company with whom individuals contract specifically in order to obtain protection from potential specified economic harm. The employer does not similarly "sell" protection to its employees; it is not providing a public service. Nor do we find convincing the idea that the employee is necessarily seeking a different kind of financial security than those entering a typical commercial contract. If a small dealer contracts for goods from a large supplier, and those goods are vital to the small dealer's business, a breach by the supplier may have financial significance for individuals employed by the dealer or to the dealer himself. Permitting only contract damages in such a situation has ramifications no different from a similar limitation in the direct employer-employee relationship.

Finally, there is a fundamental difference between insurance and employment relationships. In the insurance relationship, the insurer's and insured's interest are financially at odds. If the insurer pays a claim, it diminishes its fiscal resources. The insured of course has paid for protection and expects to have its losses recompensed. When a claim is paid, money shifts from insurer to insured, or, if appropriate, to a third party claimant.

Putting aside already specifically barred improper motives for termination which may be based on both economic and noneconomic considerations, as a general rule it is to the employer's economic benefit to retain good employees. The interests of employer and employee are most frequently in alignment. If there is a job to be done, the employer must still pay someone to do it. This is not to say that there may never be a "bad motive" for discharge not otherwise covered by law. Nevertheless, in terms of abstract employment relationships as contrasted with abstract insurance relationships, there is less inherent relevant tension between the interests of employers and employees than exists between that of insurers and insureds. Thus the need to place disincentives on an employer's conduct in addition to those already imposed by law simply does not rise to the same level as that created by the conflicting interests at stake in the insurance context. Nor is this to say that the Legislature would have no basis for affording employees additional protections. It is, however, to say that the need to extend the special relationship model in the form of judicially created relief of the kind sought here is less compelling.

We therefore conclude that the employment relationship is not sufficiently similar to that of insurer and insured to warrant judicial extension of the proposed additional tort remedies in view of the countervailing concerns about economic policy and stability, the traditional separation of tort and contract law, and finally, the numerous protections against improper terminations already afforded employees.

Our inquiry, however, does not end here. The potential effects on an individual caused by termination of employment arguably justify additional remedies for certain improper discharges. * * *

The issue is how far courts can or should go in responding to these concerns regarding the sufficiency of compensation by departing from long established principles of contract law. Significant policy judgments affecting social policies and commercial relationships are implicated in the resolution of this question in the employment termination context. Such a determination, which has the potential to alter profoundly the nature of employment, the cost of products and services, and the availability of jobs, arguably is better suited for legislative decisionmaking.

It cannot be disputed that legislation at both the state and national level has profoundly affected the scope of at-will terminations. As noted, regulation of employment ranging from workers' compensation laws to antidiscrimination enactments, fair labor standards, minimum compensation, regulation of hours, etc., all have significantly impinged on the laissez-faire underpinnings of the at-will rule. Moreover, unionization of a portion of the domestic workforce has substantial implications for the judicial development of employment termination law because the rights of such workers when terminated are often governed exclusively by the terms of applicable collective bargaining agreements. The slate we write on thus is far from clean.

We are not unmindful of the legitimate concerns of employees who fear arbitrary and improper discharges that may have a devastating effect on their economic and social status. Nor are we unaware of or unsympathetic to claims that contract remedies for breaches of contract are insufficient because they do not fully compensate due to their failure to include attorney fees and their restrictions on foreseeable damages. These defects, however, exist generally in contract situations. As discussed above, the variety of possible courses to remedy the problem is well demonstrated in the literature and include increased contract damages, provision for award of attorney fees, establishment of arbitration or other speedier and less expensive dispute resolution, or the tort remedies (the scope of which is also subject to dispute) sought by plaintiff here.

The diversity of possible solutions demonstrates the confusion that occurs when we look outside the realm of contract law in attempting to fashion remedies for a breach of a contract provision. As noted, numerous legislative provisions have imposed obligations on parties to contracts which vindicate significant social policies extraneous to the contract itself. As Justice Kaus observed in his concurring and dissenting opinion in White v. Western Title Ins. Co. (1985) 40 Cal.3d 870, 901, 221 Cal.Rptr. 509, 710 P.2d 309, "our experience * * * surely tells us that there are real problems in applying the substitute remedy of a tort recovery—with or without punitive damages—outside the insurance area. In other words, I believe that under all the circumstances, the problem is one for the Legislature. * * * "

Plaintiff may proceed with his cause of action alleging a breach of an implied-in-fact contract promise to discharge him only for good cause; his claim is not barred by the statute of frauds. His cause of action for a breach of public policy pursuant to *Tameny* was properly dismissed because the facts alleged, even if proven, would not establish a discharge in violation of public policy. Finally, as to his cause of action for tortious breach of the implied covenant of good faith and fair dealing, we hold that tort remedies are not available for breach of the implied covenant in an employment contract to employees who allege they have been discharged in violation of the covenant.

Broussard, Justice, concurring and dissenting. I maintain that we should retain the well-recognized tort cause of action for bad faith discharge. To demonstrate the point, I propose to show (1) that a tort cause of action for bad faith discharge is an established feature of California common law; (2) that the analogy between the insurance cases, in which a tort cause of action has long been recognized, justifies tort recovery for bad faith discharge; (3) that the existence of a cause of action in contract for discharge in breach of contract does not exclude a tort action for bad faith; and (4) that it is fundamentally illogical to abolish a tort cause of action on the ground that radical change in existing remedies should be left to legislative action.

A tort action for bad faith discharge * * * requires that the discharge be wrongful—that is, in breach of contract. But once that prerequisite is satisfied, it focuses not upon the employee's right to enforce a particular contractual provision, but upon society's right to deter and demand redress for arbitrary or malicious conduct which inflicts harm upon one of its members. This is the proper and traditional function of tort law.

Notes

1. *Cracks in At Will.* As the court in *Foley* indicates, common law courts have qualified the at-will doctrine in three different ways:

(a) *A Contract Implied in Fact.* As in *Foley,* a court may find or "imply" an employer's promises in its employee's manual or handbook. Torosyan v. Boehringer Ingelheim Pharmaceuticals, 234 Conn. 1, 662 A.2d 89, 96 (1995); Williams v. Riedman, 339 S.C. 251, 529 S.E.2d 28 (App. 2000).

Contract Law Interlude. Promissory Estoppel. An employee did not receive the manual until after he began to work; he could not claim that he gave consideration for the manual's protections. Promissory estoppel to the rescue: he could claim that the manual was a promise and his continuing to work and to use the manual's grievance process was detrimental reliance. United States ex rel. Yesudian v. Howard University, 946 F.Supp. 31, 34–36 (D.D.C. 1996).

Unilateral Contract. An employer's late handbook or oral representation favorable to the employee might be the employer's offer of a unilateral contract that the employee accepts by conduct, continuing to work. An employee who continues to work after an unfavorable handbook amendment, however, may not have consented to it. Torosyan v. Boehringer Ingelheim Pharmaceuticals, 234 Conn. 1, 662 A.2d 89, 96–99 (1995).

(b) *Public Policy Exception.* Courts have established an ex-employee's cause of action after his employer discharges him for a reason that is contrary to public policy. The courts that have developed a tort for an employee who is discharged in violation of public policy have had trouble finding principles of confinement that integrate this tort with traditional contract doctrines. Rodriguez–Torres v. Caribbean Forms Manufacturer, Inc., 399 F.3d 52 (1st Cir. 2005).

An employer's discharge of an employee may violate public policy in one of three ways: (i) The employer may fire the employee because the employee did something that public policy encouraged him to do; for example, suppose an employee reported the employer's use of toxic substances to the authorities. (ii) The employer may sack the employee after the employee declined to do something public policy frowns upon, for example, the employee refused use toxic substances in the factory. Or (iii), the employer may discharge the employee for a reason that is contrary to public policy, examples are below.

Public or Private? The public-private distinction has been an issue for many other whistleblowers. The California court ruled that Foley blew his whistle too privately to qualify his termination as a violation of any *public* policy. An employee's internal complaint lacks the official quality of a citizen's right to turn to public officials. An employee's internal "whistleblowing" about dangers in the workplace were not a public policy violation in Torosyan v. Boehringer Ingelheim Pharmaceuticals, 234 Conn. 1, 662 A.2d 89 (1995). If, however, the court's public-policy goal is to expose wrongdoers' criminal misconduct and to deter and apprehend miscreants, how justifiable is the public-private distinction?

Source of Policy. Sometimes an employer's violation of public policy is distinct and abrupt. One employee was fired for filing a workers' compensation claim. Ramirez v. IBP, Inc., 950 F.Supp. 1074 (D.Kan.1996). Another employer violated a public policy against allowing a hazardous environment. Cloutier v. Great Atlantic & Pacific Tea Co., 121 N.H. 915, 436 A.2d 1140 (1981). A third employer fired an employee who was a witness in prior litigation. Reust v. Alaska Petroleum Contractors, 127 P.3d 807 (Alaska 2005).

The plaintiff may have to look a little harder for a public policy. Plaintiff's daughter sued defendant for dental malpractice; defendant discharged plaintiff, an at-will employee. The judge held that plaintiff's discharge violated the state constitutional right of access to court. Fortunato v. Office of Silston, 48 Conn.Supp. 636, 856 A.2d 530, 534 (2004).

Sometimes the source of public policy has been less distinct. Plaintiffs have sought public policy in constitutions, statutes, and the common law. The *Foley* court focuses on the penal statutes. Other courts look more broadly. Employees have argued that constitutional free speech provisions establish public policy favorable to expression which is binding on private employers. A Connecticut statute establishes a cause of action for an employee who is discharged because of constitutionally protected expression. Connecticut General Statute § 31–51g.

Should an employer's professional code of ethics establish public policy? Does a law firm's discharge of an associate who blew the whistle on a partner's overbilling or conflict of interest violate public policy?

Does an employer's consent decree or an administrative regulation establish a public policy?

A Statute? Legislatures establish public policy in statutes. Civil Rights statutes forbid employment discrimination based on an employee's forbidden characteristics like gender; but the legislation also sets a size threshold for defendants, establishes administrative procedures for plaintiffs, and defines remedies. The legislature's statutory statements of the public policy against discrimination are distinct. But do the legislature's threshold, process, and remedies limit a victim of discrimination to the statute and preclude a common-law public-policy cause of action?

One answer came from the Virginia court. An employer who employed too few people to be covered under either the state or the federal civil rights statute allegedly terminated a young mother "because she was no longer dependable since she had delivered a child; that [her] place was at home with her child; that babies get sick sometimes and [she] would have to miss work to care for her child; and that [the employer] needed someone more dependable." The Virginia court thought "this basis for termination is a classic example of gender discrimination which is repugnant to Virginia's strong public policy. Additionally, * * * while the [plaintiff's] cause of action for wrongful termination based on gender discrimination arose independently from the Virginia Human Rights Act, the public policy articulation in that Act satisfies our requirement * * * for identifying a statutory embodiment of the public policy of the Commonwealth." Bailey v. Scott–Gallaher, Inc., 253 Va. 121, 123, 127, 480 S.E.2d 502, 503–04 (1997). Similar is Weaver v. Harpster, 885 A.2d 1073 (Pa.Super. 2005).

Recovery. In addition to lost wages, a plaintiff may recover mental suffering damages and punitive damages for the public policy tort of retaliatory discharge. Reust v. Alaska Petroleum Contractors, 127 P.3d 807 (Alaska 2005); Ramirez v. IBP, Inc., 950 F.Supp. 1074 (D.Kan.1996). Southwest Forest Industries, Inc. v. Sutton, 868 F.2d 352 (10th Cir.1989), cert. denied, 494 U.S. 1017 (1990); Niblo v. Parr Manufacturing, 445 N.W.2d 351 (Iowa 1989).

(c) *An Implied Covenant.* Several courts have recognized an implied covenant of good faith and fair dealing in employment contracts. If a court does recognize an employee's cause of action for the employer's breach of an implied covenant of good faith and fair dealing, is the plaintiff's cause of action a tort or a breach of contract?

Contract. The California court, dealing with a commercial contract, confirmed *Foley* and confined the "bad faith" tort to insurance contracts; this decision left plaintiff's action for breach of the implied covenant of good faith and fair dealing in contract. Freeman & Mills, Inc. v. Belcher Oil Co., 11 Cal.4th 85, 44 Cal.Rptr.2d 420, 900 P.2d 669 (1995). The California court returned to the employment relationship in 2000, holding that a discharged at-will employee did not have an independent claim for his employer's breach of the covenant of good faith and fair dealing. Guz v. Bechtel National, Inc., 24 Cal.4th 317, 100 Cal.Rptr.2d 352, 8 P.3d 1089 (2000).

Other courts have limited an ex-employee's recovery for the employer's breach of the implied covenant of the covenant of good faith and fair dealing to contract damages. Thus, no punitive damages. The Servicemaster Co. v. Martin, 252 Ga.App. 751, 556 S.E.2d 517, 522–23 (2001); Williams v. Riedman, 339 S.C. 251, 529 S.E.2d 28 (App. 2000); McKinney v. National Dairy Council, 491 F.Supp. 1108, 1122 (D.Mass.1980); Maddaloni v. Western Massachusetts Bus Lines, Inc., 386 Mass. 877, 438 N.E.2d 351 (1982); Fortune v. National Cash Register Co., 373 Mass. 96, 364 N.E.2d 1251 (1977).

Tort. A few courts, however, have treated an employer's breach of the implied covenant of good faith and fair dealing as a tort and have allowed the employee to recover punitive damages. See Flanigan v. Prudential Federal Savings & Loan Association, 221 Mont. 419, 720 P.2d 257, cert. dismissed, 479 U.S. 980 (1986); K Mart Corp. v. Ponsock, 103 Nev. 39, 732 P.2d 1364 (1987). *Ponsock* was qualified in Ingersoll–Rand Co. v. McClendon, 498 U.S. 133 (1990), where the Supreme Court held the employer's breach, termination of an employee to avoid pension payments, was preempted by federal ERISA. But the *Ponsock* decision's remedies holding persists.

Separate Tort. An employer' separate tort, like defamation, may open the door for plaintiff to recover tort damages like emotional distress. Torosyan v. Boehringer Ingelheim Pharmaceuticals, 234 Conn. 1, 662 A.2d 89, 102–03, 106 (1995).

2. *Statutory Remedies.* A wrongfully discharged employee may also have statutory remedies.

(a) *Discrimination.* Federal and state civil rights statutes prohibiting employment discrimination based on disability, age, gender, race, religion, and sexual preference have been discussed.

(b) *Sections 1983 and 1981.* When a state official violates an employee-plaintiff's constitutional rights, a successful § 1983 claim may lead to an injunction, as well as to recovery of damages and attorney fees. Some courts hold that § 1981 applies to at-will employment. McLean v. Patten Communities, Inc., 332 F.3d 714 (4th Cir. 2003). If so, § 1981 may be better for a plaintiff than Title VII; for a § 1981 plaintiff may recover for race discrimination in employment without either EEOC procedures to exhaust before suing or caps on damages. Spriggs v. Diamond Auto Glass, 165 F.3d 1015 (4th Cir. 1999).

(c) *"Whistleblower."* A potential plaintiff should also examine state and federal codes for whistleblower protection. Statutes supplement the public policy tort to protect an employee from a retaliatory discharge.

The broad federal Sarbanes–Oxley Act forbids most public companies from discharging, demoting, suspending, threatening, harassing, or discriminating against an employee who participated in protected activity; the Act protects an employee who communicates information about corporate activity that the employee reasonably believes violates criminal fraud statutes, SEC rules and regulations, and federal law that protects shareholders from fraud; the Act protects an employee's activity including litigation or furnishing information to federal authorities or to members of Congress. 18 U.S.C. § 1514A.

The federal False Claims Act forbids the retaliatory discharge of an employee of a government contractor who reports the employer for defrauding the government.

31 U.S.C. § 3730(h). The Financial Institutions Reform, Recovery, and Enforcement Act protects an employee of a depository institution from retaliatory discharge for providing information to the authorities. 12 U.S.C. § 1831j. Civil rights statutes usually forbid an employer from retaliating. State whistleblowing statutes include Cal.Lab. Code § 1102.5, which is not limited to a particular type of employer.

Even if the statute does not explicitly forbid an employer's retaliation against a whistleblowing employee, a court may read an employer's retaliation to be forbidden discrimination. "Without protection from retaliation, individuals who witness discrimination would likely not report it," Justice O'Connor wrote for the Supreme Court in Jackson v. Birmingham Board of Education, 544 U.S. 167 (2005).

A teacher who had exposed the effects of polygamy was rewarded with an unrenewed contract. She combined a Utah whistleblower statute with federal § 1983 to recover compensatory damages and potentially punitive damages. Youren v. Tintic School District, 343 F.3d 1296 (10th Cir. 2003).

(d) *Remedies Under Statutes.* Plaintiff's statutory remedies may include back pay, front pay, mental suffering damages, and punitive damages. Double damages, reinstatement, and attorney fees are additional incentives for a plaintiff to pursue a statutory remedy.

3. *Employer's Fraud in an Employment Contract.* A former employee may sue his former employer for an intentional misrepresentation. An employer promises someone employment or promises what the terms of his employment will be. If the employer's promise is not performed, the employee may sue the employer for breach of contract. If an employer promises someone employment or represents the terms of employment without present intent to perform, the employee may sue the employer for the tort of fraud. The distinction between an employer's breach of contract and its fraud is, in short, between its promise, later broken, and its knowing misrepresentation of intention. The difference between an employer's breach of contract and its fraud approaches evanescence particularly when the employee pleading the facts uses alternative pleading adroitly to allege both. A plaintiff's higher damages for the employer's tort of fraud make fraud a tempting goal, but one that the defendant will attempt to block.

The breach-fraud distinction perplexed the California court in an employment opinion written after *Foley*, Lazar v. Superior Court of Los Angeles County, 12 Cal.4th 631, 49 Cal.Rptr.2d 377, 909 P.2d 981, 990 (1996).

Lazar alleged that defendant's fraud that induced him to move from the East Coast to California to enter an employment contract with the defendant. Emphasizing the *Foley* court's statement that the employment relationship is a "fundamentally contractual" one, the defendant argued that the court ought to limit an employment-termination plaintiff to breach-of-contract damages with the single exception of the public-policy tort. In short, the court should bar a former employee from suing a former employer for promissory fraud with its more extensive compensatory damages and possible punitive damages.

The court, declining to withdraw the tort of promissory fraud from employment termination litigation, reasoned:

"[T]his area of the law traditionally has involved both contract and tort principles and procedures. For example, it has long been the rule that where a contract is secured by fraudulent representations, the injured party may elect to affirm the contract and sue for the fraud. * * *"

"More fundamentally, it is a truism that contract remedies alone do not address the full range of policy objectives underlying the action for fraudulent inducement of contract. In pursuing a valid fraud action, a plaintiff advances the public interest in punishing intentional misrepresentations and in deterring such misrepresentations in the future. Because of the extra measure of blameworthiness inhering in fraud, and because in fraud cases we are not concerned about the need for 'predictability about the cost of contractual relationships' (*Foley*) fraud plaintiffs may recover 'out-of-pocket' damages in addition to benefit-of-the-bargain damages. [citations] For example, a fraudulently hired employee, as [plaintiff] has alleged himself to be, may incur a variety of damages 'separate from the termination' itself, such as the expense and disruption of moving or loss of security and income associated with former employment."

Plaintiff could pursue the fraud compensatory damages as well as "appropriate exemplary damages."

The court of appeal later clarified that an employment fraud plaintiff's recovery of "income associated with former employment" included plaintiff's lost future income from the employer he was induced to leave to join the defendant. To recover his lost future income, plaintiff must prove that it was neither speculative nor remote. Helmer v. Bingham Toyota Isuzu, 129 Cal.App.4th 1121, 29 Cal.Rptr.3d 136 (2005).

Courts have continued to search for appropriate boundaries between contract and tort and for principles to confine tort damages. An ex-employee may sue his former employer for an intentional misrepresentation that occurred either before his employment began or after it ended. A court will limit the plaintiff to a contract action for the employer's misconduct and deception that occurred during the employment period. The plaintiff may not sue a former employer in tort for fraud that occurred during the time he was employed. The Wisconsin court held, for example, that the state has no intentional misrepresentation tort when an employer uses deception to induce an at-will employee to continue. Mackenzie v. Miller Brewing Co., 241 Wis.2d 700, 623 N.W.2d 739 (2001). Agosta v. Astor, 120 Cal.App.4th 596, 15 Cal.Rptr.3d 565 (2004). Pollock v. University of Southern California, 112 Cal.App.4th 1416, 6 Cal.Rptr.3d 122, 130–31 (2003). Betterman v. Fleming Companies, Inc., 271 Wis.2d 193, 677 N.W.2d 673 (App. 2004).

4. *Detour to the Employee's Side of the Fraud Coin: A Resume Ruse.* A potential employee with a falsified resume may commit fraud. Usually the employer's remedy is a prompt discharge. Larger issues were litigated in Food Lion v. Capital Cities/ABC. Two reporters misrepresented their backgrounds in employment applications to Food Lion, a grocery chain; after Food Lion hired them, the reporters surreptitiously recorded their "employer's" unhygienic practices for a "highly critical" *PrimeTime Live* expose'. The reporters were defendants in Food Lion's lawsuit, but the deep pocket was their other employer, Capitol Cities/ABC. A Capitol Cities attorney had advised "that, so long as the undercover reporters performed their Food Lion jobs, there would be no fraud." Food Lion's fraud theory, coupled with trespass and breach of loyalty, led to a jury verdict for $1,402 compensatory damages, broken down as $2 compensatory damages for the reporters' trespass and breach of the duty of loyalty; $1400 compensatory damages for fraud; plus punitive damages of $5,545,750 for their fraud. Eventually, however, the court of appeals reversed all of Capitol Cities' fraud damages, but it affirmed the $2 verdict for the reporters' trespass and breach of their duty of loyalty. Food Lion, Inc. v. Capital Cities/ABC, Inc., 194 F.3d 505 (4th Cir. 1999).

5. *Contract-Tort–Statute.* Contract, tort, and statute have merged as an ex-employee's remedies for an improper employment termination. In this legal revolution, the plaintiff's remedy drives substance, and remedial issues abound. What statute of limitations governs? When does the plaintiff have a duty to seek comparable employment? Is a future remedy available to the prevailing plaintiff in an

uncertain world? Will the plaintiff's remedy be reinstatement or damages based on salary? Who decides, jury or judge? Are the plaintiff's special damages limited by the contract doctrine of Hadley v. Baxendale or by tort proximate cause principles? When may the plaintiff recover for emotional distress, mental suffering, and pain and suffering? When are punitive damages available? May the plaintiff's spouse recover for lost consortium?

6. *Remedies and Litigation Finance.* Possible tort and statutory recoveries shift a plaintiff's incentives to prefer them to a breach of contract claim. The incentive is not just plaintiff's. A typical ex-employee retains an attorney with a contingency fee contract where the attorney shares a percentage of the damages the plaintiff recovers. Plaintiff's recovery of tort damages for emotional distress and perhaps punitive damages will create a fund to compensate her attorney without reducing her recovery to below her pecuniary loss. A plaintiff's recovery of attorney fees usually accompanies her success in a statutory cause of action.

7. *Abuse of Contract as a Tort?* Should a court establish a common-law tort cause of action for any person's abuse of any contract right in violation of any public policy? Joseph Perillo, Abuse of Rights: A Pervasive Legal Concept, 27 Pacific L.J. 37 (1995). From this vantage point, the courts' appear to be taking the opposite tack, that is refurbishing the fence between tort and contract. For example, the Hawai'i court abandoned earlier decisions to hold that an employer's willful and wanton breach of an employment contract does not create a tort cause of action with emotional distress damages and punitive damages. Francis v. Lee Enterprises, 89 Hawai'i 234, 971 P.2d 707 (1999).

8. *Disclaimers.* One way for an employer to forestall litigation is to draft an employment contract "at will" which excludes any broader agreement. How have courts responded?

(a) One court granted summary judgment to an employer on the basis of the following contract language: "In consideration of my employment, I agree to conform to the rules and regulations of Sears, Roebuck and Co., and my employment and compensation can be terminated, with or without cause, and with or without notice, at any time, at the option of either the Company or myself. I understand that no store manager or representative of Sears, Roebuck and Co., other than the president or vice-president of the Company, has any authority to enter into any agreement for employment for any specified period of time, or to make any agreement contrary to the foregoing." Batchelor v. Sears, Roebuck & Co., 574 F.Supp. 1480, 1483 (E.D.Mich.1983). See also, Anderson v. Douglas & Lomason Co., 540 N.W.2d 277 (Iowa 1995).

(b) Another court was less open to Howard University's disclaimer: "Howard University points to two provisions in its employee handbook which it claims constitute, as a matter of law, an effective disclaimer of all contractual obligations."

"[Howard University] relies on the sentence on page ii of the handbook that '[t]his document is not to be construed as a contract,' and on the statement on page 14 of the handbook that: 'The University reserves the right unto itself to maintain exclusive discretion to exercise the customary functions of management including, but not limited to, the discretion to select, hire, promote, demote, suspend, terminate, assign the size of and composition of the work force, to establish, change and/or abolish policies, procedures, rules, and regulations; to create, abolish, and modify positions and descriptions and job classifications; and to assign duties of employees in accordance with the needs and requirements determined by the University.'"

"When viewed in a vacuum," observed the court, "these disclaimers would seem to be sufficient. However, viewing them in conjunction with other provisions of the handbook, the Court adheres to the conclusion * * * that it is unable to rule as a matter of law that the disclaimers effectively nullified all contractual obligations.

"Immediately preceding the statement that the handbook is not to be construed as a contract, appears the statement that the handbook is a 'policy statement intended to promote a better understanding of what staff employees can expect from the University and what the University can expect from them in return.' In addition, the provisions in the handbook relating to termination of employment are phrased in such a manner as to lead an employee to believe that the University does not have unfettered discretion in its termination decisions. Section 1.11 of the manual distinguishes between temporary and probationary employees on the one hand, and regular employees, such as the plaintiff here, on the other, stating: 'Temporary and Probationary employees may be terminated at any time their services are found to be unsatisfactory, or not in the best interests of the University. A Probationary employee may be terminated at any time during the probationary period upon the recommendation of the employee's supervisor. However, in the case of Regular employees, termination on grounds of unsatisfactory work performance is in order only when employees fail to make satisfactory improvement within thirty (30) calendar days after their supervisors have given them written notice of warning.... Charges against an employee of serious neglect of duty or conduct incompatible with the welfare of the University must be substantiated by the supervisor. Failure of the employee to refute successfully such charges constitutes grounds for dismissal.' Moreover, the handbook sets out a detailed grievance procedure and states that '[e]mployees of the University who are serving on Continuing Appointments [as plaintiff was] are entitled to provisions of the Grievance Procedures, under the conditions as indicated herein.' § 1.16(D) (emphasis added). Nowhere does the manual state that a 'Regular employee' may be terminated at will and for no reason at all."

"Given the contradictory language of the manual provisions, the Court finds that the issue of whether the employee manual constituted a contract was an issue for the jury." United States ex rel. Yesudiar v. Howard University, 946 F.Supp. 31, 34–35 (D.D.C. 1996).

Similarly, a South Carolina court held that an employer's handbook's disclaimer balanced against other promises created a jury question on whether the disclaimer was effective. Williams v. Riedman, 339 S.C. 251, 529 S.E.2d 28 (App. 2000).

Contrast the way the court treated the goods seller's limitation of remedies. Note 6, pp. 627–29.

9. *Arbitration.* An arbitration clause is another way to keep an employment dispute out of court. An arbitrator's decision may be prompt and inexpensive. Are there reasons to be wary? In arbitration, the parties waive complete civil discovery, jury trial, and perhaps the right to recover punitive damages and attorney fees. The arbitrator, whose decision is secret, may lack a sense of urgency to advance statutory social policy.

Contractual and statutory employment claims are arbitrable. A court will approve an agreement to arbitrate that the parties enter after the dispute arises. A pre-dispute arbitration agreement in an employee's application or contract is harder to swallow. Mandatory arbitration of an employment dispute, including an employee's claims under civil rights statutes, has been controversial. Recent decisions support arbitration for plaintiffs' statutory and employment discrimination claims.

The Supreme Court held that a plaintiff's claim under the federal age discrimination statute was subject to a mandatory arbitration clause in his original registration application. Gilmer v. Interstate/Johnson Lane Corp., 500 U.S. 20 (1991). And the Court upheld a mandatory arbitration clause that shunted an employee's state statutory cause of action to arbitration. Circuit City Stores v. Adams, 532 U.S. 105 (2001).

In a later decision, the court of appeals upheld an agreement requiring arbitration of an employee's federal Title VII claim. EEOC v. Luce, Forward, Hamilton & Scripps, 345 F.3d 742 (9th Cir. 2003). But the parties' agreement to arbitrate a statutory cause of action cannot bar plaintiff from recovering a remedy provided in the governing statute, for example, an employee's recovery of punitive damages for an employer's employment discrimination. Where the arbitration contract had a severance clause, the court recognized divided authority but held that the trial judge could sever the improper no-punitive-damages clause from an arbitration clause and forward the dispute to arbitration. Booker v. Robert Half International, Inc., 413 F.3d 77 (D.C.Cir. 2005).

5. EMPLOYEE'S RESTITUTION

Restitution plays an important role in employment litigation. A plaintiff uses the legal restitution common count of quantum meruit to recover for the "reasonable" value of her services. The Restitution Chapter has quantum meruit decisions, for example Campbell v. Tennessee Valley Authority, p. 406, and Maglica v. Maglica, p. 415. The student will find variations in terminology, including courts that refer to a plaintiff's quantum meruit action as "unjust enrichment" or "a contract implied in law," for example the court in Kossian American National Insurance Company, p. 393.

To begin with an exception, the Connecticut court refused to approve quantum meruit for an employee working under an express contract for work that fell within the scope of that contract. The employer and employee had agreed in principle to augment the employee's income with incentive compensation, but the idea had not been translated from concept to contract. Justice Ellen Peters in Meaney v. Connecticut Hospital Association, 250 Conn. 500, 735 A.2d 813, 823 (1999).

Plaintiff's quantum meruit claim will succeed when no contract exists or when the plaintiff's services are not covered by the contract; these concepts engender inevitable disputes in home-building and remodeling. In a more interesting example, Jesse "The Body" Ventura who had contracted for live television wrestling commentary with Titan Sports sued Titan for quantum meruit for Titan's distribution of videotapes. In addition to Titan benefitting from Ventura's services beyond the parties' contract, Titan's unlicenced use of Ventura's name-likeness violated his right to publicity. Thus the "unjustness" of Titan's benefit could flow from that tort or its breach of contract. Ventura v. Titan Sports, 65 F.3d 725, 730 (8th Cir. 1995).

The *Ventura* court distinguished the rule in *Meaney*, that a plaintiff cannot recover quantum meruit where an express contract covers the subject matter. Ventura's contact for live commentary did not extend to the videotape commentary, "the benefit for which recovery is sought." Arguing, however, that "Mr. Ventura wants additional compensation for having performed no additional work," Judge Morris Arnold dissented. Ventura v. Titan Sports, 65 F.3d 725, 737 (8th Cir. 1995). Political Note: Jesse Ventura provided copious free "color commentary" during his term as governor of Minnesota from 1999–2003.

A plaintiff cannot recover quantum meruit for services performed under an illegal contract, for example to collect on a "contract" to "rough up" a dilatory debtor. But someone who performs services under an agreement that, though covered by a statute of frauds, is not written may recover quantum meruit.

For example, if a successful realtor's agreement with a lessor or seller fails the writing test in the statute of frauds, nevertheless, the realtor may recover for quantum meruit. Coldwell Banker v. Blancke, 368 N.J.Super. 382, 846 A.2d 633 (App.Div. 2004).

Although our subject below, a lawyer's contract with a client or another lawyer, differs from other employment and services contracts, we can start with a similarity. Although a lawyer-client contract for a contingency fee must be written, a court will allow a lawyer with an oral agreement for a contingency fee to recover the "reasonable" value of services in quantum meruit. To anticipate the *Chambliss* case below, A court might cap the lawyer's quantum meruit recovery of "reasonable value" at the rate in the unenforceable oral contract. Starkey, Kelly, Blaney & White v. Nicolaysen, 172 N.J. 60, 796 A.2d 238, 244–45 (2002). The lawyer's quantum meruit won't undermine the rule requiring a writing because the lawyer's contract is invalidated and he may encounter professional discipline.

Plaintiff law firm referred Client to Defendant law firm for 25% of Defendant's ultimate fee. The law firms neglected to disclose this arrangement to the client and to secure the client's written consent, professional responsibility prerequisites for a valid contract. Defendant recovered $250,000 for Client and collected a fee, nearly $74,000; but Defendant refused to share 25% of the fee with Plaintiff on the ground that Client had not consented in writing. In Plaintiff's lawsuit, the California Supreme Court held that Plaintiff could recover $5,000 quantum meruit from Defendant for the value of Plaintiff's professional services. Quantum meruit, the court said, is not a a fee division subject to the rule of disclosure and Client consent. The divided fee would have been $18,497. Plaintiff's quantum meruit recovery from Defendant would not "undermine" the requirement of Client's consent because the agreed fee would have been larger than quantum meruit. Huskinson & Brown v. Wolf, 84 P.3d 379, 32 Cal.4th 453, 9 Cal.Rptr.3d 693 (2004). (2004).

Suppose the lawyer's quantum meruit recovery of the reasonable value of his professional services would exceed his "contractual" fee? Read on.

CHAMBLISS, BAHNER & CRAWFORD v. LUTHER

Court of Appeals, Tennessee, 1975.
531 S.W.2d 108.

GODDARD, JUDGE. This is a suit by a firm of attorneys for collection of a fee for a previous lawsuit. Plaintiff–Appellant Chambliss, Bahner, and Crawford is a Chattanooga law firm whose senior partner, Jac Chambliss, represented Defendants–Appellees in a lawsuit against the Detrex Corporation in a stock securities matter.

The case arose in the following manner: Mr. Chambliss had been engaged as an attorney by Lutex, Inc. since the formation of the corporation, and owned a few shares of its stock. In 1968 Detrex, a large chemical firm, became interested in acquiring Lutex and as a result of the ensuing negotiations, Detrex absorbed the smaller concern. The absorption was accomplished by an exchange of stock, the stockholders of Lutex receiving Detrex stock in exchange for their interest in Lutex.

In the latter part of 1969, the former principal shareholders of Lutex became concerned that the stock they had received was not as valuable as they had been led to believe. They contacted Attorney Chambliss, who took the case and managed to secure a compromise settlement offer of $860,000 from Detrex. The former stockholders of Lutex were not satisfied with this offer and decided to bring suit against Detrex for a violation of securities regulations.

On June 5, 1971, Attorney Chambliss was retained to bring that suit upon a contingency fee basis. It was agreed that his fee would be 15 percent of the recovery above the compromise offer.

The stockholders became dissatisfied with his representation. About one year after the suit was filed, the stockholders suggested to Attorney Chambliss that another local attorney, John I. Foster, Jr., be associated in the case. Mr. Foster's association was with the approval of Mr. Chambliss. They agreed among themselves that the division of the 15 percent contingency fee would be 70 percent to Chambliss and 30 percent to Foster. Thereafter, Attorney Foster was made lead counsel for the litigation by the stockholders. Chambliss did not approve of this move and withdrew as counsel by letter dated May 15, 1972.
* * *

On October 31, 1972, that suit was settled for the sum of $965,150, a betterment of $105,150 over the base offer. It was agreed that Attorney Chambliss did not take part in the negotiations which led to the final settlement, although as counsel of record he approved the order of settlement and, as a stockholder, raised no objection. He received for his stock some $46,000 on an investment of $2,000.

Under the contingency fee contract, Attorney Chambliss' 15 percent would have been $15,772.50. The Chancellor in the present action held that the contract of employment had been breached by the appointment of Attorney Foster as lead counsel, but that the damages to Attorney Chambliss should be limited to the contract price. Attorney Chambliss seeks recovery in quantum meruit, claiming that he and his brother have spent over 1,000 hours on this lawsuit over the period of two years and that he is entitled to reasonable compensation for these services apart from the contract. The testimony as to the reasonable value of his services ranged from $60,000 to $175,000.

Under Tennessee law—and it appears the rule is practically universal—a client is entitled to discharge his attorney with or without cause.

Plaintiff while recognizing this rule, insists that because Defendants breached the employment contract it is entitled to proceed on the basis of quantum meruit and its recovery is not limited by the amount of the original contract.
* * *

Plaintiff cites Re Montgomery, which unquestionably stands for the proposition he propounds. In that case an attorney for an estate, who had a contract fee for a fixed amount, was discharged without cause. The Court allowed the attorney to recover a sum in excess of his contract fee on the basis of quantum meruit. In so doing, the Court of Appeals of New York reasoned:

> 'In the case at bar the recovery allowed is upon the basis of quantum meruit without regard to the contract price, and the question for determination is whether the right of the attorney to recover is limited by the contract price of $5,000.'

'Thus far it has been decided that the discharge of the attorney canceled and annulled the contract and that the contract having been canceled, it could not limit the amount of the recovery although it might be considered in fixing the amount of the reasonable value of the services rendered; the theory being that the cancellation could not be a half way cancellation.'

'Under that theory, the contract price does not constitute a limitation on the amount of an attorney's recovery, although its effect may be to enhance the amount the client may be compelled to pay and in a certain sense penalizes the client for exercising a privilege given by law to discharge an attorney at will regardless of cause.' Re Montgomery, 272 N.Y. 323, 6 N.E.2d 40, 41 (1936). * * *

[A] California Supreme Court case, Fracasse v. Brent, 6 Cal.3d 784, 100 Cal.Rptr. 385, 494 P.2d 9 (1972), uses language which we think is instructive:

'We have concluded that a client should have both the power and the right at any time to discharge his attorney with or without cause. Such a discharge does not constitute a breach of contract for the reason that it is a basic term of the contract, implied by law into it by reason of the special relationship between the contracting parties, that the client may terminate that contract at will. It would be anomalous and unjust to hold the client liable in damages for exercising that basic implied right.' * * *

The only case we can find directly in point which is supportive of defendants' position, is Moore v. Fellner, 50 Cal.2d 330, 325 P.2d 857 (1958), wherein the California Supreme Court said:

'As declared in Salopek v. Schoemann (1942), 20 Cal.2d 150, 153[1], 155[3], 124 P.2d 21 "if an attorney is discharged for sufficient cause he is entitled to no more than the reasonable value of his missing services rendered prior to his discharge," has "no cause to complain and is fully protected by payment of the reasonable value," and may not recover the full contract amount (at least if such amount exceeds the reasonable value of the services). On the other hand in a case in which the discharge appears to have been without cause, it has been held that where the contract amount is less than the reasonable value of the services, recovery is nevertheless limited to the fee fixed by the contract. [citation] In the present case plaintiff sought and was awarded judgment based on reasonable value. Under the rules above stated his recovery must not, of course, exceed the fee fixed by the employment contract, less expenses to which the client (defendant) was put by the change of counsel.'

It seems to us that a necessary corollary to the rule that a client has the unqualified right to discharge an attorney, must be that the exercise of this legal right does not subject the client to additional penalties requiring him to pay an amount above the contract price.

Plaintiff's counsel persuasively argues that the rule should be as insisted by him, especially in contingent fee cases, for the reason that a highly skilled and competent attorney might be discharged by the client, who then entrusts the case to a less skillful one. The resulting loss of the suit would preclude the first attorney from receiving any fee. This argument is certainly appealing. However, in this case we are not called upon to make a decision in regard to these assumptions.

It would seem to us that the better rule is that because a client has the unqualified right to discharge his attorney, fees in such cases should be limited to the value of the services rendered or the contract price, whichever is less. * * *

[In this case we] simply hold that under the circumstances here shown, wherein there is no claim of fraud or overreaching as to the discharged attorney, and the settlement ultimately received is not assailed as inadequate or improper, recovery is limited to the contract price.

The decision of the Chancellor in this case preserved for Attorney Chambliss every penny to which he would have been entitled had he not been discharged. Because he is an officer of the court and a minister of justice, we do not believe he should insist upon more.

To adopt the rule advanced by Plaintiff would, in our view, encourage attorneys less keenly aware of their professional responsibilities than Attorney Chambliss, as shown in this record (unfortunately, events of the last year have shown there are such), to induce clients to lose confidence in them in cases where the reasonable value of their services has exceeded the original fee and thereby, upon being discharged, reap a greater benefit than that for which they had bargained. * * *

The assignment of error is overruled and the judgment of the Trial court affirmed. * * *

Notes

1. *Professional Responsibility.* The court's parenthetical statement in the last full paragraph almost certainly refers to the Watergate scandal. Should the court reduce an honest attorney-plaintiff's recovery because in the future another attorney, this one unscrupulous, *might* behave unethically? Can't the future court deal separately with the other lawyer's possible future misconduct?

2. *Measurement of Restitution.* Under the professional responsibility Restatement, "A lawyer who has been discharged or withdraws may recover the lesser of the fair value of the lawyer's services * * * and the ratable proportion of the compensation provided by any otherwise enforceable contract between the lawyer and client for the services performed." Restatement (Third) of The Law Governing Lawyers § 40(1)(2000).

Quantum meruit protects the client from paying the lawyer breach of contract damages which may include recovery for work the lawyer has not done. Should the court use the lawyer's usual hourly rate to measure quantum meruit? If the former contract sets fees, should the court use that rate either (a) as evidence of reasonable value, or (b) to measure reasonable value? The lawyer, Judge Posner wrote, may recover the fair value of services rendered; if the contract rate is reasonable, it governs. Maksym v. Loesch, 937 F.2d 1237, 1247 (7th Cir.1991).

3. Plaintiff in *Chambliss* argued against allowing "a highly skilled and competent attorney [to] be discharged by the client, who then entrusts the case to a less skillful one. The resulting loss of the suit would preclude the first attorney from receiving any fee." "This argument," the court replied, "is certainly appealing. However, in this case we are not called upon to make a decision in regard to these assumptions."

A scenario very much like the plaintiff's hypothetical unfolded in Arkansas. After entering a contingency fee contract with a client, the plaintiff-lawyers had investigated and researched the client's case and prepared a petition. The client discharged the lawyers and filed the substantially the same pleading pro se. The lawyers sued the client for quantum meruit before the court had resolved client's claim. The court dealt with whether the discharged lawyer's recovery of quantum meruit from the client "is dependent upon the contingency originally agreed to in the contract, *i.e.,* the successful prosecution of the client's case."

"There is a split amongst the states on this issue. Some states adhere to the 'California rule,' which provides that the discharged attorney's cause of action does not accrue unless and until the occurrence of the stated contingency. [citations] Under this rule, a discharged attorney is barred from receiving any fee if the client does not recover on the underlying matter. This is true even if the attorney was discharged without cause."

"Other states subscribe to the 'New York rule,' which provides that the discharged attorney's cause of action accrues immediately upon discharge and is not dependent upon the former client's recovery. In Re: Estate of Callahan, 144 Ill.2d 32, 161 Ill.Dec. 339, 578 N.E.2d 985 (1991); Tillman v. Komar, 259 N.Y. 133, 181 N.E. 75 (1932). The courts that subscribe to this rule do so primarily for two reasons. First, they reason that when the client terminates the contingent-fee contract by discharging the attorney, the contract ceases to exist and the contingency term, *i.e.,* whether the attorney wins the client's case, is no longer operative. As the New York Court of Appeals explained: 'Either [the contract] wholly stands or totally falls.' *Tillman.* Because the contract is terminated, the client can no longer use the contract's term to prevent the discharged attorney from recovering a fee in quantum meruit. 'A client cannot terminate the agreement and then resurrect the contingency term when the discharged attorney files a fee claim.' *Estate of Callahan.*"

"The second primary reason that courts subscribe to the 'New York rule' is that they believe that forcing the discharged attorney to wait on the occurrence of the contingency is unfair in that it goes beyond what the parties contemplated in the contract. The New York Court of Appeals said it best: 'The value of one attorney's services is not measured by the result attained by another. This one did not contract for his contingent compensation on the hypothesis of success or failure by some other member of the bar. * * * In making their agreement, the parties may be deemed to have estimated this lawyer's pecuniary merit according to his own character, temperament, energy, zeal, education, knowledge and experience which are the important factors contributing to his professional status and constituting in a large degree, when viewed in relation to the volume of work performed and the result accomplished, a fair standard for gauging the value of services as prudent counsel and skillful advocate.' *Tillman.*"

"An additional reason for holding that a discharged attorney does not have to wait on the occurrence of the contingency is that the attorney is not claiming under the contingent-fee contract. The Illinois Supreme Court explained: '[Q]uantum meruit is based on the implied promise of a recipient of services to pay for those services which are of value to him. The recipient would be unjustly enriched if he were able to retain the services without paying for them. The claimants's recovery here should not be linked to a contract contingency when his recovery is not based upon the contract, but upon quantum meruit.' Estate of Callahan."

"We believe that the 'New York rule' is the better rule." Salmon v. Atkinson, 355 Ark. 325, 137 S.W.3d 383, 385–86 (2004).

Questions. Would it have been fair to measure the lawyers' quantum meruit recovery by the client's pro se representation? The concurring opinion in *Salmon* wondered whether a contingent-fee client could discharge her lawyer, decide not to sue at all, and still avoid paying her lawyer quantum meruit. Salmon v. Atkinson,

355 Ark. 325, 137 S.W.3d 383, 387 (2004). Has the *Salmon* court lost the ability to cap a lawyer's quantum meruit recovery at the contract rate?

If the *Salmon* court reasoned correctly that the contract and its contingency ceased to exist, may the client, for example in *Chambliss,* terminate a contract to exit it and then resurrect it to cap the lawyer's quantum meruit recovery? Should a court cap a plaintiff's quantum meruit at the rate in the contract that the defendant breached?

UNITED STATES v. ALGERNON BLAIR, INC.

United States Court of Appeals, Fourth Circuit, 1973.
479 F.2d 638.

CRAVEN, CIRCUIT JUDGE. May a subcontractor, who justifiably ceases work under a contract because of the prime contractor's breach, recover in quantum meruit the value of labor and equipment already furnished pursuant to the contract irrespective of whether he would have been entitled to recover in a suit on the contract? We think so * * *.

The subcontractor, Coastal Steel Erectors, Inc., brought this action under the provisions of the Miller Act, in the name of the United States against Algernon Blair, Inc. * * * Blair had entered a contract with the United States for the construction of a naval hospital in Charleston County, South Carolina. Blair had then contracted with Coastal to perform certain steel erection and supply certain equipment in conjunction with Blair's contract with the United States. Coastal commenced performance of its obligations, supplying its own cranes for handling and placing steel. Blair refused to pay for crane rental, maintaining that it was not obligated to do so under the subcontract. Because of Blair's failure to make payments for crane rental, and after completion of approximately 28 percent of the subcontract, Coastal terminated its performance. Blair then proceeded to complete the job with a new subcontractor. Coastal brought this action to recover for labor and equipment furnished.

The district court found that the subcontract required Blair to pay for crane use and that Blair's refusal to do so was such a material breach as to justify Coastal's terminating performance. This finding is not questioned on appeal. The court then found that under the contract the amount due Coastal, less what had already been paid, totaled approximately $37,000. Additionally, the court found Coastal would have lost more than $37,000 if it had completed performance. Holding that any amount due Coastal must be reduced by any loss it would have incurred by complete performance of the contract, the court denied recovery to Coastal. While the district court correctly stated the " 'normal' rule of contract damages,"[1] we think Coastal is entitled to recover in quantum meruit.

In United States for Use of Susi Contracting Co. v. Zara Contracting Co., 146 F.2d 606 (2d Cir. 1944), a Miller Act action, the court was faced with a situation similar to that involved here—the prime contractor had unjustifiably breached a subcontract after partial performance by the subcontractor. The court stated:

---

1. [Footnotes renumbered.] Fuller & Perdue, The Reliance Interest in Contract Damages, 46 Yale L.J. 52 (1936).

For it is an accepted principle of contract law, often applied in the case of construction contracts, that the promisee upon breach has the option to forego any suit on the contract and claim only the reasonable value of his performance. * * *

Further, that the complaint is not clear in regard to the theory of a plaintiff's recovery does not preclude recovery under quantum meruit. [citation] A plaintiff may join a claim for quantum meruit with a claim for damages from breach of contract.

In the present case, Coastal has, at its own expense, provided Blair with labor and the use of equipment. Blair, who breached the subcontract, has retained these benefits without having fully paid for them. On these facts, Coastal is entitled to restitution in quantum meruit.

> "The 'restitution interest,' involving a combination of unjust impoverishment with unjust gain, presents the strongest case for relief. If, following Aristotle, we regard the purpose of justice as the maintenance of an equilibrium of goods among members of society, the restitution interest presents twice as strong a claim to judicial intervention as the reliance interest, since if A not only causes B to lose one unit but appropriates that unit to himself, the resulting discrepancy between A and B is not one unit but two." Fuller & Perdue, The Reliance Interest in Contract Damages, 46 Yale L.J. 52, 56 (1936).

The impact of quantum meruit is to allow a promisee to recover the value of services he gave to the defendant irrespective of whether he would have lost money on the contract and been unable to recover in a suit on the contract. [citation] The measure of recovery for quantum meruit is the reasonable value of the performance; and recovery is undiminished by any loss which would have been incurred by complete performance. [citation] While the contract price may be evidence of reasonable value of the services, it does not measure the value of the performance or limit recovery.[2] Rather, the standard for measuring the reasonable value of the services rendered is the amount for which such services could have been purchased from one in the plaintiff's position at the time and place the services were rendered.

Since the district court has not yet accurately determined the reasonable value of the labor and equipment use furnished by Coastal to Blair, the case must be remanded for those findings. * * *

Reversed and remanded with instructions.

Notes

1. *A Good Rule for Goods?* In *Algernon Blair,* the court held that a contractor may recover more than the total contract price from a defaulting defendant. Would it be proper to extend the holding to a seller of goods like Wellston Coal, p. 763? If the value of coal Wellston Coal delivered in part performance exceeded the total contract price for full delivery, should the defaulting customer pay more restitution than it would have had to pay under the contract if all the coal had been delivered?

2. [citations] "It should be noted, however, that in suits for restitution there are many cases permitting the plaintiff to recover the value of benefits conferred on the defendant even though this value exceeds that of the return performance promised by the defendant. In these cases it is no doubt felt that the defendant's breach should work a forfeiture of his right to retain the benefits of an advantageous bargain."
Fuller & Perdue.

2. *A Bad Rule for Everybody*? Another line of decisions caps a plaintiff's restitution at the contract price. The Restatement Third has accepted this approach which it calls "restitutionary damages." A plaintiff's alternative measure of recovery for the defendant's total breach may be "the value to the defendant of the plaintiff's uncompensated contractual performance, not exceeding the price of such performance as determined by reference to the parties' agreement." Restatement (Third) of Restitution and Unjust Enrichment § 38 (Tent. Draft No. 3, 2004).

3. *Mark's Remark. Algernon Blair*, Mark Gergen observed, "is the worst possible teaching case unless the [casebook editor's] goal is to make the law seem idiotic." Mark P. Gergen, Restitution as a Bridge Over Troubled Contract Waters, 71 Fordham L.Rev. 709, 711–18, 730–31 (2002).

Well, have I succeeded? And between *Algernon Blair* and the Restatement, which do you think is the better rule on whether a plaintiff's quantum meruit restitution can exceed the rate in the contract the defendant breached?

4. *Employee's Restitution Plus.* Under what circumstances may the plaintiff rescind an employment or service contract and recover restitution plus damages? And what kind of damages may the plaintiff recover? As the following decision reveals, the answers to these apparently simple questions turn out to be complex.

RUNYAN v. PACIFIC AIR INDUSTRIES, INC.

Supreme Court of California, 1970.
2 Cal.3d 304, 85 Cal.Rptr. 138, 466 P.2d 682.

SULLIVAN, JUSTICE. * * * Defendant Pacific Air Industries, Inc. (Pacific) is a corporation engaged in the business of aerial surveying and photogrammetric services with headquarters in Long Beach. In 1965 plaintiff was, and for several years prior thereto had been, a geologist and engineer employed by Tidewater Oil Company (Tidewater). In October of that year he responded to an advertisement placed by Pacific in the Wall Street Journal announcing the availability of Pacific franchise territories in various areas of California. A number of conferences with Pacific followed. Eventually on March 9, 1966, plaintiff and Pacific entered into a written area service contract whereby, in consideration of the payment by plaintiff of $25,000, he was awarded an exclusive photogrammetric franchise for the Counties of Inyo, Kern, Kings and Tulare. In the meantime, on February 18, 1966, he had resigned his position with Tidewater Oil Company. * * *

Pacific's performance in supplying and maintaining the local office did not comply with its obligations under the contract. * * *

Despite Pacific's failure to fully perform its promises plaintiff initially made no complaint. In late summer, however, he became concerned that his franchise was being treated by Pacific merely as a commission arrangement. He complained that Pacific was making charges for "first order instrument" work at arbitrary rates. Finally, on October 7, 1966, plaintiff gave Pacific written notice of rescission of the contract of March 9, 1966, based upon failure of consideration and fraud.

Shortly thereafter plaintiff brought the instant action for restitution and consequential damages. His complaint set forth four counts: the first based on rescission for failure of consideration; the second and third based on rescission for fraud; and the fourth a common count for money lent apparently grounded on a theory of rescission. Plaintiff sought recovery not only of the consideration paid by him but also of consequential damages consisting of office expenses, training expenses and loss of salary for the period during which he had attempted to operate under the franchise.

The trial court found in favor of plaintiff on the first count but against plaintiff on the remaining three counts. The court concluded that plaintiff had rescinded the area service contract on October 7, 1966, and was entitled to recover the $25,000 franchise fee and his "net consequential damages" in the sum of $5,273.25.[1] Judgment was entered accordingly. This appeal followed.
* * *

We now take up Pacific's principal contention that the court erred in awarding consequential damages. Actually Pacific does not challenge the entire award of consequential damages. It raises no issue as to the item of $1,082 for training and office expense. It objects only to the item of "loss of income" in the sum of $7,256.25 upon the ground that there is no evidence that it had guaranteed to plaintiff a profit from the franchise equal to or greater than his former salary with Tidewater. In essence Pacific argues that plaintiff "assumed the risk" of loss which is inherent in an entrepreneurial activity. We are thus called upon to inquire into plaintiff's entitlement not only to the restitution of the $25,000 franchise fee but also to consequential damages because of the loss of his salary income.

The positions of the parties may be briefly summarized thusly: Pacific argues that damages cannot be recovered in the event of rescission since the two remedies are mutually inconsistent, a claim for damages being based upon an affirmance of the contract while rescission is predicated upon its disaffirmance. Plaintiff in response maintains that although prior to 1961 an award of damages in cases of rescission "might have been subject to serious question," nevertheless Civil Code section 1692 enacted in that year not only authorized but probably requires an award of consequential damages where relief is sought based upon a rescission.

Section 1692 which provides for relief based upon rescission was added to the Civil Code in 1961 upon the recommendation of the California Law Revision Commission. * * * We set forth section 1692 in full in the footnote.[2]

At the start it would appear that the statute compels the rejection of Pacific's argument that damages cannot be recovered in an action for relief

---

1. The findings clearly indicate that the court's award of consequential damages in the net sum of $5,273.25 was arrived at as follows:

Loss of income from 3/9/66 to 9/30/66	$7,256.25
Training expense	550.00
Office expense	532.00
	$8,338.25
Less plaintiff's gross income from activities relating to franchise	3,065.00
	$5,273.25

2. Section 1692 provides: "When a contract has been rescinded in whole or in part, any party to the contract may seek relief based upon such rescission by (a) bringing an action to recover any money or thing owing to him by any other party to the contract as a consequence of such rescission or for any other relief to which he may be entitled under the circumstances or (b) asserting such rescission by way of defense, counterclaim or cross-complaint.

"If in an action or proceeding a party seeks relief based upon rescission and the court determines that the contract has not been rescinded, the court may grant any party to the action any other relief to which he may be entitled under the circumstances.

"A claim for damages is not inconsistent with a claim for relief based upon rescission. The aggrieved party shall be awarded complete relief, including restitution of benefits, if any, conferred by him as a result of the transaction and any consequential damages to which he is entitled; but such relief shall not include duplicate or inconsistent items of recovery.

"If in an action or proceeding a party seeks relief based upon rescission, the court may require the party to whom such relief is granted to make any compensation to the other which justice may require and may otherwise in its judgment adjust the equities between the parties."

based on a rescission since the section expressly and unequivocally states that a "claim for damages is not inconsistent with a claim for relief based upon rescission" and that the aggrieved party "shall be awarded complete relief, including restitution of benefits, if any, * * * and any consequential damages to which he is entitled; * * * but * * * not * * * duplicate or inconsistent items of recovery." Our more proper inquiry then is whether the relief awarded in the instant case is that intended by the Legislature. Since the enactment of section 1692 was not an isolated event we must examine the section in the light of the historical background of rescission procedures and the purpose of the statutory changes enacted in 1961.

In California prior to 1961 there were two methods provided for in the Civil Code by which a party entitled to rescind could obtain rescissionary relief. The first, found in sections 1688–1691, specified certain instances in which a party to a contract might rescind it and provided that such rescission could be accomplished by the rescinding party by giving notice of the rescission and offering to restore everything of value which he had received. This method contemplated a rescission "by the individual act of one of the parties to the contract" and has been referred to as a unilateral rescission. McCall v. Superior Court (1934) 1 Cal.2d 527, 536, 36 P.2d 642, 646.) Having rescinded the contract by his own act, the rescinding party then brought an action to enforce the out-of-court rescission. (Philpott v. Superior Court (1934) 1 Cal.2d 512, 524, 36 P.2d 635.) Such action was considered to be one at law brought on the implied promise on the part of the nonrescinding party to repay or return the consideration received. "In reality, it is an action in which the law, in order to prevent the unjust enrichment of defendants from the property of plaintiff, itself implies a promise to repay the sum demanded. In other words, it is an action in *assumpsit* upon a promise implied by law."

The second method by which a party could obtain rescissionary relief was the action for a judicial rescission. * * * Unlike the method of unilateral rescission, however, this method was viewed as an action for specific judicial relief for the wrong giving rise to the right of rescission, and was deemed equitable in nature. * * * Significant substantive and procedural differences existed between these two methods for obtaining rescissionary relief. The right to a jury trial, the applicable statute of limitations, the availability of the provisional remedy of attachment and the possibility of joinder of other claims all depended upon which of these two methods the plaintiff elected to use in seeking rescissionary relief. The result was a body of law which was "unnecessarily complex and confusing to both courts and attorneys, to say nothing of laymen." 3 Cal.Law Revision Com.Rep. (1961).

As previously mentioned the Legislature made several changes in these procedures in 1961. Prominent among these was the addition of section 1692 and the repeal of sections 3406–3408. "This legislation, in effect, abolished the action to obtain court rescission and left only an action to obtain relief based upon a party effected rescission." (Paularena v. Superior Court (1965) 231 Cal.App.2d 906, 913, 42 Cal.Rptr. 366, 370.) * * *

We perceive in this fusing of the two former rescission procedures no intention on the part of the Legislature to disturb, much less eradicate, substantive differences theretofore underlying such procedures. Indeed the Law Revision Report which was the genesis of these statutory changes included among its specific recommendations the following: "The rescission statutes should make plain that, after rescinding a contract, a party may seek any form of relief warranted under the circumstances, whether legal or equitable. As all such actions will be to *enforce* a rescission, the right of the parties to a jury and the court in which the action must be brought will be determined by the nature of the substantive relief requested and not by the form of the complaint. For example, if a bare money judgment is sought, a justice court will have jurisdiction in appropriate cases, and the plaintiff may not convert the action into an equity action and thus deprive the justice court of jurisdiction merely by a prayer for rescission. The statute should also make plain that the court may grant any other relief that is appropriate under the circumstances if it develops at the trial that the plaintiff has mistaken his remedy and the purported rescission was not effective." * * *

Under the new statutory scheme, when a contract has been rescinded in accordance with the statutory procedure (§ 1691)[3] "any party to the contract may seek relief based upon such rescission * * *." This is accomplished by bringing an action "to recover any money or thing owing to him" and "for any other relief" to which he may be entitled. Whatever may have been the rule under former decisional law dealing with "legal" rescission, the statute now expressly provides that a "claim for damages is not inconsistent with a claim for relief based upon rescission" and that the aggrieved party "shall be awarded complete relief" including restitution and consequential damages, if any. (All quotations are from section 1692.)

Under pre–1961 law, however, an action at law to enforce an out-of-court rescission was, by its very nature, invariably restricted to the recovery of the consideration given by the rescinding party. As we have explained, it was an action in *assumpsit* upon a promise implied by law. The scope of relief was therefore limited by the promise raised by implication of law on which the action was based—namely to return the consideration;[4] there was no implied "promise" to pay damages. The decisions were replete with statements that the remedies of rescission and damages were inconsistent. * * *

However, under pre–1961 law in actions in equity to obtain a judicial rescission, monetary awards including those of consequential damages, given in conjunction with restitution, have been sustained in a variety of contexts. Thus, it was settled that a vendee of real property who rescinded a land sale contract

---

3. Section 1691 provides: "Subject to Section 1693, to effect a rescission a party to the contract must, promptly upon discovering the facts which entitle him to rescind if he is free from duress, menace, undue influence or disability and is aware of his right to rescind:

(a) Give notice of rescission to the party as to whom he rescinds; and

(b) Restore to the other party everything of value which he has received from him under the contract or offer to restore the same upon condition that the other party do likewise, unless the latter is unable or positively refuses to do so.

"When notice of rescission has not otherwise been given or an offer to restore the benefits received under the contract has not otherwise been made, the service of a pleading in an action or proceeding that seeks relief based on rescission shall be deemed to be such notice or offer or both."

4. Speaking of the action to enforce a unilateral rescission, the court in *Philpott* said: "[I]t is a case where the plaintiff has not elected to sue for damages, general or special or both, which he may have suffered from the tort inflicted upon him by defendants; likewise it is not a case where the plaintiff is seeking the application of equitable remedies to redress his grievances. All these elements, which may have been shown by appropriate allegations for such relief, are conspicuously absent. Plaintiff apparently *is content to merely seek a return from defendants of money given them,* with interest, *forgetting and foregoing all other elements of injury.* Is it not plain, therefore, that he has waived the tort of defendants and has come into court relying solely upon the promise created by law to return to him the consideration paid upon the contract?" (Italics added.) Philpott v. Superior Court.

because of the vendor's fraud could recover the purchase money paid by him and the reasonable value of improvements less the reasonable rental value of the land while in the vendee's possession. * * * An award for the value of improvements was also available in some cases where the vendee rescinded because of failure of consideration. * * * Similarly, the rescinding vendee was entitled to monetary compensation for any payments by him to reduce the amount of a mortgage imposed upon the property by the vendor. Where the vendor rescinded, the vendee was liable for the rental value of the land while he had possession. When a contract for the sale of personal property was rescinded, a rescinding vendor was also entitled to an award for the reasonable value of the use of the property by the vendee, or for its cost of replacement where the specific property could not be returned. * * *

Some of these cases refer to such monetary awards given in an action for rescission as "damages" or "consequential damages." * * * For example, we said in Hines v. Brode (1914) 168 Cal. 507, 511–512, 143 P. 729, 731, that "[T]he vendee may rescind, and, in addition to the recovery of the consideration with which he has parted, obtain recoupment for *any other special damage* to which he has been subjected by the vendor's fraud." (Italics added.) * * *[5]

The fundamental principle underlying these decisions and the awards which they upheld is that "in such actions the court should do complete equity between the parties" and to that end "may grant any monetary relief necessary" to do so. (Stewart v. Crowley, supra, 213 Cal. 694, 701, 3 P.2d 562, 565.) * * *

As the cases already cited by us illustrate, California courts applying general principles of equity have recognized that the restoration to the rescinding party of the consideration with which he originally parted does not necessarily in all instances restore him to his former position and bring about substantial justice. The rescinding vendee of land who in reliance upon the contract has placed improvements on the property must invariably be compensated for them if he is to be afforded "complete relief." In instances such an adjustment may be compelled so as to forestall unjust enrichment of the nonrescinding party through whose fault the grounds of rescission have arisen.

This prompts us to point out that restitutionary damages have not been awarded the rescinding party in every case of rescission. Such damages may be awarded in conjunction with restitution where rescission has been sought for the nonrescinding party's fraud * * * misrepresentations, * * * and, in some cases, failure of consideration * * *. We have not found nor has our attention been directed to any reported California decisions in which the courts have awarded consequential damages when rescission has been sought merely upon the grounds of illegality or mistake * * *. It appears, therefore, that California

---

5. In Lobdell v. Miller, 114 Cal.App.2d 328, 250 P.2d 357 which involved rescission for fraud, the court observed: "The remedy of rescission necessarily involves a repudiation of the contract. The remedy afforded by an action for the recovery of damages suffered by reason of fraud, * * * involves an affirmance of the contract. The measure of damages recoverable in an action for rescission is essentially different from that in a simple action for damages * * *. In the rescission action a plaintiff is entitled to recover the consideration he gave on restoration or offer of restoration of that which he received. He is also entitled to recover compensation for whatever consequential damages he may have suffered by reason of having entered into the contract."

Thus the damages available under each remedy are different. The award given in an action for damages compensates the party not in default for the loss of his "expectational interest"—the benefit of his bargain which full performance would have brought. (Fuller and Perdue, The Reliance Interest in Contract Damages: 1(1936) 46 Yale L.J. 52, 54.) Relief given in rescission cases—restitution and in some cases consequential damages—puts the rescinding party in the *status quo ante,* returning him to his economic position before he entered the contract.

decisions, in determining when restitutionary damages should be awarded, have differentiated between actions for rescission based upon a ground involving some fault on the part of the nonrescinding party, and actions based upon a ground not involving such fault. Only in the former category have courts of equity required the nonrescinding party to pay to the other restitutionary damages, for the obvious reason that otherwise he would be unjustly enriched. * * *

These traditional and deep-rooted principles of courts of equity can now be invoked through the simple procedure furnished by section 1692. * * *

Mindful of these principles and of the purpose of the statutory changes enacted in 1961, we turn to the case before us. Essentially the question we confront is whether the trial court, presumably responsive to the mandate that the aggrieved party be awarded complete relief, acted reasonably and equitably in making an award of consequential damages for plaintiff's "loss of income."

The trial court gave plaintiff relief on the first count[6] of his complaint which sought rescissionary relief based upon failure of consideration. * * * The trial court found that plaintiff had in good faith substantially performed his part of the contract, that there had been a material failure of consideration because of specified acts of Pacific, that plaintiff gave Pacific notice of rescission based on such failure of consideration, that *"In reliance* upon said contract plaintiff necessarily incurred" (italics added) certain expenses including the "loss of income" here in question, and that while the franchise was in effect plaintiff had certain gross income from his franchise activities.

As we have pointed out, the trial court awarded plaintiff the sum of $7,256.25 to compensate him for his loss of income for the period from the execution of the area service contract to the giving of the notice of rescission, this loss being measured by the salary he would have received had he remained at Tidewater. We cannot find this award unreasonable or inequitable particularly since, as the court expressly found, plaintiff relied upon the contract in severing his relationship with Tidewater. * * *

The judgment is affirmed.

Notes

1. *Does the Reason for Plaintiff's Rescission Affect the Recovery of Damages?* The *Runyan* court establishes that a rescinding plaintiff *may* recover special, consequential, or incidental damages, as distinguished from "restitutionary" damages. A word of caution: a court may grant rescission for reasons that range from defendant's tortious conduct or breach to plaintiff's innocent mistake.

2. *Restitution Plus Special Damages.* Suppose that the parties order their affairs assuming a contract was formed; then the court finds that no contract exists. While restitution normally follows rescission, the court may limit the rescinding plaintiff's damages; in a transaction rescinded because of mistake, for example, the court cannot charge the defendant with any damages, special or otherwise.

(a) *Reliance Recovery.* The sale of a mink ranch collapsed because the agreement failed to specify the parties' obligations. The seller, in reliance on the supposed contract, had purchased a home in a nearby town and moved off the ranch. In

---

6. It will be recalled that the court found that the allegations of the remaining three counts were not true.

unscrambling this aborted sale, is the seller entitled to recover house-purchase expenses as reliance or consequential damages? The court held that since no contract had been formed, the seller's only remedy was restitution which required proof that the buyer had received a benefit. Dursteler v. Dursteler, 108 Idaho 230, 697 P.2d 1244 (App.1985), aff'd, 112 Idaho 594, 733 P.2d 815 (App.1987).

(b) The sellers of a dairy canceled the sale because of the buyer's nonpayment. The court held that because the contract was canceled, the buyer was limited to quasi-contractual recovery for unjust enrichment. Hollywood Dairy, Inc. v. Timmer, 411 N.W.2d 258 (Minn.App. 1987)

(c) After a land buyer rescinded because of a cloud on the seller's title, the trial judge ordered cancellation of the buyer's notes, but denied monetary relief. The appellate court dealt with (i) expectancy damages, (ii) restitution, and (iii) reliance recovery. (i) The buyer's recovery of expectancy damages, the profit from full performance, is inconsistent with rescission which sets the parties back to the starting place as if the contract had never existed. (ii) Restitution follows rescission; but the buyer had not proved the seller had received any benefits to restore. (iii) The buyer's reliance expense, the court said, is the nonbreaching party's outlay in anticipation of the other party's performance, "reasonably related to the purposes of the contract which would not have incurred but for the contract's existence." Plaintiff's recovery of reliance expense is consistent with rescission; the plaintiff could prove reliance expense and recover it on remand. Brown v. Yacht Club of Coeur d'Alene, Ltd., 111 Idaho 195, 722 P.2d 1062 (App.1986).

3. *Measurement.* Even when a plaintiff's damages accompany restitution, the reason the court grants rescission may affect the way the court measures them. Runyan originally sued the defendant for fraud; if the court had granted him rescission for fraud, Runyan, under tort damages measures, could have recovered "proximately caused" special-consequential damages. But eventually the court granted Runyan rescission for the defendant's breach of contract, failure of consideration variety. Runyan may recover special damages, reliance variety. But under contract damages doctrine, defendant may invoke Hadley v. Baxendale. Has Runyan established that the special damages were within the parties' contemplation when the contract was made?

4. *Punitive Damages.* When defendants committed fraud in the transactions, several courts have allowed the rescinding plaintiffs to recover punitive damages in addition to granting them restitution. See Thomas Auto Co. v. Craft, 297 Ark. 492, 763 S.W.2d 651 (1989); Michaels v. Morris, 220 Cal.Rptr. 22 (1985); Indiana & Michigan Electric Co. v. Harlan, 504 N.E.2d 301 (Ind.App.1987).

In Roberts v. Estate of Barbagallo, 366 Pa.Super. 559, 531 A.2d 1125 (1987), the court said, however, that since the rescinding party cannot recover compensatory damages, there can be no punitive damages either. Where rescission was based on breach of contract, the court disallowed punitive damages in McKinney v. Gannett Co., 660 F.Supp. 984 (D.N.M.1981), appeal dismissed, 694 F.2d 1240 (10th Cir.1982). [See Note 6, p. 131].

5. *Rescission Reform.* According to the Recommendations and Study of the California Law Revision Commission, 1960, the California "unitary" system eliminates the former suit in equity to rescind. Retained are the legal prerequisites of notice of intent to rescind and offer to restore (although these may be excused), leaving plaintiff a quasi-contractual action for restoration designated as "action based on rescission."

Although the Law Revision report recommended abandonment of the legal common counts for pleading in this restitution action, a court nevertheless accepted these pleadings. Klein v. Benaron, 247 Cal.App.2d 607, 56 Cal.Rptr. 5 (1967).

The reporter also recommended jury trials in all rescission cases and a single statute of limitation, subject to the underlying requirement of plaintiff's "promptness" in effecting a rescission. A court, however, rejected a jury trial where no money claim was involved: "The [plaintiff] has confused the right to bring an action at law to recover the consideration paid or damages and the equitable action to cancel a deed." Porter v. Superior Court, 73 Cal.App.3d 793, 798–99, 141 Cal.Rptr. 59, 62 (1977).

6.   May an employee or service-provider breach his contract and nevertheless recover restitution from his employer? Read on.

LYNN v. SEBY

Supreme Court of North Dakota, 1915.
29 N.D. 420, 151 N.W. 31.

Goss, J. Plaintiff has recovered judgment against defendant for a small amount as a balance of a threshing bill. Judgment was granted upon the pleadings. In brief, plaintiff agreed to thresh all of defendant's grain. He threshed the wheat and oats, but refused to thresh the flax. Defendant was unable to procure threshing of his flax that fall, and defends and counterclaims for the amount of the resulting damage from the flax remaining unthreshed through the winter. The contract for threshing was the usual one, with no special provision whereby plaintiff agreed to be responsible in damages for more than ordinary liability. Therefore the counterclaim did not plead a cause of action for damages, under the holding in Hayes v. Cooley, 13 N.D. 204, 100 N.W. 250, for the reason that the loss of grain through resulting exposure to the elements is a remote and not a proximate consequence of the breach of contract and will not sustain a recovery, the measure of which is defined by section 7146, C.L.1913, merely declaratory of the common law. It cannot be said that such damages are those "which in the ordinary course of events would be likely to result" from the breach of the contract by plaintiff. Defendant concedes this to be the declared law of this state, but avers that the same should be either overruled, or there should be ingrafted thereon the further condition that if defendant cannot recover such damages plaintiff should not be allowed to breach his contract and also recover for the part performance by him. Or, in other words, that the parties should be left as they are found, and, if plaintiff sees fit to breach his contract, that he should go without pay for the portion performed and for which he would have received payment had he fully performed.

The question is an important one, and no doubt much can be said towards, and much authority cited sustaining, the contention of the defendant. The rule at common law was against plaintiff's recovery until the case of Britton v. Turner, 6 N.H. 481, was decided in 1834, in disregard of precedent. But the reasoning of that case is so cogent that it seems to have at least divided, if not changed, the current of authority. It first recognized the fact of the benefits of the part performance to the party who would keep such benefits, incapable of being returned, and still avoid paying anything for the benefits accrued where the contract is not fully performed. It may be remarked that, besides affecting parties similarly situated to those before us, this decision must also be a precedent upon the right of recovery of those in analogous positions, as, for instance, the farm laborer who hires for the summer and at the end of six months' labor performed quits his employment, and similar cases, where the contract is indivisible. An equitable rule has gradually developed permitting a recovery for the value of the services rendered, irrespective of the breach, giving to the other party to the contract a corresponding right of action in damages separately or in mitigation of the plaintiff's recovery, so that the rights of both may be equitably adjusted at law, notwithstanding the breach and nonperformance of the contract. This is true only where that which has been received by the employer under the partial performance has been beneficial to him.

[handwritten margin note: only true for restitution]

In this case it must be admitted that the threshing done was of substantial benefit to defendant and a partial performance of this contract. While there is a division of authority, and the weight of authority, from the number of holdings alone, would deny a right of recovery, yet we prefer to follow the other line of authority. Either rule must, under certain circumstances work injustice. Otherwise there would be no division in authorities. We elect to follow that which we believe to be the trend of authority. * * *

The judgment is affirmed.

Notes

1. *Britton's Contemporary Application.* State wage legislation compels an employer to pay an employee periodically, usually weekly, biweekly, or monthly. Many statutes require an employer to pay an employee in full on termination. Possible multiple damages and criminal sanctions encourage an employer to comply with wage statutes. *Britton* is not applicable to these employment relationships. Exceptions to wage laws, however, may exist for professionals, administrators, and executives; freelancers, consultants, and independent contractors are not covered by wage laws. Breach and restitution issues may arise under these more fluid relationships.

2. *Alternatives.* The *Lynn* court had several choices.

(a) *Opportunistic Breach?* The threshing contractor may have left the farmer's flax to spoil in the field because he had an opportunity to make more money threshing for someone else.

(b) *Restitution or Not?* Should the threshing contractor, who has breached his contract with the farmer, recover quantum meruit restitution at all?

(c) *Measurement?* If yes, how will the court measure the contractor's recovery?

The *Britton* court valued the benefit the employee conferred on the employer and subtracted the employer's damages from the employee's breach.

(i) *Employer's Benefit from an Employee's Part Performance?* Within that calculation, how should the court measure the farmer's benefit? The court may choose either the market value of the contractor's services or the actual benefit to the farmer.

(ii) *Employer's Damages from an Employee's Breach?* Next is how the court should calculate the farmer's damages. The farmer asked the court to discard a narrow and restrictive test for special damages and to allow him to recover broader special damages.

3. *Combining the Choices.* If the *Lynn* court's choice between granting and denying the contractor quantum meruit restitution is combined with its choice between awarding the farmer broad or narrow special damages, the court had four options. (a) To grant the contractor restitution and to deny the farmer an offset for broad special damages. (b) To grant the contractor restitution and to award the

farmer an offset for broad special damages. (c) To deny the contractor restitution and to retain the restrictive special damages test. (d) To deny the contractor restitution and to award the farmer broad special damages.

Questions. Which does the court choose? How well does the court's choice accommodate the goals of preventing unjust enrichment, deterring breach, and compensating loss?

4. *A Limit to Restitution?* Forest had a contract with Walters to transport logs; Forest asked his employee Kinzer to start work; unbeknownst to Forest, Kinzer instead arranged to pay Kennedy as a substitute to haul Walters's logs using Forest's truck. Several days later Kennedy had an accident on a return trip. Alleging he was Forest's employee, Kennedy filed a worker's compensation claim to recover for his injuries.

The referee and the Industrial Commission accepted Kennedy's argument for an "employment relationship" because of a contract implied in law. According to the Commission, an "implied employment contract existed between Forest and Kennedy based upon the theory of unjust enrichment." "Forest had accepted the 'benefit' of Kennedy's transportation of the three loads of logs * * * [and] would be unjustly enriched by retaining the benefit of Kennedy's services 'without liability for those services.' "

The Idaho supreme court disagreed:

"We employ the phrase 'implied-in-law contract' synonymously with quasi-contract, unjust enrichment, and restitution."

"In the worker's compensation context, an implied-in-law contract cannot form the basis for an employment relationship. First of all, an implied-in-law contract is not a contract or agreement at all and is simply a method by which the courts fashion a remedy in cases where there is no binding relationship between the parties. The definition of 'employer' in the worker's compensation statutes clearly contemplates a situation where one person employs another person or contracts to do so—as opposed to a relationship implied by the courts to do equity. Secondly, quasi-contract originates in the theory of unjust enrichment. The measure of recovery in such an action is limited to the 'value of the benefit bestowed upon the defendant which, in equity, would be unjust to retain without recompense to the plaintiff.' Gillette v. Storm Circle Ranch, 101 Idaho 663, 666, 619 P.2d 1116, 1119 (1980). A search of the case law has revealed no instance of a court awarding damages other than these in a quasi-contractual action, and no case in which a court treated a contract implied-in-law as a true contract and sought to imply terms based upon it. Thus, an implied-in-law contract cannot create an employment relationship and cannot expose Forest, as an employer, to worker's compensation liability or any other liabilities stemming from a true employment contract or agreement to hire."

"The Commission's conclusion that an implied-in-law contract exists in this instance is also incorrect. For a quasi-contractual obligation to arise, Forest would have to have been unjustly enriched by his retention of the benefits of Kennedy's services. In this case, however, Forest was not unjustly enriched. Even if Forest received a 'benefit' from Kennedy's services upon receipt of Walters' payment, Forest indirectly compensated Kennedy for his services. Upon receiving payment from Walters, Forest paid Kinzer the amount upon which they had agreed. Kinzer, in turn, paid Kennedy the amount that they had negotiated when Kennedy agreed to substitute for Kinzer. Thus, Forest already compensated Kennedy for his services and, consequently, for the value of any 'benefit' that Forest received."

The court remanded to provide Kennedy an opportunity to prove "an employment relationship based upon an implied-in-fact contract of hire." Kennedy v. Forest, 129 Idaho 584, 586–88 930 P.2d 1026, 1027–30 (1997).

6. EMPLOYEE'S REMEDIES: RECAP

FREUND v. WASHINGTON SQUARE PRESS, INC.

Court of Appeals of New York, 1974.
34 N.Y.2d 379, 357 N.Y.S.2d 857, 314 N.E.2d 419.

SAMUEL RABIN, JUDGE. * * * In 1965, plaintiff, an author and a college teacher, and defendant, Washington Square Press, Inc., entered into a written agreement which, in relevant part, provided as follows. Plaintiff ("author") granted defendant ("publisher") exclusive rights to publish and sell in book form plaintiff's work on modern drama. Upon plaintiff's delivery of the manuscript, defendant agreed to complete payment of a nonreturnable $2,000 "advance." Thereafter, if defendant deemed the manuscript not "suitable for publication," it had the right to terminate the agreement by written notice within 60 days of delivery. Unless so terminated, defendant agreed to publish the work in hardbound edition within 18 months and afterwards in paperbound edition. The contract further provided that defendant would pay royalties to plaintiff, based upon specified percentages of sales. (For example, plaintiff was to receive 10% of the retail price of the first 10,000 copies sold in the continental United States.) If defendant failed to publish within 18 months, the contract provided that "this agreement shall terminate and the rights herein granted to the Publisher shall revert to the Author. In such event all payments theretofore made to the Author shall belong to the Author without prejudice to any other remedies which the Author may have." * * *

Plaintiff performed by delivering his manuscript to defendant and was paid his $2,000 advance. Defendant thereafter merged with another publisher and ceased publishing in hardbound. Although defendant did not exercise its 60–day right to terminate, it has refused to publish the manuscript in any form.

Plaintiff * * * initially sought specific performance of the contract. The Trial Term Justice denied specific performance but, finding a valid contract and a breach by defendant, set the matter down for trial on the issue of monetary damages, if any, sustained by the plaintiff. At trial, plaintiff sought to prove: (1) delay of his academic promotion; (2) loss of royalties which would have been earned; and (3) the cost of publication if plaintiff had made his own arrangements to publish. The trial court found that plaintiff had been promoted despite defendant's failure to publish, and that there was no evidence that the breach had caused any delay. Recovery of lost royalties was denied without discussion. The court found, however, that the cost of hardcover publication to plaintiff was the natural and probable consequence of the breach and, based upon expert testimony, awarded $10,000, to cover this cost. It denied recovery of the expenses of paperbound publication on the ground that plaintiff's proof was conjectural.

The Appellate Division (3 to 2) affirmed, finding that the cost of publication was the proper measure of damages. In support of its conclusion, the majority analogized to the construction contract situation where the cost of completion may be the proper measure of damages for a builder's failure to complete a house or for use of wrong materials. The dissent concluded that the cost of publication is not an appropriate measure of damages and consequently, that plaintiff may recover nominal damages only. We agree with the dissent. In so concluding, we look to the basic purpose of damage recovery * * *.

It is axiomatic that * * * the law awards damages for breach of contract to compensate for injury caused by the breach—injury which was foreseeable, i.e., reasonably within the contemplation of the parties, at the time the contract was entered into. [citation] Money damages are substitutional relief designed in theory "to put the injured party in as good a position as he would have been put by full performance of the contract, at the least cost to the defendant and without charging him with harms that he had no sufficient reason to foresee when he made the contract." (5 Corbin, Contracts, § 1002, pp. 31–32.) In other words, so far as possible, the law attempts to secure to the injured party the benefit of his bargain, subject to the limitations that the injury—whether it be losses suffered or gains prevented—was foreseeable, and that the amount of damages claimed be measurable with a reasonable degree of certainty and, of course, adequately proven. [citations] But it is equally fundamental that the injured party should not recover more from the breach than he would have gained had the contract been fully performed. (Baker v. Drake, 53 N.Y. 211, 217; see, generally, Dobbs, Law of Remedies, p. 810.)

Measurement of damages in this case according to the cost of publication to the plaintiff would confer greater advantage than performance of the contract would have entailed to plaintiff and would place him in a far better position than he would have occupied had the defendant fully performed. Such measurement bears no relation to compensation for plaintiff's actual loss or anticipated profit. Far beyond compensating plaintiff for the interests he had in the defendant's performance of the contract—whether restitution, reliance or expectation (see Fuller & Perdue, Reliance Interest in Contract Damages, 46 Yale L.J. 52, 53–56) an award of the cost of publication would enrich plaintiff at defendant's expense.

Pursuant to the contract, plaintiff delivered his manuscript to the defendant. In doing so, he conferred a value on the defendant which, upon defendant's breach, was required to be restored to him. Special Term, in addition to ordering a trial on the issue of damages, ordered defendant to return the manuscript to plaintiff and plaintiff's restitution interest in the contract was thereby protected.

At the trial on the issue of damages, plaintiff alleged no reliance losses suffered in performing the contract or in making necessary preparations to perform. Had such losses, if foreseeable and ascertainable, been incurred, plaintiff would have been entitled to compensation for them.

As for plaintiff's expectation interest in the contract, it was basically twofold—the "advance" and the royalties. (To be sure, plaintiff may have expected to enjoy whatever notoriety, prestige or other benefits that might have attended publication, but even if these expectations were compensable, plaintiff did not attempt at trial to place a monetary value on them.) There is no dispute that plaintiff's expectancy in the "advance" was fulfilled—he has received his $2,000. His expectancy interest in the royalties—the profit he stood to gain from sale of the published book—while theoretically compensable, was speculative. Although this work is not plaintiff's first, at trial he provided no stable foundation for a reasonable estimate of royalties he would have earned had defendant not breached its promise to publish. In these circumstances, his claim for royalties falls for uncertainty.

Since the damages which would have compensated plaintiff for anticipated royalties were not proved with the required certainty, we agree with the dissent in the Appellate Division that nominal damages alone are recoverable. Though these are damages in name only and not at all compensatory, they are nevertheless awarded as a formal vindication of plaintiff's legal right to compensation which has not been given a sufficiently certain monetary valuation.

In our view, the analogy by the majority in the Appellate Division to the construction contract situation was inapposite. In the typical construction contract, the owner agrees to pay money or other consideration to a builder and expects, under the contract, to receive a completed building in return. The value of the promised performance to the owner is the properly constructed building. In this case, unlike the typical construction contract, the value to plaintiff of the promised performance—publication—was a percentage of sales of the books published and not the books themselves. Had the plaintiff contracted for the printing, binding and delivery of a number of hardbound copies of his manuscript, to be sold or disposed of as he wished, then perhaps the construction analogy, and measurement of damages by the cost of replacement or completion, would have some application.

Here, however, the specific value to plaintiff of the promised publication was the royalties he stood to receive from defendant's sales of the published book. Essentially, publication represented what it would have cost the defendant to confer that value upon the plaintiff, and, by its breach, defendant saved that cost. The error by the courts below was in measuring damages not by the value to plaintiff of the promised performance but by the cost of that performance to defendant. Damages are not measured, however, by what the defaulting party saved by the breach, but by the natural and probable consequences of the breach *to the plaintiff.* In this case, the consequence to plaintiff of defendant's failure to publish is that he is prevented from realizing the gains promised by the contract—the royalties. But, as we have stated, the amount of royalties plaintiff would have realized was not ascertained with adequate certainty and, as a consequence, plaintiff may recover nominal damages only.

Accordingly, the order of the Appellate Division should be modified to the extent of reducing the damage award of $10,000 for the cost of publication to six cents, but with costs and disbursements to the plaintiff.

Notes

1. *Freund's Goals.* What benefits did Freund seek to accomplish through the contract? After the publisher breached, what remedy or remedies should Freund be entitled to?

2. *Specific Performance?* A court will grant a plaintiff specific performance or expectancy damages to give a plaintiff either the exact benefit of the breached contract or its profit potential. The trial judge's denied Freund's request for specific performance and Freund did not cross appeal, so specific performance fell out of the appeal. Was specific performance probably the remedy that Freund preferred? What reasons might the trial judge have given to refuse Freund's request for specific performance? Are these reasons persuasive? Should the New York court have adopted the Utah court's reasoning in *Thurston*? pp. 718–21.

3. *Damages—Cost to Publish?* Freund sought to recover damages based on Washington Square's (saved) cost to publish. Would that measure have accomplished the goals of compensation and deterrence?

4. *Damages—Lost Royalties?* A plaintiff usually prefers to recover the benefit of the bargain or his expectancy. The court finds Freund's recovery of royalties to have foundered at the proof stage. What discovery might Freund have conducted to support his recovery of lost royalties? Could Freund have done a better job of proving lost royalties?

5. *Restitution and Reliance Recovery?* A plaintiff who cannot prove lost profit may pursue restitution and reliance recovery. A court may employ restitution and reliance recovery to restore the plaintiff to the world before the contract. Restitution following rescission of a contract forces the defendant to return the plaintiff's consideration; in addition to restoring the pre-contract status quo, restitution prevents the defendant's unjust enrichment. Most courts measure plaintiff's reliance recovery by his expenditures in preparing for the defendant to perform that did not benefit the defendant; but some commentators' broader definition of a plaintiff's reliance recovery includes plaintiff's foregone opportunities. A plaintiff who can choose between restitution and reliance will usually select reliance; for a plaintiff's reliance, based on the cost he incurred, includes expenditures that do not benefit or enrich the defendant.

(a) *Restitution?* What restitution occurred in *Freund*? Do you think Freund felt vindicated?

(b) *Reliance Recovery?* Consider Freund's expenses of performing. If Freund could not prove lost royalties, should he have sought to recover reliance expense as a fallback or proxy? What were Freund's out-of-pocket reliance expenses? Freund's largest cost to write the book was the value of his time in another activity, his foregone income or, an economist's term, his opportunity cost. If Freund wrote the book after he entered into the contract with Washington Square, could he have recovered, as a reliance expense, the value of the time he spent writing? Should the court assume that Freund's expectation damages were at least equal to his expenditures in performing?

6. *An Unpublished Legal Treatise.* Rafael Chodos, a California business lawyer, contracted with a legal publisher to write and publish a treatise on fiduciary duty. Chodos's royalty would have been 15%. He reduced his practice and spent several years, he estimated 3600 hours, on the book. After it received the completed 1247-page book, West, the publisher's successor, repudiated the agreement to publish it, maintaining that the book, although high quality, would not be commercially viable.

On the first appeal, the court of appeals held that the publisher had breached the contract and turned to Chodos's remedy. Specific performance, the court hinted, might have been an available remedy: "It might also be reasonably argued that West's publishing of Chodos's treatise was an additional element of consideration to which Chodos was entitled, since substantial benefits other than the royalties he would have received might have accrued to him as a result of publication, including enhanced reputation and additional client referrals."

Since Chodos's lost royalties from the unpublished book were "pure speculation" that "cannot be calculated with reasonable certainty," he could not recover his expectancy.

Chodos could, the court held, recover restitution, quantum meruit variety. The court wrote that "Chodos is entitled to sue for restitution for the time and effort he reasonably invested in writing the manuscript." Although the court's statement measures Chodos's restitution by his performance that the publisher bargained for, it might also confuse reliance, Chodos's cost, with restitution, West's benefit. The court of appeals sent the case back to the trial judge, expressing "no opinion as to how restitution should be calculated in this case; nor do we intimate any suggestion as to the appropriate amount of such recovery." Chodos v. West Publishing Co., 292 F.3d 992 (9th Cir. 2002).

The second appeal was Chodos's, from a jury's verdict for $300,000. The court of appeals affirmed the jury verdict. Although the court labeled its affirmance as "not appropriate for publication" and one that "may not be cited to or by the courts of this circuit," your editor thinks that a lengthy excerpt is warranted in this Remedies casebook, which work the editor hopes is commercially viable enough to be published by West:

"In California," the court began, " '[t]he measure of recovery in quantum meruit is the reasonable value of the services rendered, provided they were of direct benefit to the defendant.' Maglica v. Maglica, [p 415.] California courts have adopted a subsidiary definition of the reasonable value of a plaintiff's services: the amount that it would have cost the defendant to obtain the services from another person. *See Maglica,* (upholding jury instruction based on this definition). Alternatively, California courts have formulated this measure as the amount the defendant would have had to pay on the 'open market' to obtain the same services, or the 'comparable charge' for such services. *See Maglica.* California trial courts are afforded broad discretion in allowing evidence on the reasonable value of a plaintiff's services. [citations]

"Chodos objects to the jury instruction that provided: '[i]n assessing the reasonable value of plaintiff's time and effort, you may evaluate what he would have been paid if the parties had bargained for plaintiff's services in the open market.' As discussed above, however, this instruction comports with California law."

"Chodos further argues that his recovery in quantum meruit must be measured by the value to him of the time and effort he reasonably invested in preparing the manuscript, which he contends is the amount he could have earned in legal fees as a practitioner over the two years he devoted to writing his manuscript. However, the case upon which Chodos relies, Earhart v. William Low Co., 'merely held * * * that where the defendant urged the plaintiff to render services to a third party the plaintiff could still be compensated in quantum meruit for those services.' *Maglica.* *Earhart* did not address the proper measure of compensation for those who have made out a valid claim for recovery in quantum meruit."

"Chodos has pointed to no California precedent measuring recovery in quantum meruit by the plaintiff's lost business opportunities. Lost business opportunities are normally categorized as a form of reliance damages under California law. [citation] However, Chodos abandoned recovery of contract damages when he elected to plead recovery in quantum meruit."

"The district court properly allowed Chodos to present evidence of his lost business opportunities to the jury, since such evidence was relevant to a determination of what Chodos would have received if the parties had negotiated a lump sum payment for the services rendered. However, the trial judge was also correct in rejecting Chodos's proposed jury instruction, which would have required the jury to equate restitution with Chodos's lost business opportunities."

"Chodos argues the 'open market' jury instruction was erroneous because there is no actual market for the legal authorship services of practicing lawyers. Chodos cites no precedent to support his proposition that the existence of an actual, identical market for the services in question must be established through competent evidence before the jury is allowed to evaluate the reasonable value of the plaintiff's services under an open market theory. California courts have given juries discretion to choose among several possible markets in evaluating the reasonable value of the services. [citations]"

"It was within the competence of the jury to determine the value of Chodos's services based on West's testimony on the hourly or per unit compensation that West would have offered to have the treatise written and Chodos's testimony on what a practicing attorney would have accepted to produce the treatise. The district court's 'open market' jury instruction, which gave the jury discretion to do so, was not in error. * * *"

"Finally, Chodos claims that the jury verdict of $300,000 was not supported by substantial evidence. The jury considered evidence on the expected value of the contract at its inception, supplemented by Chodos's and West's conflicting testimony as to the compensation that West would have offered to pay and a practicing attorney like Chodos would have accepted to produce the treatise. The jury's estimation of the reasonable value of Chodos's services based on the extensive testimony presented was within its discretion." Chodos v. West Publishing Co., 92 Fed.Appx. 471 (9th Cir. 2004).

Questions. (a) *Granting Chodos Restitution.* Although the publisher bargained for Chodos's performance, how did his execution of the contract benefit or enrich West? If the court assumes that Chodos's expectation is at least equal to the value to West of his performance of the contract, does that justify awarding restitution to Chodos?

(b) *Measuring Chodos's Restitution.* Did the jury undervalue Chodos's expertise in his legal specialty? Assuming Chodos's estimate that he allocated 3600 hours is accurate, what hourly rate did the jury select for a lawyer proficient enough at his trade to write a 1247–page treatise on fiduciary duty? Is that adequate?

7. *Avoidable Consequences?* If Freund or Chados finds another publisher for the books, they have, it seems, avoided the consequences of the defendants' breaches.

8. *Living it Up on Nominal Damages.* Freund receives next to nothing. The publisher breached its contract with him and escaped the consequences. Does the result undermine the substantive law of contracts with its dual compensatory-admonitory goals? Should the court have permitted Freund to recover, as a surrogate for the publisher's performance and as a second-best way to measure his damages, either (a) the publisher's saved cost of publication, or (b) the value of the time he spent writing? Do the reasons for a court to order specific performance here overcome the arguments against it?

9. *Sales and Employment: Relational Contracts.* People enter into contracts to accomplish their objectives. But the types of parties' contracts and the nature of parties' objectives differ. Parties's interests coincide and diverge. Relational contracts include employment, franchises, service contracts, and many leases.

Compare a buyer's contract to pay a seller money for bricks with a lawyer's contract to teach a course in Property Law at a paralegal school. Several things distinguish the brick transaction from a relational employment contract.

(a) The buyer and seller can exchange money and bricks simultaneously. But the duration of the contract for a Property course extends over the semester.

(b) The brick contract leaves little uncertainty about what consideration each party is to furnish. But the lawyer's contract to teach Property leaves important issues open to discretion, for example what textbook to use, the assignments, the format, discussion vs. lecture.

(c) The buyer and seller can walk away from the pile of bricks leaving their future co-operation, if any, to be negotiated in a separate future contract. However the lawyer's agreement to teach Property Law anticipates cooperation during the semester. Indeed the school may have issued an employees' manual with a detailed grievance procedure to resolve disputes. People with investments specific to an agreement usually prefer to adjust differences, settle disputes, and preserve the contract.

(d) The parties' principal risks in the brick exchange, price fluctuation and changing needs, are allocated to the buyer and the seller. But a relational contract may anticipate risk sharing. One of the parties to a relational contract may have investments specifically allocated to the contract, in particular the future teacher's time spent in advance reading and preparing for the Property Law course. Since the parties' relational contract will last some time, they may form close relationships which facilitate their performance and may increase their personal satisfaction.

The relational contract concept is a useful way of looking at many contract problems. Distinguishing a relational contract from another contract is a matter of tendency and degree. Not all relational contracts have all the features of relational contracts. Freund's contract with Washington Square was probably "relational." But has the editor "pushed the envelope" to put it in the Employment Agreements Chapter?

Different types of contracts summon different features of contract law. The parties' willingness to co-operate and adjust are more important in relational than in other contracts. A duty of good faith and fair dealing may not mean much in a transaction where a seller has either delivered bricks or has not and the buyer has either paid or has not. Neither the school's assigning a teacher with emphysema to teach in a fifth-floor classroom nor the lawyer's decision to focus the future paralegals' Property course on the philosophers, Locke, Bentham, and Marx may breach any particular term of the contract.

How many of the differences between sales and employment contracts and their remedies are explained on the ground that the sales contract usually is not a relational contract while an employment contract usually is?

Chapter 9

PROPERTY INTERESTS

Our Property chapter examines an owner's remedies to protect and vindicate her interests in property. The professional skills this chapter emphasizes, choosing between remedies and measuring the remedy selected, are among the tools a lawyer uses to evaluate a client's contentions, to plan and draft pleadings, to conduct discovery, to negotiate a settlement, and finally to try a lawsuit. The adversary system and the process called characterization reward creative argumentation within available categories.

In addition to differences between remedies, the distinctions between real and personal property and between several torts affect the plaintiff's choice and measurement of remedies. The plaintiff's major personal-property torts are conversion-trover, trespass to chattels, and negligence; replevin is the name of the owner's action to recover chattels in fact. The real property torts are trespass to land, nuisance, strict liability, and negligence again; but the plaintiff's pleadings may be labeled ejectment, forcible entry, quiet title, or something else. Finally, defendant's breach of a contract may also enter remedial calculations.

The first three cases are short in length but long in learning. Planning and early decisions are crucial, because choosing one solution may eliminate others.

A. CHOOSING THE REMEDY

BARAM v. FARUGIA

United States Court of Appeals, Third Circuit, 1979.
606 F.2d 42.

ALDISERT, CIRCUIT JUDGE. In this age of space travel and computer technology, a horse named Foxey Toni requires us to return to a more tranquil era and examine elements of trover and conversion under Pennsylvania common law. * * *

Dr. Joseph Baram, appellee, acquired legal title to Foxey Toni, a bay filly race horse, for $3,000 in a claiming race at the Keystone Race Track, Bucks County, Pennsylvania. Dennis Fredella became the trainer for Foxey Toni and was given authority to enter her in races in Dr. Baram's name. Foxey Toni raced under Dr. Baram's name on October 11, October 17, and November 8, 1975. Thereafter, a Certificate of Foal Registration for the horse, issued by the Jockey Club of America, came into Fredella's possession at a time when he was indebted to appellant Robert Farugia. Without the knowledge or consent of Dr. Baram, Farugia obtained possession of the horse from Fredella and was given the foal certificate bearing the forged signature of Dr. Baram. The district court found that both Fredella and Farugia knew or should have known that the signature on the foal certificate had been forged and that Fredella had no authority to transfer Foxey Toni.

Farugia first dated the certificate, transferring the horse to himself, and then transferred her to appellant Glenn Hackett and himself. Foxey Toni was subsequently raced in Canada by the putative new owners without the knowledge or consent of Dr. Baram. After Dr. Baram learned of these events, he met with Farugia and demanded the return of Foxey Toni. Farugia refused to return the horse or pay her value of $3,000 but offered instead a modest cash settlement. Dr. Baram rejected the settlement offer and initiated litigation.

Dr. Baram filed a complaint sounding in "Trespass for Conversion," in the district court against Farugia, Hackett, and Fredella. A default judgment for failure to appear was entered against Fredella. Dr. Baram acknowledged at trial that, as a result of previous criminal proceedings against Fredella in state court, he had been paid $3,000 by Fredella covering Dr. Baram's claim "for the value of the horse, Foxey Toni," and that he "agreed to accept that." This case then proceeded as a bench trial for compensatory and punitive damages for conversion against Farugia and Hackett. The court awarded compensatory damages of $3,000 against both defendants for the value of Foxey Toni and assessed punitive damages of $5,000 against Farugia. The court dismissed the complaint against Fredella with prejudice. This appeal by Farugia and Hackett followed.

Appellants argue that the judgment must be reversed because the $3,000 payment by the converter Fredella for the value of the horse extinguished any further claim in conversion by Dr. Baram. We agree with appellants' argument. * * *

The modern law remedy for conversion has emerged from the common law action of trover, which was premised on the theory that the defendant had appropriated the plaintiff's chattel, for which he must pay. * * * A plaintiff who proved conversion in a common law trover action was entitled to damages equal to the full value of the chattel at the time and place of conversion. [citation] According to Professor Prosser, "[w]hen the defendant satisfied the judgment in trover, the title to the chattel passed to him, and the plaintiff had nothing more to do with it. The effect was that the defendant was compelled, because of his wrongful appropriation, to buy the chattel at a forced sale, of which the action of trover was the judicial instrument. [citation]" Pennsylvania courts have long recognized the forced sale aspect of conversion actions.

The title-passing and forced-sale concepts distinguished trover from the common law action of trespass, which was premised on the theory that the plaintiff remained the owner of the chattel and was entitled only to the damages he had sustained through loss of possession, and from the action of replevin, which also left title in the plaintiff and returned the chattel to his possession. The modern day tort of conversion retains the conceptual underpinnings of trover and is generally applicable only to cases such as this one in which there has been a major or serious interference with a chattel or with the plaintiff's right in it. It is the seriousness of the interference that justifies the forced judicial sale to the defendant, described by Prosser as "the distinguishing feature of the action." The Restatement (Second) of Torts preserves this conceptual basis:

> "When the defendant satisfies the judgment in the action for conversion, title to the chattel passes to him, so that he is in effect required to buy it at a forced judicial sale. Conversion is therefore properly limited, and has been limited by the courts, to those serious, major, and important interferences with the right to control the chattel which justify requiring the defendant to pay its full value."

§ 222A, Comment c (1965). Although Pennsylvania law is unclear about whether title passes on entry of judgment against the converter or only when the converter satisfies the judgment, the rule recognized in most states is that title to the chattel passes only when the judgment against the converter is satisfied. We need not venture our opinion on how the Pennsylvania courts would resolve this question, however, because in this case both the judicial order that Fredella pay the value as a condition of his probation and actual payment of $3,000 to Dr. Baram, events related to the first conversion, preceded judgment on the second claim. * * *

On receipt by Dr. Baram of the $3,000 from Fredella, and acknowledgment that this sum reflected the true value of the horse, a common law forced sale was effected, passing title from the legal owner to the converter at the time and place of the original conversion. Had the converter made no offer of an amount reflecting the horse's value, and had Dr. Baram not received full value, he could have made out a conversion action against Farugia and Hackett. But the acceptance by Dr. Baram of the horse's true market value with the resultant passage of title in the nature of "a forced judicial sale" had the effect of vesting title in Fredella retroactively from November 29, 1975, the date of the conversion. [citation] With title so vested, Fredella therefore had the right to transfer Foxey Toni on November 29, 1975, and Farugia, by the same reasoning, then took possession of the horse from a person legally entitled to possess and transfer. Dr. Baram retroactively lost his right to possession of Foxey Toni, and without a right of possession at the time of the alleged conversion could not maintain an action for conversion against Farugia and Hackett. [citation] Thus, although successive and independent actionable conversions of the same chattel are possible, satisfaction of the earlier conversion by payment in full of the value of the chattel acts as a complete bar to subsequent recoveries. * * *

Accordingly, the judgment of the district court will be reversed * * *.

Note

Election of Remedies. Although it does not mention the doctrine of election of remedies, the court appears to limit Dr. Baram to the "remedy" he first "elected." This advances the idea that the owner can recover the property's value, but only once. In the process, however, the court liberates tortfeasors from paying punitive damages to their victim. Do you think Dr. Baram understood the technical rules of conversion and title when he accepted the $3,000? What if his criminal "restitution" had been only $1,000? Did the court take its fictions too seriously?

WELCH v. KOSASKY

Massachusetts Court of Appeals, 1987.
24 Mass.App.Ct. 402, 509 N.E.2d 919.

ARMSTRONG, JUSTICE. In 1974 a thief broke into the Welches' home in Cambridge and stole twelve lots of valuable antique silver from Mrs. Welch's collection. A month later the defendant, a physician, purchased eleven of the lots from a dealer in Brookline for $2,750, items for which Mrs. Welch had paid in excess of $40,000 during the previous twelve years. There was evidence that the Brookline dealer was involved in receiving stolen goods, and the trial judge, who heard the case without a jury, concluded that the defendant, despite his denials, knew or should have known that the silver items he purchased from the Brookline dealer were stolen goods.

In 1981, the defendant approached Firestone and Parson, a Boston dealer, to sell the silver. There, nine of the eleven lots were purchased by an English dealer for $40,000. He left several items on consignment with Firestone and Parson for sale in this country. One of the two lots not purchased by the English dealer was a set of three James II castors that Mrs. Welch had purchased from a New York dealer in 1971 for $7,500. These were thought by the English dealer to have been altered in the Victorian period and, for that reason, to lack substantial value as collector's items. He recommended certain alterations (removal of feet and some chasing) to restore them to what he thought to be original form. The defendant authorized the changes, and the work was done in London.

One day in 1981, Mrs. Welch saw two of the stolen items in Firestone and Parson's window. (They were identified as the stolen items through photographs, descriptions, and hallmarks.) Through this discovery, over the next year or two, Mrs. Welch succeeded in recovering all of the stolen items that had been purchased by the defendant. The Welches then brought this action for conversion of all the items and for damages (by the alterations) to the James II castors.

The judge found for the Welches and awarded damages as follows: $10,000 for loss of use of the silver during its eight-year absence; $22,000 for diminution in the value of the James II castors; and $5,000 in consequential damages, representing in part a fee of $994.78 paid to an attorney in connection with the recovery of the castors from London, and in part a portion of a $10,000 fee paid for another attorney who performed services in seeking to locate and recover all the items stolen in the 1974 housebreak, including many works of art and antiques other than the silver items previously discussed.

The most difficult question raised by the defendant's appeal concerns the damages awarded for the diminution in value of the castors. Here the evidence conflicted sharply. The London dealer who recommended and arranged for the alterations to the James II castors testified, as would be expected, that the alterations did not diminish their value, that it simply conformed their appearance to the original and made them more aesthetically pleasing. Another expert shared the London dealer's view that the castors had been altered previously and that the latest alterations did not affect their value. The New York dealer who had sold the castors to Mrs. Welch for $7,500 in 1971 testified that the castors were then unaltered; that they were worth $7,500 in 1971; that in 1984 (two years after their recovery), when he appraised the castors again, they would have been worth $25,000 to $30,000 in their previous condition but that, as altered, they were worth only $3,000. (The London dealer agreed with the last figure.) As this was all the evidence bearing on the value of the castors, it is clear that the judge credited the testimony of the New York dealer and that the $22,000 damages awarded for diminution of value represents the difference (as found by the judge) between the value of the castors at the time they were returned and the value that they would have had at that time had they not been altered.

This, the defendant contends, is an improper measure of damages. He relies on the rule of damages in conversion cases, long settled in this State * * * that damages are measured by the value of the converted goods at the time of the conversion, with interest from that time, and that subsequent fluctuations in the value of the converted goods neither enhance nor diminish the damages recoverable. [citations] Where, as here, the rightful owner elects to receive back the converted goods, the rule of damages, as the defendant correctly observes, is still based on value at the time of the conversion, but the converter is (1) credited with the value of the returned goods at the time of their return, and (2) charged with damages for loss of use of the goods during the period of the detention. [citations] The defendant thus contends that damages applicable to the castors should have been computed as follows: value of the castors in 1974, $7,500 less their value when returned in 1982 ($3,000) for a net reduction of $4,500.

The defendant's formulation of the rule applicable to conversion cases is correct as far as it goes, but we find nothing in the decisions cited that definitively precludes the rightful owner from recovering the value of the converted property as appreciated if an independent basis for doing so appears. Typically the owner of converted goods that appreciated after the conversion would, if the goods could be located, sue in replevin rather than trover (under the common law forms of action) and would thereby recover the appreciated goods in specie. [citation] Trover (or, later, tort for conversion) was the preferred remedy when the goods depreciated or were damaged after the conversion, because the rightful owner could elect to treat the conversion as a sale and recover the undepreciated value. * * *

In Jones v. Hoar, 5 Pick. 285 (1827), it was held that, when the converter sold the converted goods, the owner, at his election, could waive the conversion and sue in contract for the purchase price (assumpsit for money had and received to plaintiff's use) and could in this manner recover the value of any appreciation after the conversion. [citations]

The cases which, on superficial reading, seem most strongly to support the defendant's contention [citations] are seen on closer reading to turn on an infelicitous election of remedies. Contrary to the defendant's contention, the general rule of substantive law, broadly stated, is: "The conscious wrongdoer cannot make a profit and is responsible for losses." Loring v. Baker, 329 Mass. 63, 66, 106 N.E.2d 434 (1952). Under this rule the Welches' damages with respect to the castors are not necessarily capped by their value on the date of the conversion.

In 1981, prior to the alteration of the castors, the Welches had a legal right to their return in specie, although they were not then able to vindicate that right because they had not yet located the castors. The value of that right, on the judge's findings, approximated $25,000. The alteration of the castors reduced their value, and correspondingly the value of the Welches' right to replevy, by

$22,000. The alteration was not authorized by the Welches. As to them it was a tortious act of trespass [to chattels] or injury to their castors, a tort distinct from the previous eight-year detention. If the defendant had then been rightfully in possession of the castors as a bailee, his act of commissioning the unauthorized alterations would give rise to an action for damages by the Welches, either for the injury to the castors (trespass [to chattels]) or for their full value prior to the alteration (conversion). [citations] It would be incongruous to hold that he escapes that liability because his possession was wrongful. The Welches may consistently seek damages for both torts. [citation] The award for damage to the castors was not error.

[The court reduced the Welches' damages for locating and returning the stolen items to] a total of $3,494.78 for all consequential damages.

The Welches cite no authority for their suggestion that consequential damages might include compensation for mental anguish. Restatement (Second) of Torts § 927 comment m (1979), seems to contemplate situations where plaintiff makes out the elements of intentional infliction of emotional distress. * * *

The judgment is to be modified to reflect the reduction in consequential damages described above, and, as so modified, the judgment is affirmed.

So ordered.

Notes

1. *Pause for a Second.* This short decision introduces most of the remedial choices in this chapter. The first choice is between recovery in fact and recovery of money.

(a) *Recovery in Fact.* The Welches had already recaptured the silver in fact when they started this lawsuit. But the court mentions replevin, the owner's statutory legal remedy to recover converted personal property in fact. Another way for an owner to regain possession of property is an injunction, an equitable remedy, that orders the defendant to return it.

(b) *Recovery of Money.* The Welches sued to recover money. Within the category of recovery of money, the plaintiffs' choice is between (i) two torts, trover-conversion and trespass to chattels, and (ii) restitution for money had and received. The Welches recover for both torts.

(i) *Tort Damages.* The court discusses two general damages measures for the tort of trover-conversion and a separate one for trespass to chattels. The Welches recover for both conversion and trespass to chattels. Do damages for both torts duplicate?

"The conscious wrongdoer," the court says, "cannot make a profit and is responsible for losses." Does the court turn the owner's damage measure on the quality of defendant's misconduct? Exactly how should the tortfeasor's mental state affect the choice of torts and the measure of damages? Does the defendant's intent affect the plaintiffs' loss and their need for compensation? Is the court's language too imprecise to be a "rule"?

Proof of Value. The next choice is how plaintiff proves value and how the court evaluates evidence of value to determine the value of the property to set the Welches' tort damages.

Lost Use. An owner's recovery for loss of use of a converted chattel has not been common, probably because it is theoretically inconsistent with the theory of a "forced sale" dating back to the time of conversion, and because of the availability of prejudgment interest. However, the Restatement Torts approves an owner's lost use damage if "not otherwise compensated." Restatement (Second) of Torts § 927(2)(d) (1979). Was lost use an appropriate item of damages for the Welches?

Special Damages. The Welches recover for their search expense, but not for emotional distress.

(ii) *Restitution.* The Welches do not recover restitution. Why not?

2. *Can Trespass to Chattels Enter the Computer Age?* When the tortfeasor is a hacker who misappropriates via computer, what is the difference between the tort of conversion and its little-brother tort, trespass to chattels? A computer hacker's use of plaintiff's long-distance phone line is not a conversion, the California court of appeal said; but hacking out free phone service is a trespass to chattels. Hacking is not a conversion because the defendant-hacker did not physically take something tangible; it is a trespass to chattels since it is "unauthorized use of personal property." The phone company's mislabeling of trespass to chattels as conversion is not fatal, since its evidence supports the former tort. Thrifty–Tel v. Bezenek, 46 Cal.App.4th 1559, 1556, 54 Cal.Rptr.2d 468, 473 (1996). The California Supreme Court declined, however, to extend the tort of trespass to chattels to include a former employee's use of his former employer's computer system to flood his former co-workers' computers with thousands of unsolicited "spam" e-mails; to trigger an injunction, the court held, his previous employer must show that the defendant's "trespass" to its computer system "injured" its property. Intel Corp. v. Hamidi, 30 Cal.4th 1342, 1 Cal.Rptr.3d 32, 71 P.3d 296 (2003).

3. The next case takes up the plaintiff's choice of remedies and damage measures for the defendant's conversion tort when the converted property's value has fluctuated.

TRAHAN v. FIRST NATIONAL BANK OF RUSTON

United States Court of Appeals, Fifth Circuit, 1982.
690 F.2d 466.

JOHN R. BROWN, CIRCUIT JUDGE: The facts in this case are not disputed. The district court found the First National Bank of Ruston liable to J. C. Trahan for the conversion of 15,000 shares of stock in Texas International Petroleum Corporation (TIPCO). The judge ordered the Bank to procure and deliver 15,000 shares of TIPCO stock to Trahan within 30 days of the date of judgment. Both parties appeal. The sole issue before this Court is whether, under Louisiana law, the trial judge used the correct measure of damages. The Bank contends that damages should be fixed at the value of the stock at the time of conversion. Trahan claims that the court should have awarded him the highest value reached by the stock between the date of conversion and the date of judgment. On March 13, 1978, the date of conversion, TIPCO stock was worth $10 per share. On January 19, 1982, the date on which judgment was entered against the Bank, the stock was worth $29.50 per share. The highest value reached by the stock between those two dates was $64.25 per share, on January 28, 1981. * * * Because we find no error, we affirm the district court's judgment.

In the fall of 1973, Trahan pledged 70,000 shares of TIPCO stock to the Bank to secure two loans. In 1977, Trahan repaid the loans and demanded the return of the stock. The Bank refused, saying that the stock had been pledged additionally to secure loans made to a corporation, Resource Exploration, Inc., which the Bank considered to be "one and the same" as Trahan. This latter obligation was evidenced by an uninitialed interlineation on the pledge agreement. When Resource Exploration defaulted on its loan, the Bank sold 15,000 shares of the stock. Trahan filed this diversity suit.

The trial judge found that the stock had not validly been pledged as security for the loan to Resource Exploration and had been wrongfully converted by the Bank. He then ordered the Bank to tender an equal number of shares of TIPCO stock to Trahan, an award with which neither party is satisfied.

The Bank points out, correctly, that the usual measure of damages for conversion in Louisiana is either the return of the property converted or the value of the property at the time of conversion. [citations]

The trial court, however, found that unusual circumstances were present to justify its unusual award. Specifically, the judge concluded that as of the date of judgment "there (had) been no final and complete alienation" of the stock in question since the Bank could possibly retrieve the stock by way of a pending state court suit between it and the purchaser. If it were to do so, the order to procure 15,000 shares of TIPCO stock would amount to nothing more than the return of the property converted, in accordance with the traditional measure of damages. Moreover, the court found that if the Bank was allowed to recover and keep the actual stock while paying only for its value at the time of conversion, "the Bank would profit tremendously by its own wrongdoing to the tune of over three hundred thousand dollars at the stock's current value. That is the difference in what Schneider paid the Bank and what is the current value of the stock." The brokerage firm of Schneider, Bernet and Hickman, Inc. was the purchaser of the stock in question and plaintiff in the pending state action. The "current value" referred to by the court is, of course, the stock's value at the time of judgment.

The court's order did not require the Bank to return the actual shares of stock which it had converted. Thus it is not strictly in accordance with the traditional measure of damages. The court ruled, however, that in unique circumstances Louisiana law does not inflexibly demand adherence to that measure. We agree that this distinguished Louisiana-trained judge read the Louisiana law correctly.

In order to reach this conclusion, we must blow a little dust from some cases decided around the turn of the century. In Leurey v. Bank of Baton Rouge, 131 La. 30, 58 So. 1022 (1912), the Louisiana Supreme Court adopted the traditional measure of damages called for here by the Bank. Upon elaboration, however, the Court recognized that particular circumstances might at times demand a different standard.

> There are, no doubt, some transactions in stocks, in which to hold a defendant liable only for the value of the stocks at the date of their actual conversion would afford a very inadequate remedy; as, for instance, where one, acting through a broker, buys stocks with the intention of holding them for a rise in the market and the broker sells them without authority and delays giving notice to his principal, so that the latter loses the opportunity of availing himself of the rise that he expected, there is a loss of profit which was within the contemplation of the contract, and which should be borne by him through whose fault it is made.... And so, where, as in the case between the plaintiff and Mayer, the element of bad faith is found.

The Bank argues that the Court meant this exception to apply solely to damages for breach of contract. The Court's language, however, plainly refutes this argument. *Leurey* instead says that in unusual situations, where justice so demands, a judge may fashion different, more appropriate remedies for the conversion of corporate stock. It then suggests two examples of such a situation.

Succession of Gragard, 106 La. 298, 30 So. 885 (1901), predates even *Leurey*. In *Gragard*, suit was successfully brought for recovery of the value of a number of bales of cotton. The Louisiana Supreme Court did not limit the plaintiff's damages to the value of the cotton at the time of conversion. "Considering that the cotton was being held for better prices, we think that the owners of it should be given the benefit of the better prices that prevailed within a few months afterwards."

Here, of course, there is no evidence that Trahan, if in possession, would have attempted to sell the stock at the higher prices which it reached after the date of conversion. Although the facts of the two cases are not identical, however, *Gragard* certainly demonstrates that Louisiana courts have not felt compelled in every situation to calculate damages for conversion strictly according to the traditional formula.

Although these decisions are, as the trial court remarked, rather "elderly," Louisiana has published no obituary of their demise. The Louisiana courts have many times since discussed the issue of damages for conversion. Neither expressly nor implicitly, however, have they repudiated either *Leurey* or *Gragard* in their holding that the unique circumstances of some transactions may call for the value of converted property to be fixed at some time other than the date of conversion. * * *

We reject the Bank's argument that the court was obligated to fix damages at the value of the stock at the time of conversion.

Trahan maintains that he should as a matter of law have received the highest value reached by the stock between the date of conversion and the date of judgment. In support of this assertion, he provides this Court with neither citations, rationale, nor argument. We see no reason to compel the imposition of the measure of damages which he seeks.

The trial court levied a damage award which was proper under Louisiana law.

Notes

1. *Damages.* The court mentions two damages measures: (a) the property's value at the time of conversion, (b) and the property's highest value between conversion and trial. A third damages measure is New York's, (c) the highest market value within a reasonable time after the owner discovers the conversion. Ahles v. Aztec Enterprises, Inc., 120 A.D.2d 903, 502 N.Y.S.2d 821, 823 (App.Div.1986); Transcontinental Oil Corp. v. Trenton Products Co., 560 F.2d 94 (2d Cir.1977); Restatement (Second) of Torts § 927(1)(b) (1977).

All three damages measures have adherents. What are the advantages and disadvantages of each? Why did the court reject (a) the stock's value at the time of conversion? (b) its highest value between conversion and trial? (c) Would the New York measure have been superior? What led the court to approve the "procure and deliver" remedy?

2. *Recapture.* An owner may recover specific property, usually through replevin; in Louisiana, as we learned, recapture is a plaintiff's alternative remedy for defendant's conversion. Under some circumstances, however, a bona fide purchaser of a security from a converter will become the "owner" of it, precluding a prior "owner" from specific recovery. This had apparently not happened at the time of the trial in *Trahan.*

3. *Injunction.* (a) Plaintiff-owner can request a temporary restraining order or preliminary injunction to forbid defendant from transferring negotiable property. (b) A give-it-back injunction serves same purpose as replevin.

4. *Restitution.* The owner may also consider restitution, to base recovery on the defendant's unjust enrichment. Suppose the Bank had sold the TIPCO stock for $64.25 per share. When would any particular damages measure encourage plaintiff to seek restitution?

5. *Damages Equal Restitution?* If the converter sells the converted chattel, the court may measure the owner's damages by the amount the converter received from the buyer. Bruner Corp. v. R.A. Bruner Co., 133 F.3d 491, 498 (7th Cir.1998). If so, are the owner's damages equal to restitution?

B. CALCULATING DAMAGES

1. GENERAL DAMAGES: DIMINISHED VALUE v. COST TO REPAIR

HEWLETT v. BARGE BERTIE

United States Court of Appeals, Fourth Circuit, 1969.
418 F.2d 654, cert. denied, 397 U.S. 1021 (1970).

ALBERT V. BRYAN, CIRCUIT JUDGE. Computation of pecuniary damages recoverable for a [barge's] injury in a maritime collision centers this cause. The minim of the injury here, however, obscures and tempts neglect of the importance of the issue.

* * * [T]he respondents confessed negligence at trial and relied exclusively on absence of injury. The admiralty court only allowed the libelant "the sum of $1.00 by way of nominal damages" with costs. He appeals.

The basis of the decision was that as the [barge] BA–1401 had been declared a constructive loss two years before, the District Court was of the opinion that a subsequent injury could not sustain a claim. The declaration followed upon her misfortune on November 11, 1958, when she foundered in Chesapeake Bay. * * * Raised and refloated by the present libelant as contractor-salvor in June 1959, the repair and recovery cost of the barge was estimated to exceed both her 1958 purchase price of $40,000.00 and current insurance of $45,000.00. In these circumstances she was released to Hewlett in satisfaction of his claim for services. After $1305.76 was expended upon her in temporary repairs, such as leak stoppages, she was brought to Norfolk.

The barge was used or useable for carrying pilings or logs—weather-proof cargo. She was engaged on one occasion as a pontoon or caisson in lifting a steamer from the river bottom. * * *

Admittedly, the barge had no market value as an instrument of navigation and could be sold only for scrap. The skin of the barge was not pierced in the collision, and the only mark of impact was a dent in her starboard side. It produced no harmful effect upon the barge's seaworthiness or carrying capacity.

Our concern is the acceptance by the instance court of the respondent's defense to the damage claim, i.e. "the barge was a constructive total loss and that no real or actual damages have been shown, thus restricting the recovery to nominal damages." The decree on review purports to fix "nominal damages," but this is in reality a dismissal of the libel, for admiralty does not recognize nominal damages. * * * Presently the Court stated, "We find no precedent for allowing damages where a vessel, deemed a constructive total loss, suffers still further damage." Apparently, the award of $1.00 was the product of this proposition. It is, we think, an untenable postulate; if accepted, it could result in unjust deprivations.

Actually, the case does not commence with the barge as a constructive loss, as the admiralty judge believed. True, that was her status more than a year previous, but only as between the owner and the salvor. Even this, however, was not a decree of outlawry. She was not a derelict, to be jostled about with impunity. Indeed, as a sheer-hulk she had a demonstrated utility for the libelant. Slightly more than a year previous to repeat, $1305.76 had been expended in restoration. The accused tugboat and tow cannot escape liability by recall of the past ill luck of the BA–1401. Nor are they relieved by showing that she has not suffered in utility value or in market value.

To illustrate, although an automobile through age or misfortune may have no value in the market save for scrap, and although still another nick in its paint or shape may not appreciably reduce the usefulness or dollar-value of the car, nevertheless its checkered career and disreputable appearance do not assure absolution to one who negligently further scars the vehicle. The owner is entitled to have the automobile free of even that dent. De minimis non curat lex does not, semble, apply to damages but only to injury.

"Restitutio in integrum" is the precept in fixing damages, and "where repairs are practicable the general rule followed by the admiralty courts in such cases is that the damages assessed against the respondent shall be sufficient to restore the injured vessel to the condition in which she was at the time the collision occurred." The Baltimore, 8 Wall. 377, 75 U.S. 377, 385 (1869).

The workable guides to this end, generally stated, are these. If the ship sinks and is beyond recovery, the damages are her value just before she sank, plus interest thereon until payment. If she is not a complete loss and repossession or repairs are both physically and economically feasible, then the reasonable cost of recovery, including repairs and an allowance for deprivation of use, is the measure. But if the reclamation expense including repairs exceeds the ship's just value at the time of the casualty, or if repairs are not both physically and economically practicable, then it is a constructive total loss, and the limit of compensation is the value plus interest. * * *

The case at bar comes closer to the second category—the loss was not complete, repairs were physically practicable, but the question remains whether they were economically so. The answer depends on whether the repair cost was more than the value of the barge. Libelant has shown a fair estimate for the repairs to be between $2895.00 and $3000.00. If this expense was beyond the fair and reasonable monetary value of the vessel to the owner, then the recovery is limited to such value.

When, as here, the tortfeasors assert that the value is less than the cost of repairs, they have the burden to establish that fact. The respondents have failed to do so. Consequently, the case stands on the proof of the repair cost, and the libelant is entitled to a decree in that amount.

The District Court made no finding of value. It merely found that the BA–1401 had no value save for sale as scrap, but this is not the equivalent of fixing a figure of value. Moreover, it is erroneous. It is refuted by the other uncontested findings of her continuing utility.

Apparently, the chief factor influencing the District Judge in this determination was the absence of any market for the sale of the barge. That problem, however, cannot justify withholding all value from libelant's vessel. The special value to the owner is a consideration of substance. * * *

Even if the cost of repairs be limited to the *diminution* in value of the ship rather than to her entire value, our decision would for at least two reasons, not be different. The first point of our conclusion here is that no such values were proved. Beyond that, however, the second point is that in admiralty, the cost of repairs is the equivalent of value-diminution. "Damage less than total loss is compensated by reference to cost of repairs." Gilmore & Black, Admiralty 436; Pan–American Petroleum & Transport Co. v. United States, 27 F.2d 684, 685 (2 Cir.1928):

> "Strictly the measure of damages in collision is the difference in value between the ship before and after the collision, but the cost of the necessary repairs and the loss of earnings while they are being made have long been regarded as its equivalent."

Furthermore, the cost of repairs is considered an accurate measure. Diminution in value is always dependent upon an opinion, while repairs are not quite so speculative. * * *

The order on appeal will be vacated, and the cause remanded with request to the District Court to enter a decree awarding the appellant Hewlett damages of $2895.00, with interest at 6% per annum from the date of the collision until paid, together with costs in the trial and appellate courts.

Reversed and remanded for entry of judgment.

HAYNSWORTH, CHIEF JUDGE (dissenting): * * * The barge in her then condition had a market value of $5,616. This was her scrap value, but it was a ready market value, and it seems to me to be a mistake to approach the case as if there were no market value when everyone agrees there was.

Everyone agrees, too, that the market value of $5,616 was not affected in the slightest by the additional dent inflicted in her side when the Barge Bertie collided with her. The already battered Barge 1401 had a scrap value after the additional dent of $5,616, just as she had before.

* * * She was as useful as a pontoon after she sustained this dent as she was before, and whatever potential she had for use in carrying deck cargo was not impaired in the slightest.

Under these circumstances, of course, the owner did not attempt to effect the repair of the barge for the repairs were estimated to cost $2,895, and that expenditure would not enhance the value of the barge or its usefulness to the libelant, or to anyone else in the slightest. No one claims that any such repairs would ever be attempted. * * *

I think the damages are to be measured by the economic loss sustained by the libelant and that no different rule can be found in admiralty by looking at isolated statements lifted from their context.

[In] Williamson v. Barrett, 54 U.S. (13 How.) 101, 110, the Court stated what until today never seems to have been doubted: "The general rule in regulating damages in cases of collision is to allow the injured party an indemnity to the extent of the loss sustained." The loss sustained, of course, is the difference in the value of the vessel before and after the collision, together with a sum to compensate for the loss of her service during the completion of repairs, if she is reparable. The particular question in *Williamson* related to the latter assessment. When repairs are economically feasible, however, the assessment of the first item of damage may not depend upon generalized appraisals of the value of the vessel before and after the collision, for the difference in fact is measured by the cost of repair. This was clearly stated in The Schooner Catharine v. Dickinson, 58 U.S. (17 How.) 170. The Catharine sank as a result of a collision just off the New Jersey coast and her owners sold her where she lay for $140. They claimed the difference between the appraised value of the vessel before the collision and $140. The fact, however, was that the schooner had been raised, repaired and returned to service. The Supreme Court held that the actual cost of raising the vessel, repairing her and returning her to service was a more accurate measure of the diminution in value than could be gotten by use of the owner's sales price before she was raised or by the general opinions of inexpert witnesses that the vessel was worth no more than the owner's appraisal before she was refloated.

Since the Supreme Court's decision in *The Catharine* one frequently encounters the expression that the cost of repairs is the equivalent of the diminution in value. This is factually true whenever repairs are economically feasible, for whatever the appraisal of the vessel's value before the collision, all practical men know that the diminution in value is measured by the reasonable cost of necessary repairs to substantially return the vessel to its former condition. That is a more accurate measure of the diminution than a comparison of appraisals by some of the precollision value with general appraisals by others of the post-collision value, as was held in *The Catharine.* * * *

There is not factual equivalency between diminution in value and the cost of repair when the cost of repair is greater than the precollision value of the vessel. In such a case, the measure of damages is clearly the precollision value of the vessel. That this truism is sometimes expressed as a limitation upon the right to recover cost of repairs does not obscure the absence of factual equivalency between diminution in value and cost of repair and the irrelevance of the cost of repair in such a situation. Cost of repair is not the measure of damages simply because in that situation it is not the factual equivalent of diminution in value.

In this case there is no factual equivalency between diminution in value and cost of repair.

If my brothers are right, the libelant is unduly enriched. He must hope greatly that another errant navigator will hit his battered barge again, and still another yet again, so that each time he may happily pocket the estimated cost of theoretical repairs which neither he nor anyone else will ever dream of undertaking while retaining all along a barge as seaworthy and useful to him and of undiminished worth if he chooses to sell it.

Notes

1. *Diminished Value vs. Cost to Repair.* A court usually thinks of plaintiff's general damages as damages measured by market value; it usually requires a reason to depart from value measures. (Editor's Aside: In personal injury parlance, plaintiff's pain and suffering is "general damages," which is a different and confusing usage of the same words.)

A dominant general damages measure for plaintiff's property is its diminished value, or the market value before the loss less its market value after. Litigants usually prove the property's values through expert witnesses. What disadvantages of the diminution measure do the majority and the dissent mention?

An alternative damages measure is the cost to repair the property. If the estimated or actual repair costs exceed the property's pre-collision value, will damages measured by cost to repair overcompensate the owner? Do the majority's damages measures overcome that argument?

You may remember, from Contracts, Groves v. John Wunder or Peevyhouse v. Garland Coal and Mining Co., which deal with the choice between diminished value and cost to restore for breach of contract.

2. *Questions.* The opinion lists three damages measures. Which does the majority favor? Which does the dissent favor? In reaching their respective conclusions, which theories of value does each emphasize? Between the policies of compensation and deterrence, which does each stress?

ORNDORFF v. CHRISTIANA COMMUNITY BUILDERS

California Court of Appeal, 1990.
217 Cal.App.3d 683, 266 Cal.Rptr. 193.

BENKE, ACTING PRESIDING JUSTICE. Plaintiffs have lived in their home since 1977. They have no plans to leave it. Unfortunately their home was built on defectively compacted soil. * * *

The Orndorffs presented evidence that further settlement was likely and that, in light of future settlement, a pier or caisson and beam system was necessary to repair their house. The Orndorffs' expert estimated it would cost $221,792.68 to install such a system. In addition to the cost of repair, the Orndorffs presented evidence they would be required to incur $21,747 in additional engineering costs, permit fees and relocation expenses while the repairs were completed. * * *

[The trial judge] found the measure of damages for construction defects was either the diminution in value or the likely repair costs and that in this case an award of repair costs, plus relocation expenses, was appropriate. He found fill settlement was likely to continue and that a pier or caisson and grade system was the most efficient method of repair. Thus he awarded the Orndorffs the $243,539.95 needed to install a pier and grade system and pay the Orndorffs' relocation expenses while the repairs were performed. * * *

On appeal the defendants argue the measure of damages in construction defect cases is the lesser of the diminution in value caused by the defect or the cost of repair. Since the Orndorffs' appraiser testified their home was worth $67,500 without repair and would be worth $238,500 following repairs, the defendants claim the trial court had no power to award more than the $171,000 diminution in value established by the Orndorffs' appraiser.

In their reply brief the defendants also argue the trial court erred because it gave the Orndorffs an amount needed to repair the defect, rather than an amount needed to repair the damage caused by the defect.

We do not find the law as rigid as the defendants suggest. Where, as here, the plaintiffs have a personal reason to repair and the costs of repair are not unreasonable in light of the damage to the property and the value after repair, costs of repair which exceed the diminution in value may be awarded. (See Heninger v. Dunn (1980) 101 Cal.App.3d 858, 863–866, 162 Cal.Rptr. 104 (*Heninger*).) In *Heninger* the defendants bulldozed a road over the plaintiffs' land. The road damaged or killed 225 of plaintiffs' trees and destroyed much vegetative undergrowth. However because of improved access the trial court found the road actually increased the value of the land from $179,000 to $184,000. The trial court also found it would cost $221,647 to replace the dead or dying trees and that the undergrowth could be restored for $19,610. Because the value of the property had been increased, the trial court denied the plaintiffs any award of damages.

The Court of Appeal reversed and remanded. In rejecting the trial court's rigid approach to damage calculation, the Court of Appeal stated: "The rule precluding recovery of restoration costs in excess of diminution in value is, however, not of invariable application. Restoration costs may be awarded even though they exceed the decrease in market value if 'there is a reason personal to the owner for restoring the original condition' (Rest.2d Torts, § 929, com. b, at pp. 545–546), or 'where there is reason to believe that the plaintiff will, in fact, make the repairs' (22 Am.Jur.2d, Damages, § 132, at p. 192)." *Heninger.* * * *

In *Heninger* the court also discussed a number of cases from other jurisdictions which allowed similar recoveries in cases involving destruction of shade or ornamental trees which were of personal value to their owners. "Where such trees or shrubbery are destroyed by a trespasser, '[s]ound principle and persuasive authority support the allowance to an aggrieved landowner of the fair cost of restoring his land to a reasonable approximation of its former condition, without necessary limitation to the diminution in the market value of the land * * *.' [citations] If restoration of the land to a reasonable approximation of its former condition is impossible or impracticable, the landowner may recover the value of the trees or shrubbery, either as timber or for their aesthetic qualities, again without regard to the diminution in the value of the land. [citations] The overall principles by which the courts are to be guided are 'flexibility of approach and full compensation to the owner, within the overall limitation of reasonableness.' [citation]" Thus the Court of Appeal in *Heninger* held that "If the trial court determined that appellants had personal reasons for restoring their land to its original condition, and that such a restoration could be achieved at a cost that was not unreasonable in relation to the damage inflicted and the value of the land prior to the trespass, the court should have exercised its discretion to award such restoration costs."

Although the Court of Appeal in *Heninger* found that it would not be reasonable to award the plaintiffs the $221,647 needed to entirely restore the land, "On retrial, the court's determination whether a reasonable restoration is possible should focus on the question whether an award of the cost of restoring the vegetative undergrowth (or some other method of covering the scar on the land and preventing further erosion) would achieve compensation within the overall limits of what the court determines to be just and reasonable."

Here the "personal reason" exception adopted in *Heninger* supports the trial court's award. Contrary to the defendants' argument, the "personal reason" exception does not require that the Orndorffs own a "unique" home. Rather all that is required is some personal use by them and a bona fide desire to repair or restore. For instance in *Heninger* the court relied on the plaintiff's simple statement that " 'I think the land is beautiful, the natural forest beautiful, and I would like to see it that way.' " According to the commentators to the Restatement, "if a building such as homestead *is used for a purpose personal to the owner,* the damages ordinarily include an amount for repairs, even though this might be greater than the entire value of the building. So, when a garden has been maintained in a city in connection with a dwelling house, the owner is entitled to recover the expense of putting the garden in its original condition even though the market value of the premises has not been decreased by the defendant's invasion." (Rest.2d., Torts § 929, com. b, p. 546, italics added.) * * *

We also find untenable the defendants' argument that by allowing recovery in excess of diminution in value we will somehow distort the loss distribution goals which the doctrine of strict liability in tort was designed to foster. * * *

By requiring that repair costs bear a reasonable relationship to value before harm and to the level of harm actually suffered, the *Heninger* case prevents the unusual or bizarre results the defendants in this case contend would occur should we stray in any manner from a diminution in value measure of damages. Contrary to the defendants' argument, application of the personal reason exception does not permit a plaintiff to insist on reconstruction of a unique product where the cost of repair will far exceed either the value of the product or the damage the defendant has caused. As we interpret *Heninger,* the owner of a unique home or automobile cannot insist on its reconstruction where the cost to do so far exceeds the value of the home or automobile. Nor are repair costs appropriate where only slight damage has occurred and the cost of repair is far in excess of the loss in value.

 Here the damages awarded are well within the limitations imposed by *Heninger*. The record establishes that the Orndorffs' home was worth $238,500 in an undamaged condition. A total award—$243,539.95—which is 2.5 percent greater than the undamaged value of the realty, is in our view, well within reason.

However, it bears emphasis that even where the repair costs are reasonable in relation to the value of the property, those costs must also be reasonable in relation to the harm caused. Here the trial court's finding that fill settlement was likely to continue and the Orndorffs' appraiser's opinion the home was worth only $67,500 in its present condition, suggest the damage sustained was indeed significant. Plainly this is not a case where the tortfeasors' conduct improved the value of the real property or only diminished it slightly. Rather we believe where, as here, the damage to a home has deprived it of most of its value, an award of substantial repair costs is appropriate.

Without citation to any case which has articulated the distinction, the defendants argue the trial court had no power to award the amount needed to cure the defect as opposed to the amount needed to repair the damage caused by the defect. In particular defendants contend the damage the Orndorffs' house has suffered could be remedied by installation of the less expensive reinforced mat.

While there may be cases where repairing damage rather than curing a defect would be appropriate, this is not one of them. As we have seen the trial court found that further settlement is likely. The Orndorffs presented evidence that in light of future settlement the only way of preventing future damage was installation of the more costly pier and grade system. In giving the Orndorffs the amount needed to install such a system it is plain the trial court accepted the Orndorffs' evidence. Thus the record demonstrates the amount needed to repair all the damage caused by the defect is the amount needed to install a pier and grade system.

Judgment affirmed.

Notes

1. *How is Realty's Value Established?* Value is an opinion which litigants will prove through expert witnesses. Appraiser-experts take three approaches. (a) Cost to reproduce less depreciation. (b) Capitalization of net income. (c) Comparable sales.

When possible, an appraiser will use all three to estimate value, but sometimes only one or two are appropriate. There are no comparable sales for specialized or public property. An owner-occupied house lacks any income.

If the damaged building has a special purpose like a boys' club or a church and no active market exists, how should damages be measured? Replacement cost less depreciation was held to be the proper measure in Gramercy Boys' Club Association v. City of New York, 74 N.Y.2d 678, 543 N.Y.S.2d 372, 541 N.E.2d 401 (1989).

Where the court uses this measure, a test of reasonableness is imposed. Trinity Church v. John Hancock Mutual Life Insurance involved damage to Trinity Church, a national historical landmark, during the construction of the John Hancock Tower in Boston. "Not only must the cost of replacement or reconstruction be reasonable, the replacement or reconstruction itself must be reasonably necessary in light of the damage inflicted by a particular defendant." Trinity Church v. John Hancock Mutual Life Insurance Co., 399 Mass. 43, 50, 502 N.E.2d 532, 536 (1987).

2. *Estimates May Vary.* Judicial and administrative findings of value occur for tax assessment and eminent domain as well as to set damages. T.W. Van Zelst, a taxpayer who had donated 93 acres of rugged Alaska land to the National Park Service, followed the government's press release praising his public spiritedness with a tax deduction of $2,750,000. Because of the size of his deduction, the tax benefits "vastly exceeded the purchase price of $30,000." Van Zelst's deduction was disallowed, and a trial was conducted in Tax Court "to fix the fair market value of the property on the date of donation." Van Zelst's appraiser's opinion was based on a value of $650,000 for mining, the balance "was attributable to the potential for a resort lodge." The Commissioner's witnesses' opinions were (a) a mine operation would have to spend "$99 per ton to extract ore worth $70 per ton" and (b) a resort was unlikely because, among other things, the land was on the north side of a mountain and received no direct sunlight in the summer. The court of appeals approved a value of $38,000. Van Zelst v. C.I.R., 100 F.3d 1259, 1260–61 (7th Cir.1996).

3. *Property with Rosy Perpetual Prospects.* Suppose that the evidence shows condemned property is used for a cemetery which has a potential 155,900 gravesites. Based on the projected rate of sales, the cemetery has an estimated "life" of 760 years. Should the appraised value of the land for cemetery purposes of between $817,000 to $3 million be accepted? The court found these appraisals speculative and ordered compensation determined on the basis of the "highest and best use for other

than cemetery purposes." Department of Transportation v. James Co., 183 Ga.App. 798, 802, 360 S.E.2d 56, 59 (1987).

4. *Business Assets' Value in Bankruptcy.* When the Rashes filed for Chapter 13 bankruptcy, they proposed to keep a mortgaged truck and to repay the truck's "value" over time. The secured creditor objected to the reduction in its secured debt. Under the Bankruptcy Code § 506(a), the value of a secured claim is "the value of such creditor's interest in the estate's interest in" the truck; moreover "value shall be determined in light of the purpose of the valuation and of the proposed disposition or use of such property."

Several possible "values" spring to mind. The Rashes planned to use the truck to generate business income; and the present value of the stream of income is one possible "value." Another is the amount the secured creditor would obtain through foreclosure, probably close to "wholesale." A third is what it would cost the Rashes to replace the truck, likely closer to "retail."

The Supreme Court favored replacement cost because, in light of "the purpose of the valuation," it best measured what it would cost the Rashes to obtain a similar vehicle. The Court mentioned, as another reason to favor the creditor, the risk that the debtor might default.

Aren't both the foreclosure sale and the replacement purchase hypothetical transactions which did not and will not occur? Isn't "the purpose of the valuation" to obtain the income stream for Rashes' going business? Could the court adjust the interest rate in light of the risk of a debtor's default? Associates Commercial Corp. v. Rash, 520 U.S. 953 (1997).

5. *Post-Repair Diminished–Value Syndrome.* Repairs may not return an owner's property to its pre-accident value.

(a) *Damages Rule.* The Iowa court's damages rules for automobiles are "(1) When the motor vehicle is totally destroyed or the reasonable cost of repair exceeds the difference in reasonable market value before and after the injury, the measure of damages is the lost market value plus the reasonable value of the use of the vehicle for the time reasonably required to obtain a replacement. (2) When the injury to the motor vehicle can be repaired so that, when repaired, it will be in as good condition as it was in before the injury, and the cost of repair does not exceed the difference in market value of the vehicle before and after the injury, then the measure of damages is the reasonable cost of repair plus the reasonable value of the use of the vehicle for the time reasonably required to complete its repair. (3) When the motor vehicle cannot by repair be placed in as good condition as it was in before the injury, then the measure of damages is the difference between its reasonable market value before and after the injury, plus the reasonable value of the use of the vehicle for the time reasonably required to repair or replace it. * * *"

"The trial court applied the second standard and used as the measure of damages the reasonable cost of repair of Papenheim's vehicle. The trial court reasoned as follows. The value of Papenheim's vehicle before the accident was $22,000. The value after the accident was $11,000, a difference of $11,000. Since the cost of repairs was $4,666.63, a figure less than the $11,000 difference, the proper rule to apply * * * was the second standard. Papenheim asserts that the trial court erred in using the second standard since substantial evidence does not support the court's determination that Papenheim's vehicle could by repair be placed in as good condition as it was in before the accident. Papenheim argues that the court should have used the third standard and awarded him the difference between the market value of the vehicle before the injury and after. Based on the [expert witness's] proof offered by Pappenheim in this case, we agree that the third standard should have been applied. * * * If repairing the vehicle does not return the car to its pre-accident condition as measured by its market value, then the owner is not compensated for the detriment caused if only awarded cost of repairs." Papenheim v. Lovell, 530 N.W.2d 668, 671–72 (Iowa 1995).

(b) *Owner's First–Party Insurance Coverage. Pappenheim*, above, was a plaintiff's lawsuit against a tortfeasor; the court decided it under the state's damages rules. What about a car owner's recovery against her own insurance carrier? The policy's language comes into play.

In a plaintiff class action of Georgia State Farm insureds with physical damages claims against State Farm, the Georgia Supreme Court approved cost of repairs plus lost value. State Farm Mutual Automobile Insurance Co. v. Mabry, 274 Ga. 498, 556 S.E.2d 114, 120–24 (2001). After the final settlement of $100 million, the state's Insurance Commissioner ordered all insurance carriers to pay diminished value. The National Law Journal, January 14, 2002, at B1.

The first-party coverage decisions are split. Construing the policy language to cover only an insured's repair cost to bring the vehicle to its pre-collision physical condition are, among others, the courts of Texas and South Dakota. American Manufacturers Mutual Insurance Co. v. Schaefer, 124 S.W.3d 154 (Tex. 2003); Culhane v. Western National Mutual Insurance Company, 704 N.W.2d 287 (S.D. 2005).

6. *Who Decides?* Maryland decisions permit an owner to recover cost to restore unless it is "disproportionate" to diminution in value; moreover, even if cost to restore is disproportionate to diminished value, an owner with a personal reason to restore the property to its pre-injury condition may recover restoration costs. Whether restoration damages are disproportionate to diminution is a jury question, as is, apparently, whether, even if cost to restore is disproportionate, the owner's personal reason to restore the property nevertheless qualifies for restoration damages. After the jury's findings, the owner "elects" between diminution and restoration and the judge determines whether, as a matter of law, restoration is disproportionate to diminution. Lexington Insurance Co. v. Baltimore Gas and Electric Co., 979 F.Supp. 360 (D.Md.1997).

7. *Public Environmental Law: Natural Resources Damages.* The common law which we have been studying evaluates damages to land from the owner's viewpoint, not from the public's. The common law's perspective is further narrowed by the "economic" arguments against requiring a tortfeasor to pay more damages to fix something than it was "worth" to the owner to sell to someone else. Common law courts ignore the land's "value" to the public and its intangible attributes as a resource, not an economic tool.

Different concepts of "value" are required when a natural resource, like wildlife, fish, water, air, groundwater, or undeveloped land is injured. What follows was intentionally written without technicality and with a minimum of citations; scholarly works bristling with technicality and loaded with footnotes are cited at the end for the interested reader to pursue.

First the parties who injure a natural resource may be charged with "response costs," the expense of efforts to contain and clean up immediately afterwards. This Chapter ends by examining the "nature" of response costs; but for now environmental response costs resemble common law cost-to-restore damages.

Environmental statutes allow government authorities as "public trustees" to recover beyond response costs for "natural resources damages" on the public's behalf. At first courts limited the successful public trustee to an injunction, observing that damages were inappropriate. Hawaii v. Standard Oil Co., 405 U.S. 251, 264–66 (1972); Georgia v. Pennsylvania Railroad, 324 U.S. 439, 453 (1945).

As the environmental movement gained momentum, it demanded a more activist judicial response than "Just say no." And it sought an answer to completed harm. One way to respond is with an injunction telling the wrongdoer to "Fix it up." Damages are another way.

As legislatures and courts began to recognize public trustees' right to recover damages, the difference in measurement between market value diminution and cost to restore became apparent. Diminution damages do not compensate for the public's loss, because, one court said, often "unspoiled natural areas of considerable ecological value have little of no commercial or market value." Puerto Rico v. SS Zoe Colocotroni, 628 F.2d 652, 673 (1st Cir.1980). Another important decision observed "natural resources have values that are not fully captured by the market system." Ohio v. United States Department of Interior, 880 F.2d 432, 462–63 (D.C.Cir.1989). So natural resources damages measurement shifted from market value to the cost of restoration.

Natural resources damages start where response costs leave off: they are money to compensate "for injury to, destruction of, or loss of natural resources," which were uncompensated by response costs. The preferred measure for natural resources damages is the cost to restore.

The next distinction to work out is the one between cost to restore and lost use. Lost use in natural resources damages is based on the way people use the resources; they harvest or consume resources through hunting and fishing; they may also use resources without "harvesting" them for example, by hiking and birdwatching.

Cost to restore is not capped by lost use. The federal government's original regulations had said natural resources damages are the lesser of, (a) cost to restore or replace, or (b) diminished use value. Lost or diminished use was, it appeared, almost always less than cost to restore. When the court struck these regulations down, it thought the statute expressed Congress's preference for cost to restore.

At some magnitude, cost to restore damages could become astronomical—too high to contemplate in a practical world—so the court developed an imprecise cutoff: If the cost to restore is "grossly disproportionate," then the damages may be measured by "lost use." Ohio v. United States Department of Interior, 880 F.2d 432 (D.C.Cir.1989). At present the transition from measuring by cost to restore to measurement by lost use remains murky and controversial.

Another difficult distinction is between natural resources injury associated with lost use and injury associated with "nonuse values." Nonuse values of natural resources are the attributes of a resource people value, but which are not the features they use.

There are four ways to articulate separate natural resources' nonuse values: option value, existence value, bequest value, and quasi-option value. The natural resource's option value is what it is worth to people to retain the "option" to use it in the future. Its existence value is the value to people of the knowledge that a particular resource is protected. The bequest value is what it is worth to people to know that a natural resource will be preserved and available to future generations. Quasi-option value is what a natural resource is worth to people because of the opportunity in the future to use it in ways not currently known, for example for an undiscovered medicine.

Measuring natural resources' nonuse values is even more arduous than stating they exist. Loss of nonuse values does not occur in money, but a human agent must convert the nonpecuniary destruction into dollars. This conversion has a subjective quality which depends on the decisionmaker and which means the final sum will be impossible to predict in advance. Quasi-option values, in particular, cannot be quantified in the present because they are based on future benefits which are by definition both unknown and unknowable. Implicit in each calculation of nonuse value is a potential for a large total amount.

Many favor contingency valuation methods to measure natural resources' nonuse values. Contingency valuation is a survey method to derive a dollar figure which reflects a public sense of harm when, for example, a species is destroyed or threatened or when human access or enjoyment is prevented by pollution. The goal is to learn the amount members of the public are willing to pay to preserve the natural resource. Social scientists develop questionnaires, administer them to a sample of the public, evaluate the answers, and use the answers to estimate the resources' value. Each member of the sample is asked what he or she would be willing to pay to preserve a particular resource. Alternatively the respondents are asked what amount they would be willing to accept in return for allowing the resource to disappear. These measurement techniques are often called WTP and WTA.

Critics of contingency valuation of nonuse values make several points. It is hypothetical; it does not ask people to commit any resources. The respondents do not state true willingness to pay; instead they play with Monopoly money. Moreover WTP and WTA vary, for it turns out that people are willing to pay less than they are willing to accept.

Defenders of contingency valuation of nonuse values reply to their critics as follows. Economists agree that contingency valuation can be accurate to estimate nonuse values. Alternatives to contingency valuation are inadequate because they are based on a market inferred where no market exists. Much of the criticism is based on flaws in specific study designs not on contingency valuation methodology as a whole. In economic theory, people want more to sell something they have than they were willing to pay for it in the first place; so although WTA is theoretically best, WTP can be used to be conservative.

Inexactness has never been fatal to damages calculation, proponents of contingency valuation point out. Future damages are inherently imprecise. Translating a plaintiff's nonpecuniary injuries like pain and suffering and emotional distress into dollars is always inexact; but the civil justice system submits both to properly instructed lay jurors. If the nonuse values of natural resources are significant, they can be appraised through a similar process, contingency valuation techniques.

Contingency valuation of nonuse losses may serve two functions in natural resources damages. (a) It may compliment restoration by measuring compensation for interim loss of to-be-restored resources. (b) Where "grossly disproportionate" restoration is too much, contingency valuation may measure compensation for lost resources. A public trustee may recover nonuse values through either (a) restoration plus compensation for interim nonuse losses; or (b) after a finding that cost to restore will be inappropriate, a trustee may recover monetary damages for lost use and nonuse values measured by contingency valuation.

While there is not much of what we think of as "hard law," natural resources damages are indeed real. At least Exxon thinks so, for after the Exxon Valdez oil spill, Exxon Corp. agreed to pay the United States and Alaska $900,000,000 to compensate for injury to the Prince William Sound's natural resources. United States v. Exxon, Inc., No. A91–082–CIV (D.Alaska 1991). Hundreds of other claims for natural resources damages have been asserted in different cases.

Questions: Should our analysis of natural resources damages start with the premise that the environment is worth more than its market value? Are the four headings of nonuse values helpful analytical concepts? Should legislatures de-empha-size amorphous civil damages concepts like nonuse values and rely more on criminal sanctions? Would multiplying restoration costs by two or three advance the deter-rence and compensation goals better than, or as well as, recovery for nonuse values? Does recovery of damages for both lost use and for nonuse values better compensate actual social injury and better deter potential future social losses? Are attempts to quantify nonuse values based on the assumption that the environment is market-able? If nonuse values are to be recognized, is measurement by contingency valuation technique an acceptable substitute for damages set by a civil jury following adversary procedure and testimony from expert witnesses?

Citations: Peter Manus, Natural Resources Damages from Rachel Carson's Perspective: A Rite of Spring in American Environmentalism, 37 Wm. & Mary L.Rev. 381 (1996); Judith Robinson, The Role of Nonuse Values in Natural Resource Damages: Past, Present, and Future, 75 Tex.L.Rev. 189 (1996); James Seevers, Jr., NOAA's New Natural Resource Damage Assessment Scheme: It's Not About Collect-ing Money, 53 Wash. & Lee L.Rev. 1513 (1996).

8. *Plaintiff's Practical Choices*. Even though the liability thresholds in federal environmental statutes are low, a plaintiff may choose, for remedial reasons, to file a common-law action with or instead of suing under environmental statutes. The common law substantive theories are contractual and tortious, the torts include strict liability for ultrahazardous activities, negligence, trespass, nuisance, and waste. Some of the plaintiff's remedial calculations are:

(a) There is no private action to recover response costs for cleaning up toxic waste under the Resource Conservation and Recovery Act; the statute allows only injunctive relief to forbid defendant's future violations or to order cleanup and disposal. Meghrig v. KFC Western, Inc., 516 U.S. 479 (1996).

(b) The plaintiff in *Meghrig* may have sued under the RCRA because the major federal cleanup statute, Comprehensive Environmental Response, Compensation, and Liability Act, CERCLA, excludes from its coverage pollution from petroleum. 42 U.S.C. § 9601(14). This exclusion shunts many pollution lawsuits into state and common law channels.

(c) Private recovery under CERCLA is for response costs, typically cleanup cost. 42 U.S.C. § 9607(a). CERCLA does not measure private recovery by diminished value or the full cost to restore; claimant cannot seek personal injury damages, "stigma" damages, special damages, or punitive damages. Thus a plaintiff may spurn CERCLA's broadened liability principles for larger common law tort recovery.

(d) Some state courts let an owner recover cleanup damages that exceed dimin-ished value. Permitting the owner's recovery of the cost to restore, one court emphasized the owner-plaintiff's potential responsibility under environmental stat-utes to restore the land. Nischke v. Farmers & Merchants Bank & Trust, 187 Wis.2d 96, 118, 522 N.W.2d 542, 551 (App.1994).

(e) Recovery under state statutes and common law decisions may, however, fall short of plaintiff's expectations. The Oklahoma court limited plaintiff's recovery of damages measured by cost to repair, estimated $1,300,000, to diminished value, an estimated $5175. Schneberger v. Apache Corp., 890 P.2d 847 (Okla.1994). The court followed its earlier decision, Peevyhouse v. Garland Coal and Mining Co., 382 P.2d 109 (Ok.1962). Should the Oklahoma court have considered whether plaintiff was potentially on the hook for $1,300,000 response costs under the environmental statutes?

9. *Stigma Damages*? A landowner argues that the public perceives an adverse effect or stigma from past or present contamination which—standing alone—has

diminished the land's value. The public fear of contamination lingers even after the contamination ends, and this stigma reduces market value. The owner seeks to recover damages for the diminution in value of land caused by the public's adverse perception. Courts' responses vary.

(a) *Yes.* The plaintiff's tract lost value because it was close to defendant's hazardous waste site which was contaminated by PCB. Plaintiffs, the court said, may recover for diminished value without showing permanent, physical damage to the land if: (i) defendants caused temporary physical damage; (ii) plaintiff proves that repairing this damage will not restore the value of the land; and (iii) plaintiff proves an ongoing risk to the land. In re Paoli Railroad Yard PCB Litigation, 35 F.3d 717, 796–98 (3d Cir.1994), cert. denied, 513 U.S. 1190 (1995). Following *Paoli* is Bradley v. Armstrong Rubber Co., 130 F.3d 168, 174–76 (5th Cir.1997).

(b) *No.* Declining to find stigma damage, another court ruled that third persons' unfounded fears of neighboring land being contaminated is not a private nuisance. Adkins v. Thomas Solvent Co., 440 Mich. 293, 311–14, 487 N.W.2d 715, 724–25 (1992). See also Adams v. Star Enterprise, 51 F.3d 417 (4th Cir.1995).

(c) *Maybe.* Another court declined stigma damages unless defendant actually encroached on plaintiff's land. Berry v. Armstrong Rubber Co., 989 F.2d 822 (5th Cir.1993), cert. denied, 510 U.S. 1117 (1994).

(d) *Sometimes.* Although North Carolina bars stigma damages for temporary or abatable nuisances, if the nuisance is permanent, stigma is one of the factors which bear on value in calculating plaintiff's diminution damages. Rudd v. Electrolux Corp., 982 F.Supp. 355, 372 (M.D.N.C.1997).

(e) *Stigma Damage in Condemnation.* One court allowed the owner of property being condemned to introduce evidence showing that the utility's use of the condemned land for overhead transmission wires would lower the market value of the owner's remaining land because of the public's "irrational fear" of electromagnetic radiation from the wires. San Diego Gas & Electric Co. v. Daley, 205 Cal.App.3d 1334, 253 Cal.Rptr. 144 (1988).

2. LOST USE

KUWAIT AIRWAYS CORP. v. OGDEN ALLIED AVIATION SERVICES

United States District Court, Eastern District of New York, 1989.
726 F.Supp. 1389.

DEARIE, DISTRICT JUDGE. This case arises out of a fender bender between two rather extraordinary fenders: one attached to a truck of the type used to hoist meals onto aircraft, the other on a Boeing 747. * * *

On May 29, 1984, a Boeing 747 aircraft owned and operated by plaintiff was, while parked at John F. Kennedy International Airport, struck by a truck owned and operated by defendant. Defendant has admitted liability for the accident and stipulated to the amount of damages for actual costs of repairing plaintiff's aircraft and accommodating plaintiff's passengers who were inconvenienced by the accident. The only dispute remaining between the parties is whether plaintiff is entitled to any damages for temporary loss of use of the aircraft and, if so, what the measure of those damages should be.

There is no question that the damaged aircraft was out of service for several days while repairs were being made. Plaintiff argues that this fact, coupled with defendant's admission of liability, entitles plaintiff to an award of damages for loss of use of the aircraft. Plaintiff moves for partial summary judgment establishing that the measure of its loss of use damages is the reasonable rental value of a replacement 747 for the time during which plaintiff's 747 was out of service.

Plaintiff concedes, however, that it did not actually rent a replacement 747. In fact, it appears that plaintiff was able to service all of the grounded plane's flights by using an A300 Airbus that was in plaintiff's fleet and was not otherwise engaged. Defendant submits evidence that, because no flights were cancelled and the Airbus had sufficient capacity to seat all passengers who would have flown on the grounded 747, plaintiff suffered no lost profits—and may indeed have benefitted financially—as a result of the 747's grounding. Absent an actual pecuniary loss resulting from the accident, defendant contends, there can be no recovery of damages for loss of use of the jumbo jet.

The present motion thus requires the Court to decide whether proof of actual pecuniary loss is required in order to recover for loss of use of a damaged chattel, and whether the reasonable cost of securing a replacement for the damaged chattel may be recovered even if no substitute is actually rented.[1] There are undoubtedly disputed, material issues of fact regarding the *amount* of loss of use damages suffered by plaintiff in this case—for example, the number of days the plane was out of service, the appropriate rental fee, and the relative net operating profit of the Airbus as compared to that of the 747. However, the appropriate *measure* of those damages—in effect, the decision whether the rental fee and operating profit are even relevant to determining damages in the factual context of this case—is purely a question of law that is appropriately addressed on a motion for summary judgment. * * *

Given this state of authority, the positions taken by the parties in the case at bar are unsurprising. Plaintiff contends that *Storms* and *K.L.M.* [Mountain View Coach Lines, Inc. v. Storms, 102 A.D.2d 663, 476 N.Y.S.2d 918 (1984); Koninklijke Luchtvaart Maatschaapij, N.V. (K.L.M. Royal Dutch Airlines) v. United Technologies Corp., 610 F.2d 1052 (2d Cir.1979)] correctly state New York law, and that it may therefore recover, as a matter of law, "the reasonable rental value of a substitute aircraft," even if plaintiff submits no proof of actual pecuniary loss, or indeed even in the face of evidence tending to negate the proposition that plaintiff suffered actual pecuniary loss. Defendant, predictably, counters that plaintiff is not entitled to summary judgment of entitlement to loss of use damages, because defendant has offered proof that at least raises a material issue of fact as to whether the collision caused plaintiff any loss of profits. Defendant argues that its showing either entirely precludes loss of use damages, or, at least, shifts the burden to the plaintiff to prove actual, rather than presumed, financial damages arising from the loss of use of the 747. Defendant relies on *CTI, Hartnett* and *Gehr* [CTI International, Inc. v. Lloyds Underwriters, 735 F.2d 679 (2d Cir.1984); Mountain View Coach Lines, Inc. v. Hartnett, 99 Misc.2d 271, 415 N.Y.S.2d 918 (1978), leave to appeal denied, 47 N.Y.2d 710, 419 N.Y.S.2d 1026 (1979); Mountain View Coach Lines, Inc. v. Gehr,

---

1. These two questions, although closely linked, are not necessarily one and the same. If a substitute is rented to replace a damaged chattel, the rental fee represents the total pecuniary effect of loss of use *only* if the net operating profit (or loss) of the substitute is identical to that of the original. Were the substitute more (or less) profitable to operate than the original, the actual pecuniary damage attributable to loss of use of the original chattel would be smaller (or larger) than the rental fee.

80 A.D.2d 949, 439 N.Y.S.2d 632 (1981)] as accurate statements of New York law.[2]

Sitting in diversity and bound to apply New York law, this Court must choose—in the absence of an applicable decision of the New York Court of Appeals—between directly conflicting doctrines followed by different Departments of this State's intermediate appellate court. * * *

This Court is convinced that the New York Court of Appeals, were it called upon to decide the issue, would adopt the *KLM–Storms* approach and reject *Gehr–Hartnett–CTI*. The approach of *Storms* and *KLM* represents sounder reasoning than the contrary decisions and are more consistent with settled principles of tort doctrine and, as discussed in *KLM*, with earlier, somewhat analogous cases.

As Judge Gurfein observed in *KLM*, loss of use damages exist to compensate for the deprivation of the owner's right to use its chattel as the owner sees fit. This right has a value, and its deprivation necessarily entails what economists call "opportunity cost." *Any* particular allocation of a resource necessarily costs the owner the opportunity to put that resource to other, competing uses. When a tortfeasor by its negligence forces a thing's owner to allocate that chattel to the singularly unsatisfying use of sitting in a repair shop for a while, that tortfeasor forecloses the owner's opportunity to put the chattel to some productive use.

The opportunity cost exists irrespective of the normal use to which the owner allocates the damaged item. For example, in the case of a vehicle that is used only for pleasure—say, a privately owned, high-powered sports car—the loss of the car's use deprives the owner of the opportunity to drive the car for pleasure during the repair period. Again invoking the economist's language, one could say that the owner has lost "utility." The value of that utility is measurable by the amount the owner is willing or required to spend to obtain it. There is no controversy, as a matter of tort doctrine, that the sports car owner so deprived is entitled to replace the lost utility directly, by renting an equivalent automobile and recovering the rental cost from the tortfeasor. No sound reason exists for denying that same recovery for the value of lost utility even if the owner does not rent a substitute car.

The result is no different in the case of a driver who owns a second, identical sports car that is kept in reserve for just such contingencies. The reserve sports car might enable the owner to do the same amount of pleasure driving after the tort as before, but the tort still carries with it an opportunity cost. The owner has lost the opportunity to lend the second sports car to a friend, or to keep one car brand-new while using the other, or simply to drive home in one car while smugly knowing that there is another in the garage. This lost opportunity also has a compensable value.

Shifting from a pleasure vehicle, maintained only to enhance its owner's utility, to a commercial vehicle that is maintained to provide a return on investment, has no effect whatever on the analysis.[3] To an airline, ownership of

<hr>

2. Defendant attempts to distinguish *Storms* based on that opinion's statement that "the parties stipulated * * * that the damages sustained for loss of use were $3,000," whereas in this case, defendant denies that *any* loss of use damages were in fact sustained. As explained [below] this distinction is illusory.

3. The sharp distinction between pleasure and profit-making vehicles is somewhat artificial. A classic sports car may be a valuable investment as well as being fun to drive. And the decision to use the car only for pleasure in fact represents a resource allocation that carries its own opportunity cost. By giving up some hours

a 747 represents a bundle of valuable opportunities. Those opportunities range from the chance to use the plane to entertain the board of directors and important shareholders, through flying the plane on regularly-scheduled routes, through leasing it to another airline, through holding it in reserve for use as a replacement in case another aircraft must be taken out of service. Those opportunities are all temporarily lost when a tortfeasor renders the aircraft unserviceable for a period of time. That opportunity cost *cannot* be valueless; it *must* be worth something. The difficulty sometimes encountered, of course, is choosing the appropriate method by which to measure that value.

In some cases, the best way to approximate that value will be perfectly obvious. If a replacement plane were actually rented, the rental fee would be an appropriate choice. Or, if, as was the case in *KLM*, the damaged plane were itself leased rather than owned by the victim of the tort, the prorated portion of the lease payments would approximate the value of the use of the plane for the time during which it was out of service.

The foregoing examples are the easy ones, because the proxy used to measure the airline's opportunity cost is in each case an actual out-of-pocket sum spent by the airline. Almost as easy is the case in which an airline, having no substitute plane available and choosing not to rent one, cancels the damaged airliner's flights. In such a case, the ready measure of the airline's loss would be the lost revenue from the cancelled flights, less operating costs saved by not flying.

Suppose, however, that an airline with no spare planes did not cancel any flights but instead met its schedules by stretching its regular fleet (minus the damaged plane) just enough to cover its needs. This is the *Brooklyn Terminal* case, and here the actual measure of damages is still more difficult to prove. Yet even in this case, the damages still exist. As Justice Cardozo pointed out, had the tugboat operator in *Brooklyn Terminal* been able to document overtime wages or "extra wear and tear" on the undamaged tugs, those damages would have been recoverable.

Finally, consider the case in which an airline maintains one or more airplanes that are normally held in reserve. When a front-line plane is damaged, the airline presses the reserves into service. As Justice Cardozo observed, that "result is all one" whether the replacement plane is rented from a lessor or moved from reserve status into active duty. The "spare boat doctrine" reasoning was adopted by *Storms*.

The concept of opportunity cost makes it easy to see how the airline using a spare plane suffers a genuine loss even though it does not spend money to rent an aircraft. Any prudent airline that is obligated to fly, say, 100 planes to meet its daily schedule, will own more than 100 airliners in recognition of the actuarial inevitability that some planes will be out of service on some days. The airline might determine, for example, that to be reasonably secure from the risk of flight cancellation, it would need to own 110 planes to cover a 100–plane daily need. The need for a 10–plane reserve arises from several sources: lost service days for regular inspection and maintenance, unforeseen breakdowns, accidents caused by the airline's own carelessness—*and* accidents caused by the negligence of others. If an airline could be certain that its planes would never be damaged

of pleasure driving, and therefore some utility,
the owner might be able to make money renting
the car for hour-long joyrides.

by the fault of tortfeasors, it would be able to get by with a smaller reserve fleet. As a practical matter, it is probably impossible to know whether one, two, or more of the spare planes must be maintained solely as insurance against negligence of others. But it is possible, after a particular accident has occurred, and the airline has utilized a particular spare airplane, to estimate the lifetime cost of owning and maintaining that spare airplane. It is also possible to calculate the percentage of the spare plane's lifetime represented by the number of days the accident causes the airline to use the spare plane. That percentage, multiplied by the lifetime cost of the plane, represents the fraction of the airline's reserve fleet costs that are directly attributable to a particular tortfeasor, and approximates the economic injury to the airline that results from loss of use of the damaged front-line plane.[4]

Tort doctrine requires full compensation for tortiously-inflicted damage. The position taken by defendant in this lawsuit would restrict parties in the position of the plaintiff in this case (and in *Gehr, Harnett,* and *Storms*) to recovery of out-of-pocket payments made to replace a damaged vehicle, or to profits lost as a result of trip cancellations. As the discussion *supra* reveals, however, a real economic loss may be incurred, and approximately measured, even in the absence of apparent pecuniary losses. Thus the doctrine of *Storms* is sound, and this Court predicts that the New York Court of Appeals, were it to decide the question, would hold that damages for loss of use of a vehicle may be recovered even absent a showing that profitable vehicle trips were cancelled or that a substitute vehicle was rented.

The story, however, cannot quite end there, because the conclusion just reached does not imply that the plaintiff is entitled to the partial summary judgment. Quite the contrary is the case.

The Court agrees with plaintiff that loss of use damages *may* be proven and recovered even though no substitute plane was actually rented. The plaintiff asks for more, however, than a determination that it is entitled to recover loss of use damages. Plaintiff also seeks a ruling "that these damages are to be measured by the reasonable rental value of a substitute aircraft." To this second requested ruling plaintiff is not entitled.

In *Storms,* the Appellate Division directed entry of judgment in the plaintiff's favor for $3,200, the stipulated rental value of a replacement for the damaged bus. Because the parties had stipulated how the loss of use damages were to be measured if recovery for loss of use were allowed, the *Storms* court had no need to consider the method of measuring damages; the Court had only to determine that the plaintiff's failure to rent a substitute bus did not bar recovery of the stipulated damages.

The present case is quite different. It is undisputed that there is no market for rental of Boeing 747's to commercial passenger airlines for six-day periods. The "reasonable rental cost" urged by plaintiff as a measure of damages is apparently the output of an economic model devised by plaintiff or by plaintiff's retained expert. The evidence presented by defendant on this motion is sufficient

4. There might be other costs as well—for example, the incremental depreciation of the spare plane that results from its being flown instead of standing idle, or profits lost from a charter that had to be foregone because the spare plane was needed to fly scheduled routes— but they are not of analytical importance. The point is not to show that prorated lifetime cost of the spare is an exclusive measure of loss of use damages in a case such as this, but rather to demonstrate that such damages exist even absent out-of-pocket expense. For the same reason, this section does not consider the possible offsetting economic benefits to the airline.

to raise a material issue of fact as to the reliability and suitability of plaintiff's analysis. Defendant is entitled to attempt to prove at trial that the "reasonable rental cost" proffered by plaintiff is nothing more than speculation and as such insufficient to support a recovery. See *Brooklyn Terminal.*

While it is appropriate at this time for the Court to determine that plaintiff may recover a reasonable measure of loss of use damages, it would be premature for the Court to hold that any particular measure of damages is the one to be applied.[5]

Finally, defendant in this case has also raised a material issue of fact as to the effect that using the Airbus had on the profitability of the route the Airbus flew in the damaged 747's stead. Defendant is wrong when it argues that if the Airbus' lower operating costs resulted in higher profits, plaintiff *necessarily* suffered no loss of use damages. However, under settled principles of tort law in New York and elsewhere, increased operating profits could partially or entirely offset the damages for loss of use (no matter how loss of use damages are calculated).[6] "Damages are to restore injured parties, not to reward them." *Hartnett.* Even if this Court agreed with plaintiff that "reasonable replacement rental value" represented the appropriate gross measure of loss of use damages, the Court could not grant the requested summary judgment in the face of a material issue of fact directly affecting the net amount of such recovery. Plaintiff is entitled to a reasonable measure of loss of use damages even absent any out-of-pocket expenditures, but those damages must be reduced to the extent, if any, that they were recouped by operating efficiencies that are proven to have resulted from the accident.[7]

5. Reasonable replacement rental cost might turn out to be the best available estimation, but other approximations are possible. The prorated lifetime cost of the spare plane, is a conceivable alternative measure, and there are doubtless others.

6. This conclusion is not inconsistent with the analysis [above. It] implicitly assumed that all the planes in the airline's primary and reserve fleets were absolutely interchangeable. In the real world, fungibility would be the exception rather than the rule. For instance, one might normally expect a reserve fleet to be populated with older, relatively inefficient aircraft. The extra fuel costs resulting from use of the older plane would then be *added* to the loss of use damages as measured by rental value or other method. Similarly, because an Airbus is smaller than a 747, in times of peak demand the use of an Airbus would likely reduce flight revenues and hence profits. The lost profits would be added to the loss of use damages. These additions make perfect sense: had the airline actually needed to rent a replacement plane, that turned out to be less profitable to fly, the damages would clearly include both the rental fee and the lost profits. So with the use of a spare plane. But with the good plaintiff must take the bad: if the replacement plane turns out to be more profitable to use than the damaged plane, the increased profits must be subtracted from the recovery.

7. In *KLM,* the Second Circuit noted that "saved operating costs and depreciation are nor-

mally deducted from rental value to arrive at damages for loss of use of an automobile" in cases where no replacement car was actually rented. The theory behind this rule is quite simple: the owner who chooses to do without the car for a time does lose all the benefits of driving it, but he also avoids the costs of filling it with gasoline, wearing down the tire tread, etc.; it is only fair that these foregone costs be deducted from the recovery. The rule of "automatically" offsetting saved operating costs should not be applied to commercial aircraft because "there is always the possibility that any operating costs and depreciation saved by loss of use of the vehicle would have been offset by revenues generated if the vehicle had been available * * *."

KLM's reasoning is sound but in this respect its facts are distinguishable from those of the case at bar. In KLM there was no replacement plane. The plane that was out of service neither cost the airline money to operate nor generated any ticket revenues for the airline. Any prediction by the Court of the net effect of lost revenues and saved expenses would have been guesswork, which the court quite properly refused to indulge. In the case before this Court, by contrast, a reserve plane was used, and the defendant has offered to prove that use of the reserve plane reduced operating costs while having no effect on revenues. If defendant can establish those facts, the recovery must be reduced by the proven amount of increased profits.

For the reasons stated above, plaintiff's motion for partial summary judgment is denied. At trial, the recoverable damages for loss of use of plaintiff's 747, if any, shall be determined in accordance with the principles set forth, supra.

SO ORDERED.

Notes

1. *Measuring Plaintiff's Lost Use.* Once the court has decided that the owner-plaintiff may recover damages for lost use, six possible ways to measure it compete for attention: (a) Plaintiff's lost actual profit. (b) The actual rent plaintiff paid for a substitute. (c) If plaintiff used a spare, the extra expense, wear and tear. (d) Even though plaintiff did not rent one, the rental value of a substitute. (e) The rental value, undamaged, of plaintiff's damaged chattel. And (f) interest on a principal sum equal to the property's value. Some of the measures may not be available in a particular dispute.

2. *Questions.* Which of the six measures is possible in *Kuwait Airlines*? In settlement negotiations after the decision, which should plaintiff prefer? Defendant? If settlement negotiations fail and the court must choose the measure, which is most just?

3. *Lost Use in Welch v. Kosasky.* In *Welch*, p. 776, the Welches recovered $10,000 for lost use of the silver. How would you develop evidence to support their recovery of damages for their lost use? Which theory of lost use do you think applied? Was $10,000 a shot in the dark?

4. *Lost Use Exceeding the Property's Value?* For defendant's conversion of plaintiff's grader, which he had purchased several years before the conversion for $19,700, the court awarded the owner $67,500 for 27 months of lost use. The court (incorrectly) analyzed plaintiff's lost use damages as "restitution." Cross v. Berg Lumber Co., 7 P.3d 922 (Wyo. 2000).

5. *Lost Use of Pleasure Vehicle.* Owner may recover lost use damages for an automobile maintained for personal pleasure even though she does not rent a substitute vehicle. "The reason a claimant does not procure a replacement vehicle does not change the nature of the claimant's loss." Kim v. American Family Mutual Insurance Co., 176 Wis.2d 890, 900, 501 N.W.2d 24, 28 (1993). Does this support Kuwait Airlines' argument to recover rental value?

Although many jurisdictions measure the automobile owner's loss by the cost of renting a substitute vehicle, a New Jersey court held that the extent of the owner's personal inconvenience is another standard which will vary depending upon her individual circumstances. Camaraza v. Bellavia Buick Corp., 216 N.J.Super. 263, 523 A.2d 669 (App.Div.1987).

6. *Lost Use After Total Destruction.* An earlier rule limited the owner's lost use damages to a repair period for damaged property; courts denied an owner lost use damages for total destruction. Courts have departed from tradition to award owners a reasonable period of lost use damages to replace destroyed property. Long v. McAllister, 319 N.W.2d 256 (Iowa 1982).

The Restatement permits the owner to recover prejudgment interest from the date the value is fixed plus loss of use not otherwise compensated. The Restatement of Torts (Second) § 927 (1979). Isn't interest on the property's value an alternative way to measure lost use?

7. *Lost Use—Avoidable Consequences.* How does an owner's responsibility to avoid the consequences of the defendant's tort affect recovery for lost use?

(a) Although a Parnell employee had rear-ended the Uricos' truck, settlement negotiations foundered; their truck sat at the garage for 26 months after repair was finished because the Uricos were unable to pay the bill.

"At trial, the Uricos sought damages for the loss of the truck's use from the time of the accident until [Parnell's insurance company] B & S made payment [of $15,102.05] for the repairs under court order. The Uricos' theory at trial was that B & S's wrongful refusal to make a reasonable settlement offer prevented them from mitigating their damages during the post-repair period. The jury found in favor of the Uricos, awarding $11,400.00 for loss of use during the repair period, and $51,100.00 for loss of use following repair. * * * [Parnell appealed.]"

"The Uricos had a clear duty to take all reasonable steps to mitigate damages. They introduced evidence as to the course of settlement negotiations in order to excuse their failure to mitigate. Their evidentiary theory at trial was that 1) their truck was damaged and could not be used by them in business, 2) the circumstance of their truck being rear ended while parked in a breakdown lane forecast the substantial likelihood of a liability finding should the issue of fault be litigated, 3) they were unable to pay for the repairs, and so could not get the truck back on the road in furtherance of their business, 4) B & S was aware that the Uricos did not have the financial means to retrieve the truck from the repairer, and 5) even though aware of these facts, B & S refused to pay for the repairs unless the Uricos waived their [lost use] claims. In short, the Uricos attempted to show that B & S unreasonably held their truck hostage in an effort to reach a total and advantageous settlement. Such evidence was clearly relevant to the factual issue of whether actions taken by B & S on behalf of Parnell unreasonably prevented the Uricos from mitigating damage to them due to loss of use. * * *"

"Ordinarily, recovery for loss of use of a damaged vehicle is limited to that period of time reasonably necessary to complete repairs. [citations] Here, the jury found that the Uricos were entitled to additional loss of use damages beyond the repair period, because of B & S's unreasonably dilatory settlement tactics."

"The extension of loss of use damages beyond the repair period raises difficult policy questions. Limiting loss of use damages to a reasonable repair period recompenses the plaintiff for a finite period in which the vehicle is simply unavailable for use. An award of loss of use damages after the vehicle had been repaired, however, is potentially boundless. Anticipation of such an award could conceivably reduce any incentive that a plaintiff might have to mitigate losses. The evidence here, however, relieves us of these theoretical concerns. The Uricos, despite their good faith best efforts, could not mitigate their losses without possession of the repaired truck. B & S knew this. Nonetheless, B & S refused to issue payment for the repairs. * * *"

"Arbitrary conduct by an insurer, which serves to prolong rather than contain the interval of loss, is an appropriate circumstance for awarding damages beyond the traditional reasonable repair period. In Valencia v. Shell Oil Co., 23 Cal.2d 840, 147 P.2d 558 (1944), defendant initially promised to pay for repairs to a truck damaged in a collision with plaintiff. Repairs were undertaken in reliance on this promise. After the repairs were completed, defendant refused to pay unless plaintiff agreed to waive all other claims. In *Valencia,* the Supreme Court of California held that where plaintiff was financially incapable of paying for the repairs, and defendant's refusal to pay caused additional losses, plaintiff could recover loss of use damages for an extended period. The application of that theory in no way diminishes the traditional requirement that plaintiffs may not recover for damages which could have been avoided by their reasonable efforts to mitigate." Urico v. Parnell Oil Co., 708 F.2d 852 (1st Cir.1983).

Could the Uricos have borrowed the money to pay to repair the truck, given the lender a security interest in the truck, and recovered the repair bill plus interest from the tortfeasor? Suppose the defendant denies liability. If it refuses to pay the plaintiff's repair bill, does it run the risk of paying a massive lost use claim if later found liable?

(b) Defendant's vehicle negligently struck plaintiff's oil spreader truck. The owner repaired the truck. The court ruled that an owner who repairs a commercial vehicle to reduce business losses may recover the cost of repairs plus any diminution in the repaired vehicle's value, even though that sum exceeded the difference between the market value of the vehicle before and immediately after the injury. Spreader Specialists, Inc. v. Monroc, Inc., 114 Idaho 15, 752 P.2d 617 (App.1987).

3. DAMAGES FOR DUMPING

Throw it away? There's no away anymore. Private litigation about material a defendant leaves on a plaintiff's land provides us an opportunity to examine some new issues. The tortfeasors in the following decisions have deposited dirt, tires and rocks, not toxic chemicals, but the courts' approaches let us consider what would happen when something toxic is left behind.

Private remedies for trespass by dumping exist in the shadow of the environmental statutes, their wide net for possible responsible defendants, their low threshold for liability, and their damages, response cost and use value. When legal rules have actually or potentially created liability for cleanup which exceeds the land's value after the cleanup is completed, the land has a negative value. Abandonment may not be an option for the owner, for the environmental authorities' lasso is long indeed.

Returning to private solutions, a list of the landowner's possible remedies for someone else's dumping on land includes damages, an injunction, and restitution.

Damages Measures. There are five possible ways to measure the owner's damages: (a) diminution, market value before the tort less market value after it; (b) the cost to restore, without any limits, response costs under CERCLA; (c) the cost to restore, not to exceed the diminution in market value; (d) the cost to restore, not to exceed the land's value before the tort; and (e) the rental value of the property.

Injunction. An injunction may take one of two forms: (a) a prohibitory injunction which tells defendant to "stop making a mess"; and (b) a mandatory injunction which tells it to "clean up your mess." Since litigants often settle private lawsuits, a prohibitory injunction may give the defendant the choice between ceasing the activity and buying from the plaintiff the right to continue it.

Restitution. Restitution is designed to prevent defendant's unjust enrichment; there are at least two ways to measure it: (a) defendant's gain or profit; and (b) defendant's savings.

Combinations. The better to achieve full redress, a landowner may combine remedies: damages measured by rental value for past invasions plus an injunction to clean the property up for the future is an obvious combination. But the landowner's remedies ought not to be duplicative; for example defendant should not be ordered to clean the tract up and pay damages for its diminution in value, because if the land is cleaned up properly, it will not be diminished in value.

Finally two other frames of reference. The first is public: it may be useful to evaluate courts' remedial responses in light of society's evolving ethic of how to protect and conserve the environment. The second considers the realm of private bargaining: an owner's right to occupy land and to exclude an invader is combined with her right to bargain for consideration in return for waiver of that right, that is to permit another to use the land. Someone who uses her land without negotiating permission has frustrated the owner's right to bargain and receive consideration to waive her rights. If, because of the defendant's tort, the owner has lost the opportunity to bargain, it may be useful to consider what a contract would have provided.

DON v. TROJAN CONSTRUCTION CO.

District Court of Appeal of California, First District, 1960.
178 Cal.App.2d 135, 2 Cal.Rptr. 626.

DEVINE, J., PRO TEM. Plaintiffs appeal from a judgment which was rendered in their favor, on the ground of inadequacy of the award. * * *

On February 21, 1957, plaintiffs, husband and wife, bought a commercially zoned lot in the city of Campbell. They intended to build a supermarket on the lot, and placed a sign on it announcing their intention to do so, but conditions on the stock market, in which they had holdings, were not favorable to them at the time, so they postponed construction of the market. They did not intend to rent the lot to anyone, and Mr. Don testified that he would not have accepted a proposal to rent although he might have allowed a brief use of the lot without charge had he been asked for it.

The land had been owned by the Trojan Construction Company, one of the defendants, but was sold on February 21, 1957, to Ad–Mor Enterprises, Inc., a corporation. That grantee immediately, and by the next deed of record conveyed the lot to plaintiffs.

On or about June 1, 1957, Trojan Construction Company was building a subdivision near the Don lot. Streets had to be built, and there was dirt to be taken away and stored somewhere. The general manager of Trojan Construction Company, Mr. Burchfield, testified that he asked a Mr. James of Ad–Mor for permission to store the dirt on the lot, but there is no fixing of the date of the conversation. Mr. Burchfield testified that Mr. James gave Ad–Mor's consent. He testified that he did not know about Mr. Don or his ownership of the property until the suit was brought.

Mr. Burchfield instructed Kebble Construction Company, which was Trojan's subcontractor for putting in the streets, to store the dirt on the lot. During June and July, 1957, dirt was being put on the land and taken off. In August, 1957, Trojan decided it did not need any of the dirt, and advertised that free dirt was available. The public began to remove the dirt. It was stipulated that in March, 1958, there was still "substantial dirt on it," but by the end of March, 1958, there was no dirt on the property. * * *

On November 26, 1957, plaintiffs filed the action, alleging that defendants Trojan and Keeble placed large quantities of dirt on plaintiffs' land, without their permission. They alleged the rental value of the land to be $750 per month, and they prayed damages in the amount of $750 per month until all the dirt should have been removed.

They alleged that the land had been rendered unusable in its state at that time for the building of the intended supermarket, and they prayed damages in the sum of $10,000 for prevention of the use of plaintiffs' property. * * *

The evidence as to rental value of the land was: (1) The testimony of plaintiff Don that he estimated the rental value to be $650 per month; (2) Testimony (it was not actually given, but defendants stipulated it would be given if the witnesses took the stand) of two real estate brokers; one, Harry Walters estimated the rental value at $550 per month, and the other, Glenn Hannard at $450 per month.

Don's reasoning was that the average value of the land during the time of the occupation was, in his estimation, $65,000, and that he thought one per cent per month was a fair rental. Walters reasoned that there was no other vacant land in the vicinity and that the highest rental use was for storing heavy equipment. Hannard reasoned that it is difficult to find a tenant for unimproved land, that an investor in unimproved commercial property should get two-thirds of one per cent plus cost. He estimated the value at $60,000 and the rental value at two-thirds of one per cent at $400, and he added $50 per month as taxes.

The court found that the value of the lot was neither greater nor less by reason of the use of the land by defendants; that the average rental value during the period when the land was used by defendants was $550 per month, and the total $5,500. However, the court found that plaintiffs would not have made any use of the land during that time, nor did they intend to rent it out for any purpose, and would not have rented it had an offer been made. The court found that the only damages "are nominal damages sustained by reason of the technical invasion of their possessory rights in the land." The court awarded damages against both defendants in the total amount of $200, and no costs to plaintiffs.

The judgment cannot be sustained. Section 3334 of the Civil Code provides that the detriment caused by the wrongful occupation of real property (except in certain cases of wilful holding over wherein the damages are higher), "is deemed to be the value of the use of the property for the time of such occupation * * *." The court found that the rental value was $5,500, but awarded $200 and stated that this amount was merely nominal damages. It is plain that the measure explicitly required by the code was not used.

The argument made by respondents throughout the trial was that the owners had lost nothing because they did not intend to rent the land out anyway. If this subject were open to be debated upon, it could be pointed out that if only nominal damages are awarded, the appropriators of the use of land could gain a virtually expense free use of property for profitable purposes on the single condition that the owner did not presently intend to lease the land or to use it himself. However, the Civil Code in section 3334 has fixed the measure of damages, and has made no exception in cases where the plaintiff did not intend to use the land or to rent it out so that the court can do no other than apply that measure, namely, the "value of the use." That the owners did not intend to make any use of the land themselves does not deprive them of their proper award. * * *

A point relative to the nature of the action is made by respondents. It is necessary, they say, for owners who wish to claim damages according to the measure established in section 3334 of the Civil Code to waive the tort and to sue in assumpsit on an implied contract. They cite the cases of Samuels v.

Singer, 1 Cal.App.2d 545 [36 P.2d 1098, 37 P.2d 1050], and Herond v. Bonsall, 60 Cal.App.2d 152 [140 P.2d 121]. In both of those cases, the action had been essentially in assumpsit, so we have no more than the statement therein that one may waive the tort and sue for the damages described in section 3334 of the Civil Code, which the landowners did, and successfully, in those two cases. * * *

The court having found that $5,500 was the fair rental value of the property for the whole period of the wrongful occupation, judgment should be entered by the court in that amount. * * *

Notes

1. *Questions.* Why don't nominal damages vindicate the Dons' property right satisfactorily? Should the court have based their damages on the landowners' proved economic loss? Does the statutory language support the rental measure? Does either policy, compensation or deterrence, support it? In view of the lack of injury to the land, the defendants' lack of intent or willfulness, and the Dons' indifference about receiving rent and their failure to seek an injunction, does the court's measure encourage landowners to let valuable resources remain idle? Would measuring the Dons' damages by diminished value have created fewer incentives to leave resources idle? In other words does the rental value measure both overcompensate the landowners and overdeter the contractor?

Was using the Dons' lot less expensive to the developer than using a lot farther from the construction site? Is the cost of storing and disposing of excess dirt part on the developer's overhead? If the landowners lacked an economic loss, why not let them recover the construction company's savings? Olwell v. Nye & Nissen Co., p. 835. Is the rent measure the court uses the practical equivalent of restitution?

2. *More Dumping Damages.* Defendant, a street contractor, "dumped upon plaintiff's land and spread out over said land a large quantity [about one thousand cubic yards] of materials which accumulated in the course of performance of the street work." "[T]he value of the land was not diminished by the deposit on the land of the earth and soil." Indeed the trial judge found its value increased.

The landowner on appeal, "contends, however, that the measure of damages in such a case as this is to be determined by the cost of removing the obnoxious materials and restoring the property to its original condition."

"[T]he materials deposited by defendant on plaintiff's land can be removed," the court of appeals observed, "at a cost less than the value of the land. To hold that [the owner] is without remedy merely because the value of the land has not been diminished, would be to decide that by the wrongful act of another, an owner of land may be compelled to accept a change in the physical condition of his property, or else perform the work of restoration at his own expense. This would be a denial of the principle that there is no wrong without a remedy. The reasonable cost of restoration may be recovered, without regard to the fact that the plaintiff has not yet removed said materials from his land. The cost, as determined by the court, will be, in effect, the amount of diminution in value of the land, resulting from the wrong committed by defendant." Dandoy v. Oswald Brothers Paving, 113 Cal.App. 570, 570, 572, 298 P. 1030, 1030–31 (1931).

Questions. Assume the landowner will leave the fill material where it is. If the fill increased the property's value, does awarding the owner the cost of hypothetical restoration add insult to overcompensation? Does the last quoted sentence make any sense? Should the court limit the landowner to an injunction?

Should the court have told the landowner to clean the tract up and recover the cost from the contractor? Both decisions in the next Note consider whether, when the owner seeks an injunction, that solution is an adequate remedy at law.

3. *Introducing Injunctions: "Clean Up Your Mess." "Clean It Up Yourself"*.

(a) *Belinsky v. Belinsky*: "This is an appeal by the plaintiffs claiming that the trial court erred in finding that they had failed to sustain their burden of proving by a fair preponderance of credible evidence that irreparable harm had been done to them sufficient to warrant the issuance of a mandatory injunction."

"The defendant, Lewis P. Belinsky, the owner of an undivided one-quarter interest in a tract of land co-owned by the plaintiffs, joined with the defendant, Stephen Hornak, Jr., in a business venture to collect, store and sell used automobile tires. The defendants stored thousands of tires on the land and many tires still remain, even though the business is no longer in existence. The plaintiffs want the defendants to remove all the tires. * * *"

"The plaintiffs presented evidence that the presence of the tires reduces the value of the land and thereby thwarts their efforts to sell the property at a reasonable price, that the presence of the tires creates a continuing zoning violation, and that the tires create a fire hazard and a condition of attractive nuisance. The plaintiffs also presented evidence that there were facilities which would take the tires, including one located in New Haven. * * *"

"A mandatory injunction will not issue where the plaintiffs have an adequate remedy at law. [citations] Testimony disclosed that the tires could be removed and that certain facilities would accept those tires. Although this may be a costly procedure for the plaintiffs, it does not deprive them of an adequate remedy at law since a suit for damages for the cost of the removal could be brought. We, therefore, do not find that the trial court erred."

Belinsky v. Belinsky, 5 Conn.App. 133, 133–35, 497 A.2d 84, 85–86 (1985).

(b) *Wheelock v. Noonan*. Is *Belinsky* consistent with the New York court's early leading decision, Wheelock v. Noonan, 108 N.Y. 179, 15 N.E. 67 (1888)?

Defendant in "a clear abuse of the license" covered six of plaintiff's lots with fourteen to eighteen foot piles of rocks, some ten to fifteen feet long. The trial court found a continuing trespass and ordered defendant to "remove the rocks." On appeal defendant argued the injunction was improper because plaintiff had "an adequate remedy at law."

"It is now said that the remedy was at law, that the owner could have removed the stone and then recovered of the defendant for the expense incurred. But to what locality could the owner remove them? He could not put them in the street; the defendant presumably had no vacant lands of his own on which to throw the burden; and it would follow that the owner would be obliged to hire some vacant lot or place of deposit, become responsible for the rent, and advance the cost of men and machinery to effect the removal. If any adjudication can be found throwing such burden upon the owner, compelling him to do in advance for the trespasser what the latter is bound to do, I should very much doubt its authority. On the contrary, the law is the other way. [citation] And all the cases which give to the injured party successive actions for the continuance of the wrong are inconsistent with the idea that the injured party must once for all remove it. Such is neither an adequate remedy nor one which the plaintiff was bound to adopt."

"But it is further said that he could sue at law for trespass. That is undoubtedly true. The case of Uline v. Railroad Co., 101 N.Y. 98, 4 N.E.Rep. 536, demonstrates upon abundant authority that in such action only the damages to its date could be recovered, and for the subsequent continuance of the trespass new actions following on in succession would have to be maintained. But in a case like the present, would that be an adequate remedy? In each action the damages could not easily be anything more than the fair rental of the lot. It is difficult to see what other damages could be allowed, not because they would not exist, but because they would be quite uncertain in amount and possibly somewhat speculative in their character. The defendant, therefore, might pay those damages, and continue his occupation, and if there were no other adequate remedy, defiantly continue such occupation, and in spite of his wrong make of himself in effect a tenant who could not be dispossessed. The wrong in every such case is a continued unlawful occupation, and any remedy which does not or may not end it is not adequate to redress the injury or restore the injured party to his rights. On the other hand, such remedy in a case like the present might result to the wrongdoer in something nearly akin to persecution. He is liable to be sued every day, *die de diem,* for the renewed damages following from the continuance of the trespass; and while, ordinarily, there is no sympathy to be wasted on a trespasser, yet such multiplicity of suits should be avoided, and especially under circumstances like those before us. The rocks could not be immediately removed. The courts have observed that peculiarity of the case, and shaped their judgment to give time. It may take a long time, and during the whole of it the defendant would be liable to daily actions. For reasons of this character it has very often been held that while, ordinarily, courts of equity will not wield their power merely to redress a trespass, yet they will interfere under peculiar circumstances, and have often done so where the trespass was a continuing one, and a multiplicity of suits at law was involved in the legal remedy."

(c) *Permanent vs. Temporary.* Both courts mention particular damages measures while deciding whether damages are an adequate remedy for the landowner. Since the *Wheelock* court found the defendant's invasion "continuing," a sketch of another distinction will be helpful. Courts characterize invasions of land as (i) permanent, or (ii) temporary, which is divided in turn into repeated and, the court's conclusion, continuing. The classification as temporary or permanent may affect the statute of limitations, the measure of damages, and abatement of the invasion.

(i) *Permanent.* If the court classifies defendant's invasion as permanent, the landowner's cause of action accrues and the statute of limitations period commences to run when the defendant's invasion begins or when plaintiff's injury is apparent. The landowner has one cause of action for past and future damages. If the statute of limitations period passes, the owner's suit is barred. The court will measure a successful owner's permanent damages by diminution, the value lost because of the invasion. The "stigma" of being contaminated is one factor which affects its value. Rudd v. Electrolux Corp., 982 F.Supp. 355, 372 (M.D.N.C.1997). Defendant acquires, in effect, an easement on plaintiff's property by paying the owner permanent damages; defendant exercises, in effect, eminent domain power over plaintiff's property. We return to this below in Goulding v. Cook, p. 903.

(ii) *Temporary.* A defendant's temporary invasion includes its repeated or continuing invasions. Each day of a temporary invasion is a self-contained cause of action for statute of limitations purposes. The owner may sue the defendant for temporary damages which occur during the statute of limitations period immediately preceding suit. Temporary damages are more likely to be measured by the cost to restore or rent than by diminution. In the future, the owner may sue defendant in a second action for damages which occur after the first judgment. Successive suits to recover damages measured by "fair rental" are the remedy at law the *Wheelock* court finds inadequate. So the owner's future remedy for defendant's continuing invasion is often an injunction to "clean up your mess" coupled with a rental measure of damages for the past invasion. Why not couple injunction with cost-to-restore damages?

(d) *Questions*. In finding damages inadequate for plaintiff, the *Wheelock* court assumes that the plaintiff's damages will be measured by rent plus successive suits to recover for future harm. Is this conservative damages measure associated with finding damages an inadequate remedy at law? Damages measured by diminution or cost to restore will eliminate the need for an owner's serial lawsuits. Would one of these more generous measures be an inadequate remedy?

Would a damages measure capping owner's cost-to-restore damages at the land's pre-injury value be inadequate and provide support for granting an injunction? In evaluating the adequacy of damages, consider Markstrom v. United States Steel where the defendant dumped 44,000 cubic yards of rock onto eight-tenths of an acre of plaintiff's land. The court reversed a judgment giving plaintiff the cost of removing the rock. The cost of repair, it held, may not exceed the market value of the affected land. Markstrom v. United States Steel Corp., 182 Mich.App. 570, 452 N.W.2d 820 (1989).

(e) *An Anachronistic Remedial Hierarchy*? Should a court's remedial hierarchy force an owner to accept money damages instead of receiving an injunction? If an owner prefers an injunction to put the initial burden to restore on the defendant, should the court respect the plaintiff's choice? Consider the environmental impact of the remedial choice. But remember plaintiff can settle private litigation by "selling" an injunction to defendant for $1 less than cost to restore.

At this writing, because discarded tires have a negative value, the tires' "owner" has to pay someone to haul them away. An inventor may develop a profitable way to burn tires to generate electricity or cook cement, transmogrifying thousands of tire dumps from fire hazards into goldmines. But don't hold your breath.

It is possible to distinguish *Belinsky* from *Wheelock*: the *Belinsky* parties were relatives, co-owners, and former business associates; a place to dispose of the tires existed; and the defendant was less brazen.

Nevertheless is *Belinsky* simply a retrograde, incorrect decision? Is more judicial emphasis on plaintiff's choice of remedy appropriate? Will an injunction do a better job of cleaning up the environment?

4. *Punitive Damages*. The owners were an encroachment-aversive retired couple named Jacque; they had earlier lost some of their land to an adverse possessor. The trespasser Steenberg was a mobile home seller; it sought to deliver a mobile home across the Jacques' land instead of using a precarious road. Negotiations came a cropper: "it was not a question of money; the Jacques just did not want Steenberg to cross their land." Over the Jacques' vigorous protest, Steenberg crossed the land to deliver the mobile home. The government imposed a $30 citation for Steenberg's offence.

In the Jacques' civil action for Steenberg's intentional trespass, the jury, after finding no actual damages, returned a verdict for $1 nominal damages and $100,000 punitive damages. The trial judge and the intermediate appellate court thought Wisconsin law rejected punitive damages when the plaintiffs only recovered nominal damages.

Nominal damages for Steenberg's trespass to plaintiffs' land, the Wisconsin supreme court held, will support their recovery of punitive damages. For the actual harm is not the injury to the land, but the owner's loss of the right to exclude others from the land. So "actual harm occurs in every trespass." Without punitive damages a frustrated landowner, "faced with a brazen trespasser," might take the law into his or her own hands. Because the criminal punishment was insufficient, punitive damages would deter intentional misconduct and create an incentive for victims to sue. Jacque v. Steenberg Homes, Inc., 209 Wis.2d 605, 611, 619, 620, 563 N.W.2d 154, 157, 160, 161 (1997). Compare Gavcus v. Potts, p. 17.

If the Jacques had recovered for their emotional distress, would adding punitive damages been even more controversial?

4.   NONPECUNIARY DAMAGES

BOND v. A.H. BELO CORP.

Court of Civil Appeals of Texas, 1980.
602 S.W.2d 105.

CARVER, JUSTICE. Becky J. Bond appeals from a judgment awarding her only the actual value of certain family papers and photographs lost while in the possession of A.H. Belo Corporation and its employee Dottie Griffith. Bond's complaint on appeal is that the trial court refused to apply the correct measure of damages under which Bond would be entitled to recover the *reasonable special value of such articles to their owner taking into consideration the feelings of the owner for such property.* We agree and accordingly reverse and remand.

In August 1976, Griffith wrote a story on unwanted children which Belo published in its newspaper "The Dallas Morning News." Bond read the story and contacted Griffith. This led to an interview at Bond's home. Bond told Griffith that she (Bond) was an adopted child who had some interesting experiences in trying to locate her biological parents and brothers. Bond exhibited a legal size envelope crammed with "pictures and birth records and newspaper clippings, copies of newspaper stories" accumulated during her search. By mutual agreement, Griffith took the envelope with her to help in writing another story. The envelope and its contents disappeared, apparently during an office shuffle at the newspaper, and the parties concede that they are irretrievable. Bond sued for damages. * * *

[T]he parties stipulated that the actual value of the lost papers was $2,500.00 but that the "sentimental value and the special value and feelings of Becky Bond for such articles" was *greater* than the actual value. The court discharged the jury, and judgment was entered for Bond for the $2,500.00 *actual value* lost. * * *

Belo and Griffith urge here, and apparently took the position in the trial court, that the correct measure of damages is to be found in Crisp v. Security National Insurance Co., 369 S.W.2d 326 (Tex.1963), which held:

> "It is a matter of common knowledge and of usual acceptation by the courts that used household goods, clothing and personal effects have no market value in the ordinary meaning of that term. They may be sold but only at considerable sacrifice which by no means represents the value of the articles to the owner. We find no recognized authority which would hold the insured to a recovery based solely on the proceeds obtainable on a second-hand market. Likewise, replacement costs do not afford a fair test. In some instances on account of obsolescence, change in style and fashion, this measure might represent an economic gain to the insured quite aside from the difficulty of application and proof. The measure of damage that should be applied in case of destruction of this kind of property is the actual worth or value of the articles to the owner for use in the condition in which they

were at the time of the fire excluding any fanciful or sentimental considerations." [citations]

We disagree. *Crisp* was a suit to recover for fire insurance and dealt only with "used household goods, clothing, and personal effects," none of which were shown to have any "sentimental" value. Bond urges that the correct measure of damages is provided by Brown v. Frontier Theatres, Inc., 369 S.W.2d 299 (Tex.1963). In *Brown* * * * the court addressed the appropriate damages for the loss of a variety of personal property. As to such personal property as may have its "primary value in sentiment" the court held:

"As a general rule recovery for sentimental value for personal property cannot be had in a suit for the loss of property for personal use such as wearing apparel and household goods. This rule has been applied in Texas so as to deny the recovery for sentimental value in a suit for the loss of heirlooms. However, in our opinion such is not the rule to be applied in a suit to recover for the loss or destruction of items which have their primary value in sentiment.

"It is a matter of common knowledge that items such as these generally have no market value which would adequately compensate their owner for their loss or destruction. Such property is not susceptible of supply and reproduction in kind, and their greater value is in sentiment and not in the market place. In such cases the most fundamental rule of damages that every wrongful injury or loss to persons or property should be adequately and reasonably compensated requires the allowance of damages in compensation for the reasonable special value of such articles to their owner taking into consideration the feelings of the owner for such property. * * * Where such special value is greater than the market value, it becomes the only criterion for the assessment of damages." [citations.]

In *Brown* the court also described some of the personal property reflected by the record stating:

"The law recognizes that articles of small market value of which their owner is despoiled may have a special value to him as heirlooms, and there is evidence in the record that with the exception of the coin collection and the land patent the primary value of these items to Mrs. Brown was their sentimental value. For example: the wedding veil, one of the emerald rings, the shoes and the point lace collar belonged to her grandmother; the pistol belonged to her grandfather; the watch belonged to her great grandmother; and the two slumber spreads were made by hand by her great, great, great grandmothers."

We hold that under the record, including the stipulations of the parties, the correct measure of damages is supplied by *Brown,* that is "the reasonable special value of such articles to their owner taking into consideration the feelings of the owner for such property." * * *

Reversed and remanded with costs assessed to Belo and Griffith.

Notes

1. *Items Owner Used.* The *Bond* court cites the *Crisp* case which deals with the value of personal items that the owner bought to use, not to resell. Valuation risks for plaintiff's personal items are, (a) on the one hand, too much recovery, damages

based on retail value for the plaintiff's loss of old items; and (b) on the other hand, too little recovery, plaintiff's damages based on "garage sale"—second hand value. Does the *Crisp* court's measurement rule help the factfinder avoid the extremes and arrive at a sensible recovery?

2. *Items Owner Treasured: "Bonding" with Objects.* *Bond* itself deals with the emotional component of ownership.

Professor Margaret Radin explains, "Most people possess certain objects they feel are almost part of themselves. These objects are closely bound up with person-hood because they are part of the way we constitute ourselves as continuing personal entities in the world. They may be as different as people are different, but some common examples might be a wedding ring, a portrait, an heirloom, or a house." Margaret Radin, Property and Personhood, 34 Stanf.L.Rev. 957, 959 (1982).

Professor Jeanne Schroeder, on the other hand, does "not feel that I identify with other objects that I own. I have some sentimental attachment to my wedding ring in the sense that I usually wear a ring as a reminder of my husband, not because I identify it with my self, but because I identify it with my husband. Wearing a wedding ring only relates to my self because, in American society, a gold ring worn on the third finger of a woman's left hand is a symbol of her status as a married woman. If I consider this status to be part of my personhood, wearing a ring may be important to my sense of self—but I do not see how or why I would identify any particular ring with my personhood." J.L. Schroeder, Virgin Territory: Margaret Radin's Imagery of Personal Property as the Inviolate Feminine Body, 79 Minn. L.Rev. 55, 75–76, n.72 (1994).

Which professor would Becky Bond's attorney prefer as a juror on remand?

3. *Who is an Expert?* Appraisals are opinions about market value. Qualified experts' opinion testimony about pre-and post-casualty value is a staple of litigation. Remember, however, both the majority and the dissent in *Barge Bertie*, p. 782, viewed experts with skepticism.

An owner who is not otherwise qualified as an expert may testify about property value. Plaintiff testified to the sentimental value of his property in Campins v. Capels, 461 N.E.2d 712 (Ind.App.1984).

"Under Maryland law, a homeowner can testify as to the fair market value of common consumer goods, which will usually be close or equal to their replacement cost. Expert testimony, however, is required to establish the value of unusual items such as rare books or art work." Were a $3,500 blouse, two $2,000 dresses, two sofas worth $25,000, and a $1,900 shower curtain "unusual items"? Although the items were "clearly expensive," the owner's testimony was admissible to establish the value of these "indisputably common household goods." Maryland Casualty Co. v. Therm–O–Disc, Inc., 137 F.3d 780, 786 (4th Cir.1998).

4. *Tort Interlude.* Emotional distress damages have been controversial because a plaintiff's anguish, defendants argue, is be easy to feign and because there is no clear stopping point to limit plaintiff's recovery. The traditional damages rule forbids an owner from recovering for emotional distress when someone negligently destroys or damages her property. Becky Bond convinced the court to classify her property as having its "primary value in sentiment" leading to a measure which included an augmented recovery.

Plaintiff-owner's tort theory may matter in qualifying the plaintiff to recover damages for feeling, sentiment, and emotional distress. So the plaintiff examines torts for a better damages measure and proceeds accordingly.

(a) *Emotional Distress for Negligence*. Some jurisdictions reject the dominant approach and let an owner recover for emotional distress for defendant's negligent harm to her property. Gandolfo v. U–Haul International, Inc., 978 F.Supp. 558, 563 (D.N.J.1996) (prediction of New Jersey measure). In most jurisdictions, plaintiff is safer with another tort.

(b) *Outrage*. Plaintiff may consider the tort of intentional infliction of mental suffering-emotional distress, sometimes shortened to outrage. After "every family's worst [moving] nightmare," the victim's claim for intentional infliction of emotional distress even survived a species of federal preemption which insulated a defendant that "represented everything wrong with a moving company" from all other state law liability. Gordon v. United Van Lines, Inc., 130 F.3d 282, 283 (7th Cir.1997).

(c) *Punitive Damages*. If defendant's tort was intentional and sufficiently aggravated to qualify for punitive damages, the jury may add them to plaintiff's recovery.

(d) *Negligent Infliction of Emotional Distress*. Some jurisdictions also permit plaintiff's tort recovery for defendant's negligent infliction of emotional distress; but the courts circumscribe this tort with prerequisites like "impact" and obvious physical symptoms. Emotional distress damages for the witness-plaintiff after defendant negligently injures another person have created tort controversies.

The torts of trespass to land and conversion may include more generous damage measures than negligence-based torts.

(e) *Trespass to Land*. In our earlier trespass to land case, Gavcus v. Potts, p. 17, the court said, "Consequential damages can also be recovered for a trespass, since a trespasser is liable in damages for all injuries flowing from his trespass which are the natural and proximate result of it. One such compensable result of a trespass is personal injury to the owner of the land. If a trespass causes mental distress, the trespasser is liable in damages for the mental distress and any resulting illness or physical harm."

(e) *Multiplied Damages*. Many states have timber trespass statutes that let a property owner recover double or triple damages for lost trees and vegetation. May a plaintiff recover multiple damages plus emotional distress damages under a timber trespass statute?

"[W]e next turn" said the Washington Supreme Court, "to the question of whether emotional distress damages are recoverable under [the multiple damages statute] for a trespass. The timber trespass statute sounds in tort. [citation] Trespass is an intentional tort. [citations] We have 'liberally construed damages for emotional distress as being available merely upon proof of "an intentional tort." "Cagle v. Burns and Roe, Inc., 106 Wash.2d 911, 916, 726 P.2d 434 (1986) (permitting damages for emotional distress in wrongful termination action)'".

"Amicus argues that in the absence of explicit language in the statute allowing emotional distress damages, 'it would be improper to conclude that the legislature intended to allow a measure of damages for willful tree trespass that was not recoverable at common law at the time the Statute was enacted.' We disagree. First, as noted, there is nothing to suggest the timber trespass statute was intended to bar other causes of action. Second, the recovery of emotional distress damages in cases of intentional torts is consistent with the modern rule. [citations]"

"We believe the correct rule is that emotional distress damages are recoverable under [the multiple damages statute] for an intentional interference with property interests such as trees and vegetation. * * * Such emotional distress damages must, of course, be based on more than mere theory or speculation." Birchler v. Castello Land Company, Inc., 133 Wash.2d 106, 115–17 942 P.2d 968, 972–73 (1997).

(f) *Conversion vs. Negligence.* After Personal Storage agents turned Lucy Gonzales's stored property over to an imposter, she sued it for breach of contract, negligence, and conversion. An issue on appeal was whether the jury should "have been permitted to award Gonzales [$232,582] damages for her emotional distress." The court distinguished negligence from conversion:

"[N]egligent damage to personal property, for which the law generally will not permit recovery of emotional distress damages [citations] is distinct from the conversion of personal property. The foundation for the action of conversion rests neither in the knowledge nor the intent of the defendant. It rests upon the unwarranted interference by defendant with the dominion over the property of the plaintiff from which the injury to the latter results. Therefore, neither good nor bad faith, neither care nor negligence, neither knowledge nor ignorance, are of the gist of the action. * * * The liability of the warehouseman for conversion arises even though there is no element of negligence involved. * * *"

"The act of dominion over the property of another which is necessary for conversion is important to consider here because it will invariably provide the converter with very direct knowledge of the likely consequences of such interference. For instance, where a converter takes possession and disposes of household goods or family heirlooms on the basis of a reasonable but erroneous belief as to title, the converter may legitimately contend that he acted without knowledge as to rightful ownership. However, the converter cannot claim he was unaware of the potential emotional harm his interference would cause. In contrast, the negligent destroyer of personal property—the defendant who fails to properly secure the bulldozer or the warehouseman who leaves paint rags next to a gas burner—has considerably less direct knowledge of the emotional consequences of his conduct. [citations] Thus, in the context of a conversion claim there is far less likelihood that allowing recovery for emotional distress damages will create liability which is out of proportion to the nature of the defendant's act. It follows that when a defendant is guilty of conversion, there is considerably less justification for imposing the limits on emotional distress damages which exist in negligence cases. * * *"

"In sum then, we conclude that notwithstanding further developments in the law of negligence, damages for emotional distress growing out of a defendant's conversion of personal property are recoverable." Gonzales v. Personal Storage, Inc., 56 Cal.App.4th 464, 471, 476–77, 65 Cal.Rptr.2d 473, 477, 480–81 (1997). (Internal quotation marks deleted.)

Questions. The *Welch* court, p. 776, curtly dismissed the Welches' request to recover for mental anguish. Was that correct?

Finally, does it make sense to hinge plaintiff's eligibility to recover for emotional distress on distinctions like those between real property and personal property and between conversion and negligence?

5. *A Pet.* If defendant's employee lost Rebecca's pet cat Fluff, she might be surprised to learn that the court (a) considers her cat to be "property," (b) bases her damage measure on Fluff's market value, and (c) excludes her emotional distress from recovery.

Andrew Gluckman, after adopting Floyd, a stray golden retriever, in Arizona, boarded Floyd on an American Airlines flight in Phoenix. The flight was delayed; the cargo hold, where Floyd was, reached 140 degrees; Floyd suffered brain damage; and he was "put to sleep the next morning." Gluckman sued the airline for several torts, none of which survived the defendant's motion to dismiss and the judge's characterization of Floyd as property.

Negligent infliction of emotional distress? "New York law does not permit recovery for mental suffering and emotional disturbance as an element of damages for loss of a passenger's property," the judge observed, quoting an earlier decision. Intentional infliction of emotional distress? The airline's "deplorable" behavior was not intentionally directed at Gluckman. Nor, it seems, was it sufficiently outrageous to qualify for the tort. Loss of companionship? Despite several aberrational decisions, pets are property and "there is no independent cause of action for loss of the companionship of a pet."

Gluckman's contract theory, based on the airline tickets, survived the airline's summary judgment motion. Gluckman v. American Airlines, 844 F.Supp. 151, 157–59 (S.D.N.Y.1994).

Carol Schuster also had three torts and a contract.

PETCO ANIMAL SUPPLIES, INC. v. SCHUSTER

Court of Appeals of Texas, 2004.
144 S.W.3d 554.

BOB PEMBERTON, JUSTICE. In this case, we consider the types of damages that Texans may recover for the loss of a pet dog. We are thus not addressing the damages recoverable for the loss of such animals as livestock, equines, or wild animals.

Carol Schuster sued Petco Animal Supplies, Inc. (Petco) after her miniature schnauzer, Licorice, was run over by traffic after escaping from a Petco groomer. Schuster took a default judgment, and the trial court awarded damages, including Schuster's replacement costs for Licorice; her out-of-pocket costs for training and microchip implantation; her wages lost while searching for Licorice after the dog escaped; Schuster's mental anguish, emotional distress and counseling costs; " 'intrinsic value' loss of companionship"; exemplary damages; and attorneys fees. Petco now brings a restricted appeal challenging the award of several of these damage elements. Because we are bound to adhere to Texas's traditional restrictive view toward damages for the loss of a dog, we will affirm in part and reverse in part.

BACKGROUND. On January 16, 2003, Schuster brought her fourteen-month-old miniature schnauzer, Licorice, to a Petco store in Austin to be groomed. As Schuster was returning to the store to pick up Licorice, she saw the dog running away from the store through the surrounding high-traffic area. Later, Schuster learned that Licorice had slipped her leash and run away from a Petco employee who had taken the dog outside for a bathroom break. Schuster and Petco employees searched for Licorice for four days until, tragically, the dog was found dead, having been run over by traffic.

Schuster sued Petco for breach of contract, gross negligence, and conversion. Petco did not answer, and Schuster took a default judgment and then offered evidence to support a range of unliquidated damages. Schuster testified that Licorice's replacement value was $500.00; that she had incurred $892.00 to send Licorice to training school and $52.40 for microchip implantation, (apparently implanted microchips are used as identifiers, essentially a high tech version of dog tags); and that she had lost $857.68 in wages while missing work to search for Licorice.

Schuster also testified that she had experienced a total of $645,000 in mental anguish while searching for Licorice and after learning of the dog's death, as well as $160 in counseling costs. Schuster also asked the district court to award $280,000 in damages for "loss of companionship of Licorice." She additionally requested $1 million in exemplary damages, plus attorneys fees.

The district court awarded Schuster the following damages:

$500.00 as the replacement value of Licorice;
$892.00 as reimbursement costs of putting Licorice through training school;
$52.40 as reimbursement for microchip implantation;
$857.68 as lost wages for Schuster when she was searching for Licorice;
$160.00 as counseling costs;
$10,000 as compensation to Schuster for mental anguish and emotional distress;
$10,000 as compensation for 'intrinsic value' loss of companionship;
$10,000 as exemplary damages; and
$6,750 as attorney's fees * * *.

The district court thus awarded Schuster the full amount of damages she had requested except reduced amounts for mental anguish, loss of companionship, and exemplary damages. The court expressed skepticism that any damages beyond replacement value for Licorice were properly recoverable. Nonetheless, it awarded $10,000 each for mental anguish, loss of companionship, and exemplary damages. The court viewed these amounts as "more appropriate and more in line with anything that might hold up." * * *

[Petco appealed.] Petco contends only that the damage award is not authorized by law or supported by the evidence. Specifically, Petco urges: (1) Texas law does not support any award for mental anguish and related counseling, loss of companionship, or lost wages for the loss of a dog; (2) there was no evidence of conduct by Petco to support imposition of exemplary damages; [and] (3) the attorney's fee award * * * was excessive * * *.

[Under Texas law, Petco may pursue a "restricted appeal" even though it defaulted at trial and filed a late notice of appeal.]

DISCUSSION. * * * In a restricted appeal, * * * we review the entire case. [citation] * * * We can thus consider Petco's challenges to the legal and factual sufficiency of the trial court's damage award in this proceeding. This includes not only the amount of damages awarded, but whether Schuster has established the required causal nexus between those damages and the event sued upon, the death of Licorice. [citations] We can also consider the related, purely legal issue of whether the various elements of the damage award are recoverable under Texas law. [citation] City of Tyler v. Likes, 962 S.W.2d 489 (Tex.1997) (* * * holding that Texas law does not permit recovery of mental anguish damages arising from loss of property). * * *

Damages for loss of a dog. Petco asserts that the district court could not, as a matter of law, award Schuster damages for mental anguish, counseling costs, " 'intrinsic value' loss of companionship," and lost wages. We agree.

Analysis of damage issues recoverable for the loss of a dog in Texas begins with Heiligmann v. Rose, 81 Tex. 222, 16 S.W. 931 (1891), a tort action arising from the poisoning deaths of several dogs. The jury, finding that the defendant poisoned the dogs intentionally and maliciously, awarded both actual and exemplary damages. * * * [T]he Texas Supreme Court articulated legal principles governing damages for the death of a dog:

The authorities well settle that dogs are property, and that an owner has his action and remedy against a trespasser for the damages resulting from injuries inflicted upon them. Some authorit[i]es hold that dogs have no market value. This may be relatively true, but it is not a rule that will govern in all cases. It may be difficult, in the majority of cases, to ascertain the market value of a dog, but such a result may, in some cases, be accomplished. The special charge * * * given by the court substantially presents the true rule in determining the value of dogs. It may be either a market value, if the dog has any, or some special or pecuniary value to the owner, that may be ascertained by reference to the usefulness and services of the dog.

The special charge [in Heiligmann v. Rose] * * * provided, in relevant part:

In order for the plaintiffs to recover, you must find from the testimony that the defendant poisoned the dogs, and that they were the property of plaintiffs; that the dogs were of some pecuniary value,—either that they had some market value at which they would sell, or that the services or use of the dogs were of some pecuniary value. * * *

Evaluating the evidence, the court noted that the dogs had been "of a fine breed, and well-trained," that the owners had taken "great pains" to raise them, and that one of the dogs had even been trained to identify, through distinguishing barks, whether persons who approached were men, women or children. The court concluded that while "[t]here is no evidence in this case that the dogs had a market value * * * the evidence is ample showing the usefulness and services of the dogs, and that they were of special value to the owner." * * *

Heiligmann remains the law today, and it stands for several key principles that govern our resolution of the damage issues in this case. First, it classifies dogs as personal *property* for damage purposes, not as persons, extensions of their owners, or any other legal entity whose loss would ordinarily give rise to personal injury damages. Texas courts have continued to classify dogs as property for damage purposes. [citations]

We do not understand Schuster to be challenging this traditional classification. Nor does Amicus Curiae Animal Legal Defense Fund. While recognizing the status of animals as property, it urges that this classification should not preclude the award of intrinsic value damages reflecting the value of animals as companions. But another Amicus Curiae, Animal Legal Reports Services, urges this Court to classify companion animals as "sentient" property, a status that recognizes the animals' own feelings and emotions.

Second, *Heiligmann* identifies only two elements that can be awarded under the "true rule" of damages for loss of a dog: (1) market value, if any, and (2) "some special or pecuniary value to the owner, that may be ascertained by reference to the usefulness and services of the dog." Third, *Heiligmann* makes clear that the "special or pecuniary value" of a dog to its owner refers solely to economic value derived from the dog's usefulness and services, not value attributed to companionship or other sentimental considerations.

With these key principles in mind, we turn to Petco's challenges to Schuster's mental anguish, counseling costs, " 'intrinsic value' loss of companionship" and lost wages damages.

Mental anguish. Petco maintains that *Heiligmann* forecloses Schuster's recovery of mental anguish damages. Though *Heiligmann* did not squarely address whether mental anguish damages are available for the loss of a dog, our sister court in El Paso has held "this longstanding Texas rule" barred recovery of damages for mental anguish, as well as pain and suffering, for the loss of a dog in a veterinary negligence case. Zeid v. Pearce, 953 S.W.2d 368, 369 (Tex.App.-El Paso 1997, no writ).

In response, Schuster points out that at least one Texas court awarded mental anguish damages in a case involving the fatal shooting of a dog. City of Garland v. White, 368 S.W.2d 12, 14–17 (Tex.Civ.App.—Eastland 1963, writ ref'd n.r.e). But the *White* court never mentions *Heiligmann* and it is unclear whether the defendants ever disputed whether mental anguish damages were properly recoverable for the death of a dog. Even if *White* might otherwise support Schuster, the case is easily distinguishable.

White involved the intentional, premeditated shooting of a dog. This Court once cited *Garland* for the proposition that "defendant who intentionally and wrongfully shot plaintiff's dog liable for unintended injuries to plaintiff in form of mental pain and suffering and physical damage to his house caused by the shotgun blast." Bennight v. Western Auto Supply Co., 670 S.W.2d 373, 378 (Tex.App.—Austin 1984, writ ref'd n.r.e).

By contrast, Schuster asserts at most gross negligence. The Texas Supreme Court, addressing property damage cases generally, held that mental anguish damages are not recoverable for negligent property damage as a matter of law. [citation] The supreme court explicitly reserved the question of whether mental anguish arising from property damage might be available where a degree of culpability higher than simple negligence is found. But the only Texas court to have subsequently addressed the question concluded that grossly negligent property damage can support a claim for mental anguish only where there is evidence of some ill-will, animus, or desire to harm the plaintiff personally. [citation] There is no such evidence here.

The only proof that Schuster offered to establish her mental anguish damages was her testimony that she had been "terror ridden" as she searched for Licorice because the dog "had never been out, never been loose" and was likely scared; "it was cold, freezing weather" and the dog had just had a short haircut; and Schuster feared that Licorice would be killed on the busy roads. Schuster then quantified her anguish as ranging between $1,000 and $20,000 per day. Nowhere in her testimony, or even in her pleadings, did Schuster claim any ill-will, animus or desire by Petco to harm her personally.

Schuster also relies on a line of cases awarding mental anguish damages when arising from the breach of duties incident to certain "special relationships," including "a very limited number of contracts dealing with intensely emotional noncommercial subjects" such as preparing a corpse for burial or delivering news of a family emergency. [citations] It is unclear whether Schuster views these cases as supporting mental anguish damages under her tort claims or breach of contract claim, or both. Regardless, Schuster does not attempt to explain how or why dog grooming falls within the narrow class of "intensely emotional noncommercial subjects" that could give rise to mental anguish damages. To the contrary, we believe Schuster's claim is governed by the general rule that mental anguish damages are not available for breach of a contract, [citation] and by the traditional limitations of *Heiligmann*. In addition, with regard to Schuster's conversion claim, we note that Texas courts have refused to award mental anguish damages for conversion. [citations]

Because there is no support in Texas law for awarding mental anguish damages for the loss of a dog, we reverse the trial court's award of mental anguish damages. [citations]

Counseling expenses. Because Schuster cannot recover for mental anguish or emotional harm arising from Licorice's death, we also reverse her award of counseling expenses. Alternatively, we agree with Petco that there is no evidence that those expenses were reasonable and necessary.

The sole evidence supporting the counseling expenses award was Schuster's own testimony. Her attorney asked her: "[h]ave you been through counseling since the death of Licorice?" She responded that she had and had spent $160 in copayments for the counseling sessions. She provided no testimony regarding reasonableness or necessity; therefore, this testimony is no evidence supporting Schuster's award for counseling costs. [citation]

" 'Intrinsic value' loss of companionship." The trial court also awarded an element of damages it termed " 'intrinsic value' loss of companionship." The sole proof Schuster offered in support of these damages related to her subjective feelings for Licorice. * * * Schuster testified that she had purchased Licorice "as a friend and companion" after most of her children had left home. Licorice, Schuster recounted,

> was with me all the time that I was home. We always joked that her name should have been Velcro instead of Licorice because she was right by my leg all the time. We went places together. If I went somewhere where she could go, she went with me. * * * She was a companion to me and I miss her.

Schuster calculated $280,000 in "loss of companionship" damages based on what she asserted was the average life expectancy of a miniature schnauzer, 14 years, times the amount of annual salary increase, $20,000, she claimed would be required to induce her to accept a job requiring her to part with Licorice.

Although it perhaps resembles her claimed mental anguish or even the "loss of companionship" that is a component of lost human consortium, Schuster conceives her "loss of companionship" damages to be a form of "intrinsic value" property damages. "Intrinsic value" damages are conceptually distinct from personal injury damages. [citation] Texas law permits the recovery of "intrinsic value" as the measure of property damages in certain instances. Porras v. Craig, 675 S.W.2d 503, 506 (Tex.1984) (intrinsic value of felled trees might be recoverable); *see also* Ives v. Webb, 543 S.W.2d 907, 910 (Tex.Civ.App.-Corpus Christi 1976, no writ) (permitting award of intrinsic value damages in pure breach of contract suit).

Broadly speaking, intrinsic value is an inherent value not established by market forces; it is a personal or sentimental value. [citation] For example, the intrinsic value of trees is said to be comprised of both an ornamental (aesthetic) value and a utility (shade) value. [citation]

Schuster relies on Porras v. Craig for the proposition that she can recover the "intrinsic value" of Licorice as a beloved companion. But, again, *Heiligmann* and its progeny preclude such a recovery. *Heiligmann's* "true rule" permitted recovery of a dog's "special or pecuniary value" ascertained solely *"by reference to the usefulness and services of the dog."* Subsequently, in Young's Bus Lines v. Redmon, which involved the death of a seeing eye dog, the court distinguished between what it termed a dog's "intrinsic or actual value" (*i.e.,* pecuniary value) which might be recoverable, and the mere "peculiar or sentimental value placed upon the dog by [the owner], or what he considered the dog worth to him," which the court deemed irrelevant and inadmissible. 43 S.W.2d 266, 267–68 (Tex.Civ.App.-Beaumont 1931, no writ). * * * *Heiligmann* precludes the award of intrinsic value damages to Schuster, as she relies solely on sentimental considerations.

The Animal Legal Defense Fund presents an amicus brief supporting Schuster by urging that such a limited concept of the intrinsic value of dogs is archaic and fails to take account of the modern view of dogs as beloved friends and companions. * * * One commentator cited in the brief went as far as to suggest Americans today view their pets as more akin to family members than mere property:

> "In the United States, there is nearly one pet for every two Americans. Further, approximately 124 million dogs and cats live in American households. In one study, forty-five percent of dog owners reported that they take their pets on vacation. Another recent survey revealed that more than half of companion animal owners would prefer a dog or cat to a human if stranded on a desert island. Another poll revealed that fifty percent of pet owners would be 'very likely' to risk their lives to save their pets, and another thirty-three percent indicated they would be 'somewhat likely' to put their own lives in danger. These statistics indicate that companion animal owners view their pets as family members, rather than personal property."

William C. Root, Man's Best Friend: Property or Family Member? An Examination of the Legal Classification of Companion Animals and its Impact on Damages Recoverable for their Wrongful Death or Injury, 47 Vil. L.Rev. 423, 423 (2002) (footnotes omitted). Indeed, within our jurisdiction, there are myriad examples that Texans today view dogs more as companions, friends, or even something akin to family than as an economic tool or benefit. * * * [E]ven Petco's counsel have publicly acknowledged "the special bond between a pet and its owner" and suggested that "it is the rare person who does not get a little teary-eyed when Old Yeller dies."

As an intermediate appellate court, we are not free to mold Texas law as we see fit but must instead follow the precedents of the Texas Supreme Court unless and until the high court overrules them or the Texas Legislature supersedes them by statute. We note that the legislature has previously enacted statutes prescribing criminal penalties for cruelty to animals. Tex. Penal Code Ann. § 42.09 (West 2003). Thus, we follow *Heiligmann* and reject Schuster's attempt to expand "intrinsic value" damages to embrace the subjective value that a dog's owner places on its companionship.

Intrinsic value damages are recoverable only where the property is shown to have neither market value nor replacement value. [citations] Schuster did not satisfy that condition. She offered no proof at all regarding Licorice's market value, or whether Licorice had any such value, and she testified that the dog's replacement value was $500.

In Williams v. Dodson, 976 S.W.2d 861, 865 (Tex.App.—Austin 1998, no pet.), this Court permitted the recovery of what it termed "intrinsic value" damages for the conversion of a bracelet without first requiring proof regarding market value or replacement value. The Court was applying a measure of damages applicable to marketable chattels held for the use and comfort of their owner. In this context, "intrinsic value" damages refer to the loss of use of the chattel to the owner, excluding fanciful or sentimental considerations. Crisp v. Security Nat'l Ins. Co., 369 S.W.2d 326, 328–29 (Tex.1963) ("The measure of damages that should be applied * * * is the actual worth or values of the articles to the owner for use in the condition they were in at the time of the fire excluding any fanciful or sentimental considerations."). Schuster does not suggest that she could recover her broader notion of "intrinsic value" damages under this theory.

Accordingly, we reverse the trial court's damage award for " 'intrinsic value' loss of companionship."

Lost wages. Heiligmann would also appear to preclude Schuster's lost wages recovery. Moreover, Schuster cites no authority allowing her to recover lost wages for property damage unrelated to her job. *Likes* informs us that "[w]hile few persons suffering serious bodily injury would feel made whole by the mere recovery of medical expenses and lost wages, many whose *property* has been damaged or destroyed will be *entirely satisfied by recovery of its value.*" We conclude that "lost wages" are not properly recoverable under Schuster's tort theories. See *Heiligmann.*

Lost wages in this case also have too attenuated a connection to Petco's conduct to be recoverable under her breach of contract theory. The supreme court has recently discussed consequential damages in a breach of contract context:

> Consequential damages are those damages that 'result naturally, but not necessarily, from the defendant's wrongful acts.' They are not recoverable unless the parties contemplated at the time they made the contract that such damages would be a probable result of the breach. Thus, to be recoverable, consequential damages must be foreseeable and directly traceable to the wrongful act and result from it.

Stuart v. Bayless, 964 S.W.2d 920, 921 (Tex.1998). We find Schuster's lost wages damages too remote to be fairly compensable. We reverse Schuster's award for lost wages.

Exemplary damages. Petco asserts in its third issue that the district court improperly awarded Schuster exemplary damages. As to her tort claim, Petco urges there is no evidence by which any grossly negligent conduct by individual employees can be attributed to Petco. As to Schuster's breach of contract claim, Petco argues that exemplary damages are not recoverable for a breach of contract. We agree. * * *

In order for exemplary damages to have been proper in this case, Schuster would have had to have shown by clear and convincing evidence that the harm that she suffered was caused by fraud or malice on the part of Petco. [citation] Further, punitive or exemplary damages may be recovered against a corporation only if the grossly negligent act is the very act of the corporation itself. [citation] If the act is that of a mere servant or employee, then it must have been previously authorized or subsequently must be approved by the corporation. [citation].

Schuster asserts that Petco approved the action of the negligent employee when it had its employees search for Schuster's pet. We cannot agree that Petco's attempt to ameliorate the consequences of its employee's negligence is an act approving or ratifying the negligent act itself. The mere fact that Petco employees searched for Schuster's dog does not suggest that Petco vouched for the employee's act of losing the dog in the first place. Further, there is no evidence in the record that the employees were searching for Schuster's dog under the direction of Petco; the employees may have been searching for Licorice on their own accord. * * *

As to the breach of contract claim, exemplary damages are not recoverable for a breach of contract, even one breached maliciously, as a matter of law. [citation] We reverse Schuster's award of exemplary damages.

Attorney's fees. [The court held that Schuster could recover for 45 hours of legal work at $150 per hour on her breach of contract theory.] * * *

Under her breach of contract theory, Schuster may recover each of the elements of damages that remain available: replacement value, reimbursement of expenses for training and microchip implantation, [and] attorney's fees. * * * [citations]

CONCLUSION. We reverse the district court's award for mental anguish damages, counseling costs, " 'intrinsic value' loss of companionship," lost wages and exemplary damages. We otherwise affirm the district court's judgment.

Notes

1. *Compensation.* Do the *Petco* court's damages rules undercompensate a plaintiff suing for the loss of a household pet?

The intermediate appellate court is careful to follow its supreme court's precedent. But is the Texas precedent archaic and inconsistent with contemporary standards and values?

2. *Property.* Is it wrong to characterize an animal as its owner's personal property? There are no statutes forbidding cruelty to a sofa.

3. *Property Damages.* The *Petco* court does not cite the prior case in this book, Bond v. Belo, also a Texas case. Would the concept of "value to the owner" in Bond v. Belo have supported Schuster's recovery for her mental anguish and counseling expenses as well as for her pet's intrinsic value?

4. *Contra.* What are the arguments for retaining the present damages rules for a lost pet? A pet owner can obtain a substitute pet easily and quickly. The definition of who can sue for a lost pet is unclear. Plaintiff's nonpecuniary damages for a lost pet are unquantifiable. Allowing plaintiffs to recover nonpecuniary damages for lost pets will lead to fraudulent claims. Different juries will make inconsistent awards to similarly situated pet owners. Some pet owners will be overcompensated. Expanded damages will burden veterinarians and pet-oriented businesses.

5. *Tort Reform.* If the damages rule is expanded, should change come from the legislature in a statute? A statute expanding pet owners' compensatory damages would be contrary to the tort-reform trend to cap and otherwise limit personal injury plaintiffs' nonpecuniary damages, particularly for pain and suffering.

Pet-medicine companies have retained lobbyist Victor Schwartz. "If soft or non-economic compensatory damages were allowed, costs of vets would zoom, and many animals would not get the care they need or would be put to sleep when not absolutely necessary," observed Lab-owner Schwartz, always on the lookout for animals' best interests. Tort Watch for Animal Lovers, The Washington Post, December 29, 2005 at A21.

5. LIMITING DAMAGES: ECONOMIC LOSS RULE

IN RE CHICAGO FLOOD LITIGATION

Supreme Court of Illinois, 1997.
176 Ill.2d 179, 680 N.E.2d 265.

JUSTICE FREEMAN delivered the opinion of the court: In April 1992, the underground freight tunnel system in the central business district of Chicago flooded. Numerous named plaintiffs (class plaintiffs) represent individuals and businesses that claim property damage and economic loss as a result. * * *

The complaints allege as follows. An old, underground freight tunnel system (tunnel) is located under the central business district of Chicago, commonly known as the Loop, and the Chicago River. Many buildings in the Loop are connected directly or indirectly to the tunnel. Before 1959, the tunnel was used to transport freight in the Loop. Since 1959, the City has owned the tunnel and, since the 1970s, has leased the tunnel to a number of utility and telecommunication companies to carry their service lines. The tunnel crosses under the Chicago River at different locations, including near the Kinzie Street bridge.

In May 1991, the City entered into a contract with Great Lakes, which provided that Great Lakes would remove and replace wood piling clusters at five Chicago River bridges, including the Kinzie Street bridge. The contract warned Great Lakes not to drive the pilings "at any other location than that specified by the City * * * [because] even slight position changes may cause serious damage to various underground * * * structures." The contract further provided that if Great Lakes failed to heed this warning, Great Lakes would be liable to repair such damages at its own expense.

By September 1991, Great Lakes informed the City that it had fully completed the work. However, Great Lakes had installed the pilings at the Kinzie Street bridge in a location other than originally designated in the contract. During pile driving at the bridge, Great Lakes caused a breach in the tunnel wall by physically breaking, weakening, or creating excessive pressure on the tunnel wall.

In January 1992, a television crew using the tunnel discovered the breach in the tunnel wall at the Kinzie Street bridge. By February 1992, the television crew notified the City of the tunnel damage. During March and early April 1992, City employees inspected the tunnel, photographed the damage, and recommended immediate repairs.

On or about April 13, 1992, the tunnel breach opened. In a sudden torrent and continuing flow, the Chicago River rushed into the tunnel and, ultimately, into buildings connected to the tunnel. Approximately 200,000 persons were evacuated from numerous Loop buildings. On April 14, the Governor of the State of Illinois declared the Loop and surrounding areas a state disaster area. The next day, the President of the United States declared the area a federal disaster area. Thousands of Loop building occupants were unable to return to their respective places of business for days or weeks thereafter while emergency repairs and cleaning took place. Class plaintiffs sought damages for various alleged losses proximately caused by the flood, including: injury to their property; lost revenues, sales, profits, and good will; lost wages, tips, and commissions; lost inventory; and expenses incurred in obtaining alternate lodging. * * *

Class plaintiffs alleged that the City failed to: (1) properly contract for, administer, and supervise Great Lakes' pile driving activities; (2) exercise ordinary care to maintain, repair, and protect the tunnel both before and after the breach (but only up to the time of the actual flood); and (3) warn class plaintiffs of the dangerous condition caused by the tunnel breach when the City learned of it. Class plaintiffs allege that these acts constitute willful and wanton misconduct and negligence. * * *

The trial court * * * ruled that the *Moorman* doctrine (see Moorman Manufacturing Co. v. National Tank Co., 91 Ill.2d 69, 61 Ill.Dec. 746, 435 N.E.2d 443 (1982)) barred from recovery those plaintiffs who did not allege physical property damage, but rather only economic loss. * * * As part of class plaintiffs' appeal, the trial court certified the following questions for review: * * * (3) whether the *Moorman* doctrine bars the claims of those plaintiffs who allege only economic loss. * * *

The appellate court upheld the trial court's rulings that the *Moorman* doctrine barred the claims of those plaintiffs who alleged only an economic loss, but did not bar the claims of those plaintiffs who suffered damage in the form of inventory lost due to interrupted utility service. * * *

Class plaintiffs contend that the appellate court erred in holding that the *Moorman* doctrine bars recovery for those plaintiffs who incurred solely economic losses. On cross-appeal, the City contends that the appellate court erred in holding that *Moorman* does not bar recovery for those plaintiffs who lost perishable inventory as a result of interrupted electrical service. * * *

At common law, solely economic losses are generally not recoverable in tort actions. [citations] The economic loss rule, as a general proposition, is "the prevailing rule in America" [citations] and is supported by "the vast majority of commentators and cases." (Moorman)

One of the policies behind the economic loss rule is the recognition that the economic consequences of any single accident are virtually limitless. As the City notes, "[i]f defendants were held liable for every economic effect of their negligence, they would face virtually uninsurable risks far out of proportion to their culpability, and far greater than is necessary to encourage potential tort defendants to exercise care in their endeavors." The economic loss rule avoids the consequences of open-ended tort liability. [citations]

In *Moorman*, this court enunciated the economic loss rule, and held that a products liability plaintiff cannot recover solely economic loss under the tort theories of strict liability, negligence, and innocent misrepresentation. This court described economic loss as " 'damages for inadequate value, costs of repair and replacement of the defective product, or consequent loss of profits—without any claim of personal injury or damage to other property * * * ' [citation]."

In Anderson Electric, Inc. v. Ledbetter Erection Corp., this court applied the economic loss rule to claims that services were performed negligently. This court also held that "[a] plaintiff seeking to recover purely economic losses due to defeated expectations of a commercial bargain cannot recover in tort, regardless of the plaintiff's inability to recover under an action in contract."

This court in *Moorman* articulated three exceptions to the economic loss rule: (1) where the plaintiff sustained damage, i.e., personal injury or property damage, resulting from a sudden or dangerous occurrence; (2) where the plaintiff's damages are proximately caused by a defendant's intentional, false representation, i.e., fraud; and (3) where the plaintiff's damages are proximately caused by a negligent misrepresentation by a defendant in the business of supplying information for the guidance of others in their business transactions. None of these exceptions are present in this case.

Class plaintiffs complain that the application of the economic loss rule to the present case "permits identically situated plaintiffs in the same case to be treated differently for recovery of their damages based solely on the fortuity that one may have suffered property damage along with economic damage." However, the tort recovery requirement of injury to person or property is not a "fortuity." As we explained in In re Illinois Bell Switching Station Litigation:

> "The Moorman holding is bottomed upon the theory that tort law affords a remedy for losses occasioned by personal injuries or damage to one's property, but contract law and the Uniform Commercial Code offer the appropriate remedy for economic losses occasioned by diminished commercial expectations not coupled with injury to person or property. The Moorman court concluded that qualitative defects are best handled by contract rather than tort law. Tort law [is] 'appropriately suited for personal injury or property damage resulting from a sudden or dangerous occurrence' whereas the remedy for a 'loss relating to a purchaser's disappointed expectations due to deterioration, internal breakdown or nonaccidental cause * * * lies in contract.' "

Class plaintiffs also characterize the flood as "sudden" or "calamitous." Thus, according to class plaintiffs, "under the recognized exception to *Moorman* for sudden, calamitous events * * * the Courts below should have ruled as a matter of law that *Moorman* does not apply to this case and is not a bar to economic damages."

We cannot accept this argument. As we earlier explained, an exception to the economic loss rule is where the plaintiff sustained personal injury or property damage resulting from a sudden or dangerous occurrence. Courts do not speak of a calamitous, sudden, or dangerous event or occurrence to avoid the economic loss rule, but rather to distinguish tort damages from mere economic loss. In other words, the event, by itself, does not constitute an exception to the economic loss rule. Rather, the exception is composed of a sudden, dangerous, or calamitous event coupled with personal injury or property damage.

Clearly, the economic loss rule applies to losses incurred without any personal injury or property damage. However, the economic loss rule applies even to plaintiffs who have incurred physical damage to their property if the damage is caused by disappointed commercial expectations, gradual deterioration, internal breakage, or other nonaccidental causes, rather than a dangerous event. [citations] For damages to be recoverable in tort, the sudden, dangerous, or calamitous occurrence must still result in personal injury or property damage. Absent injury to a plaintiff's person or property, a claim presents an economic loss not recoverable in tort. [citations] We agree with the trial and appellate courts that those plaintiffs who did not incur personal injury or property damage may not recover solely economic losses.

The trial court ruled that the economic loss rule does not bar recovery in tort for those plaintiffs who lost perishable inventory as a result of interrupted electrical service. The appellate court affirmed. We agree.

When property damage is caused by disappointed commercial expectations, the economic loss rule bars recovery in tort. Redarowicz v. Ohlendorf. Rather, "[t]o recover in negligence there must be a showing of harm above and beyond disappointed expectations." (Redarowicz) For example, in *Redarowicz*, the court held that plaintiff's property damage was caused by a construction defect, which was a disappointed commercial expectation. Thus, plaintiff's damages were solely economic losses. However, the court indicated that had plaintiff suffered personal injury or other property damage, he would have been able to recover in tort:

> "This is not a case where defective construction created a hazard that resulted in a member of the plaintiff's family being struck by a falling brick from the chimney. The adjoining wall has not collapsed on and destroyed the plaintiff's living room furniture. The plaintiff is seeking damages for the costs of replacement and repair of the defective chimney, adjoining wall and patio. While the commercial expectations of this buyer have not been met by the builder, the only danger to the plaintiff is that he would be forced to incur additional expenses for living conditions that were less than what was bargained for."

In the present case, class plaintiffs do not seek damages for the loss of continuous electrical service, which is a disappointed commercial expectation. [citations] Rather, class plaintiffs seek damages for property loss, in the form of lost perishable inventory, as a result of a tortious event. Such damages are above and beyond class plaintiffs' disappointed commercial expectation in continuous electrical service. Thus, these losses fall outside the definition of economic loss and are recoverable in tort. [citations]

In sum, we answer the certified questions as follows. The *Moorman* doctrine bars the claims of those plaintiffs who allege only economic loss. However, the *Moorman* doctrine does not bar the claims of those plaintiffs who seek tort recovery for loss of perishable inventory due to interrupted electrical service. * * *

Notes

1. *Economic Loss in Tort?* The economic loss rule originated in buyers' lawsuits to recover for product failure where, if the economic loss rule bars a product buyer's tort recovery, she may fall back on contract. The economic loss rule, however, sets up a hierarchy of plaintiff's injuries: (a) plaintiff's personal injury; (b) damages to plaintiff's "other" property; (c) something plaintiff bought with a quality defect; and (d) plaintiff's economic loss. Should courts distinguish between types of damages and treat plaintiffs' economic loss as less compelling for recovery than her personal injury and property damage?

2. *Questions.* Does the decision in *Chicago Flood* advance the policy of protecting commercial entities' bargained expectation? What policy does the result advance? Would the proximate cause rule work just as well to cut off plaintiffs' recovery of damages for remote and farfetched injuries?

If contract law provides recovery for quality defects and tort law for the results of accidents, why can't the plaintiffs recover in tort for this catastrophic flood?

Is the court saying a plaintiff with personal injury or property damages can also recover for its economic loss? If so, is it consistent with the need to cut off recovery of all disqualified loss?

3. *Problem.* Because of defendant's negligence when its truck hits the electrical service entry, electric power to an office building is shut off; Phil's Pharmacy's drugs in an uncooled cooler spoil; next door Dr. Crown's dentist's drill won't drill. If the pharmacy may recover from the defendant for the lost drugs, why can't the dentist recover lost income from cancelled appointments? If you think the distinction is arbitrary and unjust, should the line be moved to include recovery for the dentist's appointments or to exclude recovery for the pharmacy's drugs?

C. MONETARY RECOVERY TRANSCENDING COMPENSATION

The following material takes up the owner's opportunity to recover money based not only on compensation principles but also on the defendant's willfulness, a statute multiplying recovery, punitive damages, and restitution of defendant's unjust enrichment.

1. DEFENDANT'S WILLFULNESS

GRAYS HARBOR COUNTY v. BAY CITY LUMBER CO.

Supreme Court of Washington, 1955.
47 Wash.2d 879, 289 P.2d 975.

[A group of loggers inadvertently cut timber on plaintiff's land and sold it to the defendant lumber company which was unaware of any wrong. The timber had a stumpage value of $8 per thousand board feet at the time and place of the loggers' original conversion and $35 per thousand board feet at the time and place of the lumber company's conversion; the difference was the value added by the loggers' cutting and transporting the logs to the lumber company's place of business. Plaintiff sued the lumber company for conversion claiming damages measured by the enhanced value; the lumber company brought in the loggers as cross-defendants. The trial court held the lumber company liable for the enhanced value of the logs; the supreme court, however, held that stumpage was the proper measure of damages.]

ROSELLINI, JUSTICE. If the original conversion was in *mala fides,* then damages in an action against a subsequent converter should be based upon the market value of the property as of the time and place the defendant first exercised control and dominion over it, and this rule applies even though the subsequent converter is an innocent purchaser for value. E.E. Bolles Wooden–Ware Co. v. United States, 106 U.S. 432. * * *

[However, concluded the court, the loggers' original trespass here was not wilful.]

This court early committed itself to the view that the doctrine of exemplary or punitive damages is unsound in principle and that such damages cannot be recovered except when explicitly allowed by statute. * * * However, we have adopted the punitive measure of damages where a trespass or conversion is willful or in bad faith. * * *

It was recognized in the early case of Bailey v. Hayden, 65 Wash. 57, 117 P. 720, 721, an action brought under the treble-damage statute (now RCW 64.–12.030, 040), that the wrongdoer is punished and the owner more than compensated when no allowance is made for the value added by the former's labor and expenditures. We held in that case that the measure of damages to be trebled was the stumpage, not the market value after cutting and removal. In discussing the common-law rule allowing recovery of the higher value where the trespass is wilful, we stated that such damages are punitive, not merely compensatory, and quoted from Beede v. Lamprey, 64 N.H. 510, 15 A. 133, 10 Am.St.Rep. 426, as follows:

> "In cases of conversion by willful act or fraud, the value added by the wrongdoer after the conversion is sometimes given as exemplary or vindictive damages, or because the defendant is precluded from showing an increase in value by his own wrong, and from claiming a corresponding reduction of damages."

In commenting on the quoted portion of the New Hampshire case, we said:

> "But whether the larger damages be frankly called vindictive damages, or are allowed on the last-mentioned ground without any express name, their nature is the same. It is obvious that the increased measure is allowed, not as compensation to the person wronged, but as punishment to the wrongdoer. It is not a mere question of terms, but of the inherent quality of the thing. The increased measure is punitive in its very nature, in that it exceeds the true measure of compensation. It is plain that the person whose trees are cut suffers exactly the same injury where the trespass is involuntary as where it is willful. In each case he suffers the loss of his trees."

It is argued that since the owner may replevy his property wherever he may find it, he should be able to recover its value at whatever time and place he is entitled to replevy it. But this argument is equally valid in the case where the conversion was inadvertent, and yet under such circumstances the wrongdoer is not liable in damages for the increased value. The theory under which replevin is allowed bears no consistent relation to the various measures of damage allowed when the latter remedy is elected. For example, the innocent purchaser from a wilful converter is liable in damages only for the value of the goods at the time and place of his own conversion and cannot be held for any value which he may add to them by his own labors. Yet, if the owner finds the goods in the hands of an innocent purchaser after he has enhanced their value, they may be replevied, provided, of course, that the enhancement in value has not become so great as to divest the original owner of title. Meyers v. Gerhart, 54 Wash. 657, 103 P. 1114. In view of these considerations, the mere fact that the goods can be replevied does not justify the imposition of punitive damages.

Notes

1. *"Innocent" Second Converter.* An unknowing purchaser from a willful converter is liable as an innocent converter, but the courts in the timber cases continue to be divided about the measure of damages for that liability. One court held that an unknowing purchaser from a willful converter is liable only for the value of the property at the time of the original taking—i.e. stumpage. Mineral Resources, Inc. v. Mahnomen Construction Co., 289 Minn. 412, 184 N.W.2d 780 (1971). But another court held that he is liable for the delivered value. Masonite Corp. v. Williamson, 404 So.2d 565 (Miss.1981).

2. *Duplication.* After successfully proceeding to judgment against a lumber company, which was the second converter, could the owner subsequently seek recovery for the logs from the first converters, the loggers?

"A further question arises as to the effect to be given to a favorable judgment in the first action in subsequent actions brought against the other wrongdoers. Here the position taken is that not judgment alone, but only judgment and satisfaction bars further actions. Moreover, 'no matter how many judgments may be obtained for the same trespass, or what the varying amounts of those judgments, the acceptance of satisfaction of any one of them by the plaintiff is a satisfaction of all the others.' * * * The theory is that satisfaction of the judgment transfers title to the wrongdoers, such title relating back to the date of the conversion." John Bauman, Multiple Liability, Multiple Remedies, and the Federal Rules of Civil Procedure, 46 Minn. L.Rev. 729, 737 (1962):

3. *Multiple Damages in Washington.* The Washington timber trespass statute, which the court cites, lets the timber owner recover treble damages from the original tortfeasor. If the original trespass-conversion was innocent, however, the owner recovers "single damages." Wash. Rev. Code §§ 64.12.030, 040 (2005). The defense of innocent trespass is one reason the owner chose to sue the lumber company instead of suing the loggers under the statute. Are there others? Why might an owner seek damages instead of replevin?

4. *Multiple Damages in Montana.* Montana's statute provided that damage for conversion should be: "(1) the value at the time of conversion with interest from that time; or (2) where the action has been prosecuted with reasonable diligence, the highest market value of the property at any time between the conversion and the verdict, without interest, at the option of the injured party." The court held a lumber company which negligently, but not willfully, trespassed and cut timber liable under the second alternative for the market value of lumber at its mill without interest. Rickl v. Brand S. Lumber Co., 171 Mont. 528, 530, 559 P.2d 1182, 1183 (1977).

5. *Punitive Damages.* (a) *Conversion.* A punitive damages verdict for $1,750,000 for conversion by copying computer software programs was reduced to $650,000 in Management Computer Services, Inc. v. Hawkins, Ash, Baptie & Co., 206 Wis.2d 158, 557 N.W.2d 67 (1996).

(b) *Trespass to Chattels.* During a widely publicized demonstration against Forest Service logging policies, members of EARTH FIRST! chained themselves to a logging company's equipment. The company's verdict for trespass to chattels included $5,717.34 compensatory damages and $25,000 punitive damages. The Oregon supreme court rejected defendants' argument that their activity was expression, immune from punitive damages under the state and federal constitutions. Huffman & Wright Logging Co. v. Wade, 317 Or. 445, 857 P.2d 101 (1993).

6. *Multiple Damages Plus Punitive Damages?* A more difficult question is whether an owner may recover multiple damages under a timber trespass statute plus punitive damages. That's next.

2. MULTIPLE DAMAGES AND PUNITIVE DAMAGES

BULLMAN v. D & R LUMBER COMPANY

Supreme Court of Appeals of West Virginia, 1995.
195 W.Va. 129, 464 S.E.2d 771.

CLECKLEY, JUSTICE: In this case, we consider whether a plaintiff who elects to seek treble damages for the wrongful cutting of timber as provided by W.Va. Code, 61–3–48a (1983),[1] * * * Today we hold that an award of punitive damages is not precluded by the recovery of treble damages under the statute. * * *

---

1. [footnotes renumbered] W.Va.Code, 61–3–48a, states: "Any person who enters upon the   land or premises of another without written permission from the owner of the land or prem-

In September of 1994, the jury awarded Carol Sue Bullman, the plaintiff * * * $5,000 in compensatory damages and $25,000 in punitive damages for the defendant's wrongful removal of trees and excavation of a logging road on her property when it was timbering a contiguous tract. On appeal, the defendant argues in effect that by bringing the action under the treble damage statute, the plaintiff chose the remedy afforded by statute, which is itself punitive, and the punitive damage award is tantamount to double recovery. [W]e affirm the judgment of the trial court. * * *

Ray Bowers, a timber broker, purchased timbering rights from the surface owner of a 66–acre tract known as the "Leonard" tract which is adjacent to the plaintiff's property. In November of 1988, the defendant entered into a contract with Mr. Bowers to timber the Leonard tract. * * * The defendant completed timbering operations by January 30, 1989. * * *

Twenty-three trees were cut and removed from the plaintiff's property, logging roads were dug, and the debris from the timbering operation was left on the ground. Photographs of the area were admitted into evidence showing extensive damage to the property. Approximately half of the trees removed were close to the Leonard and Bullman common boundary line and half the trees were taken from well within the plaintiff's property. Six or seven acres of her property were affected, as the defendant removed only the higher quality timber in a practice known as selective cutting. The fair market value of the timber cut was approximately $1,000. The cost of repairing the land was estimated at $1,400.

The plaintiff filed this action on February 13, 1991, seeking compensatory and punitive damages for the removal of her trees and destruction of her property. The jury awarded her $3,100 which is the stumpage value of the trees removed multiplied by three, $1,400 for repairing the land, and $500 for loss of property, totalling $5,000. The plaintiff also was awarded $25,000 in punitive damages.

The defendant asserts that because the plaintiff elected to seek treble damages as provided by W.Va.Code, 61–3–48a, then punitive damages should not be available to her. The issue raised by the defendant has some merit. Under most legislative schemes, when a statute creates a cause of action and provides the remedy, the remedy is exclusive unless the statute states otherwise. Therefore, multiple damages should not be awarded in the absence of statutory authority. [citation] Thus, at the heart of this controversy is W.Va.Code, 61–3–48a, and its intended scope and coverage. To resolve this issue, this Court must determine whether the Legislature intended to preclude an award of punitive damages where treble damages are sought.

In construing this statute, we commence with the rule that courts are not at liberty to construe any statute so as to deny effect to any part of its language. * * * Another rule equally recognized is that every part of a statute must be construed in connection with the whole, so as to make all parts harmonize, if possible, and to give meaning to each. [citation] That is to say, every word used is presumed to have meaning and purpose, for the Legislature is thought by the courts not to have used language idly. We find this statute to be remedial in

ises in order to cut, damage or carry away or cause to be cut, damaged or carried away, any timber, trees, logs, posts, fruit, nuts, growing plant or product of any growing plant, shall be liable to the owner in the amount of three times the value of the timber, trees, growing plants or products thereof, which shall be in addition to and notwithstanding any other penalties by law provided."may also seek punitive damages.

nature and, as a remedial statute, it should be liberally construed to effect the purpose of the Legislature. [citation]

The defendant contends that the plaintiff should not be allowed to recover both under the statute and common law punitive damages when the two are inconsistent. [citations] The defendant's argument, to be valid, is premised on the notion that treble damages under the statute are punitive in nature. As stated above, it is necessary for us to examine the statute for the purpose of determining whether its aim is to punish the conduct of the individual to whom it is applied. As a general rule, penal and punitive statutes contain language of the character that indicates they are concerned with mens rea. Far from containing expressions of that kind, W.Va.Code, 61–3–48a, repels any inference that it is concerned with mens rea.[2] Recovery is permitted under this statute for the mere removal or cutting of someone's trees without their written consent. In any event, the literal terms of the statute are ultimately indifferent to conduct that is willful or results from the wrongdoer's careless inattention to boundary lines. By its very language, W.Va.Code, 61–3–48a, deals with trespassers who have no evil intent. The statute is concerned with the cutting, damaging, and taking of trees, not with the state of mind of the wrongdoer.

Furthermore, a treble damage award and a punitive damage award serve two distinct purposes. The treble damage award available under W.Va.Code, 61–3–48a, is to provide compensatory damages to landowners for damaged or removed trees, logs, fruit, etc. By allowing such increase of recovery from the market value of the timber removed, the Legislature provided a remedy that would more adequately compensate landowners. In adopting this legislation, the Legislature must have recognized that many times it would not be cost effective to bring a claim for damaged or removed trees or fruit when considering the market value of the item compared with the cost of litigation. In other words, the Legislature may have been persuaded to make provision for the recovery of the enhanced amount by a belief that if a victim is granted judgment for nothing more than her actual damages, she would have nothing left for herself after she paid attorney's fees. Every time a victim institutes an action for recovery of damages, she is subjected to inconvenience, annoyances, preparation for the trial, loss of time, and the payment of attorney's fees. However, the preparation for trial, loss of time, and payment of attorney's fees are usually recoverable in the damage award. Thus, the statute gives the victim an incentive, through treble damages, to assert her rights and provides her with the means of doing so.

This point cannot be rejected lightly. Under common law, a recovery for the wrongful cutting of trees was either the difference between the market value of the land immediately before and immediately after the trespass or the fair market value of the trees. [citation] In either case, it is not difficult to understand why a legislative body might conclude the victim was not made whole. At common law, the wrongdoer was not liable for all the harmful consequences of his actions, but only for those that were proximately caused by the wrong. Obviously, there is a big difference between the proximate result and what a victim would receive given the benefit of a harmful consequences rule.

2. It is to be noted that W.Va.Code, 61–3–48a, "employs no term such as 'wilful' or 'intentional' which [is] found in statutes which impose penalties." Kinzua Lumber Co. v. Daggett, 203 Or. 585, 590, 281 P.2d 221, 223 (1955). Far from employing words that evince a purpose to deal with wanton conduct and punish it, this statute plainly indicates a legislative design for its application in cases where the wrongdoer had no evil purpose. In fact, this treble damage provision is triggered in cases where the wrongdoer actually acted in good faith.

The legislative effort to permit full recovery is not, in our judgment, a punishment to the wrongdoer but rather a desire to provide full compensation to the plaintiff from the wrongdoer for the damages sustained because of the wrongful act. To recover treble damages, a plaintiff need not make a showing that the removal of the trees was in willful disregard of the landowner's property rights. The statute does not directly or indirectly speak to punishment or penalties, but refers entirely to damages suffered by the plaintiff. Thus, we find the overriding purpose of the treble damage provision is to award the victim adequate compensation. Its amerciable effect, if any, is secondary.

On the other hand, a punitive damage award, or smart money, is given to punish a defendant, to deter others from similar conduct, and to provide additional compensation to the plaintiff. [citations] Punitive damages are sums of money that are awarded in addition to actual damages. Punitive damages are assessed against wrongdoers because the law disapproves of the conduct in which the wrongdoer is engaged and seeks to stamp it out. Cases in which punitive damages are sought have a two-fold aspect: (a) recovery of redress for an injury suffered by the victim; and (b) the amercement of the wrongdoer. Obviously, it is the amercement of the wrongdoer that is the focal point of punitive damages. We believe the Legislature in enacting W.Va.Code, 61–3–48a, accepted as a base for the treble damage award the victim's actual damages and then by tripling the sum granted her a recovery so that she would have something left in her pocket after she had discharged the expenses of the litigation. As we suggested already, this award has nothing to do with punishing the wrongdoer.

There is another flaw in the defendant's reasoning. The recovery of treble damages under W.Va.Code, 61–3–48a, is for damage to things cut, damaged, or carried away. The things covered by statute are "timber, trees, logs, posts, fruit, nuts, growing plant or product of any growing plant." It does not cover any other damages resulting from a trespass. In the instant action, the plaintiff also sought recovery for the defendant's trespass for entering her property and destroying her land. The jury awarded the plaintiff $1,400 for repair to her land as a separate item of actual damages. The punitive damages may have been awarded solely or in part for wanton and willful conduct that resulted in the damage to her land. If this is so, there is no issue of double recovery at all.

Finally, the defendant's argument, we think, fails in the face of the statutory language itself. W.Va.Code, 61–3–48a, specifically states that the treble damage award "shall be in addition to and notwithstanding any other penalties by law provided." Applying the clear language of the statute, we find that a plaintiff does not foreclose his or her claim for punitive damages by seeking recovery under W.Va.Code, 61–3–48a. If the Legislature intended for treble damages to be the exclusive remedy, it would have not added such explicit language. Just as courts are not to add to statutes something the Legislature has purposely omitted, we are also obliged not to eliminate through judicial interpretation words that were purposely included. * * *

Affirmed.

Notes

1. *Litigation Finance?* If financing litigation had been the legislature's goal, could the statute have provided separately for a successful plaintiff to recover

attorney fees? Many timber trespass statutes turn multiple damages on the defendant's imprudence, intent, willfulness, or the like; if so, the multiplied part seems punitive.

2. *Punitive Damages Under Other Multiple Statutes.* (a) The multiplied part of plaintiff's recovery under the state Human Rights statute is compensatory and not duplicative of punitive damages. Phelps v. Commonwealth Land Title Insurance Co., 537 N.W.2d 271 (Minn.1995).

(b) Another court gave two reasons not to add common law punitive damages to a state antitrust statute's trebled damages. First the multiplied part above compensatory damages is a penalty and adding punitive damages would be double recovery. Second "when a statute creates a cause of action and provides the remedy, the remedy is exclusive." John Mohr & Sons v. Jahnke, 55 Wis.2d 402, 198 N.W.2d 363, 368 (1972).

3. *Multiple Damages Plus Emotional Distress?* Washington state, the *Grays Harbor*, p. 827, court said, "early committed itself to the view that the doctrine of exemplary or punitive damages is unsound in principle and that such damages cannot be recovered except when explicitly allowed by statute." The Washington timber trespass statute's trebling is an explicitly punitive statute. In *Grays Harbor* the court considered an exception, recovery of the enhanced value for willful or bad faith trespass is punitive damages.

In a later decision, the Washington court let plaintiffs add $2000 emotional distress damages to multiplied statutory timber trespass damages. Citing *Grays Harbor*, that court said the plaintiff may recover statutory trebled damages for willful trespasses, but not for innocent ones; moreover, since statutory trebled damages are not exclusive, the owners recovery could include damages for proved emotional distress. Birchler v. Castello Land Company, Inc., quoted above, p. 813. Do emotional distress damages duplicate treble damages?

4. *Punitive Damages in Property Litigation.* When a conversion, trespass, or nuisance defendant's wrongdoing is sufficiently aggravated to qualify it for punitive damages, a plaintiff suing to protect or vindicate that property interest may recover them.

In March 1989, captained by a relapsed alcoholic, the tanker *Exxon Valdez* ran aground in Prince William Sound carrying 53 million gallons of crude oil, 11 million of which spilled into the fragile environment. After Exxon's voluntary payments, settlements, and criminal prosecution, a jury in the trial of a 32,677–member punitive-damages class entered a verdict for $5 billion punitive damages against Exxon, $5000 against Captain Hazelwood. Two trips to the United States Court of Appeals later, in his third decision on Exxon's motion to reduce-remit the punitive damages, the district judge reexamined the $5 billion verdict which was a 9.74 ratio to plaintiffs' "actual harm."

"Exxon's conduct," the judge wrote, "did not simply cause economic harm to the plaintiffs. Exxon's decision to leave Captain Hazelwood in command of the *Exxon Valdez* demonstrated reckless disregard for a broad range of legitimate Alaska concerns: the livelihood, health, and safety of the residents of Prince William Sound, the crew of the *Exxon Valdez,* and others. Exxon's conduct targeted some financially vulnerable individuals, namely subsistence fishermen. Plaintiffs' harm was not the result of an isolated incident but was the result of Exxon's repeated decisions, over a period of approximately three years, to allow Captain Hazelwood to remain in command despite Exxon's knowledge that he was drinking and driving again. Exxon's bad conduct as to Captain Hazelwood and his operation of the *Exxon Valdez* was intentionally malicious. Comparing Exxon's conduct with what happened in

BMW and *State Farm*, [pp. 133–51.] Exxon's conduct was many degrees of magnitude more egregious. For approximately three years, Exxon management, with knowledge that Captain Hazelwood had fallen off the wagon, willfully permitted him to operate a fully-loaded, crude oil tanker in and out of Prince William Sound-a body of water which Exxon knew to be highly valuable for its fisheries resources. Exxon's argument that its conduct in permitting a relapsed alcoholic to operate an oil tanker should be characterized as less reprehensible than what State Farm did to the Campbells suggests that Exxon, even today, has not come to grips with the opprobrium which society rightly attaches to drunk driving. While there are surely other situations that would be more reprehensible-such as knowingly allowing a relapsed alcoholic to operate a 747 aircraft loaded with passengers-this case is in an entirely different galaxy than selling repainted cars as new, * * * or refusing for eighteen months to pay an excess judgment of $185,849. Based on the foregoing, the court finds Exxon's conduct highly reprehensible.''

Although he thought that $5 billion punitive damages was justified, the judge, following the appellate court's directions, reduced it to $4.5 billion, urging the plaintiff class to lob a cross appeal at Exxon if it appealed a third time. In re the Exxon Valdez, 296 F.Supp.2d 1071, 1097 (D.Alaska 2004). The lengthy opinion is notable for the trial judge's disagreement with an earlier Court of Appeals opinion and skepticism about the Supreme Court's ratio guideline.

3. RESTITUTION

To begin with, in all but one of the restitution decisions below, plaintiff's defendant will be a tortfeasor who has converted plaintiff's property. Plaintiff will base restitution on the defendant's tort, not just on the defendant's unjust enrichment. So plaintiff's restitution claim, which is founded on the defendant's tort, is restitution for defendant's wrong. Because of defendant's tort, plaintiff's restitution claim is not based on defendant's unjust enrichment without any other substantive breach. Moreover, plaintiff has the option of suing the defendant for either tort damages or restitution.

Although the issue of whether the court should grant the plaintiff restitution is usually straightforward, the question of how the court should measure the plaintiff's restitution will often be nettlesome.

Suppose the court will base the owner's tort damages measure on the property's value on the date of conversion but the defendant has sold it for more than its earlier value. Then plaintiff may prefer legal restitution to recover defendant's unjust enrichment, restitution measured by what the defendant received from his buyer. Plaintiff's action for legal restitution was known as waiver of tort [conversion] and suit in assumpsit [quasi-contract or contract implied in law].

Plaintiff's legal restitution traditionally could take the form of either of two common counts with different measures of recovery: (a) when the converter had sold the property to another, plaintiff used the common count of *money had and received* to recover the proceeds of the converter's sale; or (b) when the converter still had the property, plaintiff used the common count of *goods sold and delivered* to recover the property's value.

Restitution doctrine still has not extricated itself completely from these nonfunctional and confusing forms and distinctions. The Restatement of Restitution in 1937 and decisions like the next one were major steps toward a more sensible approach. Personal property restitution is more straightforward than real property restitution, which comes later.

OLWELL v. NYE & NISSEN CO.

Supreme Court of Washington, 1946.
26 Wash.2d 282, 173 P.2d 652.

MALLERY, JUSTICE. On May 6, 1940, plaintiff, E.L. Olwell, sold and transferred to the defendant corporation his one-half interest in Puget Sound Egg Packers, a Washington corporation having its principal place of business in Tacoma. By the terms of the agreement, the plaintiff was to retain full ownership in an "Eggsact" egg-washing machine, formerly used by Puget Sound Egg Packers. The defendant promised to make it available for delivery to the plaintiff on or before June 15, 1940. It appears that the plaintiff arranged for and had the machine stored in a space adjacent to the premises occupied by the defendant but not covered by its lease. Due to the scarcity of labor immediately after the outbreak of the war, defendant's treasurer, without the knowledge or consent of the plaintiff, ordered the egg washer taken out of storage. The machine was put into operation by defendant on May 31, 1941, and thereafter for a period of three years was used approximately one day a week in the regular course of the defendant's business. Plaintiff first discovered this use in January or February of 1945 when he happened to be at the plant on business and heard the machine operating. Thereupon plaintiff offered to sell the machine to defendant for $600 or half of its original cost in 1929. A counter offer of $50 was refused and approximately one month later this action was commenced to recover the reasonable value of defendant's use of the machine, and praying for $25 per month from the commencement of the unauthorized use until the time of trial. * * * The court entered judgment for plaintiff in the amount of $10 per week for the period of 156 weeks covered by the statute of limitations, or $1,560, and gave the plaintiff his costs.

Defendant has appealed to this court assigning error upon the judgment, upon the trial of the cause on the theory of unjust enrichment, upon the amount of damages, and upon the court's refusal to make a finding as to the value of the machine and in refusing to consider such value in measuring damages.

The theory of the respondent was that the tort of conversion could be "waived" and suit brought in quasi-contract, upon a contract implied in law, to recover, as restitution, the profits which inured to appellant as a result of its wrongful use of the machine. With this the trial court agreed and in its findings of facts found that the use of the machine "resulted in a benefit to the users, in that said use saves the users approximately $1.43 per hour of use as against the expense which would be incurred were eggs to be washed by hand; that said machine was used by Puget Sound Egg Packers and defendant, on an average of one day per week from May of 1941, until February of 1945 at an average saving of $10.00 per each day of use."

In substance, the argument presented by the assignments of error is that the principle of unjust enrichment, or quasi-contract, is not of universal application, but is imposed only in exceptional cases because of special facts and circumstances and in favor of particular persons; that respondent had an adequate remedy in an action at law for replevin or claim and delivery; that any damages awarded to the plaintiff should be based upon the use or rental value of the machine and should bear some reasonable relation to its market value. Appellant therefore contends that the amount of the judgment is excessive.

It is uniformly held that in cases where the defendant *tort feasor* has benefitted by his wrong, the plaintiff may elect to "waive the tort" and bring an action in assumpsit for restitution. Such an action arises out of a duty imposed by law devolving upon the defendant to repay an unjust and unmerited enrichment.

It is clear that the saving in labor cost which appellant derived from its use of respondent's machine constituted a benefit.

According to the Restatement of Restitution, § 1(b), p. 12.

> "A person confers a benefit upon another if he gives to the other possession of or some other interest in money, land, chattels or choses in action, performs services beneficial to or at the request of the other, satisfies a debt or a duty of the other, or in any way adds to the other's security or advantage. *He confers a benefit not only where he adds to the property of another, but also where he* saves the other from expense or loss. The word 'benefit,' therefore denotes any form of advantage." (Italics ours)

It is also necessary to show that while appellant benefitted from its use of the egg-washing machine, respondent thereby incurred a loss. It was argued by appellant that since the machine was put into storage by respondent, who had no present use for it, and for a period of almost three years did not know that appellant was operating it and since it was not injured by its operation and the appellant never adversely claimed any title to it, nor contested respondent's right of repossession upon the latter's discovery of the wrongful operation, that the respondent was not damaged because he is as well off as if the machine had not been used by appellant.

The very essence of the nature of property is the right to its exclusive use. Without it, no beneficial right remains. However plausible, the appellant cannot be heard to say that his wrongful invasion of the respondent's property right to exclusive use is not a loss compensable in law. To hold otherwise would be subversive of all property rights since his use was admittedly wrongful and without claim of right. The theory of unjust enrichment is applicable in such a case.

We agree with appellant that respondent could have elected a "common garden variety of action," as he calls it, for the recovery of damages. It is also true that except where provided for by statute, punitive damages are not allowed, the basic measure for the recovery of damages in this state being compensation. If, then, respondent had been *limited* to redress *in tort* for damages, as appellant contends, the court below would be in error in refusing to make a finding as to the value of the machine. In such case the award of damages must bear a reasonable relation to the value of the property. * * *

But respondent here had an election. He chose rather to waive his right of action *in tort* and to sue *in assumpsit* on the implied contract. Having so elected, he is entitled to the measure of restoration which accompanies the remedy.

> "Actions for restitution have for their primary purpose taking from the defendant and restoring to the plaintiff something to which the plaintiff is entitled, or if this is not done, causing the defendant to pay the plaintiff an amount which will restore the plaintiff to the position in which he was before the defendant received the benefit. If the value of what was received and what was lost were always equal, there would be no substantial problem as to the amount of recovery, since actions of restitution are not punitive. In

fact, however, the plaintiff frequently has lost more than the defendant has gained, and sometimes the defendant has gained more than the plaintiff has lost."

"In such cases the measure of restitution is determined with reference to the tortiousness of the defendant's conduct or the negligence or other fault of one or both of the parties in creating the situation giving rise to the right to restitution. If the defendant was tortious in his acquisition of the benefit he is required to pay for what the other has lost although that is more than the recipient benefitted. *If he was consciously tortious in acquiring the benefit, he is also deprived of any profit derived from his subsequent dealing with it.* If he was no more at fault than the claimant, he is not required to pay for losses in excess of benefit received by him and he is permitted to retain gains which result from his dealing with the property." (Italics ours) Restatement of Restitution, pp. 595, 596.

Respondent may recover the profit derived by the appellant from the use of the machine.

Respondent has prayed "on his first cause of action for the sum of $25.00 per month from the time defendant first commenced to use said machine subsequent to May 1940 (1941) until present time."

In computing judgment, the court below computed recovery on the basis of $10 per week. This makes the judgment excessive since it cannot exceed the amount prayed for.

We therefore direct the trial court to reduce the judgment, based upon the prayer of the complaint, to $25 per month for thirty-six months, or $900.

The judgment as modified is affirmed.

Questions

Should Olwell have recovered more for restitution than he offered to sell the machine to defendants for? Does the court take value created by defendants' skill in running a going business? Should the court have measured Olwell's restitution recovery by what a negotiated rent would have been?

SCHLOSSER v. WELK

Appellate Court of Illinois, 1990.
193 Ill.App.3d 448, 550 N.E.2d 241.

Justice Wombacher delivered the opinion of the court. The defendant, Rhonda Welk, appeals from a $549 judgment entered in favor of the plaintiff, Marianne Schlosser, d/b/a Select–A–Video. The record shows that the defendant was an employee of Select–A–Video until her termination on October 5, 1987. As a general policy, employees were allowed to take video tapes home for their personal use without checking the tapes out or paying a rental fee. On the day the defendant was terminated, she had placed eight video tapes in her car. At the end of the work day, the defendant was told that she was being terminated. The defendant took the tapes home and during a conversation with her husband placed them in a storage closet. She testified that a number of weeks later she discovered the tapes while cleaning. She also testified that the tapes were never viewed by her or her family while they were in her possession. She returned the video tapes to the plaintiff's store on December 10, 1987.

At the conclusion of the bench trial, the court found that an implied contract existed between the parties. The court then ruled that the plaintiff was entitled to $549, which was the amount the defendant would have owed if she had rented the tapes for the two months she kept them.

On appeal, the defendant contends that the trial court erred in granting judgment for the plaintiff, because the plaintiff failed to show that the defendant had watched the video tapes. According to the defendant, the plaintiff therefore failed to show that the defendant derived any benefit from her possession of the tapes. She claims that because the plaintiff failed to show a benefit to the defendant, the plaintiff failed to prove an essential element necessary for recovery on its unjust enrichment claim.

The theory of unjust enrichment is based upon a finding of a contract implied in law. The essential element of a contract implied in law is the receipt of benefits by one party, which it would be inequitable for him to retain without payment; it is predicated on the principle that no one should unjustly enrich himself at another's expense.

From the record, it is clear that the defendant derived a benefit from her possession of the plaintiff's video tapes and that therefore an implied contract existed between herself and the plaintiff. The tapes were available for her use. Under any other circumstances she would have had to buy or rent the tapes in order to view them. In sum, by showing that the defendant had possession of the tapes for her private use, the plaintiff proved that the defendant had derived a benefit.

The defendant next argues that the trial court erred in determining the amount of the plaintiff's recovery.

The plaintiff's recovery is limited to the reasonable amount by which the trial court finds the defendant was unjustly enriched at the expense of the plaintiff. * * *

On review of the record, we find the evidence insufficient to support the full amount of the instant award. The unrebutted evidence showed that the defendant and her family never watched the video tapes. There was no evidence that the defendant intentionally withheld the tapes from the plaintiff. Further, the plaintiff presented no evidence that it lost money because it was unable to rent the tapes to a paying customer. Under the circumstances of this case, we find it unreasonable to treat the tapes as having been rented on a day-by-day basis for the entire time the defendant had them. The inequity in such an award is at least as great as allowing the defendant to retain the tapes without paying any rental fee. A more reasonable approach is to hold that the defendant was enriched to the extent of one day's rental fee for each of the tapes in her possession. The evidence showed that the six children's tapes held by the defendant each rented for $1 a day and the two adult tapes together rented for $3 a day during the week. Therefore, the defendant was enriched to the extent of $9, and the trial court should have entered judgment for the plaintiff in that amount. Accordingly, having found the trial court's decision contrary to the manifest weight of the evidence, we modify the judgment in favor of the plaintiff, reducing the award from $549 to $9.

The judgment of the circuit court of Peoria County is affirmed as modified.

Affirmed as modified.

JUSTICE HEIPLE, concurring in part; dissenting in part. * * * The trial court found an implied contract had arisen which entitled the store to an award of $549 for lost rentals. While the majority order affirms the principle of implied contract, it reduces the damages to $9 on the grounds that there was no evidence that the defendant viewed the tapes more than once or that the plaintiff actually suffered a loss from lost rentals. I respectfully disagree with that portion of the order.

The evidence showed a daily rental rate of $1 for the six children's tapes that were taken plus $1.50 a day for each of the two adult tapes. Hence, the majority arrived at a reduced figure of $9 which assumes a single viewing of each of the eight tapes during the course of one day's rental.

The error here is that the question of whether the tapes were viewed or not and how many times they were viewed is wholly irrelevant. The fact is that the tapes were unlawfully in the possession of the defendant and available for viewing for a period of two months whether viewed in fact or not. Likewise, the plaintiff was deprived of the tapes for two months and thereby the possibility of renting them for that period of time. The benefit conferred on the defendant is the possession of the tapes for two months. Whether she viewed them once, not at all, or used them to prop up a short leg on her dining room table is really quite beside the point. She took them, kept them, had them in her possession for such use as she chose to make of them and, in fact, deprived the lawful owner of their use and potential rental for a period of two months. Therein lies the benefit and the detriment.

Notes

1. *Questions.* How much would plaintiff have recovered if it had sued for torts, conversion or trespass to chattels? How did defendant benefit from the tapes? Do you think the trial judge, confused by the terminology, converted an "implied contract" into a real or express contract? Was defendant unjustly enriched, (a) not at all, (b) one day's rent for each tape, (c) the purchase price of used tapes, (d) the purchase price of new tapes, or (e) the full rent for the full period?

2. *Preview.* In the following two cases, *Edwards* and *Raven Red Ash*, the defendant wants something that only the owner has, access to a cave and passage across land respectively. Instead of working things out, both defendants help themselves. When hailed into court, both defendants argue for the tort damages measure, but, even though the first Restitution Restatement rejected restitution under the circumstances, both courts approved it.

In *Edwards*, the next decision, prior litigation had recognized the Lees' rights to the parts of the "Great Onyx Cave" under the surface of their land. Remember "ad coelum"?

EDWARDS v. LEE'S ADMINISTRATOR

Court of Appeals of Kentucky, 1936.
265 Ky. 418, 96 S.W.2d 1028.

STITES, JUSTICE. About twenty years ago L.P. Edwards discovered a cave under land belonging to him and his wife, Sally Edwards. The entrance to the cave is on the Edwards land. Edwards named it the "Great Onyx Cave." This cave is located in the cavernous area of Kentucky, and is only about three miles distant from the world-famous Mammoth Cave. Its proximity to Mammoth Cave, which for many years has had an international reputation as an underground wonder, as well as its beautiful formations, led Edwards to embark upon a program of advertising and exploitation for the purpose of bringing visitors to his cave. Circulars were printed and distributed, signs were erected along the roads, persons were employed and stationed along the highways to solicit the patronage of passing travelers, and thus the fame of the Great Onyx Cave spread from year to year, until eventually, and before the beginning of the present litigation, it was a well-known and well-patronized cave. Edwards built a hotel near the mouth of the cave to care for travelers. He improved and widened the footpaths and avenues in the cave, and ultimately secured a stream of tourists who paid entrance fees sufficient not only to cover the cost of operation, but also to yield a substantial revenue in additional thereto. The authorities in charge of the development of the Mammoth Cave area as a national park undertook to secure the Great Onyx Cave through condemnation proceedings, and in that suit the value of the cave was fixed by a jury at $396,000. In April, 1928, F.P. Lee, an adjoining landowner, filed this suit against Edwards and the heirs of Sally Edwards, claiming that a portion of the cave was under his land, and praying for damages for an accounting of the profits which resulted from the operation of the cave, and for an injunction prohibiting Edwards and his associates from further trespassing upon or exhibiting any part of the cave under Lee's land.

* * * An injunction was granted prohibiting Edwards and his associates from further trespassing on the lands of Lee. On final hearing the chancellor stated separately his findings of law and of fact in the following language:

"The Court finds as a matter of law the plaintiff is entitled to recover of defendants the proportionate part of the net proceeds defendants received from exhibiting Great Onyx Cave from the years 1923 to 1930, inclusive, as the footage of said cave under Lee's land bears to the entire footage of the cave exhibited to the public for fees during the years 1923 to 1930, inclusive, with 6% interest on plaintiff's proportionate part of said fund for each year from the first day of the following year as set out in the memorandum opinion.

* * * "2. The Court finds as a matter of fact there was 6,449.88 feet of said cave exhibited to the public during 1923 to 1930, inclusive, and that 2,048.60 feet of said footage was under Lee's lands making plaintiff entitled to

$\frac{2048.60}{6449.88}$ or ⅓ of the Proceeds." * * *

Appellants, in their attack here on the measure of damages and its application to the facts adduced, urge: (1) That the appellees had simply a hole in the ground, about 360 feet below the surface, which they could not use and which they could not even enter except by going through the mouth of the cave on Edwards' property; (2) the cave was of no practical use to appellees without an entrance, and there was no one except the appellants on whom they might confer a right of beneficial use; (3) Lee's portion of the cave had no rental value; (4) appellees were not ousted of the physical occupation or use of the property because they did not and could not occupy it; (5) the property has not in any way been injured by the use to which it has been put by appellants, and since this is fundamentally an action for damages arising from trespass, the recovery must be limited to the damages suffered by appellees (in other words, nominal damages) and cannot properly be measured by the benefits accruing to the trespasser from his wrongful use of the property; (6) as a result of the injunction, appellees have their cave in exactly the condition it has always been, handicapped by no greater degree of uselessness than it was before appellants trespassed upon it.

Appellees, on the other hand, argue that this was admittedly a case of willful trespass; that it is not analogous to a situation where a trespasser simply walks across the land of another for here the trespasser actually used the property of Lee to make a profit for himself; that even if nothing tangible was taken or disturbed in the various trips through Lee's portion of the cave, nevertheless there was a taking of esthetic enjoyment which, under ordinary circumstances, would justify a recovery of the reasonable rental value for the use of the cave; that there being no basis for arriving at reasonable rental values, the chancellor took the only course open to him under the circumstances and properly assessed the damages on the basis of the profits realized from the use of Lee's portion of the cave. Appellees have taken a cross-appeal, however, on the theory that, since the trespass was willful, their damages should be measured by the gross profits realized from the operation of the cave rather than from its net profits.

As the foregoing statement of the facts and the contentions of the parties will demonstrate, the case is sui generis, and counsel have been unable to give us much assistance in the way of previous decisions of this or other courts. We are left to fundamental principles and analogies.

We may begin our consideration of the proper measure of damages to be applied with the postulate that appellees held legal title to a definite segment of the cave and that they were possessed, therefore, of a right which it is the policy of the law to protect. We may assume that the appellants were guilty of repeated trespasses upon the property of appellees. * * * The proof likewise clearly indicates that the trespasses were willful, and not innocent.

Appellees brought this suit in equity, and seek an accounting of the profits realized from the operation of the cave, as well as an injunction against future trespass. In substance, therefore, their action is ex contractu and not, as appellants contend, simply an action for damages arising from a tort. Ordinarily, the measure of recovery in assumpsit for the taking and selling of personal property is the value received by the wrongdoer. On the other hand, where the action is based upon a trespass to land, the recovery has almost invariably been measured by the reasonable rental value of the property. Strictly speaking, a count for "use and occupation" does not fit the facts before us because, while there has been a recurring use, there has been no continuous occupation of the cave such as might arise from the planting of a crop or the tenancy of a house. Each trespass was a distinct usurpation of the appellees' title and interruption of their right to undisturbed possession. But, even if we apply the analogy of the crop cases or the wayleave cases, it is apparent that rental value has been adopted, either consciously or unconsciously, as a convenient yardstick by which to measure the proportion of profit derived by the trespasser directly from the use of the land itself. In other words, rental value ordinarily indicates the amount of profit realized directly from the land, as land, aside from all collateral contracts. * * *

Clearly, the unjust enrichment of the wrongdoer is the gist of the right to bring an action ex contractu. Rental value is merely the most convenient and logical means for ascertaining what proportion of the benefits received may be attributed to the use of the real estate. In the final analysis, therefore, the distinction made between assumpsit concerning real and personal property thus disappears. * * *

Similarly, in illumination of this conclusion, there is a line of cases holding that the plaintiff may at common law bring an action against a trespasser for the recovery of "mesne profits" following the successful termination of an action of ejectment. Here again, the real basis of recovery is the profits received, rather than rent. In Worthington v. Hiss, 70 Md. 172, 16 A. 534, 536, 17 A. 1026, the court said:

> 'It is well settled that in an action to recover mesne profits, the plaintiff must show in the best way he can what those profits are, and there are two modes of doing so, to either of which he may resort,—he may either prove the profits actually received, or the annual rental value of the land. * * * The latter is the mode usually adopted. Where there is occupation of a farm or land used only for agricultural purposes, and the income and profits are of necessity the produce of the soil, the owner may have an account of the proceeds of the crops and other products sold or raised thereon, deducting the expense of cultivation. These are necessarily rents and profits in such cases, but even there it is more usual to arrive at the same result by charging the occupier, as tenant, with a fair annual money rent. But the proprietor of city lots, with improvements upon them, can only derive therefrom, as owner, a fair occupation rent for the purposes for which the premises are adapted. This constitutes the rents and profits, in the legal sense of the terms, of such property, and is all the owner can justly claim in this shape from the occupier.'

Finally, in the current proposed final draft of the Restatement of Restitution and Unjust Enrichment (March 4, 1936), Part I, § 136, it is stated:

> 'A person who tortiously uses a trade name, trade secret, profit a prendre, or other similar interest of another, is under a duty of restitution for the value of the benefit thereby received.'

The analogy between the right to protection which the law gives a trade-name or trade secret and the right of the appellees here to protection of their legal rights in the cave seems to us to be very close. In all of the mineral and timber cases, there is an actual physical loss suffered by the plaintiff, as well as a benefit received by the defendant. In other words, there is both a plus and a minus quantity. In the trade-name and similar cases, as in the case at bar, there may be no tangible loss other than the violation of a right. The law, in seeking an adequate remedy for the wrong, has been forced to adopt profits received, rather than damages sustained, as a basis of recovery. In commenting on the section of the Restatement quoted above, the reporter says:

> 'Persons who tortiously use trade names, trade secrets, water rights, and other similar interests of others, are ordinarily liable in an action of tort for the harm which they have done. In some cases, however, no harm is done and in those cases if the sole remedy were by an action of tort the wrongdoer would be allowed to profit at little or no expense. In cases where the damage is more extensive, proof as to its extent may be so difficult that justice can be accomplished only by requiring payment of the amount of profits. Where definite damage is caused and is susceptible of proof, the injured person, as in other tort cases, can elect between an action for damages and an action for the value of that which was improperly received. The usual method of seeking restitution is by a bill in equity, with a request

for an accounting for any profits which have been received, but the existence of a right to bring such a bill does not necessarily prevent an action at law for the value of the use. In the case of tortious interference with patents, under existing statutes there is a right to restitution only in connection with an injunction.'

Whether we consider the similarity of the case at bar to (1) the ordinary actions in assumpsit to recover for the use and occupation of real estate, or (2) the common-law action for mesne profits, or (3) the action to recover for the tortious use of a trade-name or other similar right, we are led inevitably to the conclusion that the measure of recovery in this case must be the benefits, or net profits, received by the appellants from the use of the property of the appellees. The philosophy of all these decisions is that a wrongdoer shall not be permitted to make a profit from his own wrong. Our conclusion that a proper measure of recovery is net profits, of course, disposes of the cross-appeal. Appellees are not entitled to recover gross profits. They are limited to the benefits accruing to the appellants.

* * * In determining the profits which might fairly be said to arise directly from the use of appellees' segment of the cave, the chancellor considered not only the footage exhibited, but the relative value of the particular points of interest featured in advertising the cave, and their possible appeal in drawing visitors. Of thirty-one scenes or objects in the cave advertised by appellants, twelve were shown to be on appellees' property. Several witnesses say that the underground Lucikovah river, which is under the appellees' land for almost its entire exhibited length, is one of the most attractive features of the cave, if not its leading attraction. Other similar attractions are shown to be located on appellees' property. The chancellor excluded profits received by the appellants from the operation of their hotel, and we think the conclusion that one-third of the net profits received alone from the exhibition of the cave is a fair determination of the direct benefits accruing to the appellants from the use of the appellees' property.

* * * The judgment is affirmed [with adjustments].

Notes

1. *The First Restatement.* "Disposition of and Trespass to Land." (2) A person who has trespassed upon the land of another is not thereby under a duty of restitution to the other for the value of its use.

Illustration 2: "A uses a road across B's land without B's knowledge for a period of two years in the transportation of materials, doing so without harm to the land." A saves $2,000 thereby. "A reasonable charge for the use of the road would be $200 per year. B is not entitled to recover for the use of the land in an action of assumpsit: in an action of tort he is entitled to recover only $200." Restatement of Restitution § 129 (1937).

2. *Replacing the Restatement.* Compare the third Restatement's replacement for the preceding section. A defendant "who obtains a benefit by an act of trespass * * * is accountable to the [property owner for the benefit so obtained]." Restatement (Third) of Restitution and Unjust Enrichment § 40 (Tent. Draft No. 4 2005). Edwards v. Lee's Administrator is § 40's Illustration 4.

3. *Questions.* Is the Third Restatement's section in Note 2 wiser than the first Restatement's in Note 1?

But did the Kentucky court reach the best result? Should the court have allowed more for Edwards's personal effort, energy, and initiative? Why strip Edwards of the profit? If Edwards had negotiated with the Lees in advance, would they have agreed on one third of the net profit for the Lees? Did Edwards deprive the Lees of an opportunity to develop their property commercially?

RAVEN RED ASH COAL CO. v. BALL

Supreme Court of Appeals of Virginia, 1946.
185 Va. 534, 39 S.E.2d 231.

HUDGINS, JUSTICE. Plaintiff, Estil Ball, stated, in his notice of motion, that he was entitled to recover $5,000 from the defendant for the use and occupation of an easement across his land. Defendant denied any liability. The trial court entered judgment for plaintiff in the sum of $500 on the verdict returned by the jury. From that judgment, defendant obtained this writ of error.

There is no substantial conflict in the evidence. Plaintiff proved that he is the present owner of approximately 100 acres of land lying in Russell County which was a part of a 265–acre tract formerly owned by Reuben Sparks and that Reuben Sparks and his wife, by deed dated November 19, 1887, conveyed the coal and mineral rights on the 265–acre tract to Joseph I. Doran and William A. Dick. * * *

[The deed gave Doran and Dick an easement over what is now plaintiff's (Ball's) 100 acres to haul out the coal from their mines on adjacent land totalling 3000 acres. About 2000 feet of roadway was built over Ball's 100 acres to utilize the easement. Raven Red Ash Coal bought Doran and Dick's mining interests on their original 3000 acres, and acquired the mining rights on five more small tracts (about 80 acres total) besides. The easement does not grant any right to haul coal dug from these five tracts.]

The testimony reveals that, during the past five years, defendant transported 49,016 tons of coal mined from the five small tracts over the tramway erected across plaintiff's land and transported 950,000 tons of coal mined from lands formerly owned by Doran and Dick. There remains to be mined approximately 8,000,000 tons of coal on the tracts formerly owned by Doran and Dick and 180,000 tons of coal on the other small tracts.

Defendant's six assignments of error present two questions: (1) Whether the facts entitle plaintiff to maintain an action of trespass on the case in assumpsit; and (2) the measure of damages.

Ball concedes that defendant exercised its right in transporting across plaintiff's land the 950,000 tons of coal, but contends that it violated the property rights of plaintiff in transporting the 49,016 tons of coal across plaintiff's land to defendant's tipple. This principle was settled by this court in Clayborn v. Camilla, etc., Coal Co., 128 Va. 383, 105 S.E. 117. * * *

This case holds that every use of an easement not necessarily included in the grant is a trespass to realty and renders the owner of the dominant tenement liable in a tort action to the owner of the servient tenement for all damages proven to have resulted therefrom, and, in the absence of proof of special damage, the owner of the servient tenement may recover nominal damages only.

Plaintiff did not prove any specific damage to the realty by the illegal use of the easement, and admitted that he suffered "no more damage other than the exclusion of use during that moment and that's the reason we have sued for use and occupancy."

It thus appears that plaintiff bases his sole ground of recovery on the right to maintain assumpsit for use and occupation. * * *

Assumpsit is classified as an action ex contractu as distinguished from an action ex delicto. Hence, in order to sustain the action, it is necessary for the plaintiff to establish an express contract or facts and circumstances from which the law will raise an implication of a promise to pay. In such a case, a plaintiff may waive the tort and institute his action in assumpsit for money had and received.

Where a naked trespass is committed, whether upon the person or property, assumpsit will not lie. If one commits an assault and battery upon another, it is absurd to imply a promise by the defendant to pay the victim a reasonable compensation. There is no basis for an implication of a contract where cattle inadvertently invade a neighbor's premises and trample down and destroy his crops. In each instance, a wrong and nothing more and nothing less has been committed. On the other hand, if a trespasser invades the premises of his neighbor, cuts and removes timber or severs minerals from the land and converts them to his own use, the owner may waive the tort and sue in assumpsit for the value of the materials converted. * * * Such a person has depleted the value of the owner's property and materially enhanced his own possessions.

The general rule stated in the majority of cases we have found is that, in an action for use and occupation, or for damages to realty, based on assumpsit, the plaintiff must prove that the defendant occupied the premises with his permission, either express or implied, or that the trespasser obtained something from the soil, such as growing crops, timber or ore, and appropriated the same to his own use. If the trespasser simply used the property of another to save himself inconvenience or even expenditure of money, the owner cannot maintain an action of debt or assumpsit. [The court cited Restatement of Restitution § 129 and many cases.]

The precise question has never been decided in this jurisdiction. If the rule in force in the majority of States is followed, the landowner will be placed in this position: If he maintains an action for tort, he will be limited to nominal damages only. He may obtain an injunction and restrain the defendant from the further unlawful use of the easement, and thus indirectly, perhaps force him to agree to pay for future additional burdens imposed on the easement. Such proceedings would not give the owner compensation for past illegal use of his property, although the wrongdoer had received and retained substantial benefits by reason of his own wrongs. [The court reviewed material above: Edwards v. Lee's Adm'r, Phillips v. Homfray, cited in *Edwards,* and the Reporter's notes to the first Restatement.]

The illegal transportation of the coal in question across plaintiff's land was intentional, deliberate and repeated from time to time for a period of years. Defendant had no moral or legal right to enrich itself by this illegal use of plaintiff's property. To limit plaintiff to the recovery of nominal damages for the repeated trespasses will enable defendant, as a trespasser, to obtain a more favorable position than a party contracting for the same right. Natural justice plainly requires the law to imply a promise to pay a fair value of the benefits received. Defendant's estate has been enhanced by just this much. * * *

While plaintiff offered no evidence to establish the value of the illegal use of the easement, we, as reasonable men, know that the transportation of 49,016 tons of coal over the tramroad across the plaintiff's land was a benefit to defendant. However, in the absence of proof of the value of the benefit, the court could enter no judgment for plaintiff. This proof is supplied by the testimony of the general manager on his cross-examination. The substance of his testimony on this point is that the prevailing rate of payment, or purchase of a right of way for transportation of coal across another's land, is one cent per ton, and that this purchase includes the right to construct and maintain a tramway for distances varying up to 2½ miles; but that, where the owner of the easement has already entered upon the land, and has constructed and is maintaining a tramroad for the transportation of coal from certain specified tracts, the purchase price should be much less—a small fraction of a cent per ton. The jury were instructed that they should fix the amount of damages, if any, at such as would fairly compensate plaintiff for the use and occupation of this strip of land in the hauling and transportation of 49,016 tons of coal over the same.

While the evidence on the value of the benefits retained by defendant is not as clear and full as it could be, and perhaps should have been, the jury had all the facts and circumstances before it and evidently concluded that the value of the benefit to the defendant for the illegal use of the easement should be computed at one cent per ton. Viewing the case as a whole, we find no reversible error, and the judgment of the trial court is affirmed.

Affirmed.

Notes

1. *Ball's Remedial Options.* The coal company's tort presented Ball with several possible remedies. They include (a) an injunction forbidding defendant's future misuse of the easement, (b) tort damages, and (c) restitution. How does the court evaluate (a) the injunction and (b) tort damages? (c) Why does the court approve Ball's restitution?

2. *Measuring Ball's Restitution.* There are at least three possible ways for the jury to measure Ball's restitution: (a) Ball's request, (b) the value of a new easement, and (c) the value of adding to an existing easement. The court approved the jury verdict's measure. Is that larger than the coal company's savings were? Is it more than an earlier negotiated transaction would have been?

3. *Structuring Future Negotiation.* The coal company still had quite a bit more coal which, although not covered by the easement, it needed to haul out, presumably over Ball's land. (In coal-country vernacular, coal-hauling privilege is "wheelage.") If the court had granted Ball an injunction, would that remedy encourage the coal company to bargain with Ball in the future? After this restitution decision, will the coal company probably have to pay Ball more wheelage to haul the coal out than it would have paid him in an earlier bargained transaction?

4. *Raven Red Ash* continues to present creative remedial possibilities, not all of which lawyers and judges grasp, as the following summaries reveal. Are you ready for some review, a little property technicality, and a few bad jokes?

(a) Another Virginia coal company had removed coal to construct a subterranean drainway through plaintiffs' property. Plaintiffs sued the coal operator for trespass for the coal and the use of the drainway:

"The plaintiffs have asserted the right to recover damages for the use of the drainway based upon the financial advantage which accrued to the defendant. If the plaintiffs had brought this action to recover on a theory of implied contract, the measure of damages would have been the value of the benefit received by the defendant." [Editors: The court cited and discussed *Raven Red Ash*.]

"The plaintiffs here, having chosen to bring an action for trespass, may recover only trespass damages. They may prove any damages which resulted from the use of the drainway. Absent such proof, they may recover nominal damages only."

"The court would further note that if the suit had been brought in contract the plaintiffs could not recover punitive damages. Punitive damages are not permitted in Virginia for breach of contract unless there is a separate independent tort. [citation] Here there is no separate independent tort. Since this suit is brought in tort the court is permitting the issue of punitive damages to go to the jury." Payne v. Consolidation Coal Co., 607 F.Supp. 378, 382 n. 2 (W.D.Va.1985).

Questions. But doesn't *Raven Red Ash* mean that when defendant commits the tort of trespass, the plaintiff's available remedies include both damages and restitution? Also, should the confusing label of legal restitution as an "implied contract" or a contract implied by law mean that restitution has all the attributes of contract including defendant's immunity from punitive damages? The "contract fallacy" is discussed above, p. 403.

(b) In Jantzen Beach Associates, LLC v. Jantzen Dymanic Corp., the Oregon Court of Appeals distinguished *Raven Red Ash*.

Plaintiff had a restrictive covenant on a neighboring parcel that guaranteed plaintiff's development's visibility from a highway, an interest the court called a "view easement." Defendant built a Circuit City store on the neighboring parcel.

Plaintiff alleged that the new building blocked the view in violation of the covenant. A court usually remedies a defendant's violation of a servitude with damages or an injunction, not with restitution. Defendants admitted that the Circuit City building breached the restrictive covenant and argued that plaintiff should be limited to that claim. The Circuit City building and the adjacent development, defendants maintained, increased the rental value of plaintiff's property.

Question. Does the preceding explain why plaintiff may have bypassed recognized remedies, damages and an injunction, to venture into restitution which was unknown remedial territory?

Plaintiff argued to support restitution that defendant was unjustly enriched by the amount that plaintiff could have received to release the building restriction-restrictive covenant on the parcel.

The Court of Appeals, reversing a judgment for plaintiff for $750,000, held that the trial judge should have granted the defendant judgment on the pleadings. Confining assumpsit narrowly to waiver of tort and suit in assumpsit, the court held that for a plaintiff to recover for restitution, defendant's interference with plaintiff's real property must be accompanied by a conversion of tangible property. "[A]ssumpsit is a remedy to recover on what the law implies is a contract to make restitution for something tangible that belonged to the plaintiff and was appropriated by defendants."

The Oregon court distinguished *Raven Red Ash*: First, *Raven Red Ash* represented the minority view, in contrast to the majority view which was that a defendant's interference with plaintiff's interest in real property must be accompanied by a conversion of tangible property. Second, *Raven Red Ash* involved a defendant's "naked trespass" that tortiously interfered with a plaintiff's possessory property right, not a violation of a nonpossessory, intangible restrictive covenant. Jantzen Beach Associates, LLC v. Jantzen Dynamic Corp., 200 Or.App. 457, 115 P.3d 943, 948 (2005), on rehearing, 204 Or. App. 68, 129 P.3d 186 (2006).

Questions. What was Raven Red Ash's substantive violation? Is that similar to a violation of a restrictive covenant?

As discussed above, although the 1937 Restatement of Restitution had rejected a landowner's restitution against a trespasser, the modern view, expressed in the Restatement Third, is to approve restitution. p. 843. Indeed, *Raven Red Ash* is the basis for Illustration 2 after § 40. Restatement (Third) of Restitution and Unjust Enrichment § 40, Illus. 2 (Tent. Draft No. 4 2005). *Raven Red Ash*, said Professor Palmer, is "one of the most important modern cases which has allowed quasi-contractual recovery." George Palmer, The Law of Restitution § 2.5, at 77–78 (1978).

Did the Oregon court leave the defendant unjustly enriched?

(c) Williams had a pipeline under the City of Shawnee's property. Shawnee had granted Williams an easement for the pipeline restricted to oil or oil products, gas and water. Under a license from Williams, AT & T installed a fiber optic cable for transcontinental lines in the Williams pipeline. Although Shawnee knew about the AT & T telecommunications cable, it had not granted a telecommunications easement to either Williams or AT & T. Shawnee charged AT & T with trespass and sought punitive damages. AT & T moved for summary judgment.

The court found AT & T's cable was a permanent trespass and barred Shawnee's suit against the cable as trespass under the statute of limitations. But each time AT & T transmitted a "pulse of information" under Shawnee's land, it committed an intentional and continuing trespass. "Although incorporeal electronic pulses do not necessarily come immediately to mind when one thinks of a 'thing,' the invasion of Shawnee's right to control the use of its property is no less real because the offending item is intangible. To hold otherwise would deny Shawnee its historical right as a landowner to exclude nonowners from using its property."

In response to AT & T's argument that Shawnee lacked any but nominal damage and indeed had not sought any actual damages, the court said "Shawnee may seek an injunction to prevent AT & T's continuing trespass. Thus, Shawnee has suffered an actionable injury which may support an award of punitive damages." City of Shawnee, Kansas v. AT & T Corp., 910 F.Supp. 1546, 1562, 1563 (D.Kan. 1995).

Question. Would awarding Shawnee restitution based on *Raven Red Ash* also be appropriate?

(d) Seeking certification of a plaintiff class charging that the power-company defendant had trespassed by exceeding the scope of easements for wire electric lines by installing and using a commercial fiber optic network, plaintiffs argued that "the appropriate measure of damages for unjust enrichment obtained through trespass is the value that the trespasser obtained through its unlawful use of the land, i.e., the price the trespasser would fairly have been required to pay to use the land legally." Fisher v. Virginia Electric and Power Co., 217 F.R.D. 201, 225 (E.D.Va.2003).

Question. Had the jury's measurement of Ball's restitution exceeded a landowner's usual charge for additional wheelage?

(e) Back in Virginia's coal country, defendant-Equitable Production had erroneously laid about 70 feed of natural-gas pipeline across the edge of plaintiff-Mullins's two-acre plot on Bad Ridge. Defendant had paid other landowners $1 a foot for pipeline easements, and it had removed the encroaching pipeline from plaintiff's land and relaid it where it should have been. Mullins sued Equitable Production seeking restitution and "(aided and abetted by his lawyer)" sought to recover "royalties of a million dollars for all the gas that has went through" the pipeline, citing *Raven Red Ash*.

Question. Was Mullins's demand a correct statement of the way Ball's restitution was measured?

Mullins's trespass claim for Equitable Production's initial encroachment was time-barred, and the pipeline was removed by mutual agreement. Nevertheless the defendant's line had "trespassed" on plaintiff's property for several years.

The court rejected Mullins's extravagant restitution claim and, finding that he was unable to prove "actual damages," entered summary judgment for $1 nominal damages, also citing *Raven Red Ash*. Mullins v. Equitable Production, 2003 WL 21754819 (W.D.Va.)

Question. Must a plaintiff seeking restitution for defendant's unjust enrichment prove his "actual damages"? Can we account for the "award" of nominal damages with the old saying, "Pigs get fed, hogs get slaughtered"?

(f) Brown, who owned a private road easement appurtenant to cross the Vosses' property to reach parcel B, misused the easement to transport construction material to parcel C as well. The trial judge declined to grant the Vosses' request for an injunction to stop Brown's future misuse of the easement on the ground that "the Vosses would suffer no appreciable hardship or damages if the court denied their request for an injunction." The intermediate appellate court reversed, holding an injunction must issue: "Where a continuing condition, such as the Browns' planned location for their residence, would result in frequent trespasses, an award of damages is not a sufficient remedy. Injunctive relief is far superior to a remedy at law under the circumstances." Brown v. Voss, 38 Wash.App. 777, 782–83, 689 P.2d 1111, 1114 (1984).

But the Washington Supreme Court was "persuaded that the trial court acted within its discretion." The dissent, citing *Raven Red Ash*, argued for an injunction because "damages would be difficult to measure." Brown v. Voss, 105 Wash.2d 366, 374, 715 P.2d 514, 518 (1986).

Question. Perhaps, but what about restitution?

5.   In a merged court with power to grant both legal and equitable remedies, would the coal company's misconduct in *Raven Red Ash* support both restitution for its past misuse and an injunction to prevent its future misuse?

6.   In both *Edwards* and *Raven Red Ash*, would nominal damages plus punitive damages be a better solution than restitution? See, Jacque v. Steenberg Homes, Note 4, p. 809.

2.   Restitution for converted personal property can also be equitable, with equitable restitution terminology and tracing. On with the show.

MATTSON v. COMMERCIAL CREDIT BUSINESS LOANS, INC.

Supreme Court of Oregon, In Banc, 1986.
301 Or. 407, 723 P.2d 996.

CAMPBELL, JUSTICE. This case involves conversion of lumber and the payment to defendant of the proceeds from the converted lumber. Plaintiffs, owners of the converted lumber, sought recovery of the proceeds from the sale of the lumber from the defendant creditor of the converter based on two claims for relief. The first was labeled money had and received, pursuant to which plaintiffs requested actual and punitive damages. The second, which was labeled unjust enrichment, requested a constructive trust.

Plaintiffs and West Coast Lumber Sales, which is not a party to this action, had a contract whereby West Coast would cut plaintiffs' logs at plaintiffs' site for orders pre-sold by West Coast and approved by plaintiffs. In May 1980, West Coast removed 285,000 board feet of lumber from plaintiffs' site without plaintiffs' approval. In September 1980, plaintiffs sued West Coast seeking only money damages for conversion of the lumber. Plaintiffs did not seek replevin, or an injunction to prevent the sale of the lumber, or a constructive trust on the proceeds.

In February 1981, while the litigation between plaintiffs and West Coast was pending, Commercial Credit, defendant in this action, opened a line of credit for West Coast which was secured by inventory and accounts. West Coast's attorney advised defendant of the pending litigation between plaintiffs and West Coast, but the attorney advised defendant that the existence of the litigation did not prevent defendant from making a loan to West Coast so long as plaintiffs were making no claim to the collateral on which defendant was relying in making the loan. In June 1982, plaintiffs won a judgment for $192,011.17 against West Coast for conversion. Shortly thereafter, West Coast filed a petition for bankruptcy.

Under the terms of the accounts receivable contract between West Coast and defendant, all money received by West Coast was turned over to defendant; defendant would then make fresh advances. During the one and one-half years that the contract was in operation, defendant loaned West Coast approximately $2,000,000 more than it received back. Defendant declared West Coast in default in July 1982.

During the pendency of the bankruptcy proceeding, plaintiffs learned that defendant claimed a security interest in all of West Coast's inventory, including the converted lumber and the money generated from the sales of the converted lumber. In March 1983, plaintiffs filed this action asserting a claim against the proceeds West Coast received from the sale of the converted lumber which, plaintiffs asserted, defendant received as part of the revolving credit arrangement with West Coast.

Defendant moved for summary judgment and the trial court granted the motion. The Court of Appeals affirmed without opinion. We reverse and remand.
* * *

Plaintiffs claim that summary judgment could have been based on one of two arguments which defendant presented to the trial court. First, plaintiffs were not entitled to the money generated by the sale of the converted lumber because defendant had a security interest in those proceeds under its accounts receivable financing arrangement with West Coast. Second, even in the absence of a valid security interest, plaintiffs could not recover proceeds from the sale of converted property from third parties; plaintiffs were limited either to recovering the converted lumber from third parties to whom it had been sold, or to recovering the proceeds from such sales from the converter. Plaintiffs contend that the granting of summary judgment on either of these bases was error.

[The court ruled that because West Coast did not own the lumber, it could not grant Commercial Credit a security interest in it and] defendant had no security interest which could prevail over plaintiffs' claimed rights to proceeds from the sale of the converted lumber.

The trial court may also have granted summary judgment on the basis that, even in the absence of a valid security interest, plaintiffs could not recover proceeds from the sale of the converted property from third parties. Plaintiffs assert that they are entitled to recover identifiable proceeds based on the theories of [constructive trust] tracing rights and unjust enrichment.

In moving for summary judgment, defendant argued that such tracing and recovery of proceeds are not permitted at common law. Although we have found no cases involving the precise fact situation involved here, there are cases which have permitted tracing and recovery from third parties. * * *

[T]racing doctrine operates against innocent transferees who receive no legal title and transferees who are not bona fide purchasers and receive legal but not equitable title. If either type of transferee exchanges the acquired property for other property, or receives income from the acquired property, tracing may apply.

As Professor Palmer notes, "There is no theoretical limit on the number of transactions or changes in form through which the claimant will be allowed to trace." 1 Palmer, Law of Restitution 178 (1978). For example,

> "In a decision of the Third Circuit the president of the plaintiff corporation misappropriated $170,000 of its funds, bought bonds with the money, and transferred the bonds to the two defendant corporations which he organized and controlled. The proceeds from the sale of these bonds were used in part by the defendants to develop and perfect inventions and patents; in addition, the remaining assets of the defendant corporations were found to be the product of the bonds. The court ordered specific restitution of the patents, inventions, and all other assets of the defendant corporations. [Flannery v. Flannery Bolt Co., 108 F.2d 531 (3d Cir.1939)]."

Professor Goode notes that under English law an owner may follow proceeds from the disposition of converted property into the hands of a third party. Goode, The Right to Trace and Its Impact in Commercial Transactions—I, 92 L.Q.Rev. 360, 376 (1978). Goode also provides the following example with facts similar to those involved in this case:

> 'Suppose, for example, that B, holding goods as O's bailee, wrongfully sells them to T1 and passes the proceeds to T2, who takes as a volunteer or with notice of B's breach of duty. Here there are infringements of no less than four different rights vested in O; a right to possession of the original goods against B; a like right against T1; a right to require B to account for the proceeds; and a like right against T2. Possible remedies open to O are (I) against B, a claim for damages for conversion of the goods, a personal claim at common law to the proceeds as money had and received, and a personal claim in equity to account for the proceeds as a constructive trustee; (ii) against T1, a claim for damages for conversion, or a claim for delivery up of the goods and damages for their detention; (iii) *against T2, a personal claim at common law for money had and received and a proprietary claim in equity by way of a tracing order.*'

Goode, The Right to Trace and Its Impact in Commercial Transactions—II, 92 L.Q.Rev. 528, 541 (1978). (Emphasis added.) Defendant's position in this case is analogous to "T2."

Defendant argues that the tracing of proceeds of converted goods in the hands of third party transferees should not be permitted because "the parties liable would increase like an inverted pyramid ever upward and outward" making such tracing commercially impracticable. Defendant asserts that under plaintiffs' theory if West Coast had used the proceeds from the sale of the converted lumber to pay its employees, its employees would be liable to plaintiffs. Similarly, each lumber company that bought plaintiffs' lumber presumably later resold it and used those proceeds to pay its bills. Defendant argues that under plaintiffs' theory the creditors of subsequent converters who are paid with those proceeds are also liable.

Defendant's commercial impracticability argument ignores the reality that tracing of proceeds into the hands of third, fourth, fifth, etc. party transferees is permitted under the Uniform Commercial Code. [§ 9–306(2)] indicates that tracing proceeds into the hands of remote transferees is considered commercially practicable. [§ 9–306(2)] provides:

"(2) Except where * * * otherwise provide[d], a security interest continues in collateral notwithstanding sale, exchange or other disposition thereof unless the disposition was authorized by the secured party in the security agreement or otherwise, and also continues in any identifiable proceeds including collections received by the debtor."

Tracing proceeds into the hands of third party transferees is routinely sanctioned in a variety of UCC contexts. See, e.g., In Re Guaranteed Muffler Supply Co., Inc., 1 B.R. 324, 27 UCC Rep. 1217 (Bankr.N.D.Ga.1979) (permitting secured creditor to trace proceeds from sale of debtor's inventory and accounts into hands of third-party transferee); Baker Prod. Credit v. Long Cr. Meat, 266 Or. 643, 513 P.2d 1129 (1973) (allowing creditor with security interest in farm products to recover proceeds from sale of products from third-party transferees).

Defendant's argument also ignores the fact that a bona fide purchaser would cut off plaintiffs' tracing rights. See Lane County Escrow v. Smith, Coe, 277 Or. 273, 285, 560 P.2d 608 (1977). Section 208(1) of the Restatement on Restitution provides:

"(1) Where a person wrongfully disposes of property of another knowing that the disposition is wrongful and in exchange therefore other property is transferred to a third person, the other can enforce a constructive trust or an equitable lien upon the property, unless the third person is a bona fide purchaser."

The creditors or employees of the companies that bought the lumber are analogous to purchasers in that they are exchanging their services for money. If they "purchased" in good faith without knowledge that the money they received was proceeds from stolen property, they would be like bona fide purchasers and thus would also cut off plaintiffs' tracing rights.

Whether defendant is a bona fide purchaser cutting off plaintiffs' tracing rights is a question of material fact which precludes summary judgment. An innocent purchaser is one who has no reasonable grounds to suspect that the person from whom he buys an article did not have good title. As this court noted long ago, whether one is a purchaser in good faith is an issue of fact that must be determined from many circumstances, including actual and constructive notice and suspicious circumstances. The facts surrounding the transaction, including any unusual or peculiar business methods of the vendor that were known to the purchaser, may properly be submitted to the jury to be considered on the ultimate question of good or bad faith. * * *

In addition, plaintiffs' right to recover under a tracing theory is limited by their ability to trace the proceeds from the converted lumber. If they cannot trace the proceeds to defendant then they cannot recover under this theory. Plaintiffs submitted evidentiary materials to the trial court describing how such tracing could be established. Defendant claims that the proceeds from the sale of the converted lumber have long since passed through its hands to undetermined third parties. Plaintiffs' ability to identify and trace proceeds from the sale of the converted lumber is evidentiary, a matter of proof. It is not an appropriate basis for summary judgment. * * *

In light of these genuine issues of material fact, the grant of summary judgment to defendant was error. The decision of the Court of Appeals is reversed. The case is remanded to the trial court for further proceedings.

Notes

1. *Mattson's Tactics and Options.* Why may Mattson have decided not to seek replevin? In retrospect, was Mattson's damages judgment against West Coast inferior to the constructive trust Mattson "did not seek"?

2. *Looking Ahead: What's Next for Mattson?* One who purchases a constructive trustee's legal title for value and in good faith without notice is a bona fide purchaser who takes free of the plaintiff's equitable claim. Let's unpack the preceding sentence.

(a) *Purchaser.* The court uses the word "purchaser" in the technical sense to mean one who acquires an asset not by gift or execution. Commercial Credit is a purchaser.

(b) *For Value.* The tortfeasor West Coast's money went to Commercial Credit, a creditor; the money reduced the debt West Coast owed Commercial Credit. Discharge of an antecedent debt is "value." One who receives cash "owns" it. So if Commercial Credit gave up a valid claim, its debt, in exchange for West Coast's payment of money, then Commercial Credit was a purchaser for value, and not unjustly enriched by the money.

(c) *Without Notice.* A purchaser from a wrongdoer *with* notice of plaintiff's right is not a bona fide purchaser. The question is whether Commercial Credit knew or should have known facts that would lead a reasonably diligent creditor to inquire and whether an inquiry, if undertaken, would have surfaced the facts and circumstances of the constructive trust. Should West Coast's attorney's disclosure to Commercial Credit have put Commercial Credit on inquiry?

(d) *Tracing.* Commercial Credit argues that it has spent West Coast's money. The burden of proof is on Mattson to trace its asset, the constructive trust res, into Commercial Credit's assets and to locate it there. Commercial Credit may be aided by a presumption called the low intermediate balance rule, the idea that a "trustee" would spend the trust money last. If Commercial Credit's fund balance never fell below the amount of Mattson's claim, Mattson may have traced satisfactorily.

3. *Restitution for a Tortfeasor?* We have been studying restitution for wrongs— the property-owner's restitution against a tortfeasor. Our next topic reverses the parties. Suppose Calvin builds a house by mistake on Uriah's lot. Trespass only requires the trespasser's intent to enter, so Calvin's mistake does not negate his tort. Moreover, under well-established real property doctrine, any improvement, an

"fixture," Calvin "attaches" to Uriah's real estate belongs to Uriah as the owner of the underlying fee. So much for you, Calvin?

But property law does not override restitution. A person who makes a mistake may ask the court for affirmative relief through the magic of restitution. In Jeffs v. Stubbs, below, the Utah court applies restitution principles to aid several Calvins.

The mistaken improver has also been successful in legislatures. Utah is one of the many states with an occupying claimants or betterment statute. The Utah occupying claimant statute is not an exclusive remedy; restitution exists outside the statute.

JEFFS v. STUBBS

Supreme Court of Utah, 1998.
970 P.2d 1234, cert. denied, 526 U.S. 1130 (1999).

ZIMMERMAN, JUSTICE: This case involves a dispute over the occupancy of land between twenty-one individuals ("the claimants") and the United Effort Plan Trust ("the UEP"). The claimants built improvements on land located in Hildale, Utah, and Colorado City, Arizona, which they occupy but which is owned by the UEP. Claimants filed an action in Washington County, Utah, to determine their rights in the UEP land they occupy. * * *

After trial, the court relied on an unjust enrichment theory to hold that the claimants were entitled to occupy the UEP land during their lifetimes or to receive compensation for the improvements they made. The court imposed a constructive trust in favor of the claimants. * * *

Each party appealed. The UEP argues that (I) the trial court erred in awarding claimants a continuing interest in the land on an unjust enrichment theory and (ii) giving the claimants a continuing interest in the land infringes on the remaining UEP members' free exercise of religion and therefore violates the Utah and United States Constitutions. On their cross appeal, the claimants argue that the trial court erred by applying the wrong legal standard to their claim under Utah's Occupying Claimants Act ("the Act"). * * * We reject the UEP's arguments, affirm the trial court's unjust enrichment ruling, * * * reverse its interpretation of the Utah Occupying Claimants Act, and remand for further proceedings. * * *

Sometime in the late nineteenth century, some members of the Church of Jesus Christ of Latter–Day Saints organized a movement called the Priesthood Work ("The Work") to continue the practice of plural marriage outside that church. In the early part of this century, The Work's leadership—the Priesthood Council—decided to settle its membership in an isolated area to avoid interference with their religious practices. In approximately the 1930s, The Work selected an area composed of Hildale, Utah, and Colorado City, Arizona—an area now known as Short Creek. The Priesthood Council secured a large tract of land in this area, and adherents of The Work began to settle there.

The Work continued to secure additional land in the area. Commonly, its adherents bought land and deeded it to The Work. Eventually, the leadership of The Work formed a trust to hold title to the land. * * * In 1942, the Priesthood Council signed and recorded in Mohave County, Arizona, a Declaration of Trust for the United Effort Plan. After the Priesthood Council formed the UEP, adherents deeded most of the land that had been held by the first trust to the UEP. Over the years, the UEP acquired more land as adherents obtained and deeded it to the trust. The UEP currently owns all the land occupied by the claimants.

From its inception, the UEP invited members to build their homes on assigned lots on UEP land. Through this system, the UEP intended to localize control over all local real property and to have the religious leaders manage it. Members who built on the trust land were aware that they could not sell or mortgage the land and that they would forfeit their improvements if they left the land. However, the UEP did encourage its members to improve the lots assigned to them and represented to its members that they could live on the land permanently, by using such phrases as "forever" or "as long as you wanted." The leaders also told members that having a home on UEP land was better than having a deed because creditors could not foreclose upon the land for members' debts.

Sometime during the late 1960s or early 1970s, dissension over a doctrinal issue arose among adherents of The Work, causing a split in the Priesthood Council. The dissension broke into the open in 1984 when adherents of The Work split into two groups: One group, led by Rulon T. Jeffs ("Jeffs"), acquired control of the UEP. A second group, led by J. Marion Hammon and Alma Timpson, includes most of the claimants in the present case. Some of the claimants now claim no affiliation with either group.

In 1986, Jeffs declared that all those living on UEP land were tenants at will. Before this declaration, neither the UEP nor any of its representatives had told the claimants that they were tenants at will. * * * The UEP * * * filed an unlawful detainer action and several quiet title actions against some of the claimants in state court in 1989 and 1993. * * * Shortly thereafter, the claimants filed an action in Utah's district court in Washington County. The state court consolidated their action with the UEP's previously filed unlawful detainer action and several quiet title actions.

In these consolidated actions, the claimants presented a number of claims, the most pertinent of which is that they are entitled to their lots under the Utah Occupying Claimants Act, *see* Utah Code Ann. §§ 57–6–1 to–8, and, alternatively, that the UEP has been unjustly enriched by their improvements to the land. After a bench trial, the judge made findings of fact and granted claimants relief only on their unjust enrichment claim. It found as a matter of statutory interpretation that they were not covered by the Utah Occupying Claimants Act.

On appeal, the claimants argue that the trial court erred in applying the Act. * * * For its part, the UEP asserts that the trial court erred in granting claimants equitable relief, primarily because application of equitable principles to a religious organization violates the Utah and United States Constitutions. We address each issue in turn. * * *

The first question is whether the trial court correctly interpreted the Utah Occupying Claimants Act. Section 57–6–1 of the Act provided:

> Where an occupant of real estate has *color of title* thereto, and in *good faith* has made *valuable improvements* thereon, and is afterwards in proper action found not to be the owner, no execution shall issue to put the plaintiff in possession of the same after the filing of a complaint as hereinafter provided, until the provisions of this chapter have been complied with.

Utah Code Ann. § 57–6–1 (1994) (emphasis added). This statute requires occupying claimants to show that they (i) have "color of title" and (ii) made valuable improvements (iii) in good faith. [citation] *See* Hidden Meadows Dev. Co. v. Mills, 590 P.2d 1244, 1249 (Utah 1979). The district court found that the claimants had made valuable improvements. However, it did not determine whether claimants had color of title because it had first concluded that the claimants did not make the improvements in "good faith" as required by the statute.

We address the preliminary question of whether the claimants had color of title before addressing the determination that they lacked good faith. Section 57–6–4(2)(a) (Supp.1997) of the Code defines "color of title." It states:

[A]ny person has color of title who has occupied a tract of real estate by himself, or by those under whom he claims, [i] *for the term of five years, or* [ii] who has thus occupied it for less time, if he, or those under whom he claims, *have at any time during such occupancy with the knowledge or consent, express or implied, of the real owner made any valuable improvements thereon,* or [iii] if he or those under whom he claims have at any time during such occupancy paid the ordinary county taxes thereon for any one year, and two years have elapsed without a repayment of the same by the owner, and the occupancy is continued up to the time at which the action is brought by which the recovery of the real estate is obtained. (brackets and emphasis added).

Factually, categories (i) and (ii) cover all the claimants here. They either "occupied a tract of real estate * * * for the term of five years," or they, or those under whom they claim, have made "valuable improvements" to real estate "with the owner's knowledge or consent." The facts found by the district court show that the UEP knew that all the claimants were improving the land and encouraged them to do so. In many cases, claimants obtained consent from The Work's leadership to improve the land. The claimants, therefore, have color of title.

The next requirement under section 57–6–1 is that the claimants show that they made the improvements in "good faith." The trial court found that they did not. In defining the statutory term, "good faith," the trial court relied on case law stating that "[t]he good faith of an occupying claimant must be premised upon a reasonable and honest belief of ownership." Ute–Cal Land Dev. Corp. v. Sather, 645 P.2d 665, 667 (Utah 1982). The trial court concluded that the claimants did not make the improvements in good faith because they had "not even claimed that they actually own the land they occupy" and because "they were installed upon the property of the UEP, knowingly by those who were using the land by permission." We conclude that the trial court erred in its interpretation of "belief of ownership."

The trial court appears to have assumed that "ownership" means possession of a fee simple interest in land. But it is settled law that " '[o]wnership' is a collection of rights to possess, to use and to enjoy property, including the right to sell and transmit it. * * * [T]he term owner is often used to characterize the possessor of an interest less than that of absolute ownership, such as * * * a tenant for life." 63C Am.Jur.2d *Property* § 26 (1997). We have no reason to think that when the Act was passed the legislature intended to restrict the meaning of the term "ownership" to a narrower class of interests in land than the general law would allow. The only restriction intended by the legislature is indicated by the express language stating that the Act should not be construed to create any ownership interest in a tenant against a landlord. We therefore conclude that a good faith belief in a life interest in land satisfies the good faith requirement of the Utah Occupying Claimants Act.

In the present case, the claimants acknowledged that they do not hold fee simple title. But the evidence before the trial court is entirely consistent with the claimants' having a good faith belief that they were entitled to possess the property during their lives so long as they did not abandon the property. The law describes such an interest as a life estate, and a life estate is an "ownership" interest. Because the UEP represented to claimants that they could occupy the land for their lives, so long as they did not sell, mortgage, or abandon the property, the claimants' interest is actually a life estate subject to a condition subsequent. In other words, the UEP had both a reversionary interest, which vests upon the death of a claimant, and the possibility of reverter, which would only vest if a claimant sold, mortgaged, or abandoned the property. [citation]

On this point, however, we must remand the matter for additional specific findings as to claimants' beliefs of a life estate interest.

The claimants presented evidence that the UEP represented to them that they could occupy the land for their lives or for as long as they lived on the land. And the trial court concluded that these representations "could reasonably have created in [claimants'] mind[s] an expectation that [they] would be able to live out [their] days on the [UEP] land so long as [they] did not sell the land, mortgage it or abandon its use." But because the trial court believed the Act required a good faith belief of a fee simple interest, it made no specific findings as to claimants' beliefs that they possessed a life estate interest. Absent such a belief, good faith would be lacking. * * * Because it is not our place to find facts, we remand this issue to the trial court for additional findings and, if it deems appropriate, for additional evidence on the good faith issue. If it concludes that some or all of the claimants have a life estate, then it should enter an order giving them a remedy under the Act.

The Utah Occupying Claimants Act provides the following remedy once the court determines that an occupier had color of title and made valuable improvements in good faith:

> The plaintiff in the main action may thereupon pay the appraised value of the improvements and take the property, but should he fail to do so after a reasonable time, to be fixed by the court, the defendant may take the property upon paying its value, exclusive of the improvements. If this is not done within a reasonable time, to be fixed by the court, the parties will be held to be tenants in common of all the real estate, including the improvements, each holding an interest proportionate to the values ascertained on the trial. Utah Code Ann. § 57–6–3.

This does not end this matter, however. Those claimants occupying land in Arizona have no remedy under the Utah Occupying Claimants Act. Therefore, we must still determine whether the trial court properly granted that group of claimants an equitable remedy under Arizona law. Similarly, if on remand, the trial court determines that some or all of the Utah claimants did not have a good faith belief in a life estate, we must determine if the court properly granted these claimants an enrichment equitable remedy under Utah law.

The UEP argues that the trial court erred in granting claimants equitable relief for two reasons: first, a court cannot assess the equities between religious entities; and, second, because claimants knew that the UEP owned the land,

there is nothing inequitable about the UEP's keeping the improvements without compensating the claimants. Before addressing these issues, we note that we will analyze the trial court's equity ruling under both Arizona and Utah law because the court's equitable remedy affects real property in both Arizona and Utah. [The] existence of equitable interest in land is usually governed by local law of situs of property. [citation] Therefore, we review the ruling affecting Arizona land under Arizona law and the ruling affecting Utah land under Utah law.
* * *

The UEP first argues that the religious context of this case should prohibit a court from applying unjust enrichment principles. Essentially, the UEP argues that balancing the equities between the UEP and claimants is tantamount to judging the fairness of the UEP's religious practices and is therefore prohibited. * * * [W]e find nothing that would suggest that courts are not competent to hear cases involving religious entities.

Under both Arizona and Utah law, courts have broad authority to grant equitable relief as needed. *See* Murdock–Bryant Constr., Inc. v. Pearson, 146 Ariz. 48, 703 P.2d 1197, 1202 (1985). And nothing in the general rules of equity applicable in both states prohibits a court from deciding an equity case because the parties are religious entities. The UEP has cited no Arizona or Utah law suggesting that a court should limit the application of the doctrine of unjust enrichment solely because of the religious nature of the relationship and motivation of the UEP and claimants. And federal constitutional law imposes no such limitation. United States Supreme Court precedent suggests that courts may entertain property disputes between religious organizations. [citation] [N]o question of church doctrine is central to this case. We therefore conclude that in Arizona and Utah nothing prevents a civil court from hearing an ordinary equity case between religious entities or factions, or between a religious entity and a private litigant.

The UEP's second argument is that because the claimants knew they did not own the land, there is nothing inequitable about the UEP's keeping the improvements without compensating claimants. * * *

[T]he facts underlying an unjust enrichment claim are often complex and vary greatly from case to case. Indeed, by its very nature, the unjust enrichment doctrine developed to handle fact situations that did not fit within a particular legal standard but which nonetheless merited judicial intervention. *See* Restatement of Restitution, intro. n. (1937) (noting that narrow early common law causes of actions posed difficulties and required creation of chancery courts because "there were many situations in which one justly entitled to recover was not able to do so"). * * *

It is true that the unjust enrichment doctrine has ancient roots, and courts have had a great deal of opportunity to apply it. However, the court's ability to state clearly the outcome-determinative factors remains elusive. The Arizona Supreme Court, in discussing the equitable rules it applies, and which we apply here, notes the rules' indeterminativeness:

The circumstances of this case are somewhat unique. * * * The Restatement of Restitution * * * does not cover the factual circumstances presented by the case at bench. This is not determinative, however, because the remedy of restitution is not confined to any particular circumstance or set of facts. It is, rather, a flexible, equitable remedy available whenever the court finds that "the defendant, upon the circumstances of the case, is obliged by the ties of natural justice and equity" to make compensation for benefits received.

We have also recognized the rationale for restitutionary relief, stating that restitution * * * is available "as a matter of reason and justice from the acts and conduct of the parties and circumstances surrounding the transactions, * * * and [is] imposed for the purpose of bringing about justice without reference to the intentions of the parties." Murdock–Bryant Constr. * * *

Unjust enrichment law developed to remedy injustice when other areas of the law could not. Unjust enrichment must remain a flexible and workable doctrine. Therefore, we afford broad discretion to the trial court in its application of unjust enrichment law to the facts.

We now turn to our analysis of the trial court's application of the law. Arizona recognizes the equitable remedy of unjust enrichment and generally provides that " '[a] person who has been unjustly enriched at the expense of another is required to make restitution to the other.' " Murdock–Bryant Constr. (quoting Restatement of Restitution § 1 (1937)). A person is unjustly enriched if (i) he received a benefit, and (ii) his retention of that benefit would be unjust. [citation] We find that the trial court correctly concluded that claimants proved both elements.

Regarding the first element, the trial court found: "There can be no doubt from the evidence presented that [claimant] has conferred a benefit on the UEP by improving the lot." Arizona law defines a benefit as "any form of advantage." Artukovich & Sons, Inc. v. Reliance Truck Co., 126 Ariz. 246, 614 P.2d 327, 329 (1980) (en banc). In making its finding, the court relied on evidence showing that the claimants spent a considerable amount of money and time improving the UEP land, that these improvements increased the value of the land, and that the UEP will benefit from the increased value. We agree that this evidence supports the finding that the UEP received some advantage, and, thus, a benefit.

The claimants must also show that the UEP's retention of these benefits would be unjust. The UEP argues that because the claimants knew that the UEP owned the land and because the claimants intended to "donate" the improvements, they cannot recover. We disagree.

In determining whether it would be unjust to allow the retention of benefits without compensation, Arizona law provides that:

> a court need not find that the defendant intended to compensate the plaintiff for the services rendered or that the plaintiff intended that the defendant be the party to make compensation. This is because the duty to compensate for unjust enrichment is an obligation implied by law without reference to the intention of the parties. *What is important is that it be shown that it was not intended or expected that the services be rendered or the benefit conferred gratuitously, and that the benefit was not "conferred officiously."* Murdock–Bryant Constr.

Thus, under Arizona law, the trial court had to find that (i) services were conferred, (ii) the services were not conferred "officiously," and (iii) it was not intended that the services were "gratuitously" conferred. As we explained above, the trial court found that the claimants conferred a benefit on the UEP—they rendered services by improving the UEP lots.

As to the second element, the claimants plainly did not confer the services officiously. "Officiousness means interference in the affairs of another not justified by the circumstances under which the interference takes place." Restatement of Restitution § 2 cmt. a (1937). Thus, an officious person is one who "thrust[s] benefits upon others." Here, the claimants did not interfere or thrust benefits on the UEP. To the contrary, the UEP encouraged the claimants to improve the land. The trial court found:

> There can also be no doubt that the trust was aware of the benefit as its representatives encouraged the construction and the improvement of the lot by the occupant and watched the building going in. The issue is whether, given the facts of this case, it would be inequitable to allow the UEP to retain the benefit without compensation. * * * The Court is of the opinion that such a result would be inequitable.

Finally, the claimants did not confer their services gratuitously. One renders services gratuitously if at the time they were rendered, there was no expectation of "a return benefit, compensation, or consideration." Webster's New Int'l Dictionary 992 (3d ed.1961). We conclude that because the claimants built the improvements with the intention that they could occupy them for their lifetimes, they did not confer them gratuitously.

The Restatement of Restitution * * * is instructive in determining whether one rendered services gratuitously. Section 40 provides:

> A person who has rendered services to another * * * is entitled to restitution therefor if the services were rendered * * * in the mistaken belief, of which the other knew or had reason to know, that the services would inure to the benefit of the one giving them. * * *

Thus, one who renders services with the reasonable expectation of a returned benefit does not render the services gratuitously. Section 42 of that Restatement, which limits a party's right to recovery for improvements to land, specifies that section 40 applies when the true owner, "having notice of the error and of the work being done, stands by and does not use care to prevent the error from continuing." A comment to section 40 clarifies that an owner "cannot retain a benefit which knowingly he has permitted another to confer upon him by mistake."

Section 42(1) of the Restatement of Restitution, governing improvements upon land or chattels, provides:

> Except to the extent that the rule is changed by statute, a person who, in the mistaken belief that he or a third party on whose account he acts is the owner, has caused improvements to be made upon the land of another, is not thereby entitled to restitution from the owner for the value of such improvement; but *if his mistake was reasonable,* the owner is entitled to obtain judgment in an equitable proceeding or in an action for trespass * * * only on condition that he makes restitution to the extent that the land has been increased in value by such improvements, or for the value of labor and materials employed in making such improvements, whichever is least. (emphasis added).

Thus, if a person who made improvements had a reasonable belief of ownership, the true owner may eject the party who made the improvements only after paying restitution for the improvements.

The trial court concluded that the claimants "expected to use the property into the foreseeable future" and "[a]s a result [they] invested lots of money and time in the improvement of the property." The court also found that the claimants improved the land with the knowledge and encouragement of the UEP and with the understanding that they could remain on the land for their lifetimes. The court further indicated that the UEP failed to disabuse claimants of their beliefs that they could remain on the land for their lifetimes. The court stated:

> The UEP must bear a large share of the blame for the confusion as to the terms of occupancy since it did not communicate to [claimants] directly the conditions of [their] occupancy * * * even though the trust was engaged in a long term and wide spread program of settling its people on UEP lands. It would have been easy to prepare a list of conditions of occupancy and to distribute the list to those preparing to invest heavily in improvements with the encouragement and agreement of the trust.

Applying the law to these facts, we conclude that the trial court's disposition was adequately supported by the evidence and was consistent with the Arizona substantive law. We therefore find that the trial court did not abuse its discretion in requiring the UEP to allow claimants to live on the land for their lifetimes or to compensate them for the improvements.

We next consider the trial court's unjust enrichment ruling under Utah law, as that law governs the claims of any Utah residents who may not be covered by the Occupying Claimants Act or for whom an equitable remedy is more favorable. Utah law, like Arizona's, recognizes the remedy of unjust enrichment. * * *

Here, the claimants improved the land in reliance upon the UEP's representations that they could live on the land for the rest of their lives. Even though the claimants intended to benefit from the improvements by occupying them during their lifetimes, the claimants' services still conferred a direct, not incidental, benefit on the UEP. Thus, we uphold the trial court's equitable remedy for all claimants, both those occupying land in Arizona and Utah.

The UEP next argues that the trial court's particular equitable remedy violates both article I, section 4 of the Utah Constitution and the First Amendment to the United States Constitution because the ruling burdens the free exercise of its members' religious beliefs. Specifically, the UEP asserts that the ruling is unconstitutional because it measures "religious expression against secular standards of fairness." [Most of the court's lengthy discussion of the judicial role in religious property disputes was omitted.]

[W]e find the UEP's claim would fail even if we were to adopt the test it suggests. The trial court's award was carefully crafted to be the least restrictive means available to further the state's compelling interest. The remedy provided the claimants redress for their injuries in a manner that minimizes the burden upon free exercise. The court's ruling allows the UEP to force the claimants off the UEP land at any time. The UEP need only compensate claimants first for the benefits it received. The court's adjudication of this matter did not violate [either the United States or the Utah constitution]. * * *

In conclusion, we uphold the trial court's equitable ruling allowing claimants to remain on the land for their lifetimes or requiring the UEP to compensate the claimants for the benefit it received if the UEP seeks to remove claimants. However, we find that the trial court erred in its interpretation of the Utah Occupying Claimants Act and that the findings are insufficient for us to determine whether any or all of the claimants have life estates. * * * Therefore, we remand that issue to the trial court for further proceedings consistent with this opinion.

Notes

1. *Evolution of Mistaken Improvement*. (a) *Restatement First*. The first Restatement's mistaken-improver section, which the court quotes in Jeffs v. Stubbs, is really quite narrow: normally, a court will deny restitution to a mistaken improver; but the "reasonable" mistaken improver may use restitution as a defense to the true owner's ejectment action. Under that authority, restitution is not available to the improver offensively, in a suit, for example, for restitution or a declaratory judgment. James v. Bailey, 370 F.Supp. 469 (D.V.I. 1974).

(b) *Common Law Interlude*. In Hughey v. Bennett, 264 Ark. 64, 568 S.W.2d 46 (1978), the court held that if the plaintiff in an ejectment action does not seek mesne profits or the removal of the improvement, the defendant is not entitled to a set off unless a betterment statute is affirmatively asserted.

Several courts granted affirmative relief to a good faith mistaken improver. See Duncan v. Akers, 147 Ind.App. 511, 262 N.E.2d 402 (1970) (improver entitled to equitable relief); Sugarman v. Olsen, 254 Or. 385, 459 P.2d 545 (1969) (judgment for value of improvements); Comer v. Roberts, 252 Or. 189, 448 P.2d 543 (1968) (owner compelled to convey for value); Somerville v. Jacobs, 153 W.Va. 613, 170 S.E.2d 805 (1969) (alternative judgment for value of improvement or conveyance of land for value).

(c) *Betterment Statutes* Many state legislatures have passed statutes to aid the mistaken improver. The most common statutes allow the mistaken improver a set-off when the owner sues to recover mesne damages. Even this limited remedy may not be available unless the mistaken improver can show that he made the improvements in good faith and under "color of title." Uhlhorn v. Keltner, 723 S.W.2d 131 (Tenn.App.1986). The statute may not be the improver's exclusive remedy; as in Jeffs v. Stubbs, nonstatutory restitution principles may apply.

California's expansive mistaken improver statute permits an improver to sue in an action based on the improvements; it directs the court to "effect such an adjustment of the rights, equities, and interest of the good faith improver, the owner of the land, and other interested parties * * * as is consistent with substantial justice to the parties under the circumstances of the particular case." Cal.Civ.Proc. Code, §§ 871.1–871.7. See also Southern Pacific Transportation Co. v. Superior Court, 58 Cal.App.3d 433, 129 Cal.Rptr. 912 (1976).

(d) *Restatement Third*. The Third Restatement of Restitution reverses the earlier rule: "A person who improves the real or personal property of another, acting by mistake, has a claim in restitution as necessary to prevent unjust enrichment." Restatement (Third) of Restitution and Unjust Enrichment § 40 (Tent. Draft No. 1 2001).

Question. Is the Third Restatement's solution an improvement?

2. *Remedy*. (a) *Forced Exchange*. Section 40's second sentence qualifies the Third Restatement's remedy: "A remedy for mistaken improvement that subjects the owner to a forced exchange will be qualified or limited to avoid undue prejudice to the owner."

Question. In Jeffs v. Stubbs, the trial judge had imposed an equitable remedy, a constructive trust. Did the judge's remedy "subject" the defendants to an involuntary "forced exchange"?

(b) *Equitable Restitution*. Chancellors of Equity used in an personam order to grant a plaintiff restitution where title theories would prevent legal restitution. A mistaken-improvement plaintiff lacks title to the land; plaintiff's legal restitution may founder because of the defendant's legal title. Moreover a mistaken-improvement defendant is not a wrongdoer in the sense of being a tortfeasor or contract breacher.

(c) *Constructive Trust—Restitution to the Rescue*. Nevertheless, as in Jeffs v. Stubbs, a court may hold that the defendant is a constructive trustee who owns legal title in "trust" for the plaintiff who owns the equitable title. The court may order the defendant, in personam, to convey the legal title to the plaintiff.

(d) *Equitable Lien*. An equitable lien, a second form of equitable restitution, gives the plaintiff a security interest in defendant's property for a specific amount. In contrast, a constructive trust gives plaintiff complete "equitable" title to it. The equitable lien has the constructive trust's feature of tracing; plaintiff follows his property into defendant's asset and becomes a secured creditor who may force a sale of the defendant's asset. Although the constructive trust's tracing feature captures the property's appreciation, an equitable lien for a specific amount will not. The judge may impose an equitable lien when a full-scale constructive trust would be too large.

Question. In Jeffs v. Stubbs, would an equitable lien have been a more appropriate remedy than the constructive trust?

(e) *Buy-Sell Election*. In mistaken improver remedies, a buy-sell election occurs when the court lets the owner choose between (i) paying the improver the value of the improvement; and (ii) selling the property to the improver at its unimproved value.

Question. Does the trial judge's remedy in Jeffs v. Stubbs resemble a buy-sell election?

(f). *Unclean Hands*. A plaintiff's equitable restitution claim is subject to equitable defenses, including unclean hands.

Question. Could defendants argue successfully that a mistaken improvement claimant who deeded his land to the UEP to thwart his creditors had unclean hands that barred him from equitable relief?

3. *Meanwhile Back in Texas—Mistaken Improvement of Un–Real Property*. "Storms placed a movable frame house on cement blocks on land owned by a third party." Upon discovering that utilities were not available to the property, Storms left the house on the land until it could be moved to a different location. Approximately two years later, appellee Charles Reid purchased the property without knowing that Storms owned the house. Reid subsequently spent around $18,000.00 on restoration and improvements to the house. Storms saw the restored house and demanded that Reid pay him for it. When Reid refused to do so, Storms filed suit for conversion. * * *

"Storms contends that the trial court erred in awarding him monetary damages instead of the house itself. * * *"

"Storms contends that, as the owner of converted property, he had the option to sue either for its specific recovery or for its market value. However, the cases upon which he relies all mention this point in dicta in the context of holding that a property owner cannot be forced to accept a tender of the converted goods by the wrongdoer where a money judgment was awarded against the wrongdoer. [citations]"

"[I]t would constitute unjust enrichment to award the house to Storms. The trial court assessed its fair market value at the time of conversion at $1,200.00. Reid spent $18,000.00 on it in improvements and restoration. * * * Storms would be unjustly enriched if we were to require the trial court to award him the improved house. He would receive a house worth $18,000.00 when he had only invested $1,200.00 in it. Further, Storms had virtually abandoned the house for two years. He only asserted his ownership interest after Reid spent $18,000.00 improving it. Also, there was no finding that the house was unique."

"Although * * * the plaintiff [apparently has] an election between suing for the return of the converted property or its fair market value, this election is subservient to the doctrine that the 'object is to compensate for the injury.' In conversion cases, the trial court must be given the discretion required to fashion an equitable remedy. If allowing the plaintiff to elect to recover the converted property itself will overcompensate him for his injury, then the election must be taken away from the plaintiff. The trial court cannot be forced to order an inequitably large recovery at the plaintiff's option. Here, the trial court properly limited Storms' recovery to the fair market value of the house at the time and place of conversion." Storms v. Reid, 691 S.W.2d 73 (Tex.App.1985).

In the preceding paragraph, in what sense is the court using the term "equitable remedy"? Would "equitable lien" have been a happier term? How does the Texas court's approach compare to Judge Brown's in Trahan v. First National Bank of Ruston? p. 779.

Suppose the court had decided that the house was part of the realty. Would that difference warrant a different result?

D. SPECIFIC RECOVERY: REPLEVIN AND INJUNCTION

1. STATUTORY REPLEVIN

When a tortfeasor takes and retains an owner's personal property, the tortfeasor has committed the tort of conversion and the owner may choose between regaining possession and recovering damages. This book calls the owner's lawsuit to regain chattels replevin; other names are detinue, claim and delivery, and sequestration. Statutory replevin is an action at law; specific statutes vary and should be consulted. Pursuing "equitable replevin," an owner may sue a converter for an injunction ordering the defendant to return the property. Recovery of the item is, if you like, specific restitution.

As a prerequisite, plaintiff must establish a property right in the thing defendant allegedly converted. In his famous damages action for conversion of his spleen, plaintiff Moore failed to surmount this fundamental hurdle. He asserted that defendants wrongfully converted his cells for medical research. But the California Supreme Court declined to find property in excised cell tissue; it reasoned that other legal theories are adequate to protect a patient seeking medical assistance. Moore v. Regents of University of California, 51 Cal.3d 120, 271 Cal.Rptr. 146, 793 P.2d 479 (1990), cert. denied, 499 U.S. 936 (1991).

Ownership, once established, is a powerful concept, entitled to impressive protection. A thief cannot pass good title and a purchaser from a thief cannot obtain one. U.C.C. § 2–403. The owner's suit to retake possession may, however, be barred by either (a) the doctrine of accession or (b) time-bar, the passage of time measured against either the statute of limitations or laches.

(a) *Accession*. The doctrine of accession means that someone loses "owner-ship" of something and cannot sue to recover possession. The saga of a '65 Corvette is as interesting as it is complex:

"On May 1, 1975, a 1965 Chevrolet Corvette was stolen from William T. Revis of Indianapolis, Indiana. Subsequently, it was stripped and the stripped-down hull was bought by James Billy Pack from Howard's Used Cars. Pack then sold the stripped-down hull to Doug Horn, who sold it to W.A. Sartin on August 23, 1976, for the sum of $200."

"Sartin used the stripped-down hull to build a functioning Corvette automobile with his own labor and materials and sold it to Randy Bennett for $4,750. Bennett then sold it to Robert Earheart for $4,775. Earheart then traded the car to Capitol Chevrolet on May 7, 1979, for a 1979 Corvette. Capitol allowed $6,052 on the trade-in and Earheart paid the balance by check."

"On May 9, 1979, Capitol Chevrolet sold the rebuilt 1965 Corvette to Dave Crass."

"It was stolen from Crass in Atlanta on June 12, 1979, and was recovered by the Atlanta police, who returned it to the original owner Revis on July 4, 1979. Revis had identified the car by the serial number remaining on the original hull of the car that had been stolen from him in 1975."

"Crass has never paid anything to Capitol Chevrolet on the car, alleging [apparently, because of breach of the seller's warranty of title, that] he owed nothing because the car was stolen merchandise when sold to him. Capitol sued both Crass, its vendee, and Earheart, its vendor. Third-party suits [apparently for breaches of the warranty of title] have been entered back up the chain of title as far as Pack. Crass filed a counter-complaint against Capitol for selling him a stolen car."

"The Chancellor, after a bench trial, found that all defendants were innocent purchasers acting in good faith. The Chancellor further found that Sartin acquired title by accession when he rebuilt the car, stating as follows:

'When Sartin acquired the hull salvage, it was no longer an automobile. No part was intact. By making the improvement he acquired good title which he conveyed to Bennett and the others in the chain of title.'

'Any liability would be only to the true owner of the misappropriated property and limited to the value of the property innocently used which would be the scrap value of the hull.'

'Capitol Chevrolet conveyed good title to Crass and is entitled to a judgment against him for $7,257.00, plus $2,400.00 attorney's fee and the costs.' * * *

"Our review of this record," the court of appeals said, "sustains the Chancellor's finding that Sartin acquired title to the car by accession and that all defendants herein acted in good faith. Earheart conveyed good title to Capitol Chevrolet, which conveyed the same to Crass. Crass is the owner of the car less any claim held by the original owner Revis to an amount corresponding to the value of the unimproved stripped-down hull purchased by Sartin."

As the concurring judge pointed out, Revis "the owner of the stolen part is not a party to this case, hence his rights may not be determined herein." Capitol Chevrolet Co. v. Earheart and Crass v. Bennett v. Sartin v. Horn v. Pack, 627 S.W.2d 369 (Tenn.App.1981).

Question. How does the Texas court's solution in Storms v. Reid, Note 3., p. 863, differ from the Tennessee court's conclusion that Sartin acquired title to the 1965 Corvette by accession when he rebuilt it from the stripped hull?

(b) *Time–Bar—The Replevin Statute of Limitations and Adverse Possession.* When the statute of limitations period expires, the owner's remedy, replevin or damages, is barred; moreover the owner loses "title" and the adverse possessor becomes the new owner. Controversy rages about precisely when the owner's cause of action accrues and the statute of limitations's clock begins to tick. Stolen art works and other collectibles in the hands of honest collectors have led to well-known litigation.

(i) Georgia O'Keeffe's replevin "cause of action accrued when she first knew, or reasonably should have known through the exercise of due diligence, of the cause of action, including the identity of the possessor of the paintings." O'Keeffe v. Snyder, 83 N.J. 478, 416 A.2d 862 (1980).

(ii) In awarding recovery of stolen mosaics to the plaintiff, the court followed *O'Keeffe*; the statute of limitations did not begin to run until the true owner discovered the mosaics in defendant's possession. Autocephalous Greek–Orthodox Church v. Goldberg & Feldman Fine Arts, 917 F.2d 278 (7th Cir.1990), cert. denied, 502 U.S. 941 (1991).

(iii) Rejecting *O'Keeffe* because it provides insufficient protection for owners of stolen art is Solomon R. Guggenheim Foundation v. Lubell, 77 N.Y.2d 311, 567 N.Y.S.2d 623, 569 N.E.2d 426 (1991). The replevin statute of limitations does not, the court held, begin to run until the true owner demands return and the good faith purchaser refuses.

(iv) Despite the passage of 200 years, the state of North Carolina owned two Colonial Court bills of indictment in the hands of collectors. The statute of limitations, the court said, does not run against the state. State v. West, 293 N.C. 18, 235 S.E.2d 150 (1977).

FUENTES v. SHEVIN

Supreme Court of the United States, 1972.
407 U.S. 67.

[Plaintiff sued for declaratory and injunctive relief to prevent the continued enforcement of the Florida prejudgment replevin procedures on the ground that the state statutes violated the due process clause of the fourteenth amendment.]

JUSTICE STEWART delivered the opinion of the Court. * * * Under the Florida statute challenged here, "[a]ny person whose goods or chattels are wrongfully detained by any other person * * * may have a writ of replevin to recover them * * *." Fla.Stats. § 78.01, F.S.A. There is no requirement that the applicant make a convincing showing before the seizure that the goods are, in fact, "wrongfully detained." Rather, Florida law automatically relies on the bare assertion of the party seeking the writ that he is entitled to one and allows a court clerk to issue the writ summarily. It requires only that the applicant file a complaint, initiating a court action for repossession and reciting in conclusory fashion that he is "lawfully entitled to the possession" of the property, and that he file a security bond.

       "In at least double the value of the property to be replevied conditioned that plaintiff will prosecute his action to effect and without delay and that if defendant recovers judgment against him in the action, he will return the property, if return thereof is adjudged, and will pay defendant all sums of money recovered against plaintiff by defendant in the action." Fla.Stats. § 78.07, F.S.A.

On the sole basis of the complaint and bond, a writ is issued "command[ing] the officer to whom it may be directed to replevy the goods and chattels in possession of defendant * * * and to summon the defendant to answer the complaint." Fla.Stats. § 78.08. If the goods are "in any dwelling house or other building or enclosure," the officer is required to demand their delivery; but if they are not delivered, "he shall cause such house, building or enclosure to be broken open and shall make replevin according to the writ * * *." Fla.Stats. § 78.10, F.S.A.

Thus, at the same moment that the defendant receives the complaint seeking repossession of property through court action, the property is seized from him. He is provided no prior notice and allowed no opportunity whatever to challenge the issuance of the writ. *After* the property has been seized, he will eventually have an opportunity for a hearing, as the defendant in the trial of the court action for repossession, which the plaintiff is required to pursue. And he is also not wholly without recourse in the meantime. For under the Florida statute, the officer who seizes the property must keep it for three days, and during that period the defendant may reclaim possession of the property by posting his own security bond in double its value. But if he does not post such a bond, the property is transferred to the party who sought the writ, pending a final judgment in the underlying action for repossession. Fla.Stats. § 78.13, F.S.A. * * *

Although these prejudgment replevin statutes are descended from the common law replevin action of six centuries ago, they bear very little resemblance to it. Replevin at common law was an action for the return of specific goods wrongfully taken or "distrained." Typically, it was used after a landlord (the "distrainor") had seized possessions from a tenant (the "distrainee") to satisfy a debt allegedly owed. If the tenant then instituted a replevin action and posted security the landlord could be ordered to return the property at once, pending a final judgment in the underlying action. However, this prejudgment replevin of goods at common law did *not* follow from an entirely *ex parte* process of pleading by the distrainee. For "[t]he distrainor could always stop the action of replevin by claiming to be the owner of the goods; and as this claim was often made merely to delay the proceedings, the writ *de proprietate probanda* was devised early in the fourteenth century which enabled the sheriff to determine summarily the question of ownership. If the question of ownership was determined against the distrainor the goods were delivered back to the distrainee [pending final judgment]." 3 Holdsworth, History of English Law 284 (1927).

Prejudgment replevin statutes like those of Florida * * * are derived from this ancient possessory action in that they authorize the seizure of property before a final judgment. But the similarity ends there. As in the present cases, such statutes are most commonly used by creditors to seize goods allegedly wrongfully detained—not wrongfully taken—by debtors. At common law, if a creditor wished to invoke state power to recover goods wrongfully detained, he had to proceed through the action of debt or detinue. These actions, however, did not provide for a return of property before final judgment.[1] And, more

---

1. [Footnote renumbered.] The creditor could, of course, proceed without the use of state power, through self-help, by "distraining" the property before a judgment.

importantly, on the occasions when the common law did allow prejudgment seizure by state power, it provided some kind of notice and opportunity to be heard to the party then in possession of the property, and a state official made at least a summary determination of the relative rights of the disputing parties before stepping into the dispute and taking goods from one of them.

For more than a century the central meaning of procedural due process has been clear: "Parties whose rights are to be affected are entitled to be heard; and in order that they may enjoy that right they must be notified." Baldwin v. Hale, 68 U.S. 223. * * * It is equally fundamental that the right to notice and an opportunity to be heard "must be granted at a meaningful time and in a meaningful manner." Armstrong v. Manzo, 380 U.S. 545, 552.

The primary question in the present cases is whether these state statutes are constitutionally defective in failing to provide for hearings "at a meaningful time." * * *

We hold that the Florida * * * prejudgment replevin provisions work a deprivation of property without due process of law insofar as they deny the right to a prior opportunity to be heard before chattels are taken from their possessor. Our holding, however, is a narrow one. We do not question the power of a State to seize goods before a final judgment in order to protect the security interests of creditors so long as those creditors have tested their claim to the goods through the process of a fair prior hearing. The nature and form of such prior hearings, moreover, are legitimately open to many potential variations and are a subject, at this point, for legislation—not adjudication. Since the essential reason for the requirement of a prior hearing is to prevent unfair and mistaken deprivations of property, however, it is axiomatic that the hearing must provide a real test. "[D]ue process is afforded only by the kinds of 'notice' and 'hearing' which are aimed at establishing the validity, or at least the probable validity, of the underlying claim against the alleged debtor *before* he can be deprived of his property * * *." Sniadach v. Family Finance Corp., 395 U.S. at 343 (Harlan, J., concurring).

JUSTICE WHITE, dissenting. * * * Third: The Court's rhetoric is seductive, but in end analysis, the result it reaches will have little impact and represents no more than ideological tinkering with state law. It would appear that creditors could withstand attack under today's opinion simply by making clear in the controlling credit instruments that they may retake possession without a hearing, or, for that matter, without resort to judicial process at all. Alternatively, they need only give a few days' notice of a hearing, take possession if hearing is waived or if there is default; and if hearing is necessary merely establish probable cause for asserting that default has occurred. It is very doubtful in my mind that such a hearing would in fact result in protections for the debtor substantially different from those the present law provides. On the contrary, the availability of credit may well be diminished or, in any event, the expense of securing it increased.

None of this seems worth the candle to me. The procedure which the Court strikes down is not some barbaric hangover from bygone days. The respective rights of the parties in secured transactions have undergone the most intensive analysis in recent years. The Uniform Commercial Code, which now so pervasively governs the subject matter with which it deals, provides in Art. 9, § 9–503, that:

> "Unless otherwise agreed a secured party has on default the right to take possession of the collateral. In taking possession a secured party may proceed without judicial process if this can be done without breach of peace or may proceed by action * * *."

I am content to rest on the judgment of those who have wrestled with these problems so long and often and upon the judgment of the legislatures that have considered and so recently adopted provisions that contemplate precisely what has happened in these cases.

Notes

1. *Due Process for the Debtor.* The Supreme Court's refinements of due process in debtor-creditor relations have continued. The Court has rejected creditors' procedures which lacked notice to the alleged debtor and an opportunity to be heard. In Connecticut v. Doehr, 501 U.S. 1 (1991), the Court disapproved pre-judgment attachment of real estate. In North Georgia Finishing, Inc. v. Di–Chem, Inc., 419 U.S. 601 (1975), it disapproved pre-judgment garnishment of a bank account.

In Mitchell v. W.T. Grant Co., 416 U.S. 600 (1974), which like *Fuentes*, involved a secured creditor's recovery of its collateral, the Court approved a Louisiana procedure without any preseizure notice and opportunity for an adversary hearing. Factors considered in *Mitchell* and later decisions include whether a judge evaluated the request; whether plaintiff's evidence or affidavits were factual rather than conclusions; whether the dispute was amenable to documentary, rather than testimonial, proof; whether the plaintiff had a pre-existing interest in the property; and whether defendant could schedule a post-seizure hearing immediately.

2. *Legislatures Respond.* Judicial decisions following *Fuentes* struck down states' provisional replevin procedures for lack of notice to the debtor-defendant and an opportunity to be heard. Blair v. Pitchess, 5 Cal.3d 258, 96 Cal.Rptr. 42, 486 P.2d 1242 (1971); Laprease v. Raymours Furniture Co., 315 F.Supp. 716 (N.D.N.Y.1970); Hamrick v. Ashland Finance Co., 423 F.Supp. 1033 (S.D.W.Va.1976).

Legislatures revised state statutes to comply with the decisions. Some of the statutes emphasize the *Fuentes* approach, others the more lenient *Mitchell-Doehr* factors. Consult your jurisdiction's statute for detail.

See Cal.Civ.Proc.Code § 512.020b. Excepted from the due process requirements are actions to recover stolen property, credit cards, and property about to be destroyed or removed from the state. But courts disfavor ex parte writs of possession except in the most exigent circumstances. Sea Rail Truckloads, Inc. v. Pullman, Inc., 131 Cal.App.3d 511, 182 Cal.Rptr. 560 (1982).

Plaintiff may consider seeking a temporary restraining order, which, under the federal rules, may be issued without notice to the defendant. Fed.R.Civ.P. 65(b). We return to this below with equitable replevin.

3. *Damages Instead of Return of Property.* Several states' statutes permit the plaintiff to sue for replevin, but to recover the value of the withheld property *at the time of trial* instead of specific restitution. E.g. Hallmark v. Stillings, 620 S.W.2d 436 (Mo.App.1981).

FLICKINGER v. MARK IV APARTMENTS, ASSOCIATION

Supreme Court of Iowa, 1982.
315 N.W.2d 794.

SCHULTZ, JUSTICE. On September 4, 1976, Flickinger was delinquent on her rental obligation to Mark IV [apartment association]. She returned to her apartment at approximately 9:00 p.m. but was unable to gain entrance because Mark IV had installed a new lock. Mark IV had previously utilized such a "lock-out" as a means of collecting rent from Flickinger. On this occasion, however, Flickinger did not contact Mark IV with respect to either access to the apartment or payment of the overdue rent. She left Iowa City and within a few days was arrested in Hardin County, where she was incarcerated until November 10, 1976.

Flickinger's parents, Pennsylvania residents, came to Iowa and took custody of her children. Before returning to Pennsylvania, the parents apprised Mark IV of Flickinger's situation and were allowed to remove the children's clothing and toys from the apartment. Mark IV then moved the contents of Flickinger's apartment to a locked storage facility. When she was released from jail, Flickinger made no attempt to contact Mark IV to recover her property.

In January 1977, at which time Flickinger resided in Eldora, Iowa, Mark IV obtained a default judgment against her in the Johnson District Small Claims Court in the amount of $500 for the delinquent rent. Subsequently, Flickinger moved to Pennsylvania to be with her children and parents. Telephonic and written communications followed.

During a telephone conversation in August 1977, Mark IV advised Flickinger that her property had been stored and that she could settle the default judgment for $200. On January 20, 1978, Flickinger's attorney, a staff member of Hawkeye Legal Services Society, informed her that Mark IV wanted her property removed by February 15. On February 16 Mark IV gave Flickinger written notice to remove her possessions by March 13 or to give it written permission to dispose of the property. Flickinger responded by requesting that the property be allowed to remain in storage until May, and Mark IV assented. Flickinger then sent Mark IV three checks for $20 each, to be applied toward the settlement for the delinquent rent. Flickinger did not remove her furniture in May, however, and in September Mark IV notified Flickinger that if she did not remove her property it would be given to Goodwill Industries.

[Flickinger sued Mark IV for replevin.] The evidence concerning the disposition of Flickinger's property is conflicting. Flickinger testified that she returned to Iowa City in the fall of 1978 and removed items of her property from the storage facility on three occasions. * * * Flickinger testified that she received some, but not all, of her property. She stated that during her last telephone conversation with Mark IV she was informed that her remaining property was in the process of being disposed of and would not be there when she came to claim it. * * *

Flickinger introduced into evidence a schedule of the items of personal property she allegedly did not recover from Mark IV. The trial court found as a matter of fact that all of the items on the schedule, with the exception of baby clothes, had been wrongfully detained by Mark IV. The court ordered Mark IV to return the property to Flickinger or, if it were unable to do so, to pay her damages of $2471, the value assigned to the property by the court. * * * [Both parties appeal] Flickinger assigns error to the trial court's failure to award her damages for loss of use of the property during the period of detention.

General Principles. Replevin is an action to recover specific personal property that has been wrongfully taken or wrongfully detained, with an incidental right to damages caused by reason of such detention. In Iowa the action is statutory, ch. 643, The Code; it combines the features of the common-law actions of replevin and detinue. The pleading requirements are contained in section 643.1, The Code. The petition must state, *inter alia:* facts showing the plaintiff's right to possession of the property; that the property was neither taken pursuant to court order or judgment nor attachment or execution, or, if so, that it was exempt from seizure by such process; and the alleged cause of the detention of the property. § 643.1(3)–(5), The Code.

The gist of a replevin action is enforcement of the plaintiff's right to immediate possession of the property wrongfully taken or detained. [citations] A wrongful taking need not be by forcible dispossession; any unlawful interference with, or assertion of control over, the property is sufficient. A wrongful detention occurs when the defendant wrongfully withholds or retains possession of the property sought to be recovered.

Replevin is an action at law. § 643.2, The Code. * * *

Wrongful detention. * * * Mark IV contends that the court seems to have found a wrongful taking rather than a wrongful detention. It concedes that the "lock-out" constituted a wrongful taking, since it thereby obtained control over Flickinger's property. However, it claims that, unless followed by a wrongful detention, a wrongful taking will not sustain an action in replevin.

Mark IV's assertion that the fact that Flickinger was at all times free to recover her property changed the nature of its possession from wrongful to rightful is without merit. Once there has been a wrongful taking or detention, possession does not become rightful until some form of redelivery occurs. Wrongful possession of property does not become rightful merely by agreeing to allow recovery by the party entitled to possession.

When the plaintiff in a replevin action satisfies the burden of proving a wrongful taking of property, the burden shifts to the defendant to show that he or she no longer has possession; if the defendant fails to do so, it is presumed that possession continues. * * *

Damages for loss of use. In Universal C.I.T. Credit Corp. v. Jones, 227 N.W.2d 473, 478 (Iowa 1975), this court summarized the law of damages in a replevin action as follows:

'(1) The injured party may demand the return of his property plus damages for its wrongful detention.'

(2) He may seek judgment for the money value of the property, treating the conversion as complete either at the time it was taken or at the time of trial.

(3) If the former, he may have interest on the value as determined by the trier of fact from the date of the seizure until the date of judgment and nothing more. The judgment itself, of course, bears interest thereafter.

(4) If he elects under (2) above to rely on a conversion as of the time of trial, he may have the money value of the property as of that date, plus damages for loss of use from the time it was seized until the time of trial.

Flickinger maintains that since she elected to treat the conversion as occurring at the time of trial she is entitled to loss-of-use damages from the time of the lock-out until the time of trial.

The trial court concluded that Flickinger was not entitled to damages for loss of use. The court found that she was in no position to use the property during the two-month period following the lock-out and that Mark IV did not prevent her from recovering the use of her property. Relying on *Universal* and Barry v. State Surety Co., 261 Iowa 222, 154 N.W.2d 97 (1967), however, Flickinger contends that she was not required to show that she would have used the property as a prerequisite to recovering damages for loss of use.

In *Barry* an implement company had obtained immediate possession of a tractor in a replevin action by filing a replevin bond. Judgment was later entered determining the replevin was wrongful and ordering the tractor to be returned to the plaintiffs. The plaintiffs then brought an action against the surety on the bond for wrongful seizure and detention of the tractor. The defendant surety company contended that the plaintiffs were not entitled to damages for loss of use because the evidence did not disclose any actual loss. This court stated:

> "The fact, if it be a fact, that plaintiffs here did not hire equipment to replace theirs and that they would not have used this equipment anyway, even if it had been in their possession, does not appeal to us. It was their equipment. They were entitled to its possession and to its use, and defendant's interference with that possession entitles plaintiffs to damages."

The rule authorizing recovery for loss of use when the property could not or would not have been used, is not applicable when use of the property is not prevented by the party that wrongfully seized the property, however. [citations] In *Barry* the plaintiffs' use was prevented by the implement company's replevy of the tractor pursuant to legal process; the plaintiffs could not have recovered the tractor during the pendency of the replevin action. In the present case the trial court found that Mark IV did not prevent Flickinger from recovering the use of her property. * * * We therefore hold that the court correctly denied Flickinger damages for loss of use. * * *

Affirmed.

Notes

1. *Plaintiff's Choice.* Does the statute in *Flickinger* allow the plaintiff to select the most advantageous damages elements of both replevin and conversion? Does it build in possible recovery for inflation?

2. *Landlord's Rent–Collection Techniques.* "Consumer"-oriented landlord-tenant statutes abolish both distress-distraint and the landlord's lien. Neither seems to have been involved in *Flickinger*. Distress or distraint allows, or allowed, a landlord to seize a tenant's property on the premises and keep it pending payment of rent. A landlord's lien procedure creates, or created, a lien to allow the landlord to sell the tenant's property and pay itself rent out of the proceeds. In addition to statutory revision, both procedures are vulnerable to *Fuentes*-style due process attack, particularly if a state official is involved. William Stoebuck & Dale Whitman, The Law of Property §§ 6.57–.58 (3d ed. 2000). Check "The Code," that is appropriate for your jurisdiction.

3. *Debtor's Exemptions.* State exemption statutes protect certain of a debtor's property by restricting her creditor from appropriating it to collect its judgment.

Debtor's clothing and furniture are typically exempt from collection. Even though her exemption may explain why Mark IV did not collect its $500 judgment from Ms. Flickinger's effects, Mark IV did dispose of the furniture in the end anyway.

4. *Question.* The Iowa court had announced rules in Universal C.I.T. Credit Corp. v. Jones. Did it follow them here?

5. *Confusion Between Conversion and Replevin?* Justice Newbern concurring in an Arkansas decision observed:

"My primary objection to the majority opinion is that it leaves the impression that this court fails to understand that conversion damages and incidental damages accompanying replevin are wholly inconsistent remedies. The distinguishing feature of an action for *conversion* is an interference with property so serious as to justify a forced judicial sale to the wrongdoer. [citation] The property owner is compensated by an award for value of the property at the time and place of the conversion."

"On the other hand, the primary object of a replevin action is the actual *recovery of possession* of the property. The owner cannot be required to accept the value of the item in lieu of return of possession. [citation] By statute, the property owner may, in addition to return of the item, recover damages for loss of use while it was out of his possession. Ark.Stat.Ann. § 34–2116 (Repl.1962)."

"It is generally recognized that the *value of the use* of the property converted is not recoverable in a conversion action. Ford Motor Credit Co. v. Herring, 267 Ark. 201, 589 S.W.2d 584 (1979) (measure of damages for conversion is the market value at the time and place of conversion, not the purchase, rental, or replacement cost); Hardin v. Marshall, 176 Ark. 977, 5 S.W.2d 325 (1928) (instruction allowing jury to assess as damages rental value of property converted in addition to value of property was error in a conversion cause of action)." France v. Nelson, 292 Ark. 219, 222–25, 729 S.W.2d 161, 164–65 (1987).

6. In the next decision, a litigant seeks a give-it-back injunction instead of replevin. This tactic is called equitable replevin.

2. EQUITABLE REPLEVIN

CHARLES SIMKIN & SONS v. MASSIAH

United States Court of Appeals, Third Circuit, 1961.
289 F.2d 26.

McLAUGHLIN, CIRCUIT JUDGE. * * * In April 1959, plaintiff entered into a contract with the City of Trenton, New Jersey for the construction of a Sewage Treatment Plant at Duck Island, Trenton. * * *

Plaintiff, by written agreement, subcontracted the concrete work to the defendant. During the course of performance of the subcontract, various disputes arose between the parties, and on June 10, 1960, the plaintiff gave notice of termination for the alleged default of the defendant. * * * On July 13, 1960, the plaintiff took possession of defendant's tools and equipment and assumed performance of the concrete work.

Ten days later, plaintiff instituted an action in the Superior Court of New Jersey. * * * Upon the requisite showing, the defendant removed the case to the Federal District Court. Defendant filed an answer and counterclaimed for sums allegedly due under the contract, breach of contract, conversion of the tools and equipment and injunctive relief against the plaintiff's continued use and possession of them. * * *

The district court denied defendant's petition for an injunction against plaintiff's continued possession and use of defendant's equipment and tools. We agree with the district court's conclusion.

The relief sought by the defendant is in the nature of equitable replevin. The basis for invoking this type of relief is well-settled.

> "A court of equity may compel the delivery of a specific chattel wrongfully withheld, notwithstanding replevin or trover may lie therefor, but only in cases where damages would be an inadequate redress for the injury, for instance, as in the case of heirlooms, and other articles incapable of being replaced, which are prized for their associations rather than for intrinsic value. Burr v. Bloomsburg, 101 N.J.Eq. 615 [138 A. 876]."

To support the assertion that the tools and equipment are a proper subject for equitable relief, the defendant has cited several cases. In no way do they support his position. In all of them the chattels involved were "unique" and could not be replaced by purchase on the open market. E.g., Coven v. First Savings and Loan Ass'n, Ch.1947, 141 N.J.Eq. 1, 55 A.2d 244 (an attorney's title plant); Redmond v. New Jersey Historical Society, E. & A. 1942, 132 N.J.Eq. 464, 28 A.2d 189 (Stuart's portrait of Captain Lawrence); Burr v. Bloomsburg, Ch.1927, 101 N.J.Eq. 615, 138 A. 876 (a family heirloom).

In this appeal, the tools and equipment are not "unique" but are standard-made and readily available on the open market. Items such as electric fans, electric drills, shovels, boots, wheelbarrows, rakes, scrapers, wire cutters, etc., are not within the category of personalty which affords a proper basis to invoke the remedy of equitable replevin.[1] * * *

Therefore on the defendant's appeal, the judgment of the district court will be affirmed.

Notes

1. *Questions.* Is the court's uniqueness test too restrictive? Was the court excessively technical in telling the plaintiff that it lost because it picked the wrong words to put on its request? Has the court stood idly by while a wrong occurred, content merely to charge the wrongdoer with damages?

Is there something unsettling about a remedial hierarchy that limits the judge to granting the legal remedy, replevin, unless the plaintiff shows it inadequate?

Many replevin statutes allow a defendant to post a counterbond and get the property back. Might procedural shortcuts in seeking an injunction undermine the replevin statute's protections for the defendant?

2. *Original Art.* "Because the Duerers are unique chattels the court may exercise its equitable jurisdiction to enter a judgment directing Elicofon to deliver

---

1. [Footnote renumbered.] In his brief the defendant argues: "But * * * [defendant's] remedy may not be measured by the loss of wheelbarrows and concrete mixers. It is the sum total of what was taken, embracing as it did the defendant's entire working tools and equipment, that lends significance and invokes the remedy."

This misconceives the theory that invokes equitable remedies in the case of chattels. *It is not a quantitative evaluation.* The reason for the granting of equitable relief is the inadequacy of the remedy at law. "Such a case is established, where a chattel * * * is unique, or not purchasable in the market." Williston on Contracts § 1419, p. 3954 (Rev. ed. 1937). "The equitable jurisdiction in these cases really rests upon the fact that the only relief which the plaintiff can have is possession of the *identical* thing, and this remedy cannot *with certainty* be obtained by any common-law action." Pomeroy, Equity Jurisprudence § 185, pp. 265–66 (5th ed. 1941).

the paintings to the Kunstsammlungen. N.Y.—McKinney's C.P.L.R. § 7109. * * * The contempt remedy is provided in N.Y.—McKinney's C.P.L.R. § 7109(b) to compel delivery after judgment. Thus an alternative provision for recovery of the value of the chattel need not be included in the judgment where the chattel is unique." Kunstsammlungen Zu Weimar v. Elicofon, 536 F.Supp. 829, 859 (E.D.N.Y.1981), aff'd, 678 F.2d 1150 (2d Cir.1982).

3. *TRO, Preliminary Injunction.* A court may grant an injunction or temporary restraining order to prohibit the defendant from removing chattels before a hearing. When the California replevin statute was amended to meet *Fuentes*'s due process requirements, this feature was added. See Cal.Civ.Code § 513–010.

4. *Remember McNulty?* If the litigation is in one jurisdiction and the property is in another outside the local officials' bailiwick, the judge may grant an order requiring the defendant to repatriate it. p. 234.

3. RECOVERING AND PROTECTING REAL PROPERTY

A landowner's right to exclude a trespasser while nearly absolute is burdened with historical and technical distinctions.

The owner-nonoccupant has several remedies against a defendant who is committing the tort of trespass to land.

Trespass to Land. The owner-plaintiff may sue a trespasser for trespass and seek damages and an injunction. Trespass to try title may end with nominal damages but have a declaratory judgment effect of determining ownership; this judicial imprimatur may suffice to prevent a trespasser from occupying the land during the entire period of the statute of limitations and becoming owner by adverse possession.

Forcible Entry. Forcible entry and detainer is a summary remedy to recover *possession* of land. The technical differences between an injunction and forcible entry and detainer were examined in a well-known decision in Nebraska, Warlier v. Williams, 53 Neb. 143, 73 N.W. 539 (1897).

Plaintiff alleged that defendants were squatters on plaintiff's Missouri River bottomlands; they were cultivating crops; all were insolvent; and they could claim title by adverse possession after ten years. The trial court sustained defendant's demurrer. Plaintiff appealed.

"This proceeding," the Nebraska supreme court began, "is, in effect, an application to a court of equity for a mandatory injunction to remove the defendants * * * from the real estate of the plaintiff, * * * upon which they have forcibly and wrongfully entered, and are wrongfully occupying. * * *

"A litigant cannot successfully invoke the extraordinary remedy of injunction to enforce a legal right unless the facts and circumstances in the case are such that his ordinary legal remedies are inadequate; * * * Now, the facts stated in the petition of the plaintiff * * * show simply this: That the defendants * * * have forcibly entered upon, and are occupying, his real estate. The plaintiff * * * has the legal title, and is in possession of this real estate. He might then institute against these defendants * * * an action of forcible entry and detainer, under * * * the Code of Civil Procedure, * * * which expressly provides that such an action may be brought against a defendant who is a settler or occupier of lands, without color of title, and to which the complainant in the forcible detainer suit has the right of possession. Here, then, is a plain statutory remedy for the wrong of which the plaintiff * * * complains in this action. Is this remedy an adequate one? The statute provides that this action of forcible entry and detainer may be brought before a justice of the peace, after giving the parties in possession of the land three days' notice to quit; that no continuance for more than eight days shall be granted in the case, unless the party made defendant shall give bond for the payment of rent; and, if the judgment shall be entered in favor of the plaintiff, a writ of restitution shall be awarded in his favor, unless appellate proceedings are taken by defendants, in which case they shall give a bond to pay a reasonable rent for the premises while they wrongfully detain the same. This remedy is not only an adequate one, but it is a summary and a speedy one. The relief demanded by the plaintiff * * * in this injunction proceeding is the ousting of the defendants * * * from his real estate, so that he may have the exclusive possession of it. A judgment and a writ of restitution in a forcible entry and detainer suit would afford him the same and a more speedy redress than a proceeding by injunction." Faithful to the reigning rhetoric which required a plaintiff requesting an injunction to show the remedy at law inadequate, the court rejected plaintiff's arguments based on defendants' insolvency and the necessity of multiple suits at law.

After the end of the dual court system and the forms of action, the court would be criticized for subordinating the plaintiff's preference for an injunction to a formalistic adherence to repudiated distinctions. A contemporary court would not be likely to refuse to grant plaintiff an injunction on the ground that damages are an adequate remedy.

Procedural and tactical questions about the choice between forcible entry and an injunction remain, nevertheless. Forcible entry comes before a justice of the peace; an injunction before a judge with general-equitable jurisdiction. Was the plaintiff shopping for a sympathetic judge? In an action at law, would the defendants have been entitled to demand a jury trial at some stage? Did the forcible-entry statute have specialized procedural provisions or protections for defendants that may be lost with an ex parte injunction? Might the court have been concerned about enforcing an injunction with contempt?

Ejectment. Ejectment is the name of the plaintiff's remedy designed to settle ownership—*title*—disputes. Ejectment, like replevin, an action at law, is the functional equivalent of an injunction; all three remedies allow the owner to recover the property itself. The chief procedural difference between ejectment and replevin, on the one hand, and an injunction, on the other, is the litigants' right to demand a jury for replevin and ejectment. A successful ejectment plaintiff also recovers damages for the value of using the land; these damages are called mesne profits.

Equitable Defenses to Ejectment? Although in City of Sherrill, New York v. Oneida Nation of New York, p. 323, the Supreme Court held that laches bars plaintiff's equitable claim for an injunction, the Court's decision appeared not to disturb the plaintiff's ejectment and trespass claims for damages. In Cayuga Indian Nation v. Pataki, the United States Court of Appeals dealt with the role of equitable defenses in two actions at law, ejectment and trespass to land. The Court of Appeals extended the *Oneida* court's reasoning.

The New York Cayugas were suing for ejectment, an action at law, on the State of New York's 204-year-old, 60,000–acre violation of their rights. Although the demand in the plaintiffs' ejectment action for possession had been converted to one for damages, the Court of Appeals reversed their damages verdict. It held that equitable defenses, including laches, apply to "disruptive Indian land claims more generally." The court also barred the Cayuga's trespass tort for damages because it was "predicated entirely upon plaintiffs' possessory land claim." Cayuga Indian Nation v. Pataki, 413 F.3d 266, 278 (2d Cir.2005), cert. denied, 126 S.Ct. 2021, 2022 (2006).

An Injunction. An injunction is a landowner's typical and all-purpose remedy. An injunction is an equitable remedy; defendant may argue that plaintiff's remedies at law, ejectment and forcible entry and detainer, are adequate remedies at law. The rubric that each parcel of land is unique has routed contrary doctrine; a judge will almost always grant plaintiff an injunction forbidding a defendant's trespass and nuisance. While a judge is unlikely to accept defendant's argument that damages will be an adequate remedy for a landowner, defendant's request to "balance the hardships" may succeed, as we will see below.

Quiet Title. A plaintiff not occupying, but claiming to own, land has two other equitable remedies: (a) quiet title to determine who owns land; and (b) a suit to remove a cloud on title, which means what it sounds like it means. Statutes and judicial decisions combine in each jurisdiction to form a unique concoction. Technicalities rooted in history lurk in each action and the choices between them.

When, for example, the state of New York sued in United States district court to regain possession of 612 acres of land after "forty-two members of the Mohawk Nation * * * seize[d] possession of the property and buildings thereon * * * thus dramatically ending 175 years of silent acquiescence in non-Indian ownership," the federal courts applied the "well-pleaded complaint" doctrine to New York's claim of federal question jurisdiction. The action was one "arising under" federal law, New York maintained, because of a 1798 "treaty" between New York and the Mohawk Nation. The court of appeals began its discussion of the difference between ejectment and the action to remove a cloud on title by commenting on New York's "fallacious assumption that the pleader operates free of constraints in choosing between these two related causes of action." "A bill to remove a cloud on title," the court's lecture continued, "is traditionally a suit in equity, and, as such, available only when there is no adequate remedy at law. Despite the merger of law and equity in 1938, this basic principle of federal jurisprudence retains its viability as a safeguard for the right to a jury trial guaranteed by the Seventh Amendment. Possession is the critical determinant. Since the State is concededly not in possession of the land in Herkimer County, it was obliged first to pursue the legal remedy of ejectment. Judge Port was correct in construing the State's complaint consonant with this obligation. In an action for ejectment, plaintiff need only allege that he is the owner in fee and that he has been wrongfully ousted from possession by the action of the defendants. Neither of these elements required the State to plead, as it did, the validity of the treaty of 1798. Stripped of this assertion, New York's complaint is bereft of any allusion to federal law."

The court allowed New York to amend its cloud-on-title complaint to allege its possession of other contested land. "As to land so challenged and still within the State's control, a suit to remove a cloud on title would properly lie. Moreover, in contrast to an action for ejectment, a bill to remove a cloud on title may, as the State's complaint does, introduce a question of federal law in its description of the cloud which plaintiff seeks to remove." New York v. White, 528 F.2d 336 (2d Cir.1975).

Procedure Aside: If New York's cloud-on-title complaint were characterized as one for quiet title, plaintiffs' federal-question jurisdiction may have been improper on the ground that a quiet title bill cannot allege the nature of a "cloud" or defense.

KRUVANT v. 12–22 WOODLAND AVENUE CORP.

Superior Court of New Jersey, 1975.
138 N.J.Super. 1, 350 A.2d 102.

DWYER, J.S.C. While sipping a drink and chatting with an attorney at a party about plans to develop what is labeled as Lot 1445–B in Block 152–X on the tax maps of Town of West Orange (Lot B), one of the owners was startled to hear the attorney tell him that those who had been riding horses across Lot B from the nearby stable might have acquired an easement across it because the activity had been going on for as long as the attorney could remember. Shortly thereafter the owners of Lot B demanded for the first time that the stable either pay rent or stop using Lot B. The stable refused both demands. The owners then commenced this action.

[P]laintiffs Philip Kruvant, Charles Kruvant and Bobcar Corporation are the record owners of Lot B. 12–22 Woodland Avenue Corporation, trading as Suburban Essex Riding Club (club) operates a boarding stable for approximately 100 horses, and a riding academy on premises which the club owns on the north side of Nicholas Avenue, a paper street, and which premises face Lot B located on the opposite, or south, side of Nicholas Avenue.

The matters at issue are: (1) the right of plaintiffs to terminate the club's use of the bridle trail which extends approximately 800 feet diagonally across Lot B to an oversize culvert constructed in 1939 by Essex County to permit horses to pass from that bridle trail under Prospect Street and into Eagle Rock Reservation (Reservation) where there are several miles of bridle trails, the right to terminate the club's use of certain other areas of Lot B [called the "meadow" or "dressage" area] and the right of plaintiffs to collect money damages from 1973 based on use and occupancy, and (2) the right of the club, asserted by counterclaim, to have the court declare that it has either title to said bridle trail and said certain other areas under the doctrine of adverse possession, or a prescriptive easement for the bridle trail and those other areas. * * *

The court concludes that the club has established a prescriptive easement for the bridle trail. [T]he acts of those associated with the club were sufficiently open, notorious, continuous and limited to a fixed area to put the owners of Lot B on notice to take action. This they did not do for over 20 years. The court finds that the meadow area, or dressage field, was not used until after the area was bulldozed by plaintiffs in 1959 or 1960. * * * The court concludes that the club has not established a prescriptive easement in the meadow area. * * *

This leaves the question of what damages, if any, should be awarded to plaintiffs for the meadow area and what remedy should be granted to the club.

Where a party proves that another has trespassed on his lands, he is entitled to nominal damages even if there is no proof of injury or damage to the lands.

Plaintiffs have not established that the club and its predecessors damaged the lands, other than trampling some grass and enriching the area with horse manure. Plaintiffs, therefore, are not entitled to damages. They have not proved that they were denied the use of the lands for any activity they had planned.

However, plaintiffs have borne all the carrying costs for Lot B. Without permission, the club has used the meadow area in connection with its profit-making activities.

Although counsel for plaintiffs cited no authority for the proposition that plaintiffs were entitled to recover damages on the basis of rental value or use and occupancy, plaintiffs have asserted such a claim [and] were allowed to make an offer of proof as to what a reasonable rent or charge for use and occupancy would be.

Lasser [a real estate broker] testified that the real estate taxes were $12,000 annually. In his opinion Lot B was worth $250,000. It is zoned for office/research and civic center development. The zoning ordinance calls for 5 A minimum lots with a front setback of 100 feet, side and rear-yard setbacks of 75 feet, and permits buildings to occupy 20% of the lot.

On direct examination Lasser testified that in his opinion one-sixth of the carrying charges, allowing a 10% return on the land value, would be a reasonable rent or charge for use and occupancy of the bridle trail and meadow area. On his calculations this is $500 a month. On cross-examination he admitted that he had not measured the area of the bridle trail or meadow. He said that considering the activity and the carrying charges it was his opinion that an allocation of one-sixth of the carrying charges was fair and reasonable.

The court has found no New Jersey case as to whether a landowner is entitled to recover on the basis of rent, or use and occupancy, from a trespasser who has used the property for profit-making activity.

Comment b to § 931 of Restatement, Torts (1939), states:

"The owner of the subject matter is entitled to recover as damages for the loss of the value of the use, at the rental value of the * * * land during the period of deprivation. This is true even though the owner in fact has suffered no harm through the deprivation, as where he was not using the subject matter at the time."

See also Baltimore & O. R. Co. v. Boyd, 67 Md. 32, 10 A. 315 (Ct.App.1887) (rental value of right of way for a railroad track across unimproved, unenclosed, vacant land held proper measure of damages for period of entry without permission and before condemnation).

The court concludes that where a person uses the land of another to carry on profit-making activities, without permission, the landowner should be able to recover a reasonable rent.

Plaintiffs have offered proof of taxes and that a 10% return on capital would be a fair means of calculating such a charge. They did not measure the meadow area although it is identified on a scaled map prepared for Essex County, as is the bridle trail. This map is in evidence. The club did not offer any contradictory evidence as to value because its objection was sustained. The court notes that there are tax stamps affixed to the deed in 1955 from Mayfair for Lot B. Lasser's opinion of value is substantially higher than the value reflected by the tax stamps. The court directs that parties calculate the meadow area; it will permit the club to submit evidence as to assessment value, or other value, of Lot B, and such comment by memoranda or a hearing (if it desires) as to value upon which return should be allowed. The period for which demand has been made by plaintiffs starts in July 1973 and money damages will be allowed only from that date.

Notes

1. *Preventive Remedies.* Before developing the lot, the plaintiff will now have to come to terms with the club. What might an owner have done to prevent the neighbors' apparently harmless activity from ripening into an easement?

The Restatement helps us answer: "In some situations repeated or continuing torts may, if maintained long enough, give the wrongdoer an easement by prescription. This is not, in itself, necessarily a conclusive factor in favor of injunction, because a series of damage actions, each seasonably brought, would not only give the plaintiff compensation but would also prevent prescription. However, a peculiar problem may arise in the case of a continuing or repeated tort that causes little if any immediate harm—for example, when the defendant has laid a water pipe across the plaintiff's waste land. So far as compensation is concerned, a damage action would not be worth its cost. Yet, if the plaintiff is not to suffer the acquisition of an easement he must either sue for damages or by some other means toll the prescription. Here the easement factor is material. The case does not, however, present a simple dilemma of repeated actions or injunction against the tort. Prescription may be prevented by a decree that merely enjoins the defendant from asserting an easement, or one which requires him to accept a license. This form of relief might be the most appropriate if an injunction against the tort would cause grave hardship— for example, if the water pipe in the case suggested above were necessary to the operation of the defendant's mine." Restatement (Second) of Torts § 944 comment *g* (1977).[†]

2. *Measuring Plaintiff's Damages.* If plaintiff's damages for the riding club's trespasses on the "meadow" are measured by rent, how should the court set the lot's value to calculate the "rent"? (a) The value of an urban lot, which is what the lot is. (b) The value of a similar meadow in the country, which is the way the lot was used. How does the riding club's easement affect the lot's value? Should the rent be what a contract between to lot owner and the riding club would have been? Should the owner consider seeking restitution measured by the riding club's savings?

FENTON v. QUABOAG COUNTRY CLUB

Supreme Judicial Court of Massachusetts, 1968.
353 Mass. 534, 233 N.E.2d 216.

REARDON, JUSTICE. This appeal has to do with the game of golf and in particular with the abilities of certain golfers in the county of Hampden whose alleged transgressions gave rise to a suit. The plaintiffs * * * seek an injunction designed to terminate the operation of one of the holes in the defendant's nine-hole course, together with damages for injuries to person and property. * * *

A master to whom the case was referred filed a report which illuminates the deep antagonisms which spring to life when home and family are threatened by devotees of the great outdoors. We refer to his findings.

In 1952 the plaintiffs, John F. and Miriam E. Fenton, "not familiar with the details of the game of golf," bought their house, garage and land from one Lussier and his wife. * * * The Lussiers had purchased the land from the defendant in 1944 and had, as one may gather from the report, coexisted happily with the golf club, a state of affairs no doubt enhanced by the fact that during their tenure Lussier and his family had sold soft drinks and sandwiches to golfers on the course and thus found no fault when errant golf balls descended upon their property. The club itself had a lengthy history. It opened in 1900 * * *.

Into this posture, fraught with potential trouble which only a golfer could fully appreciate, came the plaintiffs "not familiar with the details of the game of golf." Any deficiency in their knowledge was soon remedied as they immediately came under the assault of balls "hit onto and over their property." "Except for a few isolated occasions, these balls were not intentionally directed" at the Fenton estate. However, the master has provided us with some chilling statistics which cast grave doubt on the proficiency of the golfers of Hampden County, at least those who were playing the defendant's course. From 1952 an annual average number of 250 balls "were left" on the land of the plaintiffs, save for the year 1960 when a grand total of 320 such deposits were made. Over the years sixteen panes of glass in the plaintiffs' house were broken, for six of which fractures the plaintiffs have received reimbursement. The cost of such replacements apparently defied inflation and remained constant throughout the years at $3.85 for each new pane. Affairs worsened in 1961 when the defendant added a sand trap "to the northwest corner of the ninth green." Since golfers intent on achieving the green drove from the tee in a southerly direction, they were faced with alternatives. They might aim somewhat to the west and face the sand trap, or they might veer more to the east and face the Fentons. The master inclined to the belief that they were prone to make the latter choice although, as he found, this was not without hazard, for the plaintiff John F. Fenton collected "all the balls he found on his land and sold them periodically." Continued unbridled hooking and slicing caused further aggravation. Some years back the Fentons were possessed of a German Shepherd dog which developed apprehension at the approach of golfers to the point that they were forced to dispense with his companionship. In his place they acquired a Doberman evidently made of sterner stuff. The dog is still with them notwithstanding that he has been struck by a flying golf ball. On one occasion the male plaintiff himself stopped an airborne ball supposedly directed to the ninth green but winging its way off course. At another time a Fenton family steak cookout was interrupted by a misdirected ball which came to rest "just under the grill." There were additional serious evidences of mutual annoyance. In an episode "after dark, a ball was driven from the * * * [defendant's] fairway directly against the * * * [plaintiffs'] house." In another, a battered ball bearing the greeting "Hi, Johnnie" descended upon the plaintiffs' close. Hostile incidents occurred. One player venturing on the plaintiffs' property to retrieve a ball swung his club first at the Fentons' dog, then raised it at John Fenton, following which, according to the master's report, he "withdrew."

It need not be emphasized that from the year 1952 the plaintiffs were not silent in their suffering, and there was some talk about a fence. After the commencement of this suit the defendant constructed on its land a fence twenty-four feet high and three feet in from part of the boundary lines on the northern and western sides of the plaintiffs' land. The master states that while this fence has substantially, it has not entirely, abated the problem caused by the rain of golf balls. We are told that the erection of the fence in 1965 was followed by the flight of some eighty-one balls in that year onto the plaintiffs' territory. This somewhat minimized invasion the master terms "a continuing nuisance and trespass." For all of these depredations he assessed damages at $38.50 for those broken panes as yet unreimbursed, and $2,250 "for loss in the fair market value of * * * [the] property" because of the trespasses as well because the fence "seriously diminishes the value of the property aesthetically." He also found damages at $2,600 for disturbance of the plaintiffs' "peace and comfort" for the thirteen years prior to the erection of the unaesthetic fence. He placed a value on the loss of the plaintiffs' peace and comfort since the fence went up at $50.

Following confirmation of the master's report the court entered a final decree enjoining the defendant from so operating its course "as to damage the property of the Plaintiffs, or to cause golf balls to be cast upon or propelled upon or against the property of the Plaintiffs." The failure to employ the technical language peculiar to the game of golf in the decree in no sense muddies its meaning. The damages assessed by the master were awarded in the interlocutory and final decrees.

We have the case on appeals from the decrees.

We have no doubts about the propriety of the injunction. The plaintiffs are clearly entitled to an abatement of the trespasses. Stevens v. Rockport Granite Co., 216 Mass. 486, 489, 104 N.E. 371. We paraphrase the apt expression of Chief Justice Rugg in the *Stevens* case: "The pertinent inquiry is whether the noise [the invasion of golf balls] materially interferes with the physical comfort of existence, not according to exceptionally refined, uncommon, or luxurious habits of living [e.g. golf addiction], but according to the simple tastes and unaffected notions generally prevailing among plain people [nongolfers]. The standard is what ordinary people [again those who eschew golf], acting reasonably, have a right to demand in the way of health and comfort under all the circumstances." Were it not that this court cannot assume the function of a Robert Trent Jones we should make a judicial suggestion that the defendant's burden under the injunction will be considerably eased by shifting the location of the trap to the northeasterly corner of the green on the assumption, and on this the record is silent, that none exists there now.

On the damages awarded, the plaintiffs are entitled to the sum of $38.50 for the cost of replacing the glass, and also for the sum of $2,650 awarded them for their distress and discomfort over fourteen years. The master took testimony on the effect on the plaintiffs of their discomfort which was sufficient to enable him to make the award which he did. * * *

There was error, however, in the award of damages based on loss in the fair market value of the property due to what the master found to be a continuing trespass. This was a trespass of such a nature that it might be terminated by appropriate action, which is what the injunction in fact seeks to do. As such the true measure of damages is the loss in rental value of the property while injury continues. In the assessment of damages the defendant's erection of the fence on its own property can play no part. The interlocutory and final decrees are reversed. The case is remanded to the Superior Court for further proceedings consistent with this opinion.

So ordered.

Notes

1. According to the January 3, 1988 New York Times, the dispute between the Fentons and the golf club continued for twenty-two years and was resolved when the club agreed to shorten its ninth hole.

2. Do damages based on diminution in market value duplicate an injunction? Do damages for lost rental value duplicate damages for "distress and discomfort"?

3. *Detailed Instructions.* Compare the *Fenton* court's injunction to another court's golf course solution. Plaintiff alleged nuisance, trespass and negligence: "Plaintiffs are entitled to the issuance of a mandatory injunction * * * directing the defendants * * * to redesign and reconstruct the third and fourth holes of the existing golf course in such a manner as to minimize the intrusion of golf balls onto the plaintiff's adjoining property and upon completion thereof to file with the court a copy of the revised design together with evidence of the completion thereof." Sierra Screw Products v. Azusa Greens, Inc., 88 Cal.App.3d 358, 364, 151 Cal.Rptr. 799, 802 (1979).

Why not "assume the function of a Robert Trent Jones" and tell the country club how to fix the problem?

4. *Fore! Plaintiff Winged.* A plaintiff actually hit by a wandering golf ball may plead several torts, negligence, trespass, nuisance, and perhaps battery. The golfers commit the trespass; whereas the golf course commits the nuisance. Bearing in mind the in personam nature of an injunction and the need to draft an enforceable order, which tort theory is more suitable for future relief?

Ms. Hennessey, who had "paused to dally over some flowers in her front-yard garden," when she was struck by a careening golf ball sued (a) the golf club for nuisance and negligence; and (b) the golfer, who was the club's assistant pro, for nuisance, assault and battery, and negligence, but not for trespass. The Rhode Island court sent the plaintiff's lawsuit against the golfer back for trial on negligence, but not for nuisance or battery. It redefined the golfer's negligence duty as the exercise of "reasonable care for the safety of persons reasonably within the range of danger of being struck by the ball." It also deflated the golfer's defense of assumption of the risk when a plaintiff is on her own property; the court's purpose was to assure that the landowner could avoid the "Hobson's choice of home confinement in her Plexiglass bunker or of venturing outside subject to being suddenly stoned by a mishit golf ball * * * or the wearing of some type of protective armor when she ventures forth during playing hours." Hennessey v. Pyne, 694 A.2d 691, 700 (R.I.1997).

Will the golfers' negligence duty eliminate wandering golf balls more efficiently than the injunction in *Fenton*?

4. LIFE ALONG THE PROPERTY LINE: VARIATIONS ON THE OWNER'S RIGHT TO EXCLUDE

The owner of the soil owns all the way to heaven and all the way to the depths. In Latin, it is "Cuius est solum eius asque ad coelum et usque ad inferos," or just "ad coelum." This Chapter discusses how courts protect the "ad coelum" through remedies to protect the owner's right to exclude. The following material summarizes some of the ways courts have qualified and extended the owner's remedies along the borderland.

Economic considerations justify the owner's right to exclude an invader. The owner with a right to exclude has an incentive to improve and invest in property which encourages owners to use the land resource efficiently; for if an invader could swoop and grab with impunity, an owner would have no incentive to improve and exploit land.

Even a slight physical invasion under the government's aegis constitutes a "taking." Loretto v. Teleprompter Manhattan CATV Corp., 458 U.S. 419 (1982). In private litigation the owner uses trespass, nuisance and negligence and their remedies, injunctions, damages and restitution, to protect and vindicate the right to possess. An injunction makes the owner's right real.

Nature does not always cooperate with law by fitting neatly into legal definitions and categories. Should courts' remedies to protect the owner's column be carried as far as logic does, or should they be affected by policy? Remedies, the science of practical solutions, combines with torts, property law and constitutional protection for expression to provide some answers to the perplexing question.

Shrinking the Owner's Right to Exclude. Until this century the owner's column upward was benign because people lived only on the land's surface. But the Wright brothers' flight changed that. The owner's control of airspace obviously cannot be hermetic or absolute, and an airplane may cross overhead. United States v. Causby, 328 U.S. 256 (1946). Free expression and related developments in law and commerce spawned other incursions on the owner's column.

In State v. Shack, the New Jersey court let Legal Aid lawyers call on migrant farmworkers on their employer's property. The court held that the criminal trespass statute did not extend to this visit because the owner's right to control others' access "cannot include dominion over the destiny of persons the owner permits to come upon the premises." Quoting Professor Powell, the court added "time marches on toward new adjustments between individualism and the social interests." State v. Shack, 58 N.J. 297, 277 A.2d 369 (1971).

The New Jersey state constitution is not limited to protection from "state action." The New Jersey court extended outsiders' right to enter property without the owner's permission to the Princeton University campus; the court allowed them to enter the campus for political activity. State v. Schmid, 84 N.J. 535, 423 A.2d 615 (1980).

Under the New Jersey constitution, regional and community shopping centers which were equivalent to a downtown business district had to allow people access for leafleting, subject to reasonable regulations. New Jersey Coalition Against War in the Middle East v. J.M.B. Realty Corp., 138 N.J. 326, 650 A.2d 757 (1994), cert. denied, 516 U.S. 812 (1995).

The owners of a shopping mall in Portland, Oregon sought to enjoin political activists from entering the mall to obtain signatures on initiative petitions. Trespass, the court said, is not always enjoined. The court emphasized equitable flexibility, discretion, and balancing the hardships. It held that while the mall may not exclude the solicitors, it may impose reasonable restrictions on the time, place, and manner. Lloyd Corporation, Ltd. v. Whiffen, 307 Or. 674, 773 P.2d 1294 (1989).

After the California Supreme Court found that soliciting signatures for petitions in a shopping center was expression protected under the state constitution, the United States Supreme Court held that the owner's right to exclude was not so essential to the owners' use and economic value that the solicitors' state-authorized invasion constituted a "taking" warranting compensation. PruneYard Shopping Center v. Robins, 447 U.S. 74 (1980).

Most state supreme courts, however, construe their constitutions to follow the federal constitution and require "state action." Republican Party of Texas v. Dietz, 940 S.W.2d 86 (Tex.1997).

Stretching the Owner's Right to Exclude. Injunctions granted to abortion clinics expand the owners' right to exclude into the surrounding property. An injunction which forbids demonstrators from blockading the facility at the property line is not controversial. But protestors crowding entrances may prevent people from entering and render it ineffective.

The injunction in Schenck v. Pro–Choice Network contained two extensions of the owner's right to exclude: (a) A "fixed 15–foot buffer zone" against "demonstrating within fifteen feet from either side of edge of, or in front of, doorways." (b) A "floating 15–foot buffer zone" against "demonstrating * * * within fifteen feet of any person or vehicle seeking access to or leaving such facilities." Both buffer zones were qualified to allow demonstrators to conduct "sidewalk counseling" within the buffer zone unless the recipient vetoed the message.

Their right to free expression on the public street, the defendants-demonstrators maintained, meant that the injunction burdened more speech than necessary.

Because of defendants' First Amendment challenge to the injunction, the Supreme Court added "governmental interests" to plaintiffs'. These governmental interests are: "ensuring public safety and order, promoting the free flow of traffic on streets and sidewalks, protecting property rights, and protecting a woman's freedom to seek pregnancy-related services, [which] * * * also underlie the injunction here." How do these "governmental interests" affect the injunction against "demonstrating"? "[I]n combination [they] are certainly significant enough to justify an appropriately tailored injunction to secure unimpeded physical access to the clinics."

"We uphold," wrote Chief Justice Rehnquist for the majority, "the fixed buffer zones around the doorways, driveways, and driveway entrances. These buffer zones are necessary to ensure that people and vehicles trying to enter or exit the clinic property or clinic parking lots can do so. * * * [T]he record shows that protesters purposefully or effectively blocked or hindered people from entering and exiting the clinic doorways, from driving up to and away from clinic entrances, and from driving in and out of clinic parking lots. Based on this conduct * * * the District Court was entitled to conclude that the only way to ensure access was to move back the demonstrations away from the driveways and parking lot entrances. Similarly, sidewalk counselors * * * followed and crowded people right up to the doorways of the clinics (and sometimes beyond) and then tended to stay in the doorways, shouting at the individuals who had managed to get inside. In addition, as the District Court found, defendants' harassment of the local police made it far from certain that the police would be able to quickly and effectively counteract protesters who blocked doorways or threatened the safety of entering patients and employees. Based on this conduct, the District Court was entitled to conclude that protesters who were allowed close to the entrances would continue right up to the entrance, and that the only way to ensure access was to move all protesters away from the doorways. Although one might quibble about whether 15 feet is too great or too small a distance if the goal is to ensure access, we defer to the District Court's reasonable assessment of the number of feet necessary to keep the entrances clear. * * *"

"[Defendants] claim that unchallenged provisions of the injunction are sufficient to ensure this access, pointing to the bans on trespassing, excessive noise, and 'blocking, impeding or obstructing access to' the clinics. They claim that in light of these provisions, the only effect of a ban on 'demonstrating' within the fixed buffer zone is 'a ban on peaceful, nonobstructive demonstrations on public sidewalks or rights of way.' This argument, however, ignores the record in this case. Based on defendants' past conduct, the District Court was entitled to conclude that some of the defendants who were allowed within 5 to 10 feet of clinic entrances would not merely engage in stationary, nonobstructive demonstrations but would continue to do what they had done before: aggressively follow and crowd individuals right up to the clinic door and then refuse to move, or purposefully mill around parking lot entrances in an effort to impede or block the progress of cars. And because defendants' harassment of police hampered the ability of the police to respond quickly to a problem, a prophylactic measure was even more appropriate. * * * The ban on 'blocking, impeding, and obstructing access' was therefore insufficient by itself to solve the problem, and the fixed buffer zone was a necessary restriction on defendants' demonstrations. * * *

"We strike down," the Chief Justice continued, "the floating buffer zones around people entering and leaving the clinics because they burden more speech than is necessary to serve the relevant governmental interests. The floating buffer zones prevent defendants—except for two sidewalk counselors, while they are tolerated by the targeted individual—from communicating a message from a normal conversational distance or handing leaflets to people entering or leaving the clinics who are walking on the public sidewalks. This is a broad prohibition, both because of the type of speech that is restricted and the nature of the location. Leafleting and commenting on matters of public concern are classic forms of speech that lie at the heart of the First Amendment, and speech in public areas is at its most protected on public sidewalks, a prototypical example of a traditional public forum. [citations] On the other hand, we have before us a record that shows physically abusive conduct, harassment of the police that hampered law enforcement, and the tendency of even peaceful conversations to devolve into aggressive and sometimes violent conduct. In some situations, a record of abusive conduct makes a prohibition on classic speech in limited parts of a public sidewalk permissible. [citations] We need not decide whether the governmental interests involved would ever justify some sort of zone of separation between individuals entering the clinics and protesters, measured by the distance between the two. We hold here that because this broad prohibition on speech 'floats,' it cannot be sustained on this record."

"Since the buffer zone floats, protesters on the public sidewalks who wish (i) to communicate their message to an incoming or outgoing patient or clinic employee and (ii) to remain as close as possible (while maintaining an acceptable conversational distance) to this individual, must move as the individual moves, maintaining 15 feet of separation. * * * Protesters could presumably walk 15 feet behind the individual, or 15 feet in front of the individual while walking backwards. But they are then faced with the problem of watching out for other individuals entering or leaving the clinic who are heading the opposite way from the individual they have targeted. With clinic escorts leaving the clinic to pick up incoming patients and entering the clinic to drop them off, it would be quite difficult for a protester who wishes to engage in peaceful expressive activities to know how to remain in compliance with the injunction. This lack of certainty leads to a substantial risk that much more speech will be burdened than the injunction by its terms prohibits. That is, attempts to stand 15 feet from someone entering or leaving a clinic and to communicate a message-certainly protected on the face of the injunction-will be hazardous if one wishes to remain in compliance with the injunction. Since there may well be other ways to both effect such separation and yet provide certainty (so that speech protected by the injunction's terms is not burdened), we conclude that the floating buffer zones burden more speech than necessary to serve the relevant governmental interests. * * *

"We likewise strike down the floating buffer zones around vehicles. * * * [T]he 15–foot floating buffer zones would restrict the speech of those who simply line the sidewalk or curb in an effort to chant, shout, or hold signs peacefully. We therefore conclude that the floating buffer zones around vehicles burden more speech than necessary to serve the relevant governmental interests." Schenck v. Pro–Choice Network, 519 U.S. 357, 377-80 (1997).

Question. If there were no injunction, the defendants' demonstration on the public street would be expressive activity protected by the First Amendment. The injunction potentially subjects a defendant to criminal contempt punishment for what otherwise would be constitutionally protected expression in a public forum. An injunction, defendants argued, should be tailored to the plaintiff's property interest. What justifies extending the plaintiff's property right into the street?

E.   BALANCING THE HARDSHIPS—A DEFENSE TO AN INJUNCTION

HARRISON v. INDIANA AUTO SHREDDERS CO.

United States Court of Appeals, Seventh Circuit, 1975.
528 F.2d 1107.

CLARK, ASSOCIATE JUSTICE. This is an appeal from a judgment of the United States District Court for the Southern District of Indiana in a nuisance action, permanently enjoining appellant-Indiana Auto Shredders Company from operating its shredding plant for the recycling of automobiles in the Irish Hill section of Indianapolis, Indiana, and awarding $176,956 in compensatory and $353,912 in punitive damages to plaintiffs and intervenors. The suit was filed by appellee-Russell Harrison and some 33 other "claimants" who reside or work in the Irish Hill section, alleging: (1) that the dust, vibration, and noise generated by the company's shredding plant constituted a common law and statutory nuisance under Indiana law by damaging property and endangering the health and safety of residents and workers in the area; and (2) that the company's shredding plant violated various local air pollution regulations.

* * * For reasons stated below, we reverse the judgment of the district court.

* * * The concept of salvaging discarded automobiles and other metals by shredding them and recovering the ferrous metal was developed * * * in the early 1960's. Typically, a shredding machine is composed of massive rotary teeth (called "hammers") that rip off pieces of the automobile as it passes a cutting edge and then spits fist-sized chunks of metal and other matter across a series of "cascades," blowers, and magnets, which separate the ferrous metals from the non-ferrous metals and debris. A series of conveyors then carries the product and waste to storage. A "hammermill" such as the one in this case weighs 220

tons and measures approximately ten feet in width, fourteen feet in length, and nine feet in height. * * *

Most of the witnesses for the claimants were themselves residents or employers in the Irish Hill section, and they described first-hand the vibration, noise, and air pollution they had experienced. They testified that these conditions damaged their property and seriously affected their ability to live and work comfortably in the area. In presenting its defense, on the other hand, the company did not attempt to rebut this subjective evidence, but instead focused on its efforts to ameliorate the difficulties in "starting up" the shredder operation and upon its compliance with all of the applicable ordinances and regulations. In contrast to the "ordinary citizens" who testified for the claimants, most of the company's witnesses were experts and specialists in environmental, industrial, or real estate affairs.

To bolster the testimony they had given, the claimants presented various dignitaries and prominent citizens of Indianapolis who had become involved in the shredder dispute; radio and television publicity had apparently made the affair into something of a *cause celebre*. One by one, various members of the Indianapolis community testified for the claimants and corroborated their testimony about the noise, vibrations, and air pollution caused by the shredder. The Deputy Mayor of Indianapolis, the Corporation Counsel for the City of Indianapolis, a local school board member, the director of mayor's Office of Neighborhood Services, the medical community's representative to the Indianapolis Air Pollution Control Board, a local manufacturer's representative for heavy industrial equipment, and an aide to United States Senator Birch Bayh all testified to their personal observations of the shredder and the problems it caused to the Irish Hill section.

Although this testimony gave support to the claimants' characterization of the shredder as troublesome and annoying, none of it was competent to prove that the shredder constituted a threat or hazard to the health and life of the community. * * *

This case is representative of the new breed of lawsuit spawned by the growing concern for cleaner air and water. The birth and burgeoning growth of environmental litigation have forced the courts into difficult situations where modern hybrids of the traditional concepts of nuisance law and equity must be fashioned. Nuisance has always been a difficult area for the courts; the conflict of precedents and the confusing theoretical foundations of nuisance, led Prosser to tag the area a "legal garbage can."[1] In any case, environmental consciousness may be the saving prescript for our age. Thus the right of environmentally-aggrieved parties to obtain redress in the courts serves as a necessary and valuable supplement to legislative efforts to restore the natural ecology of our cities and countryside.

Judicial involvement in solving environmental problems does, however, bring its own hazards. Balancing the interests of a modern urban community like Indianapolis may be very difficult. Weighing the desire for economic and industrial strength against the need for clean and livable surroundings is not easily done, especially because of the gradations in quality as well as quantity that are involved. There is the danger that environmental problems will be

---

1. [Footnote renumbered.] Prosser, "Nuisance Without Fault," 20 Tex.L.Rev. 399, 410 (1942).

inadequately treated by the piecemeal methods of litigation. It is possible that courtroom battles may be used to slow down effective policymaking for the environment. Litigation often fails to provide sufficient opportunities for the expert analysis and broad perspective that such policymaking often requires.

As difficult as environmental balancing may be, however, some forum for aggrieved parties must be made available. If necessary, the courts are qualified to perform the task. The courts are skilled at "balancing the equities," a technique that traditionally has been one of the judicial functions. Courts are insulated from the lobbying that gives strong advantages to industrial polluters when they face administrative or legislative review of their operations. The local state or federal court, because of its proximity to the individual problem, is often in a better position to judge the effect of a pollution nuisance upon a locality. For all of these reasons, the balancing in this case, although difficult, was nonetheless a proper function for the court below to perform. All other forums for obtaining relief were cut-off from the claimants and they understandably turned to the courts for relief.

The problem of balancing the equities in this case, however, was compounded by the fact that the company was not the ordinary industrial polluter. Usually, industrial polluters bring only their proprietary rights to be balanced on the scale opposite the community interests in a cleaner environment. The polluter asks the court to give due weight to the contributions that the business enterprise makes to the community by its economic achievements: payroll, taxes, investment of profits. [The court noted that in order for defendant to comply with the injunction "it had to lay-off forty employees and it will have to expend an additional million dollars to move the shredder to some other location."] Although when contrasted with the direct damage caused by uncontrolled pollution, such contributions may seem indirect, they are nonetheless entitled to serious consideration. No court could lightly decide to shut down a business that was the sole or principal livelihood of a community's citizens. Economic and property interests are entitled to significant weight. But here, the Indiana Auto Shredders Company makes more than only those economic contributions to the Indianapolis community; it is making a direct contribution toward improving the environment and conserving its natural resources by the recycling of abandoned automobiles. In curtailing the company's operations, the court below chose a very serious course of action. It is our view that such a course of action must be based upon conspicuous facts and reasonable standards of law.

* * * At the outset, one notes that environmental litigation of this type, whether based upon the Indiana nuisance statute or the common law of nuisance, logically will involve two stages of adjudication. First, the court or trier of fact will determine whether the facts alleged actually constitute a nuisance and a nuisance of what type. Second, having determined the nature of the alleged nuisance, the court will fashion relief appropriate to the equities of the case. Each of these two stages implicate their own legal standards.

Some activities, occupations, or structures are so offensive at all times and under all circumstances, regardless of location or surroundings, that they constitute "nuisance per se." Activities that imminently and dangerously threaten the public health fall into this category. It is more often the case, however, that the activities challenged by suitors in a nuisance case fall short of this standard of imminent and dangerous harm. Such activities as cause more remote harm to people or are the source of inconvenience, annoyance and minor damage to property are labeled "nuisance in fact" or "nuisance per accidens." These latter activities are nuisances primarily because of the circumstances or the location and surrounding of the activities, rather than the nature of the activities themselves. Most air and water pollution, when their effects are only minimally or remotely harmful to the public health, will be nuisances of this second type. Obviously, it is this second type that more frequently occurs. Very often this second type will present the offensive activities of an otherwise lawful business, activities that are being conducted in such a manner so as to become a nuisance.

When there is an imminent and dangerous threat of harm from particular business activities, the determination of nuisance per se can easily be made. The second class of nuisance, on the other hand, depends for its definition on the facts and circumstances of each case. Not every instance of inconvenience or interference will constitute a nuisance. Nevertheless property owners have a right to require that an adjoining business be properly managed and conducted so as to avoid any unnecessary inconvenience or annoyance to them. Although it is only unnecessary and substantial annoyance that the law reaches out to prevent, whenever annoyances of this type exist, the sufferers are entitled to have their suffering alleviated. * * * Even when the pollution does not present imminent health hazards, those suffering the pollution ought to be allowed to show how the quality of their lives is diminished, despite any scientific expert's statement that the pollution is harmless.

Thus, in this first stage in the adjudication of environmental nuisance suits, it is for the court trier of fact to determine whether the facts of the particular case of pollution bring the activities of the polluter within the reaches of nuisance law.

If a pollution nuisance has been found to exist, the court must then decide what relief to grant to those suffering the nuisance. In this second stage in the adjudication of environmental nuisance suits, balancing the equities becomes all important. The court must decide whether injunctive relief, damages, or some combination of the two best satisfies the particular demands of the case before it. This is the difficult but necessary work the court must perform.

Of course, where the pollution from a mill or factory creates hazards that imminently and dangerously affect the public health, the appropriate relief is a permanent injunction against the continuation of the polluting activities. It would be unreasonable to allow a private interest in the profits and product of such a polluting menace to outweigh the community's interests in the health of its citizens. However, a permanent injunction that shuts down a mill or factory without consideration of the extent of the harm that its pollution caused would be equally unreasonable. Pollution nuisance cases present no special features that should exempt them from the equitable requirements for injunctive relief, including proof of irreparable harm and inadequate remedy at law. * * * Ordinarily a permanent injunction will not lie unless (1) either the polluter seriously and imminently threatens the public health or (2) he causes non-health injuries that are substantial and the business cannot be operated to avoid the injuries apprehended. Thus the particular situation facts of each pollution nuisance case will determine whether a permanent injunction should be issued. When a business' offensive activities fall short of that standard, only the combination of both reckless disregard of substantial annoyances caused to adjoining property owners plus the impossibility of mitigating the offensive characteristics of the business will justify the granting of permanent injunctive relief.

Turning then to the instant case, the decision to permanently close the Indiana Auto Shredders Company was made in error. Although the record indicates that industrial wastes are generated beyond the confines of the property, such facts are not supportive of permanent injunctive action unless injury to health, safety, or welfare is shown. All of the testimony as to appellant's violation of the regulations of the Division of Public Health and Hospital Corporation of Marion County, Indiana, and the Indiana State Board of Health has been negative. The testimony of the authorities and scientific experts was that no violation of state or local health and safety regulations has occurred. Even the claimants' own scientific tests show compliance. Thus the findings of the district court as to violations of the zoning ordinance regarding the emission of particulate matter, earth, vibrations, sound, and odorous matter in such quantities as to endanger the public health and safety are clearly erroneous. Under these circumstances and in the absence of any proof of the substantiality of the damage or the incorrigibility of the shredder's operation, the permanent injunction must be ordered withdrawn. We turn then to the specific findings made by the district court.

The evidence showed that the residences in the Irish Hill section were for the most part about one hundred years old—none being less than 50 years, and that present law prevents residential construction in the future. It showed that the area was near an interstate highway, a main line railroad and a community dumping ground. Previously a railroad roundhouse was occupying the spot where the shredder was located. The area had been zoned for industrial use for over half a century, and the rezoning of the company site for shredder use was three years before appellant began construction. The I–5–U zoning category specifically permits use of the property for metal operations.

Most significant was the fact that not a single expert or governmental official charged with enforcement duties testified to a single significant violation by appellant of any relevant zoning standard. Indeed, all of the testimony showed that the shredding operation was well within standards and that appellant obtained all governmental certificates and permits required of it. * * *

We can well appreciate and fully sympathize with the unhappiness of the appellees over their situation. However, the problem of zoning is a local one, governed by local law; it must be solved in local perspective. The appropriate local authority has zoned the property specifically for shredder use; and appellant has been issued a permit to so use the property. After careful and continued tests by reputable experts as well as public officials, appellant's operation has met all the required standards. Under these circumstances and in the absence of an imminent hazard to health or welfare—none of which was established or found present here, the appellant cannot be prevented from continuing to engage in the operation of its shredding. See Reserve Mining Co. v. United States, 514 F.2d 492 (8th Cir.1975). The national environmental policy, as announced by Congress, allows offending industries a reasonable period of time to make adjustments to conform to standards. See, e.g., Clean Air Act, 42 U.S.C.A. §§ 1857c–5 to 8 (1970); National Environmental Policy Act, 42 U.S.C.A. § 4331 (1970). Appellant is a new undertaking in Irish Hill; it too is entitled to a reasonable period of time to correct any defects not of imminent or substantial harm. If there is damage to property, of course, it is recoverable here as in any other case.

The trial court based its action on the existence of a common nuisance but even if such were present, the drastic remedy of closing down the operation without endeavoring to launder its objectionable features would be impermissible under our law. In applying the test of the cases, we find no ground on which to base a permanent injunction here.

This is not to say that those features of the appellant's operation that are found to be offensive should not be remedied. We only say that the offender shall have time to correct the evil. If the appellant does not correct the infractions presently existing within a reasonable period, the district court may take action that will require the appellant so to do. * * *

It follows that the damage awards must fall. In this connection we believe effective administration requires that we express our opinion that the permanent damage award made here was not permissible in the light of the granting of injunctive relief. The measure of damages in Indiana in private non-permanent nuisances is loss of use and it is measured in rental value.

Nor do we believe that punitive damages, as of this date, are recoverable. Our reading of the record indicates that the appellant cooperated with all government agencies. It did its best to improve the operation of its shredder so as to alleviate damage, discomfort, and inconvenience. Indeed, the district court permitted it to continue in business for 40 days after its death sentence was pronounced. On balance, we do not find grounds for punitive damages.

The judgment is reversed, the permanent injunction is dissolved, and the case is remanded for further proceedings in accordance herewith. * * *

Notes

1. *The Transition From Trespass to Nuisance.* Trespass to land blends into the related tort of nuisance, as we observed with the golf balls in *Fenton*, p. 880. Trespass to land protects the owner's land's physical integrity; a trespass involves an object, including humans, with size and weight.

An owner sues a defendant for a nuisance to protect her right to use and enjoy he property; nuisance involves less palpable invasions, for example noise, odor, and vibrations. Despite observers' sharp references to nuisance as a "legal garbage can," it was retrieved and adopted as the private-law foundation for modern environmental law.

Since a nuisance defendant is usually entitled to more lenient substantive and remedial judicial treatment than a trespass defendant, attorneys test the borderline between the categories to achieve favorable treatment for their clients. Particulate pollution, dust, smoke and gas, might fit into either. In Oregon, for example, a defendant who disseminates particulates and gasses with fluorides commits a trespass. Martin v. Reynolds Metals Co., 221 Or. 86, 342 P.2d 790 (1959), cert. denied, 362 U.S. 918 (1960).

As it does for trespass to land, the permanent-temporary distinction governs a nuisance plaintiff's (a) applicable statute of limitations, (b) choice between or combination of damages and an injunction, (c) measure of damages, and (d) vulnerability to preclusion-res judicata.

2. *Externality.* Should a homeowner who lives on the edge of a golf course be subjected to hazards and uncompensated depreciation from golfers' flying balls? An

owner's rights lead to uses which interfere with others' enjoyment of their land. In economists' parlance, an externality is an owner's activity's incidental effect on others, which legally the owner is not responsible for and may ignore. The court may create legal responsibility for the owner's activity and define consequences which force the owner to consider others; this decision will structure the owner's incentives to "internalize the externality." Courts have used both injunctions and damages to constrain exuberance from the game of golf.

Restricting or prohibiting a landowner's activity because it affects another person may be neither wise nor desirable. Adjoining landowners may adopt or may have adopted an efficient solution which maximizes the value of both tracts. Perhaps the house was cheaper or more desirable in the first place because of the golf course. A judge may compare the detriment the golf course causes its neighbors with the detriment that would occur if its activity is abolished, restricted, or circumscribed.

3. *Context Matters.* Both the substance of nuisance and its remedy depend on the particular situation. "A nuisance may be merely the right thing in the wrong place,—like a pig in the parlor instead of the barnyard." Village of Euclid v. Ambler Realty Co., 272 U.S. 365, 388 (1926).

Not even this famous generalization is always true. Witness the admirable grit and enterprising spirit of pioneer settlers who, during 1831–32, the winter of the "Deep Snow," and the family's first winter in central Illinois, kept a sow and her litter of squealing suckling pigs in the root cellar just below the family's puncheon floor. John Mack Faragher, Sugar Creek: Life on the Illinois Prairie 201 (1986).

4. *Property Rule or Liability Rule.* Under the analysis in Calabresi and Melamed's well-known "Cathedral" article, in nuisance litigation, the court has four possible solutions. 1) Find that a nuisance exists, and enjoin the defendant's activity, a "property" rule. 2) Find that a nuisance exists, require the defendant to pay the plaintiff damages, but let the defendant's activity continue, a "liability" rule. 3) Find that no nuisance exists, deny all relief, and let the defendant's activity continue. 4) Find that a nuisance exists, and enjoin the defendant's activity if plaintiff pays the defendant damages. Calabresi and Melamed, Property Rules, Liability Rules, and Inalienability: One View of the Cathedral, 85 Harv.L.Rev. 1089 (1972)

5. *Cathedral Tour?* Tours of Calabresi and Melamed's cathedral are a cottage industry in the law reviews. A strong recent example is Henry Smith, Exclusion and Property Rules in the Law of Nuisance, 90 Va.L.Rev. 965 (2004).

6. *Boomer.* Injunction v. Damages is the issue in our next case. Boomer v. Atlantic Cement, a renowned example of balancing hardships to choose between Calabresi and Melamed's solution 1), an injunction, and their solution 2), damages. Like the *Harrison* court, the *Boomer* court was reluctant to enter a permanent injunction prohibiting defendant's "useful" enterprise.

7. *No Liability—Famous Potatoes.* Solution 3), no nuisance, no substantive liability, does not present a choice of remedy. The Idaho court, for example, found that the economic value of defendant's enterprise, which outbalanced plaintiff's harm from the defendant's industrial feedlot with 9,000 "odiferous" cattle, led to neither liability nor any remedy at all. "Idaho is sparsely populated and its economy depends largely upon the benefits of agriculture, lumber, mining and industrial development," opined the majority. But, replied the dissent, "if humans are such a rare item in this state, maybe there is all the more reason to protect them," at least with damages. Carpenter v. Double R Cattle Company, Inc., 108 Idaho 602, 701 P.2d 222, 228, 229 (1985).

Another New York cement plant, this one a legal, nonconforming use, was not, the court held, a nuisance because the trial judge had found "the best and most modern equipment has eliminated most of the noise, dust and bright lights." The dissent argued that the plant was a nuisance which ought to be remedied, as in *Boomer*, by permanent damages. Benjamin v. Nelstad Materials, 214 A.D.2d 632, 625 N.Y.S.2d 281 (1995).

8.   Solution 4) is illustrated by Spur Industries v. Del E. Webb Development Co. The Del Webb Corporation built Sun City catering to retired people in what was then a sparsely populated area next to defendant's cattle feed lot. Although the retired homeowners "moved to the nuisance," they were entitled to an injunction. However, the court required the Sun City developer to pay the expenses of shutting down the defendant's feedlot and moving it. Spur Industries v. Del E. Webb Development Co., 108 Ariz. 178, 494 P.2d 700 (1972).

9.   *A Fifth Way*? The Cathedral's four rooms hardly exhaust the court's possible remedies for a defendant's nuisance. Consider the options the trial judge in *Harrison* had after the court of appeals's remand. (a) May the judge find that no nuisance exists? (b) May the judge change the earlier decision to a temporary nuisance with temporary damages dating from its beginning to the date of trial and an injunction abating the shredder in the future? (c) May the judge find a temporary nuisance, award the homeowners damages down to the date of trial, and let the plaintiffs sue for damages in the future if the nuisance continues? (d) May the judge find a permanent nuisance, refuse to grant an injunction, but award plaintiffs permanent damages for the diminished value of their property? (e) Finally does the court of appeals seem to favor an experimental injunction?

Sometimes a court may deal with a nuisance by allowing the defendant to continue operation after minimizing its offensive activity. The judge may order the defendant to deal with undesirable or unhealthy features, limit the times of operations and types of activity, require periodic reports, and set timetables and goals. Learned Hand's opinion in Smith v. Staso Milling Co., 18 F.2d 736 (2d Cir.1927), demonstrates this method of accommodating the conflicting interests of landowner and manufacturer.

10.   *Zoning.* In a court's determination of whether a defendant's activity is an enjoinable nuisance, zoning is usually only one factor. But sometimes courts and legislatures are more specific. Witness the California statute: "Whenever any city, city and county, or county shall have established zones or districts under authority of law wherein certain manufacturing or commercial or airport uses are expressly permitted, * * * no person or persons, firm or corporation shall be enjoined or restrained by the injunctive process from the reasonable and necessary operation in any such industrial or commercial zone or airport of any use expressly permitted therein." There is an exception for "an action to abate a public nuisance brought in the name of the people of the State of California." Cal.Civ.Proc.Code § 731a.

11.   *Neighbors, But Not Friends.* Although nuisances often involve plaintiffs' injuries from a defendant's commercial enterprise, neighborhood squabbles find their way into our courtrooms:

(a) *Furry Companions.* Defendants' kennel with sixteen barking dogs was a nuisance; the injunction limited defendants to two. Tichenor v. Vore, 953 S.W.2d 171 (Mo.App.1997).

The state sued to enjoin defendant from keeping a large number of cats. In her answer, defendant alleged that she kept no more than forty cats "in a perfect state of health" and "in an extremely sanitary manner." The court, finding a public nuisance, enjoined defendant from keeping or maintaining in excess of four cats on her premises. Boudinot v. State, 340 P.2d 268, 269 (Okl.1959).

(b) *Spite Fence.* Defendant's slab board fence nine feet high and 106 feet long with a red flag flying on top ran the full length of the lot adjoining plaintiff's home. Plaintiff, arguing defendant's fence was constructed solely to harass, sought an injunction. The court found that the injury to the plaintiff outweighed any benefit to the defendant; it granted an injunction compelling defendant to lower the fence to the height of the window sills on plaintiff's home. Schork v. Epperson, 74 Wyo. 286, 294–95, 287 P.2d 467, 470 (1955).

(c) *Festive Holiday Display.* Defendant's elaborate home Christmas lighting display attracted numerous sightseers into his residential neighborhood every evening during December. Neighbors sued for an injunction claiming several kinds of injury: traffic congestion which created difficulty in reaching and leaving their homes and finding parking, disruption from the display's amplified music as well as noisy and abusive visitors who deposited trash and worse on streets and lawns, and obstructions to obtaining emergency services. After protracted litigation and wide publicity, the Louisiana Supreme Court held that the neighbors' damage and irreparable injury could be prevented by enjoining defendant from maintaining a Christmas exhibition that attracts "bumper to bumper traffic and extremely large numbers of visitors to * * * [the] neighborhood."

The court rejected defendant's argument that time, place and manner limits infringed on his right to express his religious beliefs. The court specifically banned oversized, lighted snowmen and reindeer, but, in deference to defendant's religion, not "the Star of Bethlehem, nativity scene, religious tapestry and oversized lighted angels." Rodrigue v. Copeland, 475 So.2d 1071, 1080 (La.1985), cert. denied, 475 U.S. 1046 (1986).

Compare the "public" nuisance, pp. 248–67.

12. *Contorting Characterization of Contamination Cleanup.* Suppose a realty buyer discovers serious contamination left by its seller. A typical buyer litigates with the seller under either theories of fraud, breach and mistake, or environmental statutes. Nevertheless, a short statute of limitations, a waived or limited warranty, or the seller's insurance coverage may induce a purchaser to sue its seller for trespass to land and nuisance.

Since a trespass is a defendant's unauthorized entry on plaintiff's land, most courts reject the notion that an owner in lawful possession can trespass on its own land. Nuisance is a little harder. Courts employ nuisance analysis to resolve disputes between neighboring landowners about simultaneous uses. A dispute between a buyer and its seller concerns the prior owner's use of the identical parcel, not adjoining tracts or simultaneous uses. Moreover, a prospective buyer might have inspected the land and bargained for lower consideration or indemnity. The buyer and seller had an opportunity to resolve their interests and define their obligations in a negotiated agreement; in the real world with transaction costs, however, neighbors may lack the realistic ability to bargain. These arguments have convinced courts to decline to impose a nuisance-based tort duty which might upset the way the actual contract allocated the risks. Lilly Industries, Inc. v. Health–Chem Corp., 974 F.Supp. 702, 705–09 (S.D.Ind.1997).

Not so in California. In response to the seller's argument that one cannot commit a trespass or nuisance to one's own land, the court of appeal began with the idea that the seller's discharge of contaminants comprised the tort of public nuisance, and concluded that (a) the contaminants' presence is a continuing trespass, and (b) nuisances need not originate on neighboring land. Newhall Land & Farming Co. v. Superior Court, 19 Cal.App.4th 334, 23 Cal.Rptr.2d 377 (1993).

BOOMER v. ATLANTIC CEMENT CO.

Court of Appeals of New York, 1970.
26 N.Y.2d 219, 309 N.Y.S.2d 312, 257 N.E.2d 870.

BERGAN, JUDGE. Defendant operates a large cement plant near Albany. These are actions for injunction and damages by neighboring land owners alleging injury to property from dirt, smoke and vibration emanating from the plant. A nuisance has been found after trial, temporary damages have been allowed; but an injunction has been denied. * * * Cement plants are obvious sources of air pollution in the neighborhoods where they operate.

* * * The threshold question raised by the division of view on this appeal is whether the court should resolve the litigation between the parties now before it as equitably as seems possible; or whether, seeking promotion of the general public welfare, it should channel private litigation into broad public objectives.

A court performs its essential function when it decides the rights of parties before it. Its decision of private controversies may sometimes greatly affect public issues. Large questions of law are often resolved by the manner in which private litigation is decided. But this is normally an incident to the court's main function to settle controversy. It is a rare exercise of judicial power to use a decision in private litigation as a purposeful mechanism to achieve direct public objectives greatly beyond the rights and interests before the court.

Effective control of air pollution is a problem presently far from solution even with the full public and financial powers of government.

It seems apparent that the amelioration of air pollution will depend on technical research in great depth; on a carefully balanced consideration of the economic impact of close regulation; and of the actual effect on public health. It is likely to require massive public expenditure and to demand more than any local community can accomplish and to depend on regional and interstate controls.

A court should not try to do this on its own as a by-product of private litigation and it seems manifest that the judicial establishment is neither equipped in the limited nature of any judgment it can pronounce nor prepared to lay down and implement an effective policy for the elimination of air pollution. This is an area beyond the circumference of one private lawsuit. It is a direct responsibility for government and should not thus be undertaken as an incident to solving a dispute between property owners and a single cement plant—one of many—in the Hudson River valley.

The ground for the denial of injunction, notwithstanding the finding both that there is a nuisance and that plaintiffs have been damaged substantially, is the large disparity in economic consequences of the nuisance and of the injunction. This theory cannot, however, be sustained without overruling a doctrine which has been consistently reaffirmed in several leading cases in this court and which has never been disavowed here, namely that where a nuisance has been found and where there has been any substantial damage shown by the party complaining an injunction will be granted.

The rule in New York has been that such a nuisance will be enjoined although marked disparity be shown in economic consequence between the effect of the injunction and the effect of the nuisance.

The problem of disparity in economic consequence was sharply in focus in Whalen v. Union Bag & Paper Co., 208 N.Y. 1, 101 N.E. 805. A pulp mill entailing an investment of more than a million dollars polluted a stream in which plaintiff, who owned a farm, was "a lower riparian owner." The economic loss to plaintiff from this pollution was small. This court, reversing the Appellate Division, reinstated the injunction granted by the Special Term against the argument of the mill owner that in view of "the slight advantage to plaintiff and the great loss that will be inflicted on defendant" an injunction should not be granted. * * * "Such a balancing of injuries cannot be justified by the circumstances of this case," Judge Werner noted. He continued: "Although the damage to the plaintiff may be slight as compared with the defendant's expense of abating the condition, that is not a good reason for refusing an injunction."

Thus the unconditional injunction granted at Special Term was reinstated. The rule laid down in that case, then, is that whenever the damage resulting from a nuisance is found not "unsubstantial," viz., $100 a year, injunction would follow. This states a rule that had been followed in this court with marked consistency. [citations]

There are cases where injunction has been denied. McCann v. Chasm Power Co., 211 N.Y. 301, 105 N.E. 416 is one of them. There, however, the damage shown by plaintiffs was not only unsubstantial, it was non-existent. Plaintiffs owned a rocky bank of the stream in which defendant had raised the level of the water. This had no economic or other adverse consequence to plaintiffs, and thus injunctive relief was denied.

Thus if, within Whalen v. Union Bag & Paper Co., which authoritatively states the rule in New York, the damage to plaintiffs in these present cases from defendant's cement plant is "not unsubstantial," an injunction should follow.

Although the court at Special Term and the Appellate Division held that injunction should be denied, it was found that plaintiffs had been damaged in various specific amounts up to the time of the trial and damages to the respective plaintiffs were awarded for those amounts. The effect of this was, injunction having been denied, plaintiffs could maintain successive actions at law for damages thereafter as further damage was incurred.

The court at Special Term also found the amount of permanent damage attributable to each plaintiff, for the guidance of the parties in the event both sides stipulated to the payment and acceptance of such permanent damage as a settlement of all the controversies among the parties. The total of permanent damages to all plaintiffs thus found was $185,000. This basis of adjustment has not resulted in any stipulation by the parties.

This result at Special Term and at the Appellate Division is a departure from a rule that has become settled; but to follow the rule literally in these cases would be to close down the plant at once. This court is fully agreed to avoid that immediately drastic remedy; the difference in view is how best to avoid it.[1]

One alternative is to grant the injunction but postpone its effect to a specified future date to give opportunity for technical advances to permit defendant to eliminate the nuisance; another is to grant the injunction conditioned on the payment of permanent damages to plaintiffs which would compen-

---

1. Respondent's investment in the plant is in excess of $45,000,000. There are over 300 people employed there.

sate them for the total economic loss to their property present and future caused by defendant's operations. For reasons which will be developed the court chooses the latter alternative.

If the injunction were to be granted unless within a short period—e.g., 18 months—the nuisance be abated by improved methods, there would be no assurance that any significant technical improvement would occur.

The parties could settle this private litigation at any time if defendant paid enough money and the imminent threat of closing the plant would build up the pressure on defendant. If there were no improved techniques found, there would inevitably be applications to the court at Special Term for extensions of time to perform on showing of good faith efforts to find such techniques.

Moreover, techniques to eliminate dust and other annoying by-products of cement making are unlikely to be developed by any research the defendant can undertake within any short period, but will depend on the total resources of the cement industry nationwide and throughout the world. The problem is universal wherever cement is made.

For obvious reasons the rate of the research is beyond control of defendant. If at the end of 18 months the whole industry has not found a technical solution a court would be hard put to close down this one cement plant if due regard be given to equitable principles.

On the other hand, to grant the injunction unless defendant pays plaintiffs such permanent damages as may be fixed by the court seems to do justice between the contending parties. All of the attributions of economic loss to the properties on which plaintiffs' complaints are based will have been redressed.

The nuisance complained of by these plaintiffs may have other public or private consequences, but these particular parties are the only ones who have sought remedies and the judgment proposed will fully redress them. The limitation of relief granted is a limitation only within the four corners of these actions and does not foreclose public health or other public agencies from seeking proper relief in a proper court.

It seems reasonable to think that the risk of being required to pay permanent damages to injured property owners by cement plant owners would itself be a reasonable effective spur to research for improved techniques to minimize nuisance.

The power of the court to condition on equitable grounds the continuance of an injunction on the payment of permanent damages seems undoubted. * * *

It has been said that permanent damages are allowed where the loss recoverable would obviously be small as compared with the cost of removal of the nuisance (Kentucky–Ohio Gas Co. v. Bowling, 264 Ky. 470, 477, 95 S.W.2d 1).

The present cases and the remedy here proposed are in a number of other respects rather similar to Northern Indiana Public Service Co. v. W.J. & M.S. Vesey, 210 Ind. 338, 200 N.E. 620 decided by the Supreme Court of Indiana. The gases, odors, ammonia and smoke from the Northern Indiana company's gas plant damaged the nearby Vesey greenhouse operation. An injunction and damages were sought, but an injunction was denied and the relief granted was limited to permanent damages "present, past, and future."

Denial of injunction was grounded on a public interest in the operation of the gas plant and on the court's conclusion "that less injury would be occasioned by requiring the appellant [Public Service] to pay the appellee [Vesey] all damages suffered by it * * * than by enjoining the operation of the gas plant; and that the maintenance and operation of the gas plant should not be enjoined."

The Indiana Supreme Court opinion continued: "When the trial court refused injunctive relief to the appellee upon the ground of public interest in the continuance of the gas plant, it properly retained jurisdiction of the case and awarded full compensation to the appellee. This is upon the general equitable principle that equity will give full relief in one action and prevent a multiplicity of suits."

It was held that in this type of continuing and recurrent nuisance permanent damages were appropriate. See, also, City of Amarillo v. Ware, 120 Tex. 456, 40 S.W.2d 57 where recurring overflows from a system of storm sewers were treated as the kind of nuisance for which permanent depreciation of value of affected property would be recoverable.

There is some parallel to the conditioning of an injunction on the payment of permanent damages in the noted "elevated railway cases" (Pappenheim v. Metropolitan El., etc., Ry. Co., 128 N.Y. 436, 28 N.E. 518 and others which followed.) Decisions in these cases were based on the finding that the railways created a nuisance as to adjacent property owners, but in lieu of enjoining their operation, the court allowed permanent damages.

Thus it seems fair to both sides to grant permanent damages to plaintiffs which will terminate this private litigation. The theory of damage is the "servitude on land" of plaintiffs imposed by defendant's nuisance. (See United States v. Causby, 328 U.S. 256, 261, 262, 267, where the term "servitude" addressed to the land was used by Justice Douglas relating to the effect of airplane noise on property near an airport.)

The judgment, by allowance of permanent damages imposing a servitude on land, which is the basis of the actions, would preclude future recovery by plaintiffs or their grantees.

This should be placed beyond debate by a provision of the judgment that the payment by defendant and the acceptance by plaintiffs of permanent damages found by the court shall be in compensation for a servitude on the land.

Although the Trial Term has found permanent damages as a possible basis of settlement of the litigation, on remission the court should be entirely free to reexamine this subject. It may again find the permanent damage already found; or make new findings.

The orders should be reversed, without costs, and the cases remitted to Supreme Court, Albany County to grant an injunction which shall be vacated upon payment by defendant of such amounts of permanent damage to the respective plaintiffs as shall for this purpose be determined by the court. * * *

JASEN, JUDGE (dissenting). * * * I see grave dangers in overruling our long-established rule of granting an injunction where a nuisance results in substantial continuing damage. In permitting the injunction to become inoperative upon the payment of permanent damages, the majority is, in effect, licensing a continuing wrong. It is the same as saying to the cement company, you may continue to do harm to your neighbor so long as you pay a fee for it. Furthermore, once such permanent damages are assessed and paid, the incentive to alleviate the wrong would be eliminated, thereby continuing air pollution of an area without abatement. * * *

This kind of inverse condemnation * * * may not be invoked by a private person or corporation for private gain or advantage. Inverse condemnation should only be permitted when the public is primarily served in the taking or impairment of property. [citations] The promotion of the interests of the polluting cement company has, in my opinion, no public use or benefit.

Nor is it constitutionally permissible to impose servitude on land, without consent of the owner, by payment of permanent damages where the continuing impairment of the land is for a private use. [citations] This is made clear by the State Constitution (art. I, § 7, subd. [a]) which provides that "[p]rivate property shall not be taken for *public use* without just compensation" (emphasis added). It is, of course, significant that the section makes no mention of taking for a *private* use. * * *

I would enjoin the defendant cement company from continuing the discharge of dust particles upon its neighbors' properties unless, within 18 months, the cement company abated this nuisance.

Notes

1. *The Farber Fanclub.* Professor Dan Farber has favored readers with two valuable tellings of the *Boomer* story, in 1988 and 2005. His remedies solutions follow.

(a) *Farber's Injunction.* Farber argues that the judge should enjoin an egregious nuisance like the one in *Boomer* except "where the balance tilts very strongly against plaintiffs" and an injunction is "infeasible." Since "nowhere does the [*Boomer*] court explicitly state that it is overruling *Whalen,* * * * one tenable reading is that [the court] merely placed a gloss on the *Whalen* rule: the plaintiff is always prima facie entitled to an injunction, but in the case of highly disproportionate harm to the defendant or the public, the injunction can be made defeasible by a damage payment. * * *"

"[The court] refers to one third-party interest favoring the defendant—the number of employees at the plant-but ignores the third-party interest favoring the plaintiffs, the regional impact of the defendant's air pollution. * * * Moreover, the majority opinion fails to consider the possibility of [an injunction] that would mitigate the harm to the plaintiffs, such as a lower level of operation, changes in the scheduling of blasting, [or] construction of barriers between the plaintiff's land and the plant."

(b) *Farber's Damages Measure.* A judge who denies plaintiffs an injunction should measure their damages by market value for buffer rights instead of the traditional value before less value after calculation. In the end, Atlantic, perhaps prodded by the trial court's apparent buffer-zone measure of damages on remand, bought out most of the plaintiffs to create the buffer zone that Farber thinks it should have purchased before it built its cement plant. "But at age 80, Mr. Boomer himself still runs a business in the area."

(c) *Farber's Restitution.* If the trial court had meted out plaintiffs' damages by the amount an ordinary buyer would have had to pay, that measure would have been a "bargain" for a buyer like Atlantic that was assembling a large tract. Atlantic "would be unjustly enriched in the amount of the premium it would otherwise have had to pay for the buffer zone. Thus the [plaintiffs' buffer-zone] damage award can be considered a form of restitution, putting the parties in the same position that they would have been in if Atlantic had done the right thing in the first place and purchased a buffer zone."

Daniel Farber, Reassessing *Boomer:* Justice, Efficiency, and Nuisance Law, Property Law and Legal Education: Essays in Honor of John E. Cribbett 7, 17 (P. Hay & M. Hoeflich eds. 1988);

Daniel Farber, The Story of *Boomer*: Pollution and the Common Law, Environmental Law Stories, 7, 20, 22, 23 (Richard Lazarus and Oliver Houck editors 2005)(cited below as Environmental Stories).

2. *Where's the Boomer Court's Solution Now?* Farber is skeptical about Calabresi and Melamud's Solution 2), find that defendant's nuisance exists, but refuse an injunction and award plaintiff damages. Later New York decisions show that New York courts are reluctant to employ *Boomer*'s remedy, a nuisance with permanent damages and a servitude.

Courts granted injunctions when:

(a) Defendant's racetrack was a public nuisance, and *Boomer*-balancing is inapplicable. Hoover v. Durkee, 212 A.D.2d 839, 622 N.Y.S.2d 348 (1995);

(b) Defendant's activity violated a pollution permit. Flacke v. Bio–Tech Mills, Inc., 95 A.D.2d 916, 463 N.Y.S.2d 899 (1983), appeal denied, 60 N.Y.2d 553, 467 N.Y.S.2d 1028, 454 N.E.2d 1317 (1983);

(c) Less than a "vast" economic disparity existed between plaintiff and defendant. State v. Waterloo Stock Car Raceway, Inc., 96 Misc.2d 350, 409 N.Y.S.2d 40 (1978); and

(d) Defendant's activity also violated the zoning ordinance. Little Joseph Realty, Inc. v. Town of Babylon, 41 N.Y.2d 738, 395 N.Y.S.2d 428, 363 N.E.2d 1163 (1977).

3. *Does Calabresi and Melamed's Cathedral Have Empty Rooms?* (a) *Room 2).* As we noted above, common law courts' decisions implementing Calabresi and Melamed's Solution 2), find a nuisance exists, decline to enjoin and grant plaintiff damages, seem to be scarce.

(b) *Room 4).* Since the single example of *Spur*, Note 8, p. 894, Calabresi and Melamed's Solution 4), find that a nuisance exists, and enjoin the defendant's activity *if plaintiff, the victim, pays the tortfeasor-defendant damages*, is rare indeed today, perhaps extinct in private litigation. *Question.* Which is a good thing?

But the Cathedral's co-architect, Mr. Melamud cites examples based on his experience in the Antitrust Division of the Department of Justice, from the inner-beltway's world of government regulation. These examples, he says, demonstrate that "Rule 4 is alive and well—at least in Washington." A. Douglas Melamud, Remarks: A Public Law Perspective, 106 Yale L.J. 2209 (1997).

4. *The Parties' Post–Injunction Negotiation v. Unhappy Neighborhoods are All Alike.* Transaction costs, negotiations between the parties after an injunction, are a foundation of economists' analysis of nuisance remedies. Suppose Pacific's plant is worth $40, and its harm to plaintiff-Spoomer is $2. Suppose the judge finds a nuisance and grants Spoomer an injunction. Then, as the *Boomer* court mentioned, instead of shutting its plant down, Pacific might offer Spoomer enough money to persuade her to "settle this private litigation." Thus, after the court grants Spoomer an injunction, following the parties' negotiations, Pacific's plant stays open. But the injunction empowers Spoomer to threaten a shutdown and to leverage a "generous" settlement.

These considerations have generated an extensive law-and-economics literature. Many economic-oriented observers favor court-set damages, Calabresi and Melamud's Solution 2), a "liability" rule, over an injunction, their Solution 1), a "property" rule. The observers often make an exception in favor of an injunction where defendant's negotiations with a few plaintiffs are feasible because of low transaction costs. Richard Posner, Economic Analysis of Law § 3.10 (Sixth Edition 2003).

Professor Ward Farnsworth asked actual lawyers in reported nuisance litigation about whether the parties negotiated settlements after an injunction. The litigants, he learned, just didn't bargain. For an actual human being-litigant, the acrimony of a protracted dispute militates against any amicable discussion afterwards. Ward Farnsworth, Do Parties to Nuisance Cases Bargain After Judgment? A Glimpse Inside the Cathedral, 66 U.Chi.L.Rev. 373 (1999).

The parties' post-injunction negotiation joins *Spur Industries'* compensated injunction in classroom hypotheticals. But does it otherwise sit idly on the economists' shelf?

5. *Equitable Discretion.* Remember that in Weinberger v. Romero–Barcelo, p. 301, the Supreme Court cited both *Boomer* and *Spur Industries* to illustrate the judge's equitable discretion. Professor Farber wrote in 2005 that "unfortunately, the Supreme Court has done little to clarify the availability of environmental injunctions in the twenty years since *Weinberger*, so we still cannot be completely positive about the extent to which *Boomer* carries over to statutory injunctions." Environmental Stories at 29.

6. *Is the Time Ripe for Farber's Restitution Solution?* When a court discusses the choice between money and an injunction as a remedy for defendant's nuisance, should it limit plaintiff's money recovery to compensatory damages and perhaps punitive damages? Or should the court also consider awarding the plaintiff (a) restitution measured by defendant's savings, or (b) an accounting for defendant's profits? So far the answer has been "No." See 1 George Palmer, The Law of Restitution 137 (1978); Dan Friedmann, Restitution of Benefits Obtained Through the Appropriation of Property or the Commission of a Wrong, 80 Colum.L.Rev. 504, 509 (1980).

But Professor Andrew Kull maintains that "restitution for the economic benefits [defendant] derived from a private nuisance makes a perfectly intelligible claim in any case where the nuisance could have been enjoined, so long as the defendant can be shown to have acted willfully in invading the plaintiff's property." Andrew Kull, Restitution and the Noncontractual Transfer, 11 J. Contract L. 93, 104 (1997).

The Third Restatement of Restitution includes an Illustration based on *Boomer*'s facts; the illustration concludes, that for the defendant's nuisance, "the court may award [plaintiffs] restitution measured by the value of a license to continue the [defendant's] challenged operations." Restatement (Third) of Restitution and Unjust Enrichment § 44, Interferecne with Other Protected Interests, Illustration 14 (Tent. Draft No. 4 2005).

Conversion and trespass cases leading to plaintiffs' restitution are Olwell v. Nye & Nissen, p. 834, Edwards v. Lee's Adm'r., p. 839 and Raven Red Ash Coal Co. v. Ball, p. 844.

7. *Public Environmental Control.* Although the *Boomer* court lopped off the larger public issues from its decision, the "public health or other public agencies" who are not foreclosed from "seeking proper relief" have diligently pursued efforts to reduce pollution and clean up the air. Toxic substances in the air, the water, or the soil are candidates for cleanup. An industry that creates serious public health risks is

an inappropriate candidate to be allowed to continue its pollution after paying permanent damages to endangered neighbors. Cement plants are among the most heavily regulated of industries. Private nuisance litigation continues apace along with public environmental law.

8. *Farber's Finale. Boomer,* Farber concludes, lives on in law school because it is "a great teaching tool." "Generations of law students have wondered whether, in this battle between David and Goliath, Goliath should walk away so apparently unscathed, leaving a battered David with nothing but a few coins for his trouble." Environmental Stories at 42.

9. We return to litigants who are neighbors, but not friends, in

GOULDING v. COOK

Supreme Judicial Court of Massachusetts, 1996.
422 Mass. 276, 661 N.E.2d 1322.

FRIED, JUSTICE. The plaintiffs in this case (Gouldings) sought an injunction in the Land Court, enjoining the defendants (Cooks) to end a trespass on their property. The parties own neighboring residences in Scituate. When installation of another neighbor's swimming pool caused the Cooks's cesspool, which was partly under that neighbor's land, to malfunction, they were forced to find an alternative sewage disposal system. The town required a septic system, and the only suitable site for such a system was on a 2,998 square foot triangle of land that the Cooks claimed belonged to them but which the Gouldings claimed was part of their residential property. While the town was pressing them, the Cooks negotiated with the Gouldings to no avail. The matter came to litigation. The Gouldings sought a preliminary injunction against the Cooks's use of their land as well as a declaration that they were the fee simple owners of the land, free of any claims by the Cooks. The preliminary injunction was denied on August 8, 1991, and thereafter the Cooks entered on the land and installed the septic system. The Land Court entered a final judgment on October 7, 1992, finding ownership in the disputed triangle to be in the Gouldings but granting an easement to the Cooks for the maintenance of their septic system "at a price to be negotiated by the parties and with provisions for maintenance, repair and replacement as counsel so agree." The Gouldings appealed from the grant of the easement and the Appeals Court affirmed. We granted the plaintiffs' application for further appellate review.

It is commonplace today that property rights are not absolute, and that the law may condition their use and enjoyment so that the interests of the public in general or of some smaller segment of the public, perhaps even just immediate neighbors, are not unduly prejudiced. Restrictions from architectural approvals to zoning regulations are accepted features of the legal landscape. See Euclid v. Ambler Realty Co., 272 U.S. 365, 395 (1926). But, except in "exceptional" cases,[1]

---

1. [Footnote renumbered] [citations] See also Fragopoulos v. Rent Control Bd. of Cambridge, 408 Mass. 302, 309, 557 N.E.2d 1153 (1990). "In rare cases, referred to in our decisions as 'exceptional' courts of equity have refused to grant a mandatory injunction and have left the plaintiff to his remedy of damages, 'where the unlawful encroachment has been made innocently, and the cost of removal by the defendant would be greatly disproportionate to the injury to the plaintiff from its continuation, or where the sub-stantial rights of the owner may be protected without recourse to an injunction, or where an injunction would be oppressive and inequitable. But these are the exceptions. * * * What is just and equitable in cases of this sort depends very much on the particular facts and circumstances disclosed.'" (Citations omitted.) "Such cases have been based upon estoppel [citations] or on laches [citations] or on the trivial nature of the encroachment or injury. [citations]" Peters v. Archambault, 361 Mass. 91, 93 n. 2, 278 N.E.2d 729 (1972).

we draw the line at permanent physical occupations amounting to a transfer of a traditional estate in land. [citations] And certainly that line, because the interests on either side of it are themselves conventional and the creatures of the law, is often hard to draw. See Lucas v. South Carolina Coastal Council, 505 U.S. 1003 (1992). But we are committed to maintaining it, because the concept of private property represents a moral and political commitment that a pervasive disposition to balance away would utterly destroy. The commitment is enshrined in our Constitutions. Where the line is crossed and the commitment threatened, even in the interests of the general public, just compensation is required. See art. 10 of the Declaration of Rights of the Massachusetts Constitution; Fifth Amendment to the United States Constitution. And by implication, where the encroachment is not for a public use, the taking may not be justified at all. Although we deplore the disposition to turn every dispute into a Federal (constitutional) case and no constitutional claim was—or needed to be—made here, it is to these constitutional commitments that the dissent in the Appeals Court's decision referred when it observed that "[o]ur law simply does not sanction this type of private eminent domain."

No doubt the Cooks considered themselves in desperate straits, but theirs was not the kind of desperation that justifies self-help with financial adjustments thereafter. Vincent v. Lake Erie Transp. Co., 109 Minn. 456, 124 N.W. 221 (1910). It is not cynicism to suppose that some sum of money would suffice to assuage the Goulding's sense of having been imposed on and thus to suggest that one way of looking at this case is to ask who shall set that sum and where will the bargaining advantage lie. The Cooks, threatened with possible destruction of their ability to use their home at all, might have been willing to pay a very large sum to be able to obtain this needed facility from the Gouldings. The Appeals Court's disposition may be seen as moved by its revulsion at the thought that the Gouldings should be able to extract so large a rent for so minor an accommodation. The power of eminent domain is granted just to prevent private property owners from extracting such strategic rents from the public. And because of the Gouldings's "lock hand," the Land Court, by denying the Gouldings an injunction, assigned to itself the authority to establish the price at which the easement, 2,998 square feet of the Gouldings's land, shall be transferred to the Cooks.

Like most propositions in the law the one we reaffirm now has some play at the margins. Accordingly, the Appeals Court is quite right that the courts will not enjoin truly minimal encroachments, especially when the burden on a defendant would be very great. The classic example is given in Restatement (Second) of Torts § 941 comment c, supra at 583:

> "The defendant has recently completed a twenty-story office building on his lot. The work was done by reputable engineers and builders, and they and the defendant all acted in good faith and with reasonable care. It is, however, found that from the tenth floor upward the wall on the plaintiff's side bulges outward and extends over the line. The extent of the encroachment varies at different points, the maximum being four inches."

Such accommodation recognizes the necessarily approximate nature of all legal lines and principles. To extend the accommodation to this case where the defendants seek to install a potentially permanent, possibly malodorously malfunctioning septic system encroaching on a spatially significant portion of the plaintiffs' lot is not to accommodate the principle but to obliterate it in favor of a general power of equitable adjustment and enforced good neighborliness. That is particularly the case here, where the defendants' "good faith" consists at most in an honest belief supported by objective facts that they were the owners of the land. Although this claim was sharply disputed, they were told that they proceeded at their peril, and the matter was in litigation and awaiting disposition when they went ahead and acted. Although, as the Appeals Court properly noted, notice of an opposing claim is not decisive on the question of good faith, the instant case presents a situation where there was more than mere notice; the parties were in litigation over the locus. [citations] It changes nothing that what we have here is the Land Court's decision to deny injunctive relief, an equitable power which leaves much to the court's discretion, if that discretion was exercised on a legal criterion that we conclude is incorrect. To draw an analogy, it is the law in this Commonwealth that easements of necessity can only be granted in very limited circumstances of reasonable or absolute necessity. [citations] If a court were to deny an injunction against trespass on the premise that some wider rule of easements of necessity obtains, we would not hesitate to overturn that exercise of discretion. The same holds here.

As such, we hold that the Cooks must remove the septic system and pay damages.

The decision of the Land Court is vacated and remanded for proceedings consistent with this opinion.

So ordered.

Notes

1. *The "Lower" Courts.* The trial judge's conclusions included: (a) the Cooks acted in "a good faith conviction" that they owned the triangular piece; and (b) the Gouldings offered no evidence of harm from the encroachment and would suffer "imperceptibly" if it remained. The intermediate appellate court emphasized (c) the trial judge's discretion to craft an appropriate remedy, but it modified her decree so, failing a negotiated agreement between the Cooks and the Gouldings, the court would set the Gouldings' damages. Goulding v. Cook, 38 Mass.App.Ct. 92, 645 N.E.2d 54 (1995).

How does the Supreme Judicial Court deal with each of the trial judge's points? If the Supreme Judicial Court had followed that approach to equitable discretion in Weinberger v. Romero–Barcelo, p. 301 or *Navajo Academy*, p. 297, would the trial judge have been affirmed? Is Goulding v. Cook really a comparatively easy case? Does the defendant's trespass in *Goulding* distinguish it from the nuisance in *Boomer*?

2. *Variation.* If because of a developers' error before either the Cooks or the Gouldings bought their lot, the Cooks' septic system had been mislocated under 200 square feet of the Gouldings' lawn, would the court decline to grant the Gouldings an injunction? What if, in addition, the Gouldings were demanding $25,000, the value of a vacant building lot, for an easement?

3. *Intentional Encroachment and Balancing the Hardships.* Ordinarily a court will disqualify an intentional encroacher for the benefits of the doctrine of relative hardship. See Welton v. 40 East Oak Street Building Corp., 70 F.2d 377 (7th Cir.1934), cert. denied, 293 U.S. 590 (1934); Brown Derby Hollywood Corp. v. Hatton, 61 Cal.2d 855, 40 Cal.Rptr. 848, 395 P.2d 896 (1964); Missouri Power & Light Co. v. Barnett, 354 S.W.2d 873 (Mo.1962) (order for removal of home from

power company's easement); Papanikolas Brothers Enterprises v. Sugarhouse Shopping Center Associates, 535 P.2d 1256 (Utah 1975).

But not always. Although the defendant's encroaching building extended over the boundary line 88 inches and the trial judge found that defendant had been either willful or reckless, the court, after comparing benefits and hardships, refused mandatory injunction relief and remanded for calculation of damages. Morrison v. Jones, 58 Tenn.App. 333, 430 S.W.2d 668 (1968).

4. *Post-Injunction Negotiation and Strategic Bargaining?* Professor M.T. Van Hecke studied whether mandatory injunctions against encroachment were effective and whether they had led to "extortionate" settlements. His conclusions were similar to Professor Farnsworth's study of the parties' post-injunction negotiation after nuisance injunctions were similar. P. 902.

Professor Van Hecke contacted 44 lawyers in 29 lawsuits and received replies from 31 lawyers concerning 25 injunctions. He concluded that 75% of the injunctions were effective and that little evidence existed that the injunctions had been used to coerce settlements. Attorneys who participated in "extortionate" settlements may not have responded to the survey. Van Hecke, Injunction to Remove or Remodel Structures Erected in Violation of Building Restrictions, 32 Tex.L.Rev. 521 (1954).

5. *Life Without Balancing.* Defendant's "apartment building encroaches approximately one square foot on plaintiff's land." The encroachment was apparently inadvertent. Plaintiff's tract "has never been used for any purpose, is oddly shaped, is located substantially in a creek bed, is practically unusable and consists of one-fourth to one-third of an acre." Plaintiff offered to sell his tract to defendant for "a sum in excess of $45,000.00."

After settlement negotiations failed, plaintiff sued for an injunction. The court of appeals rejected the doctrine of balancing the hardships altogether; it concluded that "since the encroachment and continuing trespass have been established, and since defendant is not a quasi-public entity, plaintiff is entitled as a matter of law to the relief prayed for, namely removal of the encroachment. Accordingly, we remand this case to the Superior Court for entry of a mandatory injunction ordering defendant to remove that part of its apartment building that sits upon plaintiff's land as shown on the plat contained in the record." Williams v. South & South Rentals, Inc., 82 N.C.App. 378, 346 S.E.2d 665 (1986).

Questions. Would this defendant's encroachment be appropriate for permanent damages and an easement under Boomer v. Atlantic Cement? Under Goulding v. Cook? Are balancing the litigants' hardships and retaining the alternative of awarding damages indispensable to fair decisions about whether to grant a trespass or nuisance plaintiff an injunction?

F. CERCLA: CLARITY OR CHAOS?

BOEING COMPANY v. AETNA CASUALTY AND SURETY COMPANY

Supreme Court of Washington, En Banc, 1990.
113 Wash.2d 869, 784 P.2d 507.

Dore, Judge. * * * In 1983, the United States Environmental Protection Agency designated the Western Processing hazardous waste facility at Kent, Washington, as one of 400 hazardous waste sites requiring cleanup. On February 25, 1983, the EPA filed a complaint against Western Processing and its owners in the United States District Court for the Western District of Washington. In

May 1983, pursuant to the Comprehensive Environmental Response, Compensation, and Liability Act of 1980 (CERCLA), 42 U.S.C. § 9601 *et seq.*, the EPA notified the appellants (hereinafter policyholders) that they were generators of hazardous waste at the Western Processing site and were responsible parties for the "response costs" at this site. * * * On April 13, 1987, the Court entered a "Consent Decree" between EPA and policyholders for the cleanup of hazardous waste contamination of the subsurface of the Western Processing site.

EPA, in its complaint, alleged that the policyholders generated or transported hazardous substances found at the site. Further, that the migration of such wastes has contaminated the groundwater, aquifer (water bearing geological zone), commercial and agricultural property adjoining the site, and nearby surface waters. It further alleged that the United States, in order to combat the effects of contaminated groundwater, aquifer and property adjoining the site, had incurred and was incurring "response costs" as defined by CERCLA for which policyholders were liable. CERCLA defines the costs of "response" to include costs of removal of hazardous substances from the environment and the costs of other remedial work. CERCLA provides that any person or business entity responsible for a release or threatened release of hazardous substances "shall be liable for * * * all costs of removal or remedial action incurred by the United States Government or a State. * * *" Pursuant to the action by EPA, the policyholders have paid and will continue to pay environmental response costs relating to the Western Processing hazardous waste facility.

During the period of time that the policyholders generated and transported hazardous wastes to Western Processing, they carried Comprehensive General Liability (CGL) insurance purchased from the respondents (hereinafter insurers). The operative coverage provision of four of the policies provide that the insurer " 'will pay on behalf of the insured all sums which the insured shall become obligated to pay *as damages* because of bodily injury or property damage to which this policy applies, caused by an occurrence * * *.' " * * * The policies do not specifically define "damages."

The policyholders sued the insurers for indemnification for the "response costs" they incurred relating to the Western Processing facility. In each case, motions for summary judgment were filed in the United States District Court. Since the motions raised a determinative question of state law, the question of whether "response costs" constitute "damages" within the CGL policies issued by insurers, this question was certified to this court. * * * In order for the policyholders to be indemnified, the plain meaning of the contract must provide coverage for the subject "response costs."[1] Alternatively, before the insurers can avoid indemnifying the policyholders, this court must be satisfied that the plain meaning of "damages," as it would be understood by the average lay person, unmistakably precludes coverage for response costs, and any ambiguity is to be construed against the insurer.

The insurers have attempted to meet this burden by drawing lines, increasingly limited, around the word "damages." First, insurers draw a bright line between law remedies and equity remedies under common law. They assert that the legal technical meaning of "damages" includes monetary compensation for

---

1. It is important to note the absence of public policy in the construction of insurance contracts. While this case implicitly presents a grave question of policy, namely who should bear the cost of polluting our environment, the task presently before this court only requires us to construe the terms of the policies under Washington law. Washington courts rarely invoke public policy to override express terms of an insurance policy. [citations]

injury but not monetary equitable remedies such as sums paid to comply with an injunction or restitution. The insurers conclude that costs incurred under CERCLA are like injunction and restitution costs; therefore, they are equitable rather than legal and they are not "damages" within the policy language because equity does not award damages. The linchpin to insurers' argument is that "damages" should be given its legal technical meaning. Next, they draw a line between law remedies, excluding restitution-type law damages, such as remedies like CERCLA. Finally, they draw a line through the available common law damages and exclude everything except the tort-type damages.

The court is not persuaded that, under the rules of insurance contract analysis in Washington, the words "as damages" communicate these restrictions. * * *

Undefined terms in an insurance contract must be given their "plain, ordinary, and popular" meaning. * * *

The plain, ordinary meaning of damages as defined by the dictionary defeats insurers' argument. Standard dictionaries uniformly define the word "damages" inclusively, without making any distinction between sums awarded on a "legal" or "equitable" claim. For example, Webster's Third New International Dictionary 571 (1971) defines "damages" as "the estimated reparation in money for detriment or injury sustained". See also The Random House Dictionary of the English Language 504 (2d ed. 1987) (cost or expense). Indeed, even the insurers' own dictionaries define "damages" in accordance with the ordinary, popular, lay understanding: "Damages. Legal. The amount required to pay for a loss." Merit, Glossary of Insurance Terms 47 (1980). Even a policyholder with an insurance dictionary at hand would not learn about the coverage-restricting connotation to "damages" that the insurers argue is obvious.

Numerous federal and sister-state decisions (counsel at oral argument stated over 56 judges across the country) agree that "damages" include cleanup costs. [citations] This persuasive authority includes federal district courts in California, Colorado, Michigan, Pennsylvania, New Jersey, Missouri, Massachusetts, New York, Texas, and Delaware and state appellate courts in Wyoming, New Jersey, North Carolina, Michigan and Wisconsin.

These cases have found that cleanup costs are essentially compensatory damages for injury to property, even though these costs may be characterized as seeking "equitable relief." [citations] Or put another way, "coverage does not hinge on the form of action taken or the nature of relief sought, but on an actual or threatened use of legal process to coerce payment or conduct by a policyholder." Fireman's Fund Ins. Cos. v. Ex–Cell–O Corp., 662 F.Supp. 71, 75 (E.D.Mich. 1987). * * * According to * * * United States Aviex Co. v. Travelers Ins. Co., 125 Mich.App. 579, 589–90, 336 N.W.2d 838 (1983), the environmental cleanup costs are covered because they are equivalent to "damages" under state law:

> "If the state were to sue in court to recover in traditional 'damages,' including the state's costs incurred in cleaning up the contamination, for the injury to the ground water, defendant's obligation to defend against the lawsuit and to pay damages would be clear. It is merely fortuitous from the standpoint of either plaintiff or defendant that the state has chosen to have plaintiff remedy the contamination problem, rather than choosing to incur the costs of clean-up itself and then suing plaintiff to recover those costs. The damage to the natural resources is simply measured in the cost to restore the water to its original state."

Courts consistently agree that the "common-sense" understanding of damages within the meaning of the policy "includes a claim which results in causing [the policyholder] to pay sums of money because his acts or omissions affected adversely the rights of third parties * * * [*i.e.*, the public.]" United States Fid. & Guar. Co. v. Thomas Solvent Co., 683 F.Supp. 1139, 1168 (W.D.Mich.1988). * * *

In contrast to the plain ordinary meaning accorded to damages by courts across the country, insurers insist upon an accepted technical and legal meaning of damages. Insurers rely * * * on * * * Continental Ins. Cos. v. Northeastern Pharmaceutical & Chem. Co., 842 F.2d 977 (8th Cir.1988), and Maryland Cas. Co. v. Armco, Inc., 822 F.2d 1348 (4th Cir.1987), cert. denied, 484 U.S. 1008 (1988).

The definition of damages used by *Armco* was taken from Aetna Cas. & Sur. Co. v. Hanna, 224 F.2d 499, 503 (5th Cir.1955) (damages include "only payments to third persons when those persons have a legal claim for damages."). As a very recent case stated "[i]t is not clear why the *Armco* court turned to a 30–year–old case for a definition of 'damages,' a definition which is essentially a tautology defining damages as payment to a person who has 'a legal claim for damages.' "*Aerojet–General Corp.* The *Armco* court did express the opinion that it is a "dangerous step" for courts to construe insurance policies to cover "essentially prophylactic" or "harm avoidance" costs. However, a construction of "damages" which includes equitable relief "is not a boundless universe—such 'damages' still must be 'because of' property damage. Thus *Armco's* conclusion that an insurer would be held liable for prophylactic safety measures, taken in advance of any damage to property, is not applicable to the policies under review." *Aerojet– General Corp.*

In *Northeastern Pharmaceutical,* the Eighth Circuit in a sharply divided en banc decision reached a similar result as in *Armco.* The majority relied primarily on the narrow, technical decision espoused in *Armco* and *Hanna.* As with the *Armco* court, the *Continental* majority was concerned that absent a limited definition of damages, " 'all sums which the insured shall become legally obligated to pay *as damages*' "would be reduced to " '*all sums* which the insured shall become legally obligated to pay.' "*Northeastern Pharmaceutical.* However, both *Armco* and *Northeastern Pharmaceutical* effectively sever "damages" from the additional restrictive phrase "because of property damage." *Northeastern Pharmaceutical, Armco* and insurers are in effect trying to write out of the CGL policy a concept that is expressly stated—that damages paid as a consequence of property damage caused by an occurrence are covered by the policy—and to write into the policy a condition that is not there—that such sums are covered only if they have been imposed pursuant to a "legal", as opposed to an "equitable" basis for liability. * * *

[T]hese cases are not helpful to the insurers' position because they are inconsistent with Washington law. In this state, legal technical meanings have never trumped the common perception of the common man. "[T]he proper inquiry is not whether a learned judge or scholar can, with study, comprehend the meaning of an insurance contract" but instead "whether the insurance policy contract would be meaningful to the layman * * * "Dairyland Ins. Co. v. Ward, 83 Wash.2d 353, 358, 517 P.2d 966 (1974). * * *

Insurers * * * argue that when legal words are used in a document, this court applies their usual legal interpretations. [citation] However, before an insurance company can avail itself of a legal technical meaning of a word or words, it must be clear that *both* parties to the contract intended that the language have a legal technical meaning. [citations] * * *

Here, there is nothing about the language from the subject standard form policies that indicates the parties intended a legal meaning to apply to the disputed term. Therefore, the words "as damages" should be interpreted in accordance with its plain, ordinary meaning, as dictated by the well established rules of construction under Washington law.

Insurers also try to argue that this court, when it is dealing with corporations, analyzes the contract language and determines its meaning without reference to what the average lay person might understand. * * *

[O]n the facts of this case, it is questionable whether these standard rules of construction are no less applicable merely because the insured is itself a corporate giant. The critical fact remains that the policy in question is a standard form policy prepared by the company's experts, with language selected by the insurer. The specific language in question was not negotiated, therefore, it is irrelevant that some corporations have company counsel. Additionally, this standard form policy has been issued to big and small businesses throughout the state. Therefore it would be incongruous for the court to apply different rules of construction based on the policyholder because once the court construes the standard form coverage clause as a matter of law, the court's construction will bind policyholders throughout the state regardless of the size of their business. * * *

[T]he substance of the claim for response costs in the present case concerns compensation for restoration of contaminated water and real property. The cost of repairing and restoring property to its original condition has long been considered proper measure of damages for property damage. Consequently, the substance of the claim for response costs constitutes a claim for property damage and falls within the scope of coverage afforded by a CGL policy. * * *

The policy defines property damage as "physical injury to or destruction of tangible property, which occurs during the policy period. * * * " "Property damage" includes discharge of hazardous waste into the water. In Port of Portland v. Water Quality Ins. Syndicate, 796 F.2d 1188, 1196 (9th Cir.1986), the court held that the discharge of pollution into water caused "damage to tangible property," within the meaning of the policy defining property damage as physical injury to or destruction of tangible property. * * *

The issue of when costs are or are not incurred "because of" property damage is illustrated in *Aerojet* by the following hypothetical:

"Petitioners have two underground storage tanks for toxic waste. Tank #1 has leaked wastes into the soil which have migrated to the groundwater or otherwise polluted the environment. Tank #2 has not leaked, but government inspectors discover that it does not comply with regulatory requirements, and could eventually leak unless corrective measures are taken. Response costs associated with Tank #1 will be covered as damages, because pollution has occurred. Tank #2 would not be covered. Likewise, the expense of capital improvements to prevent pollution in an area of a facility where there is none, or improvements or safety paraphernalia required by government regulation and not causally related to property damage, would not be covered as 'damages.' "

Aerojet–General Corp. v. San Mateo Cy. Superior Court, 209 Cal.App.3d 973, 211 Cal.App.3d 216, 257 Cal.Rptr. 621, 635 (1989). Thus, costs owing because of property damages are remedial measures taken after pollution has occurred, but preventive measures taken before pollution has occurred are not costs incurred because of property damage.

The occurrence of the hazardous wastes leaking into the ground contaminating the groundwater, aquifer and adjoining property constituted "property damage" and thus triggered the "damages" provision of the policies carried by the policyholders. The costs assessed against the policyholders by the underlying lawsuits are covered by the subject policies to the extent that these costs are because of property damage. This duty to pay money is no different from the legal obligation that burdens a party who has been held liable to restore property to the condition it was in prior to the occurrence of the tortfeasor's conduct or damages consisting of amounts necessary to restore property to its status quo.

Response costs in response to actual releases of hazardous wastes are "damages" within the meaning of CGL coverage clauses at issue. The term "damages" does not cover safety measures or other preventive costs taken in advance of any damage to property. Consequently, we concur with the great majority of judges across the country that response costs incurred under CERCLA are "damages" to the extent that these costs are incurred "because of" property damage within the meaning of the CGL coverage clauses at issue. * * *

CALLOW, CHIEF JUSTICE (dissenting). * * * The majority's contrary holding upsets settled rules of insurance construction, violates controlling precedent, and contravenes public policy.

Washington law defines damages as:

[T]he sum of money which the law imposes or awards as compensation, or recompense, or in satisfaction for an injury done, or a wrong sustained as a consequence, either of a breach of a contractual obligation or a tortious act or omission.

Puget Constr. Co. v. Pierce Cy., 64 Wash.2d 453, 392 P.2d 227 (1964).

Damages for injury to property are measured in terms of the amount necessary to compensate for the injury to the property interest. Therefore, damages for injury to property are limited under Washington law to *the lesser of* diminution in value of the property or the cost to restore or replace the property. [citations] Damages compensate for the injured party's loss.

Restitution stands "in bold contrast" to damages, because it is based upon a benefitted party's gain. D. Dobbs, Remedies § 3.1, at 137 (1973). Restitutionary recovery is appropriate when the defendant has received a benefit under circumstances which make it unjust for him to retain it.

"A person confers a benefit upon another if he gives to the other possession of or some other interest in money, land, chattels, or choses in action, *performs services beneficial to or at the request of the other,* satisfies a debt or a duty of the other, or in any way adds to the other's security or advantage. He confers a benefit not only where he adds to the property of another, *but also where he saves the other from expense or loss.* The word 'benefit,' therefore, denotes any form of advantage."

Restatement of Restitution, § 1(b), at 12 (1937). The measure of recovery is the reasonable value of the benefit received by the defendant. Unlike compensatory damages, the amount of a restitutionary recovery can therefore greatly exceed the value of any property harmed. Olwell v. Nye & Nissen Co., [p. 835.]

CERCLA authorizes the President, acting through the Environmental Protection Agency (EPA), to respond to the release or the substantial threat of a release of any hazardous substance or any pollutant or contaminant which may present an imminent and substantial danger to public health or welfare. The EPA has broad authority to take whatever response measures it deems necessary to remove or neutralize hazardous waste. Alternatively, the EPA may seek injunctive relief to compel "responsible parties" to take necessary response action. Private citizens also have standing to sue to force compliance with CERCLA.

CERCLA permits certain governmental bodies (but not private citizens) to recover "damages for injury to, destruction of, or loss of natural resources." CERCLA does *not* provide for compensation to private individuals for personal injury, property damages and economic losses resulting from releases of hazardous substances. * * *

Natural resource damages are essentially a compensatory remedy. The measure of natural resource damages is *"the lesser of:* restoration or replacement costs or diminution of use values". (Italics mine.) 43 C.F.R. § 11.35(b)(2). Natural resource damages must be based on actual injury or loss. They are available only to governmental bodies "act[ing] on behalf of the public as trustee" of the natural resources. Total liability is limited to the value of the injured property. 42 U.S.C. § 9651(c); 43 C.F.R. § 11.35(b)(2).

In addition to natural resource damages, CERCLA permits both the EPA and other parties to recover costs which they have incurred as a result of a response action from "responsible parties." Responsible parties include hazardous waste generators, hazardous waste transporters, and hazardous waste disposal facility owners and operators.

CERCLA defines the term "response" to mean "removal * * * and remedial action * * * includ[ing] enforcement activities related thereto." Among the many safety measures identified as potential response actions are monitoring, security fencing, dikes, on-site treatment or incineration, recycling, provision of alternative water supplies, and related enforcement activities.

CERCLA response cost liability is essentially restitutional:

> "When a party, governmental or non-governmental, incurs response costs it is performing the duty of the responsible party. In seeking recovery of those costs, that party is asking for the return of money spent on behalf of the responsible party to safeguard public health. Thus, response cost recovery restores the status quo by returning to the plaintiff what rightfully belongs to it, rather than compensating the plaintiff for loss sustained to its interest as a result of the responsible parties' wrongful conduct, and is a classic example of equitable restitution."

(Footnotes Omitted.) Brett, Insuring Against the Innovative Liabilities and Remedies Created by Superfund, 6 J.Envtl.L. 1, 35 (1986).

The contrast between natural resource damage liability and response cost liability further indicates that CERCLA response costs are a restitutionary remedy. First, a responsible party can be held liable for response costs even though there is no property damage to compensate, because no actual release has yet occurred. Second, parties without an economic interest in the affected property can maintain an action for response costs. Finally, liability for response costs can greatly exceed the economic value of the affected property. See Abraham, Environmental Liability and the Limits of Insurance, 88 Colum.L.Rev. 942, 969 (1988).

The contrast between response costs and natural resource damages makes clear that response costs are an equitable restitutionary remedy, not a compensatory damage remedy. Verlan, Ltd. v. John L. Armitage & Co., 695 F.Supp. 950 (N.D.Ill.1988). Every court that has examined the nature of Superfund response costs liability outside of the insurance context has held that such costs are a form of equitable restitution. [citations] In fact, this authority is so overwhelming that *even the policyholders admit that "the governmental remedy under CERCLA is equitable."* Brief of Policyholders. Therefore, this court must also hold that CERCLA response costs are a restitutionary remedy.

The insurance policies in this case provide that the insurer "will pay on behalf of the insured all sums which the insured shall become legally obligated to pay as damages * * * because of * * * property damage. * * *" This language unambiguously extends coverage only to compensatory "damages" liability, not claims for restitutionary CERCLA response cost liability.

The majority makes several arguments attempting to show that this language is ambiguous. * * *

[It] asserts that because standard dictionaries do not explicitly distinguish between "legal" and "equitable" claims, the "as damages" clause can reasonably be interpreted to provide coverage for CERCLA response costs. Standard dictionary definitions of "damages," *including the definition cited by the majority,*[1] in fact unambiguously distinguish damages from restitution. *"Damages" are compensatory*—reparation for detriment or injury sustained. *CERCLA response cost liability, in contrast, is restitutionary*—reimbursement of a benefit unjustly retained by a responsible party.

Of course, no dictionary explicitly defines damages as "not equitable relief." Dictionaries define what a word means, not everything a word does not mean. But standard dictionaries' definitions of "damages" do establish that the "plain, ordinary, and popular meaning" of "damages" *is* reparation for detriment or injury sustained. Because CERCLA response costs are not reparation for detriment or injury sustained, they do not fall within the "plain, ordinary and popular meaning" of damages. * * *

Unlike the majority, the policyholders recognized that if the word "damages" is given this plain, ordinary meaning, the insurance policies will not cover their CERCLA response cost liabilities. They therefore vigorously advocate an alternative "cost or expense" interpretation of the word "damages."

---

1. [Footnotes renumbered.] "Standard dictionaries uniformly define the word 'damages' inclusively, without making any distinction between sums awarded on a 'legal' or 'equitable' claim. For example, Webster's Third New International Dictionary 571 (1971) defines 'damages' as 'the estimated reparation in money for detriment or injury sustained.' "[as cited by the Majority]

This dictionary's complete entry for "damages" is: "damages pl: the estimated reparation in money for detriment or injury sustained: compensation or satisfaction imposed by law for a wrong or injury caused by a violation of a legal right (bring a suit for) (was awarded compensatory s of $4000)—compare damnum absque injuria; see compensatory damages, general damages, nominal damages, punitive damages, special damages 4: expense, cost, charge, syn see injury" Webster's Third New International Dictionary 571 (1981).

The majority does cite *The Random House Dictionary of the English Language* in an attempt to show that damages can also mean "cost or expense." The majority neglects to mention that this dictionary labels the "cost or expense" definition informal. The entire definition reads:

> 2. damages, law. the estimated money equivalent for detriment or injury sustained. 3. Often, damages. informal. cost; expense; charge: What are the damages for the lubrication job on my car?

The Random House Dictionary of the English Language 365 (1973).

This court should reject the "cost or expense" definition for several reasons. First, the phrase "legally obligated to pay as damages" lies at the heart of a legal document, insuring against legal liability. Every dictionary cited indicates that the "compensation" definition is appropriate to a legal context. In contract, every dictionary that evaluates usage describes "cost or expense" as informal, colloquial or slang.[2]

Second, the "compensation" definition gives meaning to the "as damages" clause while the "cost or expense" definition renders "as damages" redundant. The "as damages" clause qualifies the phrase "all sums which the insured shall become legally obligated to pay." Amounts payable in reparation for detriment or injury sustained constitute a subset of the amounts an insured is "legally obligated to pay." The "compensation" definition therefore makes the "as damages" clause meaningfully qualify its referent.

In contrast, if interpreted to mean "cost or expense" the "as damages" clause redundantly repeats its referent. Because all sums which an insured is "legally obligated to pay" already constitute a "cost or expense" to the insured, the "as damages" clause becomes "mere surplusage, because any obligation to pay would be covered." Maryland Cas. Co. v. Armco, Inc., 822 F.2d 1348, 1352 (4th Cir.1987), cert. denied 484 U.S. 1008 (1988). * * *

The majority next emphasizes that "56 judges" have held that "damages" can include CERCLA cleanup costs. While the judicial "head-count" is hardly dispositive, it is not nearly as one-sided as the majority implies. In addition to the three cases discussed by the majority, the following reported cases also hold that CERCLA response costs are not covered "as damages:" [citations] * * *

In addition, numerous cases from other jurisdictions hold that liability insurers need not indemnify their insured's restitutionary liabilities, even if payable in money. See, e.g., * * * Desrochers v. New York Cas. Co., 99 N.H. 129, 106 A.2d 196 (1954) [in which] the insureds had been enjoined to remove a culvert placed upon their land. In holding the insurer not liable for the cost of complying with the injunction, the court stated:

> 'The cost of compliance with the mandatory injunction is not reasonably to be regarded as a sum payable "as damages." Damages are recompense for injuries sustained. Restatement, Torts, § 902. They are remedial rather than preventive, and in the usual sense are pecuniary in nature. 1 Sedgwick on Damages (9th ed.) §§ 2, 29. The expense of restoring the plaintiff's property to its former state will not remedy the injury previously done, nor will it be paid to the injured parties * * *'

---

2. Only Webster's Third New International Dictionary and the related Webster's New Collegiate Dictionary do not identify the "cost or expense" definition of damages as informal, colloquial, or slang. These dictionaries do not specially identify such usages.

'In short, the expense of complying with the order is neither a sum which the insured is obligated to pay as damages, nor is it in any real sense equivalent thereto. No equitable principle requires the [insurer] to pay it, and it is not within the scope of its undertaking as a reasonable man * * * would interpret it.'

* * * The "as damages" clause in these policies unambiguously limits coverage to compensatory damage remedies, not restitutionary remedies like CERCLA response costs. However, even if the phrase "as damages" were ambiguous, this term should not automatically be construed against the insurer. The "average lay person" rule of insurance interpretation does not apply to corporate giants. * * *

The majority acknowledges that at least some of the policyholders in the present case are "corporate giant[s]". Because these insureds *do* possess the ability and expertise to negotiate the language of the policy, the "average lay person" rule applicable to the typical consumer insurance contract should not extend to this case. * * *

[Finally] the majority's interpretation of these insurance policies ignores the public policy expressed by the United States Congress in enacting CERCLA.

* * * Congress clearly recognized that corporate polluters have reaped enormous benefits from their past inadequate waste disposal practices. These practices created significant short-term savings for polluters, resulting in higher profits for them, but caused enormous long-term harm in the form of environmental degradation. CERCLA response cost liability forces these polluters to disgorge these profits.

The insurers from whom these polluters now seek indemnification, in contrast, did not charge a premium to cover response cost liability. See Note, CERCLA Cleanup Costs Under Comprehensive General Liability Insurance Policies: Property Damage or Economic Damage, 56 Fordham L.Rev. 1169, 1176 (1988). * * * By requiring these insurers to indemnify the corporate polluters for the cost of cleanup, the majority permits the polluters to both reap the benefits and avoid the costs attributable to their pollution. This directly violates the congressional intent that polluters internalize their pollution costs. See Brett, Insuring Against the Innovative Liabilities and Remedies Created by Superfund, 6 J.Envtl.L. 1, 52 (1986).

The majority holding also violates public policy because it requires insurers to insure liability which is fundamentally uninsurable. The innovative new features of CERCLA's liability scheme simply prevent insurers from calculating and charging premiums that bear any real relation to the risk of CERCLA liability.

CERCLA's liability provisions differ from ordinary tort liability in many important respects. First, CERCLA imposes an especially strict liability upon responsible parties. Liability attaches even to those who nonnegligently dispose of a hazardous substance using state of the art procedures.

Second, CERCLA liability is retroactive. Responsible parties who disposed of hazardous waste in a completely legal, non-actionable manner before the enactment of CERCLA are now potentially liable for response costs.

Third, CERCLA regularly makes individuals liable for harms they did not cause. CERCLA imposes joint and several liability upon every responsible party connected with a hazardous waste site. Therefore, both the government and private parties may recover response costs from a "responsible party" with virtually no showing of causation.

Fourth, private citizens without any proprietary interest in the property harmed have standing to sue to enforce CERCLA. To recover response costs, a private party need only show an outlay of costs and that the costs were incurred consistently with the National Contingency Plan promulgated by the EPA.

Fifth, CERCLA authorizes the initiation of response action in response to the *threat* of a hazardous waste release. For example CERCLA authorizes the government to recoup the costs of health assessment and health effects studies. Therefore, responsible parties may be held liable for CERCLA response costs even in the absence of any actual harm to persons or property.

Sixth, CERCLA response cost liability is inevitable. Every hazardous waste containment system eventually will leak. Because CERCLA imposes liability even if hazardous waste is disposed of in a state of the art manner, every responsible party should expect eventually to be subject to CERCLA response liability.

Seventh, CERCLA response cost liability is essentially boundless, both in amount and duration. The EPA has an almost unfettered discretion to incur and recoup whatever response cost it believes are necessary to clean up a site. Moreover, because the EPA currently refuses to grant settling parties releases from further litigation, a responsible party's liability exists indefinitely into the future regardless of how much it has paid to clean up a site.

CERCLA's broadly worded provisions mean that insurers have no way of predicting what insured conduct may lead to liability. * * *

A congressionally authorized study group report on the availability of private insurance for CERCLA liability recognizes that CERCLA's radically unique approach to the imposition of response costs renders the insured's potential liability so limitless that such liability cannot be assessed by prospective insurers seeking to set premium levels. * * * A Report in Compliance With Section 301(b) of P.L. 96–105, at 83–87 & 94–95 (June 1983). In fact, since the enactment of CERCLA, pollution insurance has become unavailable in any insurance market. * * *

Congress enacted CERCLA's innovative response cost liability provisions in order to properly address the threat posed by inadequate past hazardous waste disposal practices. CERCLA liability accordingly differs substantially from ordinary tort liability. Normal tort liability results in a compensatory "damages" remedy. CERCLA response cost liability, in contrast, results in a restitutionary remedy.

The insurance policies at issue in this case require the insurer to indemnify the insureds for "all sums which the insured shall be legally obligated to pay as damages. * * *" The plain, ordinary and popular meaning of damages, as recognized by the majority, is "reparation for detriment or injury sustained." Because CERCLA response costs do not constitute reparation for detriment or injury sustained, they do not constitute "damages" within the meaning of these policies. * * *

I respectfully dissent.

DOLLIVER, J., concurs.

Notes

1. *Pressure on the Rules.* Because of the billions of dollars of liability exposure for environmental cleanup, property owners' insurance coverage for CERCLA and related environmental claims has been vigorously litigated. The adversary system has put intense pressure on basic remedial concepts. How well have the concepts stood up to the pressure? The principal decision represents the majority view.

2. *Characterization of Response Costs.* Response costs require the owner to pay to clean up contamination. That owner has an incentive to spend on prevention to avert pollution in the future to avoid payment for response costs.

(a) *Damages?* Do response costs fit the definition of compensatory damages? Are response costs retrospective and past oriented or prospective and future oriented? Restoring, remediating, and damages held the Wisconsin court. Johnson Controls, Inc. v. Employers Ins. of Wausau, 665 N.W.2d 257, 270–81 (Wis. 2003), cert. denied, 541 U.S. 1027 (2004).

Another insured's policy language, "as damages" did not mean that its insurance carrier was responsible for its liability for CERCLA "response costs." The court gave two reasons: (i) Response costs are equitable orders to pay money. (ii) CERCLA distinguishes between response-cleanup costs and damages. Floyd's Sales & Service, Inc. v. Universal Underwriters Insurance Co., 910 F.Supp. 464, 465–68 (D.Neb.1995).

(b) *Restitution?* How does the *Boeing* court deal with the insurance company's argument that polluter's savings was restitution because the savings unjustly enriched the polluter? Has a polluter saved prevention costs? Is the polluter unjustly enriched by that savings in the same way Nye & Nisson were unjustly enriched by using Olwell's egg washing machine? p. 835. If response costs are restitution for unjust enrichment, then how much of what we now call damages is also restitution?

(c) *Injunction?* Are the insured's expenditures to prevent future casualties more like injunctions? Are prevention expenditures prospective-future oriented or retrospective-past oriented?

(d) *Investigation?* Are an owner's costs to investigate whether contamination exists "damages"? Not, the federal court said, under Wisconsin common law, which said then that response costs are not "damages." "[D]amages are what you pay to the other side, not what you pay to a lawyer or consultant for assistance in your tussle with the other side, unless the payment benefits the insurance company by reducing its potential liability." Wisconsin Power and Light Co. v. Century Indemnity Co., 130 F.3d 787, 791 (7th Cir.1997).

(e) *Public Policy.* Are the parties' public policy arguments persuasive? Insurance coverage for pollution distributes the cost around the insurance pool among the group which can prevent pollution and pass on the expense as a cost of doing business. If a polluter can forward losses to an insurance company, will that reduce response costs' deterrence features? Will large unpredicted response cost liabilities crush insurance companies?

(f) *Plain Language?* To reach the desired result, does the court redefine legal "damages"? Or does it manipulate the canons of insurance policy interpretation? Is "plain language" an oxymoron after all?

*

Index

References are to Pages

†